ScottForesman

PASSING THE GED

Revised Edition

A Complete Preparation Program
for the High School Equivalency Examination

HarperPerennial
A Division of HarperCollins*Publishers*

Copyright Acknowledgements appear on pages 768-772.

First Harper Perennial Edition published 1991

Library of Congress Cataloging-in-Publication Data

Passing the GED.
Includes index.

1. General educational development tests—Study guides. I. Scott, Foresman and Company. II. Scott, Foresman and Company. Lifelong Learning Division.
LB3060.33.G45P36 1987 373.12'62 86-31564
ISBN 0-673-24314-1

ISBN 0-06-276052-1 (pbk.)

99 00 01 WEB 11 10 9

Contents

Section 5 Social Studies 249

Section 6 Science 329

Section 8 The Posttests 589

What You Should Know About the GED Test

What Is the GED Test?
The initials GED stand for General Educational Development. You may have heard the GED Test referred to as the High-School Equivalency Test. This is because the test measures your ability against that of graduating high-school students and gives you a chance to earn a certificate that is the *equivalent* of a high-school diploma. And you do not have to go back to school to get it. That's quite an opportunity!

A Bit of History The GED Test was created in 1942 during World War II. Originally it was meant to allow veterans to quickly get a credential that would be equivalent to a high-school diploma so that they could go on to college. Later it was made available to all adults. Since then, millions of people have taken the GED Test, passed it, and earned their high-school equivalency credential.

Why Take the Test? Every state in the Union, as well as the District of Columbia, six United States territories or possessions, and many Canadian provinces use GED Test results as the basis for giving high-school equivalency credentials. Those credentials are accepted as the equivalent of a high-school diploma for purposes of employment, promotion, and licensing.

Another good reason for taking the test is that many colleges and universities now accept satisfactory GED Test scores in place of completed high-school grade transcripts for admissions purposes.

Did you know that some labor unions even require their members who do not have high-school diplomas to take the GED Test?

How Much Does It Cost to Take the Test?
In many states there is no fee at all for taking the GED Test. States that do require a fee charge between two and ten dollars. In some cases, the fee may even be different in one part of a state from what it is in another. Check with a local high school or test center to find out the fee, if any, for your area. The table on pages 4–5 will give you the separate fee, if any, for issuing the GED credential in each state.

Where to Take the Test The GED Test must be taken at one of more than 3,000 official testing centers in the United States and Canada. You may not realize it, but there is probably an official testing center quite close to where you live.

Who Takes the Test? Did you know that in this country there are about 44 million people over eighteen who do not have a high-school diploma? This means that about 26 percent of the adult population of the United States has not graduated from high school.

In recent years, more than one-half million GED Tests have been taken annually. It seems that a lot of people think it makes good sense to have a high-school equivalency credential.

All adult citizens of the United States are eligible to take the GED Test provided they meet the age and residence requirements for their own state, territory, or district—or, in the case of citizens of Canada, province. If you are interested in knowing if there are any special requirements for your area, you should call an adult education center or the office of the superintendent of schools in your district for more information.

What's the GED Test Like? Most questions on the GED Test are multiple-choice, and there are five answer choices for each question. You will need to mark one of the five answer spaces for each question. You will also have to write a short essay for the Writing Skills Test.

The GED Test measures how well you have mastered the skills and general knowledge that are acquired in a four-year high-school education. However, the GED Test does not expect you to remember many details, definitions, or facts. Therefore, it should not be a handicap at all if you have been out of school for some time.

The GED Test does not base your score on your ability to race against the clock, as some tests do. You may be relieved to know that ample time is allowed for you to be able to finish each subject test. Just the same, you will want to work steadily and not waste any time.

How Does the GED Test Evaluate Test-Takers?
Every ten years the GED Test itself is "put to the test." Sample GED Tests are given to 7,000 high-school seniors who are ready to graduate. The GED Testing Service in Washington, D.C.,

makes sure it has a true representation of the United States population; it uses students from across the entire country—from urban, suburban, and rural areas. After studying the answers from those students, the GED Testing Service makes up tests that two out of three high-school students could pass.

What's on the Test? The five subtests in the GED Test have been created to test whether an adult has the knowledge and skills that the average high-school graduate does in these five areas:

Test 1: Writing Skills
Test 2: Social Studies
Test 3: Science
Test 4: Interpreting Literature and the Arts
Test 5: Mathematics

The Writing Skills Test measures your ability to recognize and write standard English. What does the term *standard* mean? It refers to the kind of English used for writing compositions, reports, or business letters. There are two parts to the Writing Skills Test, a multiple-choice section and an essay. The first part tests sentence structure, usage, spelling, punctuation, and capitalization. You will be given some fairly long passages and asked to identify and correct errors in them. All you have to do is choose one of the five answers for each test item and mark the correct answer space. In the second part of the Writing Skills Test you will have to write a short essay about a topic with which most adults are familiar. You will be asked to explain a situation or give an opinion about it. The readers who score your essay will check to see if your thoughts are organized and your writing is clear and correct.

Page 153 will give you more information about the Writing Skills Test.

The Social Studies Test is made up of questions from the areas of United States history, political science, economics, geography, and the behavioral sciences. You will be asked questions about maps, graphs, charts, and even cartoons—political cartoons, that is. You may be asked to read several quotations and to draw conclusions from them. Or you may be required to read a rather long passage from a book or an article about some social issue. Many of the questions, however, are based on a very short definition or quotation. A few questions may test your knowledge of broad concepts or trends.

If you want to read more about the Social Studies Test, turn to page 249 of this book.

The Science Test includes questions on biology, earth science, chemistry, and physics. This test is like the Social Studies Test in some ways. It, too, tests your ability to understand readings in a specialized field. In the Science Test, however, in addition to questions about science-related readings, you will be asked questions about scientific diagrams. You will also find quite a few short questions that are not related to either a passage or a diagram. Many of the questions will allow you to demonstrate your commonsense general knowledge of how science works. They are often related to basic scientific principles of which your everyday experience has made you aware.

On page 329 of this book, there is additional information about what the Science Test is like.

The Test of Interpreting Literature and the Arts has reading selections of several different types. You will find questions on passages from short stories, essays, novels, plays, poetry, and quite possibly, a review of a movie or television show. You will be asked what a passage, or part of a passage, means or what conclusions you might draw from it. You might also be asked to decide what the feeling or mood of the selection is or what you think one word in the selection means.

On page 73 of this book, you will find more details about the Test of Interpreting Literature and the Arts.

Finally, on the Mathematics Test half of the questions will be arithmetic problems. The other half will be algebra and geometry problems. If you are not familiar with these last two subjects, don't let this frighten you. Just remember that if you can answer most of the arithmetic problems correctly, you will need to get only a small number of the algebra and geometry problems right to pass the test. But if you study the entire *Mathematics* section of this book, you'll be able to get not just a passing score, but a very good one. Because math is such an important part of everyday life, this is a subject worth studying for a top score.

For more information about the Mathematics Test, turn to page 409 of this book.

How Long Is the Test? It will take you about 7½ hours to complete all five GED subtests. That may seem like a long time, but it's really not; a few years ago, it took 10 hours! The chart below shows you the time you will have for each of the five tests. It also shows you how many questions there are in a test.

Subtest	Time Allowed	Number of Questions
Writing Skills	2 hours	
Multiple-Choice	1 hour and 15 minutes	55
Essay	45 minutes	about 200 words
Social Studies	1 hour and 25 minutes	64
Science	1 hour and 35 minutes	66
Interpreting Literature and the Arts	1 hour and 5 minutes	45
Mathematics	1 hour and 30 minutes	56

In the Social Studies, Science, and Literature and the Arts tests, you often have to read a fairly long passage before answering the questions. The time you need for completing that reading is figured into the total test time.

Getting Ready for the GED Test If you are not already enrolled in a GED preparation program and would like help preparing for the test, you should make some phone calls. The office of the superintendent of schools or your local vocational education center, community college, high school, or adult school are good places to contact. Ask if there are GED preparation courses available in your neighborhood. A call or two should be enough to get the information.

Many people prefer to study on their own rather than in a class. But even if you are one of those independent spirits, you can benefit from calling one of the places suggested above. They will be likely to have printed information on the GED Test and can tell you about fees, application forms, and test times. If, however, you find they can't provide that information, you can still get it by writing to the following address:

General Educational Development
GED Testing Service of the
American Council on Education
One Dupont Circle
Washington, D.C. 20036

When to Take the Test A good time to take the GED Test is right after you get a good score on the *Posttests* at the very end of this book. If you wait too long after taking the *Posttests*, your test-taking skills may not be as finely tuned as they were. After all, you want to get the maximum benefit from all the practice you'll be doing on the pages ahead in this book.

How Is the Test Scored? In most states, you must get a total minimum standard score of 225 points to pass the GED Test. This means that you need an average standard score of 45 on each of the subject tests. Getting a few more than half of the questions right on most of the subject tests will give you a score of 45. Some good news about the scoring is that you don't have to get a score of 45 on every one of the five tests. What you need is an *average* score of 45. This means that if you get, for example, 37 on the Science Test, and if you get 53 on, say, the Social Studies Test, those two scores would average out to 45. If you get a score of less than 35 on any subject test, however, you will have to take that test over no matter how well you do on all the others.

Minimum passing scores vary from state to state. The table on pages 4 and 5 will give you the information you need for your own state.

How Many Tests at Once? Every state has its own policy for taking the GED Test. Some prefer that you take the entire group of five subtests in one day. Some will allow you to break your GED Test into two parts; they might let you take two tests on one day and the other three on another. Very few will allow you to take just one test at a time.

Getting the Results How you find out your test scores will vary from testing center to testing center. Some centers let you know immediately; most will have your scores mailed to your home, and this can take two to eight weeks. You should ask at the center where you take the GED Test and how and when you'll receive the results.

Trying Again If you don't pass one of the tests—or even all five of them—you can take the ones you didn't pass over again. Each time you take a test, you will have a different set of questions.

Current State Policies for Issuing High School Equivalency Credentials (Revised 2/86)

State	Minimum Scores[1]	Minimum Age for Credential	Residency Required	Fee for Issuing Credential[2]
Alabama	35 and 45	18	30 days	$8.00
Alaska	35 and 45	18	30 days	None
Arizona	35 and 45	18	Yes	None
Arkansas	35 and 45	17	30 days	None
California	40 and 45	18	Yes (b)	$8.00
Colorado	35 and 45	17	Yes	None
Connecticut	35 and 45	19	Yes	None
Delaware	40 and 45	17	6 months	None
District of Columbia	35 and 45	18	Yes	$3.00
Florida	40 and 45	16	Yes (c)	$5.00 (e)
Georgia	35 and 45	18	Yes	None
Hawaii	35 and 45	17	No (h)	$2.00
Idaho	35 and 45	19	6 months	$2.00
Illinois	35 and 45	18 (a)	30 days	$10.00
Indiana	35 and 45	18 (a)	30 days	None
Iowa	35 and 45	18	No	$5.00
Kansas	35 and 45	18	6 months	$3.00
Kentucky	35 and 45	17	Yes	None
Louisiana	40 or 45	17	Yes	None
Maine	35 and 45	18	Yes	$3.00
Maryland	40 and 45	16	3 months	$5.00
Massachusetts	35 and 45	18 (a)	6 months	$5.00
Michigan	35 and 45	18	No	None
Minnesota	35 and 45	19	Yes	None
Mississippi	40 or 45	17	30 days	None
Missouri	35 and 45	16	Yes	$6.50 (f)
Montana	35 and 45	18	Yes	None
Nebraska	40 or 45	18	30 days	$5.00
Nevada	35 and 45	17	Yes	None
New Hampshire	35 and 45	18	Yes	$10.00 (e)
New Jersey	40 and 45 (k)	18 (i)	No	$5.00
New Mexico	40 or 50	18 (a)	Yes	None
New York	40 and 45	19 (a)	30 days	None
North Carolina	35 and 45	16	Yes	None
North Dakota	40 or 50	19	Yes	None
Ohio	35 and 45	18	Yes	$7.00
Oklahoma	40 and 45	17	Yes	None
Oregon	40 each test	18	Yes	$5.00
Pennsylvania	35 and 45	18	Yes	None
Rhode Island	35 and 45	18 (a)	Yes	$3.00
South Carolina	45 average	19	Yes	$5.00
South Dakota	40 or 50	18	Yes (d)	None
Tennessee	35 and 45	18 (j)	Yes	None
Texas	40 or 45	17	Yes	$5.00
Utah	40 and 45	18	Yes	$3.00
Vermont	35 and 45	16	Yes	None
Virginia	35 and 45	18 (a)	30 days	$10.00
Washington	35 and 45	19 (a)	Yes (l)	None
West Virginia	40 or 45	18	Yes	None
Wisconsin	35 and 45	18	Yes	None
Wyoming	35 and 45	18	Yes	None

Canadian Province or Territory	Minimum Scores (1)	Minimum Age for Credential	Residency Required	Fee for Issuing Credential(2)
Alberta	45 each test	18	Yes	None
British Columbia	45 each test	19	6 months	None
Manitoba	45 each test	19	6 months	None
New Brunswick	35 and 45 (French) 45 each test (Eng.)	19	6 months	None
Newfoundland	40 and 45	19	6 months	None
Northwest Territories	40 and 45	18	6 months	None
Nova Scotia	45 each test	19	No	None
Prince Edward Island	40 and 45	19	6 months	None
Saskatchewan	45 each test	19	Yes	None
Yukon Territory	45 each test	19	6 months	$5.00
U.S. Territory or Other				
American Samoa	40 each test	18	Yes	None
Guam	35 and 45	19	Yes	None
Kwajalein Island	35 and 45	19	No	None
Panama	40 and 45	19	Yes	$2.00 (g)
Puerto Rico	35 and 45	18	Yes	None
Republic of Palau	40 each test	18	Yes	None
Trust Territory of the Pacific Islands	35 each test	18	Yes	$2.00
Virgin Islands	35 and 45	18	Yes	$5.00
Marshall Islands (Majuro)	40 each test	18	Yes	$2.00
Commonwealth of the Northern Mariana Islands	35 and 45	18	Yes	$2.00

1. Minimum standard scores of 35 *or* 45: no test score less than 35 *or*, if one or more scores are less than 35, an average no lower than 45 for the battery. Minimum standard scores of 35 *and* 45: no test scores less than 35 and an average no lower than 45 for the battery.

2. States often assess a fee for testing if examinee takes the GED Test at a state Official GED Testing Center. Information on testing fee (if any) separate from fee for issuing the credential should be obtained from the local testing center.

Notes

(a) Certain exceptions are made that permit credentials to be issued to persons at ages below those listed.
(b) Person must have an address of record in California.
(c) Person must live in Florida at time of application.
(d) Person must physically reside in South Dakota.
(e) Person must be in military or have taken test in another state.
(f) Fee is included in application fee.
(g) Fee if tested locally.
(h) Person must have transcript from last high school attended.
(i) If tested in Spanish, must pass Test 6.
(j) Birth certificate must be submitted with application.
(k) Test 6 is required for Spanish and French batteries.
(l) Person must have an address of record in Washington.

Think Positively, Study Right

Capitalize on Your Life Experiences If you have been out of school for quite a while, it's likely that you may be anxious about preparing for the GED Test. You may think you've forgotten how to study. Or you may feel you're not good at reading books.

If that sounds like the kind of thinking you've been doing, you're forgetting a very important fact. You should realize that one of the most important advantages you have at this point in your life is all the experiences you've accumulated. Many of the questions asked on the GED Test require you to rely on general knowledge—the kind of knowledge you acquire by talking to other people about what's going on in the country or in the world. It's also the kind of knowledge you might pick up automatically by reading maps—road maps, for example. You may be able to answer a question correctly just because you understand why the government withholds taxes from your paycheck. Or you may be able to get math problems right just because you know how to calculate how many feet of wood you need to frame a picture of a certain width and height, or how many tiles of a certain size you need to cover a floor. Try circling the correct answers for the three GED sample test questions below. Notice how skills and knowledge that people acquire in everyday life are tested.

If you do much shopping for your family, for example, you probably won't have difficulty quickly finding the answer to this math problem.

■ If apples are $1.80 a bag, and Mr. Belli buys two bags, how much change does he get from a $5.00 bill?

(1) $1.40 (2) $2.20 (3) $2.40 (4) $3.20 (5) $4.10

If you glance at political cartoons in newspapers or news magazines once in a while, you shouldn't have much of a problem with this question.

Next!

■ There is evidence in the cartoon to indicate that the cartoonist would agree with all of the following statements about Standard Oil EXCEPT

(1) It was a powerful organization.
(2) It had control over parts of the federal government.
(3) It should be encouraged to grow.
(4) It hurt many small businesses.
(5) It should be regulated.

If you have a general knowledge about different kinds of exercise, you have a head start in answering this question.

■ Aerobic exercise is any exercise that uses many muscles continuously over a period of time to increase the flow of oxygen and thereby strengthen the heart. Which of the following is NOT an example of aerobic exercise?

(1) swimming (2) bicycling (3) running (4) golf (5) rowing

The answer to the first question is (1). You should have picked (3) as the answer to the second question. And the third question's answer is (4). Were you able to get two or even all three of them right? If so, you have benefited from your life experiences and will be able to use those experiences to make your preparation for the GED Test produce good results.

Positive Thinking Can Raise Your Scores In the years you've been away from school, you've accomplished many things to take care of yourself and be of help to family and friends. These accomplishments demonstrate your basic strengths. You may have held down a job; received raises or promotions; had children; supported a family; bought, built, or rented a home; saved some money; done some traveling; acquired interesting hobbies; or made worthwhile friends. Sometimes, however, although you realize you've done some admirable things, you probably tend to forget that fact when approaching a new challenge like taking a test. You may feel unsure of yourself because now you're entering new territory—and the ground begins to feel shaky! This inability to recognize your own strong points can end up making you think negatively about yourself and your ability to pass the GED Test.

Take time now and write down on the Accomplishments Chart below five things you've done since you left high school that you feel good about having done. Don't think, "I'm proud of that, but it's too ridiculous (or too insignificant) to write down." You can be honest and put down whatever you want. After all, no one except you has to see your list.

Once you've written your list, ask yourself if accomplishing any of those things took hard work, courage, patience, or experience. Then put a check on the chart in each box where you deserve one.

When you start feeling negative about your abilities, come back to this chart and take another good look at those checks. Then tell yourself that thinking negatively about yourself is not even being logical or honest, let alone helpful.

Finally, allowing yourself to feel depressed or anxious actually takes a surprising amount of energy. You will find that by thinking positively, it will be easier to concentrate and to prepare for a new challenge in a steady, organized way.

Relax! Following that order is not always as easy as it might seem. People can relax passively—without trying—when they are having a good time, feeling satisfied, doing something they like to do, or talking to a person or persons they like. But you cannot always be lucky enough to find yourself in those situations. The real trick is to train yourself to stay calm at times when things are not so "rosy." If you are one of the many people who feel that a test-taking situation is one of those times, there are several things you can do. First, you admit to yourself that you may tend to get nervous preparing for a test. Second, you learn to relax actively—that is, you work at relaxing. Here are a few suggestions for doing just that.

Exercise is one of the best ways to relax. So it stands to reason that exercise combined with positive thinking about the GED Test can gradually make you lose your nervousness about the exam. You might, for example, try jogging for fifteen minutes after each study session. As you jog, avoid thinking about specific topics or questions you came across in your study session. Just think about how you have been working steadily and how you eventually are going to pass the GED Test. Keep your mind on that thought. If other thoughts come into your mind, push them away. For this short period of time, think only about how your steady effort is preparing you to pass the GED Test.

Another way that you can do the same sort of positive relaxation is to find a quiet spot where you can be alone for fifteen minutes after every one of your study sessions. You might sit in a comfortable chair. Or you could sit cross-legged on the floor. If your quiet spot is at home, you

Accomplishment	Hard work	Courage	Patience	Experience
1.				
2.				
3.				
4.				
5.				

could even lie on the floor. It is better not to lie in your bed because it is too easy to fall asleep. Your mind should remain alert during your relaxation. If you can relax better when listening to music, do so. It's best to find instrumental music without lyrics so that your concentration isn't broken. Close your eyes and think about how you are working steadily to pass the GED Test. Think about how you will soon achieve your goal. These are the only thoughts that should occupy your mind during your relaxation session. If you find it hard to think only about that, try repeating to yourself, "I am working hard to pass the GED Test, and I am going to pass it soon."

One more technique that might help you learn active relaxing is to tense and then relax your muscles. There are many ways to do this, and you can experiment to find the one that helps you most. For example, you can begin by tensing the muscles in your toes. Hold them tense for a few seconds and then relax them completely. Try to appreciate how good the relaxation feels after the tension. Then, when about thirty seconds have passed, tense the muscles in your feet and then relax them in the same way. Move on up your whole body, tensing and relaxing each group of muscles. All the time you are doing this, you should be thinking positively about yourself and the GED Test. You might try tensing your muscles while saying to yourself, "I am working hard to pass the GED Test." Then relax your muscles and say to yourself, "And I am going to pass it soon." Each time, appreciate the relaxation for a little while and think about how good it feels to be working toward something you want.

Research proves that people tend to forget less of what they have studied if they relax or do some physical activity immediately after studying. That's another good reason to plan to do one of the relaxation activities right after studying for the GED Test.

The Endurance Factor This book has already mentioned the importance of having a positive attitude and the need for learning to concentrate. Some people confuse two things: studying in a steady, systematic way and studying until they are exhausted or bored, or both. Doing the latter will not help you learn more. You actually will be wasting a lot of your time if you drag on your study sessions for too long or if you study at times when your power of concentration is not at its peak.

It's a good idea first of all to decide before you begin your program of study what hours you will set aside each day to prepare for the GED Test. Probably you should decide to spend between forty-five minutes and two hours per session. You can choose to have one session per day, or, if you have the time, two or even three.

Try to set up your schedule so that you can use your own periods of greatest energy for study. Usually one of those periods is the early morning hours. You will have to decide on the times that will work in with your own schedule.

If you are employed, try to make the best use of periods such as your lunch hour and coffee breaks. If you take a bus or train to work, you can use your travel time for study. If you manage to do this regularly, chances are you'll be able to squeeze in a surprising amount of extra study time.

Remember, when you feel yourself concentrating poorly or when you feel tired, close your book and try doing a different type of activity. You might try some relaxation exercises of the types mentioned on this page.

The Time Management Chart on the next page should help you organize your study. Complete it in pencil so that you can make changes if you find that things are not working to your best advantage. Here's how you can set up an organizational plan.

After you complete the *Pretest* on pages 18–60 and analyze your scores according to the instructions on page 61, give yourself a number grade on each of the five subject areas. Grade yourself 1 *(Good),* 2 *(Fair),* or 3 *(Risky)* for each area and write that grade on the chart below across from the subject area it represents. If your score was *Exceptional,* you don't need to write a number on the chart.

Grade Chart

Subject	1 (Good)	2 (Fair)	3 (Risky)
A. Writing Skills			
B. Social Studies			
C. Science			
D. Lit. & the Arts			
E. Mathematics			

As soon as you have an idea of when you will be taking the GED Test—or when you would like to take it—write that date after *Test Date* on the last line of the chart below. Then count how many weeks you have to study before that date. Suppose you have ten weeks. Now look again at your scores on the first chart. A grade of 3 *(Risky)* means that you should try to spend three times as many hours studying that subject as you should studying one on which you got a 1 *(Good).* If you gave yourself scores of 3–2–2–2–1, you could spend three weeks on one subject, one week on another, and two weeks on each of the other three. Of course, your scores and the number of weeks you have to study probably will not work out quite as neatly as this. You may have to divide up some of your weeks between two different subjects. But try to give yourself twice as much study time for a *Fair* subject as you did for a *Good* one, and three times as much study time for a *Risky* subject as you did for a *Good* one.

Notice the label *Study Times* in the upper left-hand corner of the chart below. In the tall boxes to the right of it, write the hours you plan to study each day. For instance, if on Mondays you have time to study for the GED Test from 6:30 to 7:15 A.M. and from 8:00 to 10:00 P.M., write those times in two of the four boxes under *Monday.* Four sessions a day, by the way, are enough for even the most determined student!

Now instead of just putting *X*s on your chart in the boxes below your daily study times, try coding your study according to the subject areas you will be concentrating on. On the Grade Chart on the previous page, each subject area was given a letter code. For example, you can use the letter *A* to mark every session in which you plan to study the *Writing Skills* section. To make the subject divisions on your chart even clearer, you could also write each letter with a different-colored marking pen.

It's a good idea to pick one day—or at least a few sessions—of every week as a review period to go over the areas you've already covered. Mark those sessions with an *R* on your chart.

Below you will find suggestions for a logical order in which to study the five subject areas. However, the Time Management Chart has been set up so that you can choose your own order. After all, you are the best judge of what works for you.

Which Subject First? You can organize your study of the five subject areas for the GED Test in the way you consider will be most helpful for you. Here are a few suggestions to consider, however, when you decide what order to follow.

In this book the five GED Test subject areas are arranged in the order you probably will want to follow when you study. Keep in mind that the

Time Management Chart

Study Times		Monday	Tuesday	Wednesday	Thursday	Friday	Saturday	Sunday
Week	Dates							
1								
2								
3								
4								
5								
6								
7								
8								
9								
10								
11								
12								
13								
14								
15								
16								
Test Date:								

GED Test is basically a test of your ability to read and think. For this reason, it's a good idea to begin your study with *Interpreting Literature and the Arts.* The reading skills you acquire in that section, such as how to find the main idea of a passage or how to draw conclusions, will help you a great deal in the *Social Studies* and *Science* sections also. But before you study those two areas, you'll want to complete the second section of the book, *Writing Skills.* In *Writing Skills* you'll learn how to improve your sentences and write logical, well-organized paragraphs and essays. Then in *Social Studies* and *Science* you can practice your skills by writing sentences or short paragraphs about a specific science or social studies topic you've just studied. You'll also build on the reading skills you mastered in *Interpreting Literature and the Arts* by applying what you've read to new situations and analyzing and evaluating passages. The last section of the book, *Mathematics,* is an area for which you'll need those reading skills again. Remember that a big part of getting word problems right is being able to read and understand them. On the Mathematics Test there is even a special type of problem set in which you'll have to read a fairly long passage about a real-life situation involving math. Then you'll answer several word problems based on the information in the passage.

Tools for Success—A Notebook, A Dictionary A number of questions on the GED Test will measure your ability to restate the meaning of a word that is used in a passage. A better vocabulary is a goal worth trying to achieve as you prepare for the test.

Try to make a habit from now on of underlining or highlighting any unfamiliar words you come to in your reading. The best place to start doing that is here in this book if it belongs to you. The advantage of underlining the words you find here is that most of them will be just the type of term you'll find on the GED Test itself. You should also get used to underlining when you read your own newspapers, magazines, or books.

Buy yourself a small pocket-size notebook and jot down every one of those unfamiliar words when you run into them. It's not always easy to try to remember a word later if you don't have a record of it.

Now you can use the help of a dictionary. You may already have one. If you don't, you might want to buy a paperback dictionary that you can carry around with you. That way you can check a definition immediately when you come upon a new word. It's easier to understand the dictionary meaning of an unfamiliar term when you can see that word used in a sentence or paragraph. Write the definition in your notebook and review these additions to your vocabulary at least twice a week. It would be a good idea to mark down at least one vocabulary-review session per week on your Time Management Chart on page 9.

What to Expect from This Book This book is designed specifically to prepare you to pass the GED Test. It is not meant to teach you everything you would learn in four years of high-school classes. *Passing the GED* is not going to give you any information on world history, for example, because the GED Test does not include that subject. This book will teach you *only* what you need to know about the subjects that *are* covered on the test in order to pass the GED Test. Although there are certain types of algebraic equations to which pages and pages could easily be devoted, *Passing the GED* teaches you only what you need to know about those equations to answer correctly the kinds of questions you will find on the GED Test.

Using This Book

Something for Everyone This book is designed to meet the needs of both people who need a great deal of in-depth preparation for the GED Test and people who need only a quick refresher course in the five subject areas. It is also meant to work for all those people who find themselves somewhere between those two extremes. Every reader can use this book in a different way, depending on his or her own strengths and weaknesses. Here's how to make it work for you.

The tinted inner columns on many of the pages in *Passing the GED* contain information and exercises that will help you answer the sample test items (in the white outer columns) that are similar to what you would find in a GED Test. For this reason, **unless you're told otherwise, read the tinted inner column of a page before working on any of the sample test questions in the white outer column.**

Some subject areas will naturally be easier for you than others. Suppose that you read through several pages in a subsection of one subject—say, economics within the *Social Studies* section of your book—and you find that you are doing very well answering the outer-column questions. You might then try skimming the inner-column information, or perhaps skipping it altogether, for the next two pages and answering only the white-column items. You can keep doing this with each new page until you find yourself missing white-column answers more frequently. Then stop and, once again, begin each page by reading the tinted inner column carefully before looking at the white outer column. By working through the entire book this way, you will be able to progress according to your own specific abilities, giving enough attention to the areas in which you need extra help.

This book has been carefully designed to help you in doing just what its title says, *Passing the GED.* The rest of these introductory pages will explain how you can get the most out of your book. If you understand how to use the different sections and components, you will be better prepared to approach the study pages for each subject area.

Where to Begin: The Pretest You will do yourself a big favor if you begin at the beginning. Following these introductory pages you will find a set of subject tests that make up the Pretest. The Pretest will give you an idea of what kind of score you would get on the GED Test if you took it right now—before doing the kind of serious preparation you will be doing with this book. It will also predict which of the five areas will be easy for you and which will require extra study. Once you know that, you can concentrate your energy on the portions of the book that represent your problem areas.

The Pretest has about one-half the number of questions you will find on the actual GED Test. Try to work on the Pretest at a time when you are quite sure you will not be interrupted for about four hours. (Three hours and 45 minutes is about half the time you'll have to do the actual test.) You may find it difficult to put aside so much time for yourself. If this is the case, at least be sure to allow enough time to do one entire subject subtest at one time. The amount of time needed for each subtest is given at the beginning of that test.

Remember as you work through the Pretest to do your best and not to become discouraged. If you don't know an answer, always make a guess. If you use basic common sense when guessing, chances are good that you will pick the correct answer. *Never* leave an answer space blank. On the Pretest you may want to mark the items you guess on so you can read the answer explanations carefully. Then on similar items for other tests in this book, you may not have to guess and will know the answer.

When you complete the Pretest, you will be shown how to interpret your scores. Then you will be given an individualized method for using this book to your best advantage. This will help you make the most of your study time and to progress in a logical way toward your ultimate goal of passing the GED Test.

Following the Pretest you will find the real "meat" of this book, the pages that cover the five subject areas. Take a minute now to notice how those pages are marked, or coded, to make it easier for you to keep track of where you are. The colored strip on the outside of each page marks a subject area; five different colors are used for this purpose. A sixth color is used on these introductory pages.

This coding should make it easy for you to find sections when paging through the book. Another guide for you is given at the top of each page. For example, if you turn to page 305 of the *Social Studies* section, you will notice that the head at the top reads U.S. History/Industrialization. If you turn to page 107 in the *Interpreting Literature and the Arts* section, you will find the head Fiction/Setting. In these heads, the first term is a reference to a subtopic of that test. (Fiction, for example, is a subtopic of the Test of Interpreting Literature and the Arts.) The second term is a reference to the part of the subtopic covered on that particular page. The setting of novels, short stories, and other works of fiction is the subtopic being discussed on that page.

Subject Section "Opener" Pages The very first page in every one of the five subject sections gives you general information about that subject and about the relevant GED Test. It explains any special elements that you will find only in that section of your book.

Overview Pages Following this "opener" page you are likely to find some color-tinted overview pages. These pages will give you a preview of the kinds of questions you'll be dealing with in the pages that follow. The overview pages include plenty of suggestions on how to approach those questions and lots of examples with explanations. These pages are designed to start you out on the right foot in that subject. They often include special sections that explain unique features of certain subtests. For example, the *Science* overview has several pages on answering questions about diagrams because there are so many questions of that type on the GED Science Test. The *Social Studies* overview gives you a chance to work with every type of graph you'll find on the GED Social Studies Test (and there are plenty of graphs on that test!). In this way, you'll already feel comfortable with graphs before you begin dealing with information about, say, economics or political science.

Instructional—Test Practice Pages Once you've carefully read the overview pages for a subject, you're ready to begin the pages that give you background information on a topic, exercises to reinforce that learning, and practice with sample GED questions about that topic. These are the pages in your book that have a color-tinted inner column and a white outer column. The tinted column contains information that you need to study in order to be familiar with important general concepts about a subject. The outer column gives you practice in answering sample GED questions about the same topic you just studied. Remember to read the tinted column first unless you're told otherwise.

You'll find several kinds of instructional information in the color-tinted inner columns. Every element of the instructional information is designed to help you quickly understand the basics of a subject and to remember what you learn about it in an organized way.

First the tinted columns give you important general background information on the subject. For example, in *Interpreting Literature and the Arts* you will read explanations and study examples of how to find the main idea, or of what to look for when you read a poem or a play. In the *Writing Skills* section you will learn how to create effective sentences, paragraphs, and essays. You will also be given examples of good writing. In the *Social Studies* section an example of background information is the summary of a chapter in our nation's past that you are given on each page of U.S. history. In the *Science* section an example would be the traits of different forms of life you'll find in the biology subsection. Both social studies and science are fields with specialized vocabularies. Reading the background information will help you approach those vocabularies with confidence. And in the *Mathematics* section, the background information consists of step-by-step instructions on how to do various types of problems. The best news about all these readings is that they are interesting and informative, not dry or dull.

The headings that follow indicate the other kinds of instructional information you'll find in the tinted columns.

Warm-up

Following an instructional section, you will often find a *Warm-up*. The Warm-up allows you to practice what you have just learned and to prove to yourself that you really have learned it. You may be asked to write summaries or to answer questions. The Warm-up questions will reinforce what you've just learned in the information section before you try the sample GED questions on the same subject in the white outer column.

If you miss any Warm-up questions, you should go back and carefully review the previous section where the information is found. Make sure you understand why your answer was wrong before going on to the additional instructional information that follows. Remember that the Warm-up exercises are meant to be "self-checks." They let you know if you have understood what you just read. If you don't take the time to go back and find out what caused your error, chances are that you will make another one on a similar question later on as a result of the same misunderstanding. That same error will appear in your answers to the sample GED questions in the outer column of the same page as the Warm-up exercise or on the Posttests or, worse yet, maybe in an answer on the actual GED Test.

Warm-up Answers

You can check the answers you have given for each Warm-up quickly and easily in the *Warm-up Answers* listed at the bottom of the same tinted column. You do not have to turn pages to find answers for Warm-up questions. Because they are really drills to prepare you for "the real thing," the sample GED questions in the white columns of the page, the answers are right there where you can check them immediately and then move to the sample GED questions. If there are many possible right answers for a Warm-up, answers will be labeled *Sample Warm-up Answers.* You *will* have to flip pages to find the answers for the sample GED questions in the outer white columns of the page, although you need not look at those answers until you have completed the questions on two facing pages of your book.

Coming to Terms

You will not find long lists of definitions in this book. This is because the GED questions are worded so that you don't have to memorize many terms ahead of time. For that reason, you should not use your study time to do that sort of thing. On some pages, however, you will find a *Coming to Terms* component that presents definitions to some basic specialized words. It may also give suggestions for how to approach unfamiliar words in a selection.

You do not have to memorize these terms. You should, however, try to learn the meaning of each one. You can do this by reading the definition twice, thinking about it, and then reading it again.

Sometimes the *Coming to Terms* component will be followed by a Warm-up exercise. This allows you to check whether you have really understood the definitions by asking you to apply them to real-life situations. If you turn to page 274 of the *Social Studies* section, you will find a Warm-up exercise for the *Coming to Terms* component on that same page. Notice that the answers for that Warm-up can be found in the Warm-up Answers section at the bottom of the page.

☑ Test-Taking Tips

Another component you will find in the tinted column of your instructional pages is *A Test-Taking Tip* or *Test-Taking Tips.* These tips are practical suggestions about how to approach a certain type of question. They often show you how to use plain common sense to arrive at an answer, even when the subject isn't your favorite or your best. The Test-Taking Tip on page 349 is an example of the sort of thing you can expect to find under that heading.

With all these "helps" in the tinted columns, you can move to the white test-item columns confident that you are prepared to deal with those passages, visuals, and questions, all of which are the same kind you will find on the actual GED Test. The white-column items are designed to *look* like those on the real test. After all, you don't need to have any surprises—even small ones—on the day you take the test.

The only difference you *will* find on that day is that you will be asked to mark your answer for each question that appears in the test booklet on a separate answer sheet (one for each of the five subject areas). The answer sheet will have five numbered ovals for every question on that part of the test.

If you flip through this book now, you will notice that right after each question in the white test columns there are five numbered ovals for your answer.

Need a Hint?

Some test questions will, naturally, be more difficult than others. Often, however, you could find the correct answer to a real "stickler" if you just had a little nudge in the right direction. This nudge is what you get in the component called *Need a Hint?* that precedes Warm-up Answers in the tinted columns of some pages. The hint is never a "giveaway." Rather, it offers you a chance to use your thinking skills to reason out an answer. It often asks you another question or reminds you of a way to think about a problem.

The *Need a Hint?* component at the bottom of page 426 in the *Mathematics* section is a good example of this sort of nudge. Notice that you can tell for which question or test item the hint is being given by the heading—in this case, Need a Hint for Number 10?

These hints will always appear in a white box near the bottom of the tinted column. If you are having real problems with a sample GED question in a white column, check to see if you can find a hint for it on the same page. If you can answer the test-column questions without much difficulty, try to overlook any hints in the tinted columns. You don't want to become too dependent on this extra help.

Later on, in the sections of this book called Minitests and at the end of the book in the Posttests, you will not be given any hints. There you will be checking your performance answering questions under conditions as similar as possible to those of the actual GED Test.

Answers for Sample Test Items
The *Answers* section for all the white-column sample test questions in each subject section is at the end of that section. There you can find not only each correct answer, but also an explanation of why it makes sense. You may want to read each explanation, even if you get the answer right. This helps you check your own thought processes and reinforces what you have already learned. And finally, it gives you additional confidence in your ability to make sound judgments.

It's always best to check your test-column answers every time you finish two columns. If you do, you'll know right away if you're running into difficulties. If you are, you can devote more attention to the instructional information in the tinted columns of those two pages.

Minitests
After you've completed all the components of one of the subject areas, you will have a chance to deal with passages, visuals, and questions from all those components at once, just as you will be doing on the GED Test. The *Minitests* section for each subject gives you the opportunity to do just that. Before taking the final tests, the Posttests, you will be able to measure how much you have learned and whether you need to review more before attempting them.

There are several Minitests for each subject within the Minitests section. Each Minitest is, as the name suggests, short—only about three pages. But each includes the same mix of questions from the different topics covered in a subject area that will appear on the real GED Test.

How should you use the Minitests? You may want to take one or two of the Minitests and then, after checking your answers at the end of the Minitests for that subject area and determining your score, you can review the material, or portions of it, for that subject area. Then, when you feel you have overcome your weaknesses, you can take another Minitest to see if your score improves. Continue this check-and-review process until you complete all the Minitests and have continued to raise your scores on them by reviewing the kinds of questions that gave you problems.

Another good way to use the Minitests is to take just one or two of them when you finish your study of one of the five subject areas. Then "save" the others for review sessions, days on which you come back to subject areas you've already studied to refresh your memory.

Where to End: The Posttests After you've finished studying all the subject areas and completed the Minitests that are in your course of study, you should make an appointment with yourself to take the first Posttest. When you finish, check your answers. Then find your score and the explanation of your results. If you didn't pass, you can review those sections of the book for which you still need practice. The second Posttest can be used to sharpen your test-taking skills.

Twenty-four Tips for Passing the GED Test

In addition to the Test-Taking Tips you'll find scattered throughout the tinted columns of the pages to come, here are some ideas about ways to guarantee your success on the GED Test. Some involve planning you can do far in advance of the test, others relate to ways you can strengthen your position immediately before the exam, and the last group of suggestions is for you to follow during the actual GED Test.

Long-Range Planning

1. Give yourself plenty of time to prepare for your GED Test. Don't be overconfident and think you can do all your studying in one weekend. Your mind can't continue to function at its peak if you cram too much into it at once.

2. When deciding what areas to study and when, always remember to set aside certain sessions to review the material you have already covered. Another good reason, then, to do the *Interpreting Literature and the Arts* section first is that you will be able to review the reading skills frequently. You can never devote too much time to this section because you need to keep those skills sharp for the Social Studies and Science tests as well.

3. If you can, have your eyes checked before you begin your preparation for the GED Test. All your knowledge and ability may not help you if you have a vision problem and end up misreading some of the questions.

4. Try starting out by working through about four to six pages of this book at one sitting. Don't spend more than an hour each time until you are sure that studying this amount of material doesn't upset you or wear you out. Begin slowly and build your endurance. Preparing for the GED Test is, in this sense, like preparing for running a marathon race.

5. Every person studies best at a different speed. For this reason, only you can decide how long to spend on each section of this book. You may be able to do ten pages in one area much more quickly than you can do ten pages in another. How can you evaluate your progress and decide if you are moving through a section at the right speed? If you are answering most of the test-column questions correctly, you are mastering the material.

6. It's always better to feel overprepared than underprepared. You will tend to be more nervous if you think you haven't prepared enough, and you may miss questions just because of that anxiety.

Short-Range Planning—The Last 24 Hours

1. If you have prepared for a long time in advance, as you should have, it's a good idea to do something relaxing the night before the test to get your mind off your study. You might want to go to a movie or to a sports event.

2. Getting a good night's sleep before the exam is one of the best things you can do for yourself. Cramming or studying too much in a short time is not a wise strategy for any exam. It doesn't make sense at all for one like the GED Test. For the GED Test you must rely primarily on your ability to read and think carefully and to use good common sense. A good night's sleep will help you to do just that.

3. Eat a good nutritious meal before showing up for the test. You won't do yourself any favors by eating a candy bar at the last minute after not having eaten well for hours. The protein in foods such as meat, milk, eggs, or yogurt will keep you alert during the exam. (Research has proven that it's not true that drinking milk makes people sleepy.) Avoid starches and carbohydrates—foods like french fries, noodles, cookies, and cakes. These foods may give you a quick burst of energy, but after that, you will find yourself feeling run down. And that's not the way you want to feel during a long exam. It's not smart to drink too much coffee either. After an initial "high," you'll be left feeling nervous and tired.

4. Don't dress too warmly when you go to take the test. Psychologists have found that if people feel slightly cool, they tend to do better on a test. You may become drowsy if you are too warm.

5. Show up for the test on time, but try not to arrive early. If you have to be at the test center early, don't get involved talking with others about the test. You will only increase your own tension by talking to others about their anxieties.

6. Try to sit near a window if possible. This way you may be able to open the window if you get warm. Fresh air will help keep you alert. In addition, if you're taking your test during the daylight hours, you'll have the advantage of being able to read by natural light, which is always easier on your eyes than artificial light.

During the Test

1. Always be sure to read the directions at the beginning of each section of your GED Test because the directions are not quite the same in every section. It is important to understand exactly what you should be looking for in each test item.

2. Be sure to answer *every* question on the test. Your scores will be based on the number of answers you get right; you do not get any points taken off for marking wrong answers. *Never leave a question unanswered at the end of your exam.*

3. Read the questions carefully. If necessary, read each question more than once before going on to read the answer options. If you don't understand the question, almost any answer can end up looking right.

4. Try to answer the question for yourself *before* you read the five possible choices. After you decide what you think the answer should be, match your idea to the possibilities and pick the one that is more similar.

5. For each of the tests, you may first want to go through and answer the questions that are easy for you. You can then go back and answer those that you thought would take you more time. *Warning:* If you follow this suggestion, be very careful to mark the answer space whose number is the same as that of the question you are answering. Test-takers tend to skip one question, say number 19, but they forget to skip an answer on the answer sheet. Then, when they mark the answer for question number 20, they put that answer by mistake in the next space—the space for number 19. You can probably guess what happens next—their answers to all the following problems are also in the wrong spaces. If they don't catch the problem, they can actually fail the test just because of this mix-up. Don't let it happen to you. *Make sure that you have the right answer in the right answer space.*

6. The authors of the GED Test have tried to choose passages that are not dull. However, no one can please all the people all the time. Remember that if you come to an especially difficult passage, or to one that just isn't of much interest to you, you should try extra hard. It's just human nature to want to skip over parts of reading material that don't really have any appeal, but if you allow yourself to do that on the GED Test, you could lose points and risk not getting a passing score.

7. From time to time breathe deeply and stretch. Did you know that stretching is the most natural exercise to help you feel refreshed and relaxed?

8. When you come to a reading passage followed by questions, try reading the questions (not the answer options) first. Then when you read the passage, you will know what to look for as you go. This approach will make it easier for you to choose answers quickly and, consequently, will give you some extra time to think more about questions that are difficult.

9. In multiple-choice tests that have five answer options, like the GED Test, you can usually eliminate three of the options quite easily. Then it becomes a problem of deciding between two very logical-looking options. If you really can't make up your mind about which of two good options is best, make a good guess. Remember that by answering this way, you have a better than 50 percent chance of getting the right answer because hunches, after all, are one way of arriving at legitimate conclusions.

10. Some GED questions are missed only because test-takers don't mark answer sheets correctly. In some places the answers are corrected by a machine that can recognize only a completely filled-in space as a correct answer. If the machine sees an answer that is marked in some other way—like this (1), or like this (●), or like this (X)—it cannot count that mark as a correct answer.

Remember that the machine is fair. However, if you confuse it with markings that it does not understand, it will mark your answer wrong even if it is correct. To avoid this, fill in the space so that the answer is definitely clear, but not so hard that you can't erase later if you want to change an answer. Check to make sure you have not made any extra marks near that answer or filled in any other space in that row of choices.

When you write your GED essay, make sure your handwriting is neat enough to be read. It doesn't have to look perfect, and you can cross out words and phrases, but if the scorers can't read your essay, they have to give a score of 0.

11. Try to stick to your first impressions. Don't change your answers once you've marked them unless you have lots of uncertainties about any one you've marked. Only when you have very strong doubts is your second answer likely to be correct.

12. Some people work faster, though not necessarily more accurately, than others. If you manage to finish early, don't turn in your test. Use every minute you have to go back and check your answers.

The Pretest

The *Pretest* on the following pages has one-half as many questions for each subject as the official GED Test, as well as a full-length essay assignment. Each subject test also takes half the time to complete as the official test does, except for the Writing Skills Test; you will be given the full amount of time to write your essay. Be sure to notice the time limits given at the beginning of the five subject tests, and don't let yourself go beyond those limits. You want to make certain that your scores accurately reflect your ability, so it is important to work straight through each test in the time given.

After you have taken each test and scored it using the Answer Key that follows the tests, you will find a special feature of this book very helpful—the Answer Explanations for the *Pretest* on pages 65–72. Read all the explanations, even the ones for the answers you marked correctly. They will give you worthwhile tips about how to approach the kinds of questions that will appear on the GED Test.

TEST 1: WRITING SKILLS PRETEST

Directions

The *Writing Skills Pretest* consists of 28 multiple-choice questions and an essay. It is intended to measure your ability to use clear and effective English. It is a test of English as it is usually written, not as it might be spoken. Specific directions are given at the beginning of each part. Read these directions carefully before you begin.

You should take approximately 40 minutes to complete the multiple-choice questions. There is no penalty for guessing. Try to answer as many questions as you can. Work rapidly but carefully, without spending too much time on any one question. If a question is too difficult for you, skip it and come back to it later.

For each answer, mark one answer space.

EXAMPLE

The intelligens of computers is different from that of human beings.

What correction should be made to this sentence?

(1) change the spelling of intelligens to intelligence
(2) change is to are
(3) change the spelling of different to diffrent
(4) insert a comma after that
(5) no correction is necessary

● (2) (3)  

The correct answer is (1); therefore, answer space (1) has been marked.

You should take no more than 45 minutes to complete the essay section of the test. Space is provided for writing your essay, or you can use a separate sheet of paper.

When you have completed the test, check your answers against the Answer Key on page 61. Explanations for the answers and a sample essay are on pages 65–67.

Part I

Directions: The following items are based on paragraphs that contain numbered sentences. Some of the sentences contain errors in sentence structure, usage, or mechanics. A few sentences, however, are correct as written. Read each paragraph and then answer the items based on it. For each item, choose the answer that would result in the most effective writing of the sentence or sentences. The best answer must be consistent with the meaning and tone of the rest of the paragraph.

Items 1–10 refer to the following paragraph.

(1) How will our ever-increasing technology change the job scene in the latter part of this century? (2) Of course we know that, computers will change the way most of us make a living. (3) Computerized robots are already taking over many factory jobs, we are all familiar with this trend. (4) But there is many jobs on the way out that are not so obviously connected to technology. (5) Believe it or not, computer programmers have become obsolete because a new generation of computers capable of programming themselves will be built. (6) The farm laborers of the future will be an automated army of robot field hands and the farmer of the future will sit in a computerized control tower to schedule plantings and harvests. (7) Many lumberjacks will be jobless, as you will be using computers, rather than paper, to store information such as books, magazines, and newspapers. (8) Even doctors will be affected by computerized technology. (9) The University of Pittsburgh is experimenting with a program called "Doctor on a Chip" to help in diagnosing illnesses and prescribing treatments. (10) Fast-food restaurants are increasing in numbers, but fast-food workers will lose their jobs as they become more automated. (11) The hamburger will be "your way," but it will be cooked, packaged, and ready to deliver by a worker built of aluminum and guided by a microchip. (12) For better or worse, technology will definately change our lives, but by planning ahead, we can keep from joining the unemployment line.

1. Sentence 2: **Of course we know that, computers will change the way most of us will make a living.**

   What correction should be made to this sentence?

   (1) change the spelling of course to coarse
   (2) insert a comma after course
   (3) remove the comma after that
   (4) insert a comma after us
   (5) no correction is necessary

   (1) (2) (3) (4) (5)

2. Sentence 3: **Computerized robots are already taking over many factory jobs, we are all familiar with this trend.**

   Which of the following is the best way to write the underlined portion of this sentence? If you think the original is the best way to write the sentence, choose option (1).

   (1) jobs, we
   (2) jobs because we
   (3) jobs, however, we
   (4) jobs since we
   (5) jobs; we

   (1) (2) (3) (4) (5)

3. Sentence 4: **But there is many jobs on the way out that are not so obviously connected to technology.**

   What correction should be made to this sentence?

   (1) replace there with they're
   (2) change is to are
   (3) insert a comma after jobs
   (4) replace that with who
   (5) no correction is necessary

   (1) (2) (3) (4) (5)

4. Sentence 5: **Believe it or not, computer programmers have become obsolete because a new generation of computers capable of programming themselves will be built.**

   What correction should be made to this sentence?

   (1) change the spelling of Believe to Beleive
   (2) replace have with will
   (3) insert a comma after obsolete
   (4) replace because with whenever
   (5) replace built with builded

   (1) (2) (3) (4) (5)

GO ON TO THE NEXT PAGE.

5. Sentence 6: **The farm laborers of the future will be an automated army of robot field hands and the farmer of the future will sit in a computerized control tower to schedule plantings and harvests.**

   Which of the following is the best way to write the underlined portion of this sentence? If you think the original is the best way to write the sentence, choose option (1).

   (1) hands and
   (2) hands, yet
   (3) hands; and
   (4) hands, and
   (5) hands because

   (1) (2) (3) (4) (5)

6. Sentence 7: **Many lumberjacks will be jobless, as you will be using computers, rather than paper, to store information such as books, magazines, and newspapers.**

   Which of the following is the best way to write the underlined portion of this sentence? If you think the original is the best way to write the sentence, choose option (1).

   (1) as you will be
   (2) as they will be
   (3) as we will be
   (4) as one will be
   (5) as each will be

   (1) (2) (3) (4) (5)

7. Sentence 8: **Even doctors will be affected by computerized technology.**

   What correction should be made to this sentence?

   (1) change doctors to Doctors
   (2) insert a comma after doctors
   (3) remove the word will
   (4) replace affected with effected
   (5) no correction is necessary

   (1) (2) (3) (4) (5)

8. Sentence 10: **Fast-food restaurants are increasing in numbers, but fast-food workers will lose their jobs as they become more automated.**

   What correction should be made to this sentence?

   (1) change are to is
   (2) remove the comma after numbers
   (3) replace but with since
   (4) replace they with restaurants
   (5) change become to have become

   (1) (2) (3) (4) (5)

9. Sentence 11: **The hamburger will be "your way," but it will be cooked, packaged, and ready to deliver by a worker built of aluminum and guided by a microchip.**

   If you rewrote sentence 11 beginning with

   A hamburger ordered "your way" will be cooked, packaged, and

   the next word should be

   (1) delivered
   (2) will
   (3) ready
   (4) could
   (5) be

   (1) (2) (3) (4) (5)

10. Sentence 12: **For better or worse, technology will definately change our lives, but by planning ahead, we can keep from joining the unemployment line.**

    What correction should be made to this sentence?

    (1) remove the comma after worse
    (2) change the spelling of definately to definitely
    (3) remove the comma after lives
    (4) replace but with which
    (5) replace we with you

    (1) (2) (3) (4) (5)

GO ON TO THE NEXT PAGE.

Items 11–19 refer to the following paragraph.

(1) There have never been a sight to match it: silently, gracefully, the huge, majestic airships glided overhead. (2) The age of the zeppelin was brief, it was glorious. (3) It began when a German graf, or count, Ferdinand von Zeppelin, took a balloon ride in St. Paul, Minnesota, shortly after the Civil War. (4) Graf von Zeppelin returned to Europe after his trip to the United States. (5) And then after he returned, he began to draw up plans for a dirigible. (6) A dirigible is a rigid, steerable, lighter-than-air aircraft far superior to the traditional "pressure" airships known as blimps. (7) Perhaps the most successful airship of them all was the *Graf Zeppelin,* built in Germany in 1924. (8) Almost 800 feet long and 100 feet in diameter, the *Graf* was beautifully designed reliable, and probably the greatest mail carrier ever known. (9) On its first flight to the United States in 1928, it carried 65,714 pieces of mail and on its return it brought 101,683 letters and postcards. (10) The *Graf* was also a fine passenger ship, with accommodations far more spacious and luxurious than those of today's jumbo jets. (11) Passengers cruising around the world in the *Graf* felt almost no motion and had unparalleled, close-range views of the terrain below. (12) Will the day of the zeppelin ever return? (13) The zeppelin does seem well-suited to the 1980s and 1990s because they are fuel-efficient, relatively nonpolluting, almost noiseless, and able to take off and land in a small area.

11. Sentence 1: **There have never been a sight to match it: silently, gracefully, the huge, majestic airships glided overhead.**

    What correction should be made to this sentence?

    (1) replace There with They're
    (2) change have to has
    (3) remove the word have
    (4) replace sight with site
    (5) no correction is necessary

    (1) (2) (3) (4) (5)

12. Sentence 2: **The age of the zeppelin was brief, it was glorious.**

    Which of the following is the best way to write the underlined portion of this sentence? If you think the original is the best way, choose option (1).

    (1) brief, it
    (2) brief it
    (3) brief. It
    (4) brief since it
    (5) brief, but it

    (1) (2) (3) (4) (5)

13. Sentence 3: **It began when a German graf, or count, Ferdinand von Zeppelin, took a balloon ride in St. Paul, Minnesota, shortly after the Civil War.**

    What correction should be made to this sentence?

    (1) change began to begun
    (2) change took to takes
    (3) change the spelling of balloon to baloon
    (4) change War to war
    (5) no correction is necessary

    (1) (2) (3) (4) (5)

14. Sentences 4 and 5: **Graf von Zeppelin returned to Europe after his trip to the United States. And then after he returned, he began to draw up plans for a dirigible.**

    The most effective combination of sentences 4 and 5 would include which of the following groups of words?

    (1) Upon returning to Europe, he began
    (2) returned to Europe and then began
    (3) returning to Europe and drawing up plans
    (4) Plans were drawn up after he returned
    (5) He returned to Europe, beginning to

    (1) (2) (3) (4) (5)

GO ON TO THE NEXT PAGE.

15. Sentence 7: **Perhaps the most sucessful airship of them all was the *Graf Zeppelin*, built in Germany in 1924.**

What correction should be made to this sentence?

(1) change the spelling of sucessful to successful
(2) change was to were
(3) change was to be
(4) change Germany to germany
(5) no correction is necessary

(1) (2) (3) (4) (5)

16. Sentence 8: **Almost 800 feet long and 100 feet in diameter, the *Graf* was beautifully designed reliable, and probably the greatest mail carrier ever known.**

What correction should be made to this sentence?

(1) insert a comma after long
(2) remove the comma after diameter
(3) change the spelling of beautifully to beautifuly
(4) insert a comma after designed
(5) no correction is necessary

(1) (2) (3) (4) (5)

17. Sentence 9: **On its first flight to the United States in 1928, it carried 65,714 pieces of mail and on its return it brought 101,683 letters and postcards.**

Which of the following is the best way to write the underlined portion of this sentence? If you think the original is the best way, choose option (1).

(1) mail and on
(2) mail, and on
(3) mail on
(4) mail, on
(5) mail, yet on

(1) (2) (3) (4) (5)

18. Sentence 11: **Passengers cruising around the world in the *Graf* felt almost no motion and had unparalleled, close-range views of the terrain below.**

Which of the following is the best way to write the underlined portion of this sentence? If you think the original is the best way, choose option (1).

(1) and had
(2) or had
(3) yet had
(4) having
(5) and will have

(1) (2) (3) (4) (5)

19. Sentence 13: **The zeppelin does seem well-suited to the 1980s and 1990s because they are fuel-efficient, relatively nonpolluting, almost noiseless, and able to take off and land in a small area.**

Which of the following is the best way to write the underlined portion of this sentence? If you think the original is the best way, choose option (1).

(1) they are
(2) they is
(3) it be
(4) it is
(5) one is

(1) (2) (3) (4) (5)

GO ON TO THE NEXT PAGE.

Items 20–28 refer to the following paragraph.

(1) There exists, in nutrition needs, a real gender gap, even though this is an age of equality. (2) Recent studies emphasize that both men and women in the United States commonly consume less than the average reccommended calorie intake, yet they maintain normal weight or may even be overweight. (3) Why this is so is not clear, whatever the reason, this lower-than-average calorie intake poses more of a weight problem for women than for men. (4) A man who consumes 2,400 calories a day can obtain all necessary nutrients more easily than a woman who consumes 1,600 calories or less daily. (5) Consequently, women should eat food that is more nutrient-dense. (6) The difference in the calorie needs of women and men lies in differences in body size, in body composition, and in the amount of energy expended through physical activity. (7) Researchers have found a lot of interesting information. (8) They say that it is more likely that women will tend to be overweight or obese more so than men. (9) This finding probably explains why dieting has become so common among them. (10) The social advantages of being slender are well known, and the health risks connected with obesity are many, including higher incidences of diabetes, getting heart disease, and cancer. (11) But dieters should bear in mind that the safest and most effective way to loose weight is to eat a balanced diet but to eat less, while increasing physical activity. (12) The Food and Nutrition Board has stated that diets below 1,200 calories a day should be used only under the guidance of a physician or other health professional, because it is difficult to select a diet providing all essential nutrients at this calorie level.

20. Sentence 1: **There exists, in nutrition needs, a real gender gap, even though this is an age of equality.**

    If you rewrote sentence 1 beginning with

    Even in this age of equality, a real gender gap

    the next words should be

    (1) exists there
    (2) there exists
    (3) exists in
    (4) really exists
    (5) is really existing

    (1) (2) (3) (4) (5)

21. Sentence 2: **Recent studies emphasize that both men and women in the United States commonly consume less than the average reccommended calorie intake, yet they maintain normal weight or may even be overweight.**

    What correction should be made to this sentence?

    (1) change the spelling of emphasize to emfasize
    (2) change consume to consumes
    (3) change consume to consuming
    (4) change the spelling of reccommended to recommended
    (5) change the spelling of reccommended to reccomended

    (1) (2) (3) (4) (5)

22. Sentence 3: **Why this is so is not clear, whatever the reason, this lower-than-average calorie intake poses more of a weight problem for women than for men.**

    Which of the following is the best way to write the underlined portion of this sentence? If you think the original is the best way, choose option (1).

    (1) clear, whatever
    (2) clear whatever
    (3) clear. Whatever
    (4) clear because whatever
    (5) clear, and whatever

23. Sentence 6: **The difference in the calorie needs of women and men lies in differences in body size, in body composition, and in the amount of energy expended through physical activity.**

    What correction should be made to this sentence?

    (1) insert a comma after women
    (2) change lies to lie
    (3) remove the comma after size
    (4) change the spelling of amount to ammount
    (5) no correction is necessary

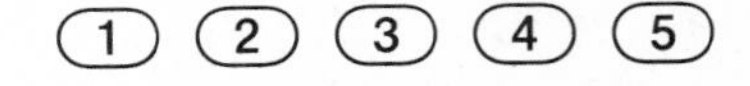

GO ON TO THE NEXT PAGE.

24. Sentences 7 and 8: **Researchers have found a lot of interesting information. They say that it is more likely that women will tend to be overweight or obese more so than men.**

The most effective combination of sentences 7 and 8 would include which of the following groups of words?

(1) found that women are more likely to
(2) finding out
(3) interesting information is
(4) men will tend
(5) obesity and women

(1) (2) (3) (4) (5)

25. Sentence 9: **This finding probably explains why dieting has become so common among them.**

What correction should be made to this sentence?

(1) change explains to had explained
(2) insert a comma after explains
(3) change become to became
(4) change the spelling of among to amung
(5) replace them with women

(1) (2) (3) (4) (5)

26. Sentence 10: **The social advantages of being slender are well known, and the health risks connected with obesity are many, including higher incidences of diabetes, getting heart disease, and cancer.**

What correction should be made to this sentence?

(1) change are to is
(2) replace and with however
(3) remove the word getting
(4) change the spelling of disease to desease
(5) change cancer to Cancer

(1) (2) (3) (4) (5)

27. Sentence 11: **But dieters should bear in mind that the safest and most effective way to loose weight is to eat a balanced diet but to eat less, while increasing physical activity.**

What correction should be made to this sentence?

(1) insert a comma after mind
(2) change the spelling of effective to affective
(3) replace loose with lose
(4) change the spelling of balanced to ballanced
(5) change to eat to eating

(1) (2) (3) (4) (5)

28. Sentence 12: **The Food and Nutrition Board has stated that diets below 1,200 calories a day should be used only under the guidance of a physician or other health professional, because it is difficult to select a diet providing all essential nutrients at this calorie level.**

Which of the following is the best way to write the underlined portion of this sentence? If you think the original is the best way, choose option (1).

(1) professional, because
(2) professional because
(3) professional. Because
(4) professional; because
(5) professional because,

(1) (2) (3) (4) (5)

GO ON TO THE NEXT PAGE.

Part II

Directions: This is a test to find out how well you write. The test has one question that asks you to present an opinion on an issue or to explain something. In preparing your answer for this question, you should take the following steps:

1. Read all of the information accompanying the question.
2. Plan your answer carefully before you write.
3. Use scratch paper to make any notes.
4. Write your answer.
5. Read carefully what you have written to make any changes that will improve your writing.
6. Check your paragraphing, sentence structure, spelling, punctuation, capitalization, and usage, and make any necessary corrections.

You will have 45 minutes to write on the question you are assigned. Write legibly and use a ballpoint pen.

More and more people change jobs every few years. Discuss the advantages and disadvantages of changing jobs frequently as opposed to staying with one company. Write your ideas in a 200-word essay.

END OF EXAMINATION

TEST 2: SOCIAL STUDIES PRETEST

Directions

The *Social Studies Pretest* consists of 32 multiple-choice questions. Some of the questions are based on maps, graphs, charts, cartoons, and short reading passages—all related to the social studies. Read the passage or study the material first and then answer the questions following it. You may refer to these materials as often as necessary to answer the questions. You will find that some of the questions will require considerable deliberation and frequent rereading of the passage or reexamination of the material presented.

This is a test of your ability to understand, analyze, and evaluate what you see and read. In general, the test will not penalize you seriously for having forgotten many of the detailed facts you once knew, if you have retained the important generalizations and are able to use them intelligently.

You should take approximately 45 minutes to complete this test. There is no penalty for guessing. Try to answer as many questions as you can. Work rapidly but carefully, without spending too much time on any one question. If a question is too difficult for you, omit it and come back to it later.

For each answer, mark one answer space. See how the following example is done.

EXAMPLE

Zoning laws are passed by local governments to ensure the orderly development of land and property. Zoning boards divide cities into zones that group together similar uses. For example, there might be one zone for homes, another for business, another for industry, and so on. Certain types of construction are allowed in some zones but not in others.

According to the passage, which of the following cases would come under local zoning laws?

(1) A driver must pay toll charges to use a state highway.
(2) A property owner must pay taxes to the state.
(3) A mountainous region in Colorado is designated a wilderness area by the U.S. Department of the Interior.
(4) A homeowner must pay for garbage pickup.
(5) A department store wants to expand by building an addition.

Options (1), (2), and (3) concern state or national governments not local ones. Option (4) does not relate to zoning laws, but to sanitation. Only option (5), which involves construction, relates to zoning laws. Answer space (5) has been marked.

Answers to the questions are in the Answer Key on page 61. Explanations for the answers are on pages 67–68.

Directions: Choose the one best answer to each question.

Items 1–2 refer to the following passage.

The first tall buildings, often rising to ten or more stories, were built in the traditional way, with thick walls supporting the weight of the building. As the buildings became taller, the walls had to become thicker. The end of the line was reached in Chicago in 1886. The Monadnock Building soared to sixteen stories and required walls six feet thick on the ground level. These immense walls of stone and brick used up valuable floor space throughout the building. But in 1883, William LeBaron Jenney developed a solution to the problem: the steel-frame building. With the weight of the building supported on a metal skeleton, walls could be thinner and windows larger. Other improvements quickly followed, enabling buildings to reach higher and higher into the sky.

1. Which statement below best explains what is meant by the sentence "The end of the line was reached in Chicago in 1886"?
   (1) Architects could not make the walls any thicker than six feet.
   (2) Building mishaps caused an end to the construction of tall buildings in Chicago.
   (3) For the last time, thick-walled construction was used to build a tall building.
   (4) Traditional construction methods took up too much floor space.
   (5) Traditional building methods made interiors dark because buildings could have no windows.

   ① ② ③ ④ ⑤

2. Which of the following facts probably contributed to this new construction method?
   (1) By 1900, 40 percent of the U.S. population lived in cities.
   (2) In the late 1800s, new techniques made the production of large quantities of fine quality steel possible.
   (3) Architect Frank Lloyd Wright was born in 1869.
   (4) Andrew Carnegie became the leading producer of steel and dominated the industry by 1890.
   (5) After the great Chicago Fire of 1871, cities developed building codes that required more fireproof construction.

   ① ② ③ ④ ⑤

Items 3–4 refer to the following passage.

Whatever the individual styles of Presidents, the presidency is still held in awe by most Americans. Its powers have been expanded far beyond the brief and somewhat vague words of the Constitution. This expansion of presidential powers is due to a number of factors: the actions and outlooks of individual Presidents, the expanded federal role in domestic and economic affairs, the emergence of the United States as a world power in the nuclear age, and a rise in public expectations concerning the presidency in an era of mass communication.

3. Which statement below best expresses the author's conclusion?
   (1) This expansion of presidential powers is due to a number of factors.
   (2) There is an expanded federal role in domestic and economic affairs.
   (3) The United States has emerged as a world power.
   (4) The powers of the presidency have been expanded far beyond the brief, vague words of the Constitution.
   (5) Mass communication has caused a rise in public expectations concerning the presidency.

   ① ② ③ ④ ⑤

4. Based on the information in the passage, what would you predict regarding presidential powers?
   (1) The presidency will retain its expanded powers.
   (2) The Supreme Courts will curb the powers of the presidency.
   (3) Future Presidents will serve more than two terms, thus increasing their power.
   (4) Congress will limit the President's powers and expand its own.
   (5) Voters will demand a constitutional amendment defining the powers of the President.

   ① ② ③ ④ ⑤

GO ON TO THE NEXT PAGE.

Items 5–7 refer to the following information.

A neurosis is an emotional disturbance or disorder characterized by extreme anxiety or fear. Below are the names and definitions of several types of neuroses.

(1) obsession—a thought or mental image that won't go away and becomes so insistent and disturbing that it interferes with a person's life

(2) compulsion—behavior consisting of repetitive, ritualistic actions that serve no rational purpose

(3) phobia—an unreasonable fear or dread of something that most people find tolerable and that persists even when there is no actual danger

(4) hypochondriasis—an unrealistic fear of disease, often involving imaginary illness accompanied by actual pains

(5) depression—an emotional state of dejection, gloomy rumination, and feelings of worthlessness

Decide which type of neurosis is illustrated in each of the following situations.

5. Nicholas has persistent headaches, a cough, and frequently feels faint, but doctor after doctor has examined him and found nothing physically wrong.

(1) obsession
(2) compulsion
(3) phobia
(4) hypochondriasis
(5) depression

① ② ③ ④ ⑤

6. Maria feels such panic in any enclosed area that she climbs the stairs to her twelfth-floor office rather than ride in the elevator.

(1) obsession
(2) compulsion
(3) phobia
(4) hypochondriasis
(5) depression

① ② ③ ④ ⑤

7. Willie spends an hour each morning arranging the objects on his desk in just the right order and seeing that all small objects—pens, paper clips, and such—are in groups of three.

(1) obsession
(2) compulsion
(3) phobia
(4) hypochondriasis
(5) depression

① ② ③ ④ ⑤

Items 8–9 are based on the maps below.

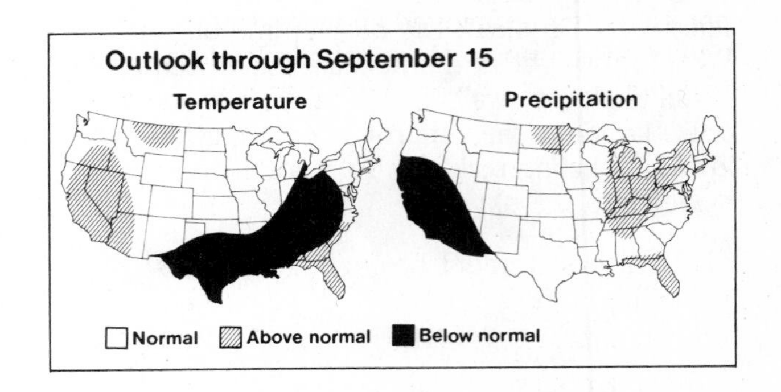

8. Which of the following states is expected to have below normal temperatures and normal rainfall?

(1) California
(2) Nevada
(3) Texas
(4) Kansas
(5) Florida

① ② ③ ④ ⑤

9. Based on these maps, in which of the following states might there be a danger of forest fires?

(1) Florida
(2) California
(3) Texas
(4) Alaska
(5) Maine

① ② ③ ④ ⑤

GO ON TO THE NEXT PAGE.

Items 10–11 refer to the passage below.

As the nature of the workplace changed, workers' organizations, or unions, changed too. A union was formed by workers to protect them when employers lowered wages or increased working hours. The idea behind the union was that one worker alone was weak, but many workers together were strong enough to stand up against an employer. Before the Civil War, unions were largely local organizations, made up of skilled workers in the same trade who lived in the same city or neighborhood. But by 1870 these small local unions found that they could not hope to bargain with the huge national corporations that employed an increasing percentage of American workers. Union leaders realized that workers, too, would have to organize on a national level.

10. Which of the following best summarizes the passage?

(1) The Civil War resulted in higher wages for workers.
(2) Organizing a union begins at the local level.
(3) The first unions included everyone in a factory.
(4) National unions grew with businesses after the Civil War.
(5) Unions help workers stand up to an employer.

(1) (2) (3) (4) (5)

11. Based on the information above, which of the following is the most reasonable prediction?

(1) Unions will return to being local organizations of workers living in the same city or neighborhood.
(2) Unions will disappear as the conditions that caused them, low wages and long working hours, have disappeared.
(3) In an effort to destroy unions, employers will raise wages and cut working hours.
(4) The growth of multinational and international corporations will cause the growth of international unions.
(5) Unions will be outlawed in more and more states.

(1) (2) (3) (4) (5)

Items 12–13 are based on the passage below.

The Fourth Amendment to the U.S. Constitution guards Americans against being arrested, having their homes searched, or having their papers or other property taken except when there is a good reason to do so and a proper warrant has been issued. Courts can issue search and arrest warrants, but only after the person asking for the warrant explains exactly why it is needed and describes exactly the person or property to be seized or searched.

12. Which of the following would be prohibited under the Fourth Amendment?

(1) A person accused of a crime is not allowed to talk to a lawyer.
(2) Police suspect a person of a crime and break into her house looking for evidence.
(3) Police with an arrest warrant seize the person described in the warrant.
(4) A person is sued because of something she wrote in a newspaper article.
(5) A person is denied a jury trial although he asks for one.

(1) (2) (3) (4) (5)

13. Which of the following was the intention of the Fourth Amendment?

(1) to expand the powers of the police
(2) to define crimes against the state
(3) to limit the powers of Congress
(4) to preserve states rights from the federal government
(5) to protect the individual against the power of the state

(1) (2) (3) (4) (5)

GO ON TO THE NEXT PAGE.

Items 14–19 refer to the following graph.

Based on current trends, here are regional population projections for the final two decades of the century.

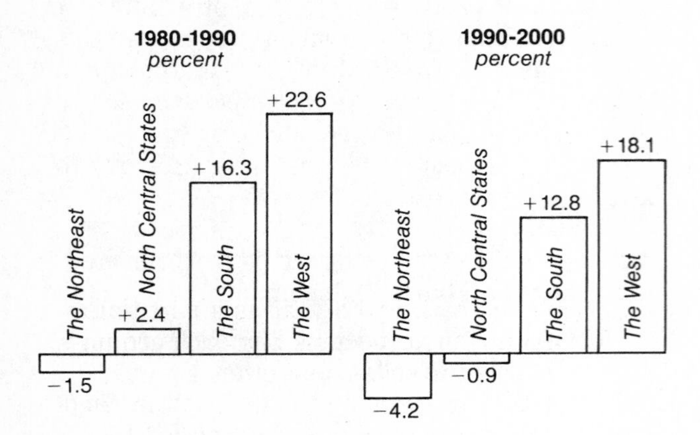

14. Which statement below best summarizes the information on the graph?

    (1) Between now and 2000 most of the country's population growth will be in the South and West, while Northeast and North Central states will have mostly negative growth.
    (2) In the final two decades of this century, the South and West will experience a population growth of about 20 percent.
    (3) Between 1980 and 2000 the Northeast and North Central states will lose population.
    (4) By 2000 the West will have a larger population than the South.
    (5) Between 1990 and 2000 the Northeast and North Central states will lose about 5 percent of their population.

    ① ② ③ ④ ⑤

15. Officials of an electric utility company serving the western U.S. could conclude from these figures that the company will need to

    (1) convince more customers to use its service
    (2) triple the amount of electricity it now generates
    (3) generate more electricity through the rest of the century
    (4) build more nuclear power plants before 2000
    (5) sell its excess electricity to utility companies in the Northeast and North Central states

    ① ② ③ ④ ⑤

16. Which of the following is an opinion, not a fact according to the graph?

    (1) The South will gain population at a rate greater than any region except the West.
    (2) In the South and West the population growth rate will slow somewhat between 1990–2000 as compared to 1980–1990.
    (3) The Northeast states are projected to lose nearly six percent of their population by 2000.
    (4) People are moving from the Northeast and North Central states to the South and the West because of the economy.
    (5) Between 1980 and 2000 the population of the West is expected to grow by more than 40 percent.

    ① ② ③ ④ ⑤

GO ON TO THE NEXT PAGE.

17. Which of the following will probably NOT occur in the Northeast and North Central states as a result of their loss of population?

(1) a loss of jobs
(2) a loss of tax revenue
(3) a younger population
(4) less congressional representation
(5) fewer new homes being built

(1) (2) (3) (4) (5)

18. Based on the graph, which of the following predictions is most likely?

(1) More women will enter the work force than ever before.
(2) New transportation systems will be built to connect the regions.
(3) The cost of living will fall in the South and West.
(4) The cost of living will rise most in the Northeast and North Central states.
(5) More houses will be built in the West between now and the year 2000.

(1) (2) (3) (4) (5)

19. Which of the following conclusions can NOT be made from the graph?

(1) Horace Greeley's advice, "Go West, young man," is still apt.
(2) Weather is the most important factor in where people choose to live.
(3) The Rust Belt is losing population to the Sun Belt.
(4) California is more likely to gain residents than New York.
(5) At some point between 1980 and 2000, population growth in the North Central states will hit zero.

(1) (2) (3) (4) (5)

Items 20–21 refer to the following table.

The Earnings of Wives
Median income in 1984 compared to husbands

HUSBANDS	WIVES
no income	$8,859
$5-5,999	$5,785
$10-12,499	$8,436
$15-17,499	$9,905
$20-24,999	$10,259
$30-34,999	$10,706
$75,000 and up	$10,678

20. Ralph earns $5,500 a year as a part-time school bus driver. Frank and Rick are unemployed and receive no other income. Frank's wife, Doris, earns $11,000 a year as a property manager. If Ralph and Rick's wives, Alice and Louise, earn exactly what the above table lists as median income for wives, which couple earns the most per year?

(1) Ralph and Alice
(2) Frank and Doris
(3) Rick and Louise
(4) they all earn the same
(5) it cannot be determined

(1) (2) (3) (4) (5)

21. Which prediction can you make based on the figures above?

(1) Laws requiring equal pay for equal work will soon be passed.
(2) The incomes of working wives are so low that many women will soon stop working.
(3) Husbands whose wives work suffer more illnesses than those whose wives stay home.
(4) When working women are divorced their standard of living declines.
(5) Children whose parents both work have more problems in school than those with one parent at home.

(1) (2) (3) (4) (5)

GO ON TO THE NEXT PAGE.

Items 22–24 refer to the following passage.

With passage of the Trade Act of 1934, Congress handed over its constitutional power to regulate trade with foreign nations to the President. The act recognized that trade policy and foreign policy cannot be separated.

22. The passage implies that foreign policy is conducted mainly by

    (1) the President
    (2) Congress
    (3) the Senate Foreign Relations Committee
    (4) public opinion polls
    (5) the Trade Act of 1934

    1 2 3 4 5

23. Which of the following is the most obvious example of the relationship between trade policy and foreign policy?

    (1) In 1982, the President sends the U.S. Marines to Lebanon on a "peacekeeping" mission.
    (2) The Philippine Islands received their independence from the United States in 1946.
    (3) To protest the South African government's racial policies, Congress and the President banned U.S. imports of South African coal.
    (4) In 1985, the United States bought \$148.5 billion more goods from foreign nations than it sold.
    (5) An American corporation decides to close its Amsterdam office as a cost-cutting measure.

    1 2 3 4 5

24. What is one assumption behind the Trade Act of 1934?

    (1) Trade policy and foreign policy are not related.
    (2) Trade with foreign nations is closely related to interstate commerce.
    (3) Foreign nations that trade with the United States will eventually achieve statehood.
    (4) Trade with enemy nations should be limited.
    (5) Nations will change their foreign policies to gain trade advantages or to avoid trade penalties.

    1 2 3 4 5

(SALLY FORTH by Greg Howard. ©News America Syndicate, 1986. Permission of News America Syndicate.)

25. Based on evidence in the cartoon above, what does the cartoonist believe?

    (1) Husbands are contributing more time and effort to household management.
    (2) Most companies allow working parents time off to have children.
    (3) Businesses are not concerned with the social lives of their employees.
    (4) To aid their careers, many employees will decide not to have children.
    (5) Arranging child care is often a problem for working parents.

GO ON TO THE NEXT PAGE.

Items 26–29 refer to the following information.

In a suit before a state Supreme Court, the plaintiff declared that the state's seat belt law was an unconstitutional violation of personal rights. Attorneys arguing against the law cited a 1985 study by the National Highway Traffic Safety Administration which found that there were slightly more head injuries among lap belt users than among passengers using no belt. The legislature, they said, can't force a person to do something that may cause injury.

Attorneys arguing for the law pointed out that the same study found fewer head, chest, and leg injuries when a lap-and-shoulder belt was used. They argued also that seat belts can prevent injuries to pedestrians and other motorists by helping a motorist keep control of the car.

26. The state seat belt law was probably intended to

(1) violate personal rights
(2) prevent injuries caused by auto accidents
(3) test the issue in the Supreme Court
(4) prevent head injuries among lap belt users
(5) help motorists keep control of their cars

① ② ③ ④ ⑤

27. Which of the following statements is best supported by evidence in the passage?

(1) Seat belts can prevent injuries to other motorists and pedestrians.
(2) Seat belts help motorists keep control of the car.
(3) The legislature can't force a person to do something that may cause injury.
(4) There are fewer head, chest, and leg injuries when a lap-and-shoulder belt is used.
(5) The state's seat belt law is an unconstitutional violation of personal rights.

① ② ③ ④ ⑤

28. Attorneys who favor the law implied that some personal rights are less important than

(1) federal laws
(2) public safety
(3) Supreme Court decisions
(4) the Constitution
(5) the rights of minorities

① ② ③ ④ ⑤

29. Basing its decision only on the information in this article, a public interest group promoting highway safety would probably recommend

(1) the use of lap-and-shoulder belts
(2) the use of lap belts
(3) that the seat belt law be repealed
(4) that government stay out of highway safety issues
(5) that individual freedom is more important than highway safety

① ② ③ ④ ⑤

GO ON TO THE NEXT PAGE.

Items 30–32 are based on the passage below.

Like nine out of ten American colonists, the typical New Englander was a farmer. But farming in New England was difficult and not very productive. New England's climate was harsh, its soil rocky and often infertile. And because of the region's topography, or shape of the land, New England had no navigable rivers flowing to the ocean. Without them, farmers could not get their crops to buyers quickly or cheaply. As a result of these things, New England farmers lived in a subsistence economy. That is, they used all that they produced for their families' daily existence. There was no surplus for sale and no profit made.

30. New England's farms were unproductive because of

(1) unfair taxes
(2) a lack of technology
(3) the region's geography
(4) a lack of navigable rivers
(5) England's restrictive trade policies

(1) (2) (3) (4) (5)

31. Which statement below is the author's main conclusion?

(1) New England has no navigable rivers flowing to the ocean.
(2) Farmers could not get their crops to buyers quickly or cheaply.
(3) The typical New Englander was a farmer.
(4) New England's climate was harsh, its soil rocky and often infertile.
(5) New England farmers lived in a subsistence economy.

(1) (2) (3) (4) (5)

32. Which of the following groups probably lived in a subsistence economy?

(1) the English of American colonial times
(2) pre-colonial American Indian tribes
(3) slaves in the American South
(4) merchants in colonial New York
(5) tobacco planters of America's southern colonies

(1) (2) (3) (4) (5)

END OF EXAMINATION

TEST 3: SCIENCE PRETEST

Directions

The *Science Pretest* consists of 33 questions most of which contain reading passages. Each passage is followed by a number of multiple-choice questions related to its content. Read the passage first and then answer the questions following it. Refer to the passage as often as necessary to answer the questions.

You should take approximately 45 minutes to complete this test. There is no penalty for guessing. Try to answer as many questions as you can. Work rapidly but carefully, without spending too much time on any one question. If a question is too difficult for you, omit it and come back to it later.

For each answer, mark one answer space. See how the following example is done.

EXAMPLE

A physical change is one in which the chemical composition of a substance is not altered. A chemical change, in contrast, results in one or more new substances with different chemical makeups.

Which of the following is an example of a physical change?

(1) butter melting
(2) tarnish on silverware
(3) gasoline being used in a car engine
(4) photographic film being developed
(5) photosynthesis in plants

 (2) (3) (4) (5)

The answer is "butter melting"; therefore, answer space (1) has been marked.

When you have completed the test, check your answers against the Answer Key on page 61. Explanations for the answers are on pages 68–69.

Directions: Choose the one best answer to each question.

Items 1–5 are based on the following passage.

Axel Heiberg Island is less than 700 miles from the North Pole. It is a dry, frozen region with almost no vegetation. Surprisingly, in the middle of this island stands a massive dead forest of fallen logs and old stumps that are 45 million years old. This suggests that the climate of this area was much different in the past than it is today.

As the scientists began their study of this "forest," they made an incredible discovery. Contained within this forest are 19 distinct layers of stumps. Each layer indicates a forest that developed, lived for centuries, and was suddenly buried alive beneath floods of sediment. This process occurred again and again over a period of several hundred thousand years and resulted in the preservation of the forests as they existed 45 million years ago. It is as though the forests were mummified.

Since the forests exist almost as they did eons ago, it is possible to study a prehistoric forest. How the trees grew, how dense they were, and how productive the forest was can all be determined. It also gives us a much better understanding of the plants that grew in the high latitudes at that time, the kind of environment they lived in, and how they relate to plant forms today.

The discovery of the forests has great scientific value. It may also have economic importance. One hypothesis that has been advanced is that the resins in these ancient trees account for the rich oil deposits of the Arctic Ocean. If so, knowledge of the climate and vegetation in the past may contribute to estimating the gas and oil potential of the area.

1. The word "mummified" as used in the passage most probably means

(1) preserved
(2) decomposed
(3) decayed
(4) turned into rock
(5) destroyed

(1) (2) (3) (4) (5)

2. Which of the following statements represents a conclusion drawn by the author?

(1) Scientists can determine the density of plants which grew in the prehistoric period.
(2) The soil of the forest can be examined in detail.
(3) The discovery of the prehistoric forest gives scientists the opportunity to determine the plant life and environmental conditions in the Arctic 45 million years ago.
(4) Scientists know the conditions of sunlight which existed near the North Pole 45 million years ago.
(5) The floor of the prehistoric forest has decayed very little.

(1) (2) (3) (4) (5)

3. Which of the following statements probably best explains why the forests did not decay when they were buried?

(1) New seeds were present in the topsoil.
(2) Rapid burial probably excluded air and prevented decay processes.
(3) The warm, moist climate of the period kept the wood fresh.
(4) Rapid burial prevented erosion of topsoil.
(5) New forests grew on top of the old ones.

(1) (2) (3) (4) (5)

4. Based on the article, which of the following represents a hypothesis rather than a fact?

(1) Several layers of forest have been found on the island.
(2) The forests grew actively 45 million years ago.
(3) The repeated growth and destruction of the forests continued for several hundred thousand years.
(4) Resins from the trees formed oil deposits.
(5) Axel Heiberg Island is located near the North Pole.

(1) (2) (3) (4) (5)

GO ON TO THE NEXT PAGE.

5. Over 45 million years ago, the climate of the earth, particularly of the northern latitudes, was much warmer.

   Based on the passage, which of the following statements would best justify the conclusion above?

   (1) Tree species which were once widespread exist now in only a few isolated areas.
   (2) Lush forests once grew near the North Pole in areas that are now frozen wastelands.
   (3) Erosion was responsible for the destruction of many forests on Axel Heiberg Island.
   (4) Tree stumps and logs have been well preserved in their frozen environment.
   (5) The earth's atmosphere probably was warmer 45 million years ago due to the presence of high levels of carbon dioxide.

   (1) (2) (3) (4) (5)

6. The freezing point of a substance is the temperature at which the liquid becomes a solid. Fats have a higher freezing point than water.

   A chef wants to remove the fat from some gravy. Based on the above information, which of the following is a simple way of doing this?

   (1) Strain the gravy through cheesecloth.
   (2) Boil the gravy for 15 minutes.
   (3) Chill the gravy and pour the fat off.
   (4) Add ice cubes and let the fat solidify on them.
   (5) Increase the heat very slowly.

   (1) (2) (3) (4) (5)

7. Each material has a unique capacity to gain or to lose heat depending on the temperature of its surroundings.

   A child playing outside complains that the metal parts of the swing set are always cold in the early morning, but that the wooden seat on the swing does not feel cold.

   Based on the information above, what is the most likely explanation for this observation?

   (1) The wood concentrates heat.
   (2) The metal parts gain heat more readily than the wood.
   (3) The metal parts magnify the sun's rays.
   (4) The metal parts are larger than the wooden seat.
   (5) The wood holds heat better because of its darker color.

   (1) (2) (3) (4) (5)

8. A hormone in the body is often regulated by the substance it causes to be produced. When the substance reaches a high level in the body, it "feeds back" and shuts off production of the hormone. Thyroid stimulating hormone is produced by the pituitary gland. This hormone causes the thyroid to produce several other substances that play a role in the body's metabolism.

   What would shut off the production of more thyroid stimulating hormone?

   (1) the pituitary gland
   (2) the thyroid gland
   (3) high levels of substances produced by the thyroid
   (4) high levels of pituitary hormones
   (5) high levels of thyroid stimulating hormone itself

   (1) (2) (3) (4) (5)

GO ON TO THE NEXT PAGE.

Items 9–11 refer to the following diagram.

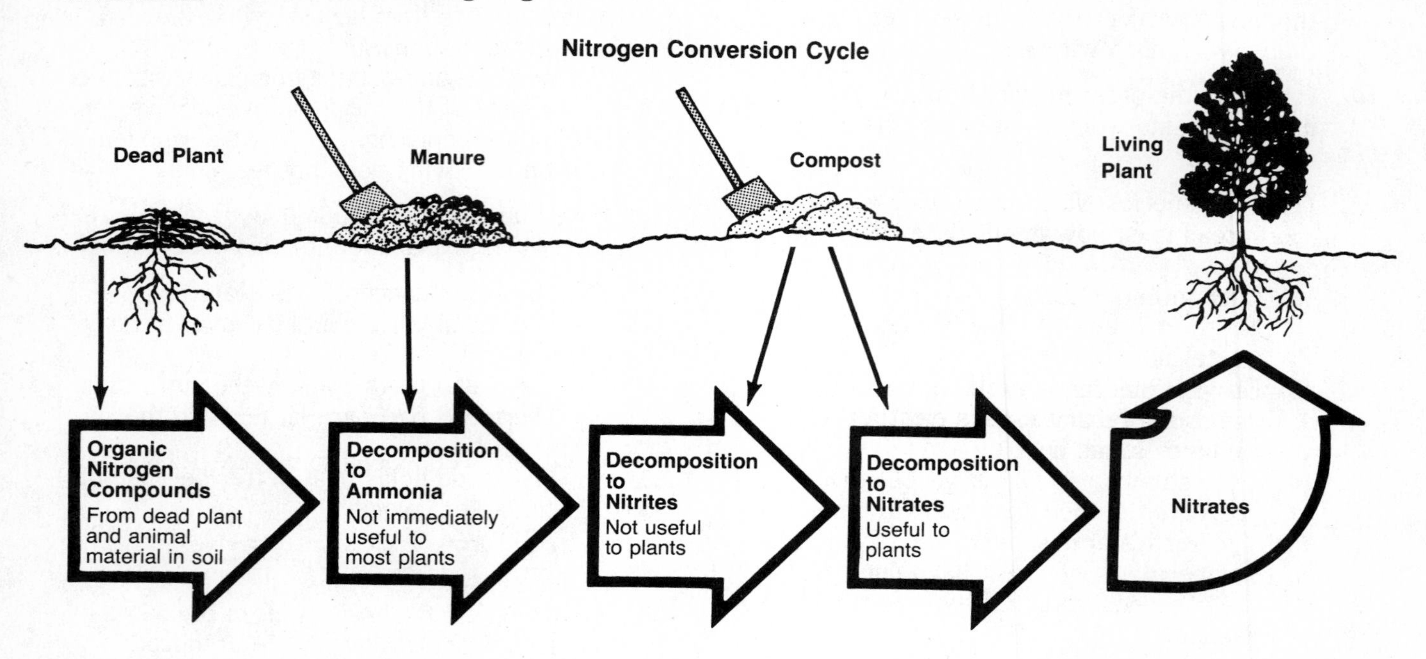

Nitrogen is used in very large quantities by plants. As a result, if plants are to grow well, nitrogen must be added to the soil from time to time. It usually comes from decaying organic material, but the process is complex because pure nitrogen cannot be used directly by plants. First, it must be converted by soil organisms (fungi, molds, bacteria) into chemical forms which can be taken up by plant roots.

9. The information given above implies that the decomposition of organic nitrogen compounds to nitrates is a series of processes which

   (1) occur only when chemicals are added to the soil
   (2) are carried out by plants
   (3) are carried out by bacteria and other soil microorganisms
   (4) are not immediately useful to plants
   (5) produce pure nitrogen

   (1) (2) (3) (4) (5)

10. A man decides to fertilize his garden with a nitrogen source which will be immediately available to the plants. Which of the following compounds should he use?

    (1) dead plant material
    (2) manure
    (3) ammonium sulfate
    (4) ammonium nitrite
    (5) calcium nitrate

    (1) (2) (3) (4) (5)

11. Clover is often planted in a field every other year because it enriches the soil in usable nitrogen. Based on the information above, which of the following statements justifies this conclusion?

    (1) Clover contains no nitrogen.
    (2) Bacteria which break down nitrate thrive on clover.
    (3) Clover plants encourage the growth of soil organisms which produce nitrates fron nitrogen.
    (4) Clover converts ammonia to nitrites.
    (5) Clover requires high nitrate levels in the soil to grow.

    (1) (2) (3) (4) (5)

GO ON TO THE NEXT PAGE.

<u>Items 12–15</u> are based on the following information.

Electricity has many properties. Five of these are defined below.

charge—the accumulation of electrons on a surface

current—the movement of electrons through a wire

kilowatt-hour—the amount of electricity required to run an appliance

resistance—the hindrance to the flow of electrons through a wire that causes electrical energy to be given off as heat

voltage—the force or pressure that causes electrons to move through a wire

Each of the following items describes a situation based on one of the terms defined above. For each item choose the one term that best describes the situation. Each of the terms may be used more than once or not at all.

12. After a child rubs an inflated balloon against his clothes, it will cling to a wall. The balloon clings to the wall due to

(1) charge
(2) current
(3) kilowatt-hours
(4) resistance
(5) voltage

13. A family's electric bill goes up when the clothes washer and dryer are used more often.

The electric bill probably goes up due to use of more

(1) charge
(2) current
(3) kilowatt-hours
(4) resistance
(5) voltage

1 2 3 4 5

14. A person checks some flashlight batteries at the store, and each appears to be good because the measured voltage is correct. When they are put into a good flashlight, however, the bulb only glows dimly.

Probably the bulb glows dimly because the batteries are not producing sufficient

(1) charge
(2) current
(3) kilowatt-hours
(4) resistance
(5) voltage

15. A heater is supposed to require 1200 watts of electricity to operate. However, careful measurements indicate that when the heater is used with an extension cord, 1202 watts of electricity are needed.

Probably the use of two additional watts is due to

(1) charge
(2) current
(3) kilowatt-hours
(4) resistance
(5) voltage

GO ON TO THE NEXT PAGE.

Items 16–18 are based on the following passage.

The small airplane flew slowly over the livestock grazing below. Inside the plane an entomologist, a scientist specializing in the study of insects, tore open paper sacks and dropped them through a pipe extending below the plane.

In one of the first experiments of its kind, scientists were trying to control an insect by natural means. The insect was the screwworm fly, which lays its eggs in the open sores of animals such as sheep, goats, and cattle. When the eggs hatch, the young offspring feed on the animals' flesh.

The sacks that were dropped from the airplane contained screwworm flies that had been sterilized by exposure to radiation. The scientists hoped that when the sterilized male flies mated with wild, untreated female flies, the females' eggs would not be fertilized and would never hatch.

The experiment worked. Repeated releases of sterilized screwworm flies have almost eliminated these insects where they were once abundant. Such natural means of insect control have become popular because chemical pesticides can kill not only the intended insects but also other insects and even animals.

16. According to the passage, natural means of insect control are being used more and more because they

(1) kill only the intended insect species
(2) are cheaper than chemical means
(3) work faster than chemical controls
(4) kill a wide variety of insects and even animals
(5) are applied more easily than chemicals

1 2 3 4 5

17. Because the experiment described was successful, which of the following can be assumed?

(1) The female flies exposed to radiation were unable to mate.
(2) Many of the male flies exposed to radiation were unable to mate.
(3) The radiation dose used was sufficient to sterilize the male flies dropped from the airplane.
(4) The wild, untreated flies would not mate with the treated ones.
(5) The offspring of the irradiated flies were infertile.

1 2 3 4 5

18. Which of the following statements best represents the hypothesis of the screwworm fly experiment?

(1) Natural means of pest control are better than chemical means because they do not affect other insects and flies.
(2) Sterilized male screwworm flies can be used to control the number of screwworm flies in an area.
(3) The screwworm flies have almost been eliminated by the use of natural control methods.
(4) Males sterilized by radiation are infertile.
(5) Insects can be artificially sterilized by dropping them from an airplane.

GO ON TO THE NEXT PAGE.

Items 19–21 refer to the following graph.

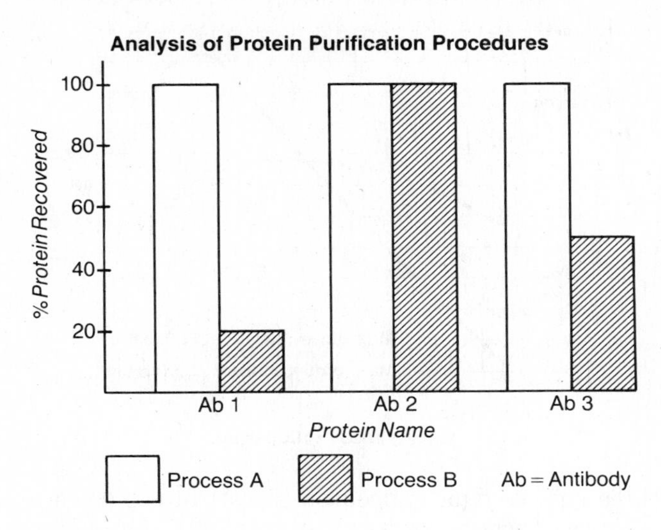

Many proteins are present in normal blood. Antibodies are blood proteins which some companies purify for use as drugs. The proteins can be purified using various procedures. Depending on the procedure used, some of the protein in the original sample may be lost during the purification step. The above graph compares the percentage of three proteins that can be recovered from a sample using two different procedures.

19. Which of the following statements best summarizes the information contained in the graph above?

(1) Greater percentages of all proteins tested are recovered when Process A is used.
(2) Processes A and B are equally efficient in their ability to recover protein from a sample.
(3) Process A results in the recovery of equal or greater percentages of any tested protein than does Process B.
(4) Using Process A 100 percent of all proteins is recovered.
(5) Less than half of the protein present in a sample is recovered using Process B.

(1) (2) (3) (4) (5)

20. A researcher is given a 5 gram sample of blood known to contain antibody. She decides to use Process A for the purification procedure. She is interested in answering the following questions:

A. What percentage of Ab 1, Ab 2, and Ab 3 in the original sample will be recovered using Process A?

B. How many grams of antibody were present in the sample?

C. How many different proteins were present in the original sample?

Which of these questions can she answer directly from the graph?

(1) A
(2) B
(3) C
(4) A and B
(5) B and C

21. A new technologist in a medical laboratory is unaware of the information provided by the above graph. He uses Process B to recover proteins from a patient's blood. After completing the process, he determines how much Ab 1 and Ab 2 are present. He reports that Ab 2 levels are normal in the patient, but that the amount of Ab 1 is dramatically decreased. What logical error has he made?

(1) Ab 2 cannot be recovered from blood using Process B.
(2) He assumed that 100 percent of both proteins was recovered using Process B.
(3) He assumed there were no other proteins present in the sample.
(4) He assumed that blood contains more Ab 2 than Ab 1.
(5) He assumed that the sample contained only protein.

(1) (2) (3) (4) (5)

GO ON TO THE NEXT PAGE.

Item 22 is based on the following map.

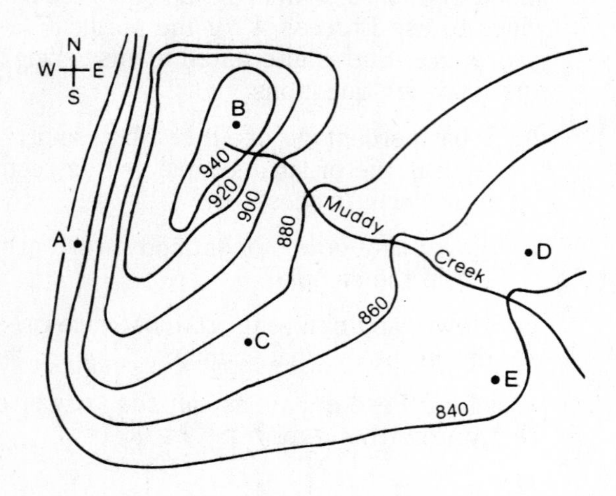

The map above represents Cedar Springs, Michigan. The dark, wavy lines show where 20-foot changes in elevation occur. The number on the line represents the lowest elevation in each area.

22. On the map above, the range of possible elevations at point C is

    (1) 840–880 ft
    (2) 860–880 ft
    (3) 860–900 ft
    (4) 880–900 ft
    (5) 940 ft

    (1) (2) (3) (4) (5)

23. Below are listed 5 statements about fiber in the diet. Some of the statements are facts which can be scientifically verified. Which one of the following statements is based on opinion?

    (1) Dietary fiber is plant material that is largely undigested and unabsorbed by the body.
    (2) Fiber has no nutritional value but does affect the body's use of food.
    (3) Foods which are rich in fiber are low in fat.
    (4) People need to include more fiber in their diets.
    (5) Soluble fiber found in citrus fruits, oat bran, and legumes makes it difficult for the body to digest fat.

    (1) (2) (3) (4) (5)

Items 24–25 refer to the following graph.

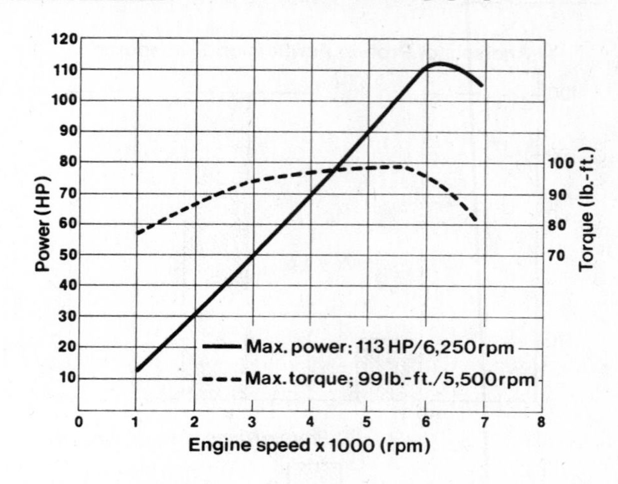

The above figure appeared as part of the promotional brochure for a new sports car. The figure provides information about the engine.

24. Which of the following statements best summarizes the power (HP) information given in the graph?

    (1) The power changes little over a wide range of engine speeds.
    (2) Power is measured in horsepower.
    (3) The engine develops approximately 70 horsepower at all rpm.
    (4) The horsepower increases as engine rpm increase and reaches a maximum at 6,250 rpms.
    (5) The maximum horsepower achieved is 113 HP.

    (1) (2) (3) (4) (5)

25. What information can NOT be derived from the graph?

    (1) the maximum horsepower the engine develops
    (2) the torque which develops at a certain engine speed
    (3) the speed of the car at a certain engine speed
    (4) the change in torque over a range of engine speeds
    (5) the units of measure for torque and power

    (1) (2) (3) (4) (5)

GO ON TO THE NEXT PAGE.

26. Symbiosis is a relationship in which two organisms live together for the mutual benefit of both.

The American beech tree requires a forest environment for normal growth. Beech roots can absorb minerals from the soil only if a particular fungus grows nearby. This fungus thrives in forest soil but dies when the forest is gone and the land becomes an open area.

Based on this information, which of the following will probably occur when a beech tree is transplanted into a yard?

(1) The tree will die within a few years.
(2) The tree will grow well if forest soil is transplanted with it.
(3) Frequent fertilization will be necessary.
(4) The tree will suffer root damage when transplanted.
(5) The beech tree will produce a fungus.

27. In nature an animal may closely resemble another organism or particular object in its environment. This resemblance may protect the organism from predators in some way.

Which of the following is an example of protective resemblance?

(1) A opossum pretends to be dead when a dog comes near.
(2) With their wings folded, some butterflies resemble brown leaves.
(3) A squid squirts an inky black fluid into the surrounding water when an enemy approaches.
(4) The orange and black stripes of a tiger allow it to blend with the grasses and shadows of its environment.
(5) Squirrels hide deep in the branches of trees to escape owls and other predators.

(1) (2) (3) (4) (5)

28. There are certain nutrients that the body needs, but these nutrients must be supplied in the diet. Some vitamins, minerals, and essential amino acids fall into this category. What assumption is made by a person who becomes a strict vegetarian?

(1) The body can manufacture all its own nutrients.
(2) Food is strictly an energy source.
(3) Vegetables are a calorie-free source of nutrients.
(4) Variety in the diet is a matter of taste.
(5) Vegetables can supply all essential nutrients.

(1) (2) (3) (4) (5)

29. When a solid is added to water, some or all of it will dissolve in the water. Eventually the amount of dissolved solid reaches a maximum. When this occurs, the solution is said to be saturated.

Additional sugar is added to a sugar-saturated glass of iced tea. Based on the above information, which of the following is most likely to occur?

(1) The amount of dissolved sugar will increase.
(2) The amount of dissolved sugar will decrease.
(3) The amount of dissolved sugar will not change.
(4) The sugar that is already dissolved will not stay in solution.
(5) All of the sugar in the tea will collect on the bottom of the glass.

(1) (2) (3) (4) (5)

GO ON TO THE NEXT PAGE.

Items 30–32 are based on the following information.

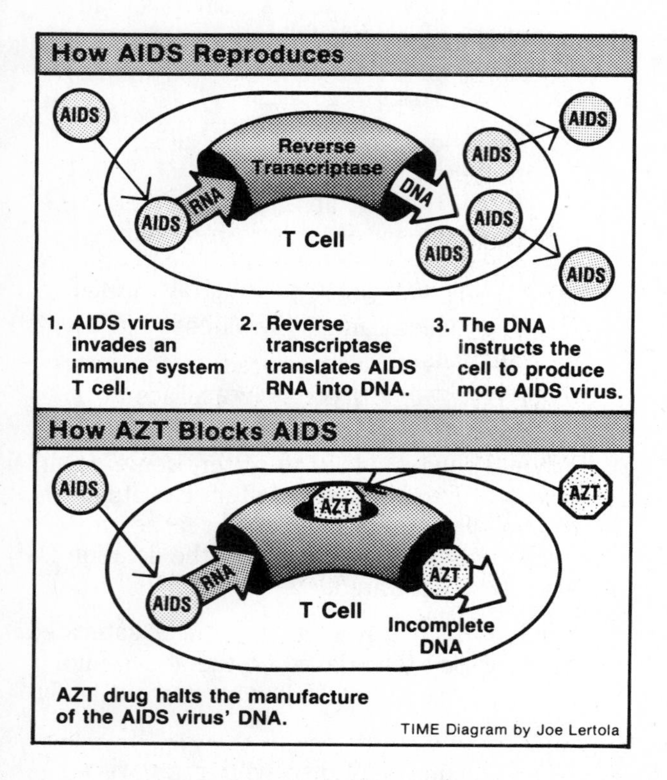
How AIDS Reproduces
AIDS
Reverse Transcriptase
RNA
DNA
T Cell
1. AIDS virus invades an immune system T cell.
2. Reverse transcriptase translates AIDS RNA into DNA.
3. The DNA instructs the cell to produce more AIDS virus.
How AZT Blocks AIDS
AZT
Incomplete DNA
AZT drug halts the manufacture of the AIDS virus' DNA.
TIME Diagram by Joe Lertola

Some viruses consist of a segment of double-stranded DNA surrounded by a protein skin. When they invade a cell, the DNA takes over the cell's genetic machinery and orders it to produce copies of the virus, which escape to infect other cells. The victim cell is often killed in the process. But the AIDS virus is a so-called retrovirus and contains single-stranded RNA. Alone, RNA lacks the ability to conquer cells, but retroviruses carry an enzyme called reverse transcriptase. When the AIDS virus invades an immune-system T cell, the enzyme enables the viral RNA to convert to DNA, take over the cell's machinery, produce copies of itself and disable the cell. . . .

When AZT enters a human cell, it is converted by a human enzyme into a "false sugar" that resembles, but is not identical to, the sugar used by the AIDS virus' reverse transcriptase to help build a DNA strand. If the AIDS enzyme mistakenly adds a false sugar molecule to the DNA chain, DNA synthesis is halted. So, . . . further reproduction of the virus . . . [is] stopped.

30. Based on the information in the passage and the diagrams, how does the AIDS retrovirus reproduce itself in a cell?

(1) Inside the cell the virus changes RNA to DNA and then uses the cell's own system to reproduce itself.
(2) The RNA of the virus is copied again and again by the cell.
(3) The DNA contained in the AIDS virus escapes and kills many cells.
(4) A special enzyme contained in human T cells converts the viral RNA to DNA.
(5) Viral RNA takes over the reproductive machinery of the cell and produces many copies of itself.

1 2 3 4 5

31. Which of the following statements represents a conclusion that can be drawn from the above information?

(1) AZT acts like a false sugar in the DNA copy process.
(2) AZT stops viral reproduction by causing errors in the DNA strand copied from the viral RNA.
(3) When AZT enters the body it must be converted to a sugar the cell machinery will recognize.
(4) If DNA synthesis stops, viral reproduction stops also.
(5) The viral enzyme reverse transcriptase assembles sugars and other compounds to form a strand of DNA.

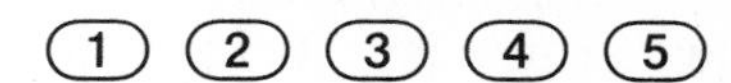
1 2 3 4 5

GO ON TO THE NEXT PAGE.

32. Clinical evaluation tests must be carried out on each new drug before it is approved for routine public use. These tests include groups of patients which receive the experimental drug and, for purposes of comparison, one control group which receives a placebo. Members of the placebo group believe they are receiving the experimental drug, but actually they are receiving a pill which has no curative value.

A physician involved in administering the clinical tests for the experimental AZT drug firmly believes that AZT is the miracle drug which will cure AIDS patients of their fatal disease. Which of the following represents a question which arises because of the physician's personal values?

(1) How many patients should receive each dose of the drug?
(2) How many doses of the drug should be tested?
(3) How many injections of the drug should the patients receive?
(4) Can anyone suffering from AIDS be refused the drug in order to include an untreated group in the study?
(5) Over what time period should the study be conducted?

(1) (2) (3) (4) (5)

33. Hemophilia is a hereditary disease in which blood does not clot normally. In the past, hemophilia was a fatal disease; victims died before reaching their teenage years. Because they died without having children, the disease remained quite rare in our population. The disease still cannot be cured, but due to medical advances hemophilia is now considered a "treatable" disease rather than a fatal disease. With proper treatment, hemophiliacs are living longer, and many of them are having children. What will be the probable effect of this on our population?

(1) The disease will be cured.
(2) There will be more hemophiliacs in our population.
(3) The number of people with hemophilia will not change.
(4) Children of hemophiliacs will not have the disease.
(5) The number of hemophiliacs will decrease.

(1) (2) (3) (4) (5)

END OF EXAMINATION

TEST 4: INTERPRETING LITERATURE AND THE ARTS PRETEST

Directions

The *Interpreting Literature and the Arts Pretest* consists of 22 multiple-choice questions based on selections from various kinds of reading materials. The selections are from literary works such as books, journals, and magazine or newspaper commentaries. One or more questions follow each selection. The best procedure for you to follow is to read the selection through once, then read all the questions based on the selection, answering as many questions as you can. Then reread the selection as many times as necessary to answer the more difficult questions.

You should take approximately 35 minutes to complete this test. There is no penalty for guessing. Try to answer as many questions as you can. Work rapidly but carefully, without spending too much time on any one question. If a question is too difficult for you, skip it and come back to it later.

For each answer, mark one answer space. See how the following example is done.

EXAMPLE

Often I think of the beautiful town
That is seated by the sea;
Often in thought go up and down
The pleasant streets of that dear old town,
  And my youth comes back to me.

In the poem above, the author is writing about

(1) an imaginary town
(2) a town that he dislikes
(3) the town he lives in
(4) a town he once visited
(5) the town he grew up in

① ② ③ ④ ●

The answer is "the town he grew up in"; therefore, answer space (5) has been marked.

When you have completed the test, check your answers against the Answer Key on page 61. Explanations for the answers are on pages 69–70.

Directions: Choose the one best answer for each item.

Items 1–4 are based on the following passage.

How does the author describe the experience of coping with unemployment?

Now, our ballooning hopes that we would quickly land a job are running into some frigid air, so we decide to confess at last our need of help—to some of our more prosperous friends in the business world (if we have such) who *surely* know what we should do at this point. The windmill is tiring us. What would they suggest we do?

"What kind of a job are you looking for?"

Ah, *that*, again! "Well, you know me well, what do you think I can do? I'll do almost anything," we say, now that the hour of desperation is snapping at our heels. "You know, with all the *kinds* of things I've done—" we say; "I mean, I've done this and that, and here and there, it all adds up to a kind of kaleidoscope. Well, anyway, there must be *something* I can do?"

"Have you tried the want-ads?" asks our friend. "Have you gone to see Bill, and Ed, and John, and Frances and Marty? Ah, no? Well, tell them I sent you."

So, off we go—now newly armed. We study the want-ads. Gad, what misery is hidden in those little boxes. Misery in miserable jobs which are built as little boxes. We dutifully send our resume, such as it is, to every box that looks as though it might not be a box.

1. The word "we" in the passage refers to

(1) prosperous friends
(2) balloonists
(3) employers
(4) job hunters
(5) students

① ② ③ ④ ⑤

2. The comment "desperation is snapping at our heels" compares desperation to

(1) a lonely feeling
(2) an attacking dog
(3) panic
(4) a frightening event of the past
(5) a job hunter

① ② ③ ④ ⑤

3. The narrator of the passage can best be described as feeling

(1) self-confident
(2) successful
(3) hopeful
(4) discouraged
(5) furious

① ② ③ ④ ⑤

4. The author uses the words "box" and "boxes" to mean both want-ads and

(1) shipping cartons
(2) newspaper stands
(3) resumes
(4) secret locations
(5) job traps

① ② ③ ④ ⑤

GO ON TO THE NEXT PAGE.

Items 5–8 refers to the following poem.

What does the poet think life *should* be like?

Where?

There's a place the man always say
Come in here, child
No cause you should weep
Wolf never catch the rabbit
Golden hair never turn white with grief
Come in here, child
No cause you should moan
Brother never hurt his brother
Nobody here ever wander without a home
There must be some such place somewhere
But I never heard of it.

5. The poem is mainly about
   (1) the poet's neighborhood
   (2) the United States
   (3) an imaginary, ideal place
   (4) a child's view of the world
   (5) an animal's world

   (1) (2) (3) (4) (5)

6. The final line of the poem suggests
   (1) eager anticipation
   (2) cheerfulness
   (3) doubtfulness
   (4) fear
   (5) whimsy

   (1) (2) (3) (4) (5)

7. The line "Wolf never catch the rabbit" means
   (1) a rabbit is faster than a wolf
   (2) wolves are not as cunning as rabbits
   (3) life's pace is slow
   (4) it is possible to keep a rabbit as a pet
   (5) no one becomes a victim

   (1) (2) (3) (4) (5)

8. The mood of the poem is
   (1) wishful
   (2) emotional
   (3) cautious
   (4) fearful
   (5) humorous

   (1) (2) (3) (4) (5)

Items 9–11 refer to the following passage.

What is Mr. Sparkins's effect on everyone?

The appearance of Mr. Horatio Sparkins at the assembly, had excited no small degree of surprise and curiosity among its regular frequenters. Who could he be? He was evidently reserved, and apparently melancholy. Was he a clergyman?—He danced too well. A barrister?—He said he was not called. He used very fine words, and talked a great deal. Could he be a distinguished foreigner, come to England for the purpose of describing the country, its manners and customs; and frequenting public balls and public dinners, with the view of becoming acquainted with high life, polished etiquette, and English refinement?—No, he had not a foreign accent. Was he a surgeon, a contributor to the magazines, a writer of fashionable novels, or an artist?—No; to each and all of these surmises, there existed some valid objection.—'Then', said everybody, 'he must be *somebody.*'—'I should think he must be,' reasoned Mr. Malderton, within himself, 'because he perceives our superiority, and pays us so much attention.'

9. The nature of the assembly mentioned above is primarily
   (1) governmental
   (2) educational
   (3) religious
   (4) commercial
   (5) social

   (1) (2) (3) (4) (5)

10. The appearance of Sparkins excited curiosity primarily because he was
    (1) a minister
    (2) a stranger
    (3) a good dancer
    (4) an artist
    (5) a foreigner

    (1) (2) (3) (4) (5)

GO ON TO THE NEXT PAGE.

11. If Malderton is a typical example of the assembly, they think of themselves as

(1) keepers of the flame
(2) social-climbing workers
(3) poor blighters
(4) socially superior
(5) professionals

(1) (2) (3) (4) (5)

Items 12–13 refer to the following commentary.

What are the strengths and weaknesses of TV news reports?

With the aid of far-flung organizations and Star Trek technology, today's breaking news is expertly covered by television journalists. Recording sound and fury is what we do best. Unfortunately, it frequently seems uncaring. *Soul* is the missing ingredient in television journalism. Too often the news is presented with such premeditated detachment it borders on frigid indifference.

"Behind me, the nation of Ethiopia is starving . . ."

"Here in Iraq the war rages on . . ."

"Twenty-nine more were killed today in South Africa . . ."

Listening to the reports, you would be justified in thinking that among newscasters passion is a dirty word. I call it the Edward R. Murrow Complex. During the Second World War and throughout the adolescence of the television news business, that CBS News icon painted fire with his word pictures and captured emotion in his messages. But because he was stone-faced, succeeding generations of reporters have mistakenly assumed he did his job untouched by the maelstrom he was observing.

Countless of his professional progeny have attempted to mimic his style. Coolness has become synonymous with objectivity, aloofness with professionalism. Let the story tell itself. Don't get involved. Don't get down and dirty.

12. Which of the following changes in television news reporting would the author most likely welcome?

(1) more pictures of newsworthy events
(2) fewer pictures of newsworthy events
(3) newscasters who are less emotional
(4) newscasters who seem to care about people in the news
(5) fewer sensational stories

(1) (2) (3) (4) (5)

13. Why does the author describe newscaster Edward R. Murrow as "stone-faced"?

(1) to contrast Murrow with today's emotional newscasters
(2) to give the impression that Murrow was stern and unpleasant
(3) to suggest that Murrow's face did not reveal the emotions that he really felt
(4) to show that Murrow was not really interested in the news he reported
(5) to point out how all newscasters should appear when they report news stories

(1) (2) (3) (4) (5)

GO ON TO THE NEXT PAGE.

Items 14–16 refer to the following dramatic passage.

What attitudes toward romance does Helen reveal?

Helen and Seth stopped by a fence near where a low, dark building faced the street. The building had once been a factory for the making of barrel staves but was now vacant. Across the street upon the porch of a house a man and woman talked of their childhood, their voices coming clearly across to the half-embarrassed youth and maiden. There was the sound of scraping chairs, and the man and woman came down the gravel path to a wooden gate. Standing outside the gate, the man leaned over and kissed the woman. "For old times' sake," he said and, turning, walked rapidly away along the sidewalk.

"That's Belle Turner," whispered Helen, and put her hand boldly into Seth's hand. "I didn't know she had a fellow. I thought she was too old for that." Seth laughed uneasily. The hand of the girl was warm and a strange, dizzying feeling crept over him. Into his mind came a desire to tell her something he had been determined not to tell. "George Willard's in love with you," he said, and in spite of his agitation his voice was low and quiet. "He's writing a story, and he wants to be in love. He wants to know how it feels. He wanted me to tell you and see what you said."

14. In the second paragraph of the passage, Helen assumes that Belle Turner

    (1) is having a romance with her companion
    (2) is younger than she looks
    (3) is older than she looks
    (4) is lonely
    (5) is married to another man

    (1) (2) (3) (4) (5)

15. Why are Helen and Seth half-embarrassed when they hear Belle Turner's voice?

    (1) Belle may think they are prying into her life.
    (2) They feel they've overheard a private conversation.
    (3) Belle may gossip about their growing friendship.
    (4) Helen and Seth don't want anyone to see them together.
    (5) Belle may suspect that George Willard is in love with Helen.

    (1) (2) (3) (4) (5)

16. George Willard's feelings of love for Helen are primarily

    (1) based on admiration for her beauty
    (2) a result of Helen's love for him
    (3) based on respect for her kindness
    (4) contrived; he wonders what love is like
    (5) just a lie that Seth has made up

GO ON TO THE NEXT PAGE.

Items 17–19 refer to the following dramatic passage.

What sort of future do the local children have to look forward to?

MR. JONES. Round here [they] are only children till they are twelve. Then they are sent away over the hills to the mine, and in one week they are old men.

MISS MOFFAT. I see. How many can read or write?

MR. JONES. Next to none.

MISS RONBERRY. Why do you ask?

MISS MOFFAT. Because I am going to start a school for them.

MISS RONBERRY. *(coldly)* Start a school for them? What for?

MISS MOFFAT. What for? See these books? Hundreds of 'em, and something wonderful to read in every single one—these nippers are to be cut off from all that for ever, are they? Why? Because they happen to be born penniless in an uncivilized countryside, coining gold down there in that stinking dungeon for some beefheaded old miser!

MR. JONES. [*rouses*] That's right!

MISS MOFFAT. The printed page, what is it? One of the miracles of all time, that's what! . . .

17. The twelve-year-old children that Mr. Jones refers to become "old men" quickly because they

    (1) mature physically very rapidly
    (2) learn their job skills so quickly
    (3) must work hard under bad conditions
    (4) are in bad health
    (5) are from poor families

18. Why does Miss Moffat want to open a school for local children?

    (1) She feels everyone should be able to enjoy books.
    (2) She secretly hopes to get some gold from the local mine.
    (3) Miss Ronberry and Mr. Jones have asked her to open a school.
    (4) The poverty-stricken area will benefit financially from having a school.
    (5) Miss Moffat is lonely and has nothing better to do.

19. Why might Miss Moffat believe the printed page is "one of the miracles of all time"?

    (1) It can heal injuries the children may suffer working in the mines.
    (2) It can transport the reader to different places and times.
    (3) It can educate the children to read and write.
    (4) It will help the poor make more money.
    (5) It can give people supernatural powers.

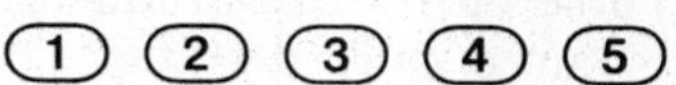

GO ON TO THE NEXT PAGE.

Items 20–22 refer to the following passage.

What sorts of thoughts ran through Charles Lindbergh's mind on that first solo transatlantic flight, more than sixty years ago?

The haze continues to clear. I can see cloud formations farther away, fly closer to their walls, follow a straighter course through their valleys. There's another mushroomed column, miles ahead. Its top silhouettes against a star-brightening sky. I bank toward the southern edge, and settle back in my cockpit.

In keeping his heading by the stars, a pilot must remember that they move. In all the heavens, there is only one he can trust, only one that won't lead him off his course—Polaris, faint star of the northern pole. Those other more brilliant points of light, which at first seem motionless too, sweep through their arcs so rapidly that he can use them only as temporary guides, lining one up ahead, letting it creep to the side, dropping the first to pick a second; then the second for a third; and so on through the night.

As a child, I'd lie on my bed in Minnesota and watch the stars curve upward in their courses—the box-like corners of Orion's belt—Sirius's piercing brilliance—rising over treetops, climbing slowly toward our roof. I would curl up under my blankets and web the constellations into imaginary scenes of celestial magnitude. . . . I'd make my wishes on the stars, and drift from wakefulness to sleep as I desired. Dreams of day and dreams of night would merge, while a planet's orbit had no effect on my security. There was no roar of an engine in my ears, no sound above the wind in leaves except the occasional whistle of a train, far away across the river.

20. "I would curl up under my blankets and web the constellations into imaginary scenes. . . ."

    In the comment above, the word "web" most nearly means

    (1) walk
    (2) move
    (3) paint
    (4) weave
    (5) watch a spider turn

    ① ② ③ ④ ⑤

21. Which of the following would the author most likely recommend to a sailor who must use the stars to plan a course?

    (1) Rely on the northern lights.
    (2) Remember that Polaris remains steady.
    (3) Always watch a small, bright star.
    (4) Always keep Sirius ahead of you.
    (5) Use the moon as your guide.

    ① ② ③ ④ ⑤

22. According to the passage, how did the author's stargazing as a child contrast with his use of stars as a pilot?

    (1) As a pilot, his life depends on the stars.
    (2) As an adult, he has lost interest in stars.
    (3) From a cockpit, stars look bigger.
    (4) As a pilot, he is unafraid.
    (5) As an adult, he no longer daydreams.

    ① ② ③ ④ ⑤

END OF EXAMINATION

TEST 5: MATHEMATICS PRETEST

Directions

The *Mathematics Pretest* consists of 28 problems. Whenever possible, you should arrive at your own answer to a question before looking at the choices; otherwise, you may be misled by plausible mistakes.

You should take approximately 45 minutes to complete this test. There is no penalty for guessing. Try to answer as many questions as you can. Work rapidly but carefully, without spending too much time on any one question. If a question is too difficult for you, omit it and come back to it later.

For each answer, mark one answer space. See how the following example is done.

EXAMPLE

A secretary bought a desk calendar for $5.95 and a pencil container for $1.89. How much change did she get from a ten-dollar bill?

(1) $7.84
(2) $8.84
(3) $2.61
(4) $8.74
(5) $2.16

The amount is $2.16; therefore, answer space (5) has been marked.

Answers to the questions are in the Answer Key on page 61. Explanations for the answers are on pages 70–72.

Directions: For all problems choose the one best answer.

1. Four hardware stores gave Ed the following prices for a certain size bolt:

   Store A: 8 for 13¢
   Store B: 2 for 3¢
   Store C: 4 for 7¢
   Store D: 10 for 16¢

   Which of the following sequences correctly lists the stores in order of bolt price, from lowest to highest?

   (1) B, C, A, D
   (2) B, D, A, C
   (3) C, A, D, B
   (4) C, B, D, A
   (5) D, A, C, B

   (1) (2) (3) (4) (5)

2. Four pounds of grapes and 3 pounds 4 ounces of sugar can be made into 8 cups of jelly. If you had 48 pounds of grapes, how many pounds of sugar would it take to make all the grapes into jelly?

   (1) $14\frac{4}{5}$
   (2) 26
   (3) 39
   (4) 143
   (5) Insufficient data is given to solve the problem.

   (1) (2) (3) (4) (5)

3. A discount shoe store sells everything for 10% off the list price. During a special after-Christmas sale, it took an additional $\frac{1}{4}$ off. If the list price of a pair of shoes is $40, what did the shoes cost during the special after-Christmas sale?

   (1) $4
   (2) $9
   (3) $13
   (4) $27
   (5) $36

   (1) (2) (3) (4) (5)

Items 4–5 refer to the following graph.

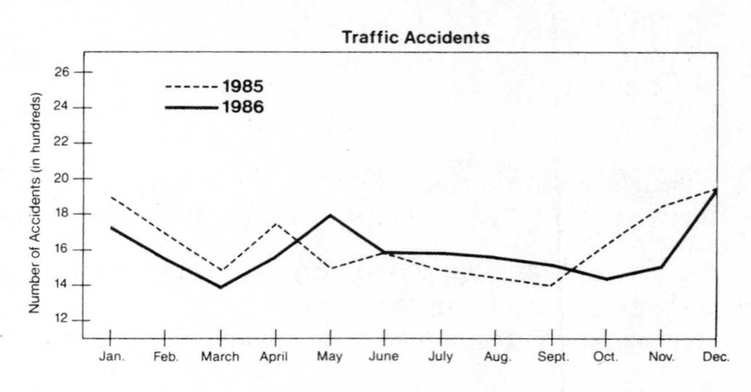

4. Compare the number of accidents for May 1985 and May 1986. How many more or fewer accidents were there in May 1986?

   (1) 300 fewer
   (2) 30 fewer
   (3) 3 fewer
   (4) 3 more
   (5) 300 more

   (1) (2) (3) (4) (5)

5. If the month of June represented the average number of accidents for 1986, what was the approximate total number of accidents for the year?

   (1) 16
   (2) 160
   (3) 190
   (4) 1,600
   (5) 19,200

   (1) (2) (3) (4) (5)

6. Phyllis Meyers bought a train ticket to New Orleans for $230. If the train travels at the rate of 50 miles per hour, how many miles will it go in 36 minutes?

   (1) 30
   (2) 36
   (3) 38
   (4) 42
   (5) 45

   (1) (2) (3) (4) (5)

GO ON TO THE NEXT PAGE.

7. A charity organization is having a dinner. Sixty people are expected to attend, of whom fifteen will be children. The following options for pricing tickets are being considered:

   A. \$3.50 per person

   B. \$4.00 per adult and children $\frac{1}{2}$ price

   C. \$5.00 per adult and \$1.50 per child

   D. \$6.00 per adult and children free

   Which of the above options will earn the most for the charity?

   (1) A
   (2) B
   (3) C
   (4) D
   (5) Insufficient data is given to solve the problem.

   ① ② ③ ④ ⑤

8. The average distance from the earth to the sun is approximately 150,000,000 kilometers. Which of the following expresses this distance in scientific notation?

   (1) 150×10^6
   (2) 15×10^7
   (3) $15 + 10^7$
   (4) 1.5×10^7
   (5) 1.5×10^8

   ① ② ③ ④ ⑤

9. Six ounces of brand-name cough medication costs \$1.95. Ten ounces of a generic cough medication costs \$2.25. How much more or less did the brand-name medication cost per ounce?

   (1) 23 cents less
   (2) 10 cents less
   (3) 5 cents more
   (4) 10 cents more
   (5) 23 cents more

   ① ② ③ ④ ⑤

10. Which of the following is equal to $52(37 - 12)$?

   (1) $52 \times 37 - 12$
   (2) $52(25)$
   (3) $52(49)$
   (4) $89 - 64 + 52$
   (5) $52(89) - 64$

   ① ② ③ ④ ⑤

11. Peter checked the prices of blenders at a discount store. Four brands sold for \$30 each, two brands sold for \$24 each, and one brand sold for \$21. What was the median price of the blenders?

   (1) \$24
   (2) \$25
   (3) \$27
   (4) \$30
   (5) \$37

   ① ② ③ ④ ⑤

12. In a school board election, Candidate A received twice as many votes as Candidate B. After the polls closed, the polltakers estimated a 40 percent voter turnout for the district. If Candidate A received 576 votes, what was the total number of votes cast in the election?

   (1) 230
   (2) 288
   (3) 720
   (4) 864
   (5) 1,152

   ① ② ③ ④ ⑤

GO ON TO THE NEXT PAGE.

Items 13–15 refer to the following situation.

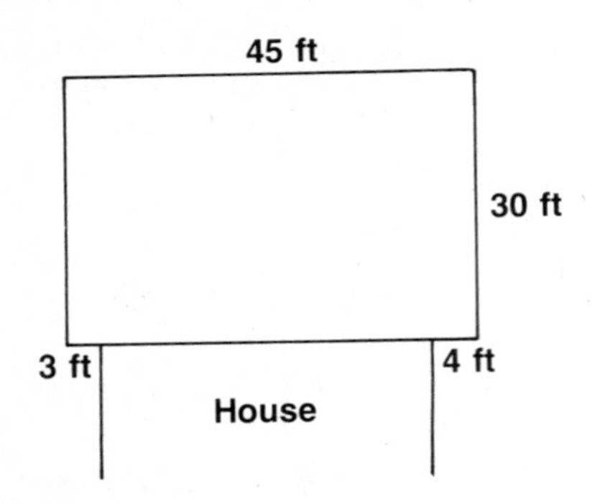

The Smiths plan to fence in their rectangular yard, shown in the figure above, and to fertilize the lawn. No fencing is needed where the yard borders the house, and a gate is to be placed on the 4-foot section of land next to the house. Store A will install the fence for $6.20 per foot and a gate for $72. A 10-pound bag of fertilizer at Store A costs $9.80. At Store B, fencing installation is discounted 10 percent for orders over 125 feet. Installation of gates costs $68 each. Store B offers a lawn service which will apply fertilizer and weed killer for $95 per year.

13. At Store A, which of the following expressions gives the cost of installing one gate and a fence around the Smiths' yard?

(1) 78(6.20 + 72)
(2) 108(6.20) + 72
(3) 112(6.20) + 72
(4) 108(6.20 + 72)
(5) Insufficient data is given to solve the problem.

① ② ③ ④ ⑤

14. At Store B, what would be the cost of installing a fence and one gate around the Smiths' yard, to the nearest dollar?

(1) $165
(2) $193
(3) $603
(4) $671
(5) Insufficient data is given to solve the problem.

① ② ③ ④ ⑤

15. What would be the approximate cost per square foot if the Smiths use Store B's lawn service for their yard?

(1) $0.07
(2) $0.63
(3) $1.58
(4) $14.21
(5) Insufficient data is given to solve the problem.

① ② ③ ④ ⑤

16. Mrs. Rodgers purchased a $1,500 lawn tractor. She made a down payment of $150 and agreed to pay a 1 percent finance charge per month on any unpaid balance. How much did she owe at the end of the first month?

(1) $1,250.50
(2) $1,336.50
(3) $1,350.00
(4) $1,363.50
(5) $1,365.50

① ② ③ ④ ⑤

17. A one-pound package of cereal costs $2.72. At that price per pound, which of the following expressions gives the cost of a 10-ounce package of cereal?

(1) 2.72/10
(2) (2.72 × 10)/16
(3) (2.72 × 12)/10
(4) (2.72 × 16)/10
(5) 2.72 × 10

① ② ③ ④ ⑤

18. When the Knox County courthouse was built in 1836, a clock was installed atop it. The clock cost $1,100 and had a radius of 72 feet. To the nearest *square yard,* what was the area of the clock?

(1) 16,278
(2) 11,094
(3) 5,184
(4) 1,809
(5) 576

① ② ③ ④ ⑤

GO ON TO THE NEXT PAGE.

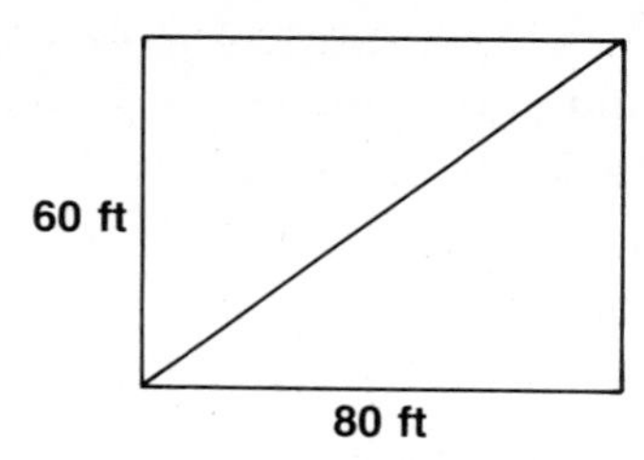

19. A city minipark is shown in the figure above. How many feet shorter is it to cross the park diagonally than to walk around the two sides?

(1) 35
(2) 40
(3) 55
(4) 60
(5) 70

Item 20 is based on the following diagram.

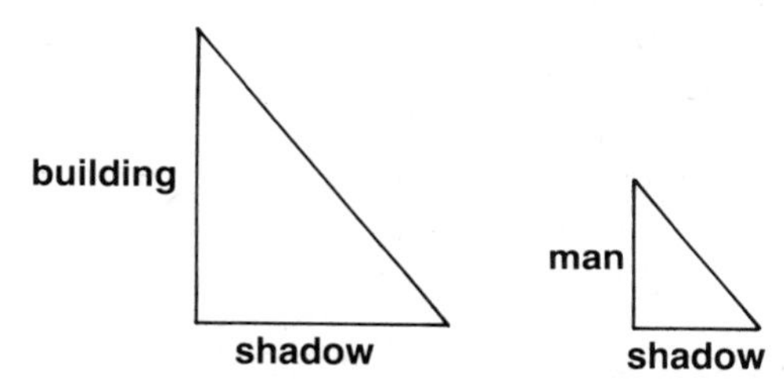

20. A man 6 feet tall casts a shadow 5 feet long. Two miles away, the shadow of a building is 60 feet long. How many feet tall is the building?

(1) 50
(2) 72
(3) 120
(4) 300
(5) 360

21. Mr. Rivera is building a new house. How much will it cost to excavate for the basement at \$1.75 per *cubic yard* if the basement is 36 feet by 24 feet by 7 feet?

(1) \$893.00
(2) \$605.00
(3) \$483.75
(4) \$425.50
(5) \$392.00

Item 22 is based on the following diagram.

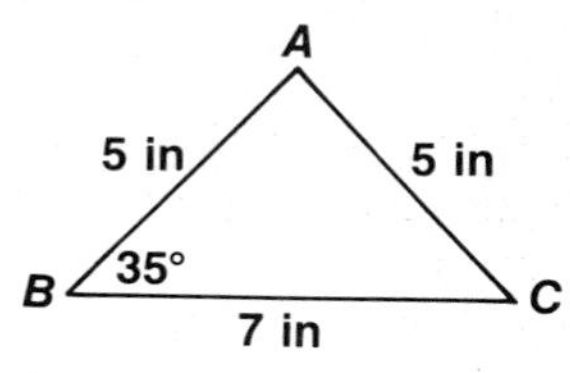

22. In triangle *ABC*, what is the measure of angle *A*?

(1) 35°
(2) 55°
(3) 70°
(4) 110°
(5) 145°

1 2 3 4 5

23. What is the distance in feet across a round pool if it is 242 feet around the edge? (Use $\pi = 3\frac{1}{7}$.)

(1) $38\frac{1}{2}$
(2) 42
(3) $59\frac{1}{2}$
(4) 68
(5) 77

GO ON TO THE NEXT PAGE.

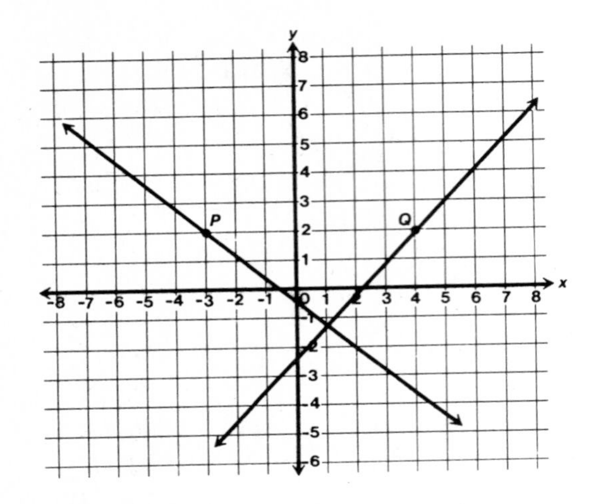

24. How many units of distance between points P and Q is shown on the figure above?

(1) 6
(2) 7
(3) 10
(4) 11
(5) 16

1 2 3 4 5

25. Let L stand for Larry's age. His grandmother's age is 3 years more than 4 times Larry's age. Which of the following expressions represents his grandmother's age?

(1) $3L + 4$
(2) $4L + 3$
(3) $7L$
(4) $6L$
(5) $4 - 3L$

1 2 3 4 5

26. A softball team played 18 games last year. If its ratio of wins to losses was 1:2, how many games did the team lose?

(1) 2
(2) 6
(3) 9
(4) 12
(5) 15

1 2 3 4 5

27. Which of the following would NOT be a correct replacement for x in the inequality $x + 3 \geq 5$?

(1) 4
(2) 3
(3) $2\frac{1}{2}$
(4) 2
(5) 1

1 2 3 4 5

28. If $x^2 - x - 30 = 0$, then x equals

(1) -6 only
(2) -5 only
(3) -6 or $+5$
(4) -5 or $+6$
(5) $+5$ only

1 2 3 4 5

END OF EXAMINATION

Pretests—Answer Key

Writing Skills

1. (3)
2. (5)
3. (2)
4. (2)
5. (4)
6. (3)
7. (5)
8. (4)
9. (1)
10. (2)
11. (2)
12. (5)
13. (5)
14. (1)
15. (1)
16. (4)
17. (2)
18. (1)
19. (4)
20. (3)
21. (4)
22. (3)
23. (5)
24. (1)
25. (5)
26. (3)
27. (3)
28. (2)

Social Studies

1. (3)
2. (2)
3. (4)
4. (1)
5. (4)
6. (3)
7. (2)
8. (3)
9. (2)
10. (4)
11. (4)
12. (2)
13. (5)
14. (1)
15. (3)
16. (4)
17. (3)
18. (5)
19. (2)
20. (1)
21. (4)
22. (1)
23. (3)
24. (5)
25. (5)
26. (2)
27. (4)
28. (2)
29. (1)
30. (3)
31. (5)
32. (2)

Science

1. (1)
2. (3)
3. (2)
4. (4)
5. (2)
6. (4)
7. (2)
8. (3)
9. (3)
10. (5)
11. (3)
12. (1)
13. (3)
14. (2)
15. (4)
16. (1)
17. (3)
18. (2)
19. (3)
20. (1)
21. (2)
22. (2)
23. (4)
24. (4)
25. (3)
26. (1)
27. (2)
28. (5)
29. (3)
30. (1)
31. (2)
32. (4)
33. (2)

Interpreting Literature and the Arts

1. (4)
2. (2)
3. (4)
4. (5)
5. (3)
6. (3)
7. (5)
8. (1)
9. (5)
10. (2)
11. (4)
12. (4)
13. (3)
14. (1)
15. (2)
16. (4)
17. (3)
18. (1)
19. (2)
20. (4)
21. (2)
22. (1)

Mathematics

1. (2)
2. (3)
3. (4)
4. (5)
5. (5)
6. (1)
7. (4)
8. (5)
9. (4)
10. (2)
11. (4)
12. (4)
13. (2)
14. (5)
15. (1)
16. (4)
17. (2)
18. (4)
19. (2)
20. (2)
21. (5)
22. (4)
23. (5)
24. (2)
25. (2)
26. (4)
27. (5)
28. (4)

To find your score, cross out the numbers above of all the questions you answered incorrectly or did not answer at all. Then count the number you have answered correctly for each test and write that number in the chart below. Look for the number of that score after the name of the test on the three parts of the Study Plan Chart on the next page. Then read the suggestions, based on that score, for what you need to study for passing the GED Test.

Writing Skills	Social Studies	Science	Interpreting Literature and the Arts	Mathematics

Study Plan Chart for Passing the GED

Use the chart on page 61 to find your score below.

Score: **Exceptional**		
Test	*Score*	*Study Plan*
Writing Skills	25 or more correct*	If your score on any of these individual tests is exceptional, you can take the Posttests for that subject. After you take each Posttest, study the answer explanations for every item you got wrong.
Social Studies	29 or more correct	
Science	29 or more correct	
Literature and the Arts	21 or more correct	
Mathematics	26 or more correct	

Score: **Good**		
Writing Skills	18 to 24 correct*	If your score on any one of the Pretests is good, you will need to read the opener and overview pages at the beginning of the section for that subject. Then skip to the Minitests at the end of the section. If you do well on the Minitests, you can take the two Posttests for that subject. Be sure to read all the answer explanations for the Pretest, Minitest, and Posttest items you missed.
Social Studies	21 to 28 correct	
Science	19 to 28 correct	
Literature and the Arts	17 to 20 correct	
Mathematics	15 to 25 correct	

Score: **Fair**		
Writing Skills	8 to 17 correct*	If your score on any one of the Pretests is in the range of correct answers shown at the left, you came close to a passing score but need further study and practice before taking the Minitests and Posttests. After you read the section opener and overview, answer all the items in the white test columns of the pages that follow. If you miss more than half the items on a page, read the tinted inner column before trying the white outer-column questions again. Then do the outer-column questions on the next page. If you miss more than half of them, read the tinted columns of the rest of the pages in that subsection. Continue in this manner until you finish the entire section. Then do the Minitests. Carefully study the answer explanations for every one of the test items. Then you can take the Posttests.
Social Studies	9 to 20 correct	
Science	9 to 18 correct	
Literature and the Arts	6 to 16 correct	
Mathematics	7 to 14 correct	

Score: **Risky**		
Writing Skills	7 or fewer correct*	With a score on any of the individual Pretests as shown at the left, you'll need to study quite a bit to prepare for that particular GED subject test. Start by reading the opener and overview. Next work slowly and carefully through the tinted and white columns of each page. Then take the Minitests. Read very carefully the answer explanation for every test item you missed. Finally do the two Posttests.
Social Studies	8 or fewer correct	
Science	8 or fewer correct	
Literature and the Arts	5 or fewer correct	
Mathematics	6 or fewer correct	

*Number of items you answered correctly on the multiple-choice section of the Writing Skills Test. See page 63 for information on how to score your essay.

Scoring Your Essay The essay is the one part of the Pretest that you cannot correct yourself. A sample essay appears on page 66 that you can use as a model. But you will also need someone to help you score your own essay.

If you're in a GED class, your teacher will be able to read your paper and help you plan a course of study. If you're studying alone, however, you'll need to find someone to read and score your essay. Choose someone who you know is a good writer—a teacher, your boss, a friend—someone you trust to be honest with you about your abilities.

First give the person you have chosen the checklist below to preview, so that he or she can understand better what is needed. (In fact, the scorer might want to read this whole section, "Scoring Your Essay," before beginning in order to fully understand what is going on.)

Essay Scoring Checklist

To the scorer: Preview this entire checklist before you read and score the essay.

Read the essay topic on page 26. Next, read the essay written on that topic *quickly.* Take no more than two minutes. Try to achieve an overall impression of the writing. Then put the essay aside and, without referring back to it, rate it using the following criteria.

	Exceptional **4**	Good **3**	Fair **2**	Risky* **1**
Message— the presence of a clear, controlling idea	☐	☐	☐	☐
Details— the use of examples and specific details to support the message	☐	☐	☐	☐
Organization— a logical presentation of ideas	☐	☐	☐	☐
Expression— the clear, precise use of language to convey the message	☐	☐	☐	☐
Mechanics— knowledge of the conventions of standard English (grammar, punctuation, and so on)	☐	☐	☐	☐
Sentence Structure— the use of complete sentences that avoid a repetitive, singsong rhythm	☐	☐	☐	☐

*Weak enough that taking an essay test at this point would not be advisable

Once the scorer has previewed the checklist, give him or her the topic assignment and then your essay to read. The scorer should read your essay *very quickly;* it should take no more than a minute or two. Then, *putting the essay aside and not looking back at it,* the scorer should record his or her impressions on the checklist. You can then use the checklist to plan your course of study as follows.

Count up your score using this method: Add 4 points for every checkmark in the Exceptional column, 3 for every mark under Good, 2 for every mark under Fair, and 1 for every mark under Risky. Your total should be from 6 to 24.

Now find your total on the chart below, and read the corresponding study plan.

Exceptional 21–24	You might first want to read pages 153–156 in the *Writing Skills* section to learn more about the GED Test itself and how the GED essay will be administered and scored. Then you can go to the Posttests and get extra practice with the essay topics there. But see below if there were any areas for which you received less than an exceptional score.
Good 16–20	If your score is in the range of good, read the *Writing Skills* opener and overview on pages 153–156 and then use the Minitests and the Posttests to improve your skills even more. See the instructions below if you scored less than good in any particular area.
Fair 10–15	A fair score means you are close but not guaranteed of writing a successful GED essay. Be sure to read the *Writing Skills* opener and overview on pages 153–156. Take the time to study the tinted explanations about writing essays on pages 204–215 and choose topics from the white columns in that section for practice. Then go on to the Minitests and Posttests.
Risky 6–9	A risky score means you'd be wise to start with the opener and overview on pages 153–156 and then study the sections on writing paragraphs and essays. Try to write as many essays about the topics in the white columns as you can, and study the sample essay answers. Then try your skills on the Minitests and Posttests.

In addition to the study plans above, you may want to use the checklist to see how you scored in particular areas. Even if you got an overall exceptional or good score, you may want additional practice in areas where you received a score of fair or risky. Here's a chart showing you which pages give explanations and practice in particular areas.

Message	197, 204
Details	197, 205, 210
Organization	198, 206
Expression	190, 195–196, 212–213
Sentence Structure	157–159, 165–167, 173–174, 182–183, 185, 187, 211
Mechanics	160–164, 168–172, 175–181, 184, 186, 188–189, 191–194

Answer Explanations—Pretest

Writing Skills
pages 19–27

1. (3) No comma is needed after *that.* No comma is needed after *course* because there is no pause between *course* and *we.*

2. (5) This is a comma splice. The best way to join these two closely related sentences is to use a semicolon.

3. (2) *There* is not the subject of the sentence. Since *jobs* (meaning more than one) is the subject, it must agree with the verb *are* (also meaning more than one).

4. (2) This passage tells about a future event. *Will become* correctly expresses future time. Since no pause occurs between *obsolete* and the dependent part of the sentence, no comma is needed.

5. (4) When *and* joins two complete sentences, a comma is inserted before *and.* The same is true for *or, but, so, yet,* and *for.*

6. (3) The passage is written with substitute words like *we, our,* and *us. You, they, one,* and *each* do not follow through with this pattern.

7. (5) No error. *Doctors* is only capitalized when it is used with a person's name (Doctor Lenore Jenkins).

8. (4) It is not clear what *they* refers to. Replacing *they* with *restaurant* clarifies the meaning.

9. (1) *A hamburger ordered "your way" will be cooked, packaged, and delivered by a worker built of aluminum and guided by a microchip. Delivered* is the only option that matches the other two verbs, *cooked* and *packaged.*

10. (2) *Definitely* is one of the most misspelled words in English. *For better or worse* is an introductory phrase and needs a comma after it.

How will our ever-increasing technology change the job scene in the latter part of this century? Of course we know that computers will change the way most of us make a living. Computerized robots are already taking over many factory jobs; we are all familiar with this trend. But there are many jobs on the way out that are not so obviously connected to technology. Believe it or not, computer programmers will become obsolete because a new generation of computers capable of programming themselves will be built. The farm laborers of the future will be an automated army of robot field hands, and the farmer of the future will sit in a computerized control tower to schedule plantings and harvests. Many lumberjacks will be jobless, as we will be using computers, rather than paper, to store information such as books, magazines, and newspapers. Even doctors will be affected by computerized technology. The University of Pittsburgh is experimenting with a program called "Doctor on a Chip" to help in diagnosing illnesses and prescribing treatments. Fast-food restaurants are increasing in numbers, but fast-food workers will lose their jobs as restaurants become more automated. A hamburger ordered "your way" will be cooked, packaged, and delivered by a worker built of aluminum and guided by a microchip. For better or worse, technology will definitely change our lives, but by planning ahead, we can keep from joining the unemployment line.

11. (2) *There* is not the subject of sentence 1. *Sight* (the subject) agrees with *has* (the verb). *Sight* is correct because it refers to something you can see. *Site* refers to a location.

12. (5) This is an example of a comma splice. Two complete sentences cannot be connected with a comma. Option (2) is a run-on. *But* is needed as a connecting word to express the contrast between the two sentences. Therefore, option (3) is incorrect.

13. (5) No error. *Begun* must always be used with a helper. The action in this passage occurred in the past.

14. (1) *Upon returning to Europe, he began to draw up plans for a dirigible.* Option (4) does not correctly express the sequence of events. He returned to Europe first. Option (5) is incorrect because the phrase *beginning to . . .* cannot describe Europe.

15. (1) *Successful* is spelled with two *c*'s and two *s*'s. The names of countries *(Germany)* are always capitalized.

16. (4) Commas are needed to separate items in a list *(designed, reliable,* and *mail carrier).*

17. (2) A comma is placed before *and* when it connects two complete sentences. (3) is a run-on. (4) is a comma splice.

18. (1) *Or* and *yet* do not logically express the relationship between the two verbs *(felt* and *had).* Option (4) creates a descriptive phrase *(having unparalled, close-range views of the terrain below)* that incorrectly describes *motion.*

19. (4) The substitute word *it* correctly takes the place of *zeppelin* because they both mean one thing. *They* can only substitute for words meaning more than one thing.

There has never been a sight to match it: silently, gracefully, the huge, majestic airships glided overhead. The age of the zeppelin was brief, but it was glorious. It began when a German graf, or count, Ferdinand von Zeppelin, took a balloon ride in St. Paul,

Minnesota, shortly after the Civil War. Upon returning to Europe, he began to draw up plans for a dirigible. A dirigible is a rigid, steerable, lighter-than-air aircraft far superior to the traditional "pressure" airships known as blimps. Perhaps the most successful airship of them all was the *Graf Zeppelin,* built in Germany in 1924. Almost 800 feet long and 100 feet in diameter, the *Graf* was beautifully designed, reliable, and probably the greatest mail carrier ever known. On its first flight to the United States in 1928, it carried 65,714 pieces of mail, and on its return it brought 101,683 letters and postcards. The *Graf* was also a fine passenger ship, with accommodations far more spacious and luxurious than those of today's jumbo jets. Passengers cruising around the world in the *Graf* felt almost no motion and had unparalleled, close-range views of the terrain below. Will the day of the zeppelin ever return? The zeppelin does seem well-suited to the 1980s and 1990s because it is fuel-efficient, relatively nonpolluting, almost noiseless, and able to take off and land in a small area.

20. (3) *Even in this age of equality, a real gender gap exists in nutrition needs.* The original sentence is awkward. Option (3) clarifies the main idea of the sentence. Options (1) and (2) are not logical. Options (4) and (5) contain extra words.

21. (4) *Recommended* is the correct spelling. If you chose option (2), you may have thought that *studies* was the subject of *consume;* in fact, *men and women* is the subject.

22. (3) The original wording is a comma splice. (2) is a run-on. *Whatever* and *and whatever* are not needed to connect the two sentences.

23. (5) No error. Commas are not used to connect two things *(women* and *men). Difference* is the subject of the sentence.

24. (1) *Researchers have found that women are more likely to be overweight or obese than men.* The original sentence is too wordy. *A lot of interesting information* is not needed. The revised sentence is an example of clear, concise writing.

25. (5) See the explanation for question 8.

26. (3) The items in a list should match. *Diabetes, heart disease,* and *cancer* are all things. *Getting heart disease* is not.

27. (3) *Loose* and *lose* look similar, but they are pronounced differently and have different meanings. *Loose* could describe your trousers after you *lose* thirty pounds.

28. (2) When a dependent part comes at the end of a sentence, do not insert a comma before the connecting word unless you can hear a pause before the connecting word.

Even in this age of equality, a real gender gap exists in nutrition needs. Recent studies emphasize that both men and women in the United States commonly consume less than the average recommended calorie intake, yet they maintain normal weight or may even be overweight. Why this is so is not clear. Whatever the reason, this lower-than-average calorie intake poses more of a weight problem for women than for men. A man who consumes 2,400 calories a day can obtain all necessary nutrients more easily than a woman who consumes 1,600 calories or less daily. Consequently, women should eat food that is nutrient-dense. The difference in the calorie needs of women and men lies in differences in body size, in body composition, and in the amount of energy expended through physical activity. Researchers have found that women are more likely to be overweight or obese than men. This finding probably explains why dieting has become so common among women. The social advantages of being slender are well known, and the health risks connected with obesity are many, including higher incidences of diabetes, heart disease, and cancer. But dieters should bear in mind that the safest and most effective way to lose weight is to eat a balanced diet but to eat less, while increasing physical activity. The Food and Nutrition Board has stated that diets below 1,200 calories a day should be used only under the guidance of a physician or other health professional because it is difficult to select a diet providing all essential nutrients at this calorie level.

Sample essay:

These days more and more people change jobs every few years. Sometimes they move for advancement, sometimes from necessity. At times, it seems, people change jobs from pure restlessness.

For an ambitious person, a new job may present a chance for advancement that is not available with the old employer. By moving around, a person can learn new ways of doing things, gain skills, and become a more valuable employee.

Moving around may also help a person find the "right" position. Job hunting can involve a lot of trial and error. After a few tries, a good career may fall into place.

However, changing jobs also has costs. One is loss of benefits, such as vacation pay and pension rights. Learning the job takes time and effort, and it takes time before a new employee is really productive.

In addition, changing jobs is stressful, not only for the employee but often for his or her family as well. If the change requires moving to a new location, everyone must make new friends and adjust to a different way of life.

Whether or not changing jobs is desirable, for most people it is sometimes necessary. Our economy is changing so rapidly that "permanent" jobs disappear, and sometimes a whole line of work becomes outmoded. Like it or not, many of us will be faced with changing jobs in the future.

Social Studies
(pages 28–36)

1. (3) The statement implies that it was pointless to construct tall buildings using the usual construction methods because it reduced the amount of floor space available. Options (1), (2), and (5) were not stated in the passage. (4) doesn't explain the sentence.

2. (2) Without an ample supply of steel, the new construction method could not be used. Options (1), (3), and (5) are irrelevant. Carnegie's control of the steel industry did not affect its production (4).

3. (4) All the other options support the conclusion in (4).

4. (1) Since the factors that contributed to the expanded powers still exist, there is no reason to believe that presidential powers will be limited as options (2), (4), and (5) state. The passage makes no mention of future presidents (3).

5. (4) Nicholas imagines his actual headaches and cough are serious even though physicians can find nothing.

6. (3) Maria has a fear of taking the elevator, which most people ride in comfortably.

7. (2) Willie's actions are a daily occurrence that serves no real purpose.

8. (3) California and Nevada will have normal temperatures and below normal rainfall. Kansas and Florida will have normal temperatures and precipitation.

9. (2) Since California is expected to have higher temperatures and little rainfall, there is a chance of forest fires.

10. (4) Options (1), (2), and (3) are not stated in the passage. (5) does occur, but it does not summarize the entire paragraph.

11. (4) Since unions have created national organizations to respond to large, national corporations, it is safe to predict that unions will become international as business does. There is no basis in the information to predict (1), (2), (3), or (5).

12. (2) Options (1), (4), and (5) pertain to other constitutional rights, not ones detailed in the Fourth Amendment. The action described in (3) is how the Fourth Amendment specifies an arrest warrant should be used.

13. (5) The first sentence of the passage states the Fourth Amendment "guards Americans against being arrested, having their homes searched, or having their papers or other property taken except when there is good reason to do so and a proper warrant has been issued."

14. (1) The projected population growth for the South and West combined is 38.9% between 1980–1990 and 30.9% for 1990–2000. Options (2)–(5) do not summarize all of the information.

15. (3) Because the population is expected to increase in the West, electric company officials foresee an increase in energy use. There will be no need for (1) or (5). Options (2) and (4) outline specific ways of generating more electricity.

16. (4) The graph indicates regional population projections only, not why people will move from one region to another.

17. (3) The population that remains in the Northeast and North Central states will most likely be older than the population of the South and West. All the other options probably will result from projected loss of people in the Northeast and North Central.

18. (5) The West will probably need more housing to accommodate its population increase. If the population of a region increases, the cost of living usually rises, (3) and (4). Options (1) and (2) are irrelevant.

19. (2) Weather as a factor in population growth cannot be determined from the graph. All the other options pertain to information on the graph.

20. (1) Ralph and Alice's combined income is $11,285, which is $285 more than (2) and $2,426 more than (3).

21. (4) If working wives had to live entirely on their own incomes, their standard of living would be much less than the standard of living based on the spouses' combined income. Options (2), (3), and (5) are irrelevant, and (1) has no basis in the figures provided.

22. (1) The first sentence of the passage states that the Trade Act of 1934 gave the President power to regulate foreign trade. The second sentence tells you that trade policy and foreign policy are inseparable. The President, therefore, has the power to conduct foreign policy.

23. (3) Option (3) is the only example that relates to both foreign and trade policies.

24. (5) Options (1) and (3) are false. Options (2) and (4) may be true but cannot be inferred from the passage. Option (5) relates directly to the link established between foreign policy and trade policy.

25. (5) The cartoon shows an employed couple coping with an ill child. There is no evidence to support Options (1), (2), or (3). Option (4) may be true, but the cartoon does not confirm it.

26. (2) Based on the passage there is no reason to believe the writers of the law had anything in mind other than preventing auto injuries of all kinds. Option (2) is more inclusive than (4) and (5). There is no evidence to suggest (1) or (3) is correct.

27. (4) Options (1), (2), (3), and (5) can be inferred from arguments made by lawyers in the case, but (4) is the only conclusion drawn directly from an official study.

28. (2) Traffic accidents threaten the safety of the public. If a mandatory seat belt law reduces serious accidents, then those in favor of the law believe public safety is more important than any right to drive without a seat belt.

29. (1) The passage indicates that lap-and-shoulder belts are safer than lap belts and no belts.

30. (3) The passage states that New England's harsh climate and rocky, infertile soil limited productivity.

31. (5) Options (1)–(4) support the conclusion in (5).

32. (2) The passage defines a subsistence economy as one where all that is produced is used for daily existence so that no profit is made from sales of the surplus products. Options (1), (4), and (5) produced profits. Option (3) were workers in a profit-making business.

Science
(pages 37–47)

1. (1) The forests are preserved as they existed 45 million years ago. All other answer options indicate some sort of change in the forest and are false.

2. (3) Only option (3) is a conclusion stated in the passage. Options (1), (2), (4), and (5) are all detailed statements which support option (3).

3. (2) Oxygen present in the air is necessary for most decay processes. Options 1, 4, and 5 are true but irrelevant. Option 3 is false.

4. (4) The article states that oil formation from resins is a hypothesis.

5. (2) Little or no vegetation grows in the harsh climate which exists on Axel Heiberg Island today. The fact that it once did grow there indicates a time when the climate was milder. While all other options are true statements, they do not support the stated conclusion.

6. (4) The fat will solidify around the ice cubes, but the rest of the gravy will remain a liquid because fat becomes a solid at a higher temperature than water does. The solidified fat can easily be removed. Increasing heat will do nothing to separate fat and water, (2) and (5). Option (3) is a reversal of the correct answer. Option (1) will have no effect.

7. (2) Metal loses and gains heat much more readily than wood does. The metal parts of the swing set seem cold to the child because the metal absorbs the heat from the child's hand. Options (1), (3), and (5) are false. Option (4) is irrelevant.

8. (3) The information states that hormones are regulated by the substances they cause to be produced. Thyroid stimulating hormone causes the production of several thyroid hormones. These hormones feed back and shut off the production of more thyroid stimulating hormone.

9. (3) Nitrates are the only chemical form of nitrogen which can be used by the plants. Organic nitrogen compounds must be reduced to ammonia, to nitrites, and finally to nitrates by bacteria, molds, and fungi living in the soil. All other options are false statements contradicted by the information given.

10. (5) The diagram indicates that nitrate is the only nitrogen form which plants can immediately use. Options (1)–(4) specify substances which must first be changed to nitrates by the action of soil organisms.

11. (3) If more soil organisms are present, more nitrates will be produced, and plants will grow better. Options (1), (2), and (5) would use up available nitrogen in the soil. Option (4) is false because nitrites are not usable forms of nitrogen.

12. (1) Charge is the only term which allows electrons to accumulate on a surface and which does not require electricity to move through a wire.

13. (3) Running the appliances more requires a greater amount of electricity. Option (2) might cause some confusion, but an appliance draws the same amount of current regardless of how long it is used. Options (1), (4), and (5) can be ruled out by rereading the definitions.

14. (2) The flow of electrons is insufficient to make the bulb glow brightly. Voltage, or pressure, can exist in the battery, but this does not mean the battery supplies enough electrons to light the bulb.

15. (4) The extension cord offers resistance to the electron flow. When the cord is used, additional electricity is required to overcome this resistance.

16. (1) Insect control programs such as those in the passage affect only the species involved. Chemical controls may kill other insects and animals (4). Options (2), (3), and (5) are not mentioned.

17. (3) If the dose of radiation were not sufficient and the males were not sterilized, offspring would have resulted from the matings. Option (1) is incorrect because only males were irradiated. The fact that the experiment worked indicates that mating did occur, (2) and (4). The matings resulted in infertile eggs and no offspring were produced.

18. (2) The purpose of the experiment was to determine if introducing sterilized males to a population of screwworm flies could control the fly population. Option (1) represents an opinion. Option (3) is the result of the experiment, not the hypothesis. *Sterilized* means infertile; as stated, (4) is a fact, not a hypothesis. Option (5) is an incorrect statement of the sterilization procedure.

19. (3) In each of the three examples on the graph, the percentage of protein recovered using process A is as high as (Ab 2) or higher than (Ab 1, Ab 3) the percentage recovered using Process B. Options (1), (2), and

(5) are incorrect. Option (4) is true for the three proteins tested, but it is incomplete because no information about Process B is included.

20. (1) The graph tells only what percentage of the original protein can be recovered (question A). The graph does not tell us what percentage of the original sample was composed of antibody (question B). The information states that the graph shows results for only 3 of the many proteins normally present in a blood sample (question C). Because options (2)–(5) all indicate that questions B and/or C can be answered, they are incorrect.

21. (2) He assumed that the amount of each protein recovered represented 100 percent of that protein present in the sample. He did not consider that perhaps less than 100 percent of the protein was recovered by the process he used. Option (1) is false. Options (3), (4), and (5) are irrelevant.

22. (2) Point C is between the lines labeled 860 and 880.

23. (4) Only this statement reflects an opinion. All other options are facts.

24. (4) Only option (4) is a correct statement which also summarizes the horsepower information on the graph. Options (1) and (3) are false. Options (2) and (5) do not summarize the graph.

25. (3) The graph tells nothing about the speed of the car, so option (3) cannot be determined. All other options can be determined from the graph.

26. (1) The tree will die without the fungus. Even if forest soil is transplanted with the tree (2), the fungus will not survive in the soil outside of the forest environment. Fertilization (3) will not keep the tree alive. Option (4) may be true but is irrelevant. Option (5) is a false statement.

27. (2) Only a brown leaf is a particular object or organism that is found in the butterfly's environment. Options (1), (3), (4), and (5) are other means of protection.

28. (5) A vegetarian assumes that she can obtain all necessary nutrients from vegetables. This is true, however, only if she carefully selects a wide variety of vegetables.

29. (3) Because the tea is already sugar-saturated, no more sugar will dissolve. Option (1), then, is false. But the addition of more sugar will not affect the amount of sugar that is already in solution. Therefore, options (2), (4), and (5) are false.

30. (1) Cell machinery cannot copy RNA. Therefore, the virus must use its own enzyme reverse transcriptase to change its RNA to DNA, a form which the cell machinery can recognize and copy. Options (2), (4), and (5) are false. Option (3) is also false because the virus does not contain DNA, only RNA.

31. (2) This statement summarizes the various steps by which the drug stops production of new viruses. All other options name one of these specific steps.

32. (4) This question involves the physician's ethics. Can he refuse a patient a curative medication for the sake of the scientific study? Furthermore, can he do so without informing the patient? The placebo group is actually deceived, because they believe they are receiving the experimental drug. All other options do not involve value judgments.

33. (2) Hemophilia is a hereditary disease. If people who have the disease have children, they will pass the genetic defect on to their children. It can be expected that more people in the population will have hemophilia. This also explains why options (3), (4), and (5) are false. Option (1) is incorrect because the information given states that hemophilia still cannot be cured.

Interpreting Literature and the Arts
(pages 48–54)

1. (4) The author has chosen to write as if he personally is experiencing the events he refers to. He describes the feelings and frustrations of a person looking for a job.

2. (2) Using the process of elimination can help you select the best answer to this question. Options (1), (3), (4), and (5) can be eliminated because they do not fit the meaning of the sentence. Only option (2) fits the meaning of the sentence and refers to something that might snap at a person's heels.

3. (4) The author describes many unsuccessful and unhappy attempts at finding a job. The many frustrations lead to discouragement.

4. (5) The "little boxes" are the job descriptions in the newspaper. But the author also uses the word "boxes" to refer to a job so unrewarding that the worker feels trapped.

5. (3) The poem describes a place—clearly imaginary—where all the residents live in harmony, no one ever feels grief, and everyone has a home and is kind to everyone else.

6. (3) In the final line the poet admits that, while there *should* be a place like the one described, it probably doesn't really exist.

7. (5) The wolf and the rabbit represent the predator and the intended victim. The poet means that in a perfect life, no one would ever be injured or mistreated.

8. (1) The poet does some wishful thinking in the poem—the mood is one of wishing and longing.

9. (5) It is a social occasion because the fifth sentence states that Sparkins danced too well. None of the other options would feature dancing at them.

10. (2) The other people were speculating on Sparkins's occupation because they did not know him. Although (3) is true, it's not the primary cause of their curiosity.

11. (4) Malderton says to himself that Sparkins "perceives our superiority." None of the other options refer to the passage.

12. (4) The author complains that today's newscasters seem to be cold and unemotional, quite unaffected by the news they report. Most likely, he would be pleased to have newscasters reveal, either by their words or expressions, that they felt the appropriate emotions as they reported the news.

13. (3) While Murrow's face did not reveal his emotion, his words and expressions made it clear that he felt strongly about the tragedies and triumphs of World War II.

14. (1) Helen's words reveal she assumed that Belle's companion is a romantic interest, not simply a relative or old friend.

15. (2) There is no evidence in the passage to suggest that options (3), (4), and (5) are true. Only Options (1) and (2) are real possibilities. Since there is no indication that Belle realizes Helen and Seth are there, Option (2) is the best answer.

16. (4) The answer is given in the last few lines of the paragraph. Seth explains that George Willard wants to know what it's like to be in love so that he can write his story. Apparently he has chosen Helen as the object of his contrived affections.

17. (3) Miss Moffat calls the mine a "stinking dungeon." There is no basis for (1) or (4), and (2) and (5) would not, by themselves, turn children into old men.

18. (1) You can tell from the passage that Miss Moffat thinks books are important. She said, "there's something wonderful to read in every single one." There is no evidence of (2)–(5).

19. (2) She said earlier that there is something wonderful to read in every book. She also implied that the children would be cut off from that if they didn't learn to read.

20. (4) To find the best answer, try substituting each of the five choices for the word *web* in the sentence. Option (4), *weave,* meaning "combine," is the best choice.

21. (2) The author discusses his use of stars to determine the direction of his flight. He points out that Polaris is the only star that remains steady. Therefore, he would probably recommend that sailors use Polaris as a guide in navigating.

22. (1) The answer is given near the end of the passage; in the days when he was a boy, he could afford to fantasize about the stars, since he didn't need to use them to steer a safe course.

Mathematics
(pages 55–60)

1. (2) B,D,A,C

First, find the cost of one bolt in each store. Divide the total cost by the number of bolts: a bolt at Store A costs $\frac{13}{8}$, at Store B $\frac{3}{2}$, at Store C $\frac{7}{4}$, and at Store D $\frac{16}{10}$ or $\frac{8}{5}$. To compare the fractions, find the least common denominator (40), change the fractions, and compare the numerators.

A $\frac{13}{8} \times \frac{5}{5} = \frac{65}{40}$ B $\frac{3}{2} \times \frac{20}{20} = \frac{60}{40}$

C $\frac{7}{4} \times \frac{10}{10} = \frac{70}{40}$ D $\frac{16}{10} \times \frac{4}{4} = \frac{64}{40}$

From smallest: $\frac{60}{40}, \frac{64}{40}, \frac{65}{40}, \frac{70}{40}$

2. (3) 39

4 lb of grapes is to 3 lb 4 oz (52 oz) of sugar as 48 lb of grapes is to an unknown quantity of sugar. Since 48 is 12 × 4, you need 12 times as much sugar: 12 × 52 oz = 624 oz. 624 oz divided by 16 oz = 39 lb. This problem can also be done as a proportion problem.

$$\frac{\overset{1}{\cancel{4}}}{\underset{12}{\cancel{48}}} = \frac{52}{x}$$

Cross multiply:
$x = 624 \text{ oz} = 39 \text{ lb}$

3. (4) $27

First compute the usual 10% discount off the $40 shoes and subtract the discount from $40.

$$\begin{array}{r} \$40 \\ \times\ .10 \\ \hline 4.00 \end{array} \qquad \begin{array}{r} \$40 \\ -\ \ 4 \\ \hline \$36 \end{array}$$

Next, compute the special after-Christmas discount of $\frac{1}{4}$ more off. Subtract this amount from the $36 discount price.

$$\frac{1}{\underset{1}{\cancel{4}}} \times \frac{\overset{9}{\cancel{36}}}{1} = \frac{1}{1} \times \frac{9}{1} = 9$$

$$\begin{array}{r} \$36 \\ -\ \ 9 \\ \hline \$27 \end{array}$$

4. (5) 300 more

First find the month of May on the graph. Then find the broken line, representing 1985, above May. Follow the 1985 point on the May line to the numbers on the left of the graph. The number is between 14 and 16, but a little less than halfway between. If the line were halfway between, it would be 15. Notice the accident figures are "in hundreds." So halfway between 14 and 16, would be 1,500 accidents.

Second, find the solid line above May that represents 1986. Follow the 1986 point to the left and find what numbers it falls between. It is almost to 18, which would be 1,800 accidents.

Finally, subtract 1,500 from 1,800.

5. (5) 19,200

First find the line that represents June 1986 on the graph. Notice that this falls on 16. Since the number of accidents is "in hundreds," the approximate number of accidents for June 1986 is 1,600. To find the total number of accidents for the year, multiply 1,600 by 12.

6. (1) 30

50 miles is to 60 minutes as *x* miles is to 36 minutes. Set up a proportion, cross multiply, and solve for *x,* which is the number of miles traveled in 36 minutes.

$$\frac{x}{50} = \frac{36}{60}$$

$$60x = 1800$$

$$\frac{\cancel{60}x}{\cancel{60}} = \frac{\cancel{1800}^{30}}{\cancel{60}_{1}}$$

$$x = 30 \text{ mi}$$

Or use the formula $d = rt$.
Change 36 min to $^{36}/_{60}$ hr.
Solve $d = (50)(^{36}/_{60}) = {}^{1800}/_{60} = 30$

7. (4) D

If 15 of the 60 people are children, then 45 are adults. Work out each option:

A: $3.50 × 60 = $210
B: $4.00(45) + $2.00(15) = $180 + $30 = $210
C: $5.00(45) + $1.50(15) = $225 + $22.50 = $247.50
D. $6.00(45) = $270

8. (5) 1.5×10^8

First, introduce a decimal to get a number between 1 and 10. This would be 1.5 (0.15 is too small and 15 is too large.) To get 150,000,000, the number 1.5 must be multiplied by 100,000,000 or 10^8.

9. (4) 10 cents more

Find the cost per ounce of the brand-name medication by dividing $1.95 by 6. Find the cost per ounce of the generic brand by dividing $2.25 by 10. Then compare the cost per ounce.

```
    .325 = .33        $ .225 = .23
6)$1.950          10)$2.250
   1 8                2 0
     15                 25
     12                 20
      30                 50
      30                 50
       0                  0
```

```
  $.33
 − .23
  $ 10
```

10. (2) 52(25)

First compute the operation within the parentheses; then multiply the answer by 52.

52(37 − 12) = 52(25)

11. (4) $30

Arrange the blender prices in order from highest to lowest, then find the middle number. Be sure to write $30 four times and $24 twice.

$30,$30,$30,<u>$30</u>,$24,$24,$21

The underlined value is the median since three numbers are above and three numbers are below it. Option (3) is the mean.

12. (4) 864

Since 576 is twice as many votes as Candidate B received, divide 576 by 2.
You can also use an equation to solve: $2x = 576$

$$\frac{2x}{2} = \frac{576}{2}$$

$$x = 288$$

Then add 288 to 576 for the total votes cast, 864.

13. (2) 108(6.20) + 72

First find the number of feet of fencing needed: 45 + 30 + 30 + 3 = 108 ft. Be sure to include 30 ft on both sides of the yard and to omit the 4 ft for the gate. Multiply this by $6.20 to get the cost of the fencing; then add $72 for the gate.

14. (5) Insufficient data is given

To find the cost of the fencing, the number of feet of fencing is multiplied by the cost per foot. Since the cost per foot at Store B is not given, there is insufficient data to solve the problem.

15. (1) $0.07

First find the number of square feet in the Smiths' lawn: 45(30) = 1,350 sq ft. Then divide the cost of the service by the number of square feet.

```
            .070 = $0.07
1,350)95.00
       0
      95 00
      94 50
         500
         500
```

16. (4) $1,363.50

$1,500	cost of tractor
− 150	down payment
$1,350	balance
$1,350	balance
× .01	rate of finance charge
$13.50	finance charge
$1,350.00	balance
+ 13.50	finance charge
$1,363.50	amount owed

17. (2) (2.72 × 10)/16

First convert 1 lb to 16 oz. Then set up a proportion: 16 ounces is to $2.72 as 10 ounces is to x. Cross multiply and solve for x, the cost of the 10 ounce cereal.

$$\frac{16}{2.72} = \frac{10}{x}$$

$$16x = 2.72(10)$$

$$\frac{16x}{16} = \frac{2.72(10)}{16}$$

$$x = \frac{2.72(10)}{16}$$

18. (4) 1,809

First convert the feet to yards then use the formula $A = \pi r^2$ to compute the area of the clock.

72 ft ÷ 3 = 24 yd
$A = \pi r^2$
$A = 3.14\ (24)^2$
$A = 3.14\ (576)$

```
    5 76
  × 3.14
   23 04
   57 6
 1728
 1808.64 or rounded to
          1,809 sq yd
```

19. (2) 40

Use the Pythagorean theorem to find the length of the diagonal path.

$c^2 = a^2 + b^2$

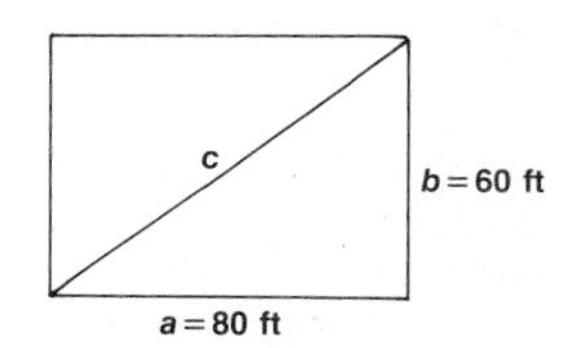

Side b = 60 ft because opposite sides of a rectangle are equal.

$c^2 = (80)^2 + (60)^2$
$c^2 = 6{,}400 + 3{,}600$
$c^2 = 10{,}000$
$c = 100$ ft

To walk around the park (60 ft + 80 ft) is 140 feet. To walk diagonally across the park is 100 feet. 140 feet minus 100 feet is 40 feet.

20. (2) 72

The triangles are similar so their sides are proportional:

$$\frac{\text{building height}}{\text{building shadow}} = \frac{\text{man's height}}{\text{man's shadow}}$$

$\frac{x}{60} = \frac{6}{5}$

Cross multiply and solve.

$5x = 360$

$\frac{5x}{5} = \frac{360}{5}$

$x = 72$ ft

If your answer was (1), the proportion was set up incorrectly.

21. (5) $392.00

First convert the feet to yards then compute the volume using the formula $V = lwh$.

36 ft ÷ 3 = 12 yd

24 ft ÷ 3 = 8 yd

7 ft ÷ 3 = $2\frac{1}{3}$ yd

$V = 12 \times 8 \times 2\frac{1}{3}$

$V = \frac{\overset{32}{\cancel{96}}}{1} \times \frac{7}{\cancel{3}_1}$

$V = 224$ cu yd

Then multiply the basement volume by the cost of excavation.

$$\begin{array}{r} 224 \text{ cu yd} \\ \times\ \$1.75 \text{ per cu yd} \\ \hline 11\ 20 \\ 156\ 8\ \ \\ 224\ \ \ \ \\ \hline \$392.00 \end{array}$$

22. (4) 110°

Sides *AB* and *AC* are equal. Thus $\angle C = 35°$ because angles are equal if they are opposite equal sides. The three angles of a triangle measure 180°, so to find $\angle A$, add $\angle B$ and $\angle C$ and subtract from 180°:

$\angle B + \angle C = 35° + 35° = 70°$
$\angle A = 180° - 70° = 110°$.

23. (5) 77

Use $C = \pi d$, where $\pi = 3\frac{1}{7} = \frac{22}{7}$.

Substitute: $242 = \frac{22}{7}d$

Solve for *d*: $d = \frac{242}{\frac{22}{7}}$

$d = 242 \div \frac{22}{7}$

$d = \overset{11}{\cancel{242}} \times \frac{7}{\cancel{22}_1} = 77$

24. (2) 7

Point *P* is −3 on the *x*-axis. Point *Q* is +4 on the *x*-axis. The distance between the two is 4 + 3 = 7 units.

25. (2) $4L + 3$

Let *L* stand for Larry's age. His grandmother is 4 times Larry's age plus 3 years, or $4L + 3$.

26. (4) 12

The ratio 1:2 can be written as $1x:2x$, where $1x$ or x represents the games won and $2x$ represents games lost. The games won plus the games lost is equal to the total number of games played (18), or

$x + 2x = 18$.

Combine like terms: $3x = 18$.

Divide by 3: $\frac{3x}{3} = \frac{18}{3}$.

So $x = 6$ and $2x$, the number of games lost, is $2(6) = 12$.

27. (5) 1

Solve the inequality for *x*.

$x + 3 \geq 5$
$x \geq 5 - 3$
$x \geq 2$

Or you can substitute each number into the inequality:

(1) $4 + 3 \geq 5$
$7 \geq 5$
True

(2) $3 + 3 \geq 5$
$6 \geq 5$
True

(3) $2\frac{1}{2} + 3 \geq 5$
$5\frac{1}{2} \geq 5$
True

(4) $2 + 3 \geq 5$
$5 \geq 5$
True

(5) $1 + 3 \leq 5$
$4 \leq 5$
False

The only option that gives a false statement is (5).

28. (4) −5 or +6

Factor the quadratic equation and solve for zero.

$x^2 - x - 30 = 0$
$(x - 6)(x + 5) = 0$
$(x - 6) = 0$
$x = +6$
$(x + 5) = 0$
$x = -5$

The GED Test of Interpreting Literature and the Arts

The GED Test of Interpreting Literature and the Arts measures your ability to understand different kinds of reading passages. The skills you develop for this test will help you with other sections of the GED Test as well. So the time you spend in this first part of the book will be an especially good investment.

On the GED Test of Interpreting Literature and the Arts, you will be given a number of different reading selections, each about 200 to 400 words long. (The poems are from 8 to 25 lines long.) A question is given before each selection; you can keep the question in mind as you read to help guide your reading. Each passage is then followed by 4 to 8 test items—sentences to complete or questions to answer on the basis of information in the passage. There are 45 items in all, and you will be given 65 minutes to answer them. The test items all use a multiple-choice format and cover three content areas:

Popular Literature	50%
Classical Literature	25%
Commentary	25%

What is popular literature? It is writing by modern authors that is generally accepted as high quality. Some of the popular literature selections on the GED Test are nonfiction—essays or articles that deal with real people and events. Other selections are from fiction—stories that writers have made up. Still other selections are poems or parts of plays.

What is classical literature? The passages from classical literature may seem similar to those from popular literature. Both kinds can be fiction, nonfiction, poetry, or drama. Both are writing of high quality. However, classical literature has withstood the test of time. Classical passages were written a fairly long time ago and have served as models of good writing for years.

What is commentary? Writings about art, dance, music, literature, theater, and television are called commentary. The commentary passages on the GED Test are usually from reviews and are carefully chosen so that you do not need to be an expert on the arts. With just basic knowledge and good reading skills, you should be able to complete the commentary items successfully.

Get off to a good start by carefully studying the next nine pages in this book. They will give you the foundation you need to build your reading skills. Pages 83–132 will help you build your skills and your confidence. Notice that each skill-building page has a tinted inner column that gives an explanation, a Warm-up practice, perhaps a vocabulary aid, and sometimes a Test-Taking Tip. The white outer column gives practice with passages and items like the ones you'll find on the GED Test of Interpreting Literature and the Arts. Unless you are told otherwise *be sure that you complete the tinted column of each page before going on to the white column.*

Inference—What's That? What do you think will happen next in this picture?

Did you notice the bucket above the door, the string attached to it, and the man attached to the string? You can *infer* that he will pull the string and dump water on the second man as he walks through the door. But notice also that the second man is carrying an exploding cigar. A good *inference* is that he will be able to get back at his friend by giving him one.

An inference is a guess based on information that has been given. For example, if you saw smoke pouring out of a building and several fire trucks at the front door, you probably would infer that the building was on fire. You would be using your observations to make that inference.

Think about the many ways people use inference every day. A good automobile mechanic can infer whether a car's engine is operating correctly from its sound. An experienced cook can infer whether a dish is ready to serve from its appearance or smell. In many other ways, people use information from observations or reliable sources to make inferences that affect their lives.

Inferences can be useful in reading as well. As people read, they constantly make inferences, and they often are not even aware that they are doing so. You'll need to infer many ideas as you read passages on the GED Test of Interpreting Literature and the Arts.

See how well you infer information from your reading. First, read the following passage carefully. Look for words and phrases that refer to an event that just happened.

> You idiot! Why don't you watch where you're going? Look at my truck! I'll never be able to finish my deliveries now! Haven't you ever heard of turn signals? You kids think you're so smart, but you don't know much about driving!

Can you "put two and two together" and guess what happened before this scene? You probably can infer that there was a collision and that the speaker is very angry. Now read the following question and five answer choices. Decide which answer you think is best.

On the basis of details in the passage, which of the following statements is probably correct?

(1) The speaker's truck has just hit a child.
(2) A driver has failed to stop where he was supposed to.
(3) The speaker's truck has collided with another vehicle.
(4) A young woman has collided with a vehicle driven by an old man.
(5) The driver of a delivery truck has just been fired.

If you decided that (3) is the best answer, you are correct. Answers (1), (4), and (5) can be eliminated immediately because there is no evidence to support them. To choose between answers (2) and (3), you may need to reread the passage. Notice that the speaker refers to "my truck" and "my deliveries." These details help you determine, or infer, that (3) is the best answer.

On the GED Test of Interpreting Literature and the Arts, you will make inferences from all kinds of reading. The following passage is from a play. Read it twice—once to find out what the two men are discussing and then a second time to determine each man's attitude.

WILL. It's an emergency! We're lost and Lieutenant Bridges wants you to be the radio operator and find out where we are! It's up to you to save the plane and us and everythin'!

BEN. Me?

WILL. They heared what a good soldier you was. *(Drags* BEN *to his feet and leads him to radio equipment.)*

BEN. Me? . . . Oh golly . . . oh Lord . . .

WILL. *(Picks up pamphlet, looks at it.)* Here's some instructions . . .

BEN. *(Sitting at equipment)* Good. Read them off. . . .

Based on the passage, what is probably true of Ben and Will?

(1) Ben and Will are experienced radio operators.
(2) Ben refuses to admit to Will that he's an expert radio operator.
(3) Will treats Ben roughly.
(4) Ben is uncertain that he can do what Will expects of him.
(5) In his sleep, Will has been talking to Ben.

A couple of details from the passage help you infer the best choice. First, Ben speaks in a halting manner, as if he isn't confident. Then he asks Will to read the instructions for operating the radio. These clues point to answer number (4). Keep in mind that making an inference is *not* the same as making a wild guess. An inference is an educated guess that you can support with information from the passage.

Building Your Vocabulary You may be surprised to find that you are familiar with thousands of words. Most people generally can read a great many more words than they speak.

Since you probably know more words than you might guess, think of your present vocabulary as a good foundation. But to understand passages on the GED Test, you need the materials to build a stronger, even more useful vocabulary on that foundation. Don't think that you have to memorize list after list of long, impressive words and their meanings. That won't help much, if at all. A more efficient way to increase your vocabulary is to use clues as you read.

Context Clues. One type of clue is a context clue. The context of a word is made up of the words and sentences that surround it. There are many different kinds of context clues. Some are shown in the examples below. See if you can infer the meaning of each **boldfaced** word from its context. Write what you think the meaning is on the line that follows the sentence.

1. The explorers landed in an **alien** environment, a place both foreign and strange to them.

____

The context clue in this sentence is a definition. The words following the comma actually define the word *alien,* which means "strange" or "foreign."

2. The bubbles in soda pop and other **effervescent** beverages can tickle your nose.

____

The clue in this sentence is an example. Soda pop is an effervescent beverage because it is bubbly. *Effervescent* means "bubbly."

3. The smell of the flower was as **compelling** as the pull of a magnet on a paper clip.

____

The clue here is a comparison. The smell of the flower is compared to the strong attraction of a magnet. *Compelling* in this particular context means "attracting."

4. My horse has been **irascible** today, even though she is usually good-tempered.

____

The clue here is a contrast. The words *even though* hint that the next part of the sentence will mean the opposite of the first part. *Irascible* means "bad-tempered" or "easily angered."

5. The wolves appeared **hostile** as the hunters approached the den. The animals bared their teeth and crouched as if preparing to spring.

____

The clue here is a set of details. The second sentence describes hostile actions. *Hostile* means "unfriendly" or "threatening." Remember that context can include sentences before and after a word. It can even involve an entire passage.

You have seen how context clues can help you discover the meanings of unfamiliar words. Context clues can also help you in another way.

Many words in the English language have more than one meaning. Context clues show you which meaning of a word is intended. Using context clues can help you answer vocabulary questions on the GED Test of Interpreting Literature and the Arts. Here's an example.

> In the early 1960s, when the Beatles were big with American audiences, other fresh musical talents arrived from overseas. Françoise Hardy came from France, and several promising rock bands came from West Germany. But it was from England that wave after wave of hopeful young musicians rushed to U.S. shores.
>
> What does the word "big," as used in the first sentence, mean?
>
> (1) large (2) generous (3) powerful
> (4) popular (5) important
>
> (1) (2) (3) (4) (5)

Replace "big" in the sentence with each of the choices. You'll find that "popular" makes the most sense. So (4) is the correct answer.

> According to the news reports of the day, several sensitive documents on the subject of national defense had been "misplaced." It was clear that an investigation was needed—and soon.
>
> What does the word "sensitive" mean in this passage?
>
> (1) painful and sore
> (2) careful not to hurt others' feelings
> (3) involving access to secret data
> (4) easily hurt or offended
> (5) susceptible to allergy or disease
>
> (1) (2) (3) (4) (5)

Ask yourself which meaning could describe documents about national defense. Choices (1), (2), (4), and (5) would apply only to living things. So (3) is the answer.

Word-Part Clues Did you know that *smog* comes from the words *smoke* and *fog*? And that *transistor* was coined from the words *transfer* and *resistor*? *Smog* and *transistor* illustrate one way words are formed in English—by combining whole words or word parts. When you recognize the words or word parts that form a new word, you often can discover what the new word means. For example, all the following terms contain the same familiar shorter word. What is it?

personalized	personify
impersonator	personnel
personal	salesperson
personality	persona non grata

The answer, of course, is *person.* Each word in the list above is called a derivative because it is derived, or formed, from another word. That word—*person*, in this case—is called the root word. Notice how derivatives of *person* are used in the sentences below.

Warren has some *personalized* notepaper with his initials for *personal* correspondence, but he uses plain stationery for business letters.

The clever *impersonator* perfectly captured the voice, gestures, and expressions—almost the whole *personality*—of the famous star she was mimicking.

One customer *personified* rudeness. The salespeople considered her *persona non grata* and groaned inwardly whenever she entered the store.

The meaning of a derivative usually is taken from the meaning of the root. For example, each *italicized* word above has something to do with the meaning of *person.* When you combine that knowledge with context clues from the sentence, you should be able to infer the meaning of each derivative.

A word part added to the beginning of a root word is called a prefix. A word part at the end is called a suffix. You don't need to know these terms, but it will help to know that prefixes and suffixes help form new words. Because many prefixes and suffixes and even some root words we use in English often have come from other languages, their meanings may not be obvious to you. Look at the lists of prefixes and suffixes below to see how many you already know.

Prefixes
ad- = to, toward
con- = together
inter- = between or among
post- = after
pre- = before
trans- = across

Suffixes

-able = (or *-ible*) able to, capable of
-ence = state, quality
-less = without
-ment = condition, act of
-ous = full of, having
-tion = act of, process of

Combine word-part and context clues to infer the meanings of the **boldfaced** words in the following sentences. Write your answers on the lines that follow the sentences, and then check your answers against the answers below.

1. High winds battered the tiny ship throughout the **transatlantic** journey.

2. Fortunately, I can **presoak** my white linen dress to get out the ink I spilled.

3. The **fearless** lion tamer placed her head inside the big cat's mouth.

4. You should have told me that the check you wrote was **postdated**.

5. Colorful flowers were **intermingled** with the shrubbery around the sun porch.

What's the Big Idea? On the GED Test of Interpreting Literature and the Arts, you will be asked which of five choices is the main idea of a paragraph or of an entire passage made up of several paragraphs. The main idea of a paragraph often is stated in the first sentence. But a writer may state the main idea in the middle of a paragraph or, for greater emphasis, may even put it in the last sentence. In some paragraphs, the main idea is implied; it is left up to you to infer the main idea as you read.

The best way to choose the main idea is to ask yourself, What is the topic of the paragraph? Then try to determine the most important idea that is stated about the topic. That point will be the main idea. Try using this two-step process to choose the main idea of the passage below.

Starlings are notoriously difficult to "control." The story is told of a man who was bothered by starlings roosting in a large sycamore near his house. He said he tried everything to get rid of them and finally took a shotgun to three of them and killed them. When asked if that discouraged the birds, he reflected a minute, leaned forward, and said confidentially, "Those three it did."

Which of the following sentences best states the main idea of the passage?

(1) Starlings are seldom quiet.
(2) Guns should be outlawed.
(3) Starlings are very hardy birds.
(4) Starlings are difficult to keep away.
(5) The starling population is increasing.

You are correct if you answered that (4) states the main idea best. The passage is about starlings. They are its topic. The opening sentence used different words to state the idea that starlings are difficult to keep away. That is the main idea. All the other sentences support, or help explain, that idea. Those sentences are the supporting details.

Just as each paragraph has a main idea and supporting details, so does a passage made up of several paragraphs. In fact, the main idea of a paragraph in a passage may be a detail that supports the main idea of the entire passage.

When you are asked to choose the main idea of a passage on the GED Test, use the same steps that you use to infer the main idea of a paragraph. Find the topic of the passage; then find the most important idea about the topic. That idea will be the main idea of the passage.

Details, Details, Details! Another skill you will use extensively on the GED Test of Interpreting Literature and the Arts is locating and understanding supporting details. Keep in mind the image of a superhighway with many smaller roads leading to it. The highway appears larger and more important, yet the small roads support the superhighway by bringing it traffic. Without the smaller roads, the highway would have no real purpose.

Answers
1. *transatlantic* = across the Atlantic Ocean **2.** *presoak* = to leave an item in a cleaning solution for a time before laundering it **3.** *fearless* = without fear; unafraid
4. *postdated* = bearing a date later than the true date
5. *intermingled* = placed in among

In a similar way, the details in a paragraph connect with and support the main idea, thereby helping you understand it.

In the paragraph below, watch for details that support the main idea, which is expressed in the first sentence. Then answer the question that follows.

The cowboy is a working man, yet he has little in common with the urban blue-collar worker. . . . Since he lives where he works, and since he deals with animals instead of machines, the cowboy is never really off work. He is on call 24 hours a day, 7 days a week, 365 days a year. The work is not always hard, but as a friend once observed to me, "It's damned sure steady." A calving heifer, a prairie fire, a sick horse may have him up at any hour of the day or night, and in this business there is no such thing as time-and-a-half for overtime.

Which of the following details is used to support the idea that a cowhand's job is different?

(1) The work of a cowhand is dangerous.
(2) A cowhand's job requires much exhausting work.
(3) A cowhand gets paid a high salary for little work.
(4) A cowhand's work never ends.
(5) Cowhands are gradually disappearing.

The choice that comes closest in meaning to one of the sentences in the paragraph and supports the idea that a cowhand's job is different from a blue-collar worker's job is the correct answer. "A cowboy's work never ends" is another way of saying "He is on call 24 hours a day, 7 days a week, 365 days a year." Most blue-collar workers are not. So (4) is the correct answer.

Drawing Conclusions There are other things you can infer besides the main idea of a passage. Whenever you draw a conclusion using information you've read, you are inferring. Drawing conclusions is a skill you will need when you take the GED Test of Interpreting Literature and the Arts.

Some questions on the test will require you to draw conclusions. In the following passage, the writer tells you about Maria's hopes for the future and then about her reactions to some news. Use those clues to draw the conclusions you need to answer the question below.

The first envelope Maria saw in the mailbox was from the city hospital. She knew instantly that it would tell her whether she would be a nurse's aide. She had heard that the work was exhausting and the hours were long, but she wanted that job more than any other. Eagerly Maria tore open the envelope and read the letter. Her face fell and, speechless with disappointment, she sank into a chair.

Based on Maria's reaction to the letter, what conclusion can you draw?

(1) She had become ill.
(2) She could not read the letter.
(3) She was no longer interested in becoming a nurse's aide.
(4) She had been rejected for the job.
(5) She had been offered the job.

Clues in the paragraph tell you that Maria wants to be a nurse's aide and that the letter contains either a job offer or a rejection. But you learn in the last sentence how disappointed Maria seems after she reads the letter. From those clues, you can conclude that she has *not* been offered the job and that answer (4) is the best choice. Sometimes an author implies a thought to build suspense. At other times, an author may imply an idea to give it more impact. Often you remember an idea more clearly if you discover it yourself. Read this next passage carefully. What conclusion can you draw about the possible fate of a city police officer?

■ Imagine yourself a cop in a major urban area. When you put on that uniform in the morning and leave the house, you never know if you will make it back home in the evening.

The author implies that a police officer could be killed in the line of duty. Leaving that thought unfinished for you to infer gives the idea much more impact.

As you read the next passage, notice sentences in which the author seems to criticize his employers. Then use those details to infer the answer to the question below.

I make my living humping cargo for Seaboard World Airlines, one of the big international airlines at Kennedy Airport. They handle strictly all cargo. I was once told that one of the Rockefellers is the major stockholder for the airline, but I don't really think about that too much. I don't get paid to think. The big thing is to beat that race with the time clock every morning of your life so the airline will be happy. The worst thing a man could ever do is to make suggestions about building a better airline. They pay people $40,000 a year to come up with better ideas. It doesn't matter that these ideas never work; it's just that they get nervous when a guy from South Brooklyn or Ozone Park acts like he actually has a brain.

Based on the passage, why is the author unhappy with the airline?

(1) The airline listens to suggestions only from stockholders.
(2) The airline values the opinions of its employees too much.
(3) The airline discourages many employees from suggesting changes.
(4) The airline wants to switch over to using robots.
(5) The airline does not train its employees well.

All the author says about stockholders is that he knows nothing about them. You can discount (1). There are no references to robots or training in the passage, so eliminate (4) and (5). Reread the passage and then ask yourself, Which of the remaining choices would the author agree with? Most likely, he or she would agree with (3).

Understanding Consequences When you understand the consequences of an action, you're really understanding a cause-and-effect relationship. Writers of passages on the GED Test often will discuss causes and effects. As a reader, you can tell when cause-and-effect relationships are being discussed because words and phrases such as *since, therefore, consequently, because, if . . . then,* and *as a result* signal such relationships. This is very often true in nonfiction.

In other types of reading you'll find on the GED Test, such as drama and fiction, understanding what event or action leads to another is sometimes difficult. That is especially so when the topic is human behavior and motivation. Often you have to infer what effects characters' actions and attitudes have. A good example is the following passage.

After my grandfather died, my grandmother lived, more than ever, through her children. When she came to visit, I would hide my diary. . . . She couldn't bear it if my mother left the house without her.

What happened when the grandmother began to live through others? For one, the granddaughter hid her diary during her grandmother's visits. Although the author does not explicitly point out a cause-and-effect relationship, you can infer from the paragraph that the grandmother probably would have picked up and read the girl's diary. A second effect of the grandmother's attitudes was that she wanted to be with her daughter constantly.

Practice your skill in understanding causes and effects by answering the question below.

Based on the passage, what probably caused the grandmother to live "through her children"?

(1) loneliness after her husband's death
(2) her children's dependence on her
(3) a fear of growing old
(4) boredom with her home and job
(5) a belief that she was helping others

Although the author does not state outright that widowhood caused the grandmother's behavior, the order of details in the paragraph leads you to believe so. Answer (1) is the best choice.

Putting Knowledge to Work It's one thing to know some information. It's another thing to *apply* it. Applying information means that you can use it in different situations. Practice this skill by applying old, familiar sayings to modern-day situations. For instance, take the saying "People who live in glass houses shouldn't throw stones." It means that a person with obvious faults should not criticize others. How can you apply this saying to the incident described below?

■ Al complained bitterly to his landlord about the people in the apartment next door. "They're really thoughtless," Al said. "Their TV makes so much noise at night that my friends and I have to keep turning up my stereo."

Al was complaining about, or "throwing stones" at, his neighbors, although he himself "lived in a glass house" because he, too, was thoughtless and noisy.

On the GED Test of Interpreting Literature and the Arts, some questions will require you to read a passage and then apply an idea from that passage to a different situation. You can practice with the following activity. Read the passage first and then choose the best answer to the question below.

Respect for law and order can never be expected until a climate of justice is created which encompasses both the cop and the man in the ghetto. The cop has to be an authority before he gets into the neighborhood. He must be trained to be an expert in understanding human behavior. He must be skilled in the art of human relationships. He must be a general practitioner trained to doctor social ills. If the cop is not adequately trained, he may be doing the very best he can, given the condition of his job; but his best is still wrong. A man does not become a brain surgeon by receiving on-the-job training in the emergency room of a hospital.

Which of the following professionals would the author probably criticize?

(1) a doctor who recently has lost a patient
(2) a teacher who has taken no education courses
(3) a lawyer who defends known criminals
(4) an actor who never has performed on Broadway
(5) a broadcaster who speaks with an accent

The passage states that police officers should be trained adequately. So the best answer to this question would apply this attitude to an untrained professional on whom people depend. The only choice that does this is (2).

Here's another chance for you to practice applying ideas. The following classical passage is from an essay entitled "Civil Disobedience" by Henry David Thoreau. You can answer the question if you (1) understand what the author believes about government and (2) predict how he would respond to government policies today.

I heartily accept the motto—"That government is best which governs least"; and I should like to see it acted up to more rapidly and systematically. Carried out, it finally amounts to this, which I also believe—"That government is best which governs not at all"; and when men are prepared for it, that will be the kind of government which they will have. Government is at best but an expedient, but most governments are usually, and all governments are sometimes, inexpedient.

Which policy of the United States government today would Thoreau most likely approve of?

(1) reserving land for national parks
(2) regulating large businesses
(3) collecting income taxes
(4) removing price controls on fuel
(5) lending money to failing manufacturers

The author believes that the less government interferes with people, the better. You can see that all the policies except that described in (4) are examples of government involvement in people's lives. So the author would most likely approve of answer (4).

Taking a Closer Look Just as a painter has brushes, a doctor has medicines, and a carpenter has saws and hammers, a writer has special tools. You use many tools of the writer in everyday speech. For instance, when you want to describe a very exciting experience, don't you choose words and details that will excite your listener? The writer does the same thing.

Careful selection of words and details is one important tool of a writer. Another tool is quotations. In a discussion, people sometimes rely on quotations from newspapers, books, TV, or other sources to support their points of view. In the same way, writers often use quotations to explain or support their points of view.

Remember that a writer sometimes leaves a thought unfinished to give the idea more impact. How good are you at inferring a writer's meaning? Test yourself with the following passage. It was taken from a commentary about modern television. As you read the passage, see if you can find phrases that cause you to react with resentment, scorn, or some other feeling. Then answer the question below.

But why is television so afraid to admit its mistakes? Why is there no regularly scheduled, prime-time self-examination on television? Television is the most pervasive and the most powerful medium in the history of mankind. It brings the entire range of human experience into virtually every living room in the country every day. But television tells viewers very little about itself and how it does its job.

Which of the following phrases from the passage might make readers look down on television?

(1) "afraid to admit its mistakes"
(2) "no regularly scheduled, prime-time self-examination"
(3) "the most powerful medium in the history of mankind"
(4) "brings the entire range of human experience into . . . every living room"
(5) "tells viewers very little about itself"

Ask yourself, If the phrases referred to a person, which would make me look on that person with scorn? Choices (2) and (5) would suggest only that the person is private. Choices (3) and (4) suggest someone who is powerful and maybe even worthy of respect. That leaves choice (1), which suggests a coward, as the answer.

Not only writers of nonfiction make careful word choices. Writers of stories, drama, and poetry also select words and build sentences to bring about special effects. The poem below is an example. Carefully read the question in the first line. Then notice the words and images, or word-pictures, the poet uses to answer the question.

Harlem

What happens to a dream deferred?

Does it dry up
like a raisin in the sun?
Or fester like a sore—
And then run?
Does it stink like rotten meat?
Or crust and sugar over—
like a syrupy sweet?

Maybe it just sags
like a heavy load.

Or does it explode?

The poem opens by asking what happens when people have a dream or goal that is deferred, or postponed, seemingly forever. Perhaps you noticed that the poet never actually answers that question; instead, the first question is followed by more questions. The effect of all those questions is to lead you to consider, one by one, some possible results of having dreams or goals put off.

Now try to picture in your mind each image that the poet has chosen—the dried raisin, the festering sore, and others. Would you say that they are all unpleasant images? Don't they imply that putting off a dream forever is not a very good thing to do? That is the effect they have.

Now read the question below about the poet's use of a special technique and select the answer you think is best.

What is the effect of setting off the last line of the poem in special type?

(1) It indicates that that line should be read more quickly than the others.
(2) It makes readers think carefully about the possibility suggested in that line.
(3) It lends an attractive visual device to the poem.
(4) It clarifies the idea in the preceding line.
(5) It concludes an otherwise negative poem on a positive note.

Did you feel the importance, the power, that the final line has in meaning? The poet wanted to stress that importance even more, so the line is *italicized* to bring it to readers' attention. Choice (2) is the best answer.

Tips for Taking the Test

As you prepare to take the GED Test of Interpreting Literature and the Arts, keep in mind that what you are learning will benefit you for life, not just the hours that you are taking the test. Certainly passing the test is foremost in your mind right now, and it should be. But don't assume that once the test is over, you will no longer have a use for what you are learning. Gain the full benefit from your investment of time and effort by considering the skills you are now mastering to be a permanent part of your life. This attitude will give you a sense of purpose as you prepare for the GED Test.

What do you need to know in order to do your best on the test? Below are four important tips. Read them carefully and use them as you do the practice items in this section.

Read and follow directions carefully. Are you good at following directions? Try the sample test below and see.

This is a test to see how well you follow directions. Before beginning, read the test through once carefully to make sure you understand all the directions.

1. In the paragraph above, circle every word that begins with the letter *a*.
2. Underline two nouns in the paragraph above.
3. Cross out all commas in the first two lines of the paragraph.
4. Fill in the center of each letter *o*.
5. Write down the number of three-letter words in sentence 1 above.
6. Do not follow the first five numbered directions. Do not make a mark on this page.

This test often fools people. They start with item 1 and work right through to item 6 without reading all the directions first, as they are told to do at the beginning. So, remember, when you begin *any* test, follow directions carefully. The directions on the GED Test of Interpreting Literature and the Arts will help you complete each test item correctly. Don't try to "outsmart" the test with shortcuts or tricky formulas. Those shortcuts usually shortchange you. Follow the directions and consider each test item an individual challenge.

Try to be flexible; be ready to move easily from one kind of test item to another. On the GED Test of Interpreting Literature and the Arts, you will find different kinds of reading, such as poetry and classical nonfiction, grouped together. However, the basic skills you develop will help you regardless of the kind of item you work on.

The Minitests on pages 137–152 of this book will give you a chance to work all kinds of test items together. If you discover that adjusting is not easy for you, look up from the page and close your eyes for a moment. Or take a deep breath to mark the end of each item before you go on.

Use the purpose questions. There will be a purpose question before each passage on the GED Test of Interpreting Literature and the Arts. The question will ask about information in the selection. While looking for the information, you will focus on your reading better. This added concentration will make answering the test items easier than if you had no purpose for reading.

Budget your time wisely. Keep a steady pace, but do not rush. You will be given 65 minutes to complete the 45 items on the GED Test of Interpreting Literature and the Arts. Most people can complete the test in that amount of time. If you are concerned about whether you can work quickly enough, time yourself when you take the Posttests in this book. If you find your mind wandering, press yourself to read more quickly. This strategy can improve your concentration.

If you complete the GED Test of Interpreting Literature and the Arts before the end of the allotted time, go back and double-check your answers. Since there is no penalty for guessing, make certain you have answered *every* question, even those you're not sure about.

The thorough preparation you are giving yourself is your best guarantee of success. Knowing that you are well prepared will give you confidence. Last-minute cramming for the test is not a good idea because it can make you tense and may block your thinking. Your careful preparation and the resulting confidence are what you need to work toward a good, solid score on the GED Test of Interpreting Literature and the Arts.

Popular and Classical Nonfiction

Finding the Main Idea Some people think that reading means understanding written words. That is partly true, but a more accurate definition of reading is the process of understanding written *ideas*—facts, opinions, or impressions that the author shares with you.

To get the most out of your reading, you need to find the **main idea**. The main idea is the most important point that the author makes. Sometimes the main idea is stated clearly at the beginning of a paragraph. Then the rest of the paragraph gives **supporting details**—small pieces of information that support, or explain, the main idea.

Sometimes the main idea is stated somewhere in the middle or at the end of a paragraph. Placing the main idea at the end gives it emphasis.

Coming to Terms

main idea the single most important point that an author makes in a paragraph or selection
supporting details small pieces of information that support, or explain, the main idea

Warm-up

Look for the main idea as you read the paragraph below.

■ The members of the company's coed softball team were filled with mixed emotions before the championship game. They were excited and enthusiastic, but they were a little nervous too. Some were even concerned that perhaps they were not good enough to be playing for the championship.

Write the main idea in a complete sentence.

____

____

Sample Warm-up Answer
The softball team had different feelings about playing in the championship.

Directions: Choose the one best answer to each question. Answers are on page 133.

Items 1–2 refers to the following passage.

Were Grandma's stories for entertainment only?

Grandma was a wonderful storyteller, and she had a set of priceless, individually tailored anecdotes with which American grandparents of her day brought up children. There was the story of the little boys who had been taught absolute, quick obedience. One day when they were out on the prairie, their father shouted, "Fall down on your faces!" They did, and the terrible prairie fire swept over them *and they weren't hurt.* There was also the story of three boys at school, each of whom received a cake sent from home. One hoarded his, and the mice ate it; one ate all of his, and he got sick; and who do you think had the best time?—why, of course, the one who shared his cake with his friends.

1. Which of the following sentences best states the main idea?

   (1) Children must obey their parents quickly.
   (2) The author remembers many of her grandmother's wonderful stories.
   (3) The grandmother was a good storyteller.
   (4) People should share with others.
   (5) The grandmother's stories helped teach the children morals and good manners.

2. Which of the following details support the main idea of the passage?

   (1) Grandma told a story about three boys at school.
   (2) The grandmother told stories.
   (3) Each of the three boys received a cake.
   (4) The children were saved from the prairie fire because they followed directions.
   (5) The prairie fire raged across the countryside.

Directions: Choose the one best answer to each question. Answers are on page 133.

Items 3–4 refer to the following passage.

What details in the passage help you understand how strong and resourceful Momma was?

And Momma came home one hot summer day and found we'd been evicted, thrown out into the streetcar zone with all our orange-crate chairs and secondhand lamps. She flashed that big smile and dried our tears and bought some penny Kool-Aid. We stood out there and sold drinks to thirsty people coming off the streetcar, and we thought nobody knew we were kicked out—figured they thought we *wanted* to be there. And Momma went off to talk the landlord into letting us back in on credit.

But I wonder about my Momma sometimes, and all the other Negro mothers who got up at 6 A.M. to go to the white man's house with sacks over their shoes because it was so wet and cold. I wonder how they made it. They worked very hard for the man. . . . They didn't have much time for us.

I wonder about my Momma, who walked out of a white woman's clean house at midnight and came back to her own where the lights had been out for three months, and the pipes were frozen and the wind came in through the cracks.

3. Which sentence best states the main idea of the first paragraph?

(1) The landlord had evicted the family.
(2) The family sold cold drinks.
(3) Thirsty people bought the cold drinks.
(4) No one knew the family was evicted.
(5) The mother cleverly cheered up her evicted family.

4. Which sentence best states the main idea of the entire passage?

(1) The author's family sold Kool-Aid.
(2) The mother's income was too low to pay the rent.
(3) The author wonders how his mother felt toward her rich employers.
(4) The mother worked hard in a depressing place.
(5) The author resents his earlier poverty.

Inferring an Unstated Main Idea In some paragraphs the main idea is not stated in any single sentence. Instead, you need to examine the details and to **infer** the main point. To *infer* means "to make an educated guess on the basis of information you have been given."

When the main idea is not stated, ask yourself two questions. First, "What is the general topic?" That is, "What is the paragraph about?" Then, "What is the most important thing that the author says about the topic?" Combine your answers to determine the main idea.

☑ A Test-Taking Tip

Whenever you need to infer a main idea on the GED Test, ask yourself the questions in the paragraph above. Then combine the answers for a statement of the main idea.

Coming to Terms

infer make an educated guess on the basis of information you have been given

Warm-up

Examine the details in the following paragraph and infer the main idea. The questions below will help. Answer them in complete sentences.

■ More and more often it happened the store of Berry & Lincoln was locked for the day; customers went to other stores; Lincoln took jobs splitting fence-rails, worked at the sawmill, harvested hay and oats, and helped out when there was a rush of customers at the store of Samuel Hill. He now saw that honesty and hard work are not enough in order to win respect as a merchant; he didn't have the trader's nose for business; he lacked the gumption to locate where trade had to come and then to use customers so they would come back. The store was a goner. "It winked out."

1. What is the general topic? ____________

____

2. What is the main point the author makes about the topic? ____________

____

3. What is the main idea of the passage?

____

____

Sample Warm-up Answers
1. Lincoln is the general topic. **2.** He was not successful as a store owner. **3.** Lincoln was not successful as a store owner.

Recognizing Supporting Details The main idea of the paragraph below is in the first sentence. As you read the paragraph, notice that all the remaining sentences help you understand and picture the main idea.

■ On Sunday mornings Momma served a breakfast that was geared to hold us quiet from 9:30 A.M. to 3 P.M. She fried thick pink slabs of home-cured ham and poured the grease over sliced red tomatoes. Eggs over easy, fried potatoes and onions, yellow hominy and crisp perch fried so hard we would pop them in our mouths and chew bones, fins, and all. Her cathead biscuits were at least three inches in diameter and two inches thick. The trick to eating catheads was to get the butter on them before they got cold—then they were delicious. When, unluckily, they were allowed to get cold, they tended to a gooeyness, not unlike a wad of tired gum.

Each sentence after the first describes part of the breakfast that kept the author's family from getting hungry too soon. Don't the supporting details help you understand why the family was "quiet from 9:30 A.M. to 3 P.M."? Each detail strengthens the main idea.

Warm-up

One sentence in the following paragraph states the main idea clearly. What details in the rest of the paragraph help you understand the main idea? Answer the questions below in complete sentences.

■ Basketball is the city game. Its battlegrounds are strips of asphalt between tattered wire fences or crumbling buildings; its rhythms grow from the uneven thump of a ball against hard surfaces. It demands no open spaces or lush backyards or elaborate equipment. Its simple motions swirl into intricate patterns; its brief soaring moments merge into a fascinating dance.

1. What is the main idea? ______________________

____

2. Give two details from the paragraph that support the main idea. ______________________

____

____

Sample Warm-up Answers
1. Basketball is a city game. **2a.** It can be played on asphalt. **b.** It doesn't require large spaces or elaborate equipment.

Item 5 refers to the following passage.

What did the campers do during the week?

We had a good week at the camp. The bass were biting well and the sun shone endlessly, day after day. We would be tired at night and lie down in the accumulated heat of the little bedrooms after the long hot day and the breeze would stir almost imperceptibly outside and the smell of the swamp would drift in through the rusty screens. Sleep would come easily and in the morning the red squirrel would be on the roof, tapping. . . .

5. According to the author, why was the camping trip pleasant?
   (1) The campers were tired at night.
   (2) The smell of the swamp was very enjoyable.
   (3) The cabin was cool and comfortable.
   (4) The campers fished successfully by day and slept soundly at night.
   (5) The campers could photograph squirrels and other wild animals.

Item 6 refers to the following passage.

Does the author enjoy his work?

Treating guide dogs for the blind has always seemed to me to be one of a veterinary surgeon's most rewarding tasks. To be in a position to help and care for these magnificent animals is a privilege, not just because they are highly trained and valuable but because they represent in the ultimate way something which has always lain near the core and centre of my life: the mutually depending, trusting and loving association between man and animal.

6. Why does the author like to treat guide dogs for the blind?
   (1) The dogs are usually worth a lot.
   (2) They represent the trust and love between people and animals.
   (3) They are good-looking dogs.
   (4) He likes to help blind people.
   (5) Guide dogs are exceptionally well trained.

Directions: Choose the one best answer to each question. Answers are on page 133.

Item 7 refers to the following passage.

Why was the woman in the passage so nervous?

The startled movement of a young woman in one corner of the bus shelter indicated that something was wrong. She moved again, a gesture of discomfort, even fear. Then I saw what troubled her: an infant rodent—perhaps mouse, perhaps rat—a small ball of brown cotton, with a toothpick for a tail. It had somehow crossed Seventh Avenue, climbed the curb and was moving through the shelter and across the sidewalk.

7. Which of the following statements best summarizes the passage?
   (1) A young woman was waiting in a bus shelter.
   (2) The animal in the bus shelter was a young mouse or rat.
   (3) The rodent was small and brown.
   (4) A small rodent startled a woman in a bus shelter.
   (5) The animal crossed the street.

Item 8 refers to the following passage.

What advice does the author give?

However mean your life is, meet it and live it; do not shun it and call it hard names. It is not so bad as you are. It looks poorest when you are richest. The fault-finder will find faults even in paradise. Love your life, poor as it is. You may perhaps have some pleasant, thrilling, glorious hours, even in a poor-house. The setting sun is reflected from the windows of the alms-house as brightly as from the rich man's abode.

8. Which of the following summarizes the author's advice?
   (1) Strive to improve your standard of living.
   (2) Help people who are poor.
   (3) Recognize the value of your life.
   (4) Try to live as your neighbors do.
   (5) Don't find fault with other people.

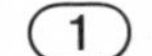

Summarizing Have you ever read through one or more paragraphs and then forgotten what you read? You can get more out of your reading by **summarizing.** *Summarizing* means restating, in your own words, the important ideas and facts in a passage. Summarizing helps you focus on what is most important and also helps you remember what you have read.

Warm-up

Below is part of a speech given by an American Indian chief to a group of U.S. government officials. After you finish reading, think about the important points that the speaker makes. On a separate sheet of paper, summarize the passage in two or three sentences.

■ I have heard that you intend to settle us on a reservation near the mountains. I don't want to settle. I love to roam over the prairies. There I feel free and happy, but when we settle down, we grow pale and die. I have laid aside my lance, bow, and shield, and yet I feel safe in your presence. I have told you the truth. I have no little lies hid about me, but I don't know how it is with the commissioners. Are they as clear as I am? A long time ago this land belonged to our fathers; but when I go up to the river, I see camps of soldiers on its banks. These soldiers cut down my timber; they kill my buffalo; and when I see that, my heart feels like bursting; I feel sorry. I have spoken.

Coming to Terms

summarizing restating, in your own words, the most important ideas and facts in a selection

☑ A Test-Taking Tip

On the GED Test of Interpreting Literature and the Arts, you will not be asked to write your own summary. Instead, you will choose the one statement out of five that best summarizes a passage. You'll feel more confident about making that choice if you have learned to summarize.

Sample Warm-up Answer
The speaker is opposed to living on a reservation. He is being honest with the commissioners but is not certain they are being truthful with him. And he is saddened by the destruction of the forests and buffalo.

Using Word-part Clues If you come across an unfamiliar word, you sometimes can determine its meaning by examining its parts. For instance, if you know the meanings of the prefixes and suffixes in the "Coming to Terms" section below, you probably can discover the meanings of many unfamiliar words. (For a more complete listing of different word parts, see pages 76 and 77 of this book.)

Coming to Terms

A prefix is added to the beginning of a word. A suffix is added to the end of a word. Both form new words with different meanings. For instance, if you add the prefix *un-* to *cover,* you get *uncover.* Because the prefix *un-* means "not," *uncover* means the opposite of the root word *cover.* Here are some other commonly used prefixes and suffixes:

dis- not
Example: I disagree with his ideas.
-ee person who is or is given *(something).*
Example: An employee of the company.
-en (1) made of (2) to become
Example: The wooden horse was heavy.
hyper- over, extra, more than usual
Example: The hyperactive child could not sit still.
hypo- under, less than
Example: A hypodermic injection is given just under the skin.
ped- having to do with the feet
Example: A pedestrian travels on foot.
re- again
Example: He refinishes old furniture.
sub- under
Example: A submarine is a ship that travels under water.

Warm-up

Use what you have learned about prefixes and suffixes to determine the meaning of each word below. In the spaces, write your definitions. On a separate sheet of paper, use each word in a complete sentence.

1. insufficient ______________________

2. absentee ______________________

3. subzero ______________________

4. leaden ______________________

Sample Warm-up Answers
1. not enough **2.** one who is absent **3.** below zero **4.** made of lead or looks like lead

Items 9–10 refer to the following passage.

Why does Grant Avenue seem like a city in China?

To the casual tourists, Grant Avenue is Chinatown, just another colorful street in San Francisco; to the overseas Chinese, Grant Avenue is their showcase, their livelihood; to the refugees from the mainland, Grant Avenue is Canton. Although there are no pedicabs, no wooden slippers clip-clapping on the sidewalks, yet the strip of land is to the refugee the closest thing to a home town. The Chinese theatres, the porridge restaurants, the teahouses, the newspapers, the food, the herbs . . . all provide an atmosphere that makes a refugee wonder whether he is really in a foreign land.

9. Who are the refugees discussed in the passage?

(1) confused persons
(2) people given shelter
(3) tourists visiting the area
(4) San Francisco natives
(5) Chinese theatergoers

10. What are the pedicabs mentioned in the passage?

(1) sidewalks along the avenue
(2) taxis powered by foot pedals
(3) types of wooden shoes
(4) small children
(5) people strolling by

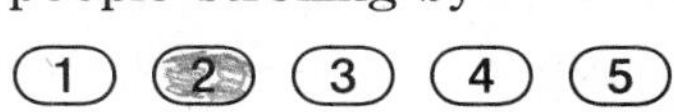

Directions: Choose the one best answer to each question. Answers are on page 133.

Items 11–12 refer to the following passage.

Why does the young man in the passage decide to visit the school infirmary?

Deerfield had an infantile paralysis case that spring, and as is the custom of the school with its strict standards, all parents were notified at once. Then in the third week of April I had a wire from the school doctor, Johnson, saying that Johnny was in the infirmary but, though he had a stiff neck, there was no indication of polio and we were not to worry. Nothing at all alarming was indicated. Boys get stiff necks and Charley horses all the time. In fact, Dr. Johnson said, he was informing us of Johnny's complaint only because, knowing of the polio scare and hearing that he was in the infirmary, we might think that he did have polio, which he didn't. I called Johnny up, and we talked briefly. He was lonely and fretful at missing a week of class work, but otherwise nothing seemed to be amiss. . . . Later we found that Johnny might not have gone to the infirmary at all, since he would never admit it when he was ill and never complained, except that one of his classmates, observing his stiff neck, insisted on his seeing a doctor. Then, wisely, Dr. Johnson held him for observation. Had this not happened, he might have died then and there.

11. What was Dr. Johnson referring to when he spoke of Johnny's "complaint"?
    (1) his protest about the school's medical services
    (2) his criticism of one of his classmates
    (3) his statement of dissatisfaction
    (4) his small physical ailment
    (5) his severe, disabling illness

    (1) (2) (3) (4) (5)

12. When Dr. Johnson referred to the "polio scare," he meant that
    (1) polio victims were afraid of dying
    (2) doctors feared polio would spread
    (3) people were mistaken when they thought polio was fatal
    (4) people were frightened that they would get polio
    (5) patients were being mistakenly diagnosed as having polio

    (1) (2) (3) (4) (5)

Using Context Clues Many words in English have more than one meaning, and some of the meanings are not even closely related. Often, in order to know which meaning of a word the author intends, you need to use context clues. (If you would like to review context clues, see page 75 of this book.)

What do you think of when you see the words *pitcher, batter,* and *plate?* Perhaps you immediately think of baseball and softball. But you may think of fixing pancakes or waffles. If the word in question is in a sentence, the **context,** or words or sentences that surround the word, help you decide on the appropriate meaning.

The word *run* is a good example. It has seventy-eight meanings. With that many possible meanings, how can you know which one is intended? Usually the context can tell you. See how the context of *run* in each item below helps you know which meaning is appropriate.

a home run	Run to the store.
a run of bad luck	Cars run on gas.

Coming to Terms

context the words and sentences that surround a particular word

☑ A Test-Taking Tip

You won't be able to use a dictionary when you take the GED Test of Interpreting Literature and the Arts. Therefore, you will find that using context clues will be very helpful for determining the meanings of words.

Warm-up

Use context clues to decide what the *italicized* word in each sentence means. Then write the letter of the appropriate definition in the blank.

1. ______ The actor wore a *bow* tie.
2. ______ X-rays can't travel through *lead*.
3. ______ Please *lead* us in singing.
4. ______ Did he *bow* to the audience?

a. a heavy metal
b. bend down from the waist
c. behave in a way that others can follow
d. loops on the ends of strings or ribbons that have been tied together

Warm-up Answers
1. d **2.** a **3.** c **4.** b

Understanding Figures of Speech You already have dealt with unfamiliar words in your reading (page 88). On the GED Test, you also will find a different type of word-meaning problem—figures of speech.

A **figure of speech** expands a word or phrase beyond its ordinary meaning, usually by making a comparison. For instance, a friend may describe his or her job as a "jungle." You know that the person is comparing the difficulties on the job to the dangers of a *jungle.* The speaker is using *jungle* as a figure of speech.

Sometimes a figure of speech may seem senseless if you apply only the ordinary meaning of each word. But it may make sense if you use your imagination. For example, when you say "bite the bullet," you simply mean that you will have to face a problem or unpleasant situation.

Coming to Terms

figure of speech an expression in which the ordinary meaning of the words is expanded, usually by making a comparison.

Warm-up

This exercise will give you practice with figures of speech similar to the ones you might find in the nonfiction section on the GED Test of Interpreting Literature and the Arts. You will learn about figurative language in poetry on page 129.

Circle the letter of the best meaning for each figure of speech in *italics*.

1. The coach was *on cloud nine* the day our team won its first game.
 a. extremely happy
 b. feeling insecure
 c. somewhere else

2. The whole team was *on pins and needles* before the game.
 a. using equipment with sharp edges
 b. having their uniforms mended and altered
 c. nervous and fidgety

3. Someone finally managed to *light a fire under* our unenthusiastic quarterback.
 a. inspire
 b. dismiss
 c. warm up

Warm-up Answers
1. a **2.** c **3.** a

Items 13–14 refer to the following passage.

Can you picture the storm described in the passage?

Mrs. Ottawa Benson had no reason to expect a visitor the night of February 25, 1963. In the best of weather her doorstep was little frequented by society. Her husband kept the lighthouse on the southwest promontory of Grand Manan Island in the Bay of Fundy. And this particular winter's eve, the eye of the lighthouse turned its great glance through blearing masses of cloud.

From Maine to Nova Scotia the bay was lashed by storm. Sixty-mile winds stampeded through the night, howling like all creation in torment. The temperature was below freezing and going down, the stars and moon invisible above the black veils, the darkness all but absolute.

13. What does the phrase "the eye of the lighthouse turned its great glance through blearing masses of cloud" mean?

 (1) Someone in the lighthouse looked through the clouds.
 (2) The beam of light shone through the clouds.
 (3) The foghorn penetrated the clouds.
 (4) In a mysterious way, the lighthouse could see.
 (5) Clouds could be seen through the windows of the lighthouse.

14. In the sentence "Sixty-mile winds stampeded through the night" what is the wind compared to?

 (1) clouds (2) surf (3) cars
 (4) animals (5) people

 (1) (2) (3) (4) (5)

Directions: Choose the one best answer to each question. Answers are on page 133.

Items 15–16 refer to the following passage.

What are some behavior patterns of the condor?

Early settlers of the American Southwest grew to realize that the appearance of the California condor signaled death. The condor soared on air currents searching for food. His food was the flesh of dead animals. In nourishing himself, the condor cleaned away dead flesh that would otherwise spread disease.

The settlements of the Southwest developed into villages; villages became cities and then massive metropolitan areas. The growth of the metropolis gradually but relentlessly diminished the area in which the condor—who needed to range freely—could breed and raise young. Farmers' pesticides and hunters' lead bullets found their way into the food chain. Because of the loss of territory and the poisons in the environment, the entire species of condor began to die out.

The early settlers realized that the appearance of the condor signaled death; they failed to see that their own appearance very likely signaled the death of the condor.

15. To early settlers, the California condor signaled death because these birds

(1) came to eat dead animals
(2) always accompanied a drought
(3) stalked and attacked humans
(4) spread disease
(5) preyed upon the settlers' farm stock

16. According to the passage, how did the growth of cities affect the California condor?

(1) City people removed the food supply of the condors.
(2) Hunters from the city shot condors for sport.
(3) Cities reduced the amount of space where condors could raise young.
(4) City people demanded that farmers use pesticides.
(5) Cities produced air pollution that poisoned the condors.

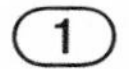

Understanding Consequences In fantasy and science fiction, events often do not follow the usual cause-and-effect relationships we expect in the real world. Instead, a secret formula or supernatural agent can cause incredible changes to occur. A human being may change into a monster, or a character may build a machine that takes him into the past. Since you know that the story is fantasy, you can accept and enjoy the unrealistic events.

However, in the real world, strong emphasis is placed on understanding consequences. You want to know how events or other people may affect your life. Parts of the GED Test of Literature and the Arts, will involve understanding consequences.

Warm-up

Read the following paragraph and then complete the sentence below.

■ A barbed wire fence was cheap to buy, erect, and maintain over the big acreages required in the West, and cattle shied from it once they ran against it. In the 1870s some animals cut themselves to death on it, and one rancher said that at first he could hardly drive a cow between two posts.

The rancher had a hard time driving some cows between posts because ______________________________
______________________________.

☑ A Test-Taking Tip

The GED Test of Interpreting Literature and the Arts may include questions that require you to determine the consequences of some events. Before you mark the answer you think is best, read the *entire* selection at least once. Then, if you are still not certain, read the passage again. Remember that the test is planned to give you a reasonable length of time to make your choices.

Sample Warm-up Answer
the cows had cut themselves on barbed wire before, and they were afraid they would be cut whenever they went between two posts

Drawing Conclusions Can you read between the lines? Reading between the lines means that you detect ideas that the writer suggests but does not state outright. In other words, you infer the author's point from information given in the passage.

Why would an author leave an important idea unstated? Sometimes he or she does so to emphasize the idea. An idea that you infer probably will stay with you longer than one that is spelled out for you. In some cases, an author only suggests an idea that should not, for some reason, be openly stated.

Warm-up

The brief passage below discusses the aftermath of the atomic bomb blast in Hiroshima, Japan. What conclusion can you draw from the passage? When you finish reading, complete the sentence that follows.

■ A year after the bomb was dropped, Miss Sasaki was a cripple; Mrs. Nakamura was destitute; Father Kleinsorge was back in the hospital; Dr. Sasaki was not capable of the work he once could do; Dr. Fujii had lost the thirty-room hospital it took him many years to acquire, and no prospects of rebuilding it; Mr. Tanimoto's church had been ruined and he no longer had his exceptional vitality. The lives of these six people, who were among the luckiest in Hiroshima, would never be the same.

From the information in the passage, you can infer that other people in Hiroshima

____

____.

A Test-Taking Tip

The GED Test of Interpreting Literature and the Arts may include many questions that ask you to infer an opinion or idea. Since the test has a multiple-choice format, your task will be easier than it sounds. Instead of having to make up your own answer, you simply will choose one answer from the five given in each item. Try to eliminate the two or three choices that seem obviously wrong. Then choose the best of the remaining answers.

Sample Warm-up Answer
suffered even worse than the six described

Item 17 refers to the following passage.

Why did the family become homeless?

It's known as the North Gila Valley, about fifty miles north of Yuma. My dad was being turned out of his small plot of land. He had inherited this from his father, who had homesteaded it. I saw my two, three other uncles also moving out. And for the same reason, the bank had foreclosed on the loan.

If the local bank approved, the Government would guarantee the loan and small farmers like my father would continue in business. It so happened that the president of the bank was the guy who most wanted our land. . . . Of course, he wouldn't pass the loan.

One morning a giant tractor came in, like we had never seen before. My daddy used to do all his work with horses. So this huge tractor came in and began to knock down this corral, this small corral where my father kept his horses.

17. Why did the bank refuse to approve the family's loan?

(1) The bank president wanted the land.
(2) The U.S. government forced him.
(3) The family had made no payments.
(4) The land was of no value.
(5) He did not like the family.

Item 18 refers to the following passage.

How does this Civil War nurse spend her days?

Up at six, dress by gaslight, run through my ward and throw up the windows, though the men grumble and shiver; but the air is bad enough to breed a pestilence; and as no notice is taken of our frequent appeals for better ventilation, I must do what I can. Poke up the fire, add blankets, joke, coax, and command; but continue to open doors and windows as if life depended on it.

18. What does the author reveal about conditions in the hospital?

(1) The U.S. government monitored them carefully.
(2) They were improving gradually.
(3) They were as good as could be.
(4) They endangered patients and staff.
(5) The hospital was fresh and pleasant.

Directions: Choose the one best answer to each question. Answers are on page 133.

Item 19 refers to the following passage.

According to the passage, why do people set up governments?

We hold these truths to be self-evident: that all men are created equal; that they are endowed by their Creator with certain inalienable Rights; that among these are Life, Liberty, and the pursuit of Happiness. That, to secure these Rights, Governments are instituted among Men, deriving their just powers from the consent of the governed.

19. Which of the following events would the writers of the passage probably approve of?

(1) A ruler declares himself president for life.
(2) An army general forcibly takes over a corrupt government.
(3) A prime minister is elected by voters in a nation.
(4) A government takes possession of private property.
(5) A dictator runs a country wisely and justly.

Item 20 refers to the following passage.

Does the author object to living alone?

For me the most interesting thing about a solitary life, and mine has been that for the last twenty years, is that it becomes increasingly rewarding. When I can wake up and watch the sun rise over the ocean, as I do most days, and know that I have an entire day ahead, uninterrupted, in which to write a few pages, take a walk with my dog, lie down in the afternoon for a long think (why does one think better in a horizontal position?), read and listen to music, I am flooded with happiness.

20. What would the author probably prefer to do?

(1) attend a writers' convention
(2) play a competitive sport
(3) go to a private beach to read
(4) speak before a large audience
(5) attend a small party

Applying Ideas In the 1700s the English writer Samuel Johnson gave this advice:

■ The next best thing to knowing something is knowing where to find it.

Don't you think this idea is still useful? Although it was written in the 1700s, we can put it to use today.

Applying facts, opinions, and ideas such as the one above is an important skill, especially when reading nonfiction. For example, suppose you have read that the young Henry Ford had devised a plan to make pocket watches on a production line. According to his plan, each worker would complete a step in putting the watch together and then pass it to another worker, who would complete the next step. If you later read about the assembly lines at Ford's automobile plants, you could recall and apply what you had learned from earlier reading.

☑ A Test-Taking Tip

The GED Test of Interpreting Literature and the Arts probably will have some questions that require you to apply information from your reading to a new and different situation. Before you answer such a question, read the entire passage and summarize it in your mind. Then decide which of the five possible answers best fits the facts, ideas, and opinions in the passage.

Warm-up

Read the passage below and decide how the author might complete the sentences.

■ Washing machines, garbage disposals, lawn mowers, light bulbs, automatic laundry dryers, water pipes, furnaces, electrical fuses, television tubes, hose nozzles, tape recorders, slide projectors—all are in league with the automobile to take their turn at breaking down whenever life threatens to flow smoothly for their human enemies.

1. Elevators often ______________________ to inconvenience their "human enemies."

2. Toasters may ______________________ when you're hungry for breakfast.

3. Vending machines ______________________ ______________________ just to annoy the customers.

Sample Warm-up Answers
1. get stuck between floors **2.** burn the toast **3.** break down

Author's Style and Craft Speakers can emphasize points or express feelings with facial expressions, loud and soft tones, and body language. However, authors cannot communicate in these ways. So authors often use other techniques to make or emphasize a point. Some of these techniques are described below.

Using a quotation Sometimes an author quotes the words of an expert or well-known person, or uses an old saying. This can help focus your attention and give support to the writer's ideas. Here is an example:

■ According to an old saying, "The closer you come to the top of a hill, the harder the climbing becomes." In other words, as you near a goal, greater effort is needed to reach it.

Using a rhetorical question A rhetorical question does not need an answer; it is meant to make readers think about an issue or idea. Here is an example:

■ Do your tax dollars *really* help you? Have you ever taken the time to find out how the taxes you pay enrich your life?

Using a contrary-to-belief statement To focus attention on a topic, a writer may open with a statement that is the *opposite* of his or her main point. After capturing your attention, the author then explains his or her true feelings about the topic. Here is an example:

■ Our schools do not teach the basics any more. At least that's what some people think. But the truth is that. . . .

Warm-up

Read the paragraph and answer the questions that follow in complete sentences.

■ *Nobody* likes spiders. That's what I used to think. Then, for an assignment, I read several books about spiders. I was amazed at how beautiful and fascinating these tiny creatures can be. Now I find that spiders are among my favorite of nature's creatures.

1. How does the author feel about spiders now? ______________________

2. What effect does the opening sentence have? ______________________

____

Sample Warm-up Answers
1. The author has positive feelings now. **2.** It captures your attention and focuses it on the topic of spiders.

Item 21 refers to the following passage.

How did the Depression affect farmers?

There's a saying: "Depressions are farm led and farm fed." That was true in the Thirties. As farmers lost their purchasing power, the big tractors piled up at the Minneapolis-Moline plant in the Twin Cities. One day they closed their doors and turned their employees out to beg or starve. My cousin was one of them. I took my truck to Minneapolis and brought him and his family out to my farm for the duration. They stayed with us until the company opened up again, two to three years later.

21. Why did the author use the quotation in the first sentence?

    (1) to suggest the great number of people that the Depression affected
    (2) to focus attention on how farmers' economic problems can affect the nation
    (3) to point out that only farm failures can lead to a depression
    (4) to encourage support for farmers
    (5) to blame farmers for the Depression

Item 22 refers to the following passage.

How does the author remind people that they often take their vision for granted?

How much easier, how much more satisfying it is for you who can see to grasp quickly the essential qualities of another person by watching the subtleties of expression, the quiver of a muscle, the flutter of a hand. But does it ever occur to you to use your sight to see into the inner nature of a friend? Do not most of you seeing people grasp only casually the outward features of a familiar face and let it go at that?

22. What is the purpose of the two questions at the end of the paragraph?

    (1) to elicit information about how people see
    (2) to instruct people about the nature of sight
    (3) to obtain information about visual handicaps
    (4) to suggest that vision can help people understand others
    (5) plead for more research into the causes of blindness

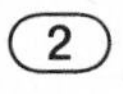

Directions: Choose the one best answer to each question. Answers are on page 133.

Items 23–24 refer to the following passage.

What does this "daily timetable" reveal about the life of a World War II family living secretly above a warehouse-and-office building?

Monday, 23 August, 1943

Dear Kitty,

Continuation of the "Secret Annexe" daily timetable. As the clock strikes half past eight in the morning, Margot and Mummy are jittery: "Ssh . . . Daddy, quiet, Otto, ssh . . . Pim." "It is half past eight, come back here, you can't run any more water; walk quietly!" These are the various cries to Daddy in the bathroom. As the clock strikes half past eight, he has to be in the living room. Not a drop of water, no lavatory, no walking about, everything quiet. As long as none of the office staff are there, everything can be heard in the warehouse. The door is opened upstairs at twenty minutes past eight and shortly after there are three taps on the floor: Anne's porridge. I climb upstairs and fetch my "puppy-dog" plate. Down in my room again, everything goes at terrific speed: do my hair, put away my noisy tin pottie, bed in place. Hush, the clock strikes! Upstairs Mrs. Van Daan has changed her shoes and is shuffling about in bedroom slippers. Mr. Van Daan, too; all is quiet.

23. The schedule in the passage most likely describes events that

(1) happen day after day
(2) could happen to the writer's family at some future time
(3) occur on the last day in hiding
(4) could never really happen
(5) take place just on a particular Monday

24. When must the occupants of the "secret annexe" be absolutely quiet?

(1) both day and night
(2) in the morning, before the office workers arrive
(3) during the night hours
(4) before the clock strikes eight-thirty
(5) whenever anyone else is in the building

Patterns of Details A well-written article follows a pattern that helps you sort out the details and see how they relate to each other. The pattern is like a blueprint. You can use it to understand and remember information from the article. Some of the more frequently used patterns are (1) time order, (2) comparison, (3) contrast, (4) a combination of comparison and contrast, and (5) cause and effect. Time order is discussed on this page. The other patterns are discussed on following pages.

Time Order In the time-order pattern, events are related in the order they occurred, or steps in a process are listed in the order they must develop. For instance, history books frequently use time order to describe what led up to a particular event. A biography that describes the events in a person's life just as they happened uses time order. And a selection that explains a process such as passing a law or refinishing wood uses time order. Sometimes time order is used to show how a person behaves or thinks, or to add humor.

Warm-up

Read the following paragraph. In the blanks below, tell why you think the author used the time-order pattern. Be sure to use complete sentences.

■ When my boss makes a decision, she begins by taking a mental inventory of the situation. Next, she writes down every possible option. She then calculates, with her unique logic, the probable outcome of each plan of action. This step is usually accompanied by much sighing, advice-seeking, and nail-chewing. Last, she inevitably proceeds to do exactly what she felt like doing in the first place.

____

____

____

☑ A Test-Taking Tip

Several words and phrases can alert you to a series of events when you read a passage on the GED Test. Some of these key words and phrases are *first, second, next, before, afterward, during, while, as, finally,* and *meanwhile.*

Sample Warm-up Answer

The steps that the boss takes to make a decision reveal that she tries to be well-organized and logical, but she actually makes decisions rather illogically.

Understanding Comparisons A comparison shows how two things are similar, or like each other. A comparison can be a few words, or it can be several paragraphs. Longer comparisons may be used to point out ways in which two different things have similar features. The paragraph below compares two different people who helped a Mexican boy learn about his new homeland.

■ I did not think of 418 L Street and the Lincoln School as in any way alike, but both had a principal, Miss Hopley and Mrs. Dodson. From Miss Hopley I learned that the man with the black beard and the sad eyes pictured on her wall was Abraham Lincoln, for whom our school was named. From Mrs. Dodson I found out that the picture of the nude lady [on the wall in her home] was September Morn and that it was a famous painting. Miss Hopley conducted me firmly and methodically through the grades into the new world of books and manners she called America. Mrs. Dodson adopted us into the odd company of the rooming house, from which I found my way through the *barrio*.

☑ A Test-Taking Tip

The following words and phrases can help you recognize comparison: *like, as, just as, similar, similarly,* and *in the same way*.

Warm-up

Read the passage below. Then answer the question that follows in one or two sentences.

■ An abstract process becomes easier to understand when it is compared to a more familiar one. The United States, with its mixture of different immigrant people is often compared to a melting pot. In cooking, many different ingredients, each with its own flavor and texture, melt and blend together into a new and interesting combination. In the same way, people from many different nations have come together in the U.S., blending their beliefs and customs with those of other countries to produce a new and interesting culture.

Why does the writer compare the mix of new immigrants in the United States to cooking?

____

____

Sample Warm-up Answer
The author compares an unfamiliar process to a simple, familiar process. The comparison makes the first process easier to understand.

Item 25 refers to the following passage.

How did Thomas Jefferson and Alexander Hamilton contribute to the nation?

Thomas Jefferson and Alexander Hamilton were fellow patriots and fellow statesmen. Men of true brilliance, the powerful influence that they exerted upon the Republic at the beginning of its history had an effect that has persisted to the present day. To them we owe some of our greatest historical documents—to Jefferson the Declaration of Independence and to Hamilton a number of the famous *Federalist* papers.

25. According to the author, what did Jefferson and Hamilton have in common?
    (1) They belonged to the Federalist party.
    (2) They were brilliant political leaders.
    (3) They came from the same state.
    (4) They wrote the Declaration of Independence together.
    (5) They had the same political views.

Item 26 refers to the following passage.

What does the author compare to a house?

Some years ago a famous novelist died. Among his papers was found a list of suggested plots for future stories, the most prominently underscored being this one: "A widely separated family inherits a large house in which they have to live together." This is the great new problem of mankind. We have inherited a house, a great "world house" in which we have to live together—black and white, Easterner and Westerner, Gentile and Jew, Catholic and Protestant, Moslem and Hindu—a family unduly separated in ideas, culture and interest, who, because we can never again live apart, must learn somehow to live with each other in peace.

26. What idea does the author illustrate with his comparison?
    (1) Different nations are like rooms of a house.
    (2) All people of the world are related.
    (3) We need to take better care of our "home."
    (4) There's enough space for everyone.
    (5) People must learn to live in peace.

Directions: Choose the one best answer to each question. Answers are on page 133.

Item 27 refers to the following passage.

How were Bing Crosby and Elvis Presley different?

There were similarities that ought to tell us something. Both [Bing Crosby and Elvis Presley] came from obscurity to national recognition while quite young and became very rich. Both lacked formal music education and went on to movie careers despite lack of acting skills. Both developed distinctive musical styles which were originally scorned by critics and subsequently studied as pioneer developments in the art of popular song.

The difference between Presley and Crosby, however, reflected generational differences which spoke of changing values in American life. Crosby's music was soothing. Presley's was disturbing. It is too easy to be glib about this, to say that Crosby was singing to, first, Depression America and, then, to wartime America, and that his audiences had all the disturbances they could handle in their daily lives without buying more at the record shop and movie theater.

27. How does the passage describe the difference between Crosby's and Presley's singing?

    (1) It was almost impossible to detect.
    (2) It was due to singing in different eras.
    (3) It was due to differences in training.
    (4) It reveals that one was a greater success.
    (5) It shows that one was a better singer.

Understanding Contrast A contrast points out differences. When opposites, such as day and night, or large and small, are contrasted, the differences are obvious. But finding differences in basically similar things is more interesting and challenging. For example, identical twins may be alike in appearance but very different in personality.

An advertisement may use contrast to show that a product is superior to competing products. In a similar way, an author may contrast two things or persons to show that one is preferable to the other.

A contrast may take a sentence or many paragraphs. Contrast and comparison are often combined to show how two items or people are alike and different. An example of combining contrast and comparison is the passage for item 28 on this page.

☑ A Test-Taking Tip

On the GED Test of Interpreting Literature and the Arts, the following words can alert you to a contrast in a passage: *however, on the other hand, yet, in contrast,* and *but.*

Warm-up

Read the following paragraph. Then answer the questions below in complete sentences.

■ To the untrained eye, popcorn seems identical to sweet corn. Both are harvested on the cob, and both are popular foods. However, popcorn kernels have a tough outer shell that sweet corn kernels don't have. This hard shell holds in moisture. When popcorn kernels are heated, the moisture turns to steam. The kernels burst with a popping sound into white, fluffy snacks.

1. How is popcorn different from sweet corn?

____

2. What word alerts you to the contrast?

____

Need a Hint for Number 27?
The passage combines comparison with contrast. To find the contrast, look for a key word.

Sample Warm-up Answers
1. Popcorn has a tough outer shell that holds in moisture.
2. The key word is *however.*

Cause and Effect as a Pattern A certain folk story clearly shows the relationship between cause and effect, that is, how one thing can lead to another. According to the story, a knight was riding to battle when a nail came out of his horse's shoe. Because the knight was in a great hurry, he rode on. Soon the shoe fell off, and the horse became lame. Still the knight pressed on. When he reached the battlefield, other knights were waiting for him—they depended on his leadership. As the knight plunged toward the enemy, his horse stumbled, and the knight was thrown to the ground. The fall killed the knight instantly. Without his leadership, the other knights turned and fled. The battle was lost, and the enemy took over the kingdom—all because of the loss of a horseshoe nail!

☑ A Test-Taking Tip

The GED Test probably will include questions that require you to understand cause-and-effect relationships. For example, a question may ask how one event in a story leads to another. Certain clues can help you identify a cause or result. *Because, therefore, consequently, caused by, so that, brought about by,* and *as a result* are examples of such clues.

Warm-up

Read the following account of a Russian immigrant. Then answer each question below with a complete sentence.

■ I never got rich. My wife and I raised six children. When my sisters and brothers got married, my father came to live with us. Then one of my sisters died and her children came to live with us. Then my wife brought her parents to America and they lived with us. Then we wanted our children to have an education, so we sent them to college. There never was enough money left to start any kind of business. But I feel that we made a good investment.

1. Why didn't the speaker start a business?

____

2. Why does he say that he made a good investment?

____

____

Sample Warm-up Answers
1. He used his money for his family. **2.** He feels that sending his children to college was a wise use of his money.

Items 28–29 refer to the following passage.

What happened to the author's mother?

As a nine-year-old boy struggling with the English language, I felt helpless against the fact of my mother's death. It was not something that I could talk about to anyone. There seemed to be nothing I could do to make up for her sacrifice except to hope that my sisters were right, that God would ultimately punish those who had betrayed, tortured and murdered her.

Then, in the seventh grade, a teacher assigned me to write about my life in Greece. It was one of the first days of spring. I looked out the school window, remembering our mountainside blazing with purple Judas trees, the Easter kid roasting on a spit outside each house, my mother boiling the eggs in a vat of blood-red dye.

I wrote how, in the spring of my eighth year, I overheard two guerrillas say they were going to take the village children away from their parents and send them behind the Iron Curtain. I ran to tell my mother what I had heard and she began to plan our escape, setting in motion the events that would end in her execution four months later.

The essay won a certificate of merit, and I realized that I was not as helpless as I had thought. I would learn to write and eventually describe what was done in that ravine in 1948 and by whom.

28. The author began to feel he could do something about his mother's death only after

(1) he wrote a successful essay about her
(2) he learned to speak English
(3) his sisters persuaded him that he could
(4) his memories no longer haunted him
(5) he turned eight and overheard two guerrillas

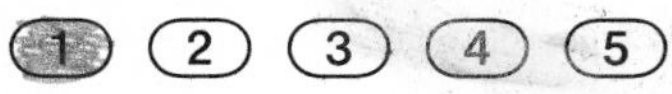

29. What event led to the mother's death?

(1) Children were taken from their parents.
(2) The family was celebrating Easter.
(3) The author wrote about his mother.
(4) The author's essay won a prize.
(5) The author overheard two guerrillas.

Directions: Choose the one best answer to each question. Answers are on page 134.

Item 1 is based on the following passage.

How did Charlie Chaplin behave when he was directing a film?

Chaplin showed the cameraman, Rollie Totheroh, where to set up the stationary camera. He looked through the finder and told Rollie to lock it off. The camera seldom moved in Chaplin's films. He then did his part. He showed us how he would walk, how he would twirl his cane, how he would tip his hat, how he would smile at Virginia Cherrill, and so on. Then he became Virginia Cherrill, the beautiful blind girl, and the tramp at the same time, jumping from one position to the other, twirling his cane, holding his hands out in front of his "sightless" eyes, then smiling, first as the tramp and then as the blind girl.

As he passed in front of our corner, Austin Jewell and I raised our peashooters. Chaplin said, "No, wait!" and promptly stopped being the tramp and the blind girl and became two newsboys blowing peashooters. He would blow a pea and then run over and pretend to be hit by it, then back to blow another pea. He became a kind of dervish, playing all the parts, using all the props, seeing and cane-twirling as the tramp, not seeing and grateful as the blind girl, peashooting as the newsboys. Austin and I and Miss Cherrill watched while Charlie did his show. Finally, he had it all worked out and reluctantly gave us back our parts. I felt that he would much rather have played all of them himself.

1. Which of the following best states the main idea of the passage?

   (1) The author was one of Chaplin's actors.
   (2) Charlie Chaplin taught Virginia Cherrill how to act.
   (3) Chaplin demonstrated exactly what each member of the crew should do.
   (4) Each member of Chaplin's crew was encouraged to suggest new ideas for the film.
   (5) Although he enjoyed acting, Charlie Chaplin also understood the cameraman's job.

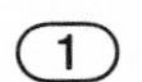    

Commentary

Inferring the Main Idea Commentary is a special type of nonfiction in which the author describes and evaluates a film, play, television program, or piece of music or art. Locating the main idea in commentary is like finding the main idea in nonfiction.

Sometimes the main idea is stated clearly within the selection. However, often the main idea is unstated. Then you need to infer it from the details of the selection. To do this, first, ask yourself what the topic of the selection is. Then ask what is the single most important point that the author makes about the topic. Combine your answers to discover the main idea.

☑ A Test-Taking Tip

The commentary in the GED Test of Interpreting Literature and the Arts is selected for an average reader, not for an expert on arts and entertainment. The passages probably will describe the person or item being discussed to help you understand the author's opinions. Deal with the test questions on commentary as you would questions on any other type of nonfiction.

Warm-up

Read the following passage from a review of a musical. Then answer the question below.

■ What do you like most in a musical—toe-tapping music? eye-catching costumes and scenery? a spirited story line? You'll find all these in the new hit musical "City Secrets." But what you probably will find most dazzling is that this musical comedy is written, produced, and performed entirely by amateurs.

What is the main idea of the paragraph?

____

____

Need a Hint?
The information in the first two paragraphs in the outer column will help you to infer the main idea.

Sample Warm-up Answer
The successful musical "City Secrets" is written, produced, and performed by amateurs.

Understanding Supporting Statements In commentary an author gives his or her views on a piece of art, music, or literature and then gives statements that support, or explain, these views. What type of information is used in supporting statements? Some give *descriptive details* that help you visualize a dance, play, or a piece of art. Some supporting statements give background about the item or person being discussed. Other supporting statements are explanations—reasons a film became extremely popular, for example.

☑ A Test-Taking Tip

When reading descriptive details in a commentary on the GED Test, picture in your mind the item or person being described. For instance, if an author describes the texture of a piece of pottery, imagine how the pottery would feel. If an author describes the movements of a dancer, visualize the performance. Using your imagination will help you understand and remember what you read. It also will help explain the author's opinions.

Warm-up

The following paragraph describes a performance of the classical ballerina Anna Pavlova. Picture the descriptive details as you read.

■ She never appeared to rest static, some part of her trembled, vibrated, beat like a heart. Before our dazzled eyes, she flashed with the sudden sweetness of a hummingbird in action too quick for understanding . . . , in action sensed rather than seen. The movie cameras of her day could not record her. . . . Her feet and hands photographed as a blur.

What fact supports the opinion that Pavlova was "too quick for understanding"?

____

____

Sample Warm-up Answer
The movie cameras of her day photographed her movements as a blur.

Items 2–3 refer to the following passage.

What kinds of music did Sam Cooke sing?

The Man and His Music is the second release in RCA's four-part reissue tribute to Sam Cooke. The first, *Sam Cooke Live at the Harlem Square Club 1963,* was issued last year. It captured Cooke at his "Having a Party" peak, all fire and brimstone and rock & roll—a sure-'nuff revelation for anyone who remembers Cooke only for sugarcoated pop with a dash of soul. *The Man,* with a few exceptions, isn't so revealing. It's essentially a "best of" package with some added attractions, such as three sides from his gospel group, the Soul Stirrers, including the doo-wopish "Touch the Hem of His Garment." Then comes the hit parade—from "You Send Me" to "Shake"—plus an assortment of B sides generally proving that Cooke's voice could redeem even the kitschiest arrangements ("Rome Wasn't Built in a Day," "Everybody Loves to Cha Cha Cha").

2. Which of Sam Cooke's songs supports the idea that he could sing rock?

   (1) "Having a Party"
   (2) "Touch the Hem of His Garment"
   (3) "You Send Me"
   (4) "Rome Wasn't Built in a Day"
   (5) "Everybody Loves to Cha Cha Cha"

3. The author believes that the second album does not reveal as much of Cooke's talents as the first because the second album includes many

   (1) B sides
   (2) gospel hymns
   (3) well-known hits
   (4) rock-and-roll songs
   (5) soul times

Directions: Choose the one best answer to each question. Answers are on page 134.

Item 4 refers to the following passage.

What is "Running Scared" about?

"Running Scared," about a pair of young Chicago detectives handling one last case before early retirement, has neither the explosive laughter nor the explosive gunplay of "48 HRS.," a similar buddy-action film.

Instead, despite its R-rating for language and violence, "Running Scared" tries to be a light comedy in a violent, comic-book world. . . .

The detectives are played by Gregory Hines and Billy Crystal, both of whom come to the movies from other mediums—dance theater and comedy, respectively.

It may be too early in their acting careers for them to pull off a credible buddy act that makes us believe they are Chicago detectives and not just Heckle and Jeckle in plainclothes.

4. What elements make "Running Scared" a "buddy-action" film?

   (1) violence and two detectives
   (2) explosive laughter and gunplay
   (3) dance theater and comedy
   (4) R-rated scenes and dialog
   (5) Heckle and Jeckle

Item 5 refers to the following passage.

What subjects did Rivera paint?

Rivera's legacy to Mexican art is perhaps without peer. He painted the people, the history, the passion of his land as few others have. He painted the politics and politicians. He painted those he loved and those at whom he scoffed. He painted seven days a week, all hours there was light. And after years of experimentation with different styles and media, he found his artistic voice in what was to become a quintessentially Mexican form of expression—muralism.

5. In the passage, what does "voice" mean in the phrase "he found his artistic voice"?

   (1) a political opinion
   (2) a kind of paint
   (3) a type of style
   (4) a way to communicate
   (5) a daily work schedule

The Vocabulary of Commentaries The world changes quickly, and people need words to describe how it changes. In fact, new words are coined, or invented, almost daily to refer to new ideas, styles, and products. Some are combinations of old words, some are taken from people's names, and some are simply made up. New words in the fields of art and entertainment appear at a particularly fast pace. They are frequently used in spoken and printed commentaries long before they appear in dictionaries. To find the meanings of new words in the commentaries on the GED Test, you can use word-part clues.

For example, a sitcom is a type of television show involving amusing situations. You probably can tell that *sitcom* is made up of the words *situation* and *comedy.* Word-part clues also are helpful with *docudrama,* which is made up of the words *documentary* and *drama.* From this you can infer that a docudrama combines documented facts with a dramatic story.

Along with word-part clues, context clues also reveal the meanings of unfamiliar words in commentary. In fact, you can use context clues to check yourself on whether you've correctly inferred the meaning of a word using its parts. See page 88 to refresh your memory on how to use context clues.

Warm Up

Use word-part clues and context clues to infer the meaning of the **boldfaced** word below. Then write a definition of the word.

■ When television was new, it was welcomed as a member of the family. The TV joined people at their meals, entertained them during long evenings, and even joined them on vacation.

But today's parents increasingly view the TV as the black sheep of the family. Alarmed by programs with violence and sexual innuendos, they have developed a severe case of **videophobia.**

What does videophobia mean? ______________

____

____

____

Sample Warm-up Answer
Videophobia means "fear of the effects of watching television."

Drawing Conclusions Writers sometimes give just enough information so readers can draw their own conclusions. In the commentary below, the writer leads you to conclude that Ray Charles's life experiences have strongly influenced his music without actually stating the idea.

> Any discussion of jazz-blues—rhythm 'n' blues-gospel and soul has to come finally to rest on Ray Charles, for he is the man who has put it all together better than anyone else. Perhaps he has felt it more deeply than anyone else: the sadness, the jazz, the beat. He was blind at six, orphaned at fifteen, became a narcotics addict by the time he was sixteen, but emerged from the dark world of drugs by his own strength of character and will-power when he was thirty-two.

The passage suggests that the singer's blindness, the death of his parents, and his experiences with drugs have contributed to the deep emotions and strong rhythms in his music. Yet the writer actually does not state this.

Warm-up

Read this passage from a review of two dance performances. Then answer the question below.

■ An enthusiastic crowd watched the Prybyk Ukrainian Dance Troupe last night at the city's ethnic festival. The troupe has perfected a variety of lively dances and then added style and humor. The performance was a complete success. Unfortunately, the square dances that followed the Ukrainians do not deserve the same high praise. Their act is best left undescribed.

What can you conclude about the quality of the square dancers' performance?

____

____

____

Sample Warm-up Answer
The square dancers' performance was not good.

Item 6 refers to the following passage.

What kind of show is "Pippin"?

"Pippin" originally ran on Broadway without an intermission during a brief fad for non-stop musicals. Luckily a break has been inserted into Circle Theatre's production, but its drawback is that the show never quite regains its momentum. We get scenes of dull domesticity as Pippin marries a young widow . . . who has a small son.

6. Why are non-stop musicals most likely no longer staged?

   (1) They could never regain momentum.
   (2) They were too expensive to produce.
   (3) Their music was unpopular.
   (4) People wanted an intermission.
   (5) Broadway will no longer allow them.

Item 7 refers to the following passage.

What kind of man was Fred Waring?

He was turned down by the glee club when he was a student at Pennsylvania State University, but Fred Waring knew how to exact the sweetest revenge. He organized his own band and singing group, the Pennsylvanians, left school without graduating and won national acclaim for his smooth melodies and rich orchestrations.

Along the way, the band scored a string of firsts—the first electronic recording of a song, the first all-musical motion picture, the first vocal band to have a national radio show, the first to have its own TV show. . . .

Death came to Waring, 84, just two days after he conducted a youth choral group at Penn State. Not good enough for the school's glee club, he demonstrated that talent, given the proper showcase, can master the world.

7. Which of the following conclusions can be drawn about Fred Waring?

   (1) Fred Waring did not allow one rejection to end his musical career.
   (2) Waring would have been even more successful if he had stayed in school.
   (3) Waring was not a good musician.
   (4) Waring died because he had returned to his old school.
   (5) Waring thought a successful music career was less important than a college education.

Directions: Choose the one best answer to each question. Answers are on page 134.

Item 8 refers to the following message.

What is wrong with modern writing?

As I have tried to show, modern writing at its worst does not consist in picking out words for the sake of their meaning and inventing images in order to make the meaning clearer. It consists in gumming together long strips of words which have already been set in order by someone else, and making the results presentable by sheer humbug. The attraction of this way of writing is that it is easy. It is easier—even quicker, once you have the habit—to say *In my opinion it is a not unjustifiable assumption that* than to say *I think.*

8. What advice would the author give new writers?

(1) Use phrases that others put together.
(2) Use words of many syllables.
(3) Use short words with clear meanings.
(4) Use many words to describe each idea.
(5) Avoid using images in your writing.

Item 9 refers to the following passage.

For what type of music is Brahms remembered?

The four symphonies Brahms wrote are worthy successors to those of his hero, Beethoven (born some 60 years earlier). Indeed, the Brahms First Symphony has been referred to as "The Tenth" because it carries on the great tradition of Beethoven's nine symphonies. . . .

Listeners will recognize the hand of a master in all his music. He loved folk melodies and created many folk-like melodies of his own, expressing in these simple songs the tender feelings and family affection missing from his personal life.

9. Which of the following songs would Brahms probably like most?

(1) a rousing national anthem
(2) an old, traditional lullaby
(3) a dance number from a musical
(4) a rock-and-roll hit
(5) a religious hymn

Applying Ideas Read the following passage to find out how the reviewer feels about the film he's discussing.

■ Steven Spielberg's *Indiana Jones and the Temple of Doom* is one of the greatest Bruised Forearm Movies ever made. You know what a Bruised Forearm Movie is. That's the kind of movie where your date is always grabbing your forearm in a viselike grip, as unbearable excitement unfolds on the screen. After the movie is over, you've had a great time but your arm is black-and-blue for a week. This movie is one of the most relentlessly nonstop action pictures ever made, with a virtuoso series of climactic sequences that must last an hour and never stop for a second. It's a roller coaster ride, a visual extravaganza, a technical triumph, and a whole lot of fun.

How would you describe the reviewer's attitude: approving? enthusiastic? positive?

However, would the reviewer recommend this film to someone who likes quiet, relaxing entertainment? Definitely not!

By answering the above questions you have applied information from a reading passage to a new situation.

Warm Up

In the following passage, look for judgments the reviewer has made. Then answer the question below.

■ Lloyd Carnahan's recent book, *Coins of the Past,* has a colorful and inviting cover. But aside from the cover, the book has little merit. In fact, Carnahan gives the impression that he isn't very interested in old coins.

While the publisher claims that the book has been researched carefully, a quick examination suggests that the research was superficial; Carnahan incorrectly names several coins, and he often gives questionable dates.

How do you think the reviewer would feel about a book called *Stamps of the Past* by the same author?

____

____

____

Sample Warm-up Answer
The reviewer probably would doubt the book's accuracy.

Understanding Tone You know how to tell a good deal just by a person's "tone of voice." The tone can tell you whether the speaker approves or disapproves of the subject being discussed, whether he or she is enthusiastic or hostile.

Similarly, the tone of a piece of writing can tell you a great deal. **Tone** is the author's attitude toward a subject. Newspaper reports, business reports, and technical reports should give information, not opinions. So the authors usually try to keep their attitudes and feelings out of their writing.

However, commentary is a more personal form of writing. It *is* opinion, with facts to back it up. The purpose of commentary is to let you know how the author honestly feels about a person or a piece of art, music, literature, or other work. Don't be surprised if you read commentary that is unflattering and negative, even strongly so. Critics are meant to "tell it like it is."

Coming to Terms

tone the author's attitude toward the subject he or she is discussing.

Warm-up

Decide what the author's tone is as you read this excerpt from a movie review.

■ It took *Dune* about nine minutes to completely strip me of my anticipation. This movie is a real mess, an incomprehensible, ugly, unstructured, pointless excursion into the murkier realms of one of the most confusing screenplays of all time. Even the color is no good; everything is seen through a sort of dusty yellow filter, as if the film was left out in the sun too long.

What adjectives in the review help you sense the author's tone? ______________________

____

Need a Hint?
Before answering item 11, picture each performer listed working at his or her craft. Ask yourself if the tone of the review would fit each performance.

Warm-up Answers
incomprehensible, ugly, unstructured, pointless, murkier, confusing

Items 10–11 refer to the following passage.

Who are the Latin American String Quartet?

Clad in T-shirt and sneakers, the sandy-haired violinist arches a bow over his instrument and nods to three bearded companions. Suddenly the air is filled with the lilting strains of a Brahms string quartet. Smiles quickly replace looks of concentration when they finish playing, and the four young musicians talk easily with the crowd that lingers to glean a few musical insights.

"You must not be afraid of the music," advises Arón Bitrán. His listeners take careful note, for despite their casual dress, these are no street musicians entertaining noontime passersby. Indeed, the foursome is Mexico's internationally acclaimed Latin American String Quartet, and they are teaching a master's class at a leading U.S. university. . . .

The Latin American String Quartet surely has come a long way in a few short years, but they prefer to think more about future challenges than past successes. "We'd like to be known someday for our own style of playing," says cellist Alvaro Bitrán. The rest of the group nods in agreement, thinking of the time when other aspiring musicians will study their technique the way they, themselves, have studied the world's greatest string quartets.

One gets the impression they will not have that long to wait.

10. What is the author's attitude toward the Latin American String Quartet?

(1) respectful (2) bored
(3) shocked (4) neutral
(5) hostile

11. The tone in this article probably would NOT be appropriate for a review of a

(1) classical pianist
(2) Shakespearean actor
(3) a circus act
(4) ballet dancer
(5) opera singer

Directions: Choose the one best answer to each question. Answers are on page 134.

Item 12 is based on the following passage.

What type of fiction does Colwin write?

Laurie Colwin's fiction has always been distinguished by glistening wit, warmth, and good humor and by her evolving fascination with the theme of romantic love—the heady, hard-core stuff strong enough to isolate her characters almost entirely from the world outside their passion.

Her sixth book in twice that many years occupies the now-fashionable ground between short-story collection and novel.

12. Which of the following words best describes the tone of the passage?

    (1) disapproving (2) approving
    (3) objective (4) sarcastic
    (5) humorous

Item 13 refers to the following passage.

Why is African news difficult to cover?

Clearly, Africa is not a top priority of television news. Most often, though, it's not for lack of skill or good intentions—it's time and money. In the mid-1970s all three networks had bureaus in Kenya. But air routes between African countries are few, and reporters often had to fly up to Europe and back down into Africa to travel from one country to another. That proved both expensive and slow. So none has a bureau in black Africa now. And many correspondents find this to be the greatest obstacle to in-depth coverage. "I would love to spend a year there," says ABC's Karen Burnes. "You just cannot understand it otherwise." The problems are many-faceted and the countries richly diverse; Nigerians alone speak some 250 languages and dialects.

13. What is the tone of the passage?

    (1) enthusiastic (2) angry
    (3) objective (4) discouraged
    (5) puzzled

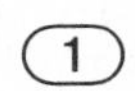

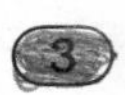

Identifying Tone Descriptive words are often clues to the tone of an article. If the author describes an artist or work of art as *refreshing, beneficial,* or *delightful,* the tone is probably approving.

However, pleasant words can express displeasure when the tone is sarcastic. **Sarcasm** says one thing and means the opposite. For example, if you call a snowy, cold day "delightfully tropical," you are using sarcasm.

If you read a passage with negative words, such as *shoddy, messy,* and *unscrupulous,* you can tell that the author's attitude is disapproving. The number and nature of the negative words will tell you just how strongly the author disapproves.

The lack of descriptive words is also a clue. That is a characteristic of objective writing.

Another clue to the tone of an article is the details an author chooses. Details help you sense whether the tone is amused, enthusiastic, or disgusted, for example.

Coming to Terms

sarcasm saying one thing and meaning the opposite

☑ A Test-Taking Tip

If you cannot answer a question about tone on the GED Test, eliminate the choices that seem obviously wrong. Then reread the selection and decide which of the remaining choices is best.

Warm-up

Read the following passage and then answer the question below.

■ But with all that is said about the shortcomings of rock, and much of this valid criticism, the fact remains that rock music has a vitality, power and excitement that other pop music forms lack. And it has been the most important form of expression for an entire generation. This alone makes it a very powerful force in our culture.

What is the author's attitude toward rock music?

Sample Warm-up Answer
The author obviously approves of rock music.

Author's Purpose and Special Techniques

The more commentary you read, the more aware you will become of special techniques that reviewers use. You already may have noticed one technique. Some commentaries in this section quote a well-known artist or performer. You also may have noticed that reviewers often ask rhetorical questions. This technique focuses attention on an idea or issue. Review the use of quotations and rhetorical questions on page 93.

As you continue to read commentary, you will become aware of a third technique: a brief reference to a well-known artist or famous work. Frequently, this reference helps you understand a new or less familiar artist or work. For instance, if a critic were reviewing a full-length cartoon, he or she might mention an old Walt Disney film. Since most readers are familiar with Disney cartoons, the reference would help form their impressions of the new film.

Warm-up

Read the following paragraph. Then answer the question below.

■ Carl Ogden, lead actor in the drama "Willow Whistle," has all the sophistication of the Three Stooges. Ogden's expressions and gestures are no more flexible than those of a wooden marionette; in short, he would do well to become a bootmaker.

How do you know that the reviewer feels Ogden's performance is unsophisticated?

____

____

As you prepare to take the GED Test, read a movie, art, music, or drama review each day. The few minutes you spend reading may give you the confidence you need to answer questions on commentary.

Sample Warm-up Answer
The writer likens Ogden to the Three Stooges, who are known for their clumsy, slapstick humor.

Item 14 refers to the following passage.

What is Pete Carson's problem?

What would you get if you crossed Robin Hood, Superman, and Chicken Little? You'd get a crusader with superhuman powers, but absolutely no courage. And that describes the main character in Jody Tripp's new novel, *The Opal Charm*. Pete Carson, Tripp's version of Robin Hood, would like to embezzle money from the village treasury in order to fund a sweeping welfare program intended to benefit jobless youth. But the problem is that Carson simply lacks the courage. He wants to be Robin Hood, but feels like Caspar Milquetoast.

14. What does the reference to Chicken Little suggest about Pete Carson?

(1) He enjoys children's stories.
(2) He is good hearted.
(3) He is not well organized.
(4) He raises poultry.
(5) He is cowardly.

Item 15 refers to the following passage.

Why are movie monsters so long-lived?

Monsters are long-lived. Monster films made in the early days of sound still go round the scream circuit, earning money years after their reputable competition has been forgotten. All the classics of horror have triggered off chains of sequels, so that the monsters stay among us. For instance, the original Mummy was followed, during the 1940s by *The Mummy's Hand, The Mummy's Ghost,* and *The Mummy's Curse;* finally even Abbott and Costello met the Mummy. The Frankenstein monster and Dracula, as well as the less important Wolfman (who has never had a feature film to himself) have all been through widely distributed repeat performances.

15. Why does the writer refer to Abbott and Costello?

(1) because they both played the Mummy
(2) because they were responsible for the success of the Mummy movies
(3) for the sake of mentioning another popular movie of the 1940s
(4) to stress how so many Mummy sequels were made
(5) to prove that Mummy movies were better than other monster movies

Directions: Choose the one best answer to each question. Answers are on page 134.

Item 1 refers to the following passage.

Did the narrator kill Phillips?

"I never saw Phillips before today," I said. "I don't count that he said he saw me up in Ventura once, because I don't remember him. I met him just the way I told you. He tailed me around and I braced him. He wanted to talk to me, he gave me his key, I went to his apartment, used the key to let myself in when he didn't answer. He was dead. The police were called and through a set of events or incidents that had nothing to do with me, a gun was found under Hench's pillow. A gun that had been fired."

1. According to the narrator, when did he first meet Phillips?
   (1) after he went to Phillips's apartment
   (2) before Phillips tailed him
   (3) when Phillips was in Ventura
   (4) the day Phillips died
   (5) at a time he couldn't quite remember

Item 2 refers to the following passage.

How long had Louisa and Joe waited to be married?

They were to be married in a month, after a singular courtship which had lasted for a matter of fifteen years. For fourteen out of the fifteen years the two had not once seen each other, and they had seldom exchanged letters. Joe had been all those years in Australia, where he had gone to make his fortune, and where he had stayed until he made it. He would have stayed fifty years if it had taken so long, and come home feeble and tottering, or never come home at all, to marry Louisa.

2. Why had Louisa and Joe's engagement lasted so long?
   (1) Joe had become ill for a while.
   (2) Joe had not been able to find a job.
   (3) Travel to Australia took many years.
   (4) Joe had taken a long time to become successful.
   (5) Louisa had never written to Joe to set a date.

Popular and Classical Fiction

Plot and Sequence Fiction includes novels, short stories, and other writings that tell about imaginary people and events. The plan or main story in a piece of fiction is called its **plot.** Understanding the order of events in a plot is important when you are reading a passage on the GED Test. You probably expect the **narrator,** or storyteller, to start at the beginning of the plot, go on to the middle, and then to the ending. But not all stories are written in **sequence,** or the order in which the events occur.

An author may choose to open a story at a very exciting moment—even if that moment is toward the middle or end of the plot. The author then may go back and explain what led up to that exciting moment. Some stories never do give the ending; instead the author leaves it to the reader to infer what happened.

✓ Test-Taking Tip

When you read a passage on the GED Test, keep a mental list of the events that happen and the order in which they happened. To help you tell which event came first, second, third, and so on, watch for key words and phrases.

Coming to Terms

narrator the voice that tells a story
plot the plan or main story in a piece of fiction
sequence the order in which the events occur

Warm-up

Write the letters of the events below in the order in which the events occurred.

1. b **2.** a **3.** c **4.** d

a. We reserved the church and asked Reverend Nelson to marry us.
b. Stan and I set a wedding date.
c. It was time for the ceremony to begin, but we waited and waited and waited.
d. Reverend Nelson had overslept; he arrived an hour late.

Warm-up Answers
1. b **2.** a **3.** c **4.** d

Setting The setting of a story is the time and place in which the events occur. Think of a movie or TV show that you have watched recently. Was the story about people today or about people from the past or future? How did you recognize the time period? Did the characters' clothing, hairstyles, and speech tell you? Or did the buildings and kinds of transportation give away the period?

The same details that helped you know when the story occurred also may have helped you infer where the action occurred. Sounds of howling winds and pictures of nothing but huge snow fields would have shown you that the story took place in or near a polar region. Palm trees and sandy beaches, on the other hand, would have been clues that the story's setting was the tropics.

When you are reading, you do not have the visual clues you do in a film or on TV. You must use the author's descriptions of the background and characters to picture the setting of the story.

Coming to Terms

setting the time and place in which the action of a story occurs

Warm-up

Read the following paragraph and then answer the questions below.

■ The melodic songs of thrushes floated on the warm breeze. Lush, lacy ferns swayed gently. Tall trees rose majestically above all. In the cool clear mountain stream a rainbow trout jumped, its bright shimmering scales reflecting the rich rays of the setting sun.

1. The time is ______________________.

2. The place is ______________________.

Warm-up Answers
1. dusk on a summer day **2.** a stream on a forested mountain

<u>Items 3–4</u> refer to the following passage.

Why are the time and the place in which Mrs. Wang lives dangerous?

Old Mrs. Wang knew of course that there was a war. Everybody had known for a long time that there was a war going on and that Japanese were killing Chinese. But still it was not real and no more than hearsay since none of the Wangs had been killed. The Village of Three Mile Wangs on the flat banks of the Yellow River, which was old Mrs. Wang's clan village, had never even seen a Japanese. This was how they came to be talking about Japanese at all.

It was evening and early summer, and after her supper Mrs. Wang had climbed the dike steps, as she did every day, to see how high the river had risen. She was much more afraid of the river than of the Japanese. She knew what the river would do. And one by one the villagers had followed her up the dike, and now they stood staring down at the malicious yellow water, curling along like a lot of snakes, and biting at the high dike banks.

"I never saw it as high as this so early," Mrs. Wang said. She sat down on a bamboo stool that her grandson, Little Pig, had brought for her, and spat into the water.

"It's worse than the Japanese, this old devil of a river," Little Pig said recklessly.

3. According to Mrs. Wang, the Yellow River is

   (1) higher than usual for the time of year
   (2) not so high as the years before
   (3) overflowing the dikes
   (4) filled with snakes
   (5) much less frightening than the Japanese

4. How has the war affected Mrs. Wang?

   (1) She lives in fear that the Japanese will come to her village.
   (2) She is preparing for a Japanese invasion.
   (3) She has not been affected except by rumors.
   (4) The Japanese have overrun the Village of Three Mile Wangs.
   (5) She is constantly talking of Japanese she has known.

(1) (2) (3) (4) (5)

Directions: Choose the one best answer to each question. Answers are on page 134.

Items 5–6 refer to the following passage.

How does Mrs. James feel about her daughter's plans to go out?

"I wish you'd reconsider and stay home tonight." Mrs. James regarded her daughter worriedly. "It sounds silly, I know, but I have this feeling—"

"Oh, Mom! You and your feelings!" Julie spoke the words laughingly, but she could not completely obliterate the twist of uneasiness that stirred within her. There was something oddly disturbing about her mother's premonitions. Many times, it was true, they turned out not to mean a thing, but there had been other times also. It was hard to forget the phone call that had seemed so ridiculous, but had sent her home to find a smoke-filled kitchen.

"I'm just going out for a couple of hours," she said now, reassuringly. "It's just to a movie with Bud."

"I wish you'd call it off."

5. What is Mrs. James trying to do in this conversation?

(1) warn her daughter
(2) express disapproval of her daughter's friend
(3) reassure her daughter
(4) reassure herself
(5) assert her authority over her daughter

6. How does Julie feel about her mother's uneasiness?

(1) She is angry at her mother.
(2) She is scornful of her mother's concern.
(3) She is a little disturbed by the uneasiness.
(4) She agrees with her mother and will call off the date.
(5) She would like to know more about her mother's uneasiness.

Characters Getting to know the characters in a story is like becoming acquainted with a person you have just met. It takes a little time to learn what the person is like. You learn from the person's actions and words and from what others say about the person.

☑ A Test-Taking Tip

Getting to know the characters in the reading passages on the GED Test of Interpreting Literature and the Arts will help you answer test questions about their feelings and their **motivations.** Motivations are the reasons characters behave as they do. Notice what the author says about a character, what the character says and does, and what other characters say about him or her.

Notice the author's descriptions. Sometimes an author will give important information about a character to help you understand what will happen in the story.

■ She was a quiet person. When she was a little girl she was often asked if the cat had got her tongue. Even with David she had a way of saying nothing in words. Her eyes, which could not lie, told what she felt. Before she smiled, a shadowy dimple quivered in one cheek. Her face was quiet under smooth wings of hair, and all her movements were gentle and deft. In her heart she never quite lost the wonder that she, quiet and shy and not very pretty, had won such a man as David.

Notice how each character behaves. Have you ever heard the old saying "Actions speak louder than words"? How a character behaves often will help you infer what that character is like. Notice how the author makes a character in the following passage seem threatening.

■ The first thing his eyes discerned was the largest man he had ever seen—a gigantic creature, solidly made and black-bearded almost to the waist. In his hand the man held a long-barreled revolver, and he was pointing it straight at Rainsford's heart. Out of the snarl of beard two small eyes regarded Rainsford.

Read the tinted column on the next page before you try the test items in the white columns on both pages.

Notice what the characters say What characters say and the way in which they speak can give information about them. Sometimes they will explain their feelings, ideas, and motivations openly. Other times you need to combine what they say and what you know about them, and then infer whether or not they are expressing their true feelings.

Some characters' accents can help you understand them. An accent is the manner of pronunciation heard in the speech of a person using a language not his own.

Often you can understand a character's personality by noticing what other characters say about him or her.

Warm-up

As you read this description, decide what word or phrase would best describe the wife. Then complete the sentences that follow.

■ On Wednesday night I always take my wife to the Chinese restaurant in the village, and then we go to the movies. We order the family dinner for two, but my wife eats most of it. She's a big eater. She reaches right across the table and grabs my egg roll, empties the roast duck onto her plate, takes my fortune cookie away from me, and then when she's done she sighs a deep sigh and says, "Well, you certainly stuffed yourself." On Wednesdays I always eat a big lunch in town, so I won't be hungry. I always have the calf's liver and bacon or something like that, to fill me up.

1. The husband eats a big lunch on Wednesdays because ______________________

2. At dinner each Wednesday the wife shows that she is ______________________

Coming to Terms

motivation a goal that prompts a character to behave in a certain way; a reason for a character's behavior

Warm-up Answers
1. his wife will eat most of his dinner **2.** greedy and thoughtless (or some other appropriate description)

Items 7–8 refer to the following passage.

What games did Cal and his two sons, Conrad and Jordan, play?

Howard rubs his palms together briskly. "Let's get this show on the road, folks!"

They exchange glances, he [Cal] and Conrad; then they look away. Cal is reminded of the game they used to play: Grandfather Trivia. "What does he say after a horseshoe ringer?" "That's one for the good guys!" "What time does he get up in the morning?" "At the crack o'dawn!" "When will he eat liver?" "When hell freezes over!" Jordan had invented it, with his eye for detail, his unmerciful memory. And another game. Nicknames. He had nicknames for everyone; new ones each week. His grandfather, the Kid, his grandmother, the Girl Friend. "Here comes the Kid in the Mercedes, he's got the Girl Friend with him!"

7. How would Conrad and Jordan probably have described their grandfather?
   (1) athletic
   (2) lazy
   (3) inventive
   (4) merciless
   (5) predictable

8. Which of the following words best describes Jordan?
   (1) brisk
   (2) timid
   (3) inventive
   (4) kind
   (5) depressing

Directions: Choose the one best answer to each question. Answers are on page 134.

Items 9–11 refer to the following passage.

How does Ariadne feel about the narrator?

A window slammed open, and the face of Ariadne appeared above me. Her dark hair tumbled about her ears.

"Go away!" she shrieked. "Will you go away!"

"Ariadne," I said loudly. "I have come as I promised. I have spoken to your father. I wish to call on you. . . . Stop this nonsense and let me in."

She pushed farther out the window and showed me her teeth.

"Be careful, beloved," I said. "You might fall."

She drew her head in quickly, and I turned then to the assembled crowd.

"A misunderstanding," I said. "Please move on." Suddenly old Mr. Langos shrieked. A moment later something broke on the sidewalk a foot from where I stood. A vase or a plate. I looked up, and Ariadne was preparing to hurl what appeared to be a water pitcher.

9. What would the narrator of the story like to do?

(1) break in through Ariadne's window
(2) meet Ariadne's father
(3) call on Ariadne to court her
(4) escape from the crowd in the street
(5) argue with Ariadne

10. Which of the following sentences best states the main idea of the passage?

(1) Ariadne is pleased to have an admirer but too shy to visit with him.
(2) A young man has come to call on Ariadne; the neighbors disapprove.
(3) Ariadne is dreadfully clumsy.
(4) Ariadne's father wants her to marry.
(5) An admirer has come to call on Ariadne; she tries to drive him off.

11. Which word best describes the narrator?

(1) persistent (2) rude (3) confused
(4) weak-willed (5) uninterested

Finding the Main Idea You have practiced locating the main idea in a nonfiction passage. However, finding the main idea of a fiction passage may be more difficult. Often the main idea is an impression or feeling, not a clear statement or message. What do you think is the main idea of the passage below?

■ Paul knew nearly nothing of his father until he found the box of photographs on the back stairs. From then on he looked at them all day and every evening, and when his mother Ethel talked to Edith Gainesworth on the telephone. He had looked amazed at his father in his different ages and stations of life, first as a boy his age, then as a young man, and finally before his death in his army uniform.

What parts of the passage suggest that the photographs were important to Paul? The main idea is that Paul spent all his time learning about his father from the photographs. But the paragraph never actually states that. You have to infer it.

Warm-up

What is the main idea in the passage below? Read the entire passage before you decide. Then write your answer in a complete sentence.

■ Everyone who knew Horace Denby thought that he was an honest, decent, respectable citizen. In business he gave a square deal, and he was always good for a donation to the Boy Scouts.

He was a bachelor, somewhere in his early fifties. Except for his hay fever which got bad during July, he looked the picture of health. He was pink-faced, a little plump, with a little bounce to his walk, and a warm glow to his eyes. He was a locksmith and prosperous enough to employ two assistants. A decent, respectable citizen—but not entirely honest.

____

____

____

Sample Warm-up Answer
Horace Denby appeared to be a model citizen, but he was actually not quite what he appeared to be.

Vocabulary Review Just as clothing and hairstyles change from time to time, so does language. Some words that were common fifty or one hundred years ago have gone out of fashion and are seldom used today. For example, *spectacles* have become *glasses* and *wireless* has become *radio.* Other words are still used but have changed in meaning.

☑ A Test-Taking Tip

On the GED Test, you can expect to find a few passages that were written over a hundred years ago. These passages may contain unfamiliar words that people no longer use or that have developed new meanings. Since you may not use a dictionary during the test, you will have to figure out the meanings of unfamiliar words from context clues and word-part clues. Review the material on pages 75, 87, and 88.

Warm-up

In the passages below, notice words that are unfamiliar or that have unexpected meanings.

■ "There's the village," said the driver, pointing to a cluster of roofs some distance to the left; but if you want to get to the house, you'll find it shorter to get over this stile, and so by the footpath over the fields. There it is, where the lady is walking."

"And the lady, I fancy, is Miss Stoner," observed Holmes, shading his eyes. "Yes, I think we had better do as you suggest."

We got off, paid our fare, and the trap rattled back on its way to Leatherhead.

"I thought it as well," said Holmes, as we climbed the stile, "that this fellow should think we had come here as architects, or on some definite business. It may stop his gossip . . ."

Using context clues, word-structure clues, or a combination of the two, write a brief definition of each of these words as it is used in the story.

1. stile ____________________

2. fancy ____________________

3. observed ____________________

4. trap ____________________

Warm-up Answers
1. a way of getting up and over something (A stile is a set of stairs used to get over a fence.) **2.** imagine; guess; think that **3.** commented **4.** small carriage

Items 12–13 refer to the following passage.

How did the youth react when he heard the sounds of battle?

The trees began softly to sing a hymn of twilight. The sun sank until slanted bronze rays struck the forest. There was a lull in the noises of insects as if they had bowed their beaks and were making a devotional pause. There was silence save for the chanted chorus of the trees.

Then, upon this stillness, there suddenly broke a tremendous clangor of sounds. A crimson roar came from the distance.

The youth stopped. He was transfixed by this terrific medley of all noises. It was as if worlds were being rended. There was the ripping sound of musketry and the breaking crash of artillery.

His mind flew in all directions. He conceived the two armies to be at each other panther fashion. He listened for a time. Then he began to run in the direction of the battle. He saw that it was an ironical thing for him to be running thus toward that which he had been at such pains to avoid. But he said, in substance, to himself that if the earth and the moon were about to clash, many persons would doubtless plan to get upon the roofs to witness the collision.

12. What did the sudden noise of battle make the youth do?
    (1) rip apart his gun
    (2) fly in all directions
    (3) sing a hymn
    (4) stop and stand still
    (5) flinch in pain

13. Why was it ironic that the youth ran toward the battle?
    (1) He wanted to see the battle from a roof.
    (2) He had tried hard to escape the fighting.
    (3) The earth and the moon were about to collide.
    (4) He was in considerable pain.
    (5) He could not concentrate on where he was going.

Directions: Choose the one best answer to each question. Answers start on page 134.

Item 14 refers to the following passage.

How is the boy feeling?

He turned slowly to go upstairs. His heart was not like a basketball but like a fast, jazz drum, beating faster and faster as he climbed the stairs. His feet dragged as though he waded through knee-deep water and he held on to the banisters. The house looked odd, crazy.

14. How does the author help you understand the character's feelings?

(1) by placing him in an "odd" house
(2) by sending the character upstairs
(3) by comparing his heart to a drum
(4) by having him wade through water
(5) by likening his heart to a basketball

Item 15 refers to the following passage.

How does the old priest feel about his work?

In the middle of the night the ring of the doorbell roused him from restless sleep. His housekeeper, old Mrs. Calchas, answered. Word was carried by a son or a daughter or a friend that an old man or an old woman was dying and the priest was needed for the last communion. He dressed wearily and took his bag and his book, a conductor on the train of death who no longer esteemed himself a puncher of tickets.

He spent much time pondering what might have gone wrong. He thought it must be that he had been a priest too long. Words of solace and consolation spoken too often became tea bags returned to the pot too many times. Yet he still believed that love, all forms of love, represented the only real union with other human beings.

15. Why are the priest's words of sympathy compared to tea bags?

(1) Tea and sympathy represented love.
(2) The words and tea bags had lost their strength.
(3) He drank tea as he thought.
(4) He brought tea bags to parishioners.
(5) Words and tea were his only real ties to others.

Figurative Language Which sentence below better describes how swiftly the tap dancer's feet moved?

- The dancer's feet tapped rapidly.
  The dancer's feet sounded like busy typewriters.

Wouldn't you agree that the second sentence gives a better idea of how the dancer's feet moved? It creates a word picture; it allows you to imagine the dancer's feet by comparing their sound to that of typewriters.

Authors sometimes use **figurative language,** such as the comparison above, to help you understand a character's feelings, picture objects, or imagine actions in a story.

There are several types of figurative language. Sometimes comparisons include a signal word such as *like* or *as.* Look at this example:

- That small boy flew past me on his skateboard like a rocket.

Other comparisons don't use any signal word such as *like* or *as.*

- That small boy rocketed past me on his skateboard.

✓ A Test-Taking Tip

When you take the GED Test of Interpreting Literature and the Arts, you will not need to identify different types of figurative language. However, you will have to recognize when an author is using figurative language, what that figurative language means, and what effect it has on the selection you are reading.

Coming to Terms

figurative language comparisons that expand words beyond their ordinary meanings

Warm-up

Underline the word that helps you picture how full of energy Ms. Peters is.

- The new employee, Ms. Peters, has turned out to be a dynamo.

Warm-up Answer
dynamo

Applying Ideas You had some practice applying information to new situations when you studied nonfiction. You can apply ideas from fiction too. For instance, you know that information about a character's background, personality, or motivation is sometimes implied in a passage. You can infer that information and use it to predict how that person would probably react under changed circumstances. For example, do you remember the legend of Robin Hood, who stole money from the rich to give to the poor? If Robin Hood were alive today, how might he react to a rich landlord charging poor tenants outrageously high rent?

☑ A Test-Taking Tip

When you are asked on the GED Test to decide how a fictional character would think and feel in a new situation, you may find it helpful to put yourself in the place of that character. Keep in mind what the character's attitudes and background are. Imagine how you would react if you were that person.

Warm-up

Below is a brief retelling of a well-known fable. As you read the fable, try to imagine how the country mouse felt and why he wanted to return home. Then answer the question that follows.

■ A poor country mouse, who had to work hard just to find food for his meager meals, went to visit his wealthy cousin who lived in a very fine house in a large city. The tasty goodies in the city mouse's pantry made the country mouse very envious—that is, until a fierce cat appeared, forcing the mice to run for their lives.

"You can keep your fancy living," said the country mouse. "I'm going home, where I can live a peaceful, if humble, life."

With which of the following sayings would the country mouse most likely agree? Put a check next to your answer.

1. ___ The early bird gets the worm.

2. ___ Better late than never.

3. _✓_ Better safe than sorry.

Warm-up Answer
3.

<u>Items 16–17</u> refer to the following passage.

How does each character feel about labor unions?

The girl came close to him and stopped just opposite his chair.

"Bigger, do you belong to a union?" she asked.

"Now Mary!" said Mr. Dalton, frowning.

"Well, Father, he should," the girl said, turning to him, then back to Bigger. "Do you?"

"Mary. . . ." said Mr. Dalton.

"I'm just asking him a question, Father!"

Bigger hesitated. He hated the girl then. Why did she have to do this when he was trying to get a job?

"No'm," he mumbled, his head down and his eyes glowering.

"And why not?" the girl asked.

Bigger heard Mr. Dalton mumble something. He wished Mr. Dalton would speak and end this thing. He looked up and saw Mr. Dalton staring at the girl. She's making me lose my job! he thought. . . .

"We can settle about the union later, Mary," said Mr. Dalton.

"But you wouldn't mind belonging to a union, would you?" the girl asked.

"I don't know, mam," Bigger said.

"Now, Mary you can see that the boy is new," said Mr. Dalton. "Leave him alone."

The girl turned and poked out a red tongue at him.

"All right, Mr. Capitalist!" She turned again to Bigger. "Isn't he a capitalist, Bigger?"

16. What would Mary probably do if she were a worker?

    (1) join a labor union
    (2) aid the owners of big corporations
    (3) improve the relationship between her employer and other employees
    (4) discourage others from joining unions
    (5) talk respectfully to her employer

17. What would Mr. Dalton probably do if Mary were rude in front of the family cook?

    (1) shout at her angrily
    (2) send her to her room
    (3) discuss the matter with her later
    (4) chuckle at her bad manners
    (5) say nothing

Directions: Choose the one best answer to each question. Answers are on page 135.

Items 18–19 refer to the following passage.

What do the people described below enjoy?

For all such people the country became the last refuge. They bought little farms in Connecticut or Vermont, and renovated the fine old houses with just a shade too much of whimsey or of restrained good taste. Their quaintness was a little too quaint, their simplicity a little too subtle, and on the old farms that they bought no utilitarian seeds were sown and no grain grew. They went in for flowers, and in time they learned to talk very knowingly about the rarer varieties. They loved the simple life, of course. They loved the good feel of "the earth." They were just a shade too conscious of "the earth," and George had heard them say, the women as well as the men, how much they loved to work in it.

18. How does the narrator feel toward the people he describes?

    (1) pitying
    (2) indifferent
    (3) loving
    (4) disgusted
    (5) critical

19. Which of the following descriptions best suits the people that the passage is about?

    (1) phony
    (2) old-fashioned
    (3) hard working
    (4) quaint
    (5) knowing

Tone The attitude an author or narrator takes toward the subject he or she is writing about is called the tone of the passage. As you read the passage below, decide what attitude you think the author shows toward the stray dog.

■ She didn't belong to anybody; she didn't even have a name. Nobody knew where she was spending the long, chilly winters or what she ate. She couldn't get close to the warm cottages for fear of angry watchdogs. Kids would chase her off the streets with stones or sticks, and adults would frighten her with shrill whistles. After darting from side to side, bumping against fences or people's legs, she'd manage to tear away and take cover in a large orchard, in a hideout she knew.

Does the author feel sympathy for the dog? Details such as long, chilly winters, angry watchdogs, and unkind children and adults give this impression. Nobody even cares enough about the dog to give her a name. The author has chosen these details in order to help you feel sympathy for the dog. Another author could have made the same dog appear unattractive by changing a few words or key details.

Warm-up

Read the passage below. Determine the author's feelings toward the war that is mentioned.

■ In the fall the war was always there, but we did not go to it anymore. It was cold in the fall in Milan and the dark came very early. Then the electric lights came on, and it was pleasant along the streets looking in the windows.

1. Does the speaker seem concerned about the war?

____

2. What does the speaker do on pleasant evenings in Milan?

____

3. Circle the word that best describes the speaker's attitude toward the war.

concerned   enthusiastic   uninterested

Warm-up Answers
1. no **2.** look in the windows along the streets
3. uninterested

Mood How would you describe the feeling you get as you read the following passage?

■ Did a twig snap? Dixon looked back and thought he saw a dark shape melt into the underbrush. Instantly he froze, staring back through the green-boled trees. There was a complete and expectant silence.

Does the passage seem mysterious and suspenseful? Does it make you wonder what will happen next? The details in the passage help to create an atmosphere of suspense.

The **mood** of a piece of writing is the feeling, or atmosphere, that the author creates through the careful choice of details and words. The sights, sounds, and scents that the author chooses to mention can create a mood of mystery, merriment, chaos, or peace.

Warm-up

Read the passage below and answer the question that follows.

■ It was late in the afternoon, and the light was waning. There was a difference in the look of the tree shadows out in the yard. Somewhere in the distance, cows were lowing and a little bell was tinkling; now and then a farm wagon tilted by, and the dust flew; some blue-shirted laborers with shovels over their shoulders plodded past; little swarms of flies were dancing up and down before the people's faces in the soft air.

Use words from the list below to complete the following sentence.

chaotic	frightening	tense	peaceful	calm
comic	mysterious	lonely	tranquil	sad

Three words that describe the mood of the passage are __Peackul__, __Clam__, and __tranquil__.

☑ A Test-Taking Tip

On the GED Test you may need to infer the mood of a passage. Simply think about what feeling you get as you read the passage.

Coming to Terms

mood the feeling or atmosphere an author creates through the choice of details and words

Warm-up Answers
peaceful, calm, tranquil

Items 20–21 refer to the following passage.

Why did the narrator park near the exit?

It's ten o'clock, closing time, when I push my loaded shopping cart out of the supermarket. The parking lot is almost deserted. There is only one delivery truck by the side of the building and a few cars near the exit, mine one of them. Not a person is in sight.

I start thinking, *How stupid to have parked so far away. The lot wasn't full when I drove in. Just habit, I guess. I've parked near the exit ever since the car was rammed that day. It seemed safer. It never seemed far, either. Now it looks a mile away. I'd better get a move on.*

The moon hangs low in the sky, with dark clouds blowing over it.

This is an eerie place at night, I think, as I push the cart hurriedly past the truck.

20. What is the mood of the passage?
    (1) cheerful (2) sad (3) tense
    (4) angry (5) tranquil

    (1) (2) (●3) (4) (5)

21. Which details help create the mood?
    (1) The shopping cart is loaded.
    (2) A delivery truck is parked by the building.
    (3) There are a few cars near the exit.
    (4) The car had been rammed once.
    (5) Dark clouds are blowing over the moon.

Item 22 refers to the following passage.

Where does McDunn work?

Out there in the cold water, far from land, we waited every night for the coming of the fog, and it came, and we oiled the brass machinery and lit the fog light up in the stone tower. Feeling like two birds in the gray sky, McDunn and I sent the light touching out, red, then white, then red again, to eye the lonely ships. And if they did not see our light, then there was always our Voice, the great deep cry of our Fog Horn shuddering through the rags of mist to startle the gulls away like decks of scattered cards and make the waves turn high and foam.

22. What is the mood of the passage?
    (1) joyful (2) pleasant (3) solemn
    (4) horrifying (5) chaotic

    (1) (2) (●3) (4) (5)

Directions: Choose the one best answer to each question. Answers are on page 135.

Items 23–24 refer to the following passage.

How did the narrator feel about Bashele and Shosha?

Yppe and Teibele were too young for me, but Shosha was just right. Neither of us went down to play in the courtyard, which was controlled by rough boys with sticks. They bullied any child younger or weaker than they. Their talk was mean. They singled me out in particular because I was the rabbi's son and wore a long gaberdine and velvet cap. They taunted me with names like "Fancypants," "Little Rabbi," "Mollycoddle." If they heard me speak to Shosha, they jeered and called me "Sissy." I was teased for having red hair, blue eyes, and unusually white skin. Sometimes they flung a rock at me, a chip of wood, or a blob of mud. Sometimes they tripped me so I fell into the gutter. Or they might sic the house watchman's dog on me because they knew I was afraid of it.

But inside Bashele's I received neither teasing nor roughness. The moment I arrived Bashele offered me a plate of groats, a glass of borscht, a cookie. Shosha took down her toy box with her dolls, doll-sized dishes and cooking things, her collection of human and animal figurines, shiny buttons, gaudy ribbons. We played jacks, knucklebones, hide-and-seek, husband and wife. . . . Once I played the role of a blind man and Shosha let me touch her forehead, cheeks, mouth. She kissed the palm of my hand and said, "Don't tell Mama."

23. The author tells the story from the point of view of a
    (1) scared young boy
    (2) man reminiscing about his childhood
    (3) kind mother and daughter
    (4) ridiculed blind man
    (5) reporter describing persecution

24. The narrator enjoyed playing with Shosha because Shosha
    (1) played rough games
    (2) prepared meals for them
    (3) was giving and loving
    (4) protected children from the bullies
    (5) could keep a secret

Point of View In some stories the authors write as if one of the characters was telling the story. That character narrates the events from his or her own point of view. As the narrator describes the events and the other characters, you can find out about his or her opinions and emotions.

Sometimes the author chooses to tell a story from the point of view of an outsider—someone who observes the action but is not part of it. This technique gives a general overview of the action and all the characters because the story is not limited to one person's point of view.

The following passage from the story "You" by Joyce Carol Oates has still another point of view. Do you think this point of view could help you thoroughly understand the main character in this story?

■ You are reading a river of words. People watch you, amazed by you. Your energy, your bouncy face, your tireless voice. You will be recorded on tape for a television show you won't even bother to watch.

Warm-up

Read the following paragraph. Imagine how the action would look from Sue's point of view.

■ As Bob searched the underbrush for small sticks to burn, *he* glanced back to watch Sue tending the campfire. A furtive movement in the woods behind her caught *his* eye. Instantly, *he* realized that someone had been watching *them.*

Now pretend you are Sue and rewrite the story.

____

____

____

____

____

____

Sample Warm-up Answer

While Bob searched the underbrush for small sticks to burn, I tended the campfire. I looked up to see Bob watching me. Suddenly, Bob seemed to glance at something in the woods behind me. I turned to find out what he had seen.

Popular and Classical Drama

Reading a Drama When you read a play, you have to visualize the characters, the costumes, and the scenery. You can do this by carefully reading dialogue and stage directions.

The speeches of the characters are written in dramatic **dialogue.** Quotation marks are not used. Instead, the name of the character is listed first, then the words being spoken.

HENRY. Nathan! Nate! Martha, have you seen that boy? I told him ten times to lock the pasture gate. And look at it now—swinging wide open.

MARTHA. Don't be hard on him, Henry. The boy's still trying to get over losing that old dog of his.

Sometimes the dialogue is interrupted by **stage directions,** or suggestions that help actors speak their lines or act out their parts. Stage directions are easy to find, because they usually are placed in parentheses like this:

HENRY. *(teeth clenched, shaking his fist at Martha)* You spoiled that boy, Martha!

(They look warily at each other, both afraid to speak the next word.)

Warm-up

Read the next few lines from the play about Henry and Martha.

Henry again shakes his fist angrily at Martha.

MARTHA: *(sweetly)* Henry, Henry. Have patience. Nate is just a boy.

1. Based on the stage directions, how does Henry feel toward Martha? ______________________

____

2. How does Martha feel toward Nate?

____

Coming to Terms

dialogue conversations in a play

stage direction a suggestion for an actor as he or she acts out the part

Sample Warm-up Answers

1. Henry is angry at Martha. **2.** Martha is sympathetic toward Nate.

Item 1 refers to the following passage.

Why does Laura stop going to her business classes?

AMANDA. Laura, where have you been going when you've gone out pretending that you were going to business college?

LAURA. I've just been going out walking.

AMANDA. That's not true.

LAURA. It is. I just went walking.

AMANDA. Walking? Walking? In winter? Deliberately courting pneumonia in that light coat? Where did you walk to, Laura?

LAURA. All sorts of places—mostly in the park.

AMANDA. Even after you'd started catching that cold?

LAURA. It was the lesser of two evils, Mother. [*Screen image:* Winter scene in a park.] I couldn't go back there. I—threw up—on the floor!

AMANDA. From half past seven till after five every day you mean to tell me you walked around in the park, because you wanted to make me think that you were still going to Rubicam's Business College?

LAURA. It wasn't as bad as it sounds. I went inside places to get warmed up.

AMANDA. Inside where?

LAURA. I went in the art museum and the bird houses at the Zoo. I visited the penguins every day! Sometimes I did without lunch and went to the movies. Lately I've been spending most of my afternoons in the Jewel Box, that big glass house where they raise the tropical flowers.

AMANDA. You did all this to deceive me, just for deception? *Laura looks down.* Why?

LAURA. Mother, when you're disappointed, you get that awful suffering look on your face, like the picture of Jesus' mother in the museum!

1. Laura had kept quiet about dropping out of business school because she

   (1) hopes to return to classes soon
   (2) is afraid her mother will be angry
   (3) doesn't want to disappoint Amanda
   (4) can't decide on a career
   (5) wants to keep her visits to the zoo a secret

Directions: Choose the one best answer to each question. Answers are on page 135.

Items 2–3 refer to the following passage.

Where is Hodel planning to go?

[*The exterior of the railroad station. Morning.* HODEL *enters and walks over to a bench.* TEVYE *follows, carrying her suitcase.*]

HODEL. You don't have to wait for the train, Papa. You'll be late for your customers.

TEVYE. Just a few more minutes. Is he in bad trouble, that hero of yours? *(She nods.)* Arrested? *(She nods.)* And convicted?

HODEL. Yes, but he did nothing wrong. He cares nothing for himself. Everything he does is for humanity.

TEVYE. But if he did nothing wrong, he wouldn't be in trouble.

HODEL. Papa, how can you say that, a learned man like you? What wrongs did Joseph do, and Abraham, and Moses? And they had troubles.

TEVYE. But why don't you tell me where he is now, this Joseph of yours?

HODEL. It is far, Papa, terribly far. He is in a settlement in Siberia.

TEVYE. Siberia! And he asks you to leave your father and mother and join him in that frozen wasteland, and marry him there?

HODEL. No, Papa, he did not ask me to go. I want to go. I don't want him to be alone. I want to help him in his work. It is the greatest work a man can do.

2. What are Hodel and her father talking about?

   (1) why Joseph and Moses were in trouble
   (2) where Siberia is located
   (3) why Hodel is traveling to Siberia
   (4) why Tevye need not wait for the train
   (5) how Tevye feels about Hodel's marriage

   (1) (2) (3) (4) (5)

3. What happened to Hodel's fiancé?

   (1) Bad companions led him astray.
   (2) He was elected leader.
   (3) His father and mother left him.
   (4) He was arrested and sent to Siberia.
   (5) He ran away to Siberia to be alone.

   (1) (2) (3) (4) (5)

Identifying the Topic Imagine that you have arrived late at a party. People are talking and laughing and obviously having great fun. You quickly move to a group of your friends, but before saying anything, you pause to find out what they're discussing. You catch the following phrases:

. . . "in perfect condition" . . . "price is a little high" . . . "all new tires and battery" . . . "gets thirty miles per gallon around town" . . . "driven only twenty thousand miles" . . . "four-door sedan" . . .

What are your friends talking about? You would probably conclude that they are discussing a used car.

In a similar way, you can find out the topic of a dramatic passage. As you read what a character says, note key words and phrases. Then pay close attention as other characters respond to the first speaker. Each part of the conversation gives a little more information. Combine the ideas from each speaker to determine the topic.

Warm-up

Read the dialogue to discover what the characters are discussing.

MARTY. . . . *(Offstage)* This is the stairway. You know, I used to slide down this banister. Very good for that.

JILL. *(Offstage)* Is that stained glass?

MARTY. *(Offstage)* Oh . . . Yeah. We're very religious—That's the den down there. And—this is the dining room.

JILL. *(Offstage)* Oooooh. Look at that chandelier.

What is Marty probably describing, and why do you think he is doing so? ______________________

____

Sample Warm-up Answer

Marty probably is describing his house because Jill has not seen it before.

Plot Every play tells a story. It may be an action-packed story, full of chills and excitement, or just a quiet, tense story of people discovering why they love or hate or mistrust each other. The plot of a drama is the story it tells.

Because each drama passage on the GED Test is just part of a play, it cannot include *all* the events of the plot. But each passage *is* complete in itself. You are not expected to have prior knowledge of the play; the excerpt is all you need to answer any test question.

☑ A Test-Taking Tip

As you read drama passages, watch for phrases that signal the passage of time. They will help you sort out the events in passages and remember the order in which they happened.

Warm-up

After reading the following dialogue, answer the questions below.

ARMSTRONG. Mrs. Reston, would you please tell the Court what happened to your daughter on the night the *William Brown* was struck by the iceberg . . .

MRS. RESTON. Well, she was left behind on the sinking ship . . .

ARMSTRONG. What did you do when you discovered this?

MRS. RESTON. Well, I was like out of my mind . . . I cried out for help. . . . And, praise God, one of the seamen, he climbed back on to the ship just as she was keeling over and rescued my daughter. Oh, I'll never forget it. That seaman didn't even know me, yet he risked his life.

1. What happened to the *William Brown?*

____

2. How was Mrs. Reston's daughter saved?

____

Need a Hint for Number 4?
Remember that stage directions can fill you in on information.

Sample Warm-up Answers
1. The ship struck an iceberg. **2.** A sailor climbed back on the ship as it was about to sink and rescued the girl.

Item 4 is based on the following passage.

Does Raquel decide to help the revolutionary army?

RAQUEL. And you believe in the Revolutionary cause?

CLETO. Yes, señora. I am a poor peasant, that's true. But still I have a right to live like a man, with my own ground, and my own family, and my own future. *(He stops speaking abruptly.)* . . . I must go and find my captain. *(He goes out.)*

RAQUEL. *(rests her face against her hand).* He's so young. But Tomás was no older. . . . *(She straightens abruptly, takes the bottle of poison from the desk drawer and stares at it. Then she crosses to the decanter and laces the wine with the poison. She hurries back to the desk and is busy writing when Andrés and Cleto return.*

ANDRÉS. You'll have to hurry that letter. The district is clear now.

RAQUEL. I'll be through in just a moment. You might as well finish the wine while you're waiting.

ANDRÉS. Thank you. A most excellent idea. *(He pours himself a glass of wine. As he lifts it to his lips she speaks.)*

RAQUEL. Why don't you give some to—Cleto?

ANDRÉS. This is too fine a wine to waste on that boy.

RAQUEL. He'll probably never have another chance to taste such wine.

ANDRÉS. Very well. Pour yourself a glass, Cleto.

CLETO. Thank you. *(He pours it.)* Your health, my captain.

4. Raquel has devised a plan to

(1) commit suicide by drinking poison
(2) knock her enemies out for the night
(3) poison the revolutionary soldiers
(4) hide the revolutionary soldiers
(5) join the revolutionary army

Directions: Choose the one best answer to each question. Answers are on page 135.

Item 5 refers to the following passage.

Who is George Spencer?

SPENCER. *(into mike)* This is Flight 714, Maple Leaf Air Charter, in distress. Come in anyone. Over.

VOICE ON RADIO. *(immediately, crisply)* This is Calgary, 714. Go ahead!

VOICE ON RADIO. (VANCOUVER OPERATOR) Vancouver here, 714. All other aircraft stay off the air. Over.

SPENCER. Thank you, Calgary and Vancouver. This message is for Vancouver. This aircraft is in distress. Both pilots and some passengers . . . *(To stewardess)* How many passengers?

STEWARDESS. It was seven a few minutes ago. It may be more now.

SPENCER. Correction. At least seven passengers are suffering from food poisoning. Both pilots are unconscious and in serious condition. We have a doctor on board who says that neither pilot can be revived. Did you get that, Vancouver? *(Pause)* Now we come to the interesting bit. My name is Spencer, George Spencer. I am a passenger on this airplane. Correction: I *was* a passenger. I have about a thousand hours' total flying time, but all of it was on single-engine fighters. And also I haven't flown an airplane for ten years.

5. Where does the action in this passage take place?

(1) at a Vancouver control tower
(2) by a Calgary airport
(3) in a plane over Canada
(4) aboard a single-engine fighter
(5) in the emergency room of a hospital

Setting The time and place of the action in a drama is the setting. The setting gives background information to help you understand events and why the characters react to the events as they do. In some cases, the setting may influence the events.

During a play, the setting may change. For example, if the action takes place at different times of day, stage directions alert you to a change, like this:

■ (Evening of the same day. Clouds fill the sky.)

Stage directions also will tell you if the action of the play changes from one place to another.

Warm-up

Read the following stage directions from a TV drama to discover the time and place of the action. Because it was written for TV, the stage directions include instructions for the camera person, such as "fade in."

FADE IN: A wooden sign swaying ever so little in a May morning breeze. . . . The sign is old and battered, and the words "Emperor Press" are barely discernible.

The camera moves slowly down across a store window so dirty you can hardly see through it. Again dimly visible, "Emperor Press." The window display is a number of samples of the printer's work—all printed at least ten years ago, the edges curling up, and covered with dust.

NARRATOR. *In* 1939 *when I was seventeen years old, I went to work in a print shop on West Twenty-sixth Street in New York . . .*

From the directions and the dialogue, what can you tell about the setting of the play? What about the time? What can you infer about the print shop? Tell as much about the setting as you can, using your reading and inference skills. Answer on your own paper.

Sample Warm-up Answers

The time is a morning in May.

The place is a print shop on West Twenty-sixth Street in New York. The sign on the print shop is old and battered, and the samples of printing are all old. Apparently it is long after 1939, and the print shop is falling into neglect since the narrator first worked there.

Getting to Know the Characters A very important part of any play is the characters. Without characters, in fact, there would be no play. You can follow the events that unfold in a drama through the characters' speeches. You also can find out how the characters feel about one another and about themselves from their conversations. By reading what the characters say and do, you will learn what they are really like. Be especially alert to what characters say about themselves and what they observe about other characters.

Warm-up

Read the brief passage below and then answer the questions that follow. Be sure to use complete sentences.

FATHER. See here! I told you when you married my daughter that you weren't to bother us. For any reason! Ever!

JAY. You've got to listen. It's about Tina. I'm calling from City Hospital. Tina is here. She's going to have a brain operation. It will cost a lot of money. Mr. Whitney? Answer me, please! Tina needs you. Look, I know how you feel about me. Just come and help her and I'll get out of her life. *(Jay hears a click, followed by silence.)* Mr. Whitney? Mr. Whitney?

1. Based on information in the passage, how does the father-in-law feel about Jay?

____

____

2. How would you describe Mr. Whitney?

____

____

Sample Warm-up Answers

1. Mr. Whitney dislikes Jay. **2.** Mr. Whitney seems stubborn and cold.

<u>Items 6–7</u> refer to the following passage from a movie script.

What sort of people are Art and Gil?

TETLEY. We'll stop here, gentlemen, and breathe our horses.

Close shot—Tetley.

TETLEY. Winder, take one man with you and go up to the top of the ridge and see what you can see.

Small Clearing near Top of Pass—Wide Angle. The men are but faintly seen as they come out of the pass and pull up and climb down. Close shot—Art—as he gets off his horse and stands swinging his arms against his chest. Other men about him are doing likewise. Gil rides up, dismounts, and pulls out a bottle.

GIL. Doing this in the middle of the night is crazy.

ART. I thought you liked excitement.

GIL. I got nothin' particular against hangin' a murderin' rustler. It's just that I don't like it in the dark. *(After taking a pull at the bottle.)* There's always some fool to lose his head and start hangin' everybody in sight.

6. What do the characters intend to do?

(1) steal cattle
(2) take a horseback ride
(3) hang a rustler
(4) hang everyone they meet
(5) join a group of rustlers

7. Why does Gil feel it is foolish to carry out their plans at night?

(1) He doesn't like excitement.
(2) The sheriff will be looking for them.
(3) His horse may run off.
(4) Someone may hang innocent victims.
(5) They need daylight to see what they are doing.

Directions: Choose the one best answer to each question. Answers are on page 135.

Items 8–9 refer to the following passage.

Why are Oscar's friends at his apartment?

ROY. *(opens the betting):* You still didn't fix the refrigerator? It's been two weeks now. No wonder it stinks in here.

OSCAR. *(picks up his cards):* Temper, temper. If I wanted nagging I'd go back with my wife. *(Throws them down.)* I'm out. Who wants food?

MURRAY. What have you got?

OSCAR. *(looks under the bread):* I got brown sandwiches and green sandwiches. Well, what do you say?

MURRAY. What's the green?

OSCAR. It's either very new cheese or very old meat.

MURRAY. I'll take the brown.

(OSCAR *gives* MURRAY *a sandwich.*)

ROY. (*glares at* MURRAY): Are you crazy? You're not going to eat that, are you?

MURRAY. I'm hungry.

ROY. His refrigerator's been broken for two weeks. I saw milk standing in there that wasn't even in the bottle.

OSCAR. (*to* ROY): What are you, some kind of a health nut? Eat, Murray, eat!

8. Which of the following phrases best describes Oscar?

(1) a health nut
(2) a witty slob
(3) a good host
(4) a gourmet cook
(5) a card shark

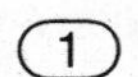

9. How might Roy describe Murray?

(1) foolish
(2) cautious
(3) sickly
(4) vicious
(5) intellectual

Inferences About Characters When you watch a play or movie, you learn a great deal from the actors' voices, gestures, and expressions. The acting helps you understand how the characters feel, what they do, and why they behave that way. But when reading a play, or a passage from one, you have to gather this type of information from the dialogue and stage directions.

Stage directions suggest motions, expressions, and gestures that help actors interpret characters for the audience. When you read rather than watch a play, stage directions help you interpret the characters for yourself. Notice the stage directions in the passage below.

HESTER. You hate this house. I know that.

RUTH. No. *(Facing* HESTER *firmly.)* But I think Bruce ought to sell.

The stage directions in Ruth's lines indicate that she is speaking firmly and quietly. In complete control of her own emotions, Ruth refuses to be intimidated by Hester.

From just a few lines, you learn a great deal about the two characters. You can tell that Ruth wants her husband to sell the house.

Warm-up

As you read the dialogue below, decide what type of person Epifania is.

EPIFANIA. My father was the greatest man in the world. And he died a pauper. I shall never forgive the world for that.

SAGAMORE. A pauper! You amaze me. It was reported that he left you, his only child, thirty millions.

EPIFANIA. Well, what was thirty millions to him? He lost a hundred and fifty millions. He had promised to leave me two hundred millions. I was left with a beggarly thirty. It broke his heart.

Describe Epifania in a sentence using two of the words below.

sweet timid spoiled kindly rich humble

____

____

____

____

Sample Warm-up Answers
Epifania is a **spoiled, rich** girl.

Applying Ideas Some questions on the GED Test will ask you how a character from a drama might react if he or she were placed in a different situation.

Read the following conversations. Try to understand what Mr. Kelly's attitudes are.

MR. KELLY. *(examining a small picture on the wall)* Dreadful! Absolutely shocking!
MRS. KELLY. What are you talking about?
MR. KELLY. This painting—displayed right here in a public room. It shows a *(coughing in embarrassment)* naked person.
MRS. KELLY. But it's not meant to be shocking.
MR. KELLY. *(glaring)* That's no excuse.

Do you have a clear idea of how Mr. Kelly feels about the painting? Suppose he were invited to see an R-rated movie, one that had some strong language and some nude scenes. Would he go to the movie or avoid it? If you apply your knowledge of his attitudes toward a nude figure in a painting, you will agree that he would most likely *not* want to see the movie.

Warm-up

Read the following passage and then answer the question below.

(*The mother darts a quick, sharp look at the girl—then looks back to her hands, which are beginning to twist nervously.*)
MOTHER. You don't think my sister Catherine should live in her daughter-in-law's house?
GIRL. Well, I don't know the people, of course, but, as a rule, I don't think a mother-in-law should live with a young couple.
MOTHER. Where do you think a mother-in-law should go?
GIRL. I don't think a mother should depend so much upon her children for her rewards in life.

Which of the following statements would the girl most likely agree with? Explain your choice.

a. Mother knows best.
b. You are your own best friend.

____

____

____

Sample Warm-up Answer
Most likely, the girl would agree with the second statement because she feels that mothers should depend on themselves, not their children, for their rewards in life.

Items 10–11 refer to the following passage.

Are Hedda and Aunt Rina close?

HEDDA. *(handing [a letter] to him).* It came early this morning.
TESMAN. It's from Aunt Julia! What can it be? *(He lays the packet on the other footstool, opens the letter, runs his eye through it, and jumps up.)* Oh, Hedda—she says that poor Aunt Rina is dying!
HEDDA. Well, we were prepared for that.
TESMAN. And that if I want to see her again, I must make haste. I'll run in to them at once.
HEDDA. *(suppressing a smile).* Will you run?
TESMAN. Oh, my dearest Hedda—if you could only make up your mind to come with me! Just think!
HEDDA. *(rises and says wearily, repelling the idea).* No, no, don't ask me. I *will* not look upon sickness and death. I loathe all sorts of ugliness.
TESMAN. Well, well, then . . . ! *(Bustling around.)* My hat . . . ? My overcoat . . . ? Oh, in the hall . . . I do hope I mayn't come too late, Hedda! Eh?

10. What would Hedda most likely do if Tesman became ill?
(1) deny that he was ill
(2) take him to a hospital
(3) wish that she was in his place
(4) try to avoid him
(5) remain constantly by his sickbed

11. Which of the following statements is true of Hedda?
(1) Hedda is sick but refuses to admit she is not perfect.
(2) Hedda is amused that someone else is sick.
(3) Hedda is unsympathetic and cold.
(4) Hedda is unselfish and tries to help others.
(5) Hedda does not understand how serious the situation is.

Directions: Choose the one best answer to each question. Answers are on page 135.

Item 12 refers to the following passage.

Where are Karen and Charles spending the night?

KAREN. You know, Charles, this really is a spooky place. I actually began to get the creeps this morning—burying Uncle Claude in the rain and watching the old sunken graves fill in with water—remembering the Swamp Woman's story.

CHARLES. Yes, there's nothing like an old ghost legend to start the imagination working.

KAREN. I could almost feel the spirits of all the other Lacombes drifting in the mist around us—

CHARLES. And now this gloomy old house with the storm outside, and the lights gone out. It doesn't help to make things more cheerful!

12. What is the mood of the passage?

    (1) humorous (2) eerie
    (3) whimsical (4) nostalgic
    (5) peaceful

Item 13 refers to the following passage.

How does Biff feel about himself and Willy?

WILLY. *(with hatred, threateningly)* The door of your life is wide open!

BIFF. Pop! I'm a dime a dozen, and so are you!

WILLY. *(turning on him now in an uncontrolled outburst)* I am not a dime a dozen! I am Willy Loman, and you are Biff Loman!

(Biff starts for Willy, but is blocked by Happy. In his fury, Biff seems on the verge of attacking his father.)

13. Which of the following terms best describes the mood of the passage?

    (1) humorous (2) explosive
    (3) mysterious (4) tranquil
    (5) sentimental

Mood The feeling that a dramatic passage gives you is the mood it creates. The plot, the setting, and the characters' speeches and actions all can contribute to the mood.

The setting can establish the mood even before the characters come onstage. For example, an opening of a storm-darkened sky over a large abandoned house can give you an eerie feeling. In contrast, an opening with an afternoon picnic on a sunny beach prepares you for a light-hearted scene.

The characters also are very important in establishing the mood of a dramatic passage. What they say and how they behave, as indicated in the stage directions, can influence the mood strongly.

Warm-up

Read the brief dialogue below. Try to feel the mood of the passage.

BEN. You told me a hundred times, Uncle Willie. Words with a "K" in it are funny.

WILLIE. Words with a "K" in it are funny. You didn't know that, did you? If it doesn't have a "K," it's not funny. I'll tell you which words always get a laugh. *(He is about to count on his fingers.)*

BEN. Chicken.

WILLIE. Chicken is funny.

BEN. Pickle.

WILLIE. Pickle is funny.

BEN. Cupcake.

WILLIE. Cupcake is funny . . . Tomato is *not* funny. Roast beef is *not* funny.

Write a sentence that tells the mood of the passage.

____

____

Sample Warm-up Answer
The passage has a light-hearted, amusing mood.

Popular and Classical Poetry

Reading a Poem Poetry is not always easy to read. A short poem may take longer to read than a full page of prose. That is because poetry is compact. In a well-written poem, each word and phrase, rhythm and rhyme, is chosen carefully to produce a particular idea, image, thought, or emotion.

☑ A Test Taking Tip

When you read a poem, keep the following in mind.

1. Read a poem, including its title, twice before answering any questions. From the first reading, you get a general impression of the mood and images. During the second reading, you note the details and how they contribute to the mood and images. After two readings, try to answer the questions. Don't hesitate to reread a part or all of the poem a third time.

2. Read the poem slowly. As you read, imagine how the words sound so that you can hear them in your head as well as see them. Some poems can be read quickly and enjoyed immediately. However, not all poems reveal their secrets so easily. Allow time to read poetry at a leisurely pace.

3. If you have difficulty understanding lines in a poem, try writing out the lines as if they were sentences in a letter. Sometimes when you see lines of poetry written out in a more familiar way, you grasp their meaning more completely.

Warm-up

Use the tips above as you read the following poem. Then answer the question below in a complete sentence.

Apartment House

A filing-cabinet of human lives
Where people swarm like bees in tunneled
  hives,
Each to his own cell in the towered comb,
Identical and cramped—we call it home.

Why is it important to read the title of this poem?

____

____

Sample Warm-up Answer
The topic of the poem is in the title.

Item 1 refers to the following poem.

What kind of dream is the poet writing about?

Dreams

Hold fast to dreams
For if dreams die
Life is a broken-winged bird
That cannot fly.

Hold fast to dreams
For when dreams go
Life is a barren field
Frozen with snow.

1. Which of the following choices most accurately states what the poem is about?

   (1) Dreams enrich our lives.
   (2) It is best to dream quickly.
   (3) Dreams can only deceive us.
   (4) Dreams can foretell the future.
   (5) When you wake from a dream, life is sad.

Item 2 refers to the following poem.

How did the father treat his child?

Those Winter Sundays

Sundays too my father got up early
and put his clothes on in the blueblack cold,
then with cracked hands that ached
from labor in the weekday weather made
banked fires blaze. No one ever thanked him.

I'd wake and hear the cold splintering,
  breaking.
When the rooms were warm, he'd call,
and slowly I would rise and dress,
fearing the chronic angers of that house.

Speaking indifferently to him,
who had driven out the cold
and polished my good shoes as well.
What did I know, what did I know
of love's austere and lonely offices?

2. Which of the following choices best states what the poem is about?

   (1) The father arose early on Sunday.
   (2) The child slept late on Sunday.
   (3) The father was unappreciated.
   (4) The father and his child did not speak.
   (5) The father was a laborer.

Directions: Choose the one best answer to each question. Answers are on page 135.

Item 3 refers to the following poem.

What planet is the astronomer from?

Earth

"A planet doesn't explode of itself," said drily
The Martian astronomer, gazing off into the air—
"That they were able to do it is proof that highly
Intelligent beings must have been living there."

3. What event is the astronomer commenting on?

   (1) Earth has exploded by itself.
   (2) People from Earth have colonized Mars.
   (3) Mars has just exploded.
   (4) Martians have destroyed Earth.
   (5) Earthlings have blown up their planet.

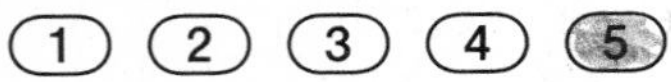

Item 4 refers to the following poem.

What kind of person is speaking in this poem?

Nobody

I'm Nobody! Who are you?
Are you—Nobody—too?
Then there's a pair of us!
Don't tell! they'd banish us—you know!

How dreary—to be—Somebody!
How public—like a Frog—
To tell your name—the livelong June—
To an admiring Bog!

4. The poem expresses the opinion that being famous is

   (1) what most people want
   (2) a good way to gain self-confidence
   (3) what the poet would like
   (4) an undesirable situation
   (5) a lonely way of life

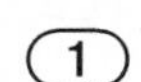   

Grasping the Meaning When you read poetry, you sometimes need to make careful inferences, because the ideas in a poem are not always spelled out. (To refresh your memory on the subject of inferences, see page 2.) You often may find that a poem's central message or main idea is not stated outright. Instead, the poet skillfully uses images, word sounds, rhythm, rhymes, and sentence patterns to help you infer the meaning.

Warm-up

As you read the following poem, decide why the poet left the last line incomplete. Then answer the question below in a complete sentence.

Not Me

The Slithergadee has crawled out of the sea.
He may catch all the others, but he won't catch me.
No you won't catch me, old Slithergadee,
You may catch all the others, but you wo—

Why did the poet leave the last line incomplete?

____

____

☑ A Test-Taking Tip

If you are not absolutely certain which answer is correct, mark the one you *think* is best. You will not be penalized for guessing on the GED Test of Interpreting Literature and the Arts. So try to answer every question.

When a test question puzzles you, carefully read over the five possible answers. Look for choices that you *know* are incorrect. Eliminate those and then decide which of the remaining choices is the most reasonable.

Need a Hint for Number 3?
Apply the steps mentioned above in the Test-Taking Tip to this question.

Sample Warm-up Answer
The last line is cut short to imply that the Slithergadee *has* caught the speaker, putting an end to the boasting.

Unusual Sentence Patterns Sentences in ordinary spoken and written language generally follow predictable patterns. However, the sentences in a poem can be puzzling. You'll learn about three types of unusual sentences on this page. They are not the only unusual sentence patterns found in poetry, but they are three of the most common ones.

Inverted Sentences In an inverted sentence, the verb comes before the subject—just the opposite order you would expect. A poet chooses this type of sentence pattern for several reasons, such as to emphasize a point or to fit the rhyme or rhythm of a poem. In the verse below, the poet put *sleeps* before *dog* so that the lines would rhyme.

Couched in his kennel, like a log,
With paws of silver sleeps the dog;

Abbreviated Sentences A poet may omit words or phrases from a sentence or use just one word in place of a complete sentence. He or she may want to imitate natural speech, to suit the poem's rhyme or rhythm, or to produce suspense, as in the following lines:

I was sure I heard a ghost on the stair.
Bravely I peeked. Nobody there.

Run-on lines You might expect each line in a poem to be a single sentence. But in some poems, a sentence may be carried over from one line to another and possibly throughout the entire poem. The first poem in the outer column is an example of a poem with run-on lines.

Warm-up

Some sentences in poetry are extremely long and complicated. Slowly read the following sentence from a poem about the beginning of the Revolutionary War. Then, on a separate sheet of paper, explain what you think the sentence means.

Concord Hymn

By the rude bridge that arched the flood,
  Their flag to April's breeze unfurled,
Here once the embattled farmers stood
  And fired the shot heard round the world.

Sample Warm-up Answer
Near an old bridge farmers started a battle that would affect the world.

Item 5 refers to the following poem.

How does the poet view his work?

Literature: The God, Its Ritual

Something strange I do not comprehend
Is this: I start to write a certain verse
But by the time that I come to its end
Another has been written that is worse
Or possibly better than the one I meant,
And certainly not the same, and different.

I cannot understand it—I begin
A poem and then it changes as I write,
Never have I written the one I thought I
  might,
Never gone out the door that I came in,
Until I am perplexed by this perverse
Manner and behavior of my verse.

I've never written the poem that I intended;
The poem was always different when it ended.

5. What happens while the poet is writing?

   (1) The poet changes.
   (2) The poem changes.
   (3) The poet becomes frustrated.
   (4) The poem's ending displeases the poet.
   (5) The poem takes longer than expected to write.

Item 6 refers to the following poem.

What distinguishes the bat and the possum from other animals?

Point of View

The little bat hangs upside down,
And downside up the possum.
To show a smile they have to frown,
Say those who've run across 'em.

6. Which of the following choices best restates the last two lines of the poem?

   (1) When upside down, the possum appears to smile.
   (2) People who have seen upside-down bats and possums claim their smiles are really frowns.
   (3) Those who study possums and bats say the animals smile when people frown at them.
   (4) Some animals seem to frown at times.
   (5) Upside-down bats and possums appear to have human expressions.

Directions: Choose the one best answer to each question. Answers are on page 136.

Items 7–9 refer to the following poem.

What kind of person was Richard Cory?

Richard Cory

Whenever Richard Cory went down town,
We people on the pavement looked at him:
He was a gentleman from sole to crown,
Clean-favored, and imperially slim.

And he was always quietly arrayed,
And he was always human when he talked;
But still he fluttered pulses when he said,
"Good-morning," and he glittered when he walked.

And he was rich—yes, richer than a king—
And admirably schooled in every grace:
In fine, we thought that he was everything
To make us wish that we were in his place.

So on we worked, and waited for the light,
And went without the meat, and cursed the bread;
And Richard Cory, one calm summer night,
Went home and put a bullet through his head.

7. What does the poet suggest by using words like "crown," "imperially," and "glitter" to describe Richard Cory?

   (1) Cory was like a king.
   (2) People admired Cory's jewelry.
   (3) Cory dressed in fancy clothing.
   (4) Cory came from a royal family.
   (5) Cory acted as if he owned the town.

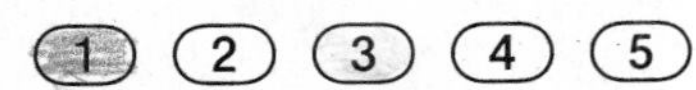

8. What does "schooled in every grace" say about Cory?

   (1) He had gone to a church school.
   (2) He danced well.
   (3) He studied different religions.
   (4) He was very courteous.
   (5) He showed off his knowledge.

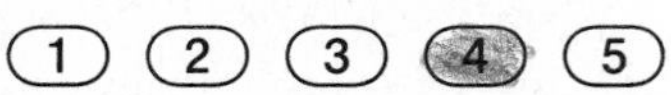

9. What did the people do when they "cursed the bread"?

   (1) avoided bread
   (2) insulted the baker
   (3) complained about their food
   (4) ate only fruits and vegetables
   (5) asked for a pay raise

Vocabulary in Poetry When reading a poem, pay close attention to the words. Poets carefully select words to suit different purposes. For example, a poet may choose a particular word to produce a harsh or soft sound, to fit the rhythm or rhyme of the poem, or to elicit a particular emotion.

☑ A Test-Taking Tip

On the GED Test of Interpreting Literature and the Arts, you may find a poem in which the poet has changed the spelling of a word or used a word in an unusual way. Because of such variations, context and word parts may not give clues to the meaning of unfamiliar words in poetry. If context and word-part clues fail to help you understand a word, sound out the word in your mind. Often the sounds of words in poems will give you clues to meaning.

Read the following poem through once to get a general idea of what it is about.

The Cobra

This creature fills its mouth with venum
And walks upon its duodenum.
He who attempts to tease the cobra
Is soon a sadder he, and sobra.

Notice that the first two and last two lines in the verse above rhyme. To produce a rhyme for *venum,* the poet used a far-fetched synonym for stomach—*duodenum,* which means "lower intestine." The poet had to try even harder to find a rhyme for cobra. However, this "word play" is what makes the verse funny.

Warm-Up

Now read the verse again to find a word that the poet deliberately misspelled. Then answer the following questions.

1. Which of the following choices best defines *sobra* in the last line?
sillier more serious snakelike

____

2. Why did the poet misspell the last word?

____

Warm-up Answers
1. more serious **2.** to make the last two lines rhyme

Figurative Language Do you ever feel as mad as a hornet? Are you cool as a cucumber? As happy as a clam? Comparisons like these are figurative language. Figurative language is often used by poets. Two types of figurative language, simile and metaphor, will be discussed on this page. A third type, personification, is discussed on the next page.

A simile (SIM uh lee) is a comparison using *like* or *as*. The comparisons above are similes; they point out *similarities* between two basically different things. For example, if someone compared shoe leather to a piece of meat, he or she would be using their toughness as a basis for comparison.

A metaphor is a comparison that does not use *like* or *as*. Have you ever heard someone say, "My job is a pain in the neck"? This metaphor compares the unpleasantness of the job to the discomfort of a sore neck.

Be especially alert to figurative language you hear every day. This practice will help you recognize the more unusual figurative language you find in poetry.

A Test-Taking Tip

On the GED Test of Interpreting Literature and the Arts, you will not have to know the definitions of *simile* and *metaphor,* and you won't need to identify examples. But you *will* need to interpret figurative language in some of the poems on the test. You will need to understand what things are being compared and how they are similar.

Warm-up

Read the poem and then answer the question in complete sentences.

Life

Life is a leaf of paper white
Whereon each one of us may write
His word or two; and then comes night.

Though thou have time
But for a line, be that sublime;
Not failure, but *low aim* is crime.

1. What is life compared to? ______________

2. What comparison is made in the third line?

____

____

Sample Warm-up Answers

1. Life is compared to a piece of blank paper, ready for people to "record" their deeds. **2.** Death is compared to night.

Item 10 refers to the following poem.

How does the poet feel about the white butterfly?

White Butterfly

What wisdom do you offer me,
Little white butterfly?
You open your wordless pages, and
Close again your wordless pages.

In your opened pages:
Solitude;
In your closed pages:
Solitude.

10. To what is the poet comparing a butterfly?

    (1) a wise idea
    (2) a blank book
    (3) a wind-blown piece of paper
    (4) the feeling of solitude
    (5) a small white insect

Item 11 refers to the following poem.

What does the poet hear?

The Garden Hose

In the gray evening
I see a long green serpent
With its tail in the dahlias.

It lies in loops across the grass
And drinks softly at the faucet.

I can hear it swallow.

11. Which choice best tells what the poem is about?

    (1) A snake is in the flower bed.
    (2) A snake can drink from a faucet.
    (3) The hose looks like a snake.
    (4) Snakes appear in the evening.
    (5) Snakes help flowers grow.

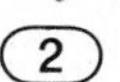

Directions: Choose the one best answer to each question. Answers are on page 136.

Item 12 refers to the following poem.

Why is the boat whistling?

Lost

Desolate and lone
All night long on the lake
Where fog trails and mist creeps,
The whistle of a boat
Calls and cries unendingly,
Like some lost child
In tears and trouble
Hunting the harbor's breast
And the harbor's eyes.

12. What does the poem compare the boat's whistle to?

    (1) a lonely person crying
    (2) a mother searching for her child
    (3) a foghorn
    (4) a child's cries for its mother
    (5) a train whistle in the night

Item 13 is based on the following poem.

Where is it raining?

Rhyme of Rain

"Fifty stories more to fall,
Nothing in our way at all,"
Said a raindrop to its mate,
Falling near the Empire State.
Said the second, "Here we go!
That's Fifth Avenue below."
Said the first one, "There's a hat.
Watch me land myself on that.
Forty stories isn't far—
Thirty seven—here we are—
Twenty, sixteen, thirteen, ten—"
"If we make this trip again,"
Said the second, "we must fall
Near a building twice as tall."
"What a time to think of that,"
Said the first, and missed the hat.

13. In the poem, what has human characteristics?

    (1) the Empire State building
    (2) a hat
    (3) Fifth Avenue
    (4) raindrops
    (5) New York City

Personification Figurative language that compares something nonhuman to a human is called *personification.* For instance, in the poem below, the continent of Africa is described as if it were a woman.

As you read the poem, watch for examples of personification.

Africa

Thus she had lain
sugar cane sweet
deserts her hair
golden her feet
mountains her breasts
two Niles her tears
thus she has lain
Black through the years.

Over the white seas
rime white and cold
brigands ungentled
icicle bold
took her young daughters
sold her strong sons
churched her with Jesus
bled her with guns.
Thus she has lain.

Now she is rising
remember the pain
remember her losses
her screams loud and vain
remember her riches
her history slain
now she is striding
although she had lain.

Warm-up

Read the poem "Africa" again to see how skillfully the details of the comparison are developed. Then answer the questions below.

1. What part of Africa is compared to a woman's tears? ____________

2. Does the poem mean that Africa's land is rising? Explain. ____________

____

A Test-Taking Tip

Often you can get a good idea of what a poem is about by looking carefully at its title.

Sample Warm-up Answers

1. the two branches of the Nile River **2.** No; it means the people of Africa are demanding justice.

Analyzing Poetic Devices Just as a poet selects words carefully (see page 128 for a review), so he or she also may choose to use certain devices for a particular purpose. For instance, some poets omit punctuation and capitalization as a matter of style. The lack of punctuation even may become these poets' personal trademark. Other poets occasionally use informal, nonstandard language for certain effects. For example, a poet may want to make a poem appear to be the words of a small child or of a person with an unusual accent, or to give the poem a folksy flavor.

Warm-up

The poem "rain or hail" is quoted below. Read it carefully and then answer the question that follows in a complete sentence.

rain or hail

rain or hail
sam done
the best he kin
till they digged his hole

:sam was a man

stout as a bridge
rugged as a bear
slickern a weazel
how be you

(sun or snow)

gone into what
like all them kings
you read about
and on him sings

a whippoorwill;

heart was big
as the world aint square
with room for the devil
and his angels too

yes, sir

What devices does the poet use to make "rain or hail" informal and conversational?

____

____

Sample Warm-up Answer
The poet omits punctuation and capitalization and uses nonstandard English, (such as *aint* and *kin)* to make the poem appear to be the words of a person unfamiliar with the rules of written English.

Item 14 refers to the following poem.

What is the poet asking for?

A Christmas Tree

Star,
If you are
A love compassionate,
You will walk with us this year.
We face a glacial distance, who are here
Huddled
At your feet.

14. What device does the poet use to carry out the idea in the poem's title?

(1) misspellings
(2) unexpected capitalization
(3) varied line lengths
(4) unusual punctuation
(5) inverted sentence pattern

Item 15 refers to the following poem.

What must everyone do?

Fable

Does everyone have to die? *Yes, everyone.*
Isn't there some way I can arrange
Not to die—cannot I take some strange
Prescription that my physician might know of?

No. I think not, not for money or love; Everyone has to die, yes, everyone.

Cannot my banker and his bank provide,
Like a trust fund, for me to live on inside
My warm bright house and not be put into
A casket in the clay, can they not do
That for me and charge a fixed per cent
Like interest or taxes or the rent?

No Madame, I fear not, and if they could
There might be more harm in it than good.

15. Five lines of the poem have words set off in a special way in order to

(1) make the poem look attractive
(2) help show that the poem is a conversation
(3) show which words should be read aloud
(4) exhibit the poet's personal style
(5) distinguish the poet's thoughts about death

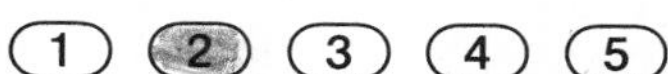   

Directions: Choose the one best answer to each question. Answers are on page 136.

Item 16 refers to the following poem.

What things can be found in the back yard?

Puppy
Catch and shake the cobra garden hose.
Scramble on panicky paws and flee
The hiss of tensing nozzle nose,
Or stalk that snobbish bee.

The back yard is vast as park
With belly-tickle grass and stun
Of sudden sprinkler squalls that are
Rainbows to the yap yap sun.

16. What is the mood of the poem?

(1) lively (2) reflective (3) sarcastic
(4) sad (5) tense

Item 17 refers to the following poem.

What is the poet considering doing?

Too Blue
I got those sad old weary blues.
I don't know where to turn,
I don't know where to go.
Nobody cares about you
When you sink so low.

What shall I do?
What shall I say?
Shall I take a gun and
Put myself away?

I wonder if
One bullet would do?
Hard as my head is,
It would probably take two.

But I ain't got
Neither bullet nor gun—
And I'm too blue
to look for one.

17. What is the mood of the poem?

(1) optimistic (2) depressed
(3) angry (4) eerie (5) joyous

Mood A smile, frown, or puzzled expression can express a person's mood. Similarly, poetry expresses different moods. A poet helps you sense the mood of a poem in many different ways. He or she sometimes develops the mood through an image or series of images that give the reader a special feeling.

The sounds of some words strengthen the mood of a poem. A line of words with soft sounds such as *m, n,* and *l* can create a drowsy mood. A line of many short, sharp words, such as *scat, shot,* and *zip,* can lend a feeling of speed and excitement.

☑ A Test-Taking Tip

After you have read a poem, ask yourself what *you* are feeling. Your own feelings are usually a good guide to the mood of a poem.

Warm-Up

Read the following poem, including the title, at least once before you answer the questions below on a separate sheet of paper. Use complete sentences.

The Latest Latin Dance Craze
First
You throw your head back twice
Jump out onto the floor like a
Kangaroo
Circle the floor once
Doing fast scissor work with your
Legs
Next
Dash towards the door
Walking in a double cha cha cha
Open the door and glide down
The stairs like a swan
Hit the street
Run at least ten blocks
Come back in through the same
Door
Doing a mambo-minuet
Being careful that you don't fall
And break your head on that one
You have just completed your first
Step.

1. What kind of feelings do the poem's short, one-syllable words, especially the action words, suggest?
2. What is the mood of the poem?

Sample Warm-up Answers
1. The short words suggest speed and excitement.
2. The mood of the poem is lively.

Answers—Interpreting Literature and the Arts

Sample Test Items

Popular and Classical Nonfiction (pages 83–97)

1. (5) The main idea is stated in the first sentence. Answer (5) is a rewording of that sentence.

2. (4) The main idea—that Grandma helped teach the children morals and good manners—is supported by this detail.

3. (5) The topic of the paragraph is the writer's mother. The details show that she cleverly kept her children happy while she dealt with their landlord.

4. (3) The topic of the passage is the writer's mother. The details show that she had to clean rich people's houses while she and her family lived in poverty. Twice the author says, "I wonder about my Momma."

5. (4) The supporting details show that the campers' trip was pleasant because they fished successfully, had good weather, and slept well.

6. (2) The main idea is stated in the first sentence. The supporting details explain why the author finds treating guide dogs is rewarding.

7. (4) Answer (4) includes the main idea and most important details in the passage: a rodent startled a woman in a bus shelter.

8. (3) In many different ways, the paragraph repeats the idea that people should recognize the value of their own lives, no matter what their lives are like.

9. (2) *Refuge* means "shelter," and *-ee* means "someone who is given something." A *refugee* is "someone who is given shelter."

10. (2) The inner column tells you that *ped-* means "having to do with the feet." You can infer that pedicabs are vehicles powered by a person on foot.

11. (4) The early sentences all refer to Johnny's stiff neck and explain that it was a minor ailment. You can infer that *complaint,* in this context, means "minor ailment."

12. (4) Parents were concerned that their children might get polio. You can infer that *scare,* in this context, means "concern about becoming ill."

13. (2) *The great eye of the lighthouse* is a figurative expression comparing the beam of light to a large eye peering through the clouds.

14. (4) The word *stampeded* is used figuratively, comparing the sound of the wind to the sound of animals running frantically.

15. (1) The condor's food is the meat of dead animals. Since the condor constantly searched for dead animals, it represented death.

16. (3) The second paragraph states the cause-and-effect relationship clearly: the growth of cities reduced the area where the condor could raise young.

17. (1) Unless the bank approved a loan, the family would lose its land. "Of course" the bank did not approve a loan, since the bank president wanted the land for himself.

18. (4) Details explain that the ward was poorly ventilated and that hospital administrators ignored the requests for better ventilation.

19. (3) The final sentence states that governments are formed by the people and derive their powers from the people. Only answer (3) describes a situation in which the citizens grant power to the government.

20. (3) The author explains why living alone is rewarding. Of the five answer choices, only (3) describes an activity that could be enjoyed alone.

21. (2) The quotation means that the failure of farms often leads to depression and then causes the depression to deepen. The quote calls attention to the way in which farmers' economic problems affect everyone.

22. (4) The author, who is blind, asks two rhetorical questions to focus readers' attention on ways in which sight helps people understand others.

23. (1) The writer calls the schedule a "daily timetable," as if the events occur in the same order and about the same time each day.

24. (2) The writer explains that warehouse workers can hear the sounds of daily living before the office staff arrives.

25. (2) There is no evidence to support answers (1), (3), (4), or (5). The process of elimination reveals that (2) is what Jefferson and Hamilton have in common.

26. (5) With his comparison, the author illustrates the idea that the people of the world are like residents of a large house who are forced by circumstances to learn how to get along.

27. (2) Bing Crosby sang for a generation that had economic and wartime problems; by contrast, Elvis sang for a generation that no longer faced those problems. The author implies that the generations differed in their values too.

28. (1) When the essay about the author's mother won an award, he realized that his writing could tell the world about the injustice of her death.

29. (5) The writer overheard two guerrillas saying that they would kidnap the village children. Because his mother tried to prevent the kidnapping, she was eventually killed.

Commentary
(pages 98–105)

1. (3) The topic of the passage is Charlie Chaplin. The details in the passage all illustrate how Chaplin demonstrated everyone's job, pointing out exactly what each should do.

2. (1) The third sentence mentions that "Having a Party" is one of the songs that Sam Cooke sang at his peak and also that it is "all . . . rock 'n' roll."

3. (3) The author says the second album is a "best of" album with Sam Cooke's "hit parade." That is why it isn't as revealing as the first album. It contains songs already heard by many people.

4. (1) The words *buddy* and *action* are combined to make up a new word that describes a film in which the detectives are good friends and lots of violent action occurs.

5. (4) The line means that Rivera found a means of expressing his political beliefs.

6. (4) The passage does not state why, but the author implies why with such phrases as "a brief fad" and "luckily a break has been inserted into Circle Theatre's production."

7. (1) Fred Waring had a very successful musical career, which proves that he was not stopped by the rejection of the glee club.

8. (3) Only (3) presents a solution to the "worst writing" that the author describes in the second sentence.

9. (2) The passage explains that Brahms loved folk music and wrote many melodies that were similar to folk tunes. Most likely he would probably prefer an old, traditional lullaby over the other choices given.

10. (1) Terms of admiration and respect help you sense that the author respects the quartet.

11. (3) The tone is respectful, serious, even solemn. A review of a circus act would probably use a more energetic, excited tone.

12. (2) Descriptive words such as *glistening wit, warmth, good humor,* and *now-fashionable* give clues that the author's attitude is one of approval.

13. (3) The lack of strongly emotional words helps you sense that the tone is objective.

14. (5) Often the word *chicken* is used to describe a fearful person. Chicken Little represents a silly, frantic little character. In addition, the passage states that Carson lacks the courage to do what he wants.

15. (4) The writer is emphasizing the extent to which the popular "Mummy" idea was exploited. Even the comedians Abbott and Costello used the far-fetched theme in a film.

Popular and Classical Fiction
(pages 106–116)

1. (4) The answer is stated in the first sentence.The narrator says that the suggestion that the two had met doesn't count.

2. (4) For fourteen years, Joe had been in Australia earning his fortune.

3. (1) Mrs. Wang says that in all her years, she has never before seen the river so high.

4. (3) Mrs. Wang has never seen a Japanese soldier, and the war does not seem real to her.

5. (1) Mrs. James speaks worriedly to her daughter; you can infer that she is concerned about something.

6. (3) Although Julie doesn't admit it, she feels uneasy. She remembers another time when her mother's premonition proved to be correct.

7. (5) The grandfather uses the same expressions so often that his grandsons can predict what he'll say in a given situation.

8. (3) Jordan made up a game called "Grandfather Trivia" and also invented nicknames for family members.

9. (3) The narrator, who calls Ariadne "beloved," explains that he has spoken to her father, suggesting that the narrator has asked for permission to court her.

10. (5) Ariadne shrieks at the visitor, ordering him to go away. To make him leave, she throws a piece of pottery at him and then prepares to throw a water pitcher.

11. (1) The narrator persists in his courtship and won't let Ariadne easily drive him away.

12. (4) The youth stops because of the noise and becomes "transfixed." The word *transfixed* means "stood still," but if you didn't know that, the context helps you out. The passage says he listens for a time and then begins running. You can infer that the youth stood still.

13. (2) It is ironic that the youth ran *toward* the battle because he had been running *away* from it. Irony involves opposites.

14. (3) Answer (3) is a comparison the author made to help readers understand the character's emotions.

15. (2) The priest compares his words, which have lost their sincerity and strength from overuse, to tea bags, which lose their flavor the same way.

16. (1) Mary encourages Bigger to join a labor union. Since she seems to favor unions, she would probably join one herself if she were a worker.

17. (3) Mr. Dalton says that they can "settle" their disagreement later. You can predict that if Mary were rude in front of other household members, Mr. Dalton would try to avoid a confrontation and speak to her later.

18. (5) Phrases like *just a shade too much, just a shade too conscious,* and *a little too quaint* suggest the the author is critical of the people he describes.

19. (1) The passage implies that the people are interested in being fashionable, not in living in the country. They are insincere, or phony.

20. (3) The narrator seems lonely and tense. This makes the mood of the passage tense.

21. (5) A dark night with clouds over the moon usually suggests eeriness and tension.

22. (3) Using the process of elimination should have helped you select the best answer. The narrator's description does not seem joyful, pleasant, horrifying, or chaotic. You can eliminate all answers except the third one; the word *solemn* fits the mood of the passage.

23. (2) As the rabbi's son, the narrator is obviously a male. And he is talking about things that happened in the past, when he was a boy.

24. (3) Shosha shared her time and possessions with the narrator, as well as showed him some affection.

Popular and Classical Drama
(pages 117–124)

1. (3) In answer to Amanda's question, Laura replies that Amanda's look of disappointment is "awful" and "suffering," like a picture of Jesus' mother.

2. (3) Using the process of elimination, you could have selected the best answer. Although the dialog touches briefly on Hodel's fiancé and on Tevye, the conversation actually leads up to the reason that Hodel is traveling to Siberia; to be with her fiancé, who needs her.

3. (4) When Tevye asks whether the fiancé has been arrested and convicted, Hodel admits that he has been.

4. (3) The stage directions describe how Raquel puts poison into some wine while the soldiers are out of the room. A short while after the soldiers return, she encourages them to drink some of the wine.

5. (3) Spencer is frantically trying to get someone on the radio who can tell him how to fly the airplane, so it is obviously in flight. With passengers, the aircraft can't be a fighter plane.

6. (3) Gil's speech suggests that the men intend to hang a rustler.

7. (4) Gil is reluctant to continue because he is afraid that someone might get carried away and hang more people than just the rustler.

8. (2) Since Oscar doesn't mind living in a smelly apartment or serving rotten food, he is probably a slob; his comments are humorous, suggesting wit.

9. (1) Roy questions Murray's sanity because Murray is willing to eat a decaying sandwich.

10. (4) Hedda says that she won't look at sickness or death, so she would probably avoid Tesman if he were ill.

11. (3) Hedda refuses to visit Tesman's dying aunt, so Hedda is probably an unfeeling person.

12. (2) You can sense the eerie mood when Karen comments that the place gives her "the creeps" and when Charles refers to the "gloomy old house."

13. (2) The stage directions help establish the mood by saying Biff is in a fury and "seems on the verge of attacking his father."

Popular and Classical Poetry
(pages 125–132)

1. (1) The poem says that without dreams, or goals, life would be earthbound and cold.

2. (3) The poet realizes now that he never said thanks for his father's loving care.

3. (5) The title reveals that the poem is about the planet Earth. The Martian astronomer suggests that people on Earth were intelligent enough to blow up their planet.

4. (4) The fifth line says, "How dreary to be somebody." That suggests that being well known is undesirable.

5. (2) Most of lines 5–13 explain that every poem the poet creates changes during the process of writing.

6. (2) The last two lines are easier to understand if you reverse the sentence order: Those who've run across (the upside-down bat and possum) say that the animals have to frown to show a smile.

7. (1) *Crown, imperially,* and *glitter* refer to royalty and splendor; the poet uses these words to suggest that Cory was regal and majestic.

8. (4) *Schooled* means "educated" or "trained." The phrase shows that Cory knew how to be gracious and polite.

9. (3) People who could not afford meat—as Richard Cory was able to do—ate the plain food they could afford, but were unhappy with it.

10. (2) The references to opening and closing "wordless pages" brings to mind the image of a blank book. The butterfly opens and closes its wings as you would a book.

11. (3) The poet uses a metaphor that compares the hose to a long, green snake.

12. (4) The words "like some lost child" state a comparison. The poem compares the lonely sound of the boat whistle to the sad sound a lost child would make.

13. (4) The whimsical dialogue between two drops of rain is a good example of personification; the raindrops are talking like people.

14. (3) To give the visual effect of a Christmas tree, the poet varies the lengths of the lines.

15. (2) The set-off lines show the second speaker. Without them, a reader might become confused.

16. (1) If you picture each of the puppy's actions described in the poem, you will see that the mood is lively.

17. (2) The poet says he's *blue,* which means "depressed." He is also describing frustration and suicidal feelings.

Minitests—Interpreting Literature and the Arts

Minitest 1

Directions: Choose the one best answer to each item. Answers are on page 151.

Items 1–2 refer to the following passage.

How does Ivor Belli feel about his wife's death?

One Saturday in March, an occasion of pleasant winds and sailing clouds, Mr. Ivor Belli bought from a Brooklyn florist a fine mass of jonquils and conveyed them, first by subway, then foot, to an immense cemetery in Queens, a site unvisited by him since he had seen his wife buried there the previous autumn. Sentiment could not be credited with returning him today, for Mrs. Belli, to whom he had been married twenty-seven years, during which time she had produced two now-grown and matrimonially settled daughters, had been a woman of many natures, most of them trying: he had no desire to renew so unsoothing an acquaintance, even in spirit. No; but a hard winter had just passed, and he felt in need of exercise, air, a heart-lifting stroll through the handsome, spring-prophesying weather; of course, rather as an extra dividend, it was nice that he would be able to tell his daughters of a journey to their mother's grave, especially so since it might a little appease the elder girl, who seemed resentful of Mr. Belli's too comfortable acceptance of life as lived alone.

1. Why did Ivor Belli visit the cemetery?
   (1) It was his custom to decorate his wife's grave with flowers.
   (2) He wanted to get fresh air and exercise and to tell his daughters he'd been there.
   (3) He hoped a visit to the cemetery would help him forget his sadness.
   (4) His daughters had asked him especially to visit his wife's grave.
   (5) He felt guilty about adjusting so easily to life without Mrs. Belli.

   1 2 3 4 5

2. Judging from information in the passage, what kind of person was Mrs. Belli?
   (1) hard to define
   (2) mysterious
   (3) difficult to live with
   (4) sentimental
   (5) accepting

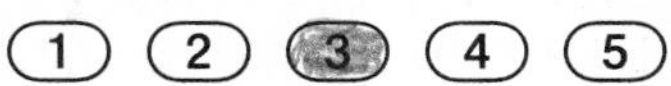

Items 3–4 refer to the following poem.

Why does the poet remind himself that he is quickly growing older?

Loveliest of Trees, the Cherry Now

Loveliest of trees, the cherry now
Is hung with bloom along the bough,
And stands about the woodland ride
Wearing white for Eastertide.

Now, of my threescore years and ten,
Twenty will not come again,
And take from seventy springs a score,
It only leaves me fifty more.

And since to look at things in bloom
Fifty springs are little room,
About the woodlands I will go
To see the cherry hung with snow.

3. The poet compares cherry blossoms to a white garment (line 4) and also to
   (1) a spring day
   (2) snow
   (3) an Easter flower
   (4) a small white room
   (5) a delicious fruit

4. What is the mood of the poem?
   (1) joyous
   (2) thoughtful
   (3) humorous
   (4) hostile
   (5) tense

Items 5–8 refer to the following passage from science fiction.

What is the object in the pit?

[Ogilvy] remained standing at the edge of the pit that the Thing had made for itself, staring at its strange appearance, astonished chiefly at its unusual shape and color, and dimly perceiving even then some evidence of design in its arrival. The early morning was wonderfully still, and the sun, just clearing the pine trees towards Weybridge, was already warm. He did not remember hearing any birds that morning, there was certainly no breeze stirring, and the only sounds were the faint movements from within the cindery cylinder. He was all alone on the common.

Then suddenly he noticed with a start that some of the grey clinker, the ashy incrustation that covered the meteorite, was falling off the circular edge of the end. It was dropping off in flakes and raining down upon the sand. A large piece suddenly came off and fell with a sharp noise that brought his heart into his mouth.

For a minute he scarcely realized what this meant, and, although the heat was excessive, he clambered down into the pit close to the bulk to see the Thing more clearly. He fancied even then that the cooling of the body might account for this, but what disturbed that idea was the fact that the ash was falling only from the end of the cylinder.

And then he perceived that, very slowly, the circular top of the cylinder was rotating on its body. It was such a gradual movement that he discovered it only through noticing that a black mark that had been near him five minutes ago was now at the other side of the circumference. Even then he scarcely understood what this indicated, until he heard a muffled grating sound and saw the black mark jerk forward an inch or so. Then the thing came upon him in a flash. The cylinder was artificial—hollow—with an end that screwed out! Something within the cylinder was unscrewing the top!

5. At first, what does Ogilvy think the cylindrical object in the pit is?

   (1) a meteorite
   (2) a large mineral deposit
   (3) a missile
   (4) a huge fossil
   (5) a living creature

    2 3 4 5

6. In lines 21–22, the author uses the phrase "brought his heart into his mouth" to indicate that Ogilvy was

   (1) ill
   (2) injured
   (3) hungry
   (4) sympathetic
   (5) startled

7. Which of the following qualities does Ogilvy seem to possess?

   (1) honesty
   (2) helpfulness
   (3) pride
   (4) curiosity
   (5) defensiveness

   1 2 3 4 5

8. What is the mood of the passage?

   (1) peaceful
   (2) nostalgic
   (3) suspenseful
   (4) humorous
   (5) sad

Items 9–10 refer to the following passage.

How does the narrator most likely feel about the father?

The boy was severely handicapped. Trying to fill a big thermos from a spring spewing out of the mountain east of Kalispell, near Hungry Horse, he laughed as the cold water splattered him, and he burbled something.

I had no idea what he said. "Very cold water indeed," I answered.

He burbled again, then lost his footing, and fell hard on the wet rocks. The gush hit the flask and kicked it away. I went to help him.

"Leave him alone!" someone shouted over the crash of water. A man who looked as if he'd swallowed a nail keg came toward us. "Let *him* do it. You'll make him weak if you do it for him. He's my son. He understands."

The boy struggled up and slipped and struggled again.

"I'll hand him the thermos."

"Let him get it." The boy retrieved the jug and went back to the big spout. He fell again, got up, and tried again.

"Grab on to the pipe!" I shouted, but he couldn't do it and hold the jug. The thermos bounced over to me. I picked it up and handed it to him.

9. Which of the following statements best summarizes the main idea of the passage?
   (1) A handicapped boy had trouble filling a thermos.
   (2) A father was cruel to his handicapped son.
   (3) Mountain spring water can be extremely cold.
   (4) A father resented a man who tried to help his handicapped son.
   (5) A man met a handicapped boy and his father east of Kalispell.

10. Why did the father shout, "Leave him alone!" (line 13)?
   (1) He thought the narrator would hurt his son.
   (2) He was punishing his son.
   (3) He wanted to help the boy himself.
   (4) He thought the boy should take care of himself.
   (5) He thought the narrator was ridiculing them.

Items 11–12 refer to the following passage.

Why is Ed Foley working in the service station?

A hot summer evening. Inside a small, dirty service station Ed Foley, an elderly man, is fumbling with the cash register, apparently trying to unlock it. The door opens and Louisa, a well-dressed, rather timid woman, enters. She looks around. Clearly, she feels uncomfortable here.

LOUISA. Pardon me—could you direct me to the Three Oaks Hotel on Serano Boulevard?

ED. What? *(looks up, startled, then notices Louisa)* Oh. Lady, I don't know nothin' about this city.

LOUISA. Perhaps I could ask the owner of this station? *(She glances around.)*

ED. You won't find the owner here tonight, lady. He took his missus to the hospital to have a baby. I'm his father, just here tonight from Grand Bend to look after the station. But I don't know nothin' about this place.

LOUISA. *(looks discouraged, then brightens)* I know. I'll call the hotel. I have the number here on the reservation slip. *(She moves to the pay phone at the back of the station, puts in a coin, and dials.)*

The door opens again. A young man enters, his expression and general attitude slightly menacing, slightly nervous. He doesn't see Louisa at the back of the room.

YOUTH. You all alone tonight, Granddad?

ED. *(not looking up)* I ain't your granddad. I ain't nobody's granddad just yet. I'm closin' up here soon. What d'ya want?

YOUTH. What I want is to talk to the owner of this gas station, old man. *(He moves toward Ed, reaching for something in his pocket.)*

LOUISA. *(Grasping the situation, she takes a step forward, still holding the phone. Her voice is loud and firm.)* I own this gas station, young man, and at the moment I'm talking with the chief of police. Please state your business quickly.

11. How could Ed Foley best be described?

(1) slow, nervous, and menacing
(2) confident and businesslike
(3) friendly and eager to help
(4) confused, impatient, and cranky
(5) frightened and shy

① ② ③ ④ ⑤

12. Louisa suspects that the youth may want to

(1) apply for a job
(2) steal money from the cash register
(3) complain about the service
(4) ask for directions to a hotel
(5) pay for gas

① ② ③ ④ ⑤

Items 13–15 refer to the following commentary.

What is the film *Round Midnight* about?

It's a USA art form, but jazz has generally been given short shrift in our movies. And sure enough, in *Round Midnight,* it is a Frenchman, director/writer Bertrand Tavernier, who pays tender homage to the lives and music of some fictional '50s jazzmen.

Tavernier has made the film breathe with authenticity by hiring real musicians to play musicians. As Dale Turner, a declining, alcoholic jazz legend working in Paris in 1959, veteran tenor saxophonist Dexter Gordon is full of wit, dignity, poignance and style. With his great, expressive face, laconically delivering lines in a voice like rocks in a blender, Gordon is a revelation in his first film.

Francois Cluzet is also winning as a French artist who crouches in the rain outside Paris' re-created Blue Note club to hear his idol play; he later sacrifices money, tears, even his own bed for Turner, in the friendship that forms the basis of *Round Midnight.*

As fellow musicians, real-life jazzmen Herbie Hancock, Bobby Hutcherson and Wayne Shorter, among others, are also effective, and film maker Martin Scorsese has a cameo as Turner's vile USA manager. Alexandre Trauner's sets are uniformly outstanding.

Hancock also composed and arranged the music for *Round Midnight,* and it's here that the film succeeds like none before it. Nightclub performances were recorded live, providing superb sound quality and a chance to hear superb jazz musicians play without the charade of syncing.

Round Midnight isn't perfect. It's a bit long (130) minutes), and a bit short on plot. But Tavernier has made a film with heart and charm—and you don't have to be a jazz aficionado to dig it.

13. Which of the following best summarizes the review of *Round Midnight?*

(1) With authentic jazz players and good music, *Round Midnight* is a warm, enjoyable film.
(2) The superb jazz music in *Round Midnight* was composed and arranged by Herbie Hancock.
(3) *Round Midnight* is the story of jazz musicians who become good friends.
(4) Frenchman Bernard Tavernier has made a film about two jazz musicians in Paris.
(5) *Round Midnight* is a little too long, and the plot is not terribly exciting.

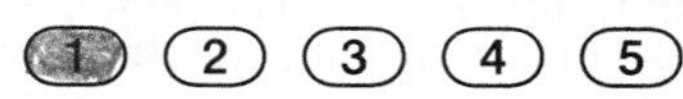

14. According to the review, musician-actor Dexter Gordon is witty and dignified and has a voice that is

(1) smooth
(2) soft
(3) melodic
(4) rough
(5) expressive

15. To which of the following types of audience would the author feel a viewer must belong in order to enjoy *Round Midnight?*

(1) authentic musicians
(2) French-speaking adults
(3) fans of fast-moving action films
(4) music lovers
(5) jazz experts

Minitest 2

Directions: Choose the one best answer to each item. Answers are on pages 151–152.

Items 1–2 refer to the following passage.

In what way is Bullard like a cannibal?

Two old men sat on a park bench one morning in the sunshine of Tampa, Florida—one trying doggedly to read a book he was plainly enjoying while the other, Harold K. Bullard, told him the story of his life in the full, round, head tones of a public address system. At their feet lay Bullard's Labrador retriever, who further tormented the aged listener by probing his ankles with a large, wet nose.

Bullard, who had been, before he retired, successful in many fields, enjoyed reviewing his important past. But he faced the problem that complicates the lives of cannibals—namely: that a single victim cannot be used over and over. Anyone who had passed the time of day with him and his dog refused to share a bench with them again.

So Bullard and his dog set out through the park each day in quest of new faces. They had had good luck this morning, for they had found this stranger right away, clearly a new arrival in Florida, still buttoned up tight in heavy serge, stiff collar and necktie, and with nothing better to do than read.

"Yes," said Bullard, rounding out the first hour of his lecture, "made and lost five fortunes in my time."

"So you said," said the stranger, whose name Bullard had neglected to ask. "Easy, boy. No, no, no, boy," he said to the dog, who was growing more aggressive toward his ankles.

1. Which of the following activities would Bullard probably enjoy most?

(1) writing his autobiography
(2) attending a party with old friends
(3) going for a walk on the beach
(4) watching an exciting movie
(5) giving a speech

1 2 3 4 5

2. Why didn't Bullard ask the stranger his name?

(1) The man seemed timid.
(2) The man offered to introduce himself.
(3) Bullard already knew the man's name.
(4) Bullard was interested only in himself.
(5) Bullard didn't want to pry.

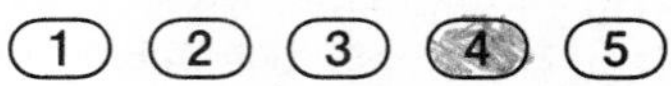

Items 3–4 refer to the following passage.

Who are the "two Abes" mentioned in the passage?

On two occasions since he had become President, Lincoln had been fired on by would-be assassins. The first of these occurred in the summer of '63. At that time, Lincoln had been daily riding the three miles between the White House and the Soldiers' Home, where the family lived through the hot-weather months. One morning as Lincoln came riding up to the White House, he met Lamon. "I have something to tell you," he said. They went to the President's office, locked the doors, and sat down.

Lamon later wrote down the talk which followed. Lincoln began: "You know I have always thought you an idiot for your apprehensions of my personal danger. Well, just now I don't know what to think.

"Last night, about eleven o'clock, I went out to the Soldiers' Home alone, riding Old Abe. When I arrived at the entrance of the Home grounds, I was jogging along, immersed in thought, when suddenly I was aroused by the report of a rifle, seemingly not fifty yards away. My erratic namesake, with one bound, separated me from my eight-dollar plug hat, and at breakneck speed we arrived in a haven of safety. I tell you there is no time on record equal to that made by the two Old Abes on that ocassion."

3. What would Lincoln most likely have done if he had been offered a bodyguard when he first became president?

(1) accepted the offer gratefully
(2) considered the matter
(3) acted insulted
(4) asked for guards for his family too
(5) said that he didn't need one

4. Details in the passage point to the conclusion that Lincoln was the kind of person who could
   (1) see the humor in every situation
   (2) see the good in all people
   (3) remain alert at all times
   (4) ride a horse expertly
   (5) detect trouble early

Items 5–7 refer to the following passage.

What surprise does Carl Tiflin have for his son Jody?

They marched past the cypress, where a singletree hung from a limb to butcher the pigs on, and past the black iron kettle, so it was not a pig killing. The sun shone over the hill and threw long, dark shadows of the trees and buildings. They crossed a stubble-field to shortcut to the barn. Jody's father unhooked the door and they went in. They had been walking toward the sun on the way down. The barn was black as night in contrast and warm from the hay and from the beasts. Jody's father moved over toward the one box stall. "Come here!" he ordered. Jody could begin to see things now. He looked into the box stall and then stepped back quickly.

A red pony colt was looking at him out of the stall. Its tense ears were forward and a light of disobedience was in its eyes. Its coat was rough and thick as an airedale's fur and its mane was long and tangled. Jody's throat collapsed in on itself and cut his breath short.

"He needs a good currying," his father said, "and if I ever hear of you not feeding him or leaving his stall dirty, I'll sell him off in a minute."

Jody couldn't bear to look at the pony's eyes any more. He gazed down at his hands for a moment, and he asked very shyly, "Mine?" No one answered him. He put his hand out toward the pony. Its gray nose came close, sniffling loudly, and then the lips drew back and the strong teeth closed on Jody's fingers. The pony shook its head up and down and seemed to laugh with amusement. Jody regarded his bruised fingers. "Well," he said with pride—"Well, I guess he can bite all right." The two men laughed, somewhat in relief. Carl Tiflin went out of the barn and walked up a side-hill to be by himself, for he was embarrassed, but Billy Buck stayed. It was easier to talk to Billy Buck. Jody asked again—"Mine?"

Billy became professional in tone. "Sure! That is, if you look out for him and break him right. I'll show you how. He's just a colt. You can't ride him for some time."

5. "Jody's throat collapsed in on itself and cut his breath short." The author includes this statement to show that
   (1) Jody was handicapped
   (2) Jody was ill
   (3) the barn was dirty and unpleasant
   (4) Jody was filled with emotion
   (5) The pony had frightened Jody

6. Which of the following descriptions best fits Carl Tiflin's manner toward his son?
   (1) gruff but loving
   (2) indulgent
   (3) cruel
   (4) neglectful
   (5) warm and kind

7. At first Jody is uncertain whether
   (1) the horse is a gift for him
   (2) Bill Buck will help him train the horse
   (3) his father is angry with him
   (4) his job is to clean the barn stalls
   (5) the horse bite is serious

① ② ③ ④ ⑤

Items 8–9 refer to the following excerpt from an article.

What makes Nancy Graves's bronze sculptures unusual?

Graves uses a mixture of bronze casting, welded assemblage and acid patination to achieve the rich effects in her new work. Much of it is produced by assembling organic parts that she has cast directly—that is, she makes molds of real pods, leaves and gourds, and those molds are filled with molten bronze to make a duplicate.

She then arranges ingenious compositions of these parts, together with manmade objects such as bicycle wheels and crowbars. Finally, she adds color to the whole creation through the innovative use of polychrome patina, paint and baked enamel.

The results are an astounding transformation of parts into a whole that seems to parallel nature and yet exists in a fantastic world of Graves' own making.

Many contemporary artists work with found objects, but the sophistication of Graves' sculptural statement puts her in another class altogether. Here, the humor and fun of discovering an ordinary ear of corn or a dangling pretzel in such an elegant context is only one note in a complex and subtle melody that is all about grace and rhythm and structure.

8. Which of the following best describes the reviewer's approach toward Graves's sculpture?

   (1) sarcastic
   (2) enthusiastic
   (3) disapproving
   (4) resentful
   (5) serious

9. Nancy Graves's sculptures combine manmade objects with

   (1) seed pods, gourds, and leaves
   (2) bronze molded into objects from nature
   (3) pieces of scrap metal welded together
   (4) duplicates of such objects
   (5) found objects

Items 10–12 refer to the following poem.

How does the speaker feel about his condition?

Organ Transplant

I drank,
my arteries filled with fat;
the ventricle went lax
and a clot stopped my heart.

Now I sit
in St. Petersburg sunshine.
No whiskey;
wearing a girl's heart.

My blood has adopted a child
who shuffles through my chest
carrying a doll.

10. Lines 1–4 of the poem tell the reader that the speaker

    (1) is an alcoholic
    (2) is fat
    (3) had a heart attack
    (4) is dead
    (5) was poisoned

11. Which of the following best restates the meaning of lines 9–11 of the poem?

    (1) The speaker has adopted a child.
    (2) The speaker still has chest pains.
    (3) The speaker thinks about the dead child.
    (4) The transplant donor was a girl.
    (5) The beat of the new heart is irregular.

12. The mood of the poem is

    (1) thankful
    (2) thoughtful
    (3) humorous
    (4) confused
    (5) hostile

Items 13–15 refer to the following passage from a play.

OSBORNE. Yes. *(Pause.)* I remember up at Wipers we had a man shot when he was out on patrol. Just at dawn. We couldn't get him in that night. He lay out there groaning all day. Next night three of our men crawled out to get him in. It was so near the German trenches that they could have shot our fellows one by one. But, when our men began dragging the wounded man back over the rough ground, a big German officer stood up in their trenches and called out: "Carry him!"—and our fellows stood up and carried the man back, and the German officer fired some lights for them to see by.

RALEIGH. How topping!

OSBORNE. Next day we blew each other's trenches to blazes.

RALEIGH. It all seems rather—*silly,* doesn't it?

OSBORNE. It does, rather. [*There is silence for a while.*]

RALEIGH. I started a letter when I came off duty last night. How do we send letters?

OSBORNE. The quartermaster sergeant takes them down after he brings rations up in the evenings. (STANHOPE *is coming slowly down the steps.* RALEIGH *rises.)*

RALEIGH. I think I'll go and finish it now—if I go on duty soon.

OSBORNE. Come and write it in here. It's more cheery.

RALEIGH. It's all right, thanks; I'm quite comfortable in there. I've rigged up a sort of little table beside my bed.

13. Osborne's story about the German officer supports the conclusion that

(1) German officers speak many languages
(2) even enemies can show compassion during a war
(3) medical help was scarce during World War I
(4) warfare is completely uncivilized
(5) officers are often kind to their troops

14. With what does Osborne contrast the actions of the German officer?

(1) Raleigh's belief that the war is silly
(2) the bravery of the men who got the injured man back
(3) the everyday act of writing a letter
(4) the heavy fighting the next day
(5) the foolishness of the German troops

15. Raleigh's reaction to Osborne's story of the German officer is one of

(1) disbelief
(2) anger
(3) approval
(4) boredom
(5) disapproval

Minitest 3

Directions: Choose the one best answer to each item. Answers are on page 152.

Items 1–3 refer to the following passage.

Was the woman in the passage truly unlucky?

There was a woman who was beautiful, who started with all the advantages, yet she had no luck. She married for love, and the love turned to dust. She had bonny children, yet she felt they had been thrust upon her, and she could not love them. They looked at her coldly, as if they were finding fault with her. And hurriedly she felt she must cover up some fault in herself. Yet what it was that she must cover up she never knew. Nevertheless, when her children were present, she always felt the center of her heart go hard. This troubled her, and in her manner she was all the more gentle and anxious for her children, as if she loved them very much. Only she herself knew that at the center of her heart was a hard little place that could not feel love, no, not for anybody. Everybody else said of her: "She is such a good mother. She adores her children." Only she herself, and her children themselves, knew it was not so. They read it in each other's eyes.

There was a boy and two little girls. They lived in a pleasant house, with a garden, and they had discreet servants, and felt themselves superior to anyone in the neighborhood.

1. According to the passage, what troubled the mother most about herself?

   (1) Her children found fault with her.
   (2) Her husband no longer loved her.
   (3) She was not capable of feeling love.
   (4) She was unlucky.
   (5) Neighbors criticized her.

2. "They lived in a pleasant house, with a garden, and they had discreet servants, and felt themselves superior to anyone in the neighborhood."

   Why does the narrator include this statement?

   (1) to establish the setting
   (2) to show how important good servants were to the family
   (3) to set up a dreamlike mood
   (4) to inform that the family had a better life than anyone else they knew
   (5) to reveal that the family was somewhat hypocritical

3. What is the narrator's attitude toward the mother?

   (1) hostile
   (2) slightly disapproving
   (3) sympathetic
   (4) admiring
   (5) frivolous

Items 4–5 refer to the following poem.

How does the mother feel toward her son?

Mother to Son

Well, son, I'll tell you:
Life for me ain't been no crystal stair.
It's had tacks in it,
And splinters,
And boards torn up,
And places with no carpet on the floor—
Bare.
But all the time
I'se been a-climbin' on,
And reachin' landin's,
And turnin' corners,
And sometimes goin' in the dark
Where there ain't been no light.
So boy, don't you turn back.
Don't you set down on the steps
'Cause you finds it's kinder hard.
Don't you fall now—
For I'se still goin', honey,
I'se still climbin',
And life for me ain't been no crystal stair.

4. The mother compares her life to a staircase in order to suggest that

   (1) she always wished for a fancy home
   (2) she was not a social climber
   (3) everyone has problems
   (4) she carries on through a hard life
   (5) life is fragile

   1 2 3 4 5

5. What does the mother in the poem urge her son to do?

   (1) live a simple, humble life
   (2) avoid a life of poverty
   (3) lend a helping hand to others
   (4) pursue goals even if discouraged
   (5) lead her up the stairs

   1 2 3 4 5

Items 6–10 refer to the following passage.

What was Florence Nightingale really like?

Everyone knows the popular conception of Florence Nightingale. The saintly, self-sacrificing woman, the delicate maiden of high degree who threw aside the pleasures of a life of ease to succour the afflicted, the Lady with the Lamp, gliding through the horrors of the hospital at Scutari, and consecrating with the radiance of her goodness the dying soldier's couch—the vision is familiar to all. But the truth was different. The Miss Nightingale of fact was not as facile fancy painted her. She worked in another fashion, and towards another end; she moved under the stress of an impetus which finds no place in the popular imagination. A Demon possessed her. Now demons, whatever else they may be, are full of interest. And so it happens that in the real Miss Nightingale there was more that was interesting than in the legendary one; there was also less that was agreeable.

Her family was extremely well-to-do, and connected by marriage with a spreading circle of other well-to-do families. There was a large country house in Derbyshire; there was another in the New Forest; there were Mayfair rooms for the London season and all its finest parties; there were tours on the Continent with even more than the usual number of Italian operas and of glimpses at the celebrities of Paris. Brought up among such advantages, it was only natural to suppose that Florence would show a proper appreciation of them by doing her duty in that state of life unto which it had pleased God to call her—in other words, by marrying, after a fitting number of dances and dinner-parties, an eligible gentleman, and living happily ever afterwards.

6. What is the author referring to when he writes that Miss Nightingale was "of high degree" (line 4)?

   (1) her level of education
   (2) her upper-class background
   (3) her high income
   (4) her good manner
   (4) her degree of intelligence

7. Which of the following best states the main idea of the first paragraph?

   (1) Florence Nightingale was a heroine.
   (2) Everyone has heard of Florence Nightingale.
   (3) The popular image of Nightingale is faulty.
   (4) Florence Nightingale saved many soldiers' lives.
   (5) Hospital conditions long ago were dreadful.

   1 2 3 4 5

8. What did the Nightingale family expect Florence to do when she reached adulthood?

   (1) marry a wealthy gentleman
   (2) remain quietly at home
   (3) manage one of the family's homes
   (4) select a ladylike career
   (5) become a battlefield nurse

9. If Florence Nightingale were living today, which of the following would she probably recommend to young women?
   (1) Always be agreeable and pleasant.
   (2) A woman's place is in the home.
   (3) Follow your dream, whatever it is.
   (4) Marry a rich gentleman.
   (5) Follow your parents' advice.

10. The writing style used in this essay would probably be appropriate in a biography of
   (1) the Marx Brothers
   (2) Paul Newman
   (3) Elvis Presley
   (4) Franklin Roosevelt
   (5) Jacqueline Kennedy Onassis

Items 11–12 refer to the following passage.

Does the tango make an interesting stage performance?

When Segovia and Orezzoli planned "Tango Argentino," they agreed on the importance of the music and brought together the best tango musicians in the world. For the entire performance, the orchestra is silhouetted in tiers at center stage, the backdrop to the dancers. The four men in front contribute the special sound of the *bandoneón,* a narrow accordion-like instrument that they collapse and expand while it lies across their knees.

Music is the soul of the rango. The violins bring their sweetness. The *bandoneones* add the melancholy, each contributing to the romantic illusion that drives the tango. The music is languorous at times, marchlike at others, lilting at still others. It is these changing moods that enables "Tango Argentino" to be a fulfilling evening in the theater. Because the evening is more than the dance. It is also music and song. When the orchestra plays its own interludes, indeed, the soul is revealed to be black, Indian and Caribbean. The singer will introduce the tango's ironic, bittersweet message, projecting the ideas that will soon find expression in arched bodies and flashing legs.

11. According to the author, what makes "Tango Argentino" satisfying entertainment?
   (1) the moods created by the combination of dance, music, and song
   (2) the interesting *bandoneón* instruments
   (3) the ethnic backgrounds of the orchestra
   (4) the idea of silhouetting the orchestra on stage
   (5) the presence of the two planners, Segovia and Orezzoli

12. Which of the following details does the author use to support the belief that music is of central importance to the tango?
   (1) Segovia and Orezzoli decided to put on a show called "Tango Argentino."
   (2) Bandoneones are musical instruments that resemble accordions.
   (3) Four men are required to play the bandoneones.
   (4) Tango dancers arch their bodies and kick their legs in a highly dramatic way.
   (5) Segovia and Orezzoli got the best tango musicians for their show.

Items 13–14 refer to the following passage.

How did the author feel about Mrs. Cullinan?

Mrs. Viola Cullinan was a plump woman who lived in a three-bedroom house somewhere behind the post office. She was singularly unattractive until she smiled, and then the lines around her eyes and mouth which made her look perpetually dirty disappeared, and her face looked like the mask of an impish elf. She usually rested her smile until late afternoon when her women friends dropped in and Miss Glory, the cook, served them cold drinks on the closed-in porch.

The exactness of her house was inhuman. This glass went here and only here. That cup had its place and it was an act of impudent rebellion to place it anywhere else. At twelve o'clock the table was set. At 12:15 Mrs. Cullinan sat down to dinner (whether her husband had arrived or not). At 12:16 Miss Glory brought out the food.

It took me a week to learn the difference between a salad plate, a bread plate and a dessert plate.

Mrs. Cullinan kept up the tradition of her wealthy parents. She was from Virginia. Miss Glory, who was a descendant of slaves that had worked for the Cullinans, told me her history. She had married beneath her (according to Miss Glory). Her husband's family hadn't had their money very long and what they had "didn't 'mount to much."

13. Which of the following conclusions could be drawn about Mrs. Viola Cullinan's character?

    (1) She was generous with her family's wealth.
    (2) She was warm only with friends.
    (3) She was inhuman.
    (4) She had a wonderful, impish sense of humor.
    (5) She was bitter about her husband's absences.

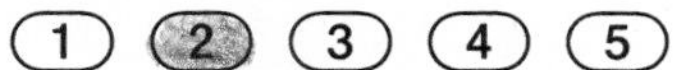

14. From the author's description, which of the following would Mrs. Cullinan probably be LEAST likely to do?

    (1) be ready for dinner on time
    (2) expect to have servants
    (3) enjoy a cool drink on the porch
    (4) insist on having the silverware polished
    (5) misplace a prized family heirloom

Items 15–20 refer to the following passage from a play.

How well does Anna like her job?

CARRIE. *(as she hears Anna moving about in the kitchen).* That you, Anna?

ANNA. *(her voice).* Just got home.

CARRIE. Hot.

ANNA. Paper says a storm.

CARRIE. I know. I'll take the plants in.

ANNA. I just put them out. Let them have a little storm air.

CARRIE. I don't like them out in a storm. Worries me. I don't like storms. I don't believe plants do, either.

ANNA. *(appears in the living room with a broom and dust rag; speaks out toward the porch).* Did you have a hard day?

CARRIE. He let me leave the office after lunch. "You're looking a little peaked, Miss Berniers, from the heat." I said I've been looking a little peaked for years in heat, in cold, in rain, when I was young and now. You mean *you're* hot and want to go home, you faker, I said. I said it to myself.

ANNA. We had a private sale at the store, coats. Coats on a day like this. There was a very good bargain, red with black braid. I had my eye on it for you all last winter. But—

CARRIE. Oh, I don't need a coat.

ANNA. Yes, you do. Did you go to the park? I wanted to, but the sale went so late. Old lady Senlis and old lady Condelet just sat there, looking at everything, even small coats. How can rich people go to a sale on a day like this?

CARRIE. I feel sorry for them. For all old ladies. Even rich ones. Money makes them lonely.

ANNA. *(laughs).* Why would that be?

CARRIE. Don't you feel sorry for old ladies? You used to.

ANNA. When my feet don't hurt and I don't have to sell them coats at a sale. Was it nice in the park?

CARRIE. I didn't go to the park. I went to the cemetery.

ANNA. *(stops dusting, sighs).* Everybody still there?

CARRIE. I took flowers. It's cool there. Cooler. I was the only person there. Nobody goes to see anybody in summer.

15. How do Anna and Carrie appear to be feeling?

    (1) angry and hostile with each other
    (2) tired and uncomfortable from the heat
    (3) resentful of their hard lives
    (4) lonely
    (5) full of good humor

16. When Carrie responds to Anna by saying only "Hot," what does she mean?

    (1) Are you hot?
    (2) Good!
    (3) The weather is very hot.
    (4) I just touched something hot.
    (5) I wish the weather would get hot.

    1 2 3 4 5

17. Why does Carrie suspect that her employer let her go home early?

    (1) because she appeared ill
    (2) because she had completed her work
    (3) so that he could leave too
    (4) because a storm was coming
    (5) so that she could visit the cemetery

    1 2 3 4 5

18. Anna believes she would be more sympathetic to rich, lonely, elderly women if

    (1) they would be more sympathetic to her
    (2) they weren't so very rich
    (3) she weren't tired and working so hard
    (4) she were also rich
    (5) they weren't so rude at sales

    1 2 3 4 5

19. After Carrie left work, she visited the cemetery. What did Anna, in contrast, do?

    (1) visited a relative
    (2) went to the park
    (3) purchased a coat
    (4) began housecleaning
    (5) took flowers to a friend

20. The author has Carrie say, "You faker, I said. I said it to myself," in order to show that she

    (1) did not want to hurt her employer's feelings
    (2) wasn't sure she was correct
    (3) was too hot to speak up
    (4) knew her employer wouldn't listen anyway
    (5) was afraid to let her employer know her thoughts

    1 2 3 4 5

Minitest Answers

Minitest 1
(pages 137–141)

1. (2) The passage mentions that after a hard winter Mr. Belli "felt in need of" exercise and fresh air. Also he would like to be able to tell his daughters he had visited their mother's grave. His older daughter apparently felt he didn't seem to mind being single now that his wife had died.

2. (3) The passage describes Mrs. Belli as "a woman of many natures, most of them trying." The word *trying* in this context means "challenging or difficult." Apparently, Mrs. Belli was hard to live with.

3. (2) The last line says the poet wants to see "the cherry hung with snow." He is comparing the white cherry blossoms to snow.

4. (2) The poet works through a complicated thought process. The poet says he's already 20 years old. Since the average person lives "threescore years and ten," or 70 years, the poet has only 50 more years to enjoy the beauty of spring cherry blossoms. Therefore, the mood is thoughtful.

5. (1) In the second paragraph, Ogilvy notices an ashy substance covering the "meteorite." Later, he discovers that "the Thing" is more than a meteorite.

6. (5) The expression means that Ogilvy is so startled that he feels as if his heart has popped into his mouth.

7. (4) Ogilvy's actions show that he is a curious man because he moves down into the pit to examine "the Thing" more closely.

8. (3) The author very carefully helps you sense the suspense of the moment with his detailed descriptions of the eerie silence and the slow, unexplained movement of the strange object.

9. (4) The topic of the passage is the handicapped boy. The details point out that the narrator tried to help him and the father resented that attempt.

10. (4) The father claims, rather gruffly, that helping the boy will "make him weak."

11. (4) Ed seems confused about how to open the cash register. Because he is confused and ill at ease, he speaks abruptly and a little impatiently.

12. (2) The youth's menacing manner and his questions ("You all alone?"), in addition to reaching for something in his pocket, all suggest that he may be planning a robbery.

13. (1) Using a process of elimination can help you select the best answer. Options (2)–(5) are too narrow; they do not refer to all the important ideas that the review (not just the plot of the movie) includes.

14. (4) The passage says that Gordon's voice sounds like "rocks in a blender"—of course, that would produce a rough sound.

15. (4) The reviewer comments on the excellent music in the film, but he adds that a person does not need to be a jazz fan to enjoy it.

Minitest 2
(pages 142–145)

1. (5) According to the author's description, Bullard loves more than anything to have someone to listen to him.

2. (4) Because he talked for a full hour about himself, you can tell that Bullard was so preoccupied with himself that he didn't care to hear anything about other people.

3. (5) According to the passage, Lincoln had—at least until the assassination attempt—felt confident that he did not need to take any measures to protect himself: "I have always thought you an idiot for your apprehensions of my personal danger." He would probably have refused a bodyguard.

4. (1) Even when an attempt was made on his life, Lincoln was able to see humor in the situation and tell the story as a joke.

5. (4) Jody is overwhelmed with excitement and joy at the sight of the colt. His short breath is a result of this strong emotion.

6. (1) Carl Tiflin has given the pony as a gift to his son. Yet he can't express his loving feelings himself, so he hides his emotions with gruffness by ordering his son about ("Come here!") and leaving the scene embarrassed.

7. (1) Twice Jody asks whether the horse is his.

8. (2) The words "ingenious," "rich effects," "astounding," "sophisticated," and "fun" help you see that the reviewer is enthusiastic about Graves's sculptures.

9. (2) The first paragraph explains that Nancy Graves makes molds out of items from nature and pours molten bronze into them to create the shapes of nature; then she combines those with parts of manmade objects.

10. (3) The words "a clot stopped my heart" indicate that the speaker in the poem had a heart attack.

11. (3) The speaker is haunted by the thought that the heart of a dead child beats in his chest.

12. (2) Surprisingly, the speaker doesn't seem especially grateful for the donated heart. But he also does not seem humorous, hostile, or confused. He is, instead, preoccupied with the thought of the transplanted heart and the child donor.

13. (2) Osborne's story tells how a German officer allowed enemy English troops to carry a wounded man into a dugout. That tends to support the conclusion that even enemies can show compassion during wartime.

14. (4) Osborne tells a story about how enemies acted quite civil one day and then shot heavily at each other the next day.

15. (3) Raleigh's comment "How topping!" is British slang, but you can tell from the context that he approves of the German officer's action.

Minitest 3
(pages 146–150)

1. (3) The woman could not feel love for anybody ("she always felt the center of her heart go hard"). That troubled her, and so she hid her coldness by pretending to be very loving and kind to her children.

2. (5) The narrator states that the family "felt themselves superior to" their neighbors. In other words, they were rather snobbish, and that helped them hide their problems from themselves.

3. (2) While the narrator does not openly criticize the mother, he suggests that she was shallow and snobbish. His attitude is not openly hostile, but it is gently disapproving.

4. (4) The mother compares life to a staircase to illustrate that her life has not been smooth and pleasant but an "uphill" struggle. It has been rough and hazardous. Then she comments that she has kept on climbing stairs—that is, she has kept on going, even through difficult times.

5. (4) The mother says, "Don't you turn back/Don't you set down." She is urging her son to keep on working toward his goal, even when life is difficult.

6. (2) The passage explains that the Nightingales were wealthy and socially influential. "Of high degree" refers to Florence Nightingale's high social standing.

7. (3) The topic of the paragraph is Florence Nightingale. The details all point out that the public tends to think of her as a delicate, self-sacrificing woman, but the real Florence Nightingale was quite different from that idea.

8. (1) In lines 36–39 the author comments that Florence Nightingale was expected to carry out her social "duty" to marry an eligible gentleman.

9. (3) The author's description points out that Nightingale seemed to be possessed by a demon. In other words, she was obssessed by a goal she wanted to achieve.

10. (4) The author's style in the passage is restrained and dignified; it would probably be appropriate for a former president but not for movie stars, singers, and other celebrities.

11. (1) The answer is found in the second paragraph. The review mentions that the music has a variety of different moods, and that this variety makes "Tango Argentino" a fulfilling evening.

12. (5) If music is of central importance, then the planners of the show would naturally want the best musicians. The other options are details from the passage, but they don't necessarily support the idea about the music.

13. (2) The author says that Mrs. Cullinan usually "rested her smile" until her friends came. That comment suggests that she wasn't particularly friendly with anyone else.

14. (5) The second paragraph describes Mrs. Cullinan's insistence on following a schedule and keeping everything in place. She also valued her family traditions. She would be unlikely to lose a family heirloom.

15. (2) Several comments in the play point out how hot the weather is. Anna mentions how tired she is after working at the coat sale.

16. (3) Carrie's line is simply an abbreviated way of saying how hot the weather is.

17. (3) Carrie says that the boss really wanted to leave the office himself ("You mean *you're* hot and want to go home").

18. (3) Anna says she feels sorry for lonely old ladies only when her feet don't hurt and she doesn't have to sell them coats.

19. (4) The stage directions explain that Anna picks up a broom and dust rag to do housecleaning.

20. (5) Carrie's rather brave but dangerous words are startling until she admits that she didn't say them aloud. She would naturally be afraid to call her employer a faker because he could fire her.

The GED Writing Skills Test

Shopping lists, notes, phone messages, postcards, greeting cards, letters, résumés—even if you feel you haven't "written anything" since you left school, everyday life has probably given you experiences that you can now use to build your skills upon as you study for the GED Writing Skills Test.

The GED Writing Skills Test is made up of two parts: a multiple-choice test, like the other GED tests, and an essay that you write on a specific topic. Many people are quite afraid of having to write the essay, but actually the multiple-choice questions account for a larger percentage of the final score.

The multiple-choice section of the GED Writing Skills Test is called the Conventions of English because it deals with the standard rules, or conventions, that are generally agreed to apply to formal English. In it you will read about six passages from ten to twelve sentences long. Each passage will be followed by eight to ten multiple-choice items that ask you to spot errors or choose the best way to rewrite sentences. You will be given 75 minutes to complete this section of the test. There are 55 items in all, and they cover these areas of the conventions of English:

Sentence Structure 35%
Usage 35%
Mechanics (capitalization, punctuation, spelling) 30%

For the essay, you will be given a specific topic and asked to write about 200 words about it; you will not have a choice in the matter. (This is actually a help to you because you won't waste time worrying about which topic to pick.) The topic will be a general subject that adults know about. Special knowledge or research will not be needed—just good thinking and writing skills. You will be given scratch paper to plan your essay and a total of 45 minutes to produce a completed one.

The *Writing Skills* section of this book will help you prepare for both sections of the GED Writing Skills Test. In the first part you will learn about writing down your ideas using good sentences. You'll be given a chance to practice both writing your own ideas and feelings and recognizing written errors in passages like those on the GED Test. Unless instructed otherwise, always read the tinted inner column on a page before you go to the practice test items in the white column. The passages in the white columns will be shorter than those on the actual test and the errors will be limited. That will give you a chance to practice what you've just studied in the tinted column as well as review material from previous tinted columns. When you go on to take the Minitests at the end of this section, you'll be able to try your skills on actual GED-length passages and a true mix of items.

In the second and third parts you can apply what you know about writing down your ideas to writing first paragraphs and then essays. The white columns in the essay section will give you topics to write about. By doing the Warm-up exercises in the tinted columns and the essay assignments in the white columns, you'll go far in increasing your chances of passing the GED Test.

The Conventions of English Test When you take the first part of the GED Writing Skills Test, you'll have to read several long passages and then answer different kinds of multiple-choice questions about them. The following is the kind of passage you will find.

> (1) Buying a home computer requires some serious thought on a consumer's part. (2) Of course, cost is always a major factor, but you must also consider one's needs. (3) You may be planning, to use the computer to budget your personal finances. (4) In that case, a computer's ability to create Graphics should be part of your consideration. (5) If you want the computer to help you write letters or reports, the cost and quality of a printer must be taken into account. (6) Or perhaps only a sophisticated toy for playing computer games is all that is wanted. (7) Whatever your needs, they must play a major role in your desision. (8) In addition, the programs you want must be able to be used with the particular computer you plan to buy. (9) In computer language, that means to make sure the software are compatible with the hardware. (10) Finally, even the best computer can be worth nothing to you. (11) It will be worthless if you cannot use it. (12) A manual that is easy to understand and your willingness to spend the time required to read and understand it are key factors to keep in mind.

Here is one kind of test item that could follow this passage. In this kind of item, the options can cover all the different areas—sentence structure, usage, capitalization, punctuation, and spelling—covered on the GED Test.

Sentence 2: **Of course, cost is always a major factor, but you must also consider one's needs.**

What correction should be made to this sentence?

(1) change the spelling of course to coarse
(2) remove the comma after course
(3) change major to Major
(4) insert a comma after but
(5) replace one's with your

   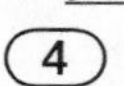 

To answer this question, look at each option and decide whether the change must be made. *Course* is spelled correctly in the sentence. The comma is needed after *course* because the phrase *of course* interrupts the message of the sentence and would be followed by a pause if spoken. The word *major* should not be capitalized in this sentence, and a comma is needed before *but* but not after it in this type of sentence. However, the word *one's* does not match the word *you,* which occurs earlier in the sentence. You should use *your* with *you* and *one's* with *one,* so option (5) is correct.

This item required that you take into account one part of the sentence to know how to fix another part. One or two items with each passage on the GED Test will also require you to take into account the entire passage in order to answer the item.

Half the items on the conventions test will be like the test item just discussed. Often the fifth option in such an item will be "no correction is necessary." And sometimes that will be the correct answer. And *no* sentence will ever have more than one mistake.

Here's a second kind of item that could be used with the passage about computers.

Sentence 5: **If you want the computer to help you write letters or reports, the cost and quality of a printer must be taken into account.**

Which of the following is the best way to write the underlined portion of this sentence? If you think the original is the best way, choose option (1).

(1) reports, the
(2) reports the
(3) reports. The
(4) reports; the
(5) reports, and the

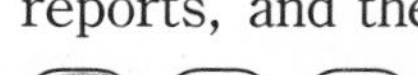  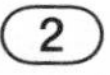  

With an item like this, option (1) is always the same as in the passage. In that sense it is very much like the option "no correction is necessary." In the sample item above option (1) is right because the sentence is correct as written. A comma is the correct mark of punctuation to use between the two parts of the sentence. But always check the other options before marking your answer. You may be overlooking something and not realize it until you read another option.

A third kind of test item can look like this.

Sentence 6: **Or perhaps only a sophisticated toy for playing computer games is all that is wanted.**

If you rewrote sentence 6 beginning with

Or perhaps you

the next word(s) should be

(1) play
(2) are playing
(3) are sophisticated
(4) want
(5) have wanted

This kind of item does not actually have an error in the original sentence, but it is written in a poor, sometimes wordy, often unclear, way. You have to figure the best way to make the sentence clearer.

How do you do that? First reconstruct the sentence in your mind before you look at the options. If the sentence began "Or perhaps you," what information from the original sentence would you need to complete the new sentence in a clear way *and* have it mean the same as the original? You're not necessarily looking for the same words; instead, you're trying to choose words that have the same *meaning.* So instead of writing "only a sophisticated toy . . . is wanted," you'd probably write "you want only a sophisticated toy. . . ." The rewritten sentence would be "Or perhaps you want only a sophisticated toy for playing computer games." Option (4) is the answer.

☑ A Test-Taking Tip

Always think through very carefully each option on a multiple-choice item on the GED Test. If, however, you've thought and thought and still can't determine the right answer, don't be afraid to guess. You won't be penalized for wrong guesses.

Finally, here's a fourth kind of GED item. In this kind of item you will be asked to choose the best way to fix two awkward sentences by combining them.

Sentences 10 and 11: **Finally, even the best computer can be worth nothing to you. It will be worthless if you cannot use it.**

The most effective combination of sentences 10 and 11 would include which of the following groups of words?

(1) Finally, it can be worth nothing
(2) Finally, even the best computer will be worthless if
(3) can be worthless, and it
(4) Even the best computer cannot be used
(5) will be worthless and be worth nothing

To answer a question like that, combine the sentences in your head *before* you look at the options. When you combine sentences, you take the necessary information from the first sentence and from the second sentence and then combine them in one smooth, concise, easy-to-understand sentence.

The important information from the first sentence is "Finally, even the best computer . . ." From the second sentence it is "will be worthless if you cannot use it." The two parts that were dropped—"can be worth nothing to you" and "It"—simply report information that has been expressed in other words. So the most effective combination would be "Finally, even the best computer will be worthless if you cannot use it." Option (2) is the correct answer.

There are four more errors in the passage on the computer. Did you spot them as you were reading? If not, can you find them now? List them on the lines below.

Sentence ____: ____________________

Sentence ____: ____________________

Sentence ____: ____________________

Sentence ____: ____________________

Pages 159–196 in this section will give you a chance to strengthen your skill at writing, correcting, and revising sentences like those on the conventions test.

Answers
Sentence 3: remove the comma after *planning*
Sentence 4: *graphics* should not be capitalized
Sentence 7: *desision* should be spelled *decision*
Sentence 9: *are* should be *is*

The Essay Test After you've taken the test of English conventions, you'll get a chance to express your ideas about a certain topic in an essay. You'll be given the topic along with a set of directions telling you to write about 200 words and to plan your essay carefully, write it, and then revise it. Scratch paper or blank pages in the test booklet will be available for you to make notes and plan what you want to write. There will be a separate answer sheet for your actual essay. After 45 minutes, you'll be asked to turn in your completed essay.

Your essay will then be holistically scored. That means that two scorers will take turns reading your essay very quickly among many other GED candidates' essays. They won't look for errors but will instead judge your essay on the overall impression they get from their rapid reading of it. They will compare it in their heads to model papers that have been assigned scores from 1 to 6. The worst paper is scored 1, the best 6. (Note that the highest score is *not* a *perfect* paper; it is merely the best of the lot.) Each scorer will then rate your paper on that same scale. Scores of 1 to 3 mean that the paper is in the lower half; scores of 4 to 6 put it in the upper half. A score of 0 will be given to an essay that is written on a topic that was not assigned, to an essay that cannot be read because of bad handwriting, and, of course, to a blank sheet of paper.

Each scorer will be unaware of how the other scorer rated your essay. Their two scores will be added. Your total essay score will then be weighted in relation to your score on the conventions test, and the two will be added and reported to you as *one* score.

☑ A Test-Taking Tip

As you write your essay, keep in mind who will be reading it. The two holistic scorers do not know you, so you'll need to be precise and explain each of your ideas clearly.

So how do you prepare to write a good essay to help your chances of passing the entire GED Writing Skills Test? First, you must be prepared to write, write, write. Be sure to complete all the Warm-up exercises and as many of the essay assignments in this section as you can. Buy a notebook or a folder with pads of paper that you can use to write all your sentences, paragraphs, and essays in. It will be satisfying to look at your collected writings at the end of this section and see how far you've come.

One thing you will soon learn, however, is that there is usually no one, right way to write. Writing is creative and personal; your thoughts are your own, and your way of expressing them is your own. So absolute answers to many of the exercises in this book cannot really be given. Instead, you'll find sample answers that you can use as guides. In addition, it is a good idea to have someone work with you to help check your writing. If you're taking a GED class, your teacher, of course, will be a great help. But if you're studying on your own, try to think of someone who can read your writing: your spouse, a close friend, a coworker, your boss, a teacher in your neighborhood, or perhaps a librarian. The person should be someone who is a good writer, not just someone who knows you and likes you.

Another way to help you learn to write a good essay is to arm yourself with a dictionary and a thesaurus as you work through this section. A dictionary will give you all sorts of useful information about words—what they mean, how to spell them, where they came from, and how to use them to convey different ideas. A thesaurus will show you different words to use to mean similar ideas. And words and ideas will be, after all, the building blocks of your essay.

In addition, you may want to get one or two books on grammar from your library or local bookstore. The librarian or store clerk should be able to recommend some. Such books will be a guide to all the points of standard English that serve as a foundation for your writing. They will also be a tremendous help if your spoken English is a *dialect,* a special form of English that is not standard. Speaking and writing are not the same. On the GED Writing Skills Test, you will need to use Standard English as it is accepted and agreed to be; you cannot write exactly as you speak. So if you talk using nonstandard phrases such as "He be sick today" instead of "He is sick today," "Sam brung it" instead of "Sam brought it," or "My brother, he can't come" instead of "My brother can't come," be sure to get a good grammar book. You can use the Warm-up exercises to see whether you need to study standard English.

These tools—the *Writing Skills* section of this book, your own writing notebook, a dictionary, a thesaurus, and possibly a grammar book—will help you prepare yourself to write a successful GED essay.

Writing Down Your Ideas

Writing Complete Sentences Artists show subjects in pictures. An artist drew this picture of a writer called Dan. Dan is jogging.

Writing is much like putting together pictures. For each sentence you select a **subject** (who or what the sentence is about, like *Dan* or *writer*) and show the subject doing something *(is jogging).* The word that shows what the subject is doing is called the **verb.** Two **complete sentences** you could write about this picture are *Dan is jogging* and *The writer is jogging.* On the GED Writing Skills Test, you'll have to recognize and write complete sentences. Complete sentences always have a subject and verb. They are always complete thoughts.

You may have noticed that the verb *is jogging* has two words. Verbs can have one to four words.

runs can condition had exercised

has been strengthened

may have been training

Sentences can be as varied as pictures, and they are limited only by the range of your thoughts and imagination. You can mix and match an endless number of subjects and verbs to create complete sentences.

You can write one kind of sentence that doesn't seem to have a subject.

■ Go running a little earlier today.

This complete sentence really means "You go running a little earlier today." But you don't have to state the subject, *you,* in this kind of command.

Coming to Terms

subject who or what a sentence is about
verb the word that tells what a subject does
complete sentence a complete thought with a subject and verb

The following subjects and verbs have to do with Dan's picture. In a notebook, write complete sentences by matching up the subjects and verbs. You may need to add a word or two to a subject, such as *the, a,* or *his.*

Subjects	**Verbs**
1. Dan	should train
2. woman	might trip
3. notebook	is soaked
4. T-shirt	has been filled

Now write a few complete sentences of your own about Dan's picture or about jogging. Be sure each has a subject and a verb.

Adding Information If you want to make your ideas clear and interesting, you will often have to add details to your sentences. *The woman should train,* for example, isn't very interesting or informative. *Dan might trip* is a better example, but a reader might like to know *why* Dan might trip. When you write, think about the person who will read your writing. Your reader can't see the picture in your mind or ask for more information. These sentences give better pictures.

■ The woman should train for the upcoming track meet.

Dan might trip on that untied shoelace.

Add details to the ends of sentences 3 and 4 you wrote above. Then rewrite all of the sentences.

Revising Incomplete Sentences Here's a common mistake you may make when adding information: *More people are running. In the morning.*

In the morning has no subject or verb. It is an incomplete sentence. If you write one of these, you need to fix, or *revise,* it. You can attach it to the sentence to form one complete sentence.

■ More people are running *in the morning.*

Sample Answers 1
1. Dan might trip. **2.** The woman should train. **3.** That notebook has been filled. **4.** His T-shirt is soaked.

Sample Answers 2
3. That notebook has been filled with Dan's writing. **4.** His T-shirt is soaked through with perspiration.

Some incomplete sentences have a subject but no verb: *That open manhole up ahead.* To fix an incomplete sentence like this, add a verb.

■ That open manhole *is* up ahead.

Other incomplete sentences have a verb but no subject: *Got some new ankle weights.* Add a subject to this kind of incomplete sentence.

■ *I* got some new ankle weights.

Sometimes you may leave out words from verbs; for example, *She been running an hour* or *I seen Julio at the gym.* These are also incomplete sentences. You can revise them by adding the missing words in the verbs.

■ She ***has*** *been running* an hour.

I ***have*** *seen* Julio at the gym.

Sometimes when you combine an incomplete sentence with a complete one, you need to reword. For example, suppose you've written *Running. It is so boring.* Rewrite it like this.

■ Running is so boring.

When you add an incomplete sentence to the front of a complete sentence, you should usually add a comma. Look at how to combine *During the winter? Only fanatics jog then.*

■ During the winter**,** only fanatics jog.

The passage below contains several incomplete sentences. Rewrite the passage, revising these sentences.

■ Jogging. It's a popular sport. Since the mid-'60s. Millions of Americans taken it up. A weight problem started me jogging. Like being outdoors too. Helps relieve stress. Doesn't take much equipment. All I need is loose clothing. And good running shoes.

What do you think of regular exercise? Write a few sentences about your opinion. Revise any incomplete sentences you may write.

Separating Run-ons You'll find that the following passage has sentences that are crammed together. Confusing sentences like these are called *run-on sentences.*

■ People don't enjoy reading two sentences crammed together it's confusing. Run-ons also sound bad to the ear try to fix them. You need to vary the rhythm of your sentences you should put in punctuation to break them up. Run-on sentences are easy to correct many people don't know how.

You will see run-ons like those above in GED multiple-choice questions, and you may accidentally write run-ons in your essay. One way you can fix a run-on is with a period. Remember to capitalize after the period.

■ People don't enjoy reading two sentences crammed together**. I**t's confusing.

Sometimes, however, you end up with choppy-sounding sentences when you fix run-ons with periods. In such cases, you can use a semicolon (;) if the sentences are closely related.

■ Run-ons also sound bad to the ear**;** try to fix them.

Or you can insert a semicolon with a connecting word such as *consequently, furthermore, however, moreover, nevertheless,* or *therefore.* Put a comma after the connecting word.

■ You need to vary the rhythm of your sentences; *furthermore,* you should put in punctuation to break them up.

Or you can put in a comma followed by a connecting word like *and, but, for, nor,* or *yet.*

■ Run-on sentences are easy to correct, *but* many people don't know how.

Separate the run-ons in the following passage in one of the ways you just read about. Rewrite your revised passage in your notebook.

■ My whole house is overdone it's not like other houses. The living room has overstuffed pillows don't miss the overstuffed armchairs in the den. The kitchen cupboards are overstuffed the kitchen counters are always loaded. The clutter makes me nervous I can't easily get over stuff.

Now write three or four sentences describing where *you* live. Check your sentences to make sure none has run-ons.

Sample Answer

Jogging is a popular sport. Since the mid-'60s, millions of Americans have taken it up. A weight problem started me jogging. I like being outdoors too. It helps relieve stress. Jogging doesn't take much equipment. All I need is loose clothing and good running shoes.

Sample Answer

My whole house is overdone; it's not like other houses. The living room has overstuffed pillows**, and** don't miss the overstuffed armchairs in the den. The kitchen cupboards are overstuffed; **consequently,** the kitchen counters are always loaded. The clutter makes me nervous, **so** I can't easily get over stuff.

Relating Ideas A GED student wanted to avoid choppy sentences by joining two complete yet related sentences. But, she didn't use a logical connecting word.

- Track meets are fun, *so* they are exciting.

So means that one thing happens because of another. At track meets, excitement and fun go hand in hand. The student can make this relationship clear by using *and* or *moreover,* which mean "in addition to."

- Track meets are fun, *and* they are exciting.

  Track meets are fun; *moreover,* they are exciting.

Did the student use *consequently,* which is used to show a result, correctly?

- We get hot in the bleachers; *consequently,* cool drinks are always on sale.

The student wants to say that fans have an alternative to the heat: cool drinks. She could use *but* or *however* to show alternatives.

- We get hot in the bleachers, *but* cool drinks are always on sale.

  We get hot in the bleachers; *however,* cool drinks are always on sale.

☑ A Test-Taking Tip

A common mistake that is tested on the GED Test is to use just a comma between two otherwise complete sentences. A comma alone is too weak for that job. You need a connecting word in addition to the comma between sentences.

Warm-up

Rewrite these sentences. Replace connecting words that are illogical. Revise complete sentences joined by commas.

- The kids loved the pole vaulters. The runway sprint takes speed, the jump takes strength. The vaulters clear that bar so gracefully, yet they can jump almost twenty feet. We all shut our eyes at the landings, the athletes don't seem worried. Someone brave might try the jump, for I'm not that brave.

Write about a sport you watch. See if you can join any sentences that have related ideas.

Sample Warm-up Answer

The kids loved the pole vaulters. The runway sprint takes speed, *and* the jump takes strength. The vaulters clear that bar so gracefully; *moreover,* they can jump almost twenty feet. We all shut our eyes at the landings, *yet* the athletes don't seem worried. Someone brave might try the jump, but I'm not that brave.

Directions: For each item, choose the answer that would result in the most effective writing. Answers are on page 220.

(1) Herbal teas are very popular these days. (2) Black tea is not an ingredient in such teas, so they don't contain caffeine. (3) Herbal teas are delicate and light in color, they are a special blend of natural ingredients. (4) They combine spices, plant leaves, seeds, roots, and flowers this blend gives them a flowery or spicy aroma.

1. Sentence 2: **Black tea is not an ingredient in such teas, so they don't contain caffeine.**

   What correction should be made to this sentence?

   (1) remove the word is
   (2) remove the comma after teas
   (3) remove the word so
   (4) replace so with yet
   (5) no correction is necessary

2. Sentence 3: **Herbal teas are delicate and light in color, they are a special blend of natural ingredients.**

   Which of the following is the best way to write the underlined portion of this sentence? If you think the original is the best way, choose option (1).

   (1) color, they (2) color they
   (3) color; nevertheless, they
   (4) color, or they (5) color, for they

3. Sentence 4: **They combine spices, plant leaves, seeds, roots, and flowers this blend gives them a flowery or spicy aroma.**

   Which of the following is the best way to write the underlined portion of this sentence? If you think the original is the best way, choose option (1).

   (1) flowers this
   (2) flowers; this
   (3) flowers and this
   (4) flowers but this
   (5) flowers; and,

Directions: For each item, choose the answer that would result in the most effective writing. Answers are on page 220.

(1) Do you suffer from extreme fatigue from carrying enormous amounts of camera equipment along on your vacation? (2) You can save yourself from all that aggravation. (3) By buying a videocassette as a record of your trip. (4) The Smithsonian Institution has them, the National Park Service has them, and soon most major tourist attractions will have them. (5) Many Americans own video-playing devices, these people are the prime market for souvenir tapes of all descriptions.

4. Sentences 2 and 3: **You can save yourself from all that aggravation. By buying a videocassette as a record of your trip.**

   Which of the following is the best way to write the underlined portion of these sentences? If you think the original is the best way, choose option (1).

   (1) aggravation. By buying
   (2) aggravation; by buying
   (3) aggravation by buying
   (4) aggravation, so buy
   (5) aggravation, and by buying

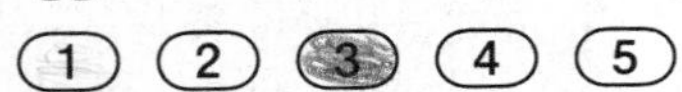

5. Sentence 5: **Many Americans own video-playing devices, these people are the prime market for souvenir tapes of all descriptions.**

   What correction should be made to this sentence?

   (1) remove the comma after devices
   (2) insert and before these
   (3) change the spelling of people to peeple
   (4) change the spelling of descriptions to decriptions
   (5) no correction is necessary

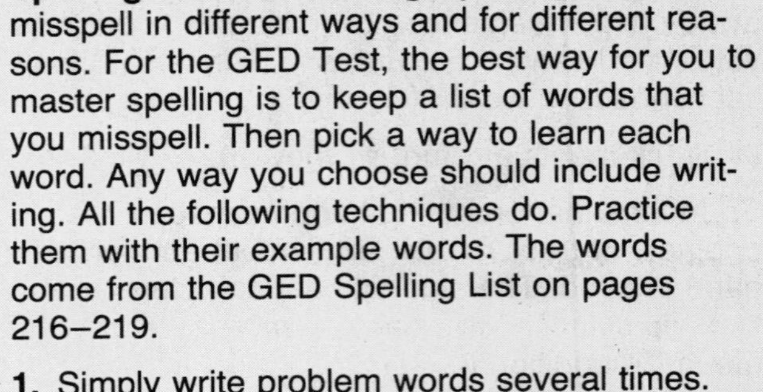

Spelling Break/Mastering Spelling Writers misspell in different ways and for different reasons. For the GED Test, the best way for you to master spelling is to keep a list of words that you misspell. Then pick a way to learn each word. Any way you choose should include writing. All the following techniques do. Practice them with their example words. The words come from the GED Spelling List on pages 216–219.

1. Simply write problem words several times.

argument, awkward, bicycle, exercise, rhythm

2. With the help of a dictionary, write long, difficult words in parts.

mis-cel-la-neous sym-met-ri-cal

3. Have someone read words aloud while you write them. You can also tape words and write them as you play back the tape.

knowledge several mischievous

4. Group similar words. Practice them together.

auth**or**/doct**or**/counsel**or**
although/**al**together/**al**ways
pre**cede**/re**cede**
pro**ceed**/suc**ceed**

5. Write sentences with spelling words. When necessary, look up meanings in a dictionary.

Katie's home **remedy** cured my hiccups.

Santa Ana had the Alamo under **siege.**

6. In one or more sentences, write similar spelling words.

Who cares **whether** the **weather** will be good?

The **stationery** is in the desk. The desks are **stationary;** they can't be moved.

7. In one or more sentences, write different forms of words.

Andy is the **twelfth** of **twelve** children!

Why don't you **decide?** The **decision** is yours, not mine. **Decisive,** you're not.

Warm-up

Use any spelling technique to master these words from the GED Spelling List.

acquaintance, descend, descent, eight, efficiency, efficient, dilemma, formal, exaggeration, predictable, former, sweet, embarrassment, peculiar, studying, weigh, Wednesday, pertain, sweat

Spelling Break/Plurals Some words, like *corporal* and *brake,* refer to only one person or thing. These words are singular. Other words, like *corporal***s** and *brake***s,** show more than one person or thing. These words are plural. You can often change singulars to plurals just by adding *-s.* But some words follow other rules. Here are the spelling rules for plurals.

1. Add *-s* to most words: invitation/invitation**s;** advantage/advantage**s.**

2. When words end in *-ch, -s, -sh, -x,* or *-z,* add *-es:* busines**s**/ business**es;** bu**sh**/ bush**es.**

3. When words end in *o,* add *-es:* potat**o**/ potato**es.**

4. When words end in *-f,* change the *-f* to *-v* before you add *-es:* loa**f**/loa**ves.**

5. When words end in *-y,* change the *-y* to *-i* before you add *-es:* compan**y**/compan**ies.**

6. When words end in *-ay* or *-ey,* add only *-s:* vall**ey**/valley**s.**

You'll find some plurals are unusual. For example, you'll need to change the basic spellings of some plural words: emphas**is**/emphas**es**.

And some words just don't follow any rule: chie**f**/chief**s;** handkerchie**f**/handkerchief**s.**

Warm-up

Rewrite these sentences. Make each *italicized* word plural.

1. Sports *hero* or not, go empty the trash.
2. Jeffrey asked the *policeman* for directions.
3. I'd like to get your *address.*
4. My doctor specializes in heart *disease.*
5. Enrique doesn't like the *arrangement.*
6. Who likes Margaret's *approach* to the problem?
7. If you want *controversy,* look at the news.
8. Here is my boss's *analysis* of the guy she hired: experienced, self-starting, good prospect.
9. The grocer cut the watermelons in *half.*
10. The whistle blew; the *holiday* had begun.

Now think of anything that you have a lot of, like dishes, weeds, friends, problems, or spelling words. Write a few sentences about your topic. Use as many plurals as you can.

Warm-up Answers
1. heroes **2.** policemen **3.** addresses **4.** diseases **5.** arrangements **6.** approaches **7.** controversies **8.** analyses **9.** halves **10.** holidays

(1) Recently, I heard many speeches given at a "Stop World Hunger" benefit I found them especially moving. (2) Two speakers offered very vivid analyses of several recent famines and I felt the need to help. (3) I made a small contribution to buy twelve loafs of bread; this donation would help feed a family of four for two weeks. (4) Many other people in the audience responded to the speakers' pleas by making donations too. (5) We all felt that we had done something positive to help feed these hungry people.

6. Sentence 1: **Recently, I heard many speeches given at a "Stop World Hunger" benefit I found them especially moving.**

   What correction should be made to this sentence?

   (1) change the spelling of speeches to speechs
   (2) change the spelling of benefit to benifit
   (3) insert a comma after benefit
   (4) insert a period after benefit
   (5) no correction is necessary

7. Sentence 2: **Two speakers offered very vivid analyses of several recent famines and I felt the need to help.**

   What correction should be made to this sentence?

   (1) change the spelling of analyses to analysises
   (2) change the spelling of several to sevral
   (3) insert a comma after famines
   (4) remove the word and
   (5) remove the word I

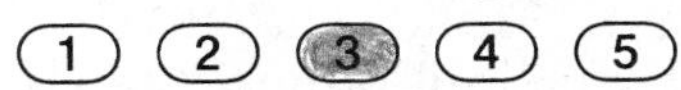

8. Sentence 3: **I made a small contribution to buy twelve loafs of bread; this donation would help feed a family of four for two weeks.**

   What correction should be made to this sentence?

   (1) change the spelling of twelve to twelfe
   (2) change the spelling of loafs to loaves
   (3) insert the word however before this
   (4) change the spelling of bread to bred
   (5) no correction is necessary

Directions: For each item, choose the answer that would result in the most effective writing. Answers are on page 220.

(1) Since 1933, many scientific expeditions have explored the island of New Guinea because the most primitive people on earth live there. (2) The natives of New Guinea live like the Stone Age people do 10,000 years ago. (3) While visiting these Stone Age villagers, the explorers introduced them to many inventions. (4) Matches, "talking boxes" (radios), and bubblegum fascinated the natives.

9. Sentence 1: **Since 1933, many scientific expeditions have explored the island of New Guinea because the most primitive people on earth live there.**

   What correction should be made to this sentence?

   (1) change have explored to will explore
   (2) change the spelling of island to iland
   (3) remove the word because
   (4) change the spelling of primitive to primative
   (5) no correction is necessary

10. Sentence 2: **The natives of New Guinea live like the Stone Age people do 10,000 years ago.**

    Which of the following is the best way to write the underlined portion of this sentence? If you think the original is the best way, choose option (1).

    (1) do (2) doing (3) did
    (4) have done (5) had done

    1 2 3 4 5

11. Sentence 4: **Matches, "talking boxes" (radios), and bubblegum fascinated the natives.**

    What correction should be made to this sentence?

    (1) change the spelling of Matches to Matchs
    (2) change the spelling of fascinated to fasinated
    (3) change fascinated to fascinate
    (4) change fascinated to will fascinate
    (5) no correction is necessary

Matching Verbs with Time Words Did you know that verbs change with the times? Here are some examples.

1. Present event: *This system* ***operates*** *like clockwork now.* Or, *This system* ***is operating*** *like clockwork now.*

2. Future event: *This system* ***will*** *soon* ***operate*** *like clockwork.* Or, *This system* ***will*** *soon* ***be operating*** *like clockwork.*

3. Past event: *This system* ***operated*** *like clockwork last week.* Or, *This system* ***was operating*** *like clockwork last week.*

4. Past-and-continuing event: *This system* ***has operated*** *like clockwork since Friday.* Or, *This system* ***has been operating*** *like clockwork since Friday.*

5. Past event before another past event: *This system broke down yesterday. It* ***had operated*** *like clockwork for a year before that.* Or, *It* ***had been operating*** *like clockwork for a year before that.*

Did you notice the time words in the sentences? The present verbs matched *now,* future verbs *soon,* and past-and-continuing verbs *last week* and *since Friday.* The past-before-another-past verb matched *for a year before.* You can use words like these to remind you of what verbs you should use in your sentences.

Warm-up

The verbs in the passage below are *italicized.* Some are wrong. Circle the time words. Then rewrite the passage with the right verbs.

■ Who *will need* clocks these days? The news *got* many people up this morning. Others *exercised* by TV even earlier. Some people already *use* certain TV commercials as go-to-work signals. And with more and more car television sets, time *is hitting* the freeways soon enough.

Almost everyone wastes time—all the time. Write three or four sentences about something that has wasted your time in the past, still does, and probably will continue to do so. Use time words in each sentence. Make sure your verbs match them.

Warm-up Answers
Verbs: needs; *got* is correct; had exercised; *use* is correct; will hit
Time words: these days; this morning; earlier; already; soon

Using Different Verb Forms Verbs are flexible; they come in many forms. You can use the different verbs to show your reader exactly what is going on in any situation you write about. You can use verbs to show action *(Sylvia **is selecting** an apple)* and conditions *(The apple **seems** ripe).* Verbs tell what might happen *(Sylvia **might buy** five pounds)* and what can happen *(Sylvia **can buy** five pounds).* Every complete sentence has a main verb: *selecting, seems, buy.* Main verbs can have helpers *(**is** selecting, **had** selected).* You also use verbs with *will, may, might, can, could, did, do, should,* and *would.* Many verbs, like *select,* change form, or *tense*, the same way: *Sylvia selects well. Sylvia select**ed** well. Sylvia **has** select**ed** well.*

Other verbs, like *buy,* change their own way in some forms: *Sylvia buys well. Sylvia **bought** well. Sylvia **has bought** well.* Several irregular verbs are listed below.

Verb	Present	Past
be	is	was/has been, had been
get	gets	got/has gotten, had gotten
go	goes	went/has gone, had gone
have	has	had/has had, had had
see	sees	saw/has seen, had seen

A Test-Taking Tip

Be alert for errors in verb use, such as *Michael **been** sick* on the GED Test. Such a sentence is incomplete because the writer left out the helper *has*.

Warm-up

Rewrite this passage. Use a correct verb form for each verb in parentheses.

■ A sport *(be)* a fruit of a different color. At one time, one kind of apple tree *(produce)* only pale, striped fruit. Then one day out *(pop)* a red apple. The grower never *(have)* better luck. He *(see)* a whole new market for the sport. Since then, grocery stores *(stock)* Red Delicious apples. And the grower *(become)* a dedicated sports fan.

Write about your favorite foods. Use different forms of verbs like *love, be,* and *eat.*

Sample Warm-up Answers
is; produced; popped; had had; saw; have stocked; has become

(1) Have you ever came home with a pair of shoes that didn't fit and wondered why you ever bought them? (2) Did the salesperson tell you that they just needed to be broke in, or did you like the style so much that you bought the shoes even though the store was out of your size? (3) Whatever the reasen, we have all fallen victim to this problem. (4) The end of your longest toe should be a thumb's width from the end of the shoe when you are standing.

12. Sentence 1: **Have you ever came home with a pair of shoes that didn't fit and wondered why you ever bought them?**

    What correction should be made to this sentence?

    (1) change came to come
    (2) change came to been coming
    (3) change fit to fitted
    (4) change bought to will buy
    (5) change bought to buyed

13. Sentence 2: **Did the salesperson tell you that they just needed to be broke in?**

    Which of the following is the best way to write the underlined portion of this sentence? If you think the original is the best way, choose option (1).

    (1) to be broke in
    (2) to be broken in
    (3) to be breaked in
    (4) to have been broken in
    (5) to been broke in

14. Sentence 3: **Whatever the reasen, we have all fallen victim to this problem.**

    What correction should be made to this sentence?

    (1) change the spelling of reasen to reason
    (2) remove the comma after reasen
    (3) change have to had
    (4) change fallen to fell
    (5) change the spelling of victim to victem

Directions: For each item, choose the answer that would result in the most effective writing. Answers begin on page 220.

(1) Queen Victoria, who ruled England from 1837 to 1901, is fatherless from infancy, but her father's brother, Leopold, provided her with fatherly advice and guidance for more than thirty years. (2) When she was eighteen, the young princess become queen of England, and her uncle immediately proposed that his nephew, Prince Albert, should marry Victoria. (3) Victoria adored her Husband, and this happy union produced nine children.

15. Sentence 1: **Queen Victoria, who ruled England from 1837 to 1901, is fatherless from infancy, but her father's brother, Leopold, provided her with fatherly advice and guidance for more than thirty years.**

What correction should be made to this sentence?

(1) change is to was
(2) remove the comma after infancy
(3) change brother to Brother
(4) change Leopold to leopold
(5) change the spelling of guidance to guidence

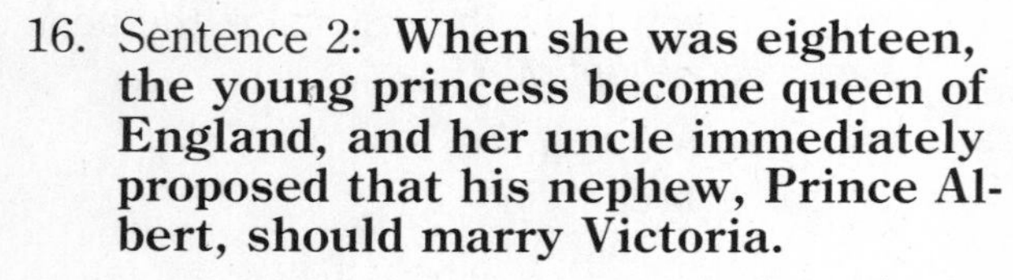

16. Sentence 2: **When she was eighteen, the young princess become queen of England, and her uncle immediately proposed that his nephew, Prince Albert, should marry Victoria.**

What correction should be made to this sentence?

(1) change become to became
(2) change uncle to Uncle
(3) change the spelling of immediately to immediatly
(4) change Prince to prince
(5) no correction is necessary

 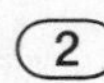   

Capitalization Break/Names Capital letters always start sentences. But you will use capitals in other ways too.

■ The name *Roosevelt* is famous. *Klaes,* the family founder, started a line of rich landowners in the 1600s. In the 1800s, *Nicholas J.* helped develop steam navigation. His great-grandnephew, *President Theodore Roosevelt,* took office in 1901. In 1905 *Uncle Teddy* walked his niece *Eleanor* down the aisle to marry his fifth cousin, *Franklin Delano Roosevelt (FDR). Franklin* became president in 1933. *Mrs. Roosevelt,* known as *"America's First Lady"* until her death in 1962, was a delegate to the *UN General Assembly* from 1945 to 1951.

When you write, remember to capitalize
1. Names, nicknames, and initials: *Roosevelt; Klaes; Nicholas J.; Theodore; Teddy; Eleanor; Franklin Delano; FDR; America's First Lady.*
2. Organizations: *UN General Assembly.*
3. Words for relatives when the words are used as names or parts of names: *Uncle Teddy.*
4. Abbreviated and other titles in front of a name: *President Theodore Roosevelt, Mrs. Roosevelt.*

 **Warm-up**

Rewrite this passage. Capitalize names and other words as needed.

■ In 1898, colonel theodore roosevelt became a hero in the cavalry unit called the rough riders. both t. r. and cousin franklin were governors. lieutenant colonel theodore roosevelt, jr., a war hero, became a famous explorer for the field museum of natural history. franklin, jr., and his brother james carried on their mother and father's political tradition as congressmen in the house of representatives.

Write three or four sentences about a public figure you support or oppose. Include information you know about the groups this person represents. Capitalize as necessary.

Warm-up Answers
In, Colonel Theodore Roosevelt, Rough Riders. Both, T. R., Cousin Franklin. Lieutenant Colonel Theodore Roosevelt, Jr., Field Museum of Natural History. Franklin, Jr., James, House of Representatives

Combining Two Verbs If a product does not appeal to you, you are unlikely to buy it. You'll find many verbs in advertisements.

Advertisers' sentences have to be smooth and interesting. So advertisers often combine verbs. You can do the same when your sentences have the same subjects but different verbs.

- Satina lotion pampers your skin. Satina lotion protects your skin. *Combined*: Satina lotion pampers and protects your skin.

The subjects don't have to be identical words.

- Tru-Color Flat paint will last longer. This paint will cost you less. *Combined;* Tru-Color Flat paint will last longer but will cost you less.

Here are more sentences with combined verbs.

- Grolger's Coffee is known worldwide yet is stocked at your local grocery.

  Either fish in our lakes or browse in our antique shops. (The subject, *you,* is understood.)

Notice that you can use the same words to combine verbs as to combine complete sentences: *and, but, yet, or.* You can also use *neither/nor* and *either/or.* Pick the word that shows the relationship, make sure the verbs are in the same form, and then combine them.

Warm-up

Combine each pair of sentences if the verbs logically go together.

1. Have a snack at the resort's Deli Depot. You can dine elegantly at the French House.
2. Speed Saw is handy around the yard. It can cut through everything from slim limbs to thick trunks.
3. Easy-Lift luggage is rugged. The brand will weigh less than competing brands.

Think of three products you've bought. Then select two verbs that tell what each one is or does. For each product, write a sentence that combines the two verbs.

Sample Warm-up Answers
1. Either have a snack at the resort's Deli Depot or dine elegantly at the French House. **2.** The thoughts are too unrelated to combine. **3.** Easy-Lift luggage is rugged yet weighs less than competing brands.

(1) In the United States, 95 percent of biting mosquitoes breed in temporary pools of water, so some varieties carry diseases. (2) Mosquitoes can ruin a camper's evening. (3) They can also make a backyard barbecue party unbearable. (4) Female mosquitoes are attracted to body warmth and moisture and are liking to bite men more than women. (5) Their bites swell and itch because they inject an enzyme to keep blood from coagulating while they enjoy their feast.

17. Sentence 1: **In the United States, 95 percent of biting mosquitoes breed in temporary pools of water, so some varieties carry diseases.**

    Which of the following is the best way to write the underlined portion of this sentence? If you think the original is the best way, choose option (1).

    (1) water, so some (2) water, some
    (3) water, but some (4) water some
    (5) water. Some

    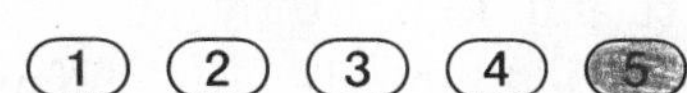

18. Sentences 2 and 3: **Mosquitoes can ruin a camper's evening. They can also make a backyard barbecue party unbearable.**

    The most effective combination of sentences 2 and 3 would include which of the following groups of words?

    (1) a camper's evening, a backyard barbecue
    (2) They can ruin and make
    (3) evening, while also making
    (4) Mosquitoes make backyard barbecues
    (5) ruin a camper's evening and make

19. Sentence 4: **Female mosquitoes are attracted to body warmth and moisture and are liking to bite men more than women.**

    What correction should be made to this sentence?

    (1) change attracted to attracting
    (2) insert a comma after moisture
    (3) change are liking to were liking
    (4) change are liking to like
    (5) no correction is necessary

Directions: For each item, choose the answer that would result in the most effective writing. Answers are on page 221.

(1) Many health-conscious people love raisins, they are wholesome, easily digested, and delicious. (2) In biblical times, raisins were used to pay taxes Hannibal fed them to his troops to give them energy as they crossed the Alps. (3) After the 1873 grape harvest was dried out by a drought the California raisin industry was born.

20. Sentence 1: **Many health-conscious people love raisins, they are wholesome, easily digested, and delicious.**

    What correction should be made to this sentence?

    (1) change the spelling of health-conscious to health-consious
    (2) remove the comma after raisins
    (3) replace the comma after raisins with because
    (4) insert and before they
    (5) change the spelling of delicious to delishious

    (1) (2) (3) (4) (5)

21. Sentence 2: **In biblical times, raisins were used to pay taxes Hannibal fed them to his troops to give them energy as they crossed the Alps.**

    Which of the following is the best way to write the underlined portion of this sentence? If you think the original is the best way, choose option (1).

    (1) taxes Hannibal
    (2) taxes, Hannibal
    (3) taxes when Hannibal
    (4) taxes. Hannibal
    (5) taxes, for Hannibal

    (1) (2) (3) (4) (5)

22. Sentence 3: **After the 1873 grape harvest was dried out by a drought the California raisin industry was born.**

    What correction should be made to this sentence?

    (1) replace After with Since
    (2) change was ruined to is ruined
    (3) insert a comma after drought
    (4) change was born to has been born
    (5) no correction is necessary

Adding Dependent Information Many things depend on one another. Take cooking. How you cook can depend on what appliance you use.

- Can't I use foil ***when*** *I microwave?*

  Use plastic wrap ***because*** *it won't melt.*

When and *because* can help you smoothly add information to your sentences. With added information, you can make your meaning clearer. Notice that the added information above depends on the first part of each sentence. By itself, the information makes no sense.

You can also use these words to add dependent information: *after, although, as, as if, as though, before, even though, if, in order that, since, so that, than, though, unless, until, whenever, wherever,* and *while.*

In the example below, information is added with *unless.*

- ***Unless*** *you're baking* potatoes.

This example has a subject and verb. But it still is not a complete sentence. To make sense, you would have to attach the example to a complete sentence. You could add it at the end, as in the first two examples, or you could add it to the beginning of a sentence.

- ***Unless*** *you're baking potatoes,* microwave them in a little water.

Since you put the dependent information first, you need to put a comma after it. Sometimes you have to use a comma even when the dependent information comes at the end. How will you know when? Say the sentence in your head. Put in a comma only when you can hear a pause before the dependent information. The second sentence below needs a comma.

- I microwaved this meatloaf ***while*** *my thoughts were elsewhere.* My family ate it, ***even though*** *the outside was rock hard.*

Sometimes you can use words that show dependence to fix run-ons.

- Run-on: Cook popcorn on the stove the microwave leaves too many kernels.

  Correct: Cook popcorn on the stove***, as*** *the microwave leaves too many kernels.*

Read the tinted column on the next page before you complete the sample test items in the white column on this page.

Warm-up 1

Rewrite this passage. Add dependent information to complete sentences. Fix run-ons.

■ I had microwave disasters. Until I read the manual. Eggs exploded, when I didn't break the yolks. Since metal twisties melt in the microwave they ruined my bagged sandwiches. A paper fire burned the oven up I finally looked in the manual. If I want to use the oven again I need to fix it. Will I? So that I can microwave once more? That depends I lost the manual.

Write three or four sentences about a problem you had with some kind of appliance. Use any of the methods you learned about to add dependent information that will make the situation clearer.

Selecting Words to Show Dependence When you add information to a sentence by using a dependent word, make sure that word is logical. Here's an illogical one.

■ People once considered men superior to women, **when** today women are equals.

A logical connecting word for this dependent part is *while.*

■ People once considered men superior to women, **while** today women are equals.

Warm-up 2

Combine these sentences. Use words that would logically show dependence.

1. The custom of shaking hands was once practical. It showed that prehistoric men carried no weapons.
2. The knights of old kissed women's hands. The women curtsied.
3. Now manners are more casual. We still have many customs.

Pick any custom you know about. Write three or four sentences on why it is fading or lasting. Add information with words that logically show dependence.

Sample Warm-up 1 Answers

I had microwave disasters until I read the manual. Eggs exploded when I didn't break the yolks. Since metal twisties melt in the microwave, they ruined my bagged sandwiches. A paper fire burned the oven up before I finally looked in the manual. If I want to use the oven again, I need to fix it. Will I, so that I can microwave once more? That depends; I lost the manual.

Sample Warm-up 2 Answers

1. practical because **2.** hands, while **3.** casual, even though

(1) Here are some tips for dressing tall and thin even whenever you are not dieting.
(2) Don't wear tight clothing; instead, wear clothes that skim your body. (3) If the elements of your outfit are in the same color family, you will look taller and slimmer. (4) Allways wear shoulder pads, even small ones, because they make clothing hang better.
(5) Buy clothes with small, subtle patterns, since large fabric designs emphasize width.

23. Sentence 1: **Here are some tips for dressing tall and thin even whenever you are not dieting.**

    What correction should be made to this sentence?

    (1) change are to were
    (2) change are to should be
    (3) change are to be
    (4) replace even whenever with even if
    (5) replace even whenever with although

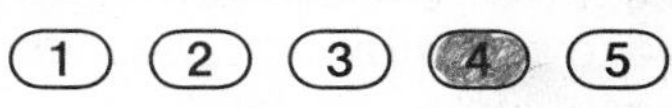

24. Sentence 4: **Allways wear shoulder pads, even small ones, because they make clothing hang better.**

    What correction should be made to this sentence?

    (1) change the spelling of Allways to Always
    (2) change the spelling of shoulder to sholder
    (3) replace because with so
    (4) remove the word because
    (5) no correction is necessary

25. Sentence 5: **Buy clothes with small, subtle patterns, since large fabric designs emphasize width.**

    Which of the following is the best way to write the underlined portion of this sentence? If you think the original is the best way, choose option (1).

    (1) patterns, since
    (2) patterns since,
    (3) patterns. Since
    (4) patterns; since
    (5) patterns; since,

Directions: For each item, choose the answer that would result in the most effective writing. Answers are on page 221.

(1) Junk mail has finally met its match, for you can recycle this "wealth" into designer stationary. (2) All you need is a blender, a small wire screen, and lots of patience. (3) Tear the junk mail into small pieces, or cover them with water in the blender. (4) After you blend this mixture for about one minute, pour the mush into a shallow pan of water. (5) Use the screen to lift out a course layer of the pulverized paper, and iron until it is dry.

26. Sentence 1: **Junk mail has finally met its match, for you can recycle this "wealth" into designer stationary.**

    What correction should be made to this sentence?

    (1) remove the comma after match
    (2) replace for with even though
    (3) replace can with could
    (4) change the spelling of stationary to stationery
    (5) no correction is necessary

27. Sentence 3: **Tear the junk mail into small pieces, or cover them with water in the blender.**

    What correction should be made to this sentence?

    (1) change the spelling of pieces to peaces
    (2) remove the comma after pieces
    (3) remove the word or
    (4) replace or with and
    (5) replace or with while

28. Sentence 5: **Use the screen to lift out a course layer of the pulverized paper, and iron until it is dry.**

    What correction should be made to this sentence?

    (1) change Use to Using
    (2) change the spelling of course to coarse
    (3) remove the comma after paper
    (4) replace is with be
    (5) no correction is necessary

Spelling Break/Words That Sound Alike You won't find a clearer example of how talking and writing differ than words that sound exactly alike but don't look the same. Here are examples from the GED Spelling List.

board/bored	council/counsel	role/roll
capital/capitol	peace/piece	sight/site
coarse/course	principal/principle	weak/week

If you misspell any of these words, learn the meanings of both. Use a dictionary. Then use the words in sentences until you master the spellings and meanings.

Warm-up

Choose the word in parentheses that fits each sentence's meaning. Use your own paper.

Do you want to see a magnificent *(capital/capitol)* ____? Look at your own in Washington, D.C. You won't be *(board/bored)* ____. Once the symbol of a *(weak/week)* ____ nation, this building today stands for a world power. The building is a fine *(peace/piece)* ____ of urban planning besides being the *(sight/site)* ____ of our national legislation. There's a small transport tunnel that links the building with *(principal/principle)* ____ Washington offices. Part of the congressional *(role/roll)* ____ call is a buzzer-and-light system in restaurants for each house of Congress. And, in the *(coarse/course)* ____ of any day, the Prayer Room is a convenient place for legislators to take *(council/counsel)* ____.

Now select three or four words you didn't use in the sentences above. Use them to write about any interesting place you have visited.

Need a Hint for Numbers 27 and 28?
You learned that it's wrong to put a comma between two verbs connected by a word like and. *However, when the subject of both verbs is the unstated* you, *you can use a comma to separate the two complete thoughts in the sentence.*

Warm-up Answers
capitol, bored, weak, piece, site, principal, roll, course, counsel

Spelling Break/Words Often Confused Some frequently misspelled words look and maybe even sound quite alike—just enough to confuse you. Here are examples from the GED Spelling List.

1. accept/except
2. advice/advise
3. affect/effect
4. angel/angle
5. breadth/breath/breathe
6. choose/chose
7. conscience/conscious
8. desert/dessert
9. later/latter
10. loose/lose
11. moral/morale
12. personal/personnel
13. quiet/quite
14. receipt/recipe
15. thorough/through

When you learn to spell these words also learn their meanings. Then practice the words together or in sentences.

Warm-up

Using words from the word pairs above, rewrite the following sentences. The numbers of the word pairs match the numbers sentences in which to use the words.

1. Why does everyone _____ Richard _____ the committee's decision?
2. We must _____ you to take our _____ seriously.
3. The computer's _____ is stunning. Who would have thought the computer could _____ so many areas of our lives?
4. The _____ is at an odd _____ on the Christmas tree.
5. With every _____ I take, I _____ a sigh of relief that I've quit smoking and probably increased the _____ of my life.
6. You _____ the smallest piece of cake. Do you wish to _____ another?
7. Good _____ won't allow _____ acts of cruelty.
8. One _____ you have to eat fast in the _____ is sherbet.

Now select one word from each word pair 9–15. Use each word in a sentence about something or someone that confuses you.

Warm-up Answers
1. except, accept **2.** advise, advice **3.** effect, affect **4.** angel, angle **5.** breath, breathe, breadth **6.** chose, choose **7.** conscience, conscious **8.** dessert, desert

(1) Last Saturday night, Uncle Miroslav's children gave him a birthday banquet that was quiet impressive. (2) Since he is Czechoslovakian, they chose recipes that represented the breath of Old World cuisine. (3) The quantity of desserts had an adverse effect on everyone's waistline. (4) At the end of the banquet, everyone needed to loosen his or her clothes in order to breathe a little easier. (5) The moral of this tale is that accepting only one dessert may not lower your morale as much as you think it would.

29. Sentence 1: **Last Saturday night, Uncle Miroslav's children gave him a birthday banquet that was quiet impressive.**

What correction should be made to this sentence?

(1) change Uncle to uncle
(2) change gave to have given
(3) change gave to will give
(4) replace quiet with quite
(5) no correction is necessary

30. Sentence 2: **Since he is Czechoslovakian, they chose recipes that represented the breath of Old World cuisine.**

What correction should be made to this sentence?

(1) change is to be
(2) remove the comma after Czechoslovakian
(3) change chose to choose
(4) replace recipes with receipts
(5) replace breath with breadth

(1) (2) (3) (4) (5)

31. Sentence 5: **The moral of this tale is that accepting only one dessert may not lower your morale as much as you think it would.**

What correction should be made to this sentence?

(1) replace moral with morale
(2) replace accepting with excepting
(3) replace morale with moral
(4) change think to will think
(5) no correction is necessary

Directions: For each item, choose the answer that would result in the most effective writing. Answers begin on page 221.

(1) The spacecraft of Captain Buck Rogers was pulled off course by a freak mishap. (2) His life-support systems were froze to temperatures beyond imagination, and his ship was lost for 500 years. (3) Then Buck approached the outer defenses of earth, and Colonel Dearing almost vaporized him. (4) Later Buck was accused of spying his only friend was Twiki.

32. Sentence 2: **His life-support systems were froze to temperatures beyond imagination, and his ship was lost for 500 years.**

What correction should be made to this sentence?

(1) change froze to frozen
(2) change the spelling of temperatures to tempertures
(3) remove the comma after imagination
(4) change was to is
(5) no correction is necessary

33. Sentence 3: **Then Buck approached the outer defenses of earth, and Colonel Dearing almost vaporized him.**

If you rewrote sentence 3 beginning with As Buck approached the outer defenses of earth, he the next word should be

(1) almost (2) vaporized
(3) is (4) was (5) vaporizes

① ② ③ ④ ⑤

34. Sentence 4: **Later Buck was accused of spying his only friend was Twiki.**

Which of the following is the best way to write the underlined portion of this sentence? If you think the original is the best way, choose option (1).

(1) spying his
(2) spying, his
(3) spying because his
(4) spying; therefore, his
(5) spying, and his

Making Two Verbs Agree On page 162, you learned how one verb in a sentence shows time. If you use two verbs in a sentence, both show time. The verbs in this GED student's sentence show present time. They *agree* with one another in this sense.

- When it **is** midnight in New York City, people **are having** lunch in Singapore.

The time word *when* is a clue that the verbs in this sentence should agree.

The GED student wanted the verbs in some of his sentences to show different times. Here, the first verb shows future time, while the second shows present. There is no time-word clue, but the verbs are logical.

- You **will have** dinner on the plane if you **take** the 5 P.M. flight.

Here's a sentence in which the student's timing is off. He should have made the verbs agree.

- On the train we **wait** until 9 A.M. before we **ate** breakfast.

The student should change *wait* to *waited* in this sentence. The time-word clue is *before: We waited* ***before*** *we ate.*

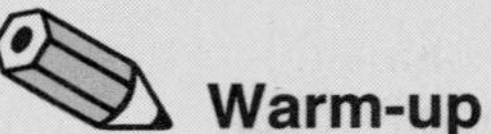

Warm-up

The verbs are **bold** in this passage. Underline any time words. Decide which verbs don't agree. Rewrite the passage using correct verbs.

- Time **waits** for no man, or so *Star Trek* **claimed.** Captain Kirk **stops** time to fix his spaceship before it **crashed** in last night's episode. Tonight he **will go** back in time to when Chicago gangsters **are having** gangland fights. **Have** you ever **wondered** whether *Star Trek*'s reruns ever **end?** They **will** not. Captain Kirk **will stop** time before they **did.**

Pretend that you are traveling. Write three or four sentences about what you are doing now, what you did to get ready, and what you'll do when you get where you're going. In each sentence, use two verbs along with time words. Make sure all your verbs show the right time.

Sample Warm-up Answers
waits is correct; claims; stopped; *crashed* is correct; *will go* is correct; had; *Have wondered* is correct; will end; *will* is correct; *will stop* is correct; do. Time words: *before, last night's, when, before*

Making Subjects and Verbs Agree On the GED Test, you'll also have to make sure verbs agree with their singular and plural subjects. Here are some examples with *be.*

- One *hummingbird* **is** the size of a bee.

  One *hummingbird* **was** the size of a bee.

  Other *hummingbirds* **are** over eight inches long.

  Other *hummingbirds* **were** over eight inches long.

You don't have to change other verbs as much as *be.* Just add *-s* or *-es* in present time.

- One lion *roar***s.**

  One chimp *go***es** bananas.

You'll never add *-s* or *-es* to your verb when your subject is plural. But usually your *subject* will end with *-s* or *-es* then.

- Two *lion***s** roar.

  Two *chimp***s** go bananas.

The *-s* usually shifts back and forth. There are two exceptions. One is plural subjects that don't end in *-s (mice squeak)*; the other is subjects that end in *-s* whether they are singular or plural *(walrus swims; walruses swim).*

Warm-up

Change the subjects in sentences 1–4 to singular. Rewrite the sentences. Make the verbs agree with the singular subjects. You'll have to start each sentence with *The* or *A.*

1. Giant tortoises live more than 100 years.
2. Pipefish swim in a sticklike position.
3. Old Egyptian cemeteries have cat mummies.
4. Bats are radar equipped.

Change these subjects to plural. Drop *The* or *A.* Then rewrite the sentences. Make the verbs agree with the singular subjects.

5. A salmon remembers odors for years.
6. The albatross courts by dancing.
7. The lizard smells by licking.

Write a few sentences with animals as subjects. First use singular subjects. Then rewrite your sentences, talking about the animal in the plural.

Warm-up Answers
1. The giant tortoise lives **2.** The pipefish swims **3.** The old Egyptian cemetery has **4.** The bat is **5.** Salmon remember **6.** Albatrosses court **7.** Lizards smell

(1) The sight of an adult wearing braces is becoming more common these days. (2) Currently, orthodontists see one adult patient in five, but by the end of the century, the number will increase to one in four. (3) One reason for the growth of this branch of dentistry is that research has proven that teeth can move no matter how old a person is. (4) Because many companies now offer health plans that include orthodontic coverage, employees are able to have their teeth straightened at little or no personal cost.

35. Sentence 2: **Currently, orthodontists see one adult patient in five, but by the end of the century, the number will increase to one in four.**

    What correction should be made to this sentence?

    (1) change see to sees
    (2) remove the comma after five
    (3) remove the word but
    (4) change will increase to increases
    (5) no correction is necessary

36. Sentence 3: **One reason for the growth of this branch of dentistry is that research has proven that teeth can move no matter how old a person is.**

    If you rewrote sentence 3 beginning with This branch of dentistry is growing the next word should be

    (1) because (2) before (3) though
    (4) until (5) although

37. Sentence 4: **Because many companies now offer health plans that include orthodontic coverage, employees are able to have their teeth straightened at little or no personal cost.**

    What correction should be made to this sentence?

    (1) change the spelling of companies to companys
    (2) change offer to offers
    (3) remove the comma after coverage
    (4) change are to is
    (5) no correction is necessary

    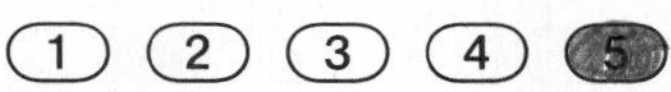

Directions: For each item, choose the answer that would result in the most effective writing. Answers are on page 222.

(1) Many have read the epic poem about Beowulf, an ancient Scandinavian warrior, especially students of Old English literature. (2) No one knows for sure whether Beowulf really existed, but the legend of his nine-hour underwater battle with a monster is still famous. (3) Beowulf's crew fought courageously with him. (4) Everyone having been rewarded handsomely for his bravery. (5) Beowulf then returned home to rule as king for fifty years.

38. Sentence 1: **Many have read the epic poem about Beowulf, an ancient Scandinavian warrior, especially students of Old English literature.**

What correction should be made to this sentence?

(1) change have to has
(2) change have to having
(3) change warrior to Warrior
(4) change the spelling of literature to litrature
(5) no correction is necessary

39. Sentence 2: **No one knows for sure whether Beowulf really existed, but the legend of his nine-hour underwater battle with a monster is still famous.**

What correction should be made to this sentence?

(1) change knows to know
(2) change existed to exists
(3) remove the comma after existed
(4) remove the word but
(5) no correction is necessary

(1) (2) (3) (4) (5)

40. Sentence 4: **Everyone having been rewarded handsomely for his bravery.**

Which of the following is the best way to write the underlined portion of this sentence? If you think the original is the best way, choose option (1).

(1) having been rewarded
(2) were rewarding (3) were rewarded
(4) was rewarding (5) was rewarded

(1) 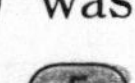 (3) (4) (5)

Using Pronoun Subjects When you write, you will want to use **pronouns.** They stand for people and things you write about. You know these pronouns from everyday conversation: *I, he, she, it, we, you, they.*

When you use pronouns, your writing will be less monotonous. You don't have to repeat the word *program,* for example, in the second sentence below.

- The **program** is going to be rebroadcast. **It** was more popular than expected.

The pronoun *It* stands for *program.* Since the pronoun is singular, you make the verb, *was,* agree.

You're no doubt also familiar with the following singular pronouns: *another, anybody, anything, each, either, everybody, everyone, everything, much, neither, nobody, none, no one, nothing, one, other, somebody, someone,* and *something*

With these pronouns; remember to use verbs that agree with singular subjects.

- *Everyone is watching* the new sitcom and that quiz show, but *neither fascinates* me.

Here are some familiar plural pronouns: *both, few, many, others, several.*

- As for the detective shows, *many are* interesting. *Several have* unique formats, even though a *few are* going to be cancelled.

Coming to Terms

pronoun a word that stands for a person or a thing

Warm-up

Rewrite these familiar sentences. Substitute each pronoun in parentheses for the boldfaced pronoun. Change verbs as needed.

1. (Several, Neither) **You** were on my mind.
2. (I, Many,) **Nothing** is certain.
3. (Others, Each) **Everybody** loves somebody sometime.
4. (a few, one) Does **anybody** really care?

Select several singular and plural pronouns. Using them as subjects of your sentences, write about people's attitudes. Use different verb forms.

Warm-up Answers
1. Several were, Neither was **2.** I am, Many are, **3.** Others love, Each loves **4.** Do a few, Does one

Combining Sentences Whenever you write, you'll want to avoid repeating yourself and boring your reader. One way you can get around this problem is to use pronouns. Another way is to combine sentences. Try the following technique when the subject and verb in two sentences mean the same thing. Notice that the combined sentence has only one subject and verb.

■ A job interview can make a person nervous. Such an interview can unnerve even a qualified applicant.

Combined: A job interview can unnerve even a qualified applicant.

In the following case, it is not just the subject or the verb that repeats information. Notice how the combination carefully chooses what is needed from both sentences and eliminates the rest.

■ The job applicant should keep one thing in mind to help make the interview successful. The one thing to remember is that the interview is his or her own chance to size up the company as well as be sized up.

Combined: To help make the interview successful, the job applicant should remember that the interview is his or her own chance to size up the company as well as be sized up.

Warm-up

Combine these sentences. Use only one subject and verb.

1. The job interviewer usually asks questions. He or she usually inquires about the applicant's experience and goals.
2. The job applicant should not become too nervous. The applicant should remain calm and confident and answer the interviewer's questions straightforwardly.
3. In addition, the applicant should have come to the interview prepared to ask his or her own questions. These questions should concern job responsibilities, room for advancement, and the company's prospects for the future.

Sample Warm-up Answers
1. The job interviewer usually inquires about the applicant's experience and goals. **2.** The job applicant should remain calm and confident and answer the interviewer's questions straightforwardly. **3.** In addition, the applicant should have come to the interview prepared to ask his or her own questions concerning job responsibilities, room for advancement, and the company's prospects for the future.

(1) Office environments can cause problems for plants. (2) These problems include poor lighting and low humidity. (3) There is another important problem to remember. (4) At nights and on weekends, ventilation and heating systems are turned down. (5) A drop in temperature results. (6) This makes the office a hostile environment for growing plants.

41. Sentences 1 and 2: **Office environments can cause problems for plants. These problems include poor lighting and low humidity.**

The most effective combination of sentences 1 and 2 would include which of the following groups of words?

(1) Things that cause
(2) offices and their problems
(3) including the problems of
(4) problems for plants, including poor
(5) to cause problems for

42. Sentences 3 and 4: **There is another important problem to remember. At nights and on weekends, ventilation and heating systems are turned down.**

The most effective combination of sentences 3 and 4 would include which of the following groups of words?

(1) remembering an important problem
(2) remember, and at nights
(3) Another important problem to remember is that
(4) problems of turning down
(5) Problems in turning down

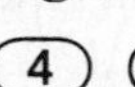

43. Sentences 5 and 6: **A drop in temperature results. This makes the office a hostile environment for growing plants.**

The most effective combination of sentences 5 and 6 would include which of the following groups of words?

(1) resulting in a temperature drop
(2) The resulting drop in temperature
(3) The office is made
(4) results and makes
(5) to make the office

Directions: For each item, choose the answer that would result in the most effective writing. Answers begin on page 222.

(1) Joggers and walkers disagree a lot about the merits of their different, yet equally enjoyable, exercise programs. (2) No one knows why some people prefer walking to jogging, but doctors and other experts have proven that walking, along with stretching exercises, puts less stress on the body's joints. (3) There is one aspect of exercise that is often overlooked. (4) It is the feeling of well-being people experience whether they have walked or run.

44. Sentence 1: **Joggers and walkers disagree a lot about the merits of their different, yet equally enjoyable, exercise programs.**

What correction should be made to this sentence?

(1) change disagree to disagrees
(2) change disagree to disagreed
(3) change the spelling of a lot to alot
(4) change the spelling of different to diffrent
(5) no correction is necessary

45. Sentences 3 and 4: **There is one aspect of exercise that is often overlooked. It is the feeling of well-being people experience whether they have walked or run.**

The most effective combination of sentences 3 and 4 would include which of the following groups of words?

(1) One aspect is the feeling
(2) One overlooked aspect of exercise is
(3) feeling well while exercising
(4) overlooked, as well as the feeling
(5) There is often overlooked the feeling

Combining Two Subjects You may sometimes find that, in two sentences, you have written the same thing about two subjects. To make your writing smoother and more pleasant, write one sentence that combines the subjects.

- Red **is** vivid. Orange **is** vivid too.
  Combined: Red **and** orange **are** vivid.

Here you combined the two subjects with *and.* Since you have two subjects in one sentence now, you need to use the plural verb *are* instead of *is.*

You can also combine subjects with terms such as *along with, as well as, in addition to,* and *like.* Look at these subjects and verbs.

- Hazardous **conditions,** as well as caution, **are signaled** by yellow.
  Caution, as well as hazardous conditions, **is signaled** by yellow.

When you put a subject after words like *as well as,* it's no longer considered a subject. So you make the verb agree with the only subject left: the first one. You also usually need to use commas when you use one of the combining terms other than *and.*

- Blue**,** as well as white**,** symbolize**s** truth.
  Emerald**,** like turquoise**,** **is** a blue-green mix.

Warm-up

Rewrite the sentences below. Combine the subjects using the word(s) in parentheses. Make verbs agree with subjects.

1. (in addition to) Medicine is packaged in white to show sterility. Some cleansers are also packaged in white to show sterility.
2. (as well as) Businesses use blue to suggest organization. And TV uses blue to suggest it.
3. (and) Safety is indicated by green. Directions are indicated by green.
4. (like) Yellow gets attention. Red gets attention also.

Write three sentences with the subject pairs listed below. Combine the subjects using terms such as *along with.* Use verbs in present time and make sure the subjects and verbs agree.

candy bars/popcorn eggs/cheese garlic/onions

Sample Warm-up Answers
1. Medicine, in addition to some cleansers, is packaged in white to show sterility. **2.** Businesses, as well as TV, use blue to suggest organization. **3.** Safety and directions are indicated by green. **4.** Yellow, like red, gets attention.

Making Sure Separated Subjects and Verbs Agree Your subjects and verbs can get separated by all kinds of words.

- Partitions **systems** like the one my office has **do** nothing to keep the noise down.
  Co-workers, for instance, **are** often unruly.

In sentences like these, you might lose track of your subject by the time you write your verb. So you have to double-check your subjects and verbs to make sure they agree.

Also keep your eye on your main subjects and verbs. Don't let ones in other sentence parts confuse you.

- Partition **systems** (like the one my *office has*) **do** nothing to keep the noise down.

A Test-Taking Tip

You saw *for instance* in the second example. It has commas around it. So usually would *for example, however, in fact,* and *of course* if you put them in the middle of a sentence. You would also use one comma if you put such a term at the beginning or end of a sentence: *For instance, coworkers are often unruly. Coworkers are often unruly, for instance.* This use of commas is tested on the GED Test.

Warm-up

Rewrite this passage. Correct any main verbs that do not agree with their subjects.

- Many people during a break in their careers feels they made an error. Others, like my friend Clara, takes the time off as a welcome relief. Your goal, more than other things, decide your attitude. Clara, who has been bored with all her jobs, want to learn a different one. Her main goal among others are to combine her work with her interests. For her, the break is worthwhile. I, on the other hand, has no choice. My unplanned baby, along with her two brothers, are separating me from my work.

Complete this sentence.

- My pet gripe, of course, is . . .

Write four or five sentences about your gripe. Use phrases in between your subjects and verbs to make your sentences more interesting, but be sure that subjects and verbs agree.

Warm-up Answers
feel; take; decides; wants; is; have; is separating

(1) A friend of mine, like all young mothers, are struggling through the "terrible twos" with her son. (2) Her son, for example, believes everything in the house is his. (3) The toys are his; the dog's bowl is his; even the remote control for the television is his. (4) One day, however she had enough and said, "William, will you please play quietly because Mommy is at the end of her rope." (5) William, with a glint in his two-year-old's eyes, looked her squarely in the face and said, "*My* rope, Mommy."

46. Sentence 1: **A friend of mine, like all young mothers, are struggling through the "terrible twos" with her son.**

    What correction should be made to this sentence?

    (1) change the spelling of friend to freind
    (2) change mothers to Mothers
    (3) change are to is
    (4) change the spelling of through to thru
    (5) replace through with thorough

47. Sentence 2: **Her son, for example, believes everything in the house is his.**

    Which of the following is the best way to write the underlined portion of this sentence? If you think the original is the best way, choose option (1).

    (1) believes (2) believe (3) believed
    (4) has believed (5) believing

48. Sentence 4: **One day, however she had enough and said, "William, will you please play quietly because Mommy is at the end of her rope."**

    What correction should be made to this sentence?

    (1) Insert a comma after however
    (2) change had to has
    (3) change the spelling of enough to enuff
    (4) change the spelling of please to pleese
    (5) replace quietly with quitely

Directions: For each item, choose the answer that would result in the most effective writing. Answers are on page 223.

(1) Like many people, you probally plan your vacation with relatives or friends, but have you ever thought of taking a learning vacation? (2) Such a vacation gives you the chance to learn or sharpen a skill. (3) Learning vacations can include lessons on cooking of the southwest or lessons with a professional photographer on trips to the Amazon Basin in South America. (4) If you are the outdoor type why not try a sailing school off the west coast of Florida?

49. Sentence 1: **Like many people, you probally plan your vacation with relatives or friends, but have you ever thought of taking a learning vacation?**

What correction should be made to this sentence?

(1) change the spelling of probally to probably
(2) remove the comma after friends
(3) remove the word but
(4) change have to has
(5) no correction is necessary

50. Sentence 3: **Learning vacations can include lessons on cooking of the southwest or lessons with a professional photographer on trips to the Amazon Basin in South America.**

What correction should be made to this sentence?

(1) change can include to included
(2) change southwest to Southwest
(3) change the spelling of professional to proffessional
(4) change Basin to basin
(5) change South to south

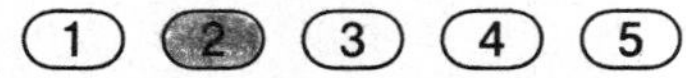

Capitalization Break/Place Names Sometimes all you'll need to grab a reader's attention is to write about a fascinating place. Just remember always to capitalize specific place names: *Madrid, Spain; Orange County, California; Catalina Island; Blue Ridge Mountains; Washington Monument; Sears Tower; Wall Street; U.S. Rte. 66; Rockland Road; Venus; Milky Way* (but not *sun, moon,* or *star*).

Watch out for direction words. You shouldn't capitalize them when you write about a general direction or geographic section: *m*idwestern Kansas, *s*outhern United States, *e*astern Asia, *n*orthwest Des Moines. You should capitalize direction words when they are part of place names: the *M*idwest, the *S*outh, the *F*ar *E*ast.

Warm-up

Rewrite these sentences. Capitalize place names and other words as needed.

1. the west has craggy peaks like the ones in the rocky mountains; the east has smoother ones.
2. the lake pontchartrain causeway near northern new orleans is the longest over-water highway.
3. in southeast georgia's okefenokee swamp, the water is good to drink but as dark as root beer.
4. the coldest weather in the arctic circle is in siberia, not at the north pole.
5. unless you have good survival skills, don't drive the lonely 287-mile stretch of u.s. hwy. 50 in nevada.

Now write some interesting sentences about each of these places. Capitalize as needed.

1. the state where you or a friend lives
2. any comet, planet, star, or other object in the sky
3. any public building

Can you write your own address correctly? Include your street, city, and state. Use abbreviations if you wish.

Warm-up Answers
1. The, West, Rocky Mountains, East **2.** The, Lake Pontchartrain Causeway, New Orleans **3.** In, Georgia's, Okefenokee Swamp **4.** The, Arctic Circle, Siberia, North Pole **5.** Unless, U.S. Hwy. 50, Nevada

Showing a Choice Between Subjects Sometimes you may want to show a choice between two subjects. You can do so by combining them with *or, either/or,* or *neither/nor.* Keep your eye on the second subject and the verb in the combined examples.

- No *student* at school *has* reason to fear computers. No *adult* at work *needs* to fear computers either.

  Combined: No student at school or *adult* at work *needs* to fear computers.

  My *savings are* one way I can pay for a computer. Or maybe a night *job is* how I'll pay for it.

  Combined: Either my savings or a night *job is* how I'll pay for my computer. *Or:* Either a night job or my *savings are* how I'll pay for my computer.

When you use *or, either/or,* or *neither/nor* to combine, make sure your verb agrees with the closest subject. As in the examples, you may need to reword to make your sentences smooth.

Warm-up

Rewrite these sentences. Combine the subjects using the words in parentheses. Reword as needed.

1. (or) No supermarket cashier works efficiently without computers. For that matter, no supermarket does either.
2. (neither/nor) Business isn't fully computerized yet. Government isn't computerized fully either.
3. (either/or) My parents are buying me a "surprise" computer for my birthday. Or maybe my wife is buying me the surprise.

Now combine these groups of words to write two sentences of your own.

4. neither/nor; desk-top computer; portable models; are
5. either/or; state legislatures; national government; have

Sample Warm-up Answers
1. No supermarket cashier or, for that matter, no supermarket works efficiently without a computer. **2.** Neither business nor government is fully computerized yet. **3.** Either my parents or my wife is buying me a "surprise" computer for my birthday. **4.** To me, neither the desk-top computer nor the portable models are worth the price. **5.** Either the national government or the state legislatures have to do something about keeping computerized records private.

(1) Often, neither readers nor writers truly understands the power of words. (2) Words not only have dictionary definitions, but they also have meanings that suggest positive or negative images. (3) For example, either "uninformed" or "stupid" are used to describe a person voting on an issue he knows nothing about. (4) Would you rather be called a fussy, scrawny person or an extremely neat, slender person? (5) One creative store owner uses the power of words to advertise her business: "We buy old furniture. We sell antiques."

51. Sentence 1: **Often, neither readers nor writers <u>truly understands</u> the power of words.**

    Which of the following is the best way to write the underlined portion of this sentence? If you think the original is the best way, choose option (1).

    (1) truly understands
    (2) truly understanding
    (3) truly understand
    (4) will truly understand
    (5) has truly understood

52. Sentence 2: **Words not only have dictionary definitions, but they also have meanings that suggest positive or negative images.**

    What correction should be made to this sentence?

    (1) change <u>only have</u> to <u>only has</u>
    (2) remove the comma after <u>definitions</u>
    (3) change <u>also have</u> to <u>also has</u>
    (4) change the spelling of <u>positive</u> to <u>posative</u>
    (5) no correction is necessary

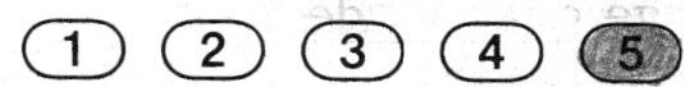

53. Sentence 3: **For example, either "uninformed" or "stupid" are used to describe a person voting on an issue he knows nothing about.**

    What correction should be made to this sentence?

    (1) remove the comma after <u>example</u>
    (2) change <u>are</u> to <u>is</u>
    (3) change <u>are</u> to <u>were</u>
    (4) change <u>knows</u> to <u>know</u>
    (5) change <u>knows</u> to <u>knew</u>

Directions: For each item, choose the answer that would result in the most effective writing. Answers are on page 223.

(1) Used to make ready-to-wear garments since the early 1900s, overlock sewing machines are now available to the home sewer. (2) There is differences between a conventional sewing machine and an overlock. (3) Most interesting are the way an overlock stitches, trims, and overcasts all in one step. (4) Overlocks sew twice as fast as conventional machines, and they make home sewing look more professional.

54. Sentence 2: **There is differences between a conventional sewing machine and an overlock.**

What correction should be made to this sentence?

(1) change is to are
(2) change is to were
(3) change is to had been
(4) change the spelling of differences to differenses
(5) change the spelling of between to betwean

55. Sentence 3: **Most interesting are the way an overlock stitches, trims, and overcasts all in one step.**

Which of the following is the best way to write the underlined portion of this sentence? If you think the original is the best way, choose option (1).

(1) are (2) is (3) be
(4) being (5) were

① ② ③ ④ ⑤

56. Sentence 4: **Overlocks sew twice as fast as conventional machines, and they make home sewing look more professional.**

If you rewrote sentence 4 beginning with With twice the speed of a conventional machine, an overlock
the next word(s) should be

(1) make (2) makes (3) made
(4) making (5) had been making

① ② ③ ④ ⑤

Writing Verbs Before Subjects The usual order of things is to put subjects before verbs. But sometimes you can make a sentence stronger by placing the verb first. Just make sure the verb and subject agree.

■ There *are* many *ways* for scriptwriters to grab an audience's attention. Here*'s one*: the unexpected *twist*. There*'s* no *question* or *argument* about how well it works. Most important, however, *is* the audience's *satisfaction* with the turn of events. Here *are* the *facts*. In public opinion, not writing tricks, *lie* the *seeds* of a writer's success.

Be careful when you are writing sentences that begin with *Here* and *There*. You read two of each in the example. Go back and find their subjects. When did the writer use *are* and *is* (*'s*)?

Warm-up

Rewrite each sentence. Use present time for the verbs in parentheses.

1. In the movie *Cocoon* (be) one good example of an older actor making a comeback.
2. In big trouble (be) the two musicians passing as showgirls in *Some Like It Hot*.
3. Skeptical but finally convinced (become) the grocery-manager-turned-prophet in *Oh, God!*
4. There (remain) neither monster nor spaceship by the end of the first *Alien* movie.
5. Here (be) two interesting twists in *Tootsie:* the actor loses the fame he wanted but finds the love he wasn't looking for.

Write four or five more sentences about movies you like or dislike. Try to switch the order of the subject and verb in two of them. Make sure that your subjects and verbs agree.

Warm-up Answers
1. is **2.** are **3.** becomes **4.** remains **5.** are

Capitalization Break/Special Days When you include the names of the days, weeks, holidays, and other special days in your writing, remember to capitalize them.

- Tuesday Friday Saturday
  June August December
  Easter Memorial Day Christmas Eve
  National Freedom Day Arbor Day
  Halloween

Use small letters for *the* and *of* when you write them in special days' names: *the Fourth of July*. You'll also have to capitalize *week* and *month,* but only when they're part of the name of a special week or month: *Pan American Week* (April), *Adult Literacy Awareness Month* (August). You don't have to capitalize the seasons: *winter/wintertime, spring, summer, fall, autumn.*

Warm-up

Rewrite these sentences. Capitalize words as needed.

1. in the united states, sunday is the only holiday recognized by law.
2. the fourth thursday in november is thanksgiving.
3. We celebrate some special birthdays on monday, though they may actually fall on another day: martin luther king's birthday (january 15) and washington's birthday (february 22).
4. three unusual special times in spring have been the national raisin week in april and yam day and national birds of prey month in may.

How do you spend special days? Write three or four sentences, each describing what you did on one holiday or special day each season this year. Make sure to capitalize properly.

Warm-up Answers
1. In, United States, Sunday **2.** The, Thursday, November, Thanksgiving **3.** We, Monday, Martin Luther King's Birthday, January, Washington's Birthday, February. **4.** Three, National Raisin Week, April, Yam Day, National Birds of Prey Month, May

(1) The word "holiday" originally meant "holy day," which was a festival to honor a sacred event or person. (2) Many countries celebrate a variety of interesting holidays, such as the Beanfeast and the Wayzgoose holidays in great Britain. (3) The Republic of Israel celebrates two independence days: passover, when the Hebrews were delivered from Egypt, and the Proclamation of the Jewish State, which took place in 1948. (4) Because of George Washington we celebrate Thanksgiving on the fourth Thursday in November, but the Pilgrims celebrated the holiday in February, July, and September.

57. Sentence 2: **Many countries celebrate a variety of interesting holidays, such as the Beanfeast and the Wayzgoose holidays in great Britain.**

    What correction should be made to this sentence?

    (1) change celebrate to celebrates
    (2) change the spelling of variety to varietie
    (3) change Beanfeast to beanfeast
    (4) change great to Great
    (5) no correction is necessary

58. Sentence 4: **Because of George Washington we celebrate Thanksgiving on the fourth Thursday in November, but the Pilgrims celebrated the holiday in February, July, and September.**

    What correction should be made to this sentence?

    (1) insert a comma after Washington
    (2) change fourth to Fourth
    (3) replace but with or
    (4) change the spelling of February to Febuary
    (5) no correction is necessary

Directions: For each item, choose the answer that would result in the most effective writing. Answers are on page 224.

(1) The advances of modern medicine is making our lives healthier than ever, but the expenses of medical care are greater than ever. (2) The more a consumer shops around for an insurance company, the easier it will be to find one with good coverage. (3) Usually, either a married couple's individual policies or a single family policy for most hospital bills.

59. Sentence 1: **The advances of modern medicine is making our lives healthier than ever, but the expenses of medical care are greater than ever.**

    What correction should be made to this sentence?

    (1) change is making to are making
    (2) change the spelling of healthier to healther
    (3) replace but with since
    (4) change are to is
    (5) change the spelling of greater to greatter

60. Sentence 2: **The more a consumer shops around for an insurance company, the easier it will be to find one with good coverage.**

    Which of the following is the best way to write the underlined portion of this sentence? If you think the original is the best way, choose option (1).

    (1) will be (2) be
    (3) will have been (4) being
    (5) has been

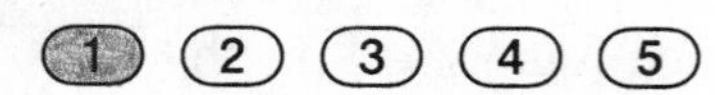

61. Sentence 3: **Usually, either a married couple's individual policies or a single family policy for most hospital bills.**

    What correction should be made to this sentence?

    (1) change the spelling of usually to usally
    (2) change couple's to couples
    (3) insert pays after policy
    (4) insert pay after policy
    (5) change hospital to Hospital

Spelling Break/Comparisons You'll want to make your GED essay as interesting as you can. One way is to compare things you write about. You can use *more* or *most* as comparing words: *mysterious, more mysterious, most mysterious.* If you're thinking in the other direction, you can use *less* or *least: mysterious, less mysterious, least mysterious.*

Another way to compare is to change the spelling of the ends of words. The GED Test has multiple-choice questions to see if you know this technique. The rules are easy. Usually you just add *-er* and *-est: straight, straighter, straightest.* If the word ends in *e,* just add *-r* and *-st: hoarse, hoarser, hoarsest.* For words that end in *-y,* change the *-y* to *-i* before you add *-er* and *-est: likely, likelier, likeliest.*

☑ A Test-Taking Tip

When you write your GED essay, use *more* and *most* with long words like *aggressive* (*more* aggressive, *most* aggressive). Use *-er* and *-est* for shorter words like *weird* (weird*er*, weird*est*).

Warm-up

Rewrite this passage. Use a logical comparing word for each word in parentheses.

■ There are three levels of makeup. Which would you rank as the (great)? The first is no makeup at all. The no-makeup people think the (plain) you look, the (pleasant) you are to look at. The in-betweens feel that the (appropriate) makeup is (heavy) than none but (light) than what some people wear. The (extreme) makeup can be a real work of art, and some people find thick makeup the (irresistible). Others disagree and say it's the (desirable), but people should seek beauty at their own level.

Here are some words from the GED Spelling List: careless, competent, courageous, efficient, fortunate, humorous, jealous, obedient, optimistic, original, precise, predictable, realistic, special, striking, successful, unusual.

Think of three people you know who are unlike one another. Then, in a few sentences, use any of the words here or in the lesson to compare them. Make sure you use all three comparing levels somewhere in your sentences.

Warm-up Answers
greatest, plainer, more pleasant, most appropriate, heavier, lighter, extremest *or* most extreme, most irresistible, least desirable

Spelling Break/Adding *-ly* When you write with words that end in *-ly,* you add a lot of meaning to your sentences. You can add *-ly* to descriptive words like *anxious, full, definite, exceptional, day,* and *comfortable.* See how important these words are to the following sentences' meanings.

■ Many GED students *anxiously* face the essay portion of the GED Writing Skills Test. If they *fully* understood the way words work, the students would *definitely* be more confident. *Exceptionally* important for students preparing for the test is to write *daily* until they can do so *comfortably.*

Here are five ways to add *-ly* to words.

1. Just add *-ly: anxious* + *-ly* = *anxiously; definite* + *-ly* = *definitely.*

2. When a word ends with two *ll*'s, add only *-y: full* + *-y* = *fully.*

3. When a word already ends in *-y,* change *-y* to *-i* and add *-ly: day* + *ly* = *daily.*

4. When a word ends in *-ble,* drop the *-e* and add *-ly; comfortable* + *-ly* = *comfortably.*

5. Memorize words like these, which follow their own rules: *whole* + *-ly* = *wholly; true* + *-ly* = *truly.*

Warm-up

Rewrite this passage. End each word in parentheses with *-ly.*

■ Writing students (*inevitable*) have to learn so many words. English students *(true)* have the biggest job, and few do it *(easy).* There are *(literal)* more words in English than any other language. Students *(sure)* try to learn as many as they can. But few people have the patience to *(dull)* plod through long vocabulary lists. Could you blame students for wanting to do away with words *(entire)*?

Here are some *-ly* words from the GED Spelling List. In three or four sentences, use the words to describe your feelings about getting ready for any part of the GED Test.

consequently especially immediately
probably scarcely severely sincerely
undoubtedly wholly

Warm-up Answers
inevitably, truly, easily, literally, surely, dully, entirely

(1) Occasionally, interesting facts about the government in Washington is reported. (2) The Office of Personnel Management was apparently interested in civil servants with unusual jobs and so decided to publish a list of federal jobs. (3) Scientificly speaking, jobs not normally associated with the government are those of astronomers and anthropologists. (4) On a recent survey list are jobs such as clothing designers, stevedores, cobblers, currency checkers, and broom makers. (5) There are sixteen butchers and nine bakers but no candlestick makers employed by the U.S. government.

62. Sentence 1: **Occasionally, interesting facts about the government in Washington is reported.**

    What correction should be made to this sentence?

    (1) change the spelling of Occasionally to Occasionaly
    (2) remove the comma after Occasionally
    (3) change Washington to washington
    (4) change is to are
    (5) no correction is necessary

63. Sentence 3: **Scientificly speaking, jobs not normally associated with the government are those of astronomers and anthropologists.**

    What correction should be made to this sentence?

    (1) change the spelling of Scientificly to Scientifically
    (2) remove the comma after speaking
    (3) change the spelling of associated to asociated
    (4) change are to is
    (5) no correction is necessary

Directions: For each item, choose the answer that would result in the most effective writing. Answers are on page 224.

(1) Not too many years ago, buying sneakers was easy. (2) The consumer's only choice was an inexpensive canvas sneaker originally designed for the tennis court. (3) Worn as a primary shoe today, the sneaker comes in a long list of types for consumers to choose from. (4) There are aerobic workout, high-top, and even snow sneakers. (5) Sold for a budget-breaking $25 and up, even infants can wear high-top sneakers.

64. Sentence 2: **The consumer's only choice was an inexpensive canvas sneaker originally designed for the tennis court.**

If you rewrote sentence 2 beginning with Originally designed for the tennis court, the next words should be

(1) the consumer's only choice was
(2) the inexpensive canvas sneaker was
(3) the inexpensiveness of canvas sneakers
(4) there was only one choice
(5) the consumer could choose only

65. Sentence 5: **Sold for a budget-breaking $25 and up, even infants can wear high-top sneakers.**

Which of the following is the best way to write the underlined portion of this sentence? If you think the original is the best way, choose option (1).

(1) even infants can wear high-top sneakers
(2) high-top sneakers are worn even by infants
(3) wearing high-top sneakers by infants
(4) and worn by infants in high-top sneakers
(5) there are infants wearing high-top sneakers

(1) (2) (3) (4) (5)

Adding Information in the Right Place You have learned the importance of putting enough information in your sentences. In the following examples, a GED student did a good job of adding information. Notice how she put in commas where adding information created a pause.

- *Using drugs, and the latest nutrition research, doctors* have brought many diseases under control.

  Patients take *drugs in pills or shots.*

  Heart transplants, *whether artificial or human,* help once-hopeless patients.

  Now implanted often, *pacemakers* keep heartbeats steady.

When you add information to your sentences, make sure to put it in the right place. The information needs to be close to the word that it is helping explain or describe. The GED student was wise to avoid writing sentences like these.

- Using drugs and the latest nutrition research, many *diseases* have been brought under control. (The student didn't mean to say that diseases use drugs and nutrition research.)

  In pills or shots, *patients* take drugs. (The patients aren't in the pills or shots.)

  Heart transplants help once-hopeless *patients*, whether artificial or human. (The patients aren't artificial or human.)

Sometimes you will have to do more than make sure all your information is in the right place. For example, how would you revise a sentence like this?

- Through constant research, more treatments are being made available to doctors.

Through constant research doesn't refer to *treatments,* nor does it refer to *doctors.* The subject of this sentence should be *scientists.* You would revise like this.

- Through constant research, *scientists* are making more treatments available to doctors.

Do the Warm-ups and read the tinted column on the next page before you try the sample test items in the white columns on this page and the next.

Warm-up 1

Rewrite each sentence. Put each phrase in an appropriate place in the sentence. Put in commas as necessary.

1. You need good nutrition and some exercise. (to keep healthy)
2. Walking can strengthen your heart. (at any pace)
3. High-fiber diets may reduce cancer risk. (followed faithfully; for some people)

Revise these sentences.

4. Whether fresh or frozen, many vitamins are in vegetables.
5. A good source is fish for getting protein into your diet.

Now write three or four sentences about your health. See if you can add information that would help a reader understand you better.

Adding Even More Information You can use just a couple of words and some commas to add information about people and things you write about. Notice where the information and commas are here.

■ Bill Chin, *my neighbor,* skydives.

Your husband's brother, *Solomon Garcia,* sold us our car.

Mercedes confides in Rosa and Carmen, *her two close friends.*

Warm-up 2

Using this lesson's examples as models, write a few sentences about friends, relatives, or other people you know. Make sure to check your commas.

Sample Warm-up 1 Answers
1. To keep healthy, you need good nutrition and some exercise. **2.** Walking at any pace can strengthen your heart. **3.** Followed faithfully, high-fiber diets may reduce cancer risk for some people. **4.** Whether fresh or frozen, vegetables have many vitamins. **5.** Fish is a good source for getting protein into your diet.

(1) The Marine Barracks in Washington, the oldest post of the Marine Corps is a registered National Historic Landmark. (2) Many tourists visit this landmark to hear the United States Marine band, "the President's Own." (3) John Philip Sousa, a famous composer, led the band during the years he composed many of his marches. (4) The Marines at the post also provide security for the president.

66. Sentence 1: **The Marine Barracks in Washington, the oldest post of the Marine Corps is a registered National Historic Landmark.**

Which of the following is the best way to write the underlined portion of this sentence? If you think the original is the best way, choose option (1).

(1) Corps is a (2) Corps, is a
(3) Corps; is a (4) Corps. Is a
(5) Corps. A

67. Sentence 2: **Many tourists visit this landmark to hear the United States Marine band, "the President's Own."**

What correction should be made to this sentence?

(1) change visit to visiting
(2) replace to hear with hearing
(3) change band to Band
(4) remove the comma after band
(5) no correction is necessary

1 2 3 4 5

68. Sentence 3: **John Philip Sousa, a famous composer, led the band during the years he composed many of his marches.**

Which of the following is the best way write the underlined portion of this sentence? If you think the original is the best way, choose option (1).

(1) Sousa, a famous composer, led
(2) Sousa, a famous composer led
(3) Sousa a famous composer, led
(4) Sousa a famous composer led
(5) Sousa, a famous composer. He led

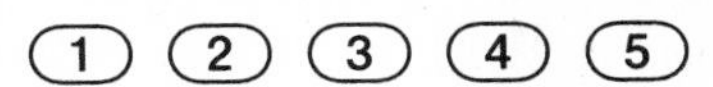

Directions: For each item, choose the answer that would result in the most effective writing. Answers begin on page 224.

(1) In the 1960s, the American alligator was in danger of becoming extinct, and they became listed with other endangered species. (2) Thanks to strict enforcement of antipoaching laws, the species has been taken off the list in Florida, Louisiana, and Texas. (3) Several other states are experiencing a population explosion of these ancient reptiles, to control their large numbers, the states hope to stage controlled hunts. (4) Their comeback has been strong, but if the alligator is killed off too quickly, it will be designated as "endangered" again.

69. Sentence 3: **Several other states are experiencing a population explosion of these ancient reptiles, to control their large numbers, the states hope to stage controlled hunts.**

Which of the following is the best way to write the underlined portion of this sentence? If you think the original is the best way, choose option (1).

(1) reptiles, to control
(2) reptiles to control
(3) reptiles, but to control
(4) reptiles; to control
(5) reptiles control

(1) (2) (3) (4) (5)

70. Sentence 4: **Their comeback has been strong, but if the alligator is killed off too quickly, it will be designated as "endangered" again.**

What correction should be made to this sentence?

(1) replace Their with Its
(2) change has been to will have been
(3) change is to were
(4) replace it with they
(5) no correction is necessary

(1) (2) (3) (4) (5)

Making Pronouns Agree with Words for Which They Stand

You have learned that pronouns like *I* and *she* are subjects. You no doubt also know these pronouns, which aren't subjects: *my, his, her, its, our, your,* and *their.* You can use these pronouns to show that words have to do with people or things you are writing about.

■ *Everett* is giving **his** testimony.

When you use pronouns, make sure they agree with the words they stand for. Sometimes the words for which they stand are in the sentence before the one in which the pronouns appear.

■ *England* was responsible for many American court practices. **It** also gave the United States a civil rights background.

You need to know one kind of word that can use either *it* (or *its*) or *they* (or *their*) as pronouns.

■ The *jury* is listening closely, and **it** will give **its** decision soon.

The first example tells you about the jury as one unit: *It is listening, and it will announce its decision.*

Warm-up

Rewrite these sentences on your own paper. Fill in each pronoun.

■ In ______ country, we're always taking oaths. By swearing allegiance to the flag, children might start as early as ______ first year in school. A couple getting married will promise that ______ will love and cherish. A club might swear in ______ officers. And the United States has ______ own oaths for everyone from the president to new citizens.

Write a few sentences about the duties or activities of any group you have belonged to or know about. Make sure to use some pronouns.

Warm-up Answers
our; their; they; its; its

Using Pronouns to Add Information Another way you can add information about people and things is with *who, whose, which,* and *that.* You can use these pronouns when you're adding information to singular or plural words.

■ **People *who*** *are having problems* need a break. Too bad everyone can't have a **Samantha, *who*** *helps her husband out of tight spots in the TV show called "Bewitched."* But there is one good luck **charm *that*** *will hang around any house.* This cloth **toy, *which*** *usually hangs from the cupboard,* is called the Kitchen Witch. You can get one to protect your stomach against cooking **disasters, *whose*** *effects can come back to haunt you.*

You need to know some rules for using these pronouns. First, use only *who* or *that* to refer to people. In the example, *people* and *Samantha* are followed by *who.* And you should use only *that* or *which* to refer to things. *Show, charm,* and toy are followed by *that* and *which. Whose* refers to persons or things, as in *disasters, whose.*

Put in commas where you hear a pause. Say all the sentences above in your head. Listen for pauses and watch for commas. Notice that *who* and *which*—never *that*—follow a comma.

Warm-up

Rewrite this passage on your own paper. Use *who, whose, which,* or *that* in the blanks. Put in commas as needed.

■ Some adults believe there are people _____ powers are supernatural. There are supposedly wizards _____ concoct love potions. And voodoo doctors are said to make voodoo dolls _____ are items into _____ people stick pins to harm enemies. One spirit _____ has made believers out of children is the tooth fairy. You might say that she has aspects _____ make her good and bad. With her, kids take a loss but wouldn't want to miss out on the financial gain _____ benefits are worth pulling teeth for.

Sample Warm-up Answers
people whose; wizards who; dolls, which; into which; spirit that; aspects that; gain, whose

(1) Dr. Helen B. Taussig, who pioneered ways to treat children born with heart defects, is known as the founder of pediatric cardiology. (2) She was the first woman to be President of the American Heart Association and to be made a full professor at the Johns Hopkins Medical School. (3) She was also the first American doctor to investigate birth defects in German babies whose mothers had taken the drug thalidomide. (4) For her work in this area, she was awarded the President's Medal of Freedom, which is the nation's highest civilian honor.

71. Sentence 2: **She was the first woman to be President of the American Heart Association and to be made a full professor at the Johns Hopkins Medical School.**

    What correction should be made to this sentence?

    (1) change President to president
    (2) insert a comma after Association
    (3) change be made to being made
    (4) change the spelling of professor to proffessor
    (5) change the spelling of professor to professer

    (1) (2) (3) (4) (5)

72. Sentence 4: **For her work in this area, she was awarded the President's Medal of Freedom, which is the nation's highest civilian honor.**

    Which of the following is the best way to write the underlined portion of this sentence? If you think the original is the best way, choose option (1).

    (1) Freedom, which is
    (2) Freedom, that being
    (3) Freedom, that is
    (4) Freedom, whose
    (5) Freedom, who is

Directions: For each item, choose the answer that would result in the most effective writing. Answers are on page 225.

(1) The people in your company's personnel office can help you in many ways. (2) It can provide information about new job openings and professional courses. (3) Many employees are eligible for education benefits once you have passed the GED Test, you might qualify for tuition assistance for college. (4) One should explore the career options available to you because learning always leads to growth.

73. Sentence 2: **It can provide information about new job openings and professional courses.**

What correction should be made to this sentence?

(1) replace It with They
(2) replace It with You
(3) change can provide to provided
(4) replace course with coarse
(5) no correction is necessary

(1) (2) (3) (4) (5)

74. Sentence 3: **Many employees are eligible for education benefits once you have passed the GED Test, you might qualify for tuition assistance for college.**

Which of the following is the best way to write the underlined portion of this sentence? If you think the original is the best way, choose option (1).

(1) benefits once
(2) benefits, once
(3) benefits, for once
(4) benefits. Once
(5) benefits; however, once

(1) (2) (3) (4) (5)

75. Sentence 4: **One should explore the career options available to you because learning always leads to growth.**

What correction should be made to this sentence?

(1) replace One with You
(2) replace One with They
(3) change the spelling of career to carear
(4) replace you with one
(5) replace you with them

(1) (2) (3) (4) (5)

Using Consistent Pronouns Do you have trouble keeping track of pronouns? See if you can tell which ones got away from the GED student who wrote this passage.

■ *I* probably like sailing more than fishing, when *one* compares the two. A fishing boat has *its* dirty work, unlike *her* cleaner cousin, the sailing boat. And a fishing pole needs *its* attention. *You* can't leave *them* alone for a minute. *One* has to watch constantly.

This GED student lost track of almost all her pronouns. She logically began with *I* because she was talking about her opinions and experiences. She should have followed through with *I* where it would be logical: *when **I** compare the two; **I** can't leave; **I** have to watch.*

Where *I* isn't logical, the student needs to use the same pronoun for the same thing: *fishing boat has **its** dirty work; unlike **its** cleaner cousin.*

The next two sentences are about a fishing pole. Since there's only one, both pronouns should be singular: *need **its** attention; can't leave **it**.*

Warm-up

Rewrite this passage. Replace the first *one* with *I*. Then correct other pronouns and verbs as needed.

■ If *one* wants to fish for trout, *they* have to do some work. First *you* have to get the right bait. *One* should use trout flies. Many people make *it* from scratch, using kits from sporting goods stores. There's a small store near *my* new house, but there *you* would have to special-order. *One* would do better to take the long trip to *our* old store because *they* have a greater selection.

Sample Warm-up Answers
I want, I, I, I, them, my (logical), I, I, my, it has

Revising Awkward Sentences The first way a writer writes a sentence is often not the best. Always look for and revise awkward sentences in your own writing. How could the following sentence be made clearer and smoother?

■ U.S. immigrants who have just arrived in this country, as you might expect, in many cases have difficulties.

Separating a subject and a verb with added information is all right, but you don't need to separate the subject and verb as much as in the example.

■ As you might expect, newly arrived U.S. immigrants in many cases have difficulties.

How could you improve this sentence?

■ People who don't speak English can't, sometimes for several years, really master the language fully.

Reorder some parts of the sentence and reduce the number of words in others.

■ Sometimes non-English speakers take several years to master the language fully.

Warm-up

Revise the sentences in this passage. Keep in mind that the answer given is a *sample;* there is more than one way to revise a sentence.

■ One Russian immigrant was, before he left Europe, told to expect to see the Statue of Liberty first, but all that he saw was a woman in the immigration office. He asked her, and he was really serious, whether she was the Statue of Liberty. The woman wanted to be kind to him and to quickly and quietly help him out of the awkward situation he had gotten himself into. She said that seeing that she was tired and somewhat poor, she supposed she qualified for, as much as anyone, the title.

Write a passage about any awkward situation you've found yourself in. Then revise any awkward sentences you find in the passage.

Sample Warm-up Answers

Before leaving Europe, one Russian immigrant was told to expect to see the Statue of Liberty first, but in reality he saw a woman in the immigration office. He asked her seriously whether she was the Statue of Liberty. The woman wanted to help him out of his awkward situation kindly, quickly, and quietly. She said that since she was tired and somewhat poor, she supposed she qualified for the title as much as anyone.

(1) The man who founded Cornell University was Ezra Cornell. (2) He made his fortune in the telegraph industry. (3) He had very little formal education, but he was a genius at inventing machines. (4) In 1844 Cornell, after a way was invented by him that helped people insulate wires on poles, also helped build the world's first telegraph line from Baltimore to Washington. (5) First he became the chief stockholder in Western Union and afterward devoted his life to farming and public service.

76. Sentences 1 and 2: **The man who founded Cornell University was Ezra Cornell. He made his fortune in the telegraph industry.**

    The most effective combination of sentences 1 and 2 would include which of the following groups of words?

    (1) Cornell, the founder of Cornell University, made
    (2) after having founded Cornell University
    (3) founded as well as made his fortune
    (4) The man who made
    (5) Cornell, and he also made

    ① ② ③ ④ ⑤

77. Sentence 4: **In 1844 Cornell, after a way was invented by him that helped people insulate wires on poles, also helped build the world's first telegraph line from Baltimore to Washington.**

    If you rewrote sentence 4 beginning with

    After inventing a way to insulate wires on poles,
    the next words should be

    (1) Cornell helped (2) people built
    (3) in 1844 (4) the world's first
    (5) also helped

    ① ② ③ ④ ⑤

Directions: For each item, choose the answer that would result in the most effective writing. Answers are on page 225.

(1) The closer it gets to Christmas, the closer many married couples come to open conflict about what gifts to buy each other. (2) Some spouses mount organized campaigns to give hints about apropriate gifts. (3) They leave notes in drawers, open catalogs to important pages, or strategically sigh when a desired gift is advertised on television. (4) The holiday spirit of both spouses rarely dissipate as the scent of victory overrides the fear of disappointment.

78. Sentence 2: **Some spouses mount organized campaigns to give hints about apropriate gifts.**

What correction should be made to this sentence?

(1) change mount to mounts
(2) change mount to will have mounted
(3) change the spelling of campaigns to campains
(4) change the spelling of apropriate to appropriate
(5) no correction is necessary

① ② ③ ④ ⑤

79. Sentence 4: **The holiday spirit of both spouses rarely dissipate as the scent of victory overrides the fear of disappointment.**

What correction should be made to this sentence?

(1) change the spelling of holiday to holliday
(2) change dissipate to dissipates
(3) change the spelling of dissipate to dissapate
(4) change the spelling of disappointment to dissappointment
(5) change the spelling of disappointment to disapointment

① ② ③ ④ ⑤

Spelling Break/Silent or Confusing Letters

You can't always trust your ears when you spell. Sometimes words have double letters, but you can hear only one: *transferred*; *dissatisfied*; *accommodate*; *excellent*. The letters *a*, *e*, and *i* sound alike in many words: *grievance/existence*; *confident/brilliant*; *available/eligible*.

There are words in which you can't hear letters at all: *muscle* (silent *c*); *autumn* (silent *n*). And you may mispronounce other words and incorrectly spell them that way: *temperature* (not *temprature*); *similar* (not *similiar*).

The rules for memorizing words like these have many exceptions. So your best strategy is to practice the words with the techniques you learned about on page 160. Make sure to do so for any words you miss in the Warm-up.

Warm-up

Spell these words according to the directions for each group. Check your spellings with the GED Spelling List on pages 216–219.

1. Add these endings to these words.

begin + *-ing* commit + *-ed*
control + *-ed* equip + *-ed*
quarrel + *-ing* refer + *-ed*

2. Add *-ance* or *-ence*.

guid perman
persever signific

3. Add *-ant* or *-ent*.

assist independ
relev superintend

4. Add *-able* or *-ible*.

advis change comfort
irresist irrit peace

5. Circle the words that are spelled wrong. Rewrite *every* word.

across already alright anser
benefitted conquer diffrent
forhead government kitchen
mispelled noticible occurred ommit
pastime preferrence prefered
quanity roomate sevral sheperd
solem suprise telefon tenent
unnecesary vacuum vegetable

Now write a sentence with each word you spelled wrong in this Warm-up.

Spelling Break/Apostrophes You can add apostrophes (') to words to show that someone or something owns something. To use apostrophes correctly, follow these guidelines.

Add *-'s* to singular words: *the magazine**'s** cover*, *the princess**'s** wedding*, *Rob**'s** basketball*, *Charles**'s** daughters*. For plural words, just add the apostrophe: *the bachelors' stag party*, *the businesses' licenses; the Martins' automobile.* If you are writing just a plural, don't use any apostrophe at all: *your neighbor*, *our neighbors*; *my address*, *their addresses*.

You can also use apostrophes to show missing letters.

■ Who*'s* (Who *is*) here?

They*'re* (They *are*) here.

No, there*'s* (there *is*) no one here.

Be careful when you spell words that have no apostrophes but sound like words that do. Many of the pronouns you studied are like that.

Warm-up

Only one of these italicized words is spelled right. With the correct spellings, rewrite the passage.

■ *Theirs* no insurance against some of *earths' danger's.* Can you believe that in 1887, 900,000 Chinese *citizen's* died in a *series'* of *floods'?* A cyclone and tidal *waves'* toll in 1970 was over 266,000 *Pakistanis'.* The United *States* highest fatalities occurred in *Texas's* devastating hurricane and storm tide that ripped through Galveston in 1900. *It's* total was over 6,000 *live's.*

Think about a storm, disaster, or other situation you've been in where damage has occurred. Write a few sentences about the people involved and the property they lost or had to repair. Try to include some words that need apostrophes to show possession or to show that a letter is missing.

☑ A Test-Taking Tip

Misusing *their* for *they're* is a common error that is often found on the GED Test. Watch for it, and be sure you know which word is correct in the particular sentence.

Warm-up Answers
There's; earth's; dangers; citizens; series; floods; wave's; Pakistanis; States'; *Texas's* is correct; Its; lives

(1) The population of the United States includes 498,000 legally blind people, with more than 11 million visually handicapped persons. (2) Several publishing companies have began to add large-print books to their inventories. (3) The main audience for these books are the growing number of older people, but many publishers believe that there's a new market for their large-print books. (4) A growing number of younger people, after working all day in front of computer screens, will find large-print books refreshing for their tired eyes.

80. Sentence 2: **Several publishing companies have began to add large-print books to their inventories.**

    What correction should be made to this sentence?

    (1) insert a comma after companies
    (2) insert the word will after companies
    (3) change have to has
    (4) change began to begun
    (5) replace their with there

    ① ② ③ ④ ⑤

81. Sentence 3: **The main audience for these books are the growing number of older people, but many publishers believe that there's a new market for their large-print books.**

    What correction should be made to this sentence?

    (1) replace these with them
    (2) change are to is
    (3) remove the comma after people
    (4) replace there's with theirs
    (5) replace their with they're

    ① ② ③ ④ ⑤

82. Sentence 4: **A growing number of younger people, after working all day in front of computer screens, will find large-print books refreshing for their tired eyes.**

    What correction should be made to this sentence?

    (1) remove the comma after people
    (2) change will find to had been finding
    (3) change will find to found
    (4) replace their with they're
    (5) no correction is necessary

Directions: For each item, choose the answer that would result in the most effective writing. Answers are on page 226.

(1) Have you ever been standing at the front door, fiddled with your keys, when you hear the telephone ring? (2) By the turn of the century, you will know who were trying to reach you. (3) The clue to the caller's identity will be in the sound of the ring. (4) You will be able to give each of your ten most frequent callers a different ring. (5) Avoiding unwanted callers and to control your time at home will be two advantages of this new telephone service.

83. Sentence 1: **Have you ever been standing at the front door, fiddled with your keys, when you hear the telephone ring?**

What correction should be made to this sentence?

(1) change Have to Has
(2) change fiddled to to fiddle
(3) change fiddled to fiddling
(4) replace when with after
(5) change hear to hearing

(1) (2) (3) (4) (5)

84. Sentence 2: **By the turn of the century, you will know who were trying to reach you.**

What correction should be made to this sentence?

(1) change century to Century
(2) change you will to one will
(3) change will know to had known
(4) change will know to knew
(5) change were to was

(1) (2) (3) (4) (5)

85. Sentence 5: **Avoiding unwanted callers and to control your time at home will be two advantages of this new telephone service.**

Which of the following is the best way to write the underlined portion of this sentence? If you think the original is the best way, choose option (1).

(1) to control (2) controlling
(3) having controlled
(4) to have controlled (5) control

(1) (2) (3) (4) (5)

Matching Forms of Words When you write a sentence that compares, contrasts, or somehow lists two things, you will need to put your words in the same form. Here is how one writer could match up words in a paragraph he wrote as part of a magazine article.

- When a couple *fails* to have a child and after *discussing* the problem with a doctor, they may decide that the wife will try fertility drugs.

  Revised: After *failing* to have a child and *discussing* the problem. . . . *Or*: After a couple *has failed* to have a child and *has discussed* the problem. . . .

  Fertility *drugs* rather than *to become pregnant* naturally mean more twins and other multiple births.

  Revised: Fertility *drugs* rather than natural *pregnancy* mean. . . . Or: *To take* fertility drugs rather than *to become* pregnant naturally means. . . .

  For some couples, *having* twins is more fun than *to have* only one.

  Revised: For some couples, *having* twins is more fun than *having*. . . . *Or*; For some couples, *to have* twins is more fun than *to have*. . . .

Warm-up

Match word forms in these sentences. Rewrite the sentences.

1. Some twins claim to feel each other's pain and that they have the same thoughts.
2. Curiosity and being clever are traits of those born under the Gemini twins' sign.
3. Twins on TV advertise gum by singing a tune and with smiles.
4. In *Return of the Jedi,* helping his twins Luke and Leia became more important to Darth Vader than to support the emperor.

Match these pairs of words in sentences of your own that discuss how parents and children can get along.

having peace of mind/to have children
patience/being understanding
when families disagreed/they could discuss

Sample Warm-up Answers
1. Some twins claim to feel each other's pain and to have the same thoughts. **2.** Curiosity and cleverness are traits of those born under the Gemini twins' sign. **3.** Twins on TV advertise gum by singing a tune and smiling. **4.** In *Return of the Jedi,* helping his twins Luke and Leia became more important to Darth Vader than supporting the emperor.

Combining Three or More You have learned that you need no commas to combine two people or things that you write about.

■ Stress can overwhelm people, and make them mentally ill. Overwork, and poor health cause stress. It also results from money problems, or divorce. Deep breathing, and good nutrition control stress.

Those unneeded commas between two things should have been left out. But when you combine three or more things you add commas, as in the next example.

■ Stress can overwhelm people, make them mentally ill, cause physical problems, and actually kill. Overwork, poor health, and past experiences cause stress. It also results from money problems, divorce, or job difficulties. Deep breathing relieves stress, good nutrition controls it, and common sense keeps it in perspective.

In your own writing you *could* leave out the comma before *and* or *or* in lists of three or more. But if you leave it out in one, you should leave it out in all.

Warm-up

Rewrite these sentences. Put in commas where you need them to combine words into lists. Be consistent with commas before *and* and *or.*

■ People with mental disorders think feel react or generally behave oddly. Some believe false things and insist they are true. Severely depressed people are sad insecure and negative. Senseless or terrifying thoughts come to certain mentally ill people. One group withdraws from reality another cannot move at all and still another group fears literally everything.

These words are in groups of twos and threes. Combine each group with *and*, *or*, and commas as appropriate. Then, with the combinations, write at least four sentences of your own about moods.

angry/frustrated/nervous — calm/contented
smile/laugh/giggle — worry/lose sleep

Sample Warm-up Answers

People with mental disorders think, feel, react, or generally behave oddly. Some believe false things and insist they are true. Severely depressed people are sad, insecure, and negative. Senseless or terrifying thoughts come to certain mentally ill people. One group withdraws from reality, another cannot move at all, and still another group fears literally everything.

(1) Many homeowners are investing in electronic security systems to make their homes safe from trespassers burglars, or other intruders. (2) Currently on the market is systems that can control up to 256 lights and appliances automatically, efficiently, and cheaply. (3) Some systems combine video cameras with computers and allow a person to monitor a summer home or a business from the owner's home. (4) Do-it-yourselfers can install most of these systems by making use of existing home wiring.

86. Sentence 1: **Many homeowners are investing in electronic security systems to make their homes safe from <u>trespassers burglars, or other intruders.</u>**

Which of the following is the best way to write the underlined portion of this sentence? If you think the original is the best way, choose option (1).

(1) trespassers burglars, or other intruders
(2) trespassers, burglars or, other intruders
(3) trespassers, burglars, or other intruders
(4) trespassers burglars or other intruders
(5) trespassers, or burglars, or other intruders

87. Sentence 2: **Currently on the market is systems that can control up to 256 lights and appliances automatically, efficiently, and cheaply.**

What correction should be made to this sentence?

(1) change <u>is</u> to <u>are</u>
(2) replace <u>that</u> with <u>which</u>
(3) replace <u>that</u> with <u>who</u>
(4) insert a comma after <u>lights</u>
(5) remove the comma after <u>automatically</u>

① ② ③ ④ ⑤

Directions: For each item, choose the answer that would result in the most effective writing. Answers are on page 226.

(1) Deep-sea diving teams methodically search for decaying wrecks of British pay ships, ancient frigates, or Pirates' galleys. (2) Interesting artifacts such as Chinese ceramics, pottery, and gold jewelry is recovered from wrecks all over the world. (3) One treasure hunter Mel Fisher, has found the remains of a Spanish galleon off the Florida Keys. (4) He and his divers have recovered treasures with an estimated value of $400 million.

88. Sentence 1: **Deep-sea diving teams methodically search for decaying wrecks of British pay ships, ancient frigates, or Pirates' galleys.**

What correction should be made to this sentence?

(1) change search to searches
(2) change British to british
(3) remove the comma after ships
(4) change Pirates' to pirates'
(5) no correction is necessary

(1) (2) (3) (4) (5)

89. Sentence 2: **Interesting artifacts such as Chinese ceramics, pottery, and gold jewelry is recovered from wrecks all over the world.**

What correction should be made to this sentence?

(1) change Chinese to chinese
(2) remove the comma after ceramics
(3) change is to are
(4) remove the word is
(5) change world to World

(1) (2) (3) (4) (5)

90. Sentence 3: **One treasure hunter Mel Fisher, has found the remains of a Spanish galleon off the Florida Keys.**

What correction should be made to this sentence?

(1) insert a comma after hunter
(2) remove the comma after Fisher
(3) change has to have
(4) change Spanish to spanish
(5) change Keys to keys

(1) (2) (3) (4) (5)

Capitalization Break/Names That Describe
You can use many names to help describe other people or things: *Texas*, *Texas chili*; *New York*, *New York skyline*; *Bogart*, *Bogart movies*; *Communist*, *Communist country*. Sometimes you need to change the name somewhat: *Europe*, *European tour*; *China*, *Chinese art*; *Episcopal*, *Episcopalian minister*; *Shakespeare*, *Shakespearean play*.

Remember to capitalize names when you use them to describe other words.

Warm-up

Rewrite this passage. Capitalize words as needed.

■ the christian christmas celebration has many customs worldwide. when mom and dad were growing up in mexico, they always had a piñata to break open on christmas eve. sinterklaas and his black companion pete give dutch children presents. argentine families have "wrapped children," which are stuffed beef rolls. in the united states, this season is one when all republican and democratic members of congress agree—to adjourn as early as possible.

Write a few sentences about a custom or activity in the United States or in another country. Use names that describe the people and things you write about. Make sure to capitalize them.

Warm-up Answers
The, Christian, Christmas; When, Mom, Dad, Mexico, Christmas Eve; Sinterklaas, Pete, Dutch; Argentine; In, United States, Republican, Democratic, Congress

Avoiding Confusing Pronouns Whenever you use a pronoun, make sure your reader can tell who or what it refers to. Whom does *his* refer to in this sentence?

■ Al went with Nick to get a video recorder for *his* apartment.

Does *his* refer to Al or Nick?

In the next example, the confusing pronoun stands for a word in another sentence.

■ Carla ordered some tapes to show her friends. However, *they* arrived late.

Were Carla's tapes or friends late?

A good way for you to fix confusing pronouns is just to repeat a word, especially if there is a chance your reader will get confused by the pronoun.

■ Al went with Nick to get a video recorder for Al's apartment.
Carla ordered some tapes to show her friends. However, the tapes arrived late.

Warm-up

Rewrite this passage. Revise unclear pronouns.

■ Although a big collection of videotapes impresses people, they cost a lot. A rental service earns its fee by providing any tape quickly and cheaply. But it can get into the wrong box. My friend Turie and her daughter Dawn were confused after she rented *The Muppet Movie* and got *Attack of the Killer Tomatoes* instead. Then they got in a stew because she refused to play the tape.

Write a few sentences about a disagreement with someone you once had. Use as many pronouns as you can to explain both sides of the argument. Check the pronouns to make sure none is confusing.

Sample Warm-up Answers
Although a big collection of videotapes impresses people, the tapes cost a lot. A rental service earns its fee by providing any tape quickly and cheaply. But a tape can get into the wrong box. My friend Turie and her daughter Dawn were confused after Turie rented *The Muppet Movie* and got *Attack of the Killer Tomatoes* instead. Then Turie and Dawn got in a stew because Turie refused to play the tape.

(1) The environmental commissioner and the governor have agreed on her policy of not building giant shopping malls in the state. (2) Both feel that business people have exaggerated the need for them. (3) Environmentalists believe that the malls cause traffic problems and strain a city's sewage and water resources. (4) Economists disagree with the views of environmentalists and argue that they generate jobs and boost a city's economy.

91. Sentence 1: **The environmental commissioner and the governor have agreed on her policy of not building giant shopping malls in the state.**

What correction should be made to this sentence?

(1) insert a comma after <u>commissioner</u>
(2) change the spelling of <u>governor</u> to <u>govenor</u>
(3) change <u>have</u> to <u>has</u>
(4) replace <u>her</u> with <u>the governor's</u>
(5) change <u>state</u> to <u>State</u>

(1) (2) (3) (4) (5)

92. Sentence 2: **Both feel that business people have exaggerated the need for them.**

What correction should be made to this sentence?

(1) insert the word <u>who</u> after <u>people</u>
(2) change <u>have</u> to <u>has</u>
(3) insert the word <u>will</u> after <u>people</u>
(4) change the spelling of <u>exaggerated</u> to <u>exagerated</u>
(5) no correction is necessary

(1) (2) (3) (4) (5)

93. Sentence 4: **Economists disagree with the views of environmentalists and argue that <u>they</u> generate jobs and boost a city's economy.**

Which of the following is the best way to write the underlined portion of this sentence? If you think the original is the best way, choose option (1).

(1) they (2) economists
(3) malls (4) environmentalists
(5) their views

(1) (2) (3) (4) (5)

Directions: For each item, choose the answer that would result in the most effective writing. Answers begin on page 226.

(1) There is always at least one neighbor whose unerring instinct leads him directly to your newly purchased hedge trimmers. (2) This means that every spring you must be possessive with your tools or pursue the tools that "walked away." (3) Maybe you should put an electronic homing device on each of your most valuable ones, which could get expensive. (4) What Shakespeare said is true: "Neither a borrower nor a lender be."

94. Sentence 2: **<u>This means that</u> every spring you must be possessive with your tools or pursue the tools that "walked away."**

Which of the following is the best way to write the underlined portion of this sentence? If you think the original is the best way, choose option (1).

(1) This means that (2) As a result,
(3) However, (4) Which is why
(5) In other words,

① ② ③ ④ ⑤

95. Sentence 3: **Maybe you should put an electronic homing device on each of your most valuable ones, which could get expensive.**

What correction should be made to this sentence?

(1) insert a comma after <u>Maybe</u>
(2) change <u>you</u> to <u>one</u>
(3) change the spelling of <u>device</u> to <u>devise</u>
(4) replace <u>your</u> with <u>his</u>
(5) replace <u>which</u> with <u>but that solution</u>

① ② ③ ④ ⑤

96. Sentence 4: **<u>What Shakespeare said</u> is true: "Neither a borrower nor a lender be."**

Which of the following is the best way to write the underlined portion of this sentence? If you think the original is the best way, choose option (1).

(1) What Shakespeare said
(2) What they say
(3) What one says
(4) You could say that this
(5) What he said

① ② ③ ④ ⑤

Avoiding Pronouns That Refer to Nothing

You know you can use the pronouns *which* and *that* to add information about specific words that come before them. You can use *this* in the same way.

■ There are many exercise *classes* **that** you can join. Some require strenuous *activity*, and you need **this** for tight muscles. Exercise also strengthens your *heart*, **which** you must take care of as you grow older.

However, when you use these words to refer to an entire thought, you aren't working hard enough.

■ Physical fitness and health aren't the same, *which* sounds like a contradiction. But *that* is true. Healthy but unfit people tire quickly. *This* also means they have less energy for other interests.

This doctor should work out a little more by getting rid of *which*, *that*, and *this* or by adding specific words that they can help describe.

■ Physical fitness and health aren't the same, and **that** *statement* is no contradiction. Healthy but unfit people tire quickly and have less energy for other interests.

The doctor also wrote these sentences. The pronoun subjects refer to nothing at all.

■ *They* say people would exercise if more leisure time was available. But *it*'s necessary to make time for good health.

Who's *they*? What's *it*?

■ *Excuse makers* say people would exercise if more leisure time was available. But *people need* to make time for good health.

Warm-up

Reword and rewrite these sentences. Get rid of any misused *which*, *that*, *this*, *they*, or *it*.

1. Physically fit people fight off disease better, and this means they recover faster.
2. Senior citizens need to keep limber. That means they need to exercise.
3. Grandfather looks half his age, and it's because he's exercised all his life.

Write four of five sentences about something you won't stand for. Use *which*, *that*, or *this*.

Sample Warm-up Answers
1. Physically fit people fight off disease better and so recover faster. **2.** Senior citizens need to exercise to keep limber. **3.** Grandfather looks half his age because he's exercised all his life.

Revising What's Nonsensical, Unneeded, or Negative The first sentence in each example below is technically correct but weakly written. The second sentence is well written. The GED Test has questions for which you're going to have to be able to tell the difference.

1. Make sure you have said what you mean.

■ Learning how other people live is interesting.

Revised: Learning about ancient peoples' bathing facilities is interesting.

2. Get rid of repeated information.

■ Archeologists have found ancient bath ruins, and ancient people seem to have had baths.

Revised: Archeologists have found ancient bath ruins.

3. Get rid of *not* and *-n't* where you can. Your sentences will be stronger.

■ In ancient Rome, average people could not (or couldn't) afford private baths.

Revised: In ancient Rome, only the wealthy could afford private baths.

4. Get rid of informal comments or slang and unneeded words.

■ To get around the problem, the Romans built public baths in just about every single city.

Revised: However, the Romans built public baths in most cities.

Warm-up

Revise these sentences. For each, use one of the techniques above.

■ During the Middle Ages, Europeans bathed less often than you could ever possibly believe. Public bathhouses where people went to bathe and wash up were called *stews.* Stews didn't have a good reputation. So government officials decided to go have a look at them.

Write a few sentences about cleaning up the place where you live or work. Then revise your sentences. Keep in mind the above techniques.

Sample Warm-up Answers

During the Middle Ages, Europeans rarely bathed. Public bathhouses were called *stews.* Stews had a bad reputation. (*Or:* Stews were disreputable.) So government officials decided to investigate them.

(1) The loudest sound ever heard on earth occurred when the volcano Krakatoa erupted in 1883. (2) This powerfully big blast, which made a really loud noise, erupted with the unbelievable force of one million atomic bombs and reduced in size an eighteen-square-mile island to only six miles. (3) Accompanying this eruption, there were earthquakes like you wouldn't believe, causing a tidal wave 200 feet high that traveled 400 miles per hour and destroyed whole towns. (4) Chunks of red-hot rocks, some eight feet thick and weighing seventy pounds, fell over an area as large as France.

97. Sentence 2: **This powerfully big blast, which made a really loud noise, erupted with the unbelievable force of one million atomic bombs and reduced in size an eighteen-square-mile island to only six miles.**

If you rewrote sentence 2 beginning with
Erupting with the force of one million atomic bombs,
the next words should be

(1) an eighteen-square-mile island was
(2) the blast was unbelievable
(3) a really loud noise was
(4) this explosion reduced
(5) and reducing in size

(1) (2) (3) (4) (5)

98. Sentence 3: **Accompanying this eruption, there were earthquakes like you wouldn't believe, causing a tidal wave 200 feet high that traveled 400 miles per hour and destroyed whole towns.**

If you rewrote sentence 3 beginning with
The earthquakes accompanying this eruption
the next words should be

(1) were unbelievably bad
(2) caused a tidal wave
(3) traveled 400 miles
(4) destroyed whole towns
(5) were caused by

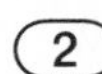

Directions: For each item, choose the answer that would result in the most effective writing. Answers are on page 227.

(1) Pets like their owners. (2) For this reason, pets make people who own them less lonely than most people without pets. (3) There are some children who arrive home before their parents do and feel safe when they have pets. (4) Human beings and dogs have been hanging out together like this for more than 30,000 years.

99. Sentence 2: **For this reason, pets make people who own them less lonely than most people without pets.**

If you rewrote sentence 2 beginning with
This loyalty helps pet owners
the next words should be

(1) feel less (2) own them
(3) and people without pets
(4) for this reason (5) make people

(1) (2) (3) (4) (5)

100. Sentence 3: **There are some children who arrive home before their parents do and feel safe when they have pets.**

If you rewrote sentence 4 beginning with
For children arriving home before their parents do,
the next words should be

(1) a pet can make them feel safe
(2) and feeling safe
(3) and for parents coming home
(4) when they have pets
(5) they feel safe

(1) (2) (3) (4) (5)

101. Sentence 4: **Human beings and dogs have been hanging out together like this for more than 30,000 years.**

Which of the following is the best way to write the underlined portion of this sentence? If you think the original is the best way, choose option (1).

(1) hanging out together like this
(2) helping each other thus
(3) the best of friends
(4) in association with one another
(5) pals

(1) (2) (3) (4) (5)

Revising What's Underlined, Overpunctuated, and Overloaded You're almost ready for the conventions of English section of the GED Writing Skills Test now. These are the last four revision techniques you need to know.

5. Get rid of unneeded underlining and exclamation marks. A good sentence stands on its own.

- The Roman bathhouses offered warm and cold baths, steam baths, and massages!

  Revised: The Roman bathhouses offered warm and cold baths, steam baths, and massages.

6. Get rid of *very, pretty, little,* and *rather* when you have used them too often to emphasize another word.

- One very big Roman bath held a rather stunning 1,600 bathers at a time.

  Revised: One enormous Roman bath held a stunning 1,600 bathers at a time.

7. Put words in front of words they describe.

- Along with ceilings that were painted, there were columns, floors, and statues of marble.

  Revised: Along with painted ceilings, there were marble columns, floors, and statues.

8. With strong verbs that involve *action,* replace long, weak wording.

- Often actors in plays were seen on stage by bathers.

  Revised: Actors often staged plays for bathers.

Warm-up

Revise these sentences.

- During the Middle Ages, what a catastrophe befell Europe. Laws that closed public baths were passed by governments. And the bottom *fell out* of the public bathing! People bathed at home pretty little. Instead, businesses that specialized in paint, powder, and perfume grew.

You've written many of your ideas in sentences. But until the last two lessons, you've concentrated on mechanics. With the eight techniques you've just learned in mind, go back and review your work. Do any of your sentences need revising?

Sample Warm-up Answers

During the Middle Ages, what a catastrophe befell Europe! Governments banned public baths. And the bottom fell out of public bathing. People seldom bathed at home. Instead, paint, powder, and perfume businesses grew.

Writing Your Ideas in Paragraphs

In the first part of this *Writing Skills* section you practiced writing down your ideas in effective sentences. In this part you can work to present those ideas by writing effective paragraphs.

A **paragraph** consists of sentences that develop a single topic.

Here's the last paragraph you worked on in the last white column. Read it from beginning to end again, and see how all the sentences talk about the topic of pets and their relationship with people.

■ Pets like their owners. This loyalty helps pet owners feel less lonely than most people without pets. For children arriving home before their parents do, a pet can make them feel safe. Human beings and dogs have been helping each other this way for more than 30,000 years.

Each sentence in that paragraph states something about pets and people.

In almost any kind of writing that you do, you will use paragraphs to organize your ideas. Certainly one of the first steps in writing a successful GED essay is developing your skill at writing a good paragraph. And the first step in writing a good paragraph is to make prewriting notes.

Coming to Terms

paragraph group of sentences about a single topic

Prewriting to Get Ideas Before you actually begin to write a paragraph, you should make *prewriting* notes. In these notes you can list your ideas and thoughts about the topic.

The purpose of making prewriting notes is simple but very important—to gather your thoughts about a topic and record them in writing. You need not write your notes in complete sentences. And don't worry about making errors in spelling, grammar, or punctuation. These kinds of errors can be corrected later, when you actually write, revise, and proofread your paragraph. When you prewrite, your goal is to get your ideas down on paper.

A GED student was asked to write a paragraph explaining why passing the GED Test was important to her. She sat and thought and made these prewriting notes.

Passing the GED Test

1. will boost my self-confidence
2. will help me move up in my job
3. want to prove to myself I can do it
4. I can begin taking college courses

After the student had completed her prewriting notes, she reread them to make sure she had included all her ideas about the topic. She decided to add the following to her notes.

5. want to set good example for my kids—show them that education is important

Below is another good example of prewriting notes. These notes, written by a career counselor, are for a paragraph explaining how a job seeker can make a good impression in a job interview.

1. try to appear relaxed, confident
2. frequent eye contact with interviewer
3. be honest—but dont volunteer negative information
4. emphasize your skills and abilities
5. don't monopolize conversation
6. don't criticize former employers
7. don't press interviewer to hire you on the spot
8. ask when you can expect answer
9. thank interviewer for his/her time

In your notebook make prewriting notes for a paragraph explaining why parents should limit the amount of time their children spend watching television. After you finish, reread your notes to make sure you have included all your ideas about the topic. Add to your notes if necessary. Sample notes appear below.

Sample Answers
1. children may neglect homework or chores **2.** may become lazy **3.** TV often presents view of life that isn't realistic **4.** danger of becoming addicted to TV **5.** time could be spent doing something more worthwhile

Prewriting to Organize Your Ideas After you've written some ideas down, the next step is to look carefully at the way you want to organize those ideas in your paragraph. You'll want to choose the most effective way of presenting the information about your topic. Keep in mind that there are various methods of organizing paragraphs. These methods of organizing paragraphs include the following.

Order of Importance In this method of organization you present your ideas in the order of their importance. You can present the most important idea first and the least important one last. Or you can start with the least important idea and work up to the most important one.

Comparison or Contrast You can present your ideas by comparing them with similar ones or by contrasting them with different ideas.

Cause-Effect You can organize your ideas by showing how a particular event or circumstance causes something else to happen.

Time Order In this method of organization you simply describe events in the order in which they happened.

The GED student decided to arrange her ideas in order of importance. She started with the most important idea and worked down to the least important one. Here is how she rearranged her notes.

1. will help me move up in my job
2. I can begin taking college courses
3. will set good example for my kids
4. will boost my self-confidence
5. want to prove to myself I can do it

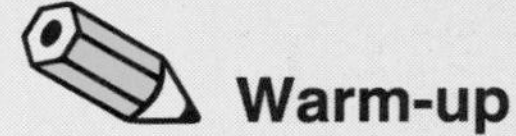

Warm-up

Look back at your own notes for your paragraph about why parents should limit the amount of time their children spend watching TV. Decide on a good method of organizing those ideas. Rearrange them if necessary.

Writing a First Draft Once you've prewritten to get and organize some ideas about your topic, it's time to write the *first draft* of your paragraph. A first draft is one of your first steps in producing a finished piece of writing. Remember the words *first step* because a first draft is never the last of your work; it's just the beginning.

Topic Sentence You can begin your first draft by writing a **topic sentence.** The topic sentence states the paragraph's main idea—that is, it tells what your paragraph is about.

The GED student mentioned above wrote this topic sentence for her paragraph about why passing the GED was important to her.

■ Passing the GED is important to me for a number of reasons.

This is a good topic sentence because it clearly states the main idea of the paragraph: why passing the GED was important to the student. After reading the topic sentence, you know exactly what her paragraph will be about.

Below is the topic sentence that the career counselor wrote for his paragraph about how to make a good impression in a job interview.

■ Every job seeker wants to make a good impression in a job interview.

After reviewing his topic sentence, the counselor realized that it really did not state the topic, or main idea, of the paragraph he wanted to write. He rewrote the sentence as follows.

■ Keep the following tips in mind if you want to make a good impression in a job interview.

Sample Warm-up Answers
Possible cause-effect relationships if parents don't limit TV watching: **1.** children might watch too much, become lazy, and neglect homework or chores **2.** TV often presents view of life that isn't realistic; children may not be prepared for real life **3.** children may become addicted to TV; won't participate in more worthwhile activities

After you finish writing the topic sentence for your paragraph, always reread it and ask yourself the following question: Does the sentence clearly state the main idea of the paragraph I'm going to write? If your answer is no, you need to rewrite the sentence.

Coming to Terms

topic sentence sentence that states the topic, or main idea, of a paragraph

Warm-up

Choose the best topic sentence for the following paragraph. Be sure that the sentence you choose clearly states the main idea of the paragraph.

■ You'll find coupons in a variety of places, including newspapers, magazines, and special racks or displays at your grocery store. Don't try to save every coupon you find. Instead, keep only those that are for products you use regularly or would like to try. This way, your coupon collection won't become so large that it's unmanageable. Once you have collected a fair number of coupons, it's best to organize them by category in a file. Doing so will make it easier to find the coupons you need when it's time to go shopping.

Circle the letter of the best topic sentence for this paragraph.

a. The only way to save money on your monthly food bill is by collecting coupons.
b. Try not to let your coupon collection get out of hand.
c. Collecting coupons is one way to save money on your monthly food bill.
d. Using coupons is more trouble than it's worth.

Now look back at your prewriting notes for your paragraph about why parents should limit the amount of time their children spend watching television. Write a topic sentence for it.

Warm-up Answers
c. Collecting coupons is one way to save money on your monthly food bill.

Sample topic sentence: Parents should limit the amount of time their children spend watching television.

Supporting Sentences After you have written a good topic sentence—one that clearly states the main idea of your paragraph—the next step is to write **supporting sentences.** These are sentences that support, or give more information about, the general idea stated in the topic sentence. They are the sentences that give your *specific* ideas about the topic—the ideas you listed in your prewriting.

When writing paragraphs, it's useful to think of the topic sentence as a promise you are making to your reader. By stating the main idea of the paragraph in the topic sentence, you are promising to explain that idea in the supporting sentences. Good supporting sentences deliver on that promise.

Always review your prewriting notes before you begin to write your supporting sentences. You may find that your notes don't include enough information to support or explain the main idea of your paragraph. If so, take the time to think some more and add to your prewriting notes.

You also may find that some of your notes do not help develop the main idea of your paragraph. In fact, some of your notes may be unrelated to your topic. That often happens; it doesn't mean you did anything wrong. But do be sure to delete those notes. Don't waste time developing ideas that don't support the main idea of your paragraph.

Here is the GED student's first draft of her paragraph about passing the GED Test. Before reading the paragraph, review the prewriting notes she made (see page 198). Can you see how she used the information in her prewriting notes to write the supporting sentences?

■ Passing the GED Test is important to me for a number of reasons. *(topic sentence)* The most important reason is that it will help me move up in my current job. *(supporting sentence)* It will allow me to begin taking college courses. *(supporting sentence)* I also want to pass the GED Test in order to set a good example for my children—to show them that education is important. *(supporting sentence)* Passing the test will give a tremendous boost to my self-confidence. *(supporting sentence)* Finally, I want to pass the GED just to prove to myself that indeed I can do it. *(supporting sentence)*

Notice that all the student's supporting sentences develop, or give more information about, the main idea stated in the topic sentence.

Here is the paragraph the career counselor wrote about how to make a good impression in a job interview. Before reading the paragraph, review the prewriting notes that he made (see page 197).

■ Keep the following tips in mind if you want to make a good impression in a job interview. *(topic sentence)* Do your best to appear relaxed and confident, no matter how nervous you feel. *(supporting sentence)* Try to make frequent eye contact with the interviewer. *(supporting sentence)* It's important for you to answer all the interviewer's questions honestly. *(supporting sentence)* But there's no need to volunteer negative information about yourself. *(supporting sentence)* Be sure to emphasize how your skills and abilities will be an asset to the company. *(supporting sentence)* Be careful, however, not to monopolize the conversation; give the interviewer a chance to talk. *(supporting sentence)* Keep in mind that criticizing former employers is never a good idea; it may make the interviewer think you're the type of employee who's never satisfied. *(supporting sentence)* Don't press the interviewer to hire you on the spot. *(supporting sentence)* Express your strong interest in the job and ask when you can expect an answer. *(supporting sentence)* At the close of the interview, be sure to thank the interviewer for his or her time. *(supporting sentence)*

The counselor's paragraph is another good example of a paragraph in which the supporting sentences develop the main idea stated in the topic sentence.

Notice that in both of the example paragraphs, the topic sentence was placed at the beginning of the paragraph. The advantage of placing the topic sentence first is that the reader immediately knows what the paragraph will be about. Although the topic sentence most commonly appears at the beginning of a paragraph, it can be placed in other positions as well.

Coming to Terms

supporting sentences sentences that support, or give more information about, the idea stated in the topic sentence of a paragraph

Warm-up

On a separate sheet of paper, write the first draft of your paragraph about why parents should limit the amount of time their children spend watching television. Include the topic sentence you wrote earlier. Before you begin to write your supporting sentences, review your prewriting notes. If necessary, add or delete information. A sample first draft appears below.

Revising You've already learned about and practiced most of the steps in the writing process. You've made prewriting notes, organized them, and have written a topic sentence and supporting sentences in your first draft. Now you're ready to move on to the next step in the writing process: revising.

You may be surprised to learn that most professional writers spend a great deal of time revising their work. Many of them consider revision to be the most important part of the writing process. The best writers revise their work again and again until they are satisfied with it.

The first step in revising a paragraph is to read it over carefully. Make sure that your topic sentence clearly states the main idea of the paragraph. Review your supporting sentences to make sure they support the main idea. If necessary, make changes in your topic sentence and supporting sentences. Also make sure that you've decided on the most effective method of organizing your paragraph. Once you're sure that your topic and supporting sentences are relevant and well organized, you can check your writing for sentence variety and transitions.

Sentence Variety Read the following paragraph. Notice the length of the sentences.

■ Joanna Stivitz owns a small clothing store. The store is on Jackson Drive. She bought the store three years ago. She had never owned a store before. She was very inexperienced. She had to work very hard to succeed. Her hard work has paid off. Joanna's store is now a great success.

Sample Warm-up Answer

Parents should limit the amount of time their children spend watching television. Children might stare at the TV for hours. They can become lazy. They may neglect their homework or their household chores. Television does not present a realistic view of life. It doesn't prepare children for real life. Many children actually become addicted to television. Television takes up so much of their time. They don't participate in more worthwhile activities.

Did you find yourself becoming bored as you read the paragraph? One problem with the paragraph is that the writer forgot to vary the length of her sentences. As a result, the paragraph sounds boring and monotonous. Below is the writer's *second* draft of the paragraph. Notice how she combined some of the shorter sentences into longer ones. Now the paragraph has sentences of varying lengths: short, medium, and long.

■ Joanna Stivitz owns a small clothing store on Jackson Drive. When she bought the store three years ago, she had never owned a store before. Because of her inexperience, she had to work very hard to succeed. Her hard work has paid off, however. Joanna's store is now a great success.

Now take another look at the first draft of the paragraph. You'll notice that the writer also forgot to vary the types of sentences she used. As you can see, all her sentences begin with the subject followed by the verb. If she had used a variety of sentence types, the paragraph would have been less boring and monotonous.

Now look again at the second draft of the paragraph to see how the writer solved this problem. You'll notice that she has used a greater variety of sentence types. Not every sentence begins with a subject followed by a verb. In rewriting the paragraph, the writer has combined sentences, added some words, and rearranged others. Here are some examples:

First draft: Joanna Stivitz owns a small clothing store. The store is on Jackson Drive.

Second draft: Joanna Stivitz owns a small clothing store on Jackson Drive.

First draft: She bought the store three years ago. She had never owned a store before.

Second draft: When she bought the store three years ago, she had never owned a store before.

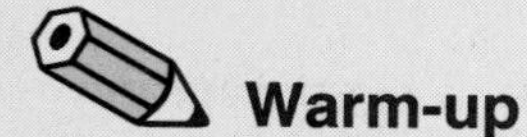

Warm-up

On a separate sheet of paper, rewrite the following paragraph so that it has sentences of varying lengths and types.

■ Goldfish make ideal pets. You don't have to walk them. They don't bark or scratch. They don't dirty the floor. It's very relaxing to watch them. They swim peacefully around the tank. Caring for goldfish is simple. Just sprinkle some food into the tank every day. Change the water several times a week.

Review the paragraph you wrote about why parents should limit the amount of time their children spend watching television. Make sure that you have included sentences of varying lengths and types. Make any necessary changes in your paragraph.

Transitions Between Sentences **Transitions** are words or groups of words that show how the ideas in a paragraph are related. Here are some examples of transitions.

To show an example—*for example, for instance*

To show cause—*because, consequently, as a result, therefore, thus*

To show differences—*instead, but, yet, besides, nevertheless, in contrast, however, on the other hand*

To show similarities—*similarly, likewise, in comparison*

To show another one—*and, also, too, in addition, as well*

To show time—*first, second, next, last, after, until, then, while, before*

To show the end—*finally, last, at last, in conclusion*

Sample Warm-up Answers

Goldfish make ideal pets. You don't have to walk them, and they don't bark, scratch, or dirty the floor. It's very relaxing to watch them swim peacefully around the tank. And caring for goldfish is simple. Just sprinkle some food into the tank every day and change the water several times a week.

Parents should limit the amount of time their children spend watching television. Staring at a television screen hour after hour can cause children to become lazy. They may neglect their homework or their household chores. Presenting an often unrealistic view of life, television does not prepare children for real life. Many children actually become addicted to television. Television takes up so much of their time that they don't participate in more worthwhile activities.

Notice how the career counselor used transitions to show how the ideas in his paragraph are related. Some transitions were used in his first draft; others he added when he revised.

■ Keep the following tips in mind if you want to make a good impression in a job interview. *First,* do your best to appear relaxed and confident, no matter how nervous you feel. Try to make frequent eye contact with the interviewer. It's *also* important for you to answer all the interviewer's questions honestly. *But* there's no need to volunteer negative information about yourself. Be sure to emphasize how your skills and abilities will be an asset to the company. Be careful, *however,* not to monopolize the conversation; give the interviewer a chance to talk. Keep in mind that criticizing former employers is never a good idea; it may make the interviewer think that you're the type of employee who's never satisfied. *And* don't press the interviewer to hire you on the spot. *Instead,* express your strong interest in the job and ask when you can expect an answer. *Finally,* at the close of the interview, be sure to thank the interviewer for his or her time.

Another way to show how the ideas in a paragraph are related is by repeating key words or groups of words. Pronouns such as *he, she, it,* and *they* also can be used as transitions. Reread the paragraph the GED student wrote. Do you see how she used repeated words and pronouns to show how the ideas in her paragraph are related?

■ *Passing the GED Test* is important to me for a number of reasons. The most important reason is that *it* will help me move up in my current job. *It* will allow me to begin taking college courses. I also want to *pass the GED Test* in order to set a good example for my children—to show them that education is important. *Passing the test* will give a tremendous boost to my self-confidence. Finally, I want to *pass the GED* just to prove to myself that indeed I can do it.

Coming to Terms

transition word or group of words that shows how ideas are related

Warm-up

Add transitions to the paragraph below. Choose from the following list of words.

because	for example	oversleeping
as a result	problem	instead

My habit of oversleeping is causing me a lot of problems at work. Last week, ______________, I was late for work three times. ______________, my boss called me into her office and warned me that I could lose my job if I didn't get to work on time. Another ______________ caused by my ______________ is the fact that I don't have time to eat breakfast. ______________ of concentrating on my work, I spend the whole morning thinking about how hungry I am. ______________ I am not getting as much work done as I should, I'm afraid I'll miss out on the promotion I'm hoping for.

Check your paragraph about why parents should limit the amount of time their children spend watching television. If needed, add transitions, including repeated words and pronouns.

Polishing In the second draft of your paragraph, you've worked to improve your topic sentence, supporting sentences, paragraph organization, transitions, and sentence variety. Now you can move on to the last step in the revision process: cleaning up and polishing your paragraph. (See pages 195–196 to review what you have already learned about revising.)

Begin by reading your paragraph again carefully. Ask yourself the following questions as you read. Then make any necessary changes in your paragraph.

1. Have I chosen words that express my meaning exactly?
2. Have I deleted repeated information?

Warm-up Answers
for example; As a result; problem; oversleeping; Instead; Because

Parents should limit the amount of time their children spend watching television. Staring at a television screen hour after hour can cause children to become lazy. *As a result,* they may neglect their homework or their household chores. Presenting an often unrealistic view of life, television does not prepare children for real life. *In addition,* many children actually become addicted to television. Television *then* takes up so much of their time that they don't participate in more worthwhile activities.

3. Have I deleted negative words whenever possible?
4. Have I deleted catchy phrases and unneeded words?
5. Have I deleted unneeded underlining and exclamation marks?
6. Have I avoided overusing the words *very, pretty, little,* and *rather?*
7. Have I put words in front of the words they describe?
8. Have I deleted weak words and used strong verbs whenever possible?

Notice how the GED student used the checklist above to clean up and polish her paragraph.

■ Passing the GED Test is important to me for a number of reasons. ~~The~~ *M*ost important~~, reason is that~~ it will help me ~~move up~~ *advance* in my current job. *Second*, it will allow me to ~~begin taking~~ *take evening* college courses. *In addition, by passing* ~~I also want to pass~~ the GED Test *I can* ~~in order to~~ set a good example for my children~~, to~~ *It will* show them that education is important. Passing the test will *also* give a tremendous boost to my self-confidence. Finally, I want to pass the GED ~~just~~ *simply* to prove to myself that (indeed) I can ^ do it.

Did you notice some of the marks she used to show her changes? Those are marks that writers and editors everywhere use to help them revise. Here's a chart showing some of the most frequently used marks.

Revision Marks

^	insert the words or punctuation written above
(delete mark)	delete
——	delete; replace with any words or punctuation written above
≡	make a capital letter (m̳ becomes M)
/	change to a small letter (M̸ becomes m)
(move mark)	move to the place shown
. , ; :	(draw in any punctuation you want to add)

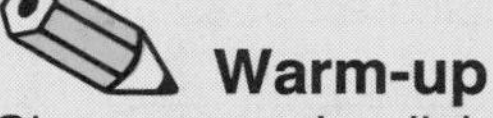

Warm-up

Clean up and polish the second draft of your paragraph about why parents should limit the amount of time their children spend watching television. As you work, refer to the checklist.

Proofreading Congratulations! You've made it to the last step in the writing process: proofreading. Here's your chance to apply everything you learned about the conventions of English to your own paragraph rather than somebody else's.

The purpose of proofreading is to find and correct any errors that you may have missed during the revision process. When you proofread, you should read your paragraph slowly and carefully. Ask yourself these questions.

1. Does my paragraph contain sentence fragments?
2. Does it contain run-on sentences?
3. Do my subjects and verbs agree?
4. Have I used pronouns correctly?
5. Do my verbs show the correct time?
6. Are all the words spelled correctly?
7. Have I used capital letters correctly?
8. Have I made any errors in grammar?
9. Do all my sentences make sense?
10. Does my paragraph read smoothly?

Warm-up

Proofread the second draft of your paragraph about why parents should limit the amount of time their children spend watching television. Make any necessary changes. Use the revision marks to help you. Then ask someone to check it for you.

Practice Makes Good If Not Perfect The best way to strengthen your skill at paragraph writing is to write paragraphs on some of the topics below or on any other topics you wish to write about. Go through all the steps you practiced here for each one—prewriting, writing, revising, proofreading. Then have someone check your work.

Why I'm Studying for the GED Test
Why I Love My Wife (or Husband, Girl Friend, or Boyfriend)
Things I'm Good at Doing
The Worst Restaurant I Ever Ate At
The Best Game I Ever Saw
How to Save Money
How to Spend Money
The Person Who Makes Me Angriest
How Parents Should Treat Their Children
How Children Should Treat Their Parents
What Is Unhappiness?
Do Things Happen for the Best?

Writing Your Ideas in Essays

On the second part of the GED Writing Skills Test, you will be required to write an *essay* about a specific topic. An essay is a short piece of writing—usually three, four, or five paragraphs—in which the writer presents ideas or personal opinions about a topic. Here is an example of an essay.

■ I believe that anyone caught drinking while driving should not be allowed to drive again. I felt this way even before my own encounter with a drunk driver.

Last year, I was severely injured when my car was struck broadside by a vehicle driven by a drunk driver. Because I was immediately knocked unconscious by the impact of the collision, I was unaware that I had even been involved in an accident until I woke up in a hosptial emergency room. When I learned of my injuries, I felt hatred toward the drunk driver who had smashed into my car. Although I feared a permanent head injury, I was lucky—within a few months, I had recovered fully.

I am, of course, only one of the many people who have been victimized by drunk drivers. And the situation seems to be getting worse, not better.

Therefore, I strongly suggest that people who are caught drinking while driving should not be allowed to drive again.

In the last part of this *Writing Skills* section, you practiced writing paragraphs. Writing an essay is a process just as writing a paragraph is. Writing an essay involves many of the same steps as writing a paragraph. In fact, you've already worked to improve many of the skills you'll need to write an effective essay.

The Controlling Idea When you studied paragraphs, you learned that the topic sentence states the main idea of the paragraph. In an essay, the *controlling idea* states the topic; it tells the reader what the essay is about. The first step in writing an essay is to write the controlling idea.

☑ A Test-Taking Tip

Remember that for the GED essay you will be given a specific topic to write about. This topic will be briefly described in a few sentences. Most or all of the information you'll need to write your controlling idea can be found in the essay assignment. In fact, writing your controlling idea may involve nothing more than restating the topic given in the essay assignment.

To see how you can get a controlling idea from an essay assignment, read the following essay assignment, which was given to a GED student.

■ Home ownership has long been considered an important part of the American dream. While there are many advantages to owning a home, there are disadvantages as well.

Write an essay discussing the advantages and disadvantages of home ownership. Be as specific as possible. Support your ideas with reasons and examples.

Notice how the student used the information given in the essay assignment to write his controlling idea.

■ Home ownership has both advantages and disadvantages.

☑ A Test-Taking Tip

After you have written the controlling idea for your essay, you should compare it with the topic given in the essay assignment. Be sure that the topic stated in your controlling idea is the same as the one given in the assignment. Don't make the mistake of writing about a different topic. If you do so on the GED essay, you'll be given a score of zero, no matter how well written your essay is.

Warm-up

Read the essay assignment. Then write a controlling idea for an essay about the topic.

■ The telephone plays an important role in modern life. There's no doubt that it has improved the quality of our lives in many ways. In other ways, however, it has had a negative effect on our lives.

Write an essay discussing both the positive and negative effects of the telephone on modern life. Support your ideas with reasons and examples. Be as specific as possible.

Sample Warm-up Answer

The telephone has improved the quality of our lives in many ways. In other ways, however, it has had a negative effect.

☑ A Test-Taking Tip

You may have heard that it's important to have a catchy opening to your essay, one that really grabs the reader's attention. That can help, but your first step should be to write a controlling idea that's direct and helps you keep your writing focused. You can always rewrite your controlling idea to be catchy and interesting when you revise.

Prewriting Once you have written the controlling idea for an essay, the next step is to make prewriting notes. The purpose of making prewriting notes for an essay is the same as it was for a paragraph: to gather your thoughts about the topic stated in your controlling idea. Remember that you don't need to write your notes in complete sentences or to worry about making errors in grammar, spelling, or punctuation. You can correct these errors later.

It's a good idea to keep your readers in mind as you prewrite. Remember that when you write your GED essay, your readers will be two people who don't know you and have never seen your writing before. They can judge your writing abilities only on the basis of your essay. Make a point to include all the important information about the topic in your prewriting notes. This way, you won't forget to include it in your essay.

Here are the prewriting notes that the GED student mentioned before made for his essay.

Controlling Idea: Home ownership has both advantages and disadvantages

1. no landlord
2. decorate to suit your tastes
3. have to fix things yourself - can't call the landlord
4. a lot of bills to pay
5. possible major purchases
6. if want to move, have to sell house
7. build equity
8. home ties you down
9. don't have to move unless you want to
10. lots of work to do around house
11. home may increase in value
12. down payment can be hard
13. put down roots

☑ A Test-Taking Tip

The worst mistake a GED examinee can make on the essay section of the test is to forget to prewrite. When people don't prewrite, their writing is often rambling. Thoughts don't connect, and a clear message just doesn't come across. You'll be given enough space on the GED Writing Skills Test for you to prewrite. Don't forget to use it.

Warm-up

On a separate sheet of paper, make prewriting notes for your essay about the positive and negative effects of the telephone. Begin by writing your controlling idea at the top of the page. After you have finished making your notes, review them to make sure that you have included all your ideas about the topic.

☑ A Test-Taking Tip

Making a list of your ideas is a good way to prewrite when you prepare your GED essay. But there are other ways to prewrite that can be useful, especially if you "freeze up" and can't think. If that happens to you on the essay test, you can try "free writing" as a way to come unblocked and get ideas to write about. When you free write, you put your pen on the paper and just keep writing. Your pen must not leave the paper or stop writing. If you can't think of anything to write about the topic, you can just write, "I can't think of anything else to write," until you *can* think of something else. After a certain time you stop writing, look at the ideas you've set down, and use the best ones in your essay.

For example, a student was asked to write an essay describing his attitudes toward money. Here is the free writing he did on the topic.

■ Money. I can't live without it. It's a hard time saving it there never seems to be enough, everything's so expensive these days

---

Sample Warm-up Answer

Controlling idea: The telephone has improved the quality of our lives in many ways. But in other ways, it has had a negative effect.

1. doing business much easier and more efficient
2. has saved lives in emergencies
3. often interrupts us
4. makes world seem smaller
5. stay in touch with friends and relatives
6. new industries, jobs
7. unwanted calls
8. fewer people write letters
9. saves time for consumer—placing orders, etc.
10. fewer people visit—they call instead
11. time-waster at home, work

wonder how much my friends make. But money isn't just a status symbol for me I really just want financial security. Right now I can't think of anything else to, oh, I know, I want to spend money and enjoy life but how much money is enough? How much do you do I need to enjoy life? Also my wife and me worry about inflation. We want to send our kids to college I know money can't buy happiness but it sure can buy freedom from worrying

That free writing may look like a jumble of poor sentences, but it's full of ideas for the student's essay. So if you become nervous during the GED Test and can't seem to list ideas for your essay, try free writing for five minutes about the topic.

Organizing Your Ideas Once you have finished making your prewriting notes, the next step is to organize the ideas in your notes. Some writers resist the idea of organizing before they begin to write. They say things such as, "Organizing is too much work. I'd rather just go ahead and write my first draft." The truth is that organizing doesn't take a great deal of time. In fact, it will save you time in the long run.

The first step in organizing an essay is to review your controlling idea and prewriting notes. Think about how the ideas in your notes can be grouped together logically. Then think of an appropriate heading for each group of ideas. Write these headings down. These headings are the main ideas that you will develop in your essay.

Next, write your controlling idea at the top of a sheet of paper. Review the headings that you just wrote down and think about the most effective method of organizing those headings. Remember that you've already learned about various methods of organizing ideas in a paragraph: order of importance, comparison or contrast, cause-effect, and time order. These same methods can be used for organizing ideas in your essay. You can also use any other method of organization that works for your topic.

Keep in mind that you can always change your method of organization later, if you decide that a different method would be more effective. You can also use different headings to fit the new method of organization that you have chosen.

Once you have decided on a method for organizing your headings, write the first one under your controlling idea. Next, list the prewriting notes that belong in that group under that heading. Then write your next main heading and appropriate notes below it. You can use numbers and letters to help you list the ideas and keep them straight. Continue in the same way until you have written all your main headings and notes.

To see how this method of organizing works, look at the steps the GED student followed. After he had reviewed his controlling idea and prewriting notes, he decided to divide his notes into four groups with the following headings.

■ Financial advantages
Financial disadvantages
Personal advantages
Personal disadvantages

After reviewing these headings, he decided to use comparison and contrast as his method of organization. Next, he listed these headings and wrote each of his prewriting notes under the appropriate heading. Notice that the student shortened some of his notes as he wrote them. He did this to save time and space. Also, he knew that he could always refer back to his prewriting notes if necessary. Notice also that the student added a sentence to his controlling idea.

■ *Controlling idea:* Home ownership has both advantages and disadvantages. These can be divided into two main categories: financial and personal.

1. Financial advantages
   a. Build equity
   b. Increase in value of home
2. Financial disadvantages
   a. Down payment
   b. Bills
   c. Major purchases
3. Personal advantages
   a. No landlord
   b. Decorate as you wish
   c. Won't be told to move
   d. Put down roots
4. Personal disadvantages
   a. Home ties you down
   b. Lots of work to do
   c. Can't call landlord to fix things
   d. To move, must find buyer for house

Once you have finished your organization, review it to make sure that all the information in it helps develop the controlling idea of your essay. Delete any information that is not related to your controlling idea. At this point you should also add any information that you may have left out.

It's also a good idea to review the method of organization that you've chosen. Is it really the most effective way to present the ideas in your essay? If not, feel free to change it. You can also change your main headings to suit your method of organization.

☑ A Test-Taking Tip

When reading your essay, the GED scorers will consider not only the ideas you have presented but also the way in which you have organized those ideas. So take the time to organize your essay. A well-organized essay will receive a higher score than a poorly organized one.

Warm-up

On a separate sheet of paper, organize the ideas for your essay about the positive and negative effects of the telephone. Follow these steps.

1. Write your controlling idea at the top of the page.
2. Review your controlling idea and prewriting notes to see how your ideas can be grouped together logically.
3. Choose an appropriate heading for each group of ideas.
4. Decide on the most effective method of organizing the ideas in your essay.
5. Follow this method of organization as you list your headings and notes.

Writing the First Draft After you have organized your ideas, you're ready to write the first draft of your essay. Keep your organizational plan and prewriting notes in front of you as you write.

Sample Warm-up Answer
Controlling idea: The telephone has improved the quality of our lives in many ways. In other ways, however, it has had a negative effect.

1. Positive effects
   - **a.** Doing business easier and more efficient
   - **b.** Saves time for the consumer
   - **c.** Makes world seem smaller
   - **d.** Can stay in touch with friends and relatives
   - **e.** New industries and jobs
   - **f.** Saves lives in emergencies
2. Negative effects
   - **a.** Time-waster
   - **b.** Frequent interruptions
   - **c.** Unwanted calls
   - **d.** Less letter writing
   - **e.** Fewer personal visits

Begin by stating your controlling idea as the first sentence or first paragraph in your essay. Then write a paragraph about the first group of ideas in your plan. In your paragraph, be sure to include all the information from your notes in that group. Next, write a paragraph about the second main group. Continue in the same way until you have written a paragraph for each of your main groups.

Don't be too concerned with errors in spelling, punctuation, or grammar when you write your first draft. You'll have a chance to find and correct them later when you proofread.

Here is the first draft of the GED student's essay. Do you see how he followed his organization plan as he wrote?

■ Home ownership has both advantages and disadvantages. These can be divided into two main categories: financial and personal.

From a financial standpoint, there are several advantages to owning a home. As you pay off your mortgage, you build equity in your home, so that one day you will own it free and clear. Also, your home will probably increase in value as well. If you decide to sell it, you can make a profit.

On the other hand, owning a home can be expensive. It may be hard to come up with a down payment. You have a lot of bills to pay. You also have to set aside money for major purchases.

Of course, money isn't the only thing about owning a home. There are personal considerations as well. When you own a home, there's no landlord. Telling you what to do and what not to do. You can decorate your home to suit your tastes. You can live in the house until you decide to move. Owning a home allows you to put down roots in a community.

On the minus side, owning a home can tie you down. Owning a home also involves a lot of work. And when something breaks, you can't call the landlord to fix it. When you decide to move you have to find someone to buy your house.

In conclusion, owning a home has both advantages and disadvantages. Everyone has to decide whether the advantages outweigh the disadvantages.

Notice that the GED student's essay has a beginning, a middle, and an end. The beginning, or **introduction,** is the first paragraph, in which the student states his controlling idea. The middle, or **body,** includes the second, third, fourth, and fifth paragraphs. In these paragraphs the student develops his controlling idea. In the last paragraph of the essay, the student has written a **summary statement.** A summary statement is a sentence or paragraph that summarizes the controlling idea developed throughout the essay.

Coming to Terms

introduction sentence or paragraph that states the controlling idea of an essay
body the paragraphs that develop the controlling idea of an essay
summary statement sentence or paragraph that ends the essay by summarizing the controlling idea

Warm-up

On a separate sheet of paper, write the first draft of your essay about the effects of the telephone. Follow these steps:

1. Keep your organizational plan and prewriting notes in front of you as you write.
2. State your controlling idea in the first sentence or paragraph as an introduction.
3. Write a paragraph about each of the main groups in your plan. In each paragraph, include all the information from your notes in that group.
4. Include a summary statement—either a sentence or a paragraph—at the end.

Sample Warm-up Answer

The telephone has improved the quality of our lives in many ways. In other ways, however, it has had a negative effect.

On the posative side, the telephone has made doing business much easier and more efficient. It has made life easier for the consumer. People can pick up the phone to place or check on an order. The telephone has also made the world seem smaller. Since it allows us to talk with people all over the country and all over the world. The telephone also helps you stay in touch with friends, and relatives, both near and far. In addition, the telephone has created many new industries and jobs. It has also saved countless lives in emergencies.

But the telephone can be a big time-waster, both at work and at home. It often interupts us and can even keep us from accomplishing our daily tasks. The telephone has also brought us plenty of unwanted calls. Because of the telephone fewer people write personal letters. The telephone can also cause people to make fewer personal visits, since they can simply talk to people on the phone.

The telephone has had many posative effects on our lives. But it has also lowered the quality of our lives in many ways.

☑ A Test-Taking Tip

When you write your GED essay, you may find that you want to write about the idea in, say, the third paragraph of your essay before the idea in the second. Perhaps it's easier for you to write about one idea before another. If that happens, go ahead and do it. Write what comes easiest first, and then go back and fill out the rest.

Revising When you studied paragraphs, you learned that many professional writers consider revision to be the most important part of the writing process. Most people who write for a living would never even consider submitting the first draft of a piece of writing. You should treat your GED essay in the same way.

When you revise your essay, read it over several times, each time looking for something different. The first step is to read it over carefully to make sure the basic organization is fine.

Review your controlling idea to make sure that it clearly states the topic of the essay. You should also make sure that your essay has a beginning, a middle, and an end.

Transitions Between Paragraphs On pages 201–202, you learned how to use transitions, including repeated words and pronouns, to show how the ideas within a paragraph are related. In essays, transitions are used within individual paragraphs for the same purpose. They are also used *between* paragraphs to show how the ideas in these paragraphs are related.

Transitions make an essay flow smoothly from paragraph to paragraph. They also help your reader see how the ideas in each of your paragraphs are related to the controlling idea of your essay. You can use words, phrases, and complete sentences as transitions in essays.

Reread the GED student's essay on page 207. Notice how he used transitions to tie his paragraphs together and to show how each paragraph is related to his controlling idea.

Controlling idea: Home ownership has both advantages and disadvantages. These can be divided into two main categories: financial and personal.

Transition between first and second paragraphs: From a financial standpoint, there are several advantages to owning a home.

Transition between second and third paragraphs: On the other hand, owning a home can be expensive.

Transition between third and fourth paragraphs: Of course, money isn't the only thing about owning a home. There are personal considerations as well.

Transition between fourth and fifth paragraphs: On the minus side, owning a home can tie you down.

Transition between fifth and sixth paragraphs: In conclusion, owning a home has both advantages and disadvantages.

Warm-up

Reread the first draft of your essay about the positive and negative effects of the telephone. Check to see that you've written a clear beginning, middle, and end. Make sure that you have included transitions between paragraphs.

☑ A Test-Taking Tip

Your GED essay must be written neatly enough so that the two scorers can read it. However, they won't except your paper to look perfect. You can use the revision marks (shown on page 203) on your essay to improve it. In fact, that use will show the scorers that you did indeed revise your writing. Copy your essay over *only* if it becomes too messy for the scorers to read.

Sample Warm-up Answer

The telephone has improved the quality of our lives in many ways. In other ways, however, it has had a negative effect.

On the posative side, the telephone has made doing business much easier and more efficient. It has made life easier for the consumer. People can pick up the phone to place or check on an order. The telephone has also made the world seem smaller. Since it allows us to talk with people all over the country and all over the world. The telephone also helps you stay in touch with friends, and relatives, both near and far. In addition, the telephone has created many new industries and jobs. It has also saved countless lives in emergencies.

On the negative side,
~~But~~ the telephone can be a big time-waster, both at work and at home. It often interupts us and can even keep us from accomplishing our daily tasks. The telephone has also brought us plenty of unwanted calls. Because of the telephone fewer people write personal letters. The telephone can also cause people to make fewer personal visits, since they can simply talk to people on the phone.

We can see, then, the role that ... *plays in*
The telephone ~~has had many posative effects on~~ our lives.
had both positive and negative effects on
~~But~~ it has ~~also lowered the quality of our lives in many ways.~~
modern life.

<u>Directions:</u> Read all the information accompanying each essay topic. Plan your answer carefully before you write. Use blank paper to make any notes. Write your essay on a separate sheet. Read carefully what you have written, and make any changes that will improve your writing. Check your paragraphing, sentence structure, spelling, punctuation, capitalization, and usage, and make any necessary corrections. Take no more than 45 minutes for each essay. Sample essays are on page 227.

1. Many states in the United States have lotteries in which a person may win a million dollars or even more. What would be the advantages of winning a million dollars? Would there be disadvantages? Write a 200-word essay explaining the advantages and disadvantages.

2. Families are having fewer and fewer children. Having even just one child can have a dramatic impact on the parents' lives. Write about this impact in about 200 words. You can discuss the negative impact, the positive impact, or both.

Directions: Read all the information accompanying each essay topic. Plan your answer carefully before you write. Use blank paper to make any notes. Write your essay on a separate sheet. Read carefully what you have written, and make any changes that will improve your writing. Check your paragraphing, sentence structure, spelling, punctuation, capitalization, and usage, and make any necessary corrections. Take no more than 45 minutes for each essay. Sample essays begin on page 228.

3. Everyone complains about taxes, yet think about what would happen if there were no longer an income tax. Discuss the positive effects of an income tax, the negative effects, or both in a 200-word essay.

4. Television is still a relatively new invention, yet it has had profound effects on America and on Americans' lives. Write about 200 words discussing the effects that television has. You can write about the good effects, the bad effects, or both.

Details After you have reviewed the basic organization of your essay, you should review the ideas, or details, that you used to develop your controlling idea. These details should be specific rather than general to help your reader get a clear picture of your message. Here are some examples of specific details that the GED student decided to add to his essay.

General detail: When you own a home, there are a lot of bills to pay.

Specific detail: When you own a home, you have to pay for all utilities, property taxes, and upkeep.

General detail: You have to set aside money for major purchases.

Specific detail: You may have to buy a new furnace, roof, water heater, or carpeting.

Notice that the general details leave the reader with unanswered questions: What kind of bills does the homeowner have to pay? What kind of major purchases are there? The specific details, on the other hand, answer those questions.

The details you choose to write about should be logical—that is, they should be clearly related to your controlling idea and should make sense to your reader. In the example below, the first detail is logically related to the controlling idea about the telephone, but the second is not.

Controlling idea: The telephone has improved the quality of our lives in many ways. In other ways, however, it has had a negative effect.

Details: The telephone has saved countless lives in emergencies such as fires and accidents. *(logical)* To save space, I decided to mount my office telephone on the wall. *(not logical)*

Warm-up

What specific details could you add to help explain the following general statement?

■ The ways people can listen to music have changed.

Sample Warm-up Answers

Listening to music—other than a live performance—used to be restricted to phonograph players and later to radios. Today the phonograph can be a stereo or a compact disc player, and the radio is either a small transistor with headphones or a huge boom box. Cassette players have also entered the scene. Even television gets into the musical act by airing music videos.

Sentence Variety You learned that it's important to vary the length of the sentences in a paragraph. You also learned that you should include a variety of sentence types in each paragraph. Otherwise, your paragraphs will sound boring and monotonous. Of course, this same advice applies to writing the paragraphs that make up your essay.

When the GED student reviewed the first draft of his essay, he noticed that the sentences in his third paragraph were all about the same length. Also, he saw that every sentence except the first one began with the subject followed by the verb. Here's how the student revised his paragraph to include sentences of varying lengths and types.

■ On the other hand, owning a home can be expensive. Coming up with the money for a down payment may be difficult. The cost of all utilities, property taxes, and upkeep comes out of your pocket. You also have to set aside money for major purchases, such as a new furnace, roof, water heater, or carpeting.

Warm-up

The sentences below can be rewritten in any number of ways. Rewrite them, either separately or by combining them, in three different ways.

■ Romance has gone out of our lives. People no longer care about it. Moonlit nights, walks in the rain, and intimate little restaurants are unimportant.

Sample Warm-up Answers

1. People no longer care about romance. Moonlit nights, walks in the rain, and intimate little restaurants are no longer important. **2.** Romance has gone out of our lives, and with it the importance of moonlit nights, walks in the rain, and intimate little restaurants. People no longer care. **3.** Moonlit nights, walks in the rain, and intimate little restaurants are unimportant, for people no longer care. Romance has gone out of our lives.

5. Most people have dreams of one day becoming rich. But does the average person have the ability to make a lot of money? Think about this question. Then write about 200 words describing your thoughts.

6. More and more people are living by themselves today. What are the advantages of living alone? What are the disadvantages? Write an essay of about 200 words explaining the advantages and disadvantages.

7. Sports are very popular in today's society. Some people believe, "Winning is the only thing." Others believe, "It's not whether you win or lose, but how you play the game." Is there a way in sports in which both opponents could "win" a game? "Lose" a game? Detail your thoughts on this issue in an essay of about 200 words.

Directions: Read all the information accompanying each essay topic. Plan your answer carefully before you write. Use blank paper to make any notes. Write your essay on a separate sheet. Read carefully what you have written, and make any changes that will improve your writing. Check your paragraphing, sentence structure, spelling, punctuation, capitalization, and usage, and make any necessary corrections. Take no more than 45 minutes for each essay. Sample essays begin on page 229.

8. Manufacturers who advertise sometimes directly name one or two of their competitors and attack their products. What are your feelings about this advertising practice? Write an essay of about 200 words describing your ideas.

9. For many years the nuclear family, consisting of father, mother, and children, was considered to be the normal family pattern in U.S. society. Yet in many other cultures and in our own in the past, three generations—grandparents, parents, and children—often have lived together. What are the advantages and disadvantages of three generations living together? Give specific examples in a 200-word composition.

Clear Expression Whenever you write for an audience—that is, for someone other than yourself—your purpose is to communicate ideas. To do this effectively, you must express your ideas clearly. In writing, it's what you say, not what you *mean* to say, that counts.

Don't expect the GED scorers to guess at your meaning; instead, do your best to make your meaning crystal clear. This will involve some work on your part. But keep in mind that even the most skilled and experienced writers don't produce perfect sentences and paragraphs on the first try.

So after you have finished the first draft of an essay, you should also review it to make sure that you've expressed all your ideas clearly. Use precise words rather than vague, general ones. Avoid slang and other informal language.

Below is an example of an essay in which the writer does not express her ideas clearly.

■ Many people think that professional athletes are really greedy and that they make way too much money. I don't.

Sure, athletes make a lot of money. But so do a lot of other people. Besides, the team owners are willing to pay these high salaries to the players. The whole situation is pretty much the owners' fault.

I don't blame the athletes for the problem. They're just looking out for themselves. They don't last very long. Why shouldn't they take the money and run?

So you can see that it's not the athletes' fault that they make these really high salaries. The owners have to take the blame for the problem.

In the tinted column on the next page is another writer's essay about the same topic. Notice how this writer uses precise rather than vague or wordy expressions (for example, "way too much money" becomes "overpaid"; "a lot of other people" becomes "employees of any organization"). She also avoids using informal language like "really greedy," "pretty much," and "really high."

■ Many people feel that professional athletes are greedy and overpaid. I disagree.

Professional athletes, like employees of any organization, are worth whatever their employers are willing to pay them. Salaries got so high in the first place because team owners kept outbidding each other to get certain players. As salaries were pushed higher and higher, the owners began to complain about the situation, but they themselves had created it.

You can't fault athletes for trying to get as much money as possible. After all, the average professional athlete's career lasts only a few years. Who can blame athletes if they try to make as much money as they can *while* they can?

To sum up, professional athletes are not greedy and overpaid. They are simply profiting from a situation that the owners created and allowed to get out of hand.

Warm-up

Review the first draft of your essay about the positive and negative effects of the telephone. Check that the details you included are specific and logical. Revise any sentence structure that is poor. Make sure that you have expressed all your ideas clearly, and be sure you've avoided language that's too informal.

Sample Warm-up Answer

The telephone has improved the quality of our lives in many ways. In other ways, however, it has had a negative effect.

On the posative side, the telephone has made doing business much easier and more efficient. ~~It has made life easier for the consumer. People~~ *Business people can call their customers rather than writing or traveling to see them. Customers* can pick up the phone to place or check on ~~an~~ order*s*. The telephone has also made the world seem smaller. Since it allows us to talk with people all over the country and all over the world. The telephone also helps you stay in touch with friends, and relatives, both near and far. In addition, the telephone has created many new industries and *thousands of new* jobs. It has also saved countless lives in emergencies *such as fires and accidents*.

~~But~~ *On the negative side,* the telephone can be a big time-waster, both at work and at home. It often interupts us and can even keep us from accomplishing our daily tasks. The telephone has also brought us ~~plenty of unwanted calls.~~ *crank calls, nuisance calls, and wrong numbers.* ~~Because of the telephone~~ fewer people write personal letters*, and* ~~The telephone can also cause~~ *fewer* people ~~to~~ make ~~fewer~~ personal visits, since they can simply talk to ~~people~~ *one another* on the phone.

We can see, then, the role that The telephone *plays in* ~~has had many posative effects on~~ our lives. ~~But~~ it has *had both positive and negative effects on modern life.* ~~also lowered the quality of our lives in many ways.~~

10. Surveys show that more people get the news by watching television than by reading the newspaper. Think about whether TV news shows are adequate as a person's only source of news. Write a composition of about 200 words that details your thoughts.

11. Some people live in one community their entire lives. Many more move at least once; some quite often. Compare and contrast moving to different parts of the country versus living in one community your entire life. Write about 200 words.

12. The automobile has had a profound effect on modern life. Some of these effects have been positive and others negative. Detail these effects in a 200-word essay.

Directions: Read all the information accompanying each essay topic. Plan your answer carefully before you write. Use blank paper to make any notes. Write your essay on a separate sheet. Read carefully what you have written, and make any changes that will improve your writing. Check your paragraphing, sentence structure, spelling, punctuation, capitalization, and usage, and make any necessary corrections. Take no more than 45 minutes for each essay. Sample essays begin on page 230.

13. Materialism means placing great importance on material things such as clothes, property, and furniture. Many people complain that modern society is too materialistic. Are people in these times "what they own" or "what they are"? Explain your thoughts on the matter in an essay of about 200 words.

14. People spend a great deal of time, money, and energy to see or read about movie stars, TV actors, and athletes. What role do such celebrities play in society? Write a composition of about 200 words. Give specific examples.

Proofreading and One Last Look After you've revised your essay, read it over slowly and carefully to find any errors that you may have missed. Check yourself on spelling, capitalization, punctuation, and grammar.

In addition, you'll want to give your essay one final reading in its entirety. That will help you see the overall impression it makes—the impression it will give the GED scorers.

Here is the final, revised version of the GED student's essay.

■ Home ownership has both advantages and disadvantages. These can be divided into two main categories: financial and personal.

From a financial standpoint, there are several advantages to owning a home. As you pay off your mortgage, you build equity in your home*.* ~~so that~~ *Therefore,* one day you will own ~~it~~ *your home* free and clear. Also, your home will ~~probly~~ *probably* increase in value ~~as well~~. If you decide to sell it, you can make a profit.

On the other hand, owning a home can be expensive. ~~It may be hard to come~~ *Coming* up with a down payment *may be difficult. In addition,* you have ~~a lot of bills~~ to pay*,* *for all utilities, property taxes, and upkeep.* You also have to set aside money for major purchases, *such as a new furnace, roof, water heater, or carpeting.*

Of course, money isn't the only ~~thing about~~ *issue involved in* owning a home. There are personal considerations as well. When you own ~~a~~ *your* home, there's no landlord *to* ~~T~~*t*ell~~ing~~ you what to do and what not to do. You can decorate your home *and landscape your property* to suit your tastes. ~~You can live in the house until you decide to move~~. *You don't have to worry about being forced to move when your lease runs out.* Owning a home *also* allows you to put down roots in a community.

On the minus side, owning a home can tie you down. ~~Owning a home~~ *It* also involves a lot of work*:* *cutting grass, shoveling snow, painting rooms.* And when something breaks, you can't call the landlord to fix it. When you decide to move, you have to find someone to buy your house.

In conclusion, owning a home has both advantages and disadvantages. *Each individual or family* ~~Everyone~~ has to decide whether ~~the advantages~~ *one side* outweigh*s* the *other.* ~~disadvantages.~~

Warm-up

Proofread the revised version of your essay about the positive and negative effects of the telephone. Make any necessary changes or corrections. Then give your essay one last reading in its entirety.

☑ A Test-Taking Tip

You'll be given 45 minutes to write your GED essay. Give yourself from 5 to 10 minutes to prewrite some ideas and to organize them. Take no more than 15 to 20 minutes for writing your first draft. That leaves 10 to 15 minutes for revising: reviewing your organization and transitions; checking your details, clearness of expression, and sentence structure; and proofreading. If you allot your time this way, you'll increase your chances of writing a successful GED essay.

Sample Warm-up Answer

The telephone has improved the quality of our lives in many ways. In other ways, however, it had has a negative effect.

On the ~~posative~~ *positive* side, the telephone has made doing business much easier and more efficient. ~~It has made life easier for the consumer.~~ *Business people can call their customers rather than writing or traveling to see them.* ~~People~~ *Customers* can pick up the phone to place or check on ~~an~~ order*s*. The telephone has also made the world seem smaller, ~~S~~since it allows us to talk with people all over the country and all over the world. The telephone also helps ~~you~~ *us* stay in touch with friends ~~A~~and relatives, both near and far. In addition, the telephone has created many *thousands of new* new industrie~~s~~ and jobs. It has also saved countless lives in emergencies, *such as fires and accidents.*

On the negative side, ~~But~~ the telephone can be a big time-waster, both at work and at home. It often ~~interupts~~ *interrupts* us and can even keep us from accomplishing our daily tasks. The telephone has also brought us ~~plenty of unwanted calls. Because of the telephone~~ *crank calls, nuisance calls, and wrong numbers.* fewer people write personal letters, ~~The telephone can also cause~~ *and fewer* people ~~to~~ make ~~fewer~~ personal visits, since they can simply talk to ~~people~~ *one another* on the phone.

We can see, then, the role that ~~T~~the telephone ~~has had many posative effects on~~ *plays in* our lives. ~~But~~ *It* has ~~also lowered the quality of our lives in many ways.~~ *had both positive and negative effects on modern life.*

15. Most people want to be successful in life, yet success can be defined in different ways. In what ways can success be defined? Write an essay of about 200 words in which you answer that question. Be specific.

16. Advertisers spend billions of dollars each year trying to persuade consumers to buy their products. How are consumers influenced by the advertising they see? In an essay of about 200 words, explain how they can be positively influenced, negatively influenced, or both.

17. Much has been written about human relationships, but humans' relationship with animals is also interesting to consider. Think of how people interact with animals in general and with specific kinds of animals. Write a 200-word essay about the role or roles animals play in human society.

GED Spelling List

The following is the list of frequently misspelled words that the GED Testing Service uses to pick the words it tests. Different forms of these words may also be tested. For example, *boundaries* could be tested as well as *boundary, awfully* as well as *awful,* and *easier* and *easiest* as well as *easy.*

Don't try to memorize the spelling of each of these words. Instead, take the time every now and then to work with one group of words at a time (there are 42 groups in all and no more than 26 words in a group). Look at each word quickly and then write it without looking at it.

If you've misspelled any words, use one of the techniques you learned about on page 160 to practice them. (Remember that *saying* the letters of a word—either aloud or to yourself—is one good way to fix the spelling of a word in your mind.) Then add any ending to the word that you can *(-s, -ly, -er,* or *-est).* The rules for adding these endings and other spelling rules are explained in the Spelling Breaks in this section.

A

a lot
ability
absence
absent
across
abundance
accept
acceptable
accident
accommodate
accompanied
accomplish
accumulation
accuse
accustomed
ache
achieve
achievement
acknowledge
acquaintance
acquainted

acquire
across
address
addressed
adequate
advantageous
advantage
advertise
advertisement
advice
advisable
advise
advisor
aerial
affect
affectionate
again
against
aggravate
aggressive
agree
aisle
all right
almost
already
although
altogether
always
amateur
American
among
amount
analysis
analyze
angel
angle
annual
another
answer
antiseptic
anxious

apologize
apparatus
apparent
appear
appearance
appetite
application
apply
appreciate
appreciation
approach
appropriate
approval
approve
approximate
argue
arguing
argument
arouse
arrange
arrangement

article
artificial
ascend
assistance
assistant
associate
association
attempt
attendance
attention
audience
August
author
automobile
autumn
auxiliary
available
avenue
awful
awkward

B

bachelor
balance
balloon
bargain
basic
beautiful
because
become
before
beginning
being
believe
benefit
benefited
between
bicycle
board
bored

borrow
bottle
bottom
boundary
brake
breadth
breath
breathe
brilliant
building
bulletin
bureau
burial
buried
bury
bushes
business

C

cafeteria
calculator
calendar
campaign
capital
capitol
captain
career
careful
careless
carriage
carrying
category
ceiling
cemetery
cereal
certain
changeable
characteristic
charity
chief

choose
chose
cigarette
circumstance
citizen

clothes
clothing
coarse
coffee
collect
college
column
comedy
comfortable
commitment
committed
committee
communicate
company
comparative
compel

competent
competition
compliment
conceal
conceit
conceivable
conceive
concentration
conception
condition
conference
confident
congratulate
conquer
conscience
conscientious
conscious
consequence
consequently
considerable
consistency
consistent

continual
continuous
controlled
controversy
convenience
convenient
conversation
corporal
corroborate
council
counsel
counselor
courage
courageous
course
courteous
courtesy

criticism
criticize
crystal
curiosity
cylinder

D

daily
daughter
daybreak
death
deceive
December
deception
decide
decision
decisive
deed
definite
delicious
dependent
deposit
derelict
descend
descent

describe
description
desert
desirable
despair
desperate
dessert
destruction
determine
develop
development
device
dictator
died
difference
different
dilemma
dinner
direction

disappear
disappoint
disappointment
disapproval
disapprove
disastrous
discipline
discover
discriminate
disease
dissatisfied

dissection
dissipate
distance
distinction
division
doctor
dollar
doubt
dozen

E

earnest
easy
ecstasy
ecstatic
education
effect
efficiency
efficient
eight
either
eligibility
eligible
eliminate
embarrass
embarrassment
emergency
emphasis
emphasize

enclosure
encouraging
endeavor
engineer
English
enormous
enough
entrance
envelope
environment
equipment
equipped
especially
essential
evening
evident

exaggerate
exaggeration
examine
exceed
excellent
except
exceptional
exercise
exhausted
exhaustion

exhilaration
existence
exorbitant
expense
experience
experiment
explanation
extreme

F

facility
factory
familiar
fascinate
fascinating
fatigue
February
financial
financier
flourish
forcibly
forehead
foreign
formal
former
fortunate
fourteen
fourth
frequent
friend
frightening
fundamental
further

G

gallon
garden
gardener
general
genius
government
governor
grammar
grateful
great
grievance
grievous
grocery
guarantee
guess
guidance

H

half
hammer
handkerchief
happiness
healthy

heard
heavy
height
heroes
heroine
hideous
himself
hoarse
holiday
hopeless
hospital
humorous
hurried
hurrying

I
ignorance
imaginary
imbecile
imitation
immediately
immigrant
incidental
increase
independence
independent
indispensable
inevitable
influence
influential
initiate
innocence
inoculate
inquiry
insistent

instead
instinct
integrity
intellectual
intelligence
intercede
interest
interfere
interference
interpreted
interrupt
invitation
irrelevant
irresistible
irritable
island
its
it's
itself

J–K
January
jealous
judgment
journal
kindergarten
kitchen
knew
knock
know
knowledge

L
labor
laboratory
laid
language
later
latter
laugh
leisure
length
lesson
library
license
light
lightening
likelihood
likely
literal
literature
livelihood
loaf
loneliness
loose
lose
losing
loyal
loyalty

M
magazine
maintenance
maneuver
marriage
married
marry
match
material
mathematics
measure
medicine
million
miniature
minimum
miracle
miscellaneous
mischief
mischievous
misspelled
mistake
momentous
monkey
monotonous
moral
morale
mortgage
mountain
mournful
muscle
mysterious
mystery

N
narrative
natural
necessary
needle
negligence
neighbor
neither
newspaper
newsstand
nickel
niece
noticeable

O
o'clock
obedient
obstacle
occasion
occasional
occur
occurred
occurrence
ocean
offer
often
omission
omit
once
operate
opinion
opportune
opportunity
optimist
optimistic
origin
original
oscillate
ought
ounce
overcoat

P
paid
pamphlet
panicky
parallel
parallelism
particular
partner
pastime
patience
peace
peaceable
pear
peculiar
pencil
people
perceive
perception
perfect
perform
performance
perhaps
period
permanence
permanent
perpendicular
perseverance
persevere
persistent
persuade
personality
personal
personnel
persuade
persuasion
pertain
picture
piece
plain
playwright

pleasant
please
pleasure
pocket
poison
policeman
political
population
portrayal
positive
possess
possession
possessive
possible
post office
potatoes

practical
prairie
precede
preceding

precise
predictable
prefer
preference
preferential
preferred
prejudice
preparation
prepare
prescription
presence
president
prevalent
primitive
principal
principle
privilege
probably
procedure
proceed

produce
professional
professor
profitable
prominent
promise
pronounce
pronunciation
propeller
prophecy
prophet
prospect
psychology
pursue
pursuit

Q
quality
quantity
quarreling
quart
quarter
quiet
quite

R
raise
realistic
realize
reason
rebellion
recede
receipt
receive
recipe
recognize
recommend
recuperate
referred
rehearsal
reign
relevant
relieve
remedy

renovate
repeat
repetition
representative
requirements
resemblance
resistance
resource
respectability
responsibility
restaurant
rhythm
rhythmical
ridiculous
right
role
roll
roommate

S
sandwich
Saturday
scarcely
scene
schedule
science
scientific
scissors
season
secretary
seige
seize
seminar
sense
separate
service
several
severely
shepherd
sheriff
shining
shoulder
shriek
sight
signal
significance
significant
similar
similarity
sincerely
site
soldier
solemn
sophomore
soul
source
souvenir
special
specified
specimen
speech
stationary
stationery
statue
stockings

stomach
straight
strength
strenuous
stretch
striking
studying
substantial
succeed
successful
sudden
superintendent
suppress
surely
surprise
suspense
sweat
sweet
syllable
symmetrical
sympathy
synonym

T
technical
telegram
telephone
temperament
temperature
tenant
tendency
tenement
therefore
thorough
through
title
together
tomorrow
tongue
toward
tragedy
transferred
treasury
tremendous
tries
truly
twelfth
twelve
tyranny

U–V
undoubtedly
United States
university
unnecessary
unusual
useful
usual
vacuum
valley
valuable
variety
vegetable
vein
vengeance
versatile
vicinity
vicious
view
village
villain
visitor
voice
volume

W
waist
weak
wear
weather
Wednesday
week
weigh
weird
whether
which
while
whole
wholly
whose
wretched

Answers—Writing Skills

Sample Test Items

Writing Sentences
(pages 159–196)

1. (5) No error. Removing *is* makes the sentence a fragment. Removing *so* makes the sentence a run-on.

2. (5) The original wording of this sentence misused a comma. Remember that two complete sentences cannot be connected with just a comma. *For* correctly expresses the relationship between the two thoughts.

3. (2) This is an example of a run-on. Since the two sentences are so closely related, a semicolon can be used to connect them.

Herbal teas are very popular these days. Black tea is not an ingredient in such teas, so they don't contain caffeine. Herbal teas are delicate and light in color, for they are a special blend of natural ingredients. They combine spices, plant leaves, seeds, roots, and flowers; this blend gives them a flowery or spicy aroma.

4. (3) *By buying a videocassette as a record of your trip* is a fragment. It lacks a subject and a verb. Adding the fragment to the end of sentence 2 completes the meaning of sentence 2. Options (2), (4), and (5) are incorrect because a semicolon, *so,* and *and* can connect only complete sentences.

5. (2) This is an example of using a comma to connect two complete sentences. Removing the comma creates a run-on.

Do you suffer from extreme fatigue from carrying enormous amounts of camera equipment along on your vacation? You can save yourself from all that aggravation by buying a videocassette as a record of your trip. The Smithsonian Institution has them, the National Park Service has them, and soon most major tourist attractions will have them. Many Americans own video-playing devices, and these people are the prime market for souvenir tapes of all descriptions.

6. (4) The original wording of this sentence is a run-on. Inserting a comma isn't enough. Adding a period after *benefit* creates two complete sentences.

7. (3) When *and* connects two sentences, you must use a comma before it.

8. (2) If a word ends in *-f,* change the *-f* to *-v* and add *-es* to make the word mean more than one. *Twelve* is often confused with *twelfth.*

Recently, I heard many speeches given at a "Stop World Hunger" benefit. I found them especially moving. Two speakers offered very vivid analyses of several recent famines, and I felt the need to help. I made a small contribution to buy twelve loaves of bread; this donation would help feed a family of four for two weeks. Many other people in the audience responded to the speakers' pleas by making donations too. We all felt that we had done something positive to help feed these hungry people.

9. (5) No error. *Will explore* indicates future time. Because the sentence begins with the time clue *Since 1933,* you know that the action took place in the past. Careful pronunciation of *primitive* will help you spell it correctly.

10. (3) *Did* is correct because of the time clue *10,000 years ago.*

11. (5) No error. Options (3) and (4) are incorrect because they do not express past time.

Since 1933, many scientific expeditions have explored the island of New Guinea because the most primitive people on earth live there. The natives of New Guinea live like the Stone Age people did 10,000 years ago. While visiting these Stone Age villagers, the explorers introduced them to many modern inventions. Matches, "talking boxes" (radios), and bubblegum fascinated the natives.

12. (1) *Came* doesn't need a helper like *have. Have come* is correct. *Buyed* is nonstandard English.

13. (2) *To be broken in* is right in both time and form.

14. (1) *Reason* is the correct spelling.

Have you ever come home with a pair of shoes that didn't fit and wondered why you ever bought them? Did the salesperson tell you that they just needed to be broken in, or did you like the style so much that you bought the shoes even though the store was out of your size? Whatever the reason, we have all fallen victim to this problem. The end of your longest toe should be a thumb's width from the end of the shoe when you are standing.

15. (1) *Was* is the correct choice because of the time clue *from 1837 to 1901. Leopold* is capitalized because it is someone's name, but *brother* is not.

16. (1) *Become* cannot be used without a helping word. *Uncle* and *nephew* are not capitalized because they are not followed by someone's name.

Queen Victoria, who ruled England from 1837 to 1901, was fatherless from infancy, but her father's brother, Leopold, provided her with fatherly advice and guidance for more than thirty years. When she was eighteen, the young princess became queen of England, and her uncle immediately proposed that his nephew,

Prince Albert, should marry Victoria. Victoria adored her husband, and this happy union produced nine children.

17. (5) *So* cannot join two unrelated ideas. The best revision is to write the original sentence as two separate sentences.

18. (5) *Mosquitoes can ruin a camper's evening and make a backyard barbecue party unbearable.* This smooth revision of sentences 2 and 3 brings the verbs together (*ruin* and *make*). The words *They can also* are not needed because they repeat information given in sentence 2.

19. (4) *Mosquitoes are attracted* and *like* make sense because both verbs are written in present time. *Mosquitoes are attracting to body warmth* is not logical. Commas are not needed after *warmth* and *moisture.*

In the United States, 95 percent of biting mosquitoes breed in temporary pools of water. Some varieties carry diseases. Mosquitoes can ruin a camper's evening and make a backyard barbecue unbearable. Female mosquitoes are attracted to body warmth and moisture and like to bite men more than women. Their bites swell and itch because they inject an enzyme to keep blood from coagulating while they enjoy their feast.

20. (3) The original sentence misuses the first comma. Commas are not strong enough to join two complete sentences. *Because* correctly expresses the relationship between the two thoughts.

21. (4) The original sentence is a run-on. The two thoughts aren't related enough to join. Option (4) is the best revision.

22. (3) Use commas after introductory dependent parts. Option (2) is incorrect because of the time clue *1873.*

Many health-conscious people love raisins because they are wholesome, easily digested, and delicious. In biblical times, raisins were used to pay taxes. Hannibal fed them to his troops to give them energy to cross the Alps. After the 1873 grape harvest was dried out by a drought, the California raisin industry was born.

23. (4) *Even if* correctly expresses the relationship between *dressing tall and thin* and *not dieting.*

24. (1) *Always* is difficult to spell because you hear the sound of *all* in front of *ways*.

25. (1) Insert a comma when you hear a pause before a dependent part. Read sentence 5 aloud and listen for the pause after *patterns.*

Here are some tips for dressing tall and thin even if you are not dieting. Don't wear tight clothing; instead, wear clothes that skim your body. If the elements of your outfit are in the same color family, you will look taller and slimmer. Always wear shoulder pads, even small ones, because they make clothing hang better. Buy clothes with small, subtle patterns, since large fabric designs emphasize width.

26. (4) These words are easy to confuse. Here's a hint. *Stationary* ends in *-ary* and means "to stay in one place." *Stationery* ends in *-ery* and means "paper for writing letters." If you remember the *a* in *-ary* along with the *a* in *stay,* and the *e* in *-ery* with the *e*'s in *letters*, you should not confuse these two words.

27. (4) The sentence tells you to do two things (*tear* and *cover*). *And* correctly joins these two verbs. If you chose option (2), remember that *tear* and *cover* express commands. Both verbs have the understood *you* as their subject. Therefore, it is correct to use a comma here because it is helping connect two complete sentences.

28. (2) *Coarse* is correct because it means "a rough or bumpy layer." A comma after *paper* is correct.

Junk mail has finally met its match, for you can recycle this "wealth" into designer stationery. All you need is a blender, a small wire screen, and lots of patience. Tear the junk mail into small pieces, and cover them with water in the blender. After you blend this mixture for about one minute, pour the mush into a shallow pan of water. Use the screen to lift out a coarse layer of the pulverized paper, and iron until it is dry.

29. (4) Correctly pronouncing *quite* and *quiet* will help you use them correctly. Uncle is always capitalized when it comes before a person's name.

30. (5) If you pronounce *breadth* with a *d* sound, you won't confuse it with *breath.* Option (1) is incorrect because *he be* is not standard English.

31. (5) No error. In this sentence, *moral* means "a lesson taught." *Morale* means "mood or spirits." *Accepting* is correct because it means "taking."

Last Saturday night, Uncle Miroslav's children gave him a birthday banquet that was quite impressive. Since he is Czechoslovakian, they chose recipes that represented the breadth of Old World cuisine. The quantity of desserts had an adverse effect on everyone's waistline. At the end of the banquet, eveyone needed to loosen his or her clothes in order to breathe a little easier. The moral of this tale is that accepting only one dessert may not lower your morale as much as you think it would.

32. (1) *Were* is a helping word. *Frozen,* not *froze,* is used after a helping word. Pronouncing *temperature* with in four parts (tem-per-a-ture) will help you remember its spelling.

33. (4) *As Buck approached the outer defenses of earth, he was almost vaporized by Colonel Dearing.* Options (2) and (5) are incorrect because *Buck* didn't vaporize anything; he *was* vaporized (or almost). *Is* indicates present time, and the passage is written in past time.

34. (5) This is an example of a run-on. Option (2) would need a connecting word along with the comma. *Because* and *therefore* usually express a cause-and-effect relationship. Being accused of spying and having Twiki as a friend do not express a cause and an effect.

The spacecraft of Captain Buck Rogers was pulled off course by a freak mishap. His life-support systems were frozen to temperatures beyond imagination, and his ship was lost for 500 years. As Buck approached the outer defenses of earth, he was almost vaporzied by Colonel Dearing. Later Buck was accused of spying, and his only friend was Twiki.

35. (5) No error. The subjects and verbs agree. The two complete thoughts are joined correctly.

36. (1) *This branch of dentistry is growing because research has proven that teeth can move no matter how old a person is.* This revision of sentence 3 gets rid of many unnecessary words. Options (2), (3), (4), and (5) do not express the cause-and-effect relationship between the growth of orthodontics and the research findings.

37. (5) No error. If you chose option (1), review the lesson on forming plurals on page 161. *Companies offer* and *employees are* agree.

The sight of an adult wearing braces is becoming more common these days. Currently, the orthodontists see one adult patient in five, but by the end of the century, the number will increase to one in four. This branch of dentistry is growing because research has proven that teeth can move no matter how old a person is. Because many companies now offer health plans that include orthodontic coverage, employees are able to have their teeth straightened at little or no personal cost.

38. (5) No error. Careful pronunciation of *literature* (lit-er-a-ture) will help you spell it correctly. The subject *Many* and the verb *have* agree because they both mean more than one thing.

39. (5) No error. *No one* and *knows* agree because they both mean one thing. Option (2) is not correct because *exists* expresses present time. Sentence 1 states that Beowulf was an *ancient* warrior. Therefore, he lived (*existed*) in the past.

40. (5) The original sentence is a fragment. *Was rewarded* correctly expresses the past time of the sentence. Option (3) is incorrect because *Everyone* and *were* do not agree.

Many have read the epic poem about Beowulf, an ancient Scandinavian warrior, especially students of Old English literature. No one knows for sure whether Beowulf really existed, but the legend of his nine-hour underwater battle with a monster is still famous. Beowulf's crew fought courageously with him. Everyone was rewarded handsomely for his bravery. Beowulf then returned home to rule as king for fifty years.

41. (4) *Office environments can cause problems for plants, including poor lighting and low humidity.* This revision gets rid of the second subject, *These problems,* because it is not necessary to repeat this information. Option (2) is not logical because it is the plants that have problems, not offices. Option (3) includes the repeated information *the problems,* which is not needed.

42. (3) *Another important problem to remember is that ventilation and heating systems are turned down at nights and on weekends.* This revision puts the subject *problem* in front of the verb, and this makes the sentence stronger. Options (1) and (2) seem to indicate that *you* are remembering an important problem or that *you* will remember to turn down the systems. *You* as a pronoun is not used anywhere in the passage.

43. (2) *The resulting drop in temperature makes the office a hostile environment for growing plants.* The first sentence is changed into a group of words that can be joined to the verb of sentence 6. This revision uses fewer words than the original two sentences. Option (3) is not the best combination of sentences 5 and 6 because the office is not really the subject of these sentences; the drop in temperature is.

Office environments can cause problems for plants, including poor lighting and low humidity. Another important problem to remember is that ventilation and heating systems are turned down at nights and on weekends. The resulting drop in temperature makes the office a hostile environment for growing plants.

44. (5) No error. *Joggers and walkers* is a subject that means more than one. *Disagree* also means more than one. Remember that verbs ending is *-s* mean one thing. *A lot* is always spelled as two words.

45. (2) *One overlooked aspect of exercise is the feeling of well-being people experience whether they have walked or run.* Notice how *that is often overlooked* was changed to one word. When you are revising your own writing, look for ways to change groups of words into one word.

Joggers and walkers disagree a lot about the merits of their different, yet equally enjoyable, exercise programs. No one knows why some people prefer walking to jogging, but doctors and other experts have proven that walking, along with stretching exercises, puts less stress on the body's joints. One overlooked aspect of exercise is the feeling of well-being people experience whether they have walked or run.

46. (3) Since *friend* is the subject, *is* (not *are*) agrees with it. Be careful when groups of words *(like all young mothers)* come between the subject and the verb. *Through* and *thorough* are often confused. In this sentence, *through* means "from the beginning to the end of." *Thorough* usually means "complete" or "very careful." Compare these: Dr. Watson helped Sherlock Holmes *through* many mysterious cases. Sherlock Holmes gave each clue a *thorough* examination.

47. (1) *Son* and *believes* both are singular, so they agree. Options (3) and (4) are in past time. Sentences 1, 2, and 3 are about something that is happening now. Option (5) makes the sentence a fragment.

48. (1) *However* interrupts the flow of the sentence. Always place commas around interrupting words. Refer to sentence 2 in the original example. *For example* is also an interrupter. Notice that sentences 4 and 5 are written about a past event. Therefore, *had* is the correct verb.

A friend of mine, like all young mothers, is struggling through the "terrible twos" with her son. Her son, for example, believes everything in the house is his. The toys are his; the dog's bowl is his; even the remote control for the television is his. One day, however, she had enough and said, "William, will you please play quietly because Mommy is at the end of her rope." William, with a glint in his two-year-old's eyes, looked her squarely in the face and said, "*My* rope, Mommy."

49. (1) Careful pronunciation of *probably* will help you spell it correctly. The comma after *friends* comes before the connecting word *but,* which joins two complete sentences.

50. (2) Words that name regions of the United States are usually capitalized (the *West,* the *South*). Points on a compass are usually not capitalized *(north, south, east, west). Basin* and *South* are capitalized because they are part of geographical names.

Like many people, you probably plan your vacation with relatives or friends, but have you ever thought of taking a learning vacation? Such a vacation gives you the chance to learn or sharpen a skill. Learning vacations can include lessons on cooking of the Southwest or lessons with a professional photographer on trips to the Amazon Basin in South America. If you are the outdoor type, why not try a sailing school off the west coast of Florida?

51. (3) When two subjects are joined by *nor,* the verb agrees with the subject closer to it. *Writers understand* is correct. The silent *t* in *often* makes it difficult to spell.

52. (5) No error. *Words have* and *they have* agree. The comma after *definitions* comes before *but,* which connects two complete sentences.

53. (2) When two subjects are joined by *or,* the verb agrees with the subject closer to it. *Stupid is used* agrees. *Knew* and *were* are not correct verb choices because they indicate past time.

Often, neither readers nor writers truly understand the power of words. Words not only have dictionary definitions, but they also have meanings that suggest positive or negative images. For example, either "uninformed" or "stupid" is used to describe a person voting on an issue he knows nothing about. Would you rather be called a fussy, scrawny person or an extremely neat, slender person? One creative store owner uses the power of words to advertise her business: "We buy old furniture. We sell antiques."

54. (1) *There* is never the subject of a sentence. *Differences* is the subject of this sentence. *Differences are* agrees. *Differences* can be pronounced with either three or four parts. To remember the correct spelling of *differences,* try pronouncing it with four parts (dif-fer-en-ces).

55. (2) To figure out the subject of this sentence, turn it around: *The way an overlock stitches, trims, and overcasts all in one step is interesting.* What is interesting? The way is.

56. (2) *With twice the speed of a conventional machine, an overlock makes home sewing look more professional.* Notice that the subject of the first sentence *(overlocks)* was made singular in the revised sentence. The revised sentence is a little smoother and clearer.

Used to make ready-to-wear garments since the early 1900s, overlock sewing machines are now available to the home sewer. There are differences between a conventional sewing machine and an overlock. Most interesting is the way an overlock stitches, trims, and overcasts all in one step. With twice the speed of a conventional machine, an overlock makes home sewing look more professional.

57. (4) *Great* should be capitalized because it is part of the geographical name *Great Britain. Countries celebrate* agrees. Even if you didn't know what Beanfeast was, you could tell from the rest of the sentence that it is the name of a holiday.

58. (1) *Because of George Washington* is an introductory phrase that needs a comma inserted after it because you would pause after *Washington* if you read the sentence aloud. *But* (not *or*) correctly shows the contrast between when *we* celebrate Thanksgiving and when the Pilgrims celebrated Thanksgiving.

The word "holiday" originally meant "holy day," which was a festival to honor a sacred event or person. Many countries celebrate a variety of interesting holidays, such as the Beanfeast and the Wayzgoose holidays in Great Britain. The Republic of Israel celebrates two independence days: Passover, when the Hebrews were delivered from Egypt, and the Proclamation of the Jewish State, which took place in 1948. Because of George Washington, we celebrate Thanksgiving on the fourth Thursday in November, but the Pilgrims celebrated the holiday in February, July, and September.

59. (1) *Advances* (not *medicine*) is the subject. Therefore, *advances are making* is correct. Option (4) is incorrect because *expenses is* would not agree.

60. (1) *Will be* is correct.

61. (3) The original sentence is a fragment because it lacks a verb. *Pays* is the correct verb choice because it agrees with *policy.* Review the rule on page 177 about two subjects joined by *or.* The verb agrees with the closer subject *(policy),* not the first subject *(policies).*

The advances of modern medicine are making our lives healthier than ever, but the expenses of medical care are greater than ever. The more a consumer shops around for an insurance company, the easier it will be to find one with good coverage. Usually, either a married couple's individual policies or a single family policy pays for most hospital bills.

62. (4) Neither *government* nor *Washington* is the subject of this sentence; the word *facts* is. Don't be tricked by words that come between the subject and the verb.

63. (1) Careful pronunciation of all six parts will help you spell *Scientifically.* This word needs *-al* added to *scientific* before you add *-ly.* Option (4) is incorrect because *jobs* is the subject, not government.

Occasionally, interesting facts about the government in Washington are reported. The Office of Personnel Management was apparently interested in civil servants with unusual jobs and so recently decided to publish a list of federal jobs. Scientifically speaking, jobs not normally associated with the government are those of astronomers and anthropologists. On a recent survey list are jobs such as clothing designers, stevedores, cobblers, currency checkers, and broom makers. There are sixteen butchers and nine bakers but no candlestick makers employed by the U.S. government.

64. (2) *Originally designed for the tennis court, the inexpensive canvas sneaker was the consumer's only choice.* The revised sentence begins with an introductory dependent part that describes the subject *(the inexpensive canvas sneaker).* In option (1), the dependent part would describe *choice;* in option (3), it would describe *inexpensiveness;* and in option (5), it would describe *consumer.*

65. (2) In the original wording, *Sold for a budget-breaking $25 and up* does not describe the subject *(infants).* Option (2) is the only answer that has the dependent part correctly describing *sneakers.*

Not too many years ago, buying sneakers was easy. Originally designed for the tennis court, the inexpensive canvas sneaker was the consumer's only choice. Able to choose from a long list of sneaker types, consumers wear sneakers as their primary shoe today. There are aerobic workout, high-top, and even snow sneakers. Sold for a budget-breaking $25 and up, high-top sneakers are worn even by infants.

66. (2) The *oldest post of the Marine Corps* provides more information about the Marine Barracks. Since a comma is placed before *the,* one must also be placed after *Corps.* Options (3), (4), and (5) create fragments.

67. (3) *Band* is capitalized because it is part of the band's name. Option (2) creates a fragment without a verb. Since *"the President's Own"* adds extra information about the United States Marine Band, it should be separated from the rest of the sentence with a comma.

68. (1) *A famous composer* adds more information to *John Philip Sousa* and must be separated from the rest of the sentence with commas. Option (5) is incorrect because *John Philip Sousa, a famous composer* would be a fragment without a verb.

The Marine Barracks in Washington, the oldest post in the Marine Corps, is a registered National Historic Landmark. Many tourists visit this landmark to hear the United States Marine Band, "the President's Own." John Philip Sousa, a famous composer, led the band during the years he composed many of his marches. The Marines at the post also provide security for the president.

69. (4) Two complete sentences are connected with a comma in the original. A comma is not strong enough to connect complete sentences, but a semicolon is.

70. (1) Since the singular *alligator* and *it* are used later in the sentence, the singular *Its* should be used.

In the 1960s, the American alligator was in danger of becoming extinct, and it became listed with other endangered species. Thanks to strict enforcement of antipoaching laws, the species has been taken off the list in Florida, Louisiana, and Texas. Several other states are experiencing a population explosion of these ancient reptiles; to control their large numbers, the states hope to stage controlled hunts. Its comeback has been strong, but if the alligator is killed off too quickly, it will be designated as "endangered" again.

71. (1) *President* would be capitalized only if it came before a person's name or if it came at the beginning of a sentence. Option (2) is wrong because a comma is used before *and* when *and* connects two complete sentences.

72. (1) *Which* is used to refer to a thing (the President's Medal of Freedom). Also, you hear a pause after *Freedom;* that's another clue that *which* with a comma before it is correct.

Dr. Helen B. Taussig, who pioneered ways to treat children born with heart defects, is known as the founder of pediatric cardiology. She was the first woman to be president of the American Heart Association and to be made a full professor at the Johns Hopkins Medical School. She was also the first American doctor to investigate birth defects in German babies whose mothers had taken the drug thalidomide. For her work in this area, she was awarded the President's Medal of Freedom, which is the nation's highest civilian honor.

73. (1) *They* is needed to refer to *people* in sentence 1. Sometimes a pronoun can refer to a word in another sentence.

74. (4) The original is a run-on. Since the second sentence contains a dependent part *(once you have passed the GED Test),* option (4) is the best choice.

75. (1) The pronoun *you* is used throughout the passage. *One* and *they* do not follow through with this usage.

The people in your company's personnel office can help you in many ways. They can provide information about new job openings and professional courses. Many employees are eligible for education benefits. Once you have passed the GED Test, you might qualify for tuition assistance for college. You should explore the career options available to you because learning always leads to growth.

76. (1) *Ezra Cornell, the founder of Cornell University, made his fortune in the telegraph industry.* In this revision, sentence 1 becomes a group of words *(the founder of Cornell University)* after the subject *(Ezra Cornell).* The verb of sentence 2 *(made)* now becomes the verb of the revised sentence.

77. (1) *After inventing a way to insulate wires on poles, Cornell helped build the world's first telegraph line from Baltimore to Washington* in 1844. The original wording of the sentence is awkward. Placing the dependent part *After inventing a way to insulate wires on poles* at the beginning of the revised sentence clarifies the meaning. Option (4) is incorrect because the introductory dependent part would describe *the world's first telegraph line,* which is not logical.

Ezra Cornell, the founder of Cornell University, made his fortune in the telegraph industry. He had very little formal education, but he was a genius at inventing machines. After inventing a way to insulate wires on poles, Cornell helped build the world's first telegraph line from Baltimore to Washington in 1844. First he became the chief stockholder in Western Union and afterward devoted his life to farming and public service.

78. (4) *Appropriate* is correct. *Campaigns* is difficult to spell because of the silent *g.*

79. (2) *Spirit,* not *spouses,* is the subject. *Spirit dissipates* agrees.

The closer it gets to Christmas, the closer many married couples come to open conflict about what gifts to buy each other. Some spouses mount organized campaigns to give hints about appropriate gifts. They leave notes in drawers, open catalogs to important pages, or strategically sigh when a desired gift is advertised on television. The holiday spirit of both spouses rarely dissipates as the scent of victory overrides the fear of disappointment.

80. (4) *Began* is never used with a helper *(have).* Always use *begun* with a helper. *Their* is used correctly to show ownership (the inventories belong to the companies).

81. (2) Even though *books* is close to the verb *are, books* is not the subject. *Audience* (the subject) agrees with *is. There's* stands for *there is.* To say *there is a new market* is correct.

82. (5) No error. *Will find* indicates a future action (an action that has not yet occurred). Options (2) and (3) indicate actions that are occurring now *(had been finding)* and actions that have already occurred *(found).*

The population of the United States includes 498,000 legally blind people, with more than 11 million visually handicapped persons. Several publishing companies have begun to add large-print books to their inventories. The main audience for these books is the growing number of older people, but many publishers believe that there's a new market for their large-print books. A growing number of younger people, after working all day in front of computer screens, will find large-print books refreshing for their tired eyes.

83. (3) *Standing* and *fiddled* don't have matching endings. Therefore, (3) is correct. *Hear* is correct, though, because it goes with *you (you hear),* not with *Have you ever been.*

84. (5) *Who* and *was* agree because in this sentence *who* is singular. Option (2) is incorrect because *one* does not follow through with the use of *you* in the rest of the passage.

85. (2) *Avoiding* and *to control* do not match, but *avoiding* and *controlling* do. Options (3), (4), and (5) also do not match *avoiding.*

Have you ever been standing at the front door, fiddling with your keys, when you hear the telephone ring? By the turn of the century, you will know who was trying to reach you. The clue to the caller's identity will be in the sound of the ring. You will be able to give each of your ten most frequent callers a different ring. Avoiding unwanted callers and controlling your time at home will be two advantages of this new telephone service.

86. (3) Commas should be used to separate the three items. In option (2) there should be no comma after *or;* in option (5) the first *or* is not needed.

87. (1) This sentence is a little tricky because the subject *(systems)* comes after the verb *(is). Systems are* is correct. Option (4) is wrong because you don't need a comma when only two things *(lights and appliances)* are mentioned.

Many homeowners are investing in electronic security systems to make their homes safe from trespassers, burglars, or other intruders. Currently on the market are systems that can control up to 256 lights and appliances automatically, efficiently, and cheaply. Some systems combine video cameras with computers and allow a person to monitor a summer home or a business from the owner's home. Do-it-yourselfers can install most of these systems by making use of existing home wiring.

88. (4) Since a specific pirate is not mentioned, there is no reason to capitalize *pirates'. Teams search* agrees. A comma is needed after *ships* because *ships* is the first item in a list *(ships, frigates, or galleys).*

89. (3) When many words come between the subject and verb, it is sometimes difficult to decide which verb form is correct. The subject *(artifacts)* agrees with *are.* Removing *is* in option (4) creates a fragment.

90. (1) *Mel Fisher* gives additional information about the word *hunter.* Therefore, *Mel Fisher* must have commas around it. *Hunter has* agrees. *Keys* is capitalized because it is part of a geographical name.

Deep-sea diving teams methodically search for decaying wrecks of British pay ships, ancient frigates, or pirates' galleys. Interesting artifacts such as Chinese ceramics, pottery, and gold jewelry are recovered from wrecks all over the world. One treasure hunter, Mel Fisher, has found the remains of a Spanish galleon off the Florida Keys. He and his divers have recovered treasures with an estimated value of $400 million.

91. (4) In the original sentence, it is not clear whether *her* refers to *commissioner* or *governor.* Option (4) is the only one that gives you a correct substitute for *her.*

92. (5) No error. Option (1) creates a fragment. *People have* agrees. Inserting the word *will* would be using the wrong time. In this sentence, it's clear that *them* refers back to shopping malls.

93. (3) In the original sentence, you can't tell what *they* refers to without stopping to think about it. Option (3) is the logical choice to replace *they.*

The environmental commissioner and the governor have agreed on the governor's policy of not building giant shopping malls in the state. Both feel that business people have exaggerated the need for them. Environmentalists believe that the malls cause traffic problems, strain a city's sewage and water resources, and often ruin large tracts of scenic land. Economists disagree with the views of environmentalists and argue that malls generate jobs and boost a city's economy.

94. (2) It is unclear what *this* refers to. *As a result,* clearly refers the reader to the actions of the neighbor in sentence 1. Options (3), (4), and (5) aren't strong enough to show the relationship between the action in sentences 1 and 2.

95. (5) Placing *which* toward the end of this sentence confuses the reader. What could get expensive? Option (5) helps the reader understand what is meant.

96. (1) *What Shakespeare said* is very specific. Options (2), (3), and (5) do not identify any speaker. Option (4) uses too many unnecessary words.

There is always at least one neighbor whose unerring instinct leads him directly to your newly purchased hedge trimmers. As a result, every spring you must be possessive with your tools or pursue the tools that "walked away." Maybe you should put an electronic homing device on each of your most valuable ones, but that solution could get expensive. What Shakespeare said is true: "Neither a borrower nor a lender be."

97. (4) *Erupting with the force of one million atomic bombs, this explosion reduced an eighteen-square-mile island to only six miles.* The original sentence contains many unnecessary words. *This powerfully big blast* can be reduced to two words *(this explosion). Which made a really loud noise* can be left out (explosions usually do make loud noises). *In size* is unnecessary because the reader knows that *eighteen to six* refers to the size of the island.

98. (2) *The earthquakes accompanying this eruption caused a tidal wave 200 feet high that traveled 400 miles per hour and destroyed whole towns.* The original sentence contains unnecessary words, some informal language, and an awkwardly placed phrase. Notice that *accompanying this eruption is* moved closer to the word it describes *(earthquakes).*

The loudest sound ever heard on earth occurred when the volcano Krakatoa erupted in 1883. Erupting with the force of one million atomic bombs, this explosion reduced an eighteen-square-mile island to only six miles. The earthquakes accompanying this eruption caused a tidal wave 200 feet high that traveled 400 miles per hour and destroyed whole towns. Chunks of red-hot rocks, some eight feet thick and weighing seventy pounds, fell over an area as large as France.

99. (1) *This loyalty helps pet owners feel less lonely than most people without pets.* The original wording of the sentence contains unnecessary words. *This loyalty* points to something specific that a reader can relate to. Notice that *people who own them* was reduced to *owners.* This revision is an example of clear, concise writing.

100. (1) *For children arriving home before their parents do, a pet can make them feel safe.* The original wording of this sentence is awkward and contains unnecessary words. Beginning a sentence with an introductory phrase adds variety to your writing.

101. (2) *Hanging out together like this* and *pals* are too informal. *The best of friends* and *in association with one another* are overused phrases that make writing uninteresting.

Pets like their owners. This loyalty helps pet owners feel less lonely than most people without pets. For children arriving home before their parents do, a pet can make them feel safe. Human beings and dogs have been helping each other thus for more than 30,000 years.

Writing Essays (pages 204–215)

1. *Sample essay:*

Every week millions of people buy lottery tickets, hoping their small investment will make them rich. They often believe that if they won a million dollars, their troubles would be over. If they actually got the money, would their dreams come true?

Whether people live "happily ever after" when they win the lottery probably depends on what their dreams are. Money can buy some things but not others.

Cash buys houses, cars, and college educations; it pays for medical treatment and clears up overdue bills. Money also purchases travel and new experiences. A million dollars could allow someone to quit a tough, boring job and try for something better. It could provide a feeling of security.

On the other hand, winning so much money could actually cause some problems. A person who quit working might eventually become bored or lose some self-respect. Family members might squabble over what should be purchased. Long-lost friends, relatives, and even complete strangers are likely to want a handout. The winner must then decide who to help and who to offend.

Despite all these drawbacks, I would rather win the money than not. The difficulties of having to manage a million dollars are troubles I would like to have.

2. *Sample essay:*

"After the baby is born, things will never be the same." People say that to expectant parents—and they are right!

It will be a long time before those parents can again sleep late in the morning. A baby wakes early, screaming for food. The toddler thinks 6 A.M. is the right time to start the day. After that come early school mornings.

It will be years before the parents can go anywhere together on the spur of the moment. Every outing must be planned ahead so that a baby-sitter can be found. The budget will be stretched, the work load will get heavier, and by the time parents can be alone, they may be too tired to talk.

Still, people want children. Why?

One reason is that children are a link to the future. They will probably be here after the parents are gone. In addition, *their* children will live after them.

A deeper reason for wanting children, perhaps, is that the more people we have to love, the more fulfilled our lives can be. By giving to a child, people enrich their own lives. In the end, we live not only for ourselves, but for others.

3. *Sample essay:*

It hurts to look at a paycheck and see how much of it was taken out for income tax. That money could have paid some important bills. It is easy to dream of doing away with the income tax and keeping all that money for ourselves.

If there were no income tax, however, the government would have a lot less to spend. The money we send to Washington seems to fall into a black hole and disappear. Actually, though, many people depend on it. The money pays the salaries of government employees, who provide services from drug control to highway building. It supports our military defense. Also, much of the money is returned to people in the form of student loans, veterans' benefits, and payments to farmers, for example. The government has been working to cut its budget lately. With every cut, someone complains loudly.

So if the income tax were eliminated, other taxes would have to make up for it. Paying those other taxes would also hurt. Sales taxes fall most heavily on poor people. Taxes on manufacturers only result in higher prices to consumers.

Income taxes are not fun to pay. But doing without them would be worse. In my opinion, income taxes should be made as fair as possible. Then we each must "bite the bullet" and do our share.

4. *Sample essay:*

Television has changed both the way we spend our time and what we know about the world. Some of the changes brought by television have improved our way of life, but others have made it worse.

People today on the average spend several hours a day watching television. In times past, they would sit on their front steps and visit on nice evenings. This neighborly visiting built close friendships, but it seldom takes place any longer. Even though families may all watch TV together, they may not communicate much. Some women have called themselves "sports widows" because their husbands spend every spare minute watching televised football, baseball, and other sports.

On the other hand, people have learned more about the world because of television. People in small towns know more about the city, and people in cities have learned about the country. Politicians, celebrities, wars, and disasters appear in the living room. Programs take viewers to the bottom of the sea, the tops of mountains, and even outer space.

Some people think television leads to violence, immorality, and greed for possessions. I am not sure whether this is ture. However, good or bad, TV is here to stay. It is up to each of us to make the most of its opportunities and avoid its problems.

5. *Sample essay:*

When lack of money prevents us from having something we want very much, it is tempting to dream of being rich. It is hard to keep in mind that Americans are already wealthy compared with people in many other parts of the world. Our modern conveniences would have been the envy of kings in times past. Just the same, most people would like a larger share of the wealth—much larger. Whether most people are capable of making a lot of money is another question.

People in average circumstances can often get ahead through education, hard work, and careful money management. But getting ahead is not the same as actually becoming rich.

Only a small percentage of Americans could be called truly wealthy. Some people joined this group from ordinary beginnings. Usually they have done it by carefully riding some major development in the economy on its way up. In the past, great fortunes have been made in oil, steel, and railroads. Recently, some people have made millions in computers and real estate.

Usually, though, it takes money to make money. Big investors often start rich and then get richer.

Most of us cannot strike oil or start the next new technical breakthrough. Most people are not born into wealthy families, either. In America it certainly is possible to become more prosperous. But unless someone wins the lottery, real wealth is not very likely to come along.

6. *Sample essay:*

You come home alone after a long day at work. You open the door to your home. No one is there. Is it blessed silence you hear—or echoing emptiness?

The millions of people who live alone today may have either experience. Some love living alone, yet others wish they didn't have to.

When they open that door at night, people who live alone do not have to put up with demands or listen to someone's noise or meet anyone's dinner deadlines. They do not have to debate about which TV program to watch or stay off the phone because someone else is expecting an important call. No one else messes up their kitchen.

But when they are sick, no one else will bring them an aspirin or call the doctor. Preparing dinner for one can be difficult, and eating dinner for one night after night can be very lonely. Perhaps no one really cares what they did all day. If they are feeling sad, there may be no one to cheer them up. Some people who live alone say the worst times come when something very good happens because there is no one to share the joy.

During the course of a lifetime, one may sometimes live with others and sometimes live alone. Each way of life has its advantages. Learning to take advantage of them is one key to contentment.

7. *Sample essay:*

Sports includes both national teams and the teams for the rest of us. The national teams are mainly concerned with winning and with money. The other teams provide different satisfactions.

Being on a team helps people learn teamwork—to rely on others and to do their own part as well. Players learn both to win and to lose. When the team loses, the members learn that they can come back from a loss. They look for the reasons they were beaten, work on their weaknesses, and try again. When the team wins, the members can learn to be gracious winners and good sports.

Sports are also for play. Most of us have work to do most of the time. Now and then we need to have fun. Sports can provide the time to relax.

If a team helps people learn to work together, lose, win, and have fun, it's a winner regardless of the score. But if players on a winning team have not worked together, if they feel that winning makes them better than others, if there was no joy in the sport, those winners are losers.

Having the winning score is important. Being a winner as a person is worth even more.

8. *Sample essay:*

Advertisers who directly attack their competitors may amuse me if they do it cleverly. However, they have probably lost me as a customer.

Companies who attack their rivals remind me of people who boost their egos by criticizing others. When people do this, I often suspect they have little to offer and may even have something to hide. I would rather find out what is good about a person, not what is bad about someone else.

Similarly, I like advertising that lets me know about products that might meet my needs. I don't place much faith in ads telling me what may be wrong with a rival product. I tend to suspect that the information could be biased.

I also believe advertisers are foolish to name their rivals because by doing so they give the competing product free publicity. If the competition is worth attacking, I tend to think it may actually have something to offer.

In advertising, as in life, I believe we should try to be the best we can be, without belittling the next person—or the rival product.

9. *Sample essay:*

Three generations living together can have both financial and personal advantages. On the other hand, it can also have personal disadvantages.

In years past and today, three generations have probably lived together mostly out of economic necessity or advantage. Sometimes a young family moves in with the older generation because the husband and wife can't afford a place of their own. Sometimes grandparents move in because they aren't well enough or can't afford to live alone anymore. Occasionally, grandparents come to take care of the children so both parents can work. In times past, and sometimes today, three generations have lived together because they all depended on the same farm or business.

Usually these arrangements do help solve financial and practical problems. Everyone has a roof over his or her head. Children and old people in need of care are likely to get it. Often a family can get ahead financially by sharing the work and the bills. In addition, a strong sense of family and of belonging can develop in everyone.

What may be harder to work out are questions of who's in charge. If grandparents don't let go of some authority, the middle generation is likely to resent it. On the other hand, ailing grandparents may force their children to be parents to them and to their own children as well. If parents and grandparents disagree on discipline, children may be confused or angry.

The personal disadvantages can be overcome. For three generations to live together successfully, everyone's needs must be respected.

10. *Sample essay:*

Television news shows are dramatic and interesting. Watching them is pleasant and does not require the effort of reading. If television did not cover the news, some people would know nothing about what is going on in the world.

However, television newscasters cover only the events that they have time for, and they prefer stories that include some dramatic pictures. Viewers are quickly bored with reporters who sit and talk into the camera. As a result, a complicated story is often cut short.

Newspapers and magazines do a better job of explaining complex events. They can include details, and a person with a special interest can take the time to read them. Others can stick to the headlines.

Reading allows more freedom of choice than television. The TV audience cannot decide which stories to watch. In broadcasting, "one size fits all." However, a person who reads newspapers and magazines can choose to spend time on business, sports, health, or the school board election, depending on special interests.

Television provides a useful glance at what's happening. However, a person who has individual interests and who wants the whole story needs newspapers and magazines as well.

11. *Sample essay:*

Some people live in one community all their lives, while others move around almost as much as nomads. Both experiences have their advantages and disadvantages.

People who stay in one spot can develop lifelong friendships, and such friends may lend a hand if trouble comes. They know each other's life history, and they judge each other for the kind of person each is, not for the image each projects.

Yet spending a lifetime in one location can also lock a person into a limited way of life. Personal change may become very difficult. People with few experiences may develop a narrow outlook and find it hard to understand those who have different ethnic, racial, or religious backgrounds.

On the other hand, moving to different parts of the country is usually stressful. A person may feel lost and uprooted in a place where streets, stores, schools, and churches all are different. At first there are no friends to help.

However, those who *do* move learn that people in other places have a variety of outlooks. There is a chance to appreciate different ways of life and even to choose the way one likes best.

For a person who moves to a different place year after year, the disadvantages of moving probably outweigh the advantages. But a few moves are probably worth the effort. By staying in each place for a length of time, people can broaden their outlook but have enough time to make adjustments and form friendships.

12. *Sample essay:*

The automobile has probably changed people's way of life more than any other invention of the last century. More than electric lights, television, air travel, or even computers, automobiles have changed where people live and work, how they make a living, and even how they find a mate.

Before there were cars, people generally traveled on foot or by horse and buggy over unpaved roads. Whether they lived in the city or the country, they rarely went farther than a few miles from home. They saw the same people and places year after year.

The car opened up whole new worlds. Roads were paved, and motorists went to see different parts of the country. Some decided to stay. People with cars could live farther from their jobs, and so the age of commuting began. New suburbs sprang up around the cities. The auto industry boomed, and millions of Americans made a living manufacturing, selling, servicing, or insuring cars.

As more people got cars, young people began driving them. No longer was courtship confined to the girl's front porch, under the watchful eye of her parents. The automobile began the sexual revolution.

Some people believe that commuting, suburban life, and courting in cars are mixed blessings. Whether the changes are good or bad, they seem to be here to stay.

13. *Sample essay:*

Many people complain that modern society is too materialistic. Other people, they say, place too great an importance on material property. Rather than value values, these critics insist, people today value things.

There is no doubt that we live in a material, consumer-oriented society. In economic terms, consumers use products; in everyday language, they acquire things: TVs, cars, clothes, furniture. This kind of materialism can actually be good for a society since it helps create jobs. When people have jobs, they acquire self-respect along with the money they need to provide the material things they and their families require.

It is true, on the other hand, that many people have taken healthy consumerism too far. Materialism is evident when an otherwise intelligent person goes into debt charging things that he or she cannot pay for. Materialism is evident when people insist on buying a particular designer label even though the same quality can be found in a cheaper product. Materialism is evident when people are judged and admired for what they own rather than what they are or can do.

Even if society has gone too far in the direction of materialism, as some say, the individual person doesn't need to surrender. He or she can still value honesty, integrity, freedom, talent, quality, and all the other values there are to value and leave the materialism to others.

14. *Sample essay:*

People spend a great deal of time, money, and energy to see or read about movie stars, TV actors, singers, and athletes. Such celebrities often become idols. Posters, T-shirts, fan clubs, and attendance at live performances prove that. What do celebrities do to merit this attention?

Celebrities create excitement. They create excitement because they have done something or can do something that supposedly not everyone else can do. Raising a child, waking early to go to work each morning, building a home and a place in the community—these achievements actually deserve more admiration than rolling through Beverly Hills in a limousine or jetting across the Atlantic to star in a new movie. Yet because these achievements are part of many people's everyday lives, they are not considered special. Celebrities help us dream by lifting us out of our everyday lives and imagining ourselves doing other than everyday activities.

Celebrities also set styles. They become models for behavior, clothing, and hairdos. Just consider Elvis Presley or the Beatles, for example. Celebrities also influence politics, as Bob Hope and Jane Fonda have done.

Celebrities' roles as "special people" and trend-setters, then, are the reason for the attention many of us lavish on them. In many ways, the celebrities of today have merely replaced the kings and queens of old.

15. *Sample essay:*

Most people want to be successful in life, but success can come about in four ways: fame, money, knowledge, and pleasure. Success is also usually characterized by the word *more;* to be successful, people feel they have to be more famous, have more money, absorb more information, or enjoy life more.

Success does not need to be characterized by *quantity,* however. Instead, you can measure the success of your life by its quality. It is not important, for example, how many people know you but who knows you and for what. Working in your community or on good relationships with family and friends can bring quality fame. Earning less money but spending it wisely and learning the joy of saving is another way to succeed. Learning more so that you can turn around and teach someone else produces quality knowledge. And finally, all the above will most likely bring you quality success in enjoying the pleasures of living.

Success, in conclusion, can be seen in different ways by different people. Only one thing is sure. No matter what other people see, the only one who knows whether you've succeeded is you.

16. *Sample essay:*

Every year billions of dollars are spent on advertising. Many approaches are used to persuade consumers to buy a product. Some seem to work better than others.

One approach, for example, is to try to make the reader or viewer identify with the people shown using the product. These people seem to be glamorous, loved, successful, elite, clever, or sexy. Supposedly, anyone who uses the product can expect the same reward. Another approach is to let the product speak for itself; people are attracted to scrumptious food, beautiful clothing, and sleek new cars. Sometimes good prices and special deals are the focus. Ads for complicated products, such as computers, may provide a lot of information. Endorsements by celebrities are especially common.

In general, many of the ads succeed. People do tend to buy what they see advertised. However, some advertising can backfire. People may be offended, for example, by ads that are overly sexy or ones that viciously or sarcastically attack competitors' products.

Advertising can be a useful aid for the consumer. It helps a person learn what is new or in style or handy to have around, what things cost, and where to buy them. To use this information effectively, however, a person must learn to look past the emotional appeals and find the facts.

17. *Sample essay:*

Some animals are pets, some are wild, and many of them provide us with food. All have a different—and important—role in our lives.

It is easy to forget that the steak at the supermarket once formed part of a steer. But without domestic animals such as chickens and cattle, we would all be vegetarians, or a great deal of our time would need to be spent hunting.

Wild animals attract sport hunters. For some people they are even an important source of food. When urban people visit the wild, deer, bears, and other wild animals remind them of an older way of life.

Pets, however, are the animals that are especially significant for most of us. They are undemanding companions; they love us when we are not at our best. A pet can be a great comfort when life seems hard.

For children, pets can be both fun and instructive. If a child cares for a pet, he or she learns to take responsibility for another being. Watching kittens or puppies being born can be a natural form of sex education. For children, as for adults, pets are loving companions and a help in tough times.

As I recall, an Indian chief once said, "Without our brothers, the animals, we would all be very lonely." I believe he was right.

Minitests—Writing Skills

Minitest 1

Directions: The following items are based on a paragraph that contains numbered sentences. Some of the sentences contain errors in sentence structure, usage, or mechanics. A few sentences, however, are correct as written. Read the paragraph and then answer the items based on it. For each item, choose the answer that would result in the most effective writing of the sentence or sentences. The best answer must be consistent with the meaning and tone of the rest of the paragraph. Answers are on pages 244–245.

(1) When passengers comment on airline service, most airlines do listen. (2) They analyze and kept track of the complaints and compliments they receive. (3) This information is used by the airlines to determine what the public wants and to identify problem areas needing special attention. (4) Like other businesses, airlines have discretion in how they respond to problems. (5) While you do have some rights as a passenger, the kind of action you get depends in large part on the way you go about complaining. (6) Start with the airline before you call or write the Department of Transportation or some other agency for help with an air travel problem, you should give the airline a chance to resolve it. (7) As a rule, airlines have trouble-shooters at the airports who can take care of most problems on the spot. (8) If you can't resolve the problem at the airport and want to file a complaint, its best to call or write the airline's consumer office. (9) Be sure to type the letter, and, if it is at all possible, try to limit it to one page in length, and also remember to be sure to include a daytime phone number where you can be reached. (10) If you clutter up your complaint with petty gripes, it can obscure what you're really angry about. (11) Say just what you expect the carrier to do to make amends. (12) If your demands are not reasonable, your letter might earn you a polite apology, and a place in the airline's crank files. (13) If you followed these guidelines, the airline will probably treat your complaint seriously.

1. Sentence 1: **When passengers comment on airline service, most airlines do listen.**

   What correction should be made to this sentence?

   (1) replace When with Because
   (2) change comment to comments
   (3) change comment to commented
   (4) remove the comma after service
   (5) no correction is necessary

   ① ② ③ ④ ⑤

2. Sentence 2: **They analyze and kept track of the complaints and compliments they receive.**

   What correction should be made to this sentence?

   (1) change the spelling of analyze to analize
   (2) insert done before kept
   (3) change kept to keep
   (4) change the spelling of compliments to complements
   (5) change receive to receives

   ① ② ③ ④ ⑤

3. Sentence 3: **This information is used by the airlines to determine what the public wants and to identify problem areas needing special attention.**

   If you rewrote sentence 3 beginning with Using this information,
   the next word(s) should be

   (1) the public
   (2) determination
   (3) the airlines
   (4) problem areas
   (5) special attention

   ① ② ③ ④ ⑤

4. Sentence 6: **Start with the airline before you call or write the Department of Transportation or some other agency for help with an air travel problem, you should give the airline a chance to resolve it.**

Which of the following is the best way to write the underlined portion of this sentence? If you think the original is the best way, choose option (1).

(1) airline before you
(2) airline, before you
(3) airline before, you
(4) airline; however, before you
(5) airline. Before you

(1) (2) (3) (4) (5)

5. Sentence 8: **If you can't resolve the problem at the airport and want to file a complaint, its best to call or write the airline's consumer office.**

What correction should be made to this sentence?

(1) replace If with Since
(2) replace you with one
(3) insert a comma after airport
(4) replace its with it's
(5) change consumer office to Consumer Office

(1) (2) (3) (4) (5)

6. Sentence 9: **Be sure to type the letter, and, if it is at all possible, try to limit it to one page in length, and also remember to be sure to include a daytime phone number where you can be reached.**

If you rewrote sentence 9 beginning with
Type the letter, limiting it to one page if possible, and
the next word(s) should be

(1) include
(2) includes
(3) to include
(4) including
(5) included

(1) (2) (3) (4) (5)

7. Sentence 10: **If you clutter up your complaint with petty gripes, it can obscure what you're really angry about.**

What correction should be made to this sentence?

(1) replace If with Even though
(2) remove the comma after gripes
(3) replace it with they
(4) replace you're with your
(5) no correction is necessary

(1) (2) (3) (4) (5)

8. Sentence 12: **If your demands are not reasonable, your letter might earn you a polite apology, and a place in the airline's crank files.**

Which of the following is the best way to write the underlined portion of this sentence? If you think the original is the best way, choose option (1).

(1) apology, and
(2) apology and
(3) apology, and,
(4) apology and,
(5) apology; and,

(1) (2) (3) (4) (5)

9. Sentence 13: **If you followed these guidelines, the airline will probably treat your complaint seriously.**

Which of the following is the best way to write the underlined portion of this sentence? If you think the original is the best way, choose option (1).

(1) you followed
(2) one follows
(3) you follow
(4) one has followed
(5) you had followed

(1) (2) (3) (4) (5)

Directions: This is a test to find out how well you write. The test has one question that asks you to present an opinion on an issue or to explain something. In preparing your answer for this question, you should take the following steps:

1. Read all of the information accompanying the question.
2. Plan your answer carefully before you write.
3. Use scratch paper to make any notes.
4. Write your answer.
5. Read carefully what you have written and make any changes that will improve your writing.
6. Check your paragraphing, sentence structure, spelling, punctuation, capitalization, and usage, and make any necessary corrections.

You will have 45 minutes to write on the question you are assigned. Write legibly and use a ballpoint pen.

The amount of leisure time—the time people have away from work and home responsibilities—has greatly increased in the last fifty years. What are some of the results of this increase in leisure time? Write an essay of about 200 words detailing your thoughts in an organized way.

Minitest 2

Directions: The following items are based on a paragraph that contains numbered sentences. Some of the sentences contain errors in sentence structure, usage, or mechanics. A few sentences, however, are correct as written. Read the paragraph and then answer the items based on it. For each item, choose the answer that would result in the most effective writing of the sentence or sentences. The best answer must be consistent with the meaning and tone of the rest of the paragraph. Answers are on page 245.

(1) Have you ever read a romance novel and thought that you could write something just as good? (2) If you love to read romances you are already part of the way toward being a romance writer. (3) What is the first step? (4) Send off for each publisher's tipsheet this paper contains its formula for writing a romance. (5) Some companies want a young, innocent heroine yet others want a mature, career-oriented one. (6) The hero must always be wealthy. (7) The hero does not have to be breathtakingly handsome. (8) He can even be younger than the heroine. (9) The Far East, Europe, or just about any faraway place will make a romantic setting. (10) Once you have chosen the right formula for you, the next step is to begin writing. (11) Some writers need a romantic setting complete with flowers and soft music; others are young mothers which can write only late at night after their children are in bed. (12) After you have finished the manuscript and the hero and heroine are living happily ever after, you should have a friend read them to correct errors. (13) When you're manuscript is free from mistakes, send it to an editor and try to wait patiently for the letter of acceptance that will make you rich and famous.

1. Sentence 2: **If you love to read romances you are already part of the way toward being a romance writer.**

   What correction should be made to this sentence?

   (1) insert a comma after read
   (2) insert a comma after romances
   (3) replace already with all ready
   (4) insert a comma after way
   (5) no correction is necessary

   ① ② ③ ④ ⑤

2. Sentence 4: **Send off for each publisher's tipsheet this paper contains its formula for writing a romance.**

   Which of the following is the best way to write the underlined portion of this sentence? If you think the original is the best way, choose option (1).

   (1) tipsheet this
   (2) tipsheet. This
   (3) tipsheet, this
   (4) tipsheet, but this
   (5) tipsheet even though this

   ① ② ③ ④ ⑤

3. Sentence 5: **Some companies want a young, innocent heroine yet others want a mature, career-oriented one.**

   Which of the following is the best way to write the underlined portion of this sentence? If you think the original is the best way, choose option (1).

   (1) heroine yet
   (2) heroine; yet
   (3) heroine, yet
   (4) heroine. Yet
   (5) heroine

   ① ② ③ ④ ⑤

4. Sentences 6 and 7: **The hero must always be wealthy. The hero does not have to be breathtakingly handsome.**

   The most effective combination of sentences 6 and 7 would include which of the following groups of words?

   (1) wealthy, and the hero
   (2) wealthy and not handsome
   (3) wealthy; however, he
   (4) Being wealthy, the hero
   (5) The wealthy hero

   ① ② ③ ④ ⑤

5. Sentence 9: **The Far East, Europe, or just about any faraway place will make a romantic setting.**

   What correction should be made to this sentence?

   (1) change Far to far
   (2) remove the comma after East
   (3) change Europe to europe
   (4) insert a comma after place
   (5) no correction is necessary

   (1) (2) (3) (4) (5)

6. Sentence 10: **Once you have chosen the right formula for you, the next step is to begin writing.**

   If you rewrote sentence 10 beginning with After choosing a formula, the next word should be

   (1) then
   (2) for
   (3) so
   (4) writing
   (5) begin

   (1) (2) (3) (4) (5)

7. Sentence 11: **Some writers need a romantic setting complete with flowers and soft music; others are young mothers which can write only late at night after their children are in bed.**

   What correction should be made to this sentence?

   (1) change need to are needing
   (2) replace which with who
   (3) change write to be writing
   (4) change night to Night
   (5) insert a comma after children

   (1) (2) (3) (4) (5)

8. Sentence 12: **After you have finished the manuscript and the hero and heroine are living happily ever after, you should have a friend read them to correct errors.**

   What correction should be made to this sentence?

   (1) remove the word are
   (2) replace are with is
   (3) remove the comma after after
   (4) change the spelling of friend to freind
   (5) replace them with it

   (1) (2) (3) (4) (5)

9. Sentence 13: **When you're manuscript is free from mistakes, send it to an editor and try to wait patiently for the letter of acceptance that will make you rich and famous.**

   What correction should be made to this sentence?

   (1) change the spelling of you're to your
   (2) change the spelling of mistakes to misstakes
   (3) replace it with them
   (4) change editor to Editor
   (5) change the spelling of patiently to pashiently

   (1) (2) (3) (4) (5)

Directions: This is a test to find out how well you write. The test has one question that asks you to present an opinion on an issue or to explain something. In preparing your answer for this question, you should take the following steps:

1. Read all of the information accompanying the question.
2. Plan your answer carefully before you write.
3. Use scratch paper to make any notes.
4. Write your answer.
5. Read carefully what you have written and make any changes that will improve your writing.
6. Check your paragraphing, sentence structure, spelling, punctuation, capitalization, and usage, and make any necessary corrections.

You will have 45 minutes to write on the question you are assigned. Write legibly and use a ballpoint pen.

Fame is desired by many people. Being a celebrity—if only for a short while—is possible for almost anyone because of television, radio, and other mass media. What would be the advantages and disadvantages of being famous? Write about 200 words detailing your thoughts on this question.

Minitest 3

Directions: The following items are based on a paragraph that contains numbered sentences. Some of the sentences contain errors in sentence structure, usage, or mechanics. A few sentences, however, are correct as written. Read the paragraph and then answer the items based on it. For each item, choose the answer that would result in the most effective writing of the sentence or sentences. The best answer must be consistent with the meaning and tone of the rest of the paragraph. Answers are on pages 245–246.

(1) During World War II, a special group of pilots was trained by a psychologist, Dr. B. F. Skinner, which was interested in animal behavior. (2) The pilots were motivated by a small tray of hemp seed suspended in front of a bull's-eye painted on the wall of Dr. Skinner's laboratory. (3) Seed was a good motivator because the pilots in this unusual group was pigeons. (4) Skinner had learned from earlier experiments that pigeons were intelligent, and had excellent eyesight. (5) To train the pilots of Project Pigeon, Skinner suspended them from the ceiling in flight jackets made from men's socks. (6) The goal was to get a bird to press bars with its beak. (7) To get a bird to do this, it would be moved closer to the food in the bull's-eye whenever it moved its head toward a bar. (8) At first neither the military nor the wartime government were interested in pigeon pilots. (9) What kind of aircraft could they fly? (10) Finally, a bomb-carrying missile called the Pelican was built. (11) That had room for three pigeons. (12) However, the highly trained pilots of Project Pigeon never had the chance to be heroes, the engineers did not trust them. (13) Twenty-four grounded pigeon pilots retired in luxury at the end of the war in a special house built for them in Skinner's minnesota backyard.

1. Sentence 1: **During World War II, a special group of pilots was trained by a psychologist, Dr. B. F. Skinner, which was interested in animal behavior.**

   What correction should be made to this sentence?

   (1) change the spelling of special to speshal
   (2) change was trained to were trained
   (3) change psychologist to Psychologist
   (4) remove the comma after psychologist
   (5) replace which with who

   (1) (2) (3) (4) (5)

2. Sentence 3: **Seed was a good motivator because the pilots in this unusual group was pigeons.**

   Which of the following is the best way to write the underlined portion of this sentence? If you think the original is the best way, choose option (1).

   (1) group was
   (2) group is
   (3) group are
   (4) group be
   (5) group were

   (1) (2) (3) (4) (5)

3. Sentence 4: **Skinner had learned from earlier experiments that pigeons were intelligent, and had excellent eyesight.**

   What correction should be made to this sentence?

   (1) change the spelling of experiments to exsperiments
   (2) replace that with which
   (3) insert a comma after pigeons
   (4) remove the comma after intelligent
   (5) no correction is necessary

   (1) (2) (3) (4) (5)

4. Sentence 5: **To train the pilots of Project Pigeon, Skinner suspended them from the ceiling in flight jackets made from men's socks.**

What correction should be made to this sentence?

(1) remove the comma after Pigeon
(2) replace them with it
(3) change the spelling of ceiling to cieling
(4) insert a comma after jackets
(5) no correction is necessary

(1) (2) (3) (4) (5)

5. Sentences 6 and 7: **The goal was to get a bird to press bars with its beak. To get a bird to do this, it would be moved closer to the food in the bull's-eye whenever it moved its head toward a bar.**

The most effective combination of sentences 6 and 7 would include which of the following groups of words?

(1) To get a bird to press
(2) The goal was to get a bird to do this
(3) by moving the bird closer
(4) with its beak, and to get a bird
(5) The goal of moving the bird

(1) (2) (3) (4) (5)

6. Sentence 8: **At first neither the military nor the wartime government were interested in pigeon pilots.**

What correction should be made to this sentence?

(1) change the spelling of neither to niether
(2) insert a comma after military
(3) change the spelling of government to goverment
(4) change were to was
(5) no correction is necessary

(1) (2) (3) (4) (5)

7. Sentences 10 and 11: **Finally, a bomb-carrying missile called the Pelican was built. That had room for three pigeons.**

Which of the following is the best way to write the underlined portion of these sentences? If you think the original is the best way, choose option (1).

(1) built. That had
(2) built with
(3) built. It had
(4) built so it had
(5) built; that had

(1) (2) (3) (4) (5)

8. Sentence 12: **However, the highly trained pilots of Project Pigeon never had the chance to be heroes, the engineers did not trust them.**

Which of the following is the best way to write the underlined portion of this sentence? If you think the original is the best way, choose option (1).

(1) heroes, the engineers
(2) heroes the engineers
(3) heroes; that is, the engineers
(4) heroes, but the engineers
(5) heroes because the engineers

(1) (2) (3) (4) (5)

9. Sentence 13: **Twenty-four grounded pigeon pilots retired in luxury at the end of the war in a special house built for them in Skinner's minnesota backyard.**

What correction should be made to this sentence?

(1) change Twenty-four to Twenty-fore
(2) insert a comma after pilots
(3) insert that after pilots
(4) change war to War
(5) change minnesota to Minnesota

(1) (2) (3) (4) (5)

Directions: This is a test to find out how well you write. The test has one question that asks you to present an opinion on an issue or to explain something. In preparing your answer for this question, you should take the following steps:

1. Read all of the information accompanying the question.
2. Plan your answer carefully before you write.
3. Use scratch paper to make any notes.
4. Write your answer.
5. Read carefully what you have written and make any changes that will improve your writing.
6. Check your paragraphing, sentence structure, spelling, punctuation, capitalization, and usage, and make any necessary corrections.

You will have 45 minutes to write on the question you are assigned. Write legibly and use a ballpoint pen.

The use of robots is increasing in certain industries, especially factory jobs such as assembly-line work. Think about the changes this increased use of robots will bring. Discuss the positive effects, the negative effects, or both in a 200-word essay.

Minitest 4

Directions: The following items are based on a paragraph that contains numbered sentences. Some of the sentences contain errors in sentence structure, usage, or mechanics. A few sentences, however, are correct as written. Read the paragraph and then answer the items based on it. For each item, choose the answer that would result in the most effective writing of the sentence or sentences. The best answer must be consistent with the meaning and tone of the rest of the paragraph. Answers are on pages 246–247.

(1) Vacationers often spend wonderful holidays with relatives, but a current trend with travelers is too spend their vacations at country inns. (2) Visiting a country inn is like being treated royally or being pampered on a luxurious cruise ship. (3) You were welcomed on Friday night with a big home-cooked dinner, usually made with the owner's favorite recipes. (4) You enjoy dessert and coffee in front of a roaring fire, you listen to homey sounds coming from the kitchen. (5) As you blissfully float downstairs in the morning, your memories are of spending the night in a cozy room full of homemade things. (6) Your tea is steeping your cherry-topped grapefruit sits on a linen-lined tray, and you're asked what you want for breakfast. (7) If you are someone which has to cook for himself or herself, such first-class service is heaven. (8) After breakfast you might be offered home-baked sticky buns, the specialty of the inn, made with pecans from its trees and honey from its beehives. (9) Sometimes an inn will include valet service your clothes are washed, ironed, and returned to your closet by a well-organized host. (10) This wonderfully relaxing weekend will end all too soon on sunday, but you know the warm afterglow will help you through the coming busy week. (11) You will probably, as you return to the city, promise yourself, the next time you need a vacation, to try another quaint little country inn.

1. Sentence 1: **Vacationers often spend wonderful holidays with relatives, but a current trend with travelers is too spend their vacations at country inns.**

   What correction should be made to this sentence?

   (1) change spend to spent
   (2) change the spelling of holidays to hollidays
   (3) remove the comma after relatives
   (4) replace too with to
   (5) no correction is necessary

   ① ② ③ ④ ⑤

2. Sentence 3: **You were welcomed on Friday night with a big home-cooked dinner, usually made with the owner's favorite recipes.**

   Which of the following is the best way to write the underlined portion of this sentence? If you think the original is the best way, choose option (1).

   (1) were welcomed
   (2) are welcomed
   (3) being welcomed
   (4) welcomed
   (5) are welcome

   ① ② ③ ④ ⑤

3. Sentence 4: **You enjoy dessert and coffee in front of a roaring fire, you listen to homey sounds coming from the kitchen.**

   What correction should be made to this sentence?

   (1) replace dessert with desert
   (2) insert a comma after dessert
   (3) remove the comman after fire
   (4) replace the comma with the word as
   (5) change listen to listened

   ① ② ③ ④ ⑤

4. Sentence 5: **As you blissfully float downstairs in the morning, your memories are of spending the night in a cozy room full of homemade things.**

   If you rewrote sentence 5 beginning with Blissfully floating downstairs in the morning, the next words should be

   (1) your memories
   (2) a cozy room
   (3) spending the night
   (4) you remember
   (5) homemade things

   (1) (2) (3) (4) (5)

5. Sentence 6: **Your tea is steeping your cherry-topped grapefruit sits on a linen-lined tray, and you're asked what you want for breakfast.**

   What correction should be made to this sentence?

   (1) insert a comma after steeping
   (2) replace sits with sat
   (3) remove the comma after tray
   (4) remove the word and
   (5) replace you're with your

   (1) (2) (3) (4) (5)

6. Sentence 7: **If you are someone which has to cook for himself or herself, such first-class service is heaven.**

   What correction should be made to this sentence?

   (1) replace which with who
   (2) replace has with have
   (3) remove the comma after herself
   (4) change heaven to Heaven
   (5) no correction is necessary

   (1) (2) (3) (4) (5)

7. Sentence 9: **Sometimes an inn will include valet service your clothes are washed, ironed, and returned to your closet by a well-organized host.**

   Which of the following is the best way to write the underlined portion of this sentence? If you think the original is the best way, choose option (1).

   (1) service your
   (2) service, your
   (3) service. Your
   (4) service; however,
   (5) service, but

   (1) (2) (3) (4) (5)

8. Sentence 10: **This wonderfully relaxing weekend will end all too soon on sunday, but you know the warm afterglow will help you through the coming busy week.**

   What correction should be made to this sentence?

   (1) replace too with to
   (2) change sunday to Sunday
   (3) replace but with as if
   (4) replace will help with had helped
   (5) replace through with threw

   (1) (2) (3) (4) (5)

9. Sentence 11: **You will probably, as you return to the city, promise yourself, the next time you need a vacation, to try another quaint little country inn.**

   If you rewrote sentence 11 beginning with As you return to the city, you will probably the next words should be

   (1) try another
   (2) the next time
   (3) promise yourself
   (4) try to promise
   (5) need a vacation

   (1) (2) (3) (4) (5)

Directions: This is a test to find out how well you write. The test has one question that asks you to present an opinion on an issue or to explain something. In preparing your answer for this question, you should take the following steps:

1. Read all of the information accompanying the question.
2. Plan your answer carefully before you write.
3. Use scratch paper to make any notes.
4. Write your answer.
5. Read carefully what you have written and make any changes that will improve your writing.
6. Check your paragraphing, sentence structure, spelling, punctuation, capitalization, and usage, and make any necessary corrections.

You will have 45 minutes to write on the question you are assigned. Write legibly and use a ballpoint pen.

Health and physical appearance are a matter of concern to many people. They devote much of their time and energy to dieting and exercising. Consider whether this concern with one's body is good, bad, or a combination of the two. Explain your thoughts in an essay of about 200 words.

Minitest Answers

Minitest 1
(pages 232–234)

1. (5) No error. *Passengers* and *comment* agree because they both are plural. The comma is needed after *service* because *When passengers comment on airline service* is an introductory dependent part.

2. (3) *Analyze* and *kept* do not match. *Analyze* shows present time, and *kept* shows past time. *Analyze* and *keep* show present time. *Compliments* and *complements* are easy to confuse. A *compliment* is something nice to say about someone or something else. A *complement* is one thing that completes the meaning of or the look of another thing. Compare these: Thank you for the *compliment* about my new suit. The colors in your tie *complement* the color of your eyes.

3. (3) *Using this information, the airlines determine what the public wants and identify problem areas.* The introductory phrase *Using this information* can describe only *the airlines.* It does not describe options (1), (2), (4), or (5).

4. (5) The error in sentence 6 is a perfect example of how a lack of punctuation can make a sentence difficult to read. *Before you call or write the Department of Transportation or some other agency for help with an airline problem* is an introductory dependent part. The clue is the comma after *problem* and the small *y* in *you.*

5. (4) *It's* is the correct word choice because it stands for *it is. Its* shows ownership. The pronoun *you* is used to address the reader throughout this passage. *One* does not follow through with this usage.

6. (1) *Type the letter, limiting it to one page if possible, and include a daytime phone number.* the verb *include* is needed to match the form and the time of *type.* Did you notice that the original sentence contained many unnecessary words?

7. (3) Good writers avoid using *it* to refer to a whole idea in the introductory part. *It* means one thing and cannot be used to substitute for *gripes,* which means more than one thing. *They,* which means more than one thing, can substitute for *gripes.*

8. (2) When *and* connects two things (*apology* and *place*), a comma is not placed before *and.* If you chose option (1), (3), or (4), you are overusing commas.

9. (3) The verb in this introductory dependent part must express present time (*follow*). *One* does not follow through with the use of *you* in the rest of the passage. Therefore, only option (3) is correct.

When passengers comment on airline service, most airlines do listen. They analyze and keep track of the complaints and compliments they receive. Using this information, the airlines determine what the public wants and identify problem areas. Like other businesses, airlines have discretion in how they respond to problems. While you do have some rights as a passenger, the kind of action you get depends in large part on the way you go about complaining. Start with the airline. Before you call or write the Department of Transportation or some other agency for help with an air travel problem, you should give the airline a chance to resolve it. As a rule, airlines have trouble-shooters at the airports who can take care of most problems on the spot. If you can't resolve the problem at the airport and want to file a complaint, it's best to call or write the airline's consumer office. Type the letter, limiting it to one page if possible, and include a daytime phone number. If you clutter up your complaint with petty gripes, they can obscure what you're really angry about. Say just what you expect the carrier to do to make amends. If your demands are not reasonable, your letter might earn you a polite apology and a place in the airline's crank files. If you follow these guidelines, the airlines will probably treat your complaint seriously.

Sample essay:

In the last fifty years there has been a great increase in leisure time for some people—but not for everyone.

There is not much leisure for working mothers, who have to put in a full day on the job and then come home and take care of their families. Other people have to work two jobs to make ends meet, and they hardly have a minute to call their own.

People who do have leisure can use it to get ahead or to make their lives more enjoyable. For example, a person could use spare time to study for the GED Test and then go on to a community college. The extra study could improve work skills or simply add interest to life.

Some people use extra time to exercise and stay in shape. They will probably improve their health and may even live longer. Others volunteer for community work or help other people who need a hand.

The increase in leisure time has also helped business, both the arts and the recreation industry. People have more time to go to the movies or museums and to go skiing, boating, or camping.

Leisure time can lead to trouble, however. Some people are bored with time on their hands. They may use it for too much drinking or get involved with drugs. They may spend the time with others who encourage harmful behavior.

Leisure time gives us choices. The way we use it can make life sweet or lead to problems.

Minitest 2
(pages 235–237)

1. (2) A comma is needed when a dependent part introduces a sentence. *Already* and *all ready* are often confused. *Already* means that an action is complete. *All ready* means that everything is in readiness or that everyone is ready. Compare these: He is *already* 10 pounds overweight. Howard and Louise are *all ready* to go to their aerobics class.

2. (2) The original wording of this sentence is a run-on. Option (3) misuses a comma. Options (4) and (5) do not logically express the relationship between the two thoughts.

3. (3) When *yet, and, nor, for,* and *but* join two complete sentences, a comma is needed before the connecting word. Since semicolons can take the place of a comma and a connecting word, option (2) is not logical.

4. (3) *The hero must always be wealthy; however, he does not have to be breathtakingly handsome.* Getting rid of repeated information is one way to revise a sentence. *The hero* should be mentioned only once. Long connecting words like *however* need a semicolon before and a comma after them.

5. (5) No error. *Far East* and *Europe* are place names and need to be capitalized. *Place* is part of the subject and should not be separated from the verb with a comma.

6. (5) *After choosing a formula, begin writing.* The original sentence is weak because it contains too many extra words. The revision is an example of clear, concise writing.

7. (2) *Which* refers to things. *Who* refers to people (*mothers*).

8. (5) *Them* seems to refer to *hero* and *heroine.* Logically, a friend would not read the hero and the heroine. Replacing *them* with *it* makes it clear that your friend will read the manuscript.

9. (1) *You're* stands for *you are. When you are manuscript* does not make sense. *Your* is used to show that one thing belongs to another.

Have you ever read a romance novel and thought that you could write something just as good? If you love to read romances, you are already part of the way toward being a romance writer. What is the first step? Send off for each publisher's tipsheet. This paper contains its formula for writing a romance. Some companies want a young, innocent heroine, yet others want a mature, career-oriented one. The hero must always be wealthy; however, he does not have to be breathtakingly handsome. He can even be younger than the heroine. The Far East, Europe, or just about any faraway place will make a romantic setting. After choosing a formula, begin writing. Some writers need a romantic setting complete with flowers and soft music; others are young mothers who can write only late at night after their children are in bed. After you have finished the manuscript and the hero and heroine are living happily ever after, you should have a friend read it to correct errors. When your manuscript is free from mistakes, send it to an editor and try to wait patiently for the letter of acceptance that will make you rich and famous.

Sample essay:

Famous people are told every day how smart, beautiful, or talented they are. They have succeeded. However, they often pay for their success by giving up what most people see as normal life.

Many famous people have fulfilled their own dream, whatever it might be. Often they have developed their talents to the fullest, whether in sports, show business, politics, science, or some other field. They are known as one of the best at what they do. There is great satisfaction in fulfilling talents and reaching goals.

Often fame brings fortune. Money enables people to acquire things they want and go where they would like to be.

But fame can also be a prison. A famous person can hardly go shopping or eat in a restaurant without coping with fans. Some must have bodyguards even in their private moments. Some of the famous—for example, Elvis Presley—find it easier just to stay home. Others manage to live almost normally.

If I had a chance for fame, would I be willing to pay the price? Probably I would, as long as the fame was earned. I believe that if I had done something very well, the satisfaction in my accomplishments would outweigh the problems of success.

Minitest 3
(pages 238–240)

1. (5) Use *who* to refer to people. Option (2) is incorrect because *group,* not *pilots,* is the subject of the sentence.

2. (5) In this sentence *pilots,* not *group,* is the subject. Don't be distracted by words between the subject and the verb.

3. (4) There should be no comma here. Commas are not used to separate verbs that have the same subject (pigeons *were* and *had*).

4. (5) No error. If you chose option (3), practice the spelling of *ceiling* and other *ei-ie* words on the spelling list. *It* in option (2) is incorrect because the pronoun *them* refers to *pilots. Them* and *pilots* both are singular.

5. (1) *To get a bird to press bars with its beak, it would be moved closer to the food in the bull's-eye whenever it moved its head toward a bar.* This combination of two sentences gets rid of unnecessary words.

6. (4) *Neither/nor* are used with the subjects, so the verb should agree with the nearest subject. Since *government* means one, the verb *was* is the correct choice.

7. (2) The second group of words is a fragment. One way to attach a fragment to a sentence is to add it on as a phrase. *With room for three pigeons* is a phrase. Option (3) is not the best choice because it makes the two sentences too choppy. Option (2) is an example of smooth, concise writing.

8. (5) Two complete sentences cannot be joined with just a comma. Using *because* expresses the cause-and-effect relationship between the two sentences.

9. (5) The names of states are always capitalized.

During World War II, a special group of pilots was trained by a psychologist, Dr. B. F. Skinner, who was interested in animal behavior. The pilots were motivated by a small tray of hemp seed suspended in front of a bull's-eye painted on the wall of Dr. Skinner's laboratory. Seed was a good motivator because the pilots in this unusual group were pigeons. Skinner had learned from earlier experiments that pigeons were intelligent and had excellent eyesight. To train the pilots of Project Pigeon, Skinner suspended them from the ceiling in flight jackets made from men's socks. To get a bird to press bars with its beak, it would be moved closer to the food in the bull's-eye whenever it moved its head toward a bar. At first neither the military nor the wartime government was interested in pigeon pilots. What kind of aircraft could they fly? Finally, a bomb-carrying missile called the Pelican was built with room for three pigeons. However, the highly trained pilots of Project Pigeon never had the chance to be heroes because the engineers did not trust them. Twenty-four grounded pigeon pilots retired in luxury at the end of the war in a special house built for them in Skinner's Minnesota backyard.

Sample essay:

Robots are replacing workers on more and more assembly lines. Not only can these robots do simple tasks, but some of them can be programmed for complex operations. Entire factories may be run with only a few human supervisors to monitor the robots.

If the robot revolution takes hold, it will have important effects on our economy. For years, assembly lines have provided fairly well-paid jobs for people without a high level of education or special skills. Thousands of men and women have spent their entire working lives on assembly lines.

Assembly-line workers who are replaced by robots may have trouble finding other work. The jobs available today are mostly in service industries. High-level service jobs, such as consulting or computer programming, require a high level of education. Low-level service jobs, such as secretarial work or keyboarding, generally pay far less than manufacturing. Also, the work is often in places far from the industrial towns where the replaced workers live. There may be some hard times ahead for these people.

For the next generation, robots could be a good thing. They eliminate tedious work that can make a person feel almost like a robot himself. Perhaps jobs of the future will be more interesting. Also, the costs of some products made by robots may decrease.

For the present, however, robots may save factories money, but workers will probably pay the price.

Minitest 4
(pages 241–243)

1. (4) *Too* usually means "also" or "in addition to." *To* often comes before verbs (*to accept, to equip, to proceed*). The comma after *relatives* separates two complete thoughts joined by *and.*

2. (2) This passage is written about present actions and with verbs that express present time (*is, are, enjoy, listen*). Therefore, *are welcomed* is correct. Option (5) is incorrect because the *-d* is left off *welcome.* If you chose option (5), be careful not to omit verb endings in your speech or writing.

3. (4) A comma is not strong enough to join two complete sentences. The connecting word *as* correctly expresses the relationship between the two sentences (*you enjoy as you listen*). Option (2) is incorrect because a comma is not used before *and* when it joins only two things (*dessert* and *coffee*).

4. (4) *Blissfully floating downstairs in the morning, you remember spending the night in a cozy room full of homemade things.* In this revision, *Blissfully floating downstairs in the morning* correctly describes *you.* This introductory phrase cannot logically describe *memories, a cozy room, spending the night,* or *homemade things.*

5. (1) This sentence contains a series of three items. Most items in a series are things or people. These three items, however, are complete thoughts. *You're* stands for *you are.* It would be correct to write *and you are asked what you want for breakfast.*

6. (1) *Who* refers to people. *Which* refers only to things.

7. (3) The original wording is a run-on. Option (2) misuses a comma because a connecting word is also needed. *However* and *but* usually connect two contrasting ideas. The ideas in these two sentences do not express a contrast. Option (3) is the only correct revision of the underlined part.

8. (2) The days of the week are always capitalized. Even though they sound alike, *through* and *threw* have different meanings. Compare these: George walked *through* the door. The chef *threw* away the leftover onion soup.

9. (3) *As you return to the city, you will probably promise yourself to try another quaint little country inn the next time you need a vacation.* The original wording of the sentence is awkward because of the position of the phrases *as you return to the city* and *the next time you need a vacation.*

Vacationers often spend wonderful holidays with relatives, but a current trend with travelers is to spend their vacations at country inns. Visiting a country inn is like being treated royally or being pampered on a luxurious cruise ship. You are welcomed on Friday night with a big home-cooked dinner, usually made with the owner's favorite recipes. You enjoy dessert and coffee in front of a roaring fire as you listen to homey sounds coming from the kitchen. Blissfully floating downstairs in the morning, you remember spending the night in a cozy room full of homemade things. Your tea is steeping, your cherry-topped grapefruit sits on a linen-lined tray, and you're asked what you want for breakfast. If you are someone who has to cook for himself or herself, such first-class service is heaven. After breakfast you might be offered home-baked sticky buns, the specialty of the inn, made with pecans from its trees and honey from its beehives. Sometimes an inn will include valet service. Your clothes are washed, ironed, and returned to your closet by a well-organized host. This wonderfully relaxing weekend will end all too soon on Sunday, but you know the warm afterglow will help you through the coming busy week. As you return to the city, you will probably promise yourself to try another quaint little country inn the next time you need a vacation.

Sample essay:

Many Americans these days are concerned with health, fitness, and physical appearance. Some spend hours each week working out at health clubs. From 5 to 6 P.M., city jogging paths are jammed. Millions have stopped smoking. Eating patterns include less red meat, more whole grains, less cholesterol, and more fiber.

Healthy bodies tend to be attractive, and people work hard to dress them well. In fact, "Dress for Success" may be the slogan of the eighties, and almost every magazine gives advice on how to do it. Both men and women are buying face-lifts, blow-dry haircuts, and designer-label clothing.

It is hard to find fault with people who guard their health. They will probably live longer and more productive lives, and they will help lower the nation's medical bill, which we all help pay through health insurance premiums.

There is a danger, however. Too much concern for one's own body can lead to self-centeredness. Appearance may become more important than a person's inner beauty. Concern with thinness can also go too far. Some people starve themselves to the point of anorexia. Others force themselves to vomit after they eat. They are harming their health.

Looking one's best, like feeling one's best, can be good for morale. In these activities, like others, moderation is a useful guideline.

The GED Social Studies Test

Are you interested in people and how they interact with the rest of the world? Do you enjoy reading about people and events in the past? Do you keep up with the news? If you answered yes to any of these questions, you are well on your way to passing the GED Social Studies Test.

The GED Social Studies Test is made up of 64 questions from five different areas. You will have 85 minutes to complete the test. The test questions are divided among the five social studies areas in the following manner:

U.S. History	25%
Economics	20%
Behavioral Science	20%
Political Science	20%
Geography	15%

History is the study of past events, people, and ideas. *Political Science* is the study of governments and the people who govern. *Economics* is the study of how people fill their physical needs and wants with goods and services. *Geography* is the study of how people affect the earth and how it affects them. *Behavioral Sciences* (psychology, sociology, and anthropology) are the study of how people meet their social and emotional needs.

The inner columns of the *Social Studies* section in this book contain concepts from each of the five social studies areas. The inner columns also offer *Warm-up* practices, hints, tips, and vocabulary reviews.

The outer columns of the *Social Studies* section provide practice questions like those on the GED Social Studies Test. These questions are keyed to the content of the inner columns.

One third of the questions on the GED Social Studies Test are single items based on brief graphics—charts, maps, graphs, tables, and cartoons—or passages of up to 40 words. These contain only enough information for one question. The rest of the questions on the test are item sets. These are six to seven questions based on detailed graphics or passages of about 250 words. The passages may be from books, articles, letters, or other sources. Some passages are very simple and clear, while others include unfamiliar words that may make the readings difficult to understand. But all the passages are written for the average person, not for experts in social studies.

The next few pages contain examples of the different types of questions on the GED Social Studies Test. The information and practice in these introductory pages can give you the skills and confidence to answer the questions in the outer columns that follow. Unless you are told otherwise, be sure that you complete the tinted column of each page before going on to the white column.

Reading Skills The questions after reading passages vary in format, that is, in the way they are set up. They also vary in difficulty. Different questions within an item set test different skills. For instance, one question may ask what the main idea is in a passage. Another question may ask you to apply that idea to a new situation. This page explains the reading skills you will need to do well on the GED Social Studies Test.

Recognizing the Main Idea and Supporting Details There is a method for successfully answering items based on passages in the GED Social Studies Test. It begins with finding the main idea of the passage. The following hints should help you:

1. If the passage has one or more paragraphs, look for a topic sentence at the beginning or end of each paragraph.

2. If the reading is a list, its main idea probably will be stated in a heading.

3. In quotations, look for an idea that includes or summarizes all the other ideas.

4. Many times the main idea is not stated. You have to sum up the reading for yourself.

If the question asks you to identify the main idea, the idea will be restated in one of the choices. Determine the main point that the author is making and then look for the option that comes closest in meaning to your answer. Often you will have to distinguish between the main idea and supporting details—ideas and examples that support the main idea. You may want to read the explanation of main ideas and supporting details in the *Interpreting Literature and the Arts* section of this book (pages 83–85).

Test your skill at recognizing the main idea and supporting details by reading the passage at the top of the next column and answering the following question.

Terrorism is a powerful weapon. Small groups using terrorist tactics have demonstrated over and over that their limited violence can produce fantastic effects. They attract attention from all over the world and force superpowers to grant their demands. In addition, they force governments to spend millions of dollars for protection against future attacks.

Which of the following statements best sums up the passage?

(1) Terrorism is often effective.
(2) Terrorists want publicity.
(3) Terrorists usually have valid requests.
(4) Fighting terrorism is expensive.
(5) Governments sometimes give in to terrorists.

You can eliminate (3) right away because the passage does not directly or indirectly state that terrorists have valid requests, although it does seem to imply that terrorists believe their requests are valid. The other answers restate ideas in the passage. However, (2), (4), and (5) all refer to examples that support (1). So (1) is the correct choice.

Drawing Conclusions from Passages Remember that conclusions are educated guesses based on information you already have. Some questions on the GED Social Studies Test will ask you to use information from a passage to decide which of five conclusions is the best. Read the passage carefully and ask yourself, "What does this all mean?" or "What will happen next?" Then work through each possible answer until you find the one that is based on evidence in the passage. Again, you may want to read the more thorough explanation of drawing conclusions in the *Interpreting Literature and the Arts* section (page 91).

Dealing with Unfamiliar Vocabulary When you come across a strange word such as *demographic* or *oligopoly* in your social studies reading, do you feel like giving up? Many people are discouraged when they come across unfamiliar words. Social studies terms can be especially troublesome because many are made up of words from Greek and Latin. However, you can overcome these reading hurdles with the help of word-part and context clues.

Word-Part Clues Knowing the English meanings of Greek and Latin word parts can help you to decode unfamiliar social studies terms and to better understand the familiar ones. Read the table below several times so you can recall it when answering questions on the GED Social Studies Test.

Word Part	Meaning	Examples
anthrop-	man	anthropology
auto-	alone	autocrat
-cracy	rule	theocracy
-foederis-	league	federation, confederation
-ology	study of	anthropology, psychology
psych-	mind	psychology
theo-	god	theocracy

Look at the definitions below. Can you fill in the correct terms from the list of examples above? Try putting together the Greek and Latin word parts to come up with the answers.

1. A lone ruler with absolute power is a(n)

________________________________.

2. A government based on religious rules is called a(n) ________________________.

The answers appear below. Now use your new knowledge of Greek and Latin to help you understand the passage at the top of the next column and answer the question about it.

Answers
1. autocrat **2.** theocracy

In 1781, the states agreed on a plan of government called the Articles of Confederation. Under the Articles, each state kept its independence. There was a national government called the Congress. The Congress was made up of one representative from each state, but it did not have much power. Over the next few years, it became clear that the Articles of Confederation did not work. The national government was too weak, and the states would not cooperate with one another.

Which of the following descriptions best fits the government under the Articles of Confederation?

(1) a central government with total power
(2) a loose league of states
(3) direct rule by the majority
(4) equal state and central governments
(5) absolute rule by a few people

① ② ③ ④ ⑤

By remembering that the root *foederis* means "league," you can easily see that option (2) is the correct answer.

Context Clues The context of a word is the sentence or sentences that surround it. If a word is unfamiliar, you often can figure out its meaning from the context. Read the sentence below. On the line, write a definition of the underlined word. Then write the clue from the sentence on which you based your definition.

The United States census is a principal source of <u>demographic</u> information such as the number of school-age Americans and the rate of unemployment.

Demographic means ________________________.

The clue is ____________________________.

____

____

Answers
Demographic means "having to do with statistics about people." The clue is "such as the number of school-age Americans and the rate of unemployment."

Answering Questions Based on Graphics
Thirty to fifty percent of the questions on the GED Social Studies Test are based on graphics. So you can see that the ability to read graphics is essential if you are to succeed on the test.

Map Questions Each map on the GED Social Studies Test probably will be followed by two or more questions. Some of the questions may ask you to choose a conclusion based on the map. Sometimes you may have to be aware of information that is not on the map to reach a conclusion.

Reading Maps If you have taken long car trips or if you use maps at your job, you already have a good working knowledge of maps. Whether you do or not, the following steps will help you become a more skillful map reader. Use these steps to study the map below.

1. First look at the map title. It will tell you what kind of information is on the map.

2. Next, look at the key or legend. The key explains the special symbols on the map.

3. Locate the north arrow or other directional clues such as latitude lines. If there are no clues, always assume that north is at the top of the map.

4. Use the map scale to help answer questions about distance. For example, what is the distance between Phoenix, Arizona, and the state capital of New Mexico? To find out, place the edge of a sheet of paper along the scale on the map below. On the paper, mark off the distances and label them. Then place your moveable scale between Phoenix and Santa Fe.

Some GED Social Studies questions test your ability to draw conclusions based on information in a map. Use the map below to answer this question:

Which of the following cities probably handles the largest volume of European imports?

(1) Seattle, Washington
(2) St. Paul, Minnesota
(3) New York, New York
(4) Galveston, Texas
(5) Columbia, South Carolina

(1) (2) (3) (4) (5)

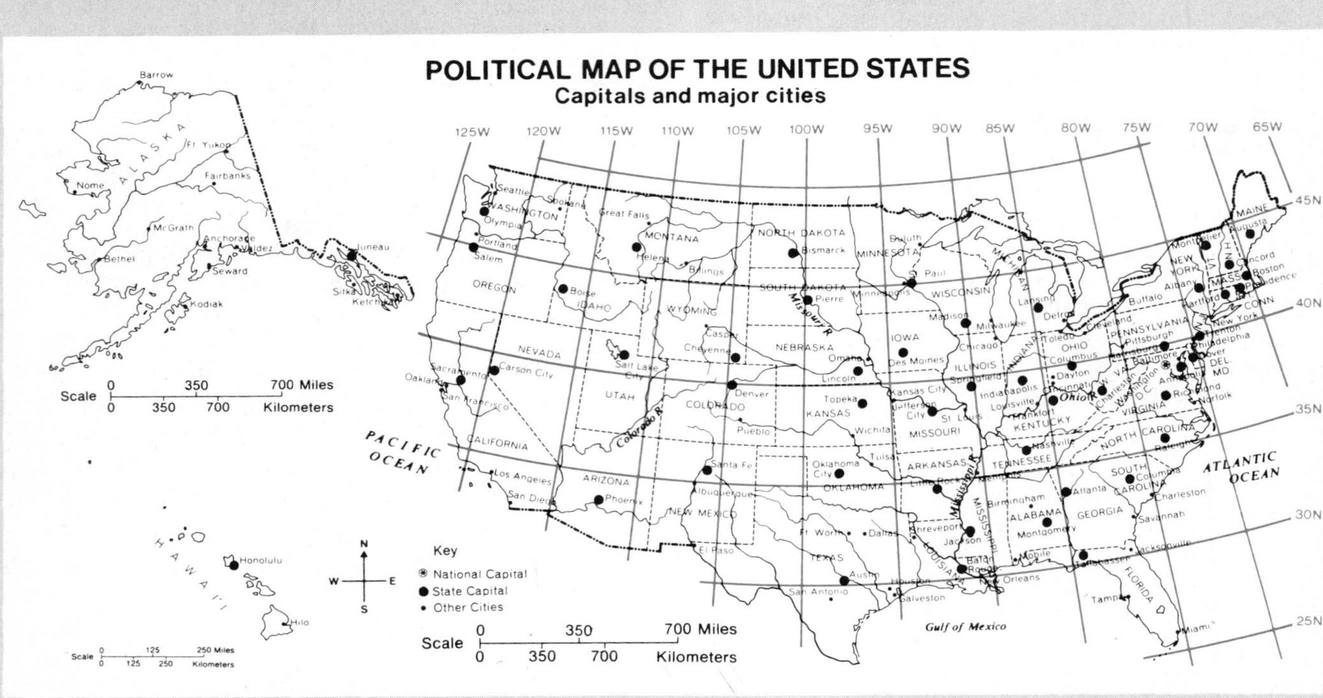

To answer this question correctly, you might reason that the city must be on the Atlantic coast, closest to Europe. That eliminates Seattle and Galveston. Columbia and St. Paul are eliminated because they are not seaports. Only New York is a port on the Atlantic coast. Therefore, (3) is the correct answer.

Special-Purpose Maps So far you've looked at a political map. The first map on this page is a special-purpose map that deals with the weather. When taking the GED Social Studies Test, read the keys on special-purpose maps carefully and quickly glance over the map before you read the questions. Practice by studying the map below and then answering the question.

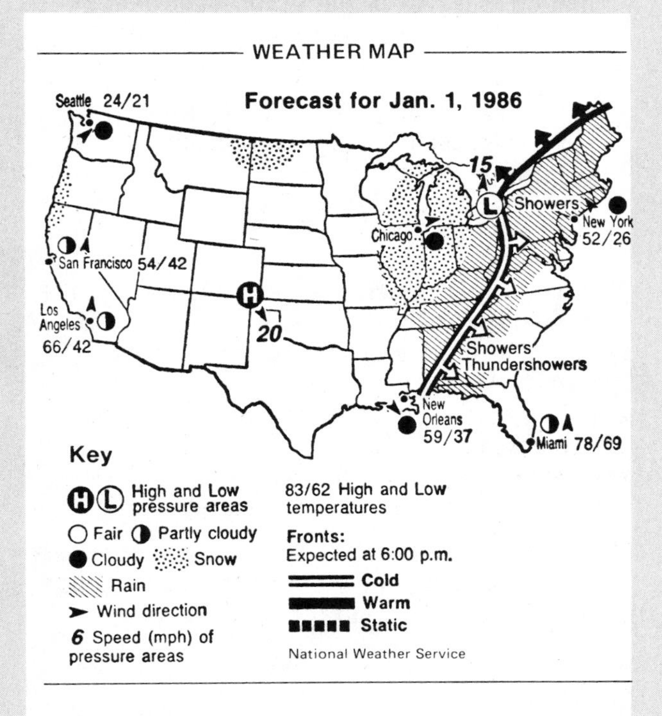

Which of the following weather conditions would cause temperatures to drop in New York City?

(1) wet winds from Miami
(2) cold winds from the Midwest
(3) blizzards in northern California
(4) snow from over the Atlantic
(5) 20 mph winds from northern Texas

Any winds from Miami would be warm, so eliminate (1). California is too far away to have an effect, weather normally doesn't move from east to west, and the winds in Texas are blowing southeast, not northeast. The winds from the snowy Midwest, however, are blowing east toward New York, so (2) is the logical answer.

The next map is a historical map. *Historical maps* show information about places in earlier periods. You need to decide just how much information this map shows to answer the following question.

Which of the following conclusions is supported by information on the map?

(1) The early Pueblo were a peaceful people.
(2) The early Cherokee had a highly developed civilization.
(3) Seafood was an important part of the early Nootkas' diet.
(4) Early Eskimos ate mainly vegetables and fruit.
(5) The early Choctaw wore warm, heavy clothing.

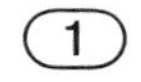

There is no information on the map to support (1) or (2). You may already know that the Pueblo were indeed a peaceful people or that the Cherokee civilization was indeed highly developed. However, keep in mind that the question is asking whether the map supports these conclusions, not whether the conclusions are facts. After studying the map, you might conclude that the opposite of (4) and (5) are true. Few fruits and vegetables grow in the Eskimos' Arctic home, and warm clothing probably is not needed in the Choctaws' southern home. On the other hand, it would be safe to assume that the Nootkas ate a lot of fish since the map shows they lived on the Pacific Coast. So (3) is the best answer.

Answering Questions Based on Graphs

The GED Social Studies Test probably will have five or six graphs. They may appear in any of the five social studies areas. Basically, there are three types of graphs—circle, bar, and line—and a standard way to read and analyze each type.

Circle Graphs The simplest type of graph is the circle, or "pie," graph. It divides a whole into parts. Portions of the circle usually are labeled with percentages. Use these steps to read the circle graph at the bottom of the column:

1. Look at the title of the graph. It will tell you what the whole circle represents.

2. Once you know what the circle represents, examine its parts. Carefully read the labels and percentages on the circle's portions.

Some circle graphs do not provide written percentages. If you come across one of these on the GED Social Studies Test, you must estimate the percentages from the size of the portions. If a question that follows the graph asks for the percentage of a portion, check the possible answers for the one closest to your estimate. Remember, the percentages must add up to 100 percent.

Some questions on the GED Social Studies Test may require you to compare portions or draw conclusions based on the portions' sizes. You may need to do simple math to arrive at the correct answers.

Now answer this question, which is based on the *Federal Budget Dollar* circle graph.

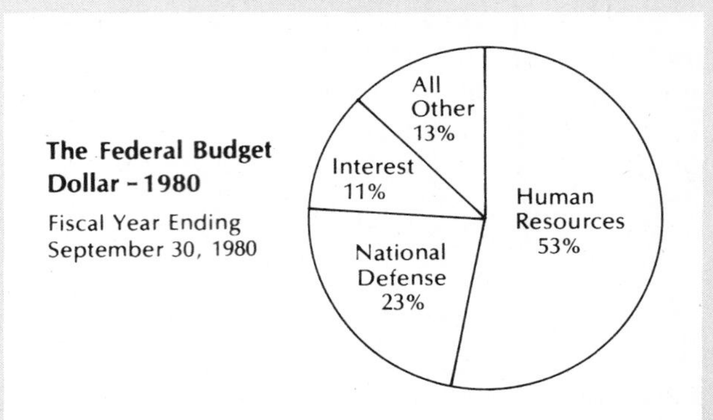

The government spent about $64 billion on interest in 1980. Based on this information and that in the graph, approximately how much was spent on human resources?

(1) $150 billion
(2) $200 billion
(3) $250 billion
(4) $300 billion
(5) $450 billion

① ② ③ ④ ⑤

To find the correct answer, you must first make your own estimate. Write $64 billion in the interest portion of the graph. Next read the percentage for human resources—53 percent. This is approximately 5 times as much as 11 percent. Multiply $64 billion by 5, and then find the response that is closest to your answer. Option (4), or $300 billion, is the correct answer.

Bar Graphs Bar graphs show simple comparisons. Use the steps given here to read the bar graph on the next page.

1. Begin by reading the title.

2. Bar graphs have two axes, or intersecting lines. One axis serves as the base, or starting point of the bars. Find that axis on the graph. Note that the labels identifying each bar appear along this line.

3. You know the topic of the graph by reading its title and the axis labels. By looking at the length of the bars, you can determine which amount is greatest, smallest, and so on. However, if it is necessary to find the exact value of a bar, you must look at the numerical scale that appears on the other axis. (Careful! This will not always be the horizontal axis. Some bar graphs have the scale on the vertical axis and the base on the horizontal axis.) Estimate the number value of the bar by running your finger from the end of the bar to the point directly opposite on the numerical scale.

Now answer the question in the next column about the bar graph on per capita income.

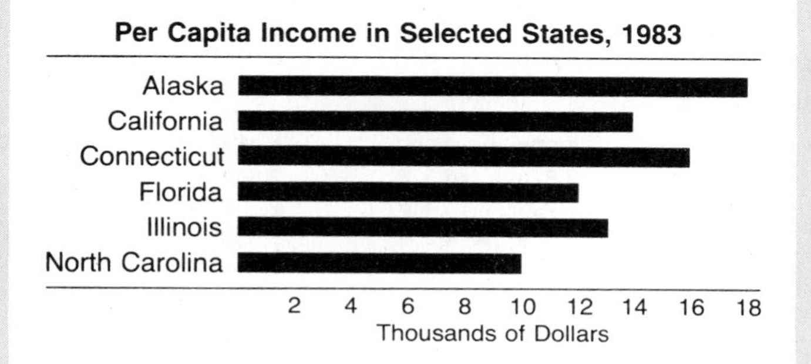

Which of the following conditions might help account for the difference in per capita income between Alaska and North Carolina?

(1) a smaller population living in Alaska
(2) a higher unemployment rate in Alaska
(3) a larger percentage of high-income jobs in North Carolina
(4) a lower rate of pay in Alaska
(5) a greater percentage of successful businesses in North Carolina

First, you have to compare the bars for Alaska and North Carolina. You can see that Alaska has the higher per capita income. Options (2) and (4) would contribute to lowering Alaska's per capita income, so they are not the right answers. Options (3) and (5) would suggest that North Carolina's per capita income is higher than Alaska's, which is not true. However, (1) suggests that fewer people live in Alaska so the demand for labor is greater than the supply of it.

Line Graphs You may find one or more line graphs on the GED Social Studies Test. Follow the steps below to read the line graph on the next page.

1. Read the title of the graph.

2. Study the axes. The horizontal axis usually represents a period of time divided into equal units such as hours, days, or years. The vertical axis generally is a scale of quantity divided into equal amounts such as ones, hundreds, or millions. The scale usually starts at zero at the point the two axes intersect.

3. The line on the graph connects points that show a certain quantity at a certain time. The graph on the next page, for example, shows that in 1929 there were more than 1 1/2 million unemployed workers. You know this because the dot directly above the year 1929 is between 1 and 2 on the quantity axis. This graph has only one line. Some graphs have more than one line; a key will show what each line (solid, dashed, dotted, and so on) measures.

Now try answering this question based on the line graph.

UNEMPLOYMENT IN THE UNITED STATES, 1929-1943

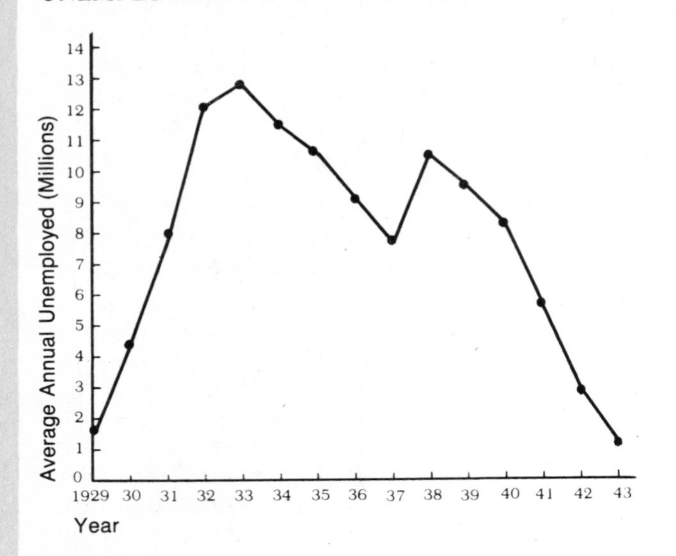

Which of the following events probably helped to increase unemployment?

(1) the stock market crash of 1929
(2) the inauguration of Franklin Roosevelt in 1933
(3) the creation of the Works Progress Administration in 1935
(4) the beginning of World War II in 1939
(5) the U.S. entrance into the war in 1941

You simply have to check the point above the year in each choice to discover that (1) is the correct answer. Among the five, the only year after which unemployment went up is 1929.

Answering Questions Based on Tables

Some questions based on tables will appear on the Test. Those questions will determine how accurately you can identify trends and otherwise use the figures on the tables. When you read a table, ask yourself the following questions:

1. What is the title of the table? The title will tell you why the information in the table is important.

2. What are the column headings? Each heading will tell you what kind of information is in the column below it.

3. What data is listed in the column on the far left? This column lists categories just as the column heads do. To read a statistic from any other column, put a finger on the head of that column and another finger on the category in the column to the far left. Move the first finger down and the other finger across until they meet. The information you find matches the column head with the category.

Use the table below to answer the question.

The Male-Female Wage Gap, 1955–1979

Year	Median Earnings*		Earnings gap in dollars	Women's earnings as % of men's
	Women	Men		
1979	$10,168	$17,062	$6,894	59.5%
1978	9,350	15,730	6,380	59.4
1977	8,618	14,626	6,008	58.9
1976	8,099	13,455	5,356	60.2
1975	7,504	12,758	5,254	58.8
1970	5,323	8,966	3,643	59.4
1965	3,823	6,375	2,552	60.0
1960	3,293	5,417	2,124	60.8
1955	2,719	4,252	1,533	63.9

*Of full-time, year-round workers

Which of the following statements is a fact supported by the table?

(1) Many women worked part-time in 1979 and that explains why men earned more than women did.
(2) Women were incapable of doing the better-paid jobs that men did.
(3) Women in 1979 made a smaller percentage of men's earnings than did women in 1955.
(4) Women in 1979 should have been pleased because their earnings had steadily increased.
(5) Men earned more than twice what women did for the entire 24-year period.

(1) (2) (3) (4) (5)

If you read the table carefully, you know it represents statistics only for full-time, year-round workers. So (1) is eliminated. Nothing in the table supports (2) and (4), which are clearly opinions. Option (5) is wrong since the table shows that women's earnings did not go below 58.8% of men's earnings between 1955 and 1979. Option (3) is the right answer because the percentage in 1979 is 4.4% lower than that in 1955.

While you're warmed up, answer two more questions about the table.

Which year would the following figures most likely apply to?

Median Earnings		Earnings Gap (in $)	Women's earnings (as % of men's)
Women	*Men*		
$4,669	$7,835	$3,116	59.6

(1) 1980 (2) 1974 (3) 1967
(4) 1964 (5) 1957

(1) (2) (3) (4) (5)

This question tests your ability to see a trend in the statistics. The median earnings during the period are always rising. So the figures given in the question most logically would fit between 1965 and 1970. Option (3) is the best answer.

Which of the following graphs best represents information in the table?

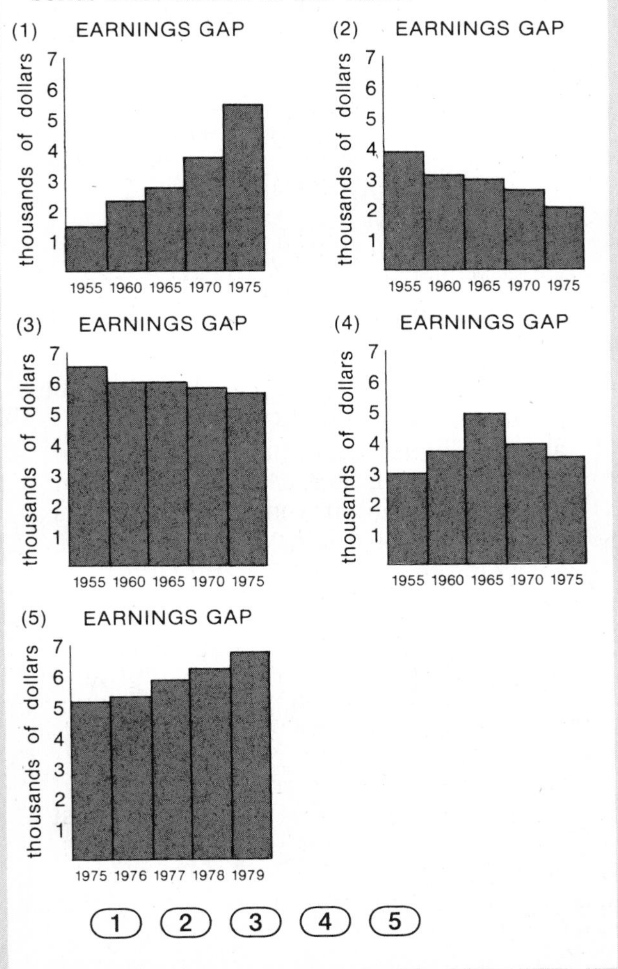

This second question tests your ability to transfer information from a table to a graph. You can eliminate (2) and (4) because the earnings gap did not decrease at any time between 1955 and 1975. Option (3) shows the percentages, not the earnings gap as indicated in the title. Option (5) shows only the figures from 1975 to 1979. Option (1) is the correct answer; it shows the earnings gap steadily widening.

Answering Questions Based on Cartoons

It should not surprise you to find a political cartoon on the Test. The cartoon probably will relate to political science or economics. You may be asked to identify the main idea of the cartoon or the cartoonist's opinion. The following steps will help you understand any cartoon on the GED Social Studies Test.

1. Read the title and caption carefully. The term "endangered species" in the title of the cartoon on the next page is used in a new context. Political cartoons typically use familiar terms in unfamiliar ways.

2. Try to recognize symbols or caricatures of important people in the cartoon. A *caricature* is a drawing that greatly exaggerates the features of a person or thing. A *symbol* is an object used to represent something else. Political cartoonists use caricatures and symbols to express opinions and concerns about issues. The eagle in the cartoon on the next page is a symbol for the United States. Other common symbols used in political cartoons are Uncle Sam, the Republican elephant, the Democratic donkey, and the Russian bear. Labels on symbols help to make the cartoonist's point more clear.

3. Determine what is happening in the cartoon. An important element of a cartoon is action—literal action and symbolic action. For example, in the cartoon on the next page, the literal action consists of shooting the eagles, whereas the symbolic action is made up of destroying privacy and liberties.

4. Guess the issue and the cartoonist's opinion from the captions, symbols, labels, and action.

Now study the cartoon below and answer the question that follows.

from Herblock's *State Of The Union* (Simon & Schuster, 1972)

Which of the following statements best expresses the cartoonist's opinion?

(1) The American eagle should be protected from hunters.
(2) Gun-control legislation would save the civil liberties of Americans.
(3) Vigorous law enforcement is needed to protect Americans from criminals.
(4) Unconstitutional law enforcement endangers all Americans' privacy and liberties.
(5) The American government should oppose criticisms made by foreign governments.

The first response might seem logical if you looked only at what was going on literally—guns shooting at eagles. Option (2) also mentions guns, but not in the symbolic way they are used in the cartoon. Option (3) expresses an opinion contrary to the one in the cartoon. Option (5) is unrelated to the cartoon topic. Only option (4) correctly expresses the opinion of the cartoonist—the tactics of law enforcement agencies endanger Americans' privacy and liberties.

Answering Application Questions Thirty percent of the questions on the Test will ask you to use information or ideas in a different way than they are used in the passages or graphics. These questions measure your skill at using what you are given or already know in new situations.

One type of item on the GED Social Studies Test defines five categories and asks you to classify new information within these categories. A sample of such an item follows. Read the definitions and test your application skills by answering the following questions.

In geography, the earth often is divided into regions that share the same kinds of vegetation. Listed below are names and descriptions of five of the earth's vegetation regions.

prairie—grassland in the midlatitudes where trees grow only along streams
tundra—dry region where short grasses, mosses, and 6-inch-tall willows grow in ground that is frozen just below the surface year round
desert—very dry region where plants conserve water in ways such as remaining leafless until rain falls or storing water in their stems
taiga forest—wet northern region of mostly evergreen, needleleaf trees
tropical rainforest—wet region on and near the equator of dense broadleaf, evergreen trees.

Each of the following statements describes a situation in one of the five regions above. Choose the region that best fits the description. The categories may be used more than once in the set of items, but no question has more than one best answer.

In an area of Brazil, the tops of the trees form a canopy that shuts out sunlight and makes it impossible for plants to grow on the ground below. Which region is this area located in?

(1) prairie (2) tundra (3) desert
(4) taiga forest (5) tropical rainforest

① ② ③ ④ ⑤

If you already know that Brazil is located on the equator, then you will know that (5) is the correct answer. Even if you are unsure about the exact location of Brazil, you can eliminate the prairie (1), tundra (2), and desert (3) as regions where too few trees would grow to form a canopy. You also could reason that the needleleaf leaves in a taiga forest (4) could not form a light-proof canopy.

Use the same vegetation categories to complete the next item.

Mesquite trees send their roots as deep as 60 feet below the surface to reach stores of underground water. In which region would you expect to find mesquite trees?

(1) prairie (2) tundra (3) desert
(4) taiga forest (5) tropical rainforest

① ② ③ ④ ⑤

The mesquite's long roots seem to be an adaptation to a dry climate, so (4) and (5) can be eliminated. Though the tundra (2) is dry, the mesquite could not send its roots through the frozen subsoil. Since trees only grow along streams in a prairie (1), the mesquite's roots would not be on the right level to take in the available water. So (3) is the best answer.

Questions That Ask for Analysis Another 30 percent of the questions on the GED Social Studies Test will ask you to break down information into ideas and to explore how those ideas are related. For example, you may be asked to distinguish facts in a passage from an opinion or to distinguish a general conclusion from supporting details. Some questions may ask you to identify causes and effects. Still others may ask you to recognize an assumption—information on which a passage is based—that is not even in the passage.

Fact or Opinion? To determine whether a statement is fact or opinion, you must read the statement critically. Look for evidence of a one-sided view and emotionalism. Opinions express people's feelings and thoughts. Watch for words like *only, must, best, worst,* and *good,* which signal an opinion. Watch for expressions such as *obviously, certainly,* and *no doubt*—attempts to make you accept the statement without question. Ask yourself, "Can research prove this statement?" A fact can be proved, but an opinion cannot. No GED question will ask for your opinion. Look for the logical answer, not the one you agree with!

Read each of the following statements. If it is an opinion, write *O*. If it is a fact, write *F*.

______ **a.** Everyone knows that Mr. Thomas is the only candidate who can do the job.

______ **b.** Mr. Thomas has served in the House of Representatives for two years.

Did you see that *Statement a* is an opinion? "Everyone knows" and "only" are meant to influence your thinking.

Now read the following passage and answer the question below.

In 1960, many Cubans who had fled to Florida planned to invade Cuba to overthrow Fidel Castro. The U.S. government gave these Cubans guns and money. When John F. Kennedy became president, he approved the government's part in the plan. The Florida Cubans landed at Cuba's Bay of Pigs. Castro's soldiers killed many of the rebels, and twelve hundred were jailed. In 1962, the United States bought back the prisoners by sending $55 million of food and medicine to Cuba.

Which of the following statements is based on fact?

(1) The Cuban soldiers acted cruelly toward the invaders.
(2) President Kennedy was obviously to blame for the invasion.
(3) The U.S. government was right to aid the rebels from Florida.
(4) Cubans should stay in Cuba.
(5) The Cuban rebels were unhappy with Castro's government.

① ② ③ ④ ⑤

Option (5) can be proved by analyzing the Cuban rebels' actions and inferring their views. Personal preference or viewpoint determines what is cruel, who is to blame for an action, whether an action is right, and what course of action some people should take. Therefore, only option (5) is a fact.

Questions That Call for Evaluation Twenty percent of the questions on the GED Social Studies Test will ask you to evaluate, or judge, information. For example, you may have to determine whether or not a graph has enough information to support a certain conclusion. Or you may have to decide if statements are accurate or logical.

Evaluating Points of View Have you ever heard the expression "Consider the source"? It means you should judge what a speaker says based on what that person knows or values. You will be asked to evaluate quotes on the GED Social Studies Test. You may have to decide whether a quote is accurate or why a person said something. Or you may have to determine what era a quote is from and what sort of person the speaker was. In these situations, you must understand the speaker's point of view. Here are some hints for doing this:

1. Read the entire quote. Then ask yourself what the main idea is and on what values the speaker is basing his or her beliefs.

2. Look for time clues—for example, the events and trends that are mentioned.

3. Read the questions and all the possible responses. Measure each response against your understanding of the quote. Eliminate responses that don't make sense and mark the best remaining answer.

Practice evaluating points of view by reading the quote below and then answering the sample question that follows.

"Redistributing income or eliminating depressions would result in less gain for the poor or the whole society than they would derive from an even relatively short period of sustained growth."

Douglas C. North

Which of the following statements would North agree with?

(1) Governments should set up welfare programs for the poor.
(2) Governments should work to prevent depressions.
(3) The gap between rich and poor can be narrowed.
(4) The overall economy is more important than the immediate needs of the poor.
(5) The situation of the needy does not improve even when the economy improves.

(1) (2) (3) (4) (5)

Options (1), (2), and (4) contradict the opinions North expresses in his quote. Option (3) is not directly related to what North has said. The correct answer is (5), because it sums up the underlying value that enables North to believe what he says.

Geography

The Earth and Its People How would you describe where you live? If you refer to the people around you—their customs or language, such as in "an English-speaking country"—you are describing your cultural region. If you answer, for example, that the area around you is hot and dry or mountainous, you are speaking of your physical region. A physical region can be defined by its climate, **landforms,** or vegetation.

Migration For thousands of years, people have moved from place to place looking for a better life. This movement is called *migration.* Waves of early people from Asia and Africa migrated to Europe. Some early Asians moved to North America and probably became the ancestors of American Indians. More recent examples of migration are the Irish who crossed the ocean to escape famine and the Forty-Niners who went west to find gold. Despite frequent migration, people have not distributed themselves evenly across the earth. Almost two-thirds of the earth's almost 5 billion people live on only one-tenth of the earth's surface. The map below represents the countries of the world according to the size of their populations rather than of their areas. As you can see, the most populated nation today is India.

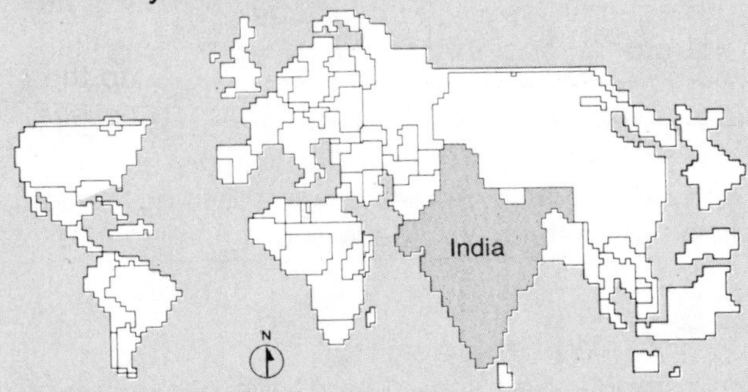

Coming to Terms

landform a physical characteristic of the land such as hills, mountains, plains, and plateaus

Warm-up

On your own paper, write two sentences describing the physical and cultural regions in which you live.

Sample Warm-up Answer
The physical region is a plain with a moderate climate. The cultural region is a middle-class suburb.

<u>Directions:</u> Choose the <u>one</u> best answer to each question. Answers are on page 312.

<u>Items 1–2</u> refer to the following map.

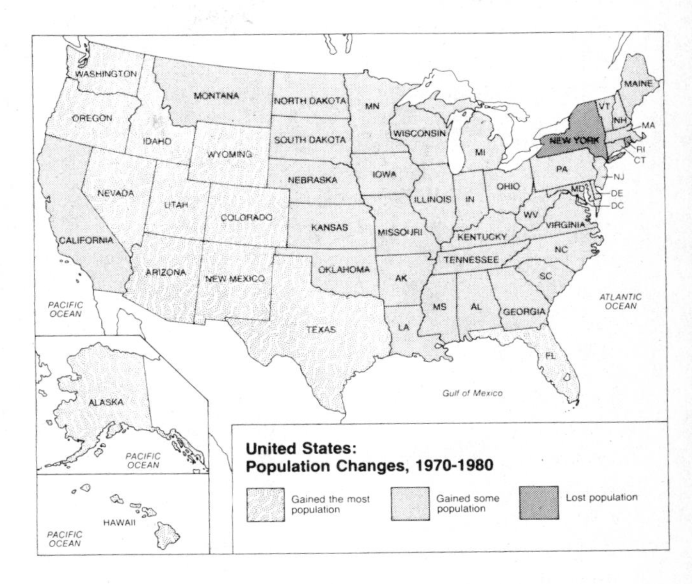

1. Which of the following conclusions is based on the map?

   (1) Texas has a larger population than New York.
   (2) The same number of people moved to Idaho and Utah.
   (3) Illinois and Indiana have the same size population.
   (4) Florida is growing at a faster rate than California.
   (5) More people recently have moved to Georgia and Maryland together than to Arizona.

   ① ② ③ ④ ⑤

2. Population implosion is a change from a pattern of thinly dispersed groups to one of densely populated communities. Which of the following states probably has experienced population implosion most recently?

   (1) New York (2) Massachusetts
   (3) California (4) Rhode Island
   (5) Alaska

Directions: Choose the one best answer to each question. Answers are on page 312.

Items 3–4 refer to the following map.

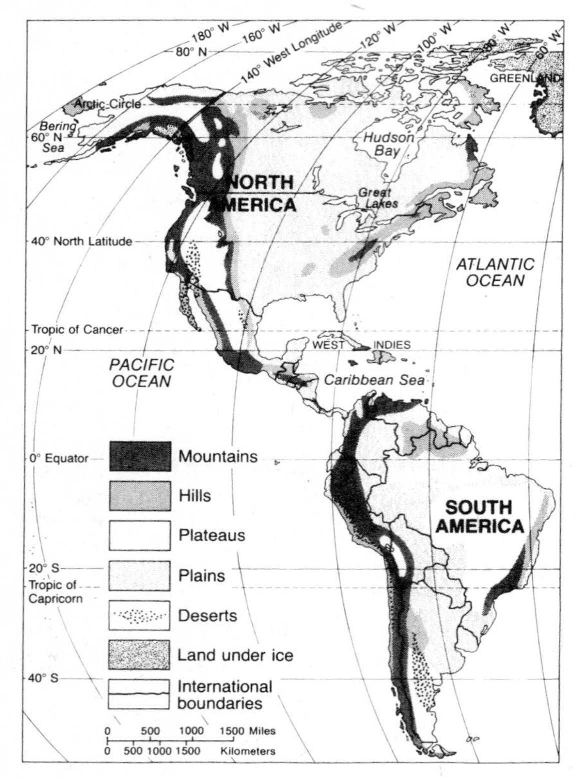

3. Where are the central plains of the United States located?
   (1) between 60° W and 80° W longitudes
   (2) above 65° N latitude
   (3) between 0° and 40° S latitude
   (4) between 30° N and 50° N latitudes
   (5) south of 20° N latitude

   1 2 3 4 5

4. Which of the following areas has a distance equal to that across the United States at 40° N latitude?
   (1) the widest part of South America
   (2) the length of South America
   (3) the widest part of the Gulf of Mexico
   (4) the land along 60° N latitude between the Bering Sea and Hudson Bay
   (5) the distance from the Great Lakes to the West Indies along 80° W longitude

Maps and Globes It has been said that if you can't map it, it isn't geography. Maps and globes help you visualize information such as location and distance. Use the map on page 252 to help you understand the following discussion.

Location Every spot on the earth has a location that can be expressed in relation to other locations with directions. For example, Seattle is north of San Francisco. Location also can be expressed with latitude and longitude. **Latitude** lines, or parallels, run east and west and are numbered north and south of the **equator.** The equator divides the earth into two halves—the northern and the southern hemispheres. Lines, or meridians, of **longitude** run north and south from pole to pole and are numbered east and west of the **prime meridian.** The prime meridian divides the earth into the eastern and the western hemispheres.

Distance The distance between two places on a map depends on the distortion of the map and its size, or map scale. This scale usually is provided in the key. It indicates how many miles on the earth's surface are represented by an inch on the map.

Coming to Terms

latitude distance in degrees north or south of the equator, as in 30° N latitude
equator imaginary line dividing the earth into the northern and the southern hemispheres
longitude distance in degrees east or west of the prime meridian, as in 90° W longitude
prime meridian imaginary line dividing the earth into the eastern and the western hemispheres

Warm-up

In complete sentences, name the hemispheres you live in, a major city you live in or near, and four other cities—one north, one south, one east, and one west of your home. Use your own paper.

Need a Hint for Number 4?
Mark the distance across the United States on the edge of a sheet of paper. Then use the paper as a ruler to compare that distance with the distances in the other options.

Sample Warm-up Answer
I live in the northern and the western hemispheres. My home is in Chicago, which is north of Tallahassee, Florida; south of Seattle, Washington; east of Denver, Colorado; and west of Boston, Massachusetts.

Climate and Natural Resources What is the weather like where you live? Is it cold or hot, wet or dry? The weather changes from day to day, but the general condition of the weather in an area remains the same over many years. This long view of the weather is called *climate*. Different climates help produce the different physical and cultural regions of the earth. Climate, in turn, is affected by winds, the elevation of the land, and the nearness of water. The map below shows U.S. climates.

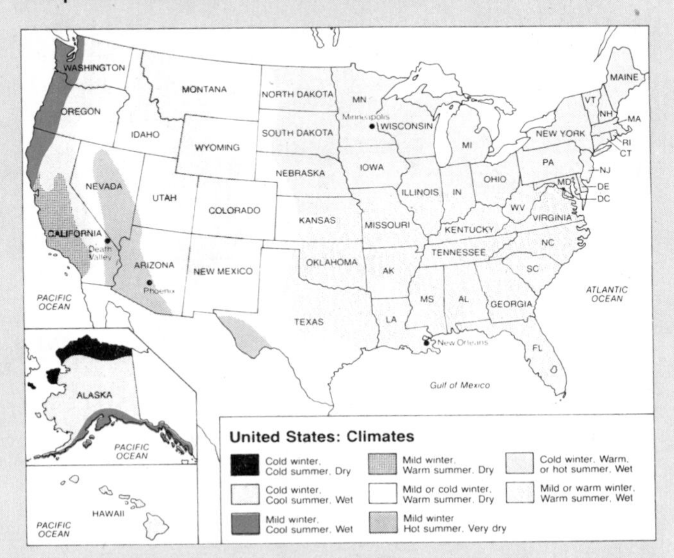

In addition to a climate, each region has resources. *Resources* are anything that people can use. Some resources, such as water, are found in nature. Other resources, such as farm crops, are produced by people. Some resources, such as forests, are renewable. Others, such as metals, are nonrenewable. There are also cultural resources, such as people's talents.

Warm-up

On your own paper, answer the questions.

1. What kinds of plants might you find in the cool, wet climate of central Washington? Explain your answer.

2. Where else pictured on the map do you think you might find similar plants? Explain your answer.

Sample Warm-up Answers

1. You might find fir trees because these trees need lots of water and can tolerate cold temperatures. **2.** Fir trees probably also grow in central Alaska, because similar climates help produce similar kinds of vegetation.

Items 5–6 refer to the following map.

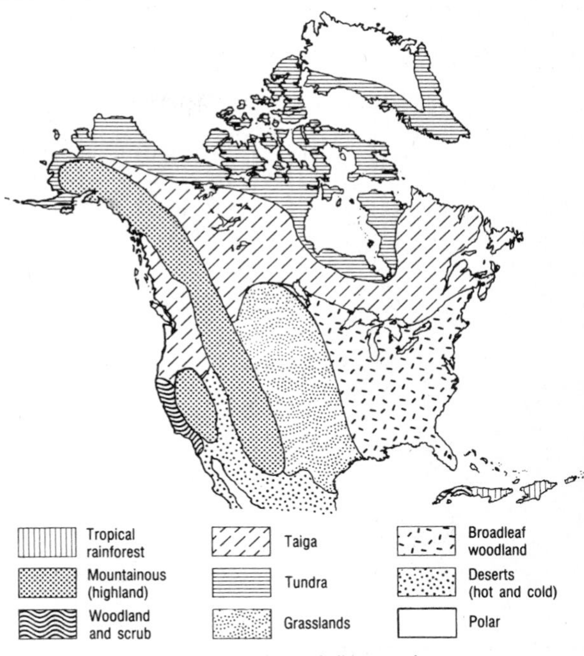

Earth's vegetation and climate regions

5. In which of the following regions is the ground just below the surface most likely to be frozen year round?
   (1) woodland and scrub (2) tundra
   (3) grasslands (4) broadleaf woodland
   (5) deserts

   (1) (2) (3) (4) (5)

6. Which of the following areas is too dry for many trees to grow?
   (1) eastern North America
   (2) around the Great Lakes
   (3) just east of the mountains
   (4) California's southern coast
   (5) near the equator

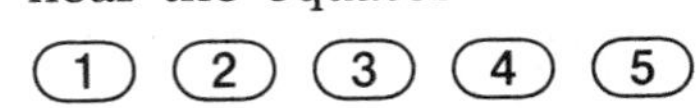

7. As people's needs and desires change, different resources become useful. Which of the following statements best illustrates this concept?
   (1) All humans must have food to survive.
   (2) Some natural resources are limited, while others are not.
   (3) As concern about being overweight increased, noncaloric sweeteners were developed.
   (4) The price of heating oil increases as the demand increases.
   (5) Cultural resources, like scientific knowledge, can be expanded.

Directions: Choose the one best answer to each question. Answers are on page 312.

Items 8–10 are based on the following map.

The Route of the Colorado River

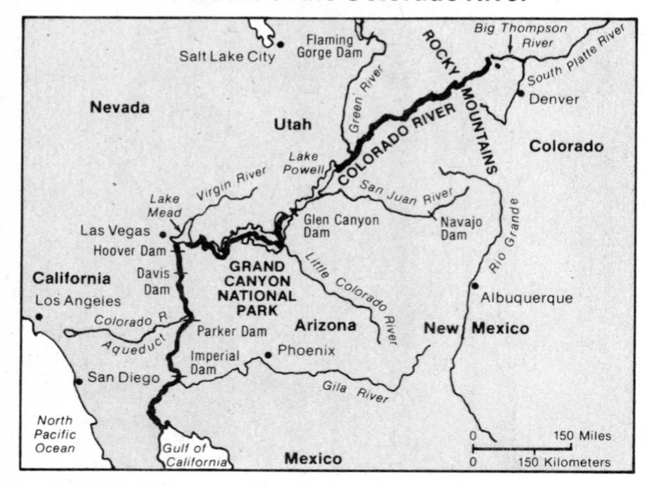

8. What three states does the Colorado River flow through?
   (1) Colorado, Nevada, and Utah
   (2) Colorado, Utah, and Arizona
   (3) California, Utah, and Arizona
   (4) New Mexico, Colorado, and Arizona
   (5) Nevada, New Mexico, and Colorado

   (1) (2) (3) (4) (5)

9. Which of the following statements about the use of the Colorado River is true?
   (1) An aqueduct delivers water from the river to Mexico.
   (2) Water is stored in reservoirs behind several dams.
   (3) People in Salt Lake City depend on the river for drinking water.
   (4) Several states east of the Rockies use Colorado River water.
   (5) Canada shares Colorado River water with the United States.

   (1) (2) (3) (4) (5)

10. Because so many people depend on the Colorado River, what problem may arise?
    (1) Little water will be left in the river when it reaches Mexico.
    (2) Too much water will flow from the United States to Mexico.
    (3) The river soon will disappear.
    (4) The river will cut the Grand Canyon even deeper.
    (5) Canada will not have enough water.

    (1) (2) (3) (4) (5)

North and South America The earth has seven great land masses called continents—Antarctica, Australia, Asia, Africa, Europe, North America, and South America. The continents of North and South America include almost every type of physical region and landform. They also contain many cultural regions, from New York City with its sophisticated urbanites to the Amazon jungle with its primitive tribes. The natural resources of this vast area are diverse.The map on this page shows the countries of the Americas.

Warm-up

Compare the eastern coasts of the United States and Brazil. Which do you think has more ports? Explain your answer. ______

______

______

______

Sample Warm-up Answer

The eastern coast of the United States has more ins and outs, so it probably has more ports.

Europe and the Middle East The large area made up of Europe and the Middle East, or southwest Asia, includes a variety of climate and landform regions. In Europe, the regions range from the cool, wet highlands of Great Britain to the warm, dry rugged land of Italy and Greece to the cold, dry Siberian plain of the Soviet Union. In the Middle East, there are plains, plateaus, and mountains. The climate is generally hot and dry.

Most people in the Middle East speak Arabic and belong to the Moslem religion. The cultural regions of Europe are more diverse. Two of the most important cultural regions are Western and Eastern Europe. The people of Western Europe speak Germanic and Romance languages, while the people of Eastern Europe speak Slavic languages. Altogether, Europeans speak more than 50 different languages. Another factor that separates Western and Eastern Europe is their governments—Western Europe is "free" while Eastern Europe is dominated by the Soviet Union. The map below shows the nations of Europe and the Middle East.

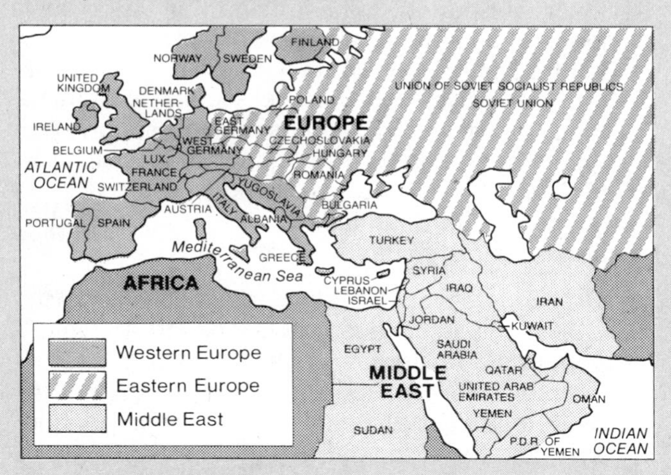

☑ A Test-Taking Tip

Questions on the GED Test may assume that you know which countries border the Atlantic Ocean and the Mediterranean Sea. The map on this page will help you.

Warm-up

Which Middle Eastern country do you think is the traditional shipping center between Europe and Asia? Explain your answer on your own paper.

Sample Warm-up Answer
Turkey, because its coasts are open to ships from other Middle Eastern countries as well as Western and Eastern Europe.

Items 11–12 refer to the following map.

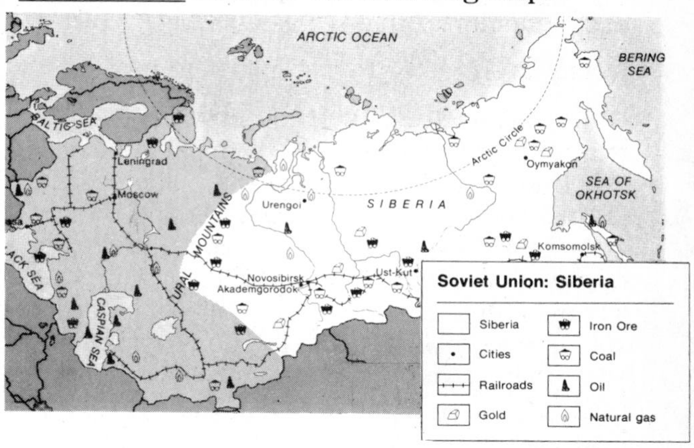

11. Which of the following Siberian cities is most likely a major transportation center?

    (1) Oymyakon (2) Urengoi
    (3) Novosibirsk (4) Ust-Kut
    (5) Komsomolsk

    ① ② ③ ④ ⑤

12. What probably happens to coal mined in northeastern Siberia?

    (1) Railroads carry it to southeast Asia.
    (2) Oymyakon and nearby towns use it.
    (3) It is shipped across the Arctic Ocean to countries further north.
    (4) People in Urengoi heat their homes with it.
    (5) Factories in Leningrad use it.

    ① ② ③ ④ ⑤

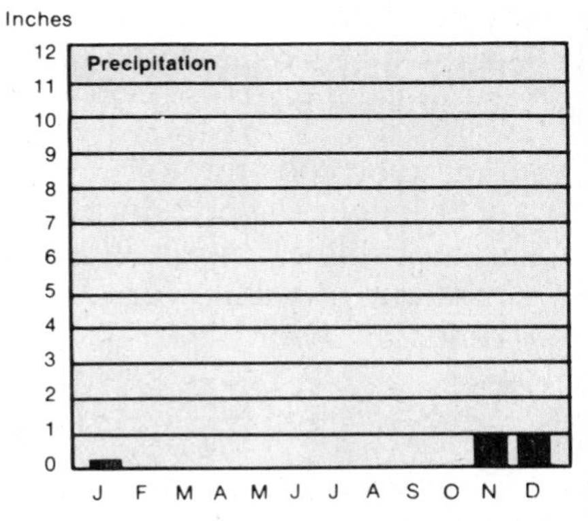

13. Which of the following statements does the above graph help to explain?

    (1) Saudi Arabia is an oil-rich country.
    (2) The camel is related to the South American llama.
    (3) Most Saudi Arabians farm.
    (4) Corn and wheat do not grow well in Saudi Arabia.
    (5) Trucks are used in the Arabian desert.

    ① ② ③ ④ ⑤

Directions: Choose the one best answer to each question. Answers are on page 312.

Items 14–15 refer to the following passage.

The Japanese view of the physical landscape is heavily influenced by Taoism, Shintoism, and Buddhism. These religions make sacred the relationship between humans and their environment. Rather than subduing the elements of the landscape into an unnatural symmetrical arrangement, therefore, the Japanese gardener will arrange plants, stones, ponds, bridges, and other garden elements into a natural pattern. Japanese gardens evoke the spirit of the landscape on a miniature scale. The arrangement of the rocks and trees is meant to encourage contemplation. Only a few objects are necessary, although the attention to detail shows the care with which these few objects are arranged.

14. How did the Japanese come to believe the environment is sacred?
    (1) from their various religions
    (2) from the superstition that plants and animals give them supernatural powers
    (3) from ignorance of scientific explanations for natural occurrences
    (4) from values taught them by early American traders
    (5) because Japan is basically a farming nation

    (1) (2) (3) (4) (5)

15. According to the passage, which of the following would a typical Japanese garden most likely include?
    (1) an outdoor cooking grill
    (2) a split-level redwood deck
    (3) shrubs trimmed into animal shapes
    (4) a meadow of wildflowers
    (5) a reflecting pool

    (1) (2) (3) (4) (5)

16. Which of the following scientific developments would people find most useful in the deserts of northern Africa?
    (1) central heating
    (2) laser weaponry
    (3) the desalination of seawater
    (4) nuclear power plants
    (5) water-generated electricity

    (1) (2) (3) (4) (5)

Asia and Africa Asia is by far the largest continent. Its area is greater than that of North and South America combined. Africa is the second-largest continent. The map below shows the countries of Asia and Africa.

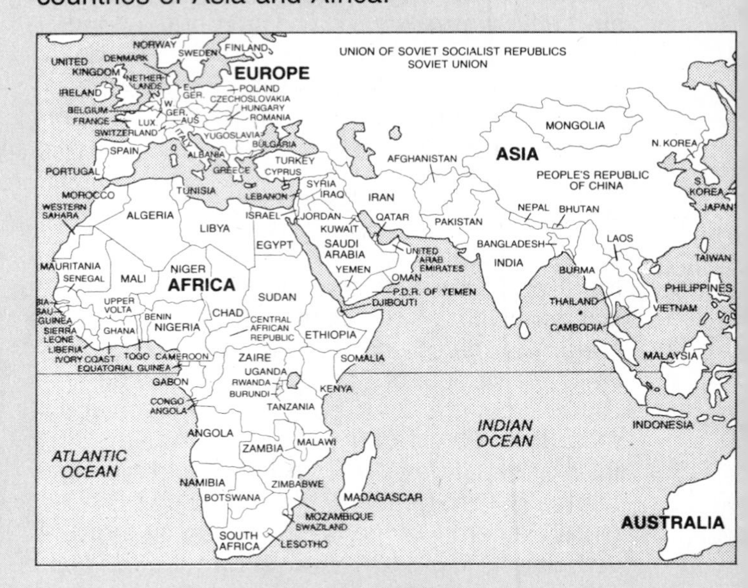

Much of South, Southeast, and Far East Asia is jungles, deserts, mountains, or frozen wasteland. Most Asians live in river valleys where they can raise crops. Asia's population of more than 2.7 billion far outstrips its food supply. As a result, hunger is widespread. Some Asian countries, such as China, are trying to improve their economies through industrialization. Today Japan is Asia's industrial giant.

Only 8 percent of Africa's land is used to raise crops. This is because barren desert and impenetrable rainforests cover much of northern and central Africa. Overgrazing the central African grasslands also affects the amount of land available for farming. Each year, hundreds of acres of what once was grassland become part of Africa's Sahara—the world's largest desert. Several oil-producing countries of northern Africa are experimenting with ways to reclaim the desert for farming.

Warm-up

On your own paper, answer the following question. Which African countries would you expect to have climate and cultural regions similar to European countries? Explain your answer.

Sample Warm-up Answer
Morocco, Algeria, Tunisia, and Libya probably are similar to nearby Mediterranean countries in Europe, because most likely, they share ideas and goods as well as sea breezes.

Resource Management A global issue of great importance today is the careful use of resources. Fishing, lumbering, farming, and ranching all strip the earth in some way. Geographers are studying ways to maintain renewable resources, such as fish and forests, so that people use the resources only as fast as they can be replaced. The oceans and poles, which belong to everyone, are of special concern to geographers, and many of them recommend that countries share the minerals under the sea and in Antarctica—the continent surrounding the South Pole.

Development The term *development* indicates the level of technology that a nation uses. A developed country, such as the United States, has many factories and depends on complex machines, such as autos and computers. Generally its people are educated and enjoy a high **standard of living.** A developing nation—Brazil, for example—has fewer and simpler machines and a lower standard of living. Fewer of its people go to school, earn good livings, or live long lives. In recent years, the economic gap between developed and developing nations has widened. At the bottom of the economic totem pole are the underdeveloped nations, often called Third World countries. To improve their economies, underdeveloped nations need to learn about technology. At the same time, they need to conserve their natural and cultural resources.

Coming to Terms

standard of living level of material comfort

Warm-up

Haiti is an underdeveloped nation where four-fifths of the people make about $125 or less a year. Haiti's government is so ill-equipped that, on hearing of a riot, Haitian soldiers flagged down cabs because they had no trucks to drive to the troubled area. Why do you think some observers argue that Haiti needs military aid before any other kind?

Sample Warm-up Answer
The government may need to settle unrest within the nation before aid programs can be carried out effectively.

Items 17–18 refer to the following map.

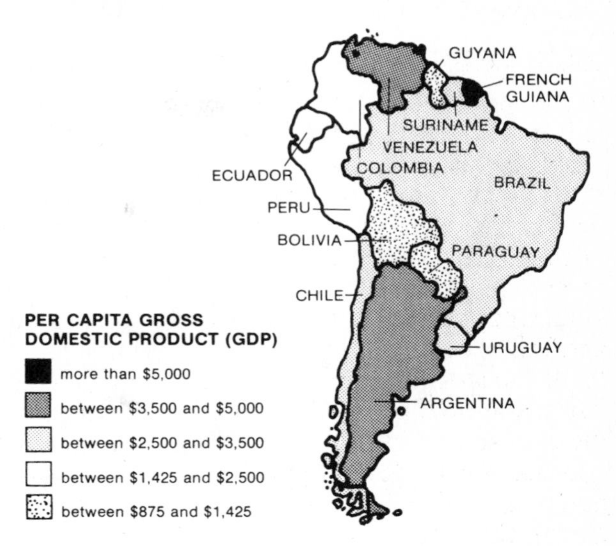

17. GDP (Gross Domestic Product) stands for the goods and services produced inside a nation. Divide the GDP by the number of people in the country and you get the per capita GDP, or average purchasing power of each individual. Which of the following countries has a per capita GDP of between $2500 and $3500?

(1) Ecuador (2) Paraguay
(3) French Guiana (4) Chile
(5) Venezuela

1 2 3 4 5

18. French Guiana's major exports are rum, shrimp, rosewood, and other timber. Which of the following events probably would lower the country's per capita GDP?

(1) an increased demand for seafood in the United States
(2) a French ban on Puerto Rican rum
(3) deforestation of French Guiana
(4) destruction of the shrimp beds in Louisiana
(5) a decrease in the popularity of glass and chrome furniture

Directions: Choose the one best answer to each question. Answers are on page 312.

19. In 1986 there was an accident at the Chernobyl nuclear power plant in the Soviet Union. Which of the following countries was unaffected by the wind-blown radiation?

(1) Poland (2) Italy (3) Holland
(4) Finland (5) Norway

① ② ③ ④ ⑤

Estimated Population Growth

Millions of people: 0, 400, 800, 1200, 1600, 2000, 2400, 2800, 3200, 3600

1984 / 2000

Africa; North America (U.S., Canada, Mexico, Central Am., W. Indies); South America; Asia; Europe; Oceania; Soviet Union (USSR)

20. In the year 2000, populations will be largest in

(1) regions with small populations in 1984
(2) the Western Hemisphere
(3) areas with controlled population growth
(4) regions having a low standard of living
(5) technically advanced countries

Preserving the World Environment Change is an important part of geography. Landforms, climate, human cultures, and technology are all changing. A world view is another basic element of geography. Geographers know that most issues today have an impact on the entire globe.

Population Growth One issue is that the ever-increasing human population is stretching the earth's resources very thin. Birth control has slowed population increases in developed nations. Despite high infant-mortality rates, populations continue to climb in developing nations, which are less equipped to care for their people.

Pollution Geographers are also studying the global long-term effects of industrial pollution in developed nations as well as in developing ones. As Third World countries try to improve their standard of living, they too are having to deal with the problems associated with industrialization.

Warm-up

Acid rain damages lakes, soils, and forests. The map below shows the origin of the pollutants in the rain.

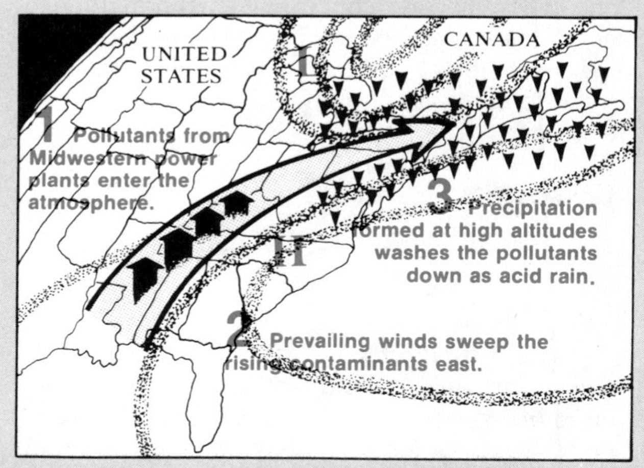

Weather Map by Ib Ohlsson from *Newsweek,* August 11, 1986, p. 53.

What can you conclude from this map about the effects of this kind of pollution? ______________________________

Sample Warm-up Answer
The effects of acid rain are far-reaching rather than local.

Behavioral Sciences

What Is Psychology? Psychology is the study of behavior. Psychologists, or experts in psychology, ask questions such as, why do most babies crawl before they walk? Why are some people shy? To find answers, psychologists examine how children learn, how people behave in groups, why people's personalities and intelligence differ, and more.

Psychology is divided into several fields. For example, experimental psychology is the study of human beings in controlled experiments, physiological psychology explores the relationships between behavior and parts of the body, and child psychology and the psychology of adolescence concentrate on children and teens.

Psychologists teach that basic needs drive people to act. Humans need rest, food, clothing, and shelter to be physically healthy. To maintain emotional health, they need things such as love and approval. Sometimes emotional needs that are unfulfilled can affect a person's physical health. The graph below illustrates one such example.

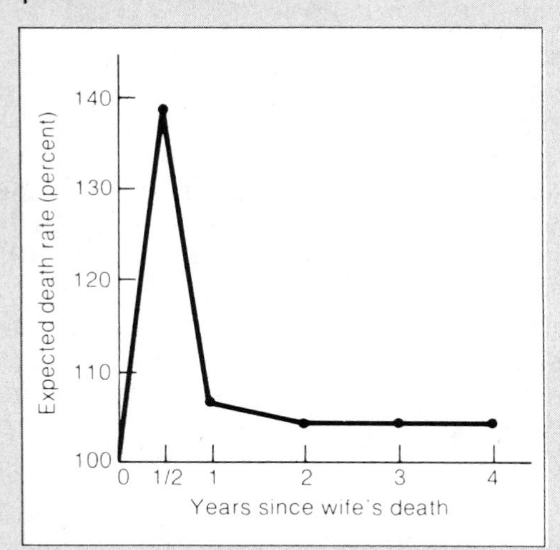

Warm-up

The graph above shows the results of a study comparing the death rates of almost 4,500 widowers with the death rates of married men at the same age. The death rate of widowers soared within six months of their wives' deaths. How might psychologists explain this in terms of emotional needs affecting physical health? Use your own paper.

Sample Warm-up Answer

Psychologists might say that the widowers died because their emotional needs were not being met.

Directions: Choose the one best answer to each question. Answers are on page 312.

Items 1–2 refer to the following study.

A study was done of six children who suffered from a special form of dwarfism. In these cases, the children came from homes where they were treated with an extreme lack of affection. The researcher found that these children gained weight and began to grow when removed from the unhappy homes. Growth slowed again if conditions were unchanged when the children returned home.

1. What did the researchers find in this study?

(1) Dwarfs come from unhappy homes.
(2) The children in this study were undernourished.
(3) The parents of dwarfs usually are not dwarfs themselves.
(4) The children studied improved when they were removed from their homes.
(5) The gains made by the children were maintained when they returned home.

2. Which of the following conclusions is best supported by the study?

(1) Curing these children would not be possible.
(2) These children were physically abused by their parents.
(3) The physical problems of the children in the study were inherited from their parents.
(4) Children from homes where they are treated with an extreme lack of affection will not gain weight.
(5) The physical problems of these children were caused by an emotionally abnormal environment.

Directions: Choose the one best answer to each question. Answers are on pages 312–313.

Items 3–4 refer to the chart below.

Percentage Agreement in How Photograph Was Judged Across Cultures

	Happiness	Disgust	Surprise	Anger	Fear
United States (*N*=99)	97%	92%	95%	67%	85%
Brazil (*N*=40)	95%	97%	87%	90%	67%
Chile (*N*=119)	95%	92%	93%	94%	68%
Argentina (*N*=168)	98%	92%	95%	90%	54%
Japan (*N*=29)	100%	90%	100%	90%	66%

3. Which emotion listed caused the most disagreement?

   (1) fear (2) anger (3) disgust
   (4) surprise (5) happiness

   ① ② ③ ④ ⑤

4. What conclusion can be drawn from this study?

   (1) Facial expressions add little meaning to language.
   (2) The ability to make and to interpret facial expressions must be taught.
   (3) Facial expressions are associated with emotions more often in Japan than in Argentina.
   (4) The rate of disagreement was highest between Brazil and the United States.
   (5) Some facial expressions convey the same emotions in many different world cultures.

   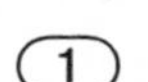

   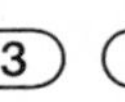

Understanding Human Behavior Do you sometimes wonder why a friend acts a certain way? You may have known this person for years yet there are some things your friend does and says that you can't explain. Understanding human behavior is a complicated task. Sometimes **heredity** or upbringing affect the way people act. But even identical twins raised together may react differently to the same experience. One reason for this is that people view their surroundings in different ways. Ask five witnesses to a crime what they saw, and you probably will hear five different stories. Each witness's experience and personality influence what he or she "sees." There are also strong outside influences on behavior. One such influence is group, or peer, pressure.

Coming to Terms

heredity qualities or characteristics of body or mind that have come to offspring from parents

Warm-up

To help explain human behavior, a researcher set up the following experiment:

Groups of students were shown cards with three lines of different lengths. They were asked to decide which of the lines was the same length as a line shown on another card. Normally, this is an easy task. In this case, however, all but one of the students were really working for the researcher who set up the experiment. The students working with the researcher would agree that an incorrect answer was the correct one. With this group pressure, it was not unusual for the lone student to agree with the majority, even though the answer was obviously wrong.

1. What influenced the student in the experiment to give the wrong answer?

____

____

2. By applying what you have learned from the passage above, write a sentence predicting what might happen when a dieter goes to a traditional Thanksgiving Day family dinner.

____

____

____

Sample Warm-up Answers
1. Group pressure influenced the student. **2.** The dieter probably will go off the diet.

Principles of Learning Learning takes place throughout the entire course of a person's life. It can be as simple as a baby's first drinking from a cup or as complex as you acquiring new skills for the GED Test. Psychologists define learning as changes in behavior resulting from experience or practice.

The simplest kind of learning is based on **stimulus** and **response.** A stimulus can make a person respond in a certain way, such as when a sudden loud noise makes someone jump.

In the early 1900s, the Russian psychologist Pavlov performed a classic experiment in learning. He trained dogs to salivate when they heard a bell. To do this, Pavlov rang a bell whenever he gave the dogs food. A dog's natural response to food is salivation. Since the dogs heard the bell whenever they were fed, they began to associate the sound with food. Eventually, the bell alone could produce the salivation response in the dogs.

☑ A Test-Taking Tip

Several questions on the GED Social Studies Test are similar to items 5–7 on this page. These items ask you to classify information. Make sure you understand the classifications before you choose an answer for each item.

Coming to Terms

stimulus something that produces behavior
response reaction to a stimulus

Warm-up

Psychologists discovered that an animal in a maze learns the beginning and end points of the maze more easily than the parts in the middle. If this were also true of the way humans learned, what would happen when a child is introduced to the alphabet?

___

___

Sample Warm-up Answer
The child would learn the first and last letters of the alphabet more quickly and easily than those in the middle.

Items 5–7 refer to the following information.

Psychologists who study learning have discovered some general rules to help a person learn.

(1) Stagger—work in short practice sessions separated by long breaks.
(2) Imitate–imitate an expert.
(3) Practice—try the task yourself rather than just watch someone do it or listen to someone explain it.
(4) Evaluate—have your performance evaluated immediately.
(5) Parcel—divide the task into steps or parts.

Each of the following statements describes a learning situation. Choose the rule that is applied in each situation.

5. Sam practices the hardest lines of the musical score first. Which rule is he following?

   (1) stagger (2) imitate (3) practice
   (4) evaluate (5) parcel

   ① ② ③ ④ ⑤

6. Right after Mercedes practices a lay-up in basketball, she asks the coach to tell her how she can improve. Which rule is she following?

   (1) stagger (2) imitate (3) practice
   (4) evaluate (5) parcel

   ① ② ③ ④ ⑤

7. Charlie plans to study half an hour before and after dinner for his Spanish test. Which rule is he following?

   (1) stagger (2) imitate (3) practice
   (4) evaluate (5) parcel

   ① ② ③ ④ ⑤

Directions: Choose the one best answer to each question. Answers are on page 313.

Items 8–9 refer to the following passage.

Hindus in India are divided into castes. A caste is an exclusive group whose members eat only with one another, marry only other members of their caste, and often do the same kind of work. Each caste is ranked as either more or less clean than other castes. Brahmans belong to the "purest" castes. Brahmans believe that unclean blood can taint their spirit. So they abstain from meat and eat only food prepared by other Brahmans. Some Brahmans will not eat even beets because they are the color of blood. At the bottom of Indian society are the Untouchables. In the 1800s, Untouchables were not allowed on the roads because they might contaminate others. Even among Untouchables, there are rankings. A leather worker would not speak to a sweeper, for instance, and a washerman is too good to eat with either one of them.

8. Which of the careers below would a conscientious Brahman most likely follow?

(1) surgeon (2) dentist (3) butcher
(4) chef (5) cobbler

① ② ③ ④ ⑤

9. Which of the following practices found in the United States is most like the caste system in India?

(1) sexism (2) ageism
(3) segregation (4) integration
(5) affirmative action

① ② ③ ④ ⑤

What Is Sociology? Sociology is the study of how people live together in social groups—history, organization, development, and problems. Sociologists are people who are experts in the field of sociology. They study how important being part of a group is to people. For example, a sociologist may examine how each member of a family relates to the group and what role he or she plays. By studying something as common as conversation at the supper table, a sociologist can discover how the group functions together.

Sociologists even study romance. Americans cringe at the idea of an arranged marriage. But it seems that we do not choose our mates as freely as we think. Studies show that most of us tend to marry people very much like ourselves in looks, attitudes, and **values.** To a large degree, group pressure and **norms** influence our choice of a husband or a wife. Marriages still are arranged in some **societies.** These societies believe that older people can make better choices than their children can. If the two do not love each other when they are married, it is believed that love will come in time. Surprisingly, studies show that arranged marriages are just as successful and happy as freely chosen marriages.

Coming to Terms

value idea about what is good or desirable. A person's values influence his or her attitudes and behavior.
norm written or unwritten rule of behavior that defines how people are supposed to behave
society people living together as a group

Warm-up

In your own words, sum up the conclusion of the studies on the two kinds of marriages described above.

____

____

____

____

Sample Warm-up Answer
The studies showed that the success and happiness of arranged and freely chosen marriages was about the same.

Groups Most human behavior is learned from other humans. A child learns how to act by watching its parents and older siblings. To keep society at large running smoothly a similar kind of socialization is necessary. It involves written rules such as traffic laws as well as unwritten rules. An example of an unwritten rule is personal space. You automatically stand just the right distance from a stranger so that he or she is not threatened or uncomfortable. But this "right" distance varies from region to region. **Socialization** has taught you the norm for personal space in your cultural region.

Someone who breaks the rules of society is considered a deviant. Some forms of deviance are tolerated, others are not and might result in the loss of friends, the loss of a job, or even imprisonment.

☑ A Test-Taking Tip

Many items on the GED Social Studies Test will require you to use graphs. Make sure that you read the label on each axis so you understand what the graph is showing.

Coming to Terms

socialization process through which a person learns skills, values, attitudes, and norms. The person also develops a sense of self and learns his or her place in society.

Warm-up

You know that you can discover the meaning of words by studying the way they are used in context. This skill will be helpful to you on the GED Test. Find *deviant* and *deviance* in the above column. Study how they are used, and then write a definition for each word.

1. deviant ______________________

____

2. deviance ______________________

____

Need a Hint for Number 10?
Notice that the question asks you to find the choice that does not *fit the role of an agent of socialization.*

Sample Warm-up Answers
1. someone who breaks the rules of society **2.** an act that goes against the norm

10. A person who teaches an individual how to become a part of society is called an "agent of socialization." Which of the following people would not be an agent of socialization for a four-year-old child?

    (1) a baby brother
    (2) parents
    (3) a baby-sitter
    (4) a nursery-school teacher
    (5) a television actor

    ① ② ③ ④ ⑤

Items 11–12 refer to the following graph.

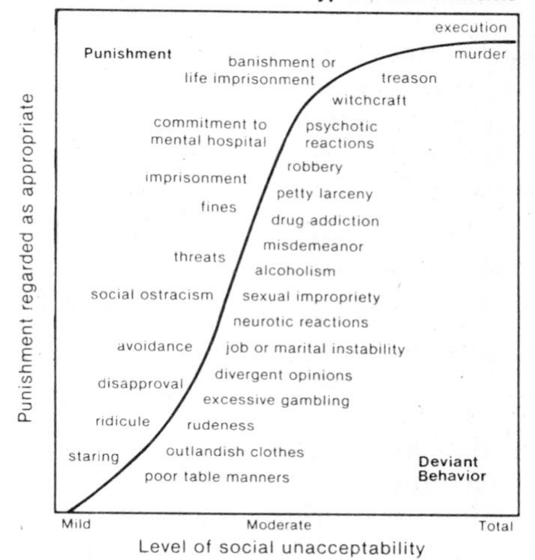

11. How are the mildest forms of deviance punished?

    (1) ridicule (2) fines (3) threats
    (4) staring (5) avoidance

    ① ② ③ ④ ⑤

12. Which of the following qualities would a society reflected in the graph value most?

    (1) courtesy (2) patriotism
    (3) sobriety (4) honesty
    (5) stability

    ① ② ③ ④ ⑤

Directions: Choose the one best answer to each question. Answers are on page 313.

13. Status is a person's position in society. Some people, like kings, are born into high-status roles. Others achieve a high status later on in life. Which of the following Americans has achieved his or her high status?

(1) a wealthy surgeon at a private hospital
(2) a Daughter of the American Revolution
(3) the heir to a candy-making company
(4) the grandson of a President
(5) the sister of an artist

(1) (2) (3) (4) (5)

14. The status of female workers is lower than that of male workers.

Which of the following pieces of evidence could be used to support this conclusion?

(1) The number of women in the work force is increasing.
(2) More men than women have low-paying jobs.
(3) Females receive about 64 percent of the salary that males with the same education receive.
(4) Women are less prepared than are men who do the same kinds of jobs.
(5) Women must often leave the work force for extended periods of time to have and raise children.

(1) (2) (3) (4) (5)

15. A person has more than one role. Role conflict develops when he or she has to fill incompatible roles at the same time. Which of the following pairs of roles would most likely cause role conflict?

(1) husband/father
(2) lawyer/grandmother
(3) single parent/flight attendant
(4) salesclerk/garden-club member
(5) widow/student in adult-education class

(1) (2) (3) (4) (5)

Social Status You have a **status,** or position, in this society. Your status is determined by the **roles** you play. You may be a student, an employee, a parent, and a baseball fan. You are born with some roles, such as being male or female. You achieve others, such as your job. Each role requires a certain kind of behavior. For instance, a worker should be prompt, honest, and industrious.

Other people have a higher or lower status than you. Your position depends on the value society places on your roles. This system that ranks people according to their roles is called **social stratification.** In the United States, roles often are ranked according to a person's salary and education rather than the importance of his or her job to society. For instance, a garbage collector usually is ranked lower than an advertising executive. However, society would suffer more if there were no garbage collectors than if there were no advertising executives.

Coming to Terms

status position in society
role a person's part or function
social stratification ranking of different roles based on factors such as birth, income, and education

Warm-up

On the lines for number 2 below, list three of your roles. On the lines for number 1, write a role with more status above each of your roles. On the lines for number 3, write a role with less status.

1. __________ __________ __________

2. __________ __________ __________

3. __________ __________ __________

Sample Warm-up Answers
1. mother doctor President
2. daughter X-ray technician citizen
3. niece nurse's aide illegal alien

What Is Anthropology? Humans all have certain needs in common. For example, we all need to eat. Yet what humans eat varies around the world. Nomads in the Middle East enjoy camel meat, and city dwellers in China consider fish eyes a delicacy. Most Americans, on the other hand, prefer beef to camel and would never eat fish eyes.

Anthropologists study the endless variety of human **cultures.** They ask how are human societies alike and how are they different? Difference in **customs** often make another culture seem strange. Anthropologists know that one culture is not better than another. Their goal is to remove the "blindfold" of their own culture and see the world from another point of view.

Coming to Terms

culture the way of life of a people. Culture is learned and covers all aspects of life in a certain group.
custom tradition of a specific culture

Warm-up

Read the following passage.

■ Cultures may differ widely, but they all have one thing in common—change. Some cultures change by picking up customs from other cultures. The American custom of eating at "fast-food" restaurants, for example, has spread throughout the world. Cultures, like Japan's, have adapted this custom to their way of life. The Japanese idea of fast food may include raw fish called sushi as well as hamburgers.

Then write a definition of *adapt* based on what you have learned from the passage.

____

____

____

____

Sample Warm-up Answer
Adapt means "to make something fit."

Items 16–17 refer to the following passage.

In our business world, we Japanese follow somewhat the same pattern as inside our families. For example, we have what is called the *oyabun-kobun.* The *oya* is the senior; the *ko* is the junior. My *oya* is the head of my department, who went to Keio University many years before I did. He has taken an interest in me ever since I entered the company. As my *oya,* he looks after my general welfare in all sorts of things. When I have personal problems, I always seek his advice. I, of course, pay great respect to my *oya.* I listen to him carefully and do as he says diligently. I do anything I can to increase his prestige.

16. Which family relationship is *oyabun-kobun* most like?

    (1) brother-brother (2) father-son
    (3) husband-wife (4) mother-uncle
    (5) brother-sister

    (1) (2) (3) (4) (5)

17. Which of the following changes would upset the relationship?

    (1) The *ko* gets a promotion above the *oya.*
    (2) The *ko* asks the *oya* for financial advice.
    (3) The *oya* becomes president of the company.
    (4) The *ko* marries the *oya*'s daughter.
    (5) The *oya* takes credit for a good sales year due mostly to the *ko*'s work.

    (1) (2) (3) (4) (5)

Directions: Choose the one best answer to each question. Answers are on page 313.

Items 18–19 refer to the following passage.

An intelligence tester among the Kentucky "poor whites" presented the following problem to a boy being tested: "If you went to the store and bought six cents' worth of candy and gave the clerk 10 cents, what change would you receive?" The boy replied, "I never had 10 cents, and if I had I wouldn't spend it for candy, and anyway candy is what your mother makes." The intelligence tester tried again, reformulating the problem as follows: "If you had taken 10 cows to pasture for your father and 6 of them strayed away, how many would you have left to drive home?" The boy replied, "We don't have 10 cows, but if we did and I lost 6, I wouldn't dare go home."

18. What do the boy's answers demonstrate?

    (1) He has no math ability.
    (2) He often solves word problems.
    (3) His experiences differ from those of the tester.
    (4) He is not as poor as the tester had thought.
    (5) His intelligence is way below the average middle-class boy.

    ① ② ③ ④ ⑤

19. Based on the boy's answers, which of the following qualities do poor whites in Kentucky probably value most?

    (1) imagination (2) common sense
    (3) sophistication (4) permissiveness
    (5) scholarship

    ① ② ③ ④ ⑤

Racism and Stereotypes Anthropologists have traditionally focused on exotic tribes living on remote islands or in tropical forests. Today, however, anthropological studies include modern communities, such as the United States, which is made up of more than one cultural group. Some of these studies are concerned with racism in society.

Racism—the idea that groups of people are naturally inferior—is centuries old. In recent times, racists point to the results of intelligence tests to support their claims that certain ethnic groups are inferior. The flaw in their arguments is that the tests measure what students have learned from experience. People in different parts of the country have different experiences.

Differences existing among groups generally prove to be cultural rather than inborn. For instance, a Hispanic student may have trouble in English class because only Spanish is spoken at home. But other students might label the Hispanic a slow learner or, worse yet, make the generalization that all Hispanics are slow. This type of broad, largely unfounded generalization is called a **stereotype.** Stereotypes can lead to **prejudice** or **discrimination.**

Coming to Terms

discrimination difference in attitude or treatment shown to different groups of people
prejudice opinion formed without taking time to learn all the facts. Prejudice usually leads to suspicion or intolerance of others.
stereotype a fixed image of the individuals in a group

Warm-up

Label each comment below with a *D* for discrimination, an *S* for stereotype, or a *P* for prejudice.

______ **1.** I don't care if it is illegal. I support segregation in schools.
______ **2.** I've seen a lot of World War II movies, and it's obvious that the enemy had little regard for human life.
______ **3.** All blacks are good dancers.
______ **4.** I'm sorry, miss. This club is for men only.

Warm-up Answers
1. D **2.** P **3.** S **4.** D

Culture and Identity Anthropologists often live with a group of people to learn about its culture firsthand. They study every aspect of the society: language, families, religion, economics, and politics. Before long, they have learned that culture's customs and how the customs differ from their own. For instance, one anthropologist learned that the Tuareg in Libya wear cotton robes dyed a dark blue that rubs off on their skin. The Tuareg are very proud of their skin's blue cast. Many Americans, on the other hand, buy only colorfast clothing because they don't like dye coming off on their underwear, much less their skin.

But anthropology is much more concerned with what people have in common than with differences. Have you ever leafed through an old family album? In one picture is a great uncle with eyes like your father's. In another is your great-grandmother with curly hair like yours. These are the kinds of things anthropologists are looking for in their studies. Why do people throughout the world love music? Why do so many groups have similar stories about how the world began? Do we share some traits and beliefs because we have common ancestors way, way back in time? Anthropologists are convinced that eventually they will find the answers.

Warm-up

Similarities between cultures abound. Read the following teaching of the Winnebago Indians.

- Be on friendly terms with everyone, and then everyone will love you.

This saying is similar to the "golden rule" in non-Indian cultures—Do unto others as you want them to do unto you.

On your own paper, write a familiar saying that means the same as this next Winnebago teaching.

- Do not imagine that you are taking your children's part if you just speak about loving them. Let them see it for themselves.

Need a Hint for Number 21?
As you read the possible answers look for a conclusion that is related to anthropology rather than to geography or psychology.

Sample Warm-up Answer
Actions speak louder than words.

Items 20–21 refer to the following passages.

In the cities along the Nile, each Egyptian pharaoh had a pyramid built for his tomb. A pyramid took 100,000 workers 20 years to build. Each stone in the pyramid weighs more than two tons, yet the stones were put together so well that, three thousand years later, you cannot slip a knife between them. Inside, the pyramids are riddled with secret passages. When a pharoah died, he was placed in his pyramid along with things he could use later on—jewelry, dishes, furniture, bows and arrows, and chariots.

About three thousand years ago, the Adena, who lived along the Ohio River, built large mounds made of earth. Inside they buried their important leaders and whatever the leaders had needed when they were alive. Among the things found were combs, hammers, flint blades, stone chisels, and bone tool-handles.

20. Which of the following things did the Egyptians and the Adena share?

    (1) desert environments
    (2) the same level of civilization
    (3) identical technology
    (4) a belief in an afterlife
    (5) similar building materials

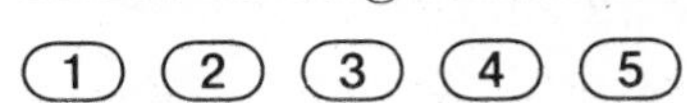

21. Which of the following conclusions would an anthropologist most likely draw from the passages?

    (1) Cultures in similar climates develop similar customs.
    (2) Recent cultures may resemble very early ones.
    (3) Some customs develop simultaneously in distant cultures.
    (4) Religion plays an important part in an individual's emotional health.
    (5) A person's status determines his or her religious beliefs.

Directions: Choose the one best answer to each question. Answers are on page 313.

Items 1–2 refer to the following passage.

Since the fall of Adam, the human race has been faced with a conflict between unlimited wants and limited resources. As individuals, we have to choose among our wants to make ourselves as well off as possible with limited amounts of income, time, and stamina. As communities, we have to choose among the needs of the community to make the community as well off as possible with its limited resources.

1. Which of the following statements best sums up the main idea of the passage?

   (1) Our economic problems started in the Garden of Eden.
   (2) Economic conflicts are caused by people wanting too much for themselves.
   (3) People and groups must prioritize their needs and wants.
   (4) People must choose between satisfying themselves or their community.
   (5) The Old Testament discusses many basic economic problems.

2. Which of the following situations involves the economic problem discussed in the paragraph?

   (1) The town of Esterville can either build a new playground or improve bicycle paths.
   (2) Chris discovers that the soccer ball he wants costs less at Sports City than at Pay Rite.
   (3) Ms. Henson's paycheck doesn't buy as much as it did last month.
   (4) Since the city of Brighton raised property taxes, fewer people are buying homes.
   (5) More companies are producing digital watches, so prices are expected to go down soon.

(1) (2) (3) (4) (5)

Economics

What Is Economics? A young tennis student won the first point of her game, and she stammered, "Uh, fifteen—um," forgetting that love is the term for zero in tennis.

"What makes the world go around?" her teacher asked.

Without any hesitation, the student responded, "Oh, fifteen—money."

That student has the makings of a good economist. Economists are experts in economics—the study of how a society fills its people's needs and wants with **goods** and **services.** This takes money, or **capital.** It also takes **technology** and natural and human resources. Sometimes a society does not have enough of these things. Then that group has a basic economic problem—scarcity.

Economic systems are ways of managing a society's or country's goods and services. In its own way, each system answers the following questions: (1) How can the greatest number of needs and wants be met? (2) What kinds and quantities of goods should be produced? (3) How should these goods be produced and for whom?

Coming to Terms

capital wealth, such as money, owned by a person or group
goods products that people use, for example, food, tires, and paper clips
services useful jobs people perform for pay
technology processes and tools used to produce goods and services

Warm-up

What factors might limit the number of goods and services in a country?

Sample Warm-up Answer
A shortage of money, resources, and technology would limit the number of goods and services.

Modern Economic Systems Goods and money are wealth. All economic systems deal with producing wealth and distributing that wealth among the people in a society.

In *market economies*, buyers and sellers compete to determine what will be produced and how. One type of market economy is *pure capitalism.* Under pure capitalism, private individuals own all the means of producing goods, and there is no limit to how much a person can own. The government doesn't interfere in business, and no welfare systems exist.

Modern capitalism, such as that in the United States, is a modified form of pure capitalism. In *modern capitalism* most property is owned privately, and there are few limits on what someone can own. There is some government regulation and some type of welfare system. Modern capitalism also is called free enterprise and is considered a mixed economy.

Another kind of mixed economy is *socialism.* Under socialism the government regulates the economy a great deal and limits how much a person can own. In fact, the government owns much property and supports a large welfare system.

Communist systems have command economies. The government controls the economy. Industry and agriculture are told what and how much to produce. The people's welfare needs are paid for totally by the government.

Warm-up

1. In two or three sentences, compare the role of government in modern capitalism, socialism, and communism.

____

____

2. In two or three sentences, compare the welfare systems under the three economies.

____

____

____

Sample Warm-up Answers
1. Under modern capitalism, government regulation of the economy is limited; under socialism, the government regulates the economy more. A communist government controls the economy completely. **2.** A capitalist government has some welfare while a socialist government has a large welfare system. A communist government pays for all its people's welfare needs.

Items 3–4 refer to the table below.

Production of Goods in U.S.S.R. 1928–1940

	1928	1933	1940
Industrial Goods			
Coal (millions of tons)	36	76	166
Steel (millions of tons)	4	7	18
Machine Tools (1000 units)	2	21	58
Trucks (1000 units)	0.7	39	136
Agricultural Goods			
Sugar (millions of tons)	2	1	3
Grain (millions of tons)	73	69	96
Cows (millions)	29	19	28

3. Which of the following statements best describes the major trend in the Soviet economy from 1928 to 1940?

(1) Both industrial and agricultural production rose sharply.
(2) Industrial and agricultural production rose slightly.
(3) Industrial production increased greatly.
(4) Agricultural production fell.
(5) Mechanization led to production increases in agriculture.

① ② ③ ④ ⑤

4. According to the table, which of the following economic plans was the Soviet Union employing from 1928 to 1940?

(1) concentration on agriculture
(2) de-emphasis on the importance of steel
(3) concentration on increasing transportation and textiles
(4) development of a strong industrial base
(5) emphasis on consumer needs

① ② ③ ④ ⑤

Directions: Choose the one best answer to each question. Answers are on page 313–314.

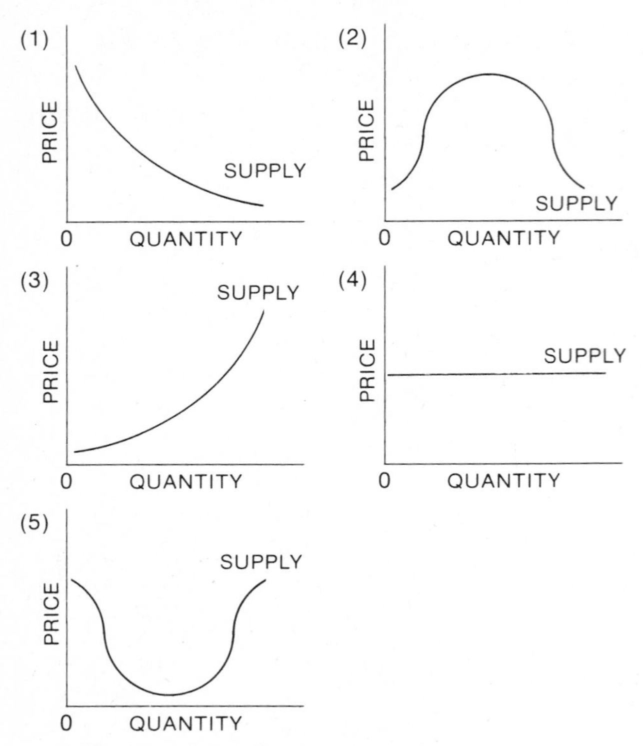

5. Which of the line graphs above represents a steady increase in supply and price?

(1) (2) (3) (4) (5)

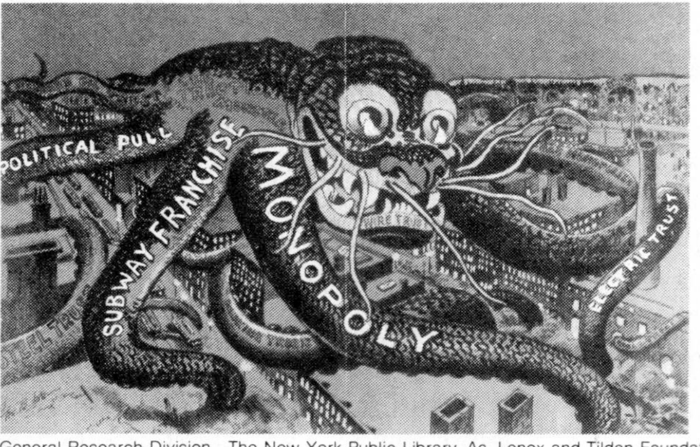

General Research Division The New York Public Library As, Lenox and Tilden Foundations

6. Which of the following statements would the cartoonist probably disagree with?
   (1) Monopolies undercut the American economic system.
   (2) Consumers are always the victims of monopolies.
   (3) Monopolies misuse political power.
   (4) Monopolies are beneficial to cities.
   (5) Government should control monopolies.

(1) (2) (3) (4) (5)

Business in a Free Enterprise System In a free enterprise system, such as that of the United States, **supply** affects prices. For example, when the supply of apples increases in the fall, their price decreases. When the supply decreases in the winter, the price increases. **Demand** also affects prices. If few consumers want a good or service, the price generally will be low to make it more attractive to buyers.

Supply and demand affect production too. Unless businesses can be reasonably sure that consumers want a product, they will not make it. In addition, businesses must set supply and prices at a level that will provide them with a profit. But the price, and, therefore, the profits, must be kept within limits.

Competition in the marketplace also affects prices. If only one company offers some good or service in demand, it is said to have a **monopoly.** That company can set its own price for the item. Most such monopolies are against the law. When several companies make the same kind of good or service, they compete in order to sell more than the next company. As a result, the price of the item goes down.

Coming to Terms

supply the available amount of a good or service at a certain price
demand the amount of a good or service people are willing to buy at a certain price
monopoly total control of a good or service

Warm-up

After reading each situation, complete the statement that follows with *increase* or *decrease.*

1. Mother's Day is this coming Sunday. The demand for flowers will ____________.

2. Recent studies show that bubble gum is hazardous to health. The price of bubble gum will ____________.

3. The price of home computers drops an average of $1000. Demand for home computers probably will ____________.

4. Deregulation causes oil prices to rise. Exploration for new sources of oil will ____________.

Warm-up Answers
1. increase **2.** decrease **3.** increase **4.** increase

Production When you buy a record, you are participating in the decision-making part of production. In a free enterprise system, consumers help decide what goods and services are offered by "voting" with their dollars. In most cases, only goods and services that they "vote" for will be produced.

Businesses determine what and how many goods and services to offer through *marketing.* Marketing is a business tool with a double edge. *Marketing research* finds out what people want, and *advertising,* the other aspect of marketing, often tells people what they want. In other words, advertising can create a demand for a good or service.

Today large numbers of goods at low prices are possible because of mass production. Mass production depends on (1) a division of labor—each worker doing one job on an **assembly line;** (2) standardization of parts—making goods so alike that their parts are interchangeable; and (3) automation—the use of machines.

☑ A Test-Taking Tip

When you come to a question on the GED Social Studies Test that refers to a passage, you may want to read the question first. Then, when you read the passage, you will know what information to look for.

Coming to Terms

assembly line arrangement of work so that it passes before several workers each of whom perform a separate task

Warm-up

How do you think assembly lines affect the care workers put into their products?

Sample Warm-up Answer
Workers probably are not committed to making a good product, because they do not have total control over how the product will come out.

7. Worst of all is the effect of advertising in making the consumer a mere target of opportunity, shamelessly manipulating his or her image of life through little dramas of sparkling kitchen floors and gleaming hair.

   Which of the following maxims exemplifies the beliefs of the advertisers referred to in the above passage?

   (1) An eye for an eye, a tooth for a tooth.
   (2) Cleanliness is next to godliness.
   (3) Do unto others as you would like them to do unto you.
   (4) The ends justify the means.
   (5) The early bird catches the worm.

Items 8–9 refer to the quotes below.

[Machines] tend to relieve the workman either from niceties of adjustment which exhaust his mind and fatigue his eyes, or from painful repetition of effort which distort or wear out his frame. Andrew Ure

Each week automation eliminates between 40,000 and 50,000 jobs . . . The loss of nearly two and a half million jobs each year, when nearly 4,000,000 young people annually enter the job market, constitutes one of the more serious problems confronting American society. Franklin D. Mitchell and Richard O. Davies

8. Which of the following statements would the authors of the two quotes most likely disagree over?

   (1) Industry fills needs and wants.
   (2) Most people require jobs to live.
   (3) Human health is of primary value.
   (4) Automation has had a tremendous impact on society.
   (5) Automation is a great boon to workers.

9. Which of the following household machines best fits Ure's description?

   (1) clothes dryer (2) dishwasher
   (3) sewing machine (4) toaster
   (5) blender

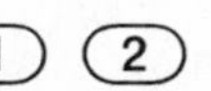

Directions: Choose the one best answer to each question. Answers are on page 314.

Items 10–11 are based on the chart below.

True Annual Percentage Rates

Lender	Dollar and Percentage Rate Charges	True Annual Percentage Rates
Credit Unions	⅔ of 1%—1% per month	8–12%
Small Loan Companies	1½%–3½% per month	18–42%
Commercial Bank	Personal loan:	
	Added-on, $6 per $100	10.90%
	Discounted, $6 per $100	11.58%
Commercial Bank	Revolving accounts and credit cards, 1%–1½% per month	12–18%
Commercial Bank	New auto loan, 5%–7% per $100	10.57–13.61%
Sales Finance Company	New auto loan, 6½%–8% per $100	12.59–15.68%
Department Stores	Revolving accounts and credit cards, 1%–1½% per month	12–18%

10. On which type of car loan could a consumer end up paying the highest rate of interest?
    (1) commercial bank loan
    (2) small loan company loan
    (3) sales finance company loan
    (4) credit union loan
    (5) loan from a relative at 3 percent a month

    (1) (2) (3) (4) (5)

11. How would a consumer with a large unpaid balance on a credit card from a department store save the most money?
    (1) paying off the debt with a credit card
    (2) making the minimum monthly payment on the balance
    (3) taking out a loan with a small loan company to pay off the balance
    (4) getting a loan from his or her credit union to pay off the balance
    (5) getting a personal loan from a commercial bank

    (1) (2) (3) (4) (5)

Consumers People have to decide how to meet their needs and wants. As consumers, Americans are bombarded by advertisements. The following laws and government and private agencies help protect consumers:

Better Business Bureau—network of local business associations that registers complaints about firms and makes that information available to the public

Consumers Union—publishes reports on the quality of products

Small Claims Court—gives consumers a way to regain damages from local businesses

Truth-in-Lending Act—says that a lender must tell a borrower exactly what credit will cost

Truth-in-Packaging Act—says that food packages must state weight and ingredients

Food and Drug Administration—protects consumers against dangerous foods, drugs, and cosmetics

Federal Trade Commission—fights false and misleading advertising

Warm-up

The Consumer Price Index (CPI) measures the average change in the prices of about 400 goods and services since 1967.

Average Consumer Price Indexes

	1978 Index	1980 Index	1982 Index	1984 Index
All items	195.3	247.0	288.6	311.1
Food, drink	206.2	248.7	278.5	295.1
Housing	202.6	263.2	314.7	336.5
Apparel upkeep	159.5	177.4	190.9	200.2
Transportation	185.8	250.5	293.1	311.7
Medical care	219.4	267.2	326.9	379.5
Entertainment	176.2	203.7	232.4	255.1
Other	183.2	213.6	257.0	307.7

On your own paper, complete the bar graph below using the data in the table. Which bar on your graph shows the greatest increase over a two-year period?

Increases in the CPI, 1978—1984

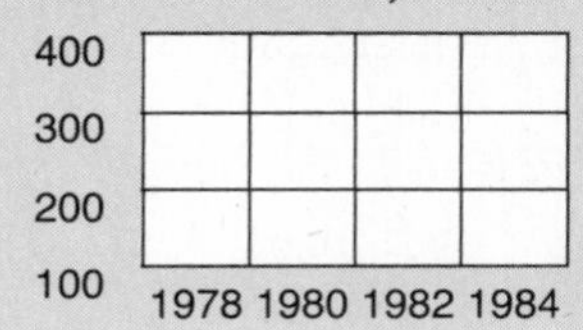

Warm-up Answers

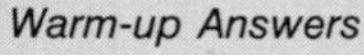

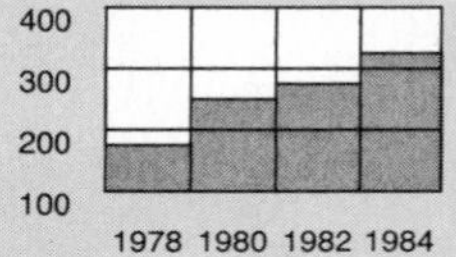

1980 shows the greatest increase over a two-year period

Financial Institutions A budget is a plan for allocating money. Most people's budgets allow them to save at least a small part of their income. The most common places for saving money are banks and savings and loan associations. These help you to manage your money in a variety of ways. For instance, you may put all your money into one of their interest-earning checking accounts. You can write checks to pay bills, and at the same time, make money on what remains in the account. Or you may choose to buy a certificate of deposit. With a certificate, your money earns a high rate of interest. But if you withdraw the deposit before an agreed-upon time, you will have to give up all or a large chunk of the interest.

Not everybody manages their money through banks. Investment firms and insurance companies offer plans like Individual Retirement Accounts (IRAs). People open IRAs because either they are not covered by pension plans at work or they want to supplement an existing pension plan. There are also Keogh retirement plans for the self-employed.

Another place to save is a **credit union.** Credit unions are sponsored by unions and companies for the use of their members and employees.

The U.S. government also encourages its people to save. One way it does this is by offering savings bonds. When you buy a **bond,** you lend money to the government, which pays back the loan with interest.

Coming to Terms

credit union group of people with a common interest that save together
bond certificate of debt issued by a private company or a government that promises to pay back a loan with interest at a certain time

Warm-up

What is one advantage of saving money at a financial institution like a bank rather than at home in a mattress?

____

____

____

Sample Warm-up Answer
Financial institutions offer interest.

Items 12–14 refer to the following information.

The items below are part of many people's budgets:

(1) fixed expense—a financial commitment that does not vary
(2) variable expense—a cost that is necessary but can be changed or controlled
(3) luxury expense—a cost that is nonessential but provides pleasure
(4) emergency—savings as protection against illness or job loss
(5) retirement—savings in addition to social security

12. Fred's grocery bills were high during the holiday season because of houseguests. Which category does the extra expense fall under?

    (1) fixed expense (2) variable expense
    (3) luxury expense (4) emergency
    (5) retirement

    ① ② ③ ④ ⑤

13. If Maria can find the time and money, she would like to take guitar lessons. Which category would the cost of the lessons be in?

    (1) fixed expense (2) variable expense
    (3) luxury expense (4) emergency
    (5) retirement

    ① ② ③ ④ ⑤

14. Each month Yoko and Cynthia pay $425 rent. Which category does this expense belong in?

    (1) fixed expense (2) variable expense
    (3) luxury expense (4) emergency
    (5) retirement

    ① ② ③ ④ ⑤

Directions: Choose the one best answer to each question. Answers are on page 314.

Items 15–16 refer to the graph below.

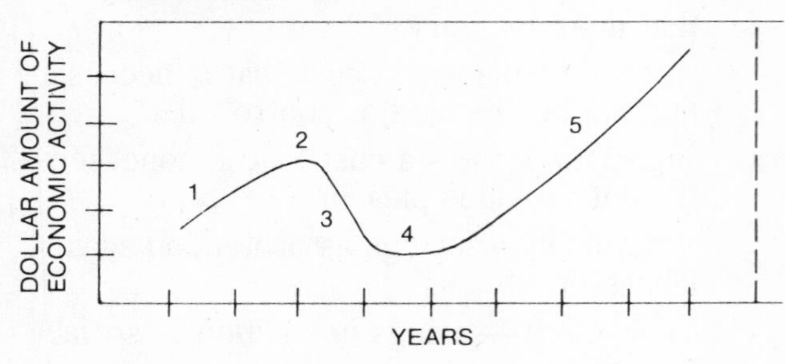

1 Recovery
2 Prosperity
3 Recession
4 Depression
5 Inflation

15. Which of the following phrases best predicts what would happen if the graph were to be continued for additional years?

(1) continued prosperity
(2) continued inflation
(3) repetition of the cycle
(4) depressed but stable economy
(5) collapse of the economy

(1) (2) (3) (4) (5)

16. Factory after factory closed down. Soon there were so few goods that prices soared. Now many companies have decided to reopen their factories to meet the increased demand. Which part of the economic cycle comes next?

(1) recovery (2) prosperity
(3) recession (4) depression
(5) inflation

How the Overall Economy Behaves In its economic history, the United States has experienced bad times and good times. Declines in employment and economic activity occur regularly. These declines are called *recessions.* During 1819, 1837, 1873, and 1893, recessions deepened into short depressions. The years between 1929 and 1940 are known as the Great Depression. There also have been periods of **inflation.** Despite this **business cycle** of recession and prosperity, the U.S. economy has grown steadily.

Coming to Terms

inflation a general rise in prices
business cycle business activity that alternates in stages of prosperity and recession

Warm-up

Study the following table showing the percentage of unemployment in the United States for certain years.

Year	% Unemployed	Year	% Unemployed
1924	5.0	1960	5.5
1928	4.2	1964	5.2
1932	23.6	1968	3.6
1936	16.9	1972	5.6
1940	14.6	1976	7.7
1944	1.2	1980	7.1
1948	3.8	1984	7.5
1952	3.0		
1956	4.1		

1. How did unemployment during the Great Depression (1932, 1936, and 1940) differ from unemployment at other times?

2. Unemployment was lowest in the wartime years of 1944, 1952, and 1968 (World War II, Korean War, and Vietnam War). Why do you think unemployment is generally low in wartime?

Need a Hint for Number 15?
From your own experience, what happens with any kind of cycle?

Sample Warm-up Answers
1. Unemployment during the Great Depression was from 2 to 20 times greater than that in any other year. **2.** Many people work for the military and in war-related industries.

Government's Role in the Economy Although the United States has a free enterprise system, the government is very much involved in the economy. It helps businesses at home and abroad; tries to avoid recessions, depressions, and inflation; helps individuals who are out of work; and protects consumers and the environment. A few examples of how government influences the economy follow.

Taxation In order to pay for government services, individuals and companies pay taxes on income, property, and purchases. Sometimes the government uses taxes to affect the spending habits of Americans. A tax cut can increase spending and business activity because people have more money to spend. A tax hike slows spending, inflation, and business activity.

Monetary Policy The Federal Reserve System is the central banking system of the United States. It controls the flow of credit and money to allow orderly economic growth.

Social Security Begun in the 1930s, social security includes welfare, Medicare, and unemployment benefits. These programs help retirees, the jobless, and the disabled.

Environmental Protection The Environmental Protection Agency, the Department of the Interior, and various state agencies monitor industrial pollution. They set guidelines for acceptable levels of pollution and suggest ways to clean up damages caused by pollution.

☑ A Test-Taking Tip

When it comes to economics, you probably know more than you think you do. You make economic decisions every day. So if a question on the GED Social Studies Test seems technical, don't panic. Use your common sense to decide the answer.

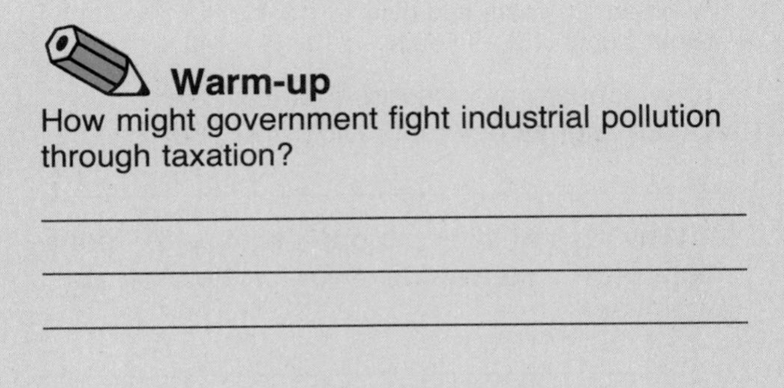

Warm-up

How might government fight industrial pollution through taxation?

Sample Warm-up Answer
The government might offer tax breaks to businesses that install pollution-reducing devices in their factories.

17. Tight money limits the loans that banks make. Borrowers find it difficult—and very expensive—to take out a loan. So businesses compete for the fewer dollars that consumers have to spend. Which of the following situations probably would result from tight money?

    (1) bargain air fares
    (2) new housing boom
    (3) flood of new restaurants
    (4) soaring automobile prices
    (5) expansion of farms

    (1) (2) (3) (4) (5)

18. Supply-side economists believe that if government cuts taxes and deregulates banks, businesses will have more money to expand and to hire new workers. Who most likely would suffer under a supply-side economy?

    (1) employees with seniority
    (2) public school children
    (3) small business owners
    (4) recent college graduates
    (5) suppliers of office furniture

    (1) (2) (3) (4) (5)

Directions: Choose the one best answer to each question. Answers are on page 314.

Items 19–20 refer to the graph below.

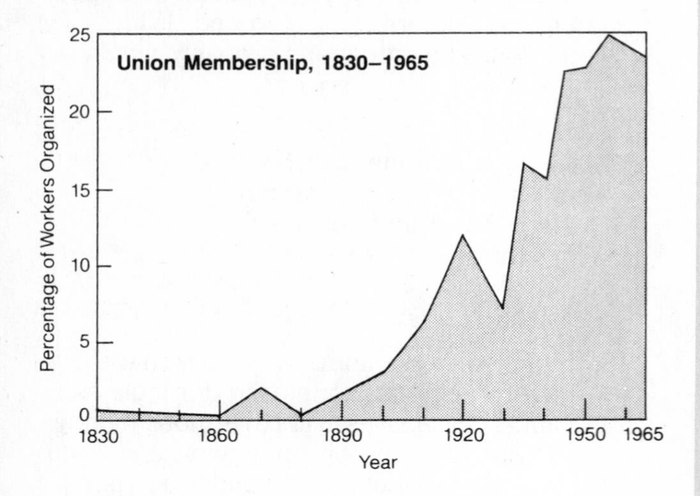

19. During which of the following years were workers probably most dissatisfied with their employers?

    (1) 1830 (2) 1860 (3) 1880
    (4) 1920 (5) 1930

    1 2 3 4 5

20. In the 1920s union leaders were accused of being agents for communist governments. What probably happened in light of the data on the above graph?

    (1) Most workers rallied around the unions.
    (2) Many members left the unions out of fear.
    (3) Thousands of immigrants from communist countries joined the unions.
    (4) The government passed a law that kept union membership intact.
    (5) The unions totally collapsed.

       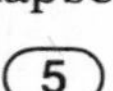 5

Labor and the Economy In the late 1930s the Wagner Act gave labor the right to organize and to negotiate contracts. This led to the use of collective bargaining as we know it today. *Collective bargaining* is the negotiating between employer and union representatives. Together they hammer out agreements on wages, working conditions, and fringe benefits. When employers and unions fail to agree, workers often strike, or stop working.

The government may step in to settle a strike. The government also sometimes sets wage and price controls. In addition, it provides unemployment benefits and enforces laws against unfair employers and unsafe working conditions.

In recent years, union membership has fallen because unemployment has remained high. The unions' main bargaining chip, a strike, is less effective when hundreds of jobless workers are willing to fill in. Besides, many workers are entering new, nonunionized fields.

☑ A Test-Taking Tip

In passages on the GED Test, look for words and phrases with meanings similar to those in the item choices. Then read the context in which these words and phrases appear. This will give you clues to the correct choice.

Warm-up

1. Study the chart and answer the question.

U.S. Labor Force Unemployment Rates

	1981	1985
White, total	6.7	6.2
Men, 20 years and older	5.6	5.2
Women, 20 years and older	5.9	5.9
Both sexes, 16–19 years	17.3	16.1
Black, total	15.6	15.6
Men, 20 years and older	13.5	13.6
Women, 20 years and older	13.4	13.7
Both sexes, 16–19 years	41.4	40.4

For which two groups did unemployment worsen slightly between 1981 and 1985?

____

2. Why do you think job opportunities for teens might have increased and not for the older unemployed?

____

____

Sample Warm-up Answers

1. black men and women **2.** Teens probably took minimum wage jobs that older workers passed up.

Foreign Trade The United States obtains goods it cannot produce through foreign trade. Our country **imports** such products as tin, rubber, tea, coffee, and bananas. The United States also **exports** products. More than one-half the wheat and soybeans grown in the United States is sold abroad. Factory workers as well as farmers depend on the sale of goods to other countries. In fact, one out of every six jobs in America is linked to foreign trade.

International trade is regulated by tariffs and quotas set by national governments. Every country would like to have a balance-of-trade surplus—that is, to export more than it imports. But since 1950, the United States has had a balance-of-trade deficit. In other words, it has bought more abroad than it has sold abroad.

Coming to Terms

imports buys goods from other countries
exports sells goods to other countries

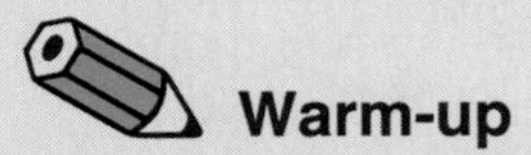

Warm-up

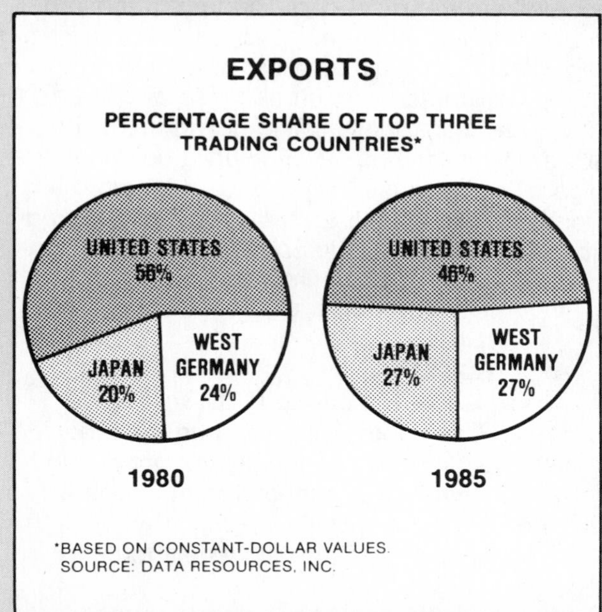

Which of the countries shown on the graphs does the caption refer to? Explain your answer.

Sample Warm-up Answer
The United States lost ground because the value of its exports decreased between 1980 and 1985.

21. Which of the people quoted below would support a protectionist policy?

    I. "Those cheap foreign cars cost me my job."—unemployed auto worker
    II. "I want the best bargain whatever the brand name is."—consumer
    III. "We've got to decrease import sales somehow—either higher tariffs or import quotas."—congressperson from Michigan
    IV. "It's not fair to make consumers pay more for an inferior product. American companies won't save jobs; they'll just make higher profits."—consumer advocate
    V. "American industry has to increase its efficiency and productivity. The challenge is to compete with foreign manufacturers, not exclude them." —economist

    (1) I, III (2) II, IV, V
    (3) I, II, III (4) V (5) II, IV

    1 2 3 4 5

U.S. sales in billions, 1980		U.S. purchases in billions, 1980	
Our Ten Best Customers		Our Ten Main Suppliers	
Canada	$35	Canada	$41
Japan	21	Japan	31
Mexico	15	Mexico	13
Britain	13	Saudi Arabia	13
West Germany	11	West Germany	12
Netherlands	9	Nigeria	11
France	8	Britain	10
Saudi Arabia	6	Taiwan	7
Italy	6	Venezuela	5
Venezuela	5	France	5

22. Based on the table above, which of the following statements was true of world trade in 1980?

    (1) The U.S. trade deficit was $20 billion.
    (2) The U.S. trade surplus was $20 billion.
    (3) The biggest U.S. trade deficit was with Canada.
    (4) The United States bought less from Mexico than it sold to that country.
    (5) The ten main U.S. suppliers are the ten main customers.

    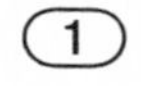    5

Directions: Choose the one best answer to each question. Answers are on page 314.

Items 1–2 are based on the following passage.

Listed below are definitions of five types of government.

(1) direct democracy—all qualified citizens can participate in lawmaking
(2) representative democracy—voters elect representatives to make the laws
(3) oligarchy—a small privileged group makes the laws
(4) constitutional monarchy—a royal family has ceremonial power but elected representatives make the laws
(5) dictatorship—one person has absolute power to make laws and all other government decisions

1. All the men in each of early Virginia's eleven settlements elected two representatives called burgesses. In 1619, the twenty-two burgesses met in Jamestown to write Virginia's laws. The type of government described is a(n)

   (1) direct democracy
   (2) representative democracy
   (3) oligarchy
   (4) constitutional monarchy
   (5) dictatorship

   (1) (2) (3) (4) (5)

2. In 1922, Benito Mussolini convinced the people of Italy that communists would take over if they did not give him complete control of the government. Once Mussolini was elected prime minister, he did away with all his political opponents. The type of government described is a(n)

   (1) direct democracy
   (2) representative democracy
   (3) oligarchy
   (4) constitutional monarchy
   (5) dictatorship

   (1) (2) (3) (4) (5)

Political Science

A word may have two very different meanings. For example, have you ever used *bad* to mean *good? Political* also has negative and positive meanings—"having to do with schemes to achieve power" and "pertaining to the science and art of government." In both senses of the word, *political* often is used to discuss governments. In fact, the study of governments is called *political science*.

Importance of Government Governments are systems of rule. At their best, governments help life run smoothly and safely for their citizens. Examples are easy to think of: traffic regulation, public education, road construction, and much more. Imagine the confusion if there were no laws or no police to enforce them. At their worst, governments destroy freedom. Many governments throughout the world today deprive individual people of liberty and even life.

Types of Government At one time, monarchies in which a king or queen held absolute power were the most common form of government. However, most monarchies today are limited. Elected officials do most of the governing. Some governments, such as those of Chile and Libya, are dictatorships. The governments of the Soviet Union and other communist countries are oligarchies because they are ruled by small groups. In the United States the majority of registered voters rules. We call our type of government *representative democracy*.

Warm-up

Many political terms on the GED Test come from the Greek and Latin. Knowing the meaning of certain word parts may help you understand unfamiliar terms. Using what you have read about different kinds of government, write each Greek or Latin word part below next to its English meaning.

oli- demo- mono- -archy

few ____________________

leader ____________________

people ____________________

alone ____________________

Warm-up Answers
oli = few; demo = people; mono = one; archy = leader

Ideals in Action The ideals of democracy are best stated in the Declaration of Independence. One well-known passage explains the people's role in government:

■ governments are instituted among men, deriving their just powers from the consent of the governed; that, whenever any form of government becomes destructive of these ends, it is the right of the people to alter or to abolish it . . .

In a democracy, the government is only as powerful as its people allow it to be. Laws must be obeyed to be effective. One law that was generally ignored was prohibition. Many people in the 1920s and early 1930s made and sold alcohol illegally. Prohibition was repealed in 1933, but, in reality, the people had done away with it long before that.

The Constitution After the War for Independence, the United States' new government under the Articles of Confederation was too weak to run the country effectively. In 1787, American leaders drew up a **federalist** plan of government—the Constitution. Anti-Federalists feared that a strong central government would eliminate the power of the states. So the authors of the Constitution listed the powers of the federal and state governments. Federal laws would affect the country at large and other nations. State laws would affect businesses, individuals, and local governments within the borders of each state. Many Americans worried that the Constitution still did not protect the rights of states and individuals. So the **Bill of Rights** was added in 1791. The Constitution works today because it provides for (1) a strong central government and (2) flexibility. The so-called "elastic clause" allows Congress "to make all laws which are necessary and proper."

Coming to Terms

federalist system in which central and state governments share power
Bill of Rights first ten amendments to the Constitution

Warm-up

Do you think the power to coin money belongs to the states or the central government? On your own paper, explain your answer.

Sample Warm-up Answer
central government, because the same money is used in all the states

<u>Items 3–4</u> refer to the following passage from the Constitution.

Section 10, Clause 2. No state shall, without the consent of Congress, lay any imposts or duties on imports or exports, except that may be absolutely necessary for executing its inspection laws; and the net produce of all duties and imposts, laid by any state on imports or exports, shall be for the use of the Treasury of the United States; and all such laws shall be subject to the revision and control of Congress.

3. What power of the states is referred to in the above clause?

   (1) levying taxes
   (2) borrowing money
   (3) chartering banks
   (4) making laws about contracts
   (5) regulating interstate trade

   (1) (2) (3) (4) (5)

4. Which of the following Constitutional principles is best illustrated by the clause?

   (1) States must not coin money.
   (2) Congress may collect taxes for defense.
   (3) National laws are above state laws.
   (4) Congress can make all necessary and proper laws.
   (5) Congress must not tax goods sent from one state to another.

   (1) (2) (3) (4) (5)

5. Amendment 1: Congress shall make no law respecting an establishment of religion, or prohibiting the free exercise thereof; or abridging the freedom of speech, or of the press; or the right of the people peaceably to assemble, and to petition the government for a redress of grievances.

   The First Amendment forbids

   (1) protests against the government
   (2) censorship of newspapers
   (3) meetings of the Communist Party
   (4) the founding of new religions
   (5) cruel and unusual punishments

Directions: Choose the one best answer to each question. Answers are on page 314.

Items 6–7 are based on the following passage.

For every 100 votes cast for the national ticket of each major political party in the United States, the Democratic 100 votes will include more young persons, more Catholics, more urban residents, more labor-union members, more southerners, more low-income persons, more Negroes, more Jews and recent immigrants in general, more lower class and more poorly educated persons than every 100 Republican votes. The 100 Republican votes would contain more older persons, Protestants, rural and small-town residents, professional and managerial persons, northerners, wealthy, whites, English, Scotch, German and Scandinavians, upper class and well educated.

6. Which of the following persons is most likely a Republican?

(1) an 18-year-old black
(2) a Cambodian refugee
(3) a Jewish Chicagoan
(4) a North Dakota minister
(5) a member of the United Auto Workers

(1) (2) (3) (4) (5)

7. Which of the following statements most accurately sums up an idea from the passage?

(1) Most Jewish Democrats are poorly educated.
(2) There are more Catholic than Protestant Democrats.
(3) Most Republicans are wealthy.
(4) Republicans over 65 outnumber those under 35.
(5) More farmers vote Republican than Democrat.

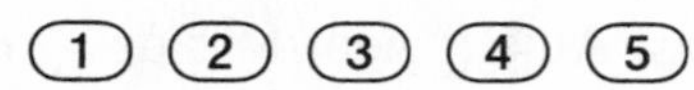

Right to Vote The most stirring definition of American democracy comes from Abraham Lincoln's Gettysburg Address: "government of the people, by the people, for the people." Ironically more than half the American people were not allowed to vote when Lincoln gave the Address. Since then, amendments to the Constitution have given blacks, women, Indians, and people between the ages of 18 and 21 the right to vote.

Political Parties The first political parties in the United States were the Federalists and Anti-Federalists. President John Adams once wrote to a friend that even though political parties existed in America since the first colonists arrived, the parties served a purpose. The parties do not cause the struggle for power, but are useful in controlling and directing that struggle.

First, political parties use the nomination process to find people capable of holding office. Second, they organize campaigns to present their candidates and their views to the voters. Third, the parties supply election officials who make voting day run smoothly. And finally, the parties recommend qualified candidates for appointive offices.

Party leaders are influenced greatly by public opinion polls when they select candidates. Polling companies like Gallup find out what a sample population of the voters thinks about candidates or issues. Parties also are influenced by special-interest groups. These groups often support a particular party in return for a promise of action on a certain issue.

Today the major political parties are the Democrats and Republicans. Democrats traditionally are middle or lower class and advocate change, while Republicans are upper or upper-middle class and oppose change. But many voters identify themselves as "independent Democrats" or "independent Republicans" and do not vote a straight party ticket.

Warm-up

Why do you think Republicans traditionally oppose change? ______________________

____

____

Sample Warm-up Answer

Change may affect their standing in the upper or upper-middle class.

Separation of Powers The federal government has three branches: executive (President), (2) legislative (Congress), and (3) judicial (Supreme Court and other federal courts). The Constitution provides a system of checks and balances that prevent any single branch of government from controlling the others.

The Executive Branch The head of the executive branch is the President. A candidate for President must be 35 years of age or older, have been born a citizen of the United States, and have lived in the United States for fourteen years. The President's main duty is to carry out laws. In addition, the President makes treaties with foreign governments, commands the armed forces, appoints judges and other officials, and pardons criminals.

The Vice-President The Vice-President succeeds the President in case he or she dies, resigns, or cannot continue in office for some other reason. As President of the Senate, the Vice-President casts the deciding vote when the senators are divided evenly on an issue.

The Cabinet The Constitution does not provide for a group of advisors to the President. But since the time of Washington, Presidents have appointed Cabinet officials to oversee different parts of the government. The Cabinet today includes the following officials: Attorney General, Secretary of State, Secretary of the Treasury, Secretary of Defense, Secretary of the Interior, Secretary of Agriculture, Secretary of Commerce, Secretary of Labor, Secretary of Health and Human Services, Secretary of Housing and Urban Development, Secretary of Transportation, Secretary of Energy, and Secretary of Education.

☑ A Test-Taking Tip

As you answer questions on the GED Test, apply generalizations. Consider the question "Which powers of the President check the legislature?" By reminding yourself that "legislatures make laws," you can narrow the choices to those that refer to lawmaking.

Warm-up

Think of projects that each Cabinet member might oversee. For instance, which Cabinet member would allocate funds for research in generating electricity with ocean tides?

____

____

Warm-up Answer
the Secretary of Energy

8. The President checks the legislature and judiciary by rejecting laws, influencing public opinion, calling special sessions of Congress, appointing judges, and pardoning criminals. Which of the following powers of the legislature and judiciary checks the President?

(1) impeaching judges
(2) interpreting laws
(3) ruling laws unconstitutional
(4) approving appointments
(5) proposing amendments

(1) (2) (3)  (5)

<u>Item 9</u> refers to the following passage.

The President is the most powerful public official in the United States. The Constitution grants the President powers to perform four roles: foreign-policy leader, commander in chief, chief executive, and chief legislator. As foreign-policy leader, the President receives foreign officials, determines how the nation acts toward other countries, and makes treaties which the Senate must approve. The President holds the title of commander in chief and is in charge of the armed forces. The President's job as chief executive is to carry out the laws passed by Congress and to appoint top government officials. As chief legislator, the President shapes what the business of Congress will be. Besides these important roles, the President has assumed other tasks that were not written into the Constitution. For example, the President plans the government budget and influences the economy. The President is also considered chief of the political party that helped elect him or her.

9. According to the passage, which of the following duties is NOT performed by the President?

(1) choosing a person to head the Department of Commerce
(2) speaking at a political party's policy meeting
(3) deciding to strengthen military bases in Western Europe
(4) hearing court cases on national issues
(5) going to Argentina to meet with the president

(1) (2)   

Directions: Choose the one best answer to each question. Answers are on page 314.

10. Each state sends two senators to Congress. Which of the following states benefits most from this system of representation?

(1) Illinois (2) New York
(3) Pennsylvania (4) California
(5) Wyoming

(1) (2) (3) (4) (5)

Items 11–12 refer to the following quotes.

"The alternative to unlimited debate is gag rule." Senator Herman Talmadge

"The Senate has a duty to debate, but. . . . We are obligated not only to pass laws, but also to pass them in time to meet the public need." Senator Jacob Javits

11. Which of the following alternatives to unlimited debate shows that Senator Talmadge's argument is flawed?

(1) set a time limit on debate
(2) encourage absentee voting
(3) pass laws without discussion
(4) discuss laws only in closed committees
(5) allow expression of only the majority opinion

(1) (2) (3) (4) (5)

12. Which of the following facts best justifies Senator Javits's point of view?

(1) The British House of Commons gave up their right to unlimited debate.
(2) Senator Thurmond once spoke for 24 hours.
(3) James Madison favored unlimited debate.
(4) Unlimited debate is a long-standing Senate rule.
(5) Limited debate gives the majority an advantage over the minority.

(1) (2) (3) (4) (5)

The Legislative Branch (Congress) The United States has a **bicameral** legislature made up of two houses: the Senate and the House of Representatives. Together the two houses are often referred to as Congress. The Senate has 100 members. A senator has to be 30 years of age or older, a U.S. citizen for at least nine years, and living in the state he or she represents. The House of Representatives has 435 members. A representative has to be 25 years of age or older, a citizen of the United States for seven years, and living in the state he or she represents.

Powers of Congress Lawmaking is the main role of Congress. **Bills** become laws only if both houses approve them. Other powers of Congress include declaring war and levying taxes. The House of Representatives has the "power of the purse strings." This means that bills to allocate money can be introduced only in the House. Also, the House of Representatives has the power to **impeach** the President and federal judges. It is the Senate, however, which holds the impeachment trials. In addition, the Senate approves appointments and treaties.

Making Laws To introduce a bill, a senator or representative sends it to the clerk of the house. The clerk forwards it to the appropriate committee. There the bill may be tabled, or killed. If the bill passes in committee, it goes to the floor, where congresspersons debate the bill and often change it. After the debate, a vote is taken. If the bill is voted down, it dies; if the bill passes, it is sent to the other house.

There the bill is again debated. If the bill is passed without changes, it goes straight to the President. If the congress members have made changes and pass the bill in its new form, the bill must go to a joint committee of senators and representatives. They hammer out a compromise bill, which is then voted on by both houses. If the majority vote in favor of the revised bill, it goes to the President.

The President may sign the bill into law or **veto** it. If the President vetoes the bill, two-thirds of the members of Congress would have to vote for the bill to make it law and to override the President's veto.

Read the inner column on the following page before attempting the questions in the outer column on this page.

☑ A Test-Taking Tip

As you learn new social studies terms, try writing each on an index card along with a definition you can easily remember. Review the terms periodically so you will remember them while taking the GED Social Studies Test.

Coming to Terms

bicameral having two legislative houses
bill proposed law
impeach accuse a public official of wrongdoing during his or her term of office
veto the power of a President to reject bills passed by a lawmaking body

Warm-up

Write the number of each of the following questions or steps in the correct space in the flowchart below. Hints: The < >'s represent questions; the [ ]'s represent steps. Also, a number can be used more than once. Some of the numbers already have been filled in for you.

1. A bill is introduced in the Senate.
2. Does the Senate pass the bill?
3. Does the committee pass the bill?
4. Does Congress approve the joint-committee version?
5. The bill dies.
6. The bill goes to the House.
7. The bill is sent to the Senate floor.
8. The bill goes to a joint committee.
9. The bill goes to a Senate committee.
10. Does the bill pass the House?
11. Has the House amended the bill?
12. The bill goes to the President.

```
(1)--->[   ]---><   >-yes->[   ]---><   >-yes->[   ]
              no                      no              |
             [   ]                   [   ]            |
                                                      v
     [   ]<-no-<   ><---[   ]<-yes-<11><-yes-<   >
                |                     no         no
                L----yes--------->[12]          [   ]
```

Warm-up Answer

```
(1)--->[ 9 ]---->< 3 >-yes->[ 7 ]---->< 2 >-yes->[ 6 ]
               no                     no              |
             [ 5 ]                  [ 5 ]             |
                                                      v
     [ 5 ]<-no-< 4 > <---[ 8 ]<-yes-<11><-yes-<10>
                |                     no         no
                L-----yes-------->[12]         [ 5 ]
```

Items 13–14 refer to the following table.

Tax Reform

Income	1-Earner Couple	2-Earner Couple
$ 25,000	−400	+350
35,000	−490	+370
45,000	−950	+230
60,000	−940	+325
80,000	−800	−100
150,000	−605	−605
630,000	−2,857	−2,857

\+ tax increase
− tax decrease

13. Which of the following groups most likely will NOT vote to reelect the members of the joint committee who put together the tax bill represented by this table?

(1) a low-income husband with a homemaker wife
(2) a working single parent
(3) a couple with two mid-sized incomes
(4) a wealthy career couple
(5) a highly paid surgeon with a retired husband

14. The above tax reforms would bring about fewer taxes over all. Which of the following situations probably would result?

(1) an increase in federal spending
(2) a decrease in federal revenues
(3) an increase in tax evasions
(4) a decrease in the deficit
(5) a decrease in consumer spending

(1) (2) (3) (4) (5)

15. Which of the following steps in the lawmaking process is necessary for a bill to become a law?

(1) debate in the Senate
(2) amendments in joint committee
(3) the President's signature
(4) approval by both houses
(5) a presidential veto

(1) (2) (3) (4) (5)

Directions: Choose the one best answer to each question. Answers are on pages 314–315.

Items 16–17 refer to the following passage.

It is the American people themselves who are in the driver's seat.
It is the American people themselves who want the furrow plowed.
It is the American people themselves who expect the third horse to pull in unison with the other two. . . .
Since the rise of the modern movement for social and economic progress through legislation, the Court has more and more often and more and more boldly asserted a power to veto laws passed by the Congress and State legislatures. . . . The Court has been acting not as a judicial body, but as a policy-making body.

16. Which of the following statements best expresses President Roosevelt's opinion?
   (1) Lawmaking is the role of the Supreme Court.
   (2) The Supreme Court has overstepped its powers.
   (3) Congress has passed several economic measures.
   (4) The Court acts in Americans' best interests.
   (5) The Court is supportive of Congress.

   (1) (2) (3) (4) (5)

17. What do the horses in the passage represent?
   (1) American farmers
   (2) the federal court system
   (3) city, state, and federal governments
   (4) the branches of government
   (5) health, education, and welfare

   (1) (2) (3) (4) (5)

18. The Supreme Court ruled that Cleveland should give preference to minorities when hiring firefighters. Which of the following persons would this decision benefit least?
   (1) a white male
   (2) a white female
   (3) a black male
   (4) an Hispanic-American
   (5) an American Indian

   (1) (2) (3) (4) (5)

The Judicial Branch The main purpose of courts is to decide disputes. In fact, the word *court* goes back to ancient times when rulers settled disputes between their subjects in open courtyards. Courts in the United States handle two kinds of cases. Civil cases involve disagreements between private citizens, generally over property rights. Criminal cases involve the government and suspected lawbreakers.

The Federal Court System U.S. federal courts are organized like a pyramid. At the bottom are 88 district courts with more than 300 judges. In the middle are 11 circuit courts. Defendants can **appeal** to a circuit judge to overturn a district court's decision. At the top is the Supreme Court. Its decisions override all other judicial rulings.

The Supreme Court The Supreme Court is made up of a chief justice and eight associate justices. The Constitution gives the Supreme Court the power to try cases of national importance, such as those between two states or between the United States and another country. The Court also hears appeals in cases that involve constitutional law. The Court's power of judicial review means that it can decide whether or not a law is constitutional.

The Supreme Court's most significant decisions have involved **civil liberties** and **civil rights.** For instance, in its famous Miranda decision, the Court ruled that police must inform accused people of their rights. And in the landmark case of *Brown* v. *Board of Education of Topeka* the court gave civil rights in America a big push. This decision made separate schools for blacks and whites illegal.

Coming to Terms

appeal apply for a retrial before a higher court
civil liberties freedom to enjoy the rights guaranteed by law
civil rights rights of a citizen, such as the right to vote

Warm-up

On your own paper, support or refute the following opinion: "The Miranda decision favors the guilty over the innocent."

Sample Warm-up Answer
Knowing their rights can help accused people who are innocent as well as those who are guilty.

Functions of State Governments State governments provide for local governments; make laws about contracts, wills, domestic relations (such as divorce); license drivers, professionals, and marriages; provide and supervise schools; regulate trade within the states; and approve constitutional amendments.

Financing State Government Most states collect income taxes. Many charge a sales tax on goods purchased in the state. Some run lotteries, which make a few lucky winners rich and provide many millions of dollars for the governments. States also receive funds from the federal government.

Governing the Communities Within a state, you find widely varying communities. Some are farm areas, some are industrial parks, some are college towns, and some are cultural centers. A state government would have a difficult time passing laws to cover all situations in every corner of the state. That is why states are divided into counties. Counties have their own governments and police forces. County laws handle those areas not governed by towns and cities. Generally there are three plans of government in towns and cities: mayor-council, commission, and council-manager. Under a mayor-council plan an elected council makes the laws and an elected mayor carries them out. In towns with a commission plan, elected commissioners make the laws and administer different departments. And under a council-manager plan an elected council makes the laws and hires a manager to carry them out.

Warm-up

In what way are all the plans of town and city government similar? Answer on your own paper.

Need a Hint for Number 20?
Remember that the city council is a lawmaking body. Which of the responses would require making a law?

Sample Warm-up Answer
In each plan, elected officials make the laws.

19. State legislators are part-time officials whose basic incomes, therefore, must come from other sources. They are rarely paid enough by their constituents to cover even the expenses of leaving their private affairs for the biennial three months in the state capital. Can we expect the lawyer, the accountant or the insurance agent turned legislator for three months to forget the client whose fees house and feed his family between sessions?

    What does the author imply in his final question?

    (1) Low pay for state legislators causes conflict of interests.
    (2) Lawyers, accountants, and insurance agents make dishonest legislators.
    (3) State legislators should work full time.
    (4) Only high-income earners should run for office.
    (5) A legislator's clients do not influence his or her official decisions.

20. In two days, vandals defaced almost 100 Chicago elevated train cars. Which of the following responses would be both within the powers of the Chicago city council <u>and</u> would most likely have an immediate effect?

    (1) make 90 arrests in five weeks
    (2) liken graffiti to folk art
    (3) ban the sale of spray paint to minors
    (4) fine offenders $500 and 80 hours of community service
    (5) photograph vandals painting cars

    ① ② ③ ④ ⑤

Directions: Choose the one best answer to each question. Answers are on page 315.

21. Social Security and Medicare are two of the federal government's fastest growing expenditures. Which of the following conditions best explains this growth?

    (1) construction of new hospitals
    (2) increased employment across the country
    (3) rising enrollment at medical schools
    (4) increased average age of the population
    (5) decreased number of corporate pension plans

    ① ② ③ ④ ⑤

22. Several states are looking to the federal government for help in cleaning up a radioactive gas called radon in their ground and water. Which of the following agencies probably would assist them?

    (1) Nuclear Regulatory Commission
    (2) Environmental Protection Agency
    (3) Consumer Product Safety Board
    (4) Federal Maritime Commission
    (5) National Science Foundation

    ① ② ③ ④ ⑤

23. If the Pony Express were active today, which government agency would it most likely be a part of?

    (1) Federal Communications Commission
    (2) Interstate Commerce Commission
    (3) U.S. Postal Service
    (4) U.S. Information Agency
    (5) Small Business Administration

    ① ② ③ ④ ⑤

Federal Expenditures The popular wisdom about government aid is that it's not free but paid for with your tax dollars. For a breakdown of what you get for your money, study the table below.

Annual Government Expenditures (in billions of dollars)

National defense	285.7
International affairs	18.3
General science	9.3
Energy	4.7
Natural resources and environment	11.9
Agriculture	12.6
Transportation	25.9
Community and regional development	7.3
Education and social services	29.3
Health	34.9
Social Security and Medicare	269.4
Other	264.4
TOTAL	973.7

Federal Agencies Part of the money spent on each of the above areas goes to indpendent federal agencies. Their activities affect the quality of your daily life. Some of these agencies are listed below.

Action—coordinates volunteers who help the needy here and abroad

The Consumer Product Safety Board—protects consumers from injury by setting safety standards for manufacturers, testing product safety, and researching the causes of injury or illness related to products on the market

The Environmental Protection Agency—sets standards for and monitors rates of pollution

The Equal Opportunity Commission—prohibits employers from discriminating against applicants or workers on the basis of sex, race, religion, or ethnic background.

Warm-up

Based on the table above, what do you think are the government's top three priorities? Explain how you reached your conclusions.

____

____

____

____

____

Sample Warm-up Answer

Defense, Social Security and Medicare, and health seem to be the government's priorities because it spends the most in these areas.

Making Foreign Policy Since the 1950s, the United States and Soviet Union have stockpiled nuclear weapons. In recent years, the two superpowers have been trying to halt the arms race. In 1979, they signed SALT II, a treaty limiting the use and number of ICBMs (intercontinental ballistic missiles). After the Soviets invaded Afghanistan, however, the Senate rejected the treaty. But Americans have continued to clamor for arms control.

Human Rights Policy In 1977 President Carter proclaimed that U.S. foreign policy would help end acts of political repression such as murder, torture, and imprisonment without trial. In addition, American human-rights groups are committed to such activities as freeing political prisoners and supplying exit visas to refugees.

Mideast Relations For a while, the U.S. government courted oil-rich Arab countries. Then oil prices began to fall, and Mideast terrorist groups began to harrass Americans. As a result, the United States cooled toward the Arab countries.

Coming to Terms

foreign policy actions and attitudes a government takes toward other nations

Warm-up

On your own paper, explain what is happening in the cartoon below.

----copyright 1979 by Herblock in The Washington Post

Sample Warm-up Answer
A symbol of death is playing containers of dangerous industrial wastes as if they were drums. The message is that the careless accumulation of waste products will have deadly results.

——from Herblock on all Fronts (New American Library, 1980)

24. Which of the following statements would the cartoonist agree with?
    (1) The Social Security system is a pillar of our society.
    (2) Employers and employees sustain the Social Security system.
    (3) Labor unions increase the Social Security system's productivity.
    (4) Most Social Security payments are to the wealthy.
    (5) Other economic sectors should not pay for Social Security.

25. The Fund for Free Expression is a human-rights group that reports on censorship and violations of free speech in countries around the world. Which of the following incidents would this group most likely get involved with?
    (1) murder of a captured guerrilla
    (2) torture of a Christian missionary
    (3) kidnapping of a CIA agent
    (4) government shutdown of a newspaper
    (5) imprisonment of an opposition leader

Directions: Choose the one best answer to each item. Answers are on page 315.

Items 1–3 refer to the following map.

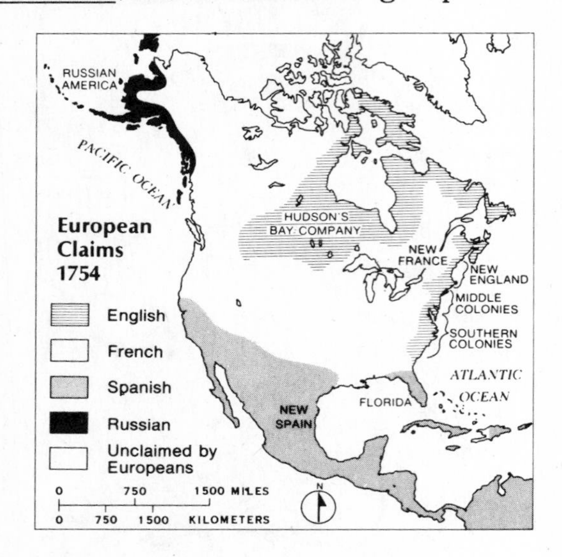

1. Which nation claimed the largest area in what is now the United States?

   (1) France (2) England (3) Spain
   (4) Hudson's Bay Company (5) Russia

   (1) (2) (3) (4) (5)

2. What was the distance between the northern and southern boundaries of the thirteen British colonies?

   (1) 750 miles (2) 1,000 miles
   (3) 1,200 miles (4) 1,500 miles
   (5) 1,800 miles

   (1) (2) (3) (4) (5)

3. Between 1754 and 1763, the British colonists fought the French in North America. What was a probable cause of that war?

   (1) French support of Russians in a boundary disagreement with the British
   (2) British need for harbors in New France
   (3) disputes over the boundaries of New France
   (4) French claims on what is now Mexico
   (5) arguments over lands on the Pacific Coast

   (1) (2) (3) (4) (5)

U.S. History

The following time line shows important dates in American history. Refer to the time line as you read pages 298–311. It may help you see relationships between events.

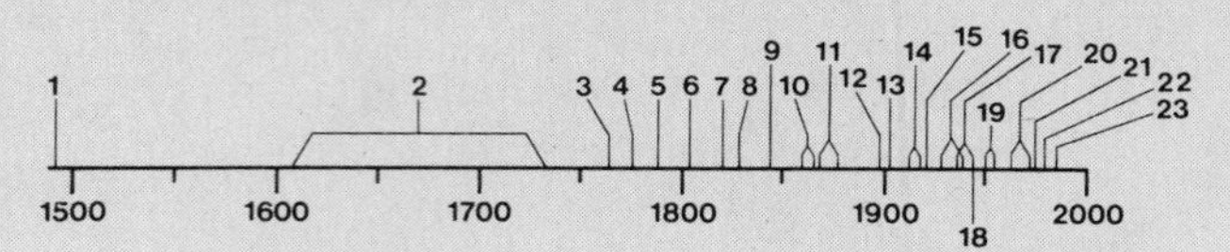

1. 1492 Columbus discovers the New World
2. 1607–1733 British settle thirteen colonies
3. 1765 Americans protest the Stamp Act
4. 1776 Declaration of Independence
5. 1789 government under the Constitution begins
6. 1803 Louisiana Purchase
7. 1820 Missouri Compromise
8. 1828 Andrew Jackson elected President
9. 1845 U.S. annexes Texas
10. 1860–1865 Civil War
11. 1867–1877 Reconstruction
12. 1898 Spanish American War
13. 1902 "trust buster" Theodore Roosevelt breaks up a few monopolies
14. 1914–1918 World War I (U.S. enters 1917)
15. 1920 Nineteenth Amendment gives women the vote
16. 1929–1940 Great Depression
17. 1939–1945 World War II (U.S. enters 1941)
18. 1945 United Nations formed
19. 1950–1953 Korean War; red scare
20. 1963–1973 Vietnam War
21. 1974 Watergate scandal; Nixon resigns
22. 1978 Camp David peace accords; American hostages in Iran
23. 1986 Tax Reform Act passed

☑ A Test-Taking Tip

Don't leave questions on the GED Test unanswered. If you cannot answer a question, guess and move on. Use your time to read carefully the questions you can answer.

Need a Hint for Number 2?
Transfer the markings from the map scale to the edge of a sheet of paper. Then use the paper to measure the length of the British colonies.

Read the inner column on the next page before attempting the questions in the outer column on this page.

A New World/A New Nation The study of American history is linked closely to the other social studies. Look for developments in geography, economics, and political science as you read the following overview.

Age of Discovery In the 1400s, Europe's economy depended on goods from far eastern countries. Europe's kings competed for trade, because the larger the share of trade, the more powerful the king. Europeans expanded their knowledge of geography to find water routes to the East. Columbus was searching for a new route when he landed in the Americas.

Between 1492 and 1700, many French, Spanish, English, and other explorers came to the New World. Settlers followed and started colonies. In 1607, England established its first permanent settlement at Jamestown, Virginia. English colonists sought land of their own, a voice in their government, and freedom to worship as they pleased. By 1733 there were thirteen British colonies and by 1763 the British ruled most of North America.

Causes of the Revolution American society differed from that in Great Britain. In America, nobility was unimportant, and many people owned land. Americans and their British rulers also disagreed on matters of economics and politics. Between 1765 and 1776, the British government imposed taxes, tried to control American trade, and reduced the power of the colonies' lawmaking bodies. Leaders in the colonies organized protests that led to fighting and to the Declaration of Independence.

Revolution and After With the help of the French and Spanish, the Americans fought the British. The American Revolution ended in 1781 with an American victory. At first, the new states could not resolve their differences, because their central government had little power. The Constitutional Convention in 1787 outlined a stronger federal government. The Constitution was ratified, or approved, and became the law of the land in 1789.

Warm-up

Why did the thirteen colonies break away from Great Britain? Answer on your own paper.

Sample Warm-up Answer
The colonists disliked Britain taxing them, interfering with assemblies, and trying to control trade.

Items 4–5 refer to the following graph.

England's Thirteen American Colonies, around 1760

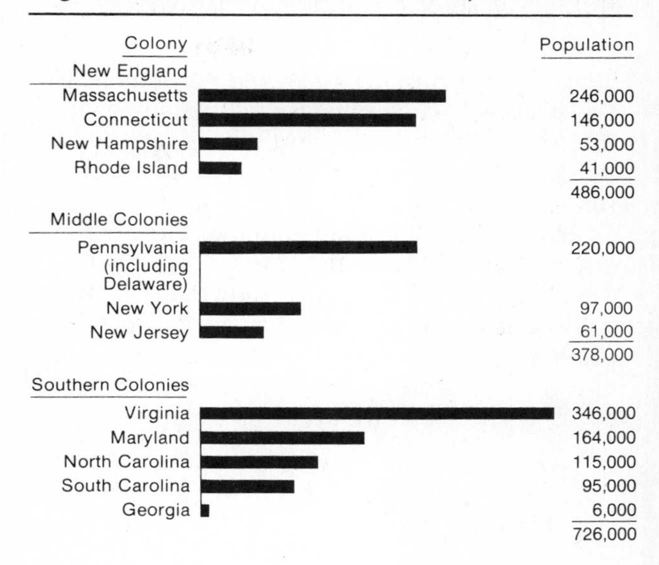

Colony
Population
New England
Massachusetts 246,000
Connecticut 146,000
New Hampshire 53,000
Rhode Island 41,000
486,000
Middle Colonies
Pennsylvania (including Delaware) 220,000
New York 97,000
New Jersey 61,000
378,000
Southern Colonies
Virginia 346,000
Maryland 164,000
North Carolina 115,000
South Carolina 95,000
Georgia 6,000
726,000

4. Which colonies probably held the greatest economic and political influence?

(1) Massachusetts, Pennsylvania, Virginia
(2) New York, Maryland, Virginia
(3) Massachusetts, New York, Georgia
(4) Virginia, New Jersey, Connecticut
(5) Virginia, North Carolina, Maryland

(1) (2) (3) (4) (5)

5. The population of New France in 1760 was 79,000. Which of the following statements is a valid comparison of New France with the thirteen British colonies?

(1) New France had more people than any one British colony.
(2) The population of the British colonies was almost ten times that of New France.
(3) New France attracted settlers as easily as the British colonies.
(4) New France had a smaller population than the British colonies because it covered a smaller area.
(5) The population of the British colonies was about twenty times that of New France.

Directions: Choose the one best answer to each question. Answers are on page 315.

Items 6–7 refer to the following passage.

An old Indian fighter, President Jackson believed that the Indians blocked settlement by the whites. Jackson wanted all Indians east of the Mississippi to give up their land to white settlers. The Indians would then settle on reservations west of the Mississippi. The Cherokees did not want to leave their home in Georgia, and the Supreme Court upheld their right to remain there; however, Jackson ignored it. He ordered the army to move the Cherokees to Oklahoma. Nearly one-quarter of the Indians died along the march, which became known as the Trail of Tears.

6. Which of the following statements best sums up President Jackson's attitude toward Indians?

   (1) They were hard workers.
   (2) They were well suited for life in Oklahoma.
   (3) They deserved the most valuable land.
   (4) They were potential supporters.
   (5) They had no rights.

   (1) (2) (3) (4) (5)

7. President Jackson's actions reflect a widely held belief of the 1800s: Manifest Destiny. Which of the following statements reflects this belief?

   (1) The United States should keep out of European affairs.
   (2) The United States has a natural right to stretch from sea to sea.
   (3) Americans should determine where they live and who will govern them.
   (4) Europeans should stay out of the Western Hemisphere.
   (5) Slavery inevitably will be abolished in the United States.

Growth and Change At first, the United States had trouble winning the respect of other nations. Both the British and French captured American ships and forced some of the sailors to join their navies. In 1812 the United States declared war on Britain over freedom of the seas. An important outcome of this war was the renown Andrew Jackson gained for his victory over the British at New Orleans.

Economic Changes After the War of 1812, U.S. trade with other countries increased. The **Industrial Revolution** began in the North, and the South found foreign markets for its cotton. President James Monroe issued the Monroe Doctrine to protect U.S. markets in Latin America. Few European countries paid attention to this decree from a country that was ill-prepared to enforce it.

Geographic Changes During the early 1800s, the United States acquired new land by buying it, fighting for it, and negotiating for it in treaties. For example, in 1846, the country went to war with Mexico over the Texas boundary. At the end of the war in 1848, Mexico ceded to the United States what is now the American Southwest. (Refer to the time line on page 298 for other examples of land acquisition.) By 1850 the United States stretched from the Atlantic to the Pacific Ocean. New roads, canals, and railroads connected the settlements in the vast new nation.

Political Changes More Americans were able to vote during the 1800s. Political campaigns often focused on popularity rather than issues. Andrew Jackson was the most popular politician of the era, which often was called the Age of Jackson. The Missouri Compromise kept the number of free and slave states equal, and this delayed violence between the North and the South.

Social Changes Nationalist artists and thinkers encouraged a uniquely American culture. Reform movements such as **abolitionism,** temperance, and women's rights were organized to improve society. However, few people could help the American Indians. Powerful leaders like Jackson were determined to move the Indians as far as possible from white settlements. On Jackson's orders, the U.S. Army forced the Cherokee Indians to march hundreds of miles to Oklahoma in 1838.

Read the inner column on the next page before attempting to answer the questions in the outer column on this page.

Coming to Terms

Manifest Destiny popular belief of the 1900s that the United States was destined, or meant, to develop all of North America
Industrial Revolution the change from hand labor to factory production
abolitionism reform movement (1830s–1860s) that called for an end to slavery

Warm-up

In 1845 President James Polk promised to support American settlers in what is now California if they rebelled against their Spanish rulers. Why do you think Polk did this?

☑ A Test-Taking Tip

Some questions on the GED Test will expect you to know the location of present-day states. Label the states on the map below with the abbreviations of their names. Look at a map to find states you don't know and to check your answers.

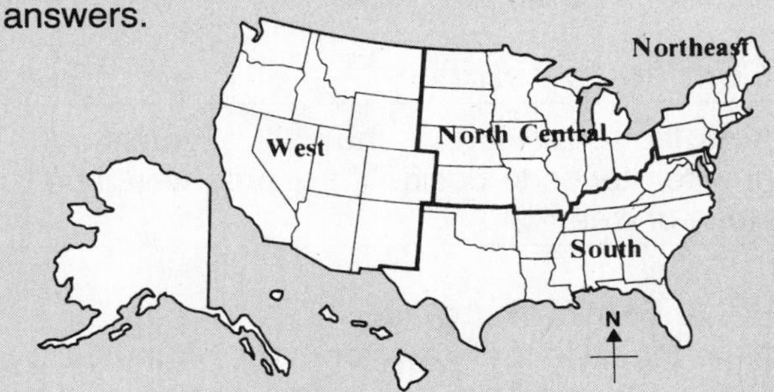

Need a Hint for Number 9?
Find the irregular boundaries on the map in "A Test-Taking Tip." Most of these are formed by rivers. Rivers determined at least part of the boundaries for most U.S. land acquisitions. Identify the Mississippi and Ohio rivers and remember the states that lie to the east and west of them.

Sample Warm-up Answer
Polk probably wanted to add California to the United States after the territory became independent.

Items 8–9 refer to the following map.

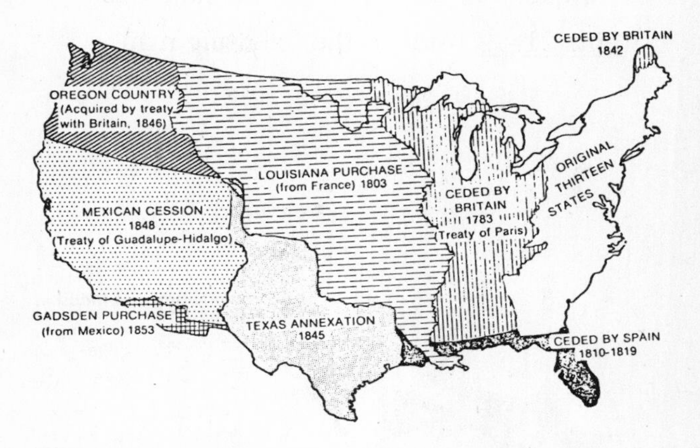

8. How did the United States acquire the territory that now makes up most of its southwestern states?
   (1) the Louisiana Purchase
   (2) the admission of Texas
   (3) war with Great Britain
   (4) peace treaty with Spain
   (5) treaty with Mexico

① ② ③ ④ ⑤

9. Which of the following pairs correctly identifies a present-day state and the way it was acquired?
   (1) Oregon—purchased from Great Britain
   (2) North Dakota—treaty with Mexico
   (3) Missouri—purchased from France
   (4) Illinois—war with France
   (5) West Virginia—treaty with Great Britain

10. President James Monroe framed the Monroe Doctrine because he believed the United States should influence other nations. Which of the following acts of other presidents would Monroe most likely disagree with?
    (1) Washington's plea to avoid foreign entanglements
    (2) Wilson's support for a League of Nations
    (3) Kennedy's creation of the Peace Corps
    (4) Nixon's visit to China in 1972
    (5) Carter's condemnation of the Russian invasion of Afghanistan

Directions: Choose the one best answer to each question. Answers are on page 315.

Items 11–12 refer to the following map.

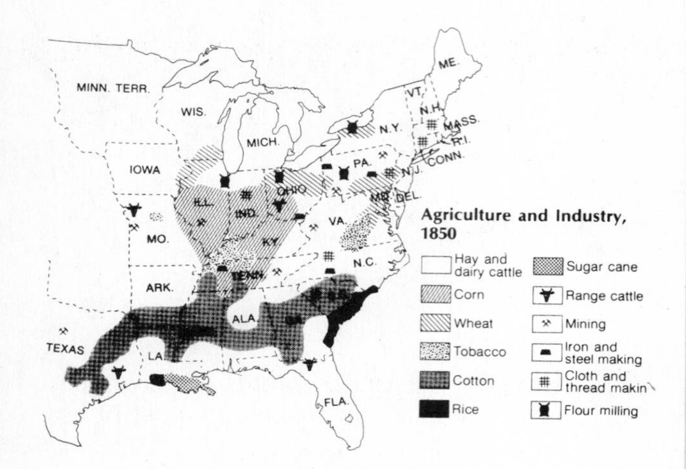

11. Which of the following statements accurately describes the cotton-growing region?

    (1) It was mainly on the East Coast.
    (2) Small pockets of cotton-growing land were found in every state.
    (3) Most cloth and thread factories were in the cotton-growing region.
    (4) It extended into the Midwest.
    (5) It was a large continuous region throughout the "Deep South."

12. Which statement best describes the economies of the North and South in the 1850s?

    (1) The North's economy was based on agriculture, and the South's centered on manufacturing.
    (2) The South grew more food crops than the North.
    (3) The North had fewer industrial centers than the South.
    (4) The South's economy depended on one cash crop, while the North had a diverse economy.
    (5) In the South, cotton was "king"; in the North, corn reigned supreme.

Conflict Between the North and South After 1850, political compromise between the North and South seemed impossible. In Kansas **popular sovereignty** led to bloodshed between antislavery and proslavery groups. The Dred Scott decision by the Supreme Court undid the Missouri Compromise and opened all territories to slavery. How had the country become so deeply divided?

Differences By 1850 the South's economy depended heavily on "King Cotton." Slaves made prosperity possible. Planters argued that slavery benefited slaves as well, because slaveowners fed, housed, and clothed their slaves. Even many small farmers who owned no slaves supported slavery. The institution of slavery allowed planters, who made up a small part of the population, to control southern society and politics. The planters upheld states' rights—the theory that each state could nullify federal laws.

Industry in the North was growing due to new inventions and improved transportation. Immigrants from Europe added to the workforce. As a result, the North had a more diverse society and economy than the South. The North did not need slavery and was ready to abolish it, or at least limit its use, by 1850.

Coming to Terms

popular sovereignty the right of voters in new territories to decide if the area would be slave or free

☑ A Test-Taking Tip

Note the titles and keys for maps on the GED Social Studies Test. The words as well as the pictures are there to help you understand the data.

Warm-up

In 1859 an abolitionist named John Brown raided an arsenal in Virginia with the intention of starting a slave uprising. Brown failed and was hanged, but many Northerners praised his motives. How do you think this affair affected Southerners' feelings for the North?

___

___

___

___

Sample Warm-up Answer
Southerners probably became even more distrustful of Northerners.

The Civil War The election of 1860 was the breaking point. The antislavery Republican Party nominated Abraham Lincoln for President. When Lincoln was elected, South Carolina seceded from the Union. Ten other southern states followed South Carolina's lead.

The Civil War divided not only the nation but also communities. Especially in the border states, neighbors and even brothers enlisted on opposite sides. Most of the war was fought in the South. Although the Confederacy had talented generals and the support of its people, it lacked the soldiers, manufactured goods, and transportation system to win the war.

Reconstruction As the war drew to a close, Lincoln planned to readmit the southern states on easy terms. But after his assassination, Congress began a harsh Reconstruction that angered the South. The Thirteenth, Fourteenth, and Fifteenth Amendments were passed to protect blacks' civil liberties. Southern leaders made their own laws to counter the amendments.

Coming to Terms

Emancipation Proclamation Lincoln's 1863 declaration freeing all slaves in the Confederacy

Reconstruction plan to set up new state governments in the southern states and to readmit the states into the Union

☑ A Test-Taking Tip

When you answer a question on the GED Social Studies Test about causes or results, remember that an event rarely has only one cause or one result. Responses that mention "the only cause" or "the one result" often will be incorrect.

Warm-up

In South Carolina after the war, a black needed a license to work at anything other than farming. Why do you think lawmakers restricted blacks this way?

____

____

____

____

Sample Warm-up Answer
The South needed farm workers because there no longer were any slaves.

13. During his presidential election campaign, Abraham Lincoln pledged to stop the spread of slavery. As a result, what happened within months after Lincoln was elected President for the first time?

    (1) South Carolina seceded from the Union, and the Civil War began soon thereafter.
    (2) Congress decided that the spread of slavery into the territories was legal.
    (3) The individual states all passed antislavery laws.
    (4) Mexico, Canada, and the United States passed a joint human rights resolution declaring slavery inhumane.
    (5) A new wave of Mexican immigrants took the jobs formerly done by slaves.

Items 14–15 refer to the following quotation.

"With malice toward none; with charity for all; with firmness in the right, as God gives us to see the right, let us strive on to finish the work we are in; to bind up the nation's wounds; to care for him who shall have borne the battle, and for his widow, and his orphan—to do all which may achieve and cherish a just and lasting peace, among ourselves, and with all nations."

—Abraham Lincoln, *Second Inaugural Address*

14. If Lincoln had lived longer, what would he probably have done?

    (1) hanged all southern leaders
    (2) rewarded Union soldiers with southern plantations
    (3) treated the defeated Southerners honorably and justly
    (4) allowed the war to spread to other nations
    (5) exiled all Southerners who fought against the Union

(1) (2) (3) (4) (5)

15. What was Lincoln's primary goal?

    (1) to guarantee disability benefits to veterans
    (2) to reward the North
    (3) to reunite the Union
    (4) to care for widows and orphans
    (5) to defeat the South

Directions: Choose the one best answer to each question. Answers are on page 315–316.

Items 16–17 refer to the following passage.

For many years, people in the United States welcomed the immigrants who came here to live. They were needed to settle the wilderness, farm the land, and work in the factories. Howevery, by the 1880s, people began to view immigrants as a threat. They believed immigrants took away jobs from American workers. The immigrants did not fit in with the American way of life, some said. They spoke a different language and had strange customs and clothes. Many people wanted the government to pass laws restricting the number of immigrants allowed to enter the country.

16. Which statement below expresses a fact rather than an opinion about immigrants?

(1) Immigrants were needed to farm the land.
(2) Immigrants were a threat to Americans.
(3) Immigrants took jobs away from Americans.
(4) Immigrants did not fit in.
(5) Immigrants had strange customs.

(1) (2) (3) (4) (5)

17. Which of the following qualities did Americans in the 1880s probably value most?

(1) tolerance (2) originality
(3) conformity (4) diversity
(5) generosity

(1) (2) (3) (4) (5)

18. Between 1862 and 1869, black, Irish, and Chinese workers laid hundreds of miles of track between Omaha and Sacramento for the first transcontinental railroad. Which of the following was NOT a result of the railroad's expansion?

(1) settlements in the West
(2) growth of the steel industry
(3) resettlement of the Plains Indians onto reservations
(4) decreased immigration
(5) decreased use of canals

(1) (2) (3) (4) (5)

Industrialization During the second half of the 1800s, America changed from a nation of farmers to one that included business tycoons, immigrant laborers, and an increasing number of city dwellers. Big business, improved transportation, new inventions, **mass production,** and rapidly growing cities all influenced one another.

Railroads After the Civil War, the railroads pushed westward. Bloody battles with American Indians did not stop this westward movement. Railroad construction encouraged the manufacture of steel and meant better transportation for all goods.

Business Large corporations were formed in every area of business, and, in some, **monopolies** eliminated competition. An example of a monopoly was the Standard Oil Trust started by John D. Rockefeller in 1882. Workers and consumers suffered as a result of the monopolies. The federal government passed the Sherman Anti-Trust Act forbidding monopolies, but did not enforce the law.

Immigrants Millions of new immigrants fleeing poverty and tyranny in their homelands worked as unskilled laborers on railroads, in factories, and in mines. American-born workers often resented the immigrants. Still the immigrants and other laborers kept crowding into cities. The crowded living conditions plus poor sanitation and lack of building codes created slums. Settlement houses were built to help the urban poor.

Warm-up

Thomas Edison invented the light bulb in 1879. Imagine that electric lighting never had been invented. How would life be different today?

____

____

____

Read the inner column on the next page before attempting the questions in the outer column on this page.

Sample Warm-up Answer

Buildings still would be built with floor-to-ceiling windows to catch all available daylight and would be lighted at night with candles or kerosene lamps.

Coming to Terms

monopoly exclusive control of a good or service
mass production the making of goods in large quantities, especially with machinery

 A Test-Taking Tip

Graphs on the GED Test do not always have a title. The labels on a graph's axes will tell you what the graph is about. Read the labels carefully. Ask yourself what is being measured, how quantities are shown, and what numerical figures represent. Only by answering these questions can you read a graph accurately.

Warm-up

Use the figures below to make a line graph.

Railroad Mileage, 1860–1900

1860	30,000 mi	1880	115,000 mi
1870	55,000 mi	1890	200,000 mi

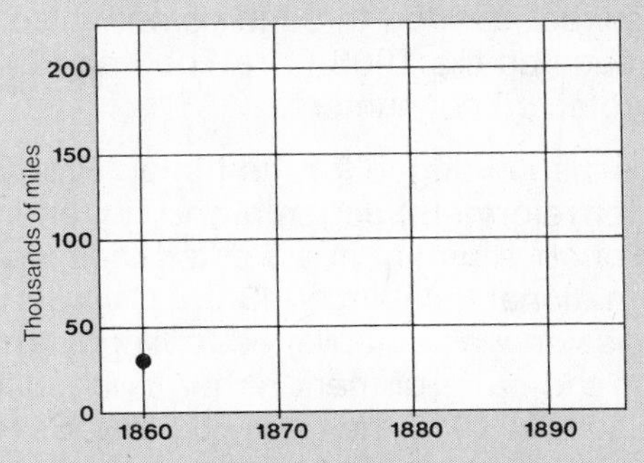

Notice that the dot above 1860 has been made for you. It is more than halfway to the 50 on the vertical axis. That 50 represents 50,000 miles, because the vertical axis is labeled *Thousands of miles.* The dot on the graph represents 30,000 miles.

Need a Hint for Number 16?
After reading each response, ask yourself, can this statement be proved? A fact can be proved with documents or statistics, an opinion cannot. Adjectives and words such as think *and* believe *often signal an opinion.*

Warm-up Answer

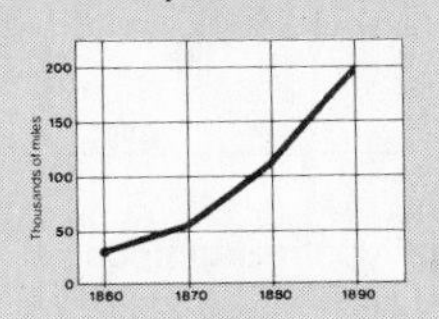

Items 19–20 refer to the graph below.

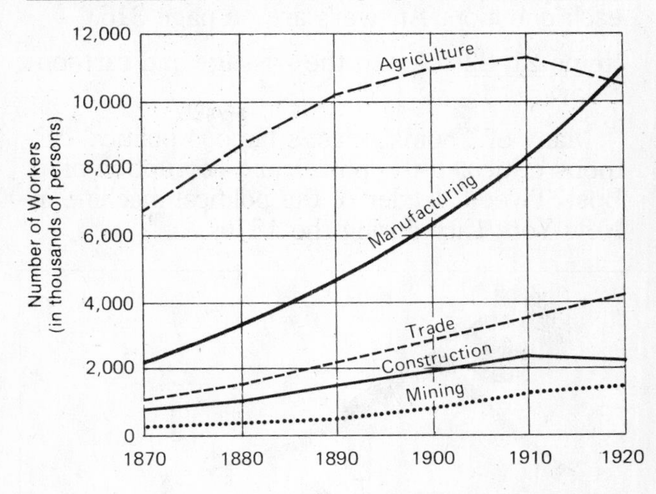

19. Based on the above graph, which of the following statements is most accurate?
    (1) The number of trade workers decreased between 1870 and 1920.
    (2) More workers were in manufacturing than in any other area of the 1920 economy.
    (3) Between 1910 and 1920, the number of farmers increased.
    (4) The number of construction workers decreased between 1870 and 1910.
    (5) The number of mining workers grew more between 1910 and 1920 than during any other decade.

20. Which of the following conclusions can you draw from the information on the graph?
    (1) Industrial growth was greater than agricultural growth.
    (2) The Industrial Revolution had not yet come to America.
    (3) The number of industrial jobs decreased, while the number of agricultural jobs increased.
    (4) During a later period of time, mining jobs would probably equal agricultural jobs.
    (5) Industrial jobs paid lower wages than agricultural jobs.

Directions: Choose the one best answer to each question. Answers are on page 316.

Items 21–22 refer to the passage and cartoon below.

Many of Thomas Nast's famous political cartoons criticized the power and corruption of Boss Tweed, leader of the political machine in New York City during the 1870s.

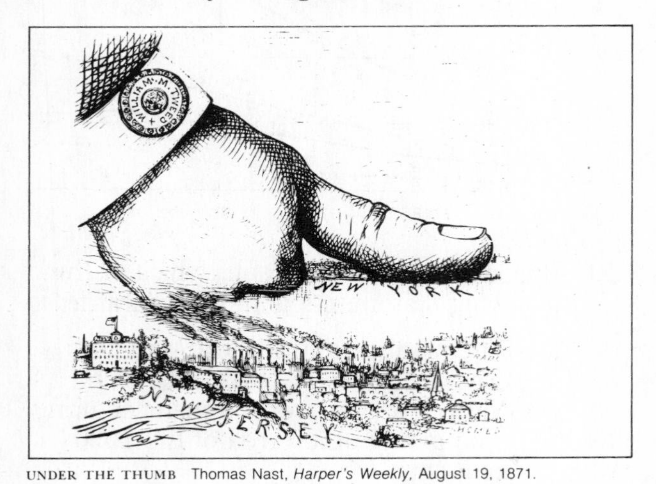

UNDER THE THUMB Thomas Nast, *Harper's Weekly*, August 19, 1871.

21. What can you conclude about Boss Tweed from this cartoon?

    (1) He was a large man.
    (2) He was very wealthy.
    (3) He was a leader in New York's high society.
    (4) He was extremely generous.
    (5) He controlled the New York City government.

    ① ② ③ ④ ⑤

22. Which of the following statements would Thomas Nast probably agree with?

    (1) New York City will never improve while under Tweed's influence.
    (2) New York should rebuild the city skyline.
    (3) Boss Tweed has little influence over New York City.
    (4) Boss Tweed has worked hard to improve New York City.
    (5) Boss Tweed will soon control New Jersey.

    ① ② ③ ④ ⑤

Crises and Reform During the decades after the Civil War, governments practiced a *laissez-faire,* or "hands-off," policy toward business. State and federal governments actually helped business by breaking strikes such as the Homestead and Pullman strikes in the early 1890s. These strikes were led by the new labor unions. Workers had organized unions to win higher wages and better working conditions. Violence between workers and police or state militia was common. Farmers demanded that the government control railroad rates and other business practices that were hurting them. Intellectuals and journalists were concerned about government's unwillingness to deal with the many problems facing the nation.

Big business gradually came under government regulation. In 1887, the federal government established the Interstate Commerce Commission, the first regulatory agency. After Theodore Roosevelt became President, he succeeded in limiting many trusts and monopolies. Some strikes were averted through compromise. New laws, such as the 1906 Pure Food and Drug Act, protected consumers.

Politics also changed for the better. Progressives, or reformers, began at the city and state levels of government and worked their way up to the national level. In 1883 the Civil Service Commission was established to fill government jobs on the basis of merit rather than political patronage. In 1913 the newly passed Seventeenth Amendment allowed direct election of senators and increased voters' influence on Congress. In 1920 the Nineteenth Amendment gave women the right to vote.

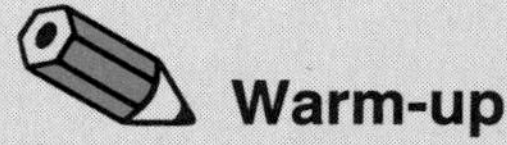

Warm-up

How does a monopoly affect consumers?

____

____

____

Need a Hint for Number 21?
Read the cartoon caption. What does this phrase mean today? Now read the passage again.

Sample Warm-up Answer
It limits competition between businesses by controlling price and production of a good or service.

Coming to Terms

Here is a review of the terms that historians use to describe time periods. Some of the terms have precise meanings while other terms are vague.

age span of time often associated with a person or distinctive condition (the Age of Discovery, the Age of Jackson); the late 1800s were called the Gilded Age because of the money made by big business
century a period of one hundred years; the 1900s are the twentieth century; Columbus made his first voyage in 1492, near the end of the fifteenth century
decade a period of ten years; recent periods often are characterized as decades (the twenties, the sixties), although events rarely fit into this neat pattern
era a period in history; an age (for example, the era of the railroads)
generation average span of time from the birth of parents to the birth of their children—about twenty-five years; members of a generation share similar historical experiences
period span of time; an age; an era (for example, the colonial period)

Warm-up

Why did farmers and city workers demand a change in government's laissez-faire policy during the Gilded Age? (Remember that *laissez-faire* is French for "leave alone.")

☑ A Test-Taking Tip

Questions on the GED Social Studies Test may refer to personalities and issues from different eras. You will feel more confident about your answers if you are familiar with the content of the items. Prepare for these questions by reading summaries of fiction and nonfiction books from several periods in American history.

Need a Hint for Number 24?
What is the main idea of the paragraph? Reread the passage with this thought in mind.

Sample Warm-up Answer
Railroad rates and other business practices were hurting farmers, and governments were siding against workers by breaking strikes.

23. In the early 1900s, Upton Sinclair wrote about meatpackers' deceitful practices such as preserving sausage with borax and then claiming the meat was smoked. Which of the following practices that food packagers use today would Sinclair most likely approve?

    (1) including the number of calories on labels
    (2) preserving meat with sodium nitrite
    (3) listing ingredients on the package
    (4) coloring food with Red Dye #2
    (5) adding BHT to cereals

Items 24–25 refer to the following passage.

During much of the nineteenth century, the U.S. government favored business. The government followed the theory of laissez-faire. According to this idea, government should not try to control business. Several high tariffs, or taxes on goods brought in from other countries, were passed to help American business. The Supreme Court said that state laws controlling businesses were unconstitutional. It also ruled that unions and strikes were not legal.

24. Which of the following opinions best sums up the government's attitude in the 1800s?

    (1) The Supreme Court has a duty to defend labor unions.
    (2) What is good for business is good for the country.
    (3) The government should lower its tariffs to please business leaders.
    (4) High tariffs mean high prices for consumers.
    (5) Laws should protect consumers in every state from monopolies.

① ② ③ ④ ⑤

25. Which of the following modern-day groups most likely shares the attitude described in the passage?

    (1) Ralph Nader's Raiders
    (2) Toyota
    (3) the Citizens Utility Board
    (4) General Electric
    (5) the United Automobile Workers

① ② ③ ④ ⑤

Directions: Choose the one best answer to each question. Answers are on page 316.

Items 26–27 refer to the graphs below.

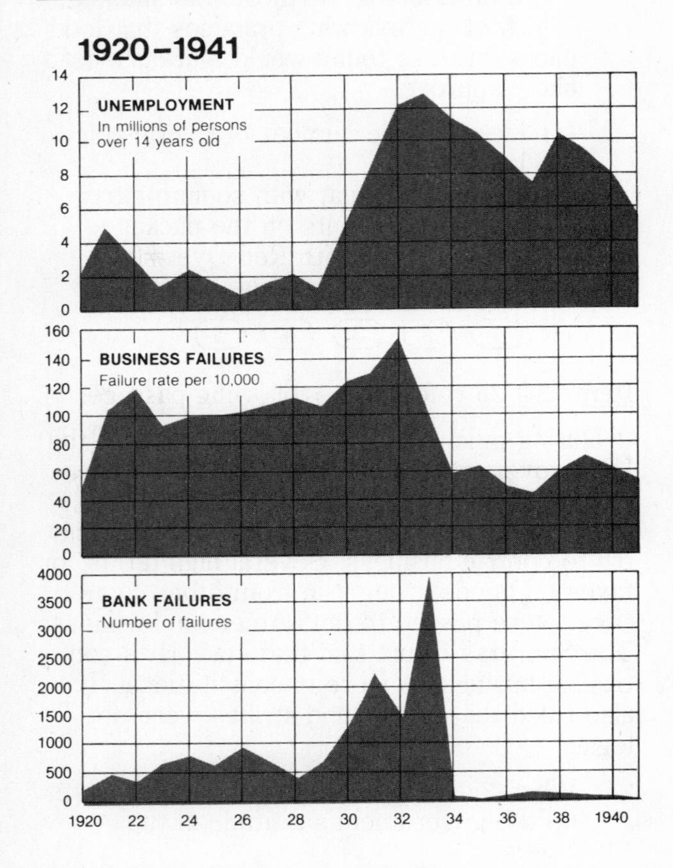

26. Based on the information in these graphs, which of the following Depression years was the worst?

(1) 1922 (2) 1930 (3) 1933
(4) 1937 (5) 1939

① ② ③ ④ ⑤

27. Based on the graphs, the New Deal program was most successful in

(1) restoring people's confidence in banks
(2) putting people back to work
(3) providing emergency relief to farmers
(4) keeping unemployment below 8 percent
(5) keeping the rate of business failures below 50 percent

Becoming a World Power As a result of the Spanish American War in 1898, the United States gained control of Cuba and acquired Puerto Rico, the Philippines, and Guam. The United States was now an imperialist nation like many European countries at that time. After a period of neutrality at the beginning of World War I, the United States entered the war as an ally of Western Europe in 1917.

America at Home As peace and prosperity returned, the growing number of city people bought more consumer goods, on credit. They also invested in the stock market, which crashed in 1929. This was the onset of the Great Depression. America now faced its greatest domestic crisis since the Civil War. After being elected President in 1932, Franklin Roosevelt initiated relief, reform, and recovery programs as part of his New Deal.

Warm-up

In 1898 Senator Albert Beveridge expressed his approval of the U.S. takeover of Cuba:

■ "Think of the hundreds of thousands of Americans who will build a soap-and-water, common-school civilization of energy and industry in Cuba, when a government of law replaces the double reign of anarchy and tyranny!"

Answer the following questions on your own paper.

1. Why might Cubans not be as pleased as Beveridge about Americans building a new civilization in Cuba?
2. Why might Cubans view their new "government of laws" as a form of tyranny?

Need a Hint for Number 27?
Take another look at the graphs. Which drops off most sharply during the New Deal? It will help if you remember what year Franklin Roosevelt was first elected President.

Sample Warm-up Answer
1. Cubans probably valued their own ways. **2.** The laws were made by Americans, not by Cubans.

The International Scene After the Japanese attacked Pearl Harbor in 1941, the United States entered World War II as an ally of Western Europe and the Soviet Union. In 1945 the **United Nations** was formed in hopes of preventing future wars. In addition, the United States, Canada, and ten Western European countries formed NATO in 1949.

After World War II, the United States perceived communist expansion as the next threat to world peace. This was the beginning of the **cold war.** The war turned hot in 1950 when the United States sent soldiers to help the South Koreans fight communist invaders. The fighting lasted into 1953 and ended with no clear victor. In 1954, the United States and seven other nations formed SEATO. The members pledged to stop the spread of communism in Southeast Asia. In the 1960s, the United States sent soldiers to fight communists in South Vietnam. The Vietnam War ended in 1973 when communists took over South Vietnam.

Coming to Terms

cold war continuing tensions between the United States and the Soviet Union since World War II

United Nations organization established as a welfare agency, a police authority, and a forum for international disputes

Warm-up

In a few sentences, describe the cold war. What countries are involved?

Sample Warm-up Answer

The cold war is the strained relationship the United States and the Soviet Union have had since 1945.

Items 28–29 refer to the following information.

Listed below are the names and descriptions of five international organizations.

UN (United Nations)—organization established as a welfare agency, a police authority, and a forum for international disputes

OAS (Organization of American States)—organization made up of the United States and 24 Latin American nations

NATO (North Atlantic Treaty Organization)—military alliance of the United States, Canada, and Western European nations

SEATO (Southeast Asia Treaty Organization)—organization including the United States and seven other nations committed to stopping the spread of communism in Southeast Asia

OPEC (Organization of Petroleum Exporting Countries)—group of oil-producing countries that try to control oil prices

Each of the following statements refer to situations involving one of the above organizations. Choose the organization that is most likely involved.

28. In 1961, President Kennedy sent additional soldiers to Western Europe when the Soviet Union demanded that troops from the United States, France, and Great Britain leave Berlin. The United States acted as a member of

    (1) UN (2) OAS (3) NATO
    (4) SEATO (5) OPEC

    (1) (2) (3) (4) (5)

29. In 1973 several Arab nations threatened to cut off oil shipments to countries that supported Israel. The Arab nations belonged to

    (1) UN (2) OAS (3) NATO
    (4) SEATO (5) OPEC

    (1) (2) (3) (4) (5)

Directions: Choose the one best answer to each question. Answers on page 316.

Items 30–31 refer to the following paragraph.

At the end of the war, many Americans resumed interrupted careers, got married, and started families. So many babies were born in the postwar period of 1946 to 1964 that it has come to be called a boom—the baby boom. The 76 million "boomers" (as babies born during this period are called) have traveled through American society with some difficulty.

30. Which of the following groups is made up of "baby boomers"?

(1) GIs from World War II
(2) parents in the early 1950s
(3) newlyweds during the years 1946 and 1954
(4) teenagers in the 1970s
(5) the kindergarten class of 1980

(1) (2) (3) (4) (5)

31. Which of the following conditions was a result of the baby boom?

(1) the end of World War II
(2) a huge drain on social security in the 1950s
(3) increased emphasis on retirees in the 1960s
(4) not enough classrooms in the late 1970s
(5) new housing boom in the 1980s

(1) (2) (3) (4) (5)

32. In 1986 analysts projected a severe teacher shortage. Which of the following conditions probably contributed to the shortage?

(1) increased teacher salaries
(2) better job opportunities in other fields
(3) increased enrollments at teacher colleges
(4) more autonomy for teachers in the classroom
(5) decreased numbers of school-age children

(1) (2) (3) (4) (5)

Contemporary Events Economic prosperity returned after World War II. The 1950s brought the **red scare,** suburban growth, a Supreme Court ruling against segregation, and organization of the black civil rights movement. Violent demonstrations for civil rights and against U.S. involvement in Vietnam took place in the 1960s and early 1970s. The Watergate scandal and President Richard Nixon's resignation marked the low point of public confidence in the federal government.

Foreign Challenges One of the biggest challenges of the last few decades has been keeping the peace. Little progress has been made in stopping the arms race. President Jimmy Carter used political influence to bring Egypt and Israel together in the Camp David Accords of 1978. The United States was challenged by the hostage crisis in Iran in 1979, and was criticized for supporting dictators in Latin America. In 1986 American planes bombed Libya after a series of attacks on Americans abroad by Mideast terrorists. That same year, Congress voted to send $100 million to **guerrillas** in Nicaragua who were trying to overthrow their communist government.

Domestic Challenges In the 1970s and early 1980s, the U.S. economy suffered from inflation and unemployment. Skyrocketing oil prices and the influx of cheap foreign goods competing with American-made products worsened the dilemma. President Ronald Reagan urged less government involvement in the economy and more dependence on business recovery. Small businesses and farmers suffered under these new government policies, but other areas of the economy improved. By 1986 oil prices were down and the value of the dollar was up. Some of the fastest growing businesses today deal in new technology in electronics, computers, and telecommunications.

☑ A Test-Taking Tip

Many of the knowledge questions on the GED Social Studies Test deal with current events and trends. To prepare yourself for these questions, read newspapers, magazines, and watch news and documentary programs on television.

Read the inner column on the next page before attempting the outer column on this page.

Coming to Terms

guerrilla fighter who harrasses the enemy by raids, ambushes, and other surprise tactics
red scare fear that communists had infiltrated American life; the scare was publicized by Senator Joseph McCarthy

Warm-up

communism—an economic system based on community or state ownership of property

capitalism—an economic system based on ownership by private individuals or groups

The following statement describes a process that takes place in one of the systems defined above. Identify the system and explain your choice.

■ Several farm villages pool their labor and land under government supervision and are paid shares of the harvest.

____

____

____

Sample Warm-up Answer
The system is communism, because the property is shared by the community and run by the state.

Items 33–34 refer to the following passage.

A serious problem in recent decades is the rapid rise in the use of illegal drugs throughout society. While alcohol has been America's most abused substance, the abuse of other, harder drugs has a sweeping impact on crime, productivity in the workplace, and U.S. relations with drug-exporting nations.

33. Which of the following is NOT seriously affected by the drug crisis?

(1) the image of professional athletes
(2) the murder rate in large cities
(3) absenteeism in the work force
(4) the disappearance of the family farm
(5) the burglary rate in the suburbs

34. The government of a drug-exporting nation might not be eager to help U.S. efforts at drug control because

(1) its leaders are addicts
(2) its leaders are unpatriotic
(3) all exports, even drugs, boost its economy
(4) they think drugs are harmless
(5) drugs are an American problem

① ② ③ ④ ⑤

Answers—Social Studies

Sample Test Items

Geography
(pages 261–268)

1. (4) Since the map only shows rates of population change and not real numbers, only (4) is based on the map information.

2. (5) Because Alaska is the only alternative to have gained the most population, it is probably the one that has experienced population implosion.

3. (4) The central plains of the United States is the region between the Appalachian Mountains and the Rocky Mountains which extends from the Gulf of Mexico to the U.S.–Canada border.

4. (1) Use a ruler or the edge of a sheet of paper to measure and compare the areas on the map. Both the United States and South America are about 1⅝ inches wide.

5. (2) The arctic region to the north has cold temperatures year round. The tundra climate is farther north than any other climate region shown on the map.

6. (4) The southern coast of California is marked as a desert on the map. The map shows the Great Lakes and eastern North America as broadleaf woodland, the area east of the mountains as grasslands, and the area near the equator, which is zero latitude, as mostly tropical rainforest.

7. (3) Options (1), (2), (4), and (5) are true statements, but they do not illustrate the concept of resources changing over time as new needs and technologies arise.

8. (2) The Colorado River starts in the northwest corner of Colorado. It is fed by the melting snow from the Rocky Mountains and threads its way through southeast Utah and Arizona. It forms the western border of Arizona and empties into the Gulf of California.

9. (2) Options (1), (3), (4), and (5) are not supported by the map. However, the map does indicate some dams on the Colorado River.

10. (1) Options (2) and (4) directly contradict the question. Option (3) is possible but would occur long after (1) did. Therefore, (1) is a more immediate and likely problem. Canada is not located near the Colorado River's path, so (5) is impossible.

11. (3) Novosibirsk can transport materials that it receives by railroad on the Ob River. Although Ust-Kut can use the Lena River for shipping, that city would not have the railway transportation to allow a wider range of goods to be transported. Komsomolsk has a railroad but is far from production centers.

12. (2) Because Oymyakon has no transportation system for sending coal to other towns, it probably uses the fuel.

13. (4) Although options (1), (2), and (5) are true, the graph does not help to explain them. Option (3) could not be true since the graph shows Saudi Arabia does not receive much rain. Because there is little rain, very few food crops can grow; therefore, (4) is the answer.

14. (1) The passage tells you that the influences of Taoism, Shintoism, and Buddhism are part of the Japanese view of the physical landscape.

15. (5) The passage states that a Japanese gardener will arrange plants, stones, ponds, bridges, and other garden elements into a natural pattern. An outdoor cooking grill, split-level deck, and shrubs trimmed into animal shapes would neither evoke the spirit of the natural landscape nor encourage contemplation of nature. The meadow of wildflowers would be natural but not symmetrical as there would be no arrangement; the field would grow wildly and naturally. A reflecting pond would encourage meditation and could symbolize an element of nature, the sea.

16. (3) Since the deserts could most use water, removing the salt from an abundant, nearby supply of it would be most useful for North Africa.

17. (4) Use the key to check each answer. Chile is marked as a country with a per capita GDP of $2,500 to $3,500.

18. (3) Options (1), (2), (4), and (5) would cause a greater demand for French Guiana's exports and increase the country's per capita GDP. Only (3) would hurt the country's economy and lower GDP.

19. (3) Use the key to check each answer. Holland has no shaded area, which means it did not receive any wind-blown radiation.

20. (4) To answer this question, you must estimate increases on the bar graph and know where developing countries are located—in Africa, Asia, and South America.

Behavioral Sciences
(pages 269–277)

1. (4) The third sentence states this finding in other words.

2. (5) Because the children improved when they were removed from the home environment and worsened when they were returned to it, you could infer that the home environment was the cause of the problem.

3. (1) The percentages matching fear ranged from 54% to 85%. No other emotion showed this much disagreement.

4. (5) The rate of agreement among the cultures listed in matching pictures with emotions such as happiness and surprise is extremely high. Some facial expressions, therefore, must mean the same thing to different cultures.

5. (5) Sam is dividing the musical score into parts.

6. (4) Mercedes is having her performance evaluated immediately.

7. (1) Charlie is staggering his learning by working in two short sessions separated by a break.

8. (4) The first three options are occupations in which a person may have to deal with blood. A cobbler is a leather worker and is, according to the passage, an Untouchable. Brahmans do, however, prepare food for other Brahmans.

9. (3) Both segregation and the caste system involve grouping people and then keeping the groups separate.

10. (1) The other options are adults who, even if it may be unintentional (as in the case of a TV actor), teach a young child how to behave in society. A baby brother could not because he knows even less. In fact, the four-year-old child would be an agent of socialization for his or her brother.

11. (4) The mildest forms of deviance are at the lower left of the curve. They are punished by the first punishment listed—staring.

12. (2) The punishment for treason is much more severe than for rudeness, alcoholism, or instability. So the society values patriotism even more than courtesy, sobriety, or stability.

13. (1) Only the wealthy surgeon has achieved his or her own status by studying at school and then practicing medicine. Options (2), (3), (4), and (5) are granted a certain amount of status only through "an accident of birth"—they didn't *do* anything to achieve it.

14. (3) Only (3) helps show that female employees have less status because they are treated unequally when it comes to pay. If their status equalled men's, they would receive equal pay for equal education and work.

15. (3) While role conflict may be present in any of the situations given, it's most likely present in (3). Trying to be a flight attendant and still find time to parent a child would be extremely difficult.

16. (2) The relationship of *oya* to *ko* is senior to junior, like father to son. Each of options (1), (3), (4), and (5) belong in the same generation.

17. (1) A promotion above the *oya* would put the *ko* in a superior position, making the senior-junior relationship difficult. The other options would keep the basic relationship intact.

18. (3) The boy can hardly imagine having ten cents let alone ten cows because he's so poor. His experience is so far different from the tester's and his or her questions that he cannot answer.

19. (2) The boy's answers reflect common sense. (If he had ten cents, he wouldn't spend it on candy, and if he lost six cows, he wouldn't go home to his angry father.)

20. (4) Both cultures included in tombs the material things that people used every day on earth. They must have believed that the dead person would still have a need for such things. He or she would have a need only if there was life after death.

21. (3) Both cultures buried their dead with material tools, even though the cultures were thousands of miles apart and had no known way of communicating with each other.

Economics
(pages 278–287)

1. (3) To answer this question, you must pick out the most valid and the most general option. Read each answer, then check to see if it makes sense as the title or topic sentence of the passage. Options (1) and (2) are valid but don't state the main idea of the passage. Option (4) is invalid, and option (5) is not discussed.

2. (1) This question asks you to apply information from the passage to a concrete situation. The correct response tells of a situation when the problem of scarcity is involved. Option (2) has to do with comparison shopping. Option (3) illustrates an effect of inflation. Option (4) is about taxation, and (5) involves supply and demand.

3. (3) Read the title and the subheads, then the question and answer. Only one will be true. Figures show that production of only industrial goods rose sharply.

4. (4) It is clear from the figures that during the period shown on the chart the Soviets concentrated their efforts on industrial rather than agricultural growth.

5. Find the price axis and quantity axis on each graph. Graph (3) has a supply curve that shows an increase in quantity and an increase in price.

6. (4) The monster in the cartoon represents the evils of monopolies and other business combinations. Option (4) speaks favorably of monopolies and is the exception you are looking for.

7. (4) The passage describes a lack of scruples in advertising best summed up by (4).

8. (5) None of the authors indicate in their quotes that they would disagree with (1) or (2). Ure would agree with (3) while the other two do not indicate that they would disagree. All three definitely agree on (4). However,

Ure believes that automation benefits workers while Mitchell and Davies blame automation for rising unemployment. They would disagree with Ure's contention in (5).

9. (3) The sewing machine is the only choice that saves the operator's eyes as well as eliminates repetitive movements.

10. (2) Compare the figures in the True Annual Percentage column and you will find the highest rates for (2).

11. (4) Compare figures as you did in item 10, and you will find the lowest rates for credit unions.

12. (2) Grocery bills, which are necessary but can be changed, are variable expenses.

13. (3) Guitar lessons are not essential but would provide pleasure for Maria; so they are a luxury expense.

14. (1) Rent is a budget expense that generally stays the same from month to month.

15. (3) Cycles are called *cycles* because they repeat themselves.

16. (1) Item 16 describes first a depression and then inflation. The next stage shown on the graph is recovery.

17. (1) Options (2), (3), (4), and (5) would be possible results of a "loose" money policy. When companies like airlines compete for consumer dollars, they lower their prices as in (1).

18. (2) People such as public school children who depend on services bought with tax dollars most likely would suffer from a tax cut.

19. (4) Unions were organized to address workers' grievances. So a peak in union membership as is evident in (4) probably would coincide with worker dissatisfaction.

20. (2) The line on the graph drops sharply between 1920 and 1930. Options (1), (3), and (4) indicate membership rose or stayed the same. Option (5) would indicate that the line should have disappeared from the graph. Only (2) explains the drop in union membership.

21. (1) To answer this question, you must know what a protectionist policy is. (See page 287.) Read each quote for comments supporting restraint or taxation of imports.

22. (4) Options (1) and (2) are incorrect because the charts do not include all U.S. imports and exports. Options (3) and (5) are disproved by the charts.

Political Science
(pages 288–297)

1. (2) The burgesses were elected representatives who made Virginia's laws.

2. (5) Although Mussolini was elected, he eliminated his political opponents so that he would have complete power.

3. (1) *Duties* and *imposts* are other words for taxes.

4. (3) This is stated in the first few lines: a state can impose no duties without Congress' consent.

5. (2) This is stated as no "abridging the freedom of speech or of the press."

6. (4) The passage generalizes that Republicans are rural and small-town residents, northerners, well educated, and Protestant, all of which fit the profile of a North Dakota minister. The people profiled in the other options would tend to be Democrats.

7. (5) Most farmers are older persons who are rural and small-town residents, characteristics which appear in the passage as describing Republicans.

8. (4) To answer this question, you must know what special powers the executive, legislative, and judicial branches have over each other. For more information, see pages 291–294.

9. (4) The President's duties may include all of the options except (4) which is in the realm of the judicial branch of government.

10. (5) Since every state is represented by two senators, states like Wyoming which are less populated have equal representation with more populated states such as New York.

11. (1) Options (2), (3), (4), and (5) would tend to eliminate or render meaningless most legitimate debate on an issue.

12. (2) Options (3), (4), and (5) argue against Senator Javits's point of view. Option (1) suggests that the British House of Commons might agree with Javits but doesn't say why. Option (2), however, suggests that the right of unlimited debate has been abused.

13. (3) Options (1), (2), (4), and (5) will experience a decrease in the amount of taxes they pay. Option (3) will pay more taxes on their combined incomes.

14. (2) Since income tax is the major source of federal revenue, a decrease in that tax would decrease federal revenues.

15. (4) To answer this question, you must know how the legislative branch operates. For more information, see pages 292–293.

16. (2) Option (2) restates the last line of the President's comments.

17. (4) Options (1), (2), (3), and (5) would not relate to President Roosevelt's comments about the Supreme Court.

18. (1) Options (2), (3), (4), and (5) are members of different minority groups, while (1) is not.

19. (1) Nothing in the passage supports (4) and (5). Options (2) and (3) add points not stated in the passage. Option (1) accurately restates the author's point.

20. (3) Options (1) and (4) are not within the powers of the city council; (2) and (5) would not effectively curtail vandalism.

21. (4) Options (1), (2), (3), and (5) do not affect growth in Social Security and Medicare expenditures.

22. (2) The EPA would assist because it deals with environmental pollution. The Nuclear Regulatory Commission licenses nuclear plants; the Consumer Product Safety Board protects consumers and tests product safety; the Federal Maritime Commission regulates shipping, and the National Science Foundation conducts scientific research.

23. (3) Because the Pony Express was a mail delivery service, it would come under the U.S. Postal Service.

24. (2) Option (2) restates the cartoon caption.

25. (4) Option (4) is the only alternative that refers to a curtailment of communication.

U.S. History
(pages 298–311)

1. (1) Match the shading on the key with the shading on the map. In the area that became the United States, France claimed more land than any other European nation.

2. (4) From the northern to the southern boundary of the colonies is about the same distance as the map scale itself, which equals 1,500 miles.

3. (3) From the map you can tell the British and French claimed land next to each other. It is likely they would fight over boundaries of their claims.

4. (1) The bar graph shows that these states had the largest populations. It is likely the greatest number of people would have the most influence.

5. (5) The sum of the populations of the three groups of colonies is about 1½ million (486,000 + 378,000 + 726,000 = 1,590,000). That is about 20 times the population of New France (79,000 is about 80,000; 80,000 × 20 = 1,600,000).

6. (5) Jackson ignored the Supreme Court's decision that the Cherokees had the right to stay in Georgia. He forced them out, so you can conclude he felt they had no rights.

7. (2) Perhaps you already knew that Manifest Destiny was the belief that the United States was destined to expand. If not, you could see that Jackson's actions helped the white settlers move west and expand the land they controlled.

8. (5) To answer this question, you must know that the Southwest is the lower left-hand portion of the map. This area was ceded, or given, to the United States by Mexico after a war.

9. (3) You need to know the general location of each state listed in order to answer this question. Missouri is in the central part of the country within the area marked "Louisiana Purchase (from France) 1803."

10. (1) The other options all deal with U.S. involvement with other nations. Washington wanted the country to remain uninvolved.

11. (5) Look at the key for cotton and find the areas on the map where cotton was grown. Knowing U.S. regions is a great help, but (5) is also the only answer that describes the fairly large, continuous area you see on the map.

12. (4) By reading each option carefully and looking at the map for data to back it up, you can see that (4) is the best description. Option (5) doesn't account for the manufacturing and mining in the North.

13. (1) You need to remember a bit of history to answer this question. South Carolina was a slave state, so it seceded from the Union soon after the antislavery Lincoln was elected. Its secession eventually led to the Civil War.

14. (3) Lincoln's speech talks of kindness ("charity for all") and healing ("bind up the nation's wounds"). It seems likely he would not want to take revenge on the South but treat it honorably and justly to achieve "a just and lasting peace."

15. (3) Again, look at the meaning of Lincoln's words: "to bind up the nation's wounds" and "achieve a just and lasting peace, among ourselves." He does speak of caring for widows and orphans, but that is only one way of achieving his primary goal of reuniting the Union.

16. (1) Remember that a fact can be proved true. The fact that there weren't enough Americans to farm the land could be proved. The other options only express many Americans' views, or opinions, on immigrants.

17. (3) You have to infer this answer. If many Americans felt the immigrants didn't fit in because of their "strange" customs, they must have respected only those who conformed to American customs.

18. (4) Think of causes and effects here. Towns would grow up along railroads because transportation would be easier (1). Steel would be needed to build railroads (2). The white man would force Indians off the land he wanted for settlements and farms (3). And the need for canals would decrease (5). Immigration would *increase* because workers for the railroad would be needed.

19. (2) You have to read each option and then check the graph to see whether it's true. Only option (2) is correct; the line for manufacturing rises above the line for agriculture right before the end of the graph.

20. (1) The number of workers in industrial jobs—manufacturing, construction, trade, and mining—increased even more than the number of agricultural workers (which actually began to decrease in the last decade shown on the map). So you can conclude that industry was growing more than farming.

21. (5) Tweed's large thumb is a symbol of his great power.

22. (1) The short paragraph tells you Nast criticized Boss Tweed for his corruption. The cartoon also implies Nast's negative view of Tweed. Nast would most likely see little chance for improvement in New York while Tweed was still in power.

23. (3) Sinclair would approve of the *honest* listing of ingredients since he disapproved of the dishonest claims of meatpackers about their products.

24. (2) Government action favored business by keeping goods from other countries expensive but not controlling U.S. businesses in any way. It must have felt that helping business would also, in turn, help the rest of the country.

25. (4) A big business would favor the pro-business attitude of the government described in the paragraph. Unions and consumer groups would not; neither would a Japanese company.

26. (3) Unemployment and bank failures were highest in 1933 (in the middle of the lines for 1932 and 1934). Business failures were higher in 1932, but they were still at a high rate in 1933.

27. (1) Look how the line representing bank failures in the third graph drops drastically after 1933, when the New Deal was in effect. People would therefore feel more confident about placing their savings in banks.

28. (3) The United States was acting with its Western European allies.

29. (5) *Oil* is the key word here. The Arab countries tried to use their oil for political rather than economic ends in this case.

30. (4) Anyone who was a teenager in the 1970s would have been born from the early 1950s to the mid-1960s, a time that falls within the baby-boom period.

31. (5) Think of what you need at different times of life. In the 1980s many baby boomers would be in their twenties and thirties—the time of life when people start their own homes in apartments and houses.

32. (2) Each of the other options would result in *more* teachers, not fewer. If other jobs are more desirable, people will pick them over teaching, and a teacher shortage will result.

33. (4) Options (1) and (3) are examples of productivity in the workplace. Options (2) and (5) are examples of impact on crime. No connection would exist between the increased use of drugs and the decreasing number of family-run farms.

34. (3) Drug exports bring money into a country, even though they are illegal. Much of the money is spent within the country and may even be invested in some legitimate businesses, bringing jobs to other people. Stopping drugs would therefore hurt the economy of the nation, and the leaders of some drug-exporting countries feel the economy is more important than putting an end to drugs.

Minitests—Social Studies

Minitest 1

Directions: Choose the one best answer to each question. Answers are on page 327.

Items 1–2 refer to the maps below.

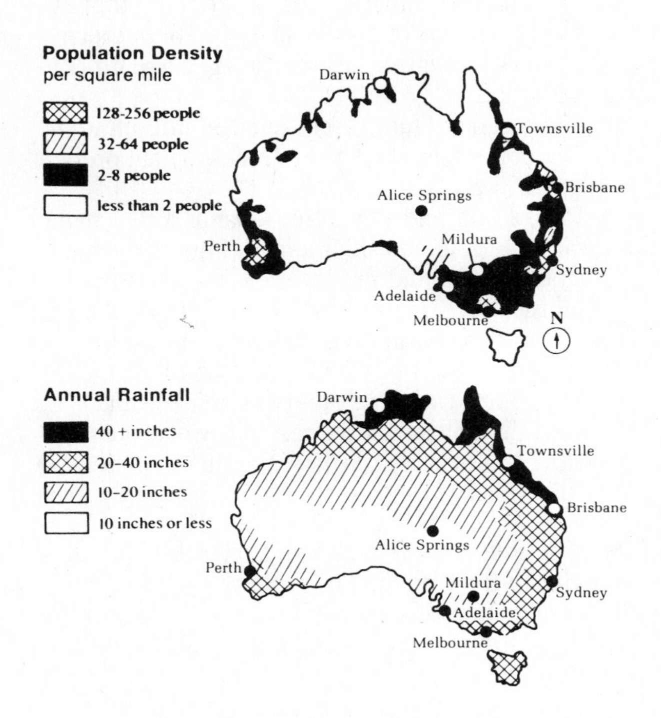

1. Which of the cities listed best fits the following description?

   coastal city in a region where population density is 128–256 people per square mile and rainfall is more than 40 inches annually

   (1) Perth
   (2) Brisbane
   (3) Sydney
   (4) Darwin
   (5) Mildura

   1 2 3 4 5

2. Which statement correctly describes a relationship between rainfall and population in Australia?

   (1) The Australian population is most dense where annual rainfall is highest.
   (2) Population density is highest along the coast where annual rainfall is low.
   (3) Population density and rainfall are inversely related. In most of the area where annual rainfall is 40 inches or more, the population is less than 8 people per square mile.
   (4) Population is very dense in and near Perth and Sydney.
   (5) Rainfall in the underpopulated south-central region of Australia averages a scant 10 inches or less annually.

Items 3–4 refer to the passage below.

The word *family* does not have the same meaning for everyone. Family patterns in the United States are changing. A nuclear family consists of one set of parents and their children. Stresses on the nuclear family are many—for instance, rising divorce rates, the increase in two-income households, and the fact that many families relocate frequently. But the increased sharing of responsibilities between spouses seems to indicate that nuclear families are adapting to these stresses.

3. Which of the following is a source of trouble to the nuclear family?

   (1) lack of day-care centers
   (2) environmental pollution
   (3) white collar crime
   (4) the rising price of oil
   (5) the threat of nuclear war

   1 2 3 4 5

4. If a nuclear family is composed of parents and children only, which of the following is part of a nuclear family?

   (1) brother
   (2) fiance
   (3) father-in-law
   (4) cousin
   (5) aunt

5. Which circle graph best shows the percentage of urban population in 1900?

U.S. RURAL AND URBAN POPULATION, 1870–1900

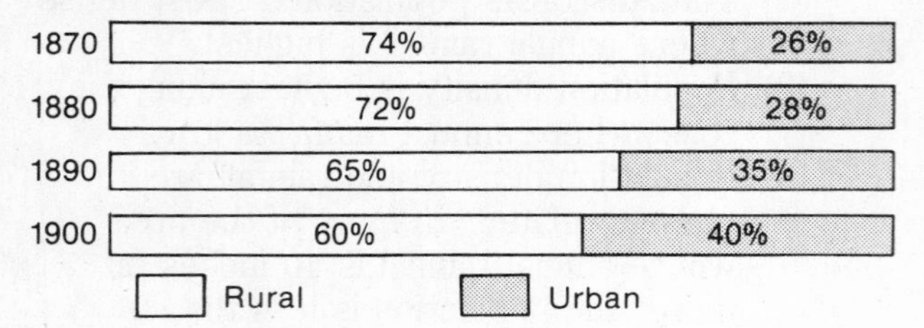

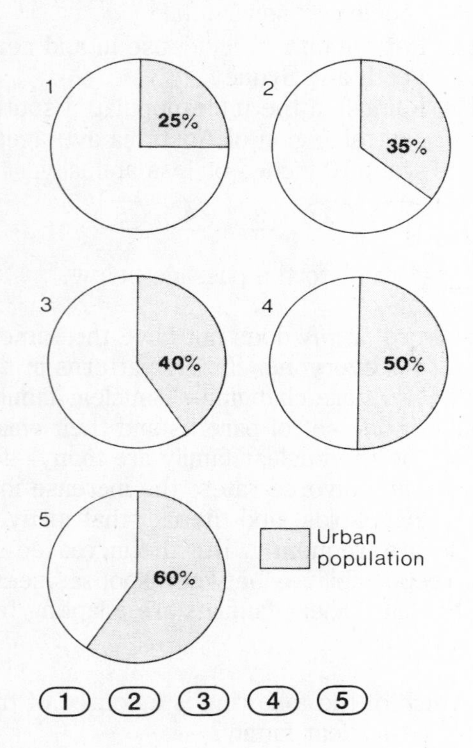

(1) (2) (3) (4) (5)

Items 6–8 are based on the following information.

Listed below are five acts that are often referred to when discussing milestones in American history.

(1) Clayton Antitrust Act—outlawed business practices that lessened competition while protecting farmer's organizations and unions
(2) National Reclamation Act—set aside money from the sale of public lands in 16 western and southwestern states to pay for dam construction
(3) Emergency Quota Act—limited immigration to quotas based on the ethnic population of the United States in 1910
(4) Pure Food and Drug Act—banned the manufacture, sale, or shipment of impure or mislabeled food and drugs in interstate commerce
(5) Interstate Commerce Act—required interstate railroads charge "reasonable" rates, prohibited rate-fixing between lines, and brought railroad activities that were outside state government jurisdiction under federal control

6. The following is a passage from Upton Sinclair's 1904 novel *The Jungle.* Its shocking description of the working conditions in Chicago's stockyards and meat-packing plants stunned the nation.

"... and as for the other men, who worked in the tank-rooms full of steam, and in some of which there were open vats near the level of the floor, their peculiar trouble was that they fell into the vats; and when they were fished out, there was never enough of them left to be worth exhibiting,—sometimes they would be overlooked for days, till all but the bones of them had gone out to the world as Durham's Pure Leaf Lard!"

Which of the following acts was most likely passed as a result of public opinion about Sinclair's writing?

(1) the Clayton Antitrust Act
(2) the National Reclamation Act
(3) Emergency Quota Act
(4) Pure Food and Drug Act
(5) Interstate Commerce Act

7. "The Grange" was an organization formed to ease the isolation of southern farm families. Each local chapter built its own Grange Hall which became the hub of social and cultural life in the rural community. The Grange urged cooperation among farmers in their efforts to combat such "eastern monopolies" as the railroads.

   Which of the following acts was passed as a result of the Grangers' influence?

   (1) Clayton Antitrust Act
   (2) National Reclamation Act
   (3) Emergency Quota Act
   (4) Pure Food and Drug Act
   (5) Interstate Commerce Act

8. Soon after Standard Oil Company gained control of the oil refining industry, other businesses began to dominate their fields successfully. For example, the McCormick Harvester Company of Chicago acquired a near monopoly of farm equipment. The American Tobacco Company and the American Sugar Refining Company almost completely controlled their industries. And the Armour and Swift companies dominated the meat packing businesses.

   Which of the following acts restricted these businesses?

   (1) Clayton Antitrust Act
   (2) National Reclamation Act
   (3) Emergency Quota Act
   (4) Pure Food and Drug Act
   (5) Interstate Commerce Act

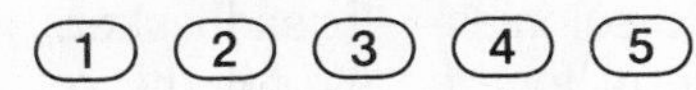

Minitest 2

Directions: Choose the one best answer to each question. Answers are on page 327.

Items 1–2 refer to the table and graph below.

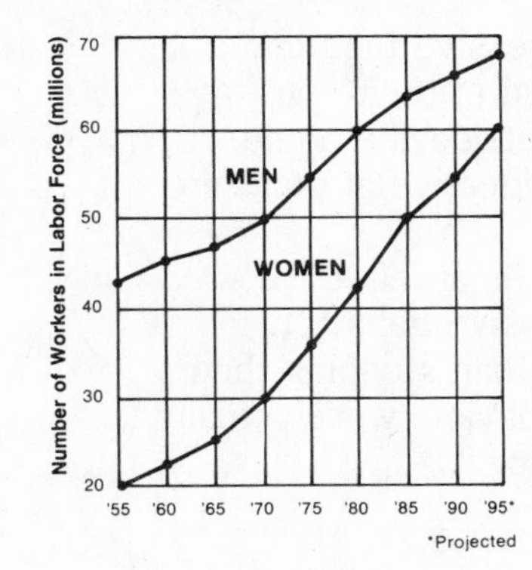

The 10 occupations with largest projected absolute growth from 1984 to 1995

Occupation	Percent women workers in 1985	Number of new jobs by 1995
Cashier	83%	556,000
Nurse	95	452,000
Cleaner	40	443,000
Truck Driver	2	428,000
Waiter/Waitress	84	424,000
Sales (Wholesale)	17	369,000
Nurse's Aide	90	348,000
Sales (Retail)	69	343,000
Accountant	44	307,000
Teacher	90	281,000

1. Which of the following conclusions is valid based on the table?

   (1) There is a low percentage of women truck drivers because it is difficult to get accepted into the Teamster's Union.
   (2) Most of the occupations with the largest projected absolute growth will be unskilled occupations.
   (3) Nursing would be a poor occupation to consider for the future since 95% of the workers are women already.
   (4) More women will be entering male-dominated occupations in the 1990s.
   (5) Teaching is the occupation with the largest projected growth from 1984 to 1995.

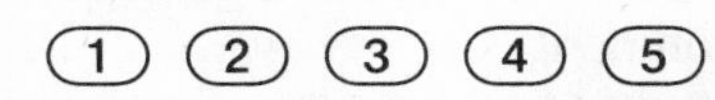

2. Based on information in the table and graph, what can be predicted about the future?

   (1) The United States needs to build more colleges to train women for new careers.
   (2) Eventually women will force men out of the work force and there will be more unemployment.
   (3) Most women will be earning less than $19,000 a year by 1995.
   (4) The Equal Rights Amendment will probably be passed due to the increase of women in the work force.
   (5) The rapid growth of occupations dominated by women means women will keep pouring into the work force and hold nearly as many jobs as men.

3. In a study of very aggressive teenage boys, it was found that they were often physically punished at home by their fathers for aggressive behavior. What is the most likely conclusion that can be drawn from this study?
   (1) Boys are more aggressive than girls.
   (2) The fathers approved of their sons' aggressive behavior outside the home.
   (3) Mothers are more effective at punishing than fathers.
   (4) Physical punishment is an effective way of preventing aggressive behavior.
   (5) The fathers, rather than stopping their sons' aggressive behavior, were actually setting an example for it.

   (1) (2) (3) (4) (5)

4. Geographers study the relationship between people and the land. Geography is a point of view, a way of looking at people and places. It focuses on two central themes: how people use the earth and how the earth influences the way people live. But its goal is always to discover the relationship between land and people.

   According to this passage, geography is
   (1) the science of the earth
   (2) the study of how people feel about themselves
   (3) an opinion about other lands and their peoples
   (4) the study of human beings in their environment
   (5) the study of the various changes the earth undergoes

   (1) (2) (3) (4) (5)

Questions 5–6 refer to the following map.

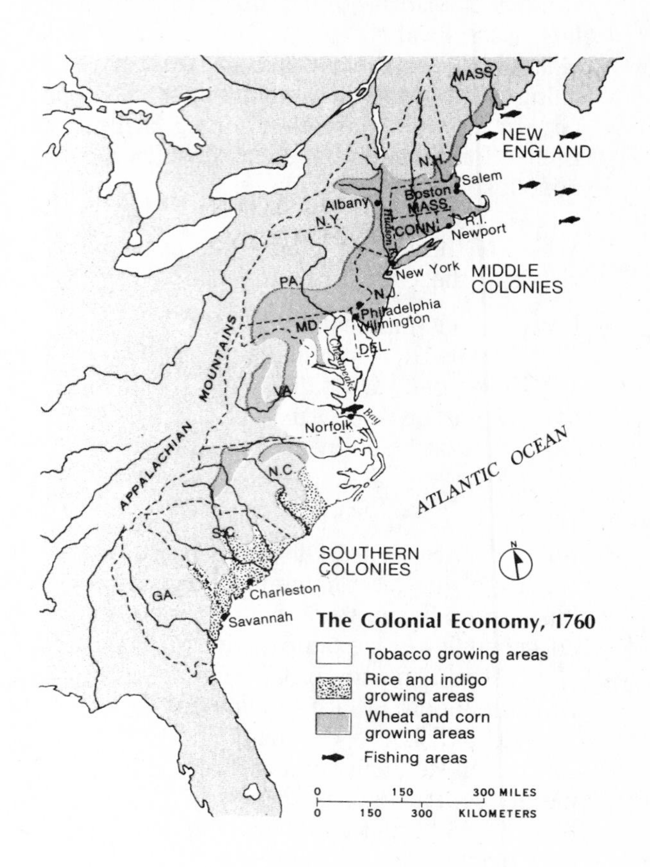

5. Which colonial region is correctly matched with a description of its economy?
   (1) Southern colonies—many small farms raising food crops
   (2) Middle colonies—few port cities
   (3) New England—rice, indigo, and tobacco cash crops on large plantations
   (4) Middle colonies—"breadbasket," or source of food crops, for the rest of the colonies
   (5) Southern colonies—fishing and whaling industries

   (1) (2) (3) (4) (5)

6. In which city would people probably rely most heavily on trade with other areas for their survival?
   (1) Newport
   (2) Philadelphia
   (3) Norfolk
   (4) Charleston
   (5) Savannah

   (1) (2) (3) (4) (5)

7. —By the age of sixty-five, the average American will have spent nine full years watching television.
—By the time our youngsters graduate from high school, they will have spent an average of 11,000 hours in the classroom and 15,000 in front of the television.
—Forty percent of the American public gets all its news from television.
—A youngster watching children's weekend programming has to wait five full weeks before seeing a woman over sixty-five in a leading role.
—One out of every six people in the world watched Prince Charles and Lady Diana get married.

What conclusion about the viewing audience can be drawn from the information given above?

(1) Children watch more television than adults.
(2) Television affects one's view of the world.
(3) Most Americans get all their news from television.
(4) Many television programs feature children.
(5) People all over the world can watch the same television programs every night of the week.

(1) (2) (3) (4) (5)

Item 8 refers to the cartoon below.

8. Which of the following can be inferred from the cartoon above?

(1) Tax reform benefited the poor and hurt the middle class.
(2) The middle class will be taking jobs away from the poor because of tax reform.
(3) Tax reform shoves the middle class "against the wall."
(4) The middle class will impersonate the poor to get better tax reforms for themselves.
(5) The poor will be so heavily taxed it wouldn't be worthwhile to keep even the simplest job.

Minitest 3

Directions: Choose the one best answer to each question. Answers are on pages 327–328.

Items 1–2 refer to the graph below.

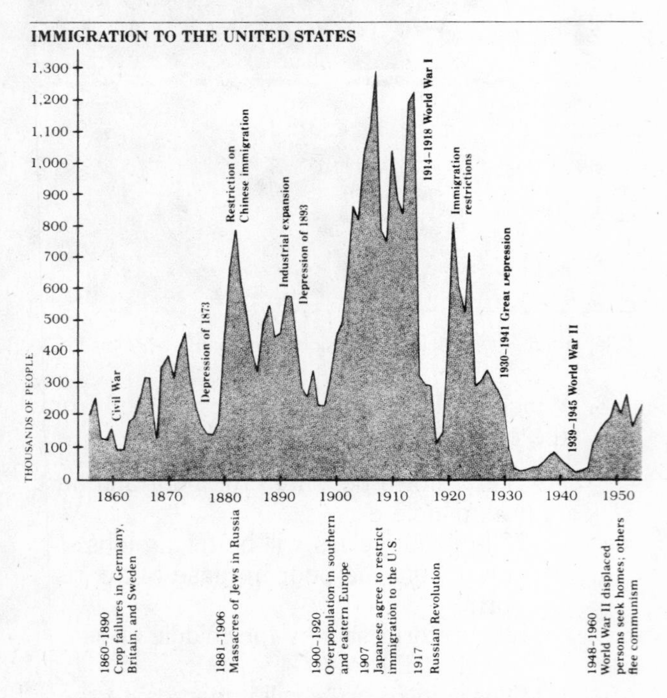

1. Which of the following events seems to reduce immigration to the United States the most?

   (1) immigration restrictions
   (2) crop failures
   (3) expanding industries
   (4) periods of persecution
   (5) wars and depressions

   (1) (2) (3) (4) (5)

2. Which of the following statements is best supported by information from the graph?

   (1) Persecution was the cause of the highest rate of immigration.
   (2) The restriction on Chinese immigrants caused the industrial expansion of 1890.
   (3) Overpopulation is the stimulus for mass immigration.
   (4) The fewest immigrants came when immigration restrictions were imposed.
   (5) Industrial growth caused the highest rate of immigration to the United States.

Listed below are brief descriptions of terms psychologists use when referring to aspects of the personality.

(1) the *id*—the primitive, unconscious part of the personality whose impulses push for expression and gratification even if what is desired is not realistic or morally acceptable
(2) the *superego*—the storehouse of an individual's values, including moral attitudes implanted by society
(3) the *ego*—the arbitrator between the conflicting id and superego. Part of the ego's job is to choose the kinds of action that will gratify id impulses without having undesirable consequences
(4) *ego ideal*—a part of the superego. It develops as a child internalizes the views of others as to the kind of person he or she should strive to become.
(5) *unconscious mind*—where memories are stored that seem to have been forgotten because they are rarely brought to the conscious mind in later life

Items 3–4 refer to one of the aspects of the personality as described above.

3. Melanie hiked to the top of a cliff. As she looked at the environment around her, she got an urge to fly by leaping off the cliff. Instead she went to an amusement park and rode a roller coaster.

   Which of the following personality factors took control of the decision-making process described above?

   (1) id
   (2) superego
   (3) ego
   (4) ego ideal
   (5) unconscious mind

4. Luca was very late driving to work. As he approached an intersection, the traffic light turned red. No other cars were around, so Luca accelerated and went through the red light.

   Which of the following personality factors was dominant in the situation above?

   (1) id
   (2) superego
   (3) ego
   (4) ego ideal
   (5) unconscious mind

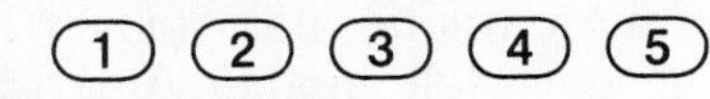

Item 5 refers to the passage below.

With 20 percent of the world's land, Africa is the second-largest continent in both the eastern hemisphere and the world. The continent is almost surrounded by water: the Mediterranean Sea to the north, the Red Sea and Suez Canal to the northeast, the Indian Ocean to the southeast, and the Atlantic Ocean to the south and west. The equator cuts Africa in half, making the countries above it part of the northern hemisphere and the ones below it part of the southern hemisphere.

5. What can be inferred from the passage?

   (1) When it is daytime in South Africa, it is nighttime in North Africa.
   (2) There is no change of seasons in Africa.
   (3) When it is winter in Egypt, it is summer in South Africa.
   (4) When it is summer in South Africa, it is winter in South America.
   (5) Africa is an island.

Items 6–7 are based on the following passage.

Juries are required to be randomly selected, except in minor cases in some states. Potential jurors' names usually are taken from voter registration lists. Even though the Supreme Court held that racial discrimination in jury selection is unconstitutional, minorities are often underrepresented. A number of professions and occupations are quite regularly excused from jury duty. One reason wage earners ask to be excused is that the fee paid for jury service seldom equals their regular pay.

6. Individuals who serve on juries

   (1) are seldom minorities
   (2) must be registered party voters
   (3) represent only a few professions
   (4) commit too many crimes in proportion to their numbers in society
   (5) usually seek to be excused from jury duty

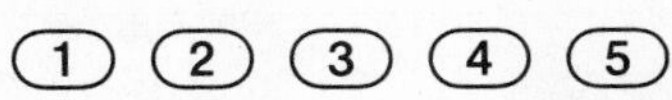

7. Juries often do not represent the adult population as a whole.

   All of the following could be used to support the conclusion above EXCEPT the fact that

   (1) certain professionals usually are excused from having to serve on juries
   (2) juries are dismissed when cases are settled out of court
   (3) voters are more likely to be called for duty than nonvoters
   (4) the number of minorities on juries is less than their occurrence in society
   (5) the jury fee is usually less than what an employed person makes

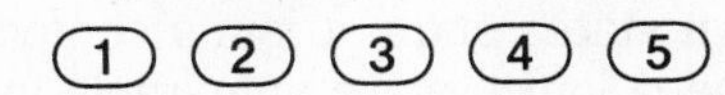

Items 8–9 refer to the following cartoons.

Cartoon A was published by Benjamin Franklin as a warning to the 13 colonies. Cartoon B was published more than 200 years later and refers to the Democratic party.

Cartoon A

Franklin's cartoon was probably based on the myth of the "snapping snake," which broke into pieces to protect itself, but had to rejoin quickly, or die.

Cartoon B

8. Which of the following does Cartoon A suggest?

   (1) The colonies should be drawn and quartered.
   (2) Eight colonies aren't enough to form a nation.
   (3) Colonial leaders wanted to govern their own states and not join a confederacy.
   (4) The colonies were vulnerable unless they united.
   (5) The New England states made it impossible for a permanent union of the colonies.

9. The cartoonist most likely modeled Cartoon B after Cartoon A because

   (1) the disjointed donkey is similar to a snapping snake which breaks into pieces to protect itself
   (2) the head of the party, the liberals, disrupted the Democratic party just as the New England states thwarted colonial efforts to unite
   (3) there are too many self-interest groups in the nation
   (4) the motto "Join or Die" is an appropriate warning to the Democrats whose lack of unity will be their ruin
   (5) the cartoonist felt another American Revolution was approaching

Minitest 4

Directions: Choose the one best answer to each question. Answers are on page 328.

Items 1–2 refer to the passage below.

In the economic war, the challengers change constantly. On the retail battleground, powerful merchants such as Sears, Montgomery Ward, and J. C. Penney lost ground to discount chains like K Mart, Venture, and Target. Corporate heavyweights like Woolco were felled. In the auto arena, the Chrysler Corporation went bankrupt while General Motors, Ford, and AMC lost sales to foreign companies who heeded the demands of American buyers for fuel-efficient cars. On the office machinery front, Xerox, which had dominated the market for photocopying equipment, is fending off competition from a host of Japanese firms and smaller American companies. Even IBM is barraged by competition from new entries and old rivals in the computer field.

1. Which of the following statements is best supported by evidence in the passage?

   (1) Consumers will shop where they can get the best value.
   (2) Companies need security systems to prevent economic ambush.
   (3) Corporate giants are not immune to market pressures.
   (4) Large corporations manipulate consumers through advertising and marketing.
   (5) Brand loyalty is a thing of the past.

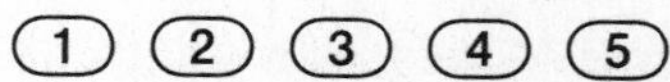

2. Which of the following titles best fits the passage?

(1) Technological Advances Spur Business Growth
(2) Business Is War
(3) The Consumer Is King
(4) The Changing Face of Big Business
(5) Competition: An Economic Spur

1 2 3 4 5

3. The following is a quote from Henry Adams in reference to scandals in President Ulysses S. Grant's administration.

"The progress of evolution from President Washington to President Grant, was alone evidence to upset Darwin."

What did Henry Adams mean?

(1) Darwin's theory of evolution was wrong, and men were evolving into apes.
(2) The United States was becoming a backward nation.
(3) Politics were having a negative rather than a positive effect on federal government.
(4) "In the struggle for existence" government shouldn't help the "unfit."
(5) Darwin's theory of evolution was unpopular among many Americans.

1 2 3 4 5

4. Asia is the largest continent in the eastern hemisphere, and it has more people than any other continent. About 60 percent of the world's people live in Asia. Compared to Asia, Europe is much smaller. Although Europe has only about 7 percent of the world's land, it has 15 percent of the world population.

Based on information in the passage, which of the following can be inferred?

(1) Europe has a higher population density than Asia.
(2) Asia has a higher population density than Europe.
(3) Europe has a higher population rate than the United States.
(4) Europe is not in the eastern hemisphere.
(5) Most economic problems would occur in Asia.

1 2 3 4 5

Items 5–6 refer to the following passage.

Stress is a demand made on a person that may result in harm to him or her or to self-esteem if he or she does not deal with the demand successfully. Sometimes such demands come from the outside world: a teacher assigns students to read "War and Peace" by Friday, or an oncoming car swerves into your path. At other times, the stress is more a matter of an individual putting demands on himself or herself.

5. Which of the following is a statement of someone suffering from self-induced stress?

(1) "We're 10 points behind and the coach told *me* to throw a touchdown pass!"
(2) "If I can't have a new dress for the prom, I'll just die."
(3) "The way this motor sounds I doubt if we'll make it to the next gas station."
(4) "The foreman just sped up the assembly line *again*!"
(5) "Clyde the bully told Cindy he's looking for me."

1 2 3 4 5

6. One specific type of stress is pressure, which requires an individual to speed up, intensify, or alter an ongoing behavior. Which of the following situations is NOT an example of pressure?

(1) John's girlfriend tells him his jokes aren't as funny as they used to be.
(2) Pat's new boss issues a memo detailing a complicated new procedure.
(3) Henry realizes he isn't reading fast enough to finish a library book before it is due.
(4) Olivia turns on the TV to watch the ballgame but discovers the set is broken.
(5) The health club instructor tells Shawn a woman her height should benchpress much more weight than she is currently.

7. Anticipating stress is itself stressful, particularly as the event comes closer in time. Which of the following events would be stressful in this way?

   (1) The neighbor's apartment is burglarized.
   (2) Becky's new car is scraped in the parking lot.
   (3) Tom is preparing for his wedding next week.
   (4) Linda finds she did not make the tennis team.
   (5) A storm interrupts the electric power in the city.

8. According to this cartoon, what would an amendment to abolish the electoral college do?

   (1) run into opposition from big states and city bosses
   (2) equalize power between large and small states
   (3) leave small states with reduced education funds
   (4) reduce the influence of small states over presidential elections
   (5) create alliances among urban and rural voting districts

Item 9 refers to the following passage.

At the end of the 1800s the farmer's condition was growing worse. Improvements in farming were one reason. An agricultural revolution of new techniques and tools had increased production in many parts of the globe. U.S. farmers were producing surpluses, and so were Canadians, Australians, Russians, and Argentines. The only steady market for surplus crops was Western Europe, where cities demanded more than local farmers could produce. But, of course, the competition for the Western European market grew more fierce each year.

9. Based on the passage, farmers in the United States were trapped by

   (1) the laws of supply and demand
   (2) the need for newer equipment
   (3) the railroads whose freight rates were so expensive
   (4) revolution that was disrupting crop yields
   (5) the urbanization of Western Europe

(1) (2) (3) (4) (5)

Minitest Answers

Minitest 1
(pages 317–319)

1. (2) Note map titles and keys. By checking each answer with the data on both maps, you can eliminate all the other cities listed.

2. (3) Options (1) and (2) are invalid, based on the data on both maps; (4) and (5) are valid statements but do not discuss the relationship between rainfall and population.

3. (1) Option (1) is the only option that has an effect on the nuclear family. The other options concern people regardless of their family ties.

4. (1) Since the nuclear family includes parents and children, a brother is part of the nuclear family by definition.

5. (3) The bar graph shows that 40 percent of the population was urban in 1900. Circle graphs (1), (2), (4), and (5) do not show the correct percentage.

6. (4) Option (4) banned the manufacture, sale, or shipment of impure or mislabeled food and drugs in interstate commerce. Although (1) outlawed certain business practices, the above passage is not about trusts. The passage does not address immigration quotas (3), dam construction (2), or railroads (5).

7. (5) The Grange was formed in sympathy with southern farmers who were victims of unfair railroad practices. Although the passage referred to "eastern monopolies," the reference was to railroads.

8. (1) Option (1) outlawed business practices that lessened competition. Options (2)–(4) do not concern business. Option (5) deals specifically with railroad business dealings.

Minitest 2
(pages 319–321)

1. (2) The majority of the occupations listed do not require college education or special skills. There is no information about unions in the table; if you choose (1), you are making an assumption. Option (3) is a misinterpretation of the table. Option (4) is not a conclusion based on information given in the table. The opposite of (5) is true.

2. (5) The projections and percentages in the table indicate that women dominate most of the occupations listed and that there is room for growth. The graph indicates women are rapidly entering the work force. The table and graph do not support (1). Option (2) is untrue because the graph shows that the percentage of men working is increasing. The information in (3) is not in the graph or table. Option (4) is an assumption with no supporting evidence.

3. (5) Options (1) and (3) are not discussed in the paragraph. Options (2) and (4) are false.

4. (4) Option (4) includes the idea that geography is a careful study, not a casual opinion (3) about the relationship between people and the land. Options (1) and (5) mention only the land, and (2) mentions only the people.

5. (4) Option (4) is the only response correctly matching a region with an economy. Note regions and key symbols to eliminate the other options.

6. (3) Norfolk is mainly in a tobacco growing area and would rely on other areas for rice, indigo, wheat, and corn.

7. (2) Check each conclusion with the reading. Option (1) might be true, but it is not a point made in the reading. Option (3) is incorrect because 40 percent is less than most. Options (4) and (5) are incorrect conclusions based on the last two points in the list.

8. (1) You can infer the poor man is happy. He no longer needs to beg since he is kicking away his means of earning a living. The middle-class man takes the poor man's place; he is now the "poor," so he was hurt by tax reform. Although the middle-class man is leaning against a wall, the interpretation of (3) is not correct. The cartoon contains no evidence from which (2) could be inferred or (4) or (5) suggested.

Minitest 3
(pages 322–324)

1. (5) Note the title, axes, and where the lowest points are on the graph. Low levels of immigration occurred in 1860, the mid-to late 1870s, the mid-1890s, between 1915 and 1920, and throughout the 1930s until about 1945.

2. (3) Find the highest point on the graph and then look to the bottom axis for the information. The greatest number of immigrants came as a result of overpopulation in southern and eastern Europe between 1900 and 1920.

3. (3) The ego acted as go-between for the id, which wanted to fly, and the superego, which realized the folly of such an act. The ego found that a roller coaster ride would satisfy both the id and the superego.

4. (1) The id wanted to keep driving even though the stoplight came on. Instead of stopping completely and waiting for the green light, Luca continued through the intersection.

5. (3) Because the equator divides Africa between the north and south hemispheres, the seasons differ. All the other options are false.

6. (2) The passage states that names of potential jurors usually are taken from voter registration lists. All four other options are not supported by evidence in the passage.

7. (2) Option (2) does not support the conclusion. Out-of-court settlements do not affect jury selection or representation. Option (4) restates the conclusion, while (1), (3), and (5) support it.

8. (4) The colonies had to unite to protect themselves from an attack by the French, and 20 years later, they would unite against the British. "Join or Die" was the motto of the American Revolution. Option (1) is an incorrect interpretation of Cartoon A. There is no evidence to imply (2) or to suggest (3) or (5) in the cartoon.

9. (4) The separate groups are similar to the separate colonies; they are vulnerable if they don't unite. Therefore, the motto is appropriate advice to the Democratic party. There is no such thing as a disjointed donkey or a snapping snake as described in (1). The myth of the snake was popular in Benjamin Franklin's time. Option (3) is wrong because the donkey represents a political party not the nation. Option (2) interprets the symbol too literally when it states liberals head the party because the donkey's head is labeled "liberals." Option (5) is not supported by the cartoon.

Minitest 4
(pages 324–326)

1. (3) Size alone does not protect modern corporations from competitive pressures. Options (1), (2), (4), and (5) are not supported by evidence in the passage.

2. (4) The passage describes how large companies are coping with new competition. There is no mention of new technology affecting business growth (1) or how consumer demands determine business activity (3). Options (2) and (5) agree with the war analogy but do not summarize the passage.

3. (3) "Upsetting Darwin" would mean going from a higher level to a lower level; the mention of scandals reinforces the idea. Options (1), (2), and (4) interpret Adams's statement too literally. Option (5) is irrelevant.

4. (1) Since 15 percent of the world's population lives on 7 percent of the world's land, there are more people per square mile in Europe than in Asia, where there are more people living on a greater amount of land. Option (2) is the opposite of the correct answer. Option (4), although true, is not alluded to in the passage. The U.S. population rate is not mentioned in the passage (3), nor are economic problems (5).

5. (2) Option (2) is the only one in which a person makes demands upon herself. The other options concern demands made by persons other than the speaker.

6. (4) Option (4) is not an example of pressure since the situation does not portray a behavior in process. Options (1) and (2) impose a change in behavior, while (3) and (5) call for people to intensify behavior in progress.

7. (3) Option (3) is the only one that has an upcoming event. The other options describe things that have already occurred.

8. (4) The small states are obviously suffering in this cartoon, and the amendment would only affect national elections, so (2), (3), and (5) can be eliminated. It is difficult to predict (1).

9. (1) As the quantity of farm products rose, the prices buyers were willing to pay fell. As world production rose, U.S. farmers found it difficult to sell their crops abroad. Options (2) and (4) are false. New farm equipment was already being used. There was no revolution in the United States during the late 1800s. The urbanization of Western Europe was a help not a hindrance to farmers since it provided the market for their crops (5). Railroad rates (3) were not a factor contributing to surplus crops.

The GED Science Test

How important is science in your daily life? If you said "Not very," think again. Without science, we wouldn't have some of the fabrics we wear, the appliances we depend on, or even many of the foods we eat. Think too about basic human curiosity. Isn't it just human nature to wonder about what lies in the reaches of outer space and how we can eliminate disease? Science influences your life every day whether you study it or not.

The GED Science Test is made up of items from just four areas of science: biology, earth science, chemistry, and physics. There are two types of items on the test. One type, called a *single item,* begins with a short statement of information or with some type of visual such as a diagram, chart, or table, and then asks a question about that material. The second type, called the *item set,* begins with a longer reading passage, for example, an essay of three or four paragraphs or a set of definitions, or possibly a combination of visual material with written material. A cluster of test items then relates to that material. All test items are in multiple-choice format. That means there is a question to answer or a sentence to complete and then five possible answer choices. You simply need to select the one choice that best completes the item.

Pages 329–386 of this book will give you important basic information to help you answer the items on the GED Science Test. Even more importantly, those pages will help you develop the reading and thinking skills you need for the test.

On each of the next ten pages you will see two columns, both in color tint. They give help in developing test-taking skills and also basic reading skills such as finding the main idea, discovering the meanings of unfamiliar words, and getting information from illustrations, tables, charts, and diagrams. They also show you how to use some important thinking skills, for instance, how to apply a new concept or idea to another situation, how to use analysis, and how to evaluate ideas and information as you read.

The next series of pages have tinted inner columns with information you need in the subject areas and some vocabulary as background for the test. There are also handy Test-Taking Tips, and Need a Hint? sections, which help you to arrive at the right answer to questions in the white outer columns. These practice test items will help you to become familiar with the kinds of questions you will find in the GED Test. Unless you are instructed otherwise, remember to read the tinted material on each page before you go on to the sample test items in the outer columns.

You . . . and Science . . . and Success
Before you begin your actual preparation for the GED Science Test, think about how much you already know about science. Are you interested in reading about new developments in medicine, air- and water-pollution control, or space exploration? Do you enjoy the outdoors and its plants and animals? Do you wish you knew more about the natural forces that influence our weather or produce earthquakes and volcanic eruptions? If you can answer yes to any of these questions, chances are that you know much more about science than you realize.

It is true, of course, that you can't possibly know all there is to learn from the millions of volumes written about scientific subjects. Nobody can. So you shouldn't feel discouraged if your present knowledge is limited. What you will need to do for the GED Test is to learn to get the most out of your reading and reasoning skills and to add as much as you can to your background of factual knowledge.

You and Your Attitudes Your attitudes, too, can affect your performance on the GED Test. Careful preparation will give you confidence, and that attitude is a big help. But certain attitudes tend to work against people. Occasionally, for instance, people find that some of the basic concepts of science may be in conflict with personal values or religious beliefs. Darwin's theory of evolution is an example. Some people believe that Darwin's theory *is* true; others hesitate to accept the theory because it conflicts with their religious beliefs. In a test-taking situation, it is important to remain objective and to remember that it *is* a test, not an attempt to persuade you to change your beliefs. The writers of the GED Test are always careful to avoid using any material that is likely to be at all offensive.

On the subject of attitudes, if you thought carefully about your own attitudes toward science, what would your feelings be about science and scientists in general? Do you think of their work as being beyond your powers of understanding? Do you tend to regard scientists as a different breed with a language of their own?

You and the Scientific Process You may feel more comfortable about science when you become more familiar with the method scientists follow. Do you know how an idea becomes an accepted fact in the scientific community? The first step the scientist must take is to identify the problem, for example, what causes cancer?

Then the scientist must decide just what it is that he or she needs to look for. A good deal of careful thought, work, and study goes into this step, which is called *developing a hypothesis.* A hypothesis is a statement of what is believed to be a reasonable explanation. Then the scientist *designs experiments* to find out whether the hypothesis is correct. A decision must be made about the best procedures to follow and the best tools to use. Data are gathered and recorded carefully. If results of the experiments support the hypothesis, then it is *accepted as a theory.* The theory may bring up more questions that lead to further tests and experiments.

Only after other scientists or scientific groups have conducted the same experiments and have duplicated the same results is the hypothesis *accepted as a fact.* This process can take many years. Sometimes long after the general public has accepted a fact, more is discovered that proves the believed fact to be wrong. Then scientists start over again with a new hypothesis.

Think about the ancient theory of how the universe is constructed. The ancients believed the earth was at the center of the universe and that the sun, stars, and planets were embedded in crystal balls, or spheres, that revolved around the earth. The movement of these spheres, they believed, created pleasant sounds that were called "the music of the spheres." You can well imagine that this delightful view of the universe could not withstand the type of testing and experimentation that is typical of science today. Now, our advanced knowledge and scientific instruments confirm the idea of the sun as the center of our solar system, with the earth and other planets circling it. This has been tested and retested. It is accepted as a fact that the sun lies at the center of our solar system.

If a scientist, or anyone else, decides how something works before it is proven by hypothesis, experiment, theory, and duplication, he or she is not using the scientific method.

☑ Test-Taking Tips

No matter how extensive or how limited your knowledge, there are some things you can do to achieve your very best possible score. The following material offers a number of hints for dealing with the GED Science Test as a whole and then for dealing with individual test items.

Be Test-wise Knowing how to take a test can be just as important as knowing what answers to mark. Being test-wise means finding out what to expect on the test and learning how to use your time and information wisely. You need to know, for instance, that the GED Test does not give penalties for incorrect answers, so you can probably raise your score by answering *all* questions on the test, even when you're not absolutely certain of some answers. Since you will not be allowed to use a dictionary on the test, you'll want to practice using context clues to discover the meanings of unfamiliar words.

Plan Your Time Most people are able to complete the GED Science Test quite comfortably in the time allowed. It is a good idea, though, to keep track of time as you work through the test. Before you begin, glance at the clock and calculate at what time you will need to hand in the test. As you take the test, check the time occasionally to see if you are moving through the items at a fast enough pace. Try to be at least halfway through the items when the time is half gone.

If you get stuck on one item and find that you are taking a long time to answer it, mark a possible answer for that item and then move on. If you place a checkmark in the margin next to the puzzling item, you can come back to it later and rethink your answer.

If you finish before the time is over, go back and check your answers carefully. Be sure to take advantage of *all* the time you are given for the test.

Focus on Careful Thinking Memorizing fact after fact is *not* the best way to prepare for the GED Test. More important than simply recalling information is being able to use it to recognize and understand different relationships among ideas as you read. Often, all the information you need is given right in the test item. Your challenge is to process the information in your mind.

Practice using your thinking skills by reading and answering the sample test item.

A person with Type A blood can receive a donation of Type A or Type O blood. A person with Type B blood can receive either Type B or Type O blood. A Type AB person can receive Type A, Type B, Type AB, or Type O blood. A Type O person can safely receive Type O blood only. A person with which blood type can be considered a universal donor?

(1) Type A (2) Type B
(3) Type AB (4) Type O
(5) All blood types can be donated to everyone.

(1) (2) (3) (4) (5)

If you understand that universal means "applying to all," you can figure out the answer. Go back and read the question again. You might even want to draw an informal diagram on scrap paper to help you process the information. Which blood type is mentioned in each sentence? Persons with all blood types can receive Type O blood, so the correct answer is option (4), Type O.

Other types of questions may require you to apply a scientific concept to an everyday situation, analyze different steps in a process, or evaluate different ideas to see how—or whether—they are useful in a particular situation.

The best way to become comfortable with these thinking skills is to practice them. Pages 334–339 will get you started with these skills, and the outer columns questions on pages 340–386 will give further practice.

Developing Reading Skills The following discussion will help you brush up on basic reading skills you'll use in science. If you want to see examples or need to practice, feel free to refer to the section on reading in this book.

Main Idea Locating the main idea will help you comprehend what you are reading, and it will help you organize your thoughts about the topic or subject of the passage. It also will help you remember later what you have read.

To find the main idea of a passage, first ask yourself what the passage is about. Then ask what the central, most important statement made about the topic is; that statement will be the main idea. In a well-written passage, all the other sentences will add examples, details, or other types of information that refer in some way to the main idea. These are *supporting details.* They help the reader understand the main idea as completely as possible.

Often, but not always, the main idea is stated in the first sentence of a paragraph. Sometimes a writer will choose to give the main idea in the last sentence, where it serves as a type of summary statement.

Sometimes a writer will choose to write a paragraph without stating the main idea. In such a case, the details will lead the reader to *infer* the main idea, that is, to figure it out for herself or himself. In any case, whether the main idea is stated at the beginning, middle, or end—or even left unstated—you can find the main idea by deciding what the topic is and then deciding what the central, most important idea developed about that topic is.

Not all passages on the GED Test will be just a single paragraph—many will have two, three, or more. Each paragraph will have its own main idea, and each paragraph will also provide supporting information about the main idea of the entire passage. To find the idea of the whole passage, use exactly the same process that you use with individual paragraphs. The process works in the same way, no matter how long or how complex the reading passage might be.

Supporting Details Details give a reader a more complete understanding of the main idea. Without them, a reading passage would have just the bare essentials. You can improve your comprehension and your ability to recall material if you can see the overall picture or pattern that the writer uses to organize the details. Some paragraphs are organized to show a comparison or contrast. Some simply list a group of reasons. Others divide a topic into categories. You will find examples of these different types of organization on the GED Test.

The paragraph below develops a contrast, showing differences between moths and butterflies. Understanding the pattern will help you organize the information in your mind.

■ There are a few differences between butterflies and moths. Butterflies are usually active during the daytime, while most moths fly at night. Moths are usually much duller in color than the brightly colored butterflies. Butterflies' antennae have knobs at the end, while those of moths do not. The bodies of butterflies are more slender than those of moths.

Take a careful look at the next sample paragraph. The main idea is stated in the first sentence, and the remaining sentences give supporting details—except for one sentence. That one sentence is really out of place in the paragraph because, while it is about the topic, it does not support the main idea stated. See if you can recognize which sentence does not belong.

■ The qualifications for becoming an astronaut early in the American space program were very strict. Applicants had to be males between the ages of twenty-five and forty. Other criteria considered essential were a willingness to accept hazardous conditions, a capacity to tolerate severe physical stress, and the ability to react quickly in a crisis. The word *astronaut* means "sailor among the stars." All of the early astronauts were former military test pilots.

Did you identify the sentence that does not belong? The next to the last sentence, although it is about astronauts, does not contribute to the main idea—that the qualifications for being an astronaut in the early days were very strict. That sentence, therefore, is not a supporting detail; it belongs in another paragraph.

Dealing with Scientific Language The following material will help you deal with words and concepts that are new to you.

Unfamiliar Words When you come across an unfamiliar word in your reading about science, a word like *pterodactyl* or *deoxygenate,* do you feel as if you'd just like to give up and read something else instead? You're not alone! Many people get nervous when they meet a long, unfamiliar word, especially one from a foreign language, printed in italics. That seems to make the word even more difficult.

The first step in overcoming that nervous feeling is to realize that you *can* overcome it. The second step is to get into the habit of using *context clues* and *word-part clues* to figure out the meanings of many new words as you are reading. The sample test items in the outer columns of this science section provide such clues so these skills will become especially useful when you are taking the GED Test.

Context Clues The *context* of a word is the set of words that surround it. Often the context will give a hint as to the meaning of an unfamiliar word. Read the following example. Below the sentence write what you think the underlined word means and then write the clue given in the sentence.

■ Many plants are phototropic; they bend or turn toward the source of light.

Phototropic means ______________________

The clue is ______________________

If you wrote that *phototropic* means "turning or bending towards the light," you were correct. The clue is the brief definition given just after the word itself. If that seems unusually easy to you, start noticing in your reading how often an unusual word is defined right within the same sentence.

What do you think is the meaning of the underlined word in the next sentence? What is the clue?

■ Dr. Wilson has spent the last two years studying how monerans, one-celled organisms better known as bacteria, can cause disease.

Monerans are ______________________

The clue is ______________________

You can mark your answer correct if you wrote that monerans are one-celled organisms or if you wrote they are bacteria. The clue, of course, is the description given just after the word *monerans*.

Now try this last sentence.

■ Chameleons, like other lizards, shed their skin regularly.

A *chameleon* is a ______________________

The clue is ______________________

A chameleon is a lizard; the clue is the comparison between chameleons and other lizards.

Read the following passage from a chapter about the human circulatory system. See if you can use context clues to figure out the meanings of *aorta, arterioles,* and *capillaries.* Write the definitions and the clues below the passage.

■ From the heart, blood is pumped into the aorta, the largest blood vessel in the body. The aorta distributes blood throughout the body. The aorta branches into arteries which turn into the smallest arteries, the arterioles. From the arterioles the blood flows into the smallest vessels, the capillaries. The capillaries carry the blood to the individual cells of the body where oxygen and food are delivered and metabolic waste products are collected for disposal.

The *aorta* is ______________________

The clue is ______________________

An *arteriole* is ______________________

The clue is ______________________

A *capillary* is ______________________

The clue is ______________________

In all three cases, the clue is a brief definition given directly before or after the word. The *aorta* is the largest artery or blood vessel; an *arteriole* is the smallest artery; and a *capillary* is the smallest blood vessel of all.

A final word about context clues: It is not always possible to figure out the meaning of a word from its context. If context clues won't work in a particular situation, you can try word-part clues, discussed next. And some readers find that if they cannot decide the meaning of a word in any other way, they simply read the sentence, skipping over the unfamiliar word, and still get the basic thought or meaning of the sentence. Keep these ideas in mind in your reading.

Word-Part Clues *Biology . . . geology . . . dermatology*—what do those three words have in common? If you said that they all end in the same five letters, you are right. And if you said that all of them name a particular area of study in the sciences, you are also correct. The ending of those words, *-ology,* comes from an ancient Greek word that means "the study of."

Sometimes you can figure out the meaning of an unfamiliar word if you know the meanings of its parts. Practice putting word parts together in the four items at the top of page 334. Each of the words you "build" ends in *-ology,* so you know that each of them means the study of something.

1. *bio* (meaning "life" or "living things") with *-ology* is *biology,* which means ______________________________

2. *geo* (meaning "earth") with *-ology* is *geology,* which means ______________________________

3. *derma* (meaning "the skin") with *-ology* is *dermatology,* which means ______________________________

4. *epi* (meaning "visit") and *demos* (meaning "people") with *-ology* is *epidemiology,* which means ______________________________

Here is another challenge. Do you think that you could figure out the meaning of the word *electroencephalogram? Encephalo-* refers to the brain and its activity. The word part *electro-* refers to electricity, while *-gram* means "a writing or recording." When you put the parts together in order, you'll find that an electroencephalogram is a recording of the electrical activity of the brain. Do you think that you could figure out the meaning of the word *cardiogram* if you knew that *cardio-* refers to the heart?

The subjects of earth science, chemistry, and physics introduce another set of word parts that will be useful to you as you read passages about the sciences. You may already be familiar with many of them and their meanings. The word parts are listed on the left, while the definitions are scrambled on the right. Try to find the definition that goes with each word part. Write the letter in the blank.

____	**1.** astro-	**a.** relating to heat
____	**2.** hydro-	**b.** relating to the stars
____	**3.** micro-	**c.** under
____	**4.** -port	**d.** far away
____	**5.** photo-	**e.** relating to light
____	**6.** tele-	**f.** to carry
____	**7.** therm-	**g.** relating to water
____	**8.** trans-	**h.** very small
____	**9.** sub-	**i.** relating to air
____	**10.** pneum-	**j.** across

Answers
1. study of life and living things **2.** study of the earth **3.** study of the skin **4.** study of diseases affecting many people

Use a combination of context clues and word-part clues to "crack" the meanings of the underlined words below. Use your own paper.

■ Yellowstone Park has a fascinating underworld—a world of subsurface hot springs, geysers, and other types of geothermal activity. Visitors to the park may feel as if they have been transported to a far corner of the earth, where the usual laws of nature don't apply. Television and photographs simply cannot do justice to the awesome landscape of Yellowstone Park.

Expanding Your Vocabulary in Other Ways In addition to using context clues and word-part clues, you could create a card file of new words and their meanings. This file would be especially helpful for new science words because you remember words better when you write them down. You can review the words in your file as a last-minute reminder of their meanings the day before you take the science section of the GED Test.

Understanding Visual Aids It has been said that a picture is worth a thousand words. An illustration, chart, or diagram that is well presented can add a great deal to your understanding of a particular concept, process, or object. For example, study the two photographs of blood cells on page 335. What can you learn from these pictures? Which do you think would give you a clearer idea of what a red blood cell looks like—a description in words or the picture? Which do you think would give you a

Answers
1. b **2.** g **3.** h **4.** f **5.** e **6.** d **7.** a **8.** j **9.** c **10.** i

Sample Answers
subsurface = under the surface; *geothermal* = heated within the earth; *transported* = carried across; *television* = vision at a great distance; *photographs* = recordings of light

clearer idea of the contrast between a normal red blood cell and a sickled red blood cell? Most likely, you would agree that the photograph gives a better understanding in both cases.

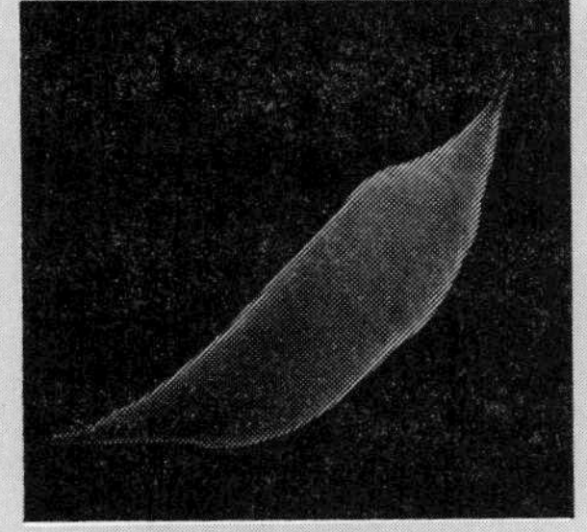

Sickled Red Blood Cell

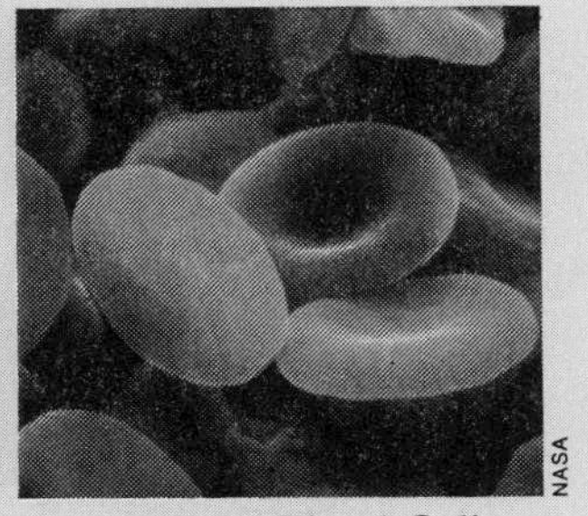

Normal Red Blood Cell

Some of the questions on the GED Science Test may require you to get information from a diagram, graph, or illustration. There are special skills in learning the art of reading visual aids, too. The following discussion will give you some tips on getting the most from visual aids.

A *diagram* is a special kind of drawing that helps make something clear by showing only the essential parts. A diagram may make a point all by itself, or it may accompany a written explanation so that the two work together to provide information. Usually a diagram illustrates a particular type of relationship. It might show the steps in a process; it might compare or contrast two things; it might show the division of a main category into smaller ones; it might show the relationships among the different parts of an object; or it might show the cross-section of an object as though it had been split down the middle to allow you to peer inside.

Below is a diagram that shows both the inside and the outside of something at the same time; one end of the object has been cut away in the drawing to allow you to see the inside.

A GED Test question about this diagram might be, What are the many small disk-shaped objects inside the chloroplast called?

Inside a chloroplast

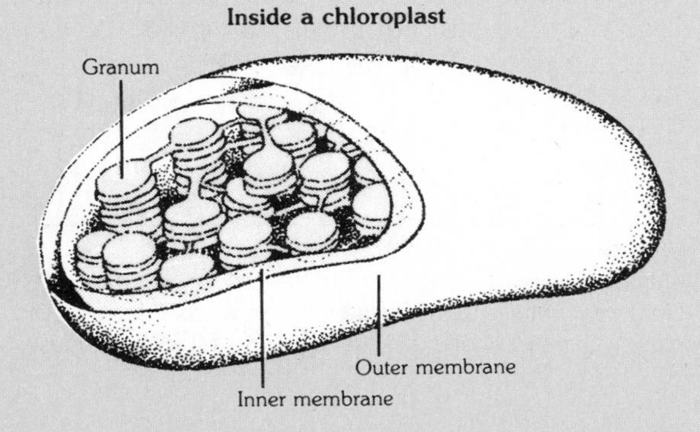

A *graph* presents information in a form that allows you to see comparisons, contrasts, relative sizes, distances, and so forth. The example given below was made by a student in a circuitry class. She wanted to compare four computers to see how fast each could process the same piece of information. Each computer she tested is represented by a bar on the graph. The number of seconds necessary to process the information is shown on the left. Which computer processed the information most rapidly? Which was slowest?

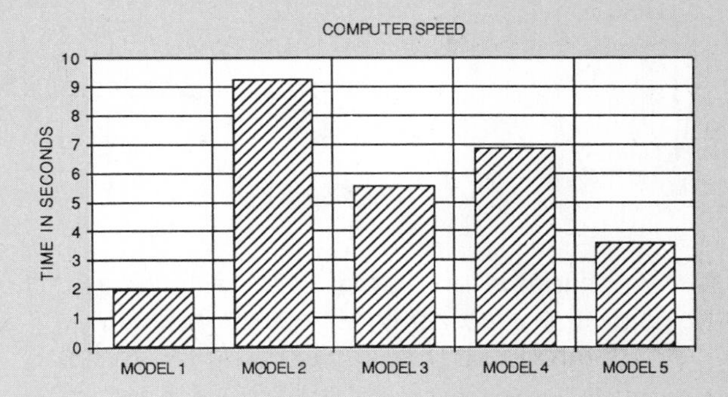

If you said that model 1 was the fastest and model 2 the slowest, you were right.

To get information from a graph quickly and efficiently, be sure to read the headings along the top or bottom and side. If you read the headings first, you will see exactly what type of information is given in the graph and in what order it is presented.

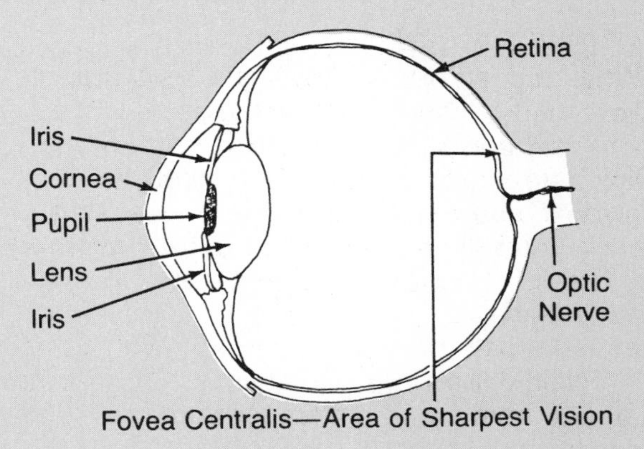

1. What is the name of the dark area in the center of the iris?

---

2. What is the area of sharpest vision on the retina called?

Answers
1. pupil **2.** fovea centralis

Sometimes when a diagram and written explanation are given together, the labels for the parts of the diagram are given in a paragraph rather than on the diagram itself. Notice how the parts of a flashlight in the diagram below are numbered. You can find the name of each part by matching the numbers with those in the written explanation.

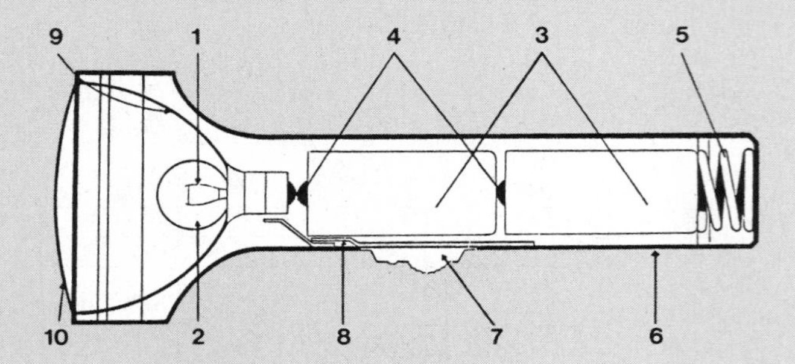

■ A flashlight is an electric light. A tiny *wire* (1) inside the *bulb* (2) lights up when electricity flows through it. Electricity comes from the *batteries* (3) through the metal pieces called *electrodes* (4) to the bulb. The batteries are behind the bulb. They are held in place by a *spring* (5) in the end of the *case* (6). The *switch* (7) on the outside of the flashlight controls the flow of electricity. When the switch is pressed, a small piece of *copper* (8) touches a battery. The electricity starts flowing. A *reflector* (9) is a cone-shaped piece of shiny metal. It is covered by a curved piece of glass called a *lens* (10).

When a chart or diagram illustrates a process, you need to figure out how the steps in the process, from first to last, are shown. Sometimes arrows or some other symbols will be given to show how the process moves, but often you will need to figure out the pattern for yourself. You will not always be able to read the diagrammed process from left to right—which is a logical pattern, since our eyes travel in that direction while we read—at times you may have to read from top to bottom, or from right to left.

Study the diagram below and then answer the questions that follow.

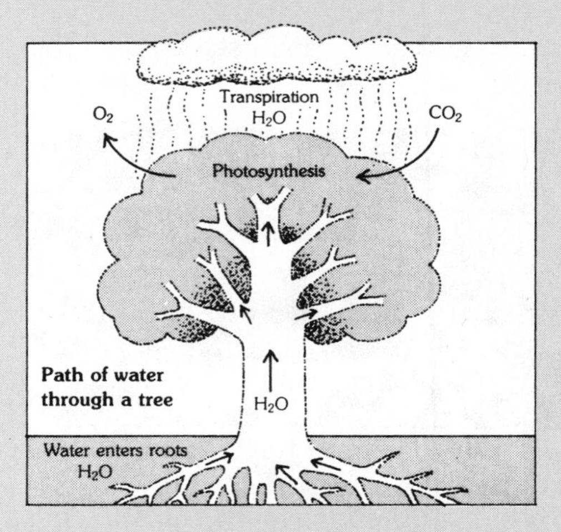

1. Where does water enter the tree?

---

2. What does H_2O mean in the diagram?

---

3. What does the cloud indicate about what happens when water leaves the tree?

Applying Information A mechanic is showing her young son how to clean a rusty, dirty piece of metal in an acid bath. Before she pours the acid into the soaking tray, she places a large box of baking soda on the workbench. She knows that the acid could injure them seriously, so she takes the safeguard of having soda nearby. In case the acid spills, the soda could neutralize the acid, making it harmless. The mechanic is applying a basic principle of chemistry in her work.

Some items on the GED Science Test will require you to apply some scientific information to a practical, everyday situation similar to the one just described. The test items will supply you with the important information; your job will be to process the information in your mind to see how it can be applied, or used, in a different situation. Some test items may simply state or explain the principle to be used. Others may illustrate the principle in a reading or in visual material.

Answers

1. Water enters at the tip of the roots. **2.** H_2O is the chemical formula for water. **3.** The water vaporizes as it travels out through the leaves and into the sky, where it forms clouds.

Try using the skill of application. First look at the diagram and read the explanation below it.

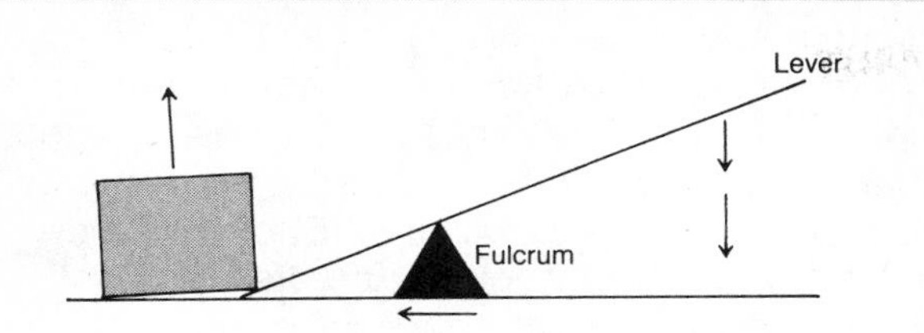

One of the oldest—and most effective—tools used to move heavy objects is a lever used over a fulcrum, which may be a rock, log, or other solid, stationary object. The closer the fulcrum is to the object that is being lifted, the greater the force that is exerted on the object by pressing on the opposite end of the lever.

Study the diagram to see how the lever and fulcrum work together. When the right end of the lever is pressed down (as indicated by the arrows in the diagram), the left end of the lever will exert upward force on the heavy object. When the fulcrum is placed closer to the heavy object, greater lifting force will be exerted.

Do you understand the principle? If you are still a little uncertain, take a moment to think about ways in which you might use the principle in your own life. In other words, imagine how you might apply the principle yourself.

Now read the question and choose the answer you think is best.

A homeowner tries to pry loose a stump using a steel rod as a lever over a cement block. On the first try the stump will not move. What might be done to increase the chances of moving the stump?

(1) move the block away from the stump
(2) move the block closer to the stump
(3) replace the block with a rock
(4) grasp the rod closer to the block
(5) reverse the rod

Option (2) is the correct choice. If the fulcrum is moved closer to the object being lifted, the lifting force will be greater. By moving the cement block closer to the stump, the homeowner will increase the chances of moving the stump.

Now try another way of applying information to a situation. Two categories of matter are defined below; these are followed by passages referring to substances that fit the categories. Compare the information given in the definitions and the passages and identify the category each substance belongs to. Explain your choice in complete sentences.

organic—related to or originating from living or once-living organisms
inorganic—composed from matter other than plant or animal

■ Coal is formed much as other fossil fuels are formed from ancient plant and animal remains. Coal, however, usually appears nearer the earth's surface.

____

____

■ Salt occurs naturally in land and water. It is used primarily to preserve and season food, although it has many other functions in industry.

____

____

The first passage tells you that coal is made from plant and animal remains, so you can identify coal as an organic substance. The second passage states that salt occurs naturally in land and water. Because it is not plant or animal matter, salt is inorganic.

☑ A Test-Taking Tip

When you answer questions that require you to use application, first check your understanding of the principle by imagining how *you* could apply it in your life.

Using Analysis *Analysis* means breaking down a process, problem, or relationship into its parts. When you use analytical thinking, you consider a topic carefully to see what its different parts are and how they fit together. Analysis involves more complicated thinking than just reading or applying a scientific principle.

The example tells how analysis helped people understand the nature of a problem they faced.

■ Oakville, a small midwestern community, suddenly experienced an enormous increase in rainfall. An investigative team was hired to find out why. After careful study, the team discovered that two factors had worked together to increase Oakville's rainfall. First, a new chemical factory several miles west of Oakville was emitting large amounts of a chemical used to "seed" clouds in order to produce rain. Second, prevailing winds swept the "seeded" clouds east, directly over Oakville. The combination of the two factors caused Oakville's rain to increase.

The GED Test will include several different types of questions that call for analytical thinking. With some items, you need to identify causes or effects. With others, you need to detect assumptions that the author has made but not stated. With still others, you will be required to distinguish between facts and opinions or between supporting evidence and a conclusion. If this sounds difficult, remember that the test item will provide you with the necessary information; you simply need to think carefully about what you read and note how different parts of the information fit together.

Try using your analytical skills with this sample test item.

In some parts of the world people are able to use geothermal energy, or heat from inside the earth. For instance, residents of Iceland have built huge cement pipes to bring water from natural hot springs into their cities. The hot water heats their homes in winter, provides all the hot water they need for home life and industry, and even supplies them with the luxury of naturally heated water for health spas and outdoor swimming pools.

Which of the following is NOT an advantage of using water from natural hot springs?

(1) It reduces air pollution caused by burning different fuels.
(2) It conserves valuable fossil fuels.
(3) It eliminates the need to buy furnaces, boilers, or water heaters.
(4) It avoids the cost of importing coal, oil, and fuels from other countries.
(5) It uses a heating system that is readily available in all parts of the world.

(1) (2) (3) (4) (5)

The correct answer is (5). Using naturally heated water would save fossil fuels, avoid pollution from those fuels, and avoid transportation costs and cost of equipment to burn fuel. With those four cause-and-effect relationships in mind, you can eliminate options (1), (2), (3), and (4). But is option (5) an advantage of using hot-spring water? No, the passage states that geothermal energy can be used in some, but not all, parts of the world. Option (5) does *not* describe an advantage of using water from hot springs; it answers the question best.

Now try another type of test item that involves using analysis. Read the passage and then think about possible answers to the question that follows.

The female sea turtle lays her eggs in sand. Because the eggs are easily found, different types of predators are able to eat many of them before they hatch. In past years, conservationists have tried to aid this endangered species by hiding the eggs in coolers, covering them with canvas, or reburying them in hidden spots until they hatch.

Recent evidence, however, suggests that sea turtle eggs which are incubated at cooler temperatures produce only males, while those that are incubated in the sun's warmth produce females. Conservationists who hide eggs in cool, hidden places may actually be further endangering the species by reducing the number of females that hatch.

Which of the following is a statement of fact?

(1) Well-meaning conservationists could actually endanger the sea turtle species.
(2) We should do more research on the sea turtle.
(3) Some types of predators eat sea turtle eggs.
(4) Temperature may determine whether sea turtle eggs produce males or females.
(5) Conservationists should be more closely controlled.

(1) (2) (3) (4) (5)

Option (3) is correct. Options (1), (2), and (5) are opinions. While nearly everyone may agree with them, they cannot be *proved* true. Option (4) is a hypothesis. Only (3) states a fact.

Using Evaluation On the GED Science Test you can expect to find questions that ask you to evaluate some statements, items, or pieces of evidence. It's especially important to realize that you need to decide on the worth of the idea or evidence *as it relates to the situation described on the test.* Instead of relying on popular ideas, hearsay, or just what "sounds best" to you, make your decisions according to information set up in the test item.

Some GED Test items may ask you to evaluate several possible pieces of evidence to determine which one best supports a particular conclusion. Here's an example for you to try.

The label on a package of a popular brand of ice cream makes these claims:

A. contains all natural ingredients
B. flavor that everyone loves
C. only 100 calories per 1/2 cup serving
D. now richer and tastier than ever

Which of the above statements could NOT be proven in laboratory analysis of the product?

(1) A only
(2) B only
(3) A and B only
(4) A and C only
(5) B and D only

The correct answer is (5). A and C are statements that are capable of being verified in a laboratory. But B and D are individual judgments or opinions. There is no way to measure that everyone enjoys a particular flavor; opinions and tastes vary from person to person.

Other types of evaluative test items ask you to decide whether evidence is relevant or whether it is accurate. Information will be given in the test item to help you make such decisions. Still other test items may ask you to detect faulty logic.

Detecting faulty thinking is not always easy. Some types of illogical thinking result from a misunderstanding of the way some words are used. Others result from believing that an opinion is a fact. Very often, illogical thinking results from overgeneralizing—from thinking that what is true of a few cases is true of all. Faulty thinking also can result from a misinterpretation of events or time relationships. For example, during the 1600s doctors thought that illness was caused by bad blood rather than viruses. Because of this faulty logic, patients were "bled" to remove bad blood from their systems. We now realize that taking blood from an ill person is harmful not helpful to recovery since the blood manufactures antibodies that fight against disease.

In the sample test item below, you need to evaluate different pieces of evidence. Be alert for an example of faulty thinking.

In some areas of Canada and the northeastern United States, rainfall with a high acid content has raised the level of acid in streams and lakes.

Which of the following pieces of evidence does NOT support the belief that something must be done to stop acid rain?

(1) Many types of desirable fish can't survive in acidic water.
(2) Tiny plants that feed many water animals can't survive in acidic water.
(3) The acid content of some rainfall is as high as that of vinegar.
(4) Many Canadian foxes became ill right after a heavy rain; acid rain caused their illness.
(5) The clear water of some northeastern lakes shows they can no longer support life.

1 2 3 4 5

The correct answer is (4). The test item asks you to judge which answer does *not* support the belief stated. Options (1), (2), (3), and (5) all *support* the belief and offer reasonable evidence. But (4) is an example of faulty thinking; it assumes that because a rain preceded the illness, it must have been the cause.

☑ A Test-Taking Tip

When you answer a GED Test item that involves use of evaluation, first examine the item carefully to see exactly what information is given and what type of answer is needed. Be on guard for examples of faulty thinking.

Biology

Life Qualities People who like raising fish, gardening, recognizing bird calls, and similar hobbies find their lives enriched by their knowledge of living things. *Biology* is the study of life and living things. Strange as it may seem, it can be hard to tell the difference between things that are alive and those that are not. Exactly what characteristics separate living from nonliving things?

Living things can usually be recognized by certain traits that they all have in common:

—Living things are made up of extremely small units called cells.

—Most living things move under their own power. Even those that do not swim, run, crawl, or fly about may move internally.

—Living things obtain and use energy. The name of the chemical processes by which a living thing converts food into energy is **metabolism.**

—Living things grow as they mature. They use some of their food to reproduce their own body cells.

—Living things eliminate waste materials.

—Living things react to stimuli. A *stimulus* is anything that causes some kind of activity.

—Living things produce offspring (reproduce).

Coming to Terms

metabolism process in living plants and animals by which food is changed into energy, new cells, waste products, etc.

☑ A Test-Taking Tip

Before you choose an answer for each GED Test item, be sure you read and understand all the answer choices given for that item.

Warm-up

Express in your own words some of the differences between living and nonliving things. Use complete sentences.

____

____

Sample Warm-up Answer

Living things are made of cells that produce change and growth. They move by themselves. They also reproduce themselves. Nonliving things do not have all of these qualities.

Directions: Choose the one best answer to each question. Answers are on page 387.

Items 1–2 are based on the following passage.

Decisions about whether something is alive or whether life exists in a particular place are not always easy to make. The problem is illustrated by the tests performed aboard the Viking landers on the planet Mars. The landers contained special instruments that searched for life. Cameras scanned the landscape for objects that appeared to be alive. They saw nothing but rocks. But could tiny living things survive in Martian soil?

To find out, the Viking landers used digging arms to obtain samples of the soil. The samples were analyzed in three miniature laboratories that were equipped to look for chemical signs of life. The search on Mars for chemical compounds similar to living things on Earth has failed so far.

1. According to the passage, the Viking landers carried on their investigation by

   (1) recording sounds on Mars' surface
   (2) photographing and analyzing Mars' soil
   (3) photographing the sky from Mars' surface
   (4) X-raying the surface
   (5) surveying Mars from above the surface only

   ① ② ③ ④ ⑤

2. Which of the following is a hypothesis investigated by Viking landers?

   (1) People have always wanted to find out more about Mars.
   (2) Tiny living things might be able to survive in Martian soil.
   (3) Viking landers contained sophisticated equipment to search for life on Mars.
   (4) We can conclude that no life has ever existed on Mars.
   (5) We must continue to search for signs of life on Mars.

   ① ② ③ ④ ⑤

Cell Structure Living things are made up of cells. These cells come in many sizes and shapes and you'd need a microscope to see most of them. Some are so small that hundreds would fit into the period at the end of this sentence. Yet, every living cell contains the same substances and is constantly doing the work of life.

All cells are made up of an outer permeable membrane that encloses a clear, jellylike fluid called cytoplasm. In more complex cells, the cytoplasm holds various structures that keep the cell functioning. Like the organs of the body, each part of the cell carries out a specific job.

The main part of a cell—and the easiest to see—is the **nucleus.** The nucleus contains a mass of fibers called **chromosomes** that direct and store instructions for the cell's activities.

Coming to Terms

nucleus structure that contains the master plan of a cell
chromosome structure that directs a cell's development and activity

Warm-up

Read the paragraph and study the diagram. Then answer the question on your own paper.

- There are more than 100 different kinds of cells in your body. Their shapes are related to their functions. Some, like red blood cells, are round. Others, like muscle cells, are long and can contract. Nerve cells have long branches with many twiglike endings that help relay messages throughout the body.

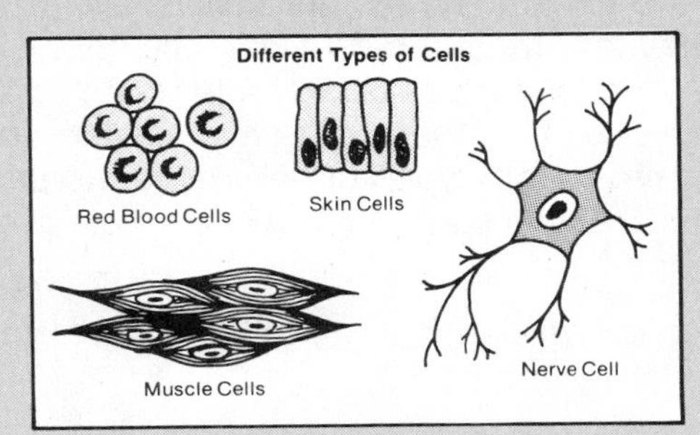

Why do cells have specialized shapes? Explain.

Sample Warm-up Answer
The shapes of cells help them to perform their functions more efficiently.

Items 3–4 refer to the following diagram.

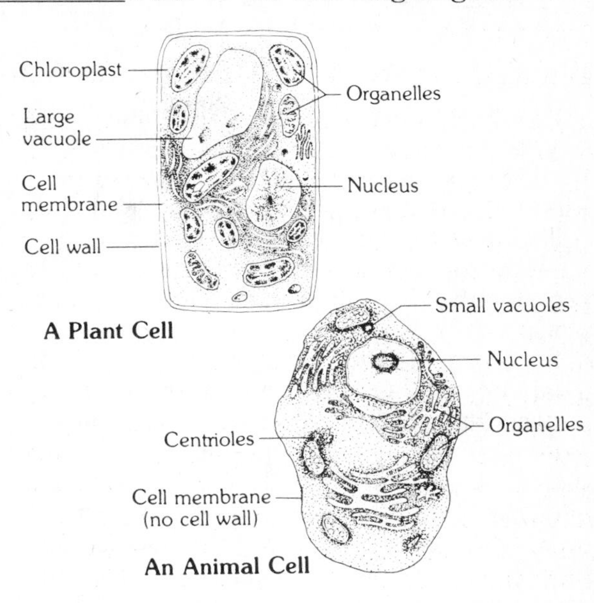

3. Which of the following pieces of information can be determined from the diagram?
   (1) Animal cells contain a cell wall.
   (2) Only the animal cell has a cell membrane.
   (3) Animal cells are perfectly round.
   (4) Animal cells contain large and small vacuoles.
   (5) Plant and animal cells contain a nucleus.

4. A farm supply company wishes to find out whether a certain mineral will strengthen the chloroplast within a cell. The researcher should use cells from
   (1) cattle (2) sheep (3) cabbage
   (4) mice (5) any living organism

Directions: Choose the one best answer to each question. Answers are on page 387.

Items 5–6 are based on the following passage.

A cell's nucleus contains the chemical deoxyribonucleic acid, or DNA. DNA controls the life processes of the cell in two ways. First, it passes on all information about the cell's heredity from one generation to the next. Second, it determines what kind of proteins the cell will produce in order to do its work.

Some one-celled plants and animals function independently. Others live in groups that have a loose interaction. But in plants and animals made up of many cells, specialized cells have their own particular jobs to do. For example, because of muscle cells attached to your eyeballs, your eyes are moving across the page. Nerve cells in your eyes carry to your brain messages about the words you are reading. Muscle cells, nerve cells, and other specialized cells are in groups that form tissues, such as muscle or nerve tissue. Different kinds of tissues form organs, such as the eyes, brain, and skin.

5. Which of the following can be used to support the conclusion that specialized cells have particular jobs to do?

(1) Nerve cells carry messages to the brain.
(2) Cells produce different types of proteins.
(3) Some organisms are made up of a single cell.
(4) Plant and animal cells contain DNA.
(5) DNA controls a cell's life processes.

① ② ③ ④ ⑤

6. Red blood cells carry oxygen throughout the body from the lungs. They do this because they are programmed by

(1) tissues of the body
(2) organs of the body
(3) the brain
(4) DNA in every cell of the body
(5) DNA in each blood cell nucleus

① ② ③ ④ ⑤

Cell Processes Cells, the "building blocks" of life, all have some things in common. They "breathe," take in food, and eliminate waste products. They also grow, reproduce their own kind, and eventually die. This is true whether an organism is made up of only one cell or of billions. What is it that provides the fuel for these processes? In green plants, of course, fuel includes sunlight as an energy source. But the cells of all living things are fueled by whatever is their food.

Think of your cells as being surrounded by a watery solution. In the solution is what you ate recently, broken down by digestion into its basic nutrients. Only those nutrients needed by a cell pass through the permeable cell membrane and circulate through the cytoplasm. And just as if each nutrient were zip-coded, it passes into that part of the cell responsible for processing it. Here, food is changed into energy and stored or used as necessary.

The control center that directs functions of the cell is the nucleus. The nucleus contains the cell's genetic program, a master plan that controls almost everything the cell does.

Warm-up

One-celled organisms such as bacteria and blue-green algae do not have a well-defined nucleus or any organelles in their cytoplasm. The cells of these small, simple organisms are called *procaryotic,* which means "before the nucleus." Cells in all other organisms have a true nucleus, and the name of this kind of cell, *eucaryotic,* means just that. Unicellular (one-celled) organisms such as diatoms and amoebas are eucaryotic. All multicellular plants and animals are made up of eucaryotic cells. Despite the differences between procaryotic and eucaryotic cells, they both have similar programming. Both types of cells have the same kind of genetic plan that directs protein production and heredity.

On your own paper, summarize this information in several sentences.

Need a Hint for Number 6?
Remember that the nucleus of every body cell contains DNA.

Sample Warm-up Answer
Although some cells have a well-defined nucleus and organelles and others do not, both kinds have a similar basic plan that directs their activities.

Genetics Each species has its own traits, or special characteristics. **Heredity** is the passing of traits from parents to offspring. **Genetics** is the study of how traits are passed on.

To understand genetics, you first think about cells. All human body cells have 23 pairs of chromosomes. These chromosomes are found within the nuclei of the cells, and they are made up of segments called genes, which are sections of DNA. The genes or DNA in the chromosomes carry instructions for how the body should develop.

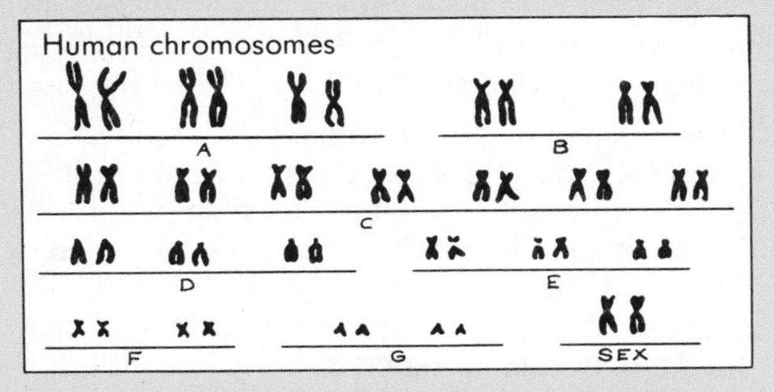

According to theory, genes determine which traits an organism will inherit from its parents' chromosomes. For one trait two genes are necessary; one comes from the male and the other from the female.

Coming to Terms

heredity passing of traits from parents to offspring
genetics study of the way organisms pass on characteristics to their offspring

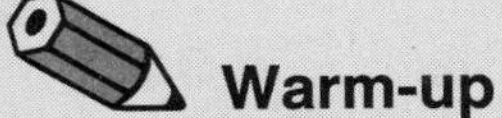

Warm-up

■ A person's sex is determined by the X and Y chromosomes. (These chromosomes are named for their shapes.) Each person receives two sex chromosomes, one from the mother's egg cell and one from the father's sperm cell. All egg cells contain one X chromosome. A male cell, however, contains either an X or a Y chromosome.

When a sperm with an X chromosome unites with an egg, a female will result. If the sperm has a Y chromosome, a male will result.

Based on the information in this passage, what decides the sex of the offspring?

Sample Warm-up Answer
The sex of the offspring depends on which kind of sperm unites with the egg.

Items 7–8 refer to the following passage.

Many people are aware that certain medications and illegal drugs are *teratogens,* agents that cause birth defects. But more babies are harmed by a substance that is widely used and often isn't thought of as a drug—alcohol.

Babies born to mothers who are heavy drinkers are often severely damaged or stillborn. There is a higher than average risk of premature birth; mental retardation; and physical deformities, such as small heads, narrow eye slits, heart defects, and joint malformations.

Dr. David Smith of the University of Washington, where fetal alcohol syndrome was first identified in the United States, estimated that about one to two of every 1,000 infants is born with some type of defect caused by the mother drinking alcoholic beverages during pregnancy. It is difficult to know what is a dangerous amount of alcohol for an expectant mother to drink, but one to two ounces a day is considered risky.

7. Which of the following best restates the first paragraph?

(1) Teratogens are substances that cause birth defects.
(2) Certain medicines and illegal drugs are teratogens.
(3) Alcoholic beverages are often unsuspected teratogens.
(4) Expectant mothers should be careful about the medicines they take.
(5) Alcoholic beverages can affect the body in unpredictable ways.

8. A woman who has just learned she is pregnant is advised by a family member to drink about 4 ounces of wine with dinner each night in order to stay relaxed throughout pregnancy. Following this advice will

(1) help keep mother and baby healthy
(2) surely cause the baby to be stillborn
(3) increase the risk of birth defects
(4) have absolutely no effect on the baby
(5) put the mother at risk, but not the baby

Directions: Choose the one best answer to each question. Answers are on page 387.

Items 9–10 refer to the following passage.

One example of how changes in the environment can affect wildlife is seen in the story of the peppered moth in Great Britain. Up until the mid-1800s, peppered moths were easily identified by their light-colored wings, which were lightly "peppered" with small black spots. Only rarely was a dark-winged peppered moth seen.

Over a period of years people in industrial areas gradually began to notice more and more of the once-rare dark peppered moths. At the same time, the lighter ones became increasingly rare. The reason became clear when researchers noticed that the trees on which the moths often gathered had been gradually blackened by soot from hundreds of coal-burning fireplaces, railway trains, and factories.

As long as tree trunks were light in color, the lighter moths were protected by their coloring. But when the tree trunks were blackened by soot, the light moths were easily seen by birds and eaten. Meanwhile, the darker moths, now protected by their coloring, survived and produced offspring like themselves.

9. Peppered moths were able to survive in British industrial areas because

   (1) They used soot as food.
   (2) Lighter moths moved away.
   (3) The species adapted.
   (4) The moths gather on tree bark.
   (5) The lighter moths were genetically stronger.

   (1) (2) (3) (4) (5)

10. When cockroaches became a problem, a bakery owner sprayed with pesticide. Most of the roaches were killed, but a few survived. Soon the offspring of the survivors became a nuisance and the baker sprayed again. This time quite a few roaches survived.

    Which of the following situations will probably be true if the baker continues to use the same spray?

    (1) All of the roaches will be killed.
    (2) The roaches will become smaller.
    (3) The roaches will migrate to other places.
    (4) More offspring will survive the spray.
    (5) The offspring will use the spray as food.

    (1) (2) (3) (4) (5)

Natural Selection and Evolution Biology deals with the *scientific* study of life. This statement means that biologists gain knowledge by observing and testing natural events under controlled conditions. Other ways of knowing about life can be equally valid. But biology deals only with the scientific methods that are used to learn about life.

Scientists developed the theory of evolution to explain how changes can occur in members of a species over a period of time. Most scientists use this theory as a basis for formulating hypotheses and conducting research. They try to discover how and why changes in the inherited makeup of an organism came about.

Changes in weather patterns, temperature, and available food and water cause organisms to **evolve,** or gradually change from simpler to more complex forms, so they can continue to live. **Adaptation** occurs when an organism changes to fit into its surroundings. When this occurs over a long period of time, it is called *natural selection.* Organisms that have some genetic trait that helps them to live in the changing condition are the ones that survive.

Coming to Terms

evolve the change in a species from simpler to more complex form

adaptation inherited trait or group of traits that increase an organism's chances of surviving and reproducing

☑ A Test-Taking Tip

Don't let your feelings or personal beliefs affect the way you answer questions on the GED Test. Even if you disagree with an author's ideas, try to understand them so you can give the answers that the questions are asking for.

Warm-up

Write a sentence in your own words answering the following question.

How does an animal's ability to respond to changing conditions relate to its survival?

___

___

___

Sample Warm-up Answer

Animals that adapt to the changes around them often survive longer than those that do not.

Classifying Living Things Until about 250 years ago, the study of biology was very confusing. People had gathered many facts about thousands of living things but every country had its own system for naming them. In 1735, the botanist Carolus Linneaus devised a method of grouping organisms into a logical order based on their similarities and differences.

His process might remind you of dividing a city into neighborhoods, then dividing the neighborhoods into blocks, blocks into houses or apartment buildings, and finally into individual rooms or apartments. Each breakdown gives you more precise information.

Linneaus started by dividing all life forms into two general groups called *kingdoms*—plant and animal. These kingdoms have "plantness" or "animalness" in common but otherwise have widely differing traits (characteristics). As Linneaus continued to subdivide the members of the kingdoms into progressively smaller groups, the traits shared by the members of each group became more numerous. The most specific grouping, *species,* includes living things that have the greatest number of similar characteristics.

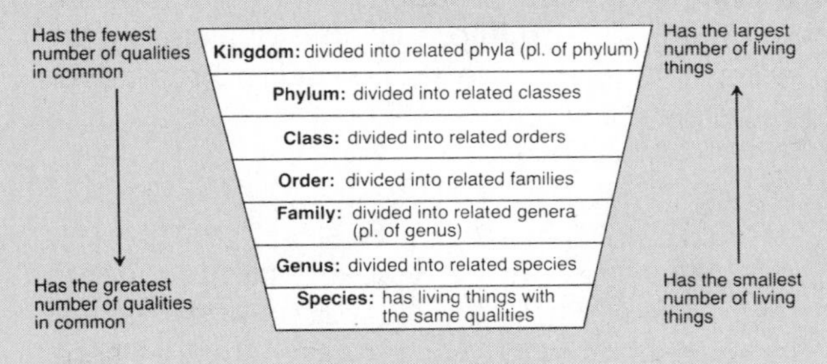

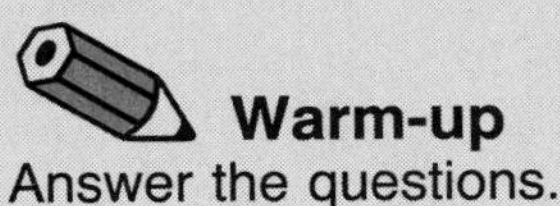

Warm-up

Answer the questions.

1. What does *classification* mean?

____

2. How did Linneaus' method of classification simplify the study of biology? ______________

____

Sample Warm-up Answers

1. Classification is a method of listing, or grouping, items.

2. When biologists use the same criteria for identifying life forms, they can communicate more easily.

Items 11–12 refer to the following chart.

Kingdom	Characteristics	Example
Monera	Most are simple, one-celled organisms Some produce own food; others take it from outside sources	staphylococci
Protista	One-celled organisms More complex cell structure than monerans Some produce own food; others take it from outside sources	Euglena
Fungi	Made up of many cells Cannot move about Obtain food by absorbing it from dead or living organisms	mold
Plantae	Made up of many cells Cells are specialized for different tasks Cannot move about Can produce own food	oak tree
Animalia	Made up of many cells Cells are specialized for different tasks Capable of moving about Obtain food from outside sources	humans

11. According to the chart, which kingdoms include members that can produce their own food?

(1) Monera, Protista, Plantae,
(2) Fungi, Plantae, Animalia,
(3) Monera, Fungi
(4) Plantae, Animalia
(5) Monera, Plantae

① ② ③ ④ ⑤

12. *Agaricus campestris* is the scientific name for an organism that lives on lawns and meadows. It does not move about but instead gets its food from the grasses in which it grows. What kingdom does *Agaricus campestris* belong to?

(1) Monera (2) Protista (3) Fungi
(4) Plantae (5) Animalia

① ② ③  ⑤

Directions: Choose the one best answer to each question. Answers are on page 387.

Items 13–14 refer to the following passage.

When you hear the word *bacteria,* do you think of disease-causing germs? Many people do, and yet the truth is that we rely on some types of bacteria for healthy living. Certain types of bacteria, in fact, play a vital role in producing our food.

Health-conscious people often add yogurt to their diets, aware that it provides protein and other valuable nutrients. Think how surprised they might be if they examined their yogurt under a high-powered microscope and found many examples of the moneran named *Lactobacillus!* These are the bacteria that turn milk into yogurt.

To make yogurt, milk is carefully brought to a temperature that will encourage the growth of bacteria, yet is not hot enough to kill them. Then a culture of living *Lactobacillus* bacteria, probably in the form of fresh yogurt, is added to the warm milk. The bacteria begin to multiply as they feed on lactose, a sugar found in milk. As they feed, they produce lactic acid. That acid causes the milk to thicken, giving it a smooth, creamy texture. The acid is also responsible for the tart, snappy taste that many people enjoy plain or combined with such fruits as bananas, cherries, and blueberries.

Although the bacterial action changes the texture and taste of the milk, it does not change the nutritional content of the milk.

13. People who must limit their intake of sugar might want to avoid yogurt because it contains

    (1) protein (2) lactose (3) bacteria
    (4) acid (5) the nutrients of fresh milk

    (1) (2) (3) (4) (5)

14. A cooking school student boiled some yogurt in preparation for making a sauce. After the yogurt had cooled, he had some left over and decided to use it as a starter culture to make his own yogurt. His attempt to make yogurt failed because he

    (1) allowed the culture to cool
    (2) did not add yeast
    (3) used the wrong type of bacteria
    (4) boiled the yogurt, killing the bacteria
    (5) did not add fruit

    (1) (2) (3) (4) (5)

Monerans What type of organism has a bigger population than any other on earth? You may suspect that the answer is houseflies—but the truth is that monerans are thought to be the most numerous. Monerans are tiny one-celled organisms, better known as *bacteria.*

A moneran's most important distinguishing feature is the simple structure of its cell. Unlike more complex cells, there is no distinct nucleus or other *organelle*—specialized part of a cell similar to an organ—within the membrane.

Most people know that bacteria can cause disease. Some bacteria, however, perform useful functions. They decompose dead plant and animal matter, which helps to build soil. They enrich soil with nitrogen compounds and make it possible for plants to grow. "Friendly" bacteria in your intestines aid digestion and destroy harmful organisms.

Although viruses are even simpler than monerans, some of their features are similar to those of bacteria. Each type of virus has a distinct shape and size, but all are too small to be seen with an ordinary microscope. A virus outside of a living organism is unable to reproduce itself. But if it is carried into a living organism, it can enter cells, infect the organism, and reproduce itself.

Warm-up

The illustration shows typical bacteria under a microscope. Study the illustration and answer the questions with one or more complete sentences.

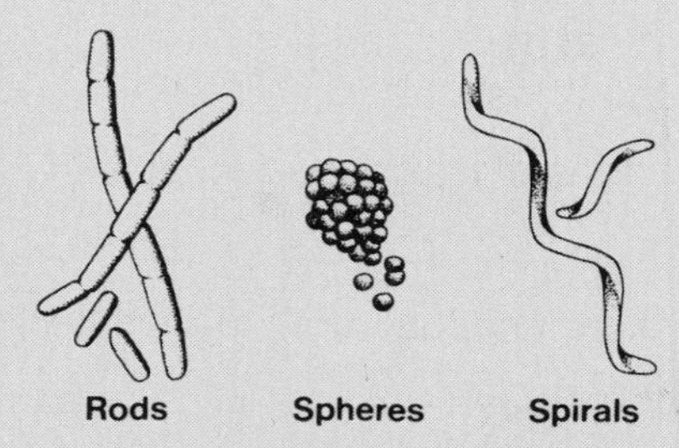

Do these bacteria have simple cells or complex cells? What makes you think so? Use your own paper.

Need a Hint for Number 14?
Reread the third paragraph of the passage to find if or how boiling the yogurt would affect the yogurt bacteria.

Sample Warm-up Answer
The absence of nuclei or other organelles shows that the bacteria are simple cells.

Protists Protists, like monerans, are one-celled organisms. A major difference between the two is that protists have a more complicated cell containing several organelles. Although they have characteristics similar to those found in both the animal and plant kingdoms, protists are neither plant nor animal. In fact, scientists have recently discovered that green algae may be more similar to the protist kingdom than to the plant kingdom.

The best-known protist is the amoeba. If you looked at an amoeba under a microscope, you would see that its tiny shape changes constantly. At one moment it may appear as a shapeless blob. Then it may extend a section of its body to make a "false foot," or pseudopod, and pull itself around that pseudopod. Since it can move itself about, the amoeba is considered to be an animal-like protist.

Other protists are more like plants. One example is the diatom. Diatoms float on the surfaces of fresh- and saltwater. Diatoms are one of the most important food sources for all animals of the sea and shore.

Warm-up

Use information from the diagram to complete the sentences that follow.

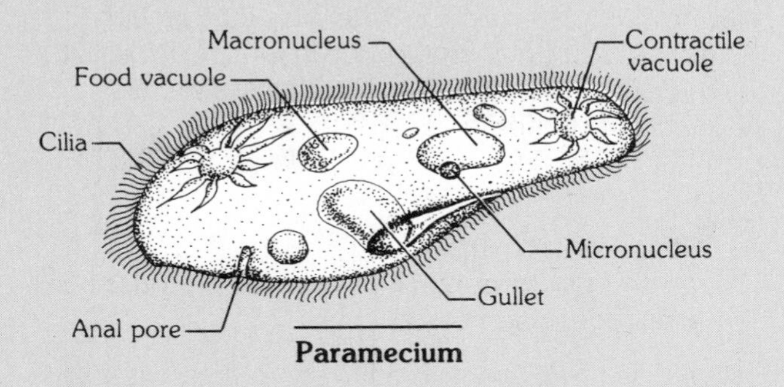

Paramecium

A paramecium is an example of a protist. The ______________________ are tiny hairlike threads along the outside of the body. They propel the organism. The paramecium takes food into its gullet and releases waste through its ______________________.

Warm-up Answers
cilia; anal pore

Items 15–16 is based on the following passage.

The one-celled organism Euglena is now classified as a member of the protist kingdom. But before the five-kingdom scheme was devised—back in the days when biologists recognized only the plant kingdom and the animal kingdom—Euglena was the object of a classification "tug-of-war." Some biologists claimed Euglena for the animal kingdom because it has some animallike traits, such as a flexible covering and special organelles for motion. At the same time it was claimed by other biologists to be part of the plant kingdom because it contains the green pigment chlorophyll.

Because of its combination of plantlike and animallike traits, Euglena is versatile in the way it lives. It can use photosynthesis to make food when light is present. But in the absence of light, it can take in material for nourishment, rather than produce its own food. This versatility has enabled Euglena to survive in a number of different environments.

15. The Euglena can adapt to different conditions because of its ability to

    (1) move about
    (2) use sunlight
    (3) take in food or make its own food
    (4) slip into small places
    (5) live without light

    ① ② ③ ④ ⑤

16. When scientists used to classify all known living things into two kingdoms, plant and animal, one problem was that some organisms did not actually fit into either kingdom. Over the years the original system has been revised. Scientists now recognize five kingdoms of living things. Yet even today, researchers continue to work on the system, trying to make it more accurate and more useful.

    Which of the following conclusions can be drawn from the evidence above?

    (1) The original system was wrong.
    (2) We should still use the original system.
    (3) Scientific ideas may need to be updated.
    (4) The present system should remain unchanged.
    (5) Some organisms are difficult to classify.

    ① ② ③ ④ ⑤

Directions: Choose the one best answer to each question. Answers are on page 387.

Items 17–18 are based on the following passage.

Alexander Fleming, a member of the British army medical corps during World War I, saw the terrible infections that could develop when soldiers were wounded. In those days, there were no antibiotics to treat such infections. After the war, Fleming dedicated himself to finding a way to help the body defend itself against infection.

In 1928, while Fleming was studying staphylococcus bacteria, he grew several specimens of the germ in culture dishes, awaiting microscopic examinations. One dish became contaminated by a mold, as was common under nonsterile laboratory conditions. The mold was a common type of fungus found on old bread and cheese, *Penicillium notatum.* Usually a contaminated specimen would have been thrown away. But this time Fleming noticed that the harmful bacteria were disappearing in the area around where the mold had grown. He realized that the mold had some qualities that caused it to weaken or destroy the bacteria in the culture dish.

Scientists now know much about the various penicillins that can be extracted from mold. The penicillins kill bacteria by preventing formation of the stiff cell wall that bacteria need to survive. Success with penicillin led to the development of many other antibiotics.

17. Which of the following statements is based on fact rather than opinion?

    (1) Fleming noticed that an ordinary mold destroyed or weakened bacteria.
    (2) Fleming was a clever scientist.
    (3) Contaminated laboratory dishes should be discarded.
    (4) Penicillin is the most important medical discovery of this century.
    (5) Penicillin is still a wonderful tool to use in healing infections.

    (1) (2) (3) (4) (5)

18. Penicillin may have affected the outcome of World War II by

    (1) providing a valuable tool for research
    (2) keeping wounded soldiers alive
    (3) providing a use for old, spoiled food
    (4) preventing soldiers' food from spoiling
    (5) keeping hospitals cleaner

    (1) (2) (3) (4) (5)

Fungi If the idea of a fungus makes you want to turn the other way, you have a surprise coming. Freshly baked bread, blue-cheese salad dressing, tender sauteed mushrooms—they all rely on fungi. The yeast that makes the bread rise, the mold that produces the distinctive cheese flavor, and, of course, the mushrooms themselves are all fungi.

Fungi are single- and multicelled organisms that appear in a variety of forms. They may be soft or firm, large or tiny, and may take on a variety of colorations. Some can be eaten; others are poisonous.

Unlike green plants, a fungus has neither flowers nor leaves. Nor can fungi produce food for themselves to live on. Some of the multicelled organisms of the fungi kingdom are **parasites** that depend on other living organisms for their food. Other fungi digest dead material. Sometimes the parasites cause diseases. Other fungi are of benefit to the **host** organism. Many forest trees are kept healthy by mushrooms that live at their base. The tree provides organic nutrients to the fungi; the fungi, in turn, send down networks of tiny threads that help the tree roots absorb water and minerals.

Coming to Terms

parasite organism that lives on or in another living thing from which it derives its nutrition

host plant or animal on or in which a parasite lives and which the parasite digests as its source of nutrients

Warm-up

Read the paragraph. Then answer the question in a complete sentence.

■ As decomposers, fungi use up the remains of dead plants and animals. They break down tissues and release the waste materials into the soil. The nutritious makeup of these materials can be reused by other organisms to build new cells.

What could happen if waste materials were not reused?

Sample Warm-up Answer

The dead bodies of plants and animals could pile up, and the soil would be depleted of nutrients. Life could not exist.

Photosynthesis The word *photosynthesis* is derived from two Greek words meaning "putting together by means of light." Green plants work together with sunlight, water, and carbon dioxide to create a life-support system for everything else that lives on the earth. If green plants could not create food from inorganic substances, life as we know it could not exist.

The food-making photosynthesis process takes place only in green plants. The simplest green plants are one-celled green algae that grow in water or damp places. The most complex are seed plants.

You could say that photosynthesis consists of three major processes: (1) The plant's vascular system (veins) carries water and minerals from the ground into the leaves. Air, containing carbon dioxide, passes into the undersides of the leaves through tiny openings. (2) Leaf cells contain small bodies that hold the green chemical compound chlorophyll. When sunlight strikes the leaf, the chlorophyll absorbs it and changes it from light energy to chemical energy. The chemical energy transforms the water and carbon dioxide into sugar and other foods. (3) As the food is manufactured, the veins carry it out of the leaves to be used or stored by the roots and other parts of the plant. Extra, unneeded oxygen re-enters the air through the underleaf openings.

☑ A Test-Taking Tip

You may want to skim a passage on the GED Test before reading it carefully. Skimming gives you a good idea of what the passage is about and helps you determine what type of information you want to gather from it. Run your finger down the page from upper left to lower right. Follow the tip of your finger with your eyes. Next read the test item, then read the passage carefully.

Warm-up

Use complete sentences to write a short summary of the process of photosynthesis.

____

____

____

____

Sample Warm-up Answer

Photosynthesis takes place in sunlight. Energy from light is stored in chlorophyll and transformed into chemical energy. The energy changes water and carbon dioxide into food for the plant.

Items 19–20 refer to the following passage and diagram.

To make the delicate process of photosynthesis possible, a plant must take in certain gases from the air and release others. Tiny openings on the surfaces of leaves allow this exchange of gases to occur. Each of those openings is called a *stoma;* the plural is *stomata.* The diagram below shows that each stoma is surrounded by two guard cells which control its opening and closing. When the guard cells absorb moisture from the leaf, they swell until they open the stoma. After they have lost moisture, the guard cells recede and close the stoma.

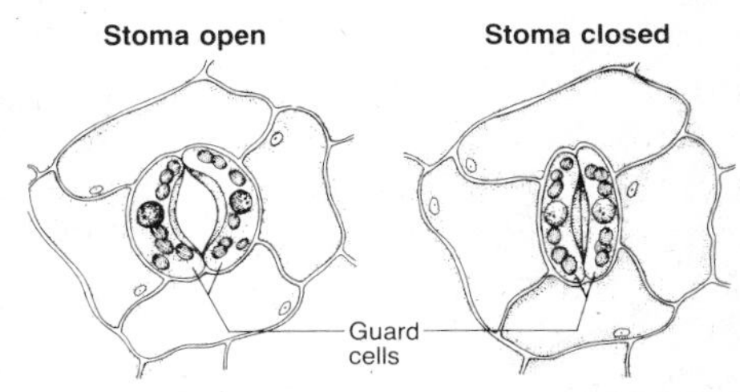

During the day, when sunlight makes photosynthesis possible, the stomata on most plants swell and open. After sunset, the stomata close and remain closed during the night.

19. A florist gave each customer a leaf spray that covered plant leaves with a thick, waxy substance that made them look glossy. Several weeks later, customers who used the spray complained that the leaves on their plants looked unhealthy.

    Which of the following most likely explains what happened to the plants?

    (1) The spray clogged the stomata.
    (2) The plants needed more water.
    (3) The plants needed more attention.
    (4) The plants received too much light.
    (5) All the plants had simply completed their life cycles.

    (1) (2) (3) (4) (5)

20. In plants such as the water lily, which has leaves that lie on top of water, you would expect to find stomata

    (1) only on the upper side of a leaf
    (2) only on the lower side of a leaf
    (3) mostly on the lower side of a leaf
    (4) evenly divided between top and bottom
    (5) not at all

    (1) (2) (3) (4) (5)

Directions: Choose the one best answer to each question. Answers are on page 387.

Items 21–22 refer to the following diagram.

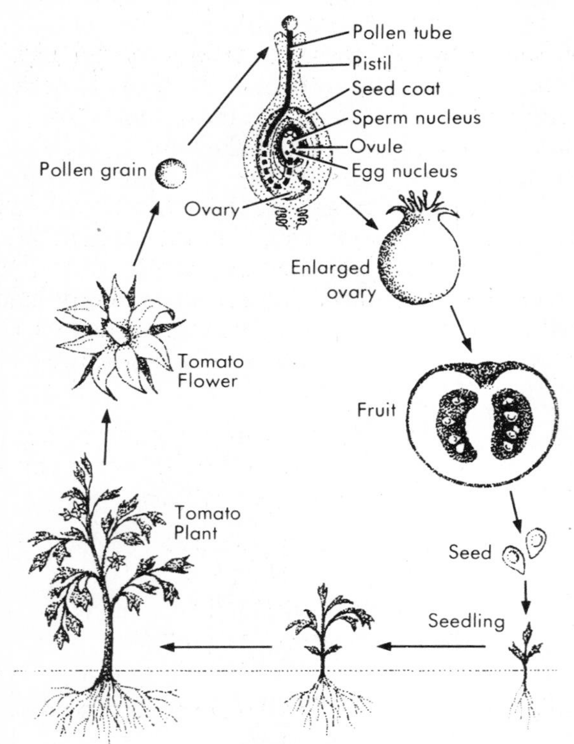

Angiosperm life cycle

21. The arrows on the chart indicate that the process
    (1) depends on strong winds
    (2) takes a long time
    (3) begins with the seedling and ends with the seed
    (4) begins with the pollen grain and ends with the flower
    (5) is a cycle with each step leading to another

    (1) (2) (3) (4) (5)

22. The delicious taste of some fruits, such as peaches, apples, and pears, helps a plant
    (1) gather nutrients
    (2) disperse seeds
    (3) absorb nutrients
    (4) fertilize the ovule
    (5) grow

    (1) (2) (3) (4) (5)

Plant Structure and Reproduction Roots anchor plants in the soil and transport water from the soil to the stems, leaves, and flowers. If you looked at a slice of a root under a microscope, you could see tubelike tissues called xylem that carry water and minerals through the stem to the leaves. Other pathways carry food from the leaves and stems down to the roots to use for growth or to store for future use.

Stems that are green and flexible are called *herbaceous.* Plants with herbaceous stems—tomatoes and celery are examples—usually live for about one growing season. Other plants, such as trees, have woody stems that are usually rigid and hard. These plants grow for years.

A plant's flowers contain its reproductive organs. The stamen, or male reproductive organ, is found just inside the petals. Pollen grains, which contain male reproductive nuclei, are made in the anther, a part of the stamen.

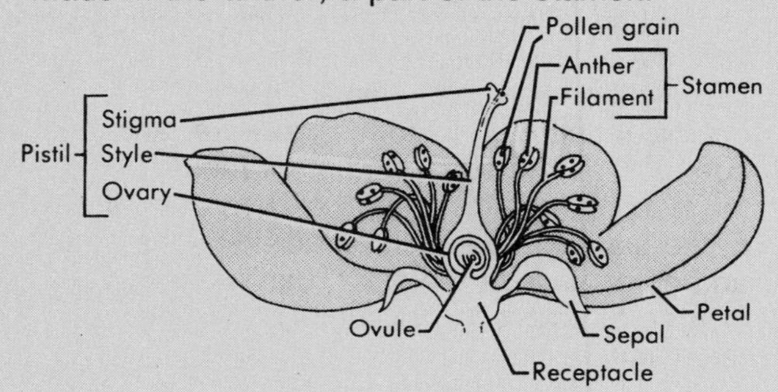

Cross section of a flower

The pistil is the female reproductive organ. It is found in the center of the flower. Its sticky stigma attracts pollen grains which then travel to the ovary and fertilize the plant ovules, which produce seeds.

Warm-up

The main parts of a plant contain specialized structures. In a sentence list the main parts of a flowering plant.

____

____

☑ A Test-Taking Tip

Before you answer a question that refers to a diagram, read the title and *all* the labels.

Sample Warm-up Answer

The main parts of a flowering plant are the roots, stem, leaves, and flowers.

The Animal Kingdom Unlike one-celled protists and monerans, animals are made up of many cells. Animals have a definite size and shape. Unlike plants, animals cannot make their own food.

Invertebrates Many animals are very different from the ones we know best. One example is the invertebrates, animals that do not have backbones. Some simple invertebrates are described below.

Most *coelenterates*—jellyfish, sea anemones, and corals, for instance—live in warm seawater. The sponges, some of them brightly colored, are attached to the ocean floor.

Flatworms and *roundworms* are bilaterally symmetrical. This means their parts have the same size, form, and arrangement on both the right and left sides. Many of these worms are parasites. Some others may cause disease.

Segmented worms, such as the earthworm, are more complex with specialized organs for digestion and reproduction. They also have simple nervous system. Snails, clams, and oysters are *mollusks.* Mollusks have soft bodies and a muscular foot used for locomotion and capturing prey.

Starfish and sea urchins are *echinoderms.* Adults have radial symmetry, with five arms, or *rays,* attached to a central disk. Many species are able to regenerate lost or injured parts.

Warm-up

The diagram below shows that sponges are attached to the ocean floor. How does that make them different from other sea animals? Answer the question with a complete sentence.

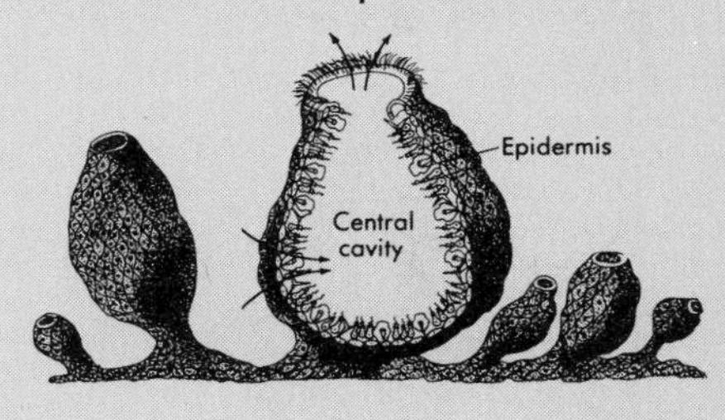

Sample Warm-up Answer
Sponges cannot move about.

Items 23–24 refer to the following passage.

Studying an animal may reveal that certain body parts do not seem to perform any function to help assure survival. These parts are called *vestigial* structures.

For example, some cave-dwelling fish and salamanders have eyes, but they cannot see with them. Vision is unnecessary in entirely dark caves, so eyes have become vestigial structures.

Probably the best-known vestigial structure in humans is the appendix. In other mammals this organ plays an important part in digestion. Other vestigial parts of humans are body hair (which does not keep us warm) and the caudal vertebrae (similar to the tails of vertebrate animals).

23. On the basis of information given in the passage, which one of the following parts of the human body is vestigial?

(1) molars (2) eyelashes
(3) little toes (4) lips
(5) muscles to move ears

24. Which of the following sentences best restates the passage?

(1) Humans have some vestigial structures.
(2) Some birds cannot fly.
(3) Some fish cannot see.
(4) Some animals have useless parts.
(5) Some body structures not useful for survival have become vestigial.

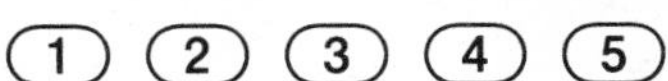

Directions: Choose the one best answer to each question. Answers are on page 387.

Items 25–26 refer to the following passage.

Communication plays an important role in the success of a society. Karl von Frisch and other biologists have done extensive research on honeybee communication. Von Frisch found that honeybees communicate with each other through a series of bee dances. When the worker bees find food, they return to the hive and are able to communicate what kind of food is available, how far away it is, and in what direction.

If the food is within 100 meters, the worker bee does a round dance on the vertical side of the hive. In the round dance, the bee makes a complete circle—first clockwise, then counterclockwise. Food that is farther away than 100 meters leads to a different movement—the waggle dance. This one has four steps: 1) The bee runs a short distance in a straight line. 2) It makes a 360-degree turn to the left. 3) It runs straight ahead again. 4) It makes a 360° turn to the right. This pattern is repeated while the bee continually wags its abdomen.

25. Which of the following statements is NOT supported by information in the passage?

(1) Worker bees search for food.
(2) Bees dance to tell others how to find food.
(3) Bees indicate that an enemy is near by doing the waggle dance.
(4) Different types of dance "steps" show how far food is.
(5) Worker bees communicate with other bees.

(1) (2) (3) (4) (5)

26. Which of the following could be used to support the hypothesis that odor is a form of communication among bees?

(1) The sweet odor of a flower attracts a worker bee.
(2) A guard bee attacks a visiting bee that has a "foreign" odor.
(3) Bees' honey attracts a bear.
(4) An angry bee stings one from another hive.
(5) Most honey smells sweet.

(1) (2) (3) (4) (5)

Invertebrates—the Arthropods Unlike people, arthropods do not have bones inside their bodies. Instead, they have a hard outer covering—an **exoskeleton.** This can range from the hard shell of a crustacean (such as lobsters, crayfish, and shrimp) to the thin, elastic shell of a fly, to the tough skin of a spider. And, arthropods all have jointed legs.

Insects make up the largest group of arthropods. More than 700,000 species have been identified so far. One reason there are so many is that they reproduce very quickly. All insects have three parts to their bodies: a *head,* a middle section called a *thorax,* and an *abdomen.* They have six legs. Some also have wings.

Insects begin their lives as tiny eggs. However, most insects change from one kind of body form to another during their lives. This change in body shape from egg to larva to pupa to adult is called **metamorphosis.**

Spiders, scorpions, ticks, mites, and daddy longlegs belong to a group of arthropods called *arachnids.* Most of these wingless creatures have two body parts: a *cephalothorax* (combined head and middle body), and an *abdomen.* They also have eight jointed walking legs. Most arachnids, especially spiders, are helpful to humans, since they eat harmful insects. Very few spiders are actually harmful to humans.

Coming to Terms

exoskeleton hard outer covering rather than internal bones
metamorphosis changes of body form

Warm-up

What body features of a crayfish identify it as an arthropod?

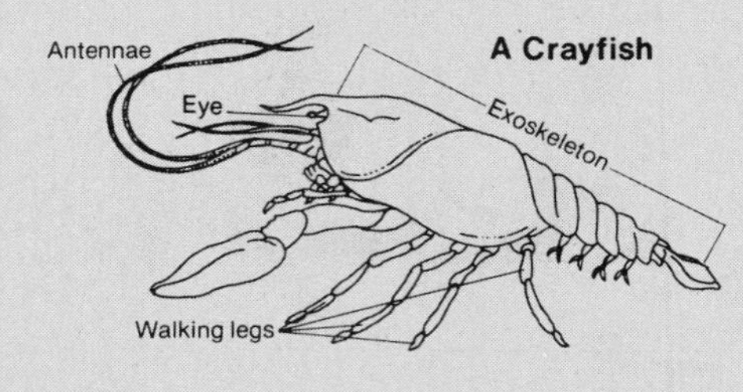

Sample Warm-up Answer
An exoskeleton and jointed legs show that a crayfish is an arthropod.

Fish There is an amazing variety of fish species—about 25,000 different kinds! Fish can vary in appearance from slippery, scaleless animals to tiny, delicately tinted tropical fish, to the large, fierce barracuda. Even the number and composition of fins varies greatly among fish.

There are, however, some characteristics that are common to all fish. All have backbones: they are **vertebrates.** They are *ectothermic,* which means that their body temperature changes with their surroundings. And they have gills, slits that enable them to get oxygen from water and release carbon dioxide.

For most fish fertilization of eggs takes place in water, not in their bodies. During spawning, the female lays thousands of eggs in the water. The male spreads sperm over the eggs. The fertilized eggs develop into embryos and then into young fish.

Coming to Terms

vertebrate animal that has a spinal column made up of small bones called *vertebrae*

☑ A Test-Taking Tip

Can you tell the difference between a fact and an opinion? A fact can be proved true or false. For example, the statement *Sharks have sharp teeth* is a fact that can be proved through observation. On the other hand, *People should learn more about sharks* is an opinion. While you may agree, you cannot prove that this statement is true. On the GED Science Test you may be asked to distinguish between facts and opinions in some of the passages.

Warm-up

Read the opinion below. Then circle the letter of the one fact that supports the opinion.

■ The sea lamprey is an undesirable fish.

A. Sea lampreys have sharp teeth and mouths like suction cups.
B. Sea lampreys swim up rivers to spawn.
C. Sea lampreys are parasites that feed on lake trout, a valuable freshwater fish.
D. Sea lampreys have no scales.

Warm-up Answer
C

Items 27–28 are based on the following passage.

The cry "Shark!" strikes fear into the hearts of many people—especially those swimming where sharks have been known to appear. The truth is, however, that few sharks will attack humans. Sharks probably have more to fear from humans than humans have to fear from sharks!

Most sharks must swim constantly to keep water moving over their gills. They use the oxygen from the water, then the used water passes out through their gill slits. Swimming also keeps them from sinking to the bottom. Most fish have a swim bladder filled with gas that helps them to remain at a certain depth. Sharks do not have this organ. Instead, some species gulp air into their stomachs to stay afloat. When they dive, they expel the air with a belch. Other species rely on oils in their livers to keep them from sinking.

Sharks have a keen sense of smell. They also are sensitive to vibrations in the water. Small pits along the sides of the body are organs that sense change in temperature, pressure, and electrical charges in the water.

Some sharks do attack humans, but their reputation as eager to eat people has been exaggerated. Reports have shown that sharks are often quite timid.

27. Which of these statements is a fact supported by the passage?

(1) Sharks look mean.
(2) Sharks are undesirable creatures.
(3) Sharks have keen vision.
(4) Sharks are not actually fish.
(5) There are two or more species of shark.

28. The oil that some shark species have in their livers keeps them afloat because it

(1) forms a slick to glide on
(2) is lighter than water
(3) is expelled with each motion
(4) is filled with air from the stomach
(5) is sensitive to vibrations

Directions: Choose the one best answer to each question. Answers are on page 387.

Items 29–30 refer to the following passage.

Most amphibians begin life in water or moist ground. As they grow into adulthood, they change into land animals. Nearly all of them, however, return to the water to mate and to bear young.

Because amphibians are ectothermic (cold-blooded), their temperatures change with their surroundings. The activity level of certain frogs decreases when the temperature drops in the autumn. The frogs bury themselves in mud and hibernate until spring.

Some kinds of amphibians are inactive in hot weather when bodies of water dry up between rains. Because their bodies can dry out quickly, some amphibians bury themselves in mud. During this period of estivation, body processes slow down, although not as much as they do in hibernation.

29. The word *amphibian,* which means "living in two ways," is an appropriate name for frogs because

(1) their temperature changes
(2) there are two species of frogs
(3) in cold weather, some frogs hibernate
(4) some frogs burrow in mud during dry weather
(5) they live both in water and on land

① ② ③ ④ ⑤

30. A small, spotted frog is a popular delicacy for the villagers of a swampy area in Central America. During the dry season, when the swamps dry up, villagers know they can find the frogs

(1) on the dry, parched ground
(2) buried in mud
(3) under small bushes and rocks
(4) higher up in the mountains
(5) only in the evening

① ② ③ ④ ⑤

Amphibians The word *amphibian* means "living in two ways." Most amphibians live part of the time in water, part of the time on land. There are about 3,000 kinds of amphibians, and they live on every continent except Antarctica. Amphibians are ectotherms. There are three major groups of amphibians: (1) frogs and toads, which have four legs and no tail when they are mature; (2) salamanders, which have four legs and long tails; and (3) caecilians, most of which live underground in the tropics and have no legs. Caecilians look like large earthworms.

Usually, amphibian young, which have gills, live in the water. They change into a land-living form that looks very different from the young. As an example, frog and toad eggs develop into tadpoles that have gills and a tail. After several weeks the gills and tail disappear as lungs and legs develop. When the metamorphosis is complete, the frog or toad can live on land.

A lot of people have trouble telling a frog from a toad. Toads have dry, bumpy skin. Frogs have smoother, moist skin. Like salamanders, both lay their eggs in water to keep them moist. Instead of having shells, frog and toad eggs are protected by a moist, jelly-like substance so they must remain in water to keep from drying out.

Warm-up

Using the information above and the diagram, answer the two questions.

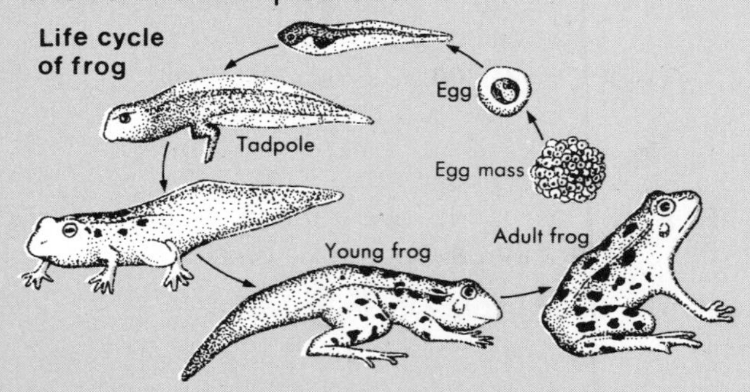

1. In which stage does the frog first develop legs?

____

2. What four major changes characterize the metamorphosis of a tadpole into an adult frog?

____

____

____

Sample Warm-up Answers

1. A frog first grows legs at the tadpole stage. **2.** The gills and tail disappear as legs and lungs develop.

Reptiles As alligators watch for fish, swimming birds, and other prey, they drift in the water with only their eyes and nostrils sticking out of the water. They are members of the *crocodile* group of reptiles, which live primarily in water. Yet, they and members of the other three main groups of reptiles all reproduce on land. Some reptiles lay eggs, but a few give birth to live young. Almost 3,000 different species of reptiles have been identified. Although reptiles vary in shape and size, they are alike in some ways. All have scaly skin and lungs and all are ectothermic.

Turtles make up a second group of reptiles. They have armorlike shells that provide protection. Although they have no teeth, many have strong, sharp beaks. Sea turtles have limbs like flippers. Some species of tortoises (land turtles) have lived in captivity for more than 150 years.

Lizards are a third group of reptiles. They are closely related to snakes, and some, like snakes, are legless. Others look like snakes but have legs. Lizards range in length from 5 centimeters to about 3 meters. Some of the larger ones resemble crocodiles. Lizards have toes with claws, ear openings, and movable eyelids. Most are meat eaters.

Snakes are a fourth group. Snakes eat other animals. They can unhinge their jaws to swallow prey larger than the diameter of their own heads. Snakes do not have limbs or ear openings. They can be found in land and water environments.

☑ A Test-Taking Tip

On the GED Test you may be asked to decide whether the evidence given in a reading passage is enough to support a particular conclusion. *Evidence* can be facts, figures, records of observations, results of experiments, or other information. Ask yourself whether the evidence given actually relates to the topic discussed.

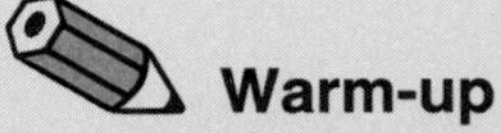

Warm-up

In a complete sentence, list the four groups of reptiles and the ways they are similar.

___

___

___

Sample Warm-up Answer
Crocodiles, turtles, lizards, and snakes all have scales, lungs, and take on the temperature of their environment.

Items 31–32 refer to the following passage.

Scientists have assumed that extinct reptiles such as dinosaurs were cold-blooded. But new evidence suggests that some were warm-blooded. Experts differ in their interpretations. Those who argue that dinosaurs were warm-blooded say many of the smaller carnivorous dinosaurs had some traits comparable to modern-day warm-blooded animals: 1) They were built for speed with powerful hind legs. 2) Fossil evidence suggests that carnivorous dinosaurs traveled in packs and attacked larger herbivores. 3) Their bones contained numerous blood vessels as do bones of modern warm-blooded animals. 4) Studies suggest that they ate more prey than necessary for cold-blooded animals.

Scientists who favor the theory that dinosaurs were cold-blooded state these reasons: 1) A warm-blooded animal the size of the 72-metric-ton *Brachiosaurus* would have to eat as much as about 12 African elephants. 2) The predator/prey ratios for the large carnivorous dinosaurs might be the same as for warm-blooded animals, so the ratios shown in fossils would not indicate warm-bloodedness. 3) A few present-day reptiles have bone structures with well-developed blood vessels, so the fossil evidence does not prove warm-bloodedness.

31. Which of the following pieces of evidence supports the theory that some dinosaurs were warm-blooded?

(1) Some dinosaurs had structures for releasing excess body heat.
(2) Since dinosaurs did not have fur, it would be difficult for them to maintain body heat.
(3) Dinosaurs are usually considered to have been reptiles.
(4) Some dinosaurs were both flesh-eaters and plant-eaters.
(5) Dinosaur remains have been found in many different areas of the world.

(1) (2) (3) (4) (5)

32. Evidence that supports the warm-blooded dinosaur theory and that *also* disagrees with it assumes that

(1) Cold-blooded creatures are faster.
(2) Warm-blooded creatures are heavier.
(3) Body temperature has no effect on speed.
(4) Plant-eaters are warm-blooded.
(5) Warm-blooded creatures eat more.

(1) (2) (3) (4) (5)

Directions: Choose the one best answer to each question. Answers are on page 387.

Item 33 refers to the following passage.

Starlings are not native to North America. Brought here from England in the 1800s, they have created problems for native birds and people too. In some areas, starlings became so numerous by the mid-1900s that they darkened the sky. Thousands fed on farmers' crops each day. People feared they could spread disease.

How could this invader become such a problem? First, starlings took the best nesting sites when native birds flew south for the winter. Second, they like to feed on the ground where the grass is short, making lawns and mowed grass along highways popular for them and the birds troublesome to citizens.

33. Which of the following is based on facts rather than opinions?

(1) Starlings are selfish birds.
(2) Flocks of starlings are a nuisance.
(3) Starlings aren't native to North America.
(4) Winter is when starlings are at their worst.
(5) Starlings' feathers are rather handsome.

Item 34 refers to the following diagram.

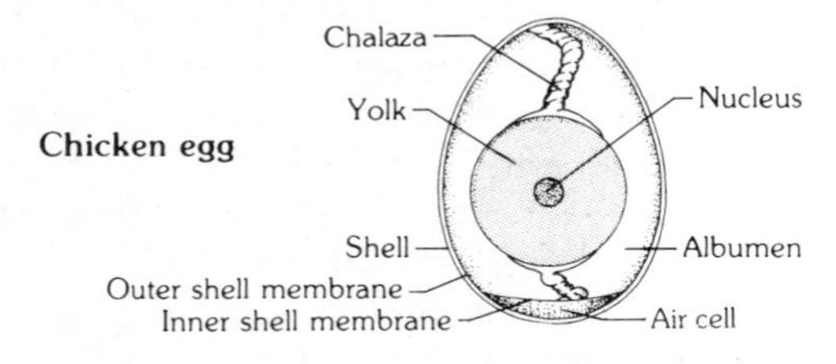

34. Judging from the diagram, it appears that the function of the chalaza is to

(1) provide a way for a chick to get out of the egg
(2) breathe for the unhatched chick
(3) supply food from the mother hen
(4) keep the yolk suspended
(5) to support the shell

1 2 3 4 5

Birds What characteristic do birds have that no other animal has? Flight? No, most birds can fly, but some, such as penguins, cannot. They lay eggs? So do snakes. Birds are endothermic (warm-blooded), which means they keep an internal body temperature that is not affected by their surroundings. But so are other animals, including humans. The one thing that all birds have that no other animal has is *feathers.*

Flight is an important characteristic of most birds, of course. The shapes of a bird's beak, neck, feathers, and tail help streamline it for flight. Its bones are hollow, and they have braces for support, making the skeleton light and strong.

In relation to their size, birds eat a very large amount of food. Food and a constant supply of oxygen provide the energy needed for flying. Birds also use food energy to provide body warmth. To retain body heat, blood vessels near the surface of a bird's body become smaller when it is cold. Birds also retain heat by fluffing their feathers for insulation.

☑ A Test-Taking Tip

After you have chosen an answer to a question on the GED Science Test, go back and read the question again carefully. Be very certain that the response you have chosen actually answers the question. Sometimes one of the wrong choices will simply repeat words from the passage, misleading you into thinking that is the best choice.

Warm-up

Write a short summary of the information you just read about birds. Use complete sentences.

____

____

____

____

____

Sample Warm-up Answer

Birds are endothermic and have feathers. Their shape and hollow bones aid in flight. Their bodies can conserve heat and they use food for energy for both flight and warmth.

Mammals You are a mammal. Mammals show the highest ability of all animals to learn in new situations and are the least dependent on instinctive behavior. As a group, mammals are the most intelligent animals on earth.

Hair has a special role for most mammals. It keeps body heat from escaping, offers protection from abrasion injuries, and, in many cases, sheds water. In whales, fat or blubber replaces hair as an insulator. The armadillo, a resident of warm climates, has no hair but is covered with bony plates.

All the species of mammals have one feature in common: mammary glands. In the females of the species, the glands secrete milk for the young. For a long time after birth, baby mammals are neither able to look for food nor to digest an adult diet. Most live on mother's milk and are protected from predators by their parents until they are fully developed.

Most mammals are *placentals,* which means the embryo develops within the mother and is nourished through a temporary organ called the placenta. *Marsupials* are mammals whose young are born partially developed and must crawl to the mother's "pouch" where they continue to develop. Kangaroos and opossums are marsupials. *Monotremes* are egg-laying mammals. There are only two known monotremes, the duck-billed platypus and the spiny anteater. Both live in Australia and on nearby islands.

The largest mammal is the blue whale; the smallest is a tiny bat that lives in Thailand and is about the size of a bumblebee.

Warm-up

People can be referred to as vertebrate, endothermic, placental mammals. In one or more sentences, explain what this means.

Need a Hint for Number 36?
Shape different letters or signals with your hands and fingers. Which of the listed characteristics would you find most helpful in signing?

Sample Warm-up Answer
People have backbones. They are warm-blooded. Before they are born they receive food through a special organ called a placenta. After they are born, they can live on mother's milk.

Items 35–36 refer to the following passage.

Humans are members of an order of mammals known as primates. Monkeys and apes are primates too. The brains of primates are more highly developed than those of any other animals. For years scientists have wondered whether primates such as chimpanzees or gorillas could learn to communicate with humans. One difference between humans and other primates is that the human vocal tract is developed for speech. For better communication with other primates, a way had to be devised that avoided speech.

Developmental psychologist Penny Patterson began work in 1972 with a one-year-old female gorilla named Koko. She attempted to show Koko how to communicate in sign language, using the gorilla's paws as "hands." At first Koko did not want to make signs. But later she became a rapid learner. By the time she was seven, Koko had a vocabulary of 375 signs.

Using signs, Koko can communicate feelings of happiness, sadness, and anger; she can discuss the past; she can lie to avoid trouble, such as a scolding (she'll blame someone else). She can ask for hugs and can make up her own insults.

35. Koko the gorilla has many emotions similar to those of humans.

    Which of the following pieces of evidence supports the conclusion stated above?

    (1) Gorillas' brains are highly developed.
    (2) Patterson taught Koko to use sign language.
    (3) Koko became an eager learner.
    (4) At age 7 Koko recognized 375 signs.
    (5) Koko signs to express anger or affection.

    (1) (2) (3) (4) (5)

36. In sign language symbols for different ideas are made by placing the fingers, thumb, hand, and arm in different positions. This means that in order for an animal to use sign language, it must have, in addition to a highly developed brain,

    (1) long fingers and toes
    (2) long arms and legs
    (3) a keen sense of touch and sound
    (4) large paws
    (5) fingers and thumbs that move separately

Directions: Choose the one best answer to each question. Answers are on page 388.

Items 37–38 refer to the following passage.

An *electroencephalograph* is an instrument used to measure the electrical activity of the brain. Recordings can be taken from both hemispheres, or halves, of the brain while various activities are being performed. Those recordings can show which hemisphere is more active during a task. When test subjects were recorded drawing a picture or humming a tune, the right half of the brain was more active. When subjects were writing, speaking, or doing tasks that required fine muscle coordination, the left hemisphere recorded the activity.

Scientists have found that the left half of the brain regulates such functions as the ability to recognize and organize words, to understand numerical relationships, to process information in a logical sequence, to pay attention, and to express thoughts in speech and writing. "Intelligence" tests usually measure primarily left-hemisphere skills, though newer tests have been devised to measure right-brain skills as well.

Although the hemispheres are specialized, they work together. When a person sees someone he or she knows, for example, recognition of the face occurs in the right hemisphere and remembrance of the name in the left.

37. According to the passage, the two hemispheres of the brain operate

(1) independently of each other
(2) only when a person is awake
(3) by helping to process words
(4) in specialized ways, but work together
(5) unpredictably

① ② ③ ④ ⑤

38. Which of the following classroom activities would probably be most difficult for a person whose right brain hemisphere had been damaged?

(1) memorizing the names of the planets
(2) preparing an outline for a speech
(3) drawing a diagram of a cell
(4) writing an essay
(5) completing a math problem

Human Anatomy *Anatomy* deals with the structures of the body. *Physiology* is the study of how the structures work together. You can't expect to learn everything about these subjects before you take the GED Test. But you will need a basic understanding of the body systems.

You probably already know that the *skeletal system* shapes and supports your body.

The *digestive system*—which includes the stomach, liver, gall bladder, pancreas and intestines—breaks down food to nourish body cells.

The *circulatory system* takes nutrients obtained through digestion to all parts of the body. It also takes oxygen to body cells and waste materials to organs that will eliminate them from the body. The circulatory system also helps defend against disease?

Eyes, ears, brain, and nerves are parts of the *nervous system.* It lets you sense, analyze, and respond to changes inside and outside your body.

The *respiratory system* allows you to breathe and take in oxygen, necessary for your life. The nose, trachea, and lungs are important parts of the respiratory system.

The many glands that are responsible for human growth, use of energy, and reproduction make up the *endocrine system.* They also produce hormones.

For a man, the *reproductive system* involves various glands that produce chemicals that nourish the sperm. In a woman, a mature egg cell is released from an ovary and, if fertilized by a sperm cell, can grow and develop in the uterus. After about 40 weeks of growth, a baby travels from the uterus through the vagina to complete the reproductive process.

In a healthy individual, all these systems work together. Each system helps to support the others and helps make it possible for them to keep functioning properly.

Warm-up

Answer the following questions on your own paper.

1. Which body system includes the skull?
2. Which part of the nervous system does the skull protect?

Sample Warm-up Answers
1. The skull is part of the skeletal system. **2.** The skull protects the brain.

Ecology To understand what ecology is, it is helpful to know the meaning of some of the words that tell about it.

Organisms of the same species that live and reproduce in a particular location make up a *population.* The number of organisms in a population may change, depending on living conditions. A group of populations that live together in the same area is called a *community.*

Communities may be made up of hundreds of different populations. In a woodland pond, for instance, you might find fish that depend on small animals for food, birds that skim the water for insects, and frogs that move from water to land as they feed on dragonflies. These and other populations make up the pond community. The populations within this community interact.

An **ecosystem** is a combination of a community and its environment. A fish tank, a pasture, a city lot, and the seaside are all ecosystems. Ecosystems vary greatly in size. The largest ecosystem is called the **biosphere.** The biosphere includes all of the communities of species on earth and extends above and below the earth's surface.

Coming to Terms

ecosystem community in interaction with the nonliving parts of its environment
biosphere the parts of the earth and air where life exists

☑ A Test-Taking Tip

Understanding the order that events occur in can be particularly important for test items about processes or cause-effect relationships. Watch for key words such as *first, next, then, prior to, following, subsequently, simultaneously,* and *preceding.*

Warm-up

Circle the number of the best definition of the word *ecology.*

1. an association of conservationists
2. changes that take place in ecosystems
3. the study of how living things and their environment interact
4. the study of the earth's features
5. members of a community living in the biosphere

Warm-up Answer
3

Items 39–40 refer to the following passage.

The United States has changed a great deal since the time of the early settlers. In those days it seemed that resources were limitless. There were endless prairies, vast forests, and abundant fresh water. Factories and industries sprang up as if by magic. It became less expensive to buy new things and discard the old than it was to make things that would last.

Today's conditions have changed. Some outcomes of a very productive society are less pleasing. Many natural resources, including minerals, water, and soil, are in short supply. Energy supplies are uncertain and very expensive. Many families are living in hastily built homes that are costly to heat. People generate so much waste that it costs $6 billion a year just to carry the waste to the dump.

Present-day conditions are very different than they were when the population was smaller. Ideas that were good in the past can no longer apply. The United States cannot afford to be a "throwaway" society. New ideas are needed for houses, more efficient ways to grow food, and better means of transportation.

39. The cost for becoming a "throwaway society" is very high.

    Which of the following could NOT be used as evidence to support the conclusion above?

    (1) Transporting refuse to disposal sites costs millions of dollars each year.
    (2) Nuclear waste, even when safely buried, remains radioactive and must be guarded.
    (3) Toxic waste has ruined the value of much formerly valuable land.
    (4) Heat from burning waste products can be used to produce steam power.
    (5) When groundwater supplies are depleted, water must be transported from other places.

40. All of the following help improve the quality of air we breathe EXCEPT

    (1) Using a bicycle for transportation
    (2) adding a filter to a car's exhaust system
    (3) incinerating rubbish
    (4) composting dead leaves
    (5) drying laundry on a clothesline

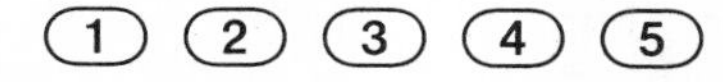

Directions: Choose the one best answer to each question. Answers are on page 388.

Items 1–2 refer to the passage below.

Modern astronomy is said to have started with Nicolaus Copernicus in the sixteenth century. He pointed out that the sun, not the earth, was the central body in the solar system. This knowledge gave later scientists, like Tycho Brahe, a basis for describing the motions of the bodies in the system.

Johannes Kepler studied Brahe's data and formulated three laws of planetary motion: (1) planetary orbits are elliptical; (2) the closer a planet is to the sun, the faster it moves around the sun; and (3) the size of a planet's orbit is related to the amount of time it takes to orbit the sun. The larger the orbit, the longer one full revolution takes.

Kepler did not try to explain the forces that acted on planets. In the seventeenth century, Isaac Newton explained why the planets move as they do by writing his laws of motion and gravitation.

1. The author assumes, but does not state, that before Copernicus' time, people thought the sun
   (1) was the center of the universe
   (2) controlled the motions of earth
   (3) controlled the motions of the stars
   (4) revolved around earth
   (5) moved in no particular pattern

   ① ② ③ ④ ⑤

2. One of Newton's principles of gravity states that objects continue to move as they have been. If they are at rest, they remain at rest. If they are moving, they keep moving at the same speed and in the same direction.

   In space, there is little to change an object's motion. Which of the following aspects of space travel illustrates the principle stated above?
   (1) A spacecraft orbits the moon.
   (2) Astronauts take their first steps on the moon.
   (3) A spacecraft returns to earth by splashing down into the ocean.
   (4) Spaceship *Voyager,* now past Saturn, will travel in the same direction for years.
   (5) Meteorites fall into Mars' atmosphere.

   ① ② ③ ④ ⑤

Earth Science

The Universe and the Solar System
Astronomers, people who study the heavens, have helped us to understand our "address" in space. Starting from the most general, we have learned that the **universe** is made up of space and everything that's in it. We live in a *galaxy* that is only one of many millions. A **galaxy** is made up of systems of stars held together by their mutual gravity. The name of our galaxy is the Milky Way. To us, the most important star in the Milky Way is our sun. The earth is in a **solar system** made up of the sun and all the bodies that orbit it, including the earth. The sun, the only star in our solar system, is its largest, heaviest, and hottest body. It is also the basic source of all heat and light in the system. Other stars, also glowing balls of super-hot, compressed gases, are far outside the solar system.

Today most scientists believe that the solar system was formed out of a large, whirling space cloud some 4.6 billion years ago. Most of the dust and gases were compressed by the force of gravity into a fiery ball, which became the sun. The remaining materials became planets and asteroids.

In order, moving outward from our sun, the nine known planets are Mercury, Venus, Earth, Mars, Jupiter, Saturn, Uranus, Neptune, and Pluto. Asteroids, rocks from one to 500 miles in diameter, also orbit the sun. Most of these chunks of rock have paths mainly between Jupiter and Mars.

Coming to Terms

universe space and everything in it
galaxy systems of stars held together by their mutual gravity
solar system group of planets and their satellites that move about a sun

Warm-up
In your own words, explain the meaning of the following statement.

■ A planetary orbit is elliptical.

___

___

Sample Warm-up Answer
A planet moving (or revolving) around the sun takes an oval-shaped path.

Tilt, Rotation, Revolution, and Seasons
Each planet has two motions. (1) *Every planet rotates, or spins, on its axis.* The time needed to make one complete rotation is called a day. Since the planets rotate at different speeds, the lengths of their days differ. Jupiter has the shortest day, Venus the longest. (2) *Every planet also revolves around the sun.* It takes the earth 365¼ days, or one year, to orbit the sun.

Imagine a line that runs through the earth from the North Pole to the South Pole. This line is called an *axis.* The axis is tilted in relation to the sun.

Since the earth always revolves around the sun at the same angle of tilt, this tilt is responsible for the changing seasons. From June 20–21 to September 22–23, it is summer in the northern hemisphere because that hemisphere is tilted toward the sun. The sun is more nearly overhead, and days are warmer and longer. During this time it is winter in the southern hemisphere, which is tilted away from the sun.

The Change of Seasons

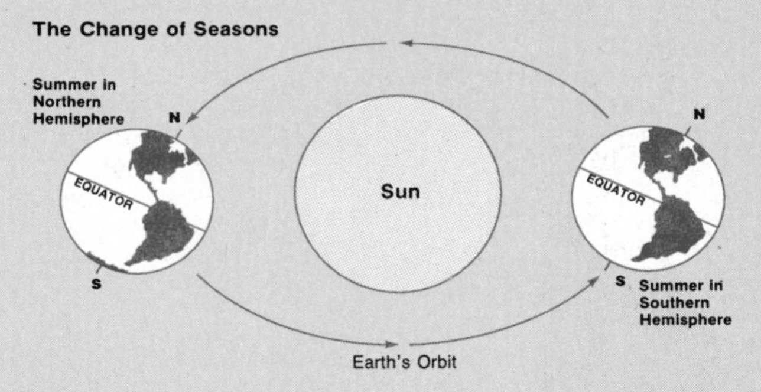

Summer begins in the southern hemisphere on December 21 or 22. At that time, the half of the earth below the equator is tilted toward the sun.

☑ A Test-Taking Tip
Directional arrows in a diagram help guide you along the steps in a process or help you see the direction in which parts of something move. To read a diagram in the most efficient manner, follow directional arrows and read the labels as you come to them.

Warm-up
Why is there little variation in the hot temperature at the equator? Base your answer on the diagram above. Use your own paper.

Sample Warm-up Answer
The sun's rays almost always hit the equator directly because of the tilt of the earth.

Items 3–4 refer to the following passage.

The succession of the seasons provides us with the great cycle we call the year. The next most important biological cycle would appear to be the twenty-eight-day lunar month. Though we moderns reckon our calendars by solar months, that is really only a bookkeeping convenience. Many animal behaviors are dominated by the phases of the moon, by the cycles of its waxing and waning; more and more human behaviors and biological processes are now considered to be affected either directly or indirectly by lunar periods. Of course the smallest and most dramatic cycle which dominates our behavior is the diurnal [daily] rotation of the earth, the alternation of night and day.

Yet we don't live our lives in accordance with this knowledge of the importance of cycles in our physiological and psychological well-being.

3. According to the passage, we fail to realize how much human behavior is influenced by

   (1) alternation of day and night
   (2) the cycle of the seasons
   (3) the cycles of the moon
   (4) relationships of the sun, earth, and moon
   (5) biological processes

4. Which of the following conclusions is supported by ideas in the passage?

   (1) Animals are more strongly affected by cycles of the moon than humans are.
   (2) People are not at all affected by cycles of the moon.
   (3) Our calendar should be based on the cycles of the moon.
   (4) The sun's daily rotation does not affect human behavior.
   (5) We should become more aware of how we are affected by cycles of the moon and sun.

Directions: Choose the one best answer to each question. Answers are on page 388.

Items 5–6 refer to the following passage.

Scientific evidence seems to indicate that the earth began to form after iron and silicate particles condensed in a large cloud of gaseous material.

As the planet grew, the force of gravity pulling on denser, iron-rich, materials increased. This is because as mass increases, so does the force of gravity. It seems that the earth's core began to develop even before the earth was fully formed. This would mean that the three layers of the earth—crust, mantle, and core—would have been differentiated very early in the earth's life cycle.

As the layers began to form and as gravitational energy was released, the planet would have heated up gradually. The heating added to the melting in the earth's core. This in turn led to greater differentiation between the layers. This process seems to indicate that the formation of the earth's core is still going on.

5. According to the passage, gravitational energy causes the earth's core to continue to

(1) decrease (2) increase
(3) melt (4) cool (5) decay

① ② ③ ④ ⑤

6. Oil from deep wells is often warm, and air in deep mines is often hot as a result of

(1) magnetic force
(2) chemicals in the earth's crust
(3) warm air from the surface
(4) heat from inside the earth
(5) the earth's rotation

① ② ③ ④ ⑤

The Earth's Layers and Magnetism Earth is the third planet from the sun. Compared with other planets it is rather small, with a diameter of about 8,000 miles.

Evidence indicates that the earth has three concentric layers: *crust, mantle,* and *core.* The crust is an outer layer of solid rock from five to thirty miles deep. Temperature and pressure increase as you move downward into the crust.

The middle layer is the mantle, which is made up of melted and solid materials.

The innermost of the earth's layers is the core. The outer core is believed to be mainly metallic iron and some other elements in a fluid state. The inner core is made up of the same materials, but they are solid.

Our planet has *magnetic poles* that are roughly similar to its geographical poles. Flares on the sun's surfaces cause "magnetic storms," or disturbances in the earth's magnetism. These disturbances start all over the earth within a minute of each other.

Warm-up

Based on what you learned above, label the various layers of the earth on the diagram below. Then answer the questions that follow.

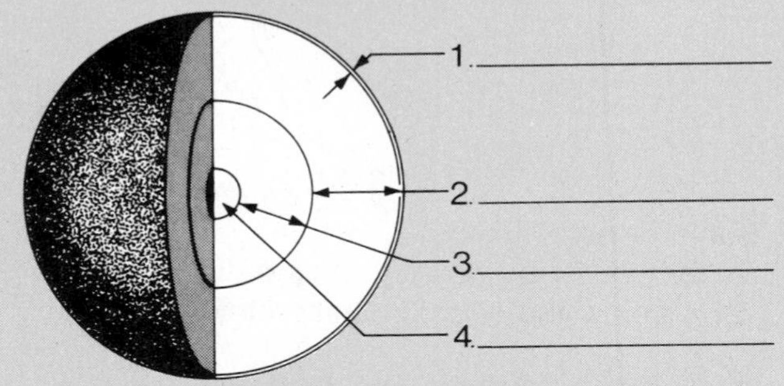

5. Which layer has the densest materials?

______

6. Why is this layer so dense? ______

______

Need a Hint for Number 5?
Skim the passage to find a reference to the key term gravitational energy. *Reread the sentence that contains that term.*

Warm-up Answers
1. crust **2.** mantle **3.** outer core **4.** inner core **5.** the core
6. Pressure increases toward the center of the earth.

Continental Drift and Mountain Formation

Although you may think of the earth's crust as being solid, geologists have found that it is made up of about 20 immense sections called tectonic plates. These plates carry the continents and ocean floors. Most of the plate edges are under the sea.

Geologists have formulated the *Continental Drift Theory* to help explain the constant motion of the tectonic plates. They believe it to be the result of tremendous pressures on the earth's crust and the upper part of the mantle. The heat from the pressure is so great that it melts rock in the upper part of the mantle. The melted rock, or magma, bursts out of the earth from between ridges at the plate edges.

When magma reaches the surface, it condenses as it cools and becomes part of the plates. The enlarged plates crush against one another, and that pressure can cause a crack in the earth's crust. If the crust moves on either side of the crack, it is called a **fault.** Most faults are at the boundaries of the plates. Rock that occurs along a fault can move up and down, from side to side, or in both directions at once. This can take place over many years; rapid motion is recorded as an earthquake.

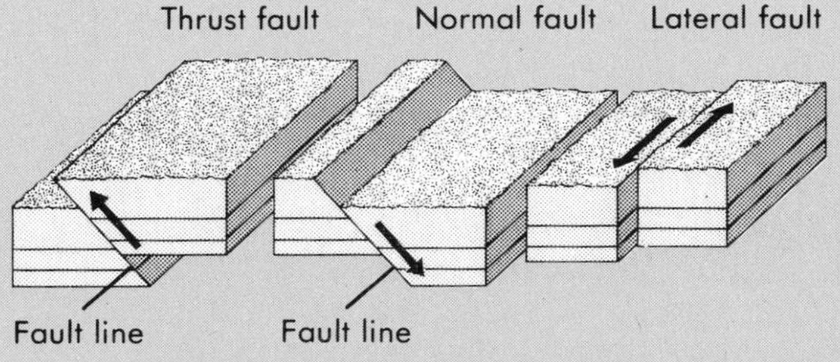

Some rock layers bend and fold rather than break when forces act on them. Most large folded mountain ranges are located where plates collide. Both the Alps and the Himalayas are becoming higher because they are on colliding plates.

Coming to Terms

fault crack caused by movement of the earth's crust

Need a Hint for Number 8?
Part A is the side view of an island. Notice how each line in Part A corresponds to a line in Part B.

Items 7–8 refer to the following passage.

Many land features are formed by the uplifting that occurs as a result of faulting and folding. Geologists believe that uplifting is caused by huge movements in the earth's mantle that force the crust to rise or sink.

A plateau is a large area of flat, uplifted land, usually of sedimentary rocks. In a moist climate, rivers and running water can carve mountains from plateaus. They may be what is left behind when water or wind wear away a plateau in a dry climate. Buttes are very small mesas. Mesas and buttes are common features in the western and southwestern parts of the United States.

7. According to the passage, uplift in the earth's crust is thought to be the result of

   (1) centrifugal force
   (2) ocean currents
   (3) rivers and running water
   (4) movement in the earth's mantle
   (5) the sun's gravitational pull

   (1) (2) (3) (4) (5)

8. Earth scientists use maps with contour lines to help them show elevation. The contour lines on the drawing below connect all points of equal elevation.

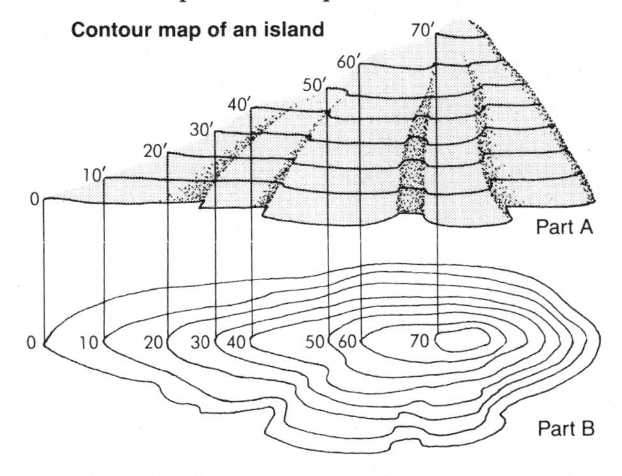

Part B of the diagram above represents

   (1) a body of water
   (2) a temperature chart
   (3) a view of the area from above
   (4) equal elevation
   (5) concentric circles

Directions: Choose the one best answer to each question. Answers are on page 388.

Items 9–10 refer to the following passage.

A government agency in China has reported that strange animal behaviors were observed just hours before an earthquake. Cattle, sheep, mules, and horses would not enter their corrals. Rats fled their homes. Hibernating snakes left their burrows early. Pigeons flew continuously and did not return to their nests. Rabbits raised their ears, jumped about aimlessly, and bumped into things. Fish jumped above water surfaces.

For years, farmers throughout the world have told stories about changes in animal behavior just before an earthquake. Scientists in many countries are interested in finding the causes for the strange behavior. They have suggested that one or more of the following may be possible causes:

1. slight change in the earth's magnetic field
2. increased amounts of electricity in the air
3. very small air pressure changes
4. changes in noise level
5. gas escaping from the ground

When scientists find the cause of the strange animal behavior, they may be able to predict earthquakes within hours.

9. According to the passage, learning the reasons for animals' behavior before an earthquake might

   (1) help predict when a quake will occur
   (2) help explain human behavior
   (3) be an inexpensive earthquake predictor
   (4) allow farmers to safeguard animals
   (5) help scientists predict the strength of a quake

   (1) (2) (3) (4) (5)

10. Which of the animal behaviors below may help predict oncoming earthquakes?

   (1) Increased noises before a quake might make wild animals uneasy.
   (2) Some domestic animals have refused to enter their corrals before a quake.
   (3) Cats are more sensitive than other animals and might detect quakes.
   (4) Smal changes in barometric pressure might alert animals to a coming quake.
   (5) Gases escaping from the ground might make animals uneasy.

   (1) (2) (3) (4) (5)

Earthquakes and Volcanoes Why do volcanoes erupt? Imagine the effects of shaking a warm bottle of pop. The cap may explode off, releasing the pop and the dissolved gas in the drink. Gas and water vapor under pressure inside a volcano can also explode.

Volcanoes often give warnings before they erupt. These include the emission of gas and smoke.

Volcanoes that have erupted recently are called *active volcanoes.* A *dormant volcano* is one that erupted in the past but has been quiet for many years. An *extinct volcano* is one that is not expected to erupt again.

Most earthquakes happen because rocks move along a fault. Rocks in the earth's crust that are under pressure bend and break. When the break occurs, energy is released. This energy makes the earth shake and is called an earthquake. Scientists study earthquakes by measuring seismic activity, the tremors and shiftings of the earth's crust. The time line shows some of the earth's major recorded earthquakes.

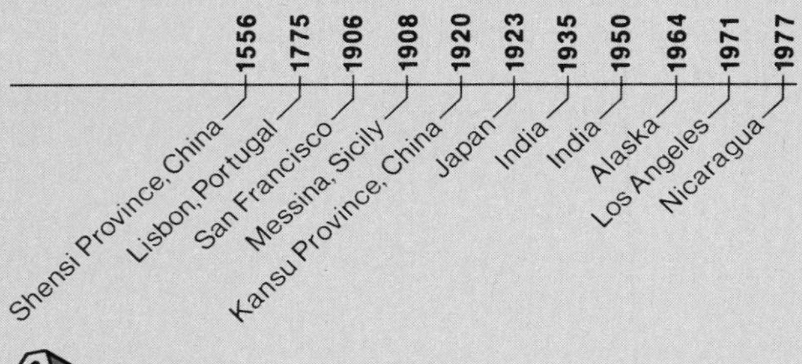

Warm-up

Study the time line and answer the questions.

1. The most deadly recorded earthquake was also one of the first to be recorded. More than 830,000 people died in 1556 as a result of this earthquake. Where did the earthquake occur?

____

2. The strongest earthquake ever in North America hit Alaska in what year? __________

☑ A Test-Taking Tip

A time line lists important events and tells when they occurred. To read a time line, first notice how many years are shown. That will help you see how each event relates to the total span of years.

Sample Warm-up Answers

1. The earthquake occurred in Shensi Province, China **2.** A strong earthquake hit Alaska in 1964.

Rocks, Minerals, and Ores The rocks that make up the earth's crust belong to three families: igneous, sedimentary, and metamorphic. *Igneous rocks* are formed from magma. As the magma forces its way up through fissures, faults, and volcanoes to the earth's surface, it cools and hardens and becomes igneous rock.

The second family is made up of *sedimentary rocks,* those that form at the earth's surface, usually by the compression of sediments. The most common kind of sedimentary rock is made up of materials carried by water, ice, or wind. Millions of years may pass before the materials are pressed together and hardened into rock. A second kind develops chemically from minerals that were once dissolved in water. A third type forms when plant and animal remains harden into rock.

Igneous and sedimentary rocks that are buried deep inside the earth may change in appearance and mineral content. The new rocks that result are called *metamorphic rocks.*

Rocks are commonly made up of mixtures of minerals. The kind and amount of minerals in any two rocks can be quite different. Any two samples of minerals, however, have exactly the same chemical compositions.

From the earth's crust we mine or extract useful organic and inorganic material. **Organic** substances originate from ancient plant or animal remains. Coal, diamonds, and limestone are examples of organic substances. **Inorganic** substances originate from sources other than plant or animal material. Iron is an example.

Rocks or minerals from which metals can be mined or extracted are known as *ore.* Platinum and copper are metals that come from ore.

Coming to Terms

organic derived from once-living materials
inorganic derived from sources other than plant or animal

Warm-up

Answer the question. What family of rocks will most likely contain fossils of water animals?

___

___

___

Sample Warm-up Answer
Fossils of water animals will most likely be found in sedimentary rock.

Items 11–12 are based on the following passage.

Two of our most widely used energy sources, oil and natural gas, are commonly found together in sedimentary rocks. Both are compounds of carbon and hydrogen similar to those found in living animals and plants. Scientists think that oil and gas form where sea life dies and drops to the bottom of ocean water. In time, animal and plant remains are covered with sediments of mud, clay, and sand that later become sedimentary rock. After millions of years, the buried remains change into oil and gas.

The muddy sediments that bury the remains often become shale. At this point, oil and gas may be squeezed into permeable rock nearby. Permeable rock, such as sandstone, has spaces that are connected. For a large deposit of oil and gas to accumulate, there must be a "trap." A bed of nonpermeable rock, such as shale, can trap the oil and gas and keep them from moving away.

11. Why is oil found in sedimentary rock rather than igneous or metamorphic?
    (1) Metamorphic rock is too deep.
    (2) Igneous rock is made from magma.
    (3) Oil forms from organic sediments.
    (4) Sedimentary rocks have no oil "seal."
    (5) Metamorphic rocks are too porous.

    (1) (2) (3) (4) (5)

12. Which of the following best describes the process by which oil formed long ago?
    (1) Time changed buried remains of sea life into oil; nonpermeable rock trapped it.
    (2) Ancient remains of sea life changed deposits of mud and clay into oil.
    (3) Mud, clay and other sediments trapped small aquatic animals and turned them to oil.
    (4) Long periods of time changed nonpermeable rock into shale and oil.
    (5) Mud and clay, trapped in nonpermeable rock, turned into oil.

Directions: Choose the one best answer to each question. Answers are on page 388.

Items 13–15 refer to the following chart.

	Paleozoic Era	Mesozoic Era	Cenozoic Era
Era began	600 million years ago	225 million years ago	65 million years ago
Climate	variable	warm, humid	cooler; several ice ages
Predominant life forms (in order of appearance)	trilobites snails ferns insects fish amphibians and reptiles	dinosaurs turtles crocodiles lizards snakes early mammals plants with seeds	large mammals woolly mammoths ancestors of modern mammals humans ancestors of modern plants

13. We [humans] have just arrived upon this Earth. How long will we stay?
—James Rettie, "But a Watch in the Night"

Which of the following justifies the conclusion in the first sentence above?

(1) The earliest humans appeared in the recent part of the Cenozoic era.
(2) Modern humans appear quite different from early ones.
(3) Humans appeared on the earth later than plants with seeds.
(4) Humans appeared on earth later than woolly mammoths.
(5) Humans appeared on earth millions of years after trilobites.

(1) (2) (3) (4) (5)

14. Which of the following could never have seen a living dinosaur?

(1) a fish (2) an amphibian
(3) an insect (4) an early human
(5) a snail

(1) (2) (3) (4) (5)

15. According to the chart, the climate during the Mesozoic era was

(1) colder than that during the Cenozoic era
(2) extremely hot and arid
(3) cold and wet
(4) variable
(5) milder than that during the Ice Ages

(1) (2) (3) (4) (5)

Geologic Eras and Fossils Scientists think that the earth is about 4.6 billion years old. They divide the history of the earth into four main geologic time periods called *eras.* The first, the *Precambrian,* was the longest and is the least understood. It includes approximately 90 percent of all the earth's history.

At the beginning of the Precambrian era, the earth was formed. Millions of years passed before the rock crust was developed. Later, oceans grew, and an atmosphere evolved around the earth. Simple life forms appeared but most were not preserved in fossil form.

The *Paleozoic* era began about 600 million years ago with the appearance of sea life, such as trilobites, snails, and sponges. Before the era ended, 225 million years ago, the first land plants had appeared.

A variety of natural resources formed during the Paleozoic era. Coal, oil, and natural gas are called fossil fuels because they formed from the remains of living organisms in the second half of the Paleozoic era.

The *Mesozoic* era followed the Paleozoic. During this time, the climate was generally quite mild. Although small mammals and birds first appeared, the era is best known for the large reptiles, or dinosaurs, that roamed the land. By the end of the era, dinosaurs had died out completely.

You are living in the *Cenozoic* era, which began about 65 million years ago, when the landforms that you see today developed. Late in the Cenozoic era, the climate began to change rapidly. Several ice ages occurred, during which large sheets of ice covered much of the land, causing changes in life forms. It was in the more recent part of the Cenozoic era that humans first appeared.

Warm-up

Why is the Precambrian period the least understood of the geologic eras described in the passage?

Sample Warm-up Answer
The period extended over millions of years; little fossil evidence remains for study.

Weather and Climate The different **weather** patterns are a combination of temperature, wind, moisture, and air pressure. During the year, weather patterns change fairly regularly all over the earth. The average of the weather conditions anywhere is called **climate.**

The basic temperature of an area—whether it is hot, cold, or in-between—is caused by the tilt of the earth in relation to the sun. The sun's rays strike the equator almost directly the year around, keeping the air hot. In the middle latitudes (sections of the earth parallel to the equator), the angle of the rays varies from more direct in the summer to more slanted in the winter. And at the poles, the air is always cold.

Many factors influence weather conditions and climate; for example, the great difference in temperatures for the equator and the poles, the earth's rotation, and the difference in land and water temperatures. These factors affect the movement of air masses. As air masses move, they bump into one another. Cold and warm air do not mix easily because their densities differ; a boundary called a **front** forms between these air masses. Fronts move from west to east, just as air masses do.

A cold front forms as a cold air mass pushes out a warm air mass. As the cold front moves into a region, it wedges under the warm air and lifts it sharply. Storms usually result. When the cold front passes, the wind changes direction and the weather becomes clear and colder.

A warm front forms as a warm air mass pushes out a cold air mass. The warm air glides up and over the cold air; rainfall or snowfall begins. As the front passes, temperatures rise and warm air replaces cold air.

Coming to Terms

weather daily condition of the atmosphere with regard to temperature, humidity, clouds, winds, and storm conditions
climate average weather condition of a place over a long period of time
front boundary between warm and cold air masses

Warm-up

In a sentence, tell what happens when a cold front passes.

Sample Warm-up Answer
Storms often clear, and the temperature drops.

Items 16–17 refer to the following weather map.

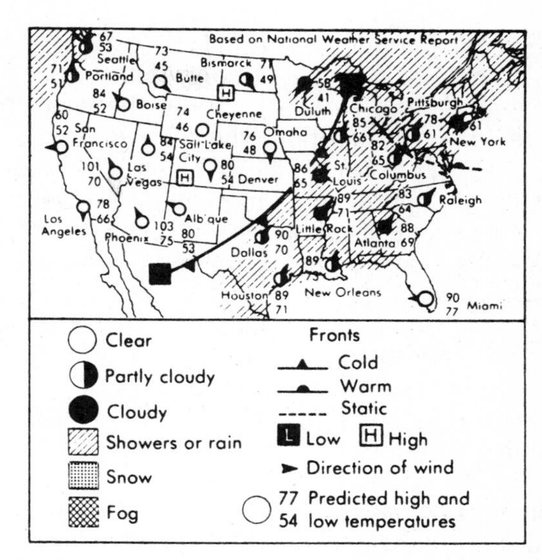

16. Which of the following *best* describes the weather conditions predicted for Atlanta?

(1) sunny with a chance for rain
(2) rain with a high of 88°F
(3) cloudy and a high of 69°F
(4) rain with partial clearing by nightfall
(5) partly cool, cloudy, rain, and a high of 85°F

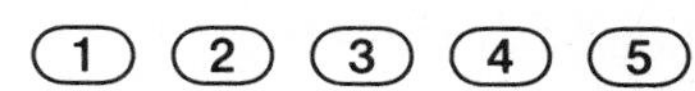

17. Cold fronts move from west to east. Which of the following describes the weather change that St. Louis can expect?

(1) sunny, clear weather
(2) cooler with continued rain
(3) cooler and foggy
(4) warmer and foggy
(5) warmer with continued rain

Directions: Choose the one best answer to each question. Answers are on page 388.

Items 18–19 refer to the following passage.

A number of elements contribute to ocean movement: the earth's rotation, the wind, the tides, rain, evaporation, river water, earthquakes, and water density. Tides, the most regular and predictable motions of seawater, are the result of primarily the moon's and also the sun's gravitational attraction on the earth. Usually the oceans' waters rise and fall twice during a period of 24 hours and 51 minutes, the time needed for the moon to return to its same position overhead. High tides occur when the moon is either overhead or halfway around the earth.

The shape of the ocean floor and the location of currents can affect the heights of tides and the times at which they appear. Some places have no tides at all because the actions of the moon and the sun are balanced by the effects of the ocean and land.

18. How long must the earth rotate before the moon returns to the same overhead position?

(1) 12 hours
(2) 24 hours and 51 minutes
(3) 72 hours and 36 minutes
(4) a day
(5) a week

① ② ③ ④ ⑤

19. The sun has much more mass than the moon and, therefore, has a much stronger gravitational force. Why is it, then, that tides are primarily a result of the moon's gravity?

(1) Ocean currents affect the sun's pull.
(2) The shape of the ocean floor affects the sun's gravitational force.
(3) The earth travels around the sun.
(4) The sun is at a greater distance from the earth than the moon is.
(5) The sun's heat weakens its gravitational force.

① ② ③ ④ ⑤

Oceans, Tides, and Currents More than 70 percent of the earth's surface is covered by oceans, which contain 97 percent of all the water on earth. Rivers, lakes, streams, and ponds hold less than 1 percent of the earth's water. The remaining 2 percent is frozen at the North and South poles.

The waters of all the oceans circulate in one gigantic ocean. Geographers divide this ocean into four separate bodies of water. The Pacific, the largest and deepest ocean, covers more than one-third of the earth's surface. Next in size comes the Atlantic. The third largest is the Indian Ocean. The Arctic is the smallest ocean.

Currents of water flow steadily, like rivers, through the seas. *Surface currents* are created and driven through the surface waters of the oceans by the direction of the constant winds. The earth's rotation also influences the currents' paths. Most currents flow in large loops, turning and flowing along coastlines. Ships use them as they sail from continent to continent.

Earth's gravity keeps the moon in orbit, but the moon also has a gravitational pull. A result of its pull on the earth is *tide,* which refers to the regular swelling and falling of seawater. High and low tide usually take place twice a day.

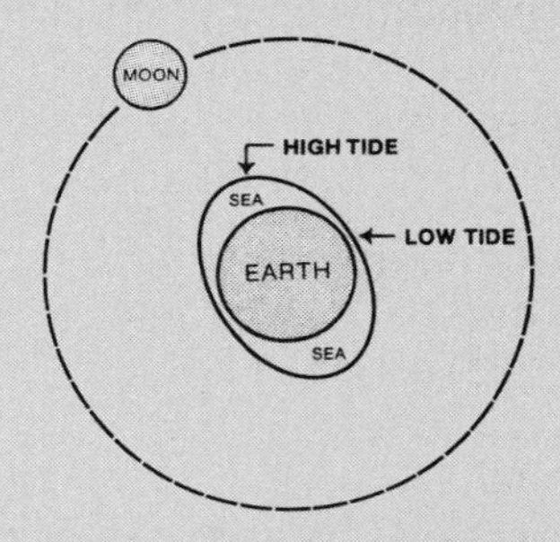

The diagram shows how the moon's gravitational pull draws the earth's waters toward the moon in a great bulge, *high tide.* The force gets weaker with distance. The least amount of pull is on the opposite side of the earth, so the water there is also at high tide.

Warm-up

Dissolved salts and minerals that come from the earth's crust dissolve in ocean water. What do you think is the most common ocean salt?

____

____

Sample Warm-up Answer
The most common ocean salt is ordinary table salt, sodium chloride.

Weathering and Erosion The earth's surface is exposed to conditions that cause the rock to break down. **Weathering** is the process by which large rocks are broken down into smaller, even tiny, pieces. This breakdown is caused by contact of the rock with water, air, and living organisms. Together these forces create soil, the smallest particles of rock. Agents of **erosion,** such as rainwater and rivers, carry the soil to other locations. Weathering and erosion change the earth's surface.

Two kinds of weathering, physical and chemical, occur at the same time. *Physical weathering* is caused by various forces that break down the rock without changing its chemical composition. Variations in temperature cause the rocks to expand and contract; cracks develop. Moisture enters the rocks and permits plant growth. As moisture seeps into the cracks, frost action causes expansion and contraction, shattering weak joints. Plant roots also exert pressure in crevices, breaking rock into smaller pieces.

Chemical weathering breaks down rocks by changing the minerals in them. The minerals react with oxygen, water, or acids to form new substances. Water may also dissolve minerals and wash them away.

Coming to Terms

weathering geologic process that changes the minerals in rocks or causes them to break apart

erosion movement of weathered rock and soil from one place to another

Warm-up

If the process of weathering had never taken place, would erosion be possible?

☑ A Test-Taking Tip

When you read a passage that describes a process or principle of science, try to imagine how it might relate to your own daily life. You might, for example, try to think of a specific example of the process or idea being described.

Sample Warm-up Answer

No. Weathering breaks large pieces of rock into tiny pieces that can be carried by the forces of erosion, such as wind and water.

Items 20–21 refer to the following passage.

Erosion is a natural process that can damage the soil. Wind can blow away the topsoil and rain can wash it away. People's actions, however, can increase the rate of erosion.

Strip-mining is the stripping of the soil and rock at the earth's surface to remove coal or mineral deposits. The removal of vegetation and soil leaves the land scarred and open to erosion. All states now require mining companies to restore the land to its original condition. This involves refilling and replanting the area that was mined.

Unwise ranching and farming methods also increase erosion. For example, allowing livestock to overgraze speeds up erosion. The animals eat the plants that hold the soil in place.

Farmers can also reduce soil erosion by planting their fields in certain ways. For example, in hilly country, farmers often make flat, steplike terraces on steep slopes to reduce water runoff.

20. Some farmers plant their crops between strips of land planted with grass or clover. The grass and clover roots help hold the soil together, break the force of raindrops, and form a layer of vegetation that absorbs water.

    Strip-farming, which is the type of planting described above, provides all the following benefits EXCEPT

    (1) preventing drought
    (2) helping water sink into the ground
    (3) preventing soil erosion by wind
    (4) preventing soil erosion by water
    (5) reducing the likelihood of floods

21. Which of the following is least likely to be disturbed by erosion?

    (1) an ocean shore
    (2) a glacier-covered mountain
    (3) an area containing a strip mine
    (4) a low swamp with no running water
    (5) a steep hill recently deforested by a fire

Directions: Choose the *one* best answer to each question. Answers are on page 388.

Items 22–23 refer to the following passage.

There are many forms of renewable energy. Living organisms store energy in their cells, so plant and animal material, or biomass, can be used to release this stored energy. For example, plants can be converted into alcohol that can be burned. Gasohol for cars and trucks is a mixture of alcohol made from grains and gasoline.

Water provides energy in many ways. The sun's energy sets the water cycle in motion. Hydroelectric energy is made at dams and waterfalls. The force of falling water turns the blades of a turbine, which, in turn, runs a generator and makes electricity. Ocean Thermal Energy Conversion (OTEC) is still in an experimental stage. Floating OTEC energy plants use the temperature differences found in ocean water to generate electricity. The process works because the water at the surface of the ocean in the tropics is warm enough to boil ammonia. The steam produced spins the blades of a turbine. Cold ocean water cools the steam, which condenses back into liquid ammonia for reuse.

22. Burning wood to cook a meal is an example of using

    (1) water power (2) fossil fuels
    (3) biomass (4) nuclear power
    (5) Ocean Thermal Energy Conversion

    (1) (2) (3) (4) (5)

23. Which of the following examples use a nonrenewable resource?

    (1) A power company operates an Ocean Thermal Energy Conversion Plant.
    (2) A youngster pedals a bicycle.
    (3) Campers use a gasoline generator to produce electricity.
    (4) A homeowner uses a woodstove to heat his house.
    (5) A windmill pumps water into a home.

    (1) (2) (3) (4) (5)

Energy Sources Just as you use food as fuel to run your body, machines need fuel to put them into motion. Fuel for mechanical energy comes from many sources, including oil, natural gas, coal, and the nuclei of atoms.

The bar graph below shows how the United States used energy resources during a recent year. As you can see, the United States used oil to meet almost half its energy needs. Most of this oil is refined into gasoline. Both oil and natural gas are used to heat homes and to run industries. Coal is also an important energy source for industry.

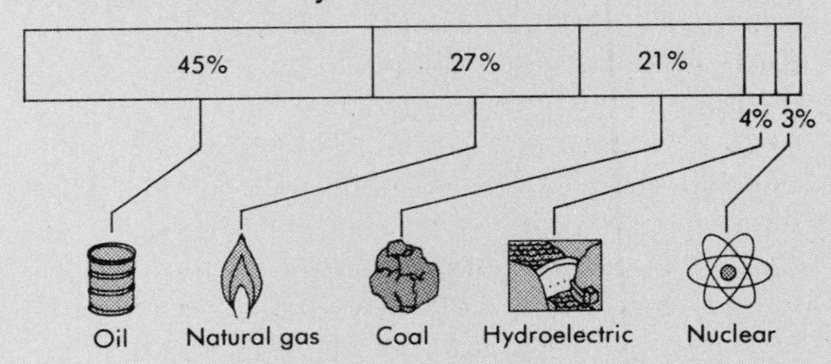

Sometimes you use energy directly, such as when you burn natural gas to cook food. Often, however, people use one energy source, such as coal or water power, to make another form of energy—electricity.

The most important sources of energy—oil, gas, and coal—are called *fossil fuels.* As you read earlier, they formed hundreds of millions of years ago from the remains of buried organisms. Once fossil fuels are used up, no more will be available. They are **nonrenewable resources.** Energy from other sources, such as the sun or wind, will not run out. They are **renewable resources.**

Coming to Terms

nonrenewable resource raw material that, when exhausted, cannot be replaced

renewable resource raw material that is not exhausted with use

Warm-up

Using the graph above, answer each question.

1. Which energy sources does the United States depend upon most? ____________

2. What renewable resource powers sailing ships? ____________

Sample Warm-up Answers

1. The United States depends primarily on oil. **2.** Sailboats depend on wind power.

Chemistry

Some people think that chemistry doesn't have much to do with everyday life. It belongs in a laboratory, they believe. Chemists *do* work in laboratories, of course, but *chemistry* is everywhere. It is part of everything in the world.

Chemistry and Matter Chemistry deals with **matter**—how it is made up and how it changes. You may not always think about it, but you see physical changes in matter all around you. For example, if you see butter melting, you don't say, "There's a change in matter," but more likely, "Who left the butter out?"

Most kinds of matter can be solid, liquid, and gas at different times. Matter changes from one of these states to another when its temperature rises or falls enough to affect the motion of particles in the substance. At low temperatures, particles in a solid vibrate in one place and stay closely joined. At higher temperatures, the particles gain energy and move more quickly and freely as a liquid. At still higher temperatures, the particles have enough energy to break away from each other, forming a gas.

Each substance has particular temperatures at which it changes state. The temperature at which a solid changes into a liquid is its *melting point*. The temperature at which a liquid changes into a solid is its *freezing point*. (Can you see that the freezing point of a substance is the same as its melting point?) When a liquid reaches the temperature of its boiling point, *vaporization* takes place. Through the process of vaporization, a liquid changes into a gas.

Coming to Terms

matter in large amounts, anything that has mass, or weight, and takes up space

Warm-up

On your own paper, describe how temperature can affect the physical states of matter.

Need a Hint for Number 1?

Remember, each substance has a particular temperature at which it changes to another state. The boiling point for water is therefore constant at each elevation, yet it may vary from elevation to elevation depending on air pressure.

Sample Warm-up Answer

At its lowest temperatures, matter is in a solid state. At higher temperatures it becomes a liquid and then a gas.

Directions: For each item, choose the one best answer. Answers are on page 388.

1. The boiling point of liquids is affected by air pressure. At high mountain altitudes, where air pressure is lower than at sea level, water comes to a boil at lower temperatures. At sea level the air pressure is higher so that water boils at a higher temperature. In order to make sure that foods are thoroughly cooked, people in mountain settings may need to

   (1) change cooking temperatures often
   (2) rely on fewer frozen foods
   (3) use lower heat settings on stoves
   (4) boil foods for longer lengths of time
   (5) vaporize more water used for cooking

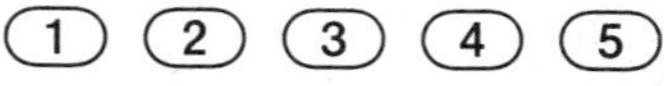

Items 2–3 refer to the passage below.

Diamonds, ice, sugar—all share a characteristic common to most solids. They are made up of crystals. Particles in a crystal are arranged in a definite, repeating pattern. A diamond is one large crystal; ice consists of many small crystals.

Crystals form when a liquid cools. As it cools, particles of a liquid slow down and move closer together. They begin to center on a particular point. From this point out, the particles arrange themselves in the crystal structure belonging to that substance.

Rate of cooling affects the forming of crystals. If a liquid cools slowly, a large single crystal may develop. If it cools quickly, many smaller crystals form.

2. According to the passage, which of the following statements is true?

   (1) Diamond crystals form very rapidly.
   (2) Size determines a crystal's shape.
   (3) Ice is a large, solid crystal.
   (4) Most solids are made up of crystals.
   (5) Particles form crystals randomly.

① ② ③ ④ ⑤

3. As crystals form, what are the number and size of the crystals affected by?

   (1) their shape
   (2) the rate of temperature decrease
   (3) the shape of their particles
   (4) the point at which particles cluster
   (5) their definite, repeating pattern

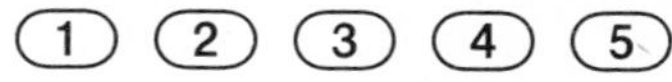

Directions: For each item, choose the one best answer. Answers begin on page 388.

Items 4–5 refer to the passage and diagrams.

Each atom of an element always contains a certain number of protons in its nucleus. The number of protons in an element's atom is its atomic number. The number of both protons and neutrons in an element's atom is its atomic mass. The atomic number of an element is always the same because its number of protons does not change. Atomic masses, however, are not always the same. Some atoms of an element have slightly different masses because they have a different number of neutrons. Atoms of one element that have different numbers of neutrons are isotopes of that element. The mass of each isotope of an element is slightly different. The diagrams below show models of an oxygen atom and the three isotopes of hydrogen.

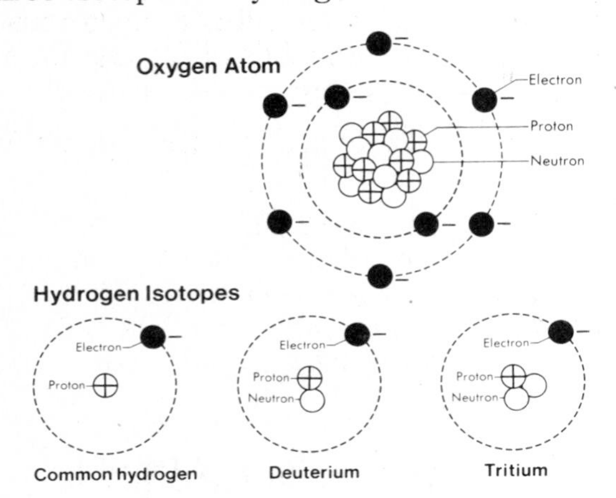

4. Based on the information in the passage and the models above, what is the atomic number for oxygen?

   (1) 2 (2) 4 (3) 8 (4) 16 (5) 32

   (1) (2) (3) (4) (5)

5. Based on the information in the passage and the models, what is the atomic mass of deuterium?

   (1) the same as its atomic number
   (2) less than that of tritium
   (3) the same as for common hydrogen
   (4) more than that of oxygen
   (5) the same as its number of electrons

Chemistry and Elements The building blocks that make up matter are **elements.** Gold and lead are elements. So are oxygen and hydrogen. No chemical means alone can separate an element into its simpler parts. The simpler parts of an element are the parts of its **atoms.**

There are more than 100 kinds of atoms. According to atomic theory, *protons* and *neutrons* make up the atom's **nucleus,** or core. *Electrons* circle the nucleus in fixed paths called *electron energy levels*. A stable atom is one that has as many electrons as protons. The negative charges of its electrons balance the positive charges of its protons. Study the model of a lithium atom below. Notice especially how the protons and neutrons cluster together to form the atom's nucleus.

Model: An atom of lithium

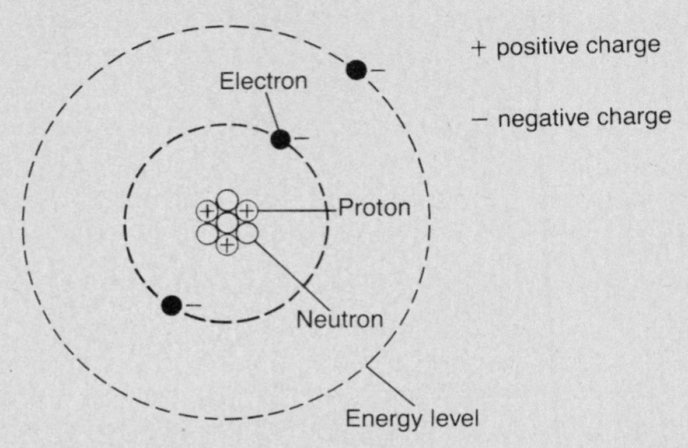

Coming to Terms

element any of the simplest substances of matter that cannot be broken down by chemical means
atom smallest bit of an element
nucleus core of an atom

Warm-up

Refer to the model above and the information in *Coming to Terms* as well as the passage you have just read. Then in a sentence or two tell why lithium is or is not a stable atom.

Sample Warm-up Answer
Lithium is a stable atom. It has three electrons to balance the three protons in the nucleus.

Chemical Change Those unwelcome brown rust spots that appear on an owner's car are the result of a **chemical change.** Chemical change occurs when the atoms in a substance regroup; a different substance results.

The behavior of electrons in atoms brings about chemical change. Each energy level in an atom can hold only a certain number of electrons. But many atoms do not have the maximum number of electrons in their outer levels. Because of this, two or more atoms may share the electrons in their outer levels. The model below shows how two hydrogen atoms and one oxygen atom share electrons to form water. The atoms come together in a *covalent bond.*

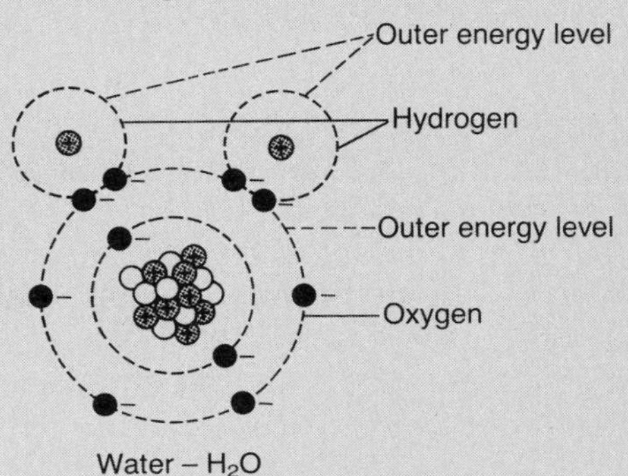

Water – H_2O

Atoms also form a bond if one atom transfers, or gives up, an electron from its outer level to the outer level of another atom. When this happens, the balance between the number of protons and electrons for each atom is upset. Each atom becomes an **ion,** or a particle with either a positive or a negative charge. Since positive and negative charges attract each other, the atoms hold together in an *ionic bond.*

Coming to Terms

chemical change regrouping of atoms in one or more substances to create new substances
ion particle that has either a positive or a negative charge

Warm-up

In what two ways do atoms bring about chemical change in substances?

____

____

____

Sample Warm-up Answer
Chemical change results when atoms form ionic or covalent bonds with their electrons.

Items 6–8 refer to the passage below.

Sodium is a silvery metal that reacts violently with water. Chlorine is a greenish-yellow, poisonous gas. When sodium and chlorine form an ionic bond, they create sodium chloride, which is much different from either sodium or chlorine. It is a white, nonpoisonous solid that dissolves easily in water. It is known as table salt.

As in other solid substances formed by ionic bonding, the ions of sodium chloride are arranged in an orderly way to form crystals. Each crystal contains billions of ions. Ionic bonds are especially strong because they extend throughout an entire crystal. Therefore, most substances with ionic bonding are hard solids at room temperature and have high melting points. Sodium chloride, for example, melts at 804°C.

In its solid form, an ionic substance does not conduct electricity. If the substance is liquid or dissolved in water, the ions separate and move freely. In these cases, ionic substances conduct electricity well.

6. Sodium chloride is a substance resulting from the ionic bonding of

(1) a liquid and a solid
(2) salt and silver
(3) a crystal and an ion
(4) water and electricity
(5) a metal and a gas

7. What will sodium chloride do if it is dissolved in water?

(1) form a new substance
(2) turn greenish-yellow
(3) cause a violent reaction
(4) group into patterns of crystals
(5) conduct electricity well

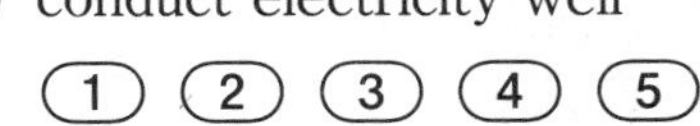

8. If the temperature is below 800°C, sodium chloride will

(1) be in a solid state
(2) melt into a liquid
(3) form new ionic bonds
(4) have freely moving ions
(5) break into sodium and chlorine

Directions: For each item, choose the one best answer. Answers are on page 389.

Items 9–10 refer to the passage below.

A solution is a special kind of mixture. In a solution each substance in the mixture breaks down into tiny particles that are evenly distributed throughout.

The most common kind of solution consists of a solid in a liquid, such as sugar in water. The sugar dissolves when individual particles break away from the lump. Attracted by the particles of water, the sugar particles spread evenly among the water particles. Even though the particles are too small to be seen, they still are not chemically combined.

Some solutions consist of one liquid dissolved in another. Water and alcohol form such a solution. Because alcohol has a lower boiling point than water, the two substances can be separated by boiling. The alcohol boils off first and leaves the water. Alcohol also has a lower freezing point than water.

9. Particles in a solution do all of the following EXCEPT

   (1) dissolve
   (2) become too small to be seen
   (3) form chemical compounds
   (4) distribute evenly
   (5) produce a physical change

   (1) (2) (3) (4) (5)

10. In cold weather alcohol is added to water in car radiators because it

    (1) has a lower freezing point
    (2) is in a solid form
    (3) does not form a solution
    (4) boils at a higher temperature
    (5) attracts particles from solids

    (1) (2) (3) (4) (5)

11. A substance that dissolves other materials is a *solvent.* Water is the most commonly used solvent, but it will not dissolve all kinds of materials. Turpentine is a solvent for oil, for instance, but water is not. If a painter needs to remove oil-based paints from brushes, which of the following might he or she need to use?

    A. water B. oil C. turpentine

    (1) A only (2) B only (3) C only
    (4) A and B (5) B and C

    (1) (2) (3) (4) (5)

Compounds and Mixtures In a supermarket you are surrounded by substances that chemists call **compounds** and **mixtures.** Table salt, made up of the elements sodium and chlorine, is an example of a chemical compound. Peanut butter, on the other hand, is made of ground peanuts, salt, and other ingredients. It is a mixture. Salad dressings, made of oil, vinegar, and seasonings, are also mixtures.

When atoms make covalent bonds, they form **molecules.** These molecules make up a chemical compound; a chemical change has taken place to form the compound. You have seen how two atoms of hydrogen and one atom of oxygen can come together in a covalent bond. This regrouping of atoms forms a molecule of water.

When substances come together in a mixture, no chemical change takes place. Their atoms stay the same; they do not bond. The physical appearance of the substances in the mixture may change, but the mixture generally has the same properties—or characteristics—as the substances that make it up. Paper, soil, gasoline—even the air—are mixtures.

Coming to Terms

compound substance formed when two or more elements bond together chemically
mixture substance formed when two or more substances intermingle without chemically bonding
molecule smallest possible particle of covalently bonded substances

☑ A Test-Taking Tip

The GED Science Test occasionally requires you to apply your understanding of chemistry to everyday situations. Be sure to call on your own experiences with such situations if you have encountered them. They may help you select the correct answer.

Warm-up

In one or two sentences of your own, explain how a compound and a mixture differ.

___

___

___

Sample Warm-up Answer
In a compound a chemical change takes place in the substances, but in a mixture there is no chemical change in the substances that make it up.

Chemical Reactions You have seen that chemical changes result in new substances with different properties. Often a chemical change consists of many different steps. A *chemical reaction* is one of those steps.

To describe how rust forms on a car, you could say that two atoms of iron (in the car's body) bond with three atoms of oxygen (from the air) to form the compound called rust. A chemist, however, could say the same thing in a shorter way with symbols and **formulas:**

$Fe_2 + O_3 \rightarrow Fe_2O_3$

Fe is the symbol for iron. The small number 2 means two atoms. The 3 and the symbol O stand for three atoms of oxygen. The arrow means "produces." Fe_2O_3 then is the formula for the compound rust resulting from the chemical reaction between the elements iron and oxygen. Taken altogether the shorthand statement is called a *chemical equation.*

During a chemical reaction atoms regroup, but the number of atoms involved always remains the same. This principle follows the law of conservation of mass, which states that matter cannot be created or destroyed.

Coming to Terms

formula symbols stating the names and number of atoms in the combination that makes up a certain compound

☑ A Test-Taking Tip

You may find symbols, formulas, or equations in some GED Test items. But you will not have to know any symbols or formulas in order to answer these questions. There will be context clues to tell what they refer to.

Warm-up

In your own words, tell how atoms behave in a chemical reaction to uphold the law of conservation of mass.

____

____

____

____

Sample Warm-up Answer

Atoms regroup during a chemical reaction but the number of atoms stays the same. This follows the principle that matter cannot be created or destroyed.

Items 12–13 refer to the passage below.

Matter is usually defined as something that has mass and takes up space. But the twentieth-century scientist Albert Einstein realized that matter is something much more than that. He recognized that matter and energy are simply different forms of each other. He discovered that a small amount of matter can change into a large amount of energy. This change is described in the equation $E = mc^2$ (E = energy; m = mass; c = the speed of light).

Einstein also realized that the total amount of energy and matter never changes. Energy and matter can change into each other, but nothing is ever lost in the change. This idea is called the Law of Conservation of Matter and Energy. Einstein's theory seemed bizarre when he first suggested it, but it has been proved many times in laboratories around the world.

12. Which of the following best restates the Law of Conservation of Matter and Energy?

    (1) Matter is increasing while energy is decreasing.
    (2) Matter and energy in the universe must be conserved.
    (3) The sum of the matter and the energy in the universe can neither increase nor decrease.
    (4) Matter can never change into energy, and energy can never change into matter.
    (5) Energy in the universe constantly increases, but matter is decreasing.

13. What does the equation $E = mc^2$ imply?

    (1) Matter and energy occur in equal amounts throughout the universe.
    (2) The larger the amount of energy, the faster the speed of light goes.
    (3) The speed of light determines how much matter is in the universe.
    (4) A small amount of matter changes into a large amount of energy.
    (5) The speed of light determines how much energy is in the universe.

Directions: For each item, choose the one best answer. Answers are on page 389.

14. Acids and bases are both chemical compounds. Acids release positive ions in water, while bases release negative ions in water. Acids and bases, therefore, are

(1) atoms (2) opposites
(3) elements (4) mixtures
(5) salts

(1) (2) (3) (4) (5)

Items 15–16 refer to the passage below.

The pH of a substance shows how acidic or basic it is. Pure water is 7, or neutral, on the pH scale. Acids have pH values of less than 7. Bases have pH values of more than 7. Human activities have begun to change the purity of rainwater. Today the pH of rain in some places is as low as 3 or 4. Such rain is more acidic than vinegar.

Many scientists believe that acid rain is caused by gases released from factories. Most factories burn coal, oil, or natural gas. Sulfur and nitrogen compounds are usually present in these fossil fuels. When these fuels burn, the sulfur and nitrogen compounds are changed into sulfur dioxide and nitrogen oxides. These gases escape from smokestacks and combine with water vapor in the air to form sulfuric acid and nitric oxides. When water falls as rain, it is acid rain.

Many lakes in certain areas are now highly acidic because of acid rain. Plants and animals in the lakes are threatened. To prevent further damage, lime—a base—has been added to the water in some lakes to neutralize the acids.

15. What is needed for sulfur dioxide to change into sulfuric acid?

(1) water vapor (2) nitrogen oxide
(3) nitric oxide (4) a fossil fuel
(5) a base

(1) (2) (3) (4) (5)

16. Which of the following could be the pH value of lime?

(1) 0 (2) 3 (3) 5 (4) 7 (5) 10

(1) (2) (3) (4) (5)

Acids, Bases, and Salts Three classes of chemical compounds appear often in your everyday life—**acids, bases,** and salts. A knowledge of acids and bases is useful for anyone who cooks or uses cleaning agents.

Many foods contain acids. Citric acid in lemons and grapefruit makes the fruit taste sour. Milk turns sour when lactose, the sugar in milk, changes to lactic acid.

Soaps and detergents are bases. Like most bases, they feel slippery. Many bases are good household cleaning agents. Sodium hydroxide is a base frequently used in soaps and drain cleaners. Ammonium hydroxide, another base, is the cleaning agent in ammonia water.

When acids and bases come together, they neutralize, or eliminate the effects of, each other. They produce a chemical reaction that forms a salt and water. You can clean up an acid spill by adding water and baking soda, a base. The acid and the baking soda will neutralize each other. You can use vinegar to clean up a base spill. The acetic acid in the vinegar will neutralize the base compound.

Coming to Terms

acid chemical compound that releases positive hydrogen ions in water. Acids taste sour and turn blue litmus paper red.

base chemical compound that releases negative oxygen-hydrogen ions in water. Bases taste bitter and turn red litmus paper blue.

Warm-up

Read *Coming to Terms* again. Then complete the sentence so that it accurately concludes the following paragraph.

Acids taste sour and bases taste bitter. Some acids and bases, however, can cause severe burns. So a chemist checking to see if a solution contains acid will probably ______________

______________.

Need a Hint for Number 16?
First ask yourself if lime is an acid or a base. Then review the first paragraph, which describes the pH values of bases and acids.

Sample Warm-up Answer
see if it turns blue litmus paper red.

Radioactivity and Half-Life It may seem that every time you pick up a newspaper, you see the word **radiation.** Sometimes the words *radiation* and *radioactivity* are used in ways that suggest they mean the same thing. However, *radiation* means, very simply, "rays." Radiation comes from the sun and from other sources of energy. Home computers, microwave ovens, and other machines and household appliances also give off radiation. Certain kinds of radiation can be harmful to living things.

What, then, is radioactivity? It is a form of disintegration—or coming apart—of the nuclei (cores) of certain atoms. Elements such as uranium and plutonium are radioactive; that is, the nucleus of the atom will disintegrate on its own, without any outside cause. In the process of disintegration, the nucleus gives off charged particles and rays of energy that can be damaging. Because it is the nucleus of the atom that is involved, the energy given off is called nuclear energy or nuclear radiation.

Scientists cannot predict *which* nuclei of a radioactive **isotope** will disintegrate, or decay. (An isotope is one among several forms of a given element). But scientists do know *how many* nuclei will decay in a certain period of time. For example, half the nuclei in a given amount of an isotope of the element strontium will decay in 28 years. Half the remainder will decay in another 28 years. This isotope of strontium, therefore, has a **half-life** of 28 years.

Coming to Terms

radiation radiant energy or charged particles released when atomic nuclei disintegrate
isotope a form of a given element; isotopes of an element have the same number of protons but different numbers of neutrons
half-life the time it takes for half the nuclei in a given quantity of a radioactive substance to decay

Warm-up

In a sentence or two, describe in your own words what happens in the nuclei of atoms during radioactive decay.

Sample Warm-up Answer
The nucleus disintegrates with no help from the outside. It gives off charged particles and radiant energy.

Items 17–18 refer to the passage below.

Radioactivity is a normal process in the natural world. Some nuclei in all matter are continually disintegrating. The amount of this natural nuclear radiation, however, is generally small.

Exposure to large doses of nuclear radiation can cause radiation sickness in humans and animals. Radiation sickness is sometimes fatal. Exposure to even small amounts of radiation can produce changes in genes, which determine inherited traits. But radiation can also be helpful if it is controlled. Sometimes radiation is used to treat cancer patients because it kills diseased cells.

Radioactive isotopes have revealed much about the earth's history. For example, scientists have measured the small amounts of uranium isotopes in rocks. By making calculations based on the half-lives of these isotopes, they have concluded that the earth is 4.6 billion years old. Such calculations are also used by scientists to determine the age of fossils, which are the preserved remains or prints of dead plants and animals.

17. Based on the information in the passage, which of the following statements is FALSE?

(1) Radiation can produce genetic changes in humans and animals.
(2) Large doses of radiation can produce dangerous illnesses.
(3) Nuclear testing and explosions introduced the world's first radioactivity.
(4) Controlled radiation can serve useful purposes among humans.
(5) Radioactivity can help scientists determine the age of fossils.

18. According to the passage, the half-lives of radioactive isotopes have been used to

(1) calculate the age of the earth
(2) treat cancer patients
(3) produce inherited traits
(4) study radiation sickness
(5) locate fossil fuel deposits

Directions: For each item, choose the one best answer. Answers are on page 389.

Item 19 refers to the passage and diagram below.

Crude oil, also called petroleum, is the source of some important fossil fuels and many other useful products. It is mainly a mixture of hydrocarbons. Before crude oil can be used, it must be separated into its different components, called *fractions.* The separation process depends on each hydrocarbon's boiling point. Fractions with the highest number of carbon atoms have the highest boiling points. The diagram illustrates this fractioning process.

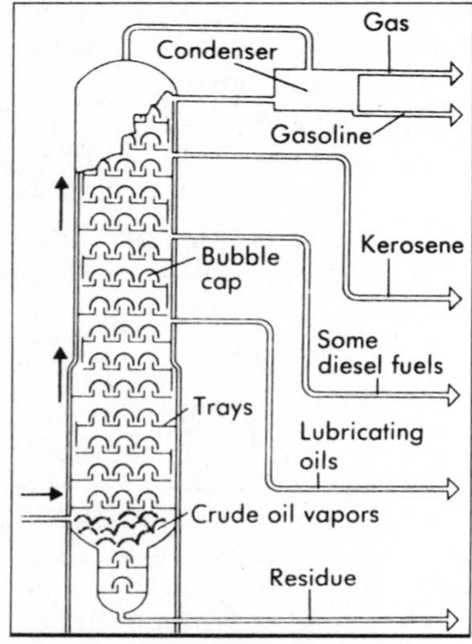

A petroleum fractionating tower

Crude oil vapors are heated and enter the tower at the bottom, as shown. As the hot vapors rise, hydrocarbons with high boiling points cool, change to a liquid state, and settle on lower trays. Fractions with low boiling points rise higher in the tower than fractions with high boiling points. Fractions with the lowest boiling points rise to the top of the tower.

19. Which of the following are gasoline and kerosene?

    (1) crude oil vapors
    (2) fractions of crude oil
    (3) petroleum residues
    (4) hydrocarbons with high boiling points
    (5) forms of the element carbon

Organic Chemistry Carbon is a very common element. It occurs naturally in more than one form. Carbon atoms are present in all living things. Carbon atoms are also special because they combine easily to form carbon compounds. Chemically, you are a collection of carbon compounds because *every* cell in your body contains molecules with carbon atoms. Because of their relationship to living things, carbon compounds are the center of studies known as *organic chemistry.*

Carbon occurs in so many different compounds for two reasons. One reason is that carbon atoms have four electrons in their outer levels to share with other atoms. Carbon can form four strong covalent bonds. The other reason is that carbon atoms can bond with each other. Linking carbon atoms in this way leads to many compounds. Most carbon compounds are made from the remains of plants and animals that lived on earth millions of years ago. These remains became today's fossil fuels.

Carbon combines with the element hydrogen to form *hydrocarbons,* or compounds that contain only hydrogen and oxygen. Natural gas used for cooking and heating is a mixture of hydrocarbons. Hydrocarbons undergo a variety of different chemical reactions. One important reaction of certain hydrocarbons is combustion, or a burning process, from which we get most of our heat. Working with the chemical reactions of hydrocarbons, industrial laboratories have developed many materials that are part of everyday life—plastics, rayon, polyester, nylon, paint.

☑ A Test-Taking Tip

To help improve your concentration when you read passages on the GED Test, make yourself read *just a little* faster than you normally would. That will help keep your mind from wandering.

Warm-up

In a sentence or two, tell what hydrocarbons are and why they are important.

Sample Warm-up Answer
Hydrocarbons are a group of compounds formed from the elements carbon and hydrogen. Hydrocarbons undergo different chemical reactions that make many useful products possible.

Physics

You see moving objects around you every day. You also know that **gravity** holds you to the earth. Did you know that the laws and principles of physics can tell how moving objects behave and measure forces such as gravity?

Scientists can measure the strength of gravity if they know the mass of two objects and the distance between them. The larger the mass of either object, the stronger the attraction between them. Your body has a certain amount of mass. Earth's gravity pulls down on this mass. Your weight is the force of gravity pulling on your body's mass.

Newton's laws of motion describe the behavior of moving objects. According to the first law of motion, a moving object will keep going at the same speed and in the same direction as long as no force acts on it. If the object is stopped, it will remain motionless unless a force acts on it again. This tendency to resist changes in motion is *inertia*.

The second law of motion states that an object accelerates because a force acts on it. The direction of the acceleration will be the same as the direction in which the force is moving. When you hit a golf ball, you accelerate it in the direction of your swing. The harder you hit the ball, the greater the acceleration.

For every force, there will be an equal and opposite force. This is the third law of motion. A rocket about to lift off pushes (exerts a force) on the burning gases in its tail assembly. The gases, however, push back (exert an equal and opposite force) and send the rocket skyward.

Coming to Terms

gravity the force that pulls any two objects together because of their masses

Warm-up

Friction from the air will eventually slow down the speed of a thrown baseball. What will a spacecraft do after it escapes the air in the earth's atmosphere? ______________________

____

Sample Warm-up Answer
According to the first law of motion, the spacecraft will keep moving at the same speed and in the same direction. There is no force changing its motion.

Directions: For each item, choose the one best answer. Answers are on page 389.

Items 1–2 refer to the passage below.

The speed at which an object travels depends on the distance traveled and the time elapsed. The greater an object's speed, the greater the distance it travels each second.

$$\text{Speed } (s) = \frac{\text{distance } (d)}{\text{time } (t)}$$

You can graph speed.

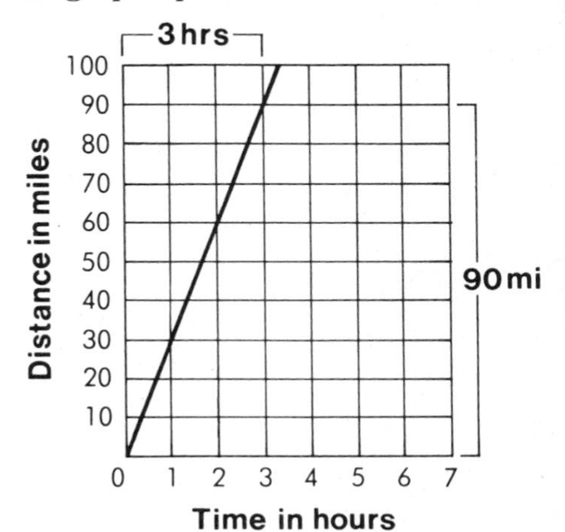

This graph shows the distance a car traveled during a trip. After three hours, the car had covered a distance of 90 miles. From the speed equation, the car's average speed was

$$s = \frac{d}{t} = \frac{90 \text{ mi}}{3 \text{ h}} = 30 \text{ mph (miles per hour)}$$

If you calculate the speed of the car at other points along the graph, you will find that it remains the same, or constant. This type of linear graph always results when an object moves at a constant speed.

1. According to the graph, what is the average speed of the car after 1 hour?

   (1) 20 mph (2) 30 mph (3) 50 mph
   (4) 60 mph (5) 90 mph

   ① ② ③ ④ ⑤

2. If an airplane is traveling at an average speed of 650 miles per hour, how many hours will it take the plane to go 2,275 miles?

   (1) 2 (2) 2.5 (3) 3.5
   (4) 5 (5) 5.5

   ① ② ③ ④ ⑤

Directions: For each item, choose the one best answer. Answers are on page 389.

Items 3–6 require the use of these equations.

A. Work = force × distance

B. M.A. (mechanical advantage) of a lever = $\frac{\text{length of effort arm}}{\text{length of resistance arm}}$

C. M.A. of an inclined plane = $\frac{\text{length}}{\text{height}}$

D. Efficiency = $\frac{\text{useful work}}{\text{work put in}} \times 100\%$

E. Power = $\frac{\text{work}}{\text{time}}$

3. Newton-meters (N · m) are units used for measuring work. A bicycle tire pump requires 16 newton-meters of work but produces 4 newton-meters of work. What is its efficiency?

(1) 5% (2) 25% (3) 40%
(4) 250% (5) 400%

① ② ③ ④ ⑤

4. Which equation should be used to find the mechanical advantage of a crowbar?

(1) A (2) B (3) C (4) D (5) E

① ② ③ ④ ⑤

5. Which equation should be used to find the amount of work done in one hour by a lawn mower using 10 watts of power?

(1) A (2) B (3) C (4) D (5) E

① ② ③ ④ ⑤

6. A 6-foot crowbar is used to pry up some boards. The fulcrum is 2 feet from the boards. What is the mechanical advantage of the crowbar? (The length of the resistance arm is the distance from the resistance to the fulcrum.)

(1) 1 (2) 2 (3) 3 (4) 6 (5) 12

① ② ③ ④ ⑤

Work and Energy If you pushed on a big rock for a long time and still had not moved it, you would feel that you had "worked" very hard. A scientist would disagree. In science, work is done only when a force that is applied to an object actually moves the object in the direction of the force. *Force* is anything that causes change in motion. *Displacement* is the distance and direction an object moves.

You already know that tools or machines can make jobs easier. Machines help do work by (1) multiplying the force exerted or by (2) changing the direction of movement. A machine that has the ability to multiply a force is said to have a *mechanical advantage (M.A.).* Machines are not 100 percent efficient because not all the work a machine does is useful. They always waste some effort by doing useless work, such as overcoming friction. Many large machines have a very low efficiency.

Work is closely related to **energy.** If you hit a tennis ball, you do work on it. Your work was a transfer of energy from yourself to the ball, which made the ball move. Scientists define energy as the ability to do work. They measure energy by the amount of work done.

Coming to Terms

energy the ability to do work. Common types of energy include mechanical energy, electrical energy, radiant energy, nuclear energy, and thermal energy, which is derived from heat.

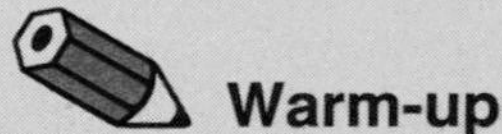

Warm-up

Suppose you pulled a wagon for two blocks up a hill. Describe the work you did in terms of force and displacement.

____

____

Need a Hint for Number 6?
Since a crowbar is a lever, you will need to use equation B. Ask yourself what numbers you need to substitute in the equation. The question tells you the length of the resistance arm in the information contained in parentheses. Now how will you find the length of the effort arm?

Sample Warm-up Answer
Pulling on the wagon provided the force. The displacement was two blocks in an uphill direction.

Electrical Circuits If the television and lights suddenly go out in a room, you may say, "Uh-oh. I think we have blown a **circuit.**" In scientific terms you are saying that there has been an interruption in the flow of electrical energy, or the **current.** Electric current flows only when it can follow a complete path back to its starting point. Such a path is a circuit.

A circuit has three basic parts. A *power source,* such as a battery or an electric power station, sends the flow of electric current. A *power-using device,* such as a lamp or TV set, uses the current. *Connectors,* such as copper wires, provide a path for the current—from the power source, through the using device, and back again to the power source.

There are two kinds of circuits. In a *series circuit,* all the parts are connected one after another. Removing any part of the series leaves a gap, or opens the circuit, and the current cannot flow. If one light bulb in a series circuit is dead, usually none of the other bulbs will light either. In *parallel circuits,* more than one path connects lights or other using devices with the power source. The circuit stays closed, and current flows no matter how many lamps or appliances are in use.

Coming to Terms

circuit closed path around which electric current flows
current flow

Warm-up

In two or three sentences describe how current flows through a circuit.

Need a Hint for Number 9?
Think for a moment about how you use appliances in your home.

Sample Warm-up Answer
Current flows from a source of power. Connectors, such as wires, carry the current around a path through power-using devices and back to the power source.

Items 7–9 are based on the two diagrams and information below.

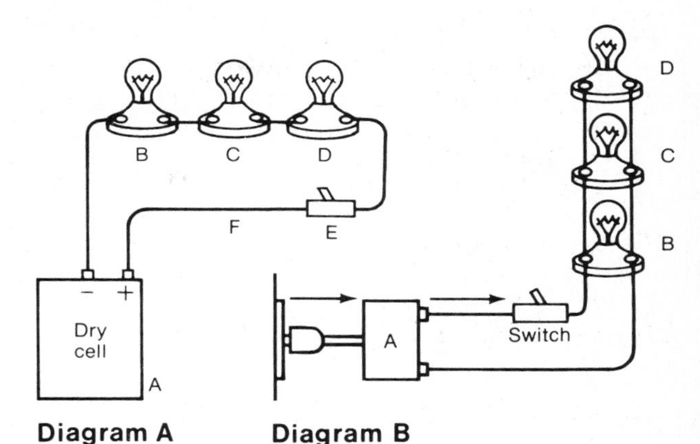

Diagram A **Diagram B**

In a series circuit a single electrical path connects several objects one after another. If one part of the series is removed, the current cannot flow. In a parallel circuit more than one electrical path connects several objects to the power source.

7. What is diagram A an example of?

   (1) a parallel circuit
   (2) a schematic for a flashlight
   (3) a series circuit
   (4) an alternating current
   (5) a complex circuit

8. If lamp B goes out in diagram B, lamp D will

   (1) go out (2) dim (3) stay on
   (4) flicker (5) brighten

9. Most homes are wired in parallel circuits. Why would this be desirable?

   (1) It is cheaper to wire in parallel circuits.
   (2) Only the appliances needed at a particular time need to be turned on.
   (3) Parallel circuits are safer than series circuits.
   (4) Lights and appliances can be used at the same time.
   (5) A parallel circuit takes less energy to power the same number of appliances.

   ① ② ③ ④ ⑤

Directions: For each item, choose the one best answer. Answers are on page 390.

10. An electric generator is a device that uses electromagnetic induction to produce an electric current in wires. To build a generator, which of the following would be needed?

(1) a coil and a magnet
(2) a wave and a current
(3) a liquid and a gas
(4) a force and a circuit
(5) a molecule and an atom

① ② ③ ④ ⑤

Items 11–12 refer to the passage below.

Magnets are objects that attract things made of iron and a few other elements by a force called *magnetism.* The region around a magnet, where magnetism acts, is called its *magnetic field.*

Even though magnets come in many shapes and sizes, every magnet has at least two poles. A suspended magnet will turn so that the same pole always points north. This is its north pole; the other end is its south pole. The north pole of one magnet and the south pole of another magnet attract each other. Two like poles push each other away. Because the poles attract and repel, scientists know that a force acts between the magnets.

11. Which of the following is true of magnets?

(1) Magnets attract all elements but no compounds.
(2) Horseshoe-shaped magnets have only a south pole.
(3) Two magnets can be used to show evidence of a magnetic field.
(4) The best magnets are usually made of iron.
(5) The earth's magnetic north pole attracts the south pole of most magnets.

① ② ③ ④ ⑤

12. The information given in the passage could be used to construct a

(1) battery (2) light bulb
(3) radio (4) compass
(5) series circuit

① ② ③ ④ ⑤

Electromagnetism Every time you listen to a tape recorder or dry your hair with a blow dryer, you are using both electricity and the force of **magnetism.** Each time you "switch on" one of these devices, electric current flows through a coiled wire inside, causing magnetism in the coil. A coil magnetized by electricity is called a *electromagnet.*

Electricity can cause magnetism, but magnetism can also produce electricity. If you move a magnet through or near a wire coil, electric current will flow in the coil. The process by which magnetism causes electric current is called *electromagnetic induction.* It occurs when a changing magnetic field and a coil are near each other. Moving either the magnet or the coil causes a change in the magnetic field. So if you moved the coil instead of the magnet, you would still cause electricity to flow in the wire.

Since electricity can cause magnetism and magnetism can cause electricity, scientists link these two forces in a single theory called *electromagnetism.* According to this theory, electricity and magnetism result from a single force. The theory also states that waves of electricity and magnetism can travel through space. Radiant energy from the sun, for example, travels through space to earth in the form of electromagnetic waves. Scientists first discovered electromagnetic waves about 100 years ago when they detected what are today called *radio waves.*

Coming to Terms

magnetism force of nature found near a magnet

Warm-up

Write a short paragraph telling how the process of electromagnetic induction works.

Sample Warm-up Answer
A magnet and a wire coil must be placed near each other. Then either the coil or the magnet must move. The motion causes a change in the magnetic field, which will cause current to flow in the wire.

Waves and Energy When a hardball is thrown to you, the moving ball carries energy from the person who threw it. You feel this energy when your hand catches the ball.

Waves also carry energy from one place to another, but matter does not move with the energy as it does with a thrown ball. Rather, a wave is a disturbance in one part of a material that is transmitted, or passed along, to another part of the material. If you tie one end of a rope to a doorknob and hold the other end in your hand at some distance from the door, you can see a wave pass down the rope as you flick your end of the rope. The rope itself, however, does not move forward. In wave action each particle of the material goes back to its original position after the energy has temporarily disturbed it.

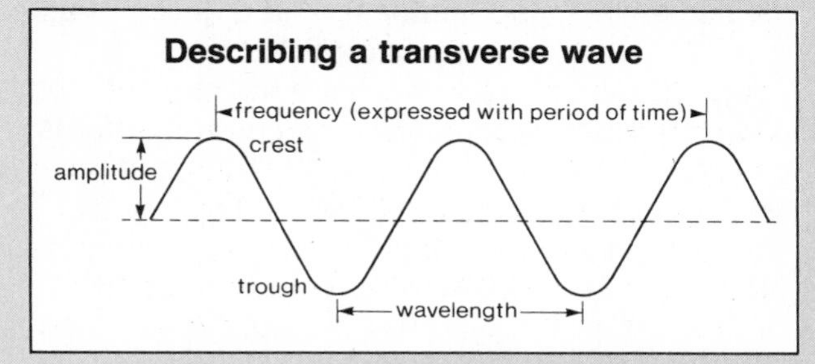

The wave shown in the diagram is a transverse wave. Transverse waves move particles of matter in a direction at right angles, or perpendicular, to the direction the wave travels. All electromagnetic waves are transverse waves. Compressional waves move particles of matter in a back and forth motion along the direction of the wave. Sound waves, for example, are compressional waves.

Coming to Terms

amplitude height of a wave from its midpoint to its crest or trough
frequency number of waves that pass a certain point in a specific time period
wavelength distance from one wave crest or wave trough to the next

Warm-up

In a sentence or two, describe briefly how a wave transmits energy.

___

___

___

Sample Warm-up Answer
A disturbance in one part of a material is transmitted to another part and so passes through it. The matter and particles, however, end up in the same place where they started.

13. The amplitude of a wave measures its height from the midpoint of its crest or its trough. The higher the wave, the greater the disturbance it creates in the material through which it is transmitted. The amplitude of a wave, therefore, can be used to tell the

(1) direction a wave is traveling
(2) amount of energy a wave is carrying
(3) result of waves crossing each other
(4) distance from one crest to another
(5) kind of matter that moves forward

① ② ③ ④ ⑤

14. Hertz and kilohertz are the units used to measure wave frequencies. One hertz equals one wave per second; one kilohertz equals 1,000 waves per second. On an AM radio dial, 67 would stand for 67 kilohertz. Sound waves from that station would travel at

(1) 67 hertz
(2) 670 waves per second
(3) 670 kilohertz
(4) 1,000 waves per 67 seconds
(5) 67,000 waves per second

① ② ③ ④ ⑤

Items 15–16 refer to the diagrams below.

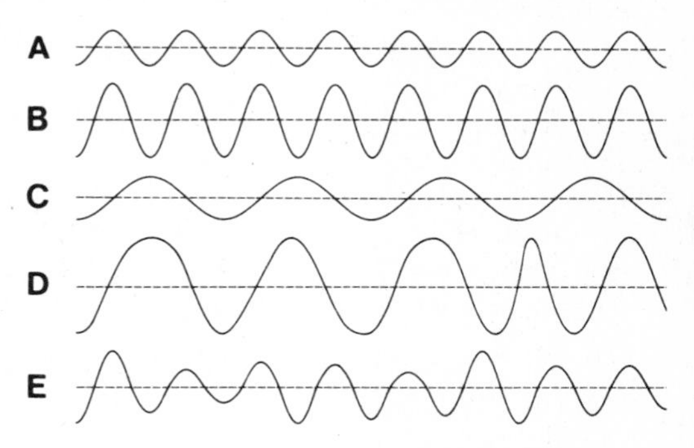

15. Which wave shows a steady frequency but a changing amplitude?

(1) A (2) B (3) C (4) D (5) E

① ② ③ ④ ⑤

16. Which wave shows a steady amplitude but a changing frequency?

(1) A (2) B (3) C (4) D (5) E

① ② ③ ④ ⑤

Directions: For each item, choose the one best answer. Answers are on page 390.

17. Unlike sound waves, light needs no medium (solid, liquid, or gas) through which to travel. It can travel in a vacuum because it is an electromagnetic wave. From outside his or her vehicle, a traveler in space would

 (1) see light but hear no sound
 (2) hear sounds before seeing light
 (3) encounter no electromagnetic waves
 (4) hear only very faint sounds
 (5) have to break a sound barrier

 ① ② ③ ④ ⑤

Items 18–20 refer to the table below.

Speed of Sound in Various Materials

Material	Speed (ft/s)
Air (68°F)	1,130
Water (59°F)	4,760
Brick	11,970
Oak	12,630
Aluminum	16,730
Steel	17,060
Granite	19,690

18. The table could be used to show that sound travels fastest in

 (1) liquids (2) dense solids
 (3) heated materials (4) gases
 (5) cooled liquids

 ① ② ③ ④ ⑤

19. An underwater swimmer and a sunbather floating on a raft are the same distance from a speeding motorboat. The swimmer will hear the sound of the boat

 (1) by rising above the surface of the water
 (2) not at all
 (3) before the sunbather does
 (4) after the sunbather does
 (5) at the same time the sunbather does

 ① ② ③ ④ ⑤

20. In which material does sound travel about 10 times as fast as in air?

 (1) water (2) steel
 (3) oak (4) brick
 (5) aluminum

 ① ② ③ ④ ⑤

Sound Waves and Light You have read that sound waves are compressional waves. The diagram below shows the disturbance pattern of sound waves. The wave condenses and then expands the molecules of a material much like the coils in a spring move back and forth.

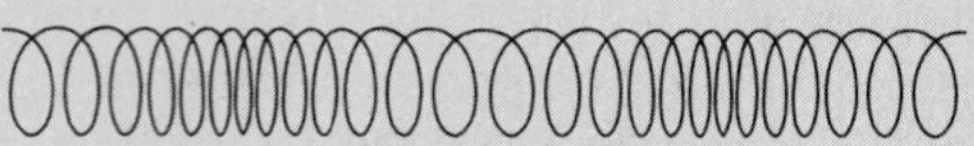

Compressional Wave

Light acts as both a wave and a particle. For a long time scientists thought that light had to be either a particle or a wave. They showed that it was a transverse wave (see page 383) when they discovered crests and troughs acting on one another.

But scientists also demonstrated that light was a particle when they discovered that electrons jump out of certain metals when light shines on them. Only energy particles given off by atoms could explain this. In its natural state, every atom has only a certain amount of energy. Heat, electricity, or other things can cause an atom to acquire extra energy. The atom then must give off this added energy. Often the energy it releases is seen as light.

Light travels very fast. When you flick on a flashlight, you see the light almost instantaneously. From very distant sources, the travel time is more noticeable. It takes light eight minutes to travel from the sun to the earth.

Light travels outward from its source in straight lines called rays. The farther the rays travel, the less light reaches a given area. The amount of light reaching an area is called its *intensity.* An object that gives off its own light, such as the sun, is called *luminous.* The moon only reflects light from the sun, so it is not luminous.

Warm-up

Write a couple of sentences stating two important differences between sound and light.

____

____

____

____

Sample Warm-up Answer
Sound waves are compressional waves, but light behaves like transverse waves. Light behaves as both a particle and a wave, but sound does not.

Behavior of Waves Waves travel through many different materials. Sometimes a wave can pass from one material into another. Diagram A below shows what happens when waves pass in a straight line from one material into another. The waves continue going straight ahead, but they change their frequency, or speed.

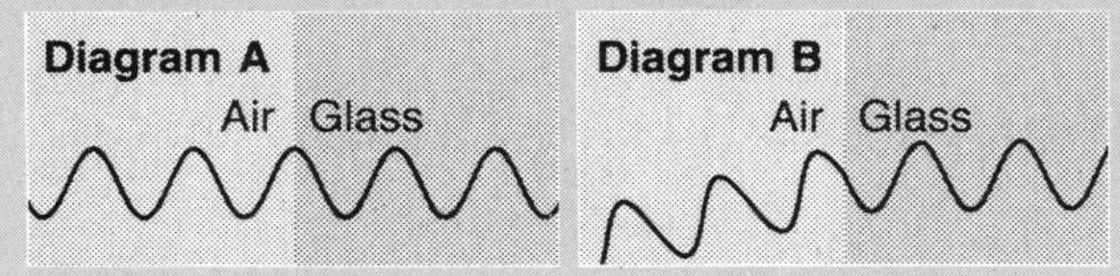

Diagram B shows what happens when waves enter a new material at an angle. They change frequency, as in Diagram A, but they also change direction. The bending of a wave as it enters a new material is called **refraction.**

Sometimes waves strike a surface and bounce back instead of passing into another material. When this happens, **reflection** occurs. Diagram C shows how a mirror reflects light rays to your eyes.

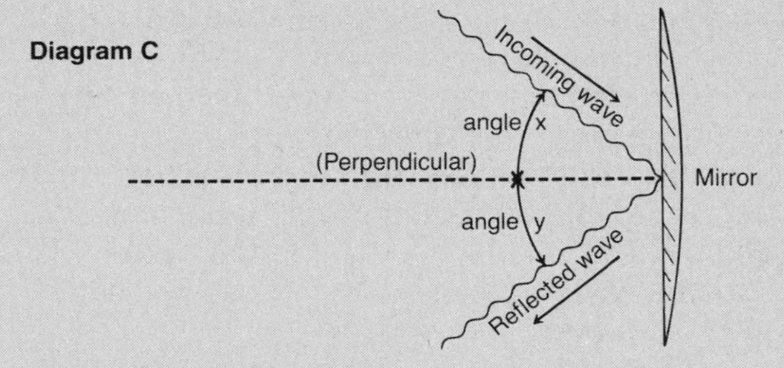

Notice the angles the incoming wave (X) and the reflected wave (Y) make with a line drawn perpendicular to the mirror's surface. The angle made by an incoming wave and the perpendicular is always equal to the angle made by the reflected wave and the perpendicular.

Coming to Terms

refraction wave's change in direction as it passes from one material to another
reflection wave's bouncing from a surface

Warm-up

On your own paper, write one or two sentences describing how a wave always changes when it passes from one material to another and how it would change if it hit the new material at an angle.

Sample Warm-up Answer
The wave will always change frequency. If it hits at an angle, it will change direction too.

Items 21–22 refer to the passage below.

Gamma rays, X rays, and ultraviolet rays are all high-energy electromagnetic waves. That is, they have very short wavelengths and very high frequencies. High-energy waves are the most harmful to humans. Yet they are very useful if exposure to them is limited. Gamma rays from radioactive cobalt are used to kill cancer cells. X rays allow doctors to "photograph" cavities in teeth, broken bones, or interior parts of the body. Ultraviolet rays can kill harmful bacteria and give skin a pleasing tan—as well as a dangerous burn.

Light, infrared rays, microwaves, and radio waves are low-energy electromagnetic waves. Infrared rays on electric heaters and in microwave ovens provide cooking conveniences. In laboratory experiments, exposure to microwaves has caused behavioral changes in animals. Some people have asked if microwaves pose a health problem for humans. Radio waves, including those that transmit TV programs, have the lowest frequencies of all electromagnetic waves. Radar uses radio waves to help pilots navigate and to detect flying objects. A radar device sends out radio waves, which are reflected back when they hit a solid object.

21. On the basis of this passage, one can conclude that radio waves are the
    (1) most abundant waves in space
    (2) least capable of traveling in water
    (3) least harmful to humans
    (4) most difficult to work with
    (5) most frequently used waves in science

22. Based on the passage, all of the following statements are true EXCEPT
    (1) X rays have higher frequencies than light.
    (2) Radio waves can be reflected.
    (3) Cobalt is a source of gamma rays.
    (4) People should use caution with ultraviolet rays.
    (5) Exposure to microwaves is harmful to people.

Directions: For each item, choose the one best answer. Answers are on page 390.

Items 23–25 refer to the passage below.

The amount of energy released in a fission reaction is enormous. Once nuclear fission starts, it can continue in a chain reaction. When a neutron splits a nucleus and releases more neutrons, one or two of these neutrons enter and break up other nuclei. Still more neutrons are produced to break up nuclei.

Whenever more than four kilograms of uranium nuclei are packed together, fission releases so much energy so quickly that it acts like a bomb. A nuclear bomb explosion is a runaway chain reaction. Nuclear chain reactions can be controlled by using such a small amount of uranium that it could never explode. Materials like cadmium or zirconium capture some of the neutrons that are created when nuclei split. The captured neutrons cannot hit other nuclei created when nuclei split, so the reaction is slowed. By capturing some—but not all—of the neutrons, scientists maintain a chain reaction at a steady rate.

23. A nuclear fission chain reaction can result from the release of

(1) electrons (2) protons
(3) cadmium (4) neutrons
(5) uranium

① ② ③ ④ ⑤

24. On the basis of the passage, one can assume that uranium is

(1) an isotope of zirconium
(2) a nuclear energy fuel
(3) a very common element
(4) a light nucleus
(5) a subatomic particle

① ② ③ ④ ⑤

25. Which one of the following statements can be supported by the information given in the passage?

(1) It is unsafe to use nuclear fission in electric generating plants.
(2) Nuclear energy is economical to use.
(3) Explosions during nuclear chain reactions can be avoided.
(4) Cadmium helps scientists predict nuclear explosions.
(5) Nuclear chain reactions occur frequently in the sun and other stars.

Nuclear Physics You have read that atomic energy comes from the nuclei of atoms. There are two processes through which nuclei release energy—*fission* and *fusion.* Nuclear fission is used in nuclear power plants and in atomic bombs. It occurs when certain heavy nuclei absorb slow-moving neutrons. (Remember that neutrons are atomic particles.) The nuclei then split into lighter nuclei.

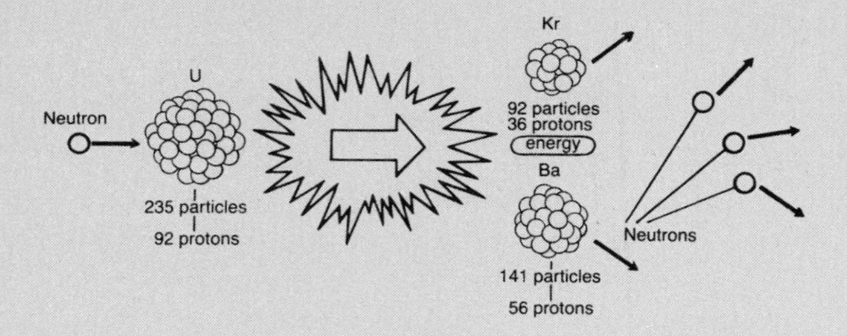

The diagram above shows a neutron splitting a uranium nucleus into two lighter elements—barium and krypton. The number of protons *after* fission (56 + 36 = 92) is the same as the number of protons *before* fission. And the total number of neutrons and other subatomic particles afterward is the same as the original number of neutrons and particles. The nuclei and particles that result, though, have slightly *less* total mass than the original uranium nucleus and the absorbed neutron. What happened to the missing mass? It became energy. This energy makes the new nuclei speed away from each other. These nuclei hit material around them and heat it.

Nuclear fusion is the opposite of nuclear fission. In nuclear fusion, two or more light nuclei "fuse," or combine, to produce a heavier nucleus. Fusion occurs continuously inside the sun and other stars. Fusion releases even more energy than fission does.

Warm-up

Study the diagram above. Then write a sentence comparing the number of neutrons before and after fission of the uranium nucleus.

____

____

Sample Warm-up Answer
After fission there are three neutrons, two more than before fission.

Answers—Science

Sample Test Items

Biology
(pages 340–359)

1. (2) The first paragraph mentions that cameras scanned the landscape; the second paragraph describes Viking's investigation of the soil.

2. (2) One purpose of Viking was to test the hypothesis that tiny organisms might live in Martian soil.

3. (5) Each cell shown in the diagram—plant and animal—contains a nucleus.

4. (3) In the diagram only the plant cell contains a chloroplast. The cabbage cells would contain chloroplasts.

5. (1) The first option gives the best example of how cells perform a particular job within an organism.

6. (5) According to the passage, DNA in every body cell determines what protein the cell makes to do its work; that decides what work each body cell does.

7. (3) Option (3) gives the most accurate summary of the ideas in the first paragraph.

8. (3) The passage states that a pregnant woman's drinking one to two ounces of alcoholic beverages daily is considered risky for her fetus.

9. (3) The change from lighter to darker color gave the moth protective coloring that helped it survive.

10. (4) Only poison-resistant individuals survived to breed, so future generations would probably have more poison-resistant roaches.

11. (1) Option (1) contains the three organisms that can make their own food.

12. (3) *Agaricus campestris,* commonly called the field mushroom, is a member of the fungi kingdom, whose members absorb food from living or dead organisms.

13. (2) Lactose is a sugar found in milk, so people who must avoid sugar will want to avoid lactose.

14. (4) Boiling killed the bacteria in the yogurt, so the starter culture failed.

15. (3) The second paragraph explains that the Euglena is versatile because of its ability to take in or produce its own food.

16. (3) The events described in the paragraph illustrate how scientific ideas may need to be revised to be useful or to include newly discovered facts.

17. (1) Options (2), (3), (4), and (5) are examples of individual opinions. Only (1) can be verified as a fact.

18. (2) By preventing death from infections, penicillin helped the British and their allies keep the army strong.

19. (1) Stomata allow a plant to "breathe." The spray clogged the stomata, preventing the normal exchange of gases.

20. (1) Plants whose leaves have only one side exposed to air will probably have stomata on that exposed side only.

21. (5) Directional arrows show that each step leads to the next, in a constant process.

22. (2) First, the taste of some fruit lures animals to eat it; then the animals carry the seeds to new places, where they generate new plants or trees.

23. (5) Since there's no need for humans to move their ears, the muscles are vestigial.

24. (5) Option (5) gives the most accurate and complete summary of the main idea and details.

25. (3) The worker bees' waggle dance indicates where food is, not an enemy.

26. (2) A bee's "foreign" odor identifies him as a member of another hive. The guard bee, receiving the message that the visitor is from another hive, attacks.

27. (5) Options (1), (2), (3), and (4) express individual opinions. Only (5) can be verified as a fact.

28. (2) Because oil is lighter than water, it helps a shark float.

29. (5) The passage describes how amphibians begin life in water, then change form to be land animals.

30. (2) In dry weather, some frogs burrow in mud for a period of estivation.

31. (1) Only the first answer describes a situation in which a dinosaur is adapted for being warm-blooded.

32. (5) Information in the passage suggests that scientists on both sides of the issue assume that warm-blooded animals eat more than cold-blooded ones.

33. (3) Options (1), (2), (4), and (5) express individual opinions, which may vary from person to person. Only (3) can be verified as fact.

34. (4) The chalaza, from its position in the diagram, appears to hold the yolk away from the shell.

35. (5) Only option (5) describes human-like emotions that Koko expresses.

36. (5) Gorillas, like humans, can move thumb and finger separately; that ability, in addition to a highly developed brain, allows them to make signs.

37. (4) Option (4) is a restatement of information given at the beginning of the third paragraph.

38. (3) The passage states that the right brain hemisphere is more active as test subjects draw; (3) is a specific example of that type of activity. If the right half of the brain were damaged, drawing is one activity that would probably be affected.

39. (4) All answers except (4) illustrate expense resulting from waste. In contrast, (4) illustrates how waste products could actually be a source of income.

40. (3) Options (1), (2), (4), and (5) all illustrate alternatives that could reduce air pollution. In contrast, incinerating rubbish puts particle waste and waste gases into the air.

Earth Science
(pages 360–370)

1. (4) The second sentence in the first paragraph suggests that people once thought the earth, not the sun, was the center of the universe.

2. (4) Voyager was launched into space. It is now so far in space that there is little that could stop it or change its course.

3. (4) The first paragraph refers to the earth's cycle around the sun, the moon's cycle around the earth, and the cycle of day and night. The second paragraph points out how little we are aware of these relationships.

4. (5) Option (5) is the only one supported by ideas in the passage, particularly the final paragraph.

5. (3) The information is given in the first two sentences of the final paragraph.

6. (4) As we dig closer to the center of the earth, the temperature rises.

7. (4) The information is found in the last line of the first paragraph.

8. (3) Part A is a side view of an island, showing its higher and lower parts. Part B shows the same island as seen in an aerial view.

9. (1) Because so many reports have been made of strange animal behavior just before an earthquake, some scientists hypothesize that we may be able to predict quakes from animal behavior.

10. (2) Options (1), (3), and (5) are hypotheses; Option (4) combines an individual opinion with a hypothesis. Only (2) is a fact that points out how animals could help us to predict earthquakes.

11. (3) The last three sentences of the first paragraph explain that scientists think oil forms from the remains of dead sea life.

12. (1) Option (1) accurately describes the process of how organic matter became oil (see answer above) *and* how permeable rock sealed the oil into a large deposit.

13. (1) Humans first appeared in the most recent part of the Cenozoic era.

14. (4) Options (1), (2), (3), and (5) are all species that appeared before dinosaurs and that continued to live through the dinosaur age into the present.

15. (5) The word *climate* under the heading Mesozoic era gives the answer.

16. (2) The map symbol for rain, slanted lines, covers the Atlanta area on the map. The two sets of figures near the Atlanta area show the high and low temperatures. The high is 88°F and the low is 69°F.

17. (1) The map shows that a cold front with clear skies is moving from the west into St. Louis.

18. (2) The information is given in the third sentence of the first paragraph.

19. (4) While the sun has a stronger gravitational force, the moon is much closer. Gravity from both affects the earth, but the moon's pull is more obvious because it is closer.

20. (1) Strip-farming encourages water to sink into the ground; that action reduces the chance of floods and erosion from running water. The roots of plants in strip-farming reduce erosion by wind. Strip-farming benefits in all ways except preventing drought.

21. (4) Wind erosion is not likely in a low area protected by water; water erosion is unlikely if the water is not moving.

22. (3) Wood is biomass that contains energy from living trees. When burned, the energy is released in the form of heat and light.

23. (3) Gasoline is a fossil fuel, which is nonrenewable; the other answers list energy sources that are renewable.

Chemistry
(pages 371–378)

1. (4) Since water boils at lower temperatures at high altitudes, the heat of the cooking water will be lower. Longer cooking time is needed to make up the difference for the reduced heat compared with the boiling point at sea level.

2. (4) The first two sentences of the passage make this statement true. There is no information in the passage to support option (2); the passage disproves the remaining options.

3. (2) The last paragraph explains that the rate of cooling (*cooling* is another way of saying "temperature decrease") helps determine whether a large single crystal or many smaller crystals develop.

4. (3) The passage defines atomic number as the number of protons in an atom. By counting the number of protons in the oxygen atom you can determine that its atomic number is 8. Option (3) is the correct answer.

5. (2) The passage defines atomic mass as the number of both the protons and the neutrons in an atom. The atomic mass for deuterium is 2 because it has one proton and one neutron. The atomic mass for tritium, with one proton and two neutrons, is 3. Therefore option (2) is the correct one.

6. (5) The answer can be found in the first three sentences of the passage.

7. (5) The first two paragraphs explain that sodium chloride is an ionic substance. The third paragraph says that ionic substances dissolved in water conduct electricity well. Therefore option (5) is correct.

8. (1) According to paragraph two, the melting point of sodium chloride is 804°C. Therefore, sodium chloride would be a solid at any lower temperature.

9. (3) The second paragraph says that particles in a solution are not chemically combined. Therefore option (3) does not accurately apply to solutions and their makeup. Think back to the definition of a *compound* if you had trouble with this question.

10. (1) The last sentence in the passage gives the information needed to answer this question. All the other options are either proved incorrect by information in the passage or are not covered in the passage.

11. (3) If you keep in mind what a solvent is—as the first sentence explains—you can reason that you would need turpentine to dissolve and thus to remove oil-based paints from brushes.

12. (3) The second paragraph explains that the *total amount* of energy and matter never changes, even though energy and matter can change into each other. This means that the total amount cannot increase or decrease.

13. (4) The answer can be found in the fourth sentence of the passage.

14. (2) Since acids release positive ions and bases release negative ions, acids and bases have to be opposites, option (2). Your familiarity with chemical terms also tells you that none of the other options could be correct.

15. (1) The fifth sentence of the second paragraph states that sulfur dioxide from smokestacks "combines with water vapor in the air to form sulfuric acid."

16. (5) The first paragraph explains that bases have pH values greater than 7. The last sentence describes lime as a base, so lime must have a pH greater than 7. Option (5) is the only answer that could be correct.

17. (3) The answer can be found in the first paragraph, which states that radioactivity is a natural occurrence. Nuclear testing and explosions are caused by humans. Information from the passage shows all the other options to be true.

18. (1) The last paragraph explains that calculations based on the half-lives of certain isotopes have led scientists to conclude that the earth is 4.6 billion years old. It then states that "Such calculations are also used . . . to determine the age of fossils."

19. (2) The diagram shows gasoline and kerosene near the top of the fractioning tower, so they have to be fractions of crude oil. All the other options contradict or are not supported by information.

Physics
(pages 379–386)

1. (2) To arrive at this answer, first locate the 1 at the bottom of the horizontal grid on the graph. Then move up the vertical grid line to the point where the diagonal line (representing speed) crosses it. You see that the car has traveled a distance of 30 mi, indicating a speed of 30 mph.

2. (3): $s = \frac{d}{t}$

$650 \text{ mph} = \frac{2{,}275}{t}$

$3.5 = t$

3. (2) Efficiency =

$\frac{4 \text{ N} \cdot \text{m}}{16 \text{ N} \cdot \text{m}} \times 100\% = 25\%$

$\text{Efficiency} = \frac{1 \text{ N} \cdot \text{m} \times 100\%}{4 \text{ N} \cdot \text{m} \times 1}$

$\text{Efficiency} = \frac{100 \text{ N} \cdot \text{m}}{4\text{N} \cdot \text{m}}\%$

$\text{Efficiency} = 25\%$

4. (2) A crowbar is a lever. Therefore,

$\text{M.A.} = \frac{\text{length of effort arm}}{\text{length of resistance arm}}$

5. (5) If $\text{power} = \frac{\text{work}}{\text{time}}$, then $\text{work} = \text{power} \times \text{time}$

6. (2) $\text{M.A.} = \frac{4 \text{ ft}}{2 \text{ ft}} = 2$

(If the fulcrum is 2 ft from the boards—the resistance—then the resistance arm is 2 ft long. If the total length of the crowbar is 6 ft, then the remaining length of the crowbar—4 ft—is the length of the effort arm.)

7. (3) In a series circuit, all the lamps are connected one after another along the same path.

8. (3) In a parallel circuit, each lamp has more than one path leading to the power source, so it can operate independently of the others.

9. (2) Parallel circuits allow you to use only the appliances you want to use without having to turn on all the others to keep from breaking the circuit. This is much more practical than a series circuit would be. So homes are wired in parallel circuits.

10. (1) Since electromagnetic induction depends on a changing magnetic field near a coiled wire, option (1) is correct. None of the other options would apply.

11. (3) By definition, the magnetic field is the region around the magnet where the force of magnetism acts. So the attracting and repelling forces of two magnets' poles would clearly demonstrate magnetic fields. All the other options can be disproved by information in the passage.

12. (4) The passage states that one pole of a suspended magnet always points north, which is the basis for constructing a compass.

13. (2) Waves carry energy in the form of disturbances that vary with amplitude. Therefore, amplitude can indicate the amount of energy a wave carries.

14. (5) If one kilohertz stands for 1,000 waves per second, 67 kilohertz would be 67,000 (67 × 1,000) waves per second.

15. (5) The widths of the waves are equal, but their heights vary.

16. (4) The heights of the waves are equal, but their widths vary.

17. (1) Since light can travel in a vacuum but sound cannot, there would be light but no sound in space, where vacuum conditions exist.

18. (2) Air is the only gas and water the only liquid shown on the table; all the other items are solids. The speeds given for sound are much greater for all the solids than they are for the gas or the liquid. Since granite is a denser solid than brick and sound travels faster in granite than in brick or any of the other solids, shown in increasing density, it follows that dense solids transmit sound waves the fastest of all mediums.

19. (3) The table shows that sound travels faster through water than it does through air; therefore, the water will carry sound to the swimmer faster than air will carry sound to the sunbather.

20. (4) Since 10 × 1,130 (the speed at which sound travels in air) is 11,300 and the speed at which sound travels through brick is 11,970, sound travels at least 10 times faster through brick than it does through air.

21. (3) The second paragraph states that radio waves have the lowest frequencies of all electromagnetic waves. The first paragraph tells you that high-energy waves—those with high frequencies—are the most dangerous. Therefore, radio waves, with the lowest frequencies of all, would be the least harmful.

22. (5) The second paragraph states only that people have questioned the safety of microwaves on the basis of laboratory experiments with animals. The questioning does not prove the point. The passage gives evidence to support the other options.

23. (4) The first paragraph states that more neutrons are released after the first neutron splits a nucleus. These neutrons go on to split other nuclei, which produces the chain reaction.

24. (2) The second paragraph describes runaway and controlled chain reactions in terms of uranium, implying that it is the fuel element involved in starting the chain reaction.

25. (3) The last part of the second paragraph describes how scientists prevent an explosion and maintain a chain reaction at a steady rate. Some of the other options might or might not have some validity, but the passage provides no evidence to support any of them.

Minitests—Science

Minitest 1

Directions: Each of the questions or incomplete statements below is followed by five suggested answers or completions. Select the one that is best in each case and then mark the corresponding answer space. Answers are on page 407.

Item 1 refers to the following diagram.

Approximate Composition of the Body

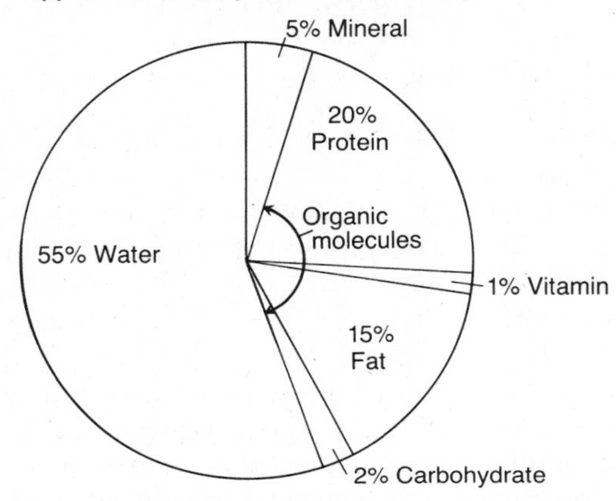

1. Organic molecules account for approximately what percentage of the composition of the body?

   (1) 55
   (2) 45
   (3) 38
   (4) 22
   (5) 17

   1 2 3 4 5

2. Matter is commonly found in one of three phases: solid, liquid, or gaseous. The process of going from one phase to another is usually the result of temperature. Phase changes do not alter the chemical identity of a substance.

   Which of the following best illustrates a change from a solid to a liquid phase?

   (1) hailstones melting on a windshield
   (2) molten lava flowing down a mountain
   (3) pudding beginning to thicken
   (4) steam rising from boiling water
   (5) burning wood turning to ashes and gas

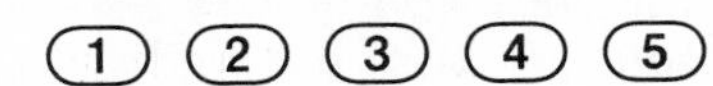

Items 3–4 are based on the following diagram and passage.

Transmission Spectra of Two Different Filters

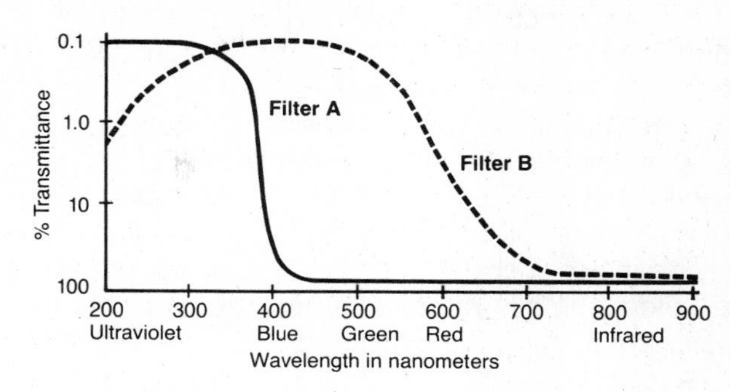

Colored glass filters are commonly used in photography to absorb certain wavelengths or colors of light and allow other wavelengths to pass and expose the film. The passage of light through a filter is called transmittance. Transmittance is expressed as the percent of light passed at each wavelength. It is determined by first measuring the brightness of light without the filter, and then measuring the brightness of the light through the filter. For example, if blue light is only half as bright when measured through a filter, then the filter has 50 percent transmittance for blue light.

3. A photographer wants to expose his film to as much light as possible above 450 nm, but to very little light below 400 nm. Based on the transmittance spectra for the two filters, which filter choice would be best?

   (1) A only
   (2) B only
   (3) A and B together
   (4) neither one
   (5) either A or B

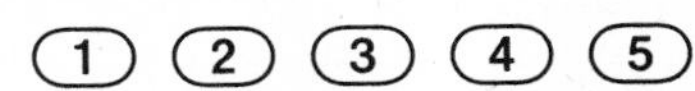

4. What information cannot be determined from the information?

   (1) wavelengths at which each filter absorbs
   (2) color the filter absorbs
   (3) comparison of transmission by two different filters
   (4) amount of light absorbed by the filter
   (5) thickness of the different filters

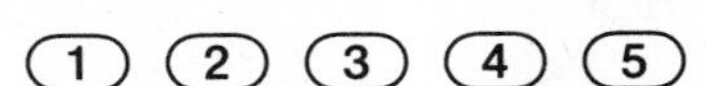

Items 5–7 are based on the following passage.

Insecticides have been developed to kill insects considered by humans to be pests. A very powerful insecticide is DDT. Houseflies were once controlled by DDT sprays. Yet houseflies from certain locations became relatively resistant to this poison. In many places DDT could no longer be relied upon to control the flies. Insects, it seems, possess traits for resistance to certain chemical poisons.

Strains of such DDT-resistant flies have been developed in laboratory experiments. A normal, sensitive strain of houseflies can be exposed to a dose of DDT that kills about 90 percent of the individuals. The survivors are used as parents of the next generation, which is also exposed to DDT. After three generations of such selection, a significant resistance to DDT appears in the housefly population.

The emergence of strains of insects resistant to various insecticides has become a major problem in recent years to those concerned with insect control. Resistance to DDT has been observed in several species of mosquitoes, body lice, cockroaches, and bedbugs. These are examples of what appears to be "microevolution" occurring in insect populations. The changes are due to gradual changes in the gene makeup of the population over a period of time.

5. Which of the following statements best summarizes the passage?

(1) Insects can no longer be killed by DDT.
(2) DDT should never be used.
(3) Houseflies thrive on doses of DDT.
(4) Exposing several generations of flies to DDT can produce a resistant strain.
(5) Resistance to DDT has developed in several different species.

(1) (2) (3) (4) (5)

6. To lessen the possibility that insect populations will develop resistance to an insecticide, which of the following might prove to be an effective pest control program?

(1) Use low doses of one insecticide.
(2) Repeatedly use one insecticide.
(3) Use several different insecticides at the same time.
(4) Avoid using all insecticides.
(5) Crossbreed the bugs with others that are not susceptible to the insecticides.

(1) (2) (3) (4) (5)

7. Which of the following statements reflects the hypothesis underlying the experiments outlined in the passage?

(1) DDT can change the flies' genetic material.
(2) DDT will kill all the flies.
(3) No insects can survive repeated doses of DDT.
(4) 90 percent of the flies will be resistant to DDT.
(5) DDT treatment can change how many individuals within a population will carry a certain trait.

(1) (2) (3) (4) (5)

Items 8–9 are based on the passage below.

Inside the cotyledon, or body of a seed, is an embryonic plant. This embryo contains genes that determine the formation of the new plant. The cotyledon provides food for the growing embryo and seedling that forms. The following experiment was carried out with kidney beans: Whole kidney beans were soaked in water. Some of the bean seeds were cut. Whole bean seeds and cut seeds were planted. Soil, light, and moisture were kept constant. After several days, seedlings that appeared from the cut seeds were smaller than the seedlings from whole seeds.

8. Based on the information given above, which of the following statements best explains this observation?

(1) Soaking the beans killed the embryos.
(2) Seedlings from cut beans require more sunlight.
(3) The seedlings from cut seeds did not have as much food stored for growth.
(4) The embryos contained all the genes for the new plant.
(5) The embryos lost half of their genetic material when the beans were cut.

9. In carrying out this experiment, what unstated assumption was made?

(1) The seedlings were measured at the same time each day.
(2) The sunlight was sufficient for growth.
(3) The food was inside the seedling.
(4) The embryo was not damaged when the seed was cut.
(5) The seedlings were watered at the same time each day.

(1) (2) (3) (4) (5)

10. A physician sees two patients. They both complain of headaches. After a complete evaluation, the physician gives both patients prescriptions but does not tell them what the prescriptions are. The first patient actually received medication to lower blood pressure. Because the physician could find nothing wrong with the second patient, this person received a placebo—a pill that does nothing. Both subsequently reported complete relief from headaches.

    Based on the information above, which of the following statements about placebos might suggest how they work?

    (1) The placebo cures the illness.
    (2) A placebo sometimes works because the patient believes it works.
    (3) A placebo lowers blood pressure.
    (4) A placebo works for most patients.
    (5) A placebo is a sugar pill.

    ① ② ③ ④ ⑤

11. Aerobic exercise is any exercise that uses many large muscles continuously over a period of at least ten minutes. This increases the heart and breathing rates and, therefore, the flow of oxygen to working muscles.

    Which of the following is an example of aerobic exercise?

    (1) a sprint
    (2) swimming
    (3) archery
    (4) golf
    (5) bowling

    ① ② ③ ④ ⑤

12. Between two objects there is a gravitational force of attraction. This force increases as the mass of the objects increases. The attraction decreases as the distance between the two objects increases.

    Two satellites in space are close together and exert a gravitational force on each other. As they move farther apart, the force of attraction between them

    (1) becomes greater
    (2) remains the same
    (3) lessens
    (4) increases then decreases
    (5) decreases then increases

    ① ② ③ ④ ⑤

Items 13–16 are based on the following passage.

In the early 1960s, scientists proposed a theory that was to change our thinking about geology. They suggested that the entire outer layer of the earth, called the crust, was slowly moving. They envisioned the continents and ocean floors to be gigantic plates of rock about 40 miles thick floating on a molten core of magma inside the earth. According to their theory, there are six major plates and numerous small plates tightly packed together. All of these plates are slowly moving and colliding, grating and ripping each other apart when they contact.

Why do these plates move? Probably several processes are involved. These include convection currents in the molten core, and the size and density of the plates. When two plates collide, the impact may be so great that they are welded together to form one larger plate. When two colliding plates are of different sizes, the larger one may dive and move underneath, thrusting the lighter one up. Alternatively, the bottom plate may sink and become part of the earth's molten core.

When the earth was young, perhaps only one super plate or continent called Pangaea existed. If this theory is correct, Pangaea broke up into several smaller plates as a result of weak areas and fractures in the earth's mantle. "Hot spots" in the molten core erupted through these weak areas. As the magma was forced up through the cracks, it cooled to form new mantle that pushed the plates apart. This process continues even today. Geologists have measured the spreading of ocean floors, changes in the position of continents and the formation of new land masses as a result of plate movements. The process is very slow by our standards, about an inch per year, but it is awesome in magnitude as eons of time pass.

13. The passage suggests that prior to 1960, all geologic theory was based on the concept that the continents and oceans were

    (1) continually changing
    (2) part of a large plate called Pangaea
    (3) moving along on top of the earth's mantle
    (4) drifting along weak spots in the earth's crust
    (5) static and unchanging

    ① ② ③ ④ ⑤

14. Which one of the following statements represents a theory which can probably never be proven or disproven?

    (1) Originally all the continents were part of one huge land mass named Pangaea.
    (2) New land masses are created from magma from the earth's core.
    (3) Ripping and tearing of our land masses coincides with plate movements.
    (4) The earth's crust is 40 miles thick surrounding a molten core.
    (5) Various techniques can be used to determine the age of the ocean floor and the continental land masses.

    1 2 3 4 5

15. Which of the following statements represents a conclusion presented by the author?

    (1) How and why the plates move is influenced by the size and density of the plates and by convection currents within the earth's molten core.
    (2) When two plates collide, the force of impact may be great enough to join the two plates together.
    (3) When a heavy plate sinks, it may melt and become part of the earth's interior.
    (4) Hot spots exist beneath the earth's crust.
    (5) The pressure of oozing magma causes the plates to change position.

    1 2 3 4 5

16. Although scientists have found rocks on land that are 3,800 million years old, the oldest rocks recovered from the ocean floor are less than 200 million years old.

    Based on the passage, which of the following statements can best explain this finding?

    (1) The earth's sea beds must be continually reforming and recycling.
    (2) Volcanoes are examples of hot spots in the earth.
    (3) Many physical forces act to shape the surface of our planet.
    (4) Magma from the earth's core fills in the gaps created by plate movement.
    (5) Plate movements can alter the shapes of existing land masses.

    1 2 3 4 5

Minitest 2

Directions: Each of the questions or incomplete statements below is followed by five suggested answers or completions. Select the one that is best in each case and then mark the corresponding answer space. Answers are on pages 407–408.

Items 1–2 refer to the following table.

Percentage of Certain Elements in the Earth's Crust			Percentage of Certain Elements in Living Cells		
Symbol	Element	Percentage	Symbol	Element	Percentage
O	Oxygen	62.5	H	Hydrogen	60.3
Si	Silicon	21.2	O	Oxygen	25.5
Al	Aluminum	6.47	C	Carbon	10.5
Na	Sodium	2.64	N	Nitrogen	2.42
Ca	Calcium	1.94	Na	Sodium	0.73
Fe	Iron	1.92	Ca	Calcium	0.226
Mg	Magnesium	1.84	P	Phosphorus	0.134
P	Phosphorus	1.42	S	Sulfur	0.132
C	Carbon	0.08	K	Potassium	0.036
N	Nitrogen	0.0001	Cl	Chlorine	0.032
Other Elements		<0.0001			

1. What percent of the earth's crust is composed of sodium (Na)?

    (1) 2.64
    (2) 2.42
    (3) 1.94
    (4) 0.73
    (5) 0.0001

2. Some chemical elements are more fit than others to make up the molecules of living organisms. Based on the information given in the table, which of the following statements would best support this conclusion?

    (1) Some elements are better suited for life processes.
    (2) O, Si, Al, and Na are the most abundant elements in the earth's crust.
    (3) Living cells must use energy to convert inorganic carbon to a usable form.
    (4) Si and C form compounds with other elements in similar ways.
    (5) C, H, and N are far more abundant in living things than in the earth's crust.

    1 2 3 4 5

Items 3–6 are based on the following diagram.

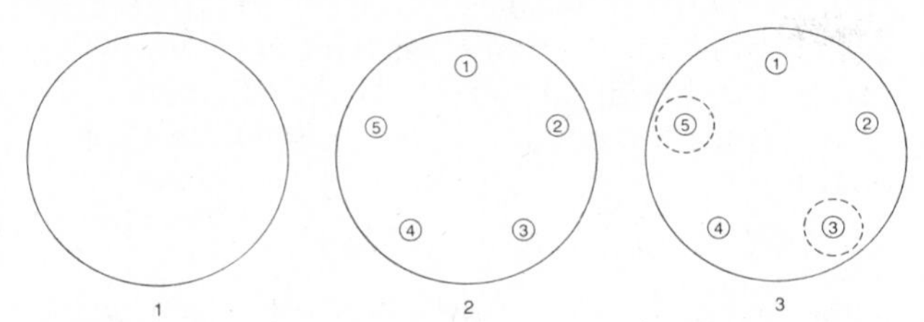

This diagram illustrates a procedure called an Antibiotic Sensitivity Test. This test is commonly used in medical laboratories. The first circle represents a small dish containing an agar growth medium. Bacteria have been spread evenly on top of the medium. The cloudiness of the plate shows that bacteria are present.

In the second dish, small paper discs (numbered 1–5) containing an antibiotic have been placed on the surface of the growth medium.

The third dish shows clear areas around discs 3 and 5. This clear zone means that the bacteria have died in the presence of the antibiotic.

3. A medical technologist is asked to determine what antibiotic will kill bacteria found in the bloodstream of a patient. Using the bacteria from the patient's blood, she set up the Antibiotic Sensitivity Test as follows: Disc 1 contains no drug. Discs 2, 3, 4, and 5 each contain a different antibiotic. The results are shown below.

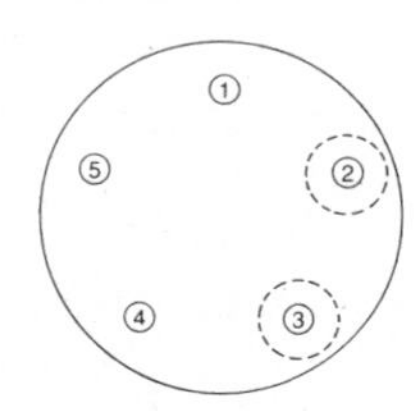

Which antibiotic will kill the bacteria in the patient's blood?

(1) 2
(2) 2 and 3
(3) 2 and 4
(4) 3 and 5
(5) 5

4. An Antibiotic Sensitivity Test is done to compare several drugs. The report states that two of the drugs were equally effective. A person reading the report would assume that

(1) all the bacteria in the plate died
(2) each drug was tested at the recommended dosage
(3) some of the drugs tested did not work
(4) all the drugs worked
(5) the two drugs were identical

5. What other information could be determined using this technique?

(1) how many bacteria were killed by the drug
(2) what disease the bacteria caused
(3) how different doses of the same drug compare
(4) what drug dosage should be used in the patient
(5) how does the antibiotic kill the bacteria

1 2 3 4 5

6. Which of the following would cause errors in interpreting the results of an Antibiotic Sensitivity Test?

(1) using a very large dish
(2) including one disc with no drug on it
(3) placing the discs too close together
(4) smearing the bacteria evenly on the agar
(5) including a drug known to kill the bacteria

1 2 3 4 5

7. An investigator of Hodgkin's disease hypothesizes that decreased growth and division of white blood cells play a part in the disease. He tests a large number of patients to see how their white blood cells respond to drugs which usually cause cells to grow and divide. The data are compared with those obtained from normal people. Some of the Hodgkin's patients show a 5 to 10 percent decrease in their response to the drugs. Which of the following statements would reflect an eagerness to prove the hypothesis?

   (1) More experiments are needed to determine if the difference is important or not.
   (2) Responses to the drugs are dramatically decreased in Hodgkin's patients.
   (3) The results are inconclusive.
   (4) White blood cells from normal people and from Hodgkin's patients have similar responses to the drugs.
   (5) There is no real difference between the two groups.

<u>Items 8–9</u> are based on the following passage.

Stomach antacids on the market make use of the fact that acids and bases neutralize each other. The digestive system of the human body is acidic. To help digest food, cells in the stomach wall produce gastric juice. This substance is composed of an enzyme and hydrochloric acid (HCl), a strong acid. The pH of gastric juice is 1.5. Tension, as well as other factors, can lead to the overproduction of hydrochloric acid, causing a high acid concentration and, consequently, an "upset" stomach.

Antacids that combat excess stomach acid contain mild bases, usually aluminum hydroxide ($Al(OH)_3$) or magnesium hydroxide ($Mg(OH)_2$). Aluminum hydroxide is a white, odorless powder. It neutralizes some of the hydrochloric acid in the stomach, producing the salt aluminum chloride and water:

$$3HCl + Al(OH)_3 \longrightarrow AlCl_3 + 3H_2O$$

Magnesium hydroxide is a white, odorless powder. Suspended in water, it has a pH of 10 and is known as milk of magnesia. Magnesium hydroxide and hydrochloric acid neutralize each other to form the salt magnesium chloride and water:

$$2HCl + Mg(OH)_2 \longrightarrow MgCl_2 + 2H_2O$$

Another common remedy to raise the stomach pH to a more normal level is sodium bicarbonate ($NaHCO_3$), or baking soda. Dissolved in water, sodium bicarbonate is a mild base with a pH of 9. It is often called bicarbonate of soda. In addition to producing the salt sodium chloride and water, the reaction between sodium bicarbonate and hydrochloric acid yields the gas carbon dioxide (CO_2):

$$HCl + NaHCO_3 \longrightarrow NaCl + H_2O + CO_2$$

8. Which of the following statements is an implication of the article above?

   (1) Pain relief by antacids is due to neutralization of stomach acidity.
   (2) Antacids work because they are white, odorless powders.
   (3) A base will neutralize an acid.
   (4) $NaHCO_3$ and $Al(OH)_3$ react with stomach acid in very different ways.
   (5) $Mg(OH)_2$ in water can be used to neutralize stomach acid because it is milk of magnesia.

   (1) (2) (3) (4) (5)

9. Which of the following statements is a conclusion drawn in the article?

   (1) Antacids are mild bases which neutralize excess HCl in the stomach.
   (2) Antacids have a pH of 9–10.
   (3) Upset stomach is the result of increased HCl in the stomach.
   (4) $Mg(OH)_2$ and $Al(OH)_3$ react with HCl to form a salt and water.
   (5) Sodium bicarbonate reacts with HCl to form CO_2.

   (1) (2) (3) (4) (5)

10. A vector is a drawing that represents both size and direction. For example, a vector can be used to describe a velocity or force exerted in a particular direction. An example of adding two vectors is shown below.

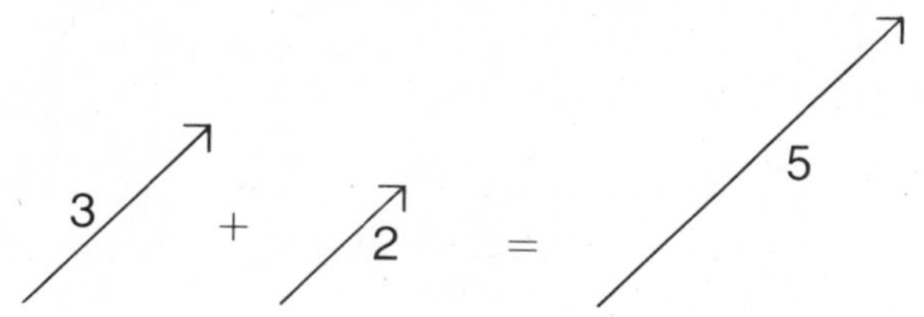

Vectors are useful because they can be added or subtracted from each other to determine the result of many different forces acting on a single object. For instance, an airplane is flying at 500 mph. It runs into a strong headwind blowing 100 mph in the opposite direction. How many miles per hour is the plane actually going?

(1) 100
(2) 300
(3) 400
(4) 500
(5) 600

① ② ③ ④ ⑤

Items 11–12 are based on the following passage.

One of the most exciting advances in recent years is the development of lasers, instruments that put light to work in fascinating ways. In the hands of surgeons, small lasers permit delicate eye and brain surgery. Uses in cancer treatment are being recognized too. But lasers have many other applications. In industry, large lasers are used to cut and weld steel. Why are lasers so powerful?

With the aid of a magnifying lens, sunlight can burn paper. Yet sunlight is not nearly as intense as laser light. What makes laser light different? Light travels in waves. Light waves from the sun move in many directions and some waves cancel out other waves. However, when the waves are all synchronized, as from a laser, the waves add to each other and the energy becomes very high.

Laser light comes from electrons of atoms or ions inside the laser. When these are energized, their electrons are excited to a high level of energy for a short time. As they fall back to their normal energy level, the electrons give off their extra energy as light. Part of the light is allowed to escape as the laser beam, and part of the light is reflected back and forth inside the laser by mirrors. The reflected light inside the laser helps to keep the process going.

11. The passage states that laser light is very intense because all the waves are synchronized. If this is correct, which of the following assumptions must be made?

(1) The lasers must contain magnifying glasses.
(2) Waves which cancel each other decrease the energy of the light beam.
(3) The laser light emits electrons.
(4) Mirrors focus the electrons.
(5) All laser light must escape from the laser.

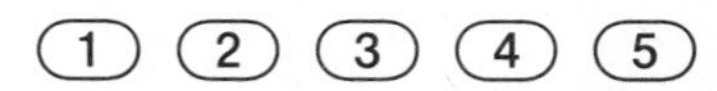

12. Which of the following statements in the passage expresses the opinion of the author?

(1) The laser is one of the most exciting recent developments in science.
(2) Lasers are widely used in eye and brain surgery.
(3) Lasers are powerful enough to cut and weld steel.
(4) Light is emitted when electrons release extra energy.
(5) Laser light is concentrated by mirrors within the laser.

Items 13–14 refer to the following information.

Groundwater is water in the ground near the earth's surface. Groundwater would dry up without rain or snow. Rainwater soaks into the soil. Plants use some of the moisture. The rest of the groundwater moves downward through soil and rock until it comes to a rock layer through which it cannot pass. Water gathers in the spaces of the soil or rocks above this line. Where these spaces are filled with water, the soil or rock is saturated. The top of this saturated soil or rock is the water table. Where the water table comes to the surface, groundwater may flow out as a spring.

Water is taken from the ground by drilling a well below the water table. Groundwater runs into the well from the saturated rock and soil around it and can then be pumped to the surface. If groundwater is used faster than it is replaced by rain or snow, however, the water table sinks farther from the surface. A lower water table causes many springs, wells, and rivers to go dry. It can take years for the water table to rise again.

13. Which of the following is the best natural example of a water table that is always at or above surface level?

(1) swamp
(2) deep well
(3) geyser
(4) irrigated farmland
(5) swimming pool

① ② ③ ④ ⑤

14. Which of the following statements best summarizes the passage?

(1) Rain and snow replenish the ground water supply.
(2) All soil below the water table is saturated with water.
(3) The water table of an area can vary widely over time.
(4) Groundwater affects our plants and rivers.
(5) The amount of groundwater determines the level of the water table.

① ② ③ ④ ⑤

15. On a clear, dry day in the desert of New Mexico, the temperature can reach 100°F. That same night, however, under a clear sky the temperature may plunge to 40°F. On a cloudy day in New Mexico, the daytime temperature may reach 70°F. That night, under a heavy cloud cover, the temperature drops only to 50°F.

Which of the following statements best explains these two frequently observed weather occurrences?

(1) Without clouds, the earth can radiate away heat and cool rapidly.
(2) Once the sun sets, the desert air turns cold.
(3) Clouds remove moisture from the air.
(4) Clouds trap the earth's heat by filtering out some of the sun's rays.
(5) The desert flatlands make weather trends unpredictable.

① ② ③ ④ ⑤

16. Enzymes are proteins which assist in chemical reactions. Enzymes usually function best within a narrow range of temperature. Fruit ripens as a process is carried out by enzymes contained within the fruit. Usually fruit ripens quickly when it is left out at room temperature.

Which of the following suggestions would probably best maintain the fruit in its present stage of ripeness?

(1) Put it in a brown paper bag.
(2) Refrigerate it.
(3) Leave it on a table.
(4) Boil it.
(5) Wrap it in a plastic bag.

① ② ③ ④ ⑤

Minitest 3

Directions: Each of the questions or incomplete statements below is followed by five suggested answers or completions. Select the one that is best in each case and then mark the corresponding answer space. Answers can be found on page 408.

1. Children ages 3–10 watch a film in which all the animals happen to have black fur. The commentary, however, repeatedly refers to the "white animals." When questioned later, the children aged 3–6 say that the animals were black. The children aged 7–10 say that the animals were white. The statements given below offer several logical explanations for this. Which one of the statements indicates that values play a part in the children's response?

   (1) Older children are generally less creative.
   (2) Younger children do not listen well.
   (3) Older children become concerned with giving the suggested answer.
   (4) Younger children rely on what they see more than on what they hear.
   (5) Verbal information is more important to children who use language well.

Items 2–5 refer to the following information.

The human body is composed of many systems which can be described in terms of their function. Listed below are five of these systems with an explanation of the functions they carry out.

respiratory—carries oxygen from the air to tissues and returns carbon dioxide from the tissues to the air

nervous—carries impulses to muscles, glands, and other tissues and carries information back to the brain about conditions internal and external to the body

skeletal—composes the body's framework and allows for its movement

digestive—absorbs water and other substances and reduces food to forms which can be used by the body to supply its nutritional needs

circulatory—distributes and transports cells, nutrients, and other substances throughout the body through a system of fluid-containing vessels

Items 2–5 each give an example of one of the functions defined above. For each item select the function which best fits the illustration given. Each function may be used more than once.

2. Saliva contains many enzymes which break down large starch molecules into small sugar units.

   Saliva is associated with the

   (1) circulatory system
   (2) digestive system
   (3) nervous system
   (4) respiratory system
   (5) skeletal system

   1 2 3 4 5

3. The end of the nose, the ear lobe, and the ends of long bones contain cartilage.

   Cartilage is part of the

   (1) circulatory system
   (2) digestive system
   (3) nervous system
   (4) respiratory system
   (5) skeletal system

   1 2 3 4 5

4. A man seriously cuts his finger while sawing wood. He no longer experiences any feeling in the tip of his finger.

   The accident apparently involved damage to his

   (1) circulatory system
   (2) digestive system
   (3) nervous system
   (4) respiratory system
   (5) skeletal system

   1 2 3 4 5

5. Nutrients will diffuse a distance of only 1 mm into tissue. Capillaries are tiny vessels which extend into tiny tissue spaces carrying food and oxygen.

   Capillaries must be part of the

   (1) circulatory system
   (2) digestive system
   (3) nervous system
   (4) respiratory system
   (5) skeletal system

   1 2 3 4 5

Items 6–7 refer to the following passage.

In 1975 automobiles were equipped with catalytic converters to meet auto-emission standards established by the U.S. government. Without these devices, cars emit poisonous carbon monoxide and other pollutants into the air.

Installed in the exhaust system of a car, a catalytic converter resembles a muffler. Its inner chamber contains heat-resistant pellets coated with catalysts, usually the two metallic elements platinum (Pt) and palladium (Pd). When a car's exhaust gases flow through the converter, these catalysts cause chemical reactions to take place quickly but the catalysts are not used up by the reactions themselves.

In one such chemical reaction, an oxidation reaction, the carbon monoxide in the exhaust reacts with oxygen to form harmless carbon dioxide:

$$2CO + O_2 \xrightarrow{\text{Pt, Pd}} 2CO_2$$

The carbon dioxide gas is then emitted through the exhaust pipe.

Cars installed with catalytic converters must use unleaded gas because lead can destroy the catalysts' effectiveness.

6. Most states require cars to pass auto emissions safety inspections. Which is the most probable cause of a car's failure to pass this inspection if it is equipped with a catalytic converter?

   (1) The muffler is defective.
   (2) CO was converted to CO_2 in the catalytic converter.
   (3) Pt and Pd combined in a chemical reaction.
   (4) The catalysts were consumed by the converter.
   (5) Leaded gasoline was used in the car.

7. Air sampling tests indicate that the chemical components of polluted air have changed since catalytic converters on cars became mandatory. Based on the information in the passage, which of the following statements best supports this conclusion?

   (1) Pt and Pd have reached high levels in our atmosphere.
   (2) Leaded gasolines are less frequently used.
   (3) Less CO is now released through car exhaust.
   (4) Poisons such as CO_2 have been eliminated.
   (5) CO_2 is being consumed by catalytic converters.

8. A lever on a fulcrum will balance if the downward force on the lever multiplied by the distance of the force from the fulcrum is equal on both sides of the fulcrum.

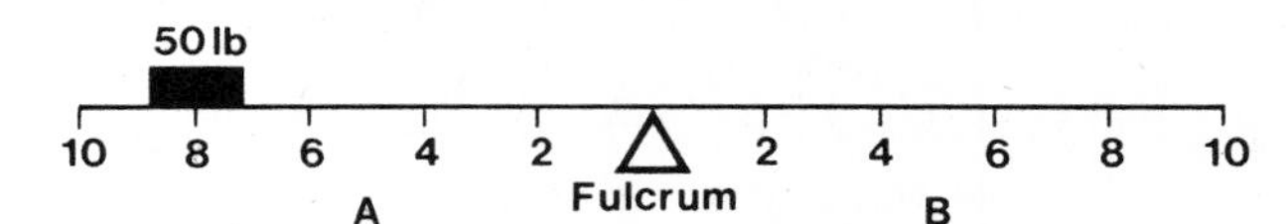

On the diagram above, at what point on side B must a 100-pound weight be placed to balance the weight on side A?

   (1) 2
   (2) 4
   (3) 6
   (4) 8
   (5) 10

① ② ③ ④ ⑤

9. Light and sound are both carried by waves. In a thunderstorm lightning is seen before thunder is heard. Which of the following statements is the best explanation of this occurrence?

   (1) Sound waves travel faster than light waves.
   (2) Light waves interfere with sound waves.
   (3) Sound waves and light waves travel at the same speed.
   (4) Light waves travel faster than sound waves.
   (5) Sound waves cannot travel in a vacuum.

① ② ③ ④ ⑤

Items 10–11 are based on the following diagram.

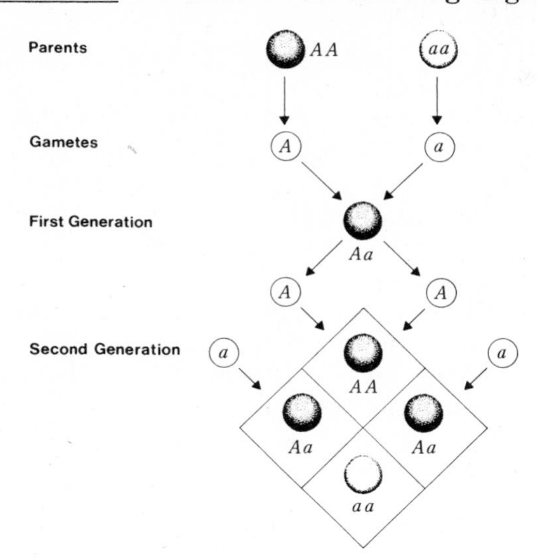

Both parents are purebred. One parent has two copies of the dominant gene "AA," and the other parent has two copies of the recessive gene "aa." Each parent forms only one type of gamete or sex cell, either an "A" or an "a." If the parents are crossed, only one type of offspring occurs. The offspring are "Aa." Because "A" is dominant over "a," the appearance of "Aa" is the same as "AA." The "A" type appearance is indicated by the dark circles, and the "a" appearance is indicated by light-colored circles.

10. If there are four second-generation offspring, how many would be expected to look like the original "AA" parent?

    (1) 0
    (2) 1
    (3) 2
    (4) 3
    (5) 4

    ① ② ③ ④ ⑤

11. A home gardener crosses two carnations, one red and one white. All of the first-generation flowers were red. He had expected them all to be pink. What factor did he overlook?

    (1) Red is dominant over white.
    (2) Neither color is dominant.
    (3) White is dominant over red.
    (4) Red is recessive to white.
    (5) The offspring inherit one gene from each parent.

    ① ② ③ ④ ⑤

12. Many scientists have tried to understand how large organic molecules found in living cells might have formed in the primitive environment of earth 3.5 billion years ago. They conducted the following experiment. Mixtures of nitrogen (N_2), hydrogen (H_2), carbon monoxide (CO), and carbon dioxide (CO_2) were exposed to sunlight, X rays, or electrical sparks. They then analyzed the resulting mixtures to determine which, if any, organic molecules were present.

    What unstated assumption did the scientists make?

    (1) The earth formed 3.5 billion years ago.
    (2) Organic molecules were always present in the earth's atmosphere.
    (3) Living cells are made up of organic molecules.
    (4) The gas mixtures were similar to the atmosphere of primitive earth.
    (5) H_2, N_2, CO, and CO_2 were formed in the atmosphere by electrical discharges.

    ① ② ③ ④ ⑤

13. The following experiment is performed to see if horizontal movement would affect downward fall. A bullet is fired horizontally from a gun held 10 feet above the ground. A small steel ball is dropped from a height of 10 feet. They reach the ground at the same time.

    Which of the following statements represents the hypothesis on which the experiment was based?

    (1) Two objects are released from the same height.
    (2) The bullet will be moving horizontally and downward at the same time.
    (3) The ball and the bullet reach the ground at the same time.
    (4) Two objects falling downward from the same height will hit the ground at the same time regardless of the horizontal forces acting on them.
    (5) Gravity is a force acting on both the ball and the bullet.

    ① ② ③ ④ ⑤

Items 14–15 refer to the following passage.

The edges of the world's oceans and sea inlets are bordered largely by a narrow green strand of wetland vegetation. Over centuries of development by humans, many of these coastal areas have been severely altered or destroyed. Historically, human settlements have thrived where rivers meet the seas. Boston, New York, San Francisco, Venice, and Amsterdam are examples of such coastal cities.

Development of coastal wetlands often results in widespread land-filling and the disappearance of marshes and swamps.

Industry buys and drains the land for factory sites. Petrochemical complexes, power stations, and huge dikes, for example, are found along the coast of northern Europe. Because the soils are fertile in wetland areas, they may also be drained and converted to productive farms. In Asia drained marshes are used for salt production or for the harvesting of timber. These activities, some critical to human welfare, affect the wetlands in which they occur.

Marshes are nurseries for many kinds of commercial fish. Without the marsh, these species will not reproduce. A major part of the commercial catch of clams, scallops, smelt, and other food species comes from the salt marshes. Wetlands also release rich organic matter into coastal waters, thus maintaining the aqua culture of shellfish such as oysters. The U.S. Department of the Interior estimates that remaining coastal marshes also produce about one million ducks each year.

In addition to being a food resource, coastal marshes scrub the contaminants from tidal waters and retain them in their muddy bottoms, thus contributing to water purification. Biologists warn that tidal wetlands are a rich but diminishing resource.

14. Which of the following statements is an implication of the passage?

(1) Humans use wetlands as a source of pure water.
(2) Once destroyed, the wetlands cannot be restored.
(3) Wetland soil makes fertile farmland.
(4) Salt can be obtained from wetland areas.
(5) Many food species live in the coastal wetlands.

1 2 3 4 5

15. Which of the following is a conclusion drawn by the author?

(1) Many species of ducks and shellfish make their homes in the coastal marshlands.
(2) Man will deplete the earth's natural resources by overdevelopment of coastal wetlands.
(3) The coastal marshes are a food resource.
(4) Without the wetlands the populations of certain fish may decrease.
(5) Coastal wetlands help control pollution of coastal ocean waters.

16. A veterinarian is examining a small puppy that is apparently ill. The puppy is listless, his eyes are dull, and his movements are jerky and somewhat uncoordinated. Which of the following can NOT be determined by the veterinarian during an examination of the puppy?

(1) The puppy's muscles are poorly developed.
(2) His diet is adequate.
(3) The pup is clear of infection.
(4) The puppy needs more affection from his owner.
(5) The pup is much smaller and thinner than normal for his age.

Minitest 4

Directions: Each of the questions or incomplete statements below is followed by five suggested answers or completions. Select the one that is best in each case and then mark the corresponding answer space. Answers are on page 408.

Items 1–4 refer to the following information. Many physical processes are involved in shaping the earth as we know it today. Five of these processes are defined below.

accretion—acquiring of new material by the earth

collision—smashing together of moving land masses to crush present land formations or uplift new ones

erosion—movement of particles, such as rock and sand, from one place to another

faulting—breaking or cracking in the earth's crust where movement has taken place

weathering—breaking down of large rocks into smaller pieces either by physical or chemical change

Items 1–4 contain an example that illustrates one of the processes defined above. For each item select the one process which is most likely responsible for the event described. More than one example of each process may be given.

1. In 1776 an earthquake occurred in Guatemala. Cracks almost the full length of the country ripped open, and in some places land on one side of the cracks slipped 3.5 meters sideways. The cracking and slipping of the earth reflect the process called

(1) accretion
(2) collision
(3) erosion
(4) faulting
(5) weathering

1 2 3 4 5

2. During the last ice age the topsoil of New England was scraped off the land and deposited off the coast of Connecticut to build up Long Island.

The force which formed Long Island was

(1) accretion
(2) collision
(3) erosion
(4) faulting
(5) weathering

3. A shooting star showers the earth with meteor dust. This is an example of

(1) accretion
(2) collision
(3) erosion
(4) faulting
(5) weathering

4. Geologists believe that the Himalayan Mountains formed when the Indian subcontinent rammed into Asia. The Himalayas were probably formed by

(1) accretion
(2) collision
(3) erosion
(4) faulting
(5) weathering

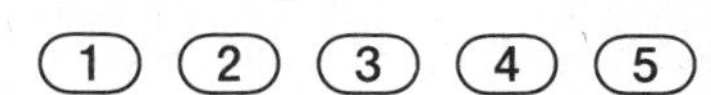

5. A small tag on a potted succulent plant gives a brief description of the plant. Which one of the following statements is based only on opinion?

(1) The plant prefers sandy soil.
(2) Plant grows best when watered infrequently.
(3) The delicate fragrance of the blooms is very pleasing.
(4) The plant is native to the deserts of New Mexico and Arizona.
(5) The plant should be placed in a warm sunlit spot.

Items 6–7 are based on the following graph. Some chemical elements are called radioactive because their atoms naturally break down or decay to form atoms of a different element. The following graph shows the schedule on which this decay happens.

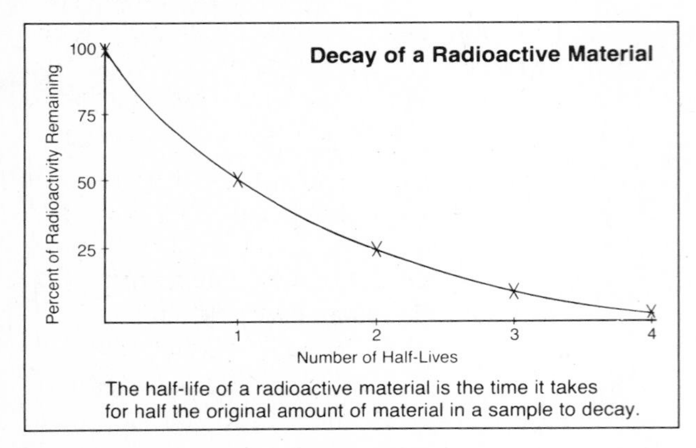

The half-life of a radioactive material is the time it takes for half the original amount of material in a sample to decay.

6. A radioactive material commonly used in medical laboratory tests is technetium–99. It has a half-life of 6 hours. If 80 grams of technetium–99 are originally present, how many grams of it remain after 12 hours?

   (1) 78
   (2) 68
   (3) 40
   (4) 25
   (5) 20

   (1) (2) (3) (4) (5)

7. An investigator has a sample of material weighing 200 grams. The half-life of the material is 3 hours. What information can NOT be derived using a graph like the one above?

   (1) how long it will take for 65 percent of the material to decay
   (2) how many half-lives will pass before 77 grams decay
   (3) how much radioactive material will remain after two hours
   (4) how long it will take for 15 grams to decay
   (5) whether the decay product is radioactive

   (1) (2) (3) (4) (5)

Items 8–9 are based on the following passage.

Acne causes many young people a good deal of unhappiness. About 80 percent of all teenagers have some form of acne. For many young people, the pimples and blemishes of acne are troublesome.

Acne occurs most often in teenagers because it begins with the rising level of hormones in the body. The hormones increase the activity of follicles in the skin. The follicles begin to produce more oil and cells than usual. Normally these materials are released through small openings in the follicles. But in cases of acne, the openings become blocked. Oil and cells collect behind the plugged openings, and the follicles swell.

Hormones and bacteria are major causes of acne. But other things, such as oil, grease, and some cosmetics, can make acne worse. Chocolate, soda pop, and emotions do not seem to be factors.

A tendency to have acne appears to be inherited, so it cannot be cured. But it can be treated. A gel containing 5 to 10 percent benzoyl peroxide is one good treatment. Another is to wash the infected area gently with mild soap and water several times a day. This removes excess oil from the skin. The best "treatment" of all is age. Acne usually clears up as teenagers become adults.

8. Which of the following statements is a conclusion that is drawn by the author?

   (1) Bacteria which accumulate below the surface of the skin can cause follicles to become blocked.
   (2) Several factors contribute to the acne problem experienced by many teenagers.
   (3) Heredity may influence the tendency to have acne.
   (4) Grease and oil may aggravate acne.
   (5) Hormonal changes occurring at puberty contribute to acne.

   (1) (2) (3) (4) (5)

9. A teenager can deal with an acne problem in several different ways. Which of the following actions indicates the influence of values in such a decision?

   (1) washing frequently with mild soap and water
   (2) using benzoyl peroxide as an effective treatment
   (3) wearing heavy makeup despite physician's warnings
   (4) gently removing excess oil from the skin
   (5) avoiding grease, oil, and cosmetics

   (1) (2) (3) (4) (5)

Items 10–11 refer to the following passage.

The German physicist Max Planck studied the distribution of energy in the radiation spectrum at the beginning of the twentieth century. As he tried to establish a mathematical relationship between the amount of energy in the different wavelengths of the spectrum, he found that the existing laws of physics were not enough to explain the facts. From this, Planck concluded that some supposedly correct laws were not altogether true. He also concluded that not all natural phenomena could be explained simply.

Planck found that radiant energy could not be explained by using the example of continuous wave motion. Instead, he postulated that energy is radiated in small bundles he called quanta. His theory was questioned at first, but today the quantum theory of radiation has become accepted.

Planck's quantum theory was the beginning of quantum mechanics, or the new physics. The new physics reflects a point of view that does not rely exclusively on a "commonsense" approach. It relies instead on mathematical logic and on deductions from observation that can be proved. While Newtonian physics still holds true for machines, the new physics deals with atoms, protons, electrons—the submicroscopic world.

10. To which of the following does Planck's quantum theory mainly apply?

(1) gravity
(2) Newtonian mechanics
(3) mathematics
(4) units of measure
(5) radiant energy

11. Which of the following statements reflects Planck's hypothesis?

(1) There are not simple explanations for all natural phenomena.
(2) Mathematical models can explain everyday occurrences.
(3) The physical principles which apply to everyday happenings do not explain subatomic events.
(4) All forms of radiant energy come in discrete packets.
(5) Quantum physics was proposed in the twentieth century.

① ② ③ ④ ⑤

12. Ripening of fruit is a process which is carried out by enzymes. Certain chemical substances produced by the fruit trigger the enzymes to begin the ripening process.

It has been observed that placing a ripe banana alongside other unripe fruits can speed up their ripening. Based on the information above, which of the following statements best explains this observation?

(1) Bananas produce too many enzymes.
(2) Many fruits do not contain ripening enzymes.
(3) The ripening chemicals produced by bananas can affect other fruit.
(4) Enzymes produce trigger substances.
(5) Bananas ripen more quickly than most fruit.

13. A gardener notes that the leaves of many of his rose bushes are turning yellow. He reads in his gardening book that yellowing usually results from a lack of iron in the soil. He purchases a liquid iron solution and with his garden sprayer applies it to all the green parts of his plants.

Which of the following statements indicates that he may have overlooked an important factor?

(1) Many soils are deficient in iron.
(2) Iron can be absorbed only through the roots of a plant, not through its leaves.
(3) Iron is necessary in plants for chlorophyll production.
(4) Iron plays a key part in photosynthesis.
(5) Without iron, plants cannot carry out their food-producing processes.

Items 14–15 refer to the following diagram.

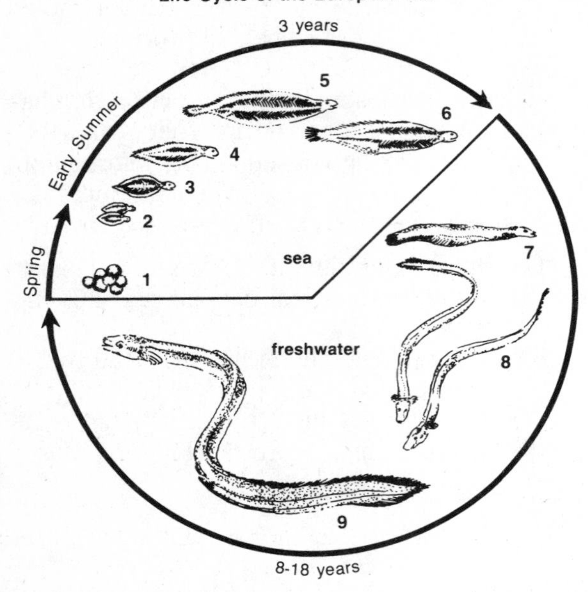

14. Which of the following is implied by the diagram above?

    (1) The larvae grow and change shape in the sea.
    (2) The adult eels die shortly after returning to the sea to spawn.
    (3) The adult eels do not survive well in freshwater.
    (4) The physical development of the eel occurs within a short time span.
    (5) The eel larvae migrate from freshwater to the sea.

    (1) (2) (3) (4) (5)

15. Which of the following statements is a conclusion that is supported by the information supplied by the diagram?

    (1) Eel eggs are laid in the spring in the sea.
    (2) Eels spend the majority of their lives in freshwater rivers.
    (3) The adults remain in freshwater before returning to the sea to lay their eggs.
    (4) In early summer the eggs hatch and gradually change shape as they drift in the seawater.
    (5) Eels can live in saltwater and freshwater at different stages of their lives.

    (1) (2) (3) (4) (5)

16. Some chemical substances pick up moisture readily from the air or from other substances. When they absorb moisture, however, they gradually change until they are chemically different from the starting material. Enzymes are included in this category. When chemical suppliers ship enzymes to buyers, they usually enclose in the package a tiny cloth bag containing a substance marked "Dessicant." The most likely purpose of the dessicant is to

    (1) keep the atmosphere in the package moist
    (2) provide extra packing material
    (3) remove moisture from the air
    (4) supply the water necessary for the breakdown of the enzyme
    (5) absorb the enzyme

    (1) (2) (3) (4) (5)

Minitest Answers

Minitest 1
(pages 391–394)

1. (3) Protein, fat, carbohydrates, and vitamins are all organic molecules. The sum of their percentages is 38.

2. (1) Option (1) shows a solid (hailstones) to liquid (water) phase change. In (2) no phase change occurs. Option (3) represents liquid to solid; (4) describes a liquid to gas. Option (5) describes a chemical change.

3. (1) Filter A transmits most of the light above 400 nm, but very little light below 400 nm. Filter B absorbs much light between 450 and 700 nm, so it is not the best choice.

4. (5) The graphs show how much light is transmitted or absorbed by the filters in terms of colors and wavelengths. Therefore, options (1), (2), (3), and (4), can all be determined from the information given.

5. (4) Options (1), (2), and (3) are false statements. Option (5) is a true statement but does not summarize the passage.

6. (3) Pests resistant to one agent may be susceptible to another. Low doses (1) may have little effect. Option (2) causes the development of resistant strains. Option (4) does not solve the pest problem. Option (5) will increase the number of resistant bugs.

7. (5) The susceptible bugs die, and survivors are resistant. Because only the survivors produce offspring, many of these offspring can be expected to be resistant also.

8. (3) The passage states that the cotyledon contains the food for the growth of the embryo and seedling. If option (1) were correct, none of the seedlings would have grown. The passage provides no information about (2). Option (4) is true, but does not explain the observation. Option (5) is false based on given information.

9. (4) Because the plants develop from the embryos, one can compare the plants only if it is assumed that all the embryos are healthy. A seedling would probably not develop from a damaged embryo. Options (1), (2), and (5) are irrelevant because the amount of sunlight and the time of measuring and watering is the same for both groups. Option (3) is false because the passage states that the cotyledon contains the food for the seedling.

10. (2) The patient is "cured" because he believes he was given an effective medication. Options (1), (3), and (4) are all incorrect statements. Option (5) is true but does not explain its effectiveness.

11. (2) Only swimming involves continuous use of large muscles.

12. (3) As the satellites move apart, the distance between them increases and the attraction decreases. Options (1), (2), (4), and (5) are false.

13. (5) The first paragraph states that the theory of plate movement changed geological thought. By implication, previous theories suggested that continents and oceans did not move or change.

14. (1) The existence of Pangaea is stated to be a theory. All other options are stated as facts and can be verified.

15. (1) The statement of how and why the plates move is a generalization supported by many specific statements in the passage.

16. (1) The rocks on the ocean floor are "young" because the ocean floor plate is continually sinking down into the earth's molten core and is recreated when new magma is forced up to fill the broken areas. Options (2), (3), (4), and (5) do not explain the difference in the ages of rocks from land and sea.

Minitest 2
(pages 394–398)

1. (1) This can be read directly from the table.

2. (5) Refer to the table. Option (1) restates the conclusion. Options (2), (3), and (4) do not support the conclusion.

3. (2) Clear zones around discs 2 and 3 indicate the bacteria have been killed by these drugs.

4. (2) The test is valid only if the drugs are used as recommended. No conclusion could be drawn if option (1) were true. Options (3), (4), and (5) do not affect the outcome of the test.

5. (3) This technique answers only one question: does the drug kill the bacteria? Several different doses of the same drug could easily be tested using this technique.

6. (3) Placing the discs too close together could cause one very large zone of clearing to hide another smaller one. Options (1) and (5) have no effect on the results. Options (2) and (4) are required for a valid test.

7. (2) Only some of the patients have decreased responses to the drugs. Option (2) interprets the data in favor of the hypothesis. Options (1), (3), (4), and (5) do not reflect an eagerness to prove the hypothesis.

8. (1) Although pain relief is not specifically mentioned, the article does indicate that an upset stomach is a consequence of excess stomach acid. Antacids neutralize stomach acid.

9. (1) Only option (1) is a conclusion.

10. (3) Since the direction of the wind is exactly opposite the direction of the plane, the wind will reduce the speed of the plane by exactly 100 mph.

11. (2) Paragraph 2 states that light from the sun is not as intense as laser light and that some light waves from the sun cancel each other out. This implies that when waves cancel each other, the light is less intense. Laser waves are synchronized so there is no cancellation of waves.

12. (1) The word *exciting* makes this a statement of opinion.

13. (1) A swamp results from water at or above the surface.

14. (5) Only option (5) is a summary statement.

15. (1) Clouds keep warmth from radiating rapidly away from the earth. Options (2) and (5) are irrelevant. Options (3) and (4) are false.

16. (2) Since enzymes work in a narrow range of temperatures, refrigerating the fruit will stop the enzymes. Options (1), (3), and (5) will allow ripening to continue. Boiling (4) will stop the enzyme, but it will also alter the fruit.

Minitest 3
(pages 399–402)

1. (3) While options (1), (2), (4), and (5) may be true, they do not reflect how values may influence decisions and behavior.

2. (2) Since saliva plays a role in the breakdown of food, it can only be assisting digestive processes.

3. (5) Cartilage gives shape to these structures and shape is a function of the skeletal system.

4. (3) The nervous system relays sensory information about the external environment to the brain.

5. (1) The circulatory system carries out its functions through a system of vessels.

6. (5) Lead coats the Pt and Pd in the catalytic converter. When this happens, the catalysts are not exposed to the exhaust gases and the chemical reactions do not occur. The other options are ruled out by information given in the passage.

7. (3) Pt and Pd are not released by the converters as is implied in Option (1). Option (2) is true but irrelevant. Options (4) and (5) are false statements.

8. (2) Read the equation explained in the passage.

9. (4) Light travels much faster than sound. Options (1), (2), and (3) are false; (5) does not explain what happens.

10. (4) The diagram indicates that if there are four second-generation offspring, one will be "AA," two will be "Aa," and one will be "aa." "AA" and "Aa" will look alike because the "A" gene is dominant. $1 + 2 = 3$.

11. (1) Only option (1) accounts for all the first-generation flowers being red.

12. (4) The scientists assumed that the compounds they put into their reaction mixture were the compounds present in the primitive atmosphere of earth. Options (1) and (3) are facts. If they assumed option (2), there would have been no reason to perform the experiment. How the starting compounds were formed is irrelevant (5).

13. (4) Only option (4) states a hypothesis that includes both directions of movement. Options (1) and (3) are observations; (2) and (5) are not hypotheses.

14. (2) The author implies that wetlands are a nonrenewable resource. Option (1) is false. Options (3), (4), and (5) are stated; they are not implications.

15. (2) Options (1), (3), (4), and (5) are specific facts which contribute to the general conclusion stated in option (2).

16. (4) Options (1), (2), (3), and (5) can be determined either by examination of the puppy or by lab tests. (4) cannot be evaluated by any of these criteria.

Minitest 4
(pages 403–406)

1. (4) Faulting is the only process which involves breaking and cracking of the earth's crust.

2. (3) Erosion is the movement of particles to a new location.

3. (1) Meteor dust comes to earth from a source other than the planet itself.

4. (2) Only collision explains the formation of a new land mass by the smashing together of two masses.

5. (3) "Pleasing fragrance" is entirely a matter of personal preference.

6. (5) Twelve hours is two half-life periods. At the end of two half-lives 25 percent of the original material will remain.

7. (5) We cannot determine the weight of the decay product because this product is often an entirely different chemical element from the starting material.

8. (2) Options (1), (3), (4), and (5) state individual factors summarized by option (2).

9. (3) Options (1), (2), (4), and (5) are all recommended procedures. Option (3) places a value on looking nice.

10. (5) Planck's quantum theory applies only to radiant energy. The first sentence of the second paragraph explains the theory.

11. (4) This is stated in the second paragraph.

12. (3) The trigger chemical produced by bananas can evaporate and influence ripening in the other fruit. Options (1), (2), and (4) are false; option (5) is irrelevant.

13. (2) His remedy for the plants will not help because the iron he puts on the leaves cannot be absorbed and used by the plants.

14. (2) No adult forms are shown living in the sea or in freshwater after the eggs are laid. Option (1) is true but is clearly illustrated. Options (3), (4), and (5) are false.

15. (5) Options (1), (2), (3), and (4) are all true about a particular phase of the eels' life. Only (5) summarizes all these statements.

16. (3) Dessicant absorbs water from the air more readily than the enzyme.

The GED Mathematics Test

Fifty-six questions appear on the GED Mathematics Test; each question has five multiple-choice options. As on all the other GED tests, there is no penalty for guessing. The math questions are broken down this way.

Type of Math	Number of Questions	Percentage of Test
Arithmetic	28	50%
Geometry	11	20%
Algebra	17	30%

The GED Mathematics Test is arranged so that the easiest questions come first and the hardest ones last. *Arithmetic, Geometry,* and *Algebra* problems are all mixed together on the test.

Each *Arithmetic* problem on the test will require at least two skills. First, you will have to be able to read and understand sentences that convey information about numbers. Second, you will have to decide what the problem is asking before you can do any computation. This math section of *Passing the GED Test* will give you plenty of help in these two areas. You will review all the basic skills needed to answer the *Arithmetic* questions correctly. These skills include adding, subtracting, multiplying, and dividing with whole numbers, fractions, decimals, and percents. You will be able to apply *Arithmetic* skills to problems relating to measurement of length, area, volume, money, and time.

Approximately five to ten questions will be based on charts, graphs, tables, diagrams, or illustrations. You may even be able to answer a few of these questions without doing any computation. You will only have to read numbers on a chart or a graph and then think about what those numbers mean.

Your chances of passing the GED Mathematics Test are greater if you understand all the material related to *Arithmetic.* To get an excellent score, you should also learn some of the basics of *Geometry* and *Algebra.* This *Mathematics* section also gives you practice you will need in basics such as computing area and volume of various shapes, using coordinate geometry, solving various types of equations, and using algebraic formulas.

Unless you are told otherwise, remember to read the tinted material of each page first. When you feel confident that you have understood the information presented there and have completed the *Warm-up* sections successfully, you can try the sample test problems in the white column of the same page or in the white columns of pages that follow. If you study the explanations and examples carefully and then work through all the practice problems, you will be quite likely to get an excellent score on your GED Mathematics Test.

Getting Mentally Ready for the GED Mathematics Test

Have you ever heard of math phobia? You probably know—or know of—people with other phobias. Some people are so afraid of heights they can't climb a ladder, and some are so afraid of math that their minds just stop working when numbers are the subject.

If you have math phobia, you could talk about your feelings with someone who really cares about your problem. Think back to your childhood days in school and jot down specific things you remember about math. You may remember being embarrassed in front of the other students during math class. Perhaps you got behind in second grade or sixth grade and felt that you never understood math well after that.

If you gave up on math long ago, you've probably decided you're no good at it. Every time math comes into your life—when you balance your checkbook or figure your income taxes—you may unknowingly send yourself the message, "I'm no good at math."

It's possible to change all this. As an adult, you've learned things every day, and you've learned many of them well. Chances are that you are now more motivated than ever before to learn math because you want to pass the GED Test. So, from now on, send yourself a new message. You don't have to tell yourself that you're great at math. Say, "I'm going to start trying to learn math. If I try, I can only get better and better."

A System for Solving Word Problems

A. Read each problem carefully to understand what you are supposed to find. *Read the problem as many times as necessary.* Sometimes it's helpful to draw or imagine a picture to help you understand the situation.

B. Figure out what information you need to answer the question and look for that information in the problem. You may find it helpful to list and label the information.

C. Decide what operation you need to use. Some problems will require more than one operation or the same operation more than once. A key word or phrase can sometimes be a clue to which operation to use. Each time you perform an operation, you take one more step toward solving the word problem. The number of steps in the problem determines the number of times you do the next three things.

D. Set up the problem.
E. Compute.
F. Check your arithmetic.
— One Step

G. See if your answer makes sense. Reread the problem to see if the number you got is logical. One way to do this is by estimating.

Estimating Answers in Word Problems You can round the numbers of a problem in your head, quickly compute, and see whether your answer comes close to your estimate. This will help you check your work and protect you from making careless mistakes. Here are two examples of how to round numbers.

1. *Round 38 to the nearest ten.* Ask yourself, is 38 closer to 30 or 40? Since 38 is closer to 40, you round up to 40. If you are rounding 35 to the nearest ten, what do you do? The rule is to round up when the number is halfway between.

2. *Round 314 to the nearest hundred.* Ask yourself, Is 314 closer to 300 or 400? Since 314 is closer to 300, round down to 300.

Using the System to Solve Word Problems
Look at the following word problem.

Mr. Wren has a dentist appointment tomorrow and wants to arrive 10 minutes early. Travel time is 20 minutes, and he needs 1 hour and 15 minutes to dress and to have breakfast. How long before his appointment should he plan to wake up?

(1) 20 minutes (2) 45 minutes
(3) 1 hour 45 minutes (4) 2 hours
(5) 2 hours 45 minutes

① ② ③ ④ ⑤

A. Read the word problem carefully. Make a mental picture.

B. Figure out what information you need. You'll have to know the amount of time each activity requires. You might want to list the times you know.

C. Decide on the operation. You know Mr. Wren needs to do a number of things before his appointment actually begins, so you will have to *add* the times for those things.

D. Set up the computation. Place the numbers in a column to be added.

```
   10 minutes           (waiting)
   20 minutes           (traveling)
+  1 hour 15 minutes    (dressing, eating)
   1 hour 45 minutes
```

E. Now add the column. The total you get is 1 hour 45 minutes.

F. Check your addition.

G. Stop for a moment and ask yourself if your answer makes sense. You can estimate your answer. Mr. Wren needs more than 1 hour but less than 2 hours to do his tasks. Of all the choices, the one closest is (3).

☑ A Test-Taking Tip

Sometimes you will be given a long, detailed situation and asked several questions about it. In these cases, be sure you know what each question is asking and use only the information necessary.

Look at the following problem.

Ms. Hallie must pay a service charge of $9 at the end of the month if the balance on her checking account is below $600 at that time. She began May with a balance of $104.68. During the month she made the following transactions: May 3, check for $22.63; May 5, deposit of $451.90; May 9, checks for $83.00 and $37.24; May 14 check for $9.25; May 22, deposit of $175.30; May 29, check for $54.00. On June 1 she withdrew 10% of her May deposits to put into her savings account.

How much money did Ms. Hallie put into her savings account?

(1) $45.19 (2) $62.72 (3) $17.53
(4) $627.20 (5) $6,272.00

① ② ③ ④ ⑤

A. Read carefully. Imagine what Ms. Hallie's checkbook looks like.

B. Look for key words and phrases. The word *deposits* tells you that you will be working with the two figures that involve deposits.

C. You will need to add the deposits and then multiply the sum by 10%. So two steps are in this problem.

Step 1

D. Set up the problem to find the total amount of her deposits.

```
  $451.90
+  175.30
```

E. Add the two deposits.

```
  $451.90
+  175.30
  $627.20
```

F. Check your arithmetic.

Step 2

D. Set up the problem to find the amount of her savings.

```
  $627.20
×     .10
```

E. Multiply carefully.

```
  $627.20
×     .10
  $62.7200
```

F. Check your arithmetic.

G. Check that your answer makes sense. $451.90 is about $500, and $175.30 is about $200. The total of the deposits is about $700, and 10% of that amount is about $70. So (2) is the correct answer.

What is Ms. Hallie's balance at the end of May?

(1) $104.68 (2) $206.12
(3) $516.76 (4) $525.76
(5) $731.88

① ② ③ ④ ⑤

A. Read the problem carefully to determine the question.

B. You will need all the numbers representing money; you will not need the dates.

C. Look for key words or phrases. The only key here is the word *balance.* When you balance a checkbook, you add deposits and subtract checks and service charges. Thus, this problem involves more than one step.

Step 1

D. Set up the problem. Start with the beginning balance and add the two deposits.

```
  $104.68
   451.90
+  175.30
```

E. Compute the problem very carefully.

$$\begin{array}{r} \$104.68 \\ 451.90 \\ +\ 175.30 \\ \hline \$731.88 \end{array}$$

F. Check your arithmetic.

Step 2
D. Set up the problem to add the checks.

$$\begin{array}{r} \$22.63 \\ 83.00 \\ 37.24 \\ 9.25 \\ +\ 54.00 \\ \hline \end{array}$$

E. Now add the amounts of the checks.

$$\begin{array}{r} \$\ 22.63 \\ 83.00 \\ 37.24 \\ 9.25 \\ +\ \ 54.00 \\ \hline \$206.12 \end{array}$$

F. Check your arithmetic.

Step 3
D. Set up the problem to subtract the amount of the checks from the amount of the deposits.

$$\begin{array}{r} \$731.88 \\ -\ 206.12 \\ \hline \end{array}$$

E. Subtract.

$$\begin{array}{r} \$731.88 \\ -\ 206.12 \\ \hline \$525.76 \end{array}$$

F. Check your arithmetic.

Step 4
Ms. Hallie's balance is less than $600, so you must subtract the service charge from the total.

D. Set up the problem.

$$\begin{array}{r} \$525.76 \\ -\quad 9.00 \\ \hline \end{array}$$

E. Compute.

$$\begin{array}{r} \$525.76 \\ -\quad 9.00 \\ \hline \$516.76 \end{array}$$

F. Check your arithmetic.

G. Check to make sure your answer makes sense.

☑ A Test-Taking Tip

Some questions on the GED Test will require that you only choose the setup of the problem. Read each question carefully so that you do not waste time computing needlessly.

There are often several parts to a problem. When the parts are expressed in math terms, parentheses are used to show which part should be done first. In the expression 49 × ($0.25 + $0.05), you would add before you multiply by 49. This kind of expression could also be written as 49($0.25 + $0.05).

☑ A Test-Taking Tip

Some questions on the GED Mathematics Test will give you more information than you actually need to solve the problem. It is your job to decide exactly what information you need.

Look at the problem below.

> Mrs. Murphy is making curtains. Each window needs two curtains. Each curtain requires 1⅔ yards of material. Each bolt of material has 20 yards. How many windows can Mrs. Murphy finish with 10 yards of material?

What information is not needed? If you said that the amount of material on each bolt is extra information, you are correct.

☑ A Test-Taking Tip

Some questions on the GED Mathematics Test will give you insufficient information to solve the problem. That is, you will be unable to compute an answer because you do not have enough information. Sometimes the wording "Insufficient data is given to solve the problem" appears as a last option. At times, this option will be the correct answer.

Look at the problem below.

> Tonya bought a skirt for $42.99, a blouse for $15.50, a belt for $12.98, and a purse for $23. How much money did she have left?

What information is missing from this question? Do you know how much money Tonya had before she started shopping? No. Yet you need that information to figure out how much she had left. Thus, the correct answer to this question would be "Insufficient data is given to solve the problem."

Basic Arithmetic
Whole Numbers

This review of whole numbers will help prepare you for the *Arithmetic* questions you'll find on the GED Mathematics Test. Before providing you with practice word problems, this book will review the basic mathematical skills you will need to do problems with whole numbers.

Adding Whole Numbers The first step in adding a group of whole numbers is to put them in a column. Line up the numbers 1, 348, 396, and 456,000 so you can add them easily. Remember, all numbers should be aligned in the ones column (the righthand column).

$$\begin{array}{r} 1 \\ 348 \\ 396 \\ +456{,}000 \\ \hline \end{array}$$

When you are thinking about a complex word problem, you shouldn't have to worry about the basic facts in addition. It would be a shame to set up a problem correctly and then get an incorrect answer because your addition wasn't perfect.

Warm-up

On a separate piece of paper, write the simple addition problems below. Then see if you can write all the answers in just thirty seconds. Follow this model.

Problem: $\begin{array}{r} 9 \\ +2 \\ \hline 11 \end{array}$ Answer: 11

If it takes you longer than thirty seconds to do these problems, put each one on a 3 × 5 card (the problem on one side, the answer on the other) and use the cards to help improve your speed.

1. 9 + 2	**6.** 4 + 8	**11.** 8 + 8
2. 8 + 9	**7.** 3 + 7	**12.** 3 + 9
3. 7 + 7	**8.** 2 + 9	**13.** 4 + 7
4. 6 + 8	**9.** 1 + 8	**14.** 6 + 6
5. 5 + 6	**10.** 5 + 7	**15.** 9 + 9

Warm-up Answers
1. 11 **2.** 17 **3.** 14 **4.** 14 **5.** 11 **6.** 12 **7.** 10
8. 11 **9.** 9 **10.** 12 **11.** 16 **12.** 12 **13.** 11 **14.** 12
15. 18

Carrying When adding large numbers, you will need to know how to carry a number from one column to the next. Look at the sample problem below.

$$\begin{array}{rrrl} \text{hundreds} & \text{tens} & \text{ones} & \\ 1 & 1 & & \leftarrow \text{carry} \\ 1 & 9 & 9 & \\ + & 7 & 6 & \\ \hline 2 & 7 & 5 & \end{array}$$

Remember to always work from right to left.

Step 1 Add the 9 to the 6 in the ones column. The total in the ones column is 15. Write 5 for the answer in the ones column. To carry the 1, write the 1 at the top of the tens column.

Step 2 Add the 9 in the tens column to the 1 you carried. This makes 10. Add the 7 in the tens column to 10. This makes 17. Write 7 for the answer in the tens column and carry the 1 to the hundreds column.

Step 3 Add the 1 in the hundreds column to the 1 you carried. Write 2 for the answer in the hundreds column.

Warm-up

First write out each problem, lining up the columns of numbers correctly.

Example: 234,098 + 34,567

Line up as follows: $\begin{array}{r} 234{,}098 \\ +\ 34{,}567 \\ \hline \end{array}$

After you write down all the problems neatly and correctly, add them as fast as you can. Practice the problems until you can add them all correctly in eight minutes or less.

1. 63 + 24	**8.** 324 + 696
2. 718 + 50	**9.** 3,196 + 845
3. 2,416 + 383	**10.** 8,456 + 778
4. 2,356 + 1,431	**11.** 5,273 + 7,128
5. 27 + 46	**12.** 69,768 + 3,649
6. 38 + 76	**13.** 433 + 796 + 564
7. 68 + 477	**14.** 379 + 52 + 2,513

Warm-up Answers
1. 87 **2.** 768 **3.** 2,799 **4.** 3,787 **5.** 73 **6.** 114
7. 545 **8.** 1,020 **9.** 4,041 **10.** 9,234 **11.** 12,401
12. 73,417 **13.** 1,793 **14.** 2,944

☑ A Test-Taking Tip

You should look for key words and phrases when you solve word problems. Certain words tell you that addition is needed. The italicized words that follow are clues that you must add: how many *in all*; what was the *combined amount*; what was the *total* cost; *altogether* the cost was; the *sum* was.

Warm-up

1. Which of the following questions cannot be solved by addition?

a. Sgt. Jackson spent $46 on a bus ticket home. His meals while on leave cost $26. How much did he spend on leave?
b. Sgt. Jackson had $585 in the bank when he went on leave. He withdrew $80. How much was left in the bank?
c. Sgt. Jackson made $600 per month, but in April he earned $85 for extra work. How much money did he earn altogether that month?

Now find the sums in the problems below.

2. A student paid $628 for tuition and books, $988 for an apartment, and $750 for food last semester. How much were her total expenses?
3. A moving van weighs 8,235 pounds when empty. It picked up two loads of furniture weighing 6,200 pounds and 1,369 pounds. How much did the van and the furniture weigh?
4. The sticker on a new car gave a suggested retail price of $6,833. Options installed on the car came to $370 for automatic transmission and $110 for whitewall tires. The destination charges were $285. What was the total cost of the car?
5. The Perez family budgets $485 for rent, $95 for utilities, $35 for transportation to work and school, and $390 for food each month. How much income do they need to cover these basic expenses?
6. Last year there were 23,600 automatic-teller machines at U.S. banks. This year 9,440 new machines were put into service. How many teller machines are available now?
7. The urban population of a small country is 7,824,080; the rural population is 4,145,768. What is the total population of the country?

Warm-up Answers
1. b. The words "how much was left" indicate that subtraction is necessary. Questions (a) and (c) ask for total amounts. Addition would be required in both of these problems.
2. $2,366 **3.** 15,804 lbs. **4.** $7,598 **5.** $1,005 **6.** 33,040
7. 11,969,848

Basic Subtraction Facts Subtraction is the opposite of addition. 9 − 5 means that you take 5 away from 9.

Warm-up

Practice the subtraction problems below until you can get them all correct in one minute.

	a	b	c	d	e	f	g	h	i	j
1.	6 −4	7 −3	5 −2	9 −6	4 −1	8 −6	2 −0	6 −5	7 −2	2 −1
2.	9 −3	7 −4	5 −5	6 −1	9 −5	3 −2	8 −7	6 −2	4 −3	1 −1

Borrowing In the problem below, how do you subtract the 9 from the 1 and the 8 from the 4? You borrow. If you have forgotten the borrowing process, carefully read the instructions below the problem.

hundreds	tens	ones
4	13	
~~5~~	~~4~~	11
	− 8	9
4	5	2

Step 1 You cannot subtract 9 from 1, so you borrow 1 from the 4 in the tens column. Cross out the 4 in the tens column and write a 3 above it. Place the 1 you borrowed from the tens column beside the 1 in the ones column. This 1 becomes 11. You can subtract 9 from 11. Write a 2 for the answer in the ones column.

Step 2 A 3 remains in the tens column, but you can't subtract 8 from it. You borrow from the 5 in the hundreds column. Draw a line through the 5 and write a 4 above it. There is now a 4 in the hundreds column. Write the 1 you borrowed beside the 3 in the tens column. Now 13 is in the tens column, and you can subtract 8 from it. Write 5 for the answer in the tens column.

Step 3 A 4 is in the hundreds column, but no number is below the 4 to subtract from it. Write 4 for the answer in the hundreds column.

Warm-up Answers

	a	b	c	d	e	f	g	h	i	j
1.	2	4	3	3	3	2	2	1	5	1
2.	6	3	0	5	4	1	1	4	1	0

☑ A Test-Taking Tip

When you have to subtract on the GED Test, you can check your work by adding the answer to the number you subtracted. For example, to check the problem you just did, add the answer to 89. The sum should equal the top number.

```
  452  (the answer)
+  89  (the number subtracted)
  541  (the number subtracted from)
```

Warm-up

Write out each problem so that the columns of numbers are correctly lined up.

Example: 34,965 − 999

Line up as follows:

```
  34,965
−    999
```

After you write down all the problems in columns, do the subtraction as fast as you can. Practice the problems again and again until you can get them all correct in eight minutes.

1. 78 − 35
2. 94 − 83
3. 34 − 9
4. 21 − 8
5. 80 − 4
6. 94 − 69
7. 50 − 19
8. 87 − 78
9. 970 − 345
10. 865 − 81
11. 7,946 − 2,871
12. 5,126 − 3,718
13. 8,103 − 1,214
14. 6,001 − 3,745
15. 4,334 − 702
16. 23,456 − 8,759

Warm-up Answers
1. 43 **2.** 11 **3.** 25 **4.** 13 **5.** 76 **6.** 25 **7.** 31 **8.** 9 **9.** 625 **10.** 784 **11.** 5,075 **12.** 1,408 **13.** 6,889 **14.** 2,256 **15.** 3,632 **16.** 14,697

☑ A Test-Taking Tip

In a word problem, words such as *difference, left, how much more, how much less,* and *how much change* usually tell you that you need to subtract.

Notice the italicized words in the questions below.

1. A department store sells a pair of shoes for $39. A discount store sells the same pair for $29. What is the *difference* in price?

2. One year we had 35 inches of rain. The next year we had 14 inches of rain. *How much less* rain did we have the second year?

Warm-up

Solve the following word problems by using subtraction.

1. One person paid cash for a TV set that cost $329. Another person bought the same TV set but bought on credit. Her total cost was $398. What was the difference in cost?

Monthly Leasing Fees

Model	12 mo.	24 mo.	30 mo.	36 mo.
Compact	$195	$147	$138	$135
Mid-sized	$212	$158	$148	$145
Full-sized	$258	$189	$178	$175

2. Using the table of leasing fees above, what are the savings per month if you lease a compact car for 36 months instead of for 12 months?

3. Marilyn had a balance of $112 in her checking account on December 15. She wrote checks for $25 and $34 on December 16. What was her balance on December 17?

4. An automobile company sold 452,280 cars and 98,126 light trucks in the United States in one year. The next year it projected sales of 475,000 cars and 125,000 trucks. How many more vehicles did it expect to sell the second year?

Warm-up Answers
1. $69 **2.** $60 **3.** $53 **4.** 49,594

Direction: For each problem, choose the one best answer. Answers are on page 545.

1. A woman leaves her estate of \$12,000 to her husband and two daughters. Her husband receives \$7,500. The oldest daughter receives \$1,250 and gives \$550 to her husband. How much will the younger daughter receive?

   (1) \$1,500 (2) \$2,700 (3) \$3,200
   (4) \$3,250 (5) \$4,250

   ① ② ③ ④ ⑤

2. Greg saved all his change for a year. At the end of the year he sorted his change and found that he had 1,603 pennies, 392 nickels, 487 dimes, 209 quarters, and 58 half dollars. How many more pennies than nickels, dimes, quarters, and half dollars combined does Greg have?

   (1) 457 (2) 1,116 (3) 1,146
   (4) 1,211 (5) 1,394

   ① ② ③ ④ ⑤

3. The 24 members of the hiking club raised \$5,012 for its 3-day trip. \$1,550 was to be used for general supplies. \$942 was to be used for food. The remaining money was to be divided among the members for their personal expenses. How much money was to be divided?

   (1) \$2,520 (2) \$2,550
   (3) \$2,580 (4) \$3,520
   (5) Insufficient data is given to solve the problem.

   ① ② ③ ④ ⑤

4. Jess has 177 books. He gives 63 books to his brother, gives some to the local library, and places the rest of the books on his 6 book shelves. How many books did he donate to the public library?

   (1) 19 (2) 63 (3) 108 (4) 114
   (5) Insufficient data is given to solve the problem.

   ① ② ③ ④ ⑤

Two-Step Word Problems A word problem with two steps is a math question in which you have to use two operations to solve the problem.

Here is a sample two-step problem followed by some ideas about solving it.

■ Mr. Cramer is a traveling salesman. He can deduct from his income the business miles he drives. From January to June he drove 6,482 miles, and from July to December he drove 8,491 miles. All but 1,239 miles were related to business. How many business miles could he deduct for the year?

This problem will require two different steps to arrive at the correct answer. First, you must find the total number of miles Mr. Cramer drove during the year. Then you can find the number of miles he can deduct.

In this problem, one key word is *deduct.* You know that Mr. Cramer will not be able to deduct from his taxes all the miles he drove. You must subtract his nonbusiness miles from the total miles. Another key word is *year.* It tells you to add the two half-years together before you subtract the nonbusiness miles.

Add the two half-year totals: 6,482 + 8,491 = 14,973. Mr. Cramer drove 14,973 miles during the year.

Now subtract his nonbusiness miles from this total: 14,973 − 1,239 = 13,734.

Mr. Cramer will be able to deduct 13,734 miles from his taxes.

You could also solve this problem by first subtracting the nonbusiness miles from the January to June total or from the July to December total. You would then add this amount to the other half-year miles. The answer would be the same as above.

Basic Multiplication Facts If you made $960 a month and wanted to figure your yearly salary, you could add $960 12 times. But it would be easier to multiply $960 by 12. Multiplying quickly and carefully is important on the GED Test.

Warm-up

Practice the multiplication problems below until you can get them all correct in one minute.

a	b	c	d	e	f	g	h	i	j
9	7	5	6	8	5	4	9	6	8
× 8	× 6	× 9	× 4	× 6	× 7	× 8	× 3	× 6	× 5

Multiplying Large Numbers Look at the problem below.

	ten-thousands	thousands	hundreds	tens	ones
			5	3	
			6	3	
			6	7	4
		x		8	9
		6	0	6	6
	5	3	9	2	
	5	9,	9	8	6

Here's how to multiply 674 by 89.

Step 1 First, multiply 674 × 9. Start on the righthand side: 9 × 4 = 36. Write 6 for the answer in the ones column. Carry the 3 and write it above the 7 in the tens column.

Step 2 Multiply 9 × 7 = 63. Add the 3 you carried (63 + 3 = 66). Write one 6 for the answer in the tens column and carry the other 6. Write the 6 you carried above the 6 in the hundreds column.

Step 3 Multiply 9 × 6 = 54. Add the 6 you carried to 54 (54 + 6 = 60). Write 0 for your answer in the hundreds column. Write the 6 that is left for the answer in the thousands column.

Step 4 Now you are multiplying 674 × 8. Start by multiplying 8 × 4 = 32. Write the 2 for the answer in the *tens* column, under the 6 that is already there. Carry the 3 and write it above the 7 in the number 674.

Step 5 Multiply 8 × 7 = 56. Add the 3 you carried (56 + 3 = 59). Write 9 for the answer in the hundreds column, under the 0 that is already there. Carry the 5 and write it above the 6 in the number 674.

Step 6 Multiply 8 × 6 = 48. Add the 5 you carried (48 + 5 = 53). Write 3 for the answer in the thousands column, under the 6 that is already there. Write 5 for the answer in the ten-thousands column.

Step 7 Add the numbers you have placed in the answer.

Multiplying by a number that ends with zeros is easy. Just multiply the other numbers first, and then write zeros after the result.

Example: Find 495 × 700.

Step 1
```
  495
×   7
3,465
```

Step 2 700 has two zeros, so add two zeros to 3,465.

Final answer: 346,500

Warm-up

Write out each problem below so the columns of numbers are lined up correctly.

Example: 456 × 43. Line up:
```
  456
×  43
```

After you write all the problems neatly and correctly, answer them as fast as you can without making mistakes. Practice until you can get the problems all correct in ten minutes or less.

1. 52 × 3
2. 63 × 5
3. 24 × 8
4. 39 × 9
5. 387 × 6
6. 548 × 7
7. 3,855 × 8
8. 3,295 × 7
9. 37 × 40
10. 65 × 90
11. 53 × 82
12. 92 × 64
13. 566 × 87
14. 727 × 94
15. 4,228 × 39
16. 2,364 × 49

☑ A Test-Taking Tip

Suppose on the GED Test you have to multiply 495 by 713. You could round 495 to 500 and 713 to 700 and get an estimate for the answer. If you were multiplying 495 by 787, you'd have to round the 787 to 800, but you could still make a quick estimate of the answer.

Warm-Up Answers

a	b	c	d	e	f	g	h	i	j
72	42	45	24	48	35	32	27	36	40

Warm-up Answers

1. 156 **2.** 315 **3.** 192 **4.** 351 **5.** 2,322 **6.** 3,836 **7.** 30,840 **8.** 23,065 **9.** 1,480 **10.** 5,850 **11.** 4,346 **12.** 5,888 **13.** 49,242 **14.** 68,338 **15.** 164,892 **16.** 115,836

Directions: For each problem, choose the one best answer. Answers are on page 545.

5. If a man earns $5 an hour, how much does he earn in a 40-hour week?

   (1) $200 (2) $210 (3) $218
   (4) $2,000 (5) $2,100

   (1) (2) (3) (4) (5)

6. How many miles can a truck driver drive if she averages 52 miles per hour for 13 hours?

   (1) 650 (2) 666 (3) 676 (4) 705
   (5) Insufficient data is given to solve the problem.

   (1) (2) (3) (4) (5)

7. If a pair of rabbits produces 24 offspring a year, how many babies will 178 pairs of rabbits have?

   (1) 4,262 (2) 4,227 (3) 4,772
   (4) 4,272 (5) 4,622

   (1) (2) (3) (4) (5)

8. A delivery cart holding 308 dozen eggs tipped, and 56 eggs were smashed. How many eggs are left?

   (1) 3,640 (2) 252 (3) 3,642
   (4) 364 (5) 3,696

   (1) (2) (3) (4) (5)

9. Mrs. Ginn bought 9 yards of material at $5 a yard and a pattern for $3. Which of the following expressions correctly represents the total of Mrs. Ginn's purchases?

   (1) 9 × $5 (2) 9($5) + $3
   (3) 9($5 + $3) (4) $5 + $3
   (5) $5 × (9 + 3)

   (1) (2) (3) (4) (5)

10. Jeff receives a commission of $78 on every set of encyclopedias he sells. In May he sold 63 sets, and in June he sold less than he sold in May. How much more money did Jeff earn in May than in June?

    (1) $468 (2) $1,468
    (3) $4,446 (4) $9,360
    (5) Insufficient data is given to solve the problem.

    (1) (2) (3) (4) (5)

Multiplication Word Problems Here is a multiplication word problem. Can you make a drawing or get a mental picture that shows multiplication is needed?

■ At a large airport, 42 flights take off every hour. If there is an average of 183 people per flight, how many people depart every hour?

Almost every minute a plane takes off from the airport. You need to know how many planes take off every hour (42) and how many people are on each plane (about 183). If you picture a crowd at an airport, you know you are seeking a large number of people. Neither adding nor subtracting will give you the answer you want. You will have to multiply 42 by 183. The answer is 7,686.

Two-Step Problems Sometimes a word problem may involve two steps before you can find the correct answer. Look at the problem below.

■ Mr. Kohn owes Mr. Arnold $28. Mr. Kohn gives Mr. Arnold a $50 bill and receives change. If Mr. Kohn then increases the amount of his change 12 times and puts it all into his savings account, how much money does Mr. Kohn deposit?

To solve this problem you will need the amount of money Mr. Kohn owes ($28), the amount of money he gives Mr. Arnold ($50) and the amount of increase Mr. Kohn plans to add to his change (12 times).

The first thing you will have to do is to subtract the amount of money Mr. Kohn owes Mr. Arnold from $50 to find the amount of change Mr. Kohn receives ($50 − $28). Mr. Kohn's change is $22. Then you will have to multiply this difference by 12 to find the amount of money Mr. Kohn saves ($22 × 12). Mr. Kohn deposits $264 into his savings account.

See if your answer makes sense. You know Mr. Kohn's change is about $20. Since 12 can be rounded to 10, you can estimate that Mr. Kohn's savings will be about $200.

Need a Hint for Number 8?
This is a two-step problem. The first step is multiplication. What is the second?

Need a Hint for Number 9?
This is also a two-step problem. What is the first step? the second step?

Three-Step Problems Look at the problem below.

■ A video club charges $2 for the first day and $1 a day for each day after that for the rental of a videotape. How much would it cost to rent a videotape for a week?

First figure out what the question is asking. You want to know the rental fee for a 7-day period. You know the fee for the first day differs from the fee for the rest of days. You will have to add these two amounts to find the correct fee. Also note that you will need more than one step to solve this problem. You will first need to find how many days have the rental fee of $1. Since the tape was rented for one week (7 days), you subtract 1 from 7 (7 − 1) to get the number of days for which the fee was $1. Then you will need to multiply 6 by $1 (6 × 1 = $6) to find the charge for the 6-day rental. Since the tape was rented for 7 days (a week), you will have to add the first-day rental fee to the rental fee for the other 6 days ($6 + $2 = $8). The charge for the week is $8.

☑ A Test-Taking Tip

Sometimes problems on the GED Mathematics Test will involve three steps. Be sure to find all the information you need and set up each part of the problem separately.

Warm-up

Solve the following problem by showing all three steps.

■ Mr. Sinclair earns $8 an hour. He works 35 hours a week for nine straight weeks. He puts $175 from his total paycheck into a retirement fund. How much money does Mr. Sinclair have left?

Warm-up Answer

Step 1: $8 × 35 = $280 (amount earned in one week)
Step 2: $280 × 9 = $2,520 (amount earned in nine weeks)
Step 3: $2,520 − $175 = $2,345 (amount Mr. Sinclair has left)

11. Mr. Dallas earns $750 every week at his regular job. He works three nights a week at another job and earns $5 an hour. How much does he earn in one work week?

    (1) $750 (2) $755
    (3) $775 (4) $785
    (5) Insufficient data is given to solve the problem.

    ① ② ③ ④ ⑤

12. At the hardware store, Mr. Ginnis bought 14 6-foot varnished boards for $12 each and 25 8-foot varnished boards for $18 each. How much money did Mr. Ginnis spend?

    (1) $216 (2) $316
    (3) $534 (4) $618
    (5) Insufficient data is given to solve the problem.

    ① ② ③ ④ ⑤

13. Mrs. Costello went to the bank to pay her electric and phone bills. Her electric bill was $177 and her phone bill was $46. If Mrs. Costello gives the bank teller 12 $20 bills, how much change will she receive?

    (1) $12 (2) $17 (3) $19 (4) $23
    (5) Insufficient data is given to solve the problem.

    ① ② ③ ④ ⑤

14. A city's budget rose from $985,000 one year to $1,112,500 the next year. The mayor wants to give each of the 15 departments $15,000. In addition, several corporations have donated $55,000 to the city. How much more money than last year does the mayor have to work with?

    (1) $82,500 (2) $127,500
    (3) $137,500 (4) $182,500
    (5) $192,500

    ① ② ③ ④ ⑤

Basic Division Facts Division is the opposite of multiplication.

$2 \times 8 = 16$

$16 \div 2 = 8$, also written: $2\overline{)16}$ with 8 above

```
  8
2)16
```

To get ready for more difficult division problems, do the *Warm-up* below.

Warm-up

Practice the division problems below until you can get them all correct in thirty seconds.

	a	b	c	d	e	f
1.	$8\overline{)72}$	$9\overline{)63}$	$7\overline{)42}$	$6\overline{)36}$	$5\overline{)35}$	$6\overline{)0}$
2.	$5\overline{)45}$	$6\overline{)48}$	$8\overline{)24}$	$9\overline{)72}$	$4\overline{)36}$	$9\overline{)0}$

Long Division Here is a slightly more difficult division problem. Note each step carefully. Find $4{,}256 \div 7$.

Step 1

```
     6
7)4,256
  4 2
```

Will 7 go into 4? No. Will 7 go into 42? Yes. $7 \times 6 = 42$

Step 2

```
     6
7)4,256
  4 2
   05
```

Subtract 42 from 42 and bring down the 5.

Step 3

```
    60
7)4,256
  4 2
   056
```

Will 7 go into 5? No. Put a zero above the 5. Bring down the 6.

Step 4

```
   608
7)4,256
  4 2
   056
    56
     0
```

Will 7 go into 56? Yes. $7 \times 8 = 56$. Write down 56 under 56 and subtract. Nothing is left.

Here is a division problem with a two-digit divisor. Note each step carefully. Find $4{,}232 \div 46$.

Step 1

```
      8
46)4,232
   3 68
```

Will 46 go into 4? No. Will 46 go into 42? No. Will 46 go into 423? Yes. To estimate how many times 46 will go into 423, round 46 to 50 and 423 to 400. 50 will go into 400 8 times. $46 \times 8 = 368$

Step 2

```
      8
46)4,232
   3 68
     55
```

Subtract 368 from 423 ($423 - 368 = 55$).

Step 3

```
      9
46)4,232
   4 14
     92
```

Will 46 go into 55? Yes. The choice of 8 in the previous step was not large enough. Change the 8 to 9 ($9 \times 46 = 414$). Write down 414 and subtract. Bring down the 2.

Step 4

```
     92
46)4,232
   4 14
     92
     92
      0
```

Will 46 go into 92? Yes. Estimate that 50 will go into 100 2 times. $46 \times 2 = 92$. Write down 92 and subtract. The remainder is 0.

☑ A Test-Taking Tip

Because there are so many steps in a division problem, it is always wise to check your work. When you have a long division problem on the GED Test, you can check your work by multiplying your answer by the number you divided by. Then add in the remainder. The answer should match the number you divided.

Long Division with a Remainder Seldom will you have a long division problem with a remainder on the GED Mathematics Test. You should, however, know how to handle this type of problem, just in case your test has one.

```
     32 R32
38)1,248
   1 14
    108
     76
     32
```

Step 1 How many times will 38 go into 124? Write a 3 in the answer, above the 4.

Step 2 $38 \times 3 = 114$. Write your answer below the 124.

Step 3 $124 - 114 = 10$.

Step 4 Bring down the 8 and write it next to the 10. Now it reads 108.

Step 5 Determine how many times 38 will go into 108.

Step 6 $38 \times 2 = 76$. Write 76 under 108 and subtract. The answer is 32.

Step 7 Notice that 38 cannot go into 32. Therefore, your remainder is 32.

Warm-up Answers

	a	b	c	d	e	f
1.	9	7	6	6	7	0
2.	9	8	3	8	9	0

Warm-up

Neatly write and solve each problem below on a sheet of paper. Give yourself enough room to check your work. It's easy to make mistakes on division problems if your paper is cluttered and the numbers don't line up correctly or clearly.

1. 76 ÷ 4
2. 81 ÷ 3
3. 876 ÷ 6
4. 344 ÷ 8
5. 8,932 ÷ 4
6. 2,142 ÷ 7
7. 32,690 ÷ 5
8. 15,712 ÷ 8
9. 96 ÷ 24
10. 84 ÷ 14
11. 258 ÷ 86
12. 938 ÷ 67
13. 5,775 ÷ 25
14. 22,644 ÷ 37

☑ A Test-Taking Tip

On the GED Mathematics Test you will come across words in problems that indicate you should divide. Words and phrases like *average, each,* and *shared equally* tell you that you should divide.

Two-Step Division Problem Look at the problem below.

■ Last year Mr. and Mrs. Washington earned $26,400 and $19,200, respectively. What was their combined monthly income?

First, figure out exactly what information you need. You know you will need to find out their combined income by adding their separate incomes ($26,400 + $19,200). So their combined yearly income is $45,600. Notice that the problem does not ask for their total yearly income. It asks for their total *monthly* income. Since 12 months are in one year, you must divide their combined income ($45,600) by 12.

```
      $3,800
  12)$45,600
      36
       9 6
       9 6
```

The Washingtons' combined monthly income is $3,800.

You could also divide each salary by 12 and then add the results together. You will get the same answer.

Warm-up Answers
1. 19 **2.** 27 **3.** 146 **4.** 43 **5.** 2,233 **6.** 306 **7.** 6,538
8. 1,964 **9.** 4 **10.** 6 **11.** 3 **12.** 14 **13.** 231 **14.** 612

<u>Directions:</u> For each problem, choose the <u>one</u> best answer. Answers are on page 545.

15. A basketball team wants to reach a city 129 miles away in 3 hours. How many miles per hour must the bus average?

(1) 33 (2) 41 (3) 43
(4) 44 (5) 65

① ② ③ ④ ⑤

16. Mrs. Wilson bought 2 dozen mechanical pencils as gifts for her students. She paid $96 for the pencils. How much did each pencil cost?

(1) $2 (2) $3 (3) $4
(4) $8 (5) $12

① ② ③ ④ ⑤

17. If an assembly line in a bottling plant can fill 156 bottles a minute and 12 bottles go into a case, how many cases are filled each minute?

(1) 12 (2) 13 (3) 15
(4) 31 (5) 1,872

① ② ③ ④ ⑤

18. Three bars of soap cost 75 cents. How much will 8 bars cost?

(1) 25 cents (2) 75 cents
(3) 80 cents (4) $1 (5) $2

① ② ③ ④ ⑤

19. A car traveled 480 miles on 15 gallons of gas. What was the average number of miles it traveled per gallon of gas?

(1) 23 mi (2) 31 mi (3) 32 mi
(4) 495 mi (5) 7,200 mi

① ② ③ ④ ⑤

20. A gardener has 168 tulip bulbs and 72 iris bulbs to plant in rows of 16. Which of the following expressions correctly represents the number of rows the gardener can plant?

(1) $16 \times (168 + 72)$ (2) $\frac{168 + 72}{16}$

(3) $168 + 72 + 16$ (4) $168 + 72 - 16$

(5) $\frac{168 - 72}{16}$

① ② ③ ④ ⑤

Directions: For each problem, choose the one best answer. Answers begin on page 545.

21. A ferry that goes to an island carries 18 cars per trip. If 3,726 cars go to the island in June and 5,778 cars go to the island in July, how many trips will the ferry have to make during the two months?

    (1) 207 (2) 321 (3) 428
    (4) 528 (5) 726

    (1) (2) (3) (4) (5)

22. Before shipping the last 17,043 telephones to the Phone Mart, a control clerk checked every 39th telephone to make sure it worked properly. The clerk discovered 17 damaged telephones. How many telephones did the clerk check that were not damaged?

    (1) 45 (2) 347 (3) 420 (4) 437
    (5) Insufficient data is given to solve the problem.

    (1) (2) (3) (4) (5)

23. A crate of 357 oranges that cost $65 is sent to an office where 17 people work. If each person eats one orange each day, how many weeks will it be before the oranges are all gone?

    (1) 3 (2) 4 (3) 12 (4) 15 (5) 21

    (1) (2) (3) (4) (5)

24. Suzanne jogged 2,184 miles last year. After she jogs 250 miles she needs to buy new jogging shoes that cost $49. How much money did she spend on jogging shoes last year?

    (1) $292 (2) $392 (3) $441
    (4) $490 (5) $500

    (1) (2) (3) (4) (5)

25. Each of the 73 members of the club donated an equal amount of money each month to pay the rent and the utility bills for the club room. If the rent was $584 and the utilities were $219 for the month, how much did each member donate this month?

    (1) $5 (2) $6 (3) $8
    (4) $10 (5) $11

    (1) (2) (3) (4) (5)

Reviewing a Multistep Word Problem Look at the following problem.

■ The library has 3,576 books that are either in need of repair or are beyond repair. The librarian decides that 888 books are beyond repair and packs the remaining books in cartons that each hold 28 books. The cartons are to be loaded into vans to be taken to the binder. If each van can hold 32 cartons, how many vans will be needed to transport the books?

You will need to know the total number of books that the library has (3,576) and the number that are beyond repair (888) to find the number of books that need to be repaired. (3,576 − 888 = 2,688).

Then you will need to divide the number of books to be repaired (2,688) by 28 (the number of books that fit into each carton) to find the number of cartons needed.

```
     96
28)2,688
   2 52
     168
     168
       0
```

And, finally, you will divide the number of cartons (96) by 32 to find out how many vans are needed. (96 ÷ 32 = 3). Three vans are needed to transport the books.

Check that your answer makes sense. You can estimate that about 3,000 books need to be repaired. Since about 30 books fit into each carton, about 100 cartons will be used. Since each van holds about 30 cartons, about 3 vans will be needed.

Warm-up

Solve this multistep problem.

■ A store clerk opens several cartons of canned soup. The cartons contain 961 cans. All but 65 of the cans are to be put on the shelves. If 28 shelves are used and 8 cans are to be in each row, how many rows of cans will be on each shelf?

Warm-up Answer
Step 1: 961 − 65 = 896 (number of cans to be shelved)
Step 2: 896 ÷ 28 = 32 (number of cans on each shelf)
Step 3: 32 ÷ 8 = 4 (4 rows of cans on each shelf)

Decimals

Decimals are parts of whole numbers. When something is divided into ten equal parts, each part is *one-tenth.* You can write the decimal 0.1 to show one-tenth. When something is divided into a hundred or a thousand equal parts, you can write the decimals 0.01 and 0.001 to show *one-hundredth* and *one-thousandth.* Notice that all decimal numbers end in *th*.

Writing amounts of money is the most familiar way of writing decimals.

\$5.36 = 5 dollars, or 5 whole units, or 5.00
+ 3 dimes, or 3 tenths of a dollar, or 0.30
+ 6 cents, or 6 hundredths of a dollar, or 0.06

On the GED Mathematics Test, *most* problems that measure your knowledge of decimals will deal with money. Decimals can, however, be used in other ways.

The weather report may say that 2.5 inches of snow fell last night. What does the 0.5 mean? It means that 2 *and* $\frac{5}{10}$ inches of snow fell. If the report said that 2.05 inches fell, it would mean that 2 and $\frac{5}{100}$ inches fell.

To understand decimals, you must realize that the value of the decimal depends on the number of digits to the right of the decimal point.

Memorize the information on the chart below so you will remember the value associated with each place. To aid your memory, just think of the way money is written: 1 cent is 0.01, and ten cents are 0.10. The chart shows whole numbers and decimal numbers.

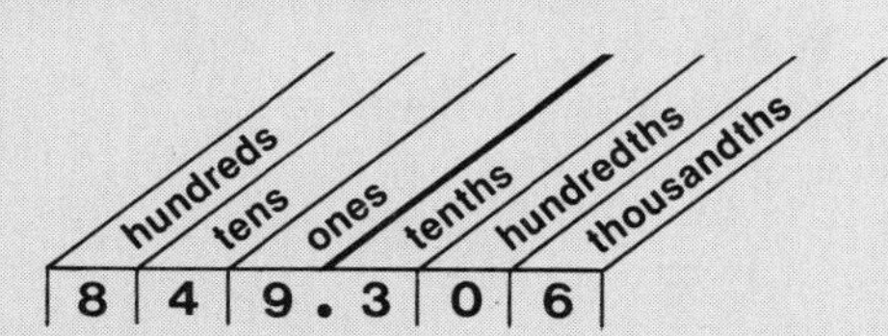

Read the whole number:	849
Read the decimal point as "and":	and
Read the decimal number:	306
Add the correct *th* word:	thousandths

The value of decimals is not changed by adding or taking away zeros from the right of the decimal number.

1.8 = 1.80 = 1.800 = 1.8000

Warm-up

Complete the sentences by referring to the illustration below.

1. The first place to the right of the decimal point is called ______________.

2. The third place to the left of the decimal point is called ______________.

3. The third place to the right of the decimal point is called ______________.

Write the decimal.

4. four tenths ______

5. five hundredths ______

6. nineteen thousandths ______

Express these decimals in words.

7. .3 ______________

8. 4.095 ______________

9. .881 ______________

10. 62.04 ______________

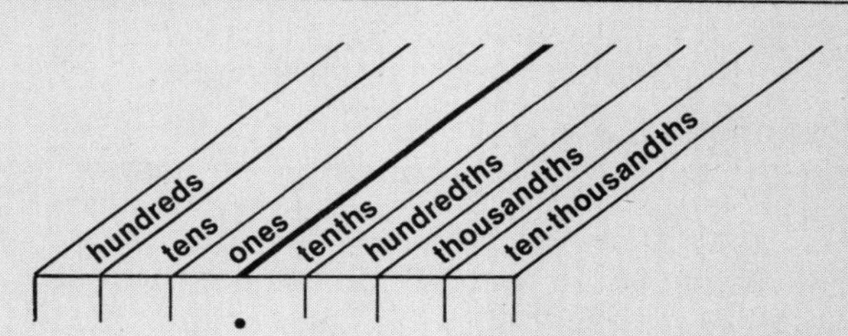

Warm-up Answers

1. tenths **2.** hundreds **3.** thousandths **4.** .4 **5.** 0.05 **6.** 0.019 **7.** three tenths **8.** four and ninety-five thousandths **9.** eight hundred eighty-one thousandths **10.** sixty-two and four hundredths

Rounding Money and decimals can be rounded in the same way as whole numbers are rounded. Money can be rounded to the nearest dime or dollar. A decimal can be rounded to the nearest tenth, hundredth, thousandth, or whatever size number you are working with.

To round decimals, look at the decimal digit to the *right* of the decimal digit you are rounding. If the digit is 5 or greater, add one to the number you are rounding. If the digit is less than 5, drop it and all other numbers to the right.

Now round 0.638 to the nearest *hundredth.*

0.638 8 is greater than 5.

Add 1 to 3 hundredths and drop the 8 thousandths. The answer is 0.64.

Round 0.638 to the nearest *tenth.*

0.638 3 is less than 5.

Drop both the 3 hundredths and the 8 thousandths. The answer is 0.6.

Now round 0.638 to the nearest *one.*

0.638 6 is greater than 5.

Add one to 0 and drop the 6 tenths, the 3 hundredths, and the 8 thousandths. The answer is 1.

How would you round 547.089 to the nearest one? Notice that 7 is in the ones column. Look at the digit to the right of the 7. Since 0 is less than 5, drop all the numbers to the right of the decimal. The answer is 547.

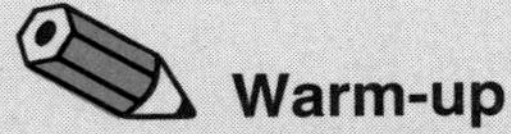

Warm-up

Round to the nearest dime.

1. $0.18 **2.** $3.47 **3.** $4.23 **4.** $.84

Round to the nearest dollar.
5. $5.67 **6.** $801.42 **7.** $0.78 **8.** $21.33

Round to the nearest tenth.
9. 0.14 **10.** 0.392 **11.** 0.277 **12.** 8.83

Round to the nearest hundredth.
13. 0.9867 **14.** 87.4091
15. 42.0026 **16.** 0.55895

Warm-up Answers
1. $.20 **2.** $3.50 **3.** $4.20 **4.** $.80 **5.** $6.00 **6.** $801.00
7. $1.00 **8.** $21.00 **9.** 0.1 **10.** 0.4 **11.** 0.3 **12.** 8.8
13. 0.99 **14.** 87.41 **15.** 42.00 **16.** 0.56

Adding Decimals The following steps show how to add sums of money.

Step 1 Write the numbers in a column, lining up the decimal points.

Step 2 Add as with whole numbers.

Step 3 Bring the decimal point straight down into the answer.

Add $15.53, 50 cents, and 5 cents.

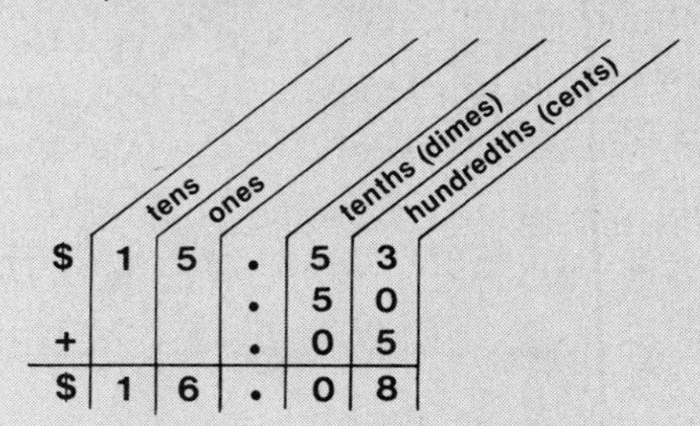

Add decimals just as you add sums of money. Write the numbers in a column, lining up the decimal points. Put a decimal point to the right of any whole number. Remember to write a decimal point in the sum.

Add the numbers 0.62, 10, 0.005, and 302.4.

$$\begin{array}{r} 0.62\mathbf{0} \\ 10.\mathbf{000} \\ 0.005 \\ +\ 302.4\mathbf{00} \\ \hline 313.025 \end{array}$$

Notice the zeros that have been added to the numbers. These zeros do not change the value of the numbers, but they do make it easier to add numbers that are in the same column. Always remember to align the decimal points.

Warm-up

Solve these addition problems.

1. 4.2 + 3.7
2. 6.4 + 3.5
3. 0.81 + 0.57
4. $2.06 + $7.29
5. $1.96 + $3.75
6. 0.062 + 0.814
7. 1.039 + 3.684
8. 0.2 + 0.6 + 0.4
9. $.09 + $3.60 + $1.50
10. 2.8 + 0.139 + 0.48

Warm-up Answers
1. 7.9 **2.** 9.9 **3.** 1.38 **4.** $9.35 **5.** $5.71 **6.** 0.876
7. 4.723 **8.** 1.2 **9.** $5.19 **10.** 3.419

Addition Word Problems Addition word problems with decimals are no different from addition word problems with whole numbers. Just remember to bring the decimal point down. Here is a sample word problem and the steps you would take to solve it.

■ Mrs. Tobias went shopping for her daughter's birthday party. She bought paper plates, a tablecloth, and napkins for $5.98, balloons for $.70, cake for $12.75, and ice cream for $3.85. What was her total bill?

(a) $0.50 (b) $23.28 (c) $25.04
(d) $35.75 (e) $40.00

Read the word problem carefully several times. Make a mental picture of the problem. Imagine each party item with a price tag. Think of the sales receipt Mrs. Tobias received from the clerk. Then picture the receipt as an addition problem.

Look for key words or phrases in the word problem. The word *total* is a key word for addition.

Find the four numbers in the problem that are to be added.

Set up the addition problem. Be sure to line up the decimal points. Then add.

$$\begin{array}{r} \$\ 5.98 \\ .70 \\ 12.75 \\ +\ 3.85 \\ \hline \$\ 23.28 \end{array}$$

The answer is (b).

Don't forget to check your arithmetic and to check that your answer makes sense.

You can estimate that $5.98 is about $6, .70 is about $1, $12.75 is about $13, and $3.85 is about $4. The total is about $24. Answers (a), (d), and (e) are too far off.

☑ A Test-Taking Tip

When taking the GED Mathematics Test, write the number of each question on your paper beside your computation for that question so you can double-check your work if you have time.

Directions: For each problem, choose the one best answer. Answers are on page 546.

1. What is the total bill for the following groceries, including sales tax: apple juice $1.49, meat $2.38, bread $1.03, bananas $.78, and soup $.39?

   (1) $5.98 (2) $6.07
   (3) $6.17 (4) $17.00
   (5) Insufficient data is given to solve the problem.

   ① ② ③ ④ ⑤

2. Before a trip, a car's odometer read 23,465.2 miles. What was the reading after the car was driven 223.8 miles?

   (1) 248 (2) 23,688.2 (3) 23,689
   (4) 23,703.8 (5) 45,090

   ① ② ③ ④ ⑤

3. A customer bought 1.62 pounds of cheddar cheese, 0.85 pounds of Edam cheese, and 2.10 pounds of Swiss cheese. How many pounds of cheese did he buy in all?

   (1) 2.6 lb (2) 4.57 lb
   (3) 8.3 lb (4) 45.7 lb
   (5) Insufficient data is given to solve the problem.

   ① ② ③ ④ ⑤

4. Pollution increased 0.034 parts per million over an earlier figure of 0.186 parts per million. What is the newer pollution count per million?

   (1) 0.11 (2) 0.152 (3) 0.21
   (4) 0.22 (5) 0.526

   ① ② ③ ④ ⑤

5. A driver going 45 miles per hour must stop suddenly. If he travels 49.3 feet during his reaction time and 112.5 feet while he is braking, how far does he travel before he stops?

   (1) 159.4 ft (2) 161.8 ft (3) 172.7 ft
   (4) 340 ft (5) 615.5 ft

   ① ② ③ ④ ⑤

Directions: For each problem, choose the one best answer. Answers are on page 546.

6. Rose bought a desk on sale for $199.49 and saved $65.51. Her charge account balance was $83.60. What was the original price of the desk?

   (1) 133.98 (2) $165.00 (3) $217.58
   (4) $265.00 (5) $348.60

   (1) (2) (3) (4) (5)

7. The balance in Sarah's checking account was $523.46. How much did she have after she wrote checks for $17.87 and $18.65?

   (1) $650.94 (2) $559.98
   (3) $586.84 (4) $568.96
   (5) $486.94

   (1) (2) (3) (4) (5)

8. Jason bought one item for $2.98 and another item for $4.88. Which of the following expressions correctly represents the change he received if he gave the clerk a $20 bill?

   (1) $7.86 + $4.88 − $20.00
   (2) $20.00 − ($2.98 + $4.88)
   (3) $20.00 − $7.86
   (4) $20.00 × ($7.86 + $4.88)
   (5) $20.00 − $4.88

   (1) (2) (3) (4) (5)

9. One dry area in the United States averages 14.2 inches of rain per year. By June, 5.3 inches of rain had fallen. How many more inches must fall before the area gets its average rainfall?

   (1) 8.9 (2) 9.5 (3) 9.9
   (4) 14.2 (5) 19.5

   (1) (2) (3) (4) (5)

10. A grocery bill amounted to $43.31. The customer had coupons worth $2.35. The sales tax was $0.86. How much did the customer pay in all?

   (1) $40.96 (2) $41.82 (3) $52.45
   (4) $53.84 (5) $75.08

   (1) (2) (3) (4) (5)

Subtracting Decimals Remember that zeros added to the right of the last digit in a decimal number do not change the value of the number. They are sometimes needed when you are subtracting decimal numbers.

Here is how to subtract decimals.

Step 1 Write the numbers in a column, lining up the decimal points. Put the larger number (the number with the highest value) on top.

Step 2 If necessary, add zeros to the right of the digits.

Step 3 Subtract as with whole numbers.

Step 4 Bring the decimal point straight down into the answer.

Subtract 89 cents from 5 dollars.

$$\begin{array}{lcrcr} \text{5 dollar} & = & \$5.00 & = & \$\overset{4}{\cancel{5}}.\overset{9}{\cancel{0}}\overset{1}{0} \\ \text{89 cents} & = & -\ .89 & = & -\ .89 \\ \cline{3-3}\cline{5-5} & & & & \$4.11 \end{array}$$

If you have forgotten how to borrow, turn to page 414 and reread the explanation. Then study the example carefully again.

Subtract 0.008 from 0.67.

$$\begin{array}{r} .67 \\ -.008 \\ \hline \end{array} \qquad \begin{array}{r} .67\mathbf{0} \\ -.008 \\ \hline \end{array} \qquad \begin{array}{r} .6\overset{6}{\cancel{7}}\overset{1}{0} \\ -.008 \\ \hline .662 \end{array}$$

Did you notice that a zero was added?

.67 = .670

Subtract 15.312 from 24.5.

$$\begin{array}{r} 24.5 \\ -15.312 \\ \hline \end{array} \qquad \begin{array}{r} 24.5\mathbf{00} \\ -15.312 \\ \hline \end{array} \qquad \begin{array}{r} 24.\overset{4}{\cancel{5}}\overset{9}{\cancel{0}}\overset{1}{0} \\ -15.312 \\ \hline .188 \end{array} \qquad \begin{array}{r} \overset{1}{\cancel{2}}\overset{1}{4}.500 \\ -15.312 \\ \hline 9.188 \end{array}$$

Before doing the word problems in the white column on this page, do the *Warm-up* problems in the tinted column on the next page. Then do the word problems on both pages.

Need a Hint for Number 10?
This is a two-step problem. Coupons decrease *the amount of a bill. Sales tax* adds *to it.*

Warm-up

Solve these subtraction problems.

1. 88.4 − 53.7
2. 74.8 − 2.5
3. $76.47 − $21.35
4. $53.07 − $21.64
5. $100 − $4.69
6. $47.79 − $.38
7. 8.537 − 4.216
8. 32.045 − 18.637
9. 87.26 − 59.8
10. 97.16 − 3.2
11. 54.07 − 6.1
12. 58.241 − 3.19
13. 71.29 − 55
14. 82.91 − 7.525
15. 50.3 − 36.218
16. 83.7 − 0.625
17. 92.1 − 17.066
18. 41 − 29.489

Complete the table. An example has been done for you. To compute your change, $4.50 was subtracted from $5.00.

	Your Bill	You Pay	Your Change
	$ 4.50	$ 5.00	$0.50
19.	$21.98	$25.03	________
20.	$32.81	$50.01	________
21.	$ 8.04	$10.00	________
22.	$ 4.23	$ 5.00	________

Need a Hint for Number 11?
This is a two-step problem. You must subtract *the restaurant's costs from $100 to find the profit. But first you must find the* total *amount of the costs.*

Need a Hint for Number 13?
The word increase *is usually a key word for addition. In this case, the phrase* amount of increase *actually means "difference," which tells you to subtract.*

Warm-up Answers
1. 34.7 **2.** 72.3 **3.** $55.12 **4.** $31.43 **5.** $95.31 **6.** $47.41 **7.** 4.321 **8.** 13.408 **9.** 27.46 **10.** 93.96 **11.** 47.97 **12.** 55.051 **13.** 16.29 **14.** 75.385 **15.** 14.082 **16.** 83.075 **17.** 75.034 **18.** 11.511 **19.** $3.05 **20.** $17.20 **21.** $1.96 **22.** $.77

11. Out of every $100 taken in, a restaurant spends $34.80 on food, $60.00 on labor, and $1.40 on advertising. Profit is what is left of the $100.00. Which of the following expressions correctly represents the profit the restaurant makes on every $100.00 it takes in?

(1) $34.86 + $60.00 + $1.40
(2) $100.00 × ($34.80 + $60.00 + $1.40)
(3) $34.80 + $60.00 + $1.40 − $100
(4) $100.00 − ($34.80 + $60.00 + $1.40)
(5) $\dfrac{\$34.80 + \$60.00 + \$1.40}{\$100.00}$

① ② ③ ④ ⑤

12. Mrs. Arndt takes a round-trip flight from Los Angeles to San Francisco that costs $138.00. Her sister, who has a fear of flying, takes the bus for $48.85 and returns by train for $63.00. How much more money does Mrs. Arndt spend?

(1) $21.95 (2) $23.95 (3) $26.15
(4) $50.65 (5) $55.75

① ② ③ ④ ⑤

13. The barometric reading was 29.437 on Monday. On Tuesday it was 30.231. What was the amount of increase?

(1) .206 (2) .794 (3) .887
(4) .894 (5) 1.674

① ② ③ ④ ⑤

14. Claude owed $10.26 for the plants he was buying at the nursery. He gave the clerk $11.00 in bills and one penny. How much change did Claude receive?

(1) $0.39 (2) $0.74 (3) $0.75
(4) $0.84 (5) $1.75

① ② ③ ④ ⑤

15. A discus thrower's record throw was 64.78 meters. His best throw in a recent competition was 4.64 meters shorter than his record. How far did he throw the discus recently?

(1) 50.20 m (2) 59.14 m
(3) 59.42 m (4) 59.865 m
(5) 60.14 m

① ② ③ ④ ⑤

Directions: For each problem, choose the one best answer. Answers begin on page 546.

16. If leaded gas costs $1.12 a gallon and unleaded gas costs $1.26 a gallon, how much would it cost to fill a 16-gallon tank?

 (1) $7.92 (2) $17.82
 (3) $17.92 (4) $25.64
 (5) Insufficient data is given to solve the problem.

 ① ② ③ ④ ⑤

17. A store has a stock of 2,240 records that cost $4.95 each. What is its inventory worth?

 (1) $23,450 (2) $15,006
 (3) $13,450 (4) $12,008
 (5) $11,088

 ① ② ③ ④ ⑤

18. How much does Miranda earn in a week if she works 37.5 hours at $7.36 an hour?

 (1) $27.60 (2) $276.00
 (3) $314.48 (4) $323.45
 (5) $604.00

 ① ② ③ ④ ⑤

19. How much is an electric bill if 197 kilowatt hours were used in one apartment and 189 kilowatt hours were used in another apartment? The cost of electric power is $0.059 per kilowatt hour.

 (1) $22.77 (2) $31.77 (3) $32.67
 (4) $42.31 (5) $56.78

 ① ② ③ ④ ⑤

20. If pineapples sell for 39 cents a pound, how much would a pineapple that weighs 3.41 pounds cost?

 (1) $4.43 (2) $2.34 (3) $1.57
 (4) $1.33 (5) $1.13

 ① ② ③ ④ ⑤

21. Luis bought a shirt for $12.50 and a tie for $5.00. To find the tax, he multiplied the total by 0.06. How much did he spend altogether?

 (1) $12.35 (2) $18.55 (3) $24.95
 (4) $28.55 (5) $108.55

 ① ② ③ ④ ⑤

Multiplying Decimals Here is how you multiply two decimals.

Step 1: Multiply as with whole numbers.

$$\begin{array}{r} 23.71 \\ \times \quad 1.5 \\ \hline 11855 \\ 2371 \\ \hline 35565 \end{array}$$

Step 2: Count the number of decimal places in *both* numbers of the problem and add them. Be sure to count to the *right* of the decimal points.

$$\begin{array}{r} 23.71 \\ \times \quad 1.5 \\ \hline \end{array} \qquad \begin{array}{r} 2 \text{ places} \\ + \ 1 \text{ place} \\ \hline 3 \text{ places} \end{array}$$

Step 3: Count off this total number of decimal places in the answer (count from right to left) and place the decimal point there.

$$\begin{array}{r} 23.71 \\ \times \quad 1.5 \\ \hline 35.565 \end{array} \quad 3 \text{ places}$$

The answer is 35,565.

When there are fewer digits in the answer than the total number of places to the right of the decimal point, add zeros to the *left* of the last digit as placeholders.

$$\begin{array}{r} 7.09 \\ \times \ .003 \\ \hline 2127 \end{array} \qquad \begin{array}{r} 2 \text{ places} \\ + \ 3 \text{ places} \\ \hline 5 \text{ places} \end{array} \qquad \begin{array}{r} 7.09 \\ \times \ .003 \\ \hline .02127 \end{array}$$

A zero is placed before the 2 so that five numbers would be to the right of the decimal. It has to be placed *before* the 2 to indicate that the number is smaller. Adding a zero after the 7 would not have lowered the decimal's value.

Warm-up

Solve these multiplication problems.

1. 40.5 × 9
2. 1.08 × 7
3. 2.16 × 3.8
4. $9.56 × 1.5
5. 5,362 × 0.08
6. 43.7 × 0.6
7. 8.33 × 2.56
8. 900 × 0.28
9. 2.31 × 0.002
10. 4.27 × 0.015

Warm-up Answers

1. 364.5 **2.** $7.56 **3.** 8.208 **4.** $14.34 **5.** 428.96 **6.** 26.22 **7.** 21.3248 **8.** 252 **9.** 0.00462 **10.** 0.06405

Multiplying Decimals by Tens If you need to use 10, 100, or 1,000 to solve a decimal word problem, try this shortcut.

Note the number of zeros in each of these numbers. 10 has one zero, 100 has two zeros, and 1,000 has three zeros. When multiplying a decimal by one of these numbers, just move the decimal point to the right as many places as there are zeros in 10, 100, or 1,000. Add zeros if necessary.

10 × 27.5 = 275
10 × 2.75 = 27.5
10 × .275 = 2.75

100 × 1.53 = 153
100 × 15.3 = 1,530
100 × 153 = 15,300

1,000 × 1.675 = 1,675
1,000 × 16.75 = 16,750
1,000 × 167.5 = 167,500

Warm-up

Solve these multiplication problems.

1. 10 × .05
2. 32.721 × 1,000
3. 1,000 × 0.13
4. 100 × 0.675
5. 0.988 × 10
6. 10,000 × 3.013

Need a Hint for Number 23?
Will the number of miles per hour be greater or less than the number of kilometers per hour? Because a mile is longer than a kilometer, a person will travel fewer miles than kilometers in an hour.

Need a Hint for Number 26?
This problem requires several operations. The question asks for the worker's total earnings in one week (addition). But first you must find how much the worker earned for 40 hours (multiplication). Then you must determine how many overtime hours were worked (subtraction) and how much was earned in overtime pay (multiplication). Then you must find the worker's total pay (addition).

Warm-up Answers
1. .5 **2.** 32,721 **3.** 130 **4.** 67.5 **5.** 9.88
6. 30,130 (There are 4 zeros in 10,000; therefore, you move the decimal point 4 places to the right.)

22. A jet plane costs $22.4 million. An airline company has ordered 18 new jets. How much are they worth?

(1) $504.3 million (2) $423.2 million
(3) $403.2 million (4) $393.4 million
(5) $1.24 million

① ② ③ ④ ⑤

23. Many people travel at 90 kilometers per hour on the West German highways. If 1 kilometer equals 0.62 miles, how many miles per hour are they driving?

(1) 48.5 (2) 51.2 (3) 55.8
(4) 60.0 (5) 82.0

① ② ③ ④ ⑤

24. Land is valued at $16.67 per square foot. How much are two lots worth that measure 427.6 square feet and 572.4 square feet?

(1) $16,670 (2) $25,000
(3) $48,900 (4) $50,210
(5) $60,400

① ② ③ ④ ⑤

25. A truck that weighs 8,000 pounds can pull a load 7.8 times its own weight. How heavy a load can it pull?

(1) 62,400 lb (2) 62,600 lb
(3) 63,800 lb (4) 624,000 lb
(5) 638,000 lb

① ② ③ ④ ⑤

26. An apprentice earns $4.30 an hour during a regular 40-hour week and is paid 1.5 times the hourly rate for overtime. Which expression correctly represents the earnings for an apprentice who works 52 hours in one week?

(1) 40 × ($4.30 × 1.5)
(2) 52 × $4.30
(3) (40 × $4.30) + (12 × $4.30)
(4) (40 × $4.30) + 12 × ($4.30 × 1.5)
(5) (40 × $4.30) − 12 × ($4.30 × 1.5)

① ② ③ ④ ⑤

<u>Directions:</u> For each problem, choose the <u>one</u> best answer. Answers begin on page 547.

27. A box of disposable diapers comes with a coupon for 2 free diapers and costs $3.24. If there are 12 diapers in each box, how much does each diaper cost?

(1) $0.27 (2) $0.35
(3) $0.48 (4) $0.53
(5) Insufficient data is given to solve the problem.

(1) (2) (3) (4) (5)

28. The profit from a dry-cleaning business for one year was $33,464.52. The next year the profit was $37,586.48. How much did each of the 2 partners earn during this 2-year period if they split the profits evenly?

(1) $4,278.50 (2) $16,732.26
(3) $18,793.24 (4) $35,525.50
(5) $38,505.45

(1) (2) (3) (4) (5)

29. Each of the 96 students who buy lunch in the school cafeteria must receive 4 ounces of vegetables daily. How many 32-ounce cans of vegetables are used each day?

(1) 7 (2) 9 (3) 12 (4) 15
(5) 394

(1) (2) (3) (4) (5)

30. At a home demonstration party, 9 guests put in orders for products. The orders totaled $96.30. What was the average amount of the orders?

(1) $9.80 (2) $10.70 (3) $15.75
(4) $19.70 (5) $43.82

(1) (2) (3) (4) (5)

31. In June a plane flew from Los Angeles to Chicago, a distance of 2,048 miles, in 3.9 hours. Another plane flew from Chicago to Los Angeles. Due to a storm, this flight took 4.2 hours. How much slower did the second plane fly than the first plane? (Round your answer to the nearest whole unit.)

(1) 25 mph (2) 37 mph (3) 400 mph
(4) 488 mph (5) 525 mph

(1) (2) (3) (4) (5)

Dividing with Decimals Divison with decimals is the same as division with whole numbers. The important thing to remember is the placement of the decimal point.

Dividing Decimals by Whole Numbers Find 78.05 ÷ 25.

Step 1 Write the problem as usual.

```
25)78.05
```

Step 2 Put the decimal point in the answer directly above its place in the problem.

```
     .
25)78.05
```

```
    3.12
25)78.05
   75
    3 0
    2 5
      55
      50
       5
```

Step 3 Divide as with whole numbers. If you have forgotten how to do division problems, reread the explanation on page 420.

```
    3.122
25)78.050
   75
    3 0
    2 5
      55
      50
       50
      550
        0
```

Remember that zeros added to the right of the decimal point do not change the value. When you have a remainder in decimal division, add a zero and continue dividing.

The answer is 3.122.

You use the same system when you divide dollars and cents by whole numbers.

A dollar amount can be changed to cents by moving the decimal point 2 places to the right: $.065 = 6.5¢

Warm-up

Divide.

1. $5.22 ÷ 3
2. 48.6 ÷ 18
3. $62.55 ÷ 9
4. 547.4 ÷ 85
5. 93.33 ÷ 15
6. 136.77 ÷ 47
7. $138.54 ÷ 23
8. 434.16 ÷ 36
9. $174.86 ÷ 14
10. $209.44 ÷ 22

Warm-up Answers
1. $1.74 **2.** 2.7 **3.** $6.95 **4.** 6.44 **5.** 6.22 **6.** 2.91 **7.** $6.02 **8.** 12.06 **9.** $12.49 **10.** $9.52

Dividing Whole Numbers by Decimals Find 68 ÷ 0.34.

Step 1 Place a decimal point after the whole number (68.). Add as many zeros as there are digits in the decimal number.

0.34)68.00

Step 2 Now move the decimal point in the number by which you are dividing (0.34) to make it a whole number (34.). Move the decimal point in the number that is being divided (68.00) the same number of places to the right (6800.). Place the decimal point in the answer directly above this one, as shown below.

34.)6800.

Step 3 Divide as with whole numbers.

```
     200.
34.)6800.
    68
     00
     00
      0
```

The answer is 200.

Use the same steps when you divide whole numbers by cents.

To divide 45 by $0.15, place a decimal point to the right of the whole number (45.). Move the decimal point in the number you are dividing by (0.15) to make it a whole number (15.), and add the same number of zeros to the nunber that is being divided (45.00). Move the decimal point to the right the same number of places (4500), and place the decimal point in the answer directly above it. Divide as with whole numbers.

```
                                  300.
$0.15)45.    $15.)45.00    $15.)4500.
                                45
                                 00
                                 00
                                  0
```

The answer is 300.

Warm-up

Divide.

1. 128 ÷ 0.16
2. 72 ÷ 0.08
3. 72 ÷ 0.8
4. 204 ÷ 1.02
5. $169 ÷ 0.13
6. $275 ÷ 2.5

Warm-up Answers
1. 800 **2.** 900 **3.** 90 **4.** 200 **5.** $1,300 **6.** $110

32. What is the hourly pay of a factory worker who earns $313.60 for a 40-hour week?

(1) $5.68 (2) $7.84 (3) $7.89
(4) $8.49 (5) $9.42

① ② ③ ④ ⑤

33. If you have 43 yards of fabric that cost $128.57, how much did each yard cost?

(1) $0.99 (2) $1.99 (3) $2.99
(4) $3.98 (5) $4.98

① ② ③ ④ ⑤

34. Fay wants to buy a new stereo that costs $639.95. She has already saved $155.45. How much will Fay have to save each week if she wants to buy the stereo for her birthday which is 19 weeks away?

(1) $20.50 (2) $21.50 (3) $22.50
(4) $25.50 (5) $30.50

① ② ③ ④ ⑤

35. If a 48-ounce box of detergent costs $1.20, what is the cost per ounce?

(1) 0.025¢ (2) 0.12¢ (3) 0.25¢
(4) 1.2¢ (5) 2.5¢

① ② ③ ④ ⑤

36. The total weight of the contents of the crates in three moving vans is 22,698.28 pounds. If each crate holds 708.9 pounds, how many crates are in each van?

(1) 18 (2) 32
(3) 1,098 (4) 7,006
(5) Insufficient data is given to solve the problem.

① ② ③ ④ ⑤

Directions: For each problem, choose the one best answer. Answers are on page 548.

37. Scientists used sound to measure the depths of three oceans. Sound travels through water at a speed of 1.5 kilometers per second. If it takes 3.8 seconds for a sound to reach the ocean bottom, how many kilometers deep is the ocean?

(1) 0.57 (2) 5.07 (3) 5.7 (4) 57
(5) Insufficient data is given to solve the problem.

① ② ③ ④ ⑤

38. Fish underwater appear to be 1.25 times larger than they really are. Scuba divers see 26 fish. One diver sees a fish that appears to be 58.25 inches. How many inches long is the fish?

(1) 4.66 (2) 32.5
(3) 46.6 (4) 1,514.5
(5) Insufficient data is given to solve the problem.

① ② ③ ④ ⑤

39. Molly uses 23.8 inches of ribbon on each package that she wraps. If she has used 404.6 inches of ribbon, how many packages has she wrapped?

(1) 17 (2) 20 (3) 21
(4) 31 (5) 41

① ② ③ ④ ⑤

40. How many monthly payments of $199.49 are needed to pay off a loan of $4,787.76?

(1) 12 (2) 16 (3) 22
(4) 24 (5) 38

① ② ③ ④ ⑤

41. A fund-raising group collected $696.50. It donated half the money to a scholarship fund and half to the library. How many library books did the donation buy if each book cost $9.95?

(1) 32 (2) 35 (3) 47
(4) 48 (5) 50

① ② ③ ④ ⑤

Dividing Decimals by Decimals Find 0.213 ÷ 0.05.

Step 1 Write the problem as usual.

.05).213

Step 2 Move the decimal point in the number you are dividing by (.05) to make it a whole number (5). Move the decimal point in the number that is being divided (.213) the same number of places to the right (21.3). Place the decimal point directly above in the answer.

50.)21.3

Step 3 Divide as with whole numbers.

```
   4.2
5)21.3
  20
   1 3
   1 0
     3
```

The answer is 4.2.

Use the same steps when you divide dollars and cents by dollars and cents.

Dividing by Tens The shortcut method you learned for multiplying decimals by 10, 100, and 1,000—moving the decimal point—is also a shortcut method for dividing decimals by 10, 100, and 1,000. When dividing, move the decimal point to the *left* the same number of places as there are zeros.

6.759 ÷ 10 = 0.6759
6.759 ÷ 100 = 0.06759
6.759 ÷ 1000 = 0.006759

Warm-up

Divide.

1. 9.6 ÷ 3.2
2. 0.639 ÷ 0.15
3. $12.65 ÷ $1.15
4. $62.90 ÷ $7.40
5. 0.1476 ÷ 3.6
6. 9.867 ÷ 10
7. 9.867 ÷ 0.10
8. 0.0735 ÷ 0.07
9. $37.24 ÷ $2.66
10. $64.50 ÷ $3.75

Warm-up Answers
1. 3 **2.** 4.26 **3.** $11 **4.** $8.50 **5.** 0.041 **6.** 0.986 **7.** 98.67 **8.** 1.05 **9.** $14 **10.** $17.20

Solving Three- and Four-Step Decimal Word Problems Here is a sample word problem that requires more than one operation to solve.

■ For a camping trip, Max Cruz and his friend bought two sleeping bags for $79.00, a tent for $64.98, and food totaling $30.52. The sales tax was $0.04 per dollar. If Max and his friend split the bill, how much did Max pay?

(a) $83.76 (b) $87.25 (c) $90.74
(d) $97.40 (e) $181.48

First, you must find the *total* of the bill before tax. Therefore, you add.

```
 $ 79.00
   64.98
  +30.52
 $174.50   (before tax)
```

Second, you must find how much tax was owed. A tax of $0.04 *per* dollar tells you to multiply.

```
 $174.50
 ×   .04
 $6.9800   (tax)
```

To find the *total* bill, add.

```
 $174.50
 +  6.98
 $181.48   (total bill)
```

Since Max and his friend split the bill, Max paid half. To find *half* of the total bill, divide by 2.

```
   $ 90.74
 2)$181.48
    18
      1 4
      1 4
        8
        8
        0
```

The answer is (c), $90.74.

☑ A Test-Taking Tip

Remember the system for solving a GED word problem.

a. Read the problem carefully to understand the question.
b. Find the information you need.
c. Decide which operation or operations to use.
d. Set up the problem.
e. Compute the problem.
f. Check your arithmetic.
g. See if your answer makes sense.

42. The women's softball team ordered the following items: 12 team shirts at $12.95 a shirt, 7 softballs at $8.49 each, and 9 mitts at $23.79 each. They were charged $10.00 for postage and handling. How much was their total bill?

(1) $45.23 (2) $55.23 (3) $428.94
(4) $438.94 (5) $439.84

① ② ③ ④ ⑤

43. Helen earns $8.38 an hour on weekdays and time and a half on Saturdays and Sundays. She works 40 hours from Monday to Friday and 9.25 hours on Saturday and Sunday. How much money does she earn? (Round to the nearest cent.)

(1) $116.27 (2) $215.79 (3) $335.20
(4) $451.47 (5) $493.40

① ② ③ ④ ⑤

44. To send a parcel 250 miles by air, the cost is $0.62 for the first pound and $0.35 for each pound after that. Susan wants to send a parcel weighing 27.6 pounds, but she only has $5.29 with her. How much more money does she need?

(1) $4.02 (2) $4.64 (3) $9.31
(4) $9.93 (5) $17.11

① ② ③ ④ ⑤

45. Section D tickets to a hockey game cost $5.25. Section E tickets cost $7.50. The box office sold 3200 section D tickets and 2000 section E tickets. If $0.40 of every dollar is going to be donated to a charity, how much money will be donated?

(1) $2,080 (2) $12,720
(3) $13,800 (4) $19,080
(5) Insufficient data is given to solve the problem.

① ② ③ ④ ⑤

46. A gallon of paint costs $12.99, a half gallon costs $7.99, and a pint costs $5.99. How much will it cost to buy 7.5 gallons of paint and three brushes?

(1) $97.43 (2) $98.92
(3) $38.97 (4) $26.97
(5) Insufficient data is given to solve the problem.

① ② ③ ④ ⑤

Fractions

Have you ever heard someone say, "I could get that job done in a *fraction* of the time"? That meant that the person thought he or she could get the job done in *part* of the time. You use fractions to think about parts of a whole. For example, a quarter is part of a dollar. There are 4 quarters in 1 dollar, so one quarter is ¼ of a dollar.

Example: 3 quarters of a dollar =
 3 quarters (part): **numerator**
 4 quarters in a dollar (whole): **denominator**

Coming to Terms

denominator bottom number in a fraction that represents the *whole* amount
numerator top number in a fraction that represents the part that is being used

Warm-up

Express each of the following as a fraction.

1. Mr. Martinez worked 5 hours of an 8-hour workday.
2. Of every 30-minute TV show, 4 minutes are commercials.
3. Three of a dozen eggs were cracked.
4. She worked 225 days out of 365 days last year.

Coming to Terms

proper fraction fraction in which the numerator is smaller than the denominator (for example, ½, ⅔, ¾). A proper fraction is always less than one whole.
improper fraction fraction in which the numerator is equal to or larger than the denominator (for example, 4⁄4, 9⁄2, 12⁄10, 15⁄15). An improper fraction always equals one whole or more than one whole.
mixed number whole number plus a fraction (for example, 4½, 16⅔, 108 4⁄9)

Warm-up Answers

1. 5 hours (part)—numerator
 8 hours in a workday (whole)—denominator
2. 4 minutes (part)—numerator
 30 minutes in a show (whole)—denominator
3. 3 eggs (part)—numerator
 12 eggs in a dozen (whole)—denominator
4. 225 days (part)—numerator
 365 days in a year (whole)—denominator

Warm-up

1. Circle the improper fractions.
 $9\frac{1}{4}$ $\frac{5}{4}$ $\frac{3}{8}$ $\frac{4}{12}$ $4\frac{1}{2}$ $\frac{17}{2}$
2. Circle the proper fractions.
 $5\frac{3}{8}$ $\frac{1}{4}$ $\frac{11}{4}$ $6\frac{1}{2}$ $\frac{5}{7}$ $\frac{3}{8}$
3. Circle the mixed numbers.
 $5\frac{4}{8}$ $\frac{8}{3}$ $\frac{2}{4}$ $7\frac{1}{4}$ $\frac{1}{2}$ $12\frac{2}{3}$

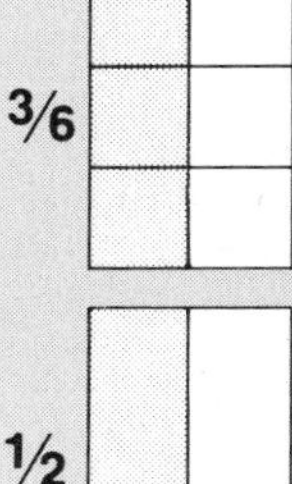

Equal Fractions The boxes to the left are equal in area. The box on the top has been divided into 6 equal parts. Three parts are shaded. The box on the bottom has been divided into 2 equal parts. One part has been shaded. You can see that the shaded portions are equal. That is because 3⁄6 and ½ are equal.

Reducing Fractions The fraction 3⁄6 is not in its lowest terms. A fraction is not in its lowest terms when the numerator and denominator can both be divided by the same number. To reduce the fraction 3⁄6 to its lowest terms, divide both the numerator and the denominator by the *same* number *evenly*. For 3⁄6, both the numerator 3 and the denominator 6 can be divided by the number 3 evenly.

$$\frac{3 \div 3}{6 \div 3} = \frac{1}{2}$$

Sometimes it is not easy to tell which number both the numerator and the denominator can be divided by evenly. You may have to use a trial-and-error approach to reduce a fraction to its lowest terms.

Example: Reduce $\frac{15}{30}$ to its lowest terms.

Step 1 If you work with numbers often, you might see that both 15 and 30 can be divided by 15 evenly. But if you cannot think of such a number right away, start with 2 and ask whether both numbers can be divided by 2 evenly. In this case, they can't (15 cannot be divided by 2 evenly). Can both numbers be divided by 3 evenly? Yes, so divide both 15 and 30 by 3.

$$\frac{15 \div 3}{30 \div 3} = \frac{5}{10}$$

Warm-up Answers

1. $\frac{5}{4}, \frac{17}{2}$ **2.** $\frac{1}{4}, \frac{5}{7}, \frac{3}{8}$ **3.** $5\frac{4}{8}, 7\frac{1}{4}, 12\frac{2}{3}$

Step 2 Ask yourself if there is any number that both 5 and 10 can be divided by evenly. Can they be divided by 2 evenly? No. Can they be divided by 3 evenly? No. Keep trying until you come to the number 5. Both 5 and 10 can be divided by the number 5 evenly. That means the fraction $5/10$ is not reduced to its lowest terms. Divide both 5 and 10 by 5.

$$\frac{5 \div 5}{10 \div 5} = \frac{1}{2}$$

Repeat these steps until both the numerator and the denominator cannot be divided evenly by any number except 1.

When the numerator and the denominator of a fraction end in zero, you can reduce by canceling the zeros. For example, $20/30$ can be reduced to $2/3$ by crossing out the zeros. What you are actually doing is dividing both 20 and 30 by 10.

☑ A Test-Taking Tip

For a fraction problem on the GED Test, the multiple-choice options will almost always be expressed in *lowest terms.* Therefore, you must be able to reduce fractions to their *lowest terms.*

Warm-up

Reduce these fractions to their lowest terms.

1. $\frac{10}{12}$ **2.** $\frac{8}{24}$ **3.** $\frac{15}{20}$ **4.** $\frac{12}{32}$ **5.** $\frac{5}{15}$

6. $\frac{6}{9}$ **7.** $\frac{12}{16}$ **8.** $\frac{6}{8}$ **9.** $\frac{3}{12}$

Warm-up Answers

1. $\frac{10 \div 2}{12 \div 2} = \frac{5}{6}$ lowest terms because no other number will go into 5 and 6 evenly

2. $\frac{8 \div 2}{24 \div 2} = \frac{4}{12}$ *not* in lowest terms because 4 will go into 4 and 12 evenly

$\frac{4 \div 4}{12 \div 4} = \frac{1}{3}$ lowest terms

3. $\frac{15 \div 5}{20 \div 5} = \frac{3}{4}$ lowest terms

4. $\frac{12 \div 4}{32 \div 4} = \frac{3}{8}$ lowest terms

5. $\frac{5 \div 5}{15 \div 5} = \frac{1}{3}$ lowest terms

6. $\frac{6 \div 3}{9 \div 3} = \frac{2}{3}$ lowest terms

7. $\frac{12 \div 4}{16 \div 4} = \frac{3}{4}$ lowest terms

8. $\frac{6 \div 2}{8 \div 2} = \frac{3}{4}$ lowest terms

9. $\frac{3 \div 3}{12 \div 3} = \frac{1}{4}$ lowest terms

Changing Improper Fractions To change an improper fraction, divide the numerator by the denominator. You will get a whole number or a whole number and a remainder. The remainder is placed over the denominator.

Example: Change $23/4$ to a whole or a mixed number.

Step 1 Divide the numerator by the denominator: $23 \div 4 = 5$, remainder 3.

Step 2 Write the whole number: 5.

Step 3 Write the remainder over the denominator: $5\,3/4$. If there is no remainder, write the answer as a whole number ($10/5 = 2$).

☑ A Test-Taking Tip

Many answers to fraction problems come out to be improper fractions. But in the answer choices on the GED Test, most improper fractions have been changed to whole or mixed numbers. Always reduce a fraction to its lowest terms and change an improper fraction to a whole or a mixed number.

Warm-up

Change these improper fractions to whole numbers or mixed numbers. Be sure to reduce the fraction part of a mixed number to its lowest terms.

1. $\frac{13}{4}$ **2.** $\frac{26}{9}$ **3.** $\frac{80}{12}$ **4.** $\frac{45}{8}$ **5.** $\frac{52}{16}$

6. $\frac{100}{25}$ **7.** $\frac{45}{6}$ **8.** $\frac{124}{10}$ **9.** $\frac{55}{7}$ **10.** $\frac{169}{13}$

Warm-up Answers

1. $3\frac{1}{4}$ **2.** $2\frac{8}{9}$ **3.** $6\frac{2}{3}$ **4.** $5\frac{5}{8}$ **5.** $3\frac{1}{4}$ **6.** 4 **7.** $7\frac{1}{2}$ **8.** $12\frac{2}{5}$ **9.** $7\frac{6}{7}$ **10.** 13

Directions: For each problem, choose the one best answer. Answers begin on page 548.

1. Marsha ate $\frac{3}{8}$ of a pizza and her sister ate $\frac{1}{8}$ of the same pizza. How much of the pizza did the women eat altogether?
   (1) $\frac{1}{4}$ (2) $\frac{3}{8}$ (3) $\frac{1}{2}$ (4) $\frac{5}{8}$
   (5) Insufficient data is given to solve the problem.
   ① ② ③ ④ ⑤

2. When he bought a compact disc player, Josh gave $\frac{2}{9}$ of his record collection to his friend Brenda and $\frac{4}{9}$ of his collection to his brother Peter. How much of his record collection did Josh give away?
   (1) $\frac{1}{6}$ (2) $\frac{2}{9}$ (3) $\frac{1}{3}$ (4) $\frac{2}{3}$ (5) $\frac{5}{6}$
   ① ② ③ ④ ⑤

3. Approximately $\frac{2}{5}$ of the U.S. population is overweight. Another $\frac{1}{5}$ is underweight. About $\frac{1}{3}$ of the underweight people are on special programs to gain weight. What portion of the U.S. population is of normal weight?
   (1) $\frac{1}{5}$ (2) $\frac{3}{10}$ (3) $\frac{2}{5}$ (4) $\frac{3}{5}$
   (5) Insufficient data is given to solve the problem.
   ① ② ③ ④ ⑤

4. Mr. T. R. Wright lives $\frac{7}{10}$ of a mile from his bank. The grocery is $\frac{3}{10}$ of a mile closer to the bank than is his house. How many miles is Mr. Wright's house from the grocery?
   (1) 1 (2) $1\frac{3}{10}$ (3) $\frac{2}{5}$
   (4) $\frac{3}{5}$ (5) $1\frac{1}{10}$
   ① ② ③ ④ ⑤

Adding and Subtracting Fractions You can't add or subtract fractions unless they have the same denominator. Fractions that have the *same* denominator are said to have a *common* denominator. Both $\frac{1}{8}$ and $\frac{3}{8}$ have the common denominator 8.

Adding Here is how you add fractions with a common denominator.

Step 1 Add the numerators.

$\frac{1}{8} + \frac{3}{8} = \frac{4}{}$

Step 2 Write the sum of the numerators over the common denominator.

$\frac{4}{8}$

Step 3 Reduce to lowest terms.

$\frac{4}{8} = \frac{1}{2}$

If your answer is an improper fraction, change it to a whole or a mixed number. For example:

$\frac{7}{10} + \frac{4}{10} = \frac{11}{10} = 1\frac{1}{10}$

Subtracting Here is how to subtract fractions with a common denominator.

Step 1 Subtract the numerators.

$\frac{3}{4} - \frac{1}{4} = \frac{2}{}$

Step 2 Write the difference over the common denominator.

$\frac{2}{4}$

Step 3 Reduce to lowest terms or change an improper fraction to a whole or a mixed number.

$\frac{2}{4} = \frac{1}{2}$

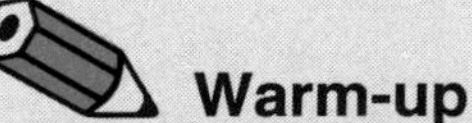

Warm-up

If you miss any of the following problems, check to see that you reduced the fractions properly.

1. $\frac{2}{4} + \frac{1}{4}$ **2.** $\frac{5}{6} - \frac{1}{6}$ **3.** $\frac{16}{20} - \frac{12}{20}$ **4.** $\frac{7}{8} - \frac{3}{8}$

5. $\frac{9}{16} + \frac{7}{16}$ **6.** $3\frac{2}{5} + 6\frac{4}{5}$ **7.** $7\frac{2}{9} + 6\frac{5}{9}$

8. $10\frac{5}{12} + 4\frac{11}{12}$

Warm-up Answers

1. $\frac{3}{4}$ **2.** $\frac{2}{3}$ **3.** $\frac{1}{5}$ **4.** $\frac{1}{2}$ **5.** 1 **6.** $10\frac{1}{5}$ **7.** $13\frac{7}{9}$ **8.** $15\frac{1}{3}$

Adding Mixed Numbers To add mixed numbers with a common denominator, follow these steps.

Step 1 Add the whole numbers.

$4\frac{1}{2} + 6\frac{1}{2} \qquad 4 + 6 = 10$

Step 2 Add the fractions.

$\frac{1}{2} + \frac{1}{2} = \frac{2}{2}$

Step 3 Reduce the sum of the fractions to its lowest terms or change an improper fraction to a whole or a mixed number.

$\frac{2}{2} = 1$

Step 4 Combine the whole number and the fraction. In this example, the whole number is 10, and the fraction equals 1: 10 + 1 = 11.

Subtracting Mixed Numbers To subtract mixed numbers with a common denominator, follow these steps:

Step 1 Subtract the whole numbers.

$9\frac{7}{8} - 5\frac{5}{8} \qquad 9 - 5 = 4$

Step 2 Subtract the fractions.

$\frac{7}{8} - \frac{5}{8} = \frac{2}{8}$

Step 3 Reduce the fraction to its lowest terms.

$\frac{2}{8} = \frac{1}{4}$

Step 4 Combine the whole number and the fraction. In this example, the whole number is 4, and the fraction is ¼. So the answer is 4¼.

Warm-up

Add or subtract the following mixed numbers.

1. $3\frac{1}{4} + 2\frac{1}{4}$ **4.** $14\frac{8}{9} - 6\frac{7}{9}$

2. $11\frac{3}{8} + 9\frac{5}{8}$ **5.** $23\frac{3}{4} - 12\frac{1}{4}$

3. $18\frac{2}{3} + 7\frac{2}{3}$ **6.** $16\frac{9}{10} - 9\frac{3}{10}$

Warm-up Answers

1. $5\frac{1}{2}$ **2.** 21 **3.** $26\frac{1}{3}$ **4.** $8\frac{1}{9}$ **5.** $11\frac{1}{2}$ **6.** $7\frac{3}{5}$

5. Over 3 days, a painter spent $8\frac{1}{4}$ hours, $6\frac{3}{4}$ hours, and 9 hours painting a house. How many hours did it take to paint the house?

   (1) $23\frac{2}{4}$ (2) $23\frac{3}{4}$ (3) 24

   (4) $24\frac{1}{2}$ (5) $24\frac{3}{4}$

   ① ② ③ ④ ⑤

6. Monte bought $1\frac{2}{3}$ pounds of roast beef, $2\frac{1}{3}$ pounds of cole slaw, and $\frac{1}{3}$ pound of Swiss cheese at a delicatessen. How many pounds of food did he buy altogether?

   (1) $3\frac{1}{6}$ (2) $3\frac{1}{3}$ (3) $3\frac{2}{3}$

   (4) $4\frac{1}{3}$ (5) $4\frac{2}{3}$

   ① ② ③ ④ ⑤

7. Tiffany rode her bike 2 miles on Monday, $2\frac{5}{8}$ miles on Tuesday, and $2\frac{1}{8}$ miles on Wednesday. How many miles did she ride in all?

   (1) 6 (2) $6\frac{1}{2}$ (3) $6\frac{3}{4}$

   (4) $6\frac{7}{8}$ (5) $7\frac{1}{8}$

   ① ② ③ ④ ⑤

8. Ms. Ames bought $5\frac{5}{6}$ yards of silk for \$6.99 a yard and $4\frac{1}{6}$ yards of cotton. Which expression correctly represents how many yards more of silk than of cotton Ms. Ames bought?

   (1) $5\frac{5}{6} \times \$6.99$

   (2) $(4\frac{1}{6} + 5\frac{5}{6}) \times \$6.99$

   (3) $5\frac{5}{6} + 4\frac{1}{6}$ (4) $4\frac{1}{6} - 5\frac{5}{6}$

   (5) $5\frac{5}{6} - 4\frac{1}{6}$

   ① ② ③ ④ ⑤

9. Mr. Farley bought $3\frac{5}{8}$ pounds of pears. He ate 2 pears; the remaining pears weighed $2\frac{3}{8}$ pounds. How many pounds did the 2 pears that Mr. Farley ate weigh?

   (1) 1 (2) $1\frac{1}{8}$ (3) $1\frac{1}{4}$

   (4) $1\frac{1}{2}$ (5) 6

   ① ② ③ ④ ⑤

Directions: For each problem, choose the one best answer. Answers are on page 549.

10. Mr. Haskell bought $1\frac{3}{4}$ ounces of dill, $2\frac{1}{4}$ ounces of rosemary, $5\frac{1}{2}$ ounces of parsley and $2\frac{1}{4}$ pounds of tomatoes at the Garden Center. How many ounces of herbs did he buy altogether?

    (1) $8\frac{1}{4}$ (2) $9\frac{1}{2}$ (3) 10

    (4) $10\frac{3}{4}$ (5) $11\frac{3}{4}$

    (1) (2) (3) (4) (5)

11. At birth one twin weighed $5\frac{1}{4}$ pounds and his brother weighed less. What was their total weight in pounds?

    (1) $9\frac{1}{8}$ (2) $9\frac{1}{4}$ (3) $9\frac{3}{8}$ (4) $10\frac{1}{8}$

    (5) Insufficient data is given to solve the problem.

    (1) (2) (3) (4) (5)

12. Mr. Fleming wants to make a suit. He needs $2\frac{1}{4}$ yards of material for the jacket, $\frac{3}{4}$ yard for the vest, and $1\frac{7}{8}$ yards for the pants. How many yards of material does he need to buy?

    (1) $3\frac{1}{4}$ (2) $3\frac{3}{8}$ (3) $4\frac{1}{4}$

    (4) $4\frac{3}{4}$ (5) $4\frac{7}{8}$

    (1) (2) (3) (4) (5)

13. Mr. Weissman worked $45\frac{3}{4}$ hours one week and $38\frac{1}{2}$ hours the next week. How many more hours did he work during the first week?

    (1) $6\frac{1}{4}$ (2) $6\frac{1}{2}$ (3) 7

    (4) $7\frac{1}{4}$ (5) $7\frac{1}{2}$

    (11) (12) (13) (14) (15)

14. Bubbles won the pie-eating contest by eating $22\frac{2}{3}$ pies. The second place winner ate $19\frac{1}{6}$ pies. How many more pies did Bubbles eat?

    (1) $3\frac{1}{2}$ (2) $3\frac{1}{3}$ (3) $3\frac{1}{6}$

    (4) $2\frac{1}{2}$ (5) $2\frac{1}{6}$

    (1) (2) (3) (4) (5)

Finding Common Denominators If you need to add or subtract fractions that do not have a common denominator, you must change one or both of the fractions so that they have a common denominator.

Changing One Fraction To add ⅓ and $\frac{2}{9}$, for example, you must first find a common denominator. You can see that 9 can be divided by 3 evenly. You can change ⅓ to a fraction with 9 as the denominator and then add.

To change ⅓, do the *opposite* of reducing the fraction; that is, *multiply* rather than divide. To keep the value of ⅓ the same, you must multiply *both* the numerator and the denominator by the same number.

Step 1 To change ⅓ to a fraction with 9 as the denominator, ask yourself how many times 3 goes into 9. The answer is 3.

Step 2 Multiply.

$$\frac{1}{3} \times \frac{3}{3} = \frac{3}{9}$$

When you multiply a fraction by a fraction, you multiply the numerator by the numerator and the denominator by the denominator. The value of ⅓ equals $\frac{3}{9}$ because $\frac{3}{3}$ equals 1. When you multiply 1 by any number, the answer is equal to the number itself.

Step 3 To check your work, reduce $\frac{3}{9}$. If you have changed the fraction correctly, it should reduce to the original fraction. In this problem, $\frac{3}{9}$ reduces to ⅓.

Step 4 Now add.

$$\frac{1}{3} + \frac{2}{9} = \frac{3}{9} + \frac{2}{9} = \frac{5}{9}$$

Warm-up

Determine each missing numerator. For example, since 15 divided by 5 equals 3, the missing numerator in the following problem can be found by multiplying $\frac{3}{5}$ by $\frac{3}{3}$.

$$\frac{3}{5} = \frac{?}{15} \qquad \frac{3}{5} \times \frac{3}{3} = \frac{9}{15}$$

1. $\frac{1}{2} = \frac{?}{16}$ **3.** $\frac{4}{5} = \frac{?}{25}$ **5.** $\frac{1}{4} = \frac{?}{8}$

2. $\frac{3}{4} = \frac{?}{12}$ **4.** $\frac{3}{6} = \frac{?}{18}$ **6.** $\frac{2}{3} = \frac{?}{12}$

Warm-up Answers

1. 8 **2.** 9 **3.** 20 **4.** 9 **5.** 2 **6.** 8

Changing Both Fractions Sometimes you need to change *both* fractions so that they have a common denominator. In the case of $\frac{1}{3} + \frac{2}{9}$, one of the denominators (9) happens to be the least common denominator.

For a problem like $\frac{1}{6} + \frac{1}{8}$, neither denominator is the least common denominator. To find the least common denominator, follow these steps.

Step 1 List the multiples of each denominator.

For $\frac{1}{6}$, these are 6, 12, 18, 24, 30, 36, . . .

For $\frac{1}{8}$, these are 8, 16, 24, 32, 40, 48, . . .

Step 2 Find the smallest number that appears in these two sets of multiples. It is 24. So 24 is the *least common denominator.*

To add $\frac{1}{6}$ and $\frac{1}{8}$, change both fractions into fractions that have denominators of 24.

$\frac{1}{6} \times \frac{4}{4} = \frac{4}{24}$ $\frac{1}{8} \times \frac{3}{3} = \frac{3}{24}$

$\frac{1}{6} + \frac{1}{8} = \frac{4}{24} + \frac{3}{24} = \frac{7}{24}$

Coming to Terms

least common denominator the smallest number that two or more denominators can be divided by evenly

Warm-up

Solve each problem by finding the least common denominator.

1. $\frac{1}{4} + \frac{2}{3}$
2. $\frac{1}{2} - \frac{1}{3}$
3. $\frac{1}{5} + \frac{1}{4}$
4. $\frac{2}{3} - \frac{5}{8}$
5. $5\frac{5}{6} - 2\frac{1}{4}$

Warm-up Answers

1. $\frac{11}{12}$ $\frac{1}{4} \times \frac{3}{3} = \frac{3}{12}$ $\frac{2}{3} \times \frac{4}{4} = \frac{8}{12}$ $\frac{3}{12} + \frac{8}{12} = \frac{11}{12}$
2. $\frac{1}{6}$ $\frac{1}{2} \times \frac{3}{3} = \frac{3}{6}$ $\frac{1}{3} \times \frac{2}{2} = \frac{2}{6}$ $\frac{3}{6} - \frac{2}{6} = \frac{1}{6}$
3. $\frac{9}{20}$ $\frac{1}{5} \times \frac{4}{4} = \frac{4}{20}$ $\frac{1}{4} \times \frac{5}{5} = \frac{5}{20}$ $\frac{4}{20} + \frac{5}{20} = \frac{9}{20}$
4. $\frac{1}{24}$ $\frac{2}{3} \times \frac{8}{8} = \frac{16}{24}$ $\frac{5}{8} \times \frac{3}{3} = \frac{15}{24}$ $\frac{16}{24} - \frac{15}{24} = \frac{1}{24}$
5. $3\frac{7}{12}$ First subtract fractions: $\frac{5}{6} \times \frac{2}{2} = \frac{10}{12}$ $\frac{1}{4} \times \frac{3}{3} = \frac{3}{12}$ $\frac{10}{12} - \frac{3}{12} = \frac{7}{12}$ Then subtract whole numbers: $5 - 2 = 3$

15. Ms. Thompson is $5\frac{1}{4}$ feet tall. Her sister is $5\frac{1}{2}$ feet tall. Her brother is $6\frac{1}{3}$ feet tall. Which of the following expressions correctly represents how much shorter Ms. Thompson is than her brother?

(1) $5\frac{1}{2} - 5\frac{1}{4}$ (2) $6\frac{1}{2} - 5\frac{1}{4}$
(3) $6\frac{1}{3} - 5\frac{1}{4}$ (4) $5\frac{1}{2} + 5\frac{1}{4}$
(5) $6\frac{1}{3} - 5\frac{1}{4} - 5\frac{1}{2}$

(1) (2) (3) (4) (5)

16. Tang Lee went camping $107\frac{1}{3}$ miles from his hometown. He traveled by train for $98\frac{1}{8}$ miles; then he had to transfer to a bus. How many miles was Tang Lee's bus trip?

(1) $8\frac{1}{24}$ (2) $9\frac{1}{5}$
(3) $9\frac{5}{24}$ (4) $10\frac{1}{12}$
(5) Insufficient data is given to solve the problem.

(1) (2) (3) (4) (5)

17. Uncle Theo gave each of his two nephews equal amounts of money as gifts. Ned put $\frac{2}{5}$ of his money in the bank, and Ed put $\frac{1}{2}$ of his money in the bank. How much more money than Ned did Ed deposit in the bank?

(1) $\frac{1}{10}$ (2) $\frac{1}{5}$ (3) $\frac{3}{10}$ (4) $\frac{2}{5}$
(5) Insufficient data is given to solve the problem.

(1) (2) (3) (4) (5)

18. Mrs. Sanchez gave a neighbor $\frac{1}{6}$ of her apple pie and $\frac{5}{9}$ of her key lime pie. How much pie did she give her neighbor altogether?

(1) $\frac{5}{12}$ (2) $\frac{4}{9}$ (3) $\frac{11}{18}$
(4) $\frac{13}{18}$ (5) $\frac{5}{6}$

(1) (2) (3) (4) (5)

Directions: For each problem, choose the one best answer. Answers are on pages 549–550.

19. Buddy Parish had $15\frac{1}{2}$ gallons of gas in his car. He used $7\frac{7}{8}$ gallons. How many gallons of gas did he have to buy to fill the tank to its capacity of 20 gallons?
(1) $7\frac{5}{8}$ (2) $11\frac{3}{8}$ (3) $12\frac{3}{8}$
(4) $12\frac{8}{10}$ (5) $13\frac{5}{8}$
① ② ③ ④ ⑤

20. A trip from Chicago to Philadelphia is about 1,026 miles. It takes $19\frac{1}{4}$ hours by train but only $2\frac{1}{2}$ hours by plane. How many more hours does it take to travel to Philadelphia by train than by plane?
(1) $16\frac{1}{4}$ (2) $16\frac{3}{4}$ (3) $17\frac{1}{4}$ (4) $17\frac{1}{2}$
(5) Insufficient data is given to solve the problem.
① ② ③ ④ ⑤

21. Marge bought 5 gallons of gas. She used $1\frac{1}{4}$ gallons for the lawn mower. How many gallons of gas does she have left?
(1) $2\frac{1}{2}$ gal (2) $2\frac{3}{4}$ gal
(3) $3\frac{1}{4}$ gal (4) $3\frac{3}{4}$ gal
(5) Insufficient data is given to solve the problem.
① ② ③ ④ ⑤

22. Ingerson's Bakery used $5\frac{7}{8}$ pounds of flour to make doughnuts. The bakery had started with $10\frac{1}{4}$ pounds of flour. How many pounds of flour were left?
(1) $4\frac{1}{4}$ (2) $4\frac{1}{2}$ (3) $4\frac{3}{8}$
(4) $5\frac{1}{8}$ (5) $15\frac{1}{4}$
① ② ③ ④ ⑤

23. Mrs. Sheridan had 5 dozen eggs. She sold $2\frac{1}{3}$ dozen and used $1\frac{1}{4}$ dozen. How many dozen did she have left?
(1) $1\frac{1}{6}$ (2) $1\frac{5}{12}$ (3) $1\frac{1}{2}$
(4) $1\frac{5}{8}$ (5) $1\frac{5}{9}$
① ② ③ ④ ⑤

Borrowing from Whole Numbers If an electrician had a 25-foot coil of wire, and he used $8\frac{1}{3}$ feet on a job. How much wire did he have left?

To answer that question, you must first subtract: $25 - 8\frac{1}{3}$. But as you can see, there is no fraction from which to subtract $\frac{1}{3}$. In this case you must borrow from the whole number. You can borrow $\frac{3}{3}$ from 25. That is the same as borrowing 1 from 25. The 25 then becomes 24.

$$24\frac{3}{3} - 8\frac{1}{3}$$

Now subtract as you normally would, first the numerators in the fractions ($\frac{3}{3} - \frac{1}{3} = \frac{2}{3}$) and then the whole numbers ($24 - 8 = 16$). The answer is $16\frac{2}{3}$.

Warm-up 1

Borrow from the whole number to compute these problems.

1. $8 - \frac{3}{4}$ **4.** $12 - 3\frac{3}{5}$ **7.** $15 - 2\frac{1}{4}$
2. $19 - 1\frac{1}{5}$ **5.** $58 - 24\frac{5}{8}$ **8.** $1 - \frac{1}{4}$
3. $6 - 5\frac{1}{2}$ **6.** $10 - 3\frac{2}{3}$

A Special Case Here is another kind of problem that requires borrowing.

$$17\frac{1}{3} - 2\frac{7}{12} = 17\frac{4}{12} - 2\frac{7}{12}$$

You cannot subtract 7 from 4, so you must borrow $\frac{12}{12}$ from 17 ($17 = 16\frac{12}{12}$).

$$17\frac{4}{12} = 16\frac{12}{12} + \frac{4}{12} = 16\frac{16}{12}$$

$$16\frac{16}{12} - 2\frac{7}{12}$$

Now you can subtract $\frac{7}{12}$ from $\frac{16}{12}$ to get $\frac{9}{12}$, or $\frac{3}{4}$. Then subtract 2 from 16 to get 14. The answer is $14\frac{3}{4}$.

Warm-up 2

Borrow to compute these problems.

1. $22\frac{1}{9} - 3\frac{4}{9}$ **4.** $82\frac{2}{5} - 32\frac{4}{5}$ **7.** $100\frac{1}{2} - 9\frac{7}{8}$
2. $9\frac{1}{6} - \frac{2}{3}$ **5.** $5\frac{1}{4} - 3\frac{3}{4}$ **8.** $5\frac{2}{3} - 1\frac{6}{7}$
3. $6\frac{3}{8} - 1\frac{7}{8}$ **6.** $15\frac{1}{3} - 9\frac{2}{3}$

Warm-up Answers 1

1. $7\frac{1}{4}$ **2.** $17\frac{4}{5}$ **3.** $\frac{1}{2}$ **4.** $8\frac{2}{5}$ **5.** $33\frac{3}{8}$ **6.** $6\frac{1}{3}$ **7.** $12\frac{3}{4}$ **8.** $\frac{3}{4}$

Warm-up Answers 2

1. $18\frac{2}{3}$ **2.** $8\frac{1}{2}$ **3.** $4\frac{1}{2}$ **4.** $49\frac{3}{5}$ **5.** $1\frac{1}{2}$ **6.** $5\frac{2}{3}$ **7.** $90\frac{5}{8}$ **8.** $3\frac{17}{21}$

Converting Fractions to Decimals To change ½ to a decimal, divide the *numerator* by the *denominator.* In this case $2\overline{)1}$ cannot be computed because 2 is larger than 1, so place a decimal point after the 1 and add a zero: $2\overline{)1.0}$. Now divide.

$$\begin{array}{r} .5 \\ 2\overline{)1.0} \end{array}, \text{ so } \frac{1}{2} = .5$$

Warm-up 1

Convert the following fractions to decimals.

1. $\frac{3}{4}$ **2.** $\frac{2}{3}$ **3.** $\frac{1}{10}$ **4.** $\frac{2}{5}$ **5.** $\frac{1}{100}$

Problems with Fractions and Decimals Sometimes you may be asked to solve a problem involving both a fraction and a decimal. For example, ⅜ × 0.64. First multiply: 3 by 0.64

$3 \times 0.64 = 1.92$

Then divide the answer by the denominator of the fraction.

$$\begin{array}{r} 0.24 \\ 8\overline{)1.92} \end{array}$$

So ⅜ × 0.64 = 0.24

If a fraction has the numerator of one, a shortcut can be used to solve the problem.

■ When the bill arrived for lunch, five friends decided that they would each pay ⅕ of the $26.75 total. How much did each person pay?

First, set up the problem: $\$26.75 \times \frac{1}{5}$

Whenever a fraction has the numerator of 1, you can simply divide the decimal by the denominator of the fraction.

$$\begin{array}{r} \$5.35 \\ 5\overline{)26.75} \end{array}$$

Each person paid $5.35.

Warm-up 2

Multiply and express the answers in decimals.

1. $\frac{1}{2} \times 0.50$ **2.** $\frac{3}{5} \times 0.70$ **3.** $\frac{1}{4} \times \$2.40$

Warm-up Answers 1

1. 0.75 $4\overline{)3.00}$ = 0.75 **2.** 0.67 $3\overline{)2.000}$ = 0.666 R2 rounded to .67

3. 0.10 $10\overline{)1.00}$ = 0.10 **4.** 0.40 $5\overline{)2.00}$ = 0.40 **5.** 0.01 $100\overline{)1.00}$ = 0.01

Warm-up Answers 2

1. 0.25 **2.** 0.42 **3.** $0.60 or 60¢

24. Of the 1,800 registered voters in Springville, only $\frac{3}{8}$ voted in the last school board election. How many people voted?

(1) 225 (2) 625 (3) 675
(4) 775 (5) 1,125

① ② ③ ④ ⑤

25. Of Sam's total income, $\frac{2}{5}$ goes for housing. Sam earns $13,800 per year. How much does he spend on housing?

(1) $1,380 (2) $2,760
(3) $3,780 (4) $5,520
(5) Insufficient data is given to solve the problem.

① ② ③ ④ ⑤

26. Agnes bought $\frac{3}{4}$ yards of gingham for $1.88 a yard. She also bought some batting for $2.98. How much did she pay for the gingham?

(1) $0.47 (2) $1.41 (3) $5.64
(4) $4.39 (5) $4.86

① ② ③ ④ ⑤

27. Brian bought sheet plastic at $4.20 per yard and 2 rolls of plastic for $7.20 a roll. How much was the total cost of the plastic?

(1) $12.80 (2) $13.20
(3) $13.65 (4) $15.50
(5) Insufficient data is given to solve the problem.

① ② ③ ④ ⑤

28. Ms. Winter bought $\frac{7}{8}$ of a yard of 2-inch thick foam padding at $2.32 a yard. How much did she pay?

(1) $0.29 (2) $1.03 (3) $1.29
(4) $2.03 (5) $2.32

① ② ③ ④ ⑤

Directions: For each problem, choose the one best answer. Answers are on page 550.

29. For a barbecue Henry bought 3 sirloin steaks. Each steak weighed $2\frac{3}{4}$ pounds. How many pounds of meat did he buy?
(1) $6\frac{1}{4}$ (2) $6\frac{3}{4}$ (3) $8\frac{1}{4}$ (4) $8\frac{1}{2}$
(5) Insufficient data is given to solve the problem.
① ② ③ ④ ⑤

30. A recipe for macaroni and cheese called for $2\frac{2}{3}$ cups of macaroni. Mrs. Harcourt wanted to triple the recipe for a potluck dinner at the PTA. How many cups of macaroni did she need?
(1) 6 (2) $6\frac{1}{2}$ (3) $7\frac{3}{4}$
(4) 8 (5) $8\frac{1}{2}$
① ② ③ ④ ⑤

31. Mr. Wong bought $3\frac{1}{2}$ pounds of hard salami at $2 per pound. He used all but $\frac{1}{7}$ of the salami for sandwiches. How many pounds of salami did Mr. Wong have left?
(1) $\frac{1}{4}$ (2) $\frac{1}{2}$ (3) $\frac{3}{4}$ (4) 1 (5) $1\frac{1}{2}$
① ② ③ ④ ⑤

32. Patrick gave $\frac{2}{5}$ of his orchid collection to Elise. Elise gave $\frac{2}{3}$ of what she received to her aunt. Which expression correctly represents the amount of Patrick's collection Elise's aunt received?
(1) $\frac{2}{3} \times \frac{2}{5}$ (2) $\frac{2}{3} \div \frac{2}{5}$ (3) $\frac{2}{3} + \frac{2}{5}$
(4) $\frac{2}{3} - \frac{2}{5}$ (5) $1 - \frac{2}{5} - \frac{2}{3}$
① ② ③ ④ ⑤

33. Ms. Dommes bought 5 yards of felt for a costume. She used $\frac{7}{8}$ of the material. How many yards of material did she use?
(1) $3\frac{1}{4}$ (2) $3\frac{2}{3}$ (3) 4
(4) $4\frac{3}{8}$ (5) $4\frac{2}{3}$
① ② ③ ④ ⑤

Multiplying with Fractions To multiply a fraction by a fraction, such as $\frac{1}{2} \times \frac{2}{3}$, follow these steps.

Step 1 Multiply the numerators.

$\frac{1}{2} \times \frac{2}{3} = \frac{2}{1}$

Step 2 Multiply the denominators.

$\frac{1}{2} \times \frac{2}{3} = \frac{2}{6}$

Step 3 Reduce to lowest terms.

$\frac{2}{6} = \frac{1}{3}$

Notice that when you *multiply* fractions, you do not need to find a common denominator.

Warm-up 1

Solve these problems. Reduce to lowest terms.

1. $\frac{1}{5} \times \frac{2}{3}$ 3. $\frac{2}{5} \times \frac{7}{8}$ 5. $\frac{4}{5} \times \frac{6}{7}$
2. $\frac{3}{4} \times \frac{5}{7}$ 4. $\frac{3}{4} \times \frac{3}{5}$ 6. $\frac{1}{8} \times \frac{4}{5}$

Whole Numbers What if you need to multiply 8 by $\frac{1}{4}$? Here is how to multiply a fraction by a whole number.

Step 1 Write the whole number as a fraction by placing it over 1. This does not change its value.

$8 = \frac{8}{1}$

Step 2 Multiply as you do with two fractions.

$8 \times \frac{1}{4} = \frac{8}{1} \times \frac{1}{4} = \frac{8}{4} = 2$

Warm-up 2

Solve these problems. Reduce to lowest terms.

1. $4 \times \frac{1}{5}$ 3. $9 \times \frac{7}{8}$ 5. $\frac{5}{7} \times 10$
2. $\frac{4}{7} \times 6$ 4. $9 \times \frac{1}{2}$ 6. $\frac{1}{4} \times 9$

Work through the tinted columns on the next page before doing the problems in the white columns on this page and on the next one.

Warm-up Answers 1

1. $\frac{2}{15}$ 2. $\frac{15}{28}$ 3. $\frac{7}{20}$ 4. $\frac{9}{20}$ 5. $\frac{24}{35}$ 6. $\frac{1}{10}$

Warm-up Answers 2

1. $\frac{4}{5}$ 2. $3\frac{3}{7}$ 3. $7\frac{7}{8}$ 4. $4\frac{1}{2}$ 5. $7\frac{1}{7}$ 6. $2\frac{1}{4}$

Mixed Numbers To multiply a fraction by a mixed number or to multiply two mixed numbers, change the mixed numbers to improper fractions and multiply as you would with any two fractions. To change a mixed number such as $2\frac{1}{5}$ to an improper fraction, follow these steps.

Step 1 Multiply the *whole number* by the *denominator:* $2 \times 5 = 10$.

Step 2 Add the *numerator* to the answer you obtained in Step 1: $10 + 1 = 11$.

Step 3 Put the answer you obtained in Step 2 over the *denominator.* In this case put 11 over 5 to get the improper fraction $\frac{11}{5}$.

Canceling. Canceling can help speed up multiplication. Here is how to use canceling to multiply $\frac{3}{4}$ by $\frac{2}{9}$ more quickly and easily. To cancel, divide any numerator and any denominator by the *same* number. As in reducing fractions, both numerator and denominator must be divided by the number *evenly.* Notice that in the fractions above, the first numerator (3) and the second denominator (9) can be divided by 3 evenly. Also, the second numerator (2) and the first denominator (4) can be divided by 2 evenly. When you cancel, cross off the numbers like this:

$$\frac{\overset{1}{\cancel{3}}}{\underset{2}{\cancel{4}}} \times \frac{\overset{1}{\cancel{2}}}{\underset{3}{\cancel{9}}} = \frac{1}{2} \times \frac{1}{3} = \frac{1}{6}$$

Here is another example: $\frac{3}{8} \times \frac{16}{27}$. The 3 and the 27 can both be divided evenly by 3; the 8 and 16 can be divided evenly by 8.

$$\frac{\overset{1}{\cancel{3}}}{\underset{1}{\cancel{8}}} \times \frac{\overset{2}{\cancel{16}}}{\underset{9}{\cancel{27}}} = \frac{1}{1} \times \frac{2}{9} = \frac{2}{9}$$

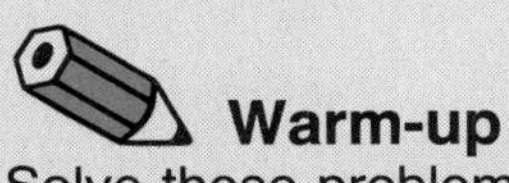

Warm-up

Solve these problems. Reduce to lowest terms.

1. $\frac{3}{12} \times \frac{2}{3}$ **4.** $28 \times \frac{3}{7}$ **7.** $3\frac{1}{5} \times 1\frac{7}{8}$

2. $4\frac{1}{5} \times 5\frac{2}{3}$ **5.** $\frac{5}{6} \times \frac{3}{10}$ **8.** $\frac{3}{5} \times 45$

3. $16 \times \frac{3}{4}$ **6.** $4\frac{1}{5} \times 7\frac{3}{7}$ **9.** $\frac{7}{8} \times \frac{4}{9}$

Warm-up Answers

1. $\frac{1}{6}$ **2.** $23\frac{4}{5}$ **3.** 12 **4.** 12 **5.** $\frac{1}{4}$ **6.** $31\frac{1}{5}$ **7.** 6 **8.** 27 **9.** $\frac{7}{18}$

34. The Wringer Company pays $7.50 an hour for overtime pay. Tom Johnson worked 40 regular hours and $9\frac{1}{2}$ hours overtime. What did he earn above his regular salary?

(1) $67.50 (2) $69.75 (3) $70.55
(4) $71.25 (5) $371.75

① ② ③ ④ ⑤

35. Pat Banner had 18 yards of ribbon. She used $\frac{3}{4}$ of it. How many yards did she have left?

(1) $4\frac{1}{2}$ (2) 6 (3) $13\frac{1}{2}$ (4) $14\frac{3}{4}$
(5) Insufficient data is given to solve the problem.

① ② ③ ④ ⑤

36. Lan bought $4\frac{2}{3}$ pounds of dried apricots and $3\frac{1}{4}$ pounds of dried figs. How much did Lan pay?

(1) $33.62 (2) $32.72
(3) $32.62 (4) $23.62
(5) Insufficient data is given to solve the problem.

① ② ③ ④ ⑤

37. On a physical map, the distance between two rivers is $3\frac{1}{4}$ inches. The scale of the map is 1 inch equals 200 miles. How many miles apart are the two rivers?

(1) 525 (2) 575 (3) 625
(4) 650 (5) 725

① ② ③ ④ ⑤

38. Erica mailed three packages to her sister. Each weighed $5\frac{2}{3}$ pounds. How many pounds did the three packages weigh?

(1) $12\frac{2}{3}$ (2) $15\frac{2}{3}$ (3) 16
(4) 17 (5) $18\frac{2}{3}$

① ② ③ ④ ⑤

Directions: For each problem, choose the one best answer. Answers are on page 550.

39. Parker's Finer Foods is selling apples at \$1.98 for $3\frac{1}{2}$ pounds. How much would 1 pound of apples cost?

(1) \$0.27 (2) \$0.48 (3) \$0.57
(4) \$0.59 (5) \$6.93

① ② ③ ④ ⑤

40. How many pieces of wood $2\frac{1}{4}$ feet long can be cut from a board 18 feet long?

(1) 6 (2) 7 (3) 8
(4) 9 (5) 10

① ② ③ ④ ⑤

41. Mariam works in the gift-wrapping department of a store. If it takes $2\frac{1}{8}$ yards of ribbon to decorate one medium-sized box, how many boxes can Mariam decorate with 68 yards?

(1) 32 (2) 33 (3) 34
(4) 35 (5) 144

① ② ③ ④ ⑤

42. A country has approximately 586,600 square miles. Each resident could live on $1\frac{2}{5}$ square miles. Which of the following expressions correctly represents the population of the country?

(1) $586{,}000 + 1\frac{2}{5}$ (2) $586{,}600 \div 1\frac{2}{5}$
(3) $586{,}600 \times \frac{7}{5}$ (4) $586{,}600 \times 1\frac{2}{5}$
(5) 586,600

① ② ③ ④ ⑤

43. The Hernandezes' electric bill was \$722 for $9\frac{1}{2}$ months of service. What was the average cost of their monthly usage?

(1) \$60.17 (2) \$65.00 (3) \$69.85
(4) \$76.00 (5) \$77.00

① ② ③ ④ ⑤

Dividing with Fractions To divide two fractions, such as $\frac{1}{2} \div \frac{3}{4}$, invert the fraction you are dividing by (the second fraction) and multiply. *Invert* means "to turn upside down."

$$\frac{1}{2} \div \frac{3}{4} = \frac{1}{2} \times \frac{4}{3} = \frac{4}{6} = \frac{2}{3}$$

To divide two mixed numbers, convert them to improper fractions and then follow the procedure for dividing fractions. For example, divide $5\frac{1}{5}$ by $2\frac{1}{6}$.

Step 1 Convert the mixed numbers to improper fractions.

$$5\frac{1}{5} \div 2\frac{1}{6} = \frac{26}{5} \div \frac{13}{6}$$

Step 2 Invert the fraction you are dividing by and multiply.

$$\frac{26}{5} \times \frac{6}{13}$$

Step 3 Cancel if possible. Notice that both 13 and 26 can be divided by 13 evenly.

$$\frac{\overset{2}{\cancel{26}}}{5} \times \frac{6}{\underset{1}{\cancel{13}}} = \frac{2}{5} \times \frac{6}{1} = \frac{12}{5} = 2\frac{2}{5}$$

To divide a fraction by a whole number, such as $\frac{3}{8} \div 6$, follow these steps.

Step 1 Convert 6 to an improper fraction.

$$\frac{3}{8} \div \frac{6}{1}$$

Step 2 Invert and multiply the second fraction on the right (the divisor).

$$\frac{3}{8} \times \frac{1}{6}$$

Step 3 Cancel if possible. Note that 3 and 6 can be divided by 3 evenly.

$$\frac{\overset{1}{\cancel{3}}}{8} \times \frac{1}{\underset{2}{\cancel{6}}} = \frac{1}{8} \times \frac{1}{2} = \frac{1}{16}$$

Warm-up

Solve these problems. Reduce your answers to lowest terms.

1. $\frac{2}{7} \div \frac{5}{7}$ 3. $\frac{7}{8} \div 6$ 5. $4\frac{1}{5} \div \frac{7}{20}$
2. $8\frac{1}{2} \div \frac{3}{4}$ 4. $\frac{3}{10} \div \frac{3}{5}$ 6. $\frac{9}{10} \div 27$

Read the tinted column on the next page before doing the problems in the white columns on these two pages.

Warm-up Answers

1. $\frac{2}{5}$ 2. $11\frac{1}{3}$ 3. $\frac{7}{48}$ 4. $\frac{1}{2}$ 5. 12 6. $\frac{1}{30}$

You may feel that memorizing the rule "Invert the second fraction and multiply" is all you want to know about dividing fractions. However, you may remember the process better if you understand *why* you invert and multiply. To understand, you must realize two concepts.

1. A problem such as ½ ÷ ¼ actually means this:

$$\frac{\frac{1}{2}}{\frac{1}{4}}$$

Notice how awkward a fraction on top of a fraction looks. To simplify this fraction, you can multiply the denominator ¼ by its opposite, called its *reciprocal.* A number multiplied by its reciprocal equals 1. The reciprocal of ¼ is 4/1 because ¼ × 4/1 = 1.

2. You need to know that whatever operation you do to the denominator of a fraction, you must also do to the numerator of the fraction. If you multiply ¼ by 4/1 to make the denominator equal 1, you must multiply the numerator by 4/1 also.

$$\frac{\frac{1}{2} \times \frac{4}{1}}{\frac{1}{4} \times \frac{4}{1}} = \frac{\frac{4}{2}}{1} = \frac{4}{2} = 2$$

Now watch what happens when you invert and multiply to compute ½ ÷ ¼.

$$\frac{1}{2} \div \frac{1}{4} = \frac{1}{2} \times \frac{4}{1} = 2$$

You can see that inverting and multiplying is just a shortcut for dividing fractions.

Warm-up

Solve these problems.

1. $\frac{2}{5} \div \frac{2}{3}$ **3.** $8 \div 4\frac{2}{3}$ **5.** $\frac{5}{6} \div 5$

2. $\frac{7}{10} \div 3\frac{1}{2}$ **4.** $4\frac{2}{3} \div 1\frac{1}{7}$ **6.** $3 \div 5\frac{1}{7}$

Warm-up Answers

1. $\frac{3}{5}$ **2.** $\frac{1}{5}$ **3.** $1\frac{5}{7}$ **4.** $4\frac{1}{12}$ **5.** $\frac{1}{6}$ **6.** $\frac{7}{12}$

44. Jamaal drove 117 miles in $2\frac{1}{4}$ hours. What was his average speed in miles per hour?

(1) 48 (2) 50 (3) 52
(4) $55\frac{1}{4}$ (5) $56\frac{1}{2}$

① ② ③ ④ ⑤

45. A dealer sold $4\frac{1}{4}$ yards of upholstery fabric and some upholstery tacks for $69.02. What was the cost of the fabric per yard?

(1) $13.99 (2) $14.88
(3) $15.62 (4) $16.24
(5) Insufficient data is given to solve the problem.

① ② ③ ④ ⑤

46. A farmer has $13\frac{1}{3}$ acres of land. He plans to sell the land to a developer who will divide the property into 40 equal lots. How many acres will each lot be?

(1) $1\frac{1}{4}$ (2) $\frac{8}{9}$ (3) $\frac{2}{5}$ (4) $\frac{3}{8}$ (5) $\frac{1}{3}$

① ② ③ ④ ⑤

47. Earlene travels $15\frac{1}{2}$ miles going back and forth to work each day. How many miles is it from her home to her job?

(1) $7\frac{1}{5}$ (2) $7\frac{3}{10}$ (3) $7\frac{1}{2}$
(4) $7\frac{3}{4}$ (5) $7\frac{7}{8}$

① ② ③ ④ ⑤

48. Glenn made 15 pieces of jewelry to sell on commission. How many rings can he make from $7\frac{1}{2}$ ounces of silver if each ring weighs $\frac{3}{4}$ ounce?

(1) 4 (2) 5 (3) 7 (4) 10
(5) Insufficient data is given to solve the problem.

① ② ③ ④ ⑤

Directions: For each problem, choose the one best answer. Answers are on page 550.

49. Mrs. Jordan makes \$165.00 a week after taxes. One week she spent $\frac{1}{3}$ of her income for food. The following week she spent $\frac{1}{4}$ of it on food. How much did she spend on food during this 2-week period?

(1) \$41.25 (2) \$55.00 (3) \$85.75
(4) \$96.25 (5) \$110.00

(1) (2) (3) (4) (5)

50. Deborah Jones is planning to make a dress. The fabric she likes costs \$4.99 per yard, and she needs $2\frac{3}{8}$ yards. She also needs $\frac{1}{2}$ yard of lining fabric at \$1.98 per yard, a zipper for \$0.89, and a spool of thread for \$0.55. Which expression correctly represents how much it will cost her to make the dress?

(1) \$4.99 + \$1.98 + \$0.89 + \$0.55
(2) $2\frac{3}{8}$ × (\$4.99 + \$1.98 + \$0.89 + \$0.55)
(3) ($2\frac{3}{8}$ × \$4.99) + ($\frac{1}{2}$ × \$1.98) + \$0.89 + \$0.55
(4) $\frac{1}{2}$ × (\$4.99 + \$1.98 + \$0.89 + \$0.55)
(5) \$4.99 × ($2\frac{3}{8}$ + $\frac{1}{2}$) + \$1.98 + \$0.89 + \$0.55

(1) (2) (3) (4) (5)

51. Alvin Doctorow works 40 hours a week for the Postal Service. He spends $\frac{1}{2}$ his time sorting mail, $\frac{2}{5}$ helping customers, and the rest doing paperwork. How many hours a week does Mr. Doctorow spend doing paperwork?

(1) 4 (2) 8 (3) 12
(4) 16 (5) 20

(1) (2) (3) (4) (5)

Solving Multistep Problems with Fractions Sometimes on the GED Mathematics Test you will be asked to solve word problems with fractions that involve more than one operation. Since you already know how to work word problems that involve several operations with whole numbers and decimals, you should have no trouble working these types of problems with fractions. Look at the problem below.

■ The doctor prescribed 50 grams of medicine for Jennifer Morris's illness. She took $2\frac{1}{2}$ grams every day for a week and $1\frac{3}{4}$ grams every day during the next week. How many grams of medicine did Jennifer have left after the second week?

(1) $19\frac{1}{4}$ g (2) $19\frac{3}{4}$ g (3) $20\frac{1}{4}$ g

(4) $21\frac{1}{4}$ g (5) $21\frac{1}{2}$ g

Find the information you need. You need to know how much medicine she started with (50 g), how much medicine she took each week, and how many days are in one week (7).

Decide what operations you will need. You know you will have to multiply to find how much medicine she took each week ($2\frac{1}{2} \times 7 = 17\frac{1}{2}$ g and $1\frac{3}{4} \times 7 = 12\frac{1}{4}$ g). Check your arithmetic.

Then you will have to add to find out how much medicine she took in the two weeks ($17\frac{1}{2} + 12\frac{1}{4}$). Be sure to change the denominators of the fractions so the denominators are the same. ($17\frac{2}{4} + 12\frac{1}{4} = 29\frac{3}{4}$ g). Check your arithmetic.

Finally, you will have to subtract to find how much medicine she has left. ($50 - 29\frac{3}{4}$). Be sure to borrow 1 from 50 before you subtract ($49\frac{4}{4} - 29\frac{3}{4} = 20\frac{1}{4}$ g). Check your arithmetic.

The correct answer is (3).

Check that your answer makes sense. You can round $2\frac{1}{2}$ to 3 and $1\frac{3}{4}$ to 2. So in the two weeks, Jennifer took about 35 grams of medicine. Since both numbers were rounded up, you know she had a little more than 15 grams of medicine left.

Percents

Working with Percents A percent compares a number with 100. The word *percent* means "hundredths." For example, 25% is the same as 25/100 or 1/4 or 0.25. One whole unit equals 100% or 100/100.

Before you can solve a problem with a percent, change the percent to a decimal or a fraction.

Changing Percents to Decimals Here's how you change 50% to a decimal.

Step 1 Drop the percent sign; change 50% to 50.

Step 2 Move the decimal point two places to the *left*: 50. = .50

If a decimal is in the percent, you still move the decimal two places to the left. For example, 25.5% = .255

If a fraction is in the percent, you ignore it and move the decimal two places to the left. For example, 25¼% = .25¼

Sometimes zeros must be added to act as placeholders. For example, 8% = .08. The zero had to be placed to the left of the 8 to express the value of 8% as hundredths.

Changing Decimals to Percents Here's how you change .08 to a percent.

Step 1 Move the decimal point two places to the *right:* .08 = 08.

Step 2 Replace the decimal point with a percent sign: 08. = 8%.

Again, zeros must sometimes be added to act as placeholders. For example, 1.2 has only one digit to the right of the decimal, so a zero must be put to the right of the 2 before you can change to a percent: 1.20 = 120%

Warm-up

Change the decimals to percents and change the percents to decimals.

1. 0.67 **2.** 19% **3.** 8.8 **4.** 109%

5. $11\frac{1}{2}$% **6.** 15.5% **7.** 0.6% **8.** 4.5

Warm-up Answers

1. 67% **2.** 0.19 **3.** 880% **4.** 1.09 **5.** $0.11\frac{1}{2}$ **6.** 0.155 **7.** 0.006 **8.** 450%

Changing Percents to Fractions Here's how you change a percent to a fraction.

Step 1 Write the number that is in front of the percent symbol as the fraction's *numerator.*

Step 2 Always write 100 as the fraction's *denominator.*

Step 3 Reduce the fraction to its lowest terms.

For example, $20\% = \frac{20}{100} = \frac{1}{5}$

☑ A Test-Taking Tip

Here are four commonly used percents written as fractions. It will save you time on the GED Test if you memorize them beforehand.

$10\% = \frac{10}{100} = \frac{1}{10}$ $25\% = \frac{25}{100} = \frac{1}{4}$

$50\% = \frac{50}{100} = \frac{1}{2}$ $75\% = \frac{75}{100} = \frac{3}{4}$

Changing Fractions to Percents The following steps show how to change a fraction to a percent.

Step 1 Change the fraction to a decimal. Divide the numerator by the denominator by adding two zeros to the right of the decimal point.

```
3      .75
- = 4)3.00
4     2 8
        20
        20
         0
```

Step 2 Write the answer as a percent by moving the decimal point two places to the right and replacing it with a percent symbol: .75 = 75%

Warm-up

Change the percents to fractions and change the fractions to percents.

1. 55% **2.** $\frac{9}{10}$ **3.** $\frac{5}{8}$ **4.** $\frac{3}{10}$ **5.** 80%

6. 25% **7.** 7% **8.** 0.5% **9.** $\frac{4}{5}$

Warm-up Answers

1. $\frac{11}{20}$ **2.** 90% **3.** 62.5% **4.** 30% **5.** $\frac{4}{5}$ **6.** $\frac{1}{4}$ **7.** $\frac{7}{100}$ **8.** $\frac{1}{200}$ **9.** 80%

Using a Grid to Set Up a Percent Problem

You can take a shortcut working percent problems by using a "grid." Often, percent problems are very confusing. By using the following method, you will be able to solve percent problems quickly and efficiently.

A grid always consists of four boxes arranged like this:

part	percent
whole	100

Each box represents a certain part of a percent problem.

All percent problems are made up of these four parts: the *part,* the *whole,* the *percent,* and *100.* A percent problem will give you the information you need to fill in three of the four boxes. Your job is to find the information that goes in the fourth box to make the box complete.

Look at the problem below.

■ Ms. Fetter bought a coat that was discounted 15%. The original price of the coat was $80. How much of a discount did Ms. Fetter receive?

Here is how to pick out the right numbers for each box.

Begin with the lower right-hand corner. The number 100 is *always* in this box.

	100

Move to the upper right-hand corner. This is the "percent" box. Since you know the percent, write 15 *without the percent sign* in this box. (The 100 beneath this number takes the place of the percent sign.)

	15
	100

Move to the lower left-hand corner. This is the "whole" box. Look for the word *of* in the word problem. The whole often comes after the word *of.* Write 80 (the original price of the coat) *without the dollar sign* in the "whole" box.

	15
80	100

Move to the upper left-hand corner. This is the "part" box. This part is another way of expressing the percent. The part is often found near the word *is.* In this problem, you would leave this box empty since this is the amount you are asked to find.

	15
80	100

Warm-up 1

Set up a grid for the following problems.

1. 12% of 58 is what number?
2. 306 is 4% of what number?
3. What percent of 720 is 80?
4. ⅖ is 30% of what number?

Solving Problems with the Grid Once you have set up the above problem, you can solve it.

Step 1 Multiply the diagonals that are known.

$80 \times 15 = 1{,}200$

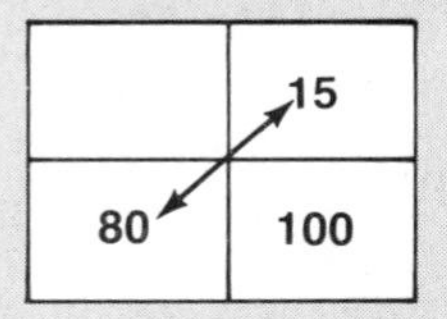

Step 2 Divide by the remaining number.

$1{,}200 \div 100 = 12$

Ms. Fetter's discount was $12.

Warm-up 2

Solve the problems in the first Warm-up.

☑ A Test-Taking Tip

Always watch for the key words *of* and *is.*

Warm-up Answers 1

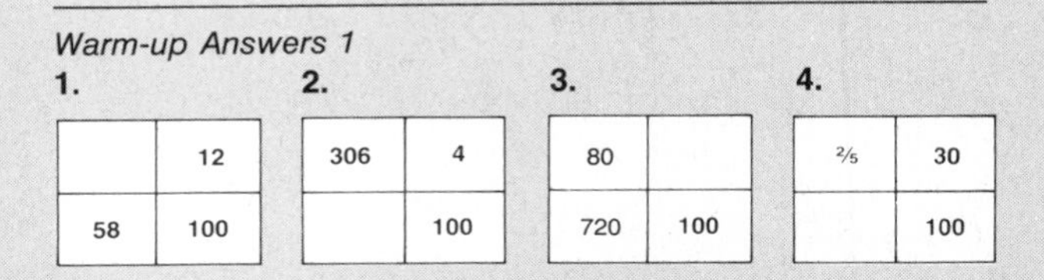

1.

	12
58	100

2.

306	4
	100

3.

80	
720	100

4.

⅖	30
	100

Warm-up Answers 2

1. 6.96 **2.** 7,650 **3.** 11.1% **4.** $1\frac{1}{3}$

Finding the Part To find the part of a number that a percent represents, set up a grid.

Look at the problem below.

■ Last year 25% of Mr. Samuels's pay went toward rent. He made $300 a week. What was his weekly rent?

First draw a grid and place the number 100 in the lower right-hand corner.

	100

Move to the upper right-hand corner. Since you know the percent, write the number 25 in the "percent" box.

	25
	100

Now, move to the lower left-hand corner. Since you know the whole amount of his weekly wages, place 300 in the "whole" box.

	25
300	100

Step 1 Multiply the diagonals that are known.

300 × 25 = 7,500

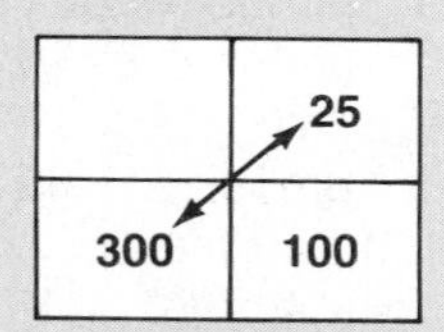

Step 2 Divide by the number that is left.

7,500 ÷ 100 = 75.

Mr. Samuels spent $75 a week on rent. Be sure to add a dollar sign in front of amounts of money.

Directions: For each problem, choose the one best answer. Answers are on page 551.

1. The Greenview Nursery Gardens sold 50 carnation plants. Of these, 20% were white. How many plants were white?

   (1) 10 (2) 12 (3) 13
   (4) 15 (5) 40

   (1) (2) (3) (4) (5)

2. In the first precinct, 9,000 voters went to the polls. The evening news reported that a high percentage of them voted for a school bond. How many voted this way?

   (1) 3,855 (2) 5,580
   (3) 5,600 (4) 5,940
   (5) Insufficient data is given to solve the problem.

   (1) (2) (3) (4) (5)

3. Harriet Barnes earned $85.75 per week before her 10% raise. How much was her weekly raise?

   (1) $10.78 (2) $8.75 (3) $8.58
   (4) $7.58 (5) $0.85

   (1) (2) (3) (4) (5)

Items 4–5 refer to the following information.

Mr. and Mrs. Nishimura earn a combined income of $25,720 per year. They have decided on a budget based on that amount.

4. The Nishimuras spend 20% of their income on rent. How much do they pay in rent per year?

   (1) $2,573 (2) $4,620 (3) $5,144
   (4) $5,145 (5) $6,086

   (1) (2) (3) (4) (5)

5. Their yearly budget for food is 17% and that for recreation is 6% of their combined income. How much do they spend on food?

   (1) $2,186.20 (2) $2,672.40
   (3) $3,400.00 (4) $4,372.40
   (5) $8,744.80

   (1) (2) (3) (4) (5)

Directions: For each problem, choose the one best answer. Answers are on page 551.

6. Agnes bought a coat for 75% of its regular price. She paid \$63.75. Which of the following expressions correctly represents the original price of the coat?

   (1) $\frac{\$63.75 \times 100}{75}$ (2) $\$63.75 \times 75$
   (3) $\frac{\$63.75 \times 75}{100}$ (4) $\frac{\$63.75}{75}$
   (5) $\$63.75 + 100\ (75)$

   (1) (2) (3) (4) (5)

7. A town reserved 5% of its property for parks. It has 120 acres of parks. How many acres of land does the town have altogether?

   (1) 2,230 (2) 2,238 (3) 2,308
   (4) 2,400 (5) 3,600

   (1) (2) (3) (4) (5)

8. Only $1\frac{1}{2}$% of the students were not inoculated for measles. These 9 children had to be vaccinated. How many students were in the school?

   (1) 600 (2) 550 (3) 500
   (4) 375 (5) 336

   (1) (2) (3) (4) (5)

9. Sales tax in the state is 6% of the total sale. Karen paid \$1.92 sales tax. What was her bill before tax was added?

   (1) \$58.45 (2) \$32.32
   (3) \$32.00 (4) \$28.00
   (5) Insufficient data is given to solve the problem.

   (1) (2) (3) (4) (5)

10. Roberto earns a $3\frac{1}{2}$% commission on all sales. Last week he earned \$52.50. Which of the following expressions correctly represents Roberto's total sales for the week?

    (1) $3\frac{1}{2} \times \$52.50$ (2) $\frac{\$52.50}{.035}$
    (3) $\frac{.035}{\$52.50}$ (4) $\$52.50 + (3\frac{1}{2} \times \$52.50)$
    (5) $\$52.50 \times .035$

    (1) (2) (3) (4) (5)

Finding the Whole To find the whole in a percent problem, set up a grid.

Look at the following problem.

■ Mr. Crown received a 25% discount on a set of new books. The price was reduced by \$25.75. What was the original price of the books?

Set up your grid with the information you know.

25.75	25
	100

Step 1 Multiply the diagonals that are known.

\$25.75 × 100 = \$2,575

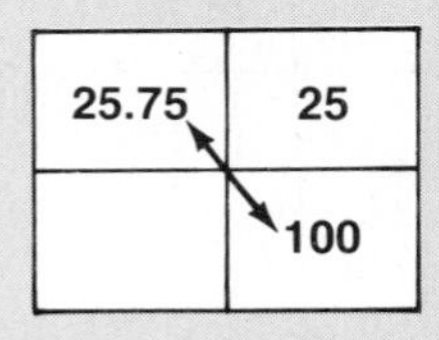

Step 2 Divide by the number that is left.

\$2,575 ÷ 25 = \$103

\$25.75 is 25% of \$103, the original price of the set of books.

Warm-up

Solve each of the following problems by using a grid. Round each of your answers to the nearest hundredth.

1. 60% of what number is 840?
2. 110% of what number is 66?
3. 16% of what number is 8?
4. 1.8% of what number is 1.134?
5. 5¼% of what number is 1.05?
6. 3.5% of what number is 4.025?
7. 23% of what number is 1,150?
8. 112% of what amount is \$504?
9. 55% of what amount is \$5,236.00?
10. 45.8% of what number is 10.076?

Warm-up Answers
1. 1,400 **2.** 60 **3.** 50 **4.** 63 **5.** 20 **6.** 115 **7.** 5,000 **8.** \$450 **9.** \$9,520.00 **10.** 22

Finding the Percent To find the percent a number represents, set up a grid.

Look at the problem below.

■ Only 5 GED students in Ms. Stevens's class of 25 are male. What percent of Ms. Stevens's class is male?

Set up your grid with the information you know.

5	
25	100

Step 1 Multiply the diagonals that are known.

$5 \times 100 = 500$

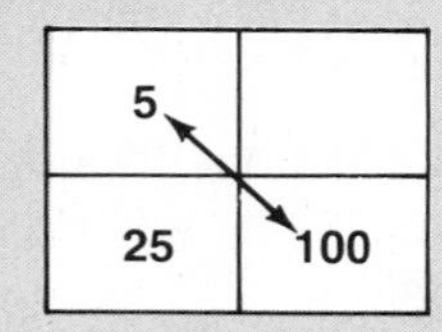

Step 2 Divide by the number that is left.

$500 \div 25 = 20$

Since you are looking for a percent, you must add a percent sign after your answer.

Ms. Stevens's class is 20% male.

Warm-up

For each problem find the percent by using a grid.

1. 50 is what percent of 500?
2. 12 is what percent of 15?
3. $0.35 is what percent of $1.75?
4. 1,275 is what percent of 8,500?
5. What percent of 125 is 65?
6. What percent of 0.5 is 1.75?
7. 125 is what percent of 125?
8. $4.75 is what percent of $25.00?
9. $3 is what percent of $12?
10. 125 is what percent of 500?

Warm-up Answers

1. 10% **2.** 80% **3.** 20% **4.** 15% **5.** 52% **6.** 350%
7. 100% **8.** 19% **9.** 25% **10.** 25%

11. To get a passing grade, Wayne needs to get 36 out of 50 questions on the exam correct. What percent of the total is that?

(1) 88% (2) 85.6% (3) 79%
(4) 72% (5) 74%

(1) (2) (3) (4) (5)

12. The Perezes just bought a home with a down payment of $3,880. The total price of the house was $48,500. What percent of the price was the down payment?

(1) 7.5% (2) 7.75%
(3) 8% (4) 8.25%
(5) Insufficient data is given to solve the problem.

(1) (2) (3) (4) (5)

13. The Kenneths' budget allows them to spend $131.67 monthly on food, $52.50 on entertainment, and $45.00 on utilities. Their monthly take-home pay is $627.00. What percent of their monthly income is spent on food?

(1) 5% (2) 21% (3) 21.5%
(4) 24% (5) 50%

(1) (2) (3) (4) (5)

14. A set of encyclopedias costs $380 and a set of sports almanacs costs $210. Manny put $190 down on one set of books. What percent of the cost did he have left to pay?

(1) 5% (2) 5.5%
(3) 45.5% (4) 50%
(5) Insufficient data is given to solve the problem.

(1) (2) (3) (4) (5)

15. Last week Loan Nguyen sold $7,200 in office machines. She earned $252 in commission. What percent of her sales is her commission?

(1) 35% (2) 4.7% (3) 4.68%
(4) 3.75% (5) 3.5%

(1) (2) (3) (4) (5)

<u>Directions:</u> For each problem, choose the <u>one</u> best answer. Answers begin on page 551.

<u>Items 16–19</u> refer to the following information.

Viewcrest Furniture Store had an inventory clearance sale that featured discounts of 25 to 60 percent. For instance, folding chairs that were originally $60 apiece were sold only in pairs at 60 percent off. Floor lamps originally priced at $85 were 25 percent off. Desks were discounted 30 percent to sell for $665. The sale lasted 10 days.

16. Which expression correctly represents the original price of a desk?

    (1) (70 × 665) ÷ 100
    (2) (100 × 70) ÷ 665
    (3) (100 × 665) ÷ 70
    (4) (30 × 665) ÷ 100
    (5) (30 × 100) ÷ 665

    ① ② ③ ④ ⑤

17. Mrs. Gronow bought two chairs, one for herself and one for a neighbor. She also bought a lamp for her neighbor. What did her neighbor owe her?

    (1) $24.00 (2) $36.00 (3) $60.00
    (4) $63.75 (5) $87.75

    ① ② ③ ④ ⑤

18. Lorraine and Martin Sarff bought a desk and a pair of chairs and charged it to their account. They wanted to pay 20 percent of the total. How much did they pay?

    (1) $70.00 (2) $95.00 (3) $124.85
    (4) $142.60 (5) $166.20

    ① ② ③ ④ ⑤

19. After six days of the sale, the store had sold 8 floor lamps, 2 sets of chairs, and 2 desks. If the store had sold $\frac{2}{5}$ of its stock of floor lamps, how many lamps remained?

    (1) 8 (2) 12 (3) 20 (4) 32
    (5) Insufficient data is given to solve the problem.

    ① ② ③ ④ ⑤

Solving Percent Problems When you read percent problems, you will have to decide whether you are trying to find the percent, the whole, or the part.

Look at the problem below.

■ Of 640 pediatricians polled, 75% recommended formula with iron for infants younger than 6 months of age. How many doctors recommend that infants use formula with iron?

Look for the information you need to answer the question. Set up a grid with the information.

	75
640	100

Notice that the 6 does not go in any box. This is just extra information that you do not need to solve the problem.

Step 1 Multiply the diagonals that are known.

640 × 75 = 48,000

	75
640	100

Step 2 Divide by the number that is left.

48,000 ÷ 100 = 480

480 pediatricians recommended that infants use formula with iron.

Warm-up

Draw a grid and solve the following problem.

■ Mr. Kamal received a $500 bonus for his outstanding work. He spent $45 of this money on some new books. What percent of his bonus did Mr. Kamal spend on books?

Warm-up Answer

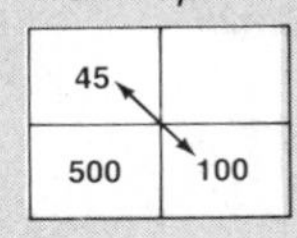

45 × 100 = 4,500
4,500 ÷ 500 = 9 9%

Solving Multistep Percent Problems No matter how many steps are in a percent problem, you will always be able to use a grid.

Look at the following problem.

■ Television sets listed at $289.95 are on sale for 7% off. The sales tax is 6%. What is the total price of each set?

Find the information you need and set up the grid to find the sale price. Round your answer to the nearest cent.

	7
289.95	100

Step 1 Multiply the diagonals that are known.

$289.95 × 7 = 2,029.65

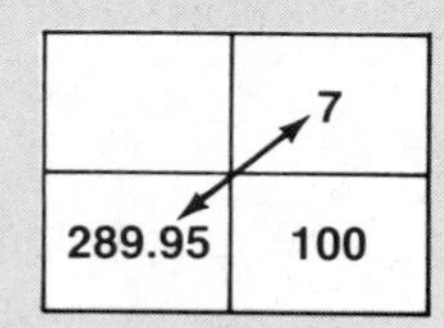

Step 2 Divide by the number that is left.

2,029.65 ÷ 100 = 20.2965 = $20.30

Step 3 Subtract to find the amount of the discount.

289.95 − 20.30 = $269.65

Now set up a grid to find the amount of the sales tax.

	6
269.65	100

Step 4 Multiply the diagonals that are known.

269.65 × 6 = 1,617.9

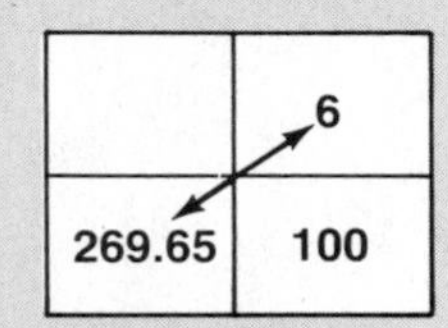

Step 5 Divide by the number that is left.

1,617.9 ÷ 100 = 16.179 = $16.18

Step 6 Add to find the final price.

$269.65 + 16.18 = $285.83

Be sure to check your arithmetic after each step.

20. Automated Service Centers announced a year-end tire sale. Super Economy radials originally selling for $63.50 were on sale for 12 percent off. What was the savings on four tires?

(1) $7.62 (2) $30.48 (3) $56.30
(4) $225.20 (5) $254.00

① ② ③ ④ ⑤

21. The Bachmans save $150 every two weeks from their combined gross salary of $1,250. What percentage of their salary do they save?

(1) 5% (2) 6% (3) 10%
(4) 12% (5) 15%

① ② ③ ④ ⑤

22. A truck driver traveled 527 miles of a 620-mile trip. What percentage of the trip was still ahead?

(1) 1.76% (2) 12.5% (3) 15%
(4) 17.6% (5) 85%

① ② ③ ④ ⑤

23. One year 7.3% of the nation's workers were unemployed. Three years later 10.1% were unemployed. What was the percentage increase in unemployment?

(1) .28 (2) .737 (3) 2.8
(4) 7.37 (5) 73.7

① ② ③ ④ ⑤

Directions: For each problem, choose the one best answer. Answers are on page 552.

Items 1–4 refer to the graph below.

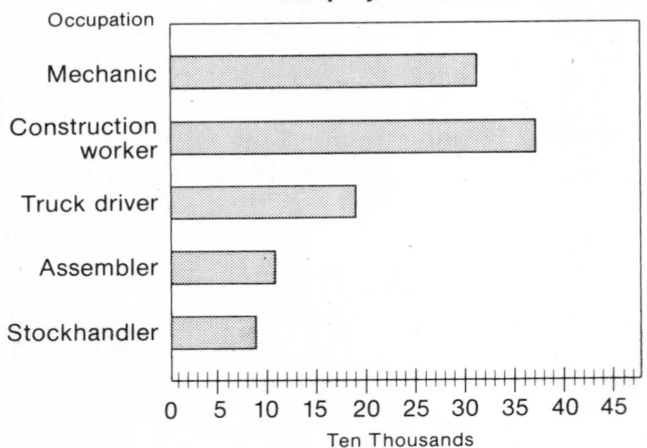

1. How many more people are construction workers than are truck drivers?

   (1) 18,000 (2) 70,000
   (3) 120,000 (4) 180,000
   (5) Insufficient data is given to solve the problem.

   ① ② ③ ④ ⑤

2. What fraction approximately represents the number of assemblers compared with the number of mechanics?

   (1) $\frac{1}{5}$ (2) $\frac{1}{4}$ (3) $\frac{1}{3}$ (4) $\frac{1}{2}$ (5) $\frac{2}{3}$

   ① ② ③ ④ ⑤

3. How many workers represent the number of general factory workers (assemblers plus stockhandlers)?

   (1) 200,000 (2) 150,000
   (3) 125,000 (4) 100,000
   (5) 20,000

   ① ② ③ ④ ⑤

4. The number of truck drivers is approximately how many more times the number of stockhandlers?

   (1) 2 (2) 4 (3) 5
   (4) 18 (5) 22

   ① ② ③ ④ ⑤

Data Analysis

Working with Graphs You will often find graphs in written material. Graphs condense information to give a quick picture of comparison. You probably see graphs in newspaper and magazine articles and on television. Several kinds of graphs may appear on the GED Test.

Bar Graphs Look at the bar graph below. Then follow the steps for reading a graph.

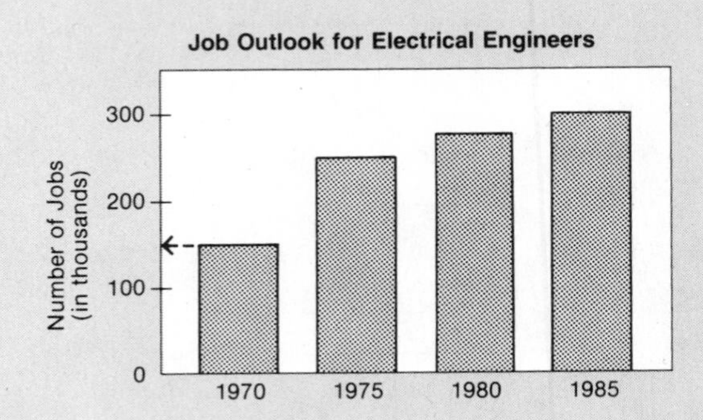

1. Read the title (Job Outlook for Electrical Engineers).
2. Look to see what is being compared (the number of jobs *in thousands* for each year).
3. To find the number of jobs in 1970, follow the bar above that year upward to the top. Then go left to determine the number of thousands. The bar stops halfway between 100,000 and 200,000, so the estimated number of jobs for electrical engineers in 1970 was 150,000.

Warm-up

Use the bar graph above to answer the following question:
What was the increase in the number of jobs from 1970 to 1980?

Warm-up Answer
First find the number of jobs in 1970 (150,000). Then find the number of jobs in 1980 (275,000). To find the difference, subtract 150,000 from 275,000. The increase was 125,000 jobs.

Double Bar Graphs The graph below is called a double bar graph. For each age group, the numbers of men and women in college are shown by two bars. The **key** shows that the open bar (☐) represents the number of women and the shaded bar (☐) the number of men.

To find the number of male students aged 21–24, first locate the right age group along the bottom scale. Follow the shaded bar to the top. Then look to the left to find the number of students in thousands (12,000).

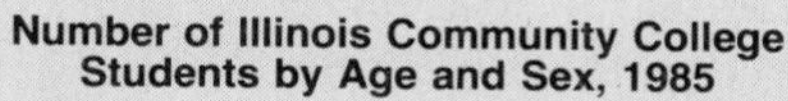

Number of Illinois Community College
Students by Age and Sex, 1985

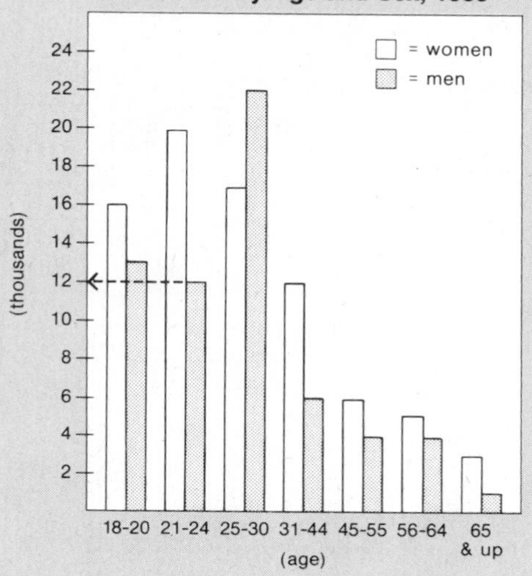

Coming to Terms

key an explanation of the meaning of each symbol or division on a graph

Warm-up

Use the graph to answer questions 1–6.

1. How many women aged 25–30 were in college in 1985? ________

2. How many more women were in age group 21–24 than in age group 18–20? ________

3. In which age group were there more men than women? ________

4. In which age group was the number of women double that of men? ________

5. What was the total number of students in the 45–55 age group? ________

____

Warm-up Answers
1. 17,000 **2.** 4,000 **3.** 25–30 age group **4.** 31–44
5. 10,000

<u>Items 5–8</u> refer to the graph below.

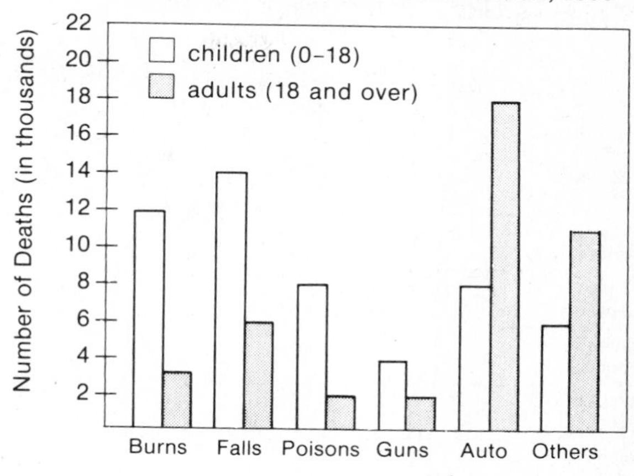

5. How many more children than adults died from burns and falls?

   (1) 2,000 (2) 5,000 (3) 7,000
   (4) 15,000 (5) 17,000

   ① ② ③ ④ ⑤

6. About how many more times are adults killed in automobile accidents than by falls?

   (1) 3 (2) 4.5 (3) 5
   (4) 6 (5) 15

   ① ② ③ ④ ⑤

7. How many accidental deaths involved children in 1986?

   (1) 14,000 (2) 34,000 (3) 42,000
   (4) 52,000 (5) 58,000

   ① ② ③ ④ ⑤

8. How many total deaths were the result of automobile accidents?

   (1) 8,000 (2) 10,000 (3) 18,000
   (4) 22,000 (5) 26,000

   ① ② ③ ④ ⑤

Directions: For each problem, choose the one best answer. Answers are on page 552.

Items 9–12 refer to the graph below.

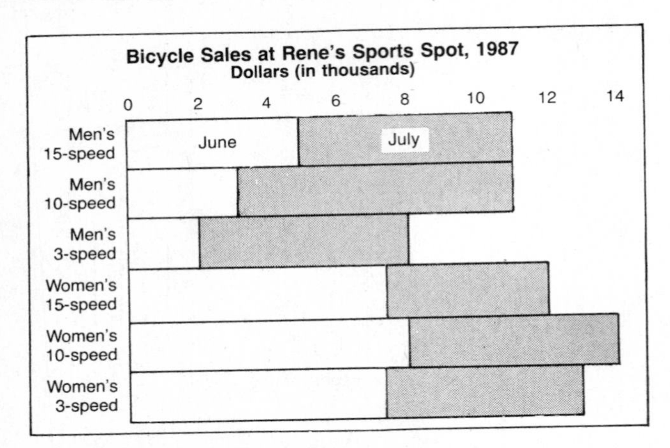

9. What was the total sales of men's 15-speed bikes in June and July?

(1) \$5,000 (2) \$6,000 (3) \$9,000
(4) \$10,000 (5) \$11,000

① ② ③ ④ ⑤

10. What was the total sales of 10-speed bikes in June and July?

(1) \$6,000 (2) \$11,000 (3) \$14,000
(4) \$23,000 (5) \$25,000

① ② ③ ④ ⑤

11. How much more money was spent on women's 3-speeds in July than in May?

(1) \$2,000 (2) \$3,000
(3) \$5,000 (4) \$8,000
(5) Insufficient data is given to solve the problem.

① ② ③ ④ ⑤

12. Which two types of bikes sold the most during June and July?

(1) men's 15-speeds and men's 10-speeds
(2) women's 3-speeds and men's 10-speeds
(3) women's 10-speeds and men's 15-speeds
(4) women's 10-speeds and women's 3-speeds
(5) men's 3-speeds and women's 3-speeds

① ② ③ ④ ⑤

Combination Bar Graph This bar graph is also a double bar graph. It also shows data about both men (male) and women (female); however, for each category the number of men and women is shown by the same bar. The end of the bar gives the total for men and women combined.

Note that the key is located in one of the bars. Read the shaded part of each bar (men) as usual. Read the light part by subtracting the number for men from the total number that the bar represents. This gives the number of women.

Employment in Major Occupational Groups by Sex, 1985

WORKERS (in millions)
0 2 4 6 8 10 12 14 16

Clerical
Professional
Male
Female
Craft
Service
Operatives
Sales

Warm-up

Use the graph to answer these questions.

1. How many people work in service occupations? ____________
2. How many men work in the service field? ____________
3. How many women work in the service field? ____________
4. In which two fields are there more women than men? ____________
5. What is the percent of women in sales? ____________

Warm-up Answers
1. 12 million **2.** 4 million **3.** 8 million **4.** clerical and service **5.** 40% ($\frac{2}{5}$)

Line Graphs A line graph is a way to show a changing amount. If the line goes up from left to right, there is an upward trend. If the line goes down from left to right, there is a downward trend.

A line graph can also be used to compare two changing amounts. This graph gives the stopping distance for a car at different speeds on a wet road and on a dry road.

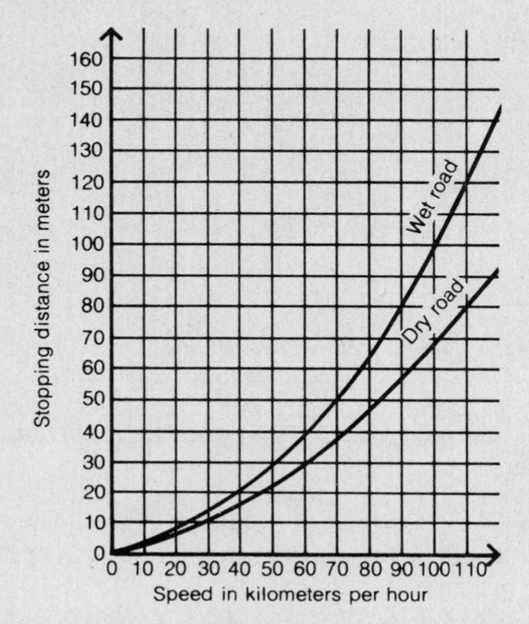

Warm-up

Answer these questions using the graph above.

1. What is the stopping distance on a dry road when a car is going 60 kilometers per hour?

____

2. What is the car's speed on a wet road when the stopping distance is 30 meters? _______

3. At 100 kilometers per hour on a dry road, can the car stop in 60 meters? _______

4. What is the approximate stopping difference in meters of a car going 90 kilometers per hour on a wet road and a similar car going 90 kilometers on a dry road? _______________

Warm-up Answers

1. 30 meters **2.** 50 kilometers per hour **3.** No **4.** 20 meters

Items 13–16 refer to the graph below.

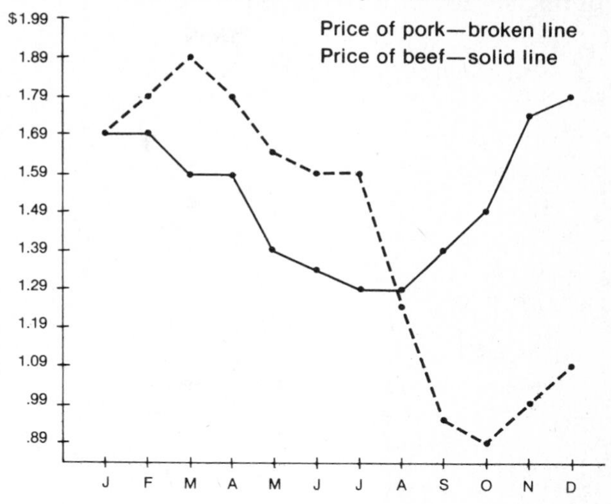

13. What was the difference in the percent of decrease in the price of pork from January to June than from July to December?

(1) 5% (2) 25% (3) 32%
(4) 36% (5) 41%

① ② ③ ④ ⑤

14. How much more was the price of pork than the price of beef in March?

(1) 20¢ (2) 25¢ (3) 30¢
(4) 35¢ (5) 40¢

① ② ③ ④ ⑤

15. The cost of beef was approximately how many times more than the cost of pork in November?

(1) 1.5 (2) 1.6 (3) 1.75
(4) 1.9 (5) 2.0

① ② ③ ④ ⑤

16. What is the percentage increase in the price of beef between the two months that had the highest price increase?

(1) 12% (2) 17% (3) 21%
(4) 27% (5) 30%

① ② ③ ④ ⑤

Directions: For each problem, choose the one best answer. Answers are on pages 552–553.

Items 17–20 refer to the graph below.

Number of Airline Passengers by Point of Origin, 1986

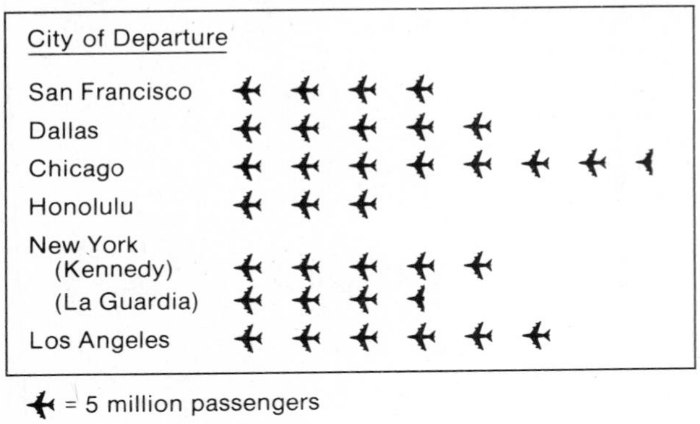
City of Departure
San Francisco
Dallas
Chicago
Honolulu
New York
(Kennedy)
(La Guardia)
Los Angeles
= 5 million passengers

17. Approximately how many passengers departed from New York in 1986?

(1) 8 million (2) 16 million
(3) 40.5 million (4) 42 million
(5) 42.5 million

1 2 3 4 5

18. How many more passengers departed from Los Angeles than from Honolulu?

(1) 2 million (2) 3 million
(3) 10 million (4) 11 million
(5) 15 million

1 2 3 4 5

19. From how many cities did more than 35 million passengers depart?

(1) 2 (2) 3 (3) 4 (4) 5 (5) 6

1 2 3 4 5

20. If 250 passengers are on each plane, how many passenger planes left San Francisco in 1986?

(1) 8,000 (2) 40,000 (3) 80,000
(4) 100,000 (5) 800,000

1 2 3 4 5

Pictographs A pictograph (picture graph) uses symbols to compare information. Partial symbols represent fractional parts of one quantity. You must count the number of symbols to determine the entire amount represented. The number you count must then be multiplied by the number represented by one symbol.

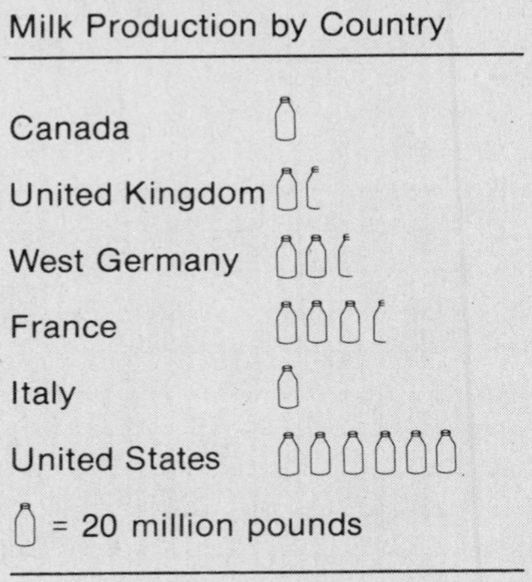
Milk Production by Country
Canada
United Kingdom
West Germany
France
Italy
United States
= 20 million pounds

The pictograph above shows milk production in different countries. To find the number of pounds of milk produced in France, count the number of symbols (3½) and multiply the number of pounds represented by one symbol (20 million): 20,000,000 × 3.5 = 70,000,000 pounds of milk were produced in France.

Warm-up

Answer these questions using the graph above.

1. How many pounds of milk were produced in the United Kingdom? ____________

2. The total production of milk in which two countries equaled the production of milk in the United States? ____________

3. Milk production in the United States is how many times its production in the United Kingdom? ____________

4. How many more pounds of milk were produced in France than in Italy? ____________

Warm-up Answers
1. 30 million pounds **2.** West Germany and France
3. 4 times **4.** 50 million pounds

Circle Graphs A circle graph is used to show the parts of a whole unit. The most common type of circle graph is divided into parts that represent percents of the whole. The sum of all the parts must add up to 100%. Sometimes a circle graph shows how one dollar is divided. Each part represents a certain number of cents and all the parts must add up to $1.00.

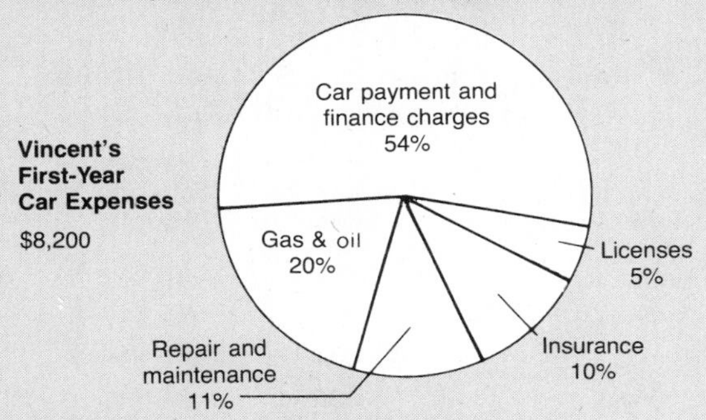

The circle graph above represents the breakdown of every dollar Vincent spent on his car during the first year he owned it. He spent a total of $8,200. To find out how much Vincent spent on repair and maintenance for the year, set up a grid and solve

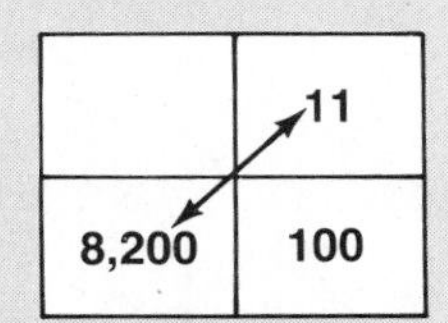

Multiply the diagonals (8,200 × 11 = 90,200). Then divide by the remaining number (90,200 ÷ 100 = 902). Vincent spent $902 on repair and maintenance.

Warm-up

Use the graph above to answer the questions.

1. Insurance and licenses represented what percent of Vincent's expenses? ______

2. Gas and oil represented what fraction of his expenses? ______

3. How much did Vincent spend for his car payment and finance charges altogether?

______

4. What was Vincent's total cost for gas and oil and repair and maintenance for the year?

______

5. Out of each dollar spent, how much did Vincent pay for gas, oil, and licenses? ______

______

Warm-up Answers

1. 15% **2.** $\frac{1}{5}$ **3.** $4,428 **4.** $2,542 **5.** 25¢

Items 21–24 refer to the graph below.

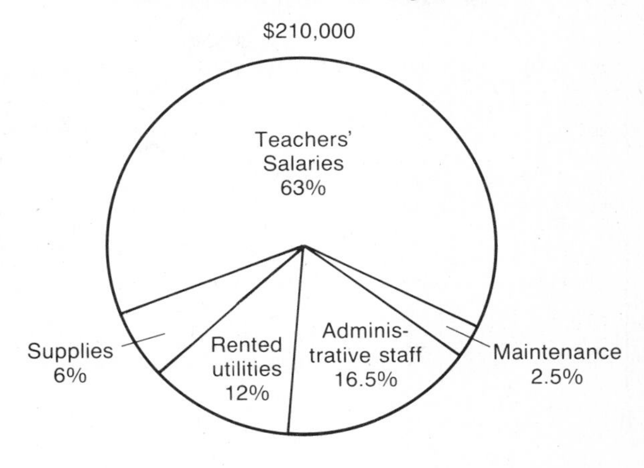

21. What was the difference between the percent spent on teachers' salaries and that spent on the administrative staff?

(1) 46% (2) 46.5% (3) 47%
(4) 56% (5) 79.5%

(1) (2) (3) (4) (5)

22. What fraction of the school's budget was spent for rent and utilities and teachers' salaries combined?

(1) $\frac{1}{4}$ (2) $\frac{2}{5}$ (3) $\frac{3}{4}$ (4) $\frac{4}{5}$ (5) $\frac{5}{6}$

(1) (2) (3) (4) (5)

23. How much money was budgeted for teachers' salaries in 1986?

(1) $13,200 (2) $131,000
(3) $132,300 (4) $133,300
(5) $148,200

(1) (2) (3) (4) (5)

24. The administrative staff consists of a president and a secretary. The secretary earns $9,525 a year. Which of the following expressions correctly represents the president's salary?

(1) $210,000 − $9,525
(2) $210,000 × 0.165
(3) ($210,000 × 16.5) − $9,525
(4) ($210,000 × 0.165) − $9,525
(5) $210,000 × (0.165 + $9,525)

(1) (2) (3) (4) (5)

Directions: For each problem, choose the one best answer. Answers are on page 553.

Items 25–28 refer to the table below.

How much will this air conditioner cost to run?

Yearly hours of use		250	750	1,000	2,000	3,000
Cost per kilowatt-hour	2¢	$7	$20	$28	$56	$84
	4¢	$14	$41	$56	$112	$168
	6¢	$20	$61	$80	$160	$240
	8¢	$27	$82	$108	$216	$324
	10¢	$34	$102	$136	$272	$408
	12¢	$41	$122	$163	$326	$489

25. If the local cost per kilowatt-hour of electricity is 8 cents and you use your air conditioner approximately 1,000 hours per year, what is your estimated yearly cost?

(1) $80 (2) $82 (3) $108
(4) $136 (5) $216

(1) (2) (3) (4) (5)

26. What is the difference in yearly cost if you run your air conditioner 1,000 instead of 3,000 hours?

(1) $136 (2) $163
(3) $272 (4) $326
(5) Insufficient data is given to solve the problem.

(1) (2) (3) (4) (5)

27. How many times as much is the cost of using your air conditioner 1,000 hours instead of 250 hours if your kilowatt cost per hour is 6 cents?

(1) 2 (2) 3 (3) 4 (4) 5 (5) 6

(1) (2) (3) (4) (5)

28. What factors will affect the individual cost per kilowatt-hour?

(1) local energy rate and product usage
(2) room capacity and local energy rate
(3) product usage and location
(4) product usage and climate
(5) Insufficient data is given to solve the problem.

(1) (2) (3) (4) (5)

Tables Like graphs, tables are a way to present information. A table usually has columns and rows of numbers that give specific information. The headings across the top of the table tell you the type of information contained in the columns. The headings down the side show you the location of the information in the rows.

Look at the following table.

Prisoner Population in Selected States, March 31, 1983

State	Prisoner population	Percent change from March 31, 1982
Alabama	9,108	16.7%
California	36,122	18.8%
Florida	27,604	12.3%
Georgia	14,686	15.1%
Illinois	13,954	3.1%
Kentucky	4,046	−2.5%
Maine	1,019	10.5%
Michigan	14,481	−5.6%
New York	28,919	9.7%
Pennsylvania	10,855	11.7%

Which state had the largest percent of increase in its prisoner population from 1982 to 1983? The headings help you find the answer. First read down the third column, "Percent change from March 31, 1982," to see that 18.8 was the largest percent of increase. Then look to the left in that row to find that the state was California.

Warm-up

Use the table above to answer these questions.

1. Which state had the smallest percentage *increase* from 1982? ______

2. Which two states had smaller prisoner populations in 1983 than in 1982?

______

3. How many more prisoners were there in Georgia than in Pennsylvania? ______

4. What was the combined prisoner population of Alabama, Florida, and Georgia?

______

Warm-up Answers
1. Illinois **2.** Kentucky and Michigan **3.** 3,831 **4.** 51,398

Reading Meters Most meters have a "hand" that points to a number in much the same way as the hands on a clock or a watch point to numbers that represent hours and minutes. When you read a meter, you must be able to tell to what number or between which two numbers the hand is pointing.

The most important thing to remember when reading a meter is that if the hand is pointing between two numbers, the *lower* of the two numbers should be recorded. If the hand points directly to a number, the exact number should be recorded.

Look at the electric meter dials below. What number of kilowatt-hours should be recorded?

On the first dial the hand points directly to 7. The reading of the second dial is 0. Read the third dial as 6. The fourth dial is 8, and the fifth dial is 4. The reading is 70,684, or 70,684 kilowatt-hours.

An altimeter, which measures the altitude of airplanes, has two hands on one meter. The shorter hand tells how many thousands of feet the airplane is above sea level, and the longer hand tells how many hundreds of feet the airplane is above sea level.

Look at this altimeter.

The short hand is pointed to the 4 and the long hand is pointing to the 7. According to the altimeter, the airplane is 4,700 feet above sea level.

☑ A Test-Taking Tip

If the GED Test gives you one meter with two hands on it, it will include directions that tell you what each hand represents. Be sure to read those directions carefully.

29. What is the reading on this gas meter?

(1) 44,067 (2) 44,077 (3) 43,067
(4) 43,078 (5) 43,068

① ② ③ ④ ⑤

30. In an altimeter, the shorter hand indicates thousands of feet above sea level. The longer hand indicates hundreds of feet above sea level. If an airplane's altimeter has the reading shown above, how many feet above sea level is the airplane flying?

(1) 6 (2) 60 (3) 600
(4) 6,000 (5) 60,000

① ② ③ ④ ⑤

31. Which number should be recorded for the dial on the meter above?

(1) 7 (2) 7.5 (3) 8
(4) 78 (5) 87

① ② ③ ④ ⑤

Directions: For each problem, choose the one best answer. Answers are on page 553.

Average sales of beachwear at Sal's Summer Shack

$15000, 14000, 13000, 12000, 11000, 10000, 9000, 8000, 7000, 6000, 5000, 4000, 3000, 2000, 1000, 0

April May June July

32. According to the chart above, how many times greater were the average sales in July than in April?

(1) 2 (2) 3 (3) 4 (4) 5 (5) 50

① ② ③ ④ ⑤

33. Temperature highs for December 12 in San Diego for five consecutive years were 62°, 71°, 78°, 69°, and 65°. What was the mean high for that date?

(1) 69° (2) 74° (3) 68°
(4) 86° (5) 345°

① ② ③ ④ ⑤

34. The quintuplets were the following lengths at birth: $15\frac{1}{4}$ inches, $15\frac{3}{8}$ inches, $14\frac{7}{8}$ inches, $15\frac{1}{4}$ inches, and $15\frac{1}{2}$ inches. What was the average length in inches of the quintuplets?

(1) $15\frac{1}{4}$ (2) $15\frac{5}{8}$ (3) $15\frac{3}{8}$
(4) $15\frac{1}{2}$ (5) $16\frac{1}{4}$

① ② ③ ④ ⑤

35. Sales receipts in a shoe store totaled $7,832 the first week, $6,445 the second week, $7,230 the third week, and $5,989 the fourth week. What were the store's mean weekly sales?

(1) $6,784 (2) $6,874 (3) $6,487
(4) $6,870 (5) $27,496

① ② ③ ④ ⑤

Finding Means (Averages) The **mean** of a group of numbers is the average of those numbers. Averages are often used in daily life. In sports you might say a baseball player has a three-hundred average. When you shop for a car, you check to see what its average gas mileage is. If you are planning a career, you may wonder what the average income is for a person in that field.

You already know how to find an average when you are given the total of something and asked to divide it by a certain number. Sometimes, however, you need to find the total yourself by adding individual items together. Then you can divide by the number of items to find the average. Here is an example of this type of two-step problem.

■ Larry Bird, a great basketball player, played 5 games in a week. He scored 24 points, 28 points, 33 points, 17 points, and 33 points. What was his average score per game that week?

First, *add* the scores. Larry scored a total of 135 points that week. Then divide by 5. You *divide* by 5 because Larry had 5 scores for the 5 games. (If you wanted to figure an average for 150 games, you'd have to add the scores for the 150 games and then divide by 150.) Larry's average (135 ÷ 5) was 27 points.

Coming to Terms

mean another word for *average*

Warm-up

Find the mean in these problems. Use the example above as a model.

1. You ask 5 plumbers what their incomes are. Here's what they say: $22,400; $27,900; $30,000; $19,000; $16,500. What is their average income?

2. To get through computer school, you ask 8 schools how many months it takes the typical student. Here's what that say: 18, 16, 30, 19, 12, 6, 10, 33. What is the mean completion time?

Warm-up Answers
1. $23,160 **2.** 18 months

Finding Medians The **median** in a set of data is the middle number. To find the median, you must arrange the data in order from least to greatest value and then find the middle number.

Look at the problem below.

- Gerry took a survey of the ages of the members of the bird watching club. Their ages are 22, 28, 23, 32, 21, 37, 41, 22, 26, 36, and 32. What is the median age of the club members?

First arrange the data in order from least to greatest:

21 22 22 23 26 28 32 32 36 37 41

Then find the middle number:

21 22 22 23 26 **28** 32 32 36 37 41

Since 28 is in the middle, the median age is 28. Just as many members are in the club who are older than 28 as are younger than 28.

If an even number of data is given, the median is the mean of the two middle numbers when all of the numbers are ordered from least to greatest.

Look at the following problem.

- In eight bowling games Steven scored the following points: 156, 148, 162, 154, 167, 149, 150, and 160. What was Steven's median score?

Arrange the data in order from least to greatest:

148 149 150 154 156 160 162 167

Since Steven played an even number of games, you must find the two middle numbers. The numbers are 154 and 156. Find the average of these numbers. (154 + 156 = 310; 310 ÷ 2 = 155). Steven's median score is 155.

Coming to Terms

median middle number in a set of data

Warm-up

Find the median in the following problem.

- Mr. Manuel earns extra money by wiring houses. He earned the following amounts of money on consecutive Saturdays: $220, $206; $185; $170; $80; $215. What were his median earnings for those weeks?

Warm-up Answer
$195.50

36. The prices for a certain car at different dealerships are $9,042, $9,036, $9,102, $9,090, $9,120, and $9,056. What is the median price of the car?

(1) $9,064 (2) $9,066 (3) $9,073
(4) $9,080 (5) $9,102

① ② ③ ④ ⑤

37. Zack received the following scores on his math tests during the last semester: 82, 83, 78, 90, 94, 91, 91, 89, 82. What was his median score?

(1) 83.5 (2) 86 (3) 86.6
(4) 89 (5) 91

① ② ③ ④ ⑤

Items 38–39 refer to the following information.

Salaries of Twelve Pro-Baseball Players

$ 92,000	$120,000	$ 96,000
$105,000	$106,000	$ 92,000
$116,000	$ 90,000	$104,000
$ 90,000	$105,000	$108,000

38. What is the median salary for the baseball players?

(1) $92,500 (2) $102,000
(3) $104,000 (4) $104,500
(5) $105,000

① ② ③ ④ ⑤

39. What is the mean salary of the baseball players?

(1) $92,500 (2) $102,000
(3) $104,000 (4) $104,500
(5) $105,000

① ② ③ ④ ⑤

40. In one week in September a thermometer recorded these temperatures: 63°, 70°, 83°, 76°, 67°, 59°, 71°. What was the median temperature for the week?

(1) 67° (2) 70° (3) 71°
(4) 76° (5) 80°

① ② ③ ④ ⑤

Directions: For each problem, choose the one best answer. Answers begin on page 553.

41. Express the ratio of 6 inches to 1 foot.

(1) 6:12 (2) 1:2 (3) 2:1
(4) 12:6 (5) 6:1

(1) (2) (3) (4) (5)

42. On an exam a student got 18 questions right and 2 questions wrong. Express the ratio of the number right to the total.

(1) 2:18 (2) 10:9 (3) 9:10
(4) 18:20 (5) 20:18

(1) (2) (3) (4) (5)

43. Alberto is 12 years old and his sister is 2 years old. Express his age to hers in ratio form.

(1) 12:2 (2) 6:1 (3) 2:12
(4) 1:6 (5) 2:6

(1) (2) (3) (4) (5)

44. Of the 240 boxes of cereal on the shelf, 144 were damaged in a flood. Express the ratio of damaged boxes to undamaged boxes. (Be sure to express the ratio in lowest terms.)

(1) 240:144 (2) 3:2 (3) 240:96
(4) 4:6 (5) 96:144

(1) (2) (3) (4) (5)

45. The ratio of rainy days to sunny days in April was 3:2. If it rained 18 days of the month, how many days were sunny?

(1) 22 (2) 18 (3) 15
(4) 12 (5) 10

(1) (2) (3) (4) (5)

Ratios A **ratio** is a comparison of two numbers. A ratio is used to compare one quantity to another. For example, if a company softball team won 5 games and lost 9 games, you could write the ratio of wins to losses in three different ways, as shown below.

5:9 $\frac{5}{9}$ 5 to 9

All three of the above expressions are read "five to nine."

A ratio is written in the order in which the information appears in the sentence. If the above example had said that the team lost 9 games and won 5, the ratio would be written as shown below.

9:5 $\frac{9}{5}$ 9 to 5

The three expressions are read "nine to five."

Since ratios are actually fractions, they are usually written in lowest terms. If the team had won 6 games and lost 8 games the ratio 6:8 would be reduced and written as 3:4. Look at it this way:

$$\frac{6}{8} = \frac{3}{4}$$

Coming to Terms

ratio comparison of two numbers that is used to compare one quantity to another

Warm-up

Express the following facts as ratios. Reduce to lowest terms. Then write each ratio in three ways.

1. 9 hours to 12 hours
2. 22 sailboats to 55 rowboats
3. \$100 to \$20
4. 3 winners to 27 losers
5. 72 feet to 16 feet

Need a Hint for Number 42?
Notice the word total *in the question. What must you do before you can write the ratio?*

Warm-up Answers

1. 3:4, $\frac{3}{4}$, 3 to 4 **2.** 2:5, $\frac{2}{5}$, 2 to 5 **3.** 5:1, $\frac{5}{1}$, 5 to 1

4. 1:9, $\frac{1}{9}$, 1 to 9 **5.** 9:2, $\frac{9}{2}$, 9 to 2

Probability If you toss a coin, it can land in one of two possible ways: a head or a tail. The chance of the coin landing as a head is 1 in 2. The *probability* of a head is 1 out of 2 or ½. The probability of a tail is also ½.

The probability of an event that can never occur is 0. The probability of an event that must occur is 1. For example, the probability that the sun will rise in the west is 0. The probability that the sun will rise in the east is 1.

You can use probability to make predictions. Suppose two squares, one triangle, three rectangles, and two stars were placed in a box. You are to pick a shape at random. But before you do, you want to predict the likelihood of selecting a triangle. Since eight objects are in the box and only one of those objects is a triangle, you have a 1 in 8 chance of choosing a triangle. In other words, the probability that you will *not* choose a triangle is ⅞ (1 − ⅛). You can predict that you are more likely not to pick a triangle than you are to pick one.

You can also reduce fractions that represent probabilities to lowest terms. For example, the probability that you will select a square in the above sample is 2/8 or ¼.

Warm-up

Find the probability of the outcome.

The letters of the word K A L A M A Z O O are placed in a bag. You choose one letter without looking. What is the probability that you choose each of the following?

1. a vowel
2. a consonant
3. an M
4. an A
5. an O
6. an L or an A

Warm-up Answers

1. $\frac{5}{9}$ **2.** $\frac{4}{9}$ **3.** $\frac{1}{9}$ **4.** $\frac{3}{9} = \frac{1}{3}$ **5.** $\frac{2}{9}$ **6.** $\frac{4}{9}$

Items 46–48 refer to the following information.

A bowl has 4 blue marbles, 4 orange marbles, 6 red marbles, and 2 green marbles. Nicholas chooses one marble from the bowl 3 different times without looking. After each selection, he returns the marble to the bowl.

46. What is the probability that Nicholas chooses a blue marble on the first draw?

(1) $\frac{1}{4}$ (2) $\frac{1}{16}$ (3) $\frac{4}{1}$

(4) 0 (5) $\frac{16}{4}$

① ② ③ ④ ⑤

47. What is the probability that Nicholas chooses a red or a green marble on the second draw?

(1) $\frac{16}{8}$ (2) $\frac{6}{16}$ (3) $\frac{3}{8}$ (4) $\frac{1}{2}$ (5) $\frac{3}{4}$

① ② ③ ④ ⑤

48. What is the probability that Nicholas chooses a blue, orange, or green marble on the third draw?

(1) $\frac{5}{10}$ (2) $\frac{5}{8}$ (3) $\frac{1}{2}$ (4) $\frac{8}{5}$ (5) $\frac{7}{16}$

① ② ③ ④ ⑤

Items 49–50 refer to the following information.

A large envelope contains some index cards all the same size. Each card indicates a prize: 25 are for tickets to a football game, 32 are movie passes, 28 are discount coupons to an ice-cream parlor, and 15 are symphony tickets. Fay chooses one card 2 different times without looking. After her first choice she does *not* return the card to the envelope.

49. On her first draw, what is the probability that Fay will draw either a ticket to a football game or to the symphony?

(1) $\frac{100}{40}$ (2) $\frac{25}{100}$ (3) $\frac{2}{5}$

(4) $\frac{1}{4}$ (5) $\frac{3}{20}$

① ② ③ ④ ⑤

50. Fay's first draw is a ticket to a football game. On her second draw, what is the probability that Fay will draw a movie pass or a discount coupon to the ice-cream parlor?

(1) $\frac{4}{5}$ (2) $\frac{20}{33}$ (3) $\frac{7}{25}$

(4) $\frac{60}{100}$ (5) $\frac{99}{60}$

① ② ③ ④ ⑤

Proportions Like a ratio, a **proportion** is a comparison. A proportion compares two equal ratios. Look at the following proportion.

$\frac{3}{4} = \frac{6}{8}$ $\quad$ 3:4 = 6:8

These ratios are a proportion because 3 has the same relationship to 4 that 6 has to 8. The 3 is ¾ of 4, and 6 is ¾ of 8.

The grid below shows the following proportion:

3:4 = 6:8

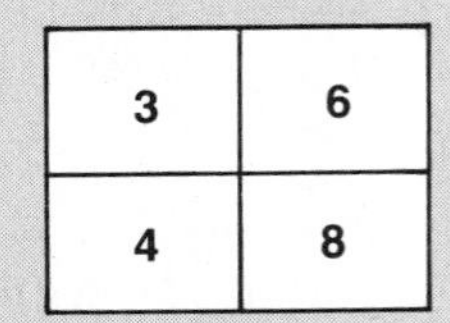

Notice the diagonals. Do you remember that when you multiplied the diagonals of a percent problem, the answers were equal? When you multiply the diagonals in a proportion, the answers are equal.

Coming to Terms

proportion a comparison that compares two equal ratios

Warm-up

Set up a grid for each of the proportions below.

1. 11:12 = 33:36
2. 100:75 = 64:48
3. 3:$2.49 = 4:$3.32
4. $\frac{1}{2}:\frac{1}{4} = \frac{3}{4}:\frac{3}{8}$

How to Use a Grid to Solve a Proportion Problem Set up a grid for a proportion problem.

■ Linda worked 48 hours in 6 days. How many hours would Hank have to work in 5 days to work the same number of hours?

Look at this grid.

hours	48		hours
days	6	5	days

Place the facts referring to Linda on the left side of the grid. Place the facts referring to Hank on the right side of the grid. Since you don't know the total number of hours Hank worked, you can place a question mark in the upper right-hand box. You find the missing number in the same way you found the missing number in a percent problem.

Step 1 Multiply the diagonals that are known.

5 × 48 = 240

Step 2 Divide by the number that is left.

240 ÷ 6 = 40

Step 3 Label your answer 40 hours.

Hank would have to work 40 hours.

Warm-up

Use the grid method to find the unknown values in each of the following proportions.

1. 20:25 + ?:45
2. ?:18 = 10:4
3. 10:? = 8:28
4. 9:3 = 57:?

Warm-up Answers

1.

11	33
12	36

2.

100	64
75	48

3.

3	4
$2.49	$3.32

4.

½	¾
¼	⅜

Warm-up Answers

1. 36. **2.** 45 **3.** 35 **4.** 19

Working with Proportions The most important part of solving a proportion problem is getting the right information into the right boxes. The top two boxes must have the same label, and the bottom two boxes must have the same label. The boxes on the left should refer to the same item, and the boxes on the right should refer to the same item.

Follow this explanation carefully to see how you can use the grid method in combination with the system to solve this type of GED Test problem.

■ If 240 calories are in 5 cookies, how many calories are in 24 cookies?

Read the problem carefully, and find the information you need. You know you need all of the information relating to calories and numbers of cookies.

You also know that since this is a proportion problem, you can use the grid method which involves multiplying and dividing.

Set up the grid.

calories	**240**		**calories**
cookies	**5**	**24**	**cookies**

Multiply the diagonals.

24 × 240 = 5,760

After checking your arithmetic, divide by the number that is left.

5760 ÷ 5 = 1,152

Twenty-four cookies have 1,152 calories.

Warm-up

Use the grid method to solve the following problems.

1. If your pulse rate is 21 beats in 15 seconds, what is your pulse rate for one minute?

2. Darryl worked for 6 days during harvest driving a truck for a wheat rancher. He earned $275. How many days would he need to work to earn $1,650?

3. A map is drawn to the scale of 1 inch to equal 75 miles. If two cities are shown as 2½ inches apart on the map, how many miles apart are they?

Warm-up Answers

1. 84 beats **2.** 36 days **3.** $187\frac{1}{2}$ miles

<u>Directions:</u> For each problem, choose the <u>one</u> best answer. Answers are on page 554.

51. If 24 tablets cost $3.36, how much will 12 tablets cost?

(1) $0.14 (2) $1.44 (3) $1.68
(4) $2.00 (5) $2.68

(1) (2) (3) (4) (5)

52. If a solution has 2 gallons of water for every quart of cleaning solution, how many quarts of cleaning solution would be needed for 12 gallons of water?

(1) 2 (2) 4 (3) 6 (4) 8 (5) 10

(1) (2) (3) (4) (5)

53. A coach timed a player who was performing knee bends. If the player performs 11 knee bends in 15 seconds, how many knee bends can she perform in one minute?

(1) 11 (2) 22 (3) 32
(4) 44 (5) 55

(1) (2) (3) (4) (5)

54. If 150 gallons of gas were pumped in one hour, how many hours would it take to pump 1,500 gallons?

(1) 12 (2) 11 (3) 10
(4) 8 (5) 6

(1) (2) (3) (4) (5)

55. If 200 compact cars can be produced in an 8-hour shift and there are 3 shifts per day at the plant, how many compact cars can be produced in a 5-day workweek?

(1) 1,000 (2) 2,000 (3) 3,000
(4) 4,000 (5) 5,000

(1) (2) (3) (4) (5)

Number Relationships

Positive and Negative Numbers Whole numbers, decimals, and fractions can all be represented on a number line.

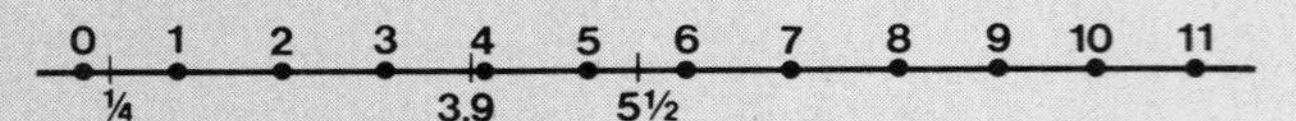

This line could go on endlessly because whole numbers, decimals, and fractions have no limit. All the numbers on this line are called **positive numbers** because all are greater than zero.

Numbers *less* than zero can also be represented on a number line. These numbers are called **negative numbers.** Positive and negative numbers are sometimes called signed numbers.

A negative number *always* has a minus sign before it. A positive number may have a plus sign before it, but any number without a sign is understood to be positive.

Zero is neither positive nor negative. Here is a number line with both positive and negative numbers and zero.

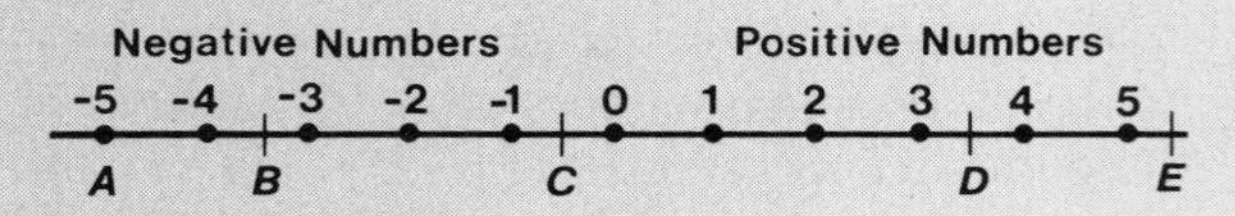

Coming to Terms

positive number any number that is greater than zero
negative number any number less than zero

Adding Two Positive Numbers Adding 5 + 6 is represented on a number line like this:

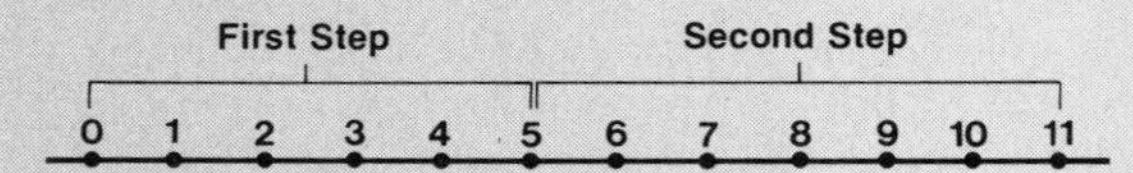

First, move 5 places to the *right.* To add 6, move 6 more places to the right. You end up at the point labeled 11.

Adding Two Negative Numbers Here is how (−5) + (−6) is represented on a number line.

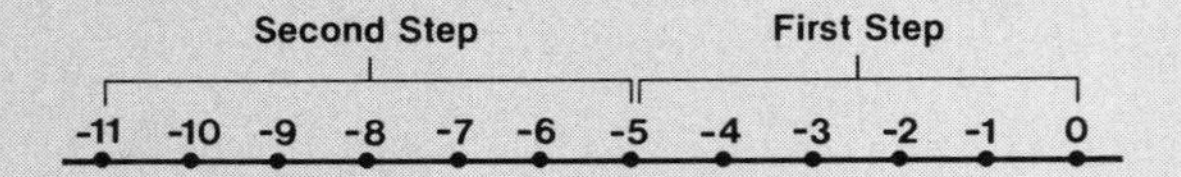

The minus sign in −5 indicates that you should move 5 places to the *left.* The minus sign in −6 indicates that you should move 6 more places to the left. You end up at the point labeled −11.

Adding Positive and Negative Numbers Adding (+5) + (−6) is represented on a number line like this:

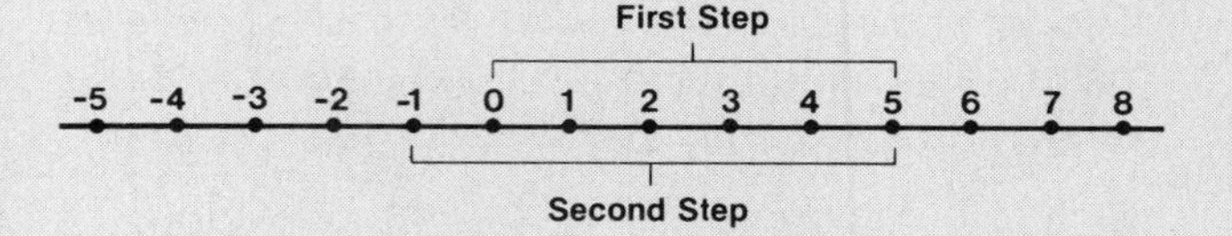

First, you move five places to the *right.* The minus sign in −6 then tells you to move to the *left.* So in your second step, move 6 places to the left. You end up at the point labeled −1.

The parentheses around +5 and −6 in the problem are used to separate the plus sign that tells you to add from the signs that indicate whether the numbers are positive (+) or negative (−).

You can add a group of positive and negative numbers without the use of a number line.

Add (+4) + (−5) + (+9) + (−14).

Step 1 Add the positive numbers and make a positive total: (+4) + (+ 9) = 13.

Step 2 Add the negative numbers and make a negative total: (−5) + (−14) = −19.

Step 3 Since the negative total is larger than the positive total, the answer is a negative number. It will have a minus sign before it.

Step 4 Subtract the smaller number from the larger one: 19 − 13 = 6. Because the answer has to be negative, the final answer is −6.

Subtracting Positive and Negative Numbers The rule for subtraction is: Change the sign of the number being subtracted and then add. For example, to subtract (−4) − (+6), you change the sign on the number being subtracted (+6 to −6) and add.

$$(-4) - (+6) = (-4) + (-6) = -10$$

To understand this better, imagine that the −4 in the problem is your checking account, which is $4 overdrawn. Imagine that the $6 is an additional check that must be subtracted from your account. If you are overdrawn by $4 and write a check for $6, you are overdrawn by $10. Your account is −$10.

To subtract $(-4) - (-6)$, you change the sign of the number being subtracted (-6 to $+6$) and then add.

$$(-4) - (-6) = (-4) + (+6) = 2$$

To understand the logic of this, imagine again that the -4 is $4 overdrawn from your checking account. You then find out that you made an error when you subtracted the amount of a check. You subtracted $6 too much. You must "take away" the subtracted $6 by adding $6. In other words, you subtract $-$6 by adding $6. You now have $2 in your account and are no longer overdrawn.

When adding and subtracting a group of positive and negative numbers, first change the signs of the numbers to be subtracted. Then add.

$$(-3) - (+4) + (-5) - (+6) =$$
$$(-3) + (-4) + (-5) + (-6)$$

The answer is -18.

Warm-up

Add the following positive and negative numbers.

1. $(-876) + (-135) =$
2. $(-12) + (-15) + (+27) =$
3. $(-12) + (8) =$
4. $(-6) + (2) + (-5) + 1 =$
5. $(3) + (-9) + (7) =$
6. $(+5) + (-\frac{9}{2}) + (+4\frac{1}{2}) =$
7. $(-12) + (3) + (-7) + (-1) =$
8. $(-8) + (-12) =$
9. $(-4) + (+9) + (3) + (1) + (-7) =$
10. $4 + (-15) + (+5) + (2) + (-7) =$

Add and subtract the following numbers.

11. $(-6) - (+18) + (-9) =$
12. $(-21) - (-4) + (-5) - (+21) =$
13. $(+12) - (+8) - (-8) + (-1) =$
14. $(+5) - (-20) + (-10) =$
15. $(-50) - (-15) + (-12) - (6) =$
16. $(-7) - (+8) - (-9) + (+4) =$
17. $(-13.5) - (-7.25) - (9.01) + (25) =$
18. $(-22) - (+4) - (\frac{1}{4}) + (-9) =$
19. $+32 - (-48) - (-13) + (+12) =$
20. $(-7) - (10) - (+15) + (-10) - (40) =$

Warm-up Answers
1. -1011 **2.** 0 **3.** -4 **4.** -8 **5.** 1 **6.** 5 **7.** -17 **8.** -20 **9.** 2 **10.** -11 **11.** -33 **12.** -43 **13.** 11 **14.** 15 **15.** -53 **16.** -2 **17.** 9.74 **18.** $-35\frac{1}{4}$ **19.** 105 **20.** -82

<u>Directions:</u> For each problem, choose the <u>one</u> best answer. Answers are on page 554.

1. A halfback carried the football 4 times. He gained 35 yards, lost 3 yards, gained 6 yards, and lost 11 yards. How many yards did he gain in all?

   (1) 18 (2) 27 (3) 38
   (4) 41 (5) 55

   ① ② ③ ④ ⑤

2. The temperature at 8:00 A.M. was 7° below zero. By noon the temperature had risen by 13°. What was the temperature at noon?

   (1) $-20°$ (2) $-6°$ (3) 6°
   (4) 13° (5) 20°

   ① ② ③ ④ ⑤

3. Mr. Hernandez opened a new checking account with $500. He wrote checks for $175, $25, $212, and $300. He then deposited $250 into the account. How much did he have in his account after depositing the $250?

   (1) $-$1,462 (2) $-$212
   (3) $-$38 (4) $38
   (5) Insufficient data is given to solve the problem.

   ① ② ③ ④ ⑤

4. Sid swam $\frac{3}{4}$ of a mile from shore, but the current pushed him back $\frac{1}{8}$ of a mile. He swam $\frac{1}{2}$ mile farther until the current pushed him back another $\frac{1}{4}$ mile. How many miles from shore was Sid?

   (1) $\frac{1}{4}$ (2) $\frac{3}{8}$ (3) $\frac{1}{2}$ (4) $\frac{5}{8}$ (5) $\frac{7}{8}$

   ① ② ③ ④ ⑤

5. Ashley returned a sweater for $24.65 and a skirt for $26.95. She bought a blouse for $18.40. How much money did Ashley have in her wallet?

   (1) $51.60 (2) $43.73
   (3) $42.73 (4) $33.20
   (5) Insufficient data is given to solve the problem.

   ① ② ③ ④ ⑤

Multiplying and Dividing How do you know what signs you should use when you multiply and divide? The rules for multiplying and dividing signed numbers are the same.

Rule 1 If *both* numbers are positive or *both* are negative, the answer is always *positive.*

Here are two examples of multiplication of signed numbers.

$(-6)(-8) = 48 \qquad (+6)(+8) = 48$

Note that when two numbers have parentheses around them and there is no operation sign between them, you multiply. That is, $(+6)(+8)$ means 6×8.

Here are two examples of division of signed numbers.

$\frac{+14}{+2} = 7 \qquad \frac{-14}{-2} = 7$

The line between the 14 and the 2 can be read as "divided by." So these problems read like this: 14 divided by 2 equals 7 and -14 divided by -2 equals 7.

Rule 2 If the numbers have *different* signs, the answer is always *negative.*

Here are examples of multiplication of signed numbers when the signs are different:

$(-6)(+8) = -48 \qquad (+6)(-8) = -48$

Here are examples of division of signed numbers when the signs are different:

$\frac{-14}{+2} = -7 \qquad \frac{+14}{-2} = -7 \qquad \frac{-2}{+14} = -\frac{1}{7}$

If more than two numbers are being multiplied in the same problem, multiply two numbers at a time and adjust the sign each time you multiply.

Example: $(-5)(+4)(-3)(5)$

Step 1 Multiply: $(-5)(+4) = -20$.
The answer is negative because the signs are *different.*

Step 2 Multiply: $(-20)(-3) = 60$.
The answer is positive because the signs are the *same.*

Step 3 Multiply: $(60)(5) = 300$.
The answer is positive because the signs are the same. Note that the 5 did not have a plus sign before it. Remember, a number without a sign is always positive.

Warm-up

Multiply the following signed numbers. Make sure the sign in the answer is correct.

1. $(-3)(7) =$
2. $(+6)(-10) =$
3. $(-\frac{1}{2})(6) =$
4. $(-\frac{1}{4})(-12) =$
5. $(-8)(2)(-4) =$
6. $(+5)(-1)(-6)(+2) =$
7. $(+2)(3) + 5 =$
8. $(-5)(3)(-4) =$
9. $(-5)(-5)(\frac{1}{25}) =$
10. $(-9)(\frac{1}{18})(2) =$

Divide the following signed numbers. Make sure the sign in the answer is correct.

11. $\frac{-12}{6} =$
12. $-25 \div 5 =$
13. $\frac{-80}{-40} =$
14. $\frac{+24}{-48} =$
15. $\frac{.144}{-.12} =$
16. $\frac{-9}{-3} =$
17. $\frac{170}{-10} =$
18. $\frac{+12}{-4} =$
19. $\frac{250}{-5} =$
20. The low temperatures for five days in January were $-5°$, $-2°$, $0°$, $-12°$, and $-11°$. What was the average low temperature?

Warm-up Answers

1. -21 **2.** -60 **3.** -3 **4.** 3 **5.** 64 **6.** 60 **7.** 11 (Note that the 5 was added, not multiplied.) **8.** 60 **9.** 1 **10.** -1 **11.** -2 **12.** -5 **13.** 2 **14.** $-\frac{1}{2}$ **15.** -1.2 **16.** 3 **17.** -17 **18.** -3 **19.** -50 **20.** $-6°$

Ordering Decimals On the GED Mathematics Test you will be asked to place decimals in order from largest to smallest or from smallest to largest.

Place the following numbers in order from largest to smallest.

0.205 0.361 0.316 0.250

Since none of the numbers has any digits to the left of the decimal, you know that all of the numbers are less than one. Now look to the right of the decimal. Which number is the largest? You can see that both 0.361 and 0.316 have a 3 in the tenths place. So both of these numbers are larger than the other two.

Now you must look in the hundredths place to decide which of the two numbers is the larger. Since 0.361 has a 6 in the hundredths place and 0.316 has a 1 in the hundredths place, 0.361 is the larger of the two numbers and is the largest of the four numbers.

You can now order 0.205 and 0.250 by the same method. On page 000 you learned that the value of a decimal is not changed by adding or taking away a zero from the right side of the decimal number. So 0.25 equals 0.250, and it is larger than 0.205.

The correct order of the numbers would be:

0.361 0.316 0.250 0.205

If you were asked to place the numbers in order from smallest to largest the order would be:

0.205 0.250 0.316 0.361

Warm-up

Circle the largest number in each set.

1. 1.5 0.15 0.015
2. 0.9 0.63 0.35
3. 0.75 0.755 7.50
4. 0.32 0.321 0.0032
5. 0.009 0.001 0.090
6. 0.534 0.657 0.982
7. 0.4582 0.5 0.09978

Warm-up Answers
1. 1.5 **2.** 0.9 **3.** 7.50 **4.** 0.321 **5.** 0.090 **6.** 0.982 **7.** 0.5

Directions: For each problem, choose the one best answer. Answers are on page 554.

6. Rainfall in Denver was measured during March, April, May, and June as 0.015 inches, 0.15 inches, 1.5 inches, and 0.105 inches. Arrange the measurements in order from the least amount to the most amount of rainfall.

(1) 0.105, 0.015, 0.15, 1.5
(2) 0.015, 0.105, 0.15, 1.5
(3) 1.5, 0.15, 0.105, 0.015
(4) 1.5, 0.105, 0.15, 0.015
(5) 0.015, 0.105, 1.5, 0.15

① ② ③ ④ ⑤

7. At the post office, Mr. Andracke mailed 4 packages with the following weights: 0.07 pounds, 7.07 pounds, 0.7 pounds, and 0.007 pounds. He handed the packages to the clerk in the order from the smallest to the largest. Which of the following correctly lists the order in which Mr. Andracke handed the packages to the clerk?

(1) 7.07, 0.7, 0.07, 0.007
(2) 7.07, 0.07, 0.7, 0.007
(3) 0.007, 0.07, 7.07, 0.7
(4) 0.007, 0.07, 0.7, 7.07
(5) 0.7, 0.07, 0.007, 7.07

① ② ③ ④ ⑤

8. On Saturday Ms. Gill walked 0.83 of a mile, Mr. Will walked 0.08 of a mile, Mr. Mill walked 0.8 of a mile, and Mrs. Hill walked 0.803 of a mile. Place their distances in order from the longest to the shortest.

(1) 0.8, 0.08, 0.83, 0.803
(2) 0.8, 0.83, 0.08, 0.803
(3) 0.83, 0.8, 0.08, 0.803
(4) 0.83, 0.08, 0.803, 0.8
(5) 0.83, 0.803, 0.8, 0.08

① ② ③ ④ ⑤

Directions: For each problem, choose the one best answer. Answers begin on page 554.

9. Derrick has $\frac{3}{10}$ of a dollar, Nate has $\frac{4}{5}$ of a dollar, and Vince has $\frac{3}{4}$ of a dollar. Place the three men in order by who has the least amount of money to who has the greatest amount of money.

(1) Derrick, Nate, Vince
(2) Derrick, Vince, Nate
(3) Vince, Derrick, Nate
(4) Vince, Nate, Derrick
(5) Nate, Vince, Derrick

① ② ③ ④ ⑤

10. A baseball coach placed 4 different bats on a bat rack from shortest to longest. Their lengths were $3\frac{1}{2}$ feet, $3\frac{5}{16}$ feet, $3\frac{1}{4}$ feet, and $3\frac{3}{8}$ feet. Place the lengths of the bats in the same order the coach did.

(1) $3\frac{1}{2}$, $3\frac{3}{8}$, $3\frac{5}{16}$, $3\frac{1}{4}$
(2) $3\frac{1}{2}$, $3\frac{5}{16}$, $3\frac{3}{8}$, $3\frac{1}{4}$
(3) $3\frac{1}{4}$, $3\frac{3}{8}$, $3\frac{5}{16}$, $3\frac{1}{2}$
(4) $3\frac{1}{4}$, $3\frac{5}{16}$, $3\frac{3}{8}$, $3\frac{1}{2}$
(5) $3\frac{5}{16}$, $3\frac{1}{4}$, $3\frac{3}{8}$, $3\frac{1}{2}$

① ② ③ ④ ⑤

11. A tailor cut material to fill some dress orders. She cut $2\frac{3}{4}$ yards of silk, $2\frac{1}{3}$ yards of cotton, $2\frac{1}{2}$ yards of polyester, and $2\frac{5}{6}$ yards of ribbon. Order the amounts of material the tailor purchased from greatest to least.

(1) $2\frac{5}{6}$, $2\frac{3}{4}$, $2\frac{1}{2}$, $2\frac{1}{3}$
(2) $2\frac{5}{6}$, $2\frac{1}{2}$, $2\frac{3}{4}$, $2\frac{1}{3}$
(3) $2\frac{1}{3}$, $2\frac{1}{2}$, $2\frac{3}{4}$, $2\frac{5}{6}$
(4) $2\frac{1}{2}$, $2\frac{1}{3}$, $2\frac{3}{4}$, $2\frac{5}{6}$
(5) $2\frac{1}{3}$, $2\frac{1}{2}$, $2\frac{5}{6}$, $2\frac{3}{4}$

① ② ③ ④ ⑤

Ordering Fractions Sometimes on the GED Mathematics Test you will be asked to place fractions in order from least to greatest or from greatest to least. You learned before that fractions can be added or subtracted only when the denominators are the same. The same is true of putting fractions in order. Before you can sequence fractions, you must first change all the denominators of the fractions to be the same. Then you can put the fractions in order.

Put the following three fractions in order from least to greatest.

$\frac{5}{9}$, $\frac{1}{3}$, $\frac{5}{6}$

Step 1 Find the least common denominator for the three fractions. Since 3, 6, and 9 are all multiples of 18, the least common denominator is 18.

Step 2 Change the three fractions.

$\frac{5}{9} = \frac{10}{18}$ $\quad \frac{1}{3} = \frac{6}{18}$ $\quad \frac{5}{6} = \frac{15}{18}$

Step 3 Place the three fractions with their common denominator in order from least to greatest. Look at the *numerators* of the three fractions and start with the smallest number.

$\frac{6}{18}$, $\frac{10}{18}$, $\frac{15}{18}$

Step 4 Reduce the fractions back to their lowest terms.

$\frac{1}{3}$, $\frac{5}{9}$, $\frac{5}{6}$

The fractions are now sequenced from least to greatest.

☑ A Test-Taking Tip

When you have a problem on the GED Test that asks you to put fractions in order, read the question carefully so you know whether you are being asked to order the fractions from least to greatest or from greatest to least.

Warm-up

Put the following mixed numbers in order from greatest to least.

1. $\frac{1}{4}$, $\frac{1}{5}$, $\frac{1}{8}$ **2.** $5\frac{2}{5}$, $5\frac{4}{15}$, $5\frac{2}{3}$

Warm-up Answer

1. $\frac{1}{4}$, $\frac{1}{5}$, $\frac{1}{8}$ **2.** $5\frac{2}{3}$, $5\frac{2}{5}$, $5\frac{4}{15}$ (You only need to change the fractions. The common denominator for the three fractions is 15.).

Comparing and Ordering Data Sometimes on the GED Test you will be asked to compare data and to put the numbers in order.

Look at the following problem.

■ Mr. Burns goes to the grocery to buy some fresh peaches. When he arrives, he sees the following three signs on three different bins:

Peaches—3 lb for $2.37
Peaches—5 lb for $3.75
Peaches—10 lb for $7.20

If Mr. Burns wants the best buy, from which bin should he buy peaches?

Step 1 Determine the price per pound from each bin by dividing the price by the weight.

$2.37 \div 3 = .79$
$3.75 \div 5 = .75$
$7.20 \div 10 = .72$

Step 2 Put the prices in order from least to greatest.

$.72 per lb, $.75 per lb, $.79 per lb

The best buy for Mr. Burns would be the peaches that sell 10 pounds for $7.20.

Warm-up

Determine the best buy of the following items.

1. a half dozen pencils for $1.26, a dozen pencils for $2.52, or two dozen pencils for $4.80

2. a 10-ounce can of tomatoes for $0.89, a 20-ounce can of tomatoes for $1.75, or a 32-ounce can of tomatoes for $2.46

Need a Hint for Number 13?
A year has 52 weeks.

Warm-up Answers
1. two dozen pencils **2.** a 32-ounce can

12. Sophia wants to buy a chair that costs $225 and a sofa that costs $625, but she cannot afford to pay for the sofa all at once. The store offers her several payment plans. Which plan would be the best for Sophia?

A. a 10% down payment, and a monthly payment of $60 for one year
B. a down payment of $100, and 12 monthly payments of $50 each
C. no down payment, and 6 monthly payments of $121 each
D. a 20% down payment, and $35 a month for a year and a half

(1) A (2) B (3) C (4) D
(5) Insufficient data is given to solve the problem.

① ② ③ ④ ⑤

13. Doug earns $350 dollars a week. He has earned a raise and has been offered the following options:

A. a raise of $1,500 a year
B. a $65-a-week raise for one year
C. a 15% raise
D. a raise of $125 every two weeks for one year

Which option should he choose?

(1) A (2) B (3) C (4) D
(5) Insufficient data is given to solve the problem.

① ② ③ ④ ⑤

14. Four different stores were offering the following prices for potatoes:

A. A 10-pound bag of potatoes
B. A bag of potatoes for $1.49
C. Two bags for $3.58
D. A 10-pound bag of potatoes for $2.76

Which would be the best buy?

(1) A (2) B (3) C (4) D
(5) Insufficient data is given to solve the problem.

① ② ③ ④ ⑤

Directions: For each problem, choose the one best answer. Answers are on page 555.

15. 5^0 =

(1) 0 (2) 1 (3) 5
(4) 10 (5) 50

① ② ③ ④ ⑤

16. 10^3 =

(1) 7 (2) 13 (3) 100
(4) 1,000 (5) 10,000

① ② ③ ④ ⑤

17. 15^2 =

(1) 7.5 (2) 30 (3) 152
(4) 225 (5) 300

① ② ③ ④ ⑤

18. 7^4 =

(1) 28 (2) 49 (3) 343
(4) 2,401 (5) 24,001

① ② ③ ④ ⑤

19. 2^5 =

(1) 10 (2) 20 (3) 32
(4) 64 (5) 128

① ② ③ ④ ⑤

20. 10^{10} =

(1) 100^1 (2) 10,000 (3) 100,000
(4) 100,000,000 (5) 10,000,000,000

① ② ③ ④ ⑤

Exponents The expression 4^3 is read "four to the third power." The 4 is called the *base,* and the 3 is called the *power* or the *exponent.* This example, 4^3, is a multiplication expression. It asks you to multiply the base, 4, times *itself* three times: $4 \times 4 \times 4 = 64$. The exponent tells you how many times to multiply the base by itself. The expression 3^2 is read "three to the second power."

Recognizing Special Cases What do you think 3^1 or 3^0 is? These are special cases. The expression 3^1 is simply 3. The expression 6^1 is 6. Just remember that when the exponent is 1, the value of the expression is the number that is the base. Every time you reduce the power of the base by one, you are dividing the value of the expression by the base. For example, $3^3 = 3^4 \div 3$. The same is true when you move from 3^1 to 3^0: $3^0 = 3^1 \div 3 = 1$. Any base, whether a positive or negative number, when raised to the zero power is 1.

Warm-up

Write the following expressions by using exponents.

1. 10×10
2. $5 \times 5 \times 5$
3. 1×1
4. $3 \times 3 \times 3 \times 3$
5. 1

Need a Hint for Number 20?
Note how exponents affect the number 10. When 10 is the base number, the exponent tells you how many zeros are to be added after the 1. For example 10^1 is 10. Since $10^2 = 10 \times 10 = 100$, the exponent 2 indicates that 2 zeros appear after the 1. Prove the idea to yourself by trying 10^3. Then compute 10^{10} for Number 21.

Warm-up Answers
1. 10^2 **2.** 5^3 **3.** 1^2 **4.** 3^4 **5.** 1^0 (or any number to the zero power)

Squares and Square Roots When the exponent of an expression is 2, the expression is called a **square.** You can call the expression 8^2 "eight to the second power" or "eight squared."

Finding the square root of a number is the opposite of squaring a number. $\sqrt{\ }$ is the symbol that means "find the square root." It looks like a division sign because finding the square root is a special kind of division. 8^2 is $8 \times 8 = 64$. The **square root** of 64, $\sqrt{64}$, asks you to find the number that, when multiplied by itself, equals the number inside the square root symbol. The expression $\sqrt{64}$ equals 8 because $8 \times 8 = 64$.

Some square roots are called *perfect* squares because the number you need to multiply by *itself* to equal the number inside the square root symbol is a whole number. It might help you on the GED Test if you know these perfect squares by heart. It's like learning the *reverse* of some multiplication problems. See the examples below.

$\sqrt{1} = 1$	$\sqrt{25} = 5$	$\sqrt{81} = 9$
$\sqrt{4} = 2$	$\sqrt{36} = 6$	$\sqrt{100} = 10$
$\sqrt{9} = 3$	$\sqrt{49} = 7$	$\sqrt{121} = 11$
$\sqrt{16} = 4$	$\sqrt{64} = 8$	$\sqrt{144} = 12$

Coming to Terms

square number that has the exponent of 2

square root number, that when multiplied by itself, equals the number inside the square root symbol

Warm-up

1. $\sqrt{9} + 7$
2. $\sqrt{25} \div 5$
3. $8^2 \div 2$
4. $\sqrt{81} \times 20$
5. $10^2 - 99$
6. $3\sqrt{144}$

Warm-up Answers
1. 10 **2.** 1 **3.** 32 **4.** 180 **5.** 1 **6.** 36

21. $\sqrt{121} + \sqrt{100} - \sqrt{81} =$

(1) 9 (2) 10 (3) 12
(4) 21 (5) 30

① ② ③ ④ ⑤

22. $4\sqrt{144} + 3\sqrt{25} =$

(1) 53 (2) 63 (3) 163
(4) 204 (5) 651

① ② ③ ④ ⑤

23. $\frac{\sqrt{64}}{2} + 4\sqrt{49} - \sqrt{16} =$

(1) 24 (2) 28 (3) 36
(4) 180 (5) 212

① ② ③ ④ ⑤

24. Which of the following is the largest number?

(1) $\frac{\sqrt{36}}{6}$ (2) $\frac{6}{\sqrt{36}}$ (3) $\frac{\sqrt{49}}{\sqrt{36}}$
(4) $\frac{\sqrt{36}}{\sqrt{64}}$ (5) $0 + \sqrt{36}$

① ② ③ ④ ⑤

Directions: For each problem, find the one best answer. Answers are on page 555.

25. Which of the following equals the scientific notation expression of 3.06×10^5?

(1) 3.06 (2) 30.6 (3) 306
(4) 30,600 (5) 306,000

① ② ③ ④ ⑤

26. Which of the following equals the scientific notation expression of 79.1×10^{-4}?

(1) 0.791 (2) 0.0791 (3) 0.00791
(4) 0.000791 (5) 0.0000791

① ② ③ ④ ⑤

27. Which of the following equals the scientific notation expression of 0.0084×10^3?

(1) 84 (2) 8.4 (3) 0.84
(4) 0.084 (5) 0.0084

① ② ③ ④ ⑤

28. Which of the following scientific notation expressions equals 92,500?

(1) 9.25×10^3 (2) 92.4×10^4
(3) 92.4×10^5 (4) 9.25×10^4
(5) 9.25×10^5

① ② ③ ④ ⑤

29. Which of the following scientific notation expressions equals 0.000806?

(1) 80.6×10^{-5} (2) 80.6×10^{-4}
(3) $.806 \times 10^{-4}$ (4) 806×10^{-5}
(5) 806×10^{-4}

① ② ③ ④ ⑤

Scientific Notation Scientific notation is a special way of working with exponents. It uses the base number 10. The expression 2.7×10 actually means 2.7×10^1. Since the exponent is 1, you are really just multiplying by 10, and you can simply move the decimal in the number one place to the *right.* So $2.7 \times 10^1 = 27$.

If you had the expression, 2.7×10^2, you would have to move the decimal two places to the *right.* If too few digits are to the right of the number, you will have to add zeros to the *right* of the number and then move the decimal. So $2.7 \times 10^2 = 270$. Remember that the exponent on the base 10 tells you how many zeros are to be added after the 1.

It's also possible to have a negative exponent. If you had the expression, 2.7×10^{-1}, you would have to move the decimal one place to the *left.* That is because you are actually multiplying by 0.10. If you had the expression, 2.7×10^{-3}, you would have to move the decimal three places to the *left.* If too few digits are to the left of the decimal, you will have to add zeros as placeholders and then move the decimal to the *left.* So $2.7 \times 10^{-3} = 0.0027$.

Since you can now compute numbers that are in scientific notation, you can also do the opposite and put any number in that form. For example, if you had to write 365 in scientific notation, you would first change the number to a number between 0 and 9.99. Then you would multiply it by 10 to whatever power would bring it back to 365. So 365 would become 3.65, and since you had moved the decimal two places to the left, you would need to multiply 3.65 by 10^2 to bring the decimal point two places back to the right. The number 365 written in scientific notation is 3.65×10^2.

Warm-up

Use scientific notation to solve the following expressions.

1. 4.6×10^5
2. 9.7×10^{-2}

Write the following numbers in scientific notation.

3. 978
4. 6,007

Warm-up Answers
1. 460,000 **2.** 0.097 **3.** 9.78×10^2 **4.** 6.007×10^3

Simplifying The word *simplify,* when used with bases and exponents, means to compute the numbers. Simplify 2^3 means "compute 2^3." Multiply the base, 2, by itself three times: $2 \times 2 \times 2 = 8$. You can also add, subtract, multiply, and divide numbers with bases and exponents. For example, you can compute $2^2 + 3^0$. If you were asked to simplify these numbers, you'd compute them, but you'd *always compute the exponents first.* First, you'd find $2^2 = 4$. Then you'd find 3^0 is equal to 1. Finally, you'd add:

$4 + 1 = 5$.

You can also simplify an expression that involves square roots and scientific notations. What would you do if you are asked to simplify the expression $\sqrt{64} + 2^5$. As in the example above, compute each part of the expressions before you add, subtract, multiply, or divide the parts. First find $\sqrt{64} = 8$. Then find $2^5 = 32$. Now you can add the two parts of the expression together: $8 + 32 = 40$.

Warm-up

Simplify the following:

1. $2^6 \times 4^2$

2. $(-5)^3 + 19^1$

3. $(\frac{1}{4})^2 \times (\frac{1}{2})^2$

4. $(0.5)^2 + (\sqrt{49})^3$

5. $\sqrt{36} \div 2$

6. $12^2 \div 2^3$

7. $8^2 - 3^3$

8. $10^2 - 20^1$

Warm-up Answers

1. First compute $2^6 = 2 \times 2 \times 2 \times 2 \times 2 \times 2 = 64$. It is easy to lose track of an operation like this, so break it down into steps. First compute $2^2 = 4$; then compute $2^3 = 4 \times 2 = 8$; next compute $2^4 = 8 \times 2 = 16$; then compute $2^5 = 16 \times 2 = 32$; finally compute $2^6 = 32 \times 2 = 64$. Multiply 64 by the answer you get when you compute $4^2 = 16$. The value of the original expression is obtained by multiplying 64×16, which equals 1,024. **2.** First compute $(-5)^3 = (-5)(-5)(-5) = -125$. The answer is negative because there was an odd number used as an exponent. Then compute $19^1 = 19$. Simplify the expression by adding the two numbers: $-125 + 19 = -106$. **3.** First compute $(\frac{1}{4})^2 = \frac{1}{4} \times \frac{1}{4} = \frac{1}{16}$. Then compute $(\frac{1}{2})^2 = \frac{1}{2} \times \frac{1}{2} = \frac{1}{4}$. Now simplify the numbers by multiplying them: $\frac{1}{16} \times \frac{1}{4} = \frac{1}{64}$. **4.** First compute $(0.5)^2 = (0.5)(0.5) = 0.25$. Then compute $(\sqrt{49})^3 = 7^3 = 343$. Now simplify the expression by adding them: $0.25 + 343 = 343.25$ **5.** Compute $\sqrt{36} = 6$; then compute $6 \div 2 = 3$. **6.** Compute $12^2 = 12 \times 12 = 144$; then compute $2^3 = 2 \times 2 \times 2 = 8$; finally compute $144 \div 8 = 18$. **7.** Compute $8^2 = 8 \times 8 = 64$; then compute $3^3 = 3 \times 3 \times 3 = 27$; finally compute $64 - 27 = 37$. **8.** Compute $10^2 = 10 \times 10 = 100$; then compute $20^1 = 20$; finally compute $100 - 20 = 80$.

30. Simplify. $4^1 \times (\frac{1}{2})^2$

(1) 0 (2) 1 (3) $4\frac{1}{4}$
(4) 5 (5) 17

(1) (2) (3) (4) (5)

31. Simplify. $(4) + (0.2)^3$

(1) 0.12 (2) 0.32 (3) 0.4
(4) 4.008 (5) 2.0

(1) (2) (3) (4) (5)

32. Simplify. $(-2)^2 - (-1)^0$

(1) -5 (2) -4 (3) 3
(4) 4 (5) 8

(1) (2) (3) (4) (5)

33. Simplify. $\sqrt{144} \times 10^3$

(1) 120 (2) 1,200 (3) 1,440
(4) 12,000 (5) 14,440

(1) (2) (3) (4) (5)

34. Simplify. $-9^0 \times 10^{-2}$

(1) 0.01 (2) 0.09 (3) 0.1
(4) 0.9 (5) 1.9

(1) (2) (3) (4) (5)

Directions: For each problem, choose the one best answer. Answers are on page 556.

1. The total distance around the Millers' yard is 187 feet. They want to install a new fence. How many yards of fencing should they buy?

   (1) 21 (2) $27\frac{1}{9}$ (3) 62

   (4) $62\frac{1}{3}$ (5) 63

   (1) (2) (3) (4) (5)

2. Edwin ran a mile five different times with the following results:

   Run A—6 minutes
   Run B—6 minutes and 12 seconds
   Run C—358 seconds
   Run D—374 seconds
   Run E—5 minutes and 51 seconds

   The coach listed Edwin's runs in order from fastest to slowest. Which of the following sequences correctly lists the order of Edwin's runs?

   (1) E, A, C, B, D (2) E, C, A, B, D
   (3) C, E, A, B, D (4) D, B, A, C, E
   (5) D, A, B, C, E

   (1) (2) (3) (4) (5)

3. Elliott bought several types of rope for his macramé projects. The ropes have the following lengths:

   Rope A—$3\frac{1}{2}$ yd
   Rope B—4 ft 3 in
   Rope C—50 in
   Rope D—$3\frac{1}{3}$ yd
   Rope E—$3\frac{3}{4}$ yd

   The salesperson placed the ropes in the bag according to length, with the longest first. Which of the following sequences correctly lists the order in which the ropes were put in the bag?

   (1) E, D, C, B, A
   (2) D, C, B, A, E
   (3) E, D, B, C, A
   (4) E, A, B, C, D
   (5) E, A, D, B, C

   (1) (2) (3) (4) (5)

Measurement

Measurement is expressed in units of length, volume, weight, and time. Standard measurements were developed so that people would have a common understanding of each unit. These pages cover measurement units used in the United States.

Length
1 mile (mi) = 1,760 yards (yd)
1 mile = 5,280 feet (ft)
1 yard = 3 feet
1 yard = 36 inches (in)
1 foot = 12 inches

Volume
1 gallon (gal) = 4 quarts (qt)
1 quart = 2 pints (pt)
1 pint = 2 cups (c)
1 cup = 8 ounces (oz)

Weight
1 ton (T) = 2,000 pounds (lb)
1 pound = 16 ounces (oz)

Time
1 year (yr) = 12 months (mo)
1 year = 52 weeks (wk)
1 year = 365 days (d)
1 week = 7 days
1 day = 24 hours (hr)
1 hour = 60 minutes (min)
1 minute = 60 seconds (sec)

Be sure to read the tinted column on the next page before you do the problems in the outer columns of both these pages.

Converting Measurements *Multiply to convert a larger measure to a smaller measure:*
How many inches are in 5 feet?
5 ft × 12 in/ft = 60 in

Divide to convert a smaller measure to a larger measure:
How many yards are in 27 feet?
27 ft ÷ 3 ft/yd = 9 yd

Converting larger to smaller:
How many pints are there in 9 quarts?
9 qt × 2 pt/qt = 18 pt

Converting smaller to larger:
How many quarts are there in 16 cups?
16 c ÷ 2 c/pt = 8 pt
8 pt ÷ 2 pt/qt = 4 qt

Note that the second problem requires two steps because you need to convert cups to pints and then pints to quarts.

Converting larger to smaller:
How many pounds are there in 3 tons?
$3\text{ T} \times 2{,}000\text{ lb/T} = 6{,}000\text{ lb}$

Converting smaller to larger:
How many pounds are there in 20 ounces?
$20\text{ oz} \div 16\text{ oz/lb} = \frac{5}{4}\text{ lb} = 1\frac{1}{4}\text{ lb}$

Converting larger to smaller:
How many hours are there in 3 days?
$3\text{ d} \times 24\text{ hr/d} = 72\text{ hr}$

Converting smaller to larger:
How many days are there in 120 hours?
$120\text{ hr} \div 24\text{ hr/d} = 5\text{ d}$

Warm-up

Convert each measure to the specified unit.

1. 108 inches = _______ yards
2. $2\frac{1}{2}$ miles = _______ yards
3. 96 inches = _______ feet
4. 5 gallons = _______ quarts
5. 24 ounces = _______ pints
6. 3 cups = _______ ounces
7. 5 pounds = _______ ounces
8. $6\frac{1}{2}$ tons = _______ pounds
9. 36 months = _______ years
10. $5\frac{1}{2}$ days = _______ hours
11. 180 seconds = _______ minutes

Warm-up Answers

1. 3 yd (108 in ÷ 36 in/yd) **2.** 4,400 yd ($2\frac{1}{2}$ mi × 1,760 yd/mi) **3.** 8 ft (96 in ÷ 12 in/ft) **4.** 20 qt (5 gal × 4 qt/gal) **5.** $1\frac{1}{2}$ pt (24 oz ÷ 8 oz/c = 3 c; then 3 c ÷ 2 c/pt = $1\frac{1}{2}$ pt) **6.** 24 oz (3 c × 8 oz/c) **7.** 80 oz (5 lb × 16 oz/lb) **8.** 13,000 lb ($6\frac{1}{2}$ T × 2,000 lb/T) **9.** 3 yr (36 mo ÷ 12 mo/yr) **10.** 132 hr ($5\frac{1}{2}$ d × 24 hr/d) **11.** 3 min (180 sec ÷ 60 sec/min)

4. Each of five families brought the following amounts of lemonade to the neighborhood picnic:

   Family A—10 qt
   Family B—3 gal 3 qt
   Family C—5 qt 6 pt
   Family D—2 gal 2 pt
   Family E—13 pt

   List the families in order according to the amount of lemonade they brought, from least to most.

   (1) E, D, C, B, A (2) E, D, C, A, B
   (3) E, C, D, A, B (4) C, E, D, A, B
   (5) B, A, D, E, C

   ① ② ③ ④ ⑤

5. An author has written five different novels. The following list shows how long she took to write each book.

   Novel A—36 mo 2 wk
   Novel B—72 wk 4 d
   Novel C—24 mo 24 wk 2 d
   Novel D—426 d
   Novel E—110 wk 6 d

   List the novels according to length of time they took to write. Put the longest first.

   (1) D, E, B, C, A (2) A, C, E, B, D
   (3) D, B, E, C, A (4) A, C, B, D, E
   (5) D, E, C, B, A

   ① ② ③ ④ ⑤

Directions: For each problem, choose the one best answer. Answers are on page 556.

6. In the charity bike-a-thon, Robert rode his bike 15 miles 1,200 yards. Raymond rode his bike 19 miles 1,500 yards. What was their combined distance if 1 mile equals 1,760 yards?

   (1) 34 mi (2) 34 mi 620 yd (3) 35 mi
   (4) 35 mi 880 yd (5) 35 mi 940 yd

   (1) (2) (3) (4) (5)

7. Miranda needed to keep a daily record of the total weight of all packages sent from the mail room. In one day, 4 packages were mailed. They weighed 5 pounds 7 ounces, 1 pound 4 ounces, 7 pounds 12 ounces, and 8 pounds 14 ounces. What was Miranda's total for that day?

   (1) 19 lb 8 oz (2) 22 lb 8 oz
   (3) 22 lb 15 oz (4) 23 lb 5 oz
   (5) 24 lb 1 oz

   (1) (2) (3) (4) (5)

8. A community organization collected paper for a fund drive. Four members collected the following amounts: 1,402 pounds 12 ounces, 1,273 pounds 8 ounces, 983 pounds 2 ounces, and 748 pounds 15 ounces. What was the total weight of their collection?

   (1) 2 tons 408 lb 5 oz
   (2) 2 tons 416 lb 12 oz
   (3) 2 tons 418 lb 6 oz
   (4) 2 tons 424 lb 4 oz
   (5) 2 tons 428 lb

   (1) (2) (3) (4) (5)

9. Mike Jackson made back-to-back delivery runs with his truck. His first delivery weighed 1 ton 500 pounds; his second weighed 1 ton 1,600 pounds. What was the total weight of his deliveries?

   (1) 2 T 200 lb (2) $2\frac{2}{3}$ T
   (3) 3 T 100 lb (4) 3 T 150 lb
   (5) $3\frac{1}{4}$ T

   (1) (2) (3) (4) (5)

Working with Measures You can add, subtract, multiply, and divide with measurement units, but for some problems you must learn new rules for borrowing and carrying.

Adding Measures What do you do if you have to add 4 feet 3 inches, 1 foot 10 inches, and 2 feet 8 inches?

Step 1 Add the feet and inches separately.

4 ft	3 in
1 ft	10 in
2 ft	8 in
7 ft	21 in

Step 2 Determine if the smaller units can be converted to the larger unit.

12 in = 1 ft, so 21 in ÷ 12 in/ft = 1 ft 9 in

Step 3 Add the converted units to the larger unit.

```
   7 ft
+  1 ft 9 in
   8 ft 9 in
```

Warm-up

Add.

1.
```
   5 mi  200 yd
 + 1 mi  632 yd
```

2.
```
   1 c   4 oz
 +       3 oz
```

3.
```
   2 gal  3 qt
   3 gal  2 qt
 + 6 gal  1 qt
```

4.
```
   7 lb   8 oz
   5 lb   7 oz
 + 8 lb  11 oz
```

5.
```
   2 yd  1 ft   2 in
   3 yd  1 ft   9 in
 + 6 yd  2 ft  11 in
```

6.
```
   4 hr  22 min  12 sec
   3 hr  39 min  46 sec
 + 3 hr  51 min  39 sec
```

Warm-up Answers
1. 6 mi 832 yd **2.** 1 c 7 oz **3.** 11 gal 6 qt = 12 gal 2 qt **4.** 20 lb 26 oz = 21 lb 10 oz **5.** 11 yd + 4 ft + 22 in = 12 yd + 2 ft + 10 in **6.** 10 hr 112 min 97 sec = 11 hr 53 min 37 sec

Subtracting Measures Here's how you could compute a problem like this: Subtract 4 gallons 3 quarts from 9 gallons 1 quart.

$$\begin{array}{r} 9 \text{ gal } 1 \text{ qt} \\ -4 \text{ gal } 3 \text{ qt} \\ \hline \end{array}$$

Step 1 You cannot subtract 3 quarts from 1 quart. Borrow 1 gallon from the 9 gallons and convert it to quarts (1 gallon = 4 quarts).

$$\begin{array}{r} \overset{8}{\cancel{9}} \text{ gal } \overset{+\,4\text{ qt}}{1 \text{ qt}} = 5 \text{ qt} \\ -4 \text{ gal } 3 \text{ qt} \\ \hline \end{array}$$

Step 2 Now subtract.

$$\begin{array}{r} 8 \text{ gal } 5 \text{ qt} \\ -4 \text{ gal } 3 \text{ qt} \\ \hline 4 \text{ gal } 2 \text{ qt} = 4\tfrac{1}{2} \text{ gal} \end{array}$$

Subtract 4 hours 30 minutes from 6 hours 15 minutes.

Step 1
$$\begin{array}{r} 6 \text{ hr } 15 \text{ min} \\ -4 \text{ hr } 30 \text{ min} \\ \hline \end{array}$$

Step 2
$$\begin{array}{r} \overset{5}{\cancel{6}} \text{ hr } \overset{+\,60\text{ min}}{15 \text{ min}} = 75 \text{ min} \\ -4 \text{ hr } 30 \text{ min} \\ \hline \end{array}$$

Step 3
$$\begin{array}{r} 5 \text{ hr } 75 \text{ min} \\ -4 \text{ hr } 30 \text{ min} \\ \hline 1 \text{ hr } 45 \text{ min} \end{array}$$

Warm-up

Subtract these answers.

1. $\begin{array}{r} 7 \text{ lb } 2 \text{ oz} \\ -2 \text{ lb } 5 \text{ oz} \\ \hline \end{array}$

2. $\begin{array}{r} 12 \text{ ft } 3 \text{ in} \\ -\ 4 \text{ ft } 8 \text{ in} \\ \hline \end{array}$

3. $\begin{array}{r} 9 \text{ yr } 12 \text{ wk} \\ -4 \text{ yr } 39 \text{ wk} \\ \hline \end{array}$

4. $\begin{array}{r} 14 \text{ hr } 22 \text{ min } 38 \text{ sec} \\ -\ 6 \text{ hr } 47 \text{ min } 51 \text{ sec} \\ \hline \end{array}$

Need a Hint for Number 11?
First find the amount of time between 9:45 a.m. and 12:00 noon. Add that amount to the amount of time between 12:00 noon and 1:43 p.m.

Warm-up Answers
1. 6 lb 18 oz − 2 lb 5 oz = 4 lb 13 oz **2.** 11 ft 15 in − 4 ft 8 in = 7 ft 7 in **3.** 8 yr 64 wk − 4 yr 39 wk = 4 yr 25 wk **4.** 13 hr 81 min 98 sec − 6 hr 47 min 51 sec = 7 hr 34 min 47 sec (Note: Although you borrowed an hour from the 13 hr and added 60 min to 22 min, you had to borrow 1 min from the 82 min. So, you are left with 81 min.)

10. Milos repainted his garage last week. He bought 4 gallons of paint but used only $2\frac{1}{2}$ gallons. How many quarts of paint did he have left?

(1) $1\frac{1}{2}$ (2) $2\frac{3}{4}$ (3) 6
(4) $6\frac{1}{2}$ (5) 26

① ② ③ ④ ⑤

11. A private plane took off from O'Hare Field at 9:45 a.m. and returned at 1:43 p.m. How long was the flight?

(1) $3\frac{3}{4}$ hr (2) 3 hr 50 min
(3) 3 hr 58 min (4) 4 hr 2 min
(5) $4\frac{1}{4}$ hr

① ② ③ ④ ⑤

12. If you need 2 hours and 20 minutes to roast a turkey and the turkey has been in the oven for 45 minutes, how much more roasting time will you need?

(1) 1 hr 15 min (2) 1 hr 30 min
(3) 1 hr 35 min (4) 1 hr 45 min
(5) 1 hr 55 min

① ② ③ ④ ⑤

13. Karen Rigger serves 36 ounces of juice to her morning kindergarten class and 52 ounces of juice to her afternoon class. How many more quarts of juice does she serve in the afternoon?

(1) $\frac{1}{2}$ (2) 1 (3) $1\frac{1}{2}$
(4) 16 (5) 26

① ② ③ ④ ⑤

Directions: For each problem, choose the one best answer. Answers begin on page 556.

14. The Escobedos needed 24 feet 4 inches of molding around each of 5 windows. How much molding did they have to buy?

(1) 100 ft 10 in (2) 121 ft 8 in
(3) 124 ft 3 in (4) 125 ft 9 in
(5) Insufficient data is given to solve the problem.

① ② ③ ④ ⑤

15. Tara exercised 7 days a week for $1\frac{1}{4}$ hours each day. At the end of 5 weeks, how much time had she spent exercising?

(1) $42\frac{1}{2}$ hr (2) 43 hr 45 min
(3) $44\frac{3}{4}$ hr (4) 45 hr
(5) Insufficient data is given to solve the problem.

① ② ③ ④ ⑤

16. A vendor sold 3 gallons and 3 quarts of lemonade a day for a week at a lunch stand. What was the total amount of lemonade sold that week?

(1) 21 gal (2) 25 gal 1 qt
(3) 26 gal 1 qt (4) 26 gal 3 qt
(5) Insufficient data is given to solve the problem.

① ② ③ ④ ⑤

17. Kellie bought 8 packages of hot dogs and several packages of ground beef. Each package of beef weighed 2 pounds and 9 ounces. How much ground beef did Kellie buy?

(1) 19 lb 8 oz (2) 20 lb
(3) 20 lb 7 oz (4) $20\frac{1}{2}$ lb
(5) Insufficient data is given to solve the problem.

① ② ③ ④ ⑤

Multiplying Measures This is how you'd solve a problem like this: Multiply 3 yards 2 feet by 5.

Step 1 Multiply the yards and feet separately.

$$\begin{array}{r} 3\text{ yd} \\ \times\ 5 \\ \hline 15\text{ yd} \end{array} \qquad \begin{array}{r} 2\text{ ft} \\ \times\ 5 \\ \hline 10\text{ ft} \end{array}$$

Step 2 Convert the smaller units to the larger unit.

3 ft = 1 yd, so
10 ft ÷ 3 ft/yd = 3 yd 1 ft

Step 3 Add the converted units to the larger unit.

$$\begin{array}{r} 15\text{ yd} \\ +\ 3\text{ yd }1\text{ ft} \\ \hline 18\text{ yd }1\text{ ft} \end{array}$$

Here's a second example. Multiply 3 hours 15 minutes by 4.

Step 1

$$\begin{array}{r} 3\text{ hr} \\ \times\ 4 \\ \hline 12\text{ hr} \end{array} \qquad \begin{array}{r} 15\text{ min} \\ \times\ 4 \\ \hline 60\text{ min} \end{array}$$

Step 2 60 min = 1 hr

Step 3

$$\begin{array}{r} 12\text{ hr} \\ +\ 1\text{ hr} \\ \hline 13\text{ hr} \end{array}$$

Warm-up

Multiply to solve these problems.

1. 4 ft 5 in × 6
2. 9 lb 11 oz × 7
3. 7 gal 3 qt × 8
4. 3 hr 32 min 28 sec × 3

Warm-up Answers
1. 24 ft 30 in = 26 ft 6 in **2.** 63 lb 77 oz = 67 lb 13 oz **3.** 56 gal 24 qt = 62 gal **4.** 9 hr 96 min 84 sec = 10 hr 37 min 24 sec (Note: After you convert the 96 min to 1 hr and 36 min, you have to convert the 84 sec to 1 min 24 sec and add accordingly.)

Dividing Measures This is how you'd solve a problem like this: Divide 11 pounds 13 ounces by 3.

Step 1
Divide 11 pounds by 3.

```
     3
  3)11 lb 13 oz
    9 lb
    2 lb
```

Step 2
Convert the remaining 2 pounds to 32 ounces and add that to the original 13 ounces. Divide the total of 45 ounces by 3.

```
     3 lb    15 oz
  3)11 lb    13 oz
     9 lb
     2 lb =  32 oz
             45 oz
             45 oz
              0
```

Here's a more complicated example. Divide 7 yards 2 feet 4 inches by 2.

Step 1

```
   3 yd
2)7 yd 2 ft 4 in
  6 yd
  1 yd
```

Step 2

```
   3 yd    2 ft
2)7 yd    2 ft 4 in
  6 yd
  1 yd  =  3 ft
           5 ft
           4 ft
           1 ft
```

Step 3

```
   3 yd    2 ft    8 in
2)7 yd    2 ft    4 in
  6 yd
  1 yd  =  3 ft
           5 ft
           4 ft
           1 ft  = 12 in
                   16 in
                   16 in
                    0
```

Note that in the addition and multiplication of measurement units, you add or multiply first and then convert the units. In subtraction and division, you convert as you work the problem.

Warm-up

1. 10 ft 6 in ÷ 3 **2.** 5 hr 27 min 16 sec ÷ 4

Warm-up Answers

```
      3 ft      6 in               1 hr   21 min    49 sec
1. 3)10 ft      6 in       2. 4)5 hr   29 min    16 sec
      9                           4
      1 ft  =  12 in              1 hr  = 60 min
               18 in                      87 min
                                          84
                                           3 min  = 180 sec
                                                    196 sec
```

18. Mr. Kelly cut a board of lumber 12 feet 9 inches long into 3 equal pieces. What was the length of each piece?

(1) 3 ft 4 in (2) 3 ft 5 in
(3) 4 ft 3 in (4) 4 ft 9 in
(5) 4 ft 11 in

① ② ③ ④ ⑤

19. In 4 days Seth spent 29 hours and 20 minutes havesting one of his fields. What was the average amount of time he harvested each day?

(1) 7 hr 44 min (2) 6 hr 20 min
(3) 7 hr 20 min (4) 6 hr 22 min
(5) 7 hr 22 min

① ② ③ ④ ⑤

20. Melissa received a $2\frac{1}{2}$-pound box of candy. She wants to share it equally with 4 of her friends. How much candy will each person receive?

(1) $\frac{1}{2}$ lb (2) $\frac{3}{4}$ lb (3) 1 lb
(4) 1 lb 3 oz (5) 1 lb 4 oz

① ② ③ ④ ⑤

21. At the 3-day bazaar the beverage booth sold 11 gallons of apple cider the first day, 23 the second day, and 14 the third day. If the cider was sold in quart containers, what was the average number of quarts of cider sold during each day of the bazaar?

(1) 12 (2) 24 (3) 48
(4) 64 (5) 192

① ② ③ ④ ⑤

Directions: For each problem, choose the one best answer. Answers are on page 557.

22. At a track meet 5 pole vaulters used 5 different poles, each of a different length:

    Pole A = 500 cm
    Pole B = 5,003 mm
    Pole C = 5.2 m
    Pole D = 0.0054 km
    Pole E = 5.02 m

    The official of the meet wanted to inspect the poles in order from shortest to longest. Which of the following sequences correctly lists the order in which the official inspected the poles?

    (1) A, B, D, C, E (2) B, A, E, C, D
    (3) A, B, E, C, D (4) D, C, E, B, A
    (5) D, C, E, A, B

    ① ② ③ ④ ⑤

23. A science teacher placed several water jugs on a table. The jugs were marked as follows:

    Jug A—2,204 mL
    Jug B—2,024 mL
    Jug C—2.104 L
    Jug D—0.00204 kL
    Jug E—21.40 dL

    The teacher asked a student to arrange the jugs in order from the one with the most water to the one with the least water. Which of the following correctly lists the order of the jugs?

    (1) A, C, E, D, B (2) A, E, C, D, B
    (3) B, D, C, E, A (4) B, D, E, C, A
    (5) D, B, E, C, A

    ① ② ③ ④ ⑤

Metric Measurement Most countries use the metric system of measurement. Since the GED Mathematics Test will ask you questions about metric measurements, you need to familiarize yourself with metrics.

The metric system is based on powers of 10.

Length The *meter* is the basic unit of length and is a little more than a yard. Here are the other units of length.

1 kilometer (km) = 1,000 meters (m)
1 hectometer (hm) = 100 m
1 dekameter (dam) = 10 m
1 decimeter (dm) = 0.1 m
1 centimeter (cm) = 0.01 m
1 millimeter (mm) = 0.001 m

The kilometer, meter, centimeter, and millimeter are the most commonly used measurements.

Volume The *liter* is the basic unit of volume and is a little more than a quart. Below are the units of volume based on the liter.

1 kiloliter (kL) = 1,000 liters (L)
1 hectoliter (hL) = 100 L
1 dekaliter (daL) = 10 L
1 deciliter (dL) = 0.1 L
1 centiliter (cL) = 0.01 L
1 milliliter (mL) = 0.001 L

The liter and the milliliter are the most commonly used measures of volume.

Weight The *gram* is the basic unit of weight in the metric system and is about the weight of a paper clip. This chart shows you the other units of weight.

1 kilogram (kg) = 1,000 grams (g)
1 hectogram (hg) = 100 g
1 dekagram (dag) = 10 g
1 decigram (dg) = 0.1 g
1 centigram (cg) = 0.01
1 milligram (mg) = 0.001 g

The kilogram, gram, and milligram are the most commonly used metric measurement units of weight.

Read the information in the tinted column on the next page before working the practice problems in the outer columns on either page.

Converting Metric Measures Since the metric system is based on powers of 10, converting measures always involves multiplying or dividing by a multiple of ten. Each unit on the charts on page 484 is always ten times the unit below it and one-tenth of the unit above it. To change from one unit to another, you must remember what the prefix means. The most common prefixes are *kilo-* (meaning 1,000), *centi-* (meaning 100), and *milli-* (meaning 1/1,000 or 0.001).

Do you remember the shortcut for multiplying and dividing by multiples of ten? Move the decimal point to the right or to the left the number of places to equal the number of zeros in 1,000, 100, or 10. This makes converting metric units very easy.

Suppose you wanted to change 6 meters into centimeters. You are going from a larger unit to a smaller unit. If you look at the chart, you will see that the centimeter and the meter are two units apart. A centimeter is 0.01 of a meter. In other words, 100 centimeters equal 1 meter. Since you are going from a larger measure to a smaller measure, you move the decimal point to the right. And since the measurements are two units apart, you move the decimal point two places to the right.

6.00 m = 600 cm

Look at the following problem: How many grams are in 392 milligrams?

Since you are converting a smaller unit to a larger unit, you move the decimal point to the left. And since the measurements are three units apart on the chart, you move the decimal point to the left three places.

392. mg = 0.392 g

Warm-up

Convert the following. Use the charts if you need them.

1. 26 mg = __ g
2. 7.3 mm = __ m
3. 22 L = __ mL
4. 6,005 mm = __ m

Warm-up Answers
1. 0.026 g **2.** 0.0073 m **3.** 22,000 mL **4.** 6.005 m

24. Five dogs in a dog show were lined up according to weight. The dogs had the following weights:

Dog A—18.8 kg
Dog B—18,080 g
Dog C—18,180,000 mg
Dog D—18.01 kg
Dog E—18,880 g

Which of the following sequences correctly lists the dogs' weights from heaviest to lightest?

(1) E, A, C, D, B (2) D, B, C, A, E
(3) D, E, A, C, B (4) E, A, C, B, D
(5) A, E, C, B, D

① ② ③ ④ ⑤

25. Nelson hiked for five days. Listed below are the distances he hiked each day.

Day A = 6.2 km
Day B = 602 dam
Day C = 6,202 m
Day D = 6.002 km
Day E = 6,022 m

Which of the following correctly lists his distances from shortest to longest?

(1) D, B, E, A, C (2) D, B, E, C, A
(3) B, D, E, A, C (4) B, D, E, C, A
(5) C, A, E, B, D

① ② ③ ④ ⑤

Directions: For each problem, choose the one best answer. Answers are on page 557.

26. Espie has a 850 mL container and a 4.5 L container. If she puts water in both containers, how many liters of water does she have?

(1) 5.35 (2) 53.5 (3) 85.45
(4) 854.5 (5) 5,350

(1) (2) (3) (4) (5)

27. Joyce rode her bike 2.6 km, jogged 1,006 m, and swam 3.9 km. How many kilometers did Joyce go?

(1) 0.7506 (2) 7.506 (3) 75.06
(4) 750.06 (5) 7,506

(1) (2) (3) (4) (5)

28. Juan bought 504 g of apples, 1.624 kg of pears, 0.988 kg of plums, and 743 g of peaches. How many grams of fruit did he buy?

(1) 0.3859 (2) 3.859 (3) 38.59
(4) 385.9 (5) 3,859

(1) (2) (3) (4) (5)

29. A mother dog weighs 4.7 kg. Her newborn puppy weighs 721 g. How many more kilograms does the mother weigh than her newborn?

(1) 3.979 (2) 5.421 (3) 39.79
(4) 54.21 (5) 397.9

(1) (2) (3) (4) (5)

Adding and Subtracting Metric Measures

Before adding or subtracting metric measurements, you must change all of the measurements to the same units. For example, if a problem uses meters and centimeters, you must change all of the measurements to either meters or centimeters. Then you can add or subtract just as you do with decimals.

Look at this example.

3L + 3402 mL =

You can change the liters to milliliters and then add.

3L = 3,000 mL
3,000 mL + 3,402 mL = 6,402 mL

Or you can change the milliliters to liters and then add.

3,402 mL = 3.402 L
3 L + 3.402 L = 6.402 L

Look at this next example.

4.08 km − 2,322 m =

You can change the kilometers to meters and then subtract.

4.08 km = 4,080 m
4,080 m − 2,322 m = 1,758 m

Or you can change the meters to kilometers and then subtract.

2,322 m = 2.322 km
4.08 km − 2.322 km = 1.758 km

☑ A Test-Taking Tip

If a problem on the GED Mathematics Test asks for the answer to be in a certain unit, such as liters, then change all of the measurements to liters before you do the problem. This will save you time.

Warm-up

Add or subtract. Give two answers for each problem.

1. 17.3 g − 422 mg
2. 7,092 mL + 7 L
3. 3.6 m + 1.7 cm
4. 46.5 kg − 656 g

Warm-up Answers
1. 16.878 g or 16,878 mg **2.** 14,092 mL or 14.092 L
3. 3.617 m or 361.7 cm **4.** 45.844 kg or 45,844 g

Multiplying and Dividing Metric Measures
Sometimes on the GED Mathematics Test you will be asked to multiply or divide measurements and then convert the measurement. Look at this example.

■ Marc bought 3 pieces of lumber. Each measured 2.6 meters. How many centimeters of lumber did Marc buy?

Step 1 Multiply 3 times 2.6 m.

$3 \times 2.6 \text{ m} = 7.8 \text{ m}$

Step 2 Convert the meters to centimeters by moving the decimal point two places to the right.

$7.8 \text{ m} = 780 \text{ cm}$

Look at this next example.

■ Kacey has 1,800 g of ice cream. If she wants to divide the ice cream into portions of 0.6 kg each, how many people can have ice cream?

Step 1 You can either convert the grams to kilograms or the kilograms to grams. But the measurements must be the same before you can divide. In the conversion below the grams have been changed to kilograms by moving the decimal point three places to the left.

$1{,}800 \text{ g} = 1.8 \text{ kg}$

Step 2 Divide 1.8 by 0.6

$$0.6\overline{)1.8}\quad = 3$$

Three people can have ice cream.

Warm-up
Multiply or divide.
1. 3.7 kg × 7
2. 22.8 km × 9
3. 6.09 g × 3
4. 2.717 m ÷ 13 cm = cm
5. 1,022.4 mL ÷ 24 L = L
6. 416 km ÷ 8,000 m = km

Warm-up Answers
1. 25.9 kg **2.** 205.2 km **3.** 18.27 g **4.** 20.9 cm **5.** .0426 L **6.** 52 km

30. Steve bought a dozen apples. Each apple weighed 109 g. How many kilograms did the apples weigh?

(1) 1,308 (2) 130.8 (3) 13.08
(4) 1.308 (5) 0.1308

① ② ③ ④ ⑤

31. If a glass holds 250 mL of milk, how many glasses of milk can be poured from four 3.5 liter bottles?

(1) 0.56 (2) 5.6 (3) 56
(4) 560 (5) 5.600

① ② ③ ④ ⑤

32. The players on a basketball team have the following heights: 2.2 m, 198 cm, 197.6 cm, 2.03 m, and 199.9 cm. What is the average height of the team members in centimeters?

(1) 0.2037 (2) 2.037 (3) 20.37
(4) 203.7 (5) 2,037

① ② ③ ④ ⑤

33. At an athletic event Bill threw the shot-put 3 different times for a total distance of 4,050 cm. The winner of the event threw the shot-put 25.8 m. How many meters shorter was Bill's average shot than the shot of the winner?

(1) 1.23 (2) 12.3 (3) 123
(4) 403.42 (5) 4,034.2

① ② ③ ④ ⑤

Directions: For each problem, choose the one best answer. Answers begin on page 557.

34. Maria wants to buy a new car. If she borrows $7,500 (the principal) at 9% per year for 4 years, how much will she pay in interest if none of the principal is paid until the end of the 4-year period? Use the following formula to compute your answer:

Interest = Principal × Rate × Time.

(1) $300 (2) $750 (3) $1,000
(4) $2,700 (5) $1,350

① ② ③ ④ ⑤

35. Mrs. Saunders deposits $3,600 in her account, which has an interest rate of $6\frac{3}{4}$%. If Mrs. Saunders leaves her money in the account for 9 months, how much interest will she earn?

(1) $82.25 (2) $182.25
(3) $192.00 (4) $192.25
(5) Insufficient data is given to solve the problem.

① ② ③ ④ ⑤

36. A loan officer told the Hamiltons that a loan of $2,000 could be paid back in 1 year or in 3 years. If the interest rate on the loan is $10\frac{1}{4}$%, how much will the Hamiltons pay in interest?

(1) $205 (2) $510
(3) $615 (4) $1,205
(5) Insufficient data is given to solve the problem.

① ② ③ ④ ⑤

37. Mr. Chen borrowed $250 at a rate of 8% for 18 months. How much interest will he pay on the loan?

(1) $16 (2) $30
(3) $240 (4) $360
(5) Insufficient data is given to solve the problem.

① ② ③ ④ ⑤

Working with Formulas A *formula* is a rule expressed in mathematical symbols. You can use formulas to solve practical problems.

☑ A Test-Taking Tip

On the GED Test you will be provided with a list of formulas. (This list appears on the inside back cover of this book.) If you learn to recognize when a word problem can be solved by using a formula, you can use this list to save you time.

Computing Interest The formula for computing interest is: Interest = principal × rate × time. To save space, the formula is usually abbreviated like this: $I = prt$. When letters are written together in math, it means you should multiply the numbers they stand for. The letters mean the following:

I (interest)—the dollar amount you earn when you invest money.
p (principal)—the amount of money borrowed or the amount of money invested.
r (rate)—this is expressed as a percent, but when you compute interest, you change this to a decimal.
t (time)—the time you take to pay back a loan or the length of time money is invested. *Time* is always expressed in years, so, for example, eighteen months would be 1½ or 1.5 years.

To use a formula, substitute the numbers provided in a problem for the letters in the formula.

Example: Find the interest on a loan of $600 when the interest rate is 12% and the duration of the loan is two years.

$I = prt$:

p is the amount borrowed, $600.
r is the interest rate, 12%.
t is the time it took to pay back the loan, 2 yr.

$I = prt$
$I = \$600 \times .12 \times 2 = \$72 \times 2 = \$144$
$144 in interest will also have to be paid.

Warm-up

Solve the following problems.

1. Mr. Grappe borrows $1,200 for 8 months at a rate of 9½%. What is the amount of interest he pays on the loan?
2. Ms. Maxwell deposits $2,500 into her savings account where it earns 7% interest. If Ms. Maxwell leaves her money in her account for 1½ years, how much interest will she earn?

Warm-up Answers
1. $76 **2.** $262.50

Figuring Costs A *unit cost* is the price per unit of an item. As a shopper, you can save money by comparing unit costs of different sizes or amounts of the same item. You can also use unit costs to figure total cost. This formula can help you find total costs when you shop and when you solve problems on the GED Test.

total *cost* = *number* of units × *rate*, or cost per unit

$c = n \times r$

For example, if one can of soup costs $0.63, three cans of soup would be $0.63 times 3, or $1.89.

You can also use the formula to find unit costs when you know the total cost. Suppose a tire store is selling 4 tires for $180. What is the cost of one tire? If the total cost is the number of items *multiplied* by the unit cost, you have to do the opposite operation to find the unit cost. You'd find the cost of one tire by *dividing the total price by the number of items.*

$180 ÷ 4 = $45

Finding Distance This distance formula can help you solve problems involving distance.

distance = rate × time

$d = rt$

Look at the following problem.

■ Mr. Adams drove at a steady speed of 55 mph for 4.75 hours. How far did Mr. Adams travel?

Step 1 Put the information you know into the formula $d = rt$.

$d = 55 \times 4.75$

Step 2 Compute your answer.

$d = 261.25$

Mr. Adams traveled 261.25 miles.

Warm-up

1. If you knew how far someone traveled and how fast she traveled, what would you do to find how long the trip took her?

2. If you knew the total cost of a purchase and the unit cost of each item, what would you do to find the number of items bought?

Warm-up Answers

1. divide the distance by the rate of speed

2. divide the total cost by the unit cost

38. Jenny bought 24 plastic hangers that cost $0.69 each, 3 garment bags that cost $11.99 each, and 8 sweater bags that cost $6.85 each. How much did Jenny spend?

(1) $87.84 (2) $97.84 (3) $107.33
(4) $107.43 (5) $108.33

① ② ③ ④ ⑤

39. Andy and Jill drive at an average steady speed of 50 mph to Jill's parents house, which is 475 miles away. How many hours will it take them to get to Jill's parents'?

(1) $9\frac{1}{2}$ (2) $9\frac{1}{4}$ (3) 9
(4) $8\frac{3}{4}$ (5) $8\frac{1}{2}$

① ② ③ ④ ⑤

40. If Mr. Caletti pays $57.60 for a dozen and a half roses, how much did he pay for each rose?

(1) $57.60 (2) $5.76 (3) $4.80
(4) $3.20 (5) $3.00

① ② ③ ④ ⑤

41. If a train travels 312 miles at a rate of 78 mph and a car travels the same number of miles at 52 mph, how many hours longer will the car take to arrive than the train?

(1) 10 (2) 6 (3) 4 (4) 2 (5) 1

① ② ③ ④ ⑤

42. A drugstore sells a 7-ounce tube of toothpaste for $1.82 and a 9-ounce tube of toothpaste for $2.16. How much cheaper is the larger tube per ounce?

(1) $0.01 (2) $0.02 (3) $0.10
(4) $0.20 (5) $0.34

① ② ③ ④ ⑤

Directions: For each problem, choose the one best answer. Answers are on page 558.

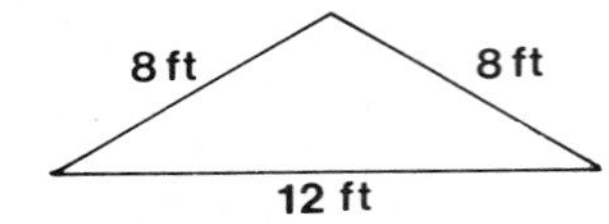

43. How many feet of fencing would you need to enclose the garden above?

(1) 20 (2) 28 (3) 32
(4) 43 (5) 97

① ② ③ ④ ⑤

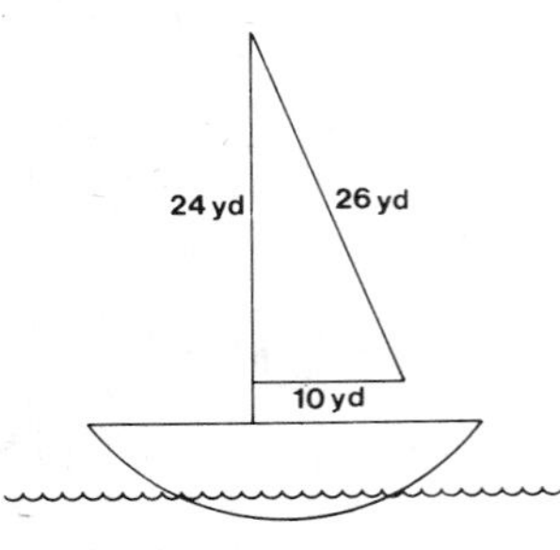

44. What is the distance in yards around the sail in the figure above?

(1) 34 (2) 50 (3) 51
(4) 60 (5) 126

① ② ③ ④ ⑤

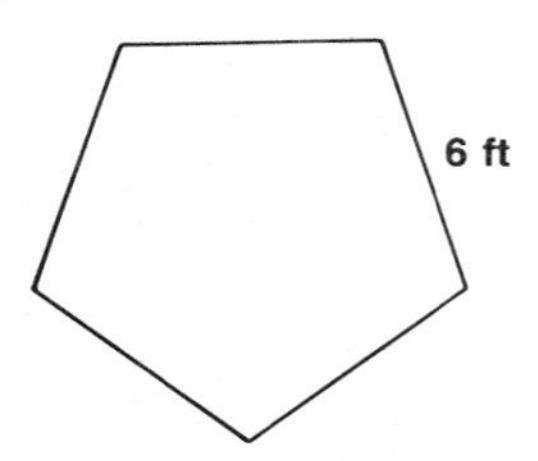

45. All the sides of the dog-show exhibition area shown above are equal. The judges want to rope off the area. How many feet of rope will they need?

(1) 12 (2) 15 (3) 24
(4) 30 (5) 72

① ② ③ ④ ⑤

46. How many feet of baseboard would you need for a room that measures 23 feet by 16 feet? Subtract 7 feet for the doorway.

(1) 39 (2) 71 (3) 78
(4) 110 (5) 124

① ② ③ ④ ⑤

Figuring the Distance Around an Area To find the distance around an area, you simply add all the sides of the area. The important thing to remember is to add *all* the sides. Some figures may have three sides of equal or unequal lengths; some figures may have six or seven sides. Be sure to find a measurement for every side before you add.

Look at the following problem.

■ Liz wants to wallpaper a border around the top of the walls in a room that measures 13 feet by 15 feet. How much border paper should she buy?

Step 1 You know that a room has 4 walls: 2 of the walls measure 13 feet and 2 measure 15 feet. So first you need to multiply each measurement by 2.

$13 \times 2 = 26$ feet
$15 \times 2 = 30$ feet

Step 2 Add the measurements together.

$26 + 30 = 56$

Liz will have to buy 56 feet of border paper.

Warm-up

Find the distance around the following:

1. a table 72 inches by 36 inches
2. a piece of paper $8\frac{1}{2}$ inches by 11 inches
3. a 6-sided shape with equal sides of 2.5 feet
4. a 5-sided shape with 2 sides of 4 inches and 3 sides of 1.5 inches
5. a picture frame that measures $12\frac{1}{2}$ inches by $6\frac{1}{2}$ inches
6. a stop sign that measures 14 inches on each of its 8 sides

Warm-up Answers
1. 216 in **2.** 39 in **3.** 15 ft **4.** 12.5 in **5.** 38 in **6.** 112 in

Figuring Square Measure Suppose you wanted to find the measure of an entire area that had four sides. Instead of adding all the sides of the area, you would multiply the two sides.

Look at the following problem.

■ You want to buy a piece of glass for a picture frame that measures 10 inches by 12 inches. What is the area of the glass you will have to buy?

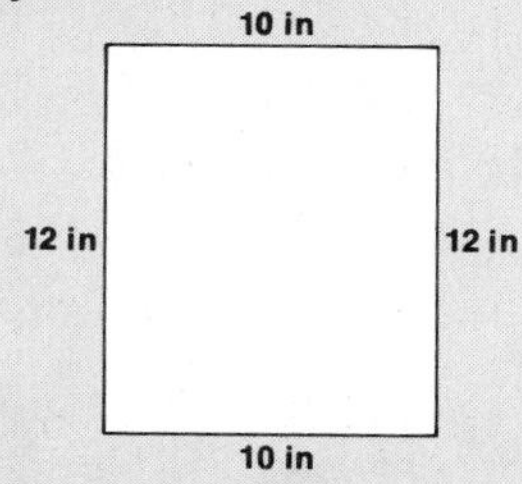

Look at the same picture frame below.

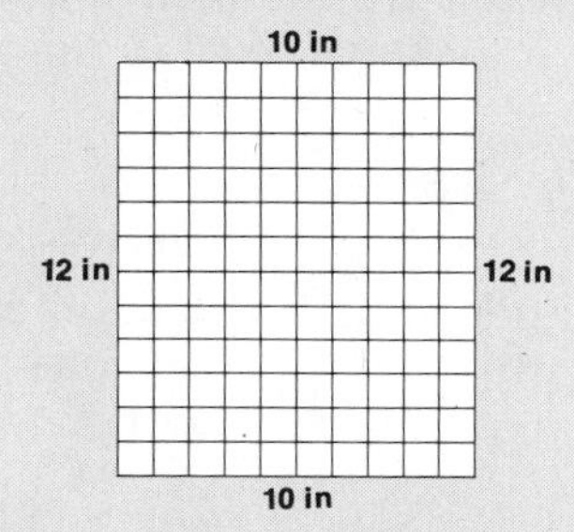

It has 12 rows with 10 squares in each row. Each square measures one inch by one inch, or one square inch. Since you want to cover the whole area of the frame with glass, you will have to multiply the measurements of the two sides.

10 in × 12 in = 120 sq in

Since you have 120 squares, the area the glass covers is 120 square inches. Area is always stated in terms of *square measure*.

Warm-up

Find the area of the following four-sided figures.

1. 23 feet by 16 feet
2. 34 yards by 28 yards
3. a 4-sided room with equal sides of 18 feet each

Need a Hint for Number 50?
Are all the measurements in the item in the same unit of measure? Change them if necessary.

Warm-up Answers
1. 368 sq ft **2.** 952 sq yd **3.** 324 sq ft

47. The Donahues want to install new wall-to-wall carpeting in their family room. The room measures 13 feet by 19 feet. How many square feet of carpeting should they order?

(1) 494 (2) 247 (3) 32 (4) 19
(5) Insufficient data is given to solve the problem.

① ② ③ ④ ⑤

48. The area of a piece of land the Anders own measures 1,600 square feet. If they enclose the area with a fence, how many feet of fencing will they need for each side?

(1) 16 (2) 100 (3) 160 (4) 1,600
(5) Insufficient data is given to solve the problem.

① ② ③ ④ ⑤

49. A large basement room has 4 walls that each measure 25 feet by 8.5 feet. If a painter uses paint that covers 300 square feet per gallon, how many gallons of paint must be bought?

(1) 1 (2) 2 (3) 3 (4) 4
(5) Insufficient data is given to solve the problem.

① ② ③ ④ ⑤

50. The area of a table top to be refinished is 7,776 square inches. If one side is 6 feet long, how many inches long is the other side?

(1) 8 (2) 12 (3) 108 (4) 1,296
(5) Insufficient data is given to solve the problem.

① ② ③ ④ ⑤

Directions: For each problem, choose the one best answer. Answers begin on page 558.

51. A box measures 17 inches by 21 inches by 6 inches. What is the capacity of the box in cubic inches?

(1) 38 (2) 44 (3) 357 (4) 2,142
(5) Insufficient data is given to solve the problem.

① ② ③ ④ ⑤

52. A large tank is 35 feet high and 26 feet wide. How many cubic feet of water can the tank hold?

(1) 61 (2) 51 (3) 810 (4) 910
(5) Insufficient data is given to solve the problem.

① ② ③ ④ ⑤

53. A wooden flower box measures 36 inches by 4 inches by 3 inches. Another box measures 28 inches by 8 inches by 6 inches. How many more cubic inches of soil can the second box hold than the first?

(1) 432 (2) 912 (3) 1,344 (4) 1,776
(5) Insufficient data is given to solve the problem.

① ② ③ ④ ⑤

54. The capacity of a wardrobe storage box is 40 cubic feet. The box is 60 inches high and 2.5 feet wide. How many feet deep is the box?

(1) 2.1 (2) 2.5 (3) 3.2 (4) 3.5
(5) Insufficient data is given to solve the problem.

① ② ③ ④ ⑤

Figuring the Capacity of an Area You have learned how to find the distance around an area and the area of a flat surface. The GED Test may also ask you to find the capacity of an area, such as a tank or a room.

Look at the drawing of the box below.

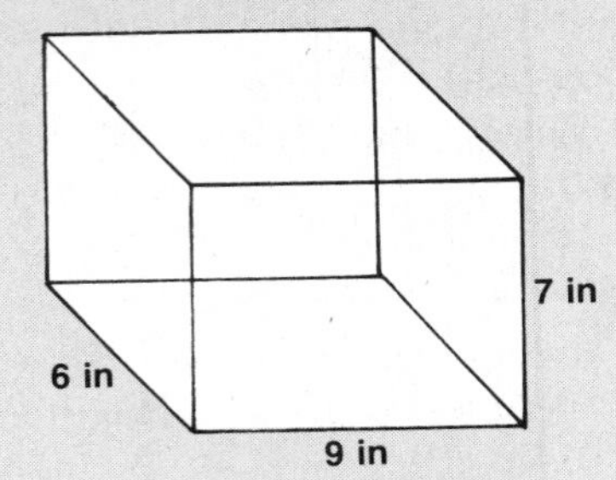

Suppose you wanted to know the capacity of the box. As you can see in the drawing, the box is 9 inches wide, 7 inches high, and 6 inches long. Since you know the measurements of all three sides, you simply multiply the three numbers.

$9 \times 7 \times 6 = 378$

The capacity of the box is 378 cubic inches. Just as area has square measure, capacity has *cubic* measure. A cubic inch is one inch wide, one inch high, and one inch long.

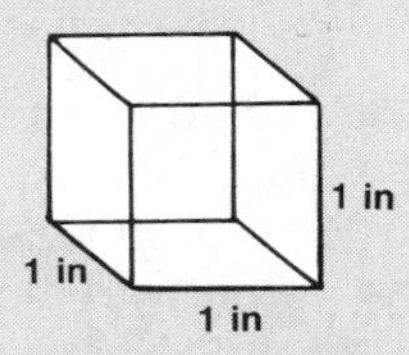

Suppose you had been told the capacity of the box was 378 cubic inches and the sides were 9 inches and 7 inches. How would you find the depth of the box? Since you know you have to multiply the three measurements together to find the capacity of the box, multiply the two measurements you know ($9 \times 7 = 63$). Then divide the capacity by this amount ($378 \div 63 = 6$).

Warm-up

Find the capacity of containers with the following measurements.

1. 12 ft × 11 ft × 4 ft
2. 26 in × 25 in × 20 in
3. 3.5 yd × 4.2 yd × 2.5 yd

Warm-up Answers
1. 528 cu ft **2.** 13,000 cu in **3.** 36.75 cu yd

Arithmetic Review

This page and the next one offer you a good chance to review the arithmetic you have already learned. These pages will also offer you practice with more GED-type word problems.

☑ A Test-Taking Tip

As a general tip for working arithmetic problems on the GED Mathematics Test, remember always to read the question carefully. If you're really stuck, don't waste time getting frustrated. Circle the number of the question you skipped, so you can come back to it later. Forget about the problem for the time being and do your best on the next problems. If you have time after you have completed the test, return to the problems you have circled and try to work them again.

Sometimes, it helps to use the process of elimination. Remember the last thing to do when solving a word problem? Check that your answer makes sense. Sometimes you may be able to look at the list of answers and know immediately that some of them do not make sense and could not possibly be answers to the problem. After you eliminate an answer or two, try again to work the problem and see if one of the remaining answers is a possible solution.

If you are ever really confused by a problem and have no idea how to work it, fill in an oval anyway—make a guess.

Need a Hint for Number 56?
Notice the word pattern *in the question. This pattern tells you that Min works the same number of hours every other week. Remember, there are 52 weeks in one year. According to Min's pattern, she works each amount of hours for 25 weeks of each year.*

Need a Hint for Number 58?
How much money does Brad earn now?

55. Bertha bought 3 bars of soap at $0.69 a bar, 6 cans of soup at $0.33 a can, 2 pounds of beef at $4.29 a pound, and a quart of milk for $0.89. How much change will Bertha get from a $20.00 bill?

(1) $14.52 (2) $13.52 (3) $7.58
(4) $6.48 (5) $5.48

① ② ③ ④ ⑤

56. Min works $38\frac{1}{2}$ hours one week and $37\frac{3}{4}$ hours the next week. If she continues this pattern for a year, and also takes a 2-week vacation, how many hours will she work in one year?

(1) $1,906\frac{1}{4}$ (2) $962\frac{1}{2}$
(3) $943\frac{3}{4}$ (4) $76\frac{1}{4}$
(5) Insufficient data is given to solve the problem.

① ② ③ ④ ⑤

57. Helen paid $25.83 for $7\frac{7}{8}$ inches of picture frame. How much did one inch cost?

(1) $3.89 (2) $3.69 (3) $3.58
(4) $3.49 (5) $3.28

① ② ③ ④ ⑤

58. Brad's boss offered him a raise of $75 a week for a year, a 12% raise, or a flat $2,200 dollar raise. How much more money would Brad receive if he chose the second offer over the first offer?

(1) $2,200 (2) $2,000
(3) $1,850 (4) $1,200
(5) Insufficient data is given to solve the problem.

① ② ③ ④ ⑤

<u>Directions:</u> For each problem, choose the <u>one</u> best answer. Answers are on page 559.

59. A store discounts everything 15% off the regular price. In addition, the store gave $\frac{1}{3}$ off the regular price. The tax was 4%. What would be the price of a set of luggage that originally cost $297.00?

(1) $143.55 (2) $153.45
(3) $159.59 (4) $158.59
(5) $159.58

(1) (2) (3) (4) (5)

60. At a local community college the ratio of teachers to students is 1 to 21.5. Approximately how many teachers should the school hire for an enrollment of 792?

(1) 21.5 (2) 30 (3) 36
(4) 37 (5) 38

(1) (2) (3) (4) (5)

61. The Chungs earn $2,580 a month. They spend 28.5% a month on a mortgage, $\frac{1}{4}$ on food for the family, and $\frac{1}{3}$ on bills and other necessities. How much money do the Chungs have left at the end of the month?

(1) $339.70 (2) $645.00
(3) $735.30 (4) $860.00
(5) $2,240.30

(1) (2) (3) (4) (5)

62. During the five business days last week, Jack's stock showed the following activity: a gain of $1\frac{1}{4}$ points, a gain of $\frac{3}{4}$ of a point, a loss of $2\frac{1}{8}$ points, a gain of $\frac{3}{8}$ of a point, and a loss of $\frac{5}{8}$ of a point. What was the net gain or loss of Jack's stock at the end of the week?

(1) $-2\frac{3}{4}$ (2) $-1\frac{3}{8}$ (3) $+\frac{3}{8}$

(4) $-\frac{3}{8}$ (5) $+2\frac{3}{8}$

(1) (2) (3) (4) (5)

Need a Hint for Number 60?
What does approximately *mean? Will you be looking for an exact answer? Be sure to round your answer to the nearest whole number. People cannot be counted in parts.*

Need a Hint for Number 61?
This problem has five steps. Be sure to check your arithmetic at each step.

Need a Hint for Number 62?
Net *is the amount you are left with after paying expenses. For example, if you earn $100, and $22 is paid in federal taxes and $8 is paid in state taxes, you net $70. Normally, you subtract to find the net. In this case, you will have to* add *and* subtract *to find the net.*

☑ A Test-Taking Tip

Here's a good way to check your answers on the GED Mathematics Test. Use the reverse operation. If you added to get an answer, subtract one of the numbers from the total, and you should get the other number.

Add	*Check*
1,289	9,272
+7,983	−7,983
9,272	1,289

If you multiplied to get an answer, divide to check.

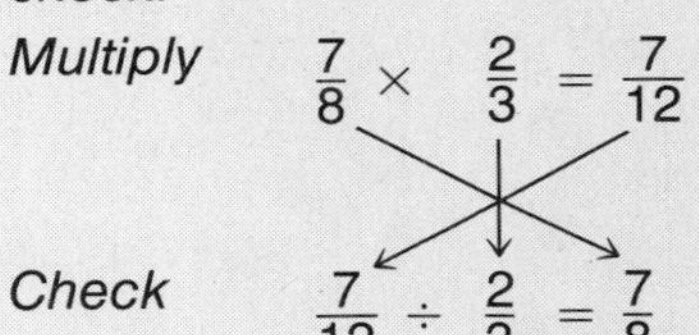

Multiply $\frac{7}{8} \times \frac{2}{3} = \frac{7}{12}$
Check $\frac{7}{12} \div \frac{2}{3} = \frac{7}{8}$

Geometry

Geometry investigates the size, shape, and position of objects in space.

The GED Test questions on geometry are divided between those that deal with plane geometry and those that deal with solid geometry. Plane geometry involves two dimensions. That is, plane geometric figures have height and width. Solid geometry involves three-dimensional figures—figures that have depth, width, and height.

When you were figuring square and cubic measures in arithmetic on pages 491 and 492, you were working with plane and solid geometric figures.

To begin your study of geometry, you must understand a few basic concepts. A **point** indicates location in space and has no size. Points are indicated by letters in geometry.

A **line** is a set of points. Lines have no width; their length is infinite. *Infinite* means "without beginning or end." A line extends infinitely far in both directions. In geometry, a line is indicated with an arrowhead at each end. Lines can be named in two ways. They can be named with a lower-case letter or by two points on the line. The line below can be called line *m* or line *AB*.

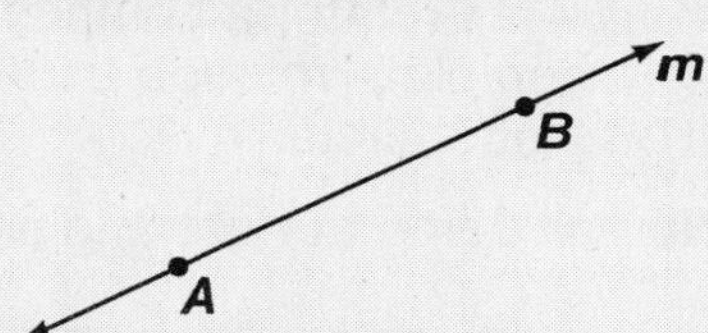

A **line segment** is a particular set of points on a line and all the points in between. $\overline{AB}$ below is a line segment. Since line segments have endpoints, a beginning and an end, their lengths can be measured.

A **ray** is part of a line. It has one endpoint and extends infinitely in the other direction. Always name the endpoint first. Ray *CD* is shown below.

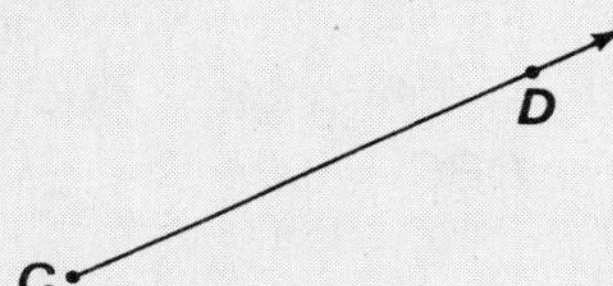

A **plane** is a set of points on a flat surface that extends to infinity.

An **angle** is formed when two rays have a common endpoint called the **vertex.**

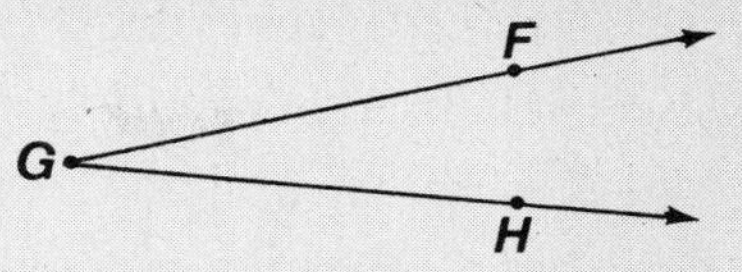

You can call this angle $\angle FGH$, $\angle HGF$, or $\angle G$. Its vertex is point *G*.

Coming to Terms

point indicator of a location in space
line set of points that extends infinitely in both directions
line segment particular set of points with two endpoints
ray part of a line with one endpoint
plane set of points on a flat surface that extends indefinitely
angle meeting of two rays with a common endpoint
vertex common endpoint of an angle

Warm-up

Warm-up questions refer to the following figures.

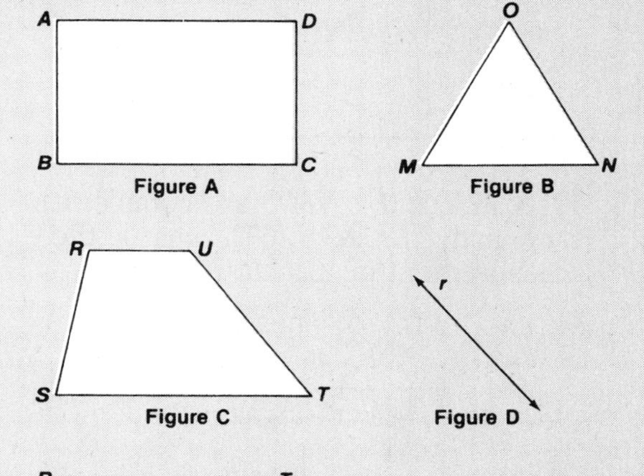

1. Which figure contains no endpoints?
2. Which of the following lists the line segments in figure C?
  a. $\overline{RU}$, $\overline{US}$, $\overline{ST}$, $\overline{RT}$
  b. $\overline{RU}$, $\overline{UT}$, $\overline{RT}$, $\overline{RS}$
  c. $\overline{RU}$, $\overline{UT}$, $\overline{ST}$, $\overline{RS}$
3. Which figure has three line segments?
4. Which figure has an infinite length?

Warm-up Answers
1. D **2.** C **3.** B **4.** D

Directions: For each problem, choose the one best answer. Answers are on page 559.

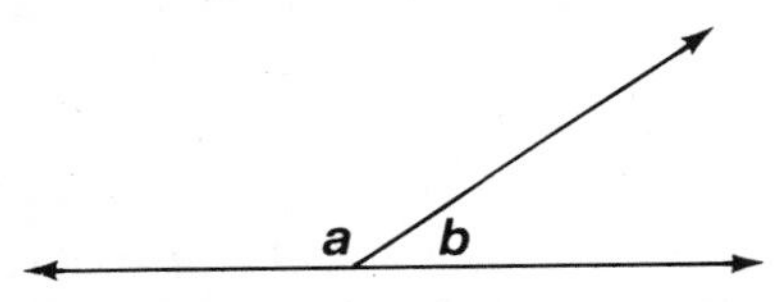

1. If $\angle a$ and $\angle b$ are supplementary, find $\angle b$ if $\angle a = 135°$.

   (1) 45° (2) 55° (3) 65°
   (4) 75° (5) 85°

   (1) (2) (3) (4) (5)

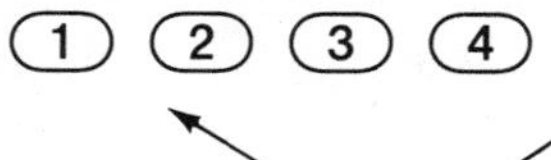

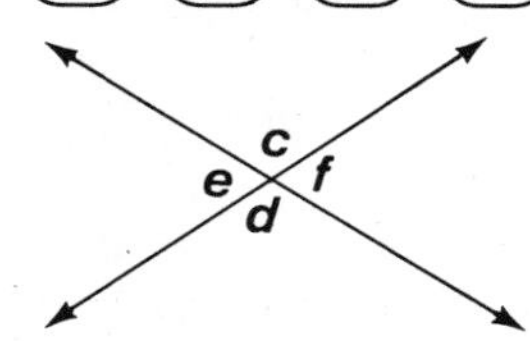

2. If $\angle c$ and $\angle d$ are vertical angles, and $\angle e$ and $\angle f$ are vertical angles, and $\angle c = 95°$, what is the measurement of $\angle f$?

   (1) 65° (2) 85° (3) 170°
   (4) 190° (5) 265°

   (1) (2) (3) (4) (5)

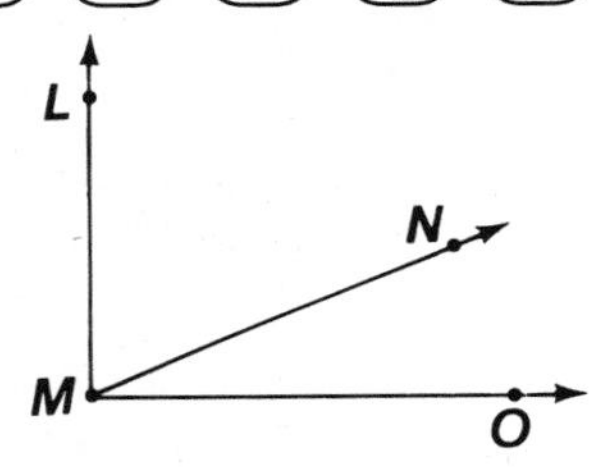

3. If $\angle LMN$ and $\angle NMO$ are complementary, and $\angle LMN = 67°$, what is the measurement of $\angle NMO$?

   (1) 13° (2) 23° (3) 33°
   (4) 113° (5) 293°

   (1) (2) (3) (4) (5)

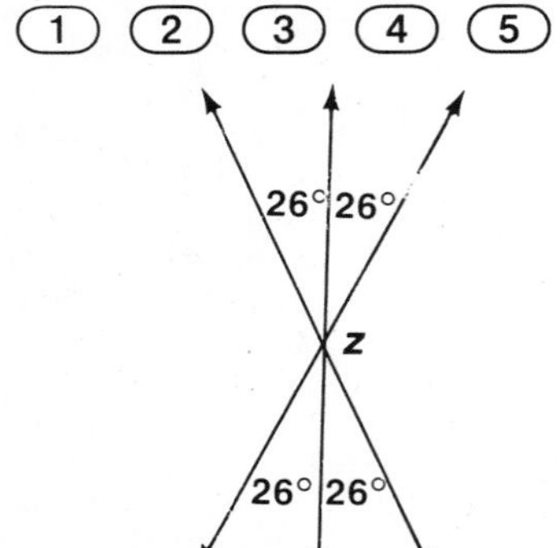

4. Find the measurement of $\angle Z$.

   (1) 26° (2) 52° (3) 76°
   (4) 128° (5) 256°

   (1) (2) (3) (4) (5)

Measuring Angles Angles are measured in units called degrees. The symbol for a degree is °.

Coming to Terms

straight angle angle that measures exactly 180°. A straight angle is a straight line.

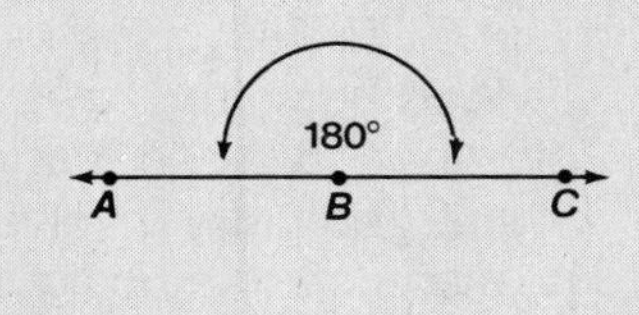

right angle angle that measures exactly 90°. The symbol for a right angle is ⌉. This symbol is placed at the vertex of the angle.

acute angle angle that measures less than 90°

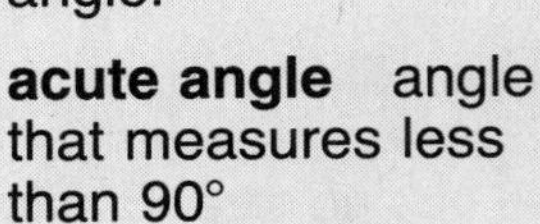

obtuse angle angle that measures more than 90° but less than 180°

reflex angle angle that measures more than 180° but less than 360°

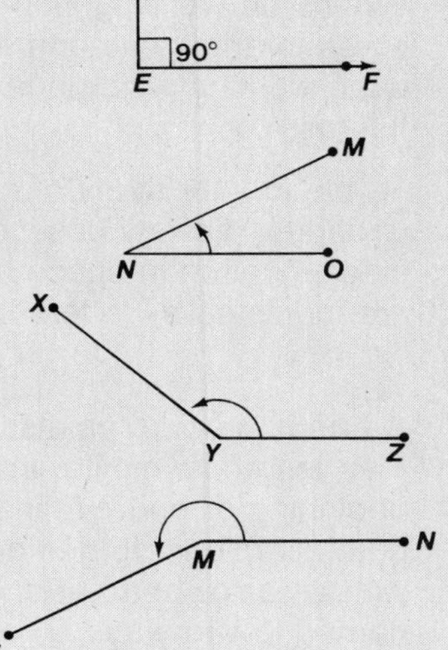

The reflex angle above indicates that when the line segments rotate, a complete circle is formed. A complete rotation is 360°. Each degree is 1/360 of a circle.

perpendicular being at right angles to a line or plane

Pairs of Angles Geometry has three common pairs of angles. These are complementary, supplementary, and vertical angles. Study the following definitions.

Complementary angles are two angles whose sum is 90°. These two angles form one right angle.

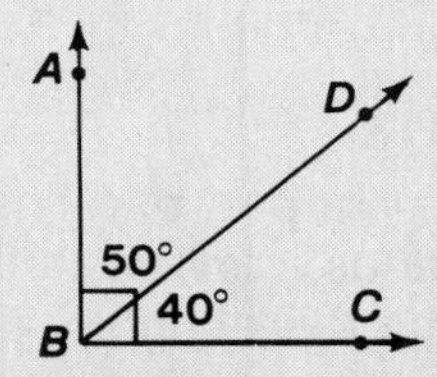

The sum of $\angle ABD$ and $\angle DBC$ is 90°. These two angles form right angle $\angle ABC$.

$$\angle ABD + \angle DBC = 90°$$
$$50° + 40° = 90°$$

Read the information in the tinted column on the next page before working the problems in the white column on either page.

Supplementary Angles are two angles whose sum is 180°. Two supplementary angles form a straight line.

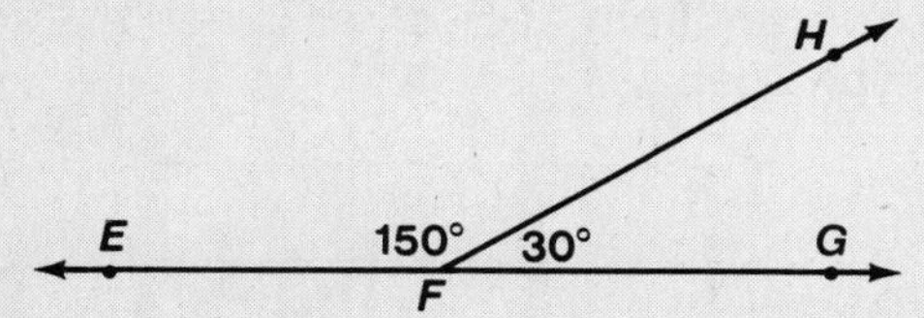

The sum of $\angle EFH$ and $\angle HFG$ is 180°. These two angles form the straight angle *EFG*.

$$\angle EFH + \angle HFG = 180°$$
$$150° + 30° = 180°$$

When two lines intersect, or cross, an *X* is formed, and four angles are created. The pairs of angles opposite each other are called *vertical angles.* The sum of the four angles equals 360°, or a complete circle. In the diagram, $\angle a$ and $\angle b$ are a pair of vertical angles; $\angle c$ and $\angle d$ are the other pair of vertical angles.

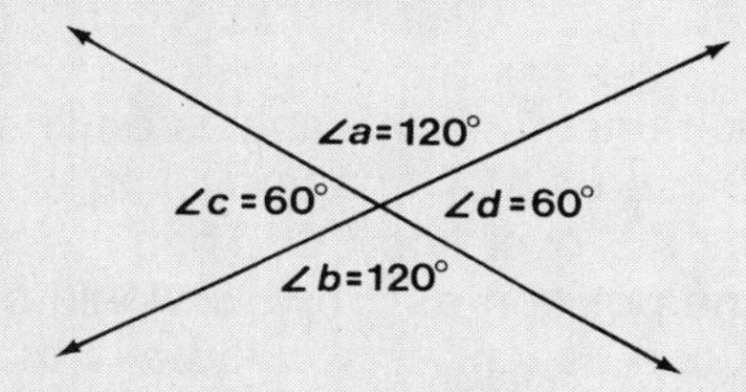

Vertical angles are equal; therefore, $\angle a$ and $\angle b$ are equal, and $\angle c$ and $\angle d$ are equal. The sum of all four angles should total 360°.

$$\angle a + \angle b + \angle c + \angle d = 360°$$
$$120° + 120° + 60° + 60° = 360°$$

Some geometric questions require you to use a number of ideas. Find the measurements of $\angle a$, $\angle b$, and $\angle c$ in the diagram.

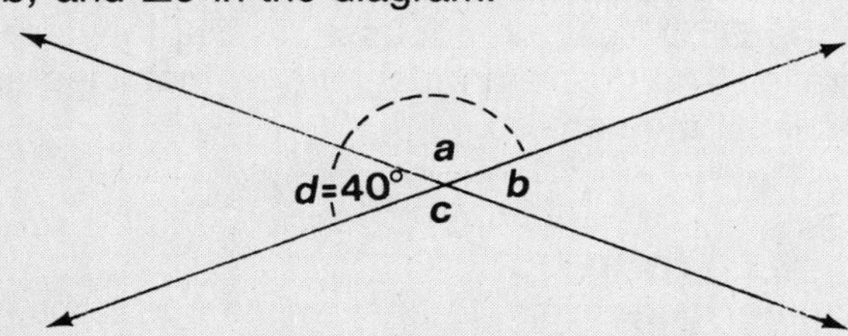

When lines cross, vertical angles are formed. The definition of vertical angles tells you that $\angle b$ is vertical to $\angle d$. Since $\angle d$ measures 40°, $\angle b$ is also 40°. If you follow the dotted arc, you'll see that $\angle d$ *and* $\angle a$ form a straight angle, or 180°.

$$\angle a = 180° - 40°$$
$$\angle a = 140°$$

$\angle a$ and $\angle c$ are vertical angles. Because vertical angles are equal, $\angle c$ equals 140°.

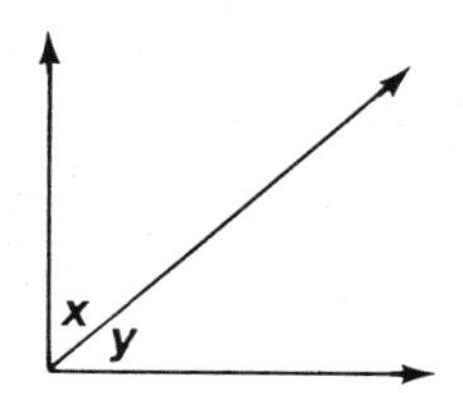

5. If $\angle x$ and $\angle y$ are complementary, find $\angle y$ if $\angle x = 55°$.

   (1) 35° (2) 45° (3) 125°
   (4) 135° (5) 145°

   ① ② ③ ④ ⑤

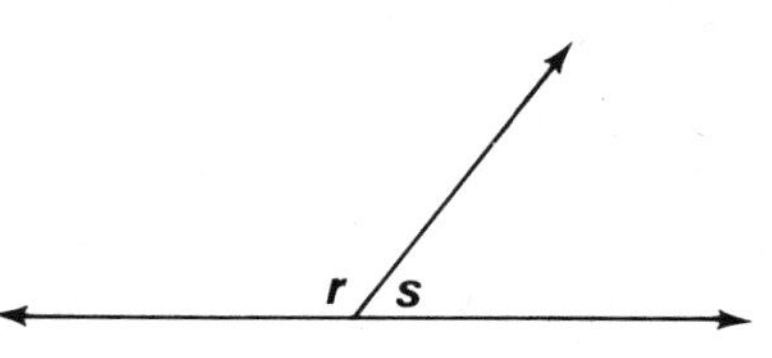

6. If $\angle s$ and $\angle r$ are supplementary, find $\angle r$ if $\angle s = 53°$.

   (1) 37° (2) 117° (3) 127°
   (4) 227° (5) 307°

   ① ② ③ ④ ⑤

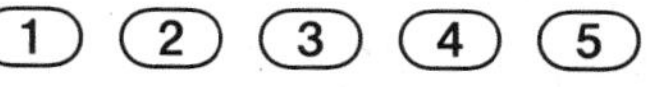

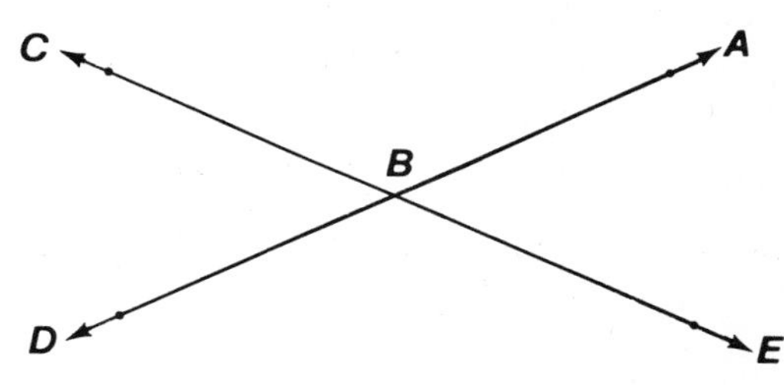

7. Find the measurement of $\angle ABC$ if $\angle ABE$ equals 50°.

   (1) 110° (2) 120° (3) 130°
   (4) 140° (5) 150°

   ① ② ③ ④ ⑤

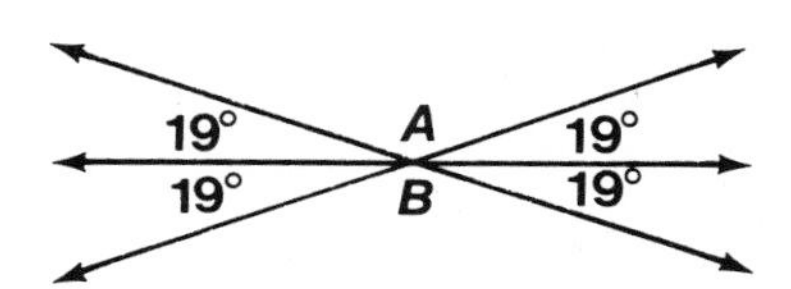

8. Find the angle measurements for $\angle A$ and $\angle B$.

   (1) Both are 104°. (2) Both are 122°.
   (3) Both are 132°. (4) Both are 142°.
   (5) Both are 144°.

   ① ② ③ ④ ⑤

Directions: For each problem, choose the one best answer. Answers are on page 559.

Items 9–12 refer to the following diagram. Lines m and n are parallel.

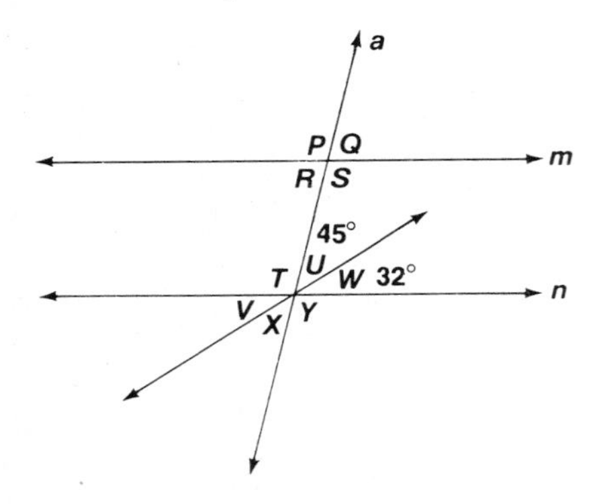

9. What is the measurement of $\angle P$ if $\angle P$ and $\angle T$ are corresponding and $\angle T$ is supplementary to $\angle U$ and $\angle W$?

   (1) 77° (2) 103° (3) 180°
   (4) 183° (5) 187°

   (1) (2) (3) (4) (5)

10. What is the measurement of $\angle X$?

    (1) 32° (2) 45° (3) 90°
    (4) 145° (5) 180°

    (1) (2) (3) (4) (5)

11. What is the measurement of $\angle Q$?

    (1) 35° (2) 47° (3) 77°
    (4) 107° (5) 283°

    (1) (2) (3) (4) (5)

12. What is the total measurement of angles T, V, X, and Y?

    (1) 77° (2) 103° (3) 273°
    (4) 283° (5) 360°

    (1) (2) (3) (4) (5)

Parallel Lines and Their Angles *Parallel lines* are lines that never meet. No matter how long the lines extend, they will always stay equally distant from each other. Lines *AB* and *CD* are parallel.

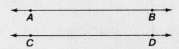

A line that cuts across several parallel lines is called a *transversal.* When a transversal cuts a pair of parallel lines, eight angles are formed.

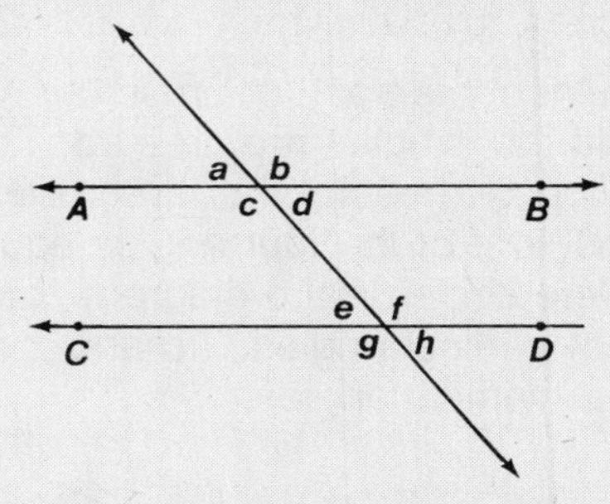

The measurements of the angles on line *AB* are equal to those on *CD.* Imagine lifting and placing line *AB* over line *CD.* Then $\angle a$ would be in the same position as $\angle e$, $\angle b$ would be in the same position as $\angle f$, $\angle c$ would be in the same position as $\angle g$, and $\angle d$ would have the same position as $\angle h$. When you match the angles one to one from line *AB* to line *CD,* you are identifying corresponding angles. Corresponding angles are equal. So, $\angle a = \angle e$, $\angle c = \angle g$, $\angle b = \angle f$, $\angle d = \angle h$.

☑ A Test-Taking Tip

When you come across lines that look parallel on the GED Test, do not assume that they are parallel. The problem must *tell* you that lines are parallel if they are so.

Warm-up

Use the figure below to answer the questions. Line segments $\overline{WX}$ and $\overline{YZ}$ are parallel.

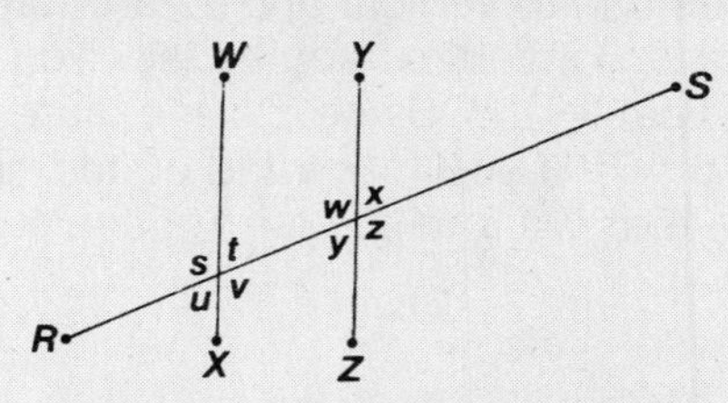

1. Name four corresponding angles.
2. Name the transversal line segment.

Warm-up Answers
1. $\angle s = \angle w$, $\angle t = \angle x$, $\angle u = \angle y$, $\angle v = \angle z$ **2.** $\overline{RS}$

More About Parallel Lines and Their Angles

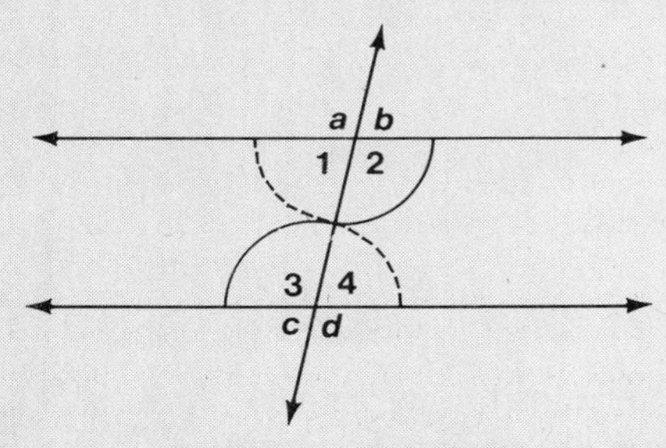

In the diagram, sections have been identified as exterior or interior. ∠*a,* ∠*b,* ∠*c,* and ∠*d* are exterior angles. ∠1, ∠2, ∠3, and ∠4 are interior angles.

Alternate interior angles are equal.
∠1 = ∠4
∠2 = ∠3

Alternate exterior angles are equal.
∠a = ∠d
∠b = ∠c

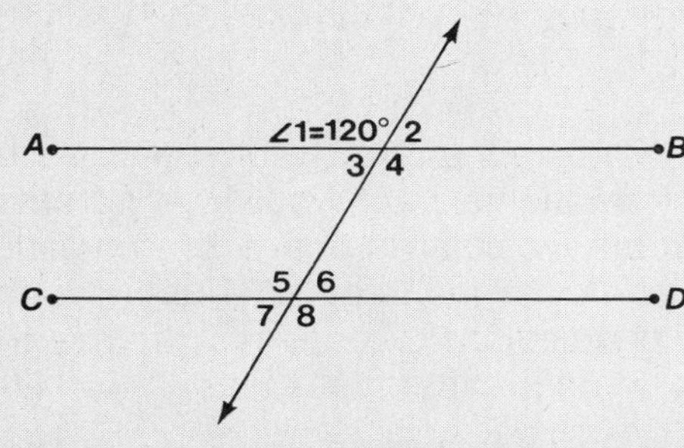

In the diagram above, $\overline{AB}$ is parallel to $\overline{CD}$.

Because ∠1 and ∠2 equal a straight line, they are supplementary. Supplementary angles are equal to 180°. If ∠1 = 120°, ∠2 = 60°. ∠3 also equals 60° because it is vertical to ∠2. ∠4 is vertical to ∠1; therefore, ∠4 = 120°.

Warm-up

Use the second diagram above to answer the following questions.

1. List the exterior angles.
2. List the interior angles.
3. List the alternate interior angles.
4. List the alternate exterior angles.

Warm-up Answers
1. ∠1, ∠2, ∠7, ∠8 **2.** ∠3, ∠4, ∠5, ∠6 **3.** ∠3 = ∠6, ∠4 = ∠5 **4.** ∠1 = ∠8, ∠2 = ∠7

Items 13–17 refer to the diagram below. Lines *c* and *b* are parallel.

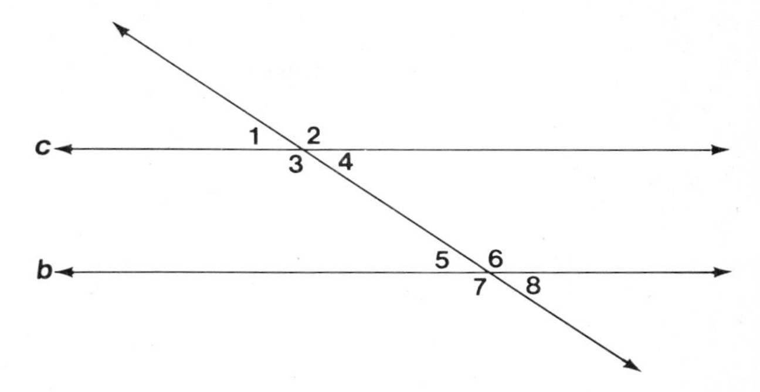

13. If ∠2 is 141°, what is the measurement of ∠1?

    (1) 39° (2) 60° (3) 90°
    (4) 120° (5) 150°

    ① ② ③ ④ ⑤

14. Which angle is equal to ∠1, ∠4, and ∠5?

    (1) ∠2 (2) ∠3 (3) ∠6
    (4) ∠7 (5) ∠8

    ① ② ③ ④ ⑤

15. Which angle is equal to ∠2?

    (1) ∠1 (2) ∠3 (3) 4
    (4) ∠5 (5) ∠8

    ① ② ③ ④ ⑤

16. The sum of ∠2 and ∠4 is

    (1) 120° (2) 180° (3) 200°
    (4) 240° (5) 280°

    ① ② ③ ④ ⑤

17. If ∠8 = 39°, what is the total of angles 5, 6, and 7?

    (1) 41° (2) 51° (3) 141°
    (4) 321° (5) 360°

    ① ② ③ ④ ⑤

Directions: For each problem, choose the one best answer. Answers are on page 559.

Items 18–19 refer to the following diagram.

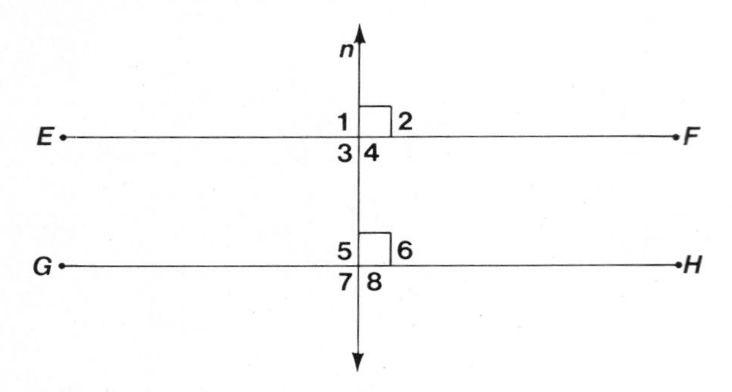

18. Line n is perpendicular to line segments $\overline{EF}$ and $\overline{GH}$. Therefore, $\overline{EF}$ and $\overline{GH}$ are

(1) perpendicular to each other
(2) straight lines
(3) infinite in length
(4) parallel to each other
(5) parallel to line n

19. What is the measure of $\angle 5$?

(1) 30° (2) 45° (3) 60°
(4) 90° (5) 120°

1 2 3 4 5

Items 20–21 refer to the following diagram.

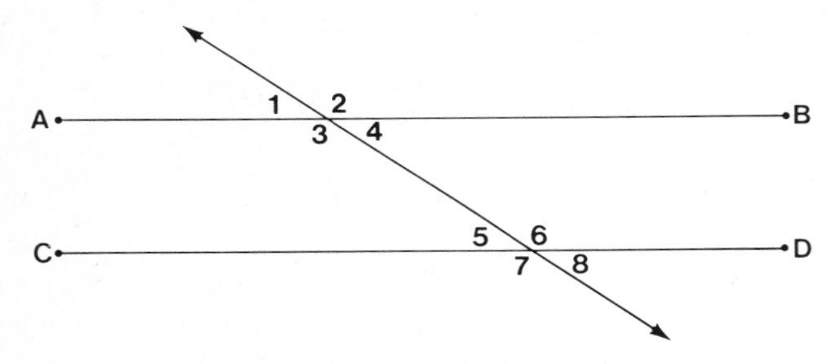

20. Which angle corresponds with $\angle 1$?

(1) $\angle 2$ (2) $\angle 3$ (3) $\angle 5$
(4) $\angle 7$ (5) $\angle 8$

1 2 3 4 5

21. Which angle is equal to $\angle 6$?

(1) $\angle 1$ (2) $\angle 4$ (3) $\angle 5$
(4) $\angle 7$ (5) $\angle 8$

1 2 3 4 5

Parallel Lines and Their Perpendiculars

Lines are said to be *perpendicular* if right angles are formed where they meet.

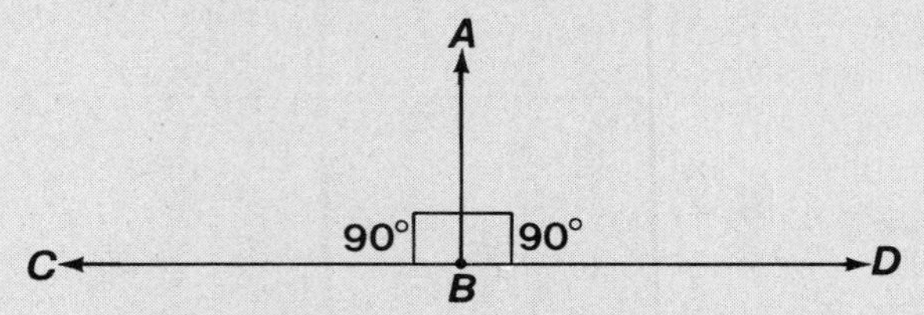

In the diagram below, line segment $\overline{AB}$ is perpendicular to line segments $\overline{CD}$ and $\overline{EF}$ because 90° angles are formed at points G and H.

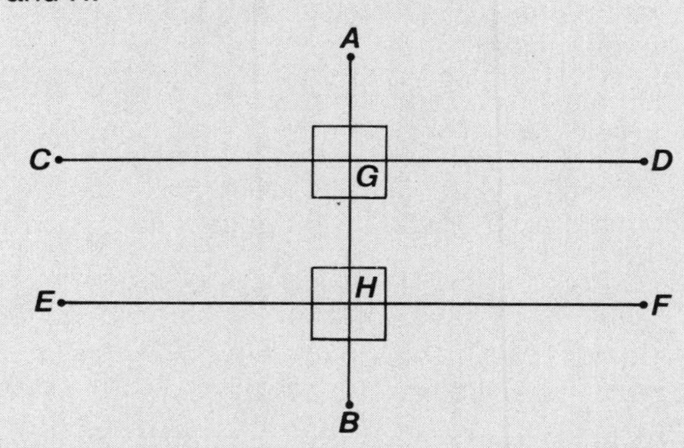

This information is useful because a transversal that is perpendicular to one of two parallel lines is perpendicular to the other. And, if two lines are perpendicular to the same line, they are parallel to each other.

Warm-up

Use what you have learned about parallel and perpendicular lines to answer the questions.

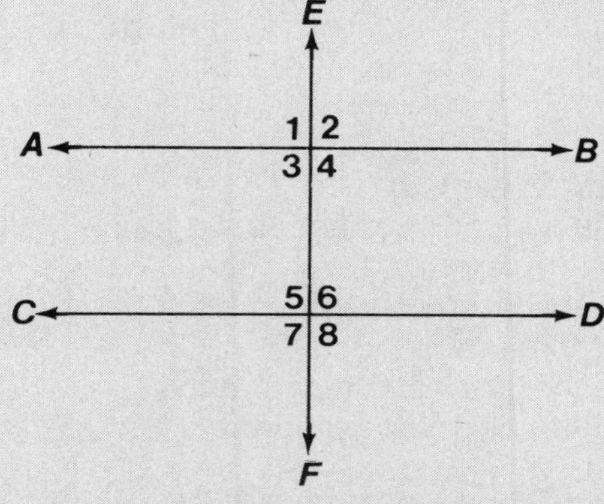

1. $\overline{EF}$ is perpendicular to $\overline{AB}$ and to $\overline{CD}$. What relationship does $\overline{AB}$ have to $\overline{CD}$?
2. What is the measure of all the angles?

Warm-up Answers
1. They are parallel. **2.** 90°

Quadrilaterals Closed figures with four sides are called quadrilaterals. You should know the following quadrilaterals. A *rectangle* is a quadrilateral with four right angles. You already learned that a right angle equals 90°. Since a rectangle has four right angles, the angles total 360° (4 × 90° = 360°). This is true of any quadrilateral. The opposite sides of a rectangle are always parallel and equal. If side $\overline{AC}$ is 6 feet long, then side $\overline{BD}$ is also 6 feet long. If side $\overline{CD}$ is 3.5 feet long, then side $\overline{AB}$ is also 3.5 feet long.

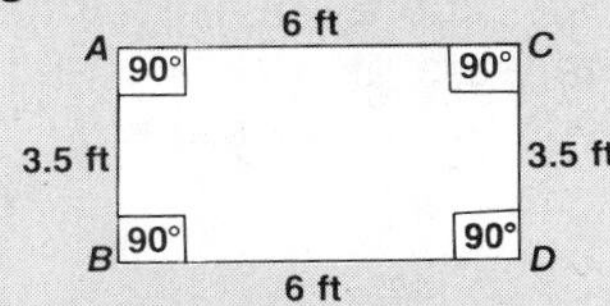

A **square** is a rectangle with four equal sides.

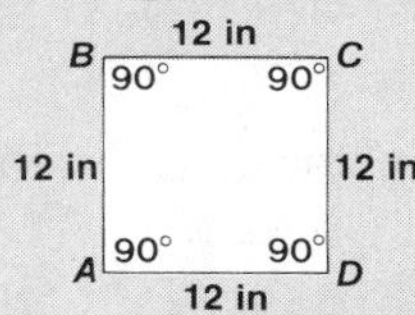

A **parallelogram** is a quadrilateral in which both pairs of opposite sides are parallel. In this figure, $\overline{CD}$ is parallel to $\overline{AB}$, and $\overline{AC}$ is parallel to $\overline{BD}$. The inside measures of angles *A, B, C,* and *D* total 360°, but each angle is not necessarily a right angle.

A **rhombus** is a parallelogram with four equal sides.

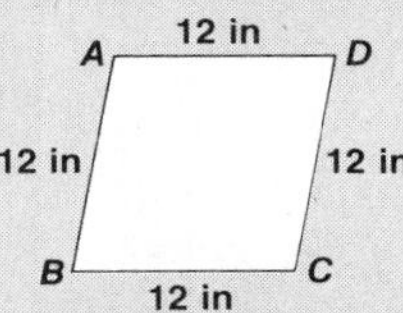

A **trapezoid** is a quadrilateral that has only one pair of parallel lines. The lengths of all four sides may differ as well.

A **diagonal** is a line that passes through two vertices that are not next to each other.

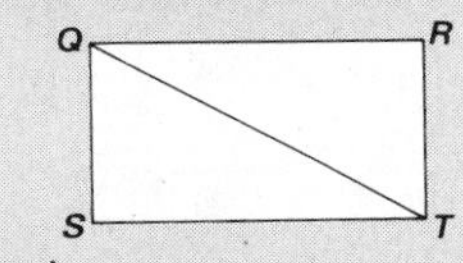

$\overline{QT}$ is a diagonal.

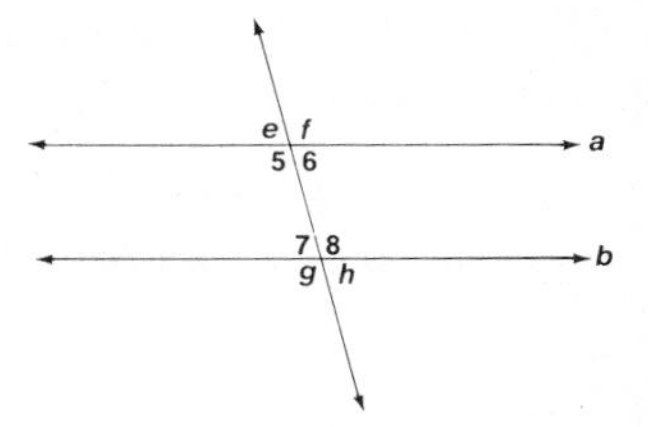

22. Line *a* and line *b* are parallel. If ∠5 = 105° and is supplementary to ∠6, what is the measurement of ∠8?

(1) 75° (2) 105° (3) 180°
(4) 255° (5) 285°

① ② ③ ④ ⑤

23. How many feet is the distance around a rectangular room that measures 32 feet by 14 feet?

(1) 46 (2) 54 (3) 76
(4) 92 (5) 108

① ② ③ ④ ⑤

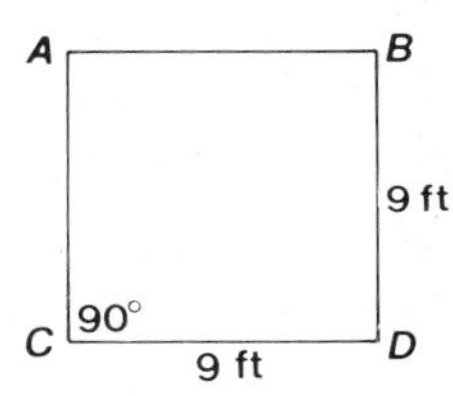

24. Figure *ABCD* above is a square. What is the measurement of ∠*BDC*?

(1) 45° (2) 90° (3) 180°
(4) 270° (5) 360°

① ② ③ ④ ⑤

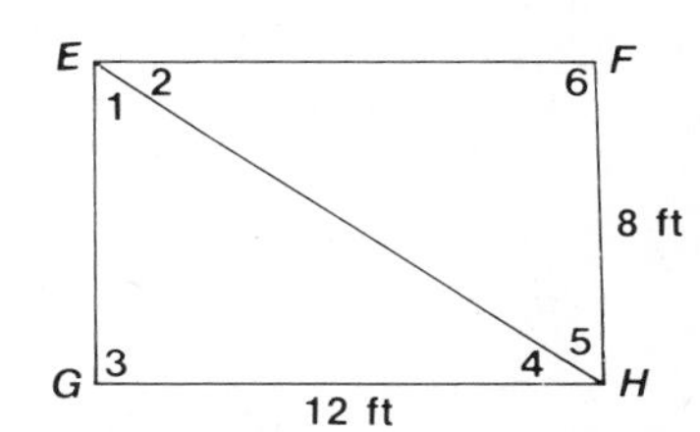

25. Figure *EFGH* is a rectangle with 4 right angles. What is the measurement of ∠6?

(1) 45° (2) 90° (3) 135°
(4) 145° (5) 180°

① ② ③ ④ ⑤

Directions: For each problem, choose the one best answer. Answers are on page 560.

26. Find the perimeter in feet of a square box if one side measures 3.5 feet.

(1) 3.5 (2) 7 (3) 10.5 (4) 14
(5) Insufficient data is given to solve the problem.

① ② ③ ④ ⑤

27. Find the perimeter in feet of a rectangular patio that is 26 feet long.

(1) 41 (2) 60 (3) 67 (4) 82
(5) Insufficient data is given to solve the problem.

① ② ③ ④ ⑤

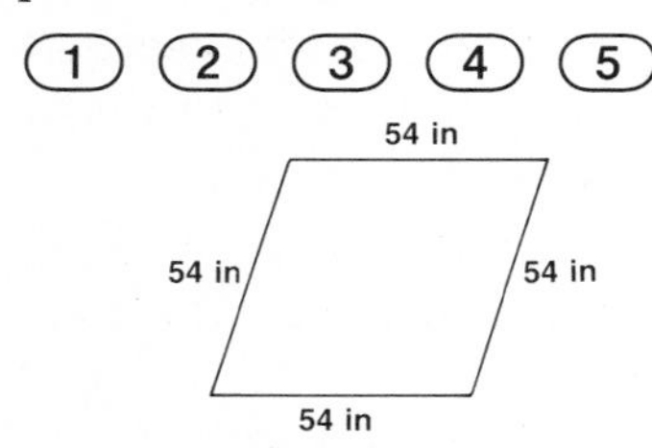

28. Find the perimeter in feet of the rhombus shown above.

(1) 12 (2) 18 (3) 72 (4) 108
(5) Insufficient data is given to solve the problem.

① ② ③ ④ ⑤

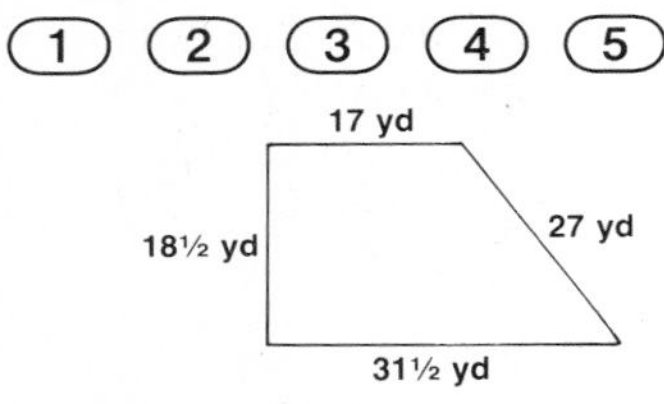

29. Find the perimeter in yards of the trapezoid shown above.

(1) $35\frac{1}{2}$ (2) $58\frac{1}{2}$ (3) 93
(4) 94 (5) 188

① ② ③ ④ ⑤

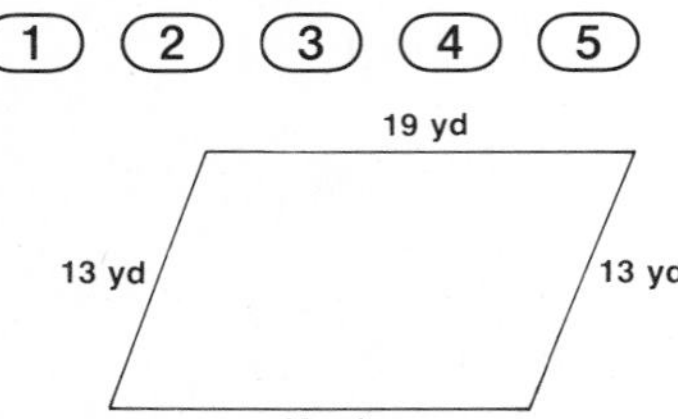

30. Find the perimeter in feet of the parallelogram shown above.

(1) 32 (2) 64 (3) 156
(4) 192 (5) 228

① ② ③ ④ ⑤

Perimeter You learned in the measurement section of arithmetic (page 490) that you find the distance around an area by simply adding the lengths of all the sides of the figure. The distance around an area is called the *perimeter.* You can use a formula for finding the perimeter of a quadrilateral even when you're not given the measures of all four sides.

The formula for finding the perimeter of a square is $P = 4s$. The letter P stands for *perimeter,* and s for *side.* So $4s$ means to multiply the measure of one side by 4. This is the same as adding the measure of one side four times. The sides of the square below are each 5 feet.

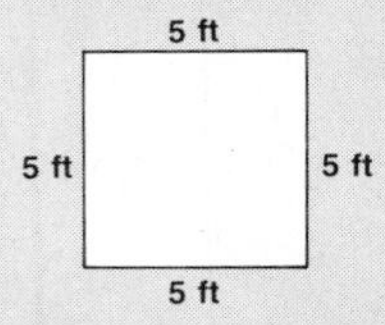

To find the perimeter, use the formula $P = 4s$.

$P = 4 \times 5 = 20$ feet

Notice that the length of the rectangle below is 14 feet and the width is 9 feet. You learned that opposite sides of a rectangle are equal. Since you know the measure of one side, you know the measure of the opposite side. Rather than add to find the perimeter ($14 + 14 + 9 + 9$), you can add twice the length (2×14) plus twice the width (2×9). That is what the formula $P = 2l + 2w$ means. The letter l stands for *length* and w for *width.* To find the perimeter, use the formula.

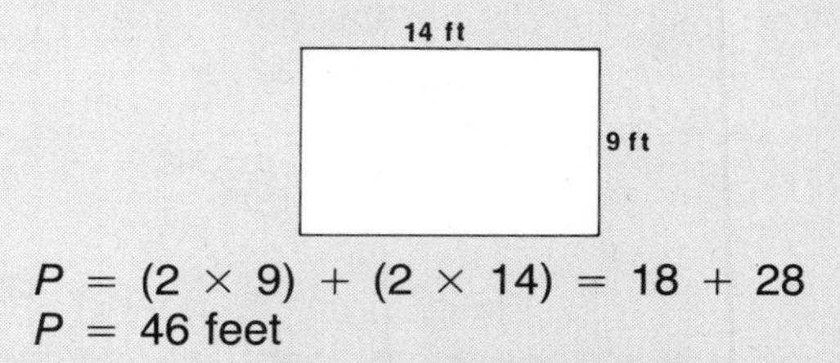

$P = (2 \times 9) + (2 \times 14) = 18 + 28$
$P = 46$ feet

If you are asked to find the perimeter of a figure that is not a square or a rectangle, add the lengths of all the sides.

Warm-up

Find the perimeter of the following figures.

1. a square book with sides 4.5 inches

2. a rectangular rug with a length of $6\frac{1}{4}$ feet and a width of $4\frac{1}{2}$ feet

Warm-up Answers

1. 18 inches **2.** $21\frac{1}{2}$ feet

Areas of Quadrilaterals When you found square measure on page 491, you were finding the area that a particular square or rectangular space covered. *Area* is actually the number of squares that can fill a certain space.

To find the area of a square, you multiply one side *(s)* by itself. The formula for finding the area of a square is $A = s^2$. Remember from your work with exponents that s^2 means $s \times s$, not $s \times 2$. All the sides of a square are equal, so if you know the length of one side, you can find the area of the square.

To find the area of a rectangle, multiply the length by the width: $A = lw$. In order to find the area, you need to know both measurements.

Here are the formulas for finding the areas of trapezoids and parallelograms.

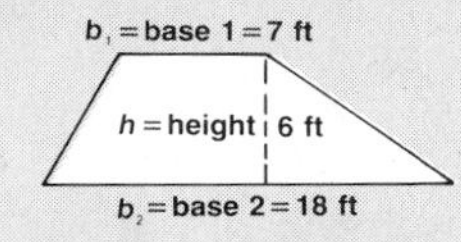

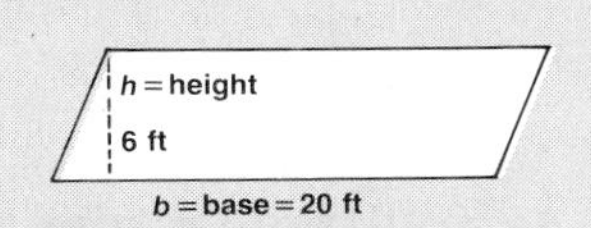

Trapezoid	**Parallelogram**
$A = \frac{1}{2}h(b_1 + b_2)$	$A = bh$
$A = \frac{1}{2} \times 6 \times (7 + 18)$ (Add the bases first.)	$A = 20 \times 6$
$A = \frac{1}{2} \times 6 \times 25$	$A = 120$ sq ft
$A = 3 \times 25$	
$A = 75$ sq ft	

A Test-Taking Tip

If you are asked to find the area of a parallelogram or trapezoid on the GED Mathematics Test, you will be given the formula right in the problem. For squares and rectangles, you can memorize the formulas or use the formula page supplied to you with the test.

Warm-up

What is the surface area of the wall below? First find the area of the rectangular wall. Then find the area of the square window. Finally, subtract the window area from the wall area to get the wall surface.

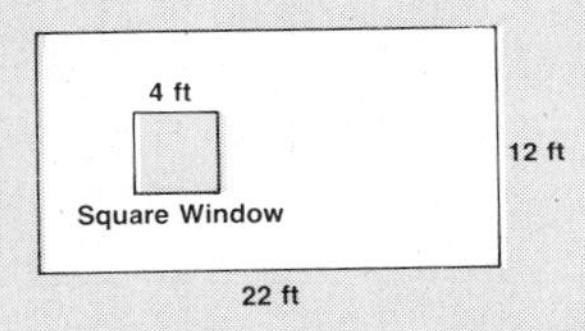

Warm-up Answer
248 sq ft

31. If a square floor measures 23 feet on one side, what is the area in square feet of the floor?

(1) 46 (2) 92 (3) 184 (4) 529
(5) Insufficient data is given to solve the problem.

(1) (2) (3) (4) (5)

32. The area of a rectangular plot of land is 60 square feet, and the width is 4 feet. What is the length in feet?

(1) 12 (2) 13 (3) 14
(4) 15 (5) 16

(1) (2) (3) (4) (5)

33. The length of a side of a rectangle is 10 inches. Find the area of the rectangle in square inches.

(1) 20 (2) 40 (3) 80 (4) 100
(5) Insufficient data is given to solve the problem.

(1) (2) (3) (4) (5)

Items 34–35 refer to the following diagram of a painting hung on a wall.

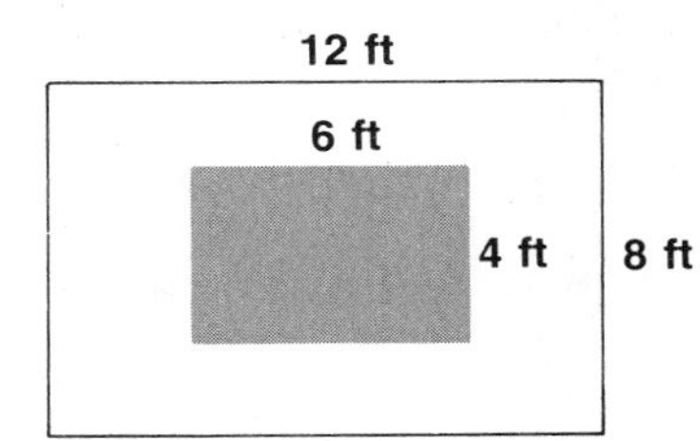

34. How many square feet is the area of the painting (the shaded portion)?

(1) 12 (2) 24 (3) 32
(4) 48 (5) 72

(1) (2) (3) (4) (5)

35. What is the area of the wall around the painting (the unshaded portion) in square feet?

(1) 24 (2) 48 (3) 54
(4) 72 (5) 96

(1) (2) (3) (4) (5)

Triangles A closed plane figure with three sides is called a triangle. A vertex in a triangle is the point at which two line segments meet to form an angle.

Triangles are classified according to (1) the number of equal sides they have or (2) their angle measures.

1. Using side measurements

An **isosceles triangle** is one in which two sides are equal.

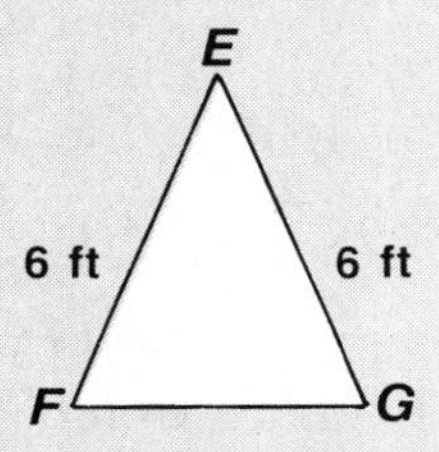

Triangle *EFG* is an isosceles triangle. Sides $\overline{EF}$ and $\overline{EG}$ are equal. The angles opposite the equal sides in an isosceles triangle are also equal.

An **equilateral triangle** has three equal sides.

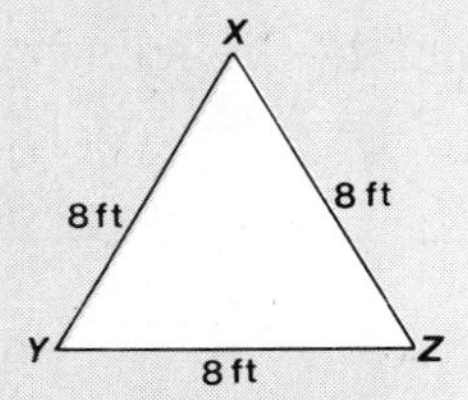

The three angles of an equilateral triangle are also equal.

2. Using angle measurements

When triangles are classified according to angle measures, the following names are used. An **acute triangle** has three acute angles. Remember that *acute* means *less than 90°* in geometry.

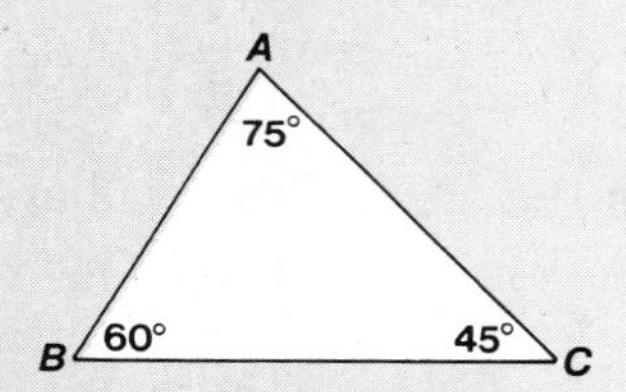

An **obtuse triangle** has one obtuse angle. An obtuse angle is greater than 90°. ∠*H* is the obtuse angle in triangle *GHI*.

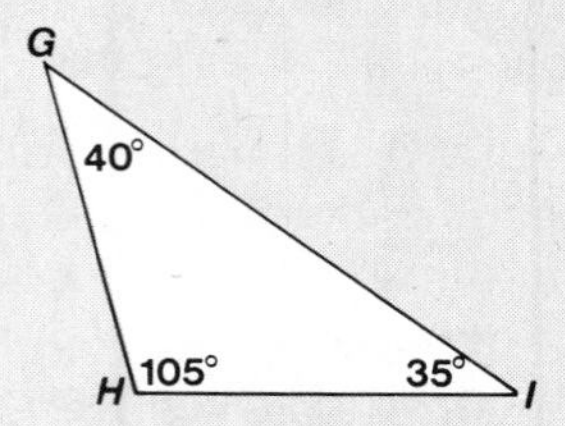

A **right triangle** has one right angle. ∠*C* is the right angle in triangle *CDE*.

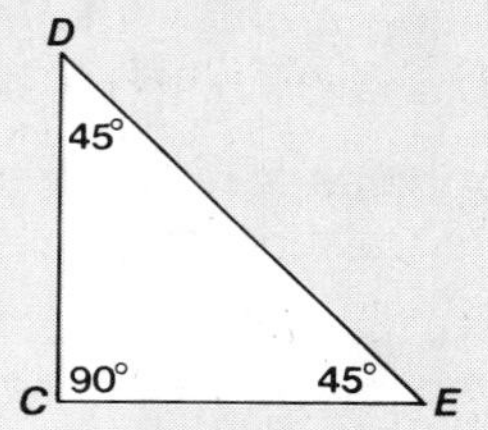

An **equiangular triangle** has three equal angles. Each angle measures 60°. The sides of an equiangular triangle are also equal.

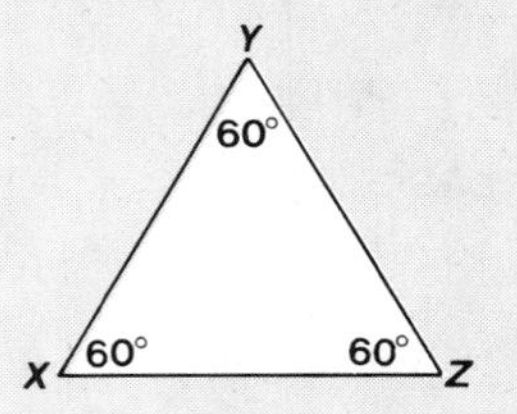

Warm-up

Answer the following questions with True (T) or False (F).

1. An acute triangle will always have one angle that equals 90°.
2. An isosceles triangle has two equal sides.
3. A right triangle must have one angle larger than 90°.
4. The sides and angles of an equilateral triangle are always equal.

Warm-up Answers
1. F **2.** T **3.** F **4.** T

Rules About Triangles The following rules about triangles are general rules. They can be applied to many problems.

Rule 1 The three interior angles of a triangle measure 180° because any triangle is actually *half* a quadrilateral. Remember the angles of a quadrilateral equal 360°.

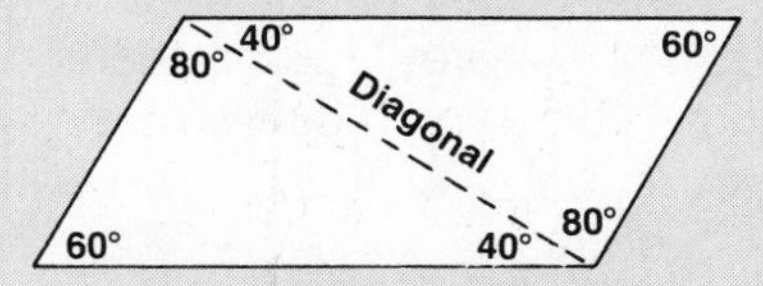

Rule 2 The sum of any two sides of a triangle is greater than the third side.

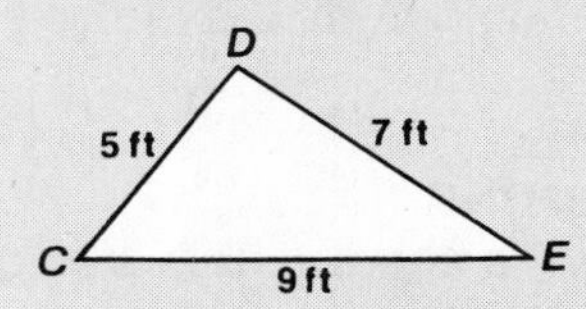

If you *add* the lengths of line segments $\overline{CD}$ and $\overline{ED}$, is their sum greater than the length of $\overline{CE}$?

5 ft + 7 ft = 12 ft
12 ft is greater than 9 ft

Rule 3 In any triangle, angles are equal if they are opposite equal sides. The reverse is also true: In any triangle, the sides are equal if they are opposite equal angles.

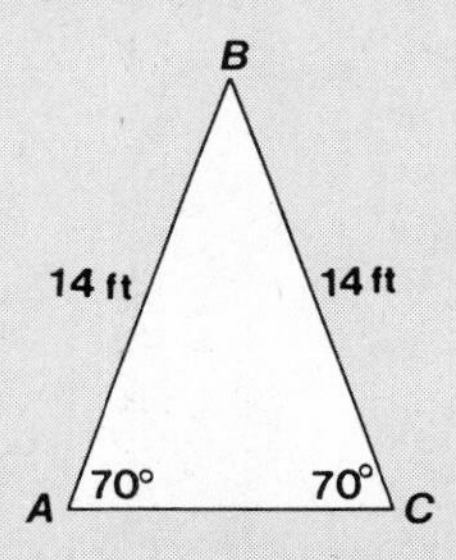

Line segments $\overline{AB}$ and $\overline{BC}$ are both 14 feet long. Therefore base angles $\angle A$ and $\angle C$ are equal. Remember $\triangle ABC$ is an *isosceles* triangle.

Rule 4 In any triangle, the largest angle is opposite the longest side, and the smallest angle is opposite the shortest side.

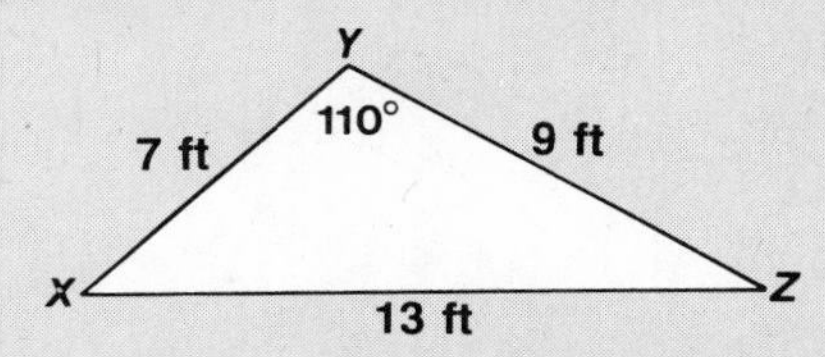

In triangle XYZ, $\angle Y$ is the largest angle, and $\overline{XZ}$ is the longest side. $\angle Z$ is the smallest angle, and $\overline{XY}$ is the shortest side.

Directions: For each problem, choose the one best answer. Answers are on page 560.

36. Find the measurement of each base angle of an isosceles triangle if the third angle is 48°.

(1) 61° (2) 66° (3) 75°
(4) 90° (5) 132°

① ② ③ ④ ⑤

37. In triangle MNO, $\angle M = 65°$ and $\angle N = 50°$. What is the measurement of $\angle O$?

(1) 25° (2) 40° (3) 50°
(4) 65° (5) 90

① ② ③ ④ ⑤

38. If the base angles of an isosceles triangle are each $47\frac{1}{2}°$, what is the measurement of the third angle?

(1) 15° (2) 75° (3) 80°
(4) 85° (5) 95°

① ② ③ ④ ⑤

39. Find the measurement of the third angle of a triangle if the first two angles of the triangle measure 102° and 34°.

(1) 24° (2) 34° (3) 44°
(4) 54° (5) 64°

① ② ③ ④ ⑤

40. Which of the following can represent the measures of the three angles of a triangle?

(1) 30°, 90°, 61° (2) 30°, 110°, 40°
(3) 55°, 45°, 90° (4) 55°, 110°, 40°
(5) 75°, 45°, 90°

① ② ③ ④ ⑤

Directions: For each problem, choose the one best answer. Answers are on page 560.

41. Triangles *ABC* and *DEF* are congruent. If ∠*B* measures 45°, what is the measurement of ∠*E*?

(1) 135° (2) 120° (3) 90°
(4) 45° (5) 30°

(1) (2) (3) (4) (5)

Items 42–44 refer to the following information.

Triangle *ABC* is congruent to triangle *DEF*.

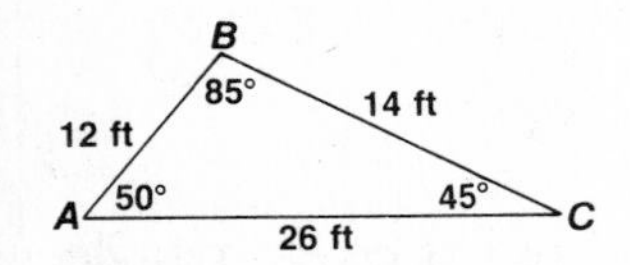

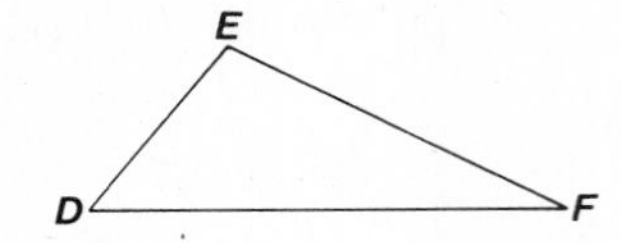

42. What is the measurement in feet of line segment $\overline{EF}$?

(1) 12 (2) 14 (3) 24
(4) 26 (5) 28

(1) (2) (3) (4) (5)

43. What is the measurement in yards of line segment $\overline{DE}$?

(1) 4 (2) 12 (3) 24
(4) 36 (5) 48

(1) (2) (3) (4) (5)

44. What is the measurement of ∠*EFD*?

(1) 45° (2) 50° (3) 85°
(4) 90° (5) 95°

(1) (2) (3) (4) (5)

Congruent Triangles

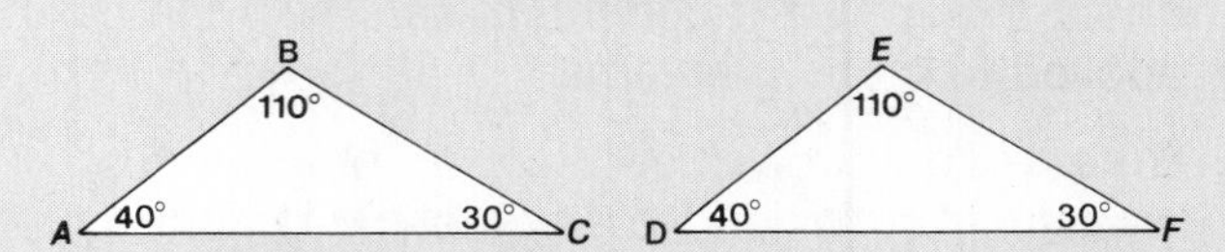

Triangles *ABC* and *DEF* are the exact same size and shape. Their angle measurements are the same. If you were to place triangle *ABC* over triangle *DEF*, you'd see that the sides $\overline{AB}$ and $\overline{DE}$ are equal. $\overline{AC}$ and $\overline{DF}$ are equal. $\overline{BC}$ and $\overline{EF}$ are equal. Triangles with corresponding side lengths and angle measurements that are equal are called *congruent triangles.* When referring to congruent triangles, you should list the corresponding vertexes in the same order.

Warm-up

Triangle *NOP* is congruent to triangle *QRS.*

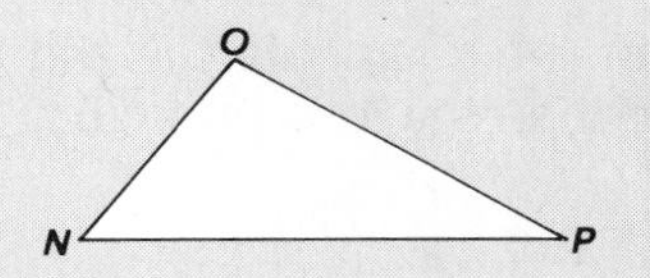

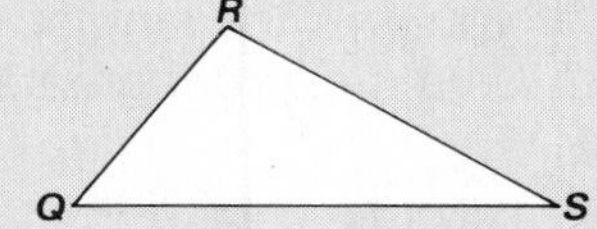

Complete.

1. ∠*N* =
2. ∠*O* =
3. ∠*P* =
4. $\overline{NO}$ =
5. $\overline{OP}$ =
6. $\overline{NP}$ =

Warm-up Answers
1. ∠*Q* **2.** ∠*R* **3.** ∠*S* **4.** $\overline{QR}$ **5.** $\overline{RS}$ **6.** $\overline{QS}$

Similar Triangles

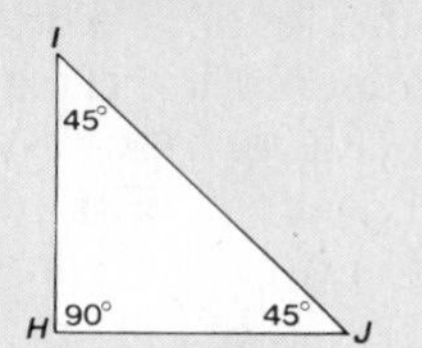

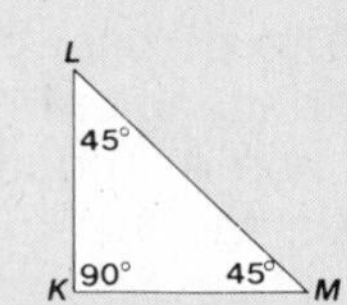

The angle measurements in triangle *HIJ* are the same as those in triangle *KLM.* These triangles are not the same size; therefore, they are not congruent. They are *similar triangles.* Similar triangles have equal angles. When angle measurements of a triangle are not given you can compare the lengths of any two corresponding sides by writing a proportional statement. If the sides are proportional, the triangles are similar.

Triangle *HIJ* is similar to triangle *KLM* if $\angle I = \angle L$, $\angle H = \angle K$, $\angle J = \angle M$, and if $\frac{\overline{IH}}{\overline{LK}} = \frac{\overline{IJ}}{\overline{LM}} = \frac{\overline{HJ}}{\overline{KM}}$.

Are triangles *ABC* and *DEF* similar?

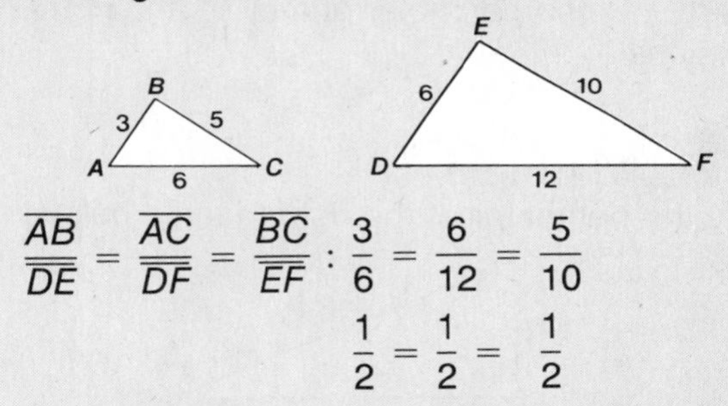

$$\frac{\overline{AB}}{\overline{DE}} = \frac{\overline{AC}}{\overline{DF}} = \frac{\overline{BC}}{\overline{EF}} : \frac{3}{6} = \frac{6}{12} = \frac{5}{10}$$

$$\frac{1}{2} = \frac{1}{2} = \frac{1}{2}$$

These two triangles are similar because their sides are proportional.

☑ A Test-Taking Tip

A question on the GED Test may ask you to find the side of a triangle when the corresponding side of a similar triangle is given. Use your skill of setting up a proportion on a grid to solve the problem.

Warm-up

Triangle *GHI* is similar to triangle *JKL.*

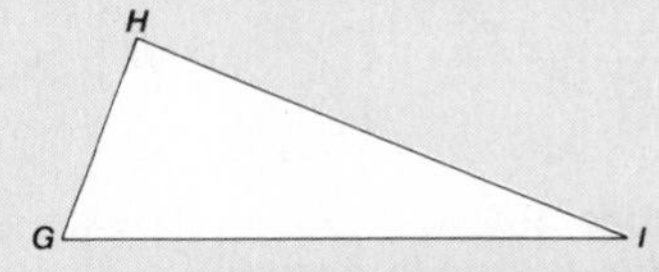

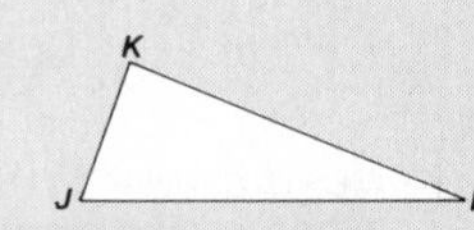

1. Name the corresponding angles.
2. Name the corresponding sides.

Warm-up Answers
1. $\angle G = \angle J$, $\angle H = \angle K$, $\angle I = \angle L$ **2.** $\overline{GH}$ is similar to $\overline{JK}$, $\overline{HI}$ is similar to $\overline{KL}$, $\overline{GI}$ is similar to $\overline{JL}$

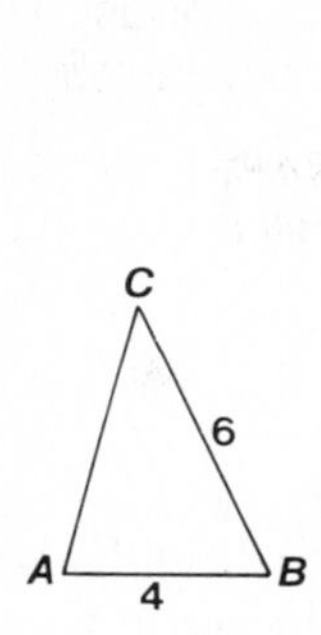

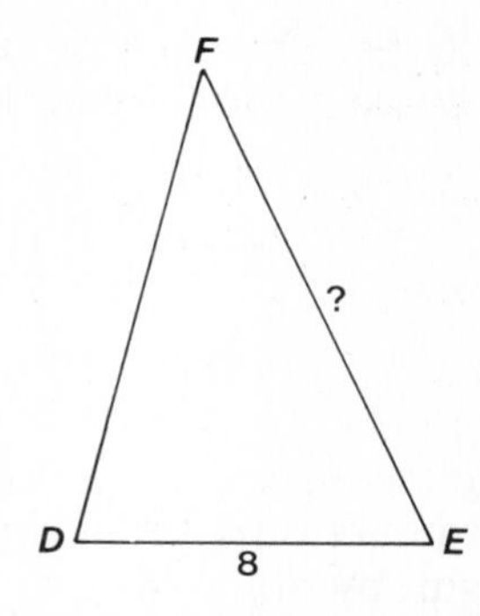

45. Triangles *ABC* and *DEF* are similar. If $\overline{AB}$ is 4 inches, $\overline{BC}$ is 6 inches, and $\overline{DE}$ is 8 inches, how many inches long is $\overline{EF}$?

(1) 8 (2) 12 (3) 24
(4) 36 (5) 48

① ② ③ ④ ⑤

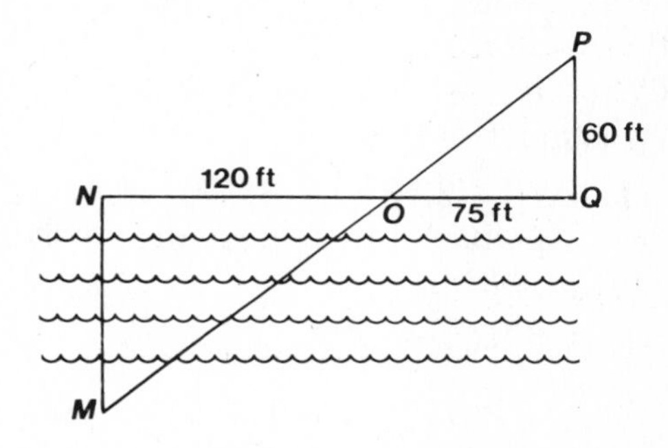

46. Triangles *MNO* and *PQO* are similar. If $\angle N = \angle Q$ and $\angle M = \angle P$, find the width of the river $(\overline{MN})$.

(1) 50 ft (2) 76 ft (3) 86 ft
(4) 90 ft (5) 96 ft

① ② ③ ④ ⑤

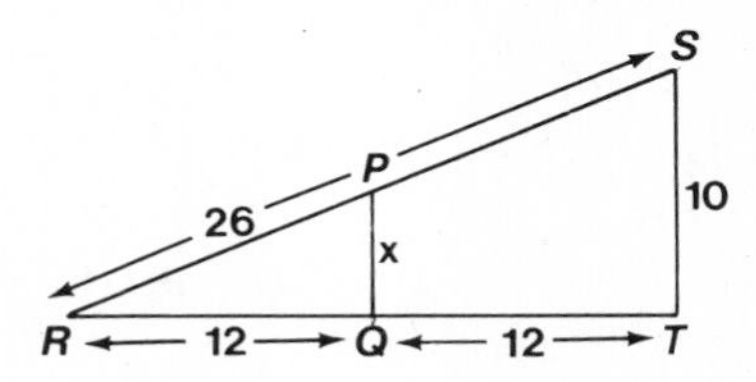

47. Find the length of $\overline{PQ}$ in the diagram above.

(1) 5 (2) 10 (3) 15
(4) 20 (5) 25

① ② ③ ④ ⑤

Directions: For each problem, choose the one best answer. Answers are on pages 560–561.

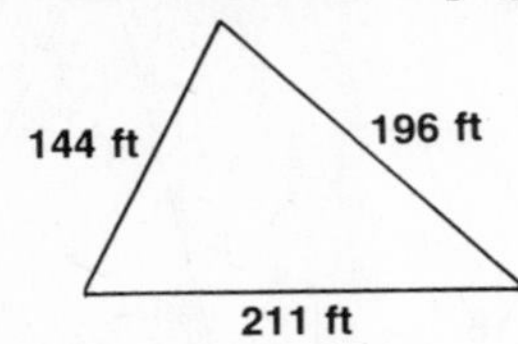

48. How many feet of fencing will be needed to enclose a triangular park with the measurements shown in the diagram?

(1) 240 (2) 340 (3) 451
(4) 551 (5) 651

(1) (2) (3) (4) (5)

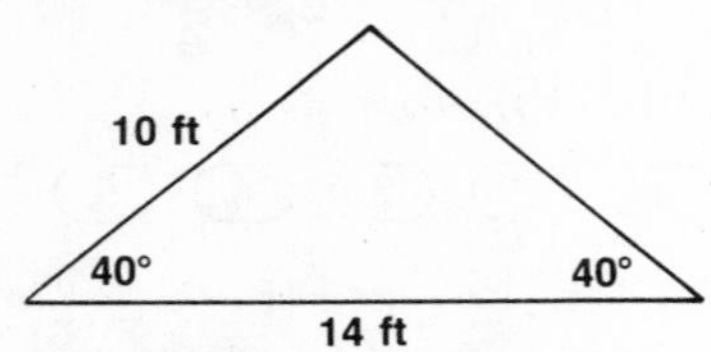

49. What is the perimeter in feet of the triangular sign above?

(1) 24 (2) 34 (3) 56 (4) 72
(5) Insufficient data is given to solve the problem.

(1) (2) (3) (4) (5)

50. What is the perimeter in inches of a triangular table with 2 sides measuring 32 inches and 23 inches?

(1) 55 (2) 58 (3) 61 (4) 71
(5) Insufficient data is given to solve the problem.

(1) (2) (3) (4) (5)

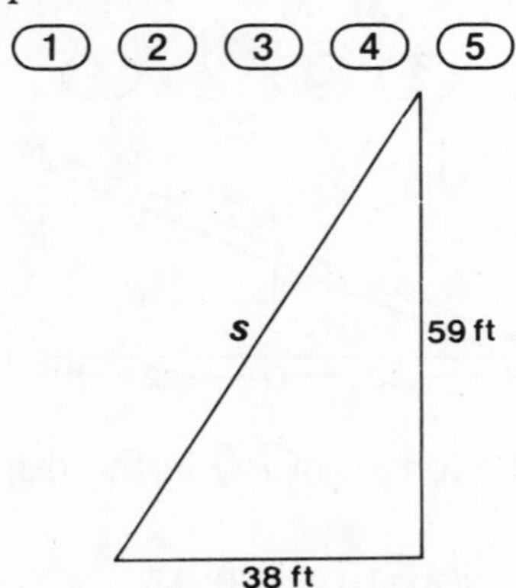

51. The perimeter of the sail is 167 feet. What is the length in feet of the missing side?

(1) 43 (2) 67 (3) 70 (4) 107
(5) Insufficient data is given to solve the problem.

(1) (2) (3) (4) (5)

The Perimeter of a Triangle The perimeter of a triangle is the sum of the lengths of its three sides. The perimeter measures the distance around a triangle. In equilateral triangle *ABC* below, side $\overline{AC}$ equals 12 inches. Find the perimeter of the triangle. It is helpful to draw a diagram.

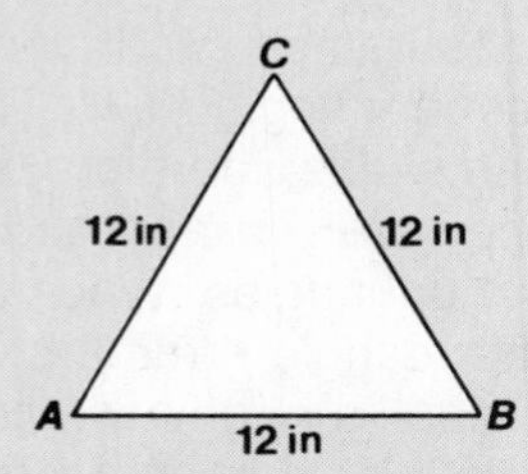

Since you know that all sides are equal in an equilateral triangle, add the side lengths of $\overline{AB}$, $\overline{BC}$, and $\overline{CA}$ together.

$$\overline{AB} + \overline{BC} + \overline{CA} = \text{perimeter}$$
$$12 \text{ in} + 12 \text{ in} + 12 \text{ in} = 36 \text{ in}$$

The formula for the perimeter of a triangle is

$$P = a + b + c$$

where P is the perimeter and a, b, and c are the sides.

Warm-up

Find the perimeter of the right triangle below.

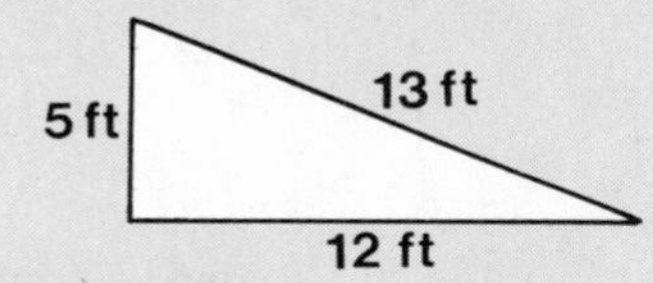

Since $P = a + b + c$
$P = 5 \text{ ft} + 13 \text{ ft} + 12 \text{ ft} = 30 \text{ ft}$

Now work the following problems.

1. What is the perimeter of a triangle with sides of 24 ft, 30 ft, and 42 ft?

2. What is the perimeter of the sail in the diagram?

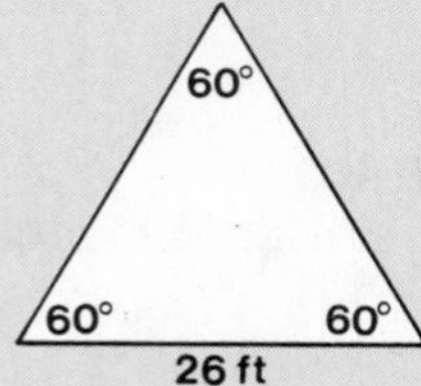

Need a Hint for Number 49?
What is true about sides opposite equal angles?

Warm-up Answers
1. 96 ft **2.** 26 ft × 3 = 78 ft

The Area of a Triangle The area, A, of a triangle is equal to one-half the length of any side times the corresponding height.

$$A = \frac{1}{2}bh$$

where b is the length of any side and h is the height.

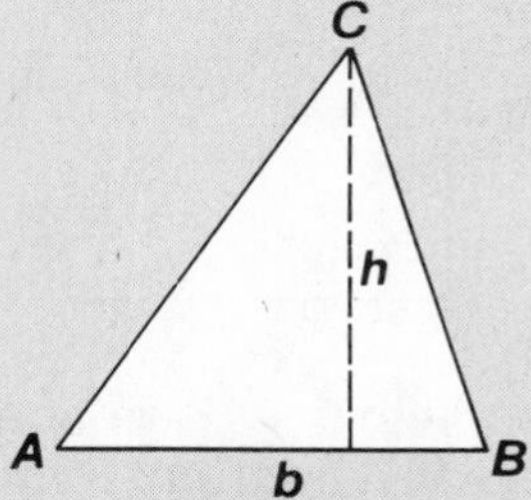

You can see that the area of a triangle is ½ the base times the height because a triangle is actually ½ of a parallelogram, and the area of a parallelogram is the base times the height.

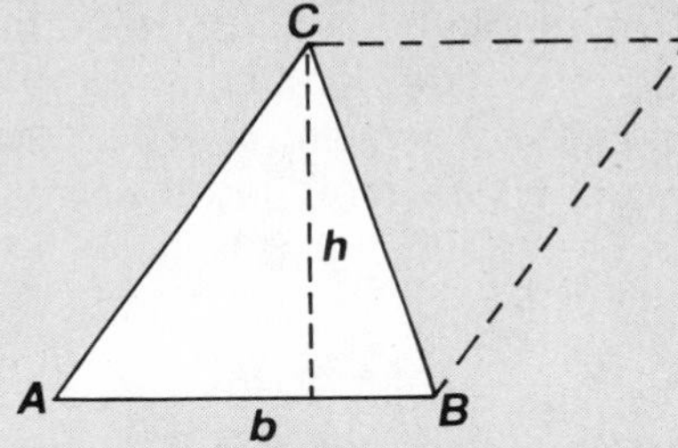

If the length of side $\overline{AB}$ equals 12 yards and the corresponding height equals 8 yards, what is the area of triangle ABC?

$$A = \frac{1}{2}(12)(8)$$

$$A = \frac{1}{2}(96)$$

$$A = 48 \text{ sq yd}$$

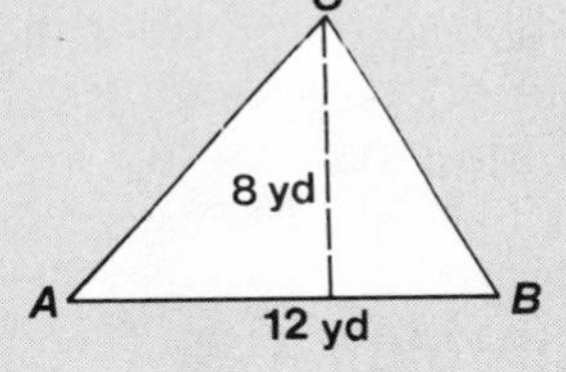

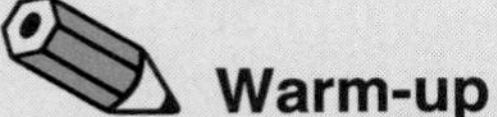

Warm-up

Find the area of each triangle shown.

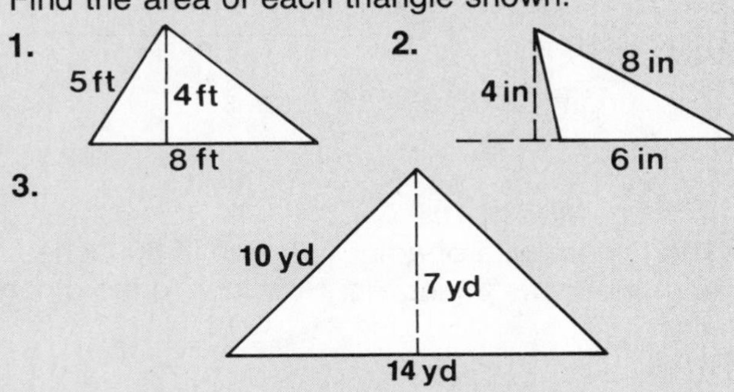

Warm-up Answers

1. $A = \frac{1}{2} \times 8 \times 4 = 16$ sq ft **2.** $A = \frac{1}{2} \times 6 \times 4 = 12$ sq in

3. $A = \frac{1}{2} \times 14 \times 7 = 49$ sq yd

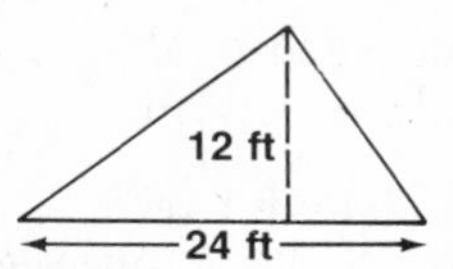

52. Find the area in square feet of the sail above.

(1) 36 (2) 72 (3) 136
(4) 144 (5) 288

(1) (2) (3) (4) (5)

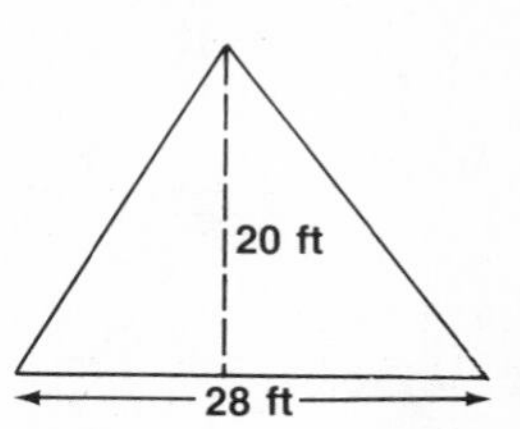

53. The library wants to replace its flag. What is the area of the flag in square feet?

(1) 48 (2) 96 (3) 198
(4) 280 (5) 560

(1) (2) (3) (4) (5)

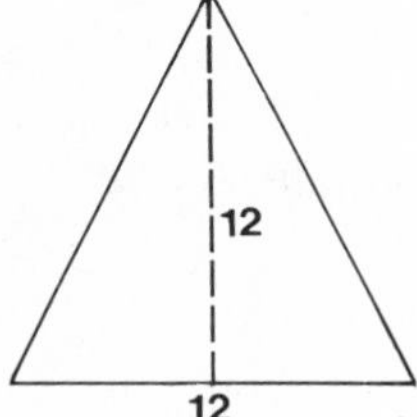

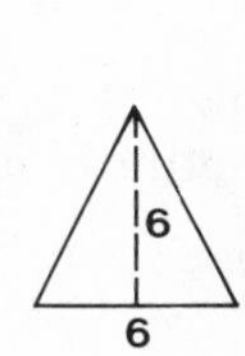

54. Write a ratio of area for the larger to the smaller triangle.

(1) 1:4 (2) 2:3 (3) 4:1
(4) 18:72 (5) 72:18

(1) (2) (3) (4) (5)

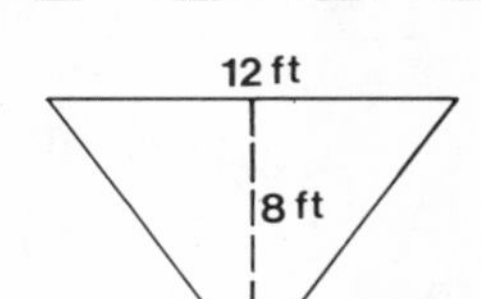

55. Mr. Sanchez is planting a triangular flower bed. How many square feet of ground will the flower bed cover?

(1) 24 (2) 48 (3) 56
(4) 72 (5) 96

(1) (2) (3) (4) (5)

Directions: For each problem, choose the one best answer. Answers are on page 561.

56. In a right triangle, how many inches is the hypotenuse if the lengths of the legs are 9 and 12 inches?

(1) 11 in (2) 12 in (3) 15 in
(4) 17 in (5) 18 in

① ② ③ ④ ⑤

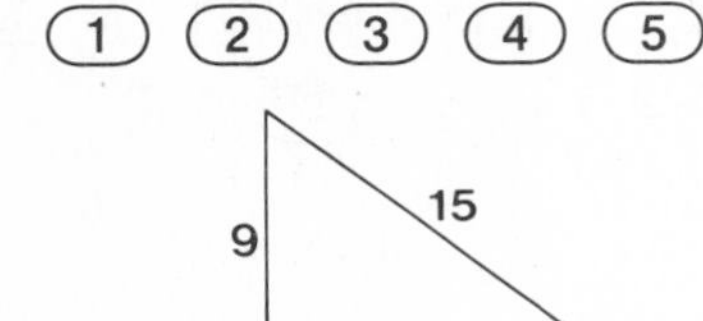

57. Given the right triangle above, find the length of leg *b*.

(1) 11 (2) 12 (3) 13
(4) 14 (5) 15

① ② ③ ④ ⑤

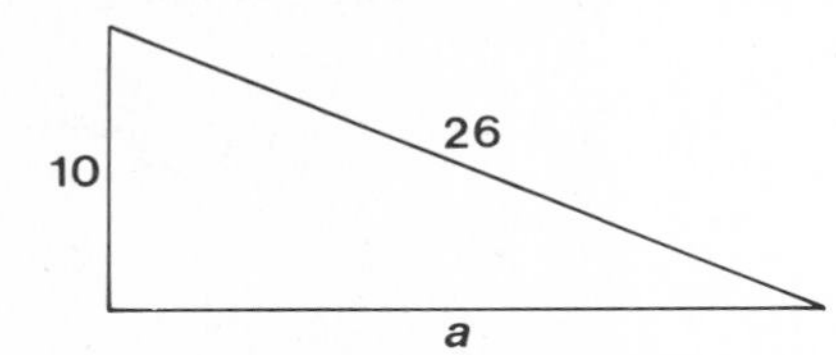

58. Given the right triangle above, find the length of leg *a*.

(1) 5 (2) 8 (3) 10
(4) 24 (5) 36

① ② ③ ④ ⑤

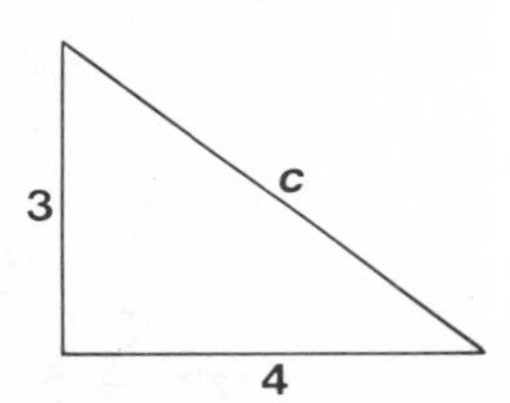

59. Given the right triangle above, find the length of the hypotenuse.

(1) 5 (2) 6 (3) 7
(4) 20 (5) 25

① ② ③ ④ ⑤

60. What is the length in yards of the other leg of a right triangle that has a hypotenuse of 26 yards and a leg of 24 yards?

(1) 5 (2) 8 (3) 10
(4) 50 (5) 100

① ② ③ ④ ⑤

The Pythagorean Theorem When you are working with right triangles, you use special terms. The side opposite the right angle is called the *hypotenuse.* The other two sides are called *legs.*

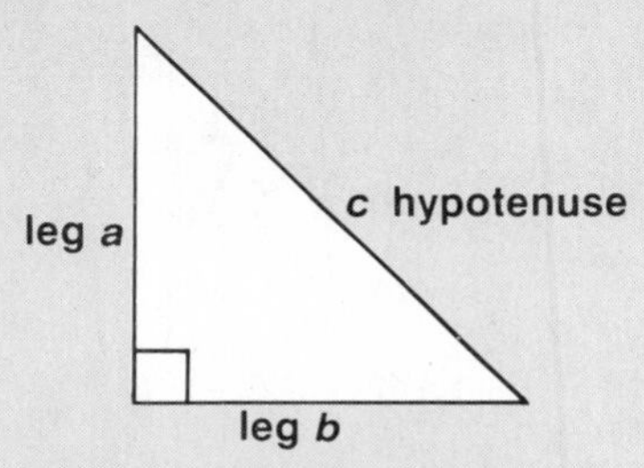

The right triangle has its own special rule called the **Pythagorean Theorem.** Pythagoras, a Greek mathematician, found that in right triangles the square of the hypotenuse is equal to the sum of the squares of the legs.

$$c^2 = a^2 + b^2$$

Study the example below. You need to use your knowledge of squares and square roots to use the Pythagorean Theorem. If leg *a* equals 5 feet and leg *b* equals 12 feet, find the length of *c*.

$$c^2 = a^2 + b^2$$
$$c^2 = 5^2 + 12^2$$
$$c^2 = 25 + 144$$
$$c^2 = 169$$
$$\sqrt{c^2} = \sqrt{169}$$
$$c = 13 \text{ ft}$$

a: 5 ft
c
b: 12 ft

You can switch the formula around to find the length of a leg when the hypotenuse is given. Find the length of leg *a* in the diagram.

$$c^2 = a^2 + b^2 \text{ so}$$
$$a^2 = c^2 - b^2$$
$$a^2 = 20^2 - 16^2$$
$$a^2 = 400 - 256$$
$$a = \sqrt{144}$$
$$a = 12 \text{ in}$$

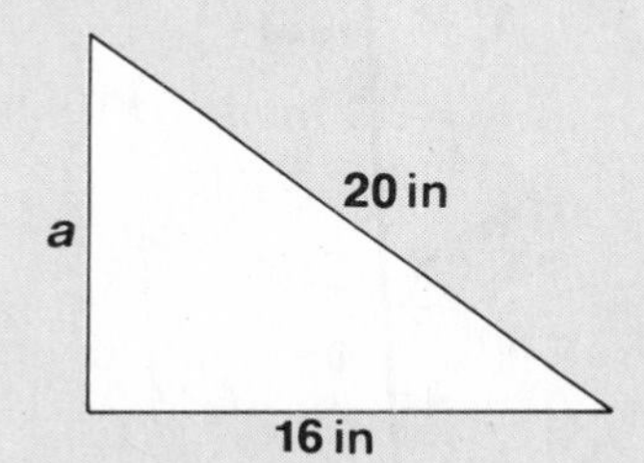

The length of leg *a* is 12 inches.

Warm-up

The hypotenuse of a right triangle is 30 inches, and one leg is 18 inches. How long is the other leg?

Warm-up Answer
24 inches

Using the Pythagorean Theorem In geometry, the Pythagorean theorem is often used to solve word problems.

- Joan wants to hike 12 miles north, then 16 miles east. If she takes the diagonal route back to her starting point, how many miles will she travel to get back?

Draw a picture to visualize what is stated.

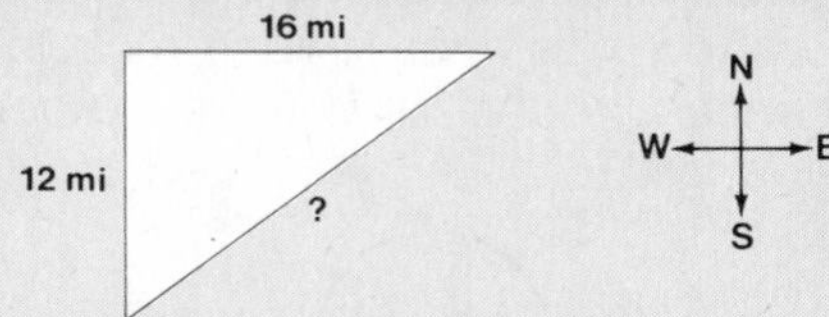

Substitute the measurements in the formula

$c^2 = a^2 + b^2.$
$c^2 = 12^2 + 16^2$
$c^2 = 144 + 256$
$c^2 = 400$
$c = \sqrt{400}$
$c = 20$ mi

The distance on the diagonal is 20 miles.

- In the drawing below, a 10-ft ladder is leaning against a wall that is 8 ft tall. Find the distance from the bottom of the wall to the bottom of the ladder.

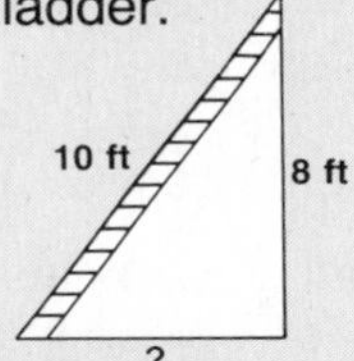

Switch the Pythagorean theorem around.

$a^2 = c^2 - b^2$
$a^2 = 10^2 - 8^2$
$a^2 = 100 - 64$
$a^2 = 36$
$a = \sqrt{36}$

$a = 6$ ft

Notice that the ladder was the hypotenuse and that the wall was one of the legs.

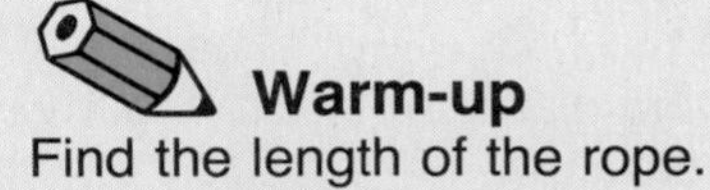

Find the length of the rope.

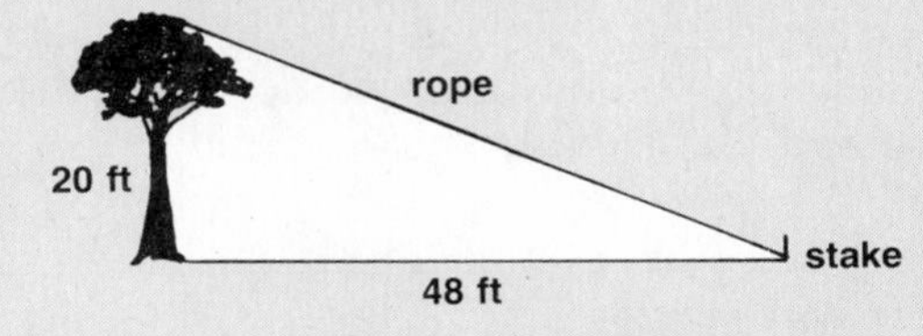

Warm-up Answer
52 ft

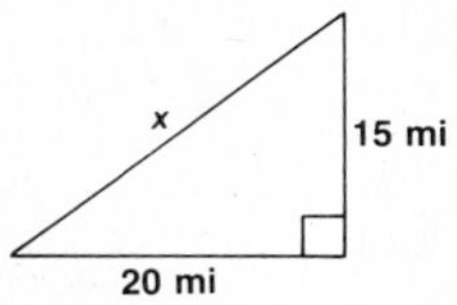

x
15 mi
20 mi

61. A cyclist rode 15 miles south, then 20 miles west. If she could travel a diagonal path, how many miles is she from the starting point?

(1) 21 (2) 23 (3) 25
(4) 35 (5) 625

(1) (2) (3) (4) (5)

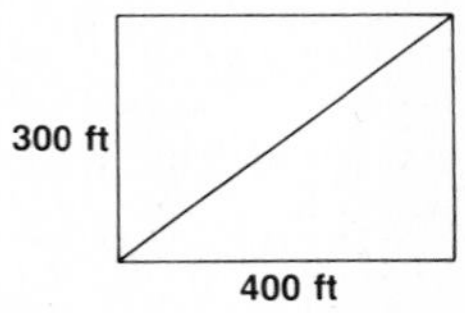

300 ft
400 ft

62. A swimmer swam the diagonal distance of the pool above. How many feet did he swim?

(1) 200 (2) 500 (3) 700
(4) 1,400 (5) 2,500

(1) (2) (3) (4) (5)

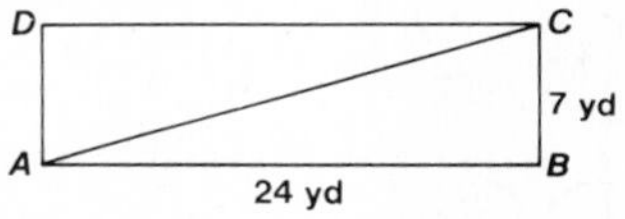

D C
7 yd
A B
24 yd

63. How many yards is the diagonal $\overline{AC}$ in the diagram above?

(1) 25 (2) 40 (3) 45
(4) 54 (5) 63

(1) (2) (3) (4) (5)

64. A man in a motorboat traveled on a diagonal 45 miles out into the lake. Then he traveled 27 miles south. How many miles west must he travel to be at the original point?

(1) 36 (2) 40 (3) 45
(4) 54 (5) 63

(1) (2) (3) (4) (5)

Directions: For each problem, choose the one best answer. Answers are on page 561–562.

65. Find the circumference in feet of a circular dance floor if the radius is 84 feet.

(1) 163.76 (2) 263.76 (3) 527.52
(4) 5,275.2 (5) 6,275.2

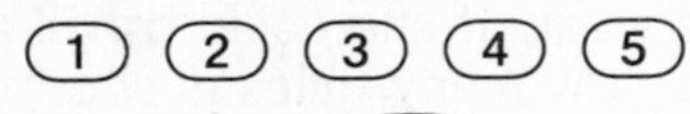

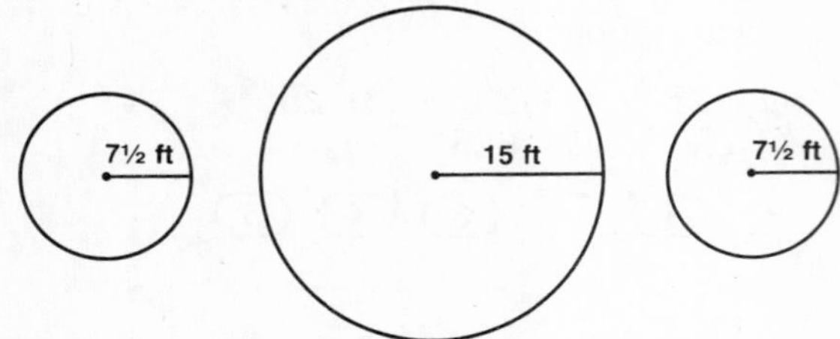

66. How many feet of fencing will be needed to enclose all three figures above?

(1) 94.2 (2) 188.4 (3) 288.4
(4) 1,884 (5) 2,884

① ② ③ ④ ⑤

67. Find the diameter in inches of a birdbath with a circumference of $81\frac{5}{7}$ inches. (Use $\frac{22}{7}$ for π.)

(1) $3\frac{1}{7}$ (2) 13 (3) 26

(4) $30\frac{2}{7}$ (5) 52

① ② ③ ④ ⑤

68. How many inches of ribbon would you need to wrap around a round tin with a diameter of 23 inches? (Use $\frac{22}{7}$ for π.)

(1) $42\frac{2}{7}$ (2) $72\frac{2}{7}$ (3) $82\frac{2}{7}$

(4) $96\frac{1}{7}$ (5) 123

① ② ③ ④ ⑤

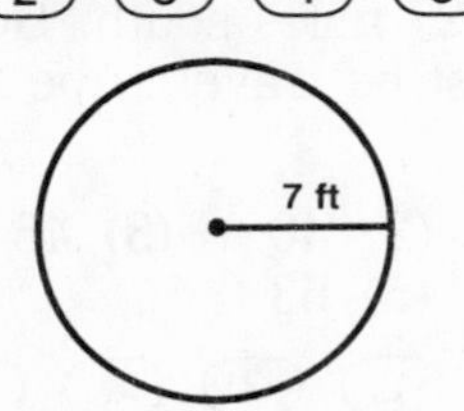

69. What is the circumference in feet of the circle above?

(1) 7 (2) 14 (3) 21.98
(4) 43.96 (5) 49.98

① ② ③ ④ ⑤

Circles A circle is a figure formed by a single closed curve. All points on a circle are the same distance from the center. You need to learn some words in order to work with circles.

Coming to Terms

diameter distance through the center of a circle
radius one-half of the diameter (plural is radii)
circumference distance around a circle (The circumference is to the circle what the perimeter is to the triangle.)

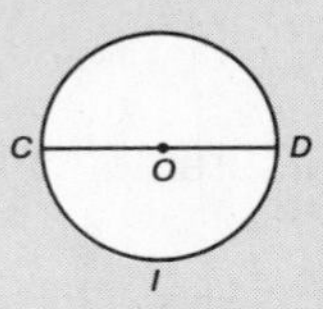

In the diagram above, line segment $\overline{CD}$ is the diameter of the circle. Line segments $\overline{OD}$ and $\overline{CO}$ are radii of the circle.

The Circumference of a Circle A common circle problem is to find the circumference of a circle. The formula for finding the circumference is $C = \pi d$, where C represents circumference, π represents a number called *pi,* and d represents the diameter. π stands for the ratio between the circumference and diameter of *every* circle and has the value of 3.14 or 22/7. The value of π never changes.

For problems relating to circles, use 3.14 as the value of π unless otherwise instructed. Also note that, since π is not a measurement, it does not carry a measurement unit.

Find the circumference of the barrel below.

$C = \pi d$
$C = 3.14 \times 14$
$C = 43.96$ ft

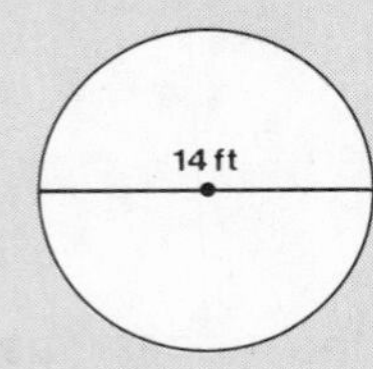

Warm-up

1. To find the circumference of a circle, you *multiply* the diameter by π: $C = \pi d$. What would you do to find the diameter if you already know the circumference?
2. The radius of a circle is one-half the diameter: $r = \frac{1}{2}d$. What would you do to find the diameter if you already knew the radius?

Warm-up Answers
1. You would divide the circumference by π. **2.** You would multiply the radius by 2.

The Area of a Circle The area of a circle is the surface inside the circle. Even though you're dealing with a circle, the area is still measured in square units. The white part of the circle below indicates the area of the circle. To find the area of a circle, use the formula $A = \pi r^2$, where A is the area, π is pi, and r is the radius of the circle.

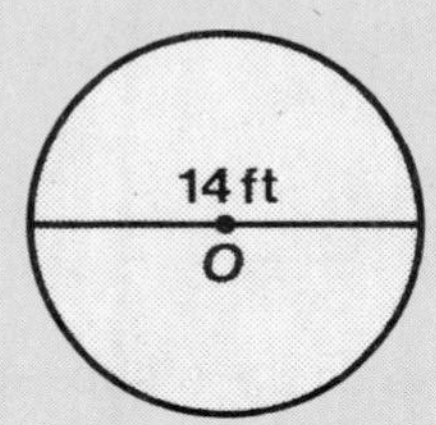

What is the area of the circle above? Since the radius is half the diameter, the radius for this circle measures 7 feet.

$A = \pi r^2$
$A = 3.14 \times 7 \times 7$
$A = 153.86$ sq ft

What is the area of the circle below?

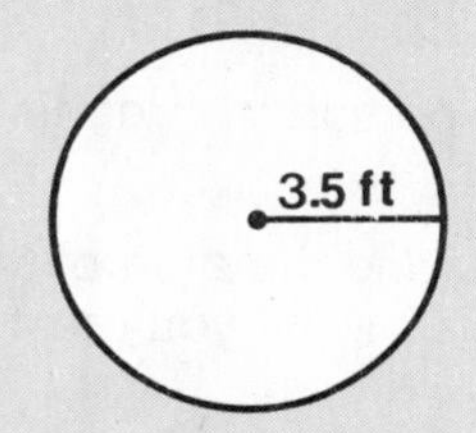

Use the formula for area.

$A = \pi r^2$
$A = 3.14 \times 3.5 \times 3.5$
$A = 38.465$ sq ft

A Test-Taking Tip

The formulas for finding the circumference and area of a circle are on the formula page of the GED Mathematics Test.

Warm-up

■ A paddle wheel has an area of 78.5 square feet. What is the radius? the diameter?

Warm-up Answers
$r = 5$ ft, $d = 10$ ft

Items 70–71 refer to the following diagram of a table with a tray on it.

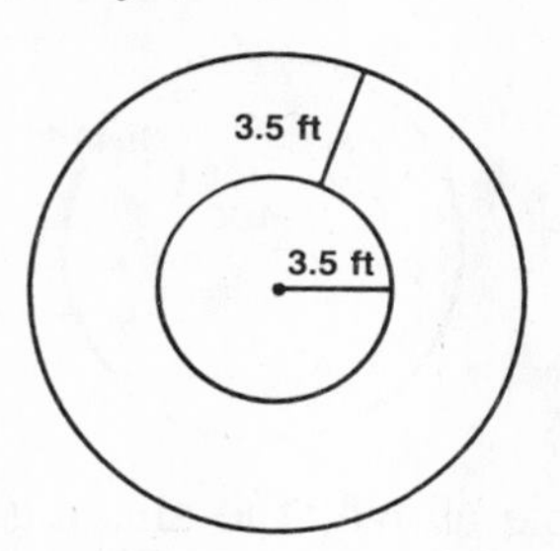

70. Find the area in square feet of the table.
    (1) 10.99 (2) 19.625 (3) 38.47
    (4) 153.86 (5) 157

    ① ② ③ ④ ⑤

71. What is the area in square feet of the tray?
    (1) 7.85 (2) 10.99 (3) 19.625
    (4) 37.625 (5) 38.465

    ① ② ③ ④ ⑤

72. If a pizza has an area of 254.34 square inches, what is its radius in inches?
    (1) 3.14 (2) 9 (3) 18
    (4) 27 (5) 81

    ① ② ③ ④ ⑤

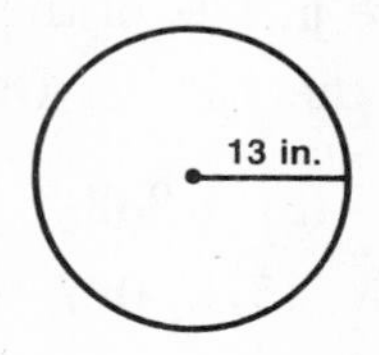

73. What is the area of the birdbath above in square inches? Round your answer to the nearest inch.
    (1) 402 (2) 531 (3) 573
    (4) 743 (5) 896

    ① ② ③ ④ ⑤

Directions: For each problem, choose the one best answer. Answers are on page 562.

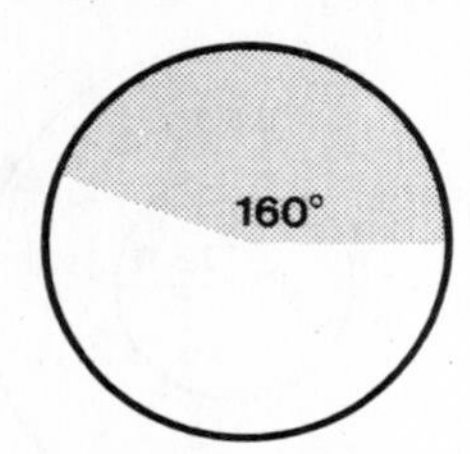

74. In the pie above, the shading shows how much has been eaten. What fraction of the pie is gone?

(1) $\frac{5}{6}$ (2) $\frac{1}{6}$ (3) $\frac{4}{9}$ (4) $\frac{5}{9}$ (5) $\frac{1}{2}$

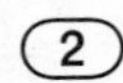

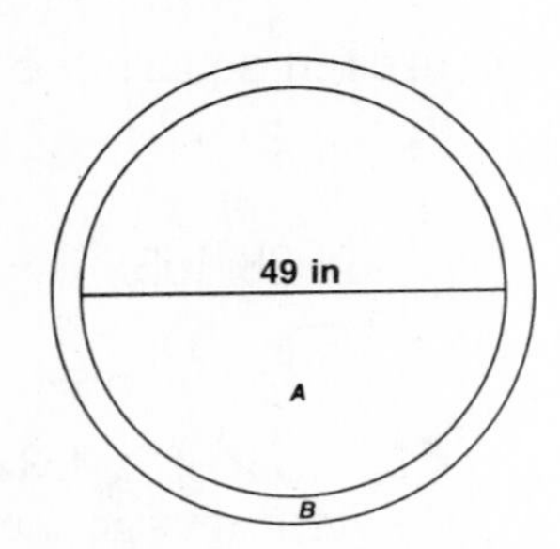

75. Circle A is a mirrored piece with a diameter of 49 inches; circle B is a wooden board with a diameter of 63 inches. How many square inches of the board is not covered by the mirror? Use $\frac{22}{7}$ for π.

(1) 1,000 (2) 1,232 (3) 1,727
(4) $3{,}113\frac{1}{2}$ (5) 3,087

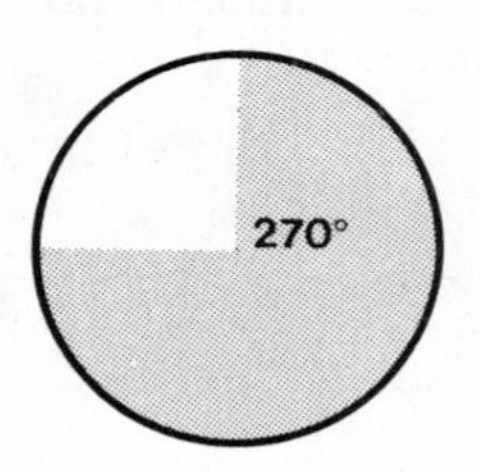

76. What fractional part of the circle is shaded?

(1) $\frac{1}{2}$ (2) $\frac{3}{4}$ (3) $\frac{3}{8}$ (4) $\frac{5}{8}$ (5) $\frac{1}{3}$

Find the Area of Part of a Circle Every circle has 360°. A question may ask you to figure out what portions of a circle are shaded or unshaded.

What portion of the circle is shaded?

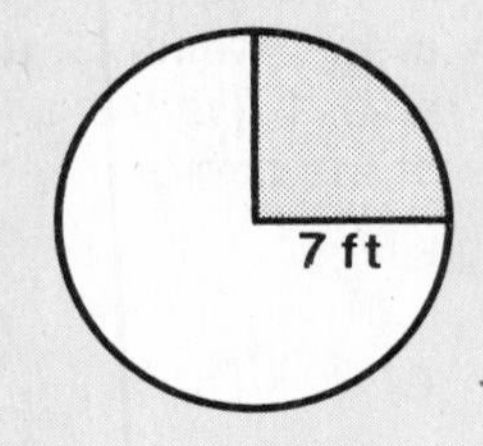

The shaded portion is a right angle. Right angles measures 90°. Therefore, you would write a fractional statement:

$$\frac{\text{shaded area}}{\text{total area}} = \frac{90°}{360°} = \frac{1}{4}$$

One-fourth of the circle is shaded. To find out what portion of the circle was unshaded, you would write another fractional statement:

$$\frac{\text{unshaded area}}{\text{total area}} = \frac{270°}{360°} = \frac{3}{4}$$

Three-quarters of the circle is unshaded. Or, you can express the unshaded portion of the circle as a ratio. The unshaded portion measures 270°. Written as a ratio, you will have

270°:90° or 3:1

The unshaded portion is three times as large as the shaded portion.

How would you find the area of the shaded portion of this circle? First, you must find the area of the entire circle.

$A = \pi r^2$
$A = 3.14 \times 7 \times 7$
$A = 153.86$ sq ft round to 154 sq ft

Then, since you know that the shaded portion of the circle is ¼ of the whole, multiply the total area by ¼.

$\frac{1}{4} \times 154$ sq ft $= 38\frac{1}{2}$ sq ft.

The area of the shaded portion is 38½ sq ft.

To find the area of the unshaded portion, simply subtract the area of the shaded portion from the area of the whole.

154 sq ft $-$ $38\frac{1}{2}$ sq ft $=$ $115\frac{1}{2}$ sq ft

The area of the unshaded portion is 115½ sq ft.

Warm-up

Three circles have the following angles in their shaded areas. What fraction of each circle is shaded? Unshaded?

1. 60° **2.** 135° **3.** 240°

Warm-up Answers

1. $\frac{1}{6}$, $\frac{5}{6}$ **2.** $\frac{3}{8}$, $\frac{5}{8}$ **3.** $\frac{2}{3}$, $\frac{1}{3}$

Composite Figures Many shapes are more complicated than a simple rectangle or square.

To work problems dealing with these more complex shapes, you must first break each shape down into its simplest parts. Then, to find the area of the whole, simply find the area of each part and add the parts together.

How would you find the area of the shape below?

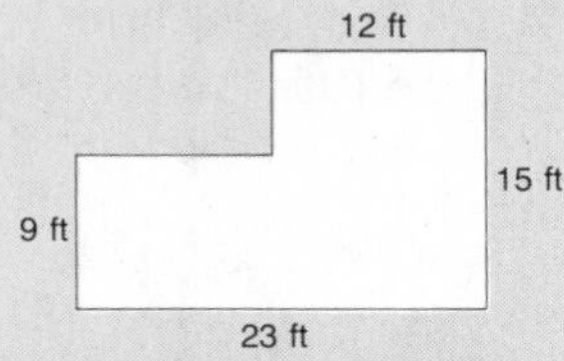

The figure can easily be divided into two separate rectangles. Both of the divisions shown are correct.

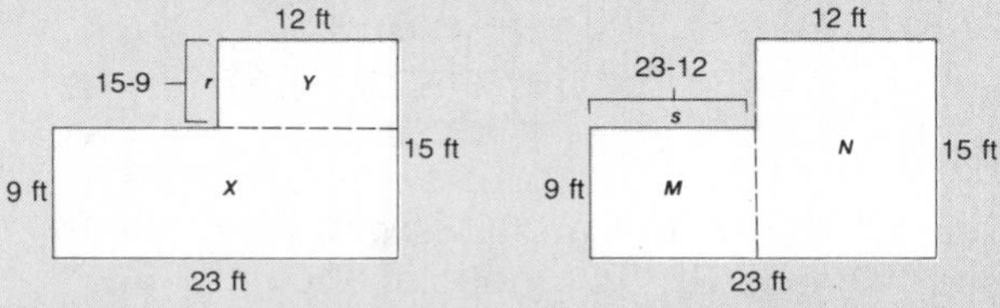

The area of a rectangle is found by multiplying length by width. Find the area of two rectangles shown at the left above.

Area rectangle $X = 23 \times 9$
$A = 207$ sq ft

Area rectangle $Y = 12 \times 6$
$A = 72$ sq ft

Then add the two areas together.

207 sq ft + 72 sq ft = 279 sq ft

The total area for the figure is 279 sq ft.

Warm-up

If you knew the length of all the line segments in these figures, how would you find the area of each figure?

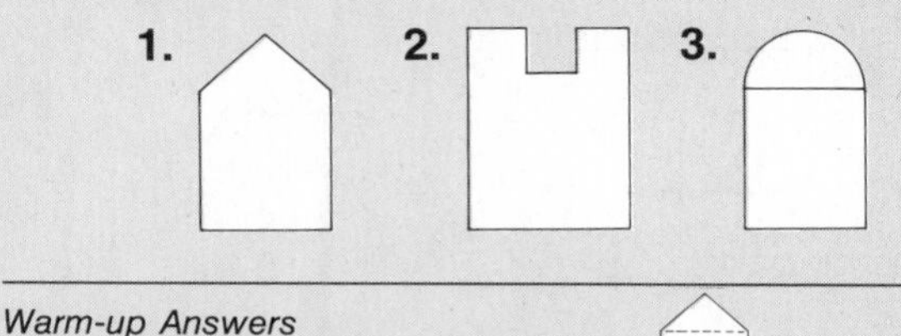

Warm-up Answers

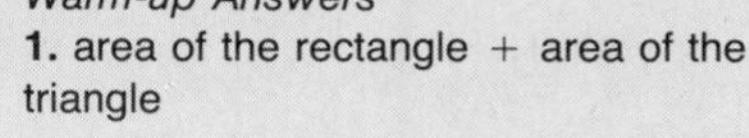
1. area of the rectangle + area of the triangle

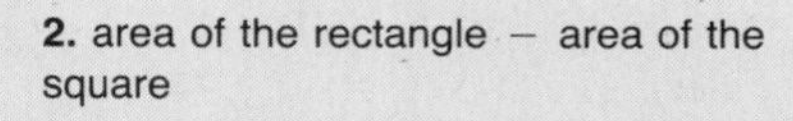
2. area of the rectangle − area of the square

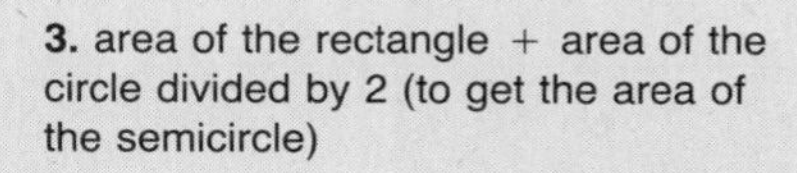
3. area of the rectangle + area of the circle divided by 2 (to get the area of the semicircle)

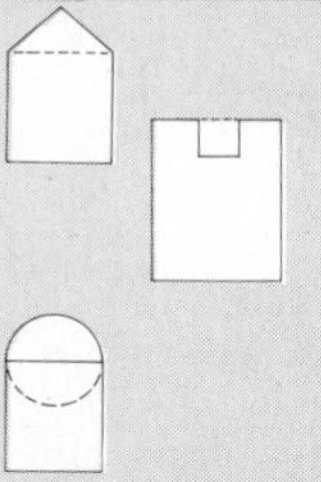

16 ft

18 ft

77. Find the area in square feet of the unshaded portion of the diagram above.

(1) 34 (2) 144 (3) 164
(4) 288 (5) 576

① ② ③ ④ ⑤

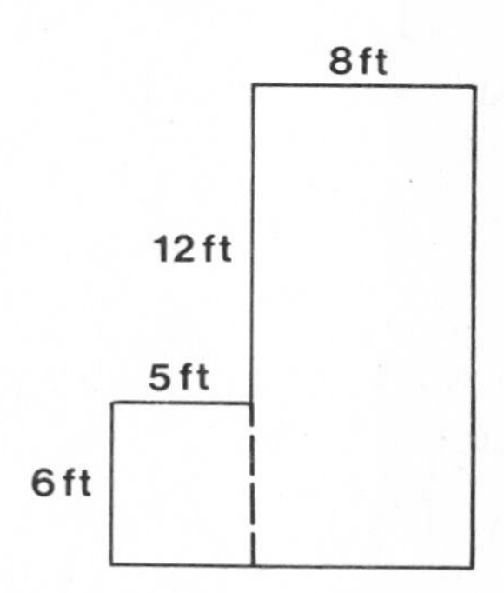

78. Find the area in square feet for the diagram above.

(1) 31 (2) 37 (3) 74
(4) 138 (5) 174

① ② ③ ④ ⑤

Items 79–80 are based on the following information.

One wallpaper square has the measurement of 12 inches by 12 inches. It costs $0.59.

79. How many squares will be needed to paper a wall 14 feet by 10 feet?

(1) 16 (2) 24 (3) 80 (4) 140
(5) Insufficient data is given to solve the problem.

① ② ③ ④ ⑤

80. How much money will be needed to buy wallpaper for a 14 foot by 10 foot wall?

(1) $9.44 (2) $14.16
(3) $47.20 (4) $82.60
(5) Insufficient data is given to solve the problem.

① ② ③ ④ ⑤

Directions: For each problem, choose the one best answer. Answers are on pages 562–563.

81. What is the volume in cubic inches of a rectangular tank with the measurements 24 inches by 48 inches?

(1) 912 (2) 1,170
(3) 9,216 (4) 20,736
(5) Insufficient data is given to solve the problem.

(1) (2) (3) (4) (5)

82. A cement sidewalk 4 feet wide, 20 feet long, and 9 inches thick contains how many cubic feet of cement?

(1) 60 (2) 80 (3) 184 (4) 720
(5) Insufficient data is given to solve the problem.

(1) (2) (3) (4) (5)

83. A rectangular container holds 720 cubic feet. Find the length in feet if it is 12 feet wide and 5 feet high.

(1) 12 (2) 13 (3) 14 (4) 15
(5) Insufficient data is given to solve the problem.

(1) (2) (3) (4) (5)

84. If a rectangular room has measurements of 18 feet by 12 feet by 18 feet, find the air space in cubic feet of the room.

(1) 234 (2) 336 (3) 363
(4) 3,224 (5) 3,888

(1) (2) (3) (4) (5)

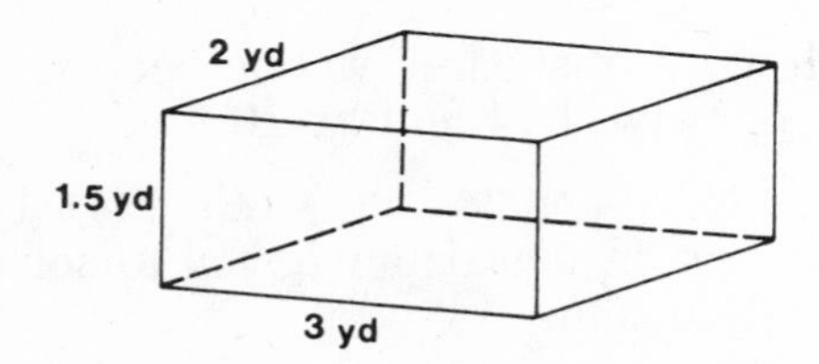

85. How many cubic yards of peat moss can be placed in a pickup truck with the measurements shown above?

(1) 3 (2) 6 (3) 7 (4) 9 (5) 12

(1) (2) (3) (4) (5)

Solid Geometry Up until this point, you have dealt with plane geometry, the study of two-dimensional figures. *Solid geometry* is the study of three-dimensional figures. These figures have depth as well as length and height.

In the arithmetic section (page 492) you learned how to find the capacity of some containers. You were actually working with solid geometry and figuring volume.

The *volume* of a solid figure is the number of cubic units of space the figure occupies. The rectangular solid shown below contains 5 horizontal layers of unit cubes. Each layer contains 3 rows of 4 cubes. Thus there are 12 cubes in each layer, so the volume of the solid is 60 cubic units.

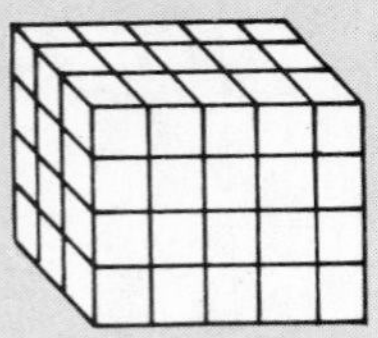

The GED Test deals mainly with three common solid shapes. Two of these shapes and the formulas for their volumes are shown below.

Cube
$V = s^3 = s \times s \times s$
$V = 4 \times 4 \times 4$
$V = 64$ cu units

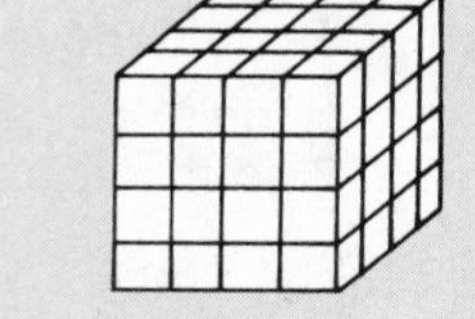

Rectangular Solid
$V = lwh$
$= 12 \times 8 \times 6$
$= 576$ cu ft

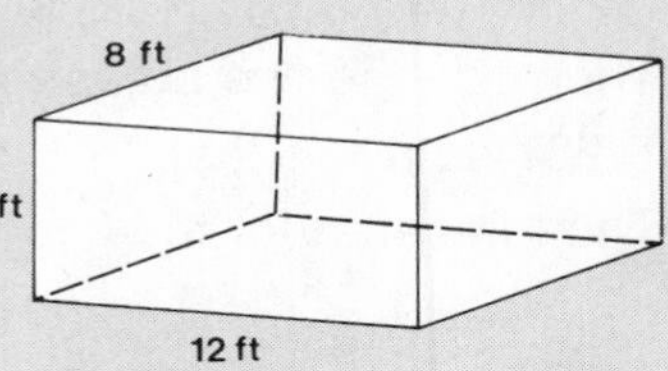

Warm-up

Use the given formulas and values to find the volumes of the shapes shown.

1.

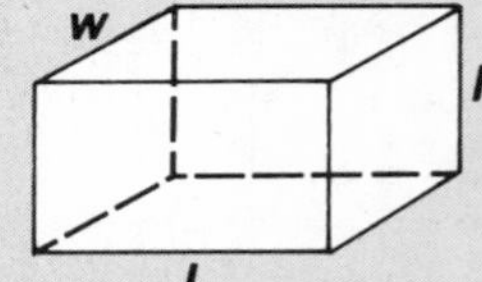

$V = lwh$
$l = 6$ in
$w = 4$ in
$h = 5$ in

2.

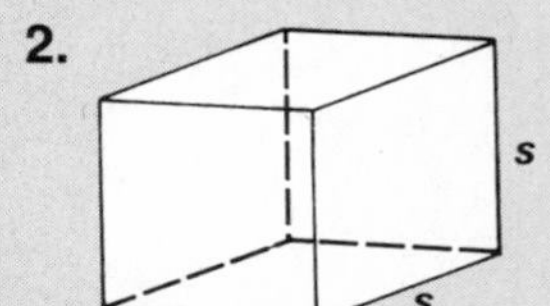

$V = s^3$
$s = 7$ ft

Warm-up Answers
1. 120 cu in **2.** 343 cu ft

Cylinder The third kind of figure for which you may be asked to find the volume is a cylinder.

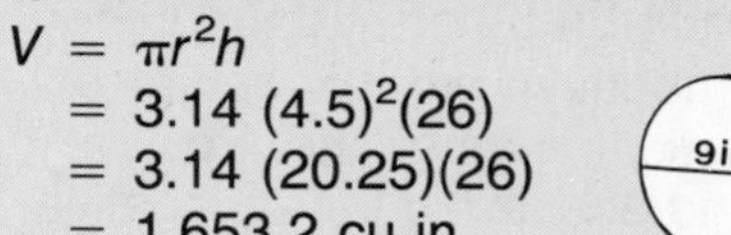

$V = \pi r^2h$
$= 3.14\ (4.5)^2(26)$
$= 3.14\ (20.25)(26)$
$= 1{,}653.2$ cu in

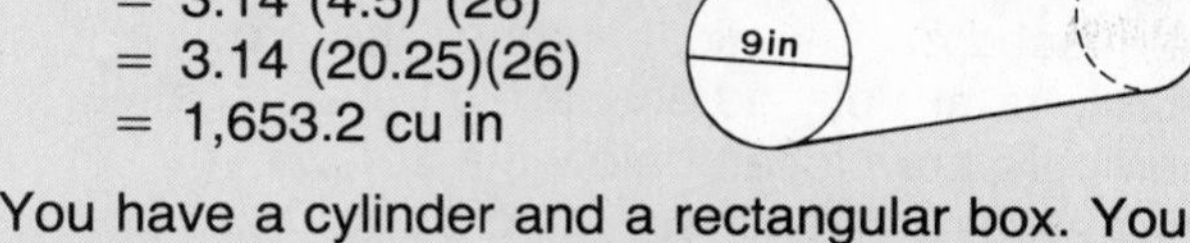

You have a cylinder and a rectangular box. You want to know which container will hold more. What do you do to compare the volumes of the two differently shaped containers?

The dimensions of the figures are as shown.

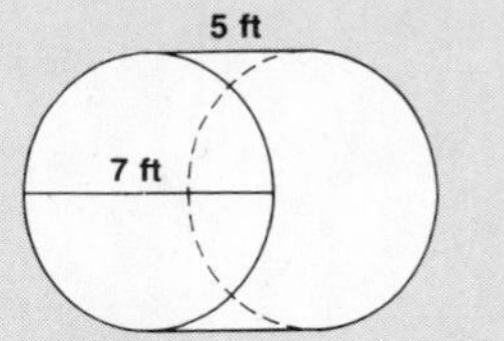

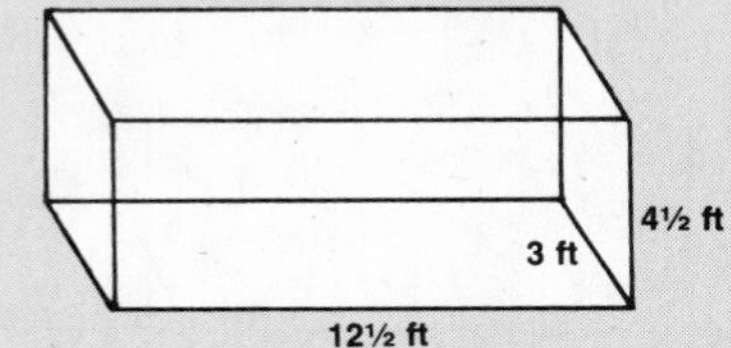

First, figure out the volume of the cylinder.

$V\ \pi r^2h$
$= 3.14 \times 3.5 \times 3.5 \times 5$
$= 192.325$ cu ft

Then, solve for the volume of the box, a rectangular solid.

$V = lwh$
$= 12.5 \times 4.5 \times 3$
$= 168.75$ or $168\frac{3}{4}$ cu ft

The cylinder holds 192⅓ cu ft. The box holds 168¾ cu ft. The cylinder holds more than the box.

☑ A Test-Taking Tip

The formula for the volume of a cube, rectangular container, and cylinder will be on the formula page of the GED Test. If you are asked to find the volume of a solid such as a prism or a pyramid, you will be given the formula to use right in the problem.

Warm-up

Use the formula given to find the volume of the following shape.

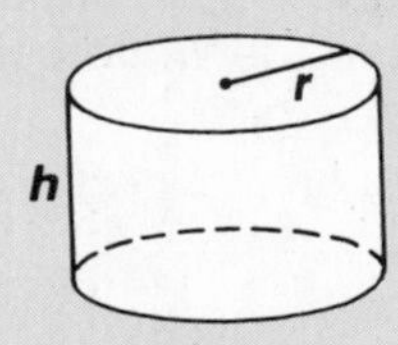

$V = \pi r^2h$
$h = 9$ yd
$r = 6$ yd

Warm-up Answer
1017.36 cu yd

86. A circular water-storage tank with a diameter of 15 feet and a height of 14 feet will have a capacity of how many cubic feet?

(1) 1,237.5 (2) 2,472.75
(3) 4,900 (4) 4,950.75
(5) 5,000.50

① ② ③ ④ ⑤

87. A large circular flower pot has a diameter of 18 inches and a height of one foot. What is the volume of the flower pot in <u>cubic inches</u>?

(1) 56.52 (2) 216 (3) 254.34
(4) 2,453.4 (5) 3,052.08

① ② ③ ④ ⑤

88. A prism has a height of 16 inches and a volume of 3584 cubic inches. If the volume equals the area of its base times height ($V = bh$), what is the area in square inches of a base?

(1) 224 (2) 236 (3) 324
(4) 356 (5) 448

① ② ③ ④ ⑤

89. A piece of metal tubing has a capacity of 1808.64 cubic inches. If the tube has a length of 3 feet, what is its radius in <u>inches?</u>

(1) 2 (2) 3 (3) 4 (4) 8 (5) 16

① ② ③ ④ ⑤

Directions: For each problem, choose the one best answer. Answers are on page 563.

Items 90–94 refer to the following coordinate grid.

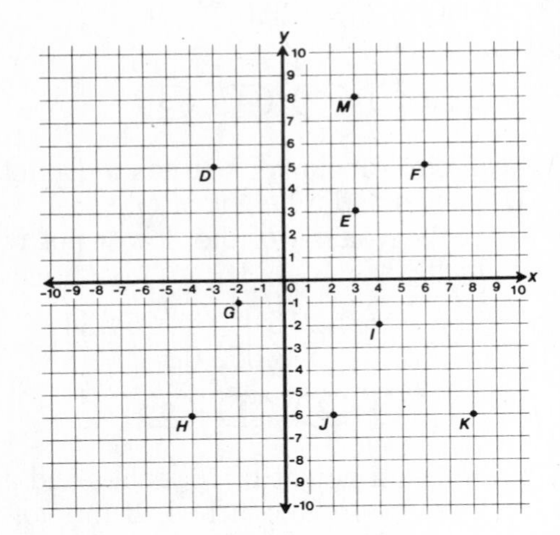

90. The ordered pair for point I is

(1) $(-2, -1)$ (2) $(4, -2)$ (3) $(2, -6)$
(4) $(-2, 4)$ (5) $(-1, -2)$

① ② ③ ④ ⑤

91. The ordered pair for point D is

(1) $(4, -3)$ (2) $(3, 3)$ (3) $(8, -6)$
(4) $(3, 8)$ (5) $(-3, 5)$

① ② ③ ④ ⑤

92. The ordered pair for point K is

(1) $(8, -6)$ (2) $(-4, -6)$ (3) $(6, 5)$
(4) $(2, -6)$ (5) $(5, 6)$

① ② ③ ④ ⑤

93. The ordered pair for point M is

(1) $(3, 3)$ (2) $(3, 8)$ (3) $(3, 5)$
(4) $(-3, 5)$ (5) $(5, -3)$

① ② ③ ④ ⑤

94. The ordered pair for point E is

(1) $(-3, 5)$ (2) $(3, 8)$ (3) $(3, 3)$
(4) $(-5, 3)$ (5) $(-3, -5)$

① ② ③ ④ ⑤

Coordinate Grids When you studied positive and negative numbers, you learned that a point could be represented on a horizontal number line. A positive or negative number can also be placed on a vertical number line. Positive numbers are placed above the zero; negative numbers are placed below the zero. If you place two number lines—a horizontal number line and a vertical number line—at right angles to each other, you will form a rectangular coordinate grid. Using such a grid, you can now represent points anywhere within a plane, not just those on a number line.

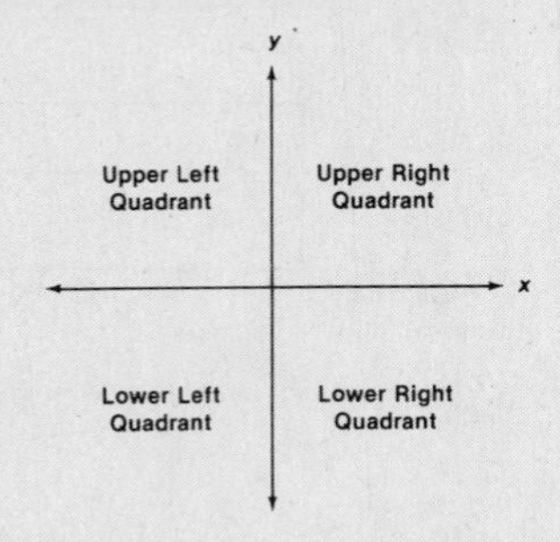

A grid has four sections, and each section is called a *quadrant.* The horizontal number line is called the *x*-axis; the vertical number line is called the *y*-axis. The *x*-axis and the *y*-axis usually meet at 0.

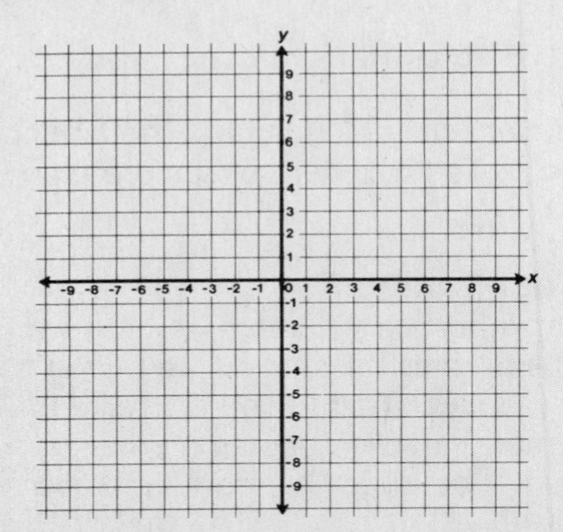

Notice that positive numbers are to the right of 0 on the *x*-axis and above the 0 on the *y*-axis. The negative numbers are to the left of 0 on the *x*-axis and below the 0 on the *y*-axis.

Read the tinted explanation on page 519 before completing the items in the white column on either this or the next page.

Ordered Pairs on a Coordinate Grid When you write the *x* and *y* coordinates, you are writing ordered pairs. Study the grid below.

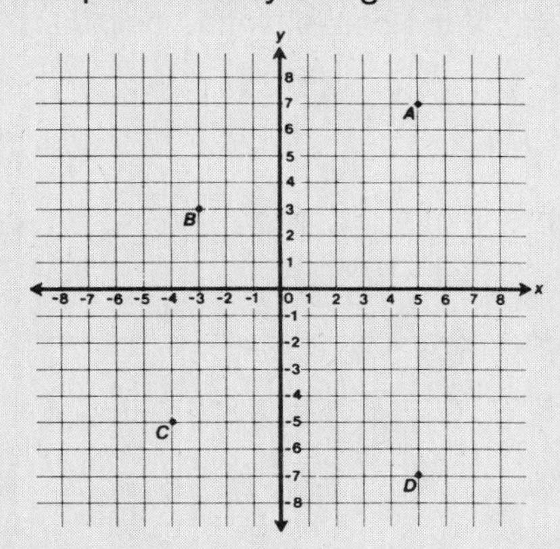

The ordered pair for point *A* is (5,7). The *x* coordinate is always written first. It is separated from the *y* coordinate by a comma. Ordered pairs are always written within parentheses.

The following steps will help you identify plotted ordered pairs. Use the grid above. To identify any point, follow these steps.

Step 1 Start at 0 on the *x*-axis; move either to the left or right on the *x*-axis. For point *B*, move 3 points to the left of 0. The *x*-axis coordinate is −3. This was a horizontal move.

Step 2 From the *x*-coordinate, move either above or below 0 on the *y*-axis. For point *B*, move 3 points above 0. The *y*-axis coordinate is +3. This was a vertical move.

Step 3 Write the two points as the ordered pair of (−3,3).

The ordered pairs for *C* and *D* are (−4, −5) and (5, −7), respectively.

Warm-up

Using the grid above, place the following points on the grid. E (6,0), F (0, −4), G(−5, −6), H(2, −7)

Warm-up Answer

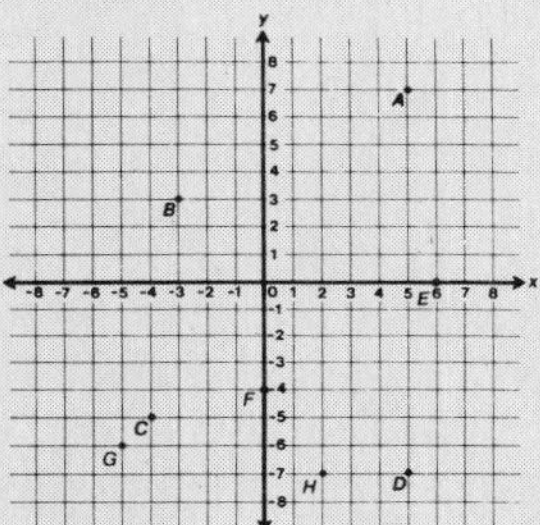

Items 95–99 refer to the following coordinate grid.

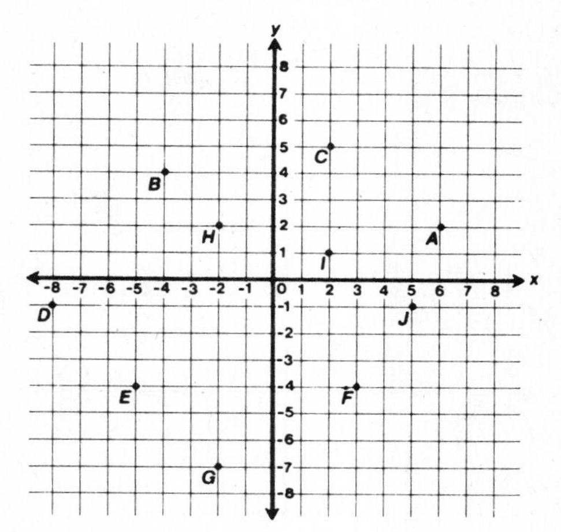

95. The ordered pair of (6,2) is for point

(1) *A* (2) *B* (3) *C*
(4) *D* (5) *F*

① ② ③ ④ ⑤

96. The ordered pair of (−8, −1) is for point

(1) *D* (2) *E* (3) *F*
(4) *A* (5) *G*

① ② ③ ④ ⑤

97. The ordered pair of (−5, −4) is for point

(1) *C* (2) *J* (3) *E*
(4) *F* (5) *G*

① ② ③ ④ ⑤

98. The ordered pair of (5, −1) is for point

(1) *E* (2) *F* (3) *G*
(4) *J* (5) *H*

① ② ③ ④ ⑤

99. The ordered pair of (−4,4) is for point

(1) *A* (2) *H* (3) *E*
(4) *B* (5) *F*

① ② ③ ④ ⑤

Directions: For each problem, choose the one best answer. Answers are on page 563.

Items 100–104 refer to the following coordinate grid.

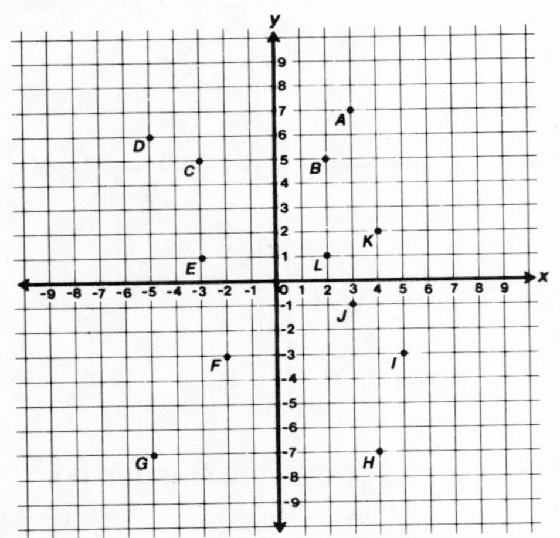

100. The distance between A (3,7) and J (3, −1) is

(1) 8 (2) 7 (3) 6
(4) 5 (5) 4

(1) (2) (3) (4) (5)

101. The distance between D (−5,6) and G (−5, −7) is

(1) 12 (2) 11 (3) 13
(4) 14 (5) 10

(1) (2) (3) (4) (5)

102. The distance between F (−2, −3) and I (5, −3) is

(1) 5 (2) 6 (3) 8 (4) 7 (5) 9

(1) (2) (3) (4) (5)

103. The distance between B (2,5) and the x-axis is

(1) 3 (2) 4 (3) 5 (4) 6 (5) 7

(1) (2) (3) (4) (5)

104. The distance between H (4, −7) and the y-axis is

(1) 4 (2) 7 (3) 9 (4) 10 (5) 11

(1) (2) (3) (4) (5)

Horizontal and Vertical Distance The distance between two points can easily be identified if both points lie on a horizontal line or on a vertical line. Study the points plotted below.

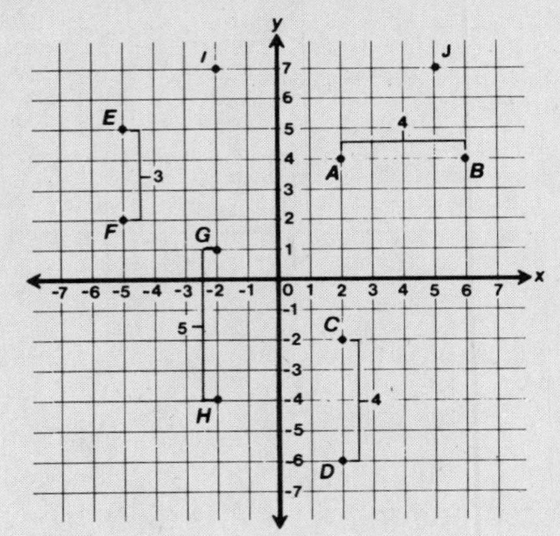

The distance between points A and B is 4. The distance between points C and D is also 4. The distance between points E and F is 3, while the distance between points G and H is 5. Although some points have negative coordinates, the distance is always indicated as a positive number.

You can also measure distances when you are given just the coordinates of the two points. If point A is located at (6, −2) and point B is located at (6,8), you simply ignore the coordinates that are the same (6) and subtract the smaller number from the larger number.

$8 - (-2) = 8 + 2 = 10$

The distance between points A and B is 10.

Warm-up

Use the coordinate system to

1. Find the distance between points I and J on the grid above.

2. find the distance between points X(7,3) and y(7, −2).

Warm-up Answers
1. 7 **2.** 5

Diagonal Distance If two points do not both lie on a single horizontal or vertical line, you can find the distance between those points by using the Pythagorean theorem formula, $c^2 = a^2 + b^2$.

To find the distance between points A and B on the graph below, note that the dotted lines are legs of a right triangle. The hypotenuse of the right triangle is the solid line between the two points.

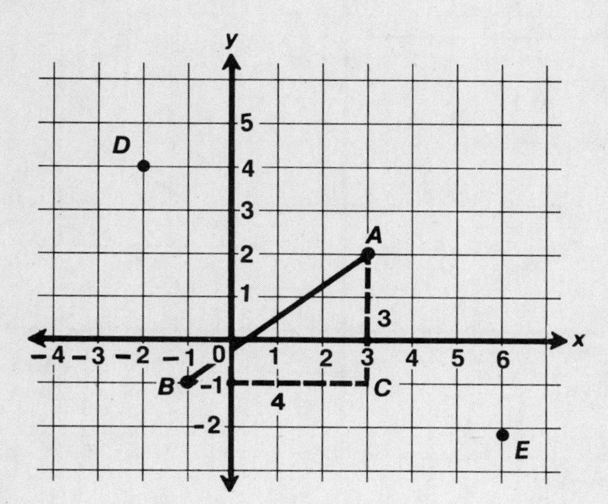

The coordinates of C are $(3, -1)$. The distance between B and C is 4, or the length of that leg. The coordinates of A are (3,2). The distance between A and C is 3, or the length of the second leg.

Use the formula.

$$c^2 = a^2 + b^2$$
$$c^2 = 4^2 + 3^2$$
$$c^2 = 16 + 9$$
$$c^2 = 25$$
$$c = \sqrt{25}$$
$$c = 5$$

The distance between points A and B is 5.

☑ A Test-Taking Tip

The GED Test will probably include a diagram with an item that asks you to find the diagonal distance. If no diagram is shown, draw the legs and the hypotenuse yourself on the scratch paper you will be given.

Warm-up

Use the grid above. Find the distance from point D to point E.

Warm-up Answer
10

Items 105–109 refer to the following coordinate grid.

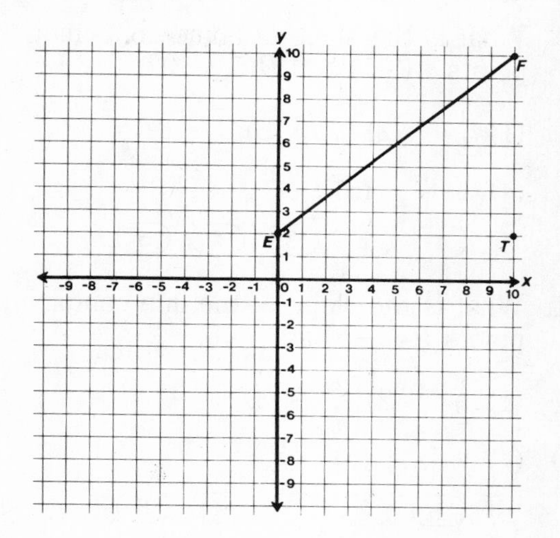

105. The coordinates of point E are
(1) (0,4) (2) (8,5) (3) $(0, -2)$
(4) (0,2) (5) $(-2,10)$

(1) (2) (3) (4) (5)

106. The coordinates of point T are
(1) (10,2) (2) $(0, -2)$ (3) (6,10)
(4) $(-8,0)$ (5) $(2, -2)$

(1) (2) (3) (4) (5)

107. The distance between points E and T is
(1) 2 (2) 4 (3) 6
(4) 8 (5) 10

(1) (2) (3) (4) (5)

108. The distance between points F and T is
(1) 4 (2) 8 (3) 10
(4) 12 (5) 15

(1) (2) (3) (4) (5)

109. The distance between points E and F is
(1) 8 (2) 10 (3) 18
(4) $\sqrt{100}$ (5) $\sqrt{164}$

(1) (2) (3) (4) (5)

Directions: For each problem, choose the one best answer. Answers are on pages 563–564.

110. What is the slope of a line containing points $A(3,7)$ and $B(5,-2)$?

(1) $\frac{1}{2}$ (2) $\frac{3}{2}$ (3) $\frac{7}{2}$
(4) $-\frac{9}{2}$ (5) $-\frac{3}{2}$

① ② ③ ④ ⑤

111. What is the slope of the line containing points $J(4,-3)$ and $K(6,-2)$?

(1) $\frac{1}{2}$ (2) $\frac{3}{2}$ (3) $\frac{5}{2}$
(4) $-\frac{1}{2}$ (5) $-\frac{5}{2}$

① ② ③ ④ ⑤

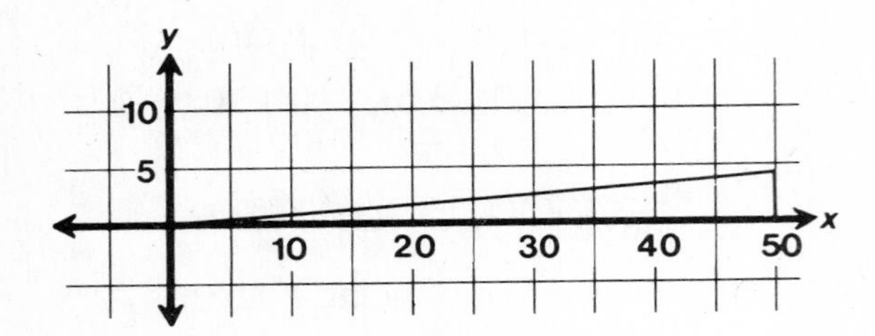

112. A car is driven up a ramp that is 50 feet long and rises 4 feet. What is the grade (slope) of the ramp?

(1) .02 (2) .08 (3) .12
(4) .18 (5) .80

① ② ③ ④ ⑤

113. The Federal Highway Commission recommends a maximum grade of 12% for a road. What is the maximum vertical rise in feet of a road covering 100 feet of horizontal distance?

(1) 6 (2) 8 (3) 10
(4) 12 (5) 16

① ② ③ ④ ⑤

114. Point $P(4,7)$ is on a line with a slope of 0. Which of the following could be the coordinates of another point on the same line?

(1) (0,8) (2) (4,6) (3) (7,0)
(4) (−3,7) (5) (−5,9)

① ② ③ ④ ⑤

The Slope of a Line You may be asked to identify the slope of a line. The *slope* of a line is the measure of the steepness of that line. You are determining the amount of a vertical distance over a horizontal distance. A line that slopes upward to the right has a positive slope. A line that slopes downward to the right has a negative slope.

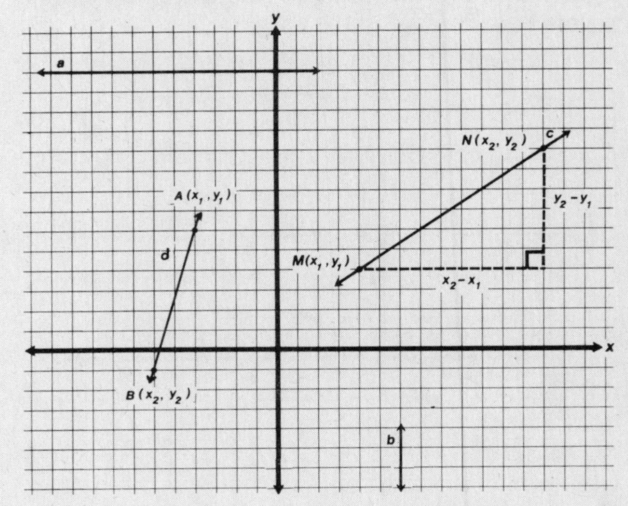

In the graph above, line *a* has a slope of 0. That is, it does not rise or descend. The slope of any horizontal line is 0. Line *b* has no slope at all. By definition, a vertical line has no slope.

Line *c* slopes upward to the right. It has a positive slope. Point *M* on line *c* has the coordinates (4,4). These can be referred to as x_1 and y_1. Point *N* (x_2 and y_2) has the coordinates (13,10). To find the slope of a line, use this formula: $m = \frac{y_2 - y_1}{x_2 - x_1}$. Use the coordinates for points *M* and *N* in the formula: $m = \frac{10-4}{13-4} = \frac{6}{9} = \frac{2}{3}$ OR $\frac{4-10}{4-13} = \frac{-6}{-9} = \frac{6}{9} = \frac{2}{3}$. The slope of line *c* is $\frac{2}{3}$.

☑ A Test-Taking Tip

If you are asked to find the slope of a line on the GED Mathematics Test, turn to the formula page. The formula you need will be listed there.

Warm-up

On line *d*, the coordinates of *A* are (−4,6). The coordinates of *B* are (−6,−1). Find the slope of line *d*.

Warm-up Answer

$\frac{7}{2}$

Geometry Review Try to remember that the sum of two complementary angles is always 90° and that the sum of two supplementary angles is always 180°. If you have trouble remembering which is which, this might help: *C,* the first letter of *complementary,* is closer to the beginning of the alphabet, so complementary angles total the lesser number of degrees. *S,* the first letter of *supplementary,* falls much later in the alphabet, so it has the greater number of degrees.

Remember that any problem involving area will have an answer in square units. Any problem involving volume will have an answer in cubic units.

Remember that you add to find perimeter. To find area and volume, you multiply.

☑ Test-Taking Tips

It is often difficult to picture geometric figures that are stated in problems. You may find it helpful to draw figures you are dealing with. Although the GED Test often includes drawings with the problems, you are also allowed to draw diagrams and compute problems on scratch paper.

Units of measurement can be confusing. If some units in a problem are stated in feet and others are in yards, look to see which unit the question actually asks for. Convert the numbers to that unit *before* you do your computations.

If a formula is not given to you, determine what figure you are dealing with and what the problem is asking for: perimeter, area, volume, and so on. Then check the formula page for the correct formula.

If a number you need to solve a problem is not stated, you might mark the answer "Insufficient data is given to solve the problem." Before you do that, think again. Perhaps you can work with the numbers you have to find the missing number. For example, if you know the length of one side of a rectangle, you know the length of the opposite side because opposite sides of a rectangle are equal. Use such relationships between the sides and angles of geometric figures to determine the numbers you need.

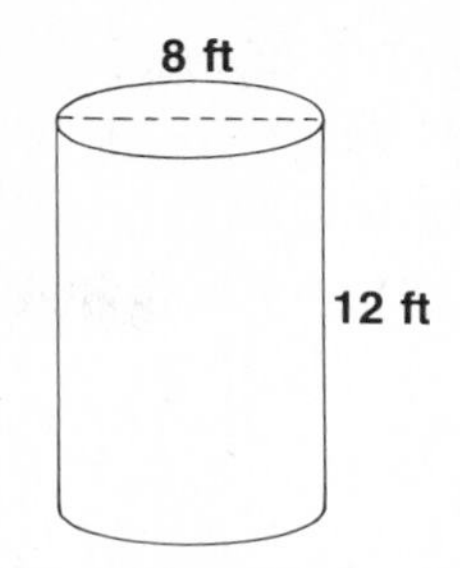

115. What is the volume in cubic feet of the cylindrical silo shown above?

(1) 62.8 (2) 96 (3) 301.44
(4) 602.88 (5) 2,411.52

① ② ③ ④ ⑤

Items 116–117 refer to the following information.

A decorator wishes to make the reception area in an office building more attractive. The dimensions of the reception area are shown below.

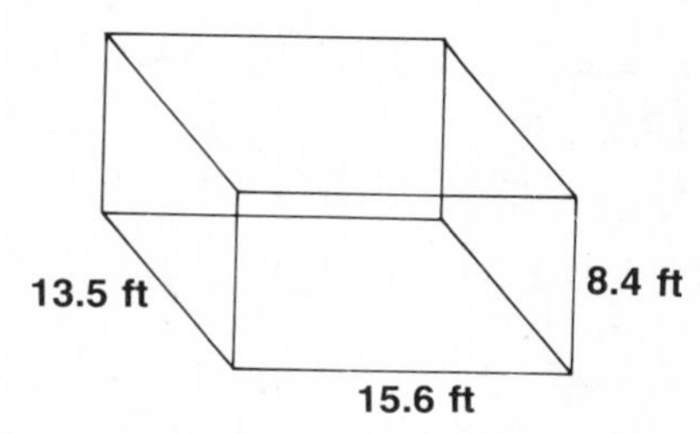

116. The floor is to be covered with wall-to-wall carpeting. How many square yards of carpeting should the decorator order?

(1) 23.4 (2) 29.1 (3) 58.2
(4) 105.3 (5) 210.6

① ② ③ ④ ⑤

117. Two adjacent walls will be papered with a mural. What is the area in square yards of the walls?

(1) 12.6 (2) 14.56 (3) 27.16
(4) 131.04 (5) 244.44

① ② ③ ④ ⑤

118. The diameter of Fred's bicycle wheel is 25 inches. How many inches will the wheel travel in 12 complete turns?

(1) 12 (2) 25 (3) 39.25
(4) 471 (5) 942

① ② ③ ④ ⑤

Directions: For each problem, choose the one best answer. Answers are on page 564.

1. Which is equal to $(4)^2 + (1)^4 - (6)(4)\frac{1}{2}$?

   (1) -8 (2) 5 (3) 8
   (4) 20 (5) 32

   (1) (2) (3) (4) (5)

2. Which is equal to $(7 - 8) + 7 - 4^2$?

   (1) -14 (2) -8 (3) 8
   (4) -10 (5) 14

   (1) (2) (3) (4) (5)

3. Which is equal to $(-\frac{1}{4})(\frac{1}{2}) + 7$?

   (1) $-7\frac{1}{8}$ (2) $-6\frac{7}{8}$ (3) $6\frac{5}{6}$
   (4) $6\frac{7}{8}$ (5) $7\frac{1}{8}$

   (1) (2) (3) (4) (5)

4. Which is equal to $-9^1 + 18$?

   (1) -27 (2) 0 (3) $+9$
   (4) 18 (5) 63

   (1) (2) (3) (4) (5)

Algebra

In algebra you'll use much of what you already learned in arithmetic and geometry. But first you need to know about the order of doing things in algebra.

Working with Order of Operations The numerical expression $5 + 3$ is one that has only one operation, addition. The numerical expression $5 + 3 \times 7$, on the other hand, contains two operations, addition and multiplication. You will get the wrong answer if you do the operations in the wrong order. Here are two ways to evaluate $5 + 3 \times 7$.

Addition First	*Multiplication First*
$5 + 3 \times 7 =$	$5 + 3 \times 7 =$
$5 + 3 = 8$	$3 \times 7 = 21$
$8 \times 7 = 56$	$5 + 21 = 26$

The correct answer is 26 because there are rules that state that you must multiply before you add. *Below is the standard set of rules that tell you the order that you must use when you are computing numerical statements with more than one operation.* These are known as the **order of operations.**

1. Do operations inside parentheses.
2. Do operations involving powers and square roots.
3. Do multiplication and division operations from left to right.
4. Do addition and subtraction operations from left to right.

The expression $5 + 3 \times 7$ could have included parentheses: $5 + (3 \times 7)$. But many numerical statements don't include parentheses. When a numerical statement does not include parentheses, compute powers and roots first, as stated in the order of operations. If parentheses, powers, and roots are not included, start by multiplying and dividing. Start by adding and subtracting only when the numerical statement you are working with does not include any of the other operations.

Before you do any of the problems in the white column on this page, read the tinted column on the next page.

Compute. $4^2 - \sqrt{25}$

Step 1 Since no numbers are inside parentheses, compute the powers and roots first: $4^2 = 16$ and $\sqrt{25} = 5$.

Step 2 Now perform the subtraction called for in the problem: $16 - 5 = 11$.

Compute. $(7 - 2)^2 + 4$

Step 1 Compute the operation inside the parentheses: $7 - 2 = 5$. $5^2 + 4$.

Step 2 Compute: $5^2 = 25$. That gives you $25 + 4$.

Step 3 Add: $25 + 4 = 29$

Compute. $(\frac{1}{2} \times \frac{1}{4})^2 \times 10 + 5^2$

Step 1 Compute the operations that are inside the parentheses: $\frac{1}{2} \times \frac{1}{4} = \frac{1}{8}$. Now the problem is $(\frac{1}{8})^2 \times 10 + 5^2$

Step 2 Compute the operations that involve powers: $(\frac{1}{8})^2 = \frac{1}{64}$; $5^2 = 25$; $\frac{1}{64} \times 10 + 25$.

Step 3 Compute the multiplication operations from left to right: $\frac{1}{64} \times 10 = \frac{10}{64} = \frac{5}{32}$; $\frac{5}{32} + 25$.

Step 4 Compute the addition: $\frac{5}{32} + 25 = 25\frac{5}{32}$.

You learned in *Geometry* that two letters written together in a formula mean to multiply. In algebra two numbers separated only by parentheses also mean to multiply.

Warm-up

Compute.

1. $3^2 + (9)(4) - 5^2$

2. $5 + 3^2 - \frac{(8 - 4)}{2}$

3. $(12 - 6) + 2^3$

4. $-5^1 + 21$

Warm-up Answers

1. The correct answer is 20. Steps to follow: *1.* Compute the numbers with powers: $3^2 = 9$; $5^2 = 25$. *2.* Multiply: $9 \times 4 = 36$. *3.* Add: $9 + 36 = 45$, and then subtract: $45 - 25 = 20$. **2.** The correct answer is 12. Steps: *1.* Compute in parentheses: $8 - 4 = 4$. *2.* Compute the numbers with exponents: $3^2 = 9$. *3.* Compute the division: $4 \div 2 = 2$. *4.* Add: $5 + 9 = 14$; subtract: $14 - 2 = 12$. **3.** The correct answer is 14. Steps: *1.* Compute the numbers in parentheses: $12 - 6 = 6$. *2.* Compute the numbers with exponents: $2^3 = 8$. *3.* No multiplication or division is called for, so compute the addition: $6 + 8 = 14$. **4.** The correct answer is 16. Steps: *1.* Compute: $-5^1 = -5$. *2.* Add: $-5 + 21 = 16$.

5. Which is equal to $6 + 2 - (7 - 5)^2$?

(1) -4 (2) -2 (3) 0
(4) 2 (5) 4

① ② ③ ④ ⑤

6. Which is equal to $3 \times 5 + 4(4 + 1)^2$?

(1) 85 (2) 100 (3) 110
(4) 115 (5) 125

① ② ③ ④ ⑤

7. Which is equal to $\frac{1}{4} \times 12 + (\frac{1}{2})^2$?

(1) 3 (2) $3\frac{1}{4}$ (3) $4\frac{1}{2}$
(4) 5 (5) 12

① ② ③ ④ ⑤

8. Which is equal to $(-4)^3 + 4^2$?

(1) -80 (2) -64 (3) -48
(4) -24 (5) -12

① ② ③ ④ ⑤

9. Which is equal to $(-1)^5 - 4 \times (4 - 2)^2$?

(1) -17 (2) -15 (3) -14
(4) 15 (5) 17

① ② ③ ④ ⑤

<u>Directions:</u> For each problem, choose the <u>one</u> best answer. Answers are on page 564.

10. Which of the following equals 25(15 + 105)?

(1) (25 + 15) + (25 + 105)
(2) (25 + 15)(25 + 105)
(3) 25(15) + 25(105)
(4) 25(15) + 105
(5) 25(105) + 15

(1) (2) (3) (4) (5)

11. Which of the following equals −22 + (8 × 9)?

(1) 22 + 72
(2) (8 × 9) + −22
(3) (8 × 9) + 22
(4) −22(9 × 8)
(5) 22(−9 × −8)

(1) (2) (3) (4) (5)

12. Which of the following equals 106 × 4 + 106 × (−12)?

(1) 106 (16)
(2) 4(−12) + 106
(3) −12(106 + 4)
(4) 106 (4 − 12)
(5) −4 (−12) − 106

(1) (2) (3) (4) (5)

13. Which of the following equals 92 × (60 × 9)?

(1) (92 × 60) × 9
(2) 92(60) + 92(9)
(3) 92(69)
(4) 92(60 + 9)
(5) (92 + 60) × 9

(1) (2) (3) (4) (5)

Laws for Numerical Expressions The laws of operation listed below will help you in your computations.

Commutative Law The commutative law states that you can reverse the numbers in an addition or a multiplication problem and still compute the same answer. For example,

22 + 46 = 68 and 46 + 22 = 68.
12 × 13 = 156 and 13 × 12 = 156.

Note that this law works only with addition and multiplication. You cannot reverse the numbers in subtraction and division problems.

Associative Law The associative law states that numbers to be added or multiplied can be grouped in different ways without changing the answer. For example,

$$(7 + 6) + 8 = 7 + (6 + 8)$$
$$13 + 8 = 7 + 14$$
$$21 = 21$$

$$(7 \times 6) \times 8 = 7 \times (6 \times 8)$$
$$42 \times 8 = 7 \times 48$$
$$336 = 336$$

You cannot apply this law when you subtract or divide.

Distributive Law The distributive law states that multiplying a sum is the same as multiplying each number that is added to make the sum. For example,

$$6(7 + 8) = 6(7) + 6(8)$$
$$6(15) = 42 + 48$$
$$90 = 90$$

Remember, you always do operations within the parentheses first.

Warm-up

Equivalent means the same thing as *equal.* On the lines below, write *equivalent* next to each pair of expressions that are equal.

1. 52 + 53 and 25 + 35 ____________

2. 2(4) + 2(6) and 2(4 + 6) ____________

3. 24 × (2 × 5) and (24 × 2) × 5 ____________

4. (5 × 7) + 3 and 5(7 + 3) ____________

Warm-up Answers
Expressions 2 and 3 are equivalent.

Working with Numerical Statements On the GED Test your ability to set up a word problem will be measured in two ways. Most of the time you will be asked to solve a math problem; sometimes, however, you will be asked to set up the *method* for working a word problem. Read the following example and select the method that you would use to solve the problem.

■ Susan purchased 6 movie tickets for $4.50 each. Which of the following would compute the cost of the tickets correctly?

1. 6 + $4.50
2. 6($4.50)
3. $\frac{\$4.50}{6}$

The question asks you to find the cost of 6 movie tickets at $4.50 each. One way to do this would be to add $4.50 together six times, but that option is not presented. *Option 2* tells you to multiply 6 by $4.50, and that would be the same as adding $4.50 six times; therefore, *option 2* is correct.

Warm-up

1. If hamburger is $1.79 per pound and buns are $0.59 per package, which expression gives the number of dollars spent for 4 pounds of hamburger and 4 packages of buns?

a. 4($1.79 + $0.59) **b.** 4($1.79) + $0.59
c. $0.59 + $1.79

2. A bicyclist pedaled 25 miles in five hours. Which statement indicates the average number of miles pedaled per hour?

a. 5(25) **b.** 5 + 25 **c.** $\frac{25}{5}$

3. If chocolates cost $1.95 per pound and hard candy costs $1.25 a pound, which numerical statement shows how to compute the combined cost of 5 pounds of chocolate candy and 8 pounds of hard candy?

a. 5($1.95) + 8($1.25)
b. 8($1.25) − 5($1.95)
c. $1.95 + $1.25

Warm-up Answers
1. *a.* The parentheses around $1.79 + $0.59 means that you multiply *both* numbers by 4 and then add. Since the question asks you to compute the total cost of four of each item, this numerical statement would solve the problem correctly. **2.** *c. Option c* shows the correct way to compute an average. You divide the total number of miles traveled by the number of hours traveled to get the *average* number of miles traveled in one hour. **3.** *a.* The key word in the question is *combined* because it tells you to add the costs of both types of candy together.

14. A television set was purchased for $229, a sewing machine for $433, and a radio for $59. If Chris made a down payment of $200 for these items, which statement expresses what his balance would be?

(1) ($229 + $433) − ($200 + $59)
(2) ($229)($433) − $200 + $59
(3) ($229 + $433 + $200) − $59
(4) ($229 + $433 + $59) − $200
(5) ($229)($433)($59) − $200

① ② ③ ④ ⑤

15. The sale price of tuna is 98 cents a can. The regular price is $1.49 per can. Which statement expresses the savings on 3 cans?

(1) 3 + ($1.49 − $0.98)
(2) (3 + $1.49) − $0.98
(3) 3($1.49 − $0.98)
(4) (3 × $0.98) − (3 × $1.49)
(5) $0.51

① ② ③ ④ ⑤

16. A new home computer can be bought for $75 down and $50 a month for one year. Which expression states this time payment plan?

(1) $75 + 12($50)
(2) $50 + 12 + $75
(3) 12($75) + $50
(4) $75($50) + 12
(5) $\frac{\$75 + \$50}{12}$

① ② ③ ④ ⑤

17. Leroy bought 10 pounds of hamburger for $\frac{1}{3}$ off the usual price of $1.59 per pound. Which of the following could be used to compute the amount Leroy saved on the hamburger?

(1) $\frac{1}{3}$($1.59) − 10($1.59)
(2) 10($1.59) ÷ $\frac{1}{3}$
(3) $\frac{10(\$1.59)}{3}$
(4) 3($1.59) − $\frac{1}{3}$(10)
(5) $1.59(10 ÷ $\frac{1}{3}$)

① ② ③ ④ ⑤

Directions: For each problem, choose the one best answer. Answers are on pages 564.

18. Three groups of hikers of equal number planned a trip. Then 6 people did not go on the trip. Represent the number of hikers who actually went on the trip.

(1) $3(n - 6)$ (2) $3n + 6$
(3) $6(3n)$ (4) $3n - 6$
(5) $n^3 - 6$

(1) (2) (3) (4) (5)

19. If Mrs. Rice received c phone calls on Monday and L phone calls on Tuesday, represent the number of calls she received.

(1) Lc (2) $c + L$
(3) $L(c + L)$ (4) cL
(5) $L - c$

(1) (2) (3) (4) (5)

20. If 5 books of equal value cost x dollars, represent the cost of one book.

(1) $\frac{5}{x}$ (2) $\frac{x}{5}$ (3) $5x$
(4) x^5 (5) $5 + x$

(1) (2) (3) (4) (5)

21. Which expression shows how to compute the number of cents in x dollars?

(1) $100x$ (2) $\frac{100}{x}$ (3) $\frac{x}{100}$
(4) $x + 100$ (5) $x - 100$

(1) (2) (3) (4) (5)

Working with Algebraic Expressions The addition, subtraction, multiplication, and division operations performed in arithmetic can be performed in algebra. The one major difference between algebra and arithmetic is that algebra uses letters to represent numerical values. The letters are often referred to as **variables** because the value of the letter varies from problem to problem.

You have been solving algebraic problems since you learned the basic addition and subtraction facts. The expression 4 + __ = 10 is read as "four plus some number equals 10." In algebra, this statement is written as $4 + a = 10$. The a represents a number that is unknown—any letter can be used. In this statement a equals 6. The a in the statement $7 + a = 11$ has the value of 4. The value varied, or changed, in each of these two examples.

You can write algebraic expressions and statements by using the four basic operational signs that are used in arithmetic.

Examples

Addition: 15 increased by a number, x:
$15 + x$

Subtraction: a number, x, decreased by nine:
$x - 9$

Multiplication: 4 multiplied by a number, y:
$4y$ (Notice that when a number is *next* to a letter, it means that you multiply them together.)

Division: a number, c, divided by 11:
$\frac{c}{11}$

Just remember that in algebra you can use any letter you want to represent the unknown number. For example, both of the following expressions are acceptable: $x + 8 = 10$ and $y + 8 = 10$.

Read the information on this and the next page before you do the problems in the white columns on these pages.

How could you write the following as an algebraic expression: 3 more than a number, *a*? The key to the algebraic expression is the word *more. More* means "add." Here's what the algebraic expression looks like: $a + 3$.

Write the following example as an algebraic expression: 25 divided by a number, *q*. Here the key is that you are dividing 25 by *q*. In algebra this is usually expressed $\frac{25}{q}$, instead of $25 \div q$ or $q\overline{)25}$.

Coming to Terms

Look for key words when converting a statement into an algebraic expression.

The **difference** between x and y: $x - y$.
Five **times** a number, w: $5w$.
Twelve **less than** x: $x - 12$.
r is **increased** by 4: $r + 4$.
z is **decreased** by 25: $z - 25$.
The **sum** of r and 9: $r + 9$.
The **product** of 9 and p: $9p$.
$10x$, **find one** x: $\frac{10x}{10}$ (*find one* means "divide").
The product of 9 and y **squared**: $9y^2$;
a **cubed**: a^3.

Warm-up

Write an algebraic expression for each of the following:

1. 5 less than a number, x
2. 7 times a number, x
3. the square of a number, x
4. 9 less than x times y
5. $\frac{1}{2}$ a number, r, plus 4
6. 40 times a number, x
7. 1 more than twice a number, b
8. five more than a number, x
9. the product of a and b, to the fifth power
10. 15 divided by x

Warm-up Answers
1. $x - 5$ **2.** $7x$ (Multiplication is shown when a number is next to a letter.) **3.** x^2 **4.** $xy - 9$ **5.** $\frac{r}{2} + 4$ **6.** $40x$ **7.** $2b + 1$ **8.** $x + 5$ **9.** $(ab)^5$ **10.** $\frac{15}{x}$

22. There were 15 people riding a bus. At the last stop x persons got off. How many people stayed on the bus?

(1) $15 - x$ (2) $x - 15$ (3) $15x$
(4) $\frac{x}{15}$ (5) $15 + x$

① ② ③ ④ ⑤

23. Gerry bought 5 postcards for her brother's collection. Which expression represents the entire collection?

(1) $\frac{x}{5}$ (2) $5 - x$ (3) $5x$
(4) $x + 5$ (5) $x + 5x$

① ② ③ ④ ⑤

24. The product of 7 and a number, a, is

(1) $a - 7$ (2) $\frac{a}{7}$ (3) $7 + a$
(4) $7a$ (5) $7 \times 7a$

① ② ③ ④ ⑤

25. A family of 6 divided x amount of pretzels. Represent each person's share.

(1) $x - 6$ (2) $\frac{x}{6}$ (3) $6x$
(4) $6 + x$ (5) $\frac{6}{x}$

① ② ③ ④ ⑤

26. If Mark weighs n pounds, represent his weight after he gains 15 pounds.

(1) $n - 15$ (2) $15(n + 15)$
(3) $15n + 15$ (4) $15n$
(5) $n + 15$

① ② ③ ④ ⑤

Directions: For each problem, choose the one best answer. Answers are on pages 564–565.

27. Simplify. $3a + a - 7a$

(1) $-11a$ (2) $-4a$ (3) $-3a$
(4) $3a$ (5) $4a$

① ② ③ ④ ⑤

28. $7rs + t - 2rs - t$ simplified is

(1) $-5rs$ (2) $5rs - 2t$ (3) $5rs$
(4) $9rs - 2t$ (5) $9rs + 2t$

① ② ③ ④ ⑤

29. Simplify. $4x - 9x + 4x - (-7x)$

(1) $-16x$ (2) $-8x$ (3) $2x$
(4) $6x$ (5) $8x$

① ② ③ ④ ⑤

30. Simplify. $4a + (-3b) - (-2a) + 6b$

(1) $6a + 3b$ (2) $-2a - 3b$
(3) $2a + 9b$ (4) $4a - 5ab + 6b$
(5) $2a + 3b$

① ② ③ ④ ⑤

31. Simplify. $c^2d^2 - 4c^2d^2$

(1) $-5c^2d^2$ (2) $-3c^2d^2$
(3) $-c^2d^2$ (4) c^2d^2
(5) $3c^2d^2$

① ② ③ ④ ⑤

Combining Like Terms: Adding and Subtracting The expression $2a$ has two parts. The 2 is called the *coefficient,* and the a is called the *variable*. Together they are called a *term.*

To find the sum of $2a + 3b + 3a + 4c - c$, you need to combine like terms. The expression has three different terms: those with a, those with b, and those with c. This expression can be simplified by combining terms with the same letters: $2a + 3a = 5a$ and $4c - c = 3c$. Now the expression is $5a + 3b + 3c$.

In $4a^2c^3 + 9a^2c^2$ the terms cannot be combined because one term has c^3 as part of it and the other has c^2 as part of it. However, if the expression read $4a^2c^3 + 9a^2c^3$, the terms could be added together to make $13a^2c^3$.

Combining these expressions can also be called adding or subtracting them, or simplifying them. The main thing to note is that the *coefficients* are added, but the variables and their exponents are left the way they are. When combining algebraic expressions, (1) notice the terms that are *exactly* alike, (2) add the coefficients, and (3) leave the exponents as you found them.

Look at the following expression:

$3ab^2 + ab^2 - 4ab^2 - ab^2$

To simplify first combine all the positive terms.

$3ab^2 + ab^2 = 4ab^2$

Remember, it is understood that ab^2 is $1ab^2$.
Next combine all the negative terms.

$-4ab^2 - ab^2 = -5ab^2$

Now combine the positive and negative terms.

$4ab^2 - 5ab^2 = -ab^2$

Notice that you subtract the coefficients, $4 - 5$, but that you don't subtract the exponents.

How do you subtract in this expression?

$4x^2 - (-9x^2)$

When you subtract negative numbers, you change the sign of the negative number and then *add.* $4x^2 + (+9x^2) = 4x^2 + 9x^2 = 13x^2$.

Warm-up

Combine, or simplify, the following terms.

1. $xy^2 + y - (-5x^2y) + 3xy^2 + x^2y =$
2. $8w - 4w + 5w - 2w =$
3. $3b - (-5a) - 9 - 2a + 4 - 56 =$
4. $2x^3 - 2x^2 + 3x - 5x =$

Warm-up Answers
1. $4xy^2 + y + 6x^2y$: $-(-5x^2y)$ becomes $+5x^2y$.
2. $7w$: $-6w + 13w$ **3.** $3b + 3a - 61$: $-(-5a) = +5a$
4. $2x^3 - 2x^2 - 2x$: $+3x - 5x = -2x$

Combining Like Terms: Multiplying and Dividing To combine like terms in the expression $3x - 6(x - 4)$, the parentheses must be removed first. To remove the parentheses, multiply the -6 by each of the terms within the parentheses. Then combine like terms. Here's how to compute the example $3x - 6(x - 4)$.

Step 1 Multiply -6 by x: $-6x$.

Step 2 Multiply -6 by -4: $+24$.

Step 3 Rewrite the terms: $3x - 6x + 24$.

Step 4 Combine the terms: $-3x + 24$.

In the example $10 - (a + 10)$, no numerical value is stated in front of the parentheses. The implied value is one. (When there is no coefficient before a term, the numerical value is one.) To remove the parentheses, place a one in front of the parentheses and multiply. The simplified expression is $-1a$, or $-a$.

To simplify $a(a + 3) - 2a$, treat the a in front of the parentheses just like a number. Multiply the a by a, which gives you a^2. The a times $3 = 3a$. The simplified expression is $a^2 + a$.

When you multiply a term like $(-4x^2)(-9x^2)$, follow the rules for multiplying negative numbers. To multiply terms with exponents, *add* the exponents together. Since both terms in $(-4x^2)(-9x^2)$ are negative, the answer is positive: $-4 \times -9 = 36$. Add the exponents in x^2 times x^2 to get x^4. The answer is $36x^4$.

When you divide a term like $\frac{10y^4z^2}{-5yz^2}$, follow the rules for dividing signed numbers. (If you need to review these rules turn to page 468.) To compute, divide the coefficients $(10 \div 5)$ and *subtract* the exponents in the denominator from the exponents in the numerator (y^{4-1} and z^{2-2}). The answer would be $-2y^3z^0$. Since any number (or letter) to the zero power equals 1, the answer would be $-2y^3$.

Warm-up

Compute the following:

1. $\frac{-27a^3bc}{9a^2bc} =$ **2.** $\frac{-27x^3y^2z^3}{9x^2y^2z^2} =$

3. $(-5a^2)(-6a^3) =$

Warm-up Answers
1. $-3a$ **2.** $-3xz$ **3.** $30a^5$

32. $2x(x + 2y + 4) =$

(1) $2x + 2y + 8$
(2) $x^2 + 2y + 8$
(3) $3x + 4xy + 6x$
(4) $2x^2 + 4xy + 8x$
(5) $3x^2 + 2xy + 4$

(1) (2) (3) (4) (5)

33. $-5(2r - 3s) - 10(r + 5s) =$

(1) $-20r - 30s$ (2) $20r - 35s$
(3) $20r + 35s$ (4) $-20r + 2s$
(5) $-20r - 35s$

(1) (2) (3) (4) (5)

34. $\frac{24a^2b^4}{-3ab} =$

(1) $-8a^3b^3$ (2) $-8ab^3$
(3) $-8ab^2$ (4) $8ab^3$
(5) $8ab$

(1) (2) (3) (4) (5)

35. $(3a^2b)(4ab^2) =$

(1) $12ab$ (2) $12a^2b^2$
(3) $12a^2b^3$ (4) $12a^3b^2$
(5) $12a^3b^3$

(1) (2) (3) (4) (5)

36. $\frac{32a^2b^3c^2}{8a^2b^2c} =$

(1) $4ab^2c$ (2) $24ab^2c$
(3) $4bc$ (4) $4abc$
(5) $4a^4b^5c^3$

(1) (2) (3) (4) (5)

Directions: For each problem, choose the one best answer. Answers are on page 565.

37. Which of the following expressions correctly factors $5x^2 - 10x$?

(1) $5(x^{22}e^2 - 10x)$ (2) $5x(x - 2)$
(3) $5(x - 2x)$ (4) $x(5x - 10)$
(5) $5x^2(1 - x)$

(1) (2) (3) (4) (5)

38. Which of the following expressions correctly factors $3a^2bc + 6ab^2c$?

(1) $abc(3a + 6b)$
(2) $3(a^2bc + 2ab^2c)$
(3) $3abc(a + 2b)$
(4) $18a^2b^2c^2$
(5) $a^2b^2c^2(3a + 6b)$

(1) (2) (3) (4) (5)

39. Which of the following expressions correctly factors $16d^2e^2 - 24de$?

(1) $8de(2de - 3)$ (2) $4(4d^2e^2 - 6de)$
(3) $8(2d^2e^2 + 3e)$ (4) $de(16de - 24)$
(5) $2de(8de + 12e)$

(1) (2) (3) (4) (5)

40. Which of the following expressions correctly factors $18x^2y - 27xy$?

(1) $9x(2xy - 3y)$ (2) $9xy(2x - 3)$
(3) $x(18xy - 27y)$ (4) $xy(18x - 27)$
(5) $9(2x^2y - 3xy)$

(1) (2) (3) (4) (5)

Factoring To factor an algebraic expression, you must state the expression as a product of other terms, called *factors*. For example, you know by the distributive law that 6(7 + 8) and 6(7) + 6(8) are equal. In the second expression, you have actually factored out the 6. Each term in the first expression has been divided by 6.

Look at the following algebraic expression.

$ab + ac$

What term is common to both expressions? Since the *a* appears in both expressions, it can be factored out. You are actually dividing each expression by *a*.

$a(b + c)$

Look at the following example.

$4x^2y + 3x^2z$

Notice that x^2 is common to both terms of the expression. To factor the expression, take the x^2 out of each term and write the expression as follows.

$x^2 (4y + 3z)$

Look at this next example.

$12d^2e + 16de^2$

To factor this expression, you need to find all the common elements to the two terms. Notice that 12 and 16 are both multiples of 4; therefore, 4 can be factored out of each expression. Also, *d* and *e* are both common to each expression, so each can be factored out.

First factor $4de$ out of $12d^2e$. Four goes into 12 three times. You also remember when you divide terms with exponents, you subtract the exponents. If you factor de out of d^2e, you are left with *d*. So your first term would be $3d$.

Next factor $4de$ out of $16de^2$. Four goes into 16 four times. If you factor de out of de^2, you are left with *e*. So,

$12d^2e + 16de^2 = 4de(3d + 4e)$

Notice that no common terms are left within the parentheses.

Read the information on this and the next page before you do the problems in the white columns on either page.

Substitution If you know the value of a variable within an algebraic expression, you can solve the expression by substituting the value for the variable. This is called evaluating the expression or *substitution.*

Examples

1. If $n = 5$, find the value of $5 + n$.

$5 + n =$
$5 + 5 = 10$

2. If $x = 3$ and $y = 2$, find the value of $3xy$.

$3xy =$
$3 \times (3)(2) = 18$

3. If $a = -27$, find the value of $\frac{a}{9}$.

$\frac{a}{9} = \frac{-27}{9} = -3$

It is important to remember that when the answer is negative, you must write the negative sign in your answer. Find the value of

$a^2 + b^2$

if $a = 3$ and $b = 5$.

$a^2 + b^2 = 3^2 + 5^2 =$
$9 + 25 = 34$

Step 1 Substitute numbers for letters: $3^2 + 5^2 =$.

Step 2 Since no numbers are in parentheses, you first square the numbers: $3^2 = 9$; $5^2 = 25$. (If you don't remember the order of operations rules, turn to page 524 and review them.) Now the problem reads $9 + 25 =$.

Step 3 Add the numbers together: $9 + 25 = 34$. The answer is 34.

Warm-up

Use substitution to solve the following:

1. If $a = 5$, $b = 7$, and $c = 4$, find the value of $6 - a(b + c)$.

2. Find the value of $cd + 2d + 3f$ if $c = 4$, $d = -10$, and $f = -5$.

3. If $m = 3$, $r = -7$, and $s = 2$, find the value of $2m - r - s$.

Warm-up Answers

1. −49. Substitute the numbers for letters: $6 - 5(7 + 4)$. First perform the operation inside the parentheses, $7 + 4 = 11$. Now the problem reads $6 - 5(11)$. Multiply: $5 \times 11 = 55$; write the problem as $6 - 55 = -49$. **2.** −75. Substitute the numbers for letters: $(4)(-10) + (2)(-10) + (3)(-5)$. Then multiply: $(-40) + (-20) + (-15) = -75$. **3.** 11. Substitute the numbers for letters: $2(3) - (-7) - 2$. Perform the multiplication operation first: $2(3) = 6$, so you have $6 - (-7) - 2$. When you subtract −7 from 6, change the −7 to +7 and add: $6 + 7 - 2 = 11$.

41. Find the value of $\frac{d^2}{e}$ if $d = 4$ and $e = -2$.

(1) −14 (2) −8 (3) −4
(4) 8 (5) 18

① ② ③ ④ ⑤

42. Evaluate $a^2 + b$ if $a = 2$ and $b = 4$.

(1) −8 (2) −1 (3) 1
(4) 4 (5) 8

① ② ③ ④ ⑤

43. If $x = 2$, $y = -4$, and $z = 6$, evaluate $-xyz - 2y$.

(1) −64 (2) −40 (3) −32
(4) +32 (5) +56

① ② ③ ④ ⑤

44. If $b = 10$ and $a = 5$, evaluate $\frac{\frac{1}{2}b}{a}$.

(1) 0 (2) 1 (3) 4
(4) 5 (5) 10

① ② ③ ④ ⑤

45. If $x = 0$ and $y = 5$, evaluate $7x^2 + 5y^2$.

(1) 17 (2) 18 (3) 25
(4) 125 (5) 132

① ② ③ ④ ⑤

Directions: For each problem, choose the *one* best answer. Answers are on page 565.

46. $n - 5 = 17$
$n =$

(1) -22 (2) -12 (3) 12
(4) 15 (5) 22

① ② ③ ④ ⑤

47. $9 + r = 18$
$r =$

(1) 2 (2) 3 (3) 6 (4) 8 (5) 9

① ② ③ ④ ⑤

48. $y + 12 = 93$
$y =$

(1) -81 (2) 18 (3) 49
(4) 81 (5) 105

① ② ③ ④ ⑤

49. $12 = x + 9$
$x =$

(1) 3 (2) 4 (3) 5
(4) 6 (5) 21

① ② ③ ④ ⑤

50. $12 = s - 8$
$s =$

(1) 4 (2) 16 (3) 20
(4) 24 (5) 36

① ② ③ ④ ⑤

Solving Equations Using Addition and Subtraction An **equation** like $5 + x = 25$ means that the two amounts—$5 + x$ and 25—are equal. The x is the unknown number. When you find the value of x, you have solved the equation. Look at $5 + x = 25$ for a moment. You may realize that $x = 20$. To check, substitute 20 for x in the equation: $5 + 20 = 25$.

When you need to solve an equation, your goal is to get the unknown on one side of the equation and all the numbers on the other side. To isolate x on one side of $5 + x = 25$, you could subtract 5 from the left side of the equation; then you'd have $x = 25$. But that's not correct because when you add 5 and 25, you don't get 25. When you solve equations, you must remember one main rule: What you do to one side of the equation you *must* do to the other side.

You can't just take 5 from one side. You must subtract 5 from both sides.

$$\begin{array}{rcr} 5 + x &=& 25 \\ -5 & & -5 \\ \hline 0 + x &=& 20 \end{array} \quad \text{or } x = 20$$

The process used to isolate an unknown on one side of an equation by itself is called the **inverse operation.**

The inverse operation of addition is subtraction. To eliminate an added number, you subtract.

The inverse operation of subtraction is addition. To eliminate a subtracted number from an equation, you add. For example, to solve the equation $z - 20 = 40$, you need to get rid of -20. So add 20 to both sides of the equation.

$$\begin{array}{rcr} z - 20 &=& 40 \\ +20 &=& +20 \\ \hline z - 0 &=& 60 \end{array} \quad \text{or } z = 60$$

Coming to Terms

equation algebraic statement that says two values are equal

inverse operation the opposite operation, used to get an unknown on one side of the equal sign

Warm-up

Solve for the unknown.

1. $a + 17 = 42$
2. $b - 9 = 21$
3. $7 + c = -26$
4. $12 - d = -6$

Warm-up Answers
1. $a = 25$ **2.** $b = 30$ **3.** $c = -33$ **4.** $d = 18$

Solving Equations Using Multiplication and Division To isolate the p in $5p = 60$, you must realize that $5p$ is a multiplication expression.

The inverse operation of multiplication is division. So you must divide both sides by 5:

$$\frac{5p}{5} = \frac{60}{5}$$
$$p = 12$$

To isolate r in $1 = r/9$, you need to realize that r is being divided by 9.

The inverse operation of division is multiplication. In the example given, multiply both sides by 9:

$$1 = \frac{r}{9}$$
$$1 \times 9 = \frac{r}{9} \times 9$$
$$9 = r$$

Warm-up

Solve the following single-operation equations.

1. $32p = 224$

2. $16 = \frac{r}{25}$

3. $95g = 570$

4. $6 = \frac{h}{17}$

5. $19t = 513$

6. $\frac{x}{9} = 31$

7. $3.6s = 4.32$

8. $\frac{w}{7.8} = 5.9$

Warm-up Answers

1. $p = 7$

$\frac{\cancel{32}p}{\cancel{32}} = \frac{\cancel{224}^{7}}{\cancel{32}}$ Divide both sides by 32. Notice that 32 cancels out on the left side.

2. $r = 400$

$16 \times 25 = \frac{r}{25} \times 25$ Multiply both sides by 25.

$16 \times 25 = r$

$400 = r$

3. $g = 6$

$\frac{\cancel{95}^{1}g}{\cancel{95}^{1}} = \frac{\cancel{570}^{1}}{\cancel{95}^{1}}$ Divide both sides by 95. Note that 95 cancels out on the left side.

4. $h = 102$

$17 \times 6 = \frac{h}{\cancel{17}^{1}} \times \frac{\cancel{17}^{1}}{1}$ Multiply each side by 17.

$17 \times 6 = h$

$102 = h$

5. $t = 27$

$\frac{\cancel{19}t}{\cancel{19}} = \frac{\cancel{513}^{27}}{\cancel{19}}$ Divide both sides by 19.

6. $x = 279$

$9(\frac{x}{9}) = 9 \times 31$ Multiply both sides by 9.

$x = 9 \times 31$

$x = 279$

7. $s = 1.2$

$\frac{\cancel{3.6}s}{\cancel{3.6}} = \frac{\cancel{4.32}^{1.2}}{\cancel{3.6}}$ Divide both sides by 3.6.

8. $w = 46.02$

$7.8 \times \frac{w}{7.8} = 5.9 \times 7.8$ Multiply both sides by 7.8.

$w = 46.02$

51. $3m = 18$
$m =$

(1) -6 (2) -5 (3) 5
(4) 6 (5) 15

① ② ③ ④ ⑤

52. $\frac{y}{2} = 5$

$y =$

(1) -11 (2) 5 (3) 10
(4) 11 (5) 12

① ② ③ ④ ⑤

53. $4a = 32$
$a =$

(1) 5 (2) 7 (3) 8
(4) 12 (5) 38

① ② ③ ④ ⑤

54. $15 = \frac{b}{3}$
$b =$

(1) 5 (2) 18 (3) 31
(4) 45 (5) 48

① ② ③ ④ ⑤

55. $93 = 3x$
$x =$

(1) 13 (2) 31 (3) 90
(4) 96 (5) 279

① ② ③ ④ ⑤

Directions: For each problem, choose the one best answer. Answers are on pages 565–566.

56. $8z + 5 = 14 + 11z$
$z =$

(1) -3 (2) -1 (3) 1
(4) 2 (5) 3

① ② ③ ④ ⑤

57. $9a - 13 = 13 - 4a$
$a =$

(1) -2 (2) 0 (3) 1
(4) 2 (5) 3

① ② ③ ④ ⑤

58. $8b - 13 + 3b = 12 + 5b - 7$
$b =$

(1) -3 (2) -1 (3) 2
(4) 3 (5) 4

① ② ③ ④ ⑤

59. $6y + 7 = 3 + 8y$
$y =$

(1) -4 (2) -3 (3) -2
(4) 2 (5) 3

① ② ③ ④ ⑤

60. $\frac{3x}{2} = 5x - 14$
$x =$

(1) 4 (2) -4 (3) 3
(4) -3 (5) -2

① ② ③ ④ ⑤

Solving Equations with Unknowns on Both Sides of the Equal Sign It takes three steps to solve equations such as $4x + 5 = 17 - 2x$ which have unknowns on both sides of the equal sign.

Step 1 Use an inverse operation to get all the unknowns to one side of the equation.

$$\begin{array}{l} 4x + 5 = 17 - 2x \\ \underline{+2x \qquad\quad + 2x} \quad \text{Add } 2x \text{ to both sides.} \\ 6x + 5 = 17 + 0 \quad \text{or } 6x + 5 = 17 \end{array}$$

Step 2 Isolate the unknown on one side by removing the 5 from the left side of the equation. Since 5 is a positive number, subtract 5 from both sides to remove it.

$$\begin{array}{l} 6x + 5 = 17 \\ \quad\ - 5 \quad -5 \\ 6x + 0 = 12 \text{ or } 6x = 12 \end{array}$$

Step 3 To find the value of one x, you must use the inverse operation of division because $6x$ is a multiplication expression.

$$\frac{6x}{6} = \frac{12}{6}$$

When $6x$ is divided by 6, the 6s cancel out.

$$\frac{6}{6} = 1.$$

12 divided by 6 $= 2$, so $x = 2$.

When solving equations, you use addition or subtraction before you use multiplication or division. To check the solution of the equation, substitute the value for x in the equation.

$$\begin{array}{r} 4x + 5 = 17 - 2x \\ 4(2) + 5 = 17 - 2(2) \\ 8 + 5 = 17 - 4 = 13. \end{array}$$

Warm-up

Solve the following equations.

1. $b + 5 = 5b - 15$ **2.** $5x + 75 = 2x + 51$

Warm-up Answers

1. $b = 5$

$$\begin{array}{rcrl} b + 5 = & & 5b - 15 & \\ \underline{-5b \qquad} & & \underline{-5b \qquad} & \text{Subtract } 5b \text{ from both sides.} \\ -4b + 5 = & & -15 & \\ \underline{\quad - 5} & & \underline{- 5} & \text{Subtract 5 from both sides.} \\ -4b & = & -20 & \\ \frac{-\not{4}b^{1}}{-\not{4}^{1}} & = & \frac{-\not{20}^{5}}{-\not{4}^{1}} & \text{Divide each side by } -4. \end{array}$$

2. $x = -8$

$$\begin{array}{rcrl} 5x + 75 = & & 2x + 51 & \\ \underline{-2x \qquad} & & \underline{-2x \qquad} & \text{Subtract } 2x \text{ from both sides.} \\ 3x + 75 = & & +51 & \\ \underline{\quad - 75} & & \underline{- 75} & \text{Subtract 75 from both sides.} \\ 3x & = & -24 & \\ \frac{\not{3}^{1}x}{\not{3}^{1}} & = & \frac{-\not{24}^{8}}{\not{3}^{1}} & \text{Divide each side by 3.} \end{array}$$

Translating Word Problems into Equations
Sometimes on the GED Mathematics Test you will be asked to set up a problem rather than solve it. You should know how to convert a word problem into an algebraic expression. If you are asked to solve the problem, you should always first set up the problem, then solve it.

To translate a word problem into an equation, follow these four rules.

Rule 1. Read the problem carefully.

Rule 2. Select a letter to represent the unknown.

Rule 3. Identify the left and right sides of the equation.

Rule 4. Write the verbal statement in algebraic form.

Look at the following example.

■ Mr. Timms divided his coin collection equally among his 5 nephews and himself. If each nephew received 17 coins, how many coins did Mr. Timms have in his collection?

Since Mr. Timms shared the coins with his nephews and also kept some of the coins, the coins were actually divided into 6 groups (his 5 nephews plus himself). You know you want to find the number of coins Mr. Timms had in his original collection. This number is the unknown. Label the unknown *c*. You know that *c* was divided by 6 to get 17. Now write that information in an equation.

$\frac{c}{6} = 17$

This is the set-up for the word problem.

Warm-up
Set up an equation for the following problem.

■ Marcy bought a sweater for $22.95. She received $17.05 in change. How much did she give the cashier?

Warm-up Answer
$x - \$22.95 = \$17.05$

61. After a weight loss of 20 pounds, Dorothy weighed 145 pounds. Which equation below would show her original weight?

(1) $20 + w = 145$ (2) $w - 20 = 145$
(3) $20 - w = 145$ (4) $145 + w = 20$
(5) $145 + 20 = w$

(1) (2) (3) (4) (5)

62. A salesclerk earned $15,000 in a year. Which equation shows his monthly salary?

(1) $12s = \$15,000$ (2) $\frac{12}{s} = \$15,000$
(3) $12 = \$15,000\,s$ (4) $s = \$15,000(12)$
(5) $s = \frac{12}{\$15,000}$

(1) (2) (3) (4) (5)

63. Two times a woman's age is 48. Which equation below shows the woman's age?

(1) $a = 48(2)$ (2) $2 = 48a$
(3) $\frac{48}{a} = 2$ (4) $2a = 48(2)$
(5) $2a = 48$

(1) (2) (3) (4) (5)

64. A large piece of cable wire was cut into 7 pieces. Each piece was 2 feet long. Which equation shows how long the original piece was?

(1) $2c = 7$ (2) $c = 7 + 2$
(3) $\frac{c}{7} = 2$ (4) $\frac{7}{c} = 2$
(5) $\frac{2}{c} = 7$

(1) (2) (3) (4) (5)

65. The price per pound for hamburger rose by $0.30. It is now $1.59. Which equation shows the original price?

(1) $p = \$1.59 + \$0.30$
(2) $p - \$0.30 = \$1.59$
(3) $p - \$1.59 = \$0.30$
(4) $p + \$0.30 = \$1.59$
(5) $p(\$0.30) = \$1.59$

(1) (2) (3) (4) (5)

Directions: For each problem, choose the one best answer. Answers are on page 566.

66. The tax on furniture is 4%. If the cost of a sofa is \$595 before the tax is added, what is the final price?

(1) \$571.20 (2) \$595.00
(3) \$618.00 (4) \$618.80
(5) Insufficient data is given to solve the problem.

(1) (2) (3) (4) (5)

67. Erica paid \$2.37 for 3 pounds of peaches. What is the price of one pound of peaches?

(1) \$0.30 (2) \$0.69
(3) \$0.79 (4) \$0.80
(5) Insufficient data is given to solve the problem.

(1) (2) (3) (4) (5)

68. Buck paid \$13.50 for 2 pairs of jeans that had been discounted. What was the original price of the jeans?

(1) \$9.00 (2) \$13.50
(3) \$17.00 (4) \$22.50
(5) Insufficient data is given to solve the problem.

(1) (2) (3) (4) (5)

69. Kacey cut some wrapping paper into lengths of $2\frac{1}{4}$ feet each. When she finished cutting, she had 13 pieces. What was the length in feet of the original piece?

(1) 27 (2) $27\frac{1}{4}$ (3) $28\frac{1}{2}$

(4) $28\frac{3}{4}$ (5) $29\frac{1}{4}$

(1) (2) (3) (4) (5)

70. Toby's manuscript cost \$997.50 to be typed. If the manuscript is 350 pages long, how much did the typist charge per page?

(1) \$3.85 (2) \$3.50 (3) \$2.85
(4) \$2.75 (5) \$2.50

(1) (2) (3) (4) (5)

Using Equations to Solve Word Problems
Now that you know how to set up a word problem as an equation, you can solve the word problem by solving the equation.

Look at the example below.

■ Mrs. Sharp received a raise of \$50 every 2 weeks for a year. By the end of the year her salary was \$26,000. What was Mrs. Sharp's salary at the beginning of the year?

You know you want to find Mrs. Sharp's salary before the raise. Assign s to represent her original salary. You know that she received \$50 every two weeks. Since 52 weeks are in one year, Mrs. Sharp received \$50 twenty-six times during the year ($52 \div 2 = 26$). You also know that by the end of the year Mrs. Sharp's salary was \$26,000. So, Mrs. Sharp's original salary (s) plus the raise ($26 \times \$50$) equals her salary at the end of the year.

$s + (26 \times \$50) = \$26,000$

Now solve the equation for s.

$s + \$1,300 = \$26,000$
$s + \$1,300 - \$1,300 = \$26,000 - \$1,300$
$s = \$24,700$

$\$24,700 + \$1,300 = \$26,000$

Mrs. Sharp's salary at the beginning of the year was \$24,700.

Warm-up
Set up and solve.

■ Theo jogs 6.5 miles a day. If he has jogged a total of 32.5 miles so far this month, how many days has he jogged?

Warm-up Answer
$6.5x = 32.5$
$\frac{6.5x}{6.5} = \frac{32.5}{6.5}$
$x = 5$ days
$6.5(5) = 32.5$

Inequalities An equation is an algebraic statement in which two values are equal. An **inequality** is an algebraic statement in which two values are *not equal.* Four symbols are used to express the fact that two values are not equal:

$<$ means less than
$>$means greater than
$\leq$ means less than or equal to
$\geq$ means greater than or equal to

To read the inequality $x \leq 20$, substitute the words *less than or equal to* for the symbol $\leq$. An equation has one correct answer, but an inequality has a **solution set,** or group of correct answers. In the inequality $x \leq 20$, x is less than or equal to 20. The *solution set* of correct answers includes 20 and all numbers *less than* 20.

To find the solution to the inequality $3 + 8x \geq 35$, you use inverse operations in exactly the same way you used them to solve equations.

$3 + 8x \geq 35$

Step 1 Subtract 3 from both sides of the inequality.

$$\begin{array}{r} 3 + 8x \geq 35 \\ \underline{-3 \qquad\; -3} \\ 8x \geq 32 \end{array}$$

Step 2 Divide both sides of the inequality by 8.

$\frac{8x}{8} \geq \frac{32}{8}$ $\qquad x \geq 4$

The answer is read, "*x* is greater than or equal to 4." The solution set includes all numbers that are equal to or greater than 4.

Coming to Terms

inequality algebraic statement in which two values are not equal
solution set group of correct answers to an inequality

Warm-up

1. Solve the inequality $6 + z \leq 8$.
   a. $z \leq 2$ **b.** $z \leq 3$ **c.** $z \leq 5$
2. Solve the inequality $x - 22 < 9$.
   a. $x < 32$ **b.** $x < 31$ **c.** $x < 30$

Warm-up Answers
1. a, any number less than or equal to 2
2. b, any number less than 31

71. Which of the following belongs to the solution set for the inequality $c + 2 \leq 10$?

    (1) 8 (2) 9 (3) 10
    (4) 11 (5) 12

    ① ② ③ ④ ⑤

72. Which of the following belongs to the solution set for the inequality $2x + 14 > 40$?

    (1) 7 (2) 9 (3) 10
    (4) 13 (5) 16

    ① ② ③ ④ ⑤

73. Find the solution to $3y + 7 \geq 40$.

    (1) $y \geq 5$ (2) $y \geq 6$
    (3) $y \geq 7$ (4) $y \geq 10$
    (5) $y \geq 11$

    ① ② ③ ④ ⑤

74. Find the solution to $5x - 9 < 36$.

    (1) $x < 45$ (2) $x < 36$
    (3) $x < 12$ (4) $x < 9$
    (5) $x < 6$

    ① ② ③ ④ ⑤

75. Find the solution to $\frac{1}{4}x + 6 < 2$.

    (1) $x < -16$ (2) $x < -4$
    (3) $x < -2$ (4) $x < 17$
    (5) $x < 32$

    ① ② ③ ④ ⑤

Directions: For each problem, choose the one best answer. Answers are on pages 566–567.

76. Fran and Steve together have \$250. Steve has 4 times as much money as Fran. How much money does Fran have?

(1) \$10 (2) \$50 (3) \$100
(4) \$150 (5) \$200

(1) (2) (3) (4) (5)

77. There were 35 people at the library. There were 1/4 as many people reading novels as there were people reading magazines. How many magazine readers were at the library?

(1) 7 (2) 9 (3) 18
(4) 28 (5) 31

(1) (2) (3) (4) (5)

78. In 16 years Terri will be 3 times as old as she is now. How old is Terri?

(1) 4 (2) 8 (3) 12
(4) 16 (5) 20

(1) (2) (3) (4) (5)

79. Elliott spent \$27.50 less on a chain saw than he spent on a drill. If he spent \$105.80 altogether, how much did each item cost?

(1) saw \$27.50, drill \$78.30
(2) saw \$39.15, drill \$66.65
(3) saw \$94.15, drill \$66.65
(4) saw \$66.65, drill \$39.15
(5) saw \$78.30, drill \$27.50

(1) (2) (3) (4) (5)

80. Felix builds decks to earn extra money. In the spring he built 4 times as many decks as he did in the summer. If he built 85 decks altogether, how many decks did he build in the summer?

(1) 17 (2) 68 (3) 85
(4) 95 (5) 98

(1) (2) (3) (4) (5)

Finding Two Unknowns Some questions on the GED Mathematics Test may require you to use an algebraic equation with two unknown numbers. The best way to develop your skill with this kind of problem is to study the explanations of the problem worked below.

■ Together Henry and Helen have \$65. If Henry has \$15 more than Helen, how much money does each one have?

Step 1 Label the two unknowns algebraically.
x = the amount of money Helen has
$x + 15$ = the amount of money Henry has

Step 2 Write an algebraic expression and solve for the unknown.

You know that the two amounts of money have the sum of \$65, so 65 is the right side of your equation. The word *together* tells you to add the two amounts on the left side.

$x + x + 15 = 65$
$2x + 15 = 65$ Combine like terms.
$-15 \quad -15$ Subtract 15 from both sides of the equation.
$2x + 0 = 50$
$\frac{2x}{2} = \frac{50}{2}$ Divide both sides of the equation by 2.
$x = 25$ the first amount
$x + 15 = 40$ the second amount

Check your work with substitution.

$x + x + 15 = 65$
$25 + 25 + 15 = 65$

Helen has \$25, and Henry has \$40.

☑ A Test-Taking Tip

On the GED Mathematics Test some questions may ask for both unknown numbers, and some may ask for only one of the numbers. When you are asked for only one number, you need to be certain that you mark the correct one.

Equations on a Grid: Point of Intersection
You can use your knowledge of geometry and coordinate grids to graph algebraic equations. As you learned, only two points are needed to draw a line on a grid. If you know two pairs of numbers that fit in an equation with two unknowns, you can consider them ordered pairs, plot those two points, and connect them to form a line. The coordinates of any point on that line would also solve the equation.

Suppose you wanted to graph two equations on the same coordinate grid. One of three things could occur.

1. The lines would be parallel and would never have a point of intersection. This means that the two equations do not share any solution.

2. The two lines might be drawn in exactly the same spot. One line would actually be on top of the other. This means all the solutions of one equation would fit into the other equation.

3. The two lines would cross, or intersect, at one point on the grid. The two lines would have only one point in common. This point is known as the **point of intersection.** The coordinates of the point of intersection make up the only solution that the two equations have in common.

Suppose you are given two equations and are asked to find the point of intersection. Look at the following two equations.

$y = 2x + 3$ $\qquad$ $y = x + 5$

What is the point of intersection?

Step 1 Set up the two equations so that they equal each other.

$2x + 3 = x + 5$

Step 2 Solve for x.

$x + 3 = 5$
$x = 2$

Step 3 Substitute 2 for x to solve for y.

$y = 2(2) + 3$
$y = 4 + 3$
$y = 7$

The common solution for the two equations is (2,7).

Coming To Terms

point of intersection point on a coordinate grid where two lines cross or intersect.

81. What is the point of intersection of the equations $y = -3x + 8$ and $y = 4x - 13$?

(1) $(-1, 3)$ (2) $(1, -3)$
(3) $(3, -1)$ (4) $(-3, 1)$
(5) $(-3, -3)$

(1) (2) (3) (4) (5)

82. What is the point of intersection of the equations $y = 2x + 3$ and $y = 3x - 2$?

(1) $(5, 13)$ (2) $(13, 5)$
(3) $(5, -5)$ (4) $(-5, 12)$
(5) $(-5, -13)$

(1) (2) (3) (4) (5)

83. What is the point of intersection of the equations $y = \frac{x}{2}$ and $y = x - 6$?

(1) $(-6, -12)$ (2) $(6, 12)$
(3) $(12, 6)$ (4) $(-12, -6)$
(5) $(6, 6)$

(1) (2) (3) (4) (5)

84. What is the point of intersection of the equations $y = 3x + 3$ and $y = 2x + 2$?

(1) $(0,0)$ (2) $(-1, -1)$
(3) $(0, -1)$ (4) $(-1, 0)$
(5) $(1, 0)$

(1) (2) (3) (4) (5)

85. What is the point of intersection of the equations $y = 3x - 1$ and $y = x - 7$?

(1) $(3, -10)$ (2) $(-3, -10)$
(3) $(-3, 10)$ (4) $(10, 3)$
(5) $(-10, -3)$

(1) (2) (3) (4) (5)

Quadratic Equations Working with quadratic equations can be very involved. You will only have to know some basics about this type of equation for the GED Mathematics Test. A **quadratic equation** is an equation that has a variable with an exponent of 2. The equation below is quadratic.

$x^2 + 3x - 7 = 0$

Multiplying To solve a quadratic equation, you first need to understand how to multiply algebraic expressions.

Suppose you were asked to multiply

$(a + b)(a + c)$.

Step 1 Multiply each letter in the second set of parentheses by the first letter in the first set of parentheses.

$a(a + c) = a^2 + ac$

Step 2 Multiply each letter in the second set of parentheses by the second letter in the first set of parentheses.

$b(a + c) = ab + bc$

Step 3 Combine the answers.

$a^2 + ac + ab + bc$

So, $(a + b)(a + c) = a^2 + ac + ab + bc$

Since the equation has the exponent of 2 in the first term, the answer is a quadratic equation.

Warm-up

Multiply.

1. $(m + n)(m + 2s)$
2. $(2p + q)(p - 3r)$

Factoring Now, suppose you are given the equation $x^2 + xz + xy + yz$ and are asked to factor it. (Review page 532 for factoring.) Factoring is actually the reverse of the multiplication that you just did.

Step 1 Look at the first two terms.

$x^2 + xz$

Factor out the common term of x. You are left with $x(x + z)$.

Step 2 Look at the second two terms.

$xy + yz$

Factor out the common term of y. You are left with $y(x + z)$.

Step 3 Combine the answers from steps 1 and 2.

$x(x + z) + y(x + z)$

Step 4 Notice that the letters in parentheses are the same. So, your answer would be

$(x + y)(x + z)$.

Coming to Terms

quadratic equation equation that has a variable with an exponent of 2. A quadratic equation usually has 2 different roots, but it may have only one.

Warm-up

Factor the following quadratic equations.

1. $d^2 + df + 2de + 2ef$
2. $g^2 - gj - hg + hj$

Warm-up Answers

1. $m^2 + 2ms + mn + 2ns$ **2.** $2p^2 - 6pr + pq - 3qr$

Warm-up Answers

1. $(d + 2e)(d + f)$ **2.** $(g - h)(g - j)$

Solving a Quadratic Equation Suppose you were asked to solve the quadratic equation $y^2 - 4y - 5 = 0$. Because the equation has a term with an exponent, the equation usually has two solutions.

Step 1 Since the first term is y^2, you know that the first term in each set of parentheses will be y. So factor out the y.

$(y \quad)(y \quad)$

Step 2 Look at the coefficient of the second term. The coefficient is -4. Now look at the last term (-5). Think of two numbers that will equal -4 when added and -5 when multiplied. The two numbers are $+1$ and -5. Place each of these numbers in the parentheses.

$(y + 1)(y - 5) = 0$

Step 3 Since the equation is equal to 0, either $y + 1$ or $y - 5$ must be equal to 0.

Write the equation $y + 1 = 0$ and solve for y.

$y + 1 = 0$
$-1 = -1$ Add -1 to both sides.
$y = -1$

Write the equation $y - 5 = 0$ and solve for y.

$y - 5 = 0$
$+5 = +5$ Add 5 to both sides.
$y = 5$

Step 4 Substitute your answers, one at a time, into the original equation $y^2 - 4y - 5 = 0$.

$-(1)^2 - 4(-1) - 5 = 0$
$1 + 4 - 5 = 0$

-1 is a correct solution for the equation.

Now substitute 5 into the original equation.

$(5)^2 - 4(5) - 5 = 0$
$25 - 20 - 5 = 0$

5 is also a correct solution for the equation.

So y can equal -1 or 5 in the equation $y^2 - 4y + 5 = 0$. The solution of the equation is both -1 and 5.

Warm-up

Solve the following quadratic equation.

1. $d^2 + d - 12 = 0$ **2.** $w^2 - 6w = -8$

Warm-up Answers

1. 3, -4 **2.** 4, 2

Directions: For each problem, choose the one best answer. Answers are on page 567.

86. Solve for x.
$x^2 + 2x - 8 = 0$

(1) -4, 2 (2) -2, -4 (3) 2 only
(4) -4, 3 (5) -3, 2

(1) (2) (3) (4) (5)

87. Solve for r.
$r^2 + 3r = 10$

(1) 3, 4 (2) 2, 0 (3) -3 only
(4) 2 only (5) 2, -5

(1) (2) (3) (4) (5)

88. Solve for w.
$w^2 - 4w + 3 = 0$

(1) 1 only (2) -3, -1 (3) 3, 1
(4) 4, 1 (5) 5, -1

(1) (2) (3) (4) (5)

89. Solve for p.
$p^2 - 2p = 15$.

(1) -3 only (2) 5 only (3) -3, 5
(4) 5, -5 (5) -5, -3

(1) (2) (3) (4) (5)

90. Solve for c.
$c^2 + 3c = 18$

(1) 3, -6 (2) -3, -6 (3) 3, 6
(4) 3 only (5) -3 only

(1) (2) (3) (4) (5)

Directions: For each problem, choose the one best answer. Answers are on page 567.

91. If $e = -9$ and $d = 20$, evaluate $d - (e^2)$.

(1) -7 (2) -20 (3) -32
(4) -61 (5) -101

(1) (2) (3) (4) (5)

92. $\frac{40abc}{-5ac} =$

(1) $-8abc$ (2) $35b$ (3) $8abc$
(4) $-8b$ (5) $35abc$

(1) (2) (3) (4) (5)

93. $3a - 10 = a$
$a =$

(1) -5 (2) -3 (3) 2
(4) 4 (5) 5

(1) (2) (3) (4) (5)

94. The ratio of snorklers to scuba divers at a resort was 8 to 1. If there were a total of 270 tourists who either snorkled or dove, how many were snorklers?

(1) 30 (2) 120 (3) 180
(4) 240 (5) 250

(1) (2) (3) (4) (5)

95. Melody had $292 in her savings account. Her bank gives $8\frac{1}{2}\%$ interest on savings accounts. How much money will Melody have in her account after she receives the interest?

(1) $316.82 (2) $299.90
(3) 292.00 (4) $290.90
(5) $282.00

(1) (2) (3) (4) (5)

96. Yolanda is half the age of her brother. Together, their ages total 15. How old is Yolanda?

(1) 5 (2) 6 (3) 10
(4) 12 (5) 15

(1) (2) (3) (4) (5)

Algebra Review

Three things to remember when you multiply variables with exponents are

1. Make sure you handle the + or − signs correctly.

2. Make sure you *multiply* the coefficients.

3. Make sure you *add* the exponents if the variables are the same.

As you used the order of operations for numerical expressions, you must use the same order of operations for algebraic expressions. You must memorize this order of operations because it will not be listed on the GED Test.

Know the ideas behind the commutative, associative, and distributive laws. On the GED Test you will not be asked to recall the names of these laws, but you will need to use them.

☑ A Test-Taking Tip

Read carefully. On the GED Mathematics Test you may be given two equations and asked the value of *either a* or *b.* Be sure to find *exactly* what the question asks for. If you are asked to find *x,* don't spend time finding *y.*

Need a Hint for Number 94?

The item tells you that the ratio of snorklers to scuba divers is 8 to 1. What would be the ratio of tourists who did both sports compared to the number of tourists who only snorkled? Use this ratio to find how many tourists were also snorklers.

Answers—Mathematics

Sample Test Items

Whole Numbers
(pages 413–422)

1. (4) $3,250

```
 $12,000
 − 7,500 amount husband
         receives
  $4,500
 − 1,250 amount oldest daughter
         receives
  $3,250 amount youngest
         daughter receives
```

2. (1) 457

```
      392 nickels
      487 dimes
      209 quarters
 +     58 half-dollars
    1,146
    1,603 pennies
 −  1,146 other coins
      457
```

3. (1) $2,520

```
 $1,550
 +  942
 $2,492 total group expenses
 $5,012
 −2,492
 $2,520 for personal expenses
```

4. (5) Insufficient data

You know nothing about the number of books he keeps or the number he gives to the library.

5. (1) $200

```
   $5.00
 ×    40 hours
 $200.00
```

6. (3) 676

```
    52 miles
 ×  13 hours
   156
   52
   676 miles
```

7. (4) 4,272

```
    178
 ×   24
    712
   3 56
  4,272 rabbits
```

8. (1) 3,640

```
   308 doz        3,696
 ×  12 eggs      −   56
   616            3,640 eggs
  3 08
 3,696 eggs
```

9. (2) (9 × $5) + $3

9 yards at $5 a yard means multiply those two numbers. Then add the $3 spent for the pattern.

10. (5) Insufficient data

You do not know how many sets were sold in June.

11. (5) Insufficient data

You do not know how many hours Mr. Dallas worked at night.

12. (4) $618

```
  $12      $18      $168
  ×14      ×25      +450
   48       90      $618
  12       36
 $168     $450
```

13. (2) $17

```
 $177                        $20
 + 46                       × 12
 $223 total of bills          40
                             20
                            $240

    3 1
  $2 4 0 total amount given to teller
  −223 total she owes
  $ 17 her change
```

14. (4) $182,500

```
 $1,112,500 new budget
 −  985,000 old budget
   $127,500 rise from last year
   $127,500
 +   55,000 donations
   $182,500
```

15. (3) 43

```
   43 mph   Divide miles by
 3)129      numbers of hours.
```

16. (3) $4

```
  12
 × 2
  24 pencils

    $4      Divide dollars by
 24)$96     pencils.
    96
     0
```

17. (2) 13

Divide the number of bottles filled in a minute by 12 to find how many cases are filled.

```
    13 cases
 12)156 bottles
    12
     36
     36
      0
```

18. (5) $2

Divide 75 cents by 3 to find the cost of one bar of soap. Then multiply by 8 to find the cost of 8 bars.

```
  25 cents         25
 3)75            ×  8
                  200 cents = $2
```

19. (3) 32

Divide the total number of miles traveled by the number of gallons of gas used to find the average number of miles per gallon.

```
     32 miles per gallon
 15)480 miles traveled
    45
     30
     30
      0
```

20. (2) $\frac{168 + 72}{16}$

First add the number of bulbs together. Then divide this total number of bulbs by 16 bulbs per row.

21. (4) 528

First add the number of cars that go to the island in June and July. Then divide by 18 to find how many trips the ferry makes.

```
   3,726              528 trips
 +5,778          18)9,504 cars
   9,504 cars       90
                     50
                     36
                     144
                     144
                       0
```

22. (3) 420

First divide 17,043 by 39 to find the number of phones that were checked. Then subtract the number of damaged phones to find the number of phones that were not damaged.

```
     437 phones      437 phones
39)17,043                checked
   156
    144           -   17 damaged
    117                  phones
     273
     273             420 phones
       0                 not
                         damaged
```

23. (1) 3

First divide the total number of oranges by the number of oranges eaten each day to find how many days it will take for the oranges to be eaten. Then divide that number by 7 to convert days to weeks.

```
    21 days              3 weeks
17)357 oranges        7)21
   34                   21
    17                   0
    17
     0
```

24. (3) $441

First divide 2,184 by 250 to find how many pairs of shoes she had to buy. Then multiply by $49 to find the cost of the shoes.

```
        8          $49
250)2184         ×   8
    2000          $392
     184         +$ 49  add'l pair
                  $441
```

Note the remainder of 184 miles. Remember, she needed to buy 1 additional pair to run the 184 miles and she still had some wear left in them.

25. (5) $11

```
 $584          $ 11   Divide
+ 219       73) 803   the total
 $803           73    bills by
                 73   73.
                 73
                  0
```

Decimals
(pages 423–433)

1. (5) Insufficient data

You do not know the amount of the sales tax.

2. (3) 23,689

```
  23,465.2 mi
+    223.8 mi
  23,689.0 mi
```

3. (2) 4.57

```
   1.62 lb
    .85 lb
+  2.10 lb
   4.57 lb
```

4. (4) .22

```
  0.186
+ 0.034
   .220 = .22 parts per million
```

5. (2) 161.8

```
  112.5 ft
+  49.3 ft
  161.8 ft
```

6. (4) $265.00

```
 $199.49 sale price
+ 65.51 savings
 $265.00 original price
```

7. (5) $486.94

```
  $17.87
+ $18.65
  $36.52 total amount of
         checks written

 $523.46 old balance
- 36.52 amount of checks
 $486.94 new balance
```

8. (2) $20 − ($2.98 + $4.88)

First you have to add the costs of the two items. You subtract *that total* from the $20 bill.

9. (1) 8.9

```
  14.2 in
-  5.3 in
   8.9 in
```

10. (2) $41.82

```
 $43.31
- 2.35 coupons
 $40.96 net amount
+  .86 tax
 $41.82 total bill
```

11. (4) $100 − ($34.80 + $60 + $1.40)

Total all the restaurant's expenses *first*. Since profit is what is *left*, subtract that total from $100.

12. (3) $26.15

```
 $63.00                 $138.00
+ 48.85               -  111.85
$111.85 sister's          $26.15
        cost              difference
```

13. (2) .794

```
  30.231
- 29.437
    .794
```

14. (3) $0.75

```
 $11.01
- 10.26
 $  .75
```

15. (5) 60.14

```
  64.78 m
-  4.64 m
  60.14 m
```

16. (5) Insufficient data

You do not know which type of gas is being used.

17. (5) $11,088

```
     2,240
  ×  $4.95
    112 00
   2 016 0
   8 960
$11,088.00
```

18. (2) $276

```
   $7.36
 × 37 .5 hr
   3 680
  51 5 2
 220 8
$276.0 00
```

19. (1) $22.77

```
   197
+  189
   386 total kilowatt-hours
   386
× $.059
  3 474
 19 30
$22.774 = $22.77
```

20. (4) $1.33

3.41 lb
×$ .39
30 69
102 3
$1.3299 = $1.33

21. (2) $18.55

$12.50 $17.50
+ 5.00 × .06
$17.50 $1.05 00
= $1.05 tax

$17.50
+ 1.05 tax
$18.55 total cost

22. (3) $403.2

$22.4 million
× 18
1792
224
$403.2 million

23. (3) 55.80

90 km
× .62
180
540
55.80 mph

24. (1) $16,670

427.6
+ 572.4
1,000.0 total sq. ft

$16.67
× 1,000
$16,670.00

25. (1) 62,400

8000
× 7.8
64000
56000
62,400.0 lb

26. (4) 40($4.30) +
12 ($4.30 × 1.5)

First find the earnings for a 40-hour week: 40 ($4.30)
Next, find the hourly overtime earnings: $4.30 × 1.5
Multiply the hourly overtime earnings by the number of overtime hours worked:
52 − 40 = 12
Add the regular and the overtime earnings.

27. (1) $0.27

$0.27
12)$3.24
2 4
84
84
0

28. (4) $35,525.50

$33,464.52
+ 37,586.48
$71,051.00

$35,525.50 for each
2)$71,051.00 partner
6
11
10
1 0
1 0
5
4
11
10
1 0
1 0
0

29. (3) 12

96 students
× 4 oz
384 oz

12 cans
32 oz)384 oz
32
64
64
0

30. (2) $10.70

$10.70 average order
9)$96.30
9
63
63
0

31. (2) 37

525.1 mph = 525 mph
3.9)2,048.00
1 95
98
78
200
195
50

487.6 mph = 488 mph
4.2)2,048.00
1 68
368
336
32 0
29 4
2 60
2 52
8

525
− 488
37 mph slower

32. (2) $7.84

To find the hourly pay, divide the weekly earnings by 40 hours.

$7.84
40)$313.60
280
33 6
32 0
1 60
1 60
0

33. (3) $2.99

$ 2.99
43)$128.57
86
42 5
38 7
3 87
3 87
0

34. (4) $25.50

$639.95 cost of stereo
− 155.45 amount saved
$484.50 left to save

$25.50 needed to be saved
19)484.50 each week
38
104
95
9 5
9 5
0

35. (5) 2.5¢

$ .025 = 2.5¢
48)$1.200
96
240
240
0

36. (5) Insufficient data

The problem only gives you information about weight.

37. (3) 5.7

3.8
× 1.5
1 9 0
3 8
5.7 0 kilometers deep

38. (3) 46.6

46.6 inches
1.25)58.25.
50 0
8 25
7 50
750
750
0

39. (1) 17

1 7 packages
23.8)404.6.
238
66 6
66 6
0

40. (4) 24

24.
$199.49.)$4,787.76.
3 989 8
797 96
797 96

41. (2) 35

$348.25
2)$696.50
6
9
8
16
16
5
4
10
10
0

35. library books
$9.95.)$348.25.
298 5
49 75
49 75
0

42. (4) $438.94

$12.95
× 12
$155.40 cost of shirts

$8.49
× 7
$59.43 cost of softballs

$23.79
× 9
$214.11 cost of mitts

$155.40
59.43
214.11
10.00 postage/handling
$438.94

43. (4) $451.47

$8.38
× 40
$335.20 earnings Mon. to Fri.

$8.38
× 1.5
4190
838
$12.570 earned per hour on Sat. and Sun.

$12.57
× 9.25
6285
2514
11313
$116.2725 = $116.27 earned on Sat. & Sun.

$335.20
+116.27
$451.47 total earnings

44. (2) $4.64

$0.62 + (26.6 × $0.35) = the cost of sending the package

26.6
× .35
1330
798
9.310

9.31
+ .62
9.93

$9.93 − $5.29 = how much more money Susan needs to send the package

$9.93
−$5.29
$4.64

45. (2) $12,720

3,200
× $5.25
16000
6400
16000
$16,800.00 total sales of Section D

2,000
× $7.50
100000
14000
$15,000.00 total sales of Section E

$16,800.00
+$15,000.00
$31,800.00 total sales

$31,800.00
× .40
$12,720.0000 donated to charity

46. (5) Insufficient data

You do not know the price of brushes.

Fractions
(pages 434–446)

1. (3) $\frac{1}{2}$

$\frac{3}{8}$
$+\frac{1}{8}$
$\frac{4}{8} = \frac{1}{2}$ of the pizza

2. (4) $\frac{2}{3}$

$\frac{2}{9}$
$+\frac{4}{9}$
$\frac{6}{9} = \frac{2}{3}$ of his collection

3. (3) $\frac{2}{5}$

$\frac{2}{5}$
$+\frac{1}{5}$
$\frac{3}{5}$ amount of population either under or over weight

1 whole population
$-\frac{3}{5}$
$\frac{2}{5}$ amount of population of normal weight

4. (3) $\frac{2}{5}$

$\frac{7}{10}$

$-\frac{3}{10}$

$\frac{4}{10} = \frac{2}{5}$ mile

5. (3) 24

$8\frac{1}{4}$ hr

$6\frac{3}{4}$ hr

$+\ 9$ hr

$23\frac{4}{4} = 24$ hr

6. (4) $4\frac{1}{3}$

$1\frac{2}{3}$ lb

$2\frac{1}{3}$ lb

$+\ \frac{1}{3}$ lb

$3\frac{4}{3}$ lb

Change $\frac{4}{3}$ lb to $1\frac{1}{3}$ lb and add it to the 3 lb for a total of $4\frac{1}{3}$ lb.

7. (3) $6\frac{3}{4}$

2 mi

$2\frac{5}{8}$ mi

$+\ 2\frac{1}{8}$ mi

$6\frac{6}{8}$ mi $= 6\frac{3}{4}$ mi

8. (5) $5\frac{5}{6} - 4\frac{1}{6}$

9. (3) $1\frac{1}{4}$

$3\frac{5}{8}$

$-\ 2\frac{3}{8}$

$1\frac{2}{8} = 1\frac{1}{4}$ pounds

10. (2) $9\frac{1}{2}$

$1\frac{3}{4}$ oz $= 1\frac{3}{4}$ oz

$2\frac{1}{4}$ oz $= 2\frac{1}{4}$ oz

$+\ 5\frac{1}{2}$ oz $= 5\frac{2}{4}$ oz

$8\frac{6}{4}$ oz

Change $\frac{6}{4}$ to $1\frac{1}{2}$ oz and add that amount to 8 oz for a total of $9\frac{1}{2}$ oz.

11. (5) Insufficient data

You do not know the weight of the second twin.

12. (5) $4\frac{7}{8}$

$2\frac{1}{4}$ yd $= 2\frac{2}{8}$ yd

$\frac{3}{4}$ yd $= \frac{6}{8}$ yd

$+\ 1\frac{7}{8}$ yd $= 1\frac{7}{8}$ yd

$3\frac{15}{8}$ yd

Change $\frac{15}{8}$ yd to $1\frac{7}{8}$ yd and add that amount to 3 yd for a total of $4\frac{7}{8}$ yd.

13. (4) $7\frac{1}{4}$

$45\frac{3}{4} = 45\frac{3}{4}$

$-\ 38\frac{1}{2} = -\ 38\frac{2}{4}$

$7\frac{1}{4}$ hours more

14. (1) $3\frac{1}{2}$

$22\frac{2}{3} = 22\frac{4}{6}$

$-\ 19\frac{1}{6} = -\ 19\frac{1}{6}$

$3\frac{3}{6} = 3\frac{1}{2}$ pies

15. (3) $6\frac{1}{3} - 5\frac{1}{4}$

Subtract Ms. Thompson's height, $5\frac{1}{4}$, from her brother's height, $6\frac{1}{3}$.

16. (3) $9\frac{5}{24}$

$107\frac{1}{3}$ mi $= 107\frac{8}{24}$ mi

$-\ 98\frac{1}{8}$ mi $= 98\frac{3}{24}$ mi

$9\frac{5}{24}$ mi

17. (1) $\frac{1}{10}$

$\frac{1}{2} = \frac{5}{10}$

$-\ \frac{2}{5}\quad -\ \frac{4}{10}$

$\frac{1}{10}$

18. (4) $\frac{13}{18}$

$\frac{1}{6} = \frac{3}{18}$

$+\ \frac{5}{9} = +\ \frac{10}{18}$

$\frac{13}{18}$ of a pie

19. (3) $12\frac{3}{8}$

$15\frac{1}{2}$ gal $= 15\frac{4}{8}$ gal $= 14\frac{12}{8}$ gal

$-\ 7\frac{7}{8}$ gal $= -\ 7\frac{7}{8}$ gal $= -\ 7\frac{7}{8}$ gal

$7\frac{5}{8}$ gal

Subtract $7\frac{5}{8}$ gal left in the tank from 20 gal to find the amount of gas that he must buy.

20 gal $= 19\frac{8}{8}$ gal

$-\ 7\frac{5}{8}$ gal $= -\ 7\frac{5}{8}$ gal

$12\frac{3}{8}$ gal

20. (2) $16\frac{3}{4}$

$19\frac{1}{4} = 19\frac{1}{4} = 18\frac{5}{4}$

$-\ 2\frac{1}{2} = -\ 2\frac{2}{4} = -\ 2\frac{2}{4}$

$16\frac{3}{4}$ hr

21. (4) $3\frac{3}{4}$

5 gal $= 4\frac{4}{4}$ gal

$-\ 1\frac{1}{4}$ gal $= -1\frac{1}{4}$ gal

$3\frac{3}{4}$ gal

22. (3) $4\frac{3}{8}$

$10\frac{1}{4} = 10\frac{2}{8} = 9\frac{10}{8}$

$-\ 5\frac{7}{8} = -\ 5\frac{7}{8} = -\ 5\frac{7}{8}$

$4\frac{3}{8}$ pounds

23. (2) $1\frac{5}{12}$

Find the number of eggs used.

$2\frac{1}{3}$ doz $= 2\frac{4}{12}$ doz eggs for Easter

$+\ 1\frac{1}{4}$ doz $= 1\frac{3}{12}$ doz eggs for salad

$3\frac{7}{12}$ doz total used

Subtract the number of eggs used from the total amount.

5 doz $= 4\frac{12}{12}$ doz

$-\ 3\frac{7}{12}$ doz $= -3\frac{7}{12}$ doz total used

$1\frac{5}{12}$ doz left

24. (3) 675

$1{,}800 \times \frac{3}{8} = \frac{1{,}800}{1} \times \frac{3}{8} = \frac{5{,}400}{8} = \frac{675}{1} = 675$ people

25. (4) $5,520

$\frac{13{,}800}{1} \times \frac{2}{5} = \frac{27{,}600}{5} = \frac{5{,}520}{1} = \$5{,}520$

26. (2) $1.41

$\frac{\$1.88}{1} \times \frac{3}{4} = \frac{5.64}{4} = \frac{1.41}{1} = \$1.41$

27. (5) Insufficient data

You do not know how much sheet plastic Brian bought.

28. (4) $2.03

$\frac{\$2.32}{1} \times \frac{7}{8} = \frac{16.24}{8} = \frac{2.03}{1} = \$2.03$

29. (3) $8\frac{1}{4}$

$3 \times 2\frac{3}{4} = \frac{3}{1} \times \frac{11}{4} = \frac{33}{4} = 8\frac{1}{4}$ lb

30. (4) 8

$2\frac{2}{3} \times 3 = \frac{8}{3} \times \frac{3}{1} = \frac{24}{3} = \frac{8}{1} =$

8 cups

31. (2) $\frac{1}{2}$

$3\frac{1}{2} \times \frac{1}{7} = \frac{7}{2} \times \frac{1}{7} = \frac{7}{14} = \frac{1}{2}$ lb

32. (1) $\frac{2}{3} \times \frac{2}{5}$

33. (4) $4\frac{3}{8}$

$5 \times \frac{7}{8} = \frac{35}{8} = 4\frac{3}{8}$ yards

34. (4) $71.25

$\$7.50 \times 9\frac{1}{2} = \frac{\overset{3.75}{\cancel{7.50}}}{1} \times \frac{19}{\underset{1}{\cancel{2}}} = \frac{71.25}{1} = \$71.25$

35. (1) $4\frac{1}{2}$

Find how many yards she used; then subtract that amount from 18 yards to find how many yards were left.

$18 \times \frac{3}{4} = \frac{\overset{9}{\cancel{18}}}{1} \times \frac{3}{\underset{2}{\cancel{4}}} = \frac{27}{2} = 13\frac{1}{2}$

$$\begin{array}{rcr} 18\text{ yd} & = & 17\frac{2}{2}\text{ yd} \\ -\ 13\frac{1}{2}\text{ yd} & = & -13\frac{1}{2}\text{ yd} \\ \hline & & 4\frac{1}{2}\text{ yd} \end{array}$$

36. (5) Insufficient data

You do not know the price of the fruit.

37. (4) 650

$3\frac{1}{4} \times \frac{200}{1} = \frac{13}{\underset{1}{\cancel{4}}} \times \frac{\overset{50}{\cancel{200}}}{1} = \frac{650}{1}$

$= 650$ mi

38. (4) 17 lb

$5\frac{2}{3} \times 3 = \frac{17}{\underset{1}{\cancel{3}}} \times \frac{\overset{1}{\cancel{3}}}{1} = \frac{17}{1} =$

17 lb

39. (3) $0.57

$\$1.98 \div 3\frac{1}{2} = \frac{1.98}{1} \div \frac{7}{2} = \frac{1.98}{1} \times \frac{2}{7} = \frac{3.96}{7} = .565 = \$0.57$

40. (3) 8

$18 \div 2\frac{1}{4} = \frac{18}{1} \div \frac{9}{4} = \frac{\overset{2}{\cancel{18}}}{1} \times \frac{4}{\underset{1}{\cancel{9}}} = \frac{8}{1} = 8$ pieces

41. (1) 32

$68 \div 2\frac{1}{8} = \frac{68}{1} \div \frac{17}{8} = \frac{\overset{4}{\cancel{68}}}{1} \times \frac{8}{\underset{1}{\cancel{17}}} = \frac{32}{1} = 32$

42. (2) $586{,}600 \div 1\frac{2}{5}$

43. (4) $76.00

$\$722 \div 9\frac{1}{2} = \frac{722}{1} \div \frac{19}{2} = \frac{\overset{38}{\cancel{722}}}{1} \times \frac{2}{\underset{1}{\cancel{19}}} = \frac{76}{1} = \$76.00$

44. (3) 52

$117 \div 2\frac{1}{4} = \frac{117}{1} \div \frac{9}{4} = \frac{\overset{13}{\cancel{117}}}{1} \times \frac{4}{\underset{1}{\cancel{9}}} = \frac{52}{1} = 52$ mph

45. (5) Insufficient data

You do not know the price of the tacks.

46. (5) $\frac{1}{3}$

$13\frac{1}{3} \div 40 = \frac{40}{3} \div \frac{40}{1} = \frac{\overset{1}{\cancel{40}}}{3} \times \frac{1}{\underset{1}{\cancel{40}}} = \frac{1}{3}$ acre

47. (4) $7\frac{3}{4}$

$15\frac{1}{2} \div 2 = \frac{31}{2} \div \frac{2}{1} = \frac{31}{2} \times \frac{1}{2} = \frac{31}{4} = 7\frac{3}{4}$

48. (4) 10

$7\frac{1}{2} \div \frac{3}{4} = \frac{15}{2} \div \frac{3}{4} = \frac{\overset{5}{\cancel{15}}}{\underset{1}{\cancel{2}}} \times \frac{\overset{2}{\cancel{4}}}{\underset{1}{\cancel{3}}} = \frac{10}{1} = 10$

49. (4) $96.25

$\$165 \times \frac{1}{3} = \frac{\overset{55}{\cancel{165}}}{1} \times \frac{1}{\underset{1}{\cancel{3}}} =$

$55 week one

$\$165 \times \frac{1}{4} = \frac{165}{1} \times \frac{1}{4} = \frac{165}{4} = \$41.25$ week two

$\$55.00 + \$41.25 = \$96.25$

50. (3) $(2\frac{3}{8} \times \$4.99 + (\frac{1}{2} \times \$1.98) + \$0.89 + \$0.55$

$2\frac{3}{8}$ yards at $4.99 a yard and $\frac{1}{2}$ yard at $1.98 a yard means to multiply those numbers to find the price of the fabric that Deborah Jones bought. Add the fabric prices together then add them to the $0.89 for the zipper and the $0.55 for thread for the total cost of the dress.

51. (1) 4

Find the amount of time spent sorting mail and helping customers; then subtract that amount of time from 40 hr.

$40 \times \frac{1}{2} = \frac{\overset{20}{\cancel{40}}}{1} \times \frac{1}{\underset{1}{\cancel{2}}} =$

20 hr sorting mail

$40 \times \frac{2}{5} = \frac{\overset{8}{\cancel{40}}}{1} \times \frac{2}{\underset{1}{\cancel{5}}} =$

16 hr helping customers

20 hr + 16 hr = 36 hr;
40 hr − 36 hr = 4 hr

Percents
(pages 447–453)

1. (1) 10

```
   50
 × .20
 10.00
```

2. (5) Insufficient data

You do not know the exact percentage.

3. (3) $8.58

```
 $85.75
 ×   .10
 $8.5750 = $8.58
```

4. (3) $5,144

```
    25,720
 ×     .20
 $5,144.00
```

5. (4) $4,372.40

```
    25,720
 ×      17
   1 800 40
   2 572 0
 $4,372.40
```

6. (1) $\frac{\$63.75 \times 100}{75}$

Work the problem as you would with a grid. Multiply the price paid, $63.75, by 100 then divide by 75 to find the original price of the coat.

7. (4) 2,400

```
        2,400.
 .05.)120.00.
       10
        20
        20
         0
```

8. (1) 600

```
          600.
 .015.)9.000.
        9 000
            0
```

9. (3) $32.00

```
        $ 32.00
 .06.)$1.92.
       1 8
         12
         12
          0
```

10. (2) $\frac{\$52.50}{.035}$

Divide the commission earned by the commission rate (.035) to find total sales.

11. (4) 72%

```
       .72 = 72%
 50)36.00
    35 0
     1 00
     1 00
        0
```

12. (3) 8%

```
              .08 = 8%
 48,500)3,880.00
        3,880 00
               0
```

13. (2) 21%

```
          .21 = 21%
 627)131.67
     125 4
       6 27
       6 27
          0
```

14. (5) Insufficient data

You do not know which set he bought.

15. (5) 3.5%

```
            .035 = 3.5%
 7,200)252.000
       216 00
        36 000
        36 000
             0
```

16. (3) (100 × 665) ÷ 70

Multiply the price paid, $665, by 100 then divide by 70 to find the original price of the desk.

17. (5) $87.75

Find the discount of one chair.
60 (60) ÷ 100 = $36

Find the sale price

```
  $60.00
 − 36.00
  $24.00
```

Find the discount on one lamp.
25 (85) ÷ 100 = $21.25

Find the sale price of the lamp.

```
  $85.00
 − 21.25
  $63.75
```

Find the total the neighbor owes.

```
  $24.00
 + 63.75
  $87.75
```

18. (4) $142.60

$665 + ($60 × 2 × .40) = total purchase
$665 + $48 = $713

```
  $7 13
 ×  .20
   0 00
 142 6
 142.60
```

19. (2) 12

Set up the problem in a grid.

$\frac{8}{?} = \frac{2}{5}$

$\frac{8 \times 5}{2} = \frac{2 \text{ x } ?}{2}$

$\frac{40}{2} = ?$

20 = ?
20 − 8 = 12

20. (2) $30.48

Find the sale.
12 (63.50) ÷ 100 = $7.62

Find the savings on 4 tires.

```
  $7.62
 ×    4
 $30.48
```

21. (4) 12%

```
        .12 = 12%
1,250)150.00
      125 0
       25 00
       25 00
           0
```

22. (3) 15%

$1 - \frac{527}{620}$ = percentage of trip remaining

```
    0.85
620)527.00
      0
    527 0
    496 0
     31 00
     31 00
```

1 − .85 = .15 or 15%

23. (3) 2.8%

10.1 − 7.3 = 2.8

Data Analysis
(pages 454–467)

1. (4) 180,000

```
  370,000
– 190,000
  180,000
```

2. (3) $\frac{1}{3}$

$\frac{110,000}{310,000} = \frac{11}{31}$ = about $\frac{10}{30} = \frac{1}{3}$

3. (1) 200,000

```
  110,000
+  90,000
  200,000
```

4. (1) 2

```
            2.1 = 2 times
90,000)190,000.0
       180 000
        10 000 0
         9 000 0
         1 000 0
```

5. (5) 17,000

```
  12,000 burns (chil.)
+ 14,000 falls (chil.)
  26,000

   3,000 burns (ad.)
+  6,000 falls (ad.)
   9,000

  26,000
–  9,000
  17,000
```

6. (1) 3

18,000 auto accidents
6,000 falls

```
          3 times
6,000)18,000
```

7. (4) 52,000

```
  12,000
  14,000
   8,000
   4,000
   8,000
+  6,000
  52,000 accidental deaths
```

8. (5) 26,000

```
  18,000 adults' auto
         accident deaths
+  8,000 children's auto
         accident deaths
  26,000 total deaths
```

9. (5) $11,000

The shaded and unshaded portions of the bar indicate $11,000.

10. (5) $25,000

```
  $11,000 men's 10-speeds
+  14,000 women's 10-speeds
  $25,000
```

11. (5) Insufficient data

You do not know how many were sold in May.

12. (4) Women's 10-speeds and women's 3-speeds

Only women's 10-speeds and 3-speeds had sales greater than $12,000.

13. (2) 25%

```
           0.059 = 6%
$1.69)$0.10.00
          8 45
          1 550
          1 521

          $0.314 = 31%
$1.59)$0.50.00
          47 7
           2 30
           1 59
             7 10
             6 36

  31%
–  6%
  25%
```

14. (3) $0.30

```
  $1.89 pork
–  1.59 beef
  $0.30
```

15. (3) 1.75

```
            1.75 times
$1.00.)$1.75.
         1 00
           750
           700
           500
           500
             0
```

16. (2) 17%

```
           0.174 = 17%
$1.49)$0.26 000
         14 9
         11 10
         10 43
            670
            596
             74
```

17. (5) 42.5 million

```
  25,000,000 Kennedy
+ 17,500,000 LaGuardia
  42,500,000
```

18. (5) 15 million

```
  30,000,000 Los Angeles
– 15,000,000 Honolulu
  15,000,000
```

19. (1) 2

Only Chicago and New York had more than 35 million departing passengers.

20. (3) 80,000

```
        80,000
250)20,000,000
    20 00
        0
```

21. (2) 46.5%

$$\begin{array}{rl} 63.0\% & \text{Teachers' salaries} \\ -\ 16.5\% & \text{Administrative salaries} \\ \hline 46.5\% & \text{difference} \end{array}$$

22. (3) $\frac{3}{4}$

$$\begin{array}{rl} 12\% & \text{Rent and utilities} \\ +\ 63\% & \text{Teachers' salaries} \\ \hline 75\% & \end{array}$$

$$= \frac{75}{100} = \frac{3}{4}$$

23. (3) $132,300

$$\begin{array}{r} \$210{,}000 \\ \times\quad .63 \\ \hline 630000 \\ 1260000 \\ \hline \$132{,}300.00 \end{array}$$

24. (4) ($210,000 × 0.165) − $9,525

Multiply the total budget by the percent of budget used for the administrative staff. Subtract the secretary's salary from that number to find the president's salary.

25. (3) $108

26. (5) Insufficient data

You do not know the rate of kilowatt-hours.

27. (3) 4

Cost of 1,000 hours = $80
Cost of 250 hours = $20

Divide to find the number of times greater.

$$\$20\overline{)\$80} = 4 \text{ times}$$

28. (1) local energy rate and product usage

Your cost will vary depending on your local energy rate and how you use the product.

29. (3) 43,067

The meter reading is 43,067.

30. (4) 6,000

The altimeter reading is 6,000 feet.

31. (1) 7

If the hand is between two numbers, record the lower one.

32. (4) 5

Divide the average July sales by the April sales.

$15,000 in July
$ 3,000 in April

$$\$3{,}000\overline{)\$15{,}000} = 5 \text{ times greater}$$
$$\begin{array}{r} 15{,}000 \\ \hline 0 \end{array}$$

33. (1) 69°

$$\begin{array}{r} 62^\circ \\ 71^\circ \\ 78^\circ \\ 69^\circ \\ +\ 65^\circ \\ \hline 345^\circ \end{array} \qquad 5\overline{)345} = 69^\circ \qquad \begin{array}{r} 30 \\ \hline 45 \\ 45 \\ \hline 0 \end{array}$$

34. (1) $15\frac{1}{4}$

Add the lengths.

$$\begin{array}{rcl} 15\frac{1}{4} & = & 15\frac{2}{8} \\ 15\frac{3}{8} & = & 15\frac{3}{8} \\ 14\frac{7}{8} & = & 14\frac{7}{8} \\ 15\frac{1}{4} & = & 15\frac{2}{8} \\ +\ 15\frac{1}{2} & = & +\ 15\frac{4}{8} \\ \hline \end{array}$$

$$74\frac{18}{8} = 76\frac{2}{8} = 76\frac{1}{4}$$

Divide the total by 5.

$$76\frac{1}{4} \div 5 =$$

$$\frac{\overset{61}{\cancel{305}}}{4} \times \frac{1}{\cancel{5}_1} = 15\frac{1}{4} \text{ inches}$$

35. (2) $6,874

To find the mean weekly sales, add the four weeks' sales and then divide by 4.

$$\begin{array}{r} 7{,}832 \\ 6{,}445 \\ 7{,}230 \\ 5{,}989 \\ \hline \$27{,}496 \end{array} \div 4 = \$6{,}874$$

36. (3) $9,073

Add the 2 middle numbers and divide by 2.

$$\begin{array}{r} \$9{,}090 \\ 9{,}056 \\ \hline \$18{,}146 \end{array} \qquad 2\overline{)18{,}146} = \$9{,}073$$

37. (4) 89

The middle number is 89.

38. (4) $104,500

Add the 2 middle numbers and divide by 2.

$$\begin{array}{r} \$104{,}000 \\ 105{,}000 \\ \hline \$209{,}000 \end{array} \qquad 2\overline{)\$209{,}000} = \$104{,}500 \qquad \begin{array}{r} 2 \\ \hline 09 \\ 8 \\ \hline 10 \\ 10 \\ \hline \end{array}$$

39. (2) $102,000

Add the salaries and then divide by 12.

$$\begin{array}{r} \$92{,}000 \\ 105{,}000 \\ 116{,}000 \\ 90{,}000 \\ 120{,}000 \\ 106{,}000 \\ 90{,}000 \\ 105{,}000 \\ 96{,}000 \\ 92{,}000 \\ 104{,}000 \\ +\ 108{,}000 \\ \hline \$1{,}224{,}000 \end{array}$$

$$12\overline{)1{,}224{,}000} = \$102{,}000 \text{ mean income} \qquad \begin{array}{r} 12 \\ \hline 24 \\ 24 \\ \hline \end{array}$$

40. (2) 70°

The middle number is 70°.

41. (2) 1:2

The ratio is

$$\frac{\text{inches}}{\text{foot}} = \frac{6 \text{ in}}{12 \text{ in}} = 1:2$$

42. (3) $\frac{9}{10}$

The ratio is

$$\frac{\text{number right}}{\text{total number}} = \frac{18}{20} = \frac{9}{10}$$

43. (2) $\frac{6}{1}$

The ratio is

$$\frac{\text{Alberto's age}}{\text{sister's age}} = \frac{12}{2} = \frac{6}{1}$$

44. (2) $\frac{3}{2}$

The ratio is

$$\frac{\text{damaged books}}{\text{undamaged books}} = \frac{144}{96} = \frac{3}{2}$$

45. (4) 12

The ratio is

$\frac{3}{2} = \frac{18}{?}$

$\frac{3}{2} = \frac{18}{12}$

It was sunny 12 days of the month.

46. (1) $\frac{1}{4}$

There is a total of 16 marbles. Since 4 marbles are blue, Nicholas has 4 chances out of 16 to select a blue marble.

$\frac{4}{16} = \frac{1}{4}$

47. (4) $\frac{1}{2}$

$\begin{array}{l} \ 6 \text{ red marbles} \\ \underline{+\ 2 \text{ green marbles}} \\ \ 8 \end{array}$

$\frac{8}{16}$ total marbles $= \frac{1}{2}$

48. (2) $\frac{5}{8}$

$\begin{array}{l} \ 4 \text{ blue marbles} \\ \ 4 \text{ orange marbles} \\ \underline{+\ 2 \text{ green marbles}} \\ 10 \text{ total marbles} \end{array}$

$\frac{10}{16} = \frac{5}{8}$

49. (3) $\frac{2}{5}$

$\begin{array}{l} \ 25 \text{ tickets to football game} \\ \underline{+\ 15 \text{ tickets to the symphony}} \\ \ 40 \text{ tickets} \end{array}$

$\frac{40}{100}$ total cards $= \frac{2}{5}$

50. (2) $\frac{20}{33}$

The total number of cards is now 99, since Fay does not return the first card to the envelope.

$\begin{array}{l} \ 32 \text{ movie passes} \\ \underline{+\ 28 \text{ coupons}} \\ \ 60 \end{array}$

$\frac{60}{99} = \frac{20}{33}$

51. (3) $1.68

The proportion is

$\frac{\text{tablets}}{\text{cost}} = \frac{\text{tablets}}{\text{cost}}$

$\frac{24}{\$3.36} = \frac{12}{x}$

$\frac{\overset{1}{\cancel{24}}x}{\underset{1}{\cancel{24}}} = \frac{\overset{1.68}{\cancel{\$40.32}}}{\underset{1}{\cancel{24}}}$

$x = \$1.68$

52. (3) 6

The proportion is

$\frac{\text{solution}}{\text{water}} = \frac{\text{solution}}{\text{water}}$

$\frac{1 \text{ qt}}{2 \text{ gal}} = \frac{x}{12 \text{ gal}}$

$\frac{\overset{1}{\cancel{2}}x}{\underset{1}{\cancel{2}}} = \frac{\overset{6}{\cancel{12}}}{\underset{1}{\cancel{2}}}$

$x = 6$ qt

53. (4) 44

The proportion is

$\frac{\text{bends}}{\text{seconds}} = \frac{\text{bends}}{\text{seconds}}$

$\frac{11}{15} = \frac{x}{60}$

$\frac{\overset{1}{\cancel{15}}x}{\underset{1}{\cancel{15}}} = \frac{\overset{44}{\cancel{660}}}{\underset{1}{\cancel{15}}}$

$x = 44$

54. (3) 10

The proportion is

$\frac{\text{gas pumped}}{\text{time}} = \frac{\text{gas pumped}}{\text{time}}.$

$\frac{150 \text{ gal}}{1 \text{ hr}} = \frac{1500 \text{ gal}}{x \text{ hr}}$

$\frac{\overset{1}{\cancel{150}}x}{\underset{1}{\cancel{150}}} = \frac{\overset{10}{\cancel{1500}}}{\underset{1}{\cancel{150}}}$

$x = 10$ hr

55. (3) 3,000

If 200 cars are produced per shift, 600 cars can be produced during a 3-shift workday. Multiply 600 cars per day by 5 days to find the total number produced in a five-day workweek: 600 × 5 = 3,000.

Number Relationships
(pages 468–477)

1. (2) 27

gained	lost	
35 yd	− 3 yd	+41 yd
+ 6 yd	−11 yd	−14 yd
41 yd	−14 yd	+27 yd

2. (3) 6°

$-7° + 13° = 6°$

3. (4) 38

Add the amounts of the checks and the deposits.

Checks:

$\begin{array}{r} \$175 \\ 25 \\ 212 \\ \underline{+\ 300} \\ \$712 \end{array}$ total checks

Deposits:

$\begin{array}{r} \$250 \\ \underline{+\ 500} \\ \$750 \end{array}$ total deposits

Subtract the total amount of the checks from the total amount of the deposits.

$\begin{array}{r} +\$750 \\ \underline{-\ 712} \\ \$\ 38 \end{array}$

4. (5) $\frac{7}{8}$

$\frac{3}{4} = \frac{6}{8}$
$-\frac{1}{8} = -\frac{1}{8}$
$\frac{5}{8}$ mile

$\frac{5}{8} = \frac{5}{8}$
$+\frac{1}{2} = +\frac{4}{8}$
$\frac{9}{8}$ mile

$\frac{9}{8} = \frac{9}{8}$
$-\frac{1}{4} = -\frac{2}{8}$
$\frac{7}{8}$ mile

5. (5) Insufficient data

You do not know how much money Ashley had in her wallet before the refund and purchase.

6. (2) 0.015, 0.105, 0.15, 1.5

7. (4) 0.007, 0.07, 0.7, 7.07

8. (5) 0.83, 0.803, 0.8, 0.08

9. (2) Derrick, Vince, Nate

10. (4) $3\frac{1}{4}$, $3\frac{5}{16}$, $3\frac{3}{8}$, $3\frac{1}{2}$

11. (1) $2\frac{5}{6}$, $2\frac{3}{4}$, $2\frac{1}{2}$, $2\frac{1}{3}$

12. (2) Plan B is the best option.

Plan A
$625
× .10
$62.50 down payment

$60
× 12
$720 total of monthly payments

$720
+ 62.50
$782.50 total cost of sofa

Plan B
$50
× 12
$600 total of monthly payments
+ $100 down payment
$700 total cost of sofa

Plan C
$121
× 6
$726 total cost of sofa

Plan D
$625
× .20
$125 down payment

$35
× 18
$630 total monthly payments

$125
+ 630
$755 total cost of sofa

13. (2) Plan B is the best option.

Plan A
$1,500 raise

Plan B
$65
× 52
130
3 25
$3,380 raise (in one year)

Plan C
$350
× 52
700
17 500
$18,200 Doug's present salary

$18,200
× .15
910 00
1 820 0
$2,730.00 raise (in one year)

Plan D
$125
× 26
750
2 50
$3,250 raise (in one yr.)

14. (5) Insufficient data

Options A, B, and C do not give you enough information to compare prices.

15. (2) 1

Any number to the zero power equals 1.

16. (4) 1,000

$10 \times 10 \times 10 = 1{,}000$

17. (4) 225

$15 \times 15 = 225$

18. (4) 2,401

$7 \times 7 \times 7 \times 7 = 2{,}401$

19. (3) 32

$2 \times 2 \times 2 \times 2 \times 2 = 32$

20. (5) 10,000,000,000

$10 \times 10 \times 10 \times 10 \times 10 \times 10 \times 10 \times 10 \times 10 \times 10 = 10{,}000{,}000{,}000$

21. (3) 12

$\sqrt{121} + \sqrt{100} - \sqrt{81} = 11 + 10 - 9 = 12$

22. (2) 63

$4\sqrt{144} + 3\sqrt{25} = 4 \times 12 + 3 \times 5 = 48 + 15 = 63$

23. (2) 28

$\frac{\sqrt{64}}{2} + 4\sqrt{49} - \sqrt{16} =$

$\frac{8}{2} + 4 \times 7 - 4 =$

$4 + 28 - 4 = 28$

24. (5) $0 + \sqrt{36}$

Convert all fractions to lowest terms and compare.

$\frac{\sqrt{36}}{6} = \frac{6}{6} = 1$

$\frac{6}{\sqrt{36}} = \frac{6}{6} = 1$

$\frac{\sqrt{49}}{\sqrt{36}} = \frac{7}{6} = 1\frac{1}{6}$

$\frac{\sqrt{36}}{\sqrt{64}} = \frac{6}{8} = \frac{3}{4}$

$0 + \sqrt{36} = 0 + 6 = 6$

25. (5) 306,000

$3.06 \times 10 \times 10 \times 10 \times 10 \times 10 = 306{,}000$ or move the decimal point 5 places to the right.

26. (3) 0.00791

79.1×10^{-4}

Move the decimal point 4 places to the left.

0 0079.1

27. (2) 8.4

0.0084×10^3

Move the decimal point 3 places to the right.

0.008 4

28. (4) 9.25×10^4

Move the decimal point 4 places to the right.
9.2500

29. (3) 8.06×10^{-4}

Move the decimal point 4 places to the left.
8.06×10^{-4}
00080.6

30. (2) 1

$4^1 \times (\frac{1}{2})^2 = \frac{4}{1} \times (\frac{1}{2}) \times (\frac{1}{2}) = \frac{4}{1} \times \frac{1}{4} = 1$

31. (4) 4.008

$(4) + (0.2)^3 = 4 \times (0.2)(0.2)(0.2) = 4 + 0.008 = 4.008$

32. (3) 3

$(-2)^2 - (-1)^0 = (-2)(-2) - (1) = +4 - 1 = 3$

33. (4) 12,000

$\sqrt{144} \times 10^3 =$
$12 \times 10^3 =$
$12 \times 10 \times 10 \times 10 = 12{,}000$

34. (1) 0.01
$-9^0 \times 10^{-2} =$
$1. \times 10^{-2} =$
0.01

Move the decimal point 2 places to the left.

Measurement
(pages 478–492)

1. (4) $62\frac{1}{3}$

Divide by 3 to convert 187 feet to yards.

$$\begin{array}{r} 62\frac{1}{3}\text{ yd} \\ 3\overline{)187\text{ ft}} \\ \underline{18}\phantom{\text{ ft}} \\ 7\phantom{\text{ ft}} \\ \underline{6}\phantom{\text{ ft}} \\ 1\phantom{\text{ ft}} \end{array}$$

2. (2) E, C, A, B, D

Run E — 351 sec
Run C — 358 sec
Run A — 360 sec
Run B — 372 sec
Run D — 374 sec

3. (5) E, A, D, B, C

Rope E — 135 in
Rope A — 126 in
Rope D — 120 in
Rope B — 51 in
Rope C — 50 in

4. (3) E, C, D, A, B

Family E — 13 pt
Family C — 16 pt
Family D — 18 pt
Family A — 20 pt
Family B — 30 pt

5. (2) A, C, E, B, D

Novel A — 3 yr 2 wk
Novel C — 2 yr 24 wk 2d
Novel E — 2 yr 6 wk 6d
Novel B — 1 yr 20 wk 4d
Novel D — 1 yr 8 wk 5d

6. (5) 35 mi 940 yd

Add the two distances.

$$\begin{array}{rl} 15\text{ mi }1{,}200\text{ yd} & \text{Robert} \\ +\ 19\text{ mi }1{,}500\text{ yd} & \text{Raymond} \\ \hline 34\text{ mi }2{,}700\text{ yd} & \end{array}$$

Convert 2,700 yards to miles.

$$\begin{array}{r} 1\text{ mi }940\text{ yd} \\ 1760\overline{)2700}\phantom{\text{ yd}} \\ \underline{1760}\phantom{\text{ yd}} \\ 940\phantom{\text{ yd}} \end{array}$$

34 mi + 1 mi 940 yd =
35 mi 940 yd

7. (4) 23 lb 5 oz

$$\begin{array}{r} 5\text{ lb }\ 7\text{ oz} \\ 1\text{ lb }\ 4\text{ oz} \\ 7\text{ lb }12\text{ oz} \\ +\ 8\text{ lb }14\text{ oz} \\ \hline 21\text{ lb }37\text{ oz} \end{array}$$

Convert 37 ounces to pounds.

$$\begin{array}{r} 2\text{ lb }5\text{ oz} \\ 16\overline{)37}\phantom{\text{ lb }5\text{ oz}} \\ \underline{32}\phantom{\text{ lb }5\text{ oz}} \\ 5\phantom{\text{ lb }5\text{ oz}} \end{array}$$

21 lb + 2 lb 5 oz = 23 lb 5 oz

8. (1) 2 tons 408 lb 5 oz

$$\begin{array}{r} 1{,}402\text{ lb }12\text{ oz} \\ 1{,}273\text{ lb }\ 8\text{ oz} \\ 983\text{ lb }\ 2\text{ oz} \\ +\ 748\text{ lb }15\text{ oz} \\ \hline 4{,}406\text{ lb }37\text{ oz} \end{array}$$

Convert 37 ounces to pounds.

$$\begin{array}{r} 2\text{ lb }5\text{ oz} \\ 16\overline{)37\text{ oz}}\phantom{\text{ 5 oz}} \\ \underline{32}\phantom{\text{ oz 5 oz}} \\ 5\phantom{\text{ oz 5 oz}} \end{array}$$

4,406 lb + 2 lb 5 oz =
4,408 lb 5 oz

Convert 4,408 pounds 5 ounces to tons.

$$\begin{array}{r} 2\text{ tons }408\text{ lb }5\text{ oz} \\ 2{,}000\overline{)4{,}408\text{ lb }5\text{ oz}} \\ \underline{4\ 000}\phantom{\text{ lb }5\text{ oz}} \\ 408\text{ lb }5\text{ oz} \end{array}$$

9. (3) 3 T 100 lb

$$\begin{array}{r} 1\text{ T }\ \ 500\text{ lb} \\ +\ 1\text{ T }1{,}600\text{ lb} \\ \hline 2\text{ T }2{,}100\text{ lb} \end{array}$$

Convert 2,100 pounds to tons.

$$\begin{array}{r} 1\text{ T }100\text{ lb} \\ 2000\overline{)2100\text{ lb}} \\ \underline{2000}\phantom{\text{ lb}} \\ 100\phantom{\text{ lb}} \end{array}$$

2 T + 1 T 100 lb = 3T 100 lb

10. (3) 6

$$\begin{array}{rcr} 4\ \text{gal} & = & 16\text{ qt} \\ -\ 2\frac{1}{2}\text{ gal} & = & -\ 10\text{ qt} \\ \hline & & 6\text{ qt} \end{array}$$

11. (3) 3 hr 58 min

$$\begin{array}{rcr} 12\text{ hr} & = & 11\text{ hr }60\text{ min} \\ -\ 9\text{ hr }45\text{ min} & = & 9\text{ hr }45\text{ min} \\ \hline & & 2\text{ hr }15\text{ min} \end{array}$$

$$\begin{array}{r} 2\text{ hr }15\text{ min} \\ +\ 1\text{ hr }43\text{ min} \\ \hline 3\text{ hr }58\text{ min} \end{array}$$

12. (3) 1 hr 35 min

$$\begin{array}{rcr} 2\text{ hr }20\text{ min} & = & 1\text{ hr }80\text{ min} \\ -\ \ 45\text{ min} & = & 45\text{ min} \\ \hline & & 1\text{ hr }35\text{ min} \end{array}$$

13. (1) $\frac{1}{2}$

$$\begin{array}{r} 52\text{ oz} \\ -\ 36\text{ 0z} \\ \hline 16\text{ oz} \end{array}$$

32 ounces are in one quart.

$\frac{16}{32} = \frac{1}{2}$ qt

14. (2) 121 ft 8 in

$$\begin{array}{r} 24\text{ ft }\ 4\text{ in} \\ \times\qquad 5 \\ \hline 120\text{ ft }20\text{ in} \end{array}$$

Convert 20 inches to feet.

$$\begin{array}{r} 1\text{ ft }8\text{ in} \\ 12\overline{)20}\phantom{\text{ ft }8\text{ in}} \\ \underline{12}\phantom{\text{ ft }8\text{ in}} \\ 8\phantom{\text{ ft }8\text{ in}} \end{array}$$

1 ft 8 in + 120 ft = 121 ft 8 in

15. (2) 43 hr 45 min

Find the amount of time spent on exercise in one week.

$7 \times 1\frac{1}{4} = 7 \times \frac{5}{4} = \frac{35}{4}$ hr

Next, find the amount of time spent on exercise in five weeks.

$\frac{35}{4} \times 5 = \frac{35}{4} \times \frac{5}{1} =$

$\frac{175}{4} = 43\frac{3}{4}$ hr

Change $\frac{3}{4}$ hour to minutes.

$\frac{3}{4} = \frac{45}{60} =$ 43 hr 45 min

16. (3) 26 gal 1 qt

$$\begin{array}{rl} 3\text{ gal }\ 3\text{ qt} & \\ \times\ 7 & \text{(days in a week)} \\ \hline 21\text{ gal }\ 21\text{ qt} & \end{array}$$

Convert quarts to gallons.

$$\begin{array}{r} 5\text{ gal }1\text{ qt} \\ 4\overline{)21}\phantom{\text{ gal }1\text{ qt}} \\ \underline{20}\phantom{\text{ gal }1\text{ qt}} \\ 1\phantom{\text{ gal }1\text{ qt}} \end{array} \qquad \begin{array}{r} 21\text{ gal} \\ +\ 5\text{ gal }1\text{ qt} \\ \hline 26\text{ gal }1\text{ qt} \end{array}$$

17. (5) Insufficient data

You do not know how many packages of ground beef Kellie purchased.

18. (3) 4 ft 3 in

```
   4 ft 3 in
3)12 ft 9 in
  12    9
        0
```

19. (3) 7 hr 20 min

Divide the total amount of time by 4 to get the average. First divide the hours.

```
   7 hr
4)29 hr
  28
   1
```

Convert the remainder of 1 hour to 60 min and add it to the 20 min (80 min) then divide.

```
  20 min
4)80 min
```

7 hr 20 min was the average harvesting time.

20. (1) $\frac{1}{2}$ lb

The candy will be divided equally among 5 people (Melissa and her 4 friends).

$2\frac{1}{2} \div 5 =$

$\frac{5}{2} \div 5 =$

$\frac{\cancel{5}}{2} \times \frac{1}{\cancel{5}} = \frac{1}{2}$ lb

21. (4) 64

```
  11
  23
+ 14
  48 total number of gal of cider
     sold
```

```
  48 gal
×  4
 192 qt sold
```

```
  64 average number of quarts
3)192 sold each day
```

22. (3) A, B, E, C, D

Pole A = 500 cm
Pole B = 500.3 cm
Pole E = 502 cm
Pole C = 520 cm
Pole D = 540 cm

23. (2) A, E, C, D, B

Jug A = 2,204 mL
Jug E = 2,140 mL
Jug C = 2,104 mL
Jug D = 2,040 mL
Jug B = 2,024 mL

24. (4) E, A, C, B, D

Dog E = 18,880 g
Dog A = 18,800 g
Dog C = 18,180 g
Dog B = 18,080 g
Dog D = 18,010 g

25. (1) D, B, E, A, C

Day D = 6,002 m
Day B = 6,020 m
Day E = 6,022 m
Day A = 6,200 m
Day C = 6,202 m

26. (1) 5.35

850 mL = 0.85 L

```
  4.5 L
+ 0.85 L
  5.35 L
```

27. (2) 7.506

1,006 m = 1.006 km

```
  1.006 km
  2.6   km
+ 3.9   km
  7.506 km
```

28. (5) 3,859

1.624 kg = 1,624 g
0.988 kg = 988 g

```
  504 g
1,624 g
  988 g
  743 g
3,859 g
```

29. (1) 3.979

721 g = 0.721 kg

```
  4.7   kg
− 0.721 kg
  3.979 kg
```

30. (4) 1.308

109 g = 0.109 kg

```
  0.109 kg
×    12
    218
   1 09
  1.308 kg
```

31. (3) 56

250 mL = 0.25 L of milk in a glass

```
 3.5
× 4
14.0 in the 4 bottles
```

```
         56 glasses
0.25)14.00.
     12 5
      1 50
      1 50
```

32. (4) 203.7

First convert all measures to centimeters.

2.2 m = 220 cm
2.03 m = 203 cm

Then add the heights.

```
  220   cm
  198   cm
  197.6 cm
  203   cm
+ 199.9 cm
1,018.5 cm
```

Then divide by 5 to find the average height.

```
   203.7 cm   average height
5)1,018.5
  1 0
     18
     15
      3 5
```

33. (2) 12.3

First convert centimeters to meters.

4,050 cm = 40.5 m

Then find the distance of Bill's average shot.

```
  13.5
3)4.0.50
  3
  10
   9
   15
```

Then subtract to find the difference.

```
  25.8
− 13.5
  12.3 m shorter
```

34. (4) $2,700

$I = p \times r \times t$

$7,500 × 0.09 × 4 yr = $2,700

35. (2) $182.25

$I = p \times r \times t$

$3,600 × 0.0675 × $\frac{9}{12}$ =
$182.25

36. (5) Insufficient data

You do not know how long it will take the Hamiltons to pay back the loan.

37. (2) $30

$I = p \times r \times t$

$250 × 0.08 × 1.5 = $301

38. (3) $107.33

First find the cost of each item; then add.

$ 0.69 × 24 = $ 16.56
$11.99 × 3 = $ 35.97
$ 6.85 × 8 = +$ 54.80
$107.33

39. (1) $9\frac{1}{2}$

$9\frac{1}{2}$ hr
50)475
450
25
$\frac{25}{50} = \frac{1}{2}$

40. (4) $3.20

$3.20
18)$57.60
54
36
36

41. (4) 2

4 hr for the train
78)312
312

6 hr for the car
52)312
312

6 hr
− 4 hr
2 hr longer

42. (2) $0.02

$0.26 per oz of 7-ounce tube
7)$1.82
1 4
42
42

$0.24 per oz of 9-ounce tube
9)$2.16
1 8
36
36

$0.26
0.24
$0.02 cheaper

43. (2) 28

Add all three sides.

8 ft + 8 ft + 12 ft = 28 ft

44. (4) 60

Add all three sides.

24 yd + 26 yd + 10 yd = 60 yd

45. (4) 30

Multiply 6 ft × 5 since all sides are equal.

6 ft × 5 = 30 ft

46. (2) 71

23 ft, 23 ft } 2 sides
16 ft, 16 ft } 2 sides
78 ft
− 7 ft − doorway
71 ft

47. (2) 247

13 × 19 = 247 sq ft

48. (5) Insufficient data

The measurements of the sides of the property are unknown.

49. (3) 3

First find the area of the 4 walls.

25 × 8.5 × 4 = 850 sq ft

One gal of paint covers 300 sq ft, 2 gal cover 600 sq ft, and 3 gal covers 900 sq ft. 3 gal will be needed.

50. (3) 108

6 ft = 72 in

108 in
72)7,776
7 2
576
576

51. (4) 2,142

17 × 21 × 6 = 2,142 cu in

52. (5) Insufficient data

You do not know the length of the tank.

53. (2) 912

First find the capacity of each box.

36 × 4 × 3 = 432 cu in
28 × 8 × 6 = 1,344 cu in

Then subtract.

1,344 cu in
− 432 cu in
912 cu in

54. (3) 32

60 in = 5 ft

First multiply the measurements you know.

5 × 2.5 = 12.5 f

Then divide to find the depth.

3.2 ft deep
12.5)40

55. (4) $6.48

First find the total amount of money spent.

$0.69 × 3 = $2.07
$0.33 × 6 = $1.98
$4.29 × 2 = $8.58
$0.89 × 1 = $0.89
$13.52

Then find the amount of change.

$20.00
−13.52
$ 6.48

56. (1) $1{,}906\frac{1}{4}$

Since there are 52 weeks in a year and Min takes a 2-week vacation, she actually works 50 weeks. According to her pattern, she works $38\frac{1}{2}$ hrs for 25 wks and $37\frac{3}{4}$ hr for 25 wks.

$38\frac{1}{2} \times 25 = 962\frac{1}{2}$ hr = $962\frac{2}{4}$ hr
$37\frac{3}{4} \times 25 = 943\frac{3}{4}$ hr = + $943\frac{3}{4}$ hr
$1{,}905\frac{5}{4} = 1906\frac{1}{4}$ hr

57. (5) $3.28

$25.83 ÷ $7\frac{7}{8}$

25.83 ÷ $\frac{63}{8}$

25.83 × $\frac{8}{63}$ = $3.28

58. (5) Insufficient data

You do not know Brad's present salary.

59. (3) $159.59

$297 × 0.15 = $44.55 discount

$297 × $\frac{1}{3}$ = $99 off reg. price

$$\begin{array}{rl} \$297.00 & \text{original price} \\ -\ 44.55 & \text{discount} \\ \hline \$252.45 & \\ -\ 99.00 & \tfrac{1}{3}\text{ off} \\ \hline \$153.45 & \end{array}$$

$153.45 × 0.04 = $6.138 = $6.14 tax

$$\begin{array}{rl} \$153.45 & \\ +\ \ 6.14 & \text{tax} \\ \hline \$159.59 & \end{array}$$

60. (4) 37

$21.5\overline{)792}$ = 36.8 = 37 teachers

61. (1) $339.70

Find the amount of each expense.

$2,580 × 0.285 = $735.30 mortgage

$2,580 × $\frac{1}{4}$ = $645 food

$2,580 × $\frac{1}{3}$ = $860 bills

Add the expenses.

$735.30 + $645 + $860 = $2,240.30

Subtract expenses from earnings.

$$\begin{array}{r} \$2,580.00 \\ -2,240.30 \\ \hline \$339.70 \end{array}$$

62. (4) $-\frac{3}{8}$

$1\frac{1}{4} + \frac{3}{4} - 2\frac{1}{8} + \frac{3}{8} - \frac{5}{8} = -\frac{3}{8}$

Geometry
(pages 495–523)

1. (1) 45°

180° − 135° = 45°

2. (2) 85°

Vertical angles = 360°
∠*c* and ∠*d* are equal.
∠*c* and ∠d each = 95°
95° × 2 = 190°

Subtract to find the total measurement of angles *e* and *f*.
360° − 190° = 170°

Divide by 2 to find the measurement of ∠*f*.

$2\overline{)170°}$ = 85°

3. (2) 23°

90° − 67° = 23°

4. (4) 128°

The four known angles equal 104° (26 × 4).

The two unknown angles are 360° − 104° = 256°.

∠*z* is one half of 256°.

$2\overline{)256}$ = 128°

5. (1) 35°

Complementary angles are two angles that have a sum of 90°.
90° − 55° = 35°

6. (3) 127°

Supplementary angles are two angles that have a sum of 180°.
180° − 53° = 127°

7. (3) 130°

$$\begin{array}{rr} \angle CBE = & 180° \\ \angle ABE = & -\ 50° \\ \hline \angle ABC = & 130° \end{array}$$

8. (4) Both are 142°.

∠*A* = 180° − 19° − 19° = 142°
∠*B* is vertical to ∠*A*. Vertical angles are equal; therefore, ∠*B* equals 142°.

9. (2) 103°

45° + 32° = 77°
180° − 77° = 103°

10. (2) 45°

Vertical angles are equal, and ∠*U* = 45°.

11. (3) 77°

45° + 32° = 77°

12. (4) 283°

103° + 45° + 32° + 103° = 283°

13. (1) 39°

∠1 and ∠2 are supplementary angles; therefore, their sum is 180°.
180° − 141° = 39°

14. (5) ∠8

Vertical angles are equal.

15. (2) ∠3

Vertical angles are equal.

16. (2) 180°

Supplementary angles equal 180°.

17. (4) 321°

Vertical angles total 360°.
360° − 39° = 321°

18. (4) parallel to each other

Perpendicular means "being at right angles to a line or plane."

19. (4) 90°

Since ∠6 = 90° and supplementary angles = 180°, ∠5 = 90°.

20. (3) ∠5

∠1 and ∠5 are corresponding angles. They are on the same side of the transversal and on the same side of the two lines that are cut by the transversal. Corresponding angles are equal.

21. (4) ∠7

Vertical angles are equal.

22. (2) 105°

∠5 and ∠*g* are corresponding angles; ∠*g* and ∠8 are vertical angles. ∠5 = ∠*g* = ∠8 = 105°

23. (4) 92

32 ft + 32 ft + 14 ft + 14 ft = 92 ft

24. (2) 90°

Angles of squares are always 90°.

25. (2) 90°

A rectangle is a quadrilateral with four right angles.

26. (4) 14

Use the formula $p = 4s$.
$3.5 \times 4 = 14$ ft

27. (5) Insufficient data

You do not know the width.

28. (2) 18

54 in = 4.5 ft
$4.5 \times 4 = 18$ ft

29. (4) 94

Add all 4 sides.

$18\frac{1}{2}$ yd + 17 yd + 27 yd + $31\frac{1}{2}$ yd = 94 yd

30. (4) 192

19 yd = 57 ft
13 yd = 39 ft
2(57 ft) + 2(39 ft)
114 ft + 78 ft = 192 ft

31. (4) 529

Use the formula $A = s^2$.
$23^2 = 529$ sq ft

32. (4) 15

Since $A = lw$, $l = \frac{A}{w}$.

$$\begin{array}{r} 15 \text{ ft} \\ 4\overline{)60} \\ 4 \\ \hline 20 \end{array}$$

33. (5) Insufficient data

You do not know the width.

34. (2) 24

Use the formula $A = lw$.

$A = 6 \text{ ft} \times 4 \text{ ft}$
$A = 24$ sq ft

35. (4) 72

Find the area of the entire diagram and subtract the area of the shaded portion from that measurement.

$A = lw$
$A = 12 \text{ ft} \times 8 \text{ ft}$
$A = 96$ sq ft

Area of the diagram:	96 sq ft
Area of the shaded portion:	− 24 sq ft
unshaded	72 sq ft

36. (2) 66°

Base angles of an isosceles triangle are equal.
$180° - 48° = 132°$
$132° \div 2 = 66°$

37. (4) 65°

The interior angles of a triangle equal 180°.

$180 - (50 + 65) =$
$180 - 115 = 65$

38. (4) 85°

$$\begin{array}{rl} & 47\frac{1}{2}° \text{ base angle one} \\ + & 47\frac{1}{2}° \text{ base angle two} \\ \hline & 94\frac{2}{2}° = 95° \end{array}$$

$180° - 95° = 85°$

39. (3) 44°

$102° + 34° = 136°$
$180° - 136° = 44°$

40. (2) 30°, 110°, 40°

The sum of the measurements of the three angles of every triangle equals 180°.
$30° + 110° + 40° = 180°$

41. (4) 45°

Congruent triangles are equal. $\angle B$ and $\angle E$ are also equal because they are corresponding angles.

42. (2) 14

Congruent triangles are exactly the same.

43. (1) 4

$$\begin{array}{r} 4 \\ 3\overline{)12} \end{array}$$

44. (1) 45°

Congruent triangles are equal.

45. (2) 12

$$\frac{\overline{AB}}{\overline{DE}} = \frac{\overline{CB}}{\overline{EF}}$$

$$\frac{4}{8} = \frac{6}{x}$$

$$\frac{\overset{12}{\cancel{48}}}{\underset{1}{\cancel{4}}} = \frac{\overset{1}{\cancel{4x}}}{\underset{1}{\cancel{4}}}$$

12 in = x

46. (5) 96 ft

Set up a proportion to find the width of the river.

$$\frac{\overline{MN}}{\overline{PQ}} = \frac{\overline{NO}}{\overline{OQ}}$$

$$\frac{x}{60} = \frac{120}{75}$$

$$\frac{\overset{1}{\cancel{75}}x}{\underset{1}{\cancel{75}}} = \frac{\overset{96}{\cancel{7200}}}{\underset{1}{\cancel{75}}}$$

$x = 96$ ft

47. (1) 5

Set up a proportion to find the length of $\overline{PQ}$.

$$\frac{\overline{RQ}}{\overline{RT}} = \frac{\overline{PQ}}{\overline{ST}}$$

$$\frac{12}{24} = \frac{x}{10}$$

$$\frac{\overset{1}{\cancel{24}}x}{\underset{1}{\cancel{24}}} = \frac{\overset{5}{\cancel{120}}}{\underset{1}{\cancel{24}}}$$

$x = 5$

48. (4) 551

Use the formula $P = s + s + s$.

$P = 144 \text{ ft} + 211 \text{ ft} + 196 \text{ ft}$
$P = 551$ ft

49. (2) 34

Use the formula $P = s + s + s$.

$P = 10 \text{ ft} + 10 \text{ ft} + 14 \text{ ft}$
$P = 34$ ft

50. (5) Insufficient data

You do not know the measurement of the third side.

51. (3) 70

Substitute the given measurements in the formula $P = s + s + s$.

$$\begin{array}{rcl} 167 \text{ ft} & = & 59 \text{ ft} + 38 \text{ ft} + s \\ 167 \text{ ft} & = & 97 \text{ ft} + s \\ -97 & = & -97 \\ \hline 70 \text{ ft} & = & s \end{array}$$

52. (4) 144

Use the formula $A = \frac{ab}{2}$.

$$A = \frac{\overset{6}{\cancel{12}} \text{ ft} \times 24 \text{ ft}}{\underset{1}{\cancel{2}}}$$

$A = 144$ sq ft

53. (4) 280

Use the formula $A = \frac{ab}{2}$.

$A = \frac{\overset{10}{\cancel{20}}\text{ ft} \times 28\text{ ft}}{\underset{1}{\cancel{2}}}$

$A = 280$ sq ft

54. (3) 4:1

Find the areas of the two triangles and then write a ratio of the area of the larger one to the area of the smaller one.

Larger Triangle	Smaller Triangle
$A = \frac{ab}{2}$	$A = \frac{ab}{2}$
$A = \frac{\overset{6}{\cancel{12}}\text{ ft} \times 12\text{ ft}}{\underset{1}{\cancel{2}}}$	$A = \frac{\overset{3}{\cancel{6}}\text{ ft} \times 6\text{ ft}}{\underset{1}{\cancel{2}}}$
$A = 72$ sq ft	$A = 18$ sq ft

The ratio is 72:18 or 4:1.

55. (2) 48

Use the formula $A = \frac{ab}{2}$.

$A = \frac{\overset{4}{\cancel{8}}\text{ ft} \times 12\text{ ft}}{\underset{1}{\cancel{2}}}$

$A = 48$ sq ft

56. (3) 15 in

Use the Pythagorean theorem to find the length of the hypotenuse.

$c^2 = a^2 + b^2$
$c^2 = 9^2 + 12^2$
$c^2 = 81 + 144$
$c^2 = 225$
$c = \sqrt{225}$
$c = 15$ in

57. (2) 12

Use the Pythagorean theorem to find the length of leg b.

$c^2 = a^2 + b^2$
$15^2 = 9^2 + b^2$
$225 = 81 + b^2$
$-81 = -81$
$144 = b^2$
$\sqrt{144} = b$
$12 = b$

58. (4) 24

Use the Pythagorean theorem to find the length of leg a.

$c^2 = a^2 + b^2$
$26^2 = a^2 + 10^2$
$676 = a^2 + 100$
$-100 \quad -100$
$576 = a^2$
$\sqrt{576} = a$
$24 = a$

59. (1) 5

Use the Pythagorean theorem to find the length of the hypotenuse.

$c^2 = a^2 + b^2$
$c^2 = 3^2 + 4^2$
$c^2 = 9 + 16$
$c^2 = 25$
$c = \sqrt{25} = 5$

60. (3) 10

Use the Pythagorean theorem to find the length of the leg.

$c^2 = a^2 + b^2$
$26^2 = 24^2 + b^2$
$676 = 576 + b^2$
$-576 \quad -576$
$100 = b^2$
$\sqrt{100} = b$
$10\text{ yd} = b$

61. (3) 25

Use the Pythagorean theorem to find the distance.

$c^2 = a^2 + b^2$
$c^2 = 20^2 + 15^2$
$c^2 = 400 + 225$
$c^2 = 625$
$c = \sqrt{625} = 25$ mi

62. (2) 500

Use the Pythagorean theorem to find the distance.

$c^2 = a^2 + b^2$
$c^2 = 300^2 + 400^2$
$c^2 = 90{,}000 + 160{,}000$
$c^2 = 250{,}000$
$c = \sqrt{250{,}000} = 500$ ft

63. (1) 25

Use the Pythagorean theorem to find the length of the diagonal.

$c^2 = a^2 + b^2$
$c^2 = 7^2 + 24^2$
$c^2 = 49 + 576$
$c^2 = 625$
$c = \sqrt{625} = 25$ yd

64. (1) 36

Use the Pythagorean theorem to find the distance that he must travel.

$c^2 = a^2 + b^2$
$45^2 = a^2 + 27^2$
$2025 = a^2 + 729$
$-729 \quad -729$
$1296 = a^2$
$\sqrt{1296} = a$
$36\text{ mi} = a$

65. (3) 527.52

Use the formula $C = \pi \times 2r$.

$C = 3.14 \times 2 \times 84$
$C = 527.52$ ft

66. (2) 188.4

To find the circumferences of the three circles, use the formula below.

Larger Circle
$C = \pi d$
$C = 3.14 \times 30$
$C = 94.2$ ft

If you add the measurements of the radii of the two smaller circles, you would find that their combined length is the same as that of the radius of the larger circle; therefore, their combined circumferences would be exactly the same measurement as the circumference of the larger circle. Multiply the larger circle's circumference by 2 to find the total amount of fencing needed.

$94.2 \times 2 = 188.4$ ft

67. (3) 26

Use the formula $C = \pi d$.

$81\frac{5}{7} = \frac{22}{7}d$

$\frac{572}{7} \div \frac{22}{7} = d$

$\frac{\overset{26}{\cancel{572}}}{\underset{1}{\cancel{7}}} \times \frac{\overset{1}{\cancel{7}}}{\underset{1}{\cancel{22}}} = 26$

$26 = d$

68. (2) $72\frac{2}{7}$

Use the formula $C = \pi d$.

$C = \frac{22}{7} \times 23$

$C = 72\frac{2}{7}$ in

69. (4) 43.96

Use the formula $C = \pi \times 2r$.
$C = 3.14 \times 2 \times 7$
$C = 43.96$ ft

70. (4) 153.86

The radius equals 7 ft.
$A = \pi r^2$
$A = 3.14 \times 7 \times 7$
$A = 153.86$ sq ft

71. (5) 38.465

The radius is 3.5 ft.
$A = \pi r^2$
$A = 3.14 \times 3.5 \times 3.5$
$A = 38.465$ sq ft

72. (2) 9

Use the formula $A = \pi r^2$.

$\frac{254.34}{3.14} = \frac{3.14}{3.14} \times r^2$ Divide both sides by 3.14

$81 = r^2$
$\sqrt{81} = r$
$9 \text{ ft} = r$

73. (2) 531

Use the formula $A = \pi r^2$.
$A = 3.14 \times 13$ in $\times 13$ in
$A = 530.66$ rounds to 531 sq in

74. (3) $\frac{4}{9}$

$\frac{160°}{360°} = \frac{4}{9}$

75. (2) 1,232

Find the area of the mirror and subtract that measurement from the area of the board. The radius of the mirror is $24\frac{1}{2}$ in.

$A = \pi r^2$

$A = \frac{\overset{11}{\cancel{22}}}{\underset{1}{\cancel{7}}} \times \frac{\overset{7}{\cancel{49}}}{\underset{1}{\cancel{2}}} \text{ in} \times \frac{49 \text{ in}}{2}$

$A = \frac{3,773}{2}$

$A = 1,886\frac{1}{2}$ sq in

The radius of the board is $31\frac{1}{2}$ in.

$A = \pi r^2$

$A = \frac{\overset{11}{\cancel{22}}}{\underset{1}{\cancel{7}}} \times \frac{\overset{9}{\cancel{69}}}{\underset{1}{\cancel{2}}} \text{ in} \times \frac{63 \text{ in}}{2}$

$A = \frac{6,237}{2}$

$A = 3,118\frac{1}{2}$ sq in

$3.118\frac{1}{2}$ sq in
$-\ 1,886\frac{1}{2}$ sq in
$1,232$ sq in

76. (2) $\frac{3}{4}$

270° shaded portion

$\frac{270°}{360°} = \frac{3}{4}$

77. (2) 144

Find the area of the shaded triangle. Subtract that measurement from the area of the rectangle.

$A = \frac{ab}{2}$

$A = \frac{16 \text{ ft} \times 18 \text{ ft}}{2}$

$A = 144$ sq ft
$A = lw$
$A = 16$ ft $\times 18$ ft
$A = 288$ sq ft

Area of the rectangle:	288 sq ft
Area of the triangle:	− 144 sq ft
unshaded:	144 sq ft

78. (5) 174

Find the areas of the rectangles and add those measurements.

Smaller Rectangle
$A = lw$
$A = 6$ ft $\times 5$ ft
$A = 30$ sq ft

Larger Rectangle:
$A = lw$
$A = 8$ ft $\times 18$ ft
$A = 144$ sq ft

Area of the smaller:	30 sq ft
Area of the larger:	+ 144 sq ft
	174 sq ft

79. (4) 140

Find the area of the wall and then divide that measurement by the area of the wallpaper squares.

Area of the wall:
$A = lw$
$A = 14$ ft $\times 10$ ft
$A = 140$ sq ft

Area of one square:
12 in $\times$ 12 in $=$
1 ft $\times$ 1 ft $=$ 1 sq ft

$\frac{140 \text{ sq ft}}{1 \text{ sq ft}} = 140$

80. (4) $82.60

```
   140
× $.59
  12 60
  70 0
$82.60
```

81. (5) Insufficient data

You need to know the depth of the tank to find its volume.

82. (1) 60

First change 9 in to $\frac{3}{4}$ ft and then use the formula $V = lwh$.

$V = 4$ ft $\times 20$ ft $\times \frac{3}{4}$ ft

$V = 60$ cu ft

83. (1) 12

Use the formula $V = lwh$.
720 cu ft $= l \times 12$ ft $\times 5$ ft

$\frac{\overset{12}{\cancel{720}}}{\underset{1}{\cancel{60}}} = \frac{\overset{1}{\cancel{60}l}}{\underset{1}{\cancel{60}}}$

$12 \text{ ft} = l$

84. (5) 3,888

Use the formula $V = lwh$.
$V = 18$ ft $\times 12$ ft $\times 18$ ft
$V = 3,888$ cu ft

85. (4) 9

Use the formula $V = lwh$.
$V = 2$ yd $\times 1.5$ yd $\times 3$ yd
$V = 9$ cu yd

86. (2) 2,472.75

Use the formula $V = \pi r^2 h$.
$V = 3.14 \times 7.5 \times 7.5 \times 14$
$V = 2,472.75$ cu ft

87. (5) 3,052.08

Use the formula $V = \pi r^2 h$.
$V = 3.14 \times 9 \times 9 \times 12$
$V = 3,052.08$ cu in

88. (1) 224

Use the formula $V = bh$.

$3{,}584 \text{ cu in} = b(16 \text{ in})$

$\frac{3{,}584 \text{ cu in}}{16 \text{ in}} = \frac{b(16 \text{ in})}{16 \text{ in}}$

$224 \text{ sq in} = b$

89. (3) 4

Use the formula $V = \pi r^2 h$.

$1{,}808.64 = 3.14 \times r^2 \times 36$ (3 ft = 36 in)

$1{,}808.64 = 113.04 \times r^2$ Divide both sides by 113.04.

$16 = r^2$

$\sqrt{16} = r$

$4 \text{ in} = r$

90. (2) (4, −2)

91. (5) (−3,5)

92. (1) (8, −6)

93. (2) (3,8)

94. (3) (3,3)

95. (1) *A*

96. (1) *D*

97. (3) *E*

98. (4) *J*

99. (4) *B*

100. (1) 8

Since the *x* coordinates are the same, ignore them. Subtract the smaller *y* coordinate from the larger. $7-(-1) = 8$

101. (3) 13

The *x* coordinates for both points are −5. Subtract the smaller *y* coordinate from the larger. $6-(-7) = 13$

102. (4) 7

The *y* coordinates for both points are −3. Subtract the smaller *x* coordinate from the larger. $5-(-2) = 7$

103. (3) 5

The coordinates for the *x* axis from *B* are (2,0). The *x* coordinates for both points are 2. Subtract the smaller *y* coordinate from the larger. $5-0 = 5$

104. (1) 4

The coordinates for the *y* axis from *H* are (0, −7). The *y* coordinates for both points are −7. Subtract the smaller *x* coordinate from the larger. $4 - 0 = 4$

105. (4) (0,2)

106. (1) (10,2)

107. (5) 10

The coordinates of *E* are (0, 2). The coordinates of *T* are (10, 2). Since the *y* coordinates of both points are 2, subtract the smaller *x* coordinate from the larger. $10 - 0 = 10$

108. (2) 8

The coordinates of *F* are (10, 10). The coordinates of *T* are (10, 2). Since the *x* coordinates of both points are 10, subtract the smaller *y* coordinate from the larger. $10 - 2 = 8$

109. (5) $\sqrt{164}$

$\overline{EF}$ is the hypotenuse of a right triangle. The distance between *E* and *T* is 10, and the distance between *F* and *T* is 8. Use the formula $c^2 = a^2 + b^2$.

$c^2 = 10^2 + 8^2$

$c^2 = 100 + 64$

$c^2 = 164$

$c = \sqrt{164}$

110. (4) $-\frac{9}{2}$

Use the formula

$m = \frac{y_2 - y_1}{x_2 - x_1}$.

$m = \frac{(-2) - 7}{5 - 3}$

$m = -\frac{9}{2}$

111. (1) $\frac{1}{2}$

Use the formula

$m \frac{y_2 - y_1}{x_2 - x_1}$.

$m = \frac{(-2) - (-3)}{6 - 4}$

$m = \frac{-2 + 3}{+2} = \frac{+1}{+2} = +\frac{1}{2}$

112. (2) .08

The bottom and the top of the ramp can be represented by the coordinates (0,0) and (50,4).

$m = \frac{y_2 - y_1}{x_2 - x_1}$

$m = \frac{4 - 0}{50 - 0}$

$m = \frac{4}{50}$

$m = .08$

113. (4) 12

The maximum rise is 100 ft × .12, or 12 ft.

114. (4) (−3,7)

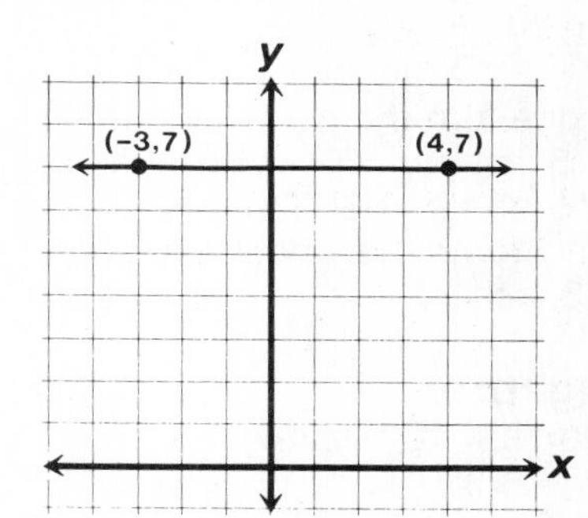

Any point that lies along this line will be the choice. There is no rise or descent of a line parallel to the *x*-axis.

115. (4) 602.88

Use the formula $V = \pi r^2 h$.

$V = 3.14 \times 4 \times 4 \times 12$

$V = 602.88 \text{ cu ft}$

116. (1) 23.4

Convert measurements to yards.
13.5 ft = 4.5 yd
15.6 ft = 5.2 yd
Use the formula $A = lw$.
$A = 4.5 \times 5.2$
$A = 23.4$ sq yd

117. (3) 27.16

Convert measures to yards.
13.5 ft = 4.5 yd
15.6 ft = 5.2 yd
8.4 ft = 2.8 yd
Use the formula $A = lw$ to find the area of each wall.
$A = 2.8 \times 4.5$
$A = 12.6$ sq yd
$A = 2.8 \times 5.2$
$A = 14.56$ sq yd
Add the areas of the two walls together: 12.6 sq yd + 14.56 sq yd = 27.16 sq yd.

118. (5) 942

Use the formula $C = \pi d$.
$C = 3.14 \times 25$
$C = 78.5$ inches
In one turn the wheel will travel 78.5 inches.
78.5 × 12 = 942 inches
In 12 turns the wheel will travel 942 inches.

Algebra
(pages 524–544)

1. (2) 5

$(4)^2 + (1)^4 - 6\,(4)\frac{1}{2} =$
$16 + 1 - 12 =$
$17 - 12 = 5$

2. (4) −10

$(7 - 8) + 7 - 4^2 =$
$-1 + 7 - 16 =$
$+7 - 17 = -10$

3. (4) $6\frac{7}{8}$

$(-\frac{1}{4})\,(\frac{1}{2}) + 7 =$
$-\frac{1}{8} + 7 = 6\frac{7}{8}$

4. (3) +9

$-9^1 + 18 =$
$-9 + 18 = +9$

5. (5) 4

$6 + 2 - (7 - 5)^2 =$
$6 + 2 - (2)^2 =$
$6 + 2 - 4 =$
$8 - 4 = 4$

6. (4) 115

$3 \times 5 + 4(4 + 1)^2 =$
$3 \times 5 + 4(5)^2 =$
$3 \times 5 + 4(25) =$
$3 \times 5 + 100 =$
$15 + 100 = 115$

7. (2) $3\frac{1}{4}$

$\frac{1}{4} \times 12 + (\frac{1}{2})^2 =$
$3 + \frac{1}{4} = 3\frac{1}{4}$

8. (3) −48

$(-4)^3 + 4^2 =$
$-64 + 16 = -48$

9. (1) −17

$(-1)^5 - 4 \times (4 - 2)^2 =$
$-1 - 4 \times (2)^2 =$
$-1 - 4 \times 4 =$
$-1 - 16 = -17$

10. (3) 25(15) + 25(105)

The distributive law states that multiplying a sum is the same as multiplying each number that is added to make the sun.

11. (2) (8 × 9) + −22

The commutative law states that you can reverse the numbers in an addition or multiplication problem and still compute the same answer.

12. (4) 106 (4 − 12)

The associative law states that numbers to be added or multiplied can be grouped in different ways without changing the answer.

13. (1) (92 × 60) × 9

The associative law says numbers to be added or multiplied can be grouped in different ways without changing the answer.

14. (4) ($299 + $433 + $59) − $200

TV + machine + radio − down payment = ($229 + $433 + $59) − $200

15. (3) 3 ($1.49 − $0.98)

3 (regular price − sale price)
3($1.49 − $0.98)

16. (1) $75 + 12($50)

Down payment + 12(monthly payment) = $75 + 12($50)

17. (3) $\frac{10\ (\$1.59)}{3}$

$\frac{10\text{ lb (cost)}}{3};\ \frac{10\ (\$1.59)}{3}$

18. (4) $3n - 6$

Six less than 3 groups of hikers:
$3n - 6$

19. (2) $c + L$

A number c phone calls increased by L phone calls:
$c + L$

20. (2) $\frac{x}{5}$

$\frac{\text{total cost of books}}{\text{total number purchased}} = \frac{x}{5} =$
cost per book

21. (1) $100x$

Each dollar has 100 cents. Multiply 100 cents by x dollars = $100x$.

22. (1) $15 - x$

15 decreased by a number x = $15 - x$.

23. (4) $x + 5$

The sum of the collection and 5:
$x + 5$

24. (4) $7a$

The product of 7 and a number, a: $7a$

25. (2) $\frac{x}{6}$

The amount, x, divided by six:
$\frac{x}{6}$

26. (5) $n + 15$

Present weight + gain:
$n + 15$

27. (3) $-3a$

$3a + a - 7a =$
$4a - 7a = -3a$

28. (3) 5 *rs*

$$\begin{array}{r} 7rs + t \\ -2rs - t \\ \hline 5rs \end{array}$$

29. (4) 6*x*

$$\begin{array}{r} 4x \\ -9x \\ 4x \\ 7x \\ \hline +6x \end{array}$$

30. (1) 6*a* + 3*b*

$$\begin{array}{l} 4a - 3b \\ 2a + 6b \\ \hline 6a + 3b \end{array}$$

31. (2) $-3c^2d^2$

$$\begin{array}{l} -4c^2d^2 \\ +\ \ c^2d^2 \\ \hline -3c^2d^2 \end{array}$$

32. (4) $2x^2 + 4xy + 8x$

$2x(x + 2y + 4) =$
$2x^2 + 4xy + 8x$

33. (5) $-20r - 35s$

$-5(2r - 3s) - 10(r - 5s) =$
$-10r + 15s - 10r - 50s =$
$-20r - 35s$

34. (2) $-8ab^3$

$$\frac{\overset{-8}{\cancel{24}}\overset{1}{a^2}\overset{3}{b^4}}{-\cancel{3}ab} = -8ab^3$$

35. (5) $12a^3b^3$

$(3a^2b)(4ab^2) = 12a^3b^3$

36. (3) 4*bc*

$$\frac{-\overset{4}{\cancel{32}}a^2\overset{b}{b^3}\overset{c}{c^2}}{-\cancel{8}a^2b^2c} = 4bc$$

37. (2) $5x(x - 2)$

Factor out 5*x*
$5x^2 - 10x$
$5x(x - 2)$

38. (3) $3abc\ (a + 2b)$

$3a^2bc + 6ab^2c$
Factor out 3*abc*.
$3abc\ (a + 2b)$

39. (1) $8de(2de - 3)$

$16d^2e^2 - 24de$
Factor out 8*de*.
$8de(2de - 3)$

40. (2) $9xy(2x - 3)$

$18x^2y - 27xy$
Factor out 9*xy*.
$9xy\ (2x - 3)$

41. (2) −8

$d^2 \div e =$
$4^2 \div -2 =$
$16 \div -2 = -8$

42. (5) 8

$a^2 + b =$
$2^2 + 4 =$
$4 + 4 = 8$

43. (5) +56

$-xyz - 2y =$
$-(2)\ (-4)\ (6) - 2(-4) =$
$48 + 8 = 56$

44. (2) 1

$$\frac{\frac{1}{2}b}{a} = \frac{\frac{1}{\cancel{2}_1} \times \frac{\overset{5}{\cancel{10}}}{1}}{5} = \frac{5}{5} = 1$$

45. (4) 125

$7x^2 + 5y^2 =$
$7(0)^2 + 5(5)^2 =$
$7(0) + 5(25) =$
$0 + 125 = 125$

46. (5) 22

$$\begin{array}{l} n - 5 = 17 \\ \ \ \ + 5\ \ \ +5 \\ \hline n\ \ \ \ \ \ = 22 \end{array}$$

47. (5) 9

$$\begin{array}{l} 9 + r = \ \ 18 \\ -9\ \ \ \ \ \ \ \ \ \ -9 \\ \hline \ \ \ \ \ \ r = \ \ \ 9 \end{array}$$

48. (4) 81

$$\begin{array}{l} y + 12 = 93 \\ \ \ \ -12\ \ -12 \\ \hline y\ \ \ \ \ \ \ \ = 81 \end{array}$$

49. (1) 3

$$\begin{array}{l} x + 9 = \ 12 \\ \ \ \ -9\ \ \ \ -9 \\ \hline x\ \ \ \ \ \ =\ \ 3 \end{array}$$

50. (3) 20

$$\begin{array}{l} s - 8 = 12 \\ \ \ + 8\ \ \ +8 \\ \hline s\ \ \ \ \ = 20 \end{array}$$

51. (4) 6

$3m = 18$

$$\frac{\overset{1}{\cancel{3}}m}{\underset{1}{\cancel{3}}} = \frac{\overset{6}{\cancel{18}}}{\underset{1}{\cancel{3}}}$$

$m = 6$

52. (3) 10

$\frac{y}{2} = 5$

$$\frac{\overset{1}{\cancel{2}}}{1} \times \frac{y}{\underset{1}{\cancel{2}}} = 5 \times 2 \qquad y = 10$$

53. (3) 8

$4a = 32$

$$\frac{\overset{1}{\cancel{4}}a}{\underset{1}{\cancel{4}}} = \frac{\overset{8}{\cancel{32}}}{\underset{1}{\cancel{4}}} \qquad a = 8$$

54. (4) 45

$15 = \frac{b}{3}$

$$\frac{\overset{1}{\cancel{3}}}{1} \times \frac{b}{\underset{1}{\cancel{3}}} = 15 \times 3 \qquad b = 45$$

55. (2) 31

$93 = 3x$

$$\frac{\overset{1}{\cancel{3}}x}{\underset{1}{\cancel{3}}} = \frac{\overset{31}{\cancel{93}}}{\underset{1}{\cancel{3}}} \qquad x = 31$$

56. (1) −3

$$\begin{array}{rcr} 8z + \ \ 5 & = & 14 + 11z \\ -14 & & -14\ \ \ \ \ \ \ \ \\ \hline 8z - \ \ 9 & = & 11z \\ -8z\ \ \ \ \ \ \ & & -8z \\ \hline -\frac{9}{3} & = & \frac{3z}{3} \\ -3 & = & z \end{array}$$

57. (4) 2

$$\begin{array}{lcl} 9a - 13 & = & 13 - 4a \\ +4a + 13 & & 13 + 4a \\ \hline \frac{\overset{1}{\cancel{13}}a}{\underset{1}{\cancel{13}}} & = & \frac{\overset{2}{\cancel{26}}}{\underset{1}{\cancel{13}}} \\ a & = & 2 \end{array}$$

58. (4) 3

$$\begin{array}{rcl} 8b - 13 + \ \ 3b & = & 12 + 5b - 7 \\ 11b - 13 & = & 5 + 5b \\ -5b\ \ \ \ \ \ \ \ \ & & \ \ \ \ \ \ -5b \\ \hline 6b - 13 & = & 5 \\ +13 & & +13 \\ \hline \frac{\overset{1}{\cancel{6}}b}{\underset{1}{\cancel{6}}} & = & \frac{\overset{3}{\cancel{18}}}{\underset{1}{\cancel{6}}} \\ b & = & 3 \end{array}$$

59. (4) 2

$$\begin{aligned} 6y + 7 &= 3 + 8y \\ -6y \quad & \quad -6y \\ 7 &= 3 + 2y \\ -3 \quad & \quad -3 \\ \frac{\overset{2}{\cancel{4}}}{\underset{1}{\cancel{2}}} &= \frac{\overset{1}{\cancel{2}y}}{\underset{1}{\cancel{2}}} \end{aligned}$$

$2 = y$

60. (1) 4

$$\begin{aligned} \frac{3x}{2} &= 5x - 14 \\ (\frac{3x}{\cancel{2}}) &= 2(5x - 14) \\ 3x &= 10x - 28 \\ 3x + 28 &= 10x \\ 3x - 3x + 28 &= 10x - 3x \\ 28 &= 7x \\ 4 &= x \end{aligned}$$

61. (2) $w - 20 = 145$

original weight − 20 = 145

$w - 20 = 145$

62. (1) $12s = \$15{,}000$

12 months × monthly salary = yearly salary

$12s = \$15{,}000$

63. (5) $2a = 48$

2 × present age = 48

$2a = 48$

64. (3) $\frac{c}{7} = 2$

$\frac{\text{cable wire}}{\text{7 pieces}} = 2$ ft

$\frac{c}{7} = 2$

65. (4) $p + \$0.30 = \$1.59$

Original price of hamburger + increase = present price

$p + \$0.30 = \$1.59$

66. (4) $618.80

Find the amount of the tax.
$595 × 0.04 = $23.80
Find the final cost.
$595 + $23.80 = $618.80

67. (3) $0.79

$$3\overline{)\$2.37}\quad = \$0.79$$

68. (5) Insufficient data

You do not know the rate of the discount.

69. (5) $29\frac{1}{4}$

$2\frac{1}{4} \times 13 = \frac{9}{4} \times 13 =$

$\frac{117}{4} = 29\frac{1}{4}$ ft

70. (3) $2.85

$$\begin{array}{r} \$2.85 \\ 350\overline{)\$997.50} \\ \underline{700} \\ 2975 \\ \underline{2800} \\ 1750 \\ \underline{1750} \end{array}$$

71. (1) 8

$$\begin{aligned} c + 2 &\le 10 \\ -2 \quad & \quad -2 \\ c &\le 8 \end{aligned}$$

72. (5) 16

$$\begin{aligned} 2x + 14 &> 40 \\ -14 \quad & \quad -14 \\ \frac{\overset{1}{\cancel{2}x}}{\underset{1}{\cancel{2}}} &> \frac{\overset{13}{\cancel{26}}}{\underset{1}{\cancel{2}}} \end{aligned}$$

$x > 13$

73. (5) $y \ge 11$

$$\begin{aligned} 3y + 7 &\ge 40 \\ -7 \quad & \quad -7 \\ \frac{\overset{1}{\cancel{3}y}}{\underset{1}{\cancel{3}}} &\ge \frac{\overset{11}{\cancel{33}}}{\underset{1}{\cancel{3}}} \end{aligned}$$

$y \ge 11$

74. (4) $x < 9$

$$\begin{aligned} 5x - 9 &< 36 \\ +9 \quad & \quad +9 \\ \frac{\overset{1}{\cancel{5}x}}{\underset{1}{\cancel{5}}} &< \frac{\overset{9}{\cancel{45}}}{\underset{1}{\cancel{5}}} \end{aligned}$$

$x < 9$

75. (1) $x < -16$

$$\begin{aligned} \frac{1}{4}x + 6 &< 2 \\ -6 \quad & \quad -6 \\ \frac{\overset{1}{\cancel{4}}}{1} \times \frac{1}{\underset{1}{\cancel{4}}}x &< -4 \times 4 \end{aligned}$$

$x < -16$

76. (2) $50

$$\begin{aligned} x &= \text{amount of money Fran has} \\ 4x &= \text{amount of money Steve has} \\ x + 4x &= \$250 \\ 5x &= \$250 \\ x &= \$50 \end{aligned}$$

77. (4) 28

$$\begin{aligned} \frac{1}{4}x + x &= 35 \\ \frac{5}{4}x &= 35 \\ (4)\ \frac{5}{4}x &= 35\ (4) \\ 5x &= 140 \\ x &= 28 \end{aligned}$$

78. (2) 8

$$\begin{aligned} x &= \text{Terri's present age} \\ 3x &= \text{Terri's age in 16 years} \\ x + 16 &= 2x \\ 16 &= 2x \\ 8 &= x \end{aligned}$$

79. (2) Saw $39.15, drill $66.65

$$\begin{aligned} x &= \text{price of drill} \\ x - \$27.50 &= \text{price of saw} \\ x + x - \$27.50 &= \$105.80 \\ 2x &= \$133.30 \\ x &= \$66.65 \text{ price of drill} \\ \$66.65 - \$27.50 &= \$39.15 \text{ price of saw} \end{aligned}$$

80. (1) 17

$$\begin{aligned} x &= \text{number of decks built in the summer} \\ 4x &= \text{number of decks built in the spring} \\ x + 4x &= 85 \\ 5x &= 85 \\ x &= 17 \text{ decks built in the summer} \end{aligned}$$

81. (3) $(3, -1)$

$$\begin{aligned} -3x + 8 &= 4x - 13 \\ -3x + 8 + 13 &= 4x - 13 + 13 \end{aligned}$$

Add 13 to both sides.

$$-3x + 3x + 21 = 4x + 3x$$

Add $3x$ to both sides.

$$\begin{aligned} 21 &= 7x \\ 3 &= x \\ y &= -3(3) + 8 \\ y &= -9 + 8 \\ y &= -1 \end{aligned}$$

$(3, -1)$

82. (1) (5,13)

$$2x + 2 = 3x - 2$$
$$2x + 3 - 3 = 3x - 2 - 3$$
Subtract 3 from both sides
$$2x - 3x = 3x - 3x - 5$$
Subtract 3x from both sides
$$-x = -5$$
$$x = 5$$
$$y = 2(5) + 3$$
$$y = 10 + 3 = 13$$
(5,13)

83. (3) (12,6)

$$\frac{x}{2} = x - 6$$
$$2(\frac{x}{2}) = 2(x - 6)$$
Multiply both sides by 2.
$$x = 2x - 12$$
Add 12 to both sides.
$$x + 12 = 2x - 12 + 12$$
Subtract x from both sides.
$$x - x + 12 = 2x - x$$
$$12 = x$$
$$y = \frac{12}{2} = 6$$
(12,6)

84. (4) (−1,0)

$$3x + 3 = 2x + 2$$
$$3x + 3 - 3 = 2x + 2 - 3$$
Subtract 3 from both sides.
$$3x - 2x = 2x - 2x - 1$$
Subtract 2x from both sides
$$x = -1$$
$$y = 3(-1) + 3$$
$$y = -3 + 3 = 0$$
(−1,0)

85. (2) (−3,−10)

$$3x - 1 = x - 7$$
$$3x - 1 + 1 = x - 7 + 1$$
Add 1 to both sides.
$$3x - x = x - x - 6$$
Subtract x from both sides.
$$2x = -6$$
Divide both sides by 2.
$$\frac{2x}{2} = \frac{-6}{2}$$
$$x = -3$$
$$y = 3(-3) - 1$$
$$y = -9 - 1$$
$$y = -10$$
(−3,−10)

86. (1) −4,2

$$(x + 4)(x - 2) = 0$$
$$x + 4 = 0$$
$$x = -4$$
$$x - 2 = 0$$
$$x = 2$$
−4 and 2 are the solutions.

87. (5) 2,−5

$$r^2 + 3r - 10 = 0$$
$$(r + 5)(r - 2) = 0$$
$$r + 5 = 0$$
$$r = -5$$
$$r - 2 = 0$$
$$r = 2$$
−5 and 2 are the solutions.

88. (3) 3,1

$$w^2 - 4w + 3 = 0$$
$$(w - 3)(w - 1) = 0$$
$$w - 3 = 0$$
$$w = 3$$
$$w - 1 = 0$$
$$w = 1$$
3 and 1 are the solutions.

89. (3) −3,5

$$p^2 - 2p - 15 = 0$$
$$(p - 5)(p + 3) = 0$$
$$p - 5 = 0$$
$$p = 5$$
$$p + 3 = 0$$
$$p = -3$$
5 and −3 are the solutions.

90. (1) 3,−6

$$c^2 + 3c - 18 = 0$$
$$(c + 6)(c - 3) = 0$$
$$c + 6 = 0$$
$$c = -6$$
$$c - 3 = 0$$
$$c = 3$$
3 and −6 are the solutions.

91. (4) −61

$$20 - (-9^2) = 20 - 81 = -61$$

92. (4) −8b

$$\frac{40\overset{8}{a}bc}{5ac} = -8b$$

93. (5) 5

$$3a - 10 = a$$
$$3a - 10 + 10 = a + 10$$
Add to both sides.
$$3a = a + 10$$
$$3a - a = a - a + 10$$
Subtract a from both sides.
$$2a = 10$$
$$\frac{2a}{2} = \frac{10}{2}$$
Divide both sides by 2.
$$a = 5$$

94. (4) 240

$$\frac{9}{8} = \frac{270}{x}$$
$$9x = 2{,}160$$
$x = 240$ snorklers

95. (1) $316.82

$292 × 0.085 = $24.82
$292 + $24.82 = $316.82

96. (1) 5

x = brother's age
$\frac{x}{2}$ = Yolanda's age
$$x + \frac{x}{2} = 15$$
$$x - x + \frac{x}{2} = 15 - x$$
Subtract x from both sides.
$$2(\frac{x}{2}) = 2(15 - x)$$
Multiply both sides by 2.
$$x = 30 - 2x$$
$$x + 2x = 30 - 2x + 2x$$
Add 2x to both sides.
$$3x = 30$$
$\frac{3x}{3} = \frac{30}{3}$ Divide both sides by 3.
$x = 10$ = brother's age
$\frac{x}{2} = \frac{10}{2} = 5$ = Yolanda's age

Minitests—Mathematics

Minitest 1

Directions: For all problems choose the one best answer. Answers are on pages 583–584.

1. The cost of a new cross-country highway was \$144,000. The city agrees to pay 4 times as much as the county to build the road. How much does each pay?

   (1) city \$104,000, county \$40,000
   (2) city \$40,000, county \$104,000
   (3) city \$28,800, county \$115,200
   (4) city \$115,200, county \$28,800
   (5) Insufficient data is given to solve the problem.

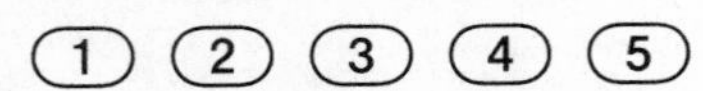

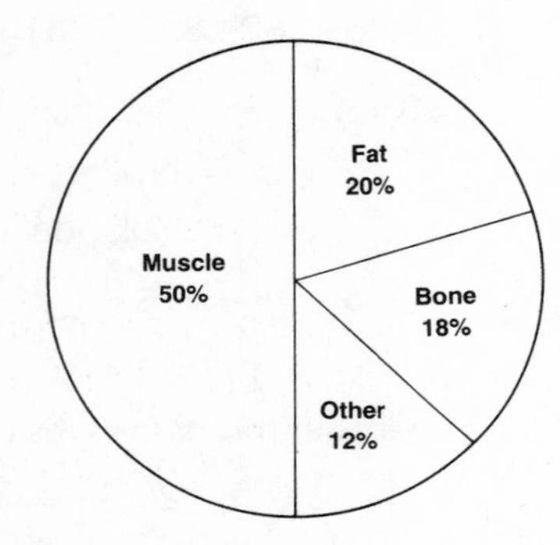

2. The graph above shows the materials that make up the human body. Muscle accounts for how many times more of the body's materials than fat?

   (1) 2
   (2) $2\frac{1}{2}$
   (3) 3
   (4) $3\frac{1}{2}$
   (5) 4

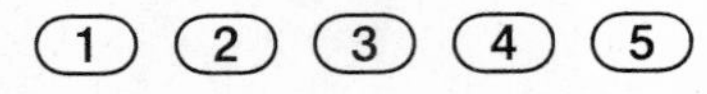

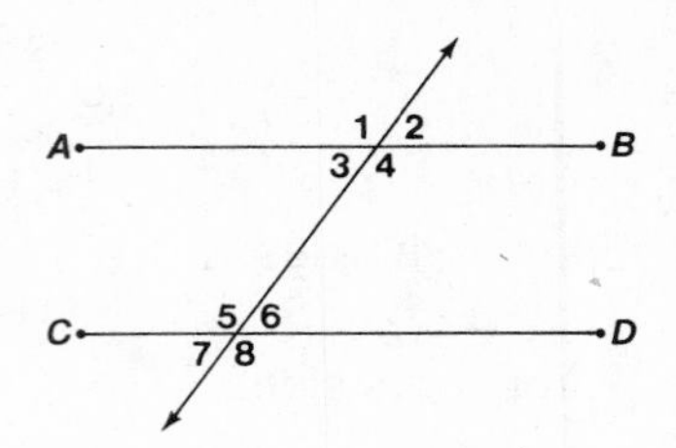

3. Line segment AB and line segment CD are parallel. If $\angle 1 = 135°$, what is the measurement of $\angle 7$?

   (1) 45°
   (2) 55°
   (3) 90°
   (4) 125°
   (5) 225°

4. Ann has 3 times as much money as Martha. Together they have \$860. Martha plans to spend \$120 on a new chair. How much money does Ann have?

   (1) \$215
   (2) \$430
   (3) \$525
   (4) \$645
   (5) Insufficient data is given to solve the problem.

   1 2 3 4 5

5. What is the combined weight of two babies if one weighs 12 pounds 3 ounces and the other weighs 8 ounces less?

   (1) 23 lb 7 oz
   (2) 23 lb 14 oz
   (3) 24 lb 8 oz
   (4) 24 lb 14 oz
   (5) Insufficient data is given to solve the problem.

   1 2 3 4 5

6. A cashier is balancing a cash register. The cash register contains 3 half-dollars, 16 quarters, 10 dimes, 5 nickels, and 3 pennies. Which of the following expressions gives the amount in dollars and cents?

   (1) 3(\$75) + 25(\$0.10) + 3
   (2) 18(\$0.75) + 15(\$0.5) + 3(\$0.01)
   (3) 3(\$0.50) + 16(\$0.25) + 10(\$0.10) + 5(\$0.05) + 3(\$0.01)
   (4) 8(\$0.5) + 26(\$0.10) + 3
   (5) 18(\$0.10) + 3(\$0.75)

   1 2 3 4 5

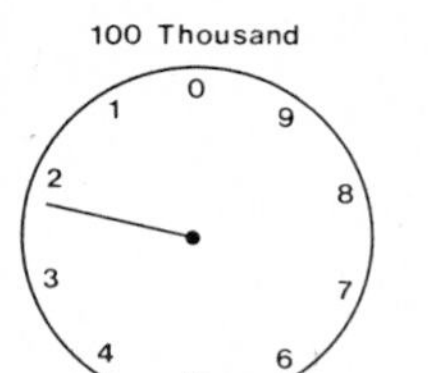

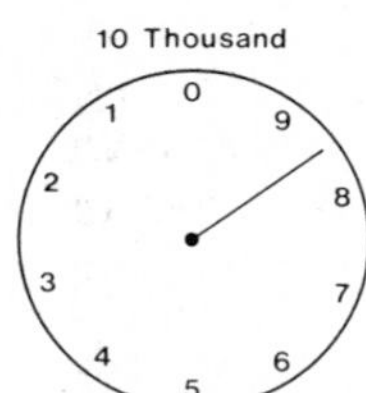

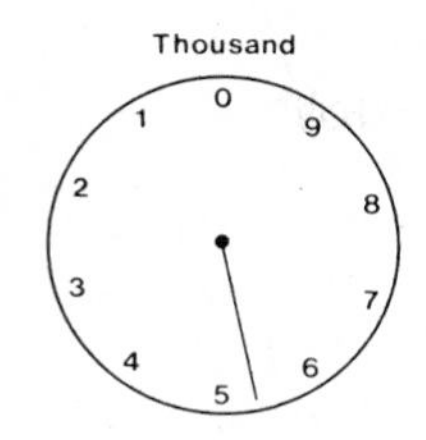

7. When the Wards' gas meter was read, the dials appeared as above. If a pointer is between two numbers, the smaller number is read. What was the gas usage in cubic feet by this family?

(1) 253,000
(2) 285,000
(3) 369,000
(4) 385,000
(5) 395,000

8. A telephone call from Miami to San Francisco costs \$3.15 for the first 3 minutes and 28 cents for each additional minute. If the tax is 78 cents, how much does a call cost?

(1) \$4.76
(2) \$5.54
(3) \$6.89
(4) \$8.69
(5) Insufficient data is given to solve the problem.

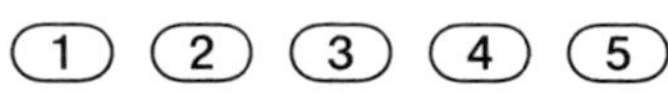

9. The simplest exponent form for $(x \cdot x \cdot x \cdot x \cdot x)(x \cdot x)$ is

(1) x^6
(2) $x^4 \cdot x^2$
(3) x^7
(4) x
(5) $7x$

10. Simplify.

$a^3bc + ab^3c + abc^3$

(1) $a^2b^2c^2\ (a + b + c)$
(2) $2abc\ (a + b + c)$
(3) $abc\ (a^2 + b^2 + c^2)$
(4) $abc\ (a + b + c)$
(5) $a^3b^3c^3\ (bc + ac + ab)$

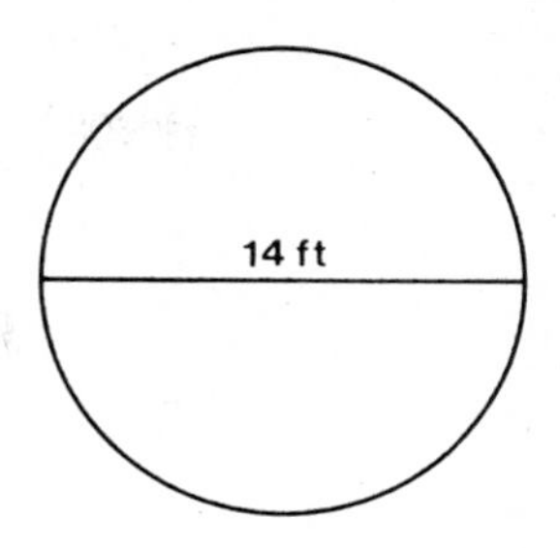

11. Mr. Simmons is planning to cement a circular patio for his barbecue pit as shown above. Each bag of cement costs \$11. What is the area in square feet that is to be cemented?

(1) 21.98
(2) 43.96
(3) 87.92
(4) 153.86
(5) 1,692.46

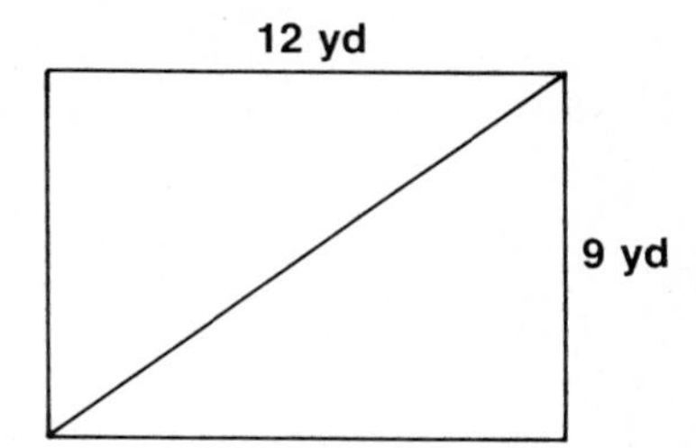

12. For a gymnastics exhibition, 4 judges placed a rope across the diagonal of the floor to separate the men's exhibition area from the women's exhibition area. How many <u>feet</u> of rope did the judges use?

(1) 5
(2) 15
(3) 21
(4) 42
(5) 45

13. At r cents an apple, which expression represents the cost in dollars of 2 dozen apples?

(1) $\frac{12r}{100}$
(2) $\frac{24r}{100}$
(3) $12r$
(4) $\frac{r}{24}$
(5) $\frac{r}{100}$

① ② ③ ④ ⑤

14. Ms. Filipa spent the following time at her part-time job this week: Monday, $5\frac{5}{6}$ hours: Tuesday, $5\frac{1}{2}$ hours; Wednesday, $5\frac{3}{4}$ hours; Thursday, $5\frac{1}{4}$ hours; Friday, $5\frac{1}{6}$ hours. Ms. Filipa's boss asked her to turn in her time sheet with the days listed in order from her shortest day to her longest day. Which of the following lists did Ms. Filipa give her boss?

A. Fri., Thurs., Tues., Wed., Mon.
B. Fri., Thurs., Tues., Mon., Wed.
C. Mon., Wed., Tues., Thurs., Fri.
D. Wed., Mon., Thurs., Fri., Tues.

(1) A
(2) B
(3) C
(4) D
(5) Insufficient data is given to solve the problem.

① ② ③ ④ ⑤

15. A baby's crib quilt measures 45 inches by 60 inches. How many <u>yards</u> of binding will be needed to finish the edges of 2 quilts with these measurements?

(1) 3
(2) 4
(3) $5\frac{5}{6}$
(4) $11\frac{2}{3}$
(5) $12\frac{2}{9}$

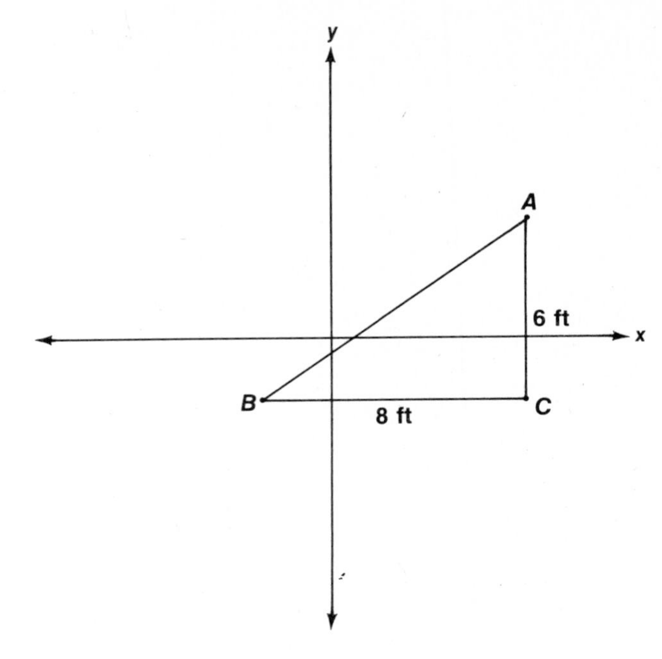

16. Line segment $\overline{AC}$ is perpendicular to $\overline{BC}$. What is the distance in feet from point A to point B on the above grid?

(1) 10
(2) 14
(3) 28
(4) 56
(5) 100

① ② ③ ④ ⑤

17. Solve for x.

$x^2 - 6x + 8 = 0$

(1) 2 and 4
(2) -2 only
(3) 4 only
(4) -2 and -4
(5) -2 and 4

① ② ③ ④ ⑤

18. If $x + y = 121$ and $x = 10y$, then $x =$

(1) 11
(2) 22
(3) 109
(4) 110
(5) 111

① ② ③ ④ ⑤

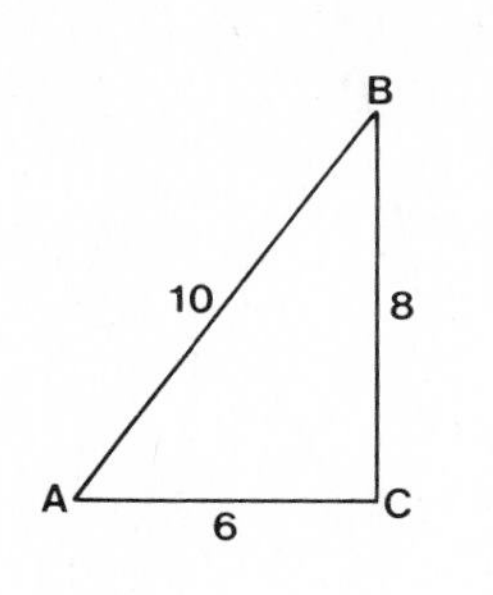

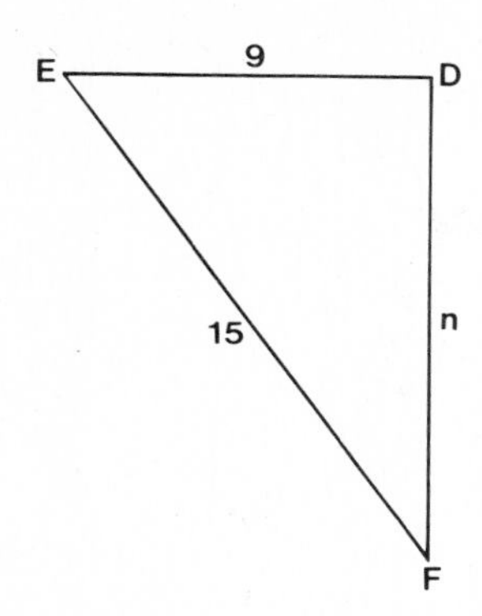

19. The two triangles above are similar. What is the value of *n*?

    (1) 2
    (2) 12
    (3) 16
    (4) 20
    (5) 24

20. The balance on Mrs. Gray's charge account was \$238. She made a payment of \$20. Then she was charged 2% on the unpaid balance. What was the new balance on her account?

    (1) \$218.76
    (2) \$220.36
    (3) \$222.36
    (4) \$222.76
    (5) \$223.76

Minitest 2

<u>Directions:</u> For all problems choose the <u>one</u> best answer. Answers are on pages 584–585.

1. The wages of 5 secretaries total \$110,000. If 4 of the secretaries are paid *y* dollars each, which of the following expressions shows how much the remaining secretary is paid?

    (1) \$110,00/4y
    (2) \$110,000 − 4y
    (3) \$110,000y
    (4) \$110,000 + 4y
    (5) Insufficient data is given to solve the problem.

2. Which of the following equals 4,692.8 expressed in scientific notation?

    (1) $10^{\circ} \times 4.6928$
    (2) 10×4.6928
    (3) $10^2 \times 4.6928$
    (4) $10^3 \times 4.6928$
    (5) $10^3 \times 46.928$

Average Weekly Earnings of Production Workers in Great Lakes States

State	1985	1986
Illinois	\$361.82	\$378.10
Indiana	380.83	401.40
Michigan	443.43	474.36
Minnesota	355.11	377.55
Wisconsin	367.59	387.36

3. In the table above, what was the approximate percentage increase in a Wisconsin worker's salary from 1985 to 1986?

    (1) 3
    (2) 5
    (3) 6
    (4) 11
    (5) 13

4. Ms. Gibson changed a dollar bill for 14 coins. The coins were all nickels and dimes. How many nickels did she receive?

    (1) 4
    (2) 6
    (3) 8
    (4) 10
    (5) 14

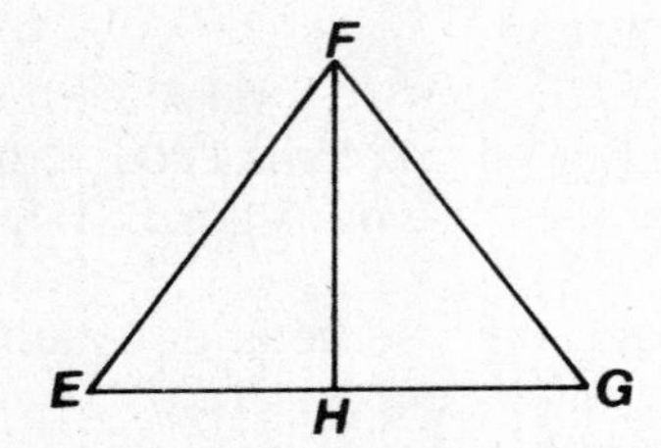

5. In the drawing above $\overline{EF}$ equals $\overline{FG}$. If $\overline{FG}$ is 5 feet long and $\overline{EG}$ is 6 feet long, how many feet long is $\overline{FH}$?

(1) 2
(2) 3
(3) 4
(4) $3\sqrt{5}$
(5) $2\sqrt{5}$

① ② ③ ④ ⑤

6. If 3 pounds of tomatoes sell for \$1.50 and 5 pounds of potatoes sell for \$1.25, what is the cost of 4½ pounds of tomatoes?

(1) \$0.50
(2) \$1.13
(3) \$2.25
(4) \$2.50
(5) \$2.75

① ② ③ ④ ⑤

7. If oranges cost 25 cents each and apples 30 cents, which expression represents the cost of 12 apples and 12 oranges?

(1) 12(\$0.30 + \$0.25)
(2) 24(\$0.30 + \$0.25)
(3) \$0.30(12) + 24(\$0.25)
(4) 24(\$0.30) + 24(\$0.12)
(5) \$0.25 + \$0.30 + 24

① ② ③ ④ ⑤

8. Factor the following equation.

$2x^2y - 4xy$

(1) $xy(2x - 4)$
(2) $2x(xy - 2y)$
(3) $2xy(x - 2)$
(4) $x^2(2xy - 4y)$
(5) $4xy(2xy)$

① ② ③ ④ ⑤

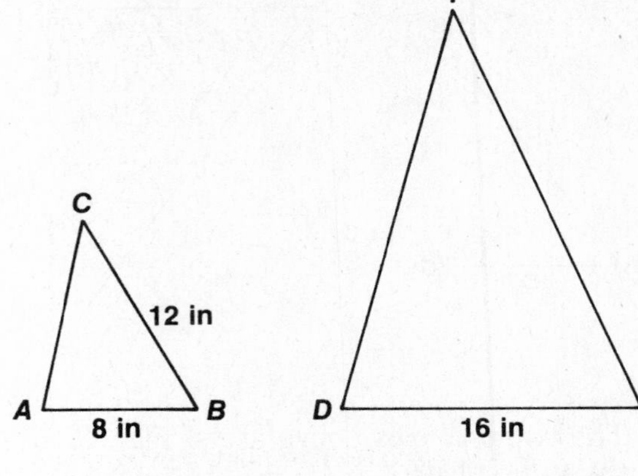

9. The triangles above are similar. How many inches long is $\overline{EF}$?

(1) 4
(2) 6
(3) 20
(4) 24
(5) 28

① ② ③ ④ ⑤

10. The numerical value of $\frac{5 \times 2^2}{2 - 1}$ is

(1) 100
(2) 25
(3) 20
(4) 10
(5) −20

① ② ③ ④ ⑤

11. Mr. and Mrs. Harwick borrowed \$5,000 from the bank to use towards a new car that costs \$8,000. They agreed to pay off the loan in 24 months. The amount of interest for each year was \$716. What was the amount of each monthly payment?

(1) \$238
(2) \$268
(3) \$348
(4) \$358
(5) \$393

① ② ③ ④ ⑤

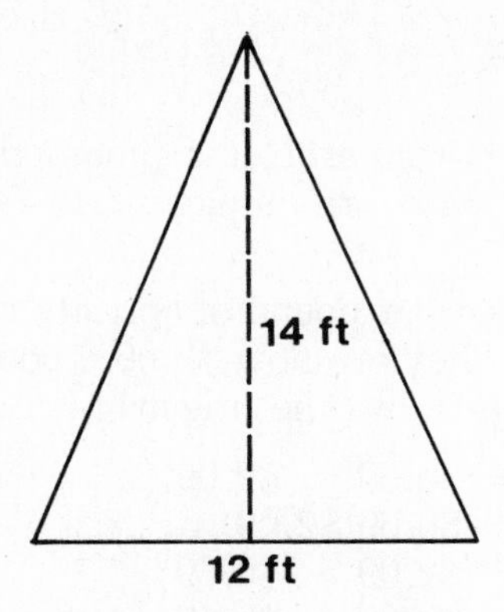

12. A landscape architect is planning to mulch the triangular plot shown in the figure above. What is the area in square feet of the plot that is to be mulched?

(1) 63
(2) 84
(3) 96
(4) 168
(5) 376

(1) (2) (3) (4) (5)

Items 13–14 refer to the following information.

Mark, a football player, is offered contracts by two professional teams. Team A offers him a yearly salary of \$56,000 with a 5% raise at the end of each of the first 2 years. He is guaranteed a 3-year contract. He will have to be on the road 18 nights of each month during the football season. Team B offers a salary of \$48,000 with a 7% raise at the end of each of the first 2 years and also guarantees Mark a 3-year contract. Team B will be on the road 21 nights of each month.

13. If Mark chooses Team A, what will be his salary at the beginning of his third year with the team?

(1) \$2,800
(2) \$56,300
(3) \$58,800
(4) \$59,115
(5) \$61,740

(1) (2) (3) (4) (5)

14. How much more will Mark's salary be at the beginning of the second year if he accepts Team A's offer rather than Team B's?

(1) \$2,800
(2) \$2,520
(3) \$7,440
(4) \$8,000
(5) \$51,360

(1) (2) (3) (4) (5)

15. Taxi fare is t cents for the first half of a mile and u cents for each additional quarter of a mile. Which of the following expressions correctly represents a fare in cents of a trip of v miles?

(1) $v(t/2 + u/4)$
(2) $t + 4u(v - \frac{1}{2})$
(3) $t + u + v$
(4) $tu + v$
(5) $v + t/2 + u/4$

(1) (2) (3) (4) (5)

16. In 6 different lab experiments, a scientist noted that the 3 chemicals A, B, and C had weights of 2.006 ounces, 2.06 ounces, and 2.66 ounces. After each experiment, the chemicals changed weight. Which of the following correctly lists the chemicals in order of lightest to heaviest after the last experiment?

(1) A, B, C
(2) A, C, B
(3) C, A, B
(4) B, C, A
(5) Insufficient data is given to solve the problem.

(1) (2) (3) (4) (5)

17. What is the least number of pieces of paneling 2 feet by 6 inches that will be required to cover a wall 12 feet by 13 feet?

(1) 150
(2) 151
(3) 152
(4) 154
(5) 156

(1) (2) (3) (4) (5)

18. The owner of a bicycle rental shop has 200 bicycles. Of this number 80 are new and 25 are children's bikes. What is the ratio of new bicycles to the total number of bicycles?

    (1) 2:5
    (2) 5:2
    (3) 2:3
    (4) 3:2
    (5) 5:1

    ① ② ③ ④ ⑤

19. If $c + d = 90$ and $c = 9d$, then $c =$

    (1) 9
    (2) 18
    (3) 27
    (4) 54
    (5) 81

    ① ② ③ ④ ⑤

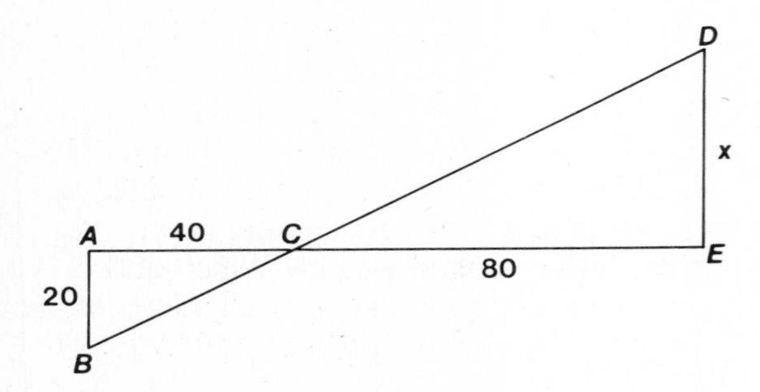

20. Given the information above, what is the value of x?

    (1) 20
    (2) 40
    (3) 100
    (4) 120
    (5) 140

    ① ② ③ ④ ⑤

Minitest 3

Directions: For all problems choose the one best answer. Answers are on pages 585–586.

1. The price per pound of apricots rose by \$0.69. They are now \$2.09 a pound. Which equation shows the original price?

    (1) $a = \$0.69 + \$2.09$
    (2) $a = \$0.69(\$2.09)$
    (3) $a = \$2.09 - \$0.69$
    (4) $a - \$2.09 = \$0.69$
    (5) Insufficient data is given to solve the problem.

    ① ② ③ ④ ⑤

2. Which of the following belongs to the solution set for the inequality $r + 7 \leq 22$?

    (1) 15
    (2) 17
    (3) 21
    (4) 22
    (5) 29

    ① ② ③ ④ ⑤

3. The Cooks' electric bill was \$52.71 more in August than in July. If the July bill was \$32.65 less than the June bill, how much was the July bill?

    (1) \$20.06
    (2) \$32.65
    (3) \$52.71
    (4) \$85.36
    (5) Insufficient data is given to solve the problem.

    ① ② ③ ④ ⑤

4. Two equal-sized gift-wrapped packages required 3 feet, 4 inches of ribbon and $2\frac{1}{4}$ square feet of wrapping paper. How much ribbon was used per package?

    (1) 1 ft $2\frac{1}{2}$ in
    (2) 1 ft 7 in
    (3) 1 ft 8 in
    (4) 1 ft 11 in
    (5) 6 ft 8 in

    ① ② ③ ④ ⑤

5. The sum of two numbers is 72. The larger number is 5 times the smaller number. What is the larger number?

(1) 12
(2) 24
(3) 36
(4) 48
(5) 60

(1) (2) (3) (4) (5)

6. The cost to rent a car for a weekend is \$95 plus 10 cents per mile. If Carl drives 350 miles, which expression tells how much he owes?

(1) \$95 + \$.10(350)
(2) \$95 − \$.10(350)
(3) \$95(10)
(4) 350(\$.10) − \$95
(5) \$95 + 350

(1) (2) (3) (4) (5)

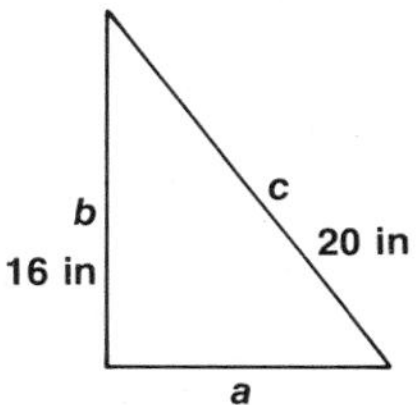

7. Mrs. Baldino is cutting a scarf for her daughter's costume. Given the measurements in the drawing above, what is the length in inches of side *a?*

(1) 4
(2) 12
(3) 36
(4) 144
(5) 656

(1) (2) (3) (4) (5)

8. Mr. Sisson wants to put $\frac{1}{4}$-inch molding beneath the baseboard in the recreation room. If the room is $8\frac{1}{2}$ feet wide and $2\frac{1}{2}$ times longer than it is wide, how many feet of molding will Mr. Sisson need?

(1) 11
(2) $29\frac{3}{4}$
(3) $42\frac{1}{2}$
(4) $59\frac{1}{2}$
(5) 68

(1) (2) (3) (4) (5)

9. What is the slope of a line containing the points $A(4, -2)$ and $B(-1, 5)$?

(1) 7/5
(2) $-\frac{7}{5}$
(3) 5/7
(4) $-\frac{5}{7}$
(5) Insufficient data is given to solve the problem.

(1) (2) (3) (4) (5)

10. $15^2 =$

(1) 30
(2) 225
(3) 250
(4) 750
(5) 1,515

(1) (2) (3) (4) (5)

11. What is the least number of pieces of sod 1 foot by 3 feet that will be required to sod a yard 20 feet by 45 feet?

(1) 30
(2) 100
(3) 200
(4) 250
(5) 300

(1) (2) (3) (4) (5)

12. During a student's week, 66 hours are spent in recreation, classes and study, and work. The ratio of time spent in these activities is 2:6:3, respectively. How many hours are spent working?

(1) 6
(2) 12
(3) 18
(4) 24
(5) 36

(1) (2) (3) (4) (5)

13. A model airplane kit contained wooden sticks in the following lengths: $2\frac{1}{4}$ in, $2\frac{3}{8}$ in, $2\frac{5}{12}$ in, and $2\frac{1}{6}$ in. Order the lengths of the sticks from longest to shortest.

(1) $2\frac{1}{6}$, $2\frac{1}{4}$, $2\frac{3}{8}$, $2\frac{5}{12}$

(2) $2\frac{1}{6}$, $2\frac{1}{4}$, $2\frac{5}{12}$, $2\frac{3}{8}$

(3) $2\frac{3}{8}$, $2\frac{5}{12}$, $2\frac{1}{4}$, $2\frac{1}{16}$

(4) $2\frac{5}{12}$, $2\frac{3}{8}$, $2\frac{1}{4}$, $2\frac{1}{6}$

(5) $2\frac{5}{12}$, $2\frac{3}{8}$, $2\frac{1}{6}$, $2\frac{1}{4}$

① ② ③ ④ ⑤

14. A waitress earned tips of \$10.35, \$7.50, \$6.10, \$5.20, and \$15.80 in 5 days. What was the average amount of her tips per day?

(1) \$7.50
(2) \$8.99
(3) \$9.00
(4) \$10.00
(5) \$44.95

① ② ③ ④ ⑤

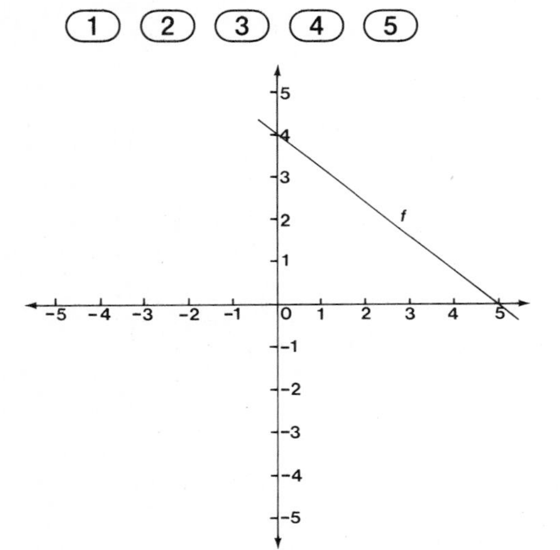

15. Line f crosses the x axis at 5 and the y axis at 4. What is the slope of the line?

(1) -4

(2) $-\frac{4}{5}$

(3) 0

(4) $\frac{3}{4}$

(5) $\frac{4}{3}$

① ② ③ ④ ⑤

16. Evaluate $4x + 3y + 2z$ if $x = 4$, $y = 6$, and $z = 5$.

(1) 22
(2) 30
(3) 44
(4) 60
(5) 120

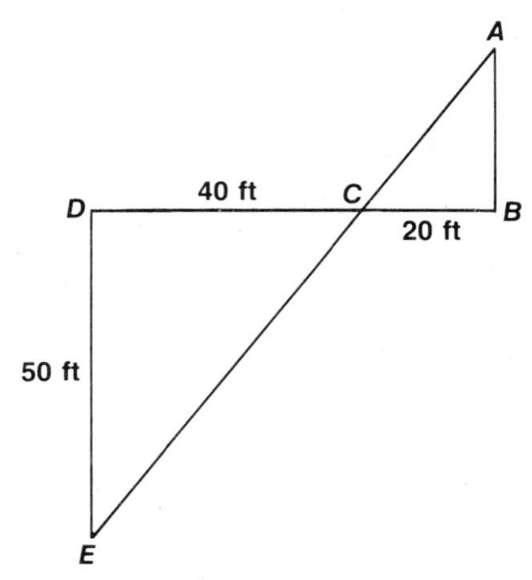

17. At a picnic area Steven stands at point A and Russ stands at point B. If Steven wants to throw a softball that will reach Russ, how many feet will he have to throw the ball?

(1) 10
(2) 20
(3) 25
(4) 30
(5) 40

① ② ③ ④ ⑤

18. Solve for x.

$x^2 - x - 42 = 0$

(1) -1 and 7
(2) 6 and -7
(3) 6 and 7
(4) -7 only
(5) -6 and 7

① ② ③ ④ ⑤

19. If $a + b = 45$ and $a = 4b$, then $a =$

(1) 9
(2) 18
(3) 27
(4) 36
(5) 45

① ② ③ ④ ⑤

20. Three circular areas are each 28 feet in diameter. How many feet of stone will be needed to enclose them? Use $\frac{22}{7}$ for π.

    (1) 84
    (2) 88
    (3) 166
    (4) 176
    (5) 264

Minitest 4

Directions: For all problems choose the one best answer. Answers are on pages 586–587.

1. Find the total cost of a car if the monthly payments are \$125 for $3\frac{1}{2}$ years.

    (1) \$3,000
    (2) \$3,250
    (3) \$4,250
    (4) \$5,250
    (5) \$7,250

    ① ② ③ ④ ⑤

2. The Wilsons needed \$6,000 but borrowed only \$3,700 from the bank for $1\frac{1}{2}$ years at a rate of 9%. How much interest did they pay on the loan?

    (1) \$399.50
    (2) \$499
    (3) \$499.50
    (4) \$810
    (5) \$3,330

    ① ② ③ ④ ⑤

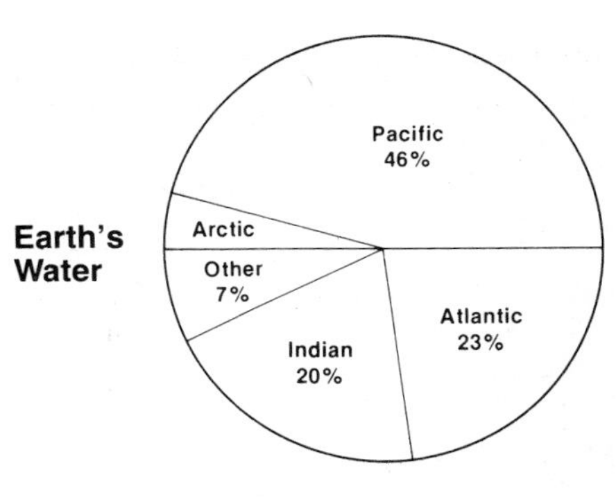

3. The graph above shows the earth's water. The Indian Ocean accounts for how many times more water than the Arctic Ocean?

    (1) 2
    (2) 4
    (3) 5
    (4) 7
    (5) 9

    ① ② ③ ④ ⑤

4. On his delivery route, Fred drove $1\frac{3}{4}$ hours on Monday, $2\frac{1}{3}$ hours on Tuesday, and $2\frac{1}{6}$ hours on Wednesday. What was his total driving time in hours?

    (1) $4\frac{1}{4}$
    (2) 5
    (3) 6
    (4) $6\frac{1}{4}$
    (5) $7\frac{1}{4}$

    ① ② ③ ④ ⑤

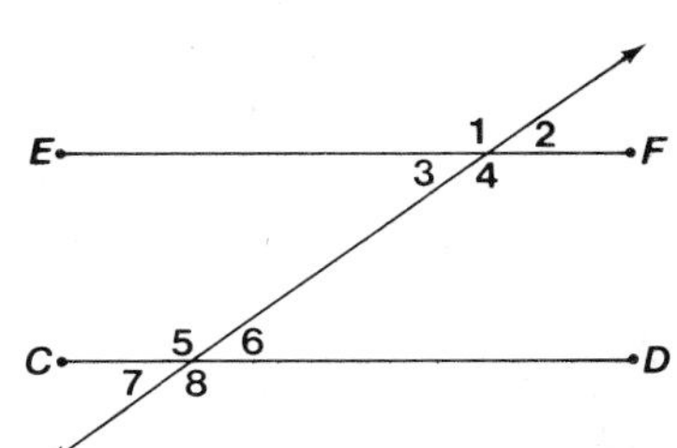

5. Line segments EF and CD are parallel. If $\angle 2$ measures 37°, what is the measurement of $\angle 5$?

    (1) 53°
    (2) 63°
    (3) 90°
    (4) 143°
    (5) 323°

    ① ② ③ ④ ⑤

6. If the sales tax in a certain state is 8%, how much would a record cost, including tax, if the price of the record is \$7.50?
   (1) \$8.00
   (2) \$8.10
   (3) \$9.00
   (4) \$9.10
   (5) Insufficient data is given to solve the problem.

   ① ② ③ ④ ⑤

7. If 1.4 pounds of meat cost \$2.52, how much does 1 pound cost?
   (1) \$1.80
   (2) \$1.90
   (3) \$2.00
   (4) \$2.05
   (5) \$2.25

   ① ② ③ ④ ⑤

8. The final cost of a tennis racket was \$59.68. This price included a 15% discount and a sales tax of \$3.63. Which equation shows the original price of the racket?
   (1) $x = \$59.68 \times 0.15$
   (2) $x = \$59.68 + 0.15x - \$3.63$
   (3) $x = \$59.68 + \$3.63$
   (4) $x = \$59.68x + \$3.63x + 0.15x$
   (5) Insufficient data is given to solve the problem.

   ① ② ③ ④ ⑤

9. Evaluate 8^4.
   (1) 32
   (2) 64
   (3) 128
   (4) 512
   (5) 4,096

   ① ② ③ ④ ⑤

10. $2^8 =$
   (1) 12
   (2) 32
   (3) 8^2
   (4) 2(64)
   (5) 2(128)

   ① ② ③ ④ ⑤

11. Find the value of x in $3(x - 5) - 2x = -7(-3)$.
   (1) 12
   (2) 24
   (3) 36
   (4) 48
   (5) 54

   ① ② ③ ④ ⑤

12. Monica is 15 years old; her father is 40 years old; and her brother is 18 years old. What is the ratio of Monica's age to her father's age?
   (1) 3:8
   (2) 5:6
   (3) 8:3
   (4) 15:40
   (5) 40:15

   ① ② ③ ④ ⑤

13. There were 2,016 people at a movie theater that can seat 2,500. The number of children was 3 times the number of adults. How many children were there?
   (1) 405
   (2) 504
   (3) 672
   (4) 1,008
   (5) 1,512

   ① ② ③ ④ ⑤

Items 14–15 refer to the following situation. A grocer can order canned soups from Distributor A or Distributor B. If she orders from Distributor A, she will have to pay \$25.50 for every 100 cans ordered. Distributor A also charges a 4% delivery fee on the total order. Distributor B charges \$28.90 for every 100 cans of soup and adds a flat fee of \$1.30 for shipping and handling for every 50 cans.

14. What will the grocer have to pay Distributor A for an order of 250 cans of soup?
   (1) \$63.75
   (2) \$66.30
   (3) \$69
   (4) \$637.50
   (5) \$663

   ① ② ③ ④ ⑤

15. How much more expensive would it be for the grocer to order 500 cans of soup from Distributor B than from Distributor A?

(1) $23
(2) $24.90
(3) $26.10
(4) $132.60
(5) $157.50

1 2 3 4 5

16. If $b = 5$, $c = 4$, and $d = 2$, find the value of $3b - 2c + 4d$.

(1) 8
(2) 7
(3) 15
(4) 23
(5) 31

1 2 3 4 5

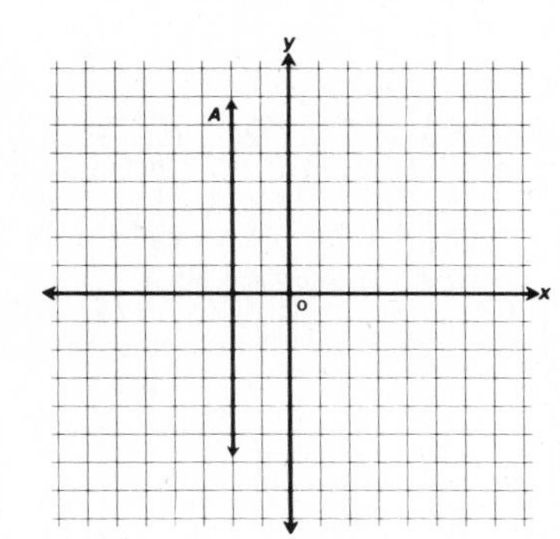

17. Line *a* crosses the *x*-axis at -2 and is parallel to the *y*-axis. What is the slope of line *a* above?

(1) 0
(2) 4
(3) 6
(4) 8
(5) no slope

1 2 3 4 5

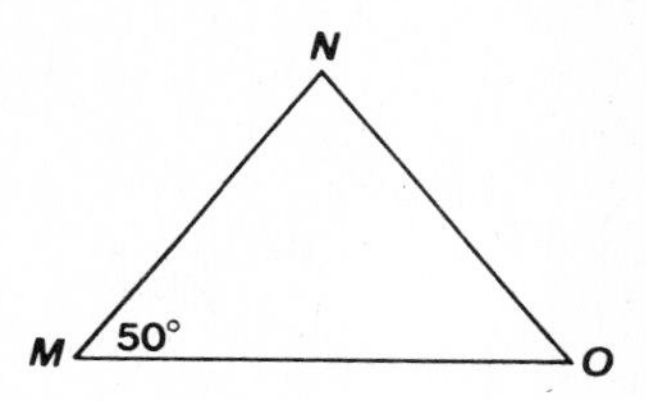

18. Triangle *MNO* is an isosceles triangle. Find the measurement of angle *N*.

(1) 50°
(2) 70°
(3) 80°
(4) 90°
(5) 100°

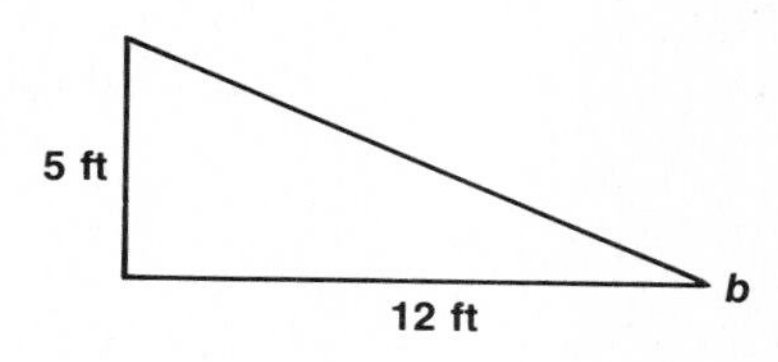

19. A telephone wire runs from the top of the pole to point *b* on the ground as shown in the diagram above. What is the distance in feet from the top of the pole to point *b*?

(1) 13
(2) 14
(3) 15
(4) 16
(5) 17

20. Ms. Timis wants to cover a square tabletop with a piece of glass. One side measures 2 feet. How many square feet of glass are needed to cover the tabletop?

(1) 0.53
(2) 1.07
(3) 4.00
(4) 6.28
(5) 12.56

1 2 3 4 5

Minitest 5

<u>Directions:</u> For all problems choose the <u>one</u> best answer. Answers are on pages 587–588.

1. Which of the following equals 320,009 expressed in scientific notation?

   (1) 3.20009×10
   (2) 3.20009×10^2
   (3) 3.20009×10^3
   (4) 3.20009×10^4
   (5) 3.20009×10^5

   ① ② ③ ④ ⑤

2. During a baseball season of 5 months, a 20-man amateur team traveled 168, 235, 363, 189, and 125 miles. What is the average number of miles traveled during the 5 months?

   (1) 216
   (2) 316
   (3) 380
   (4) 480
   (5) 1,080

   ① ② ③ ④ ⑤

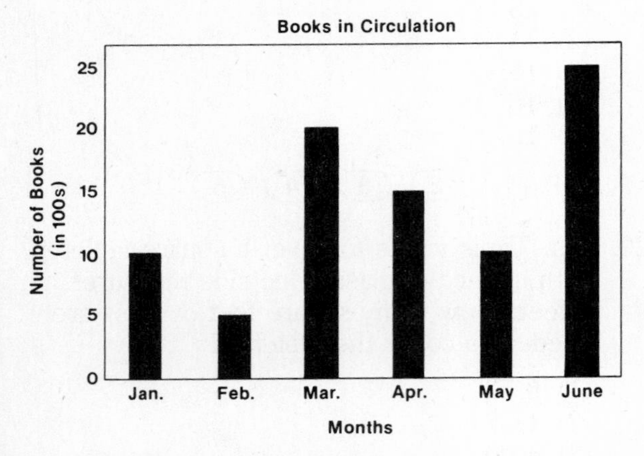

3. The difference in the number of books in circulation between the months with the greatest and least circulation is

   (1) 200
   (2) 500
   (3) 1,000
   (4) 1,500
   (5) 2,000

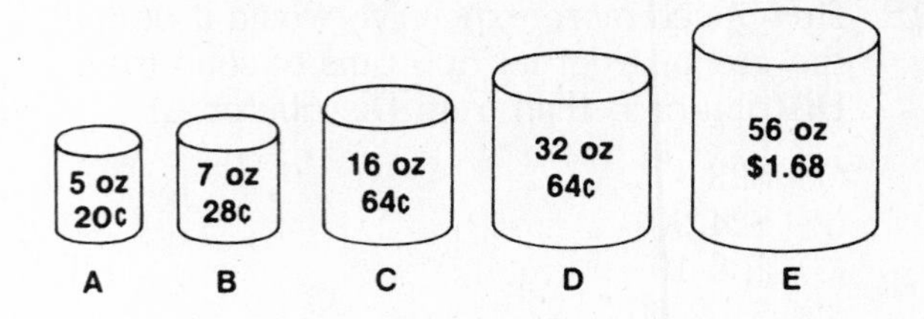

4. Which can above is the best buy?

   (1) A
   (2) B
   (3) C
   (4) D
   (5) E

   ① ② ③ ④ ⑤

5. $7^3 =$

   (1) 14
   (2) 21
   (3) 49
   (4) 163
   (5) 343

   ① ② ③ ④ ⑤

6. How much do 4 cans of vegetables cost if eight 10-ounce cans cost $5.04?

   (1) $1.52
   (2) $2.52
   (3) $3.00
   (4) $4.00
   (5) $4.50

   ① ② ③ ④ ⑤

7. What is the slope of a line that has points R (6, 0) and S (−4, −2)?

   (1) $\frac{1}{10}$
   (2) $-\frac{1}{5}$
   (3) $-\frac{2}{5}$
   (4) $\frac{1}{5}$
   (5) -5

   ① ② ③ ④ ⑤

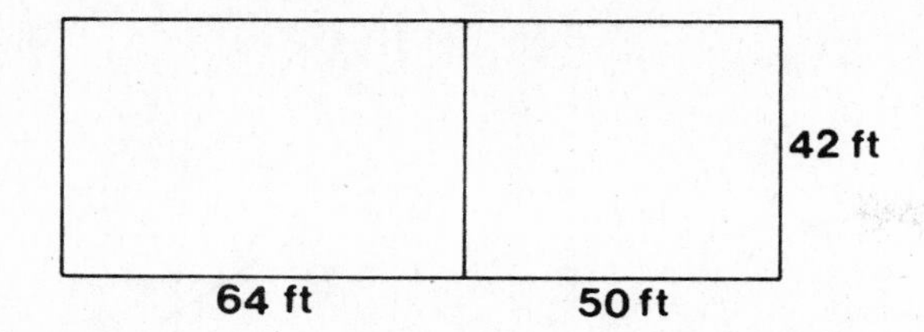

8. If a lifeguard is to be present for every 2,000 square feet of water surface, which expression gives the number of lifeguards needed for the pool above?

(1) $(42 \times 50) + (64 \times 42)$
(2) $(64 \times 42) - (42 \times 50)$
(3) $\frac{42(114)}{2{,}000}$
(4) $\frac{2{,}000}{42(114)}$
(5) $\frac{2{,}000(114)}{42}$

① ② ③ ④ ⑤

9. Write the following expression in simplest form:

$6a + b + 4c + 1\frac{1}{2}a + b + \frac{2}{3}c$

(1) $7a + 2b + 4c$
(2) $\frac{7}{2}a + 2b + \frac{4}{3}c$
(3) $7\frac{1}{2}a + 2b + 4\frac{2}{3}c$
(4) $5a + 4c$
(5) $14abc$

① ② ③ ④ ⑤

10. Takashi had $132.50 in his checking account. He wrote checks for $31.26, $57.15, and $91.89. The bank charges a $15 fee for an overdrawn check. What is the minimum amount he needs to deposit so that the account is not overdrawn?

(1) $40
(2) $47.80
(3) $62.80
(4) $70
(5) $180.30

① ② ③ ④ ⑤

11. Solve for x in $\frac{9}{25} = \frac{18}{x}$.

(1) 50
(2) 180
(3) 270
(4) 360
(5) 450

① ② ③ ④ ⑤

12. Find the value of $\frac{1}{2}p^2$ if $p = 16$.

(1) 16
(2) 32
(3) 96
(4) 128
(5) 256

① ② ③ ④ ⑤

13. A punch mixture requires 1 quart 11 ounces of ginger ale for every 4 people. If 64 people are to be served, how many quarts of ginger ale will be needed? (1 quart = 32 ounces)

(1) 16
(2) $21\frac{1}{2}$
(3) 32
(4) 64
(5) 256

① ② ③ ④ ⑤

14. Solve for x in $3(3x - 1) = 4(12 - 2x)$.

(1) 2
(2) 3
(3) 4
(4) 5
(5) 6

① ② ③ ④ ⑤

15. If an inheritance of $8,000 is divided so that the son has 3 times more than the daughter, how much more does the son get?

(1) $2,000
(2) $4,000
(3) $5,000
(4) $6,000
(5) $8,000

① ② ③ ④ ⑤

16. Solve for b in $4b - 2 \leq 6$.

    (1) $b \leq 2$
    (2) $b \leq 3$
    (3) $b \leq 4$
    (4) $b \leq 5$
    (5) $b \leq 6$

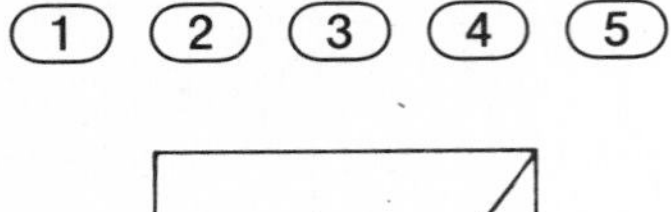

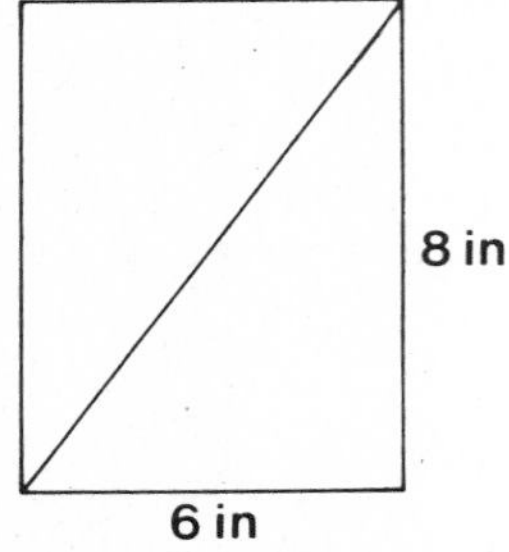

17. Find the length in inches of the diagonal in the diagram above.

    (1) 5
    (2) 10
    (3) 36
    (4) 64
    (5) 100

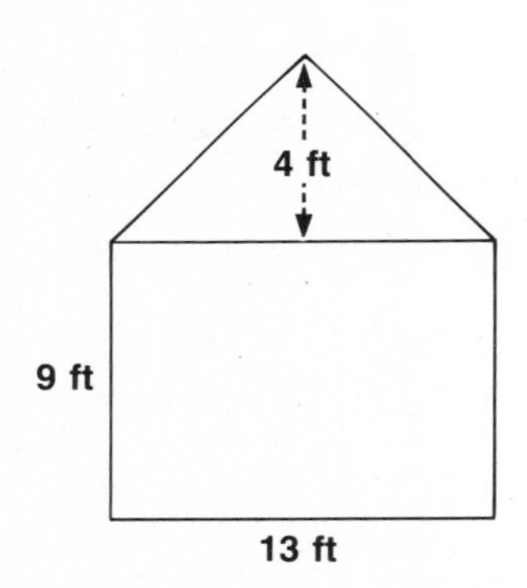

18. Mr. Cowan built his children a playhouse. The dimensions of the back are shown in the drawing above. Mr. Cowan wants to paint the back of the house red. What is the area in square feet of the back of the house?

    (1) 26
    (2) 48
    (3) 117
    (4) 143
    (5) 169

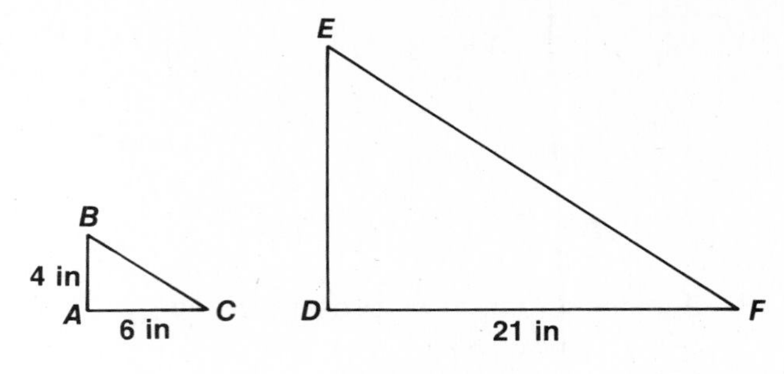

19. Triangle ABC and triangle DEF above are similar. What is the length in inches of $\overline{DE}$?

    (1) 10
    (2) 14
    (3) 24
    (4) 19
    (5) 36

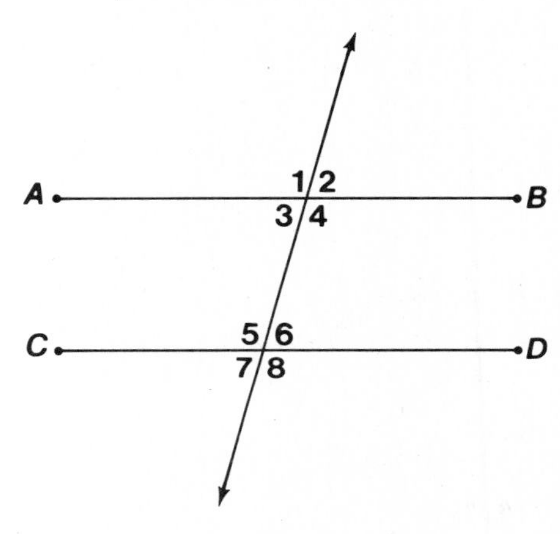

20. Line segment AB and line segment DE are parallel. If $\angle 1 = 105°$, what is the total of $\angle 6$, $\angle 7$, and $\angle 8$?

    (1) 15°
    (2) 75°
    (3) 180°
    (4) 255°
    (5) 360°

(1) (2) (3) (4) (5)

Minitest Answers

Minitest 1
(pages 568–571)

1. (4) city \$115,200 county \$28,800

x = amount county pays
$4x$ = amount city pays
$x + 4x = \$144{,}000$
$5x = \$144{,}000$
$x = \$28{,}800$ amount county pays
$5(\$28{,}800) = \$115{,}200$ amount city pays

2. (2) $2\frac{1}{2}$

Divide muscle by fat.

$2\frac{10}{20} = \quad 20\overline{)50} = 2\frac{1}{2}$
40
10

3. (1) 45°

Because ∠1 and ∠2 equal a straight line, they are supplementary. Supplementary angles equal 180°. Therefore, ∠2 = 45°. ∠3 = 45° because it is vertical to ∠2. ∠7 = 45° because it is corresponding to ∠3.

4. (4) \$645

x = amount of money Martha has
$3x$ = amount of money Anne has
$x + 3x = \$860$
$4x = \$860$
$x = \$215$ amount of money Martha has
$3x = \$645$ amount of money Anne has

5. (2) 23 lb 14 oz

12 lb 3 oz = 11 lb 19 oz
− 8 oz   − 8 oz
11 lb 11 oz weight of second baby

12 lb 3 oz
+11 lb 11 oz
23 lb 14 oz weight of both babies

6. (3) 3(\$0.50) + 16(\$0.25) + 10(\$0.10) + 5(\$0.05) + 3(\$0.01)

In each instance, multiply the number of coins by the value of the coins: 3 half-dollars = 3(\$0.50) + 16 quarters = 16(\$0.25) + 10 dimes = 10(\$0.10) + 5 nickels + 5(\$0.05) + 3 pennies + 3(\$0.01).

7. (2) 285,000

200,000
80,000
+ 5,000
285,000

8. (5) Insufficient data

You do not know the length of time of the call.

9. (3) x^7

Each x has an exponent of 1. There are 7 x's; therefore, the answer is x^7.

10. (3) $abc(a^2 + b^2 + c^2)$

a, b, and *c* are common to each term so you can factor it out. $abc(a^2 + b^2 + c^2)$

11. (4) 153.86

Use the formula $A = \pi r^2$. The diameter has to be changed to radius ($r = 1/2d$). $1/2(14) = 7$. $3.14 \times 7 \times 7 = 153.86$ sq ft

12. (5) 45

It is simpler to work this problem if you convert the yards to feet in the last step. Each exhibition area is a right triangle; therefore, use the Pythagorean theorem.

$a^2 + b^2 = c^2$
$12^2 + 9^2 = c^2$
$144 + 81 = 225$
$c^2 = 225$
$c = \sqrt{225}$
$c = 15$ yd

Then convert the yards to feet. 15 yd × 3 = 45 ft

13. (2) $\frac{24r}{100}$

12 items = 1 dozen
24 items = 2 dozen
$24r$ = the cost of 24 apples in cents
$\frac{24r}{100}$ = the cost of 24 apples in dollars

14. (1) A

Mon. $5\frac{5}{6} = 5\frac{10}{12}$
Tues. $5\frac{1}{2} = 5\frac{6}{12}$
Wed. $5\frac{3}{4} = 5\frac{9}{12}$
Thurs. $5\frac{1}{4} = 5\frac{3}{12}$
Fri. $5\frac{1}{6} = 5\frac{2}{12}$

15. (4) $11\frac{2}{3}$

First convert inches to yards. Then use the formula for finding perimeter of a rectangle.

$\frac{45}{36} = 1\frac{1}{4}$ yds $\frac{60}{36} = 1\frac{2}{3}$ yds
$p = 2l + 2w$
$p = 2(1\frac{2}{3}) = 2(1\frac{1}{4})$
$p = 2(\frac{5}{3}) + 2(\frac{5}{4})$
$p = \frac{10}{3} + \frac{5}{2}$
$p = \frac{20}{6} + \frac{15}{6}$
$p = \frac{35}{6}$
$p = 5\frac{5}{6}$ yd for one quilt
$p \times 2 = 5\frac{5}{6} \times 2 = 11\frac{2}{3}$

16. (1) 10

Use the Pythagorean Theorem.

$c^2 = a^2 + b^2$
$c^2 = 36 + 64$
$c^2 = 100$
$c = 10$ feet

17. (1) 2 and 4

$(x - 4)(x - 2) = 0$
$x - 4 = 0$
$x = 4$
$x - 2 = 0$
$x = 2$

18. (4) 110

Substitute $10y$ for x in the equation.

$x + y = 121$
$10y + y = 121$
$\frac{11y}{11} = \frac{121}{11}$
$y = 11$
$x = 10y$, so $x = 10(11) = 110$

19. (2) 12

Reverse the triangle on the right so that you can easily see the sides that are similar. Write the proportion and find the solution.

$\frac{\overline{AB}}{\overline{EF}} = \frac{\overline{BC}}{\overline{DF}}$

$\frac{10}{15} = \frac{8}{n}$

$10n = 120$

$n = 12$

20. (3) $222.36

$238
− 20
218 unpaid balance
× .02
$4.36 interest

$218.00 unpaid balance
+ 4.36 interest
$222.36

Minitest 2
(pages 571–574)

1. (2) $110,000 − 4y

If each of 4 secretaries is paid y dollars, then their total salary is $4y$. Since the total wages of the 5 secretaries is $110,000, the fifth secretary would be paid $110,000 − $4y$.

2. (4) $10^3 \times 4.6928$

$4.6928 \times 10 \times 10 \times 10 = 4{,}692.8$

3. (2) 5

Subtract the 1982 salary from the 1983 salary to find the difference:

1983 $ 387.36
1982 −367.59
$ 19.77

Divide this difference by the 1982 salary to find the increase in decimal form:

$19.77 ÷ $367.59 ≅ 0.05

Multiply 0.05 by 100 to obtain the percent: $0.05 \times 100 = 5\%$.

4. (3) 8

x = number of nickels
$14 - x$ = number of dimes
$0.05x = value of nickels
$0.10(14 − x) = value of dimes
$0.05x + $0.10(14 − x) = $1.00
$0.05x + $1.40 − $0.10x = $1.00
$1.40 − $0.05x − $1.00 = $1.00 − $1.00
$0.40 − $0.05x + $0.05x = $0.05x

$\frac{\$0.40}{\$0.05} = \frac{\$0.05x}{\$0.05}$

8 = x = number of nickels

5. (3) 4

Use the Pythagorean Theorem.

$c^2 = a^2 + b^2$

$\overline{HG}$ is half of $\overline{EG}$.

$5^2 = 3^2 + b^2$

$25 = 9 + b^2$

$25 - 9 = 9 + b^2 - 9$

$\sqrt{16} = \sqrt{b^2}$

4 feet = b

6. (3) $2.25

$0.50 the cost of one
3)$1.50 pound

$\$0.50 \times 4\frac{1}{2} = \$0.50 \times \frac{9}{2} =$

$\frac{\$4.50}{2}$ = $2.25 the cost of $4\frac{1}{2}$ pounds

7. (1) 12($0.30 + $0.25)

12($0.30) + 12($0.25)
= 12($0.30 + $0.25)

8. (3) $2xy(x - 2)$

Both terms contain $2xy$ so factor it out to make $2xy(x - 2)$.

9. (4) 24

Solve by using a ratio.

$\frac{8}{12} = \frac{16}{x}$

$8x = 12 \times 16$

$8x = 192$

$x = 24$ in

10. (3) 20

$\frac{5 \times 2^2}{2 - 1} = \frac{5 \times 4}{1} =$

$\frac{20}{1} = 20$

11. (2) $268

$ 5,000 amount of loan
+ 1,432 interest for 2 years
$ 6,432 amount to be repaid

$ 268 monthly payment
24)$6,432
48
163
144
192
192
0

12. (2) 84

Use the formula $A = \frac{bh}{2}$.

$A = \frac{14 \times 12}{2} = \frac{168}{2}$

$A = 84$ sq ft

13. (5) $61,740

$56,000 starting salary for Team A
× .05 raise at end of first
$ 2,800 year

$56,000
+ 2,800
$58,800 salary at end of first year

$58,800
× .05
$ 2,940 raise at end of second year

$58,800
+ 2,940
$61,740 salary at end of second year

14. (3) $7,440

$48,000 starting salary for Team B
× .07 raise at end of first
$ 3,360 year

$48,000
+ 3,360
$51,360 salary with Team B at end of first year

$56,000 starting salary for Team A
× .05 raise at end of first
$ 2,800 year

$$\begin{array}{r l} \$56{,}000 & \\ +\ 2{,}800 & \\ \hline \$58{,}800 & \text{salary at end of first year} \end{array}$$

$$\begin{array}{r l} \$58{,}800 & \text{Team A} \\ -51{,}360 & \text{Team B} \\ \hline \$\ 7{,}440 & \text{difference in salaries at end of first year} \end{array}$$

15. (2) $t + 4u(v - \frac{1}{2})$

t = fare for first $\frac{1}{2}$ mile

u = fare for every remaining $\frac{1}{4}$ mile

v = total miles of trip

For the first $\frac{1}{2}$ mile, the fare is t. The remaining miles of the trip can be written as $v - \frac{1}{2}$. You must convert the fare for the remaining $\frac{1}{4}$ mile so that it is also in terms of miles. Multiply u times 4. The total fare for the trip is *t plus* $4u(v - \frac{1}{2})$.

16. (5) Insufficient data

You do not know the weights of the chemicals after the last experiment.

17. (5) 156

Find the area of paneling and wall.

Step 1:
Paneling $A = lw$

$$A = \frac{2}{1} \times \frac{1}{2} = 1 \text{ sq ft}$$

Step 2:

Wall $A = lw$

$$A = 13 \times 12 = 156 \text{ sq ft}$$

Step 3: Divide the area of the wall by the area of each piece of paneling to find the number of pieces needed.

$$\begin{array}{r} 156 \text{ pieces} \\ 1\overline{)156} \\ \underline{1} \\ 5 \\ \underline{5} \\ 6 \\ \underline{6} \\ 0 \end{array}$$

18. (1) 2:5

New bicycles:
total number of bicycles
80:200

$$2:5 \text{ or } \frac{80}{200} = \frac{2}{5}$$

19. (5) 81

$$c + d = 90;\ c = 9d$$
$$9d + d = 90$$
$$\frac{10d}{10} = \frac{90}{10}$$
$$d = 9$$
$$c = 9d$$
$$c = 9(9) = 81$$

20. (2) 40

$$\frac{\overline{AC}}{\overline{CE}} = \frac{\overline{AB}}{\overline{DE}}$$
$$\frac{40}{80} = \frac{20}{x}$$
$$\frac{40x}{40} = \frac{1{,}600}{40}$$
$$x = 40$$

Minitest 3
(pages 574–577)

1. (3) $a = \$2.09 - \$0.69$

a = original price
a = present price − price of increase
= \$2.09 − \$0.69

2. (1) 15

$$r + 7 \leq 22$$
$$r + 7 - 7 \leq 22 - 7$$
$$r \leq 15$$

3. (5) Insufficient data

You do not know the amount of either the June bill or the August bill.

4. (3) 1 ft 8 in

$$\begin{array}{l} 1 \text{ ft } 8 \text{ in} \\ 2\overline{)3 \text{ ft } 4 \text{ in}} \\ \underline{2} \\ 1 \text{ ft} = 12 \text{ in} \\ \phantom{1 \text{ ft} = 1}\underline{+4} \\ \phantom{1 \text{ ft} = 1}16 \\ \phantom{1 \text{ ft} = 1}\underline{16} \\ \phantom{1 \text{ ft} = 12}0 \end{array}$$

5. (5) 60

x = the smaller number
$5x$ = the larger number
$x + 5x = 72$

$$\frac{6x}{6} = \frac{72}{6}$$

$x = 12$, the smaller number
$5x = 5(12) = 60$, the larger number

6. (1) \$95 + \$0.10(350)

The car rental cost is \$95. To that you must add the mileage cost, \$0.10 for 350 miles, or \$0.10 × 350. The total cost is \$95 + \$0.10(350).

7. (2) 12

Use the Pythagorean Theorem.
$$c^2 = a^2 + b^2$$
$$20^2 = a^2 + 16^2$$
$$400 = a^2 + 256$$
$$400 - 256 = a^2 + 256 - 256$$
$$144 = a^2$$
$$12 \text{ in} = a$$

8. (4) $59\frac{1}{2}$

First find the length of the room. Then use the formula for finding the perimeter of a rectangle.

$$l = 2\tfrac{1}{2}(8\tfrac{1}{2})$$
$$l = 21\tfrac{1}{4} \text{ ft}$$
$$p = 2l + 2w$$
$$p = 2(21\tfrac{1}{4}) + 2(8\tfrac{1}{2})$$
$$p = 42\tfrac{1}{2} + 17$$
$$p = 59\tfrac{1}{2} \text{ ft}$$

9. (2) $-\frac{7}{5}$

Use the formula
$$m = \frac{y^2 - y^1}{x^2 - x^1}.$$
$$m = \frac{5 - (-2)}{-1 - 4}$$
$$m = \frac{5 + 2}{-5}$$
$$m = -\frac{7}{5}$$

10. (2) 225

An exponent of 2 means to multiply the number by itself.
$15^2 = 15 \times 15 = 225$

11. (5) 300

Find the area of sod and yard.

Step 1: Sod $A = lw$
$A = 1 \times 3$
$= 3$ sq ft

Step 2: Yard $A = lw$
$A = 20 \times 45$
$= 900$ sq ft

Step 3: $900 \div 3 = 300$ pieces

12. (3) 18

recreation = $2x$
classes and study = $6x$
work = $3x$
total = $11x$

$\frac{11x}{11} = \frac{66}{11}$

$x = 6$ hr
work $= 3(6) = 18$ hr

13. (4) $2\frac{5}{12}, 2\frac{3}{8}, 2\frac{1}{4}, 2\frac{1}{6}$

$2\frac{1}{4}$ inches $= 2\frac{6}{24}$

$2\frac{3}{8}$ inches $= 2\frac{9}{24}$

$2\frac{5}{12}$ inches $= 2\frac{10}{24}$

$2\frac{1}{6}$ inches $= 2\frac{4}{24}$

14. (2) $8.99

$10.35
7.50
6.10
5.20
15.80
$44.95

$44.95 \div 5 = \$8.99$

15. (2) $-\frac{4}{5}$

Slope is rise over run. The x axis coordinates are (5,0). The y axis coordinates are (0,4). Use the formula to find the slope of a line.

$m \frac{y_2 - y_1}{x_2 - x_1}$

$m = \frac{4 - 0}{0 - 5}$

$m = -\frac{4}{5}$

16. (3) 44

$4x + 3y + 2z$
$4(4) + 3(6) + 2(5)$
$16 + 18 + 10 = 44$

17. (3) 25

Reverse the triangle so that you can easily see the similar sides. Write the proportion and solve.

$\frac{\overline{DE}}{\overline{AB}} = \frac{\overline{DC}}{\overline{BC}}$

$\frac{50}{x} = \frac{40}{20}$

$40x = 1{,}000$
$x = 25$

18. (5) -6 and 7

$(x - 7)(x + 6) = 0$
$x - 7 = 0$
$x = 7$
$x + 6 = 0$
$x = -6$

19. (4) 36

$a + b = 45$
$4b + b = 45$
$\frac{5b}{5} = \frac{45}{5}$
$b = 9$
$a = 4b$, so $a = 4(9) = 36$

20. (5) 264

$C = \pi d$

$\frac{22}{7} \times \frac{28}{1} = 88$ ft

If one circle requires 88 ft, 3 circles require 3(88) or 264 ft.

Mintest 4
(pages 577–579)

1. (4) $5,250

$3\frac{1}{2}$ years = 42 months

$125
× 42
250
5 00
$5,250

2. (3) $499.50

Use the formula
$i = prt.$

$i = \$3{,}700 \times 1\frac{1}{2} \times 0.09$

$i = \$3{,}700 \times \frac{3}{2} \times 0.09$ (1,850)

$i = \$499.50$

3. (3) 5

$\frac{\text{Indian Ocean}}{\text{Arctic Ocean}} = \frac{20\%}{4\%} = 5$

4. (4) $6\frac{1}{4}$

$1\frac{3}{4}$ hr $= 1\frac{9}{12}$ hr

$2\frac{1}{3}$ hr $= 2\frac{4}{12}$ hr

$+\ 2\frac{1}{6}$ hr $= 2\frac{2}{12}$ hr

$5\frac{15}{12} = 6\frac{1}{4}$ hr

5. (4) 143°

∠1 and ∠2 are supplementary and, therefore, equal 180°. Since ∠2 = 37°, ∠1 = 143°. ∠1 and ∠5 are corresponding and, therefore, are equal.

6. (2) $8.10

$7.50
× .08
.6000 = $.60 for tax

$7.50
+ .60
$8.10

7. (1) $1.80

Price per pound $= \frac{\text{cost}}{\text{weight}}$

$\$2.52 \div 1.4 = \$1.80$

8. (2) $x = \$59.68 + 0.15x - \$3.63$

The original price (x) = the present price + 15% of the original price (x) − the sales tax.
$x = \$59.68 + 0.5x - \$3.63$

9. (5) 4,096

$8 \times 8 \times 8 \times 8 = 4{,}096$

10. (5) 2(128)

$2^8 = 256$
$2(128) = 256$

11. (3) 36

$$\begin{aligned} 3(x-5) - 2x &= -7(-3) \\ 3x - 15 - 2x &= +21 \\ x - 15 &= +21 \\ +15 &= +15 \\ \hline x &= 36 \end{aligned}$$

12. (1) 3:8

$\frac{\text{Monica's age}}{\text{Father's age}} = \frac{15}{40} = \frac{3}{8}$

13. (5) 1,512

x = adults
$3x$ = children

$x + 3x = 2,016$

$\frac{\cancel{4x}}{\cancel{4}} = \frac{\cancel{2,016}}{\cancel{4}}$ (reduces to $\frac{1}{1}$ and $\frac{504}{1}$)

$x = 504$
children $= 3x = 3(504) = 1,512$

14. (2) $66.30

```
     2.5 number of 100's
100)250

 $25.50
 ×  2.5
 12 750
 51 00
$63.750   price of 250 cans

 $ 63.75 delivery fee
 ×   .04
 $2.55 00

 $63.75
 + 2.55
 $66.30 total charge for 250
        cans
```

15. (2) $24.90

```
 $ 25.50
 ×     5
 $127.50 price of 500 cans
         from Distributor A

 $127.50
 ×   .04
$   5.10 delivery fee

 $127.50
 +  5.10
 $132.60 total charge from Dis-
         tributor A

 $28.90
 ×    5
 $144.50 price of 500 cans
         from Distributor B

 $ 1.30
 ×   10
 $13.00 shipping and handling
        fee

 $144.50
 + 13.00
 $157.50 price of 500 cans
         from Distributor B

 $157.50 B's price
 − 132.60 A's price
$   24.90 difference in cost
```

16. (3) 15

$$\begin{aligned} &3b - 2c + 4d = \\ &3(5) - 2(4) + 4(2) = \\ &15 - 8 + 8 = 15 \end{aligned}$$

17. (5) no slope

Lines parallel to the y-axis have no slope.

18. (3) 80°

Isosceles triangles have equal base angles; therefore, the total for the base angles is 100°.

```
 180°
−100°
  80°
```

19. (1) 13

Use the Pythagorean Theorem.

$c^2 = a^2 + b^2$
$c^2 = 5^2 + 12^2$
$c^2 = 25 + 144$
$c = \sqrt{169}$
$c = 13$ in

20. (3) 4

Use the formula $A = s^2$.
$A = 2 \times 2$
$A = 4$ ft

Minitest 5
(pages 580–582)

1. (5) 3.20009×10^5

$3.20009 \times 10 \times 10 \times 10 \times 10 \times 10 = 320,009$

2. (1) 216

```
  168              216 miles
  235           5)1,080
  363             1 0
  189               8
+  25               5
1,080              30
                   30
```

3. (5) 2,000

```
June:   2,500 books
Feb.: −   500 books
        2,000 books
```

4. (4) D

$\frac{20¢}{5}$ = 4 cents per ounce
$\frac{28¢}{7}$ = 4 cents per ounce
$\frac{64¢}{16}$ = 4 cents per ounce
$\frac{64¢}{32}$ = 2 cents per ounce
$\frac{\$1.68}{56}$ = 3 cents per ounce

5. (5) 343

$7 \times 7 \times 7 = 343$

6. 2 $2.52

```
  $0.63 per can
8)$5.04
   4 8
     24
     24
      0
```

$0.63 × 4 cans = $2.52

7. (4) $\frac{1}{5}$

Use the formula

$m \frac{y_2 - y_1}{x_2 - x_1}.$

$m = \frac{-2 - 0}{-4 - 6}$

$m = \frac{-2}{-10}$

$m = \frac{1}{5}$

8. (3) $\frac{42(114)}{2,000}$

The number of lifeguards is given by dividing the area of the pool by 2,000.

$\frac{\text{Area of the pool}}{2,000} = \frac{42(114)}{2,000}$

9. (3) $7\frac{1}{2}a + 2b + 4\frac{2}{3}c$

$$\begin{aligned} &6a + b + 4c \\ &+ 1\tfrac{1}{2}a + b + \tfrac{2}{3}c \\ \hline &7\tfrac{1}{2}a + 2b + 4\tfrac{2}{3}c \end{aligned}$$

10. (2) $47.80

$$\begin{array}{r} \$\ 31.26 \\ 57.15 \\ +\ \ 91.89 \\ \hline \$180.30 \end{array}$$

$180.30 outstanding checks
− 132.50 balance in account
$ 47.80

11. (1) 50

$$\frac{9}{25} = \frac{18}{x}$$

$$\frac{9x}{9} = \frac{450}{9}$$

$$x = 50$$

12. (4) 128

$$\tfrac{1}{2}p^2 =$$

$$\tfrac{1}{2}(16)^2 =$$

$$\tfrac{1}{2} \times 256 = 128$$

13. (2) $21\frac{1}{2}$

$4\overline{)64}$ = 16 groups of 4

$$\begin{array}{rr} 1\text{ qt} & 11\text{ oz} \\ \times & 16 \\ \hline 16\text{ qt} & 176\text{ oz} = \\ 21\text{ qt} & 16\text{ oz} = 21\tfrac{1}{2}\text{ qt} \end{array}$$

14. (2) 3

$$3(3x - 1) = 4(12 - 2x)$$
$$9x - 3 = 48 - 8x$$
$$+8x + 3 = +3 + 8x$$
$$\frac{17x}{17} = \frac{51}{17}$$
$$x = 3$$

15. (2) $4,000

x = daughter's amount
$3x$ = son's amount
$x + 3x$ = $8,000

$$\frac{4x}{4} = \frac{\$8,000}{4}$$

x = $2,000 daughter
$3x$ = 3($2,000) = $6,000 son

$6,000 − $2,000 = $4,000

16. (1) $b \leq 2$

$$4b - 2 \leq 6$$
$$+2 \quad +2$$
$$\frac{4b}{4} \leq \frac{8}{4}$$
$$b \leq 2$$

17. (2) 10

Use the Pythagorean Theorem.

$$c^2 = a^2 + b^2$$
$$c^2 = 8^2 + 6^2$$
$$c^2 = 64 + 36$$
$$c = \sqrt{100}$$
$$c = 10 \text{ in}$$

18. (4) 143

Break the figure into a triangle and a rectangle then add the two areas together.

Area of triangle: $A = \frac{ab}{2}$

$$A = \frac{4 \times 13}{2}$$
$$A = \frac{52}{2}$$
$$A = 26 \text{ sq ft}$$

Area of rectangle: $A = lw$
$A = 9 \times 13$
$A = 117$ sq ft

Combine the areas of both.
26 sq ft + 117 sq ft = 143 sq ft

19. (2) 14

Use a ratio to solve.

$$\frac{4}{6} = \frac{x}{21}$$
$$6x = 84$$
$$x = 24 \text{ in}$$

20. (4) 255°

Alternate exterior angles are equal; therefore, $\angle 1 = \angle 8 = 105°$. $\angle 8$ and $\angle 7$ are supplementary; therefore; $\angle 7 = 180° - 105° = 75°$. Vertical angles are equal; therefore $\angle 7 = \angle 6 = 75°$.
$75° + 105° + 75° = 255°$.

The Posttests

You are now ready to take the final step in your study for passing the GED Test. Both sets of *Posttests* resemble the actual GED Test in the number and kinds of questions asked, the way the questions are placed on a page, and the time allotted for each subject. To find your *Posttests* scores in this book, you can use the Answer Keys on pages 677 and 767.

For the actual GED Test, a few testing centers offer all the subject tests on one day; many offer three on one day and two on another; and some centers will allow you to take each subject test on separate days. You need to find out the policy for your own area testing center. For taking each set of *Posttests* in this book, you should time yourself and take the tests in the same sequence of subjects and number of days as your testing center will give them to you for the actual GED Test.

Remember to guess whenever you don't know an answer. To get the best possible score, don't leave a question unanswered.

Take the first set of *Posttests.* After you have figured your scores from the Answer Key on page 677 and the information on pages 678–679, it would be a good idea to read the explanations for the answers on pages 662–676. Read not only the explanations for the answers you missed, but also the explanations for those you answered correctly. Even if you do well on the first set, you can pick up some good last-minute ideas on how to handle certain types of questions from these explanations.

If you do not do well on the first set of *Posttests,* review those subjects for which you still need practice and then take those subject tests on the second set of *Posttests.*

You may want to make arrangements to take the actual GED Test as soon as you can after achieving passing scores on the *Posttests* in this book. Your test-taking skills will be sharp, and you will feel more confident.

Posttest A

TEST 1: WRITING SKILLS POSTTEST

Directions

The Writing Skills Posttest consists of 55 multiple-choice questions and an essay. It is intended to measure your ability to use clear and effective English. It is a test of English as it is usually written, not as it might be spoken. Specific directions are given at the beginning of each part. Read these directions carefully before you begin.

You should take approximately 75 minutes to complete the multiple-choice questions. There is no penalty for guessing. Try to answer as many questions as you can. Work rapidly but carefully, without spending too much time on any one question. If a question is too difficult for you, skip it and come back to it later.

For each answer, mark one answer space.

EXAMPLE

The intelligens of computers is different from that of human beings.

What correction should be made to this sentence?

(1) change the spelling of intelligens to intelligence
(2) change is to are
(3) change the spelling of different to diffrent
(4) insert a comma after that
(5) no correction is neccessary

● (2)   

The correct answer is (1); therefore, answer space (1) has been marked.

You should take no more than 45 minutes to complete the essay section of the test. You can use a separate sheet of paper for writing your essay.

Answers to the questions are in the Answer Key on page 677. Explanations for the answers and a sample essay are on pages 662–665.

Part I

Directions: The following items are based on paragraphs that contain numbered sentences. Some of the sentences contain errors in sentence structure, usage, or mechanics. A few sentences, however, are correct as written. Read each paragraph and then answer the items based on it. For each item, choose the answer that would result in the most effective writing of the sentence or sentences. The best answer must be consistent with the meaning and tone of the rest of the paragraph.

Items 1–9 refer to the following passage.

(1) If someone mentioned the word "counterfeit," most people would automatically think of fake dollar bills. (2) In the manufacturing and consumer worlds, counterfeit means everything from fake designer jeans to bogus microchips in heart pumps. (3) Counterfeiting in almost all kinds of consumer products. (4) It costs Americans $20 billion a year and is responsible for the loss of over 750,000 jobs. (5) The dramatic increase, analysts say, is due to the average consumer's obsession with brand names. (6) To help combat this worldwide problem, the United States government has became involved.
(7) The Trademark Counterfeiting Act of 1984 calls for harsh penalties in the United States for product counterfeiting, and consumer educashun is stressed in programs provided by the International Anticounterfeiting Coalition. (8) As a consumer, what can you do to protect yourself from buying fakes? (9) It is important to shop at a store operated by a trustworthy merchant.
(10) Also, check for fuzzy or misspelled labels and tags, these are usually fake. (11) You should be careful whenever you buy something marked down more than 40 or 50 percent, especially if the seller is suspect. (12) Counterfeiting will continue to be a major problem, but being an aware consumer will help one win the battle against fakes.

1. Sentence 2: **In the manufacturing and consumer worlds, counterfeit means everything from fake designer jeans to bogus microchips in heart pumps.**

   What correction should be made to this sentence?

   (1) insert a comma after manufacturing
   (2) remove the comma after worlds
   (3) replace means with meant
   (5) change designer to Designer
   (5) no correction is necessary

   (1) (2) (3) (4) (5)

2. Sentence 3: **Counterfeiting in almost all kinds of consumer products.**

   What correction should be made to this sentence?

   (1) insert a comma after Counterfeiting
   (2) insert the word occurs after Counterfeiting
   (3) insert the word occur after Counterfeiting
   (4) change the spelling of almost to allmost
   (5) change the spelling of almost to almos

   (1) (2) (3) (4) (5)

3. Sentence 4: **It costs Americans $20 billion a year and is responsible for the loss of over 750,000 jobs.**

   What correction should be made to this sentence?

   (1) replace It with They
   (2) change Americans to americans
   (3) insert a comma after year
   (4) change the spelling of responsible to responsable
   (5) no correction is necessary

   (1) (2) (3) (4) (5)

4. Sentence 5: **The dramatic increase, analysts say, is due to the average consumer's obsession with brand names.**

   Which of the following is the best way to write the underlined portion of this sentence? If you think the original is the best way, choose option (1).

   (1) say, is
   (2) says, is
   (3) say, be
   (4) says, are
   (5) say, are

   (1) (2) (3) (4) (5)

GO ON TO THE NEXT PAGE.

5. Sentence 6: **To help combat this world-wide problem, the United States government has became involved.**

   What correction should be made to this sentence?

   (1) remove the comma after problem
   (2) change the spelling of government to goverment
   (3) change government to Government
   (4) change became to become
   (5) no correction is necessary

   (1) (2) (3) (4) (5)

6. Sentence 7: **The Trademark Counterfeiting Act of 1984 calls for harsh penalties in the United States for product counterfeiting, and consumer educashun is stressed in programs provided by the International Anticounterfeiting Coalition.**

   What correction should be made to this sentence?

   (1) change calls to will call
   (2) replace and with but
   (3) replace and with or
   (4) change the spelling of educashun to education
   (5) change is to are

   (1) (2) (3) (4) (5)

7. Sentence 10: **Also, check for fuzzy or misspelled labels and tags, these are usually fake.**

   Which of the following is the best way to write the underlined portion of this sentence? If you think the original is the best way, choose option (1).

   (1) tags, these
   (2) tags these
   (3) tags; these
   (4) tags and these
   (5) tags. Because these

   (1) (2) (3) (4) (5)

8. Sentence 11: **You should be careful whenever you buy something marked down more than 40 or 50 percent, especially if the seller is suspect.**

   If you rewrote sentence 11 beginning with

   When buying something marked down more than 40 or 50 percent,

   the next words should be

   (1) care should be taken
   (2) be careful
   (3) the seller is suspect
   (4) especially from a suspect seller
   (5) suspect the seller

   (1) (2) (3) (4) (5)

9. Sentence 12: **Counterfeiting will continue to be a major problem, but being an aware consumer will help one win the battle against fakes.**

   Which of the following is the best way to write the underlined portion of this sentence? If you think the original is the best way, choose option (1).

   (1) help one win
   (2) help you win
   (3) help them win
   (4) help it win
   (5) help us win

   (1) (2) (3) (4) (5)

GO ON TO THE NEXT PAGE.

Items 10–18 refer to the following passage.

(1) For centuries, people have tried to prove that animals can talk and to think. (2) In 1904, one such person, a german mathematics teacher named Osten, owned an unusually talented horse called Clever Hans. (3) Clever Hans became a celebrity because not only could he do simple math, but he could also add and subtract fractions. (4) Excited by the thought of a mathematical horse people traveled from all over Europe to see Clever Hans, and at the height of his popularity he was the subject of many songs. (5) Mr. Osten honestly believed in the intelligence of his horse, so one day he invited scientists to test Clever Hans. (6) They discovered that when Mr. Osten knew the question before Clever Hans was asked it, the horse almost always knew the correct answer. (7) When Mr. Osten did not know the question first, Clever Hans did not know the answer. (8) The scientists then blindfolded the horse to see if he could answer questions correctly, but Clever Hans missed them all. (9) After the scientists analyzed the results of their tests, they discovered that Mr. Osten gave nonverbal signals to the horse. (10) Mr. Osten always would have leaned forward slightly when Clever Hans began tapping out the answer with his foot. (11) When the horse had the correct answer, Mr. Osten would straighten up, and he would stop tapping. (12) Terrible disappointment was suffered by Mr. Osten at the discovery that his horse was not really a mathematician.

10. Sentence 1: **For centuries, people have tried to prove that animals can talk and to think.**

    Which of the following is the best way to write the underlined portion of this sentence? If you think the original is the best way, choose option (1).

    (1) to think
    (2) they can think
    (3) can think
    (4) think
    (5) be thinking

    ① ② ③ ④ ⑤

11. Sentence 2: **In 1904, one such person, a german mathematics teacher named Osten, owned an unusually talented horse called Clever Hans.**

    What correction should be made to this sentence?

    (1) change german to German
    (2) change mathematics to Mathematics
    (3) remove the comma after Osten
    (4) insert a comma after horse
    (5) no correction is necessary

    ① ② ③ ④ ⑤

12. Sentence 3: **Clever Hans became a celebrity because not only could he do simple math, but he could also add and subtract fractions.**

    What correction should be made to this sentence?

    (1) insert a comma after celebrity
    (2) replace because with which
    (3) remove the comma after math
    (4) remove the word but
    (5) no correction is necessary

    ① ② ③ ④ ⑤

13. Sentence 4: **Excited by the thought of a mathematical horse people traveled from all over Europe to see Clever Hans, and at the height of his popularity he was the subject of many songs.**

    What correction should be made to this sentence?

    (1) insert a comma after horse
    (2) change Europe to europe
    (3) change to see to seeing
    (4) remove the word and
    (5) change the spelling of height to heighth

    ① ② ③ ④ ⑤

GO ON TO THE NEXT PAGE.

14. Sentence 5: **Mr. Osten honestly believed in the intelligence of his horse, so one day he invited scientists to test Clever Hans.**

Which of the following is the best way to write the underlined portion of this sentence? If you think the original is the best way, choose option (1).

(1) horse, so
(2) horse, yet
(3) horse, but
(4) horse, for
(5) horse, one

(1) (2) (3) (4) (5)

15. Sentence 9: **After the scientists analyzed the results of their tests, they discovered that Mr. Osten gave nonverbal signals to the horse.**

What correction should be made to this sentence?

(1) replace their with they're
(2) remove the comma after tests
(3) insert a comma after discovered
(4) change gave to gives
(5) no correction is necessary

(1) (2) (3) (4) (5)

16. Sentence 10: **Mr. Osten always would have leaned forward slightly when Clever Hans began tapping out the answer with his foot.**

What correction should be made to this sentence?

(1) insert a comma after Osten
(2) change would have leaned to would lean
(3) insert a comma after slightly
(4) replace when with until
(5) change began to begun

(1) (2) (3) (4) (5)

17. Sentence 11: **When the horse had the correct answer, Mr. Osten would straighten up, and he would stop tapping.**

Which of the following is the best way to write the underlined portion of this sentence? If you think the original is the best way, choose option (1).

(1) and he
(2) and one
(3) and Clever Hans
(4) and Mr. Osten
(5) and they

(1) (2) (3) (4) (5)

18. Sentence 12: **Terrible disappointment was suffered by Mr. Osten at the discovery that his horse was not really a mathematician.**

If you rewrote sentence 12 beginning with

Mr. Osten was terribly disappointed

the next word should be

(1) when
(2) for
(3) so
(4) as
(5) until

(1) (2) (3) (4) (5)

GO ON TO THE NEXT PAGE.

Items 19–27 refer to the following passage.

(1) There's nothing like a Saturday night bowling tournament to create excitement among devoted bowlers. (2) This popular sport actually began 7,000 years ago with Stone Age men and boys. (3) Their sporting equiptment included pebbles and rocks to knock down their pins, which were pointed stones or sheep joints. (4) European bowling originated in German monasteries during the Middle Ages. (5) It was part of a religious ritual to persuade peasants to lead a better life. (6) The game next spread to England, where it become so popular that in 1366 the king passed a law forbidding participation in the game. (7) His people had begun to spend their free time bowling rather than to practice their archery. (8) At that time, expert archers were essential for military defense. (9) Bowling is brought to America by Dutch settlers in New York and played upon a green called a "bowling green." (10) In the 1840s ninepins, an early form of bowling reached its peak, but controversy developed when people began betting on it. (11) A law was passed, forbidding ninepins but not the game of bowling. (12) Some enterprising person added a tenth pin to the game to circumvent the law, and thus the current game was born.

19. Sentence 1: **There's nothing like a Saturday night bowling tournament to create excitement among devoted bowlers.**

    What correction should be made to this sentence?

    (1) replace There's with They're
    (2) change night to Night
    (3) insert a comma after tournament
    (4) change create to have created
    (5) no correction is necessary

    1 2 3 4 5

20. Sentence 3: **Their sporting equiptment included pebbles and rocks to knock down their pins, which were pointed stones or sheep joints.**

    What correction should be made to this sentence?

    (1) change Their to They're
    (2) change the spelling of equiptment to equipment
    (3) insert a comma after pebbles
    (4) change which to who
    (5) no correction is necessary

21. Sentence 6: **The game next spread to England, where it become so popular that in 1366 the king passed a law forbidding participation in the game.**

    What correction should be made to this sentence?

    (1) change England to england
    (2) replace it with they
    (3) change become to becomes
    (4) change become to became
    (5) change king to King

    1 2 3 4 5

22. Sentence 7: **His people had begun to spend their free time bowling rather than to practice their archery.**

    What correction should be made to this sentence?

    (1) insert a comma after people
    (2) change begun to began
    (3) replace than with then
    (4) change to practice to practicing
    (5) change to practice to having practiced

    1 2 3 4 5

GO ON TO THE NEXT PAGE.

23. Sentence 8: **At that time, expert archers were essential for military defense.**

Which of the following is the best way to write the underlined portion of this sentence? If you think the original is the best way, choose option (1)

(1) archers were
(2) archers been
(3) archers was
(4) archers could have been
(5) archers being

(1) (2) (3) (4) (5)

24. Sentence 9: **Bowling is brought to America by Dutch settlers in New York and played upon a green called a "bowling green."**

Which of the following is the best way to write the underlined portion of this sentence? If you think the original is the best way, choose option (1).

(1) is brought
(2) are brought
(3) was brought
(4) is brung
(5) was brung

(1) (2) (3) (4) (5)

25. Sentence 10: **In the 1840s ninepins, an early form of bowling reached its peak, but controversy developed when people began betting on it.**

What correction should be made to this sentence?

(1) insert a comma after bowling
(2) change its to it's
(3) change the spelling of controversy to contraversy
(4) change the spelling of developed to developped
(5) change began to begun

(1) (2) (3) (4) (5)

26. Sentence 11: **A law was passed, forbidding ninepins but not the game of bowling.**

Which of the following is the best way to write the underlined portion of this sentence? If you think the original is the best way, choose option (1).

(1) passed, forbidding
(2) passed forbidding
(3) passed. Forbidding
(4) passed; forbidding
(5) passed, and forbidding

(1) (2) (3) (4) (5)

27. Sentence 12: **Some enterprising person added a tenth pin to the game to circumvent the law, and thus the current game was born.**

If you rewrote sentence 12 beginning with

The current game of tenpins was born

the next word should be

(1) although
(2) before
(3) if
(4) when
(5) until

(1) (2) (3) (4) (5)

GO ON TO THE NEXT PAGE.

Items 28–36 refer to the following passage.

(1) Studies show that in some people stress causes physical and mental disorders. (2) Stress has been studied by Scientists for only fifty years. (3) Among the symptoms of stress they have identified are rapid heartbeat, high blood pressure, short temper, crying jags, sleeplessness, and upset stomach. (4) Stress can also weaken the body's ability to fight illness. (5) This makes a person under stress ill more often than a relaxed person. (6) But how can we possibly avoid stress, it is all around us? (7) We need not be helpless victims because it is possible to lessen the affects of stress on our lives. (8) We must first identify the sources of stress and then will try to take measures to avoid its harmful results. (9) There are many sources of stress. (10) Family problems, an unfulfilling job, weight control, and drug abuse, can all cause harmful stress. (11) As we learn to recognize the causes of stress in our lives, we can also learn to control its effects with exercise, proper diet, and to relax.

28. Sentence 2: **Stress has been studied by Scientists for only fifty years.**

    What correction should be made to this sentence?

    (1) remove has
    (2) change has to have
    (3) change has been to will have been
    (4) change Scientists to scientists
    (5) insert a comma after Scientists

    (1) (2) (3) (4) (5)

29. Sentence 3: **Among the symptoms of stress they have identified are rapid heartbeat, high blood pressure, short temper, crying jags, sleeplessness, and upset stomach.**

    What correction should be made to this sentence?

    (1) insert a comma after stress
    (2) insert a comma after identified
    (3) change are to is
    (4) change the spelling of stomach to stomache
    (5) no correction is necessary

    (1) (2) (3) (4) (5)

30. Sentences 4 and 5: **Stress can also weaken the body's ability to fight illness. This makes a person under stress ill more often than a relaxed person.**

    The most effective combination of sentences 4 and 5 would include which of the following groups of words?

    (1) which will make
    (2) weakening the body's ability
    (3) as well as make
    (4) making a person under stress ill
    (5) weaken and make ill

    (1) (2) (3) (4) (5)

31. Sentence 6: **But how can we possibly avoid stress, it is all around us?**

    Which of the following is the best way to write the underlined portion of this sentence? If you think the original is the best way, choose option (1).

    (1) stress, it
    (2) stress it
    (3) stess? It
    (4) stress; it
    (5) stress when it

    (1) (2) (3) (4) (5)

32. Sentence 7: **We need not be helpless victims because it is possible to lessen the affects of stress on our lives.**

    What correction should be made to this sentence?

    (1) replace We with You
    (2) insert a comma after victims
    (3) replace because with even though
    (4) replace lessen with lesson
    (5) replace affects with effects

    (1) (2) (3) (4) (5)

GO ON TO THE NEXT PAGE.

33. Sentence 8: **We must first identify the sources of stress and then will try to take measures to avoid its harmful results.**

Which of the following is the best way to write the underlined portion of this sentence? If you think the original is the best way, choose option (1).

(1) and then will try
(2) and then trying
(3) and then try
(4) and then tried
(5) and then to try

(1) (2) (3) (4) (5)

34. Sentence 9: **There are many sources of stress.**

What correction should be made to this sentence?

(1) replace There with They're
(2) replace There with Their
(3) change are to is
(4) change the spelling of sources to sourses
(5) no correction is necessary

(1) (2) (3) (4) (5)

35. Sentence 10: **Family problems, an unfulfilling job, weight control, and drug abuse, can all cause harmful stress.**

Which of the following is the best way to write the underlined portion of this sentence? If you think the original is the best way, choose option (1).

(1) and drug abuse, can
(2) and drug abuse can
(3) and, drug abuse can
(4) and, drug abuse, can
(5) and drug abuse should

(1) (2) (3) (4) (5)

36. Sentence 11: **As we learn to recognize the causes of stress in our lives, we can also learn to control its effects with exercise, proper diet, and to relax.**

What correction should be made to this sentence?

(1) change the spelling of recognize to reconize
(2) replace our with hour
(3) remove the comma after lives
(4) change to relax to relaxation
(5) no correction is necessary

(1) (2) (3) (4) (5)

GO ON TO THE NEXT PAGE.

Items 37–45 refer to the following passage.

(1) If you are looking for a job or plan to reenter the working world, you might find this a difficult task. (2) There is a way, however, to ease this situation and have you ever thought of working for a temporary employment agency? (3) Temporary assignments let you explore the working world before you make up your mind. (4) As a "temp," you can work in many different situations while learning new skills and meeting new people. (5) The variety of working in a different place every day or week challenge and stimulate many workers. (6) On the other hand, if you want to attend a computer seminar, lie in the sun on the first day of summer, or visit Aunt Grace on Columbus day, you can easily take the day off. (7) Some temporary agencies offer health insurance and other benefits to their workers. (8) If the one you work for does not, you will find it exspensive to provide your own health insurance. (9) Another disadvantage to temporary work is that there is no guarantee of work you do not automatically draw a paycheck every Friday. (10) Temporary work may not be appropriate for people which crave security. (11) There are risks involved with temporary work, but if you like a flexible schedule thrive on change, or need to explore different careers, this approach might be for you.

37. Sentence 1: **If you are looking for a job or plan to reenter the working world, you might find this a difficult task.**

If you rewrote sentence 1 beginning with

Looking for a job or

the next word should be

(1) finding
(2) being
(3) looking
(4) reentering
(5) working

(1) (2) (3) (4) (5)

38. Sentence 2: **There is a way, however, to ease this situation and have you ever thought of working for a temporary employment agency?**

Which of the following is the best way to write the underlined portion of this sentence? If you think the original is the best way, choose option (1).

(1) situation and have
(2) situation, and have
(3) situation, but have
(4) situation. Have
(5) situation have

(1) (2) (3) (4) (5)

39. Sentence 5: **The variety of working in a different place every day or week challenge and stimulate many workers.**

Which of the following is the best way to write the underlined portion of this sentence? If you think the original is the best way, choose option (1).

(1) challenge and stimulate
(2) will challenge and stimulate
(3) challenging and stimulating
(4) challenged and stimulated
(5) challenges and stimulates

(1) (2) (3) (4) (5)

40. Sentence 6: **On the other hand, if you want to attend a computer seminar, lie in the sun on the first day of summer, or visit Aunt Grace on Columbus day, you can easily take the day off.**

What correction should be made to this sentence?

(1) replace if with since
(2) remove the comma after seminar
(3) change summer to Summer
(4) change Columbus day to Columbus Day
(5) remove the comma after day

(1) (2) (3) (4) (5)

GO ON TO THE NEXT PAGE.

41. Sentence 7: **Some temporary agencies offer health insurance and other benefits to their workers.**

What correction should be made to this sentence?

(1) insert which after agencies
(2) change offer to offered
(3) insert a comma after insurance
(4) change the spelling of benefits to benifits
(5) no correction is necessary

(1) (2) (3) (4) (5)

42. Sentence 8: **If the one you work for does not, you will find it exspensive to provide your own health insurance.**

What correction should be made to this sentence?

(1) replace If with Since
(2) remove the comma after not
(3) change the spelling of exspensive to expensive
(4) change your to you're
(5) no correction is necessary

(1) (2) (3) (4) (5)

43. Sentence 9: **Another disadvantage to temporary work is that there is no guarantee of work you do not automatically draw a paycheck every Friday.**

Which of the following is the best way to write the underlined portion of this sentence? If you think the original is the best way, choose option (1).

(1) work you
(2) working you
(3) work. You
(4) work, you
(5) work because you

(1) (2) (3) (4) (5)

44. Sentence 10: **Temporary work may not be appropriate for people which crave security.**

What correction should be made to this sentence?

(1) insert a comma after work
(2) change the spelling of appropriate to apropriate
(3) insert a comma after people
(4) replace which with who
(5) no correction is necessary

(1) (2) (3) (4) (5)

45. Sentence 11: **There are risks involved with temporary work, but if you like a flexible schedule thrive on change, or need to explore different careers, this approach might be for you.**

What correction should be made to this sentence?

(1) change are to is
(2) replace but with and
(3) insert a comma after schedule
(4) remove the comma after careers
(5) change might be to might have been

(1) (2) (3) (4) (5)

GO ON TO THE NEXT PAGE.

Items 46–55 refer to the following passage.

(1) Today more and more people have microwave ovens and must learn a very different method of cooking. (2) Let's look, then at how microwave ovens work and how that affects their use with perishable goods. (3) Microwaves are extra-short radio waves, the movement of these waves inside the oven does the actual cooking. (4) The air in the oven usually don't heat up very much. (5) The waves inside the oven are passing through the food repeatedly, and bounce around a lot. (6) This action causes cooking to begin just below the food's surface. (7) As the heat spreads through the rest of the food, full cooking is achieved. (8) While microwaving is quick. (9) It does not always cook food evenly. (10) Before new microwave owners master their ovens, we often find that some spots in a food will overcook, while others are still not completely cooked. (11) To completely cook a particular food without overcooking these high-heat spots, many microwave Recipes call for a 10- to 15-minute standing time after the power has been turned off. (12) Because of their quick cooking times, microwave ovens have become indispensible to harried homemakers and other busy professionals.

46. Sentence 1: **Today more and more people have microwave ovens and must learn a very different method of cooking.**

    Which of the following is the best way to write the underlined portion of this sentence? If you think the original is the best way, choose option (1).

    (1) and must learn
    (2) and learned
    (3) and to learn
    (4) and have learned
    (5) and will learn

    ① ② ③ ④ ⑤

47. Sentence 2: **Let's look, then at how microwave ovens work and how that affects their use with perishable goods.**

    Which of the following is the best way to write the underlined portion of this sentence? If you think the original is the best way, choose option (1).

    (1) look, then
    (2) look, then,
    (3) look then,
    (4) look. Then
    (5) look; then,

    ① ② ③ ④ ⑤

48. Sentence 3: **Microwaves are extra-short radio waves, the movement of these waves inside the oven does the actual cooking.**

    Which of the following is the best way to write the underlined portion of this sentence? If you think the original is the best way, choose option (1).

    (1) waves, the
    (2) waves the
    (3) waves. The
    (4) waves, but the
    (5) waves, however the

    ① ② ③ ④ ⑤

49. Sentence 4: **The air in the oven usually don't heat up very much.**

    What correction should be made to this sentence?

    (1) insert a comma after air
    (2) change the spelling of usually to usualy
    (3) change don't to doesn't
    (4) change don't to do not
    (5) no correction is necessary

    ① ② ③ ④ ⑤

GO ON TO THE NEXT PAGE.

50. Sentence 5: **The waves inside the oven are passing through the food repeatedly, and bounce around a lot.**

If you rewrote sentence 5 beginning with

The waves bounce around inside the oven

the next word(s) should be

(1) passing
(2) and pass
(3) or pass
(4) are passing
(5) to pass

(1) (2) (3) (4) (5)

51. Sentence 7: **As the heat spreads through the rest of the food, full cooking is achieved.**

What correction should be made to this sentence?

(1) replace As with Whenever
(2) change spreads to is spread
(3) replace through with thorough
(4) remove the comma after food
(5) no correction is necessary

(1) (2) (3) (4) (5)

52. Sentences 8 and 9: **While microwaving is quick. It does not always cook food evenly.**

Which of the following is the best way to write the underlined portion of these sentences? If you think the original is the best way, choose option (1).

(1) quick. It
(2) quick it
(3) quick, it
(4) quick, and it
(5) quick since it

(1) (2) (3) (4) (5)

53. Sentence 10: **Before new microwave owners master their ovens, we often find that some spots in a food will overcook, while others are still not completely cooked.**

What correction should be made to this sentence?

(1) replace their with they're
(2) remove the comma after ovens
(3) replace we with they
(4) change the spelling of often to offen
(5) change are to is

(1) (2) (3) (4) (5)

54. Sentence 11: **To completely cook a particular food without overcooking these high-heat spots, many microwave Recipes call for a 10- to 15-minute standing time after the power has been turned off.**

What correction should be made to this sentence?

(1) change the spelling of particular to particuler
(2) remove the comma after spots
(3) change Recipes to recipes
(4) change call to calls
(5) change has been turned to will be turned

(1) (2) (3) (4) (5)

55. Sentence 12: **Because of their quick cooking times, microwave ovens have become indispensible to harried homemakers and other busy professionals.**

What correction should be made to this sentence?

(1) replace their with there
(2) remove the comma after times
(3) change have become to has become
(4) change the spelling of indispensible to indispensable
(5) replace harried with hurried

(1) (2) (3) (4) (5)

GO ON TO THE NEXT PAGE.

Part II

Directions: This is a test to find out how well you write. The test has one question that asks you to present an opinion on an issue or to explain something. In preparing your answer for this question, you should take the following steps:

1. Read all of the information accompanying the question.
2. Plan your answer carefully before you write.
3. Use scratch paper to make any notes.
4. Write your answer.
5. Read carefully what you have written and make any changes that will improve your writing.
6. Check your paragraphing, sentence structure, spelling, punctuation, capitalization, and usage, and make any necessary corrections.

You will have 45 minutes to write on the question you are assigned. Write legibly and use a ballpoint pen.

Computers are changing modern life, and their use is steadily increasing. Yet some people have "computer phobia"; that is, they have a great fear or dislike of computers. Why would some people feel this way about computers? Do their feelings have any merit? Detail your thoughts in a 200-word essay. Give specific examples.

END OF EXAMINATION

TEST 2: SOCIAL STUDIES POSTTEST

Directions

The Social Studies Posttest consists of 64 multiple-choice questions. Some of the questions are based on maps, graphs, charts, cartoons, and short reading passages—all related to the social studies. Read the passage or study the material first and then answer the questions following it. You may refer to these materials as often as necessary to answer the questions. You will find that some of the questions will require considerable deliberation and frequent rereading of the passage or reexamination of the material presented.

This is in part a test of your background of general knowledge in the social studies, but it is also a "study test," that is, a test of your ability to understand the important meanings in what you see and read. In general, the test will not penalize you seriously for having forgotten many of the detailed facts you once knew, if you have retained the important generalizations and are able to use them intelligently.

You should take approximately 1½ hours to complete this test. There is no penalty for guessing. Try to answer as many questions as you can. Work rapidly but carefully, without spending too much time on any one question. If a question is too difficult for you, omit it and come back to it later.

For each answer, mark one answer space. See how the following example is done.

EXAMPLE

Zoning laws are passed by local governments to ensure the orderly development of land and property. Zoning boards divide cities into zones that group together similar uses. For example, there might be one zone for homes, another for business, another for industry, and so on. Certain types of construction are allowed in some zones but not in others.

According to the passage, which of the following cases would come under local zoning laws?

(1) A driver must pay toll charges to use a state highway.
(2) A property owner must pay taxes to the state.
(3) A mountainous region in Colorado is designated a wilderness area by the U.S. Department of the Interior.
(4) A homeowner must pay for garbage pickup.
(5) A department store wants to expand by building an addition.

① ② ③ ④ ●

Options (1), (2), and (3) concern state or national governments not local ones. Option (4) does not relate to zoning laws, but to sanitation. Only option (5), which involves construction, relates to zoning laws. Answer space (5) has been marked.

Answers to the questions are in the Answer Key on page 677. Explanations for the answers are on pages 665–668.

Directions: Choose the one best answer to each question.

Items 1–2 refer to the following passage.

With the aid of federal land and money grants, the nation's railroads underwent rapid growth and improvement after the Civil War. In the process they promoted immigration through the hiring of European, Asian, and Mexican construction workers. They attracted large numbers of both American and European settlers to western lands. People in eastern cities ate beef from Texas longhorns brought across country by the railroads. New and faster methods of production were introduced in the steel industry to meet the railroads' demands for track and equipment. U.S. steel mills in 1890 were producing 60 times more steel than they were able to produce in 1870.

1. The government promoted railroad growth and expansion when it
   (1) paid high rates for troop transport
   (2) built telephone and telegraph systems
   (3) organized cattle drives
   (4) granted land and money
   (5) supported the steel mills

   ① ② ③ ④ ⑤

2. Information in the passage best supports which of the following conclusions?
   (1) The role of the federal government is to promote industrial growth and improved technology.
   (2) Growth and improvement in one industry can promote growth and improvement in related industries.
   (3) The demands of the Civil War promoted industrial growth in the United States.
   (4) The growth of U.S. industry was made possible by a huge influx of immigrant workers.
   (5) The decline of one industry encourages the growth of other industries.

   ① ② ③ ④ ⑤

Items 3–6 refer to the graph and passage below.

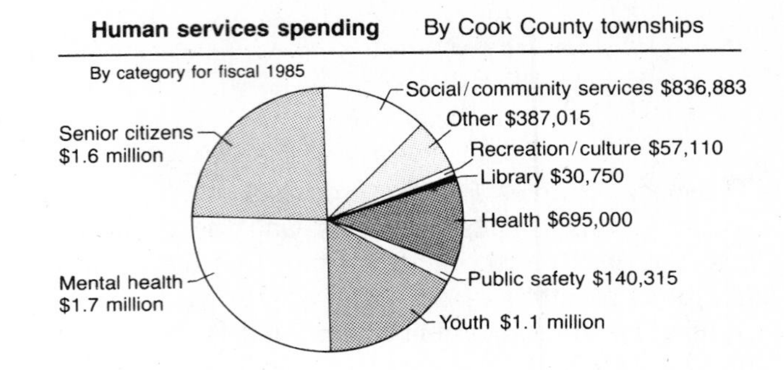

At a hearing on next year's human services budget, commissioner A recommended a cut in spending for senior citizens. Citing figures showing a projected 3 percent decline in the county's senior citizen population, commissioner A said he believed a 3-percent spending cut was warranted.

Commissioner B agreed but added that any savings should go toward increasing youth services. "If we're going to spend more," said the commissioner, "we should spend it on our young people—that is, on our workers and taxpayers."

3. Based on the data in the graph above, which of the following statements is true?
   (1) Senior citizens received the largest share of the county's human services budget.
   (2) Mental health and senior citizens received about half the county's human services budget.
   (3) The county provides more services to youth than to senior citizens.
   (4) The county has more senior citizens than young people.
   (5) Spending for health services will increase as the senior citizen population increases.

GO ON TO THE NEXT PAGE.

4. What is wrong with commissioner A's conclusion?

   (1) The number of senior citizens is only one factor that determines the cost of services to them.
   (2) A three-percent drop in the senior citizen population would require a 3-percent increase in human services spending.
   (3) The commissioner's conclusion is not based on realistic projections.
   (4) It is well known that the elderly are living longer, making a 3-percent decline in the senior citizen population unlikely.
   (5) A decline in the number of senior citizens would result in the need for fewer services, but not necessarily 3 percent fewer.

   (1) (2) (3) (4) (5)

5. What does commissioner B seem to be saying about senior citizens?

   (1) There will be more senior citizens in the year to come.
   (2) The county will spend more on senior citizens in the year to come.
   (3) Senior citizens need jobs.
   (4) Senior citizens don't work or pay taxes.
   (5) Senior citizens take jobs that should go to young people.

   (1) (2) (3) (4) (5)

6. What must commissioner B believe in order to conclude what he did?

   (1) Senior citizens are an essential element in a productive society.
   (2) Senior citizens are as valuable as young people.
   (3) Government owes equal assistance to all its citizens.
   (4) All citizens owe equal assistance to county government.
   (5) Productive citizens are more deserving than others of government services.

   (1) (2) (3) (4) (5)

7. One concept common to many theories of learning is that of stimulus and response. A stimulus is anything in the environment that brings about a reaction, or response, in a person or an animal.

   Which of the following is an example of stimulus and response?

   (1) The television weather news issues a tornado warning, but people ignore it.
   (2) A man decides to study a foreign language, perhaps Spanish.
   (3) A baby cries, but her father has just stepped outside and doesn't hear.
   (4) A young woman decides to buy a used car and so borrows the money from her parents.
   (5) Each night when a dog hears a key in the lock, it rushes to greet its owner.

   (1) (2) (3) (4) (5)

GO ON TO THE NEXT PAGE.

Items 8–12 refer to the article below.

A good layer of healthy topsoil is essential to productive agriculture. Yet the erosion of topsoil is one of our most serious problems, and a problem that is getting worse, not better.

Wind and water have always carried topsoil into the world's rivers and oceans. But human use of the land seems to have considerably speeded up the process. One geologist estimates that topsoil erosion has nearly tripled since the introduction of human agriculture and grazing.

And the problem is the same in both industrial and underdeveloped nations. In the Third World, where populations are high and land scarce, farmers use steeply sloping land, which is easily eroded by water. Or they move into semi-arid regions where the plowed earth is vulnerable to erosion by wind. Even in the American Midwest, many farmers have stopped the ecologically sound practice of long-term crop rotation in favor of planting, year after year, corn or soybeans—row crops that leave the land exposed.

Erosion has, basically, two effects on farmers' ability to grow food. When topsoil is lost or damaged, productivity decreases. Productivity may be increased by the use of fertilizer or through irrigation, but this is expensive. So farmers who lose topsoil will experience either lower crop yields or higher costs.

8. Topsoil erosion by wind and water has been speeded up by

(1) fertilizer and irrigation
(2) excessive crop rotation
(3) industrialization in the Third World
(4) human agriculture and grazing
(5) increasing costs

① ② ③ ④ ⑤

9. In an area where winds blow away topsoil, a farmer might conserve that soil by

(1) planting row crops
(2) long-term rotation of crops
(3) using fertilizer
(4) grazing sheep or cattle
(5) planting corn or soybeans

① ② ③ ④ ⑤

10. What is the most likely effect topsoil loss would have on food prices?

(1) Prices will go up because less food can be grown.
(2) Prices will come down because more food can be grown.
(3) Prices will stay the same because production can be maintained by the use of fertilizer and irrigation.
(4) Wholesale prices will increase, but retail prices will not.
(5) Retail prices will increase, but wholesale prices will not.

① ② ③ ④ ⑤

11. Which of the following is a conclusion supported in the article?

(1) Farmers who lose topsoil will experience lower crop yields or higher costs.
(2) In the Midwest many farmers have stopped the ecologically sound practice of long-term crop rotation.
(3) In the Third World farmers use steeply sloping land, which is easily eroded by water.
(4) When topsoil is lost or damaged, production decreases.
(5) Fertilizing and irrigating are expensive.

① ② ③ ④ ⑤

12. Based on the information in the article, which of the following would be the most practical, long-term way to help Third World farmers?

(1) Train farmers to do industrial and technological jobs.
(2) Invest in fertilizer and irrigation to increase production.
(3) Teach them soil conservation methods, such as terracing and crop rotation.
(4) Make available low-interest loans so farmers can buy more land.
(5) Take farming out of private hands and turn it over to the government.

① ② ③ ④ ⑤

GO ON TO THE NEXT PAGE.

Items 13–15 refer to the chart below.

Population of the World (in millions)

	1800	1940	1980	2000
Europe (including all of U.S.S.R.)	188	572	755	855
North, South, and Central America	29	277	620	915
Asia, Africa, and Oceania	702	1,396	3,000	4,500
World	919	2,245	4,375	6,270

13. An official of a European government, concluding from the chart that Europe will gain population at a slower rate than other parts of the world, orders a study to determine the reasons for Europe's declining birthrate. Why was this a poor decision?

    (1) It is not possible to determine through studies the reasons for a declining birthrate.
    (2) The chart shows that the population of Europe is growing at a faster, not a slower, rate than other parts of the world.
    (3) The decision was correct only if the population projection turns out to be accurate.
    (4) The chart shows nothing about birthrate, but instead reflects the mortality, or death, rate.
    (5) A declining birthrate is only one possible explanation for a slow rate of population growth.

    ① ② ③ ④ ⑤

14. If food shortages occur in the year 2000, where would they most likely occur?

    (1) in Europe
    (2) in North, South, and Central America
    (3) in Asia, Africa, and Oceania
    (4) in the Northern Hemisphere
    (5) equally throughout the world

    ① ② ③ ④ ⑤

15. Which of the following statements is best supported by the data on the chart?

    (1) By the year 2000, the world's supply of oil will be exhausted.
    (2) By the year 2000, farmland will be scarce in Europe and the USSR.
    (3) Sometime after the year 2000, Europe and the USSR should see an increased rate of population growth.
    (4) Between 1980 and 2000, Asia, Africa, and Oceania will add more people than they did between 1940 and 1980.
    (5) The most likely direction of human migration by the year 2000 will be from Asia, Africa, and Oceania to Europe and America.

    ① ② ③ ④ ⑤

GO ON TO THE NEXT PAGE.

Items 16–18 refer to the passage below.

A comparison of America in 1932 and in 1939 shows improvements effected by the New Deal. In agriculture, farm prices were up; in industry, profits were higher; among workers, unemployment, though still extensive, was down. Per capital income (after taxes) had risen by $246 above the 1932 level, though it still did not equal the 1929 level.

These, of course, were the gains. On the other side of the ledger were some important liabilities for which the New Deal was responsible. The Roosevelt years saw an immense increase in the federal debt. In 1930 the public debt was $16 billion; in 1940 it was $42 billion. The New Deal created a large government bureaucracy to administer the new programs and agencies. There was a great deal of waste and duplication, and some New Deal programs limited the freedom of private enterprise.

16. Which of the following statements summarizes the passage above?

(1) United States citizens were relieved of tax payments during the New Deal.
(2) New Deal economic programs were responsible for both improvements and losses.
(3) The New Deal took the United States deeper into the Depression.
(4) Many workers took jobs on farms before the New Deal ended.
(5) Programs of the New Deal were carried out economically and efficiently.

(1) (2) (3) (4) (5)

17. Which of the following is the most likely explanation for the growth of the federal debt during the New Deal years?

(1) Private industry was not allowed to make large profits.
(2) Per capita income was down, so fewer taxes were collected.
(3) Unemployment was down, but so were wages.
(4) Huge amounts of money were needed to pay for New Deal programs.
(5) Huge amounts of money were lost through fraud.

(1) (2) (3) (4) (5)

18. Which of the following statements from the article is supported by factual evidence in the article?

(1) There was a great deal of waste in New Deal programs.
(2) Many services given by New Deal programs were duplicated.
(3) The Roosevelt years saw an immense increase in the federal debt.
(4) The New Deal created a large government bureaucracy.
(5) Some New Deal programs limited the freedom of private enterprise.

(1) (2) (3) (4) (5)

Item 19 refers to the passage below.

A political party is an association of voters who wish to influence and control decision making in government by recruiting, nominating, and electing members to public office. Each party picks candidates who support its ideas to represent the party in public elections. Each party tries to persuade voters to back its candidates. Although the Constitution says nothing about political parties, during most of the nation's history there have been two major ones, the Democratic and Republican parties. Each has many supporters in all parts of the country even though George Washington once warned that parties could cause conflicts that could disrupt the nation.

19. Based on the passage, which of these tasks is likely to be performed by a political party?

(1) sell American products to foreign countries
(2) determine sites for Olympic games
(3) raise money for charities
(4) monitor polling places to ensure fair elections
(5) encourage interstate commerce

(1) (2) (3) (4) (5)

GO ON TO THE NEXT PAGE.

20. Mechanics working for International Airways Company were dissatisfied. They refused to accept a union contract that reduced health insurance and vacation benefits. Instead of going to work, the mechanics stood outside the airport terminal doors. Some workers held signs that stated their complaints against their employers. They refused to work until a conference between their representatives and their employers resulted in an acceptable contract.

Which of the following describes how the differences between the mechanics' union and International Airways are likely to be settled?

(1) The mechanics will ask the government to close down the airport.
(2) Competition with other airlines will force International Airways to satisfy the mechanics.
(3) Union representatives will negotiate with International Airways through collective bargaining.
(4) Mechanics for International Airways will be fired from their jobs.
(5) International Airways will increase vacation allowances and cancel group health insurance benefits.

(1) (2) (3) (4) (5)

Items 21–22 refer to the passage below.

In the 1896 case *Plessy* v. *Ferguson,* the Supreme Court ruled that separate public facilities for black Americans were legal so long as the facilities were equal to those provided for white citizens. In 1954, a different Supreme Court reversed this decision. In *Brown* v. *Board of Education of Topeka,* a case testing the legality of separate schools for black and white students, the Supreme Court found the separate-but-equal doctrine unconstitutional.

21. Based on the paragraph above, which of the following can be inferred about the judicial branch's power of judicial review?

(1) How the Constitution is interpreted by the Supreme Court depends largely on the individuals serving as justices.
(2) In the late 1800s, the Supreme Court upheld the civil rights of black Americans.
(3) Rulings on issues cannot be changed unless the Supreme Court changes.
(4) The Constitution has meant the same throughout the years that it has been interpreted by the Supreme Court.
(5) Traditionally, Supreme Court justices do not let personal beliefs or current events enter into their decisions.

(1) (2) (3) (4) (5)

22. In deciding *Brown* v. *Board of Education of Topeka,* the Supreme Court found which of the following most important?

(1) the right to vote
(2) the freedom to choose with whom to associate
(3) equal rights under the law
(4) the freedom to go to school in your own neighborhood
(5) the right to sue a board of education

(1) (2) (3) (4) (5)

GO ON TO THE NEXT PAGE.

Items 23–25 refer to the following map.

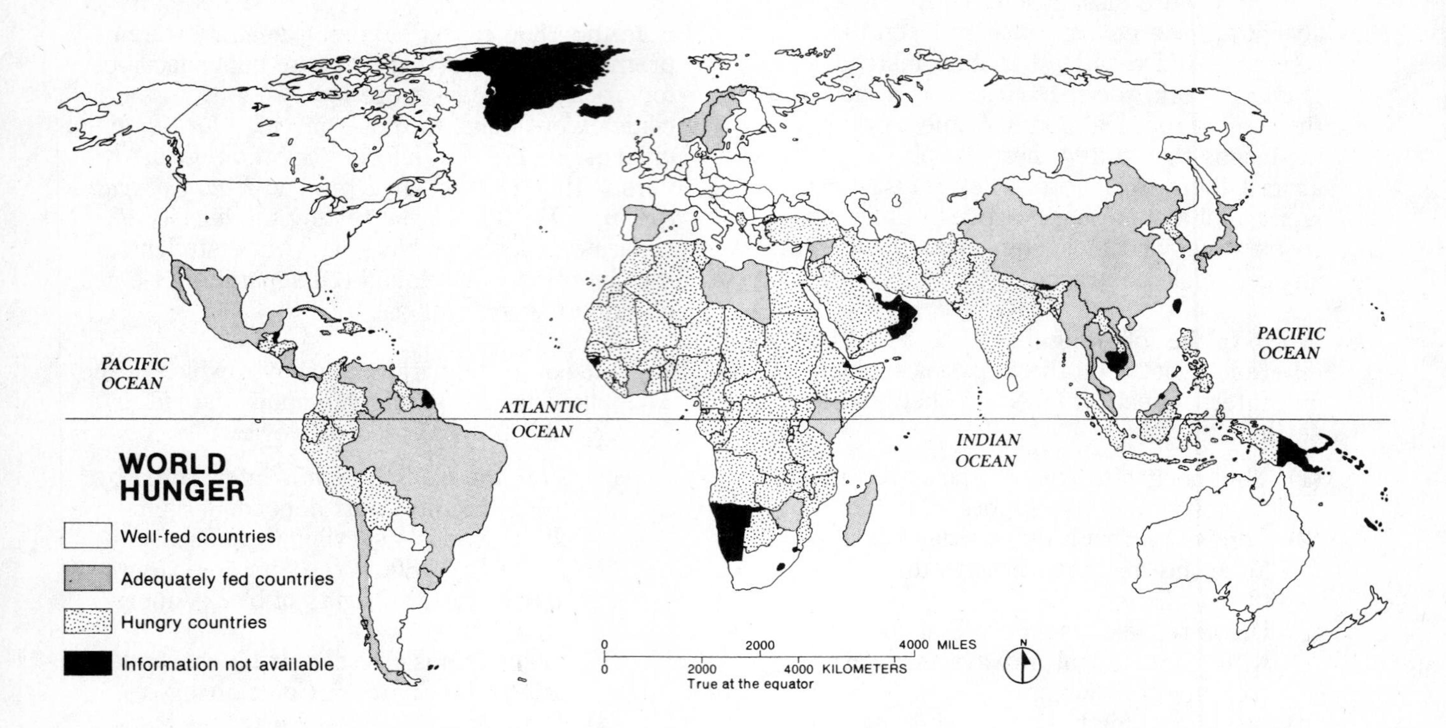

23. Which continent on the map has the largest number of hungry nations?

(1) Africa
(2) Asia
(3) South America
(4) North America
(5) Europe

(1) (2) (3) (4) (5)

24. According to the map, which of the following statements is true about "well-fed" countries?

(1) Most well-fed countries are located near the equator.
(2) Large mechanized farms are most common in well-fed countries.
(3) Most well-fed countries are in the Northern Hemisphere.
(4) There is an even distribution of well-fed countries throughout the world.
(5) Small countries cannot be well fed.

(1) (2) (3) (4) (5)

25. How might the map above be used to help solve the problem of hungry countries?

(1) to determine ways to limit population
(2) to determine the path of a satellite that could photograph and so help locate natural resources
(3) to decide which countries must begin to sell more of their food
(4) to study ways to increase crop production by the use of fertilizers
(5) to show areas where collective farming would be more efficient than farming by individual owners

(1) (2) (3) (4) (5)

GO ON TO THE NEXT PAGE.

Items 26–28 refer to the table below.

Employment of Women in Selected Occupational Groups, 1983–1984

Selected occupational groups	Total employed: Annual averages (in thousands) 1983	1984	Percent change	Women as percent of total in occupation, 1984
Women—a majority of workers				
Retail sales workers	3,839	4,033	5.1	69.0
Food preparation and service workers	3,077	3,194	3.8	64.0
Teachers, except college and university	2,386	2,481	4.0	72.1
Registered nurses	1,315	1,345	2.3	96.0
Secretaries, stenographers, and typists	4,776	4,765	−.2	97.7
Women—a minority of workers				
Supervisors and proprietors (sales)	839	955	13.8	29.7
Sales representatives, financial and business	689	764	10.9	38.4
Accountants and auditors	427	505	18.3	40.9
Computer programmers	144	179	24.3	35.4
Transportation and material moving occupations	326	369	13.2	8.3

26. The data in the table above would support which of the following conclusions?
    (1) Occupations requiring mathematics skills are not attractive to women.
    (2) Occupations requiring higher education traditionally have not attracted women.
    (3) More women are choosing to leave the work force.
    (4) More women are choosing to work in jobs traditionally done by men.
    (5) Between 1983 and 1984, fewer women went to work in jobs in which women are a majority.

    (1) (2) (3) (4) (5)

27. One economist declared that, if changes indicated by the statistics in the table became a trend, working women's incomes would rise. What is the economist assuming?
    (1) Inflation will automatically accompany the increase in the number of working women.
    (2) Husbands will demand that their working wives receive equal pay.
    (3) Jobs that have traditionally been held by men pay more.
    (4) Laws requiring equal pay for equal work will be passed.
    (5) Women will have to spend more hours working, thus earning more money.

    (1) (2) (3) (4) (5)

28. Which of the following groups could best make use of the statistics in the table?
    (1) legislators considering tax relief for retired persons
    (2) a local school board trying to predict next year's grade school enrollment
    (3) hospital administrators deciding how many nurses must be laid off in order to save money
    (4) labor union officials deciding how to invest their pension fund
    (5) curriculum planners in a vocational high school deciding which courses to expand and which to cut back

    (1) (2) (3) (4) (5)

GO ON TO THE NEXT PAGE.

Items 29–30 are based on the passage below.

One advantage that people have in facing their problems, whether large or small, is that the human brain is capable of finding many solutions to problems. People are creative beings. They can find a variety of possible paths to follow in defining problems or in seeking answers. Different human groups have developed remarkably different cultures even though they live in similar environments. Their houses and clothes, their diet and their ways of living, may be strikingly different, even though they occupy almost identical areas. Such diversity and creativity have helped increase the chances for survival when the environment changes.

29. Which of the following is an example of the human trait described above?

    (1) Workers move from an old office building into a new one and find their work productivity falling.
    (2) Islanders discover a disease killing the plant that is their main source of food. The population sickens and dies.
    (3) An Asian child adopted by an American family cannot adjust to the new diet.
    (4) A couple from New England retires to Florida. They find the climate too hot and move back north.
    (5) After years of less than normal rainfall, farmers in an area take up dry-farming, a method of covering the soil to hold in the moisture.

    (1) (2) (3) (4) (5)

30. The information in the passage above best supports which of the following hypotheses?

    (1) Humans are vulnerable.
    (2) Humans are adaptable.
    (3) Humans have large brains.
    (4) Environmental change stifles human creativity.
    (5) People who live in similar environments develop similar cultures.

    (1) (2) (3) (4) (5)

Items 31–33 refer to the map below.

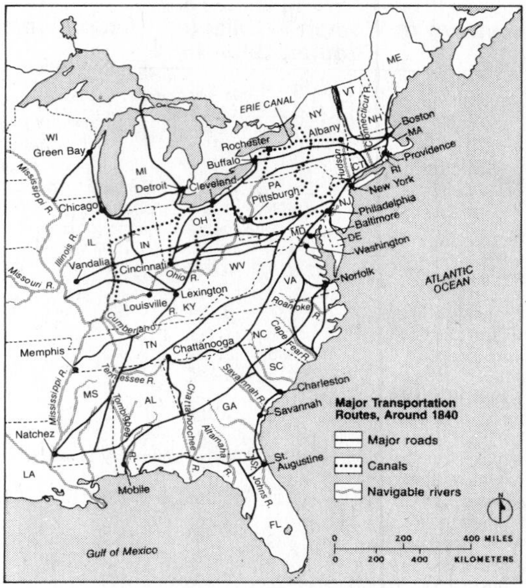

31. According to the map, which of the following statements is most likely true?

    (1) Around 1840, southern cotton growers probably moved their crops to Gulf Coast ports on navigable canals.
    (2) Around 1840, long-distance travel was easier in the North than in the South.
    (3) In general, long-distance travel was impossible in North America in 1840.
    (4) By 1840, long-distance transportation routes west of the Mississippi River were extensive and well-developed.
    (5) By 1840, long-distance rail lines crossed the nation.

    (1) (2) (3) (4) (5)

32. Which of the following statements best summarizes the information on the map?

    (1) By 1840, little had been done to develop navigable waterways.
    (2) By 1840, the South had developed an extensive network of navigable canals.
    (3) By 1840, the canals were finished; roads had taken over the business of moving people and freight.
    (4) By 1840, canals moved most of the country's people and freight.
    (5) In 1840, water was an important means of transportation in America.

    (1) (2) (3) (4) (5)

GO ON TO THE NEXT PAGE.

33. Based on the map above, which of the following is a statement of fact?

(1) By 1840, the South had begun a program of constructing navigable canals.
(2) Around 1840, southern cotton growers moved their crops to the Gulf Coast by rail.
(3) In 1840, one could travel by water from Lake Erie to Louisville, Kentucky.
(4) In 1840, a major road connected New York and Kansas City, Missouri.
(5) Soon after 1840, Americans would extend their transportation routes west of the Mississippi River.

(1) (2) (3) (4) (5)

Items 34–37 are based on the following article.

Most Americans know better but they smoke, drink, shun seat belts and don't use smoke detectors, a government survey indicates.

The study, developed by the government's National Center for Health Statistics in consultation with other agencies, concluded that most Americans know a lot about how to keep their health but many of them break the rules.

Among the specific findings:

- 80 percent understand that smoking, high cholesterol, high blood pressure and diets high in animal fat will increase chances of heart disease, the leading cause of death in America.
- About one-third of the adults responding to the survey said they smoke.
- Eight percent were heavy drinkers, 21 percent moderate drinkers and 24 percent lighter drinkers. Twelve percent said they had driven while intoxicated at least once in the past year.
- Less than one-half of the adult population exercise on a regular basis and only one-quarter have done so for five or more years.
- Forty percent said their homes did not have a working smoke detector.
- Only one-third of adults wore seat belts most of the time; another third never used seat belts.

34. According to the article, how many people in the study did not know what factors contribute to heart disease?

(1) 20 percent
(2) 80 percent
(3) 40 percent
(4) about one-third
(5) about one-half

(1) (2) (3) (4) (5)

35. A committee formed to improve Americans' health would probably conclude from the information in the article that Americans do NOT need

(1) a national seat belt law
(2) tougher drunk driving laws
(3) higher taxes on tobacco products
(4) more education about how to stay healthy
(5) a campaign to make good health more appealing

(1) (2) (3) (4) (5)

36. Which of the following is a statement of fact supported by data in the article?

(1) People who don't smoke or drink will live longer.
(2) One-third of all Americans think that seat belts are too uncomfortable.
(3) Most Americans do not have working smoke detectors in their homes.
(4) Slightly more than 50 percent of those in the study said that they drink.
(5) About one-half of those in the study have exercised regularly for five or more years.

(1) (2) (3) (4) (5)

37. The article suggests that Americans break the rules of good health

(1) for economic reasons
(2) for unknown reasons
(3) because they don't understand the rules
(4) because they enjoy taking risks
(5) because they don't trust doctors

(1) (2) (3) (4) (5)

GO ON TO THE NEXT PAGE.

Items 38–39 refer to the passage below.

The states and the federal government share some powers, such as the power to tax. A worker in New Mexico, for example, pays both federal and state income taxes. Spending is now shared, too; under a program called "revenue sharing" the federal government collects taxes and gives some of the money to state and local governments to spend. Administration of some programs is also shared. For example, Congress has adopted and partially funded a national interstate highway program, but the state governments pay part of the costs and supervise the actual construction and maintenance of the highways. There are a number of other similar programs, such as welfare assistance, health care, and unemployment compensation.

38. This paragraph demonstrates that state and federal governments
    (1) operate under a system of checks and balances
    (2) keep tax dollars separated
    (3) share overlapping powers and authority
    (4) avoid paying health care benefits
    (5) cooperate in collecting tariffs

    ① ② ③ ④ ⑤

39. According to the paragraph above, which of the following is an example of revenue sharing?
    (1) A state government collects fees from travelers on tollways.
    (2) The federal government collects taxes from workers drawing unemployment benefits.
    (3) A state government agency withholds federal income tax from paychecks of employees.
    (4) Workers in New Mexico pay both state and federal income taxes.
    (5) The federal government gives the city of St. Louis tax money to build schools.

    ① ② ③ ④ ⑤

Item 40 is based on the following graph.

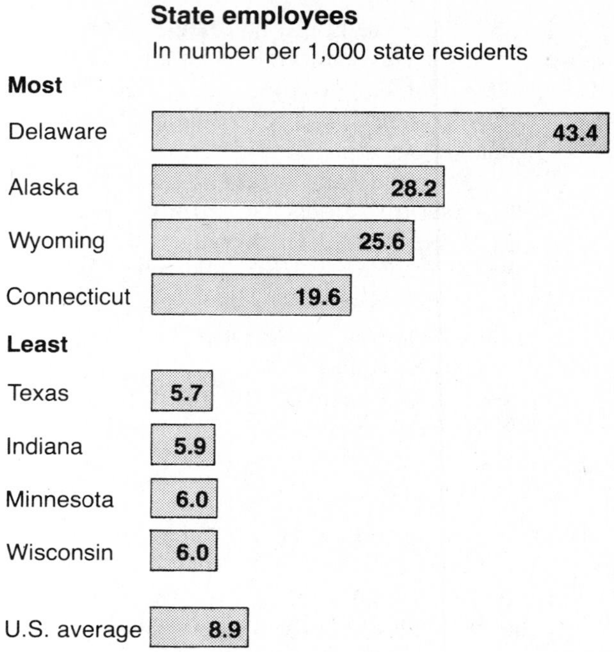

State employees
In number per 1,000 state residents

Most	Delaware	43.4
	Alaska	28.2
	Wyoming	25.6
	Connecticut	19.6
Least	Texas	5.7
	Indiana	5.9
	Minnesota	6.0
	Wisconsin	6.0
	U.S. average	8.9

40. Based on the information above, in which state would a law to reduce the pensions of state employees who retire after only 20 years of service have the least chance of passing?
    (1) Texas
    (2) Wisconsin
    (3) Connecticut
    (4) Delaware
    (5) Minnesota

    ① ② ③ ④ ⑤

GO ON TO THE NEXT PAGE.

Items 41–42 are based on the following map.

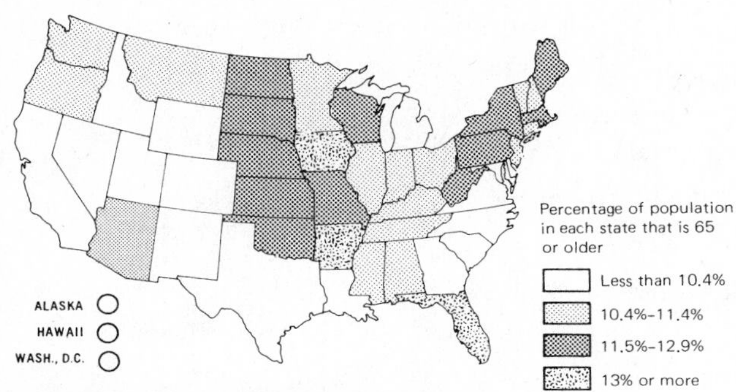

Where Older Americans Are Concentrated

41. On the national average, 10.9% of the people in the U.S. are 65 or older. According to the map, which of the following states would be in the average range?

(1) Florida
(2) California
(3) Iowa
(4) Arizona
(5) New York

42. In which of the following states would a law favoring reduced property taxes for homeowners on fixed incomes likely be most popular?

(1) Texas
(2) Illinois
(3) Arizona
(4) New York
(5) Florida

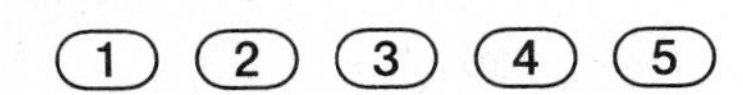

43. During the Great Depression, the years of severe economic crisis that followed the stock market crash of 1929, immigration to the United States fell to its lowest level in 100 years.

Which of the following is the most likely explanation for this fact?

(1) During the Depression, the U.S. closed its borders to immigrants.
(2) During the Depression, the U.S. sent many immigrants back to their countries of origin.
(3) People from other countries did not have enough money to immigrate.
(4) Immigrants were entering the country illegally, so their numbers could not be counted.
(5) The Depression destroyed economic opportunity, one of the main reasons for immigrating to the U.S.

1 2 3 4 5

44. Utah's legislature has approved a $55 million plan to pump record floodwaters from the Great Salt Lake into the western desert. The lake, which has risen to a record level and doubled its volume in the past four years, threatens to swamp Interstate Highway 80 and two major railroad lines.

Which of the following is the most likely explanation for the legislature's action?

(1) The lake's level and volume are expected to double in the next four years.
(2) The lake's level and volume are expected to fall in the next four years.
(3) Utah's western desert needs the water for irrigation.
(4) Serious economic loss can result if major transportation lines are cut.
(5) Serious automobile and railroad accidents will occur if major transportation lines are swamped.

1 2 3 4 5

GO ON TO THE NEXT PAGE.

Items 45–47 are based on the following data.

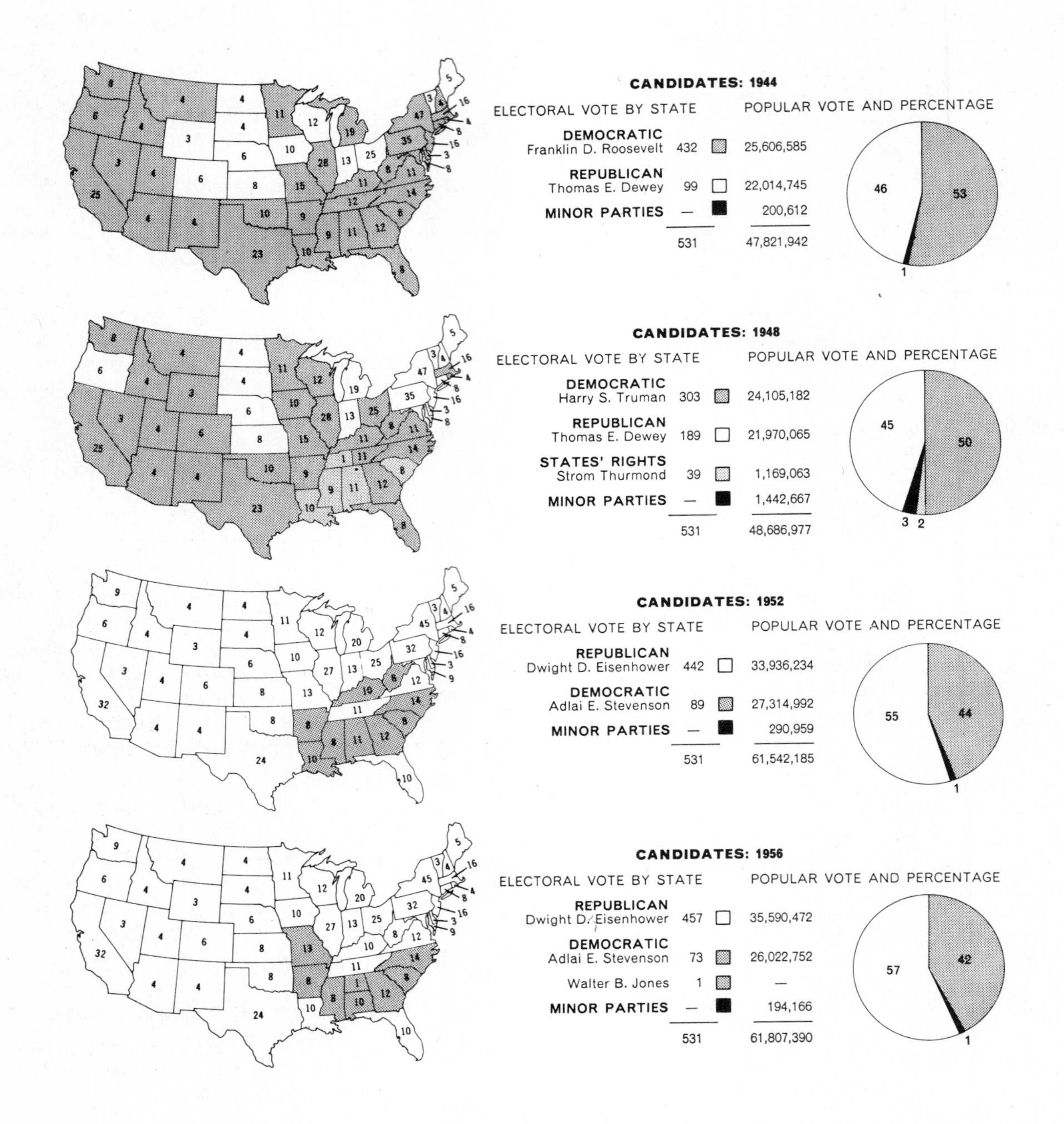
CANDIDATES: 1944
ELECTORAL VOTE BY STATE
POPULAR VOTE AND PERCENTAGE
DEMOCRATIC
Franklin D. Roosevelt 432 25,606,585
REPUBLICAN
Thomas E. Dewey 99 22,014,745
MINOR PARTIES — 200,612
531 47,821,942
46
53
1
CANDIDATES: 1948
ELECTORAL VOTE BY STATE
POPULAR VOTE AND PERCENTAGE
DEMOCRATIC
Harry S. Truman 303 24,105,182
REPUBLICAN
Thomas E. Dewey 189 21,970,065
STATES' RIGHTS
Strom Thurmond 39 1,169,063
MINOR PARTIES — 1,442,667
531 48,686,977
45
50
3 2
CANDIDATES: 1952
ELECTORAL VOTE BY STATE
POPULAR VOTE AND PERCENTAGE
REPUBLICAN
Dwight D. Eisenhower 442 33,936,234
DEMOCRATIC
Adlai E. Stevenson 89 27,314,992
MINOR PARTIES — 290,959
531 61,542,185
55
44
1
CANDIDATES: 1956
ELECTORAL VOTE BY STATE
POPULAR VOTE AND PERCENTAGE
REPUBLICAN
Dwight D. Eisenhower 457 35,590,472
DEMOCRATIC
Adlai E. Stevenson 73 26,022,752
Walter B. Jones 1 —
MINOR PARTIES — 194,166
531 61,807,390
57
42
1

GO ON TO THE NEXT PAGE.

45. Which of the following statements about the 1956 election is true?

(1) Eisenhower defeated Stevenson by a narrower margin that he did four years earlier.
(2) Minor-party candidates received more votes than they had in any of the other elections.
(3) Voters in the Great Plains voted Republican for the first time.
(4) In percentage terms, the Republicans did better than they had in the other elections.
(5) More than 80 million people voted.

(1) (2) (3) (4) (5)

46. Which of the following is a statement of facts supported by the data on page 618?

(1) In the 1948 election, Dewey would have defeated Truman if not for the votes cast for minor party candidates.
(2) The number of electoral votes that candidates receive is in direct proportion to the number of popular votes they receive.
(3) The number of votes received by minor parties in 1948 shows voters' dissatisfaction with the policies of the Republican and Democratic parties.
(4) The growing number of popular votes cast reflects the growth of U.S. population.
(5) Eisenhower received more total votes than any other candidate in any of the four elections.

(1) (2) (3) (4) (5)

47. The data on the maps will support which of the following conclusions?

(1) Minor parties have a significant influence on electoral politics.
(2) Minor parties have had little influence on electoral politics, but their influence is growing.
(3) Economics has influenced voting more than any other issue.
(4) Regional interests have at times influenced voting in presidential elections.
(5) The number of states won by Democrats in each succeeding election between 1944 and 1956 demonstrates the growing influence of that party.

(1) (2) (3) (4) (5)

48. Between 1870 and 1900, 430 million acres—more than had been settled in all the preceding years of American history—were occupied, much of it on the Great Plains. One result was a huge increase in U.S. food production. This happened at the same time that food production was increasing in other parts of the world—Canada, Australia, South America. Suddenly, agricultural overproduction was worldwide, and farmers everywhere were in trouble.

Which of the following best explains why U.S. farmers were in trouble?

(1) Overproduction would have increased the farmers' overhead costs.
(2) Overproduction would have caused food prices to rise and thus lower demand.
(3) Overproduction would have caused food prices to fall.
(4) The cost of farmland on the Great Plains would have increased.
(5) The amount of food imported from other countries would have increased.

(1) (2) (3) (4) (5)

GO ON TO THE NEXT PAGE.

Items 49–52 are based on the following information.

One theory of personality claims that people use certain unconscious mechanisms to defend against conflict and anxiety. Listed below are the names and descriptions of five common defense mechanisms.

(1) displacement—shifting anger, fear, or another emotion to an inappropriate object; to take out feelings on an innocent person or thing

(2) denial—refusing to accept a statement or situation one wishes to avoid

(3) procrastination—putting off doing what one wishes to avoid

(4) compensation—working to excel at one thing to make up for a real or imagined lack or failure in another thing

(5) rationalization—finding good, acceptable reasons for doing things one finds "bad" or unacceptable

Each of the following statements describes a person using one of the defense mechanisms above. Choose the defense mechanism that best describes each person's behavior.

49. Richard, knowing that he has to study for a difficult test, decides to watch television for a while longer. Richard's behavior is called

(1) displacement
(2) denial
(3) procrastination
(4) compensation
(5) rationalization

(1) (2) (3) (4) (5)

50. Getting into her car to drive to work, Beth discovers she has a flat tire. She goes back into the house, slamming the storm door so hard that she breaks the glass. Her behavior is called

(1) displacement
(2) denial
(3) procrastination
(4) compensation
(5) rationalization

(1) (2) (3) (4) (5)

51. Just as Susan finishes reading a magazine article identifying smoking as a cause of lung cancer, she lights a cigarette. Her behavior is called

(1) displacement
(2) denial
(3) procrastination
(4) compensation
(5) rationalization

52. Pete is resting his sprained ankle just as the doctor ordered. But he's bored. He decides to play some basketball, telling himself that a little exercise will do his ankle good. Pete's behavior is called

(1) displacement
(2) denial
(3) procrastination
(4) compensation
(5) rationalization

GO ON TO THE NEXT PAGE.

Items 53–54 are based on the following map.

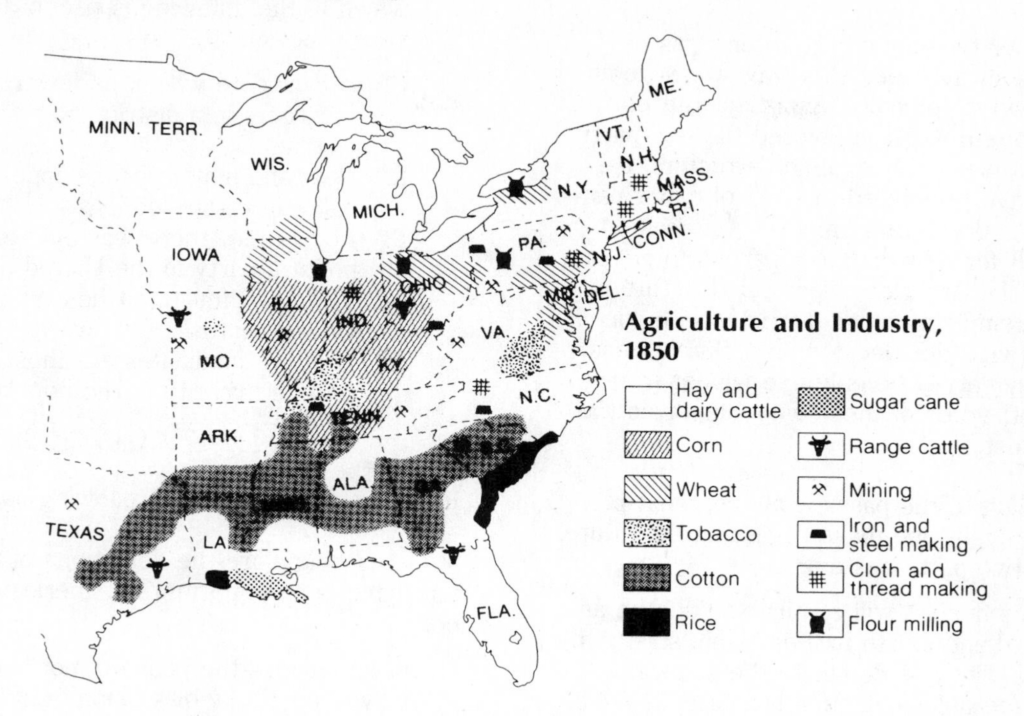

53. Based on the map, which of the following outcomes is most probable?
    (1) The North would have economic advantages over the South during the Civil War.
    (2) Control of the country's valuable tobacco lands would become a major issue during the Civil War.
    (3) The South's cotton and rice would give it an advantage over the North in the Civil War.
    (4) Mining and manufacturing in the North would hurt it during the Civil War.
    (5) The North would have political advantages over the South during the Civil War.

    (1) (2) (3) (4) (5)

54. All of the following are statements of fact that are supported by the map EXCEPT
    (1) Cotton was a major crop throughout the South in 1850.
    (2) There was little mining or steelmaking in the South in 1850 because the South has few mineral deposits.
    (3) In the 1850's, rice and sugar cane were grown along the coastal areas of the South.
    (4) In the 1850's, hay, dairy cattle, and wheat were produced mainly in the North.
    (5) Around 1850, the milling of flour was done mainly in the North.

    (1) (2) (3) (4) (5)

GO ON TO THE NEXT PAGE.

Items 55–56 are based on the following passage.

In part, our two-party system endures because it has always been that way; we have always had two major political parties. But our electoral system has also favored the two-party system because of the legal and structural barriers that have prevented the rise of minor parties. The election laws of most states make it very difficult for new or minor parties to get on the ballot. The American electoral structure is based upon single-member districts, with winner-take-all victories decided on a plurality basis. There can generally be only one winner from each district; votes of those who supported the loser are "lost."

55. According to the passage above, what prediction might one make regarding the future of the two-party system?

    (1) Its influence will continue to decline as third and fourth parties retain strength.
    (2) It is likely to dominate the political scene unless election laws are changed.
    (3) Its recent introduction to the political process will spell its failure.
    (4) It will retain its strength on the national level but lose strength at the district level.
    (5) It will create changes in vote counting in single-member districts.

    (1) (2) (3) (4) (5)

56. Based on the information in the passage, which of the following is true of the electoral process?

    (1) A candidate who wins fewer than half the votes in a district may still win the election.
    (2) New and minor parties appear on the ballot in most elections.
    (3) For a time, there was only one major political party in the United States.
    (4) Third and fourth parties are illegal in the United States.
    (5) Winning candidates are those who receive a majority of the popular vote.

    (1) (2) (3) (4) (5)

Items 57–60 refer to the following passage.

Listed below are the definitions of five terms that have been important in American foreign policy.

(1) isolationism—the policy of not becoming involved politically or economically with other nations
(2) Monroe Doctrine—a policy announced by President James Monroe declaring the Americas closed to further colonization and interference from European powers
(3) Manifest Destiny—a nineteenth-century doctrine that held Americans had a right and duty to settle the North American continent; this doctrine was later used to justify American expansion overseas
(4) containment—a policy of "containing" Soviet expansion by sending economic and military aid to threatened countries; announced by President Truman
(5) Eisenhower Doctrine—an expansion of the policy of containment; the doctrine gave President Eisenhower authority to send U.S. troops to countries asking for help to put down disorders believed inspired by communists

GO ON TO THE NEXT PAGE.

Decide which foreign policy concept is best reflected in each of the situations described below.

57. The president ordered 14,000 American troops into Lebanon, where groups thought to be supported by the Soviet Union were threatening the government.

(1) isolationism
(2) Monroe Doctrine
(3) Manifest Destiny
(4) containment
(5) Eisenhower Doctrine

(1) (2) (3) (4) (5)

58. The U.S. defeated Spain in a brief war and gained the Philippines. Some senators, eager that the U.S. should keep the islands, argued that Americans had a mission to bring civilization and democracy to the natives.

(1) isolationism
(2) Monroe Doctrine
(3) Manifest Destiny
(4) containment
(5) Eisenhower Doctrine

(1) (2) (3) (4) (5)

59. A border dispute erupted between Venezuela and British Guiana in South America. President Grover Cleveland believed England was trying to extend its colony. He told the British that the U.S. had a right to defend any nation in the Western Hemisphere.

(1) isolationism
(2) Monroe Doctrine
(3) Manifest Destiny
(4) containment
(5) Eisenhower Doctrine

(1) (2) (3) (4) (5)

60. George Washington resigned the presidency. In his farewell address he urged that Americans stay clear of "entanglements" with foreign nations.

(1) isolationism
(2) Monroe Doctrine
(3) Manifest Destiny
(4) containment
(5) Eisenhower Doctrine

(1) (2) (3) (4) (5)

GO ON TO THE NEXT PAGE.

Items 61–64 refer to the following table.

Percent Voting by Sex and Age, 1964–1982

	Congressional Elections					Presidential Elections				
	1982	1978	1974	1970	1966	1980	1976	1972	1968	1964
Population of voting age, total (millions) . . .	165.5	151.6	141.3	120.7	112.8	157.1	146.5	136.2	116.5	110.6
Percent voted, total. . .	48.5	45.9	44.7	54.6	55.4	59.2	59.2	63.0	67.8	69.3
Males	48.7	46.6	46.2	56.8	58.2	59.1	59.6	64.1	69.8	71.9
Females.	48.4	45.3	43.4	52.7	53.0	59.4	58.8	62.0	66.0	67.0
18 to 24 years old. . . .	24.8	23.5	23.8	30.4	31.1	39.9	42.2	49.6	50.4	50.9
25 to 44 years old. . . .	45.4	43.1	42.2	51.9	53.1	58.7	58.7	62.7	66.6	69.0
45 to 64 years old. . . .	62.2	58.5	56.9	64.2	64.5	69.3	68.7	70.8	74.9	75.9
65 years and over. . . .	59.9	55.9	51.4	57.0	56.1	65.1	62.2	63.5	65.8	66.3

61. Which of the following groups exercises its right to vote least often?

(1) females
(2) those 18 to 24 years old
(3) those 25 to 44 years old
(4) those 45 to 64 years old
(5) those 65 and older

(1) (2) (3) (4) (5)

62. Which of the following is a fact based on the table?

(1) More Americans vote in local than in national elections.
(2) In all but one of the elections charted, a larger percentage of men voted than women.
(3) Voters in the 45–64 age group are more interested in congressional than in presidential elections.
(4) Between 1964 and 1980, less than half the U.S. population of voting age participated in electing the president.
(5) Fewer women vote than men.

(1) (2) (3) (4) (5)

63. A candidate might decide from this table that the social issues most important to the largest block of voters would be

(1) the military draft and college loans
(2) day-care and early childhood education
(3) economic opportunities for minorities and women
(4) taxes and Social Security retirement benefits
(5) farm policy

(1) (2) (3) (4) (5)

64. Which of the following statements is supported by information on the table?

(1) Only about half of the total U.S. population has the right to vote.
(2) All Americans of voting age are required by law to vote.
(3) Those 65 and older will probably continue to be the most influential block of voters.
(4) If present trends continue, those of voting age will number less than 165 million by 1990.
(5) American citizens get the right to vote at age 18.

(1) (2) (3) (4) (5)

END OF EXAMINATION

TEST 3: SCIENCE POSTTEST

Directions

The Science Posttest consists of 66 questions most of which contain several reading passages. Each passage is followed by a number of multiple-choice questions related to its content. Read the passage first and then answer the questions following it. Refer to the passage as often as necessary in answering the questions.

You should take approximately 1½ hours to complete this test. There is no penalty for guessing. Try to answer as many questions as you can. Work rapidly but carefully, without spending too much time on any one question. If a question is too difficult for you, omit it and come back to it later.

For each answer, mark one answer space. See how the following example is done.

EXAMPLE

A physical change is one in which the chemical composition of a substance is not altered. A chemical change, in contrast, results in one or more new substances with different chemical makeups. Which of the following is an example of a physical change?

(1) butter melting
(2) tarnish on silverware
(3) gasoline being used in a car engine
(4) photographic film being developed
(5) photosynthesis in plants

● (2) (3) (4) (5)

The answer is "butter melting"; therefore, answer space (1) has been marked.

Answers to the questions are in the Answer Key on page 677. Explanations for the answers are on pages 668–672.

Directions: Choose the one best answer to each question.

Items 1–3 refer to the following diagram.

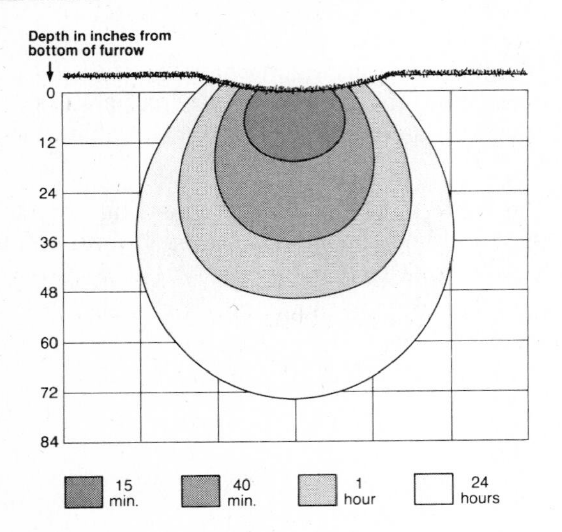

Water moves down through the soil by progressively wetting particles of soil. First, every particle of the topsoil must become thoroughly wet. When these particles can hold no more water, any additional water is free to move down into the soil and wet the next layer of soil particles. In planning a garden, the watering system used must be sufficient to soak the entire root area of the plants. Roots grow and develop only when water, soil, air, and food are available to them.

1. How many inches deep into the soil will the water have soaked after 40 minutes of watering the furrow?

(1) 12
(2) 24
(3) 36
(4) 48
(5) 60

1 2 3 4 5

2. A home gardener plants vegetables in rows. She wants to water the root area of the plants thoroughly to a depth of 12 inches. What is the shortest watering time she can use?

(1) less than 15 minutes
(2) 40 minutes
(3) 1 hour
(4) 24 hours
(5) longer than 24 hours

3. If plants are temporarily deprived of water, the ones that have been watered deeply will survive better than ones that are not usually watered deeply. Based on the information given, what statement would best explain this observation?

(1) Most deeply watered plants develop roots that can reach deep water supplies if no surface water is available.
(2) The roots of plants that are not watered deeply spread outward.
(3) Plants that are watered deeply can store more water in their roots.
(4) Plants with shallow roots do not grow well if watered deeply.
(5) Too much water deprives plants of needed oxygen.

1 2 3 4 5

GO ON TO THE NEXT PAGE.

Items 4–5 refer to the following information.

As the temperature of a liquid increases, the molecules of the liquid gain more energy and move around faster in all directions. When the temperature is high enough, the energy of the molecules becomes equal to or greater than the pressure of the air on the surface of the liquid. This temperature is called the boiling point. Therefore, the boiling point of a liquid is related to both the temperature and air pressure on the liquid.

4. In an open pot a stew is brought to the simmering point. It must simmer for 3 hours. Which one of the following procedures will best maintain the cooking temperature of the food?

   (1) Cover the pot and reduce the heat.
   (2) Cover the pot and increase the heat.
   (3) Cover the pot and turn off the heat.
   (4) Leave the pot uncovered and reduce the heat.
   (5) Leave the pot uncovered and increase the heat.

   (1) (2) (3) (4) (5)

5. A man who lives on the Eastern seacoast moves to the Rocky Mountains where the air pressure is much lower. The first meal he cooks is a spaghetti dinner. The noodles are not tender. He cannot understand what went wrong because he cooked them as long as he usually does. What factor did he forget?

   (1) Mountain air is colder than seashore air.
   (2) The starting temperature of the mountain water is colder.
   (3) Water boils at a lower temperature in the mountains.
   (4) Food cooks more slowly at low altitudes.
   (5) Water boils at a higher temperature in the mountains.

   (1) (2) (3) (4) (5)

6. T cells and macrophages are two types of white blood cells. When the two cell types are mixed together and then exposed to certain drugs, the T cells grow and divide. This forms the basis of certain medical tests. One patient's T cells failed to divide during the test period. This result was interpreted as a defect in the T cells. What other explanation is possible?

   (1) The macrophages were inactive.
   (2) The T cells were too active.
   (3) The macrophages were too active.
   (4) The drugs stimulated the macrophages.
   (5) The drugs stimulated the T cells.

   (1) (2) (3) (4) (5)

GO ON TO THE NEXT PAGE.

Items 7–10 refer to the following diagram.

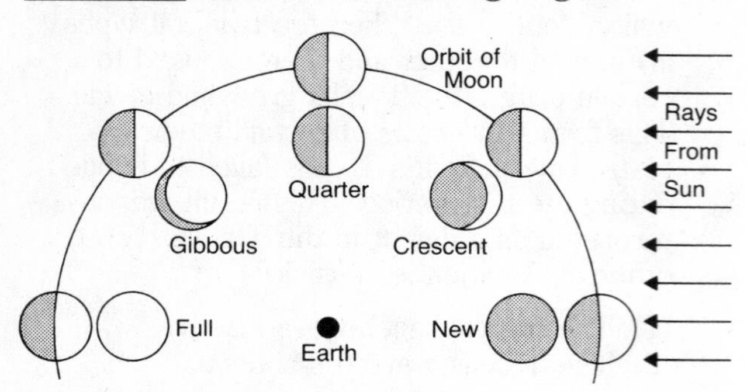

The diagram shows the moon in its different phases. The five circles along the orbit of the moon picture the lighted hemisphere on the moon. The five inner circles indicate the illumination of the moon as seen from the earth at each point. During the first half of the lunar month, a period of two weeks, the moon can be seen in the following sequence of phases: new, crescent, quarter, gibbous, and full. During the rest of the month, the sequence is reversed. The moon is seen as full, gibbous, quarter, and crescent. These changes occur because the moon revolves around the earth but receives its light from the sun. Throughout this monthly cycle, the moon appears to rise and set about 51 minutes later each day.

7. At "new moon," the moon appears from the earth to be

(1) absent from the sky
(2) crescent shaped
(3) semicircular
(4) lopsided
(5) circular

(1) (2) (3) (4) (5)

8. The full moon appeared on July 21. The next full moon would appear on approximately

(1) July 28
(2) August 5
(3) August 12
(4) August 19
(5) August 29

(1) (2) (3) (4) (5)

9. On the night of December 8, the moon rose in its first quarter phase. Two weeks later, on December 24, the moon again appeared as a quarter moon (last quarter). Which of the following statements best describes the difference between the first and last quarter moons?

(1) The last quarter phase lasted fewer days than the first quarter phase.
(2) The last quarter moon rose in the daytime sky.
(3) The last quarter moon appeared to move from west to east.
(4) The first quarter moon appeared far brighter than the last quarter moon.
(5) The first quarter moon was visible for more hours each day than the last quarter moon.

10. The moon is said to have two sides. The "dark" half is very dark and very cold. The "light" side is supposed to be bright and extremely hot. Based on the information supplied, which statement might help to explain this phenomenon?

(1) The moon goes through many phases.
(2) The same side of the moon always faces the earth.
(3) There can be no such thing: the entire surface of the moon is illuminated equally by the sun.
(4) Approximately half of the moon faces the sun at any one time.
(5) The moon goes through one complete revolution every 27 days.

(1) (2) (3) (4) (5)

GO ON TO THE NEXT PAGE.

Items 11–16 are based on the following information.

Substances can cross a cell membrane by many different processes. Five of these processes are defined below.

(1) diffusion—movement of dissolved molecules from a region of high concentration to a region of low concentration
(2) osmosis—movement of water through a membrane so that the concentration of materials dissolved in the water tends to become equal on both sides of the membrane
(3) passive transport—transfer of only certain molecules into or out of a cell, without the use of energy, by a specific carrier located in the cell membrane
(4) phagocytosis—a process by which the cell membrane moves to surround and to ingest a particle
(5) secretion—production and release of a substance by a cell

Each of the following items illustrates one of the five processes defined above. For each item choose the name of the one process that best identifies what is occurring. Each of the terms may be used more than once in the following set of items.

11. A small, single-celled animal is thrown into distilled water. It swells.

The process being described is

(1) diffusion
(2) osmosis
(3) passive transport
(4) phagocytosis
(5) secretion

① ② ③ ④ ⑤

12. Human red blood cells are suspended in a solution containing two sugars. When the cells are analyzed, only one of the sugars is found inside the cells.

The process taking place inside the cells is

(1) diffusion
(2) osmosis
(3) passive transport
(4) phagocytosis
(5) secretion

① ② ③ ④ ⑤

13. A person inhales a radioactive gas for a medical test. The gas distributes evenly throughout the lungs.

This distribution process is called

(1) diffusion
(2) osmosis
(3) passive transport
(4) phagocytosis
(5) secretion

① ② ③ ④ ⑤

14. An antibody is produced and released by certain cells of the intestine.

These cells are carrying out the process of

(1) diffusion
(2) osmosis
(3) passive transport
(4) phagocytosis
(5) secretion

① ② ③ ④ ⑤

15. A white blood cell encircles and consumes a bacterium at the site of an infection.

The white blood cell is carrying out the process of

(1) diffusion
(2) osmosis
(3) passive transport
(4) phagocytosis
(5) secretion

① ② ③ ④ ⑤

16. Some cells of the pancreas produce insulin and release it into the bloodstream.

The process occurring in these cells is

(1) diffusion
(2) osmosis
(3) passive transport
(4) phagocytosis
(5) secretion

① ② ③ ④ ⑤

GO ON TO THE NEXT PAGE.

Items 17–20 refer to the following passage.

Molybdenum is a metallic chemical element discovered in 1778. It readily forms compounds with other elements and is never found in nature in pure metallic form. Its reactivity is due to the way electrons are distributed around the nucleus.

Uses for molybdenum were not found until a century after it was discovered. Besides its reactivity, it has several characteristics that make it very useful in the world of technology. It has a high melting point (2610°C—nearly 1100°C above the melting point of iron). It is incredibly strong. When small amounts are added to hot liquid steel, the molybdenum becomes a part of the crystal-like structure of the steel. This makes the steel stronger, less brittle, and less likely to corrode. Therefore, molybdenum is alloyed with steel to produce such things as airplane landing gears which withstand high impact, high speed drills that operate at high temperatures, and stainless steel tableware which might otherwise corrode.

Molybdenum also has many applications outside the steel and iron industry. In many industrial processes, molybdenum can act as a catalyst. It can promote and speed up chemical reactions without being used up in the reaction. These processes range from refining petroleum to manufacturing formaldehyde. It can be used in place of lead and chromium to make safe paint pigments.

In microgram amounts, molybdenum is an essential factor of many enzymes of plants and animals. In addition, it has been found that tooth decay is lower in areas where the drinking water contains molybdenum.

17. Molybdenum would probably
    (1) aid a chemical reaction without being consumed
    (2) be produced during a chemical reaction
    (3) be used up in a chemical reaction
    (4) prevent a reaction from taking place
    (5) be the vessel in which a reaction occurs

    ① ② ③ ④ ⑤

18. The article suggests that whether an element combines easily with other elements is determined by its
    (1) melting point
    (2) corrosiveness
    (3) number of protons
    (4) electron arrangement
    (5) form found in nature

    ① ② ③ ④ ⑤

19. Which of the following statements is a conclusion drawn by the author of the passage?
    (1) Molybdenum has many non-steel uses.
    (2) Paints are made using molybdenum.
    (3) Petroleum refining uses molybdenum.
    (4) Molybdenum is useful in producing formaldehyde.
    (5) Some natural forms of molybdenum can be used as a lubricant.

    ① ② ③ ④ ⑤

20. Which one of the following statements is supported by information given in the article?
    (1) Each chemical element has a very limited number of uses.
    (2) A chemical element may serve important biological and physical functions.
    (3) Chemicals used for industrial technology are usually harmful to humans.
    (4) The uses of a chemical element are usually based on a single property of that element.
    (5) Reactive chemical elements are rarely useful because it is difficult to control how they will combine with other elements.

    ① ② ③ ④ ⑤

GO ON TO THE NEXT PAGE.

Items 21–24 refer to the following passage.

Adult beetles that feed on leaves usually secrete many different chemicals. These chemicals discourage attack by predators. However, the beetle larvae secrete a special mixture of chemicals called monoterpenes that deter other insects and adults of their own species from feeding on leaves occupied by the larvae.

Experiments showed that either live or dead larvae placed on a leaf protected the leaf from being eaten by the adult beetles. Also, coating the leaf with the natural secretion of the larvae protected the leaf. Other experiments performed in a similar way showed that the presence of beetle larvae inhibited the feeding of other kinds of larvae, such as caterpillars. Why do these beetle larvae carry these chemicals with them? The small insects must compete with larger ones for food resources. Therefore, the beetle larvae have evolved ways to defend their food by making it unattractive to other insects.

21. Which statement best summarizes the passage above?

(1) Beetles secrete many chemicals to protect themselves from other insect species.
(2) Chemicals from beetle larvae influence the feeding behavior of adult beetles and other insects.
(3) Beetle larvae kill other insects trying to eat the same leaf.
(4) Beetle larvae protect plants from being eaten.
(5) Larger insects and adult beetles commonly consume beetle larvae.

1 2 3 4 5

22. If the experimental results described in the passage are correct, which of the following should occur in nature?

(1) Adult and larval forms of the beetle feed on the same tree but not on the same leaf.
(2) Caterpillars and beetles eat different kinds of plants.
(3) Few beetle larvae survive in nature.
(4) Caterpillar and beetle larvae feed side by side on the same leaves.
(5) Adult beetles consume leaves on which caterpillar larvae are feeding.

1 2 3 4 5

23. The experiments described indicate that the beetle larvae discourage other insects from feeding on the leaves the larvae occupy. Which part of the experiment shows best that this is done by means of a chemical the larvae secrete?

(1) The adult beetle avoids the leaf occupied by live larvae.
(2) The adult beetle avoids the leaf occupied by dead larvae.
(3) The adult beetle avoids the leaf coated with secretions of the larvae.
(4) The caterpillars avoid the leaf occupied by live beetle larvae.
(5) The caterpillars eat leaves on which no larvae were placed.

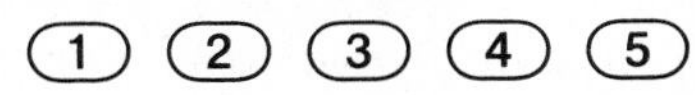

24. Within each scientific experiment there must be a "control" group. This is an untreated group against which all other data are compared. To see if the beetle larvae deterred other insects from sharing their leaves, the control would be a leaf on which

(1) live beetle larvae are placed
(2) dead beetle larvae are placed
(3) other larvae are placed
(4) the secretion from beetle larvae are placed
(5) nothing is placed

GO ON TO THE NEXT PAGE.

Items 25–28 refer to the following table.

Calorie Expenditure per Hour by a 150-pound Person in Various Activities

Activity	Calories /Hour	Activity	Calories /Hour
Backpacking (40 lb. pack)	410	Mountain Climbing	600
Badminton	340	Pool; Billiards	130
Baseball	280	Racquetball; Paddleball	600
Basketball (halfcourt)	300	Rope Jumping (continuous)	700
Bicycling (normal speed)	210	Rowing, Crew	820
Bowling	208	Running (10 m.p.h.)	900
Canoeing (4 mph)	414	Skating, Ice	350
Dance, Ballet (choreographed)	360	Skating, Roller	350
Dance, Exercise	420	Skiing, Cross-Country	700
Dance, Modern (choreographed)	360	Skiing, Downhill	600
Dance, Social	264	Soccer	540
Fitness Calisthenics	310	Softball (fast)	280
Football	300	Softball (slow)	290
Golf (walking)	250	Surfing	550
Gymnastics	310	Swimming (slow laps)	320
Handball	600	Swimming (fast laps)	630
Hiking	300	Tennis	420
Horseback Riding	240	Volleyball	350
Jogging (5½ m.p.h.)	650	Walking	318
Judo/Karate	310	Waterskiing	468
		Weight Training	470

The Calorie numbers given are for vigorous recreational play. Competitive sports may use more Calories.

25. A 150-pound man devotes one hour each day to exercise. He chooses to swim slow laps in a neighborhood pool. Approximately how many calories can he expect to burn in each exercise period?

(1) 300
(2) 400
(3) 500
(4) 600
(5) 700

(1) (2) (3) (4) (5)

26. If a person uses 3,500 calories, he will lose one pound of weight. How many hours would he have to walk to lose one pound?

(1) 2
(2) 4
(3) 6
(4) 8
(5) more than 10

(1) (2) (3) (4) (5)

27. Which of the following statements is a conclusion that can be drawn from the table?

(1) A person will consume fewer calories swimming than running at 10 mph.
(2) Swimming fast laps and playing handball require equal numbers of calories.
(3) The number of calories consumed depends on the exercise performed.
(4) Walking would burn more than half as many calories as water skiing.
(5) A person could burn more calories by cross-country skiing than by playing tennis.

28. A man claims he has several reasons for exercising. Many of them have a scientific basis. Which of the following reasons reflects the values of society rather than a health benefit?

(1) Regular exercising strengthens heart muscles.
(2) Exercise tends to make bones larger and stronger.
(3) Moderate exercise helps to control appetite.
(4) A person who exercises looks firmer and more attractive.
(5) Fat is converted to muscle through exercise.

(1) (2) (3) (4) (5)

GO ON TO THE NEXT PAGE.

Items 29–30 refers to the following passage.

Today's glaciers cover about 11 percent of the world's land. Ice sheets cover all of Antarctica and most of Greenland. In some areas the ice is 14,000 feet—nearly 3 miles—thick. The weight of these two immense ice sheets actually dents the earth's surface. Glaciers contain about 30 percent of the world's freshwater above ground. The frigid air above the vast ice sheets strongly influences worldwide weather patterns. Although glaciers are much smaller now than in prehistoric times, they still affect our world in many ways.

29. If all the glaciers melted, which of the following would probably happen?

(1) The world climate would become cooler.
(2) The depth of the oceans would decrease.
(3) New coastal lands would emerge from the sea.
(4) Usable freshwater supplies would increase.
(5) The mountains of the earth would level out.

(1) (2) (3) (4) (5)

30. Which of the following statements is a conclusion drawn from the passage?

(1) Glaciers affect where we live, our water supplies, and our weather.
(2) Glaciers cover a large portion of the earth.
(3) Glaciers affect weather trends.
(4) Glacial ice is a heavy weight on the earth's surface.
(5) Glacial ice acts as a freshwater reservoir.

(1) (2) (3) (4) (5)

31. The pilot of a hot air balloon lights the propane burner to heat the air inside the balloon. Slowly the balloon inflates. The pilot knows it will soon begin to rise. What reasonable assumption has he made?

(1) The warm air molecules inside the balloon are moving around faster than the cold air molecules outside.
(2) Warm air is lighter than cold air.
(3) There are more air molecules inside the balloon than outside.
(4) The air molecules inside the balloon are packed more closely together than in the air outside.
(5) There are fewer air molecules inside the balloon than in the air.

(1) (2) (3) (4) (5)

32. Two secretaries on their break each pour themselves a cup of coffee. One adds cream and sugar to her cup. The other adds only sugar to his. The cup to which cream is added cools more quickly. They decide that cup of coffee cooled faster because of the cream. What assumption did they make?

(1) The sugar also cooled the coffee.
(2) The coffee was hotter in one cup to start with.
(3) There was less cream than coffee in the cup.
(4) The two cups are insulated equally well.
(5) There was less coffee in one cup.

(1) (2) (3) (4) (5)

GO ON TO THE NEXT PAGE.

Items 33–36 refer to the following table.

FOOD AND SERVING SIZE

	Cholesterol (mg)	*Salt* (mg)
Beef, lean, cooked, 3 oz.	80	55
Butter, 1 Tbsp.	35	116
Cake, sponge, 1/12 cake	162	157
Cheese, cheddar, 1 oz.	25	176
Cheese, cottage, 1 cup	23	457
Chicken, cooked, 3 oz.	70	60
Eggs, 1 large	252	59
Flounder, cooked, 3 oz.	50	80
Frankfurter, 1/8 lb.	34	617
Margarine, all vegetable fat	0	14
Milk, 1 cup	14	122
Noodles, egg, cooked, 1 cup	50	2
Scallops, steamed, 3 oz.	45	225
Tomatoes, raw, 3	0	42
Tomatoes, canned, 3	0	390
Yogurt, plain, 8 oz.	17	105

The role of diet in good health has received much attention. Many researchers and physicians encourage people to eat only small amounts of certain foods or food ingredients. Cholesterol and salt have received special notice. The table lists the cholesterol and salt contents of many foods.

33. A physician prescribes low-salt and low-cholesterol diets for many of her patients. On what assumption does she base this recommendation?

    (1) Any food can be harmful if a person eats too much of it.
    (2) Both salt and cholesterol in high amounts are harmful to health.
    (3) Scientists have not proven that foods high in salt and cholesterol are harmful to health.
    (4) Too much salt causes the body to produce more cholesterol.
    (5) Salt and cholesterol are not necessary in bodily functions.

    (1) (2) (3) (4) (5)

34. Which of the following foods is relatively low in cholesterol but high in salt?

    (1) beef
    (2) cottage cheese
    (3) eggs
    (4) flounder
    (5) noodles

    (1) (2) (3) (4) (5)

35. A physician has recommended a low-salt diet. Which of the following shows the best selection of foods for such a diet?

    (1) canned rather than raw tomatoes
    (2) beef rather than scallops
    (3) scallops rather than flounder
    (4) butter rather than margarine
    (5) cottage cheese rather than milk

    (1) (2) (3) (4) (5)

GO ON TO THE NEXT PAGE.

36. If the data on tomatoes are true for other vegetables, which of the following conclusions would be correct?

    (1) Vegetables are high in cholesterol and salt.
    (2) Low-salt diets would discourage the use of fresh vegetables.
    (3) Canned vegetables contain more cholesterol than fresh vegetables.
    (4) People on low-salt diets should eat canned rather than fresh vegetables.
    (5) Canned vegetables have a much higher salt content than raw ones.

    (1) (2) (3) (4) (5)

37. Toothpaste contains many different ingredients. Most of the chemicals actually help to cleanse the teeth. Which one of the ingredients listed below helps only to make the product more pleasing?

    (1) Fluoride helps prevent tooth decay.
    (2) Foaming is due to the soap lauryl sulfate.
    (3) Toothpaste tastes sweet because of sodium saccharin.
    (4) Titanium dioxide is a whitener.
    (5) Cellulose gives the toothpaste its consistency.

    (1) (2) (3) (4) (5)

Items 38–39 refer to the following passage.

Everything around us is composed of various elements. Elements can be characterized by the number of protons and the number of neutrons in their nuclei. The sum of these numbers gives the atomic weight of the element. Isotopes of an element have the same number of protons but a different atomic weight.

38. Which of the following statements about isotopes is correct?

    (1) Isotopes have a larger number of protons and neutrons than the element itself.
    (2) Isotopes weigh more than the element.
    (3) Isotopes have fewer protons and neutrons.
    (4) Isotopes have a different number of neutrons.
    (5) There are fewer nuclear particles in isotopes.

    (1) (2) (3) (4) (5)

39. Elements are often written in the following way:

    atomic weight
    element
    proton number

    Iodine ($^{126}_{53}I$) is an element that can occur in many isotopic forms. Which of the following symbols correctly represents one of these isotopes?

    (1) $^{131}_{53}I$
    (2) $^{131}_{54}I$
    (3) $^{130}_{52}I$
    (4) $^{126}_{52}I$
    (5) $^{179}_{54}I$

    (1) (2) (3) (4) (5)

GO ON TO THE NEXT PAGE.

Items 40–44 refer to the following passage.

Whooping cough is a life-threatening respiratory disease caused by the bacterium called *Bordetella pertussis*. The sound of the victim's gasping for air between violent spasms of coughing accounts for its name.

Whooping cough was a major cause of childhood disease that often ended in death or had serious long-lasting effects. Epidemics of some diseases were eliminated by improvements in sanitation or the introduction of antibiotics. However, whooping cough was not so easily prevented. In the 1940s, a vaccine against whooping cough became publicly available, and the disease ceased to be an epidemic threat.

Usually the vaccine is given as a series of four immunizations spaced over the first 18 months of a baby's life. Some reaction to the vaccine is common in children. Redness and swelling occur at the site of immunization, and a mild fever develops.

Rarely, more serious symptoms follow the first immunization: high fever, seizures, shock, severe rash, troubled breathing, and persistent crying. Children having any of these signs should not receive the next immunization because these symptoms may become more severe.

These severe symptoms occur in fewer than 1 per 110,000 children. The occurrence of any permanent brain damage resulting from the vaccine is 1 per 300,000. The chances of suffering serious damage from whooping cough itself is 10 times as great as from the vaccine.

The publicity given to the 1 case in 300,000 has alarmed people. Despite the overwhelming odds in favor of immunization, some parents are not allowing their children to be immunized. Public health records show the impact of this. In 1982, for example, 1,895 cases of whooping cough (all in nonimmunized people) were reported in the United States. Following bad publicity about side effects, 3,275 cases were reported in 1985. Sweden, Britain, and Japan reported whooping cough epidemics following relaxation of immunization codes.

40. According to the passage, the decline in cases of whooping cough following 1940 was due to

(1) the introduction of antibiotics
(2) the beginning of routine immunization
(3) improvements in sanitation
(4) elimination of the bacterium that causes the disease
(5) public awareness of side effects

① ② ③ ④ ⑤

41. Information given by physicians indicates that the possibility of side effects from the vaccine

(A) are 10 times less than the risk due to the disease itself,
(B) may increase after the first immunization
(C) are far outweighed by the benefits of immunization.

According to the passage, which of the above statements are true?

(1) A
(2) B
(3) C
(4) A and B
(5) A, B, and C

① ② ③ ④ ⑤

GO ON TO THE NEXT PAGE.

42. Which of the following measures might satisfy both the public health authorities and alarmed parents?

    (1) eliminate the immunization series
    (2) produce a safer vaccine
    (3) pass a law requiring immunization
    (4) isolate children who have side effects
    (5) increase the length of the immunization series

    1 2 3 4 5

43. There are many flaws in the thinking of the parents who refuse to immunize their children. Which one of the following statements actually does support their thinking?

    (1) Risk associated with the disease is 10 times greater than the risk associated with the vaccine.
    (2) The current low number of cases of whooping cough will continue only if immunization requirements are not relaxed.
    (3) The current upswing in the number of cases of whooping cough is the result of not having children immunized.
    (4) Children who are not immunized are more likely to contract the disease.
    (5) There are risks associated with the immunization.

    1 2 3 4 5

44. Which of the following graphs shows the history of the occurrence of whooping cough in the United States?

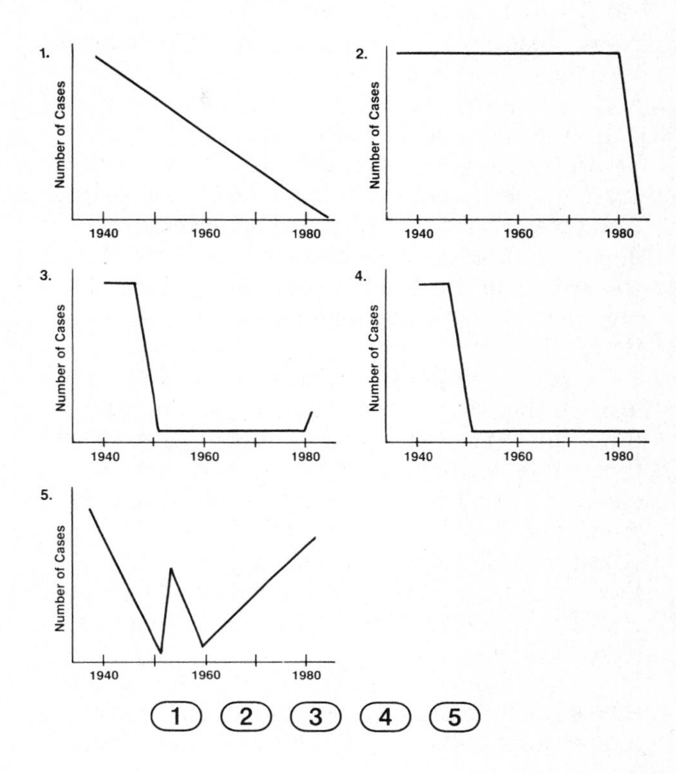

    1 2 3 4 5

GO ON TO THE NEXT PAGE.

Items 45–47 refer to the following passage.

Transistors are basic, fundamental parts of computers. Every year engineers try to make smaller transistors and place more of them onto chips of silicon. High density packing of transistors means cheaper production, faster operation, and, therefore, greater profits.

Before more advanced high density chips can be produced, physicists must learn how electric currents behave in microscopic-sized transistors. To accomplish this, experimental ones have been built that are 100 times smaller than the transistors in use today. They are so small that only one electron at a time passes through them.

What did the physicists find? First, they learned that the electrons moved through the tiny transistor at speeds different from ordinary transistors. Second, they discovered that the electrons didn't always behave as expected. Instead of moving smoothly through the new transistor, the electrons sometimes jumped from their paths and piled up in the surrounding material. This hindered the movement of other electrons trying to flow by.

The third finding was also unexpected. When certain materials are cooled to extremely low temperatures, they usually become superconductors. That means they offer no resistance to the flow of current. In these microtransistors, however, the conductivity jumped about over a wide range.

In the ordinary world, these effects are not detected. However, they become extremely important at the microscopic level because transistor technology is quickly heading in this direction. This research has led to a new branch of solid-state physics, and scientists must now try to understand and use these results.

45. According to the passage, current is due to

(1) silicon
(2) electron flow
(3) resistance
(4) superconductors
(5) transistors

1 2 3 4 5

46. Which one of the following statements best summarizes the passage?

(1) Physicists are building tiny transistors.
(2) Solid-state physics is an important area of study.
(3) Tiny scale transistors reveal new facts about how electrons behave.
(4) Silicon transistors have many industrial uses.
(5) Electrons can be studied individually.

1 2 3 4 5

47. Physicists were very surprised at some of the results they observed with the tiny transistor. Before doing the experiment, what assumption had they made?

(1) Individual electrons would behave the same way they did on a large scale.
(2) At low levels, resistance cannot be measured.
(3) At low temperatures, metals no longer conduct a current.
(4) All transistors are made of silicon.
(5) The computer industry requires small transistors.

1 2 3 4 5

48. Which of the following statements about a particular baby food is based only on opinion?

(1) The food contains no salt.
(2) There is no sugar added.
(3) No preservatives are present.
(4) It contains high levels of vitamin A.
(5) It leaves no bitter aftertaste.

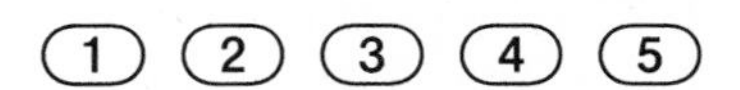

GO ON TO THE NEXT PAGE.

Items 49–53 are based on the following information.

Light can be described both as a particle and as a wave. Below are listed five properties of waves.

(1) reflection—a light wave bounces off a smooth surface at an angle equal but opposite to its original direction
(2) refraction—change in direction of a wave as it moves from one material to another
(3) diffusion—scattering of a wave by an uneven surface
(4) diffraction—change in the shape of a wave after it travels around an edge
(5) radiation—movement of waves away from their source

Each of the following items describes one of the properties of waves defined above. For each item, choose the one property that is best described. Each of the properties may be used more than once in the following set of items.

49. A pencil partially immersed in a glass of water appears to bend at the boundary between the water and the air.

The property of waves described is

(1) reflection
(2) refraction
(3) diffusion
(4) diffraction
(5) radiation

(1) (2) (3) (4) (5)

50. A laser beam from Kitt Peak Observatory is focused on a mirror left on the moon by the astronauts. The beam returns to the observers.

The property demonstrated by the laser beam is

(1) reflection
(2) refraction
(3) diffusion
(4) diffraction
(5) radiation

(1) (2) (3) (4) (5)

51. A pebble is dropped into a pond. Waves move outward from the spot where the pebble landed.

The property demonstrated by the waves is

(1) reflection
(2) refraction
(3) diffusion
(4) diffraction
(5) radiation

(1) (2) (3) (4) (5)

52. No image can be seen in a steamed-up bathroom mirror.

The property being described is

(1) reflection
(2) refraction
(3) diffusion
(4) diffraction
(5) radiation

(1) (2) (3) (4) (5)

53. A magnifying lens focuses the image of the sun to a small spot.

Focusing by the lens is due to

(1) reflection
(2) refraction
(3) diffusion
(4) diffraction
(5) radiation

(1) (2) (3) (4) (5)

GO ON TO THE NEXT PAGE.

54. Below are several statements about dogs. Which one is based on opinion rather than fact?
    (1) There are more than 70 different breeds of dogs.
    (2) Dogs were first domesticated 10,000 years ago.
    (3) Dogs are related to wolves.
    (4) Dogs are man's best friends.
    (5) Some dog breeds have been created by trait selection.

    (1) (2) (3) (4) (5)

55. A person enters a physician's office and complains of the following symptoms: fever, runny nose, sore throat, irritability, and tiredness. The doctor diagnoses a viral infection. Many things can be verified by lab tests or a physical examination. Which of the following is based only on the patient's description?
    (1) fever
    (2) irritated throat
    (3) runny nose
    (4) tiredness
    (5) viral infection

    (1) (2) (3) (4) (5)

Items 56–59 refer to the following graph and table.

Velocity of the Ball and Suitcase at One Second Intervals as They Fall through the Air

Time (sec)	Velocity of Ball (ft/sec)	Velocity of Suitcase (ft/sec)
0	0	0
1	32	32
2	64	64
3	96	95
4	128	119
5	160	138
6	192	150
7	224	158
8	256	160
9	288	162
10	320	163
11	352	163

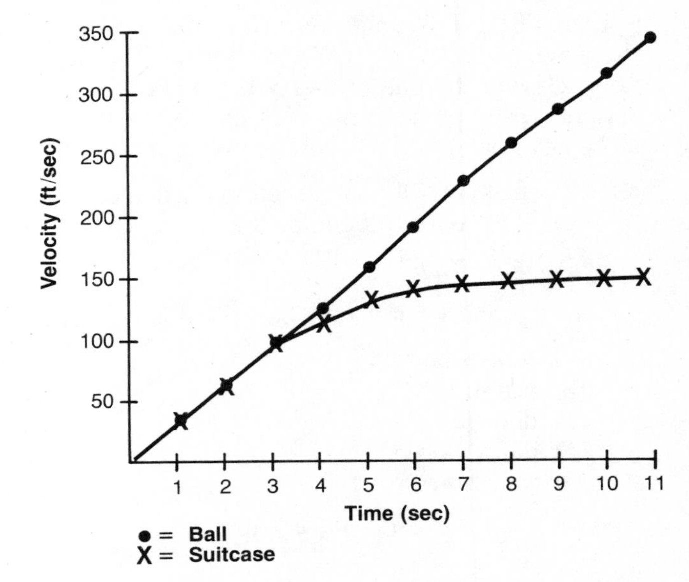

On a windy day two objects, a 5-pound steel ball and a 40-pound suitcase, were dropped at the same time from a height of 5,000 feet.

GO ON TO THE NEXT PAGE.

56. Which statement best reflects the movement of the ball 5 seconds after the two objects are dropped?

(1) It is falling faster than the suitcase.
(2) The suitcase is falling faster than the ball.
(3) Both are moving at the same velocity.
(4) The ball has stopped moving.
(5) The ball has reached the ground.

① ② ③ ④ ⑤

57. The velocity of the suitcase increases most in which time period?

(1) 1–3 seconds
(2) 3–5 seconds
(3) 5–7 seconds
(4) 7–9 seconds
(5) 9–11 seconds

① ② ③ ④ ⑤

58. The person who dropped the objects had assumed the two objects would reach the ground at the same time. They didn't. Which factor had she overlooked?

(1) air pressure
(2) wind resistance
(3) gravity
(4) starting speed
(5) weight of the objects

① ② ③ ④ ⑤

59. The velocity of the ball can best be described as

(1) increasing at a constant rate
(2) unchanging
(3) constant
(4) gradually decreasing
(5) unpredictable

① ② ③ ④ ⑤

60. An advertisement for decaffeinated coffee makes several statements about the product. Which of the following claims is based only on opinion rather than on chemical analysis?

(1) 99% caffeine free
(2) no harmful chemicals used in processing
(3) caffeine removed by water processing
(4) only Colombian coffee beans used
(5) richest coffee aroma

① ② ③ ④ ⑤

GO ON TO THE NEXT PAGE.

Item 61 refers to the following information.

Working Heart Rate Chart

Age	Maximum Heart Rate	Working Heart Rate
20	200	150
30	190	143
40	180	135
50	170	127
60	160	120

The formula (220 minus age) is used to calculate maximum heart rate. Working heart rate is 70 percent of this maximum value.

61. Members of aerobic exercise classes take their heart rates during class to make sure they are not working too hard. They are encouraged to work hard enough to reach but not exceed their working heart rate.

    Which of the following assumptions is made in using the charts?

    (1) Everyone in the class is the same age.
    (2) The maximum heart rate values are accurate for all members of the class.
    (3) Everyone can exercise for the same amount of time.
    (4) People the same age may have very different maximum heart rates.
    (5) Everyone tires at the same time.

    ① ② ③ ④ ⑤

62. Below are five statements about pearls. Many can be verified by scientific tests. Which one reflects a value judgment?

    (1) Pearls contain argonite calcium carbonate.
    (2) Historically pearls have been prized for their rarity and luster.
    (3) Secretions from the oyster's mantle create mother-of-pearl.
    (4) Bleaching pearls can lighten their color and remove dark surface impurities.
    (5) Men have learned to stimulate pearl production artificially in oysters.

    ① ② ③ ④ ⑤

Items 63–66 refer to the following passage.

Cannibalism is thought to be a practice associated with primitive peoples and rituals. Anthropology literature contains reports of people who ate human flesh. However, much of the so-called firm evidence is now being questioned. Perhaps cannibalism among humans never occurred at all.

The arguments against cannibalism can be briefly summarized. First, no society ever refers to themselves as cannibals. The cannibals are always enemies, strangers, or a very primitive group.

Second, historical eyewitness accounts of cannibalism are questionable. Old stories by travelers are not believable when examined closely. Even modern-day anthropologists who study the few remaining stone-age human societies admit that they have not actually witnessed the eating of human flesh.

Anthropologists are now reexamining prehistoric bones, burial pits, and excavation sites of early humans for evidence of cannibalism. Sophisticated scientific techniques are required for gathering these data. Bones are studied to determine if they are from humans or animals. Scratch and cut marks on the bones are examined to determine whether they were made at the time of death or resulted from damage during burial or excavation. Until these questions are answered, evidence from the past remains unclear.

GO ON TO THE NEXT PAGE.

63. Which of the following statements best summarizes this passage?
   (1) Many scientists are questioning whether cannibalism was ever practiced by primitive or modern societies.
   (2) Scientists have proven that many prehistoric societies consumed human flesh.
   (3) Using new scientific techniques researchers can prove that primitive people were not cannibals.
   (4) Human bones preserved from prehistoric times reveal much information about the people who buried them.
   (5) Whether cannibalism ever occurred cannot be documented by available scientific evidence.

   ① ② ③ ④ ⑤

64. The article suggests that cannibalism is
   (1) a ritual now carried out by primitive people
   (2) a historical fact
   (3) a myth invented about strangers
   (4) a story made for anthropologists
   (5) a scientific finding supported by documented evidence

   ① ② ③ ④ ⑤

65. Which one of the following would be the most convincing scientific evidence for the practice of cannibalism?
   (1) spoken accounts
   (2) prehistoric artwork showing cannibalism
   (3) human bones processed and disposed of as animal remains
   (4) human bones preserved and buried separately from animal bones
   (5) oral traditions

   ① ② ③ ④ ⑤

66. If cannibalism is never associated with one's own culture, then those who accused other people of cannibalism must have believed that
   (1) human life had value
   (2) human life was unimportant
   (3) people and animals were indistinguishable
   (4) animals were more important than people
   (5) vegetarianism was the best dietary choice

   ① ② ③ ④ ⑤

END OF EXAMINATION

TEST 4: INTERPRETING LITERATURE AND THE ARTS

Directions

The Interpreting Literature and the Arts Posttest consists of 45 multiple-choice questions based on selections from various kinds of reading materials. The selections are from literary works such as books, journals, and magazine or newspaper commentaries. One or more questions follow each selection. The best procedure for you to follow is to read the selection through once, then read all the questions based on the selection, answering as many questions as you can. Then reread the selection as many times as necessary to answer the more difficult questions.

You should take approximately 65 minutes to complete this test. There is no penalty for guessing. Try to answer as many questions as you can. Work rapidly but carefully, without spending too much time on any one question. If a question is too difficult for you, skip it and come back to it later.

For each answer, mark one answer space. See how the following example is done.

EXAMPLE

Often I think of the beautiful town
That is seated by the sea;
Often in thought go up and down
The pleasant streets of that dear old town,
    And my youth comes back to me.

In the poem above, what is the author writing about?

(1) an imaginary town
(2) a town that he dislikes
(3) the town he lives in
(4) a town he once visited
(5) the town he grew up in

① ② ③ ④ ●

The answer is "the town he grew up in"; therefore, answer space (5) has been marked.

Answers to the questions are in the Answer Key on page 677. Explanations for the answers are on pages 672–673.

Directions: Choose the one best answer to each question.

Items 1–6 are based on the following passage.

What do TV broadcasters need to hear?

Television is at its best when it is capturing the best things in American life.

We tend to take television so much for granted that we seldom realize its power. That came home to me one day when I was on my way to address the National Association of Broadcasters in Washington, D.C. My train stopped in Baltimore and I was looking at all those red brick houses, each one abutting the next, with everything spick-and-span. Then I noticed that every one of those houses had an antenna on top, reaching up and symbolically saying, "Come into my house." When I got down to Washington, I told the convention broadcasters about this forest of antennas in Baltimore, and said, "You people right here today have got more influence in determining the future of the U.S. than anybody, because you are constantly pouring culture and ideas and images down all those antennas and into the minds of American youth."

As we proceed into the future, I think the medium's usefulness will be greatly enhanced if broadcasters become more knowledgeable about the people they serve. Television must become humanized; it must speak to all our needs, not just our entertainment needs.

1. As used in the passage, what does the phrase "came home to me" (line 5) mean?

(1) appeared on a local television station
(2) was given to me
(3) was realized by me
(4) no longer confused me
(5) returned to my house

① ② ③ ④ ⑤

2. On TV, the author would probably welcome an increase of

(1) cartoon shows
(2) situation comedies
(3) documentaries
(4) westerns
(5) crime dramas

① ② ③ ④ ⑤

3. According to the passage, what influence do broadcasters have on the future of the United States?

(1) They try to show what the future should be like.
(2) They determine our entertainment needs.
(3) They reach homes all over the nation.
(4) They provide young people with ideas and images.
(5) They try to predict election results.

① ② ③ ④ ⑤

4. Why did the author compare the TV antennas he saw from the train to a forest?

(1) Both antennas and trees are useful to people.
(2) Both antennas and trees attract lightning.
(3) The antennas were surrounded by trees.
(4) There were so many antennas, and they rose up like trees in a forest.
(5) The antennas were part of the landscape.

① ② ③ ④ ⑤

5. Which of the following is a fact stated in the passage?

(1) Every one of the houses that the author saw in Baltimore had a TV antenna.
(2) Television is at its best when it shows the best of American life.
(3) Television must become humanized.
(4) Broadcasters should learn more about the people they serve.
(5) There are more television sets in the United States than in any other country.

① ② ③ ④ ⑤

6. This passage was most likely taken from

(1) an autobiography
(2) an article for the general public
(3) a novel
(4) a textbook on TV communications
(5) an advertising campaign

① ② ③ ④ ⑤

GO ON TO THE NEXT PAGE.

Items 7–12 are based on the following passage.

What made the career of steamboat pilot attractive to a boy?

When I was a boy, there was but one permanent ambition among my comrades in our village on the west bank of the Mississippi River. That was, to be a steamboatman. We had transient ambitions of other sorts, but they were only transient. When a circus came and went, it left us all burning to become clowns; the first Negro minstrel show that ever came to our section left us all suffering to try that kind of life; now and then we had a hope that if we lived and were good, God would permit us to be pirates. These ambitions faded out, each in its turn; but the ambition to be a steamboatman always remained. . . .

Boy after boy managed to get on the river. The minister's son became an engineer. The doctor's and the postmaster's sons became mud clerks; the wholesale liquor dealer's son became a barkeeper on a boat; four sons of the chief merchant, and two sons of the county judge, became pilots. Pilot was the grandest position of all. The pilot, even in those days of trivial wages, had a princely salary—from a hundred and fifty to two hundred and fifty dollars a month, and no board to pay. Two months of his wages would pay a preacher's salary for a year. Now some of us were left disconsolate. We could not get on the river—at least our parents would not let us.

So, by and by, I ran away. I said I would never come home again till I was a pilot and could come in glory. But somehow I could not manage it. I went meekly aboard a few of the boats that lay packed together like sardines at the long St. Louis wharf, and humbly inquired for the pilots, but got only a cold shoulder and short words from mates and clerks. I had to make the best of this sort of treatment for the time being, but I had comforting daydreams of a future when I should be a great and honored pilot, with plenty of money, and could kill some of these mates and clerks and pay for them.

7. Which of the following could be the setting of this passage?

(1) the West Coast in the early 1900s
(2) an urban area in the 1900s
(3) a village along the first continental railroad line
(4) the shores of Lake Michigan when goods were first transported by ship
(5) Missouri in the 1800s

① ② ③ ④ ⑤

8. When the narrator states, "We had transient ambitions of other sorts, but they were only transient," he means that the other ambitions of the boys were

(1) exciting
(2) realistic
(3) fleeting
(4) silly
(5) unattainable

① ② ③ ④ ⑤

9. Which of the following is an opinion expressed in the passage?

(1) A pilot made about two hundred and fifty dollars a month.
(2) A preacher works much harder than a pilot.
(3) Some boys managed to get jobs on the river.
(4) Riverboat pilot was the best job to have.
(5) Many parents would not let their children leave home to go on the river.

① ② ③ ④ ⑤

10. If the narrator were a boy today, which of the following would he most likely dream of becoming?

(1) lawyer
(2) airline captain
(3) computer programmer
(4) accountant
(5) writer

① ② ③ ④ ⑤

GO ON TO THE NEXT PAGE.

11. If the author were telling this story aloud, he would probably be

    (1) speaking angrily
    (2) laughing loudly
    (3) smiling
    (4) speaking sadly
    (5) completely serious

    ① ② ③ ④ ⑤

12. What is the main effect of the last sentence?

    (1) It foreshadows what will happen soon.
    (2) It adds humor to the writing.
    (3) It shows what a realist the author was.
    (4) It shows how desperately the author wanted to become a steamboatman.
    (5) It reveals the author's bitterness at the boys who made it to the river before he did.

    ① ② ③ ④ ⑤

Items 13–16 are based on the following poem.

How does the poet feel about the moles he watches?

Moles
William Stafford

Every day that their sky droops down,
they shrug before it can harden
and root for life, rumpling along
toward the green part of the garden.

Every day the moles' dirt sky
sags upon their shoulders,
and mine too sags on many a day,
pinned by heavy boulders.

We get tired, the moles and I,
toiling down our burrows.
They shrug dirt along their way,
and I rumple on through sorrows.

13. To what is the poet comparing moles in this poem?

    (1) the sky
    (2) boulders
    (3) himself
    (4) his sorrows
    (5) the garden

    ① ② ③ ④ ⑤

14. What is the main idea of this poem?

    (1) Moles have a hard life.
    (2) Moles burrow through the earth and ruin the poet's garden.
    (3) The poet is burdened by troubles the way the moles are burdened by dirt.
    (4) The poet wishes he could be like a mole.
    (5) Moles live underground and have dirt for a sky.

    ① ② ③ ④ ⑤

15. What does the phrase "root for life" as used in line 3 most nearly mean?

    (1) dig through the soil to survive
    (2) cheer for the living
    (3) destroy garden plants
    (4) search for food
    (5) begin to grow

    ① ② ③ ④ ⑤

16. What kind of mood does the poem create for the reader?

    (1) sentimental
    (2) funny
    (3) angry
    (4) eerie
    (5) depressing

    ① ② ③ ④ ⑤

GO ON TO THE NEXT PAGE.

Items 17–23 are based on the following passage.

Where are Irina and Arkady?

"Where do we go now?"

"You go."

"I came back for you," Irina said. "We can get away, we can stay in America."

"I don't want to stay." Arkady looked up. "I never wanted to stay. I only came because I knew Osborne would kill you if I didn't."

"Then we'll both go home."

"You *are* home. You're American now, Irina, you're what you always wanted to be." He smiled. "You're not Russian anymore. We always were different, and now I know what the difference was."

"You'll change, too."

"I'm Russian." He tapped his chest. "The longer I'm here, the more Russian I am."

"No." She shook her head angrily.

"Look at me." Arkady pulled himself to his feet. One leg was numb. "Don't cry. See what I am: Arkady Renko, former Party member and chief investigator. If you love me, tell me truthfully how American I could ever be. Tell me!" he shouted. "Tell me," he said more softly, "admit it, don't you see a Russian?"

"We came all this way. I won't let you go back alone, Arkasha—"

"You don't understand." He took Irina's face in his hands. "I'm not as brave as you are, not brave enough to stay. Please, let me go back. You will be what you already are, and I will be what I am. I will always love you."

17. What is Arkady trying to do in this passage?
    (1) ask Irina to marry him
    (2) persuade Irina to return to Russia
    (3) find a way to stay in America
    (4) convince Irina he must go back to Russia
    (5) get information about America

    (1) (2) (3) (4) (5)

18. When Arkady tells Irina, "You *are* home," (line 10) he means that
    (1) she lives in America now
    (2) she now has American attitudes
    (3) Russia will always be with her
    (4) she must learn American ways if she wants to survive
    (5) home is wherever the two of them are

    (1) (2) (3) (4) (5)

19. What is Irina's reaction when Arkady insists he is Russian?
    (1) immediate dislike
    (2) confusion
    (3) disappointment
    (4) total agreement
    (5) angry denial

    (1) (2) (3) (4) (5)

20. According to Arkady, he is unlike Irina because he is less
    (1) courageous
    (2) honest
    (3) patriotic
    (4) Russian
    (5) aggressive

    (1) (2) (3) (4) (5)

21. Which of the following questions can be answered using information from the passage?
    (1) How did Arkady and Irina get to America?
    (2) Why was Arkady's leg numb?
    (3) What position did Arkady hold in Russia?
    (4) When did Arkady and Irina first meet?
    (5) How old is Irina?

    (1) (2) (3) (4) (5)

22. The feeling the passage creates is one of
    (1) sadness
    (2) celebration
    (3) eager anticipation
    (4) bitterness
    (5) indifference

    (1) (2) (3) (4) (5)

23. This passage is most likely taken from
    (1) a magazine article about the hardships that Russian immigrants face
    (2) a novel about two Russians of different character
    (3) a letter from an immigrant to his wife in Russia
    (4) a newspaper editorial criticizing Soviet policies
    (5) an essay about political freedom

    (1) (2) (3) (4) (5)

GO ON TO THE NEXT PAGE.

Items 24–29 are based on the following passage from a play.

What does Amanda hope will happen?

AMANDA. Then he has visions of being advanced in the world! Any young man who studies public speaking is aiming to have an executive job some day! And radio engineering? A thing for the future! Both of these facts are very illuminating. Those are the sort of things that a mother should know concerning any young man who comes to call on her daughter. Seriously or—not.

TOM. One little warning. He doesn't know about Laura. I didn't let on that we had dark ulterior motives. I just said, why don't you come have dinner with us? He said okay and that was the whole conversation.

AMANDA. I bet it was! You're eloquent as an oyster. However, he'll know about Laura when he gets here. When he sees how lovely and sweet and pretty she is, he'll thank his lucky stars he was asked to dinner.

TOM. Mother, you mustn't expect too much of Laura.

AMANDA. What do you mean?

TOM. Laura seems all those things to you and me because she's ours and we love her. We don't even notice she's crippled any more.

AMANDA. Don't say crippled! You know that I never allow that word to be used!

TOM. But face facts, Mother. She is and—that's not all—

AMANDA. What do you mean "not all"?

TOM. Laura is very different from other girls.

AMANDA. I think the difference is all to her advantage.

TOM. Not quite all—in the eyes of others—strangers—she's terribly shy and lives in a world of her own and those things make her seem a little peculiar to people outside the house.

24. According to the passage, why did Tom invite a friend to dinner?

(1) to talk about engineering
(2) to offer him a family evening
(3) to examine Laura's crippled leg
(4) to meet Laura
(5) to discuss his career with Amanda

(1) (2) (3) (4) (5)

25. When Amanda tells Tom he is "eloquent as an oyster," she is

(1) praising his conversational skills
(2) telling him to keep quiet
(3) telling him he is not eloquent at all
(4) complaining about the way he talks
(5) pleased that he knows when to keep quiet

(1) (2) (3) (4) (5)

26. Which of the following best describes Tom's attitude toward Laura?

(1) scorn because she is crippled and shy
(2) anger because Laura is "peculiar"
(3) pride because Laura is so sweet
(4) concern because Laura is "different"
(5) jealous because Amanda cares more about Laura

(1) (2) (3) (4) (5)

27. What is the main topic of this passage?

(1) Laura's personality
(2) Tom's dinner guest
(3) Tom's eloquence
(4) Laura's pretty looks
(5) Amanda's opinion of public speaking

(1) (2) (3) (4) (5)

28. How would Tom most likely feel if Laura were outgoing and charming to the friend he has invited over?

(1) jealous
(2) upset
(3) indifferent
(4) guilty
(5) surprised

(1) (2) (3) (4) (5)

29. What is the most important effect of Amanda's statements, "Don't say crippled! You know that I never allow that word to be used"?

(1) It gives important information about Laura.
(2) It reveals the strong tension between Amanda and Tom.
(3) It indicates that Amanda doesn't think her daughter is crippled.
(4) It suggests what will happen to Laura.
(5) It shows how Amanda tries to deny reality.

(1) (2) (3) (4) (5)

GO ON TO THE NEXT PAGE.

Items 30–35 are based on the following passage.

What happened to the speaker while he was in prison?

I spent two days just riffling uncertainly through the dictionary's pages. I'd never realized so many words existed! I didn't know which words I needed to learn. Finally, just to start some kind of action, I began copying.

In my slow, painstaking, ragged handwriting, I copied into my tablet everything printed on that first page, down to the punctuation marks.

I believe it took me a day. Then, aloud, I read back, to myself, everything I'd written on the tablet. Over and over, aloud, to myself, I read my own handwriting. . . .

I was so fascinated that I went on—I copied the dictionary's next page. And the same experience came when I studied that. With every succeeding page, I also learned of people and places and events from history. . . .

I suppose it was inevitable that as my wordbase broadened, I could for the first time pick up a book and read and now begin to understand what the book was saying. Anyone who has read a great deal can imagine the new world that opened. Let me tell you something: from then until I left that prison, in every free moment I had, if I was not reading in the library, I was reading on my bunk. You couldn't have gotten me out of books with a wedge. Between Mr. Muhammad's teachings, my correspondence, my visitors—usually Ella and Reginald—and my reading of books, months passed without my even thinking about being imprisoned. In fact, up to then, I never had been so truly free in my life.

30. What did the speaker do to learn how to read well?

(1) He asked Mr. Muhammad to teach him.
(2) He copied and read the dictionary.
(3) He wrote and read many letters.
(4) He read books out loud.
(5) He attended a class in prison.

1 2 3 4 5

31. Which is a true statement about the speaker while he was in prison?

(1) He had a lot of time to read.
(2) He couldn't read or write when he was first imprisoned.
(3) He had no visitors.
(4) He found history boring.
(5) He planned ways to escape.

1 2 3 4 5

32. Which of the following best states the main idea of the passage?

(1) The speaker spent two days just looking through the dictionary.
(2) Studying the dictionary can help you learn new words.
(3) By teaching himself to read, the speaker freed his mind while in prison.
(4) The speaker had never been so truly free in his life.
(5) Everyone should learn to read.

1 2 3 4 5

33. In the passage, the word "free" (line 37) is used to express

(1) disappointment
(2) bitterness
(3) irony
(4) humor
(5) pride

1 2 3 4 5

34. Which of the following policies or programs would the speaker be likely to support?

(1) fixed sentences for crimes
(2) tougher laws against violent crimes
(3) censorship of certain books
(4) adult basic education programs
(5) work-release programs for prisoners

1 2 3 4 5

35. This passage was most likely taken from

(1) a novel about a daring prison escape
(2) an editorial about harsh treatment in prisons
(3) a manual on how to teach reading
(4) a letter from a prisoner to a friend
(5) an autobiography of a former convict

1 2 3 4 5

GO ON TO THE NEXT PAGE.

Items 36–40 are based on the following passage.

Why do audiences enjoy this play?

It's a bit like the old *Romeo and Juliet* shtik: Boy loves Girl, Girl loves Boy, their feuding fathers try to break it up. . . . But the similarities end there. This is *The Fantasticks,* and the old men are in cahoots, driving the kids apart to test their love. Result: Boy gets Girl. Joy abounds. Curtain. Audience departs, humming *Try to Remember,* now an American standard, and remarking about what a relief it is nowadays to see a *nice* show.

It seems odd that this spare, simple-minded musical (intrumentation: one piano, one harp) should manage to sustain for more than a week. Yet the startling fact is that *The Fantasticks,* defying bored critics and the big-bucks economics of the theater, has been playing off-Broadway for 26 years, lofting it into the pages of the *Guinness Book of World Records* as the longest running (10,864 performances) musical in stage history.

The show has put producer Lore Noto, 63, in line for a world record, too. One day 16 years ago, Noto decided to play the co-starring role of Hucklebee, the boy's father. He has been doing it ever since—harrumphing, scheming, singing and dancing through more than 5,300 performances. "When people ask how long I've been doing this," says Lore cheerfully, "I say it's a life sentence."

The Fantasticks was hardly more than a one-act experiment when Noto saw it in 1959 at Barnard College in New York and persuaded playwrights Harvey Schmidt and Tom Jones to let him produce it. Launching *Fantasticks* with a puny bankroll of $16,500, Noto coaxed it through its initial spate of tepid reviews till it became a legend. Since then, no fewer than 240 actors have played the show in New York, worldwide productions have numbered in the thousands, and Lore's backers have pocketed a 9,624 percent return on their money.

By now, Noto could probably sleepwalk through his role, but he portrays the well-meaning but bungling patriarch six days a week as if every night were his first. . . .

For Noto *The Fantasticks* is a work that crosses time and generational barriers. "It has a universality that reaches around the world," he argues. "One song says, 'Without a hurt the heart is hollow.' That's a fact. Another song says, 'What at night seems oh so scenic/May be cynic in the light.' These are statements of philosophy."

36. To what does the author compare *The Fantasticks* in order to help explain its appeal?
    (1) a long-time actor
    (2) a classic play
    (3) a lavish Broadway production
    (4) the *Guinness Book of World Records*
    (5) a popular American song

    ① ② ③ ④ ⑤

37. Which of the following statements is surprisingly true about *The Fantasticks* when one considers its long run?
    (1) It has a complicated plot.
    (2) It has been performed only in the United States.
    (3) Few actors have played in the show.
    (4) It was not very popular at first.
    (5) One of the performers sleepwalks through his role.

    ① ② ③ ④ ⑤

38. Which of the following opinions could be supported by using *The Fantasticks* as an example?
    (1) Stars should act only.
    (2) Stars who play the same role for many years soon lose their effectiveness.
    (3) Audiences are bored by productions that make philosophical statements.
    (4) It takes hundreds of thousands of dollars to launch a musical production.
    (5) Musicals don't need much instrumentation to be successful.

    ① ② ③ ④ ⑤

39. In which paragraph does the author give the most information about the plot of *The Fantasticks?*
    (1) first paragraph
    (2) second paragraph
    (3) third paragraph
    (4) fourth paragraph
    (5) last paragraph

    ① ② ③ ④ ⑤

40. How does the author feel about Noto?
    (1) She thinks Noto's acting is below par.
    (2) She is dissatisfied with the lack of recognition given Noto.
    (3) She is confused about Noto's success.
    (4) She admires his talent and versatility.
    (5) She hopes that his work will improve.

    ① ② ③ ④ ⑤

GO ON TO THE NEXT PAGE.

Items 41–45 are based on the following poem.

What is the poet's journey like?

Night Journey

Now as the train bears west,
Its rhythm rocks the earth,
And from my Pullman berth
I stare into the night
While others take their rest.
Bridges of iron lace,
A suddenness of trees,
A lap of mountain mist
All cross my line of sight,
Then a bleak wasted place,
And a lake below my knees.
Full on my neck I feel
The straining at a curve;
My muscles move with steel,
I wake in every nerve.
I watch a beacon swing
From dark to blazing bright;
We thunder through ravines
And gullies washed with light.
Beyond the mountain pass
Mist deepens on the pane;
We rush into a rain
That rattles double glass.
Wheels shake the roadbed stone,
The pistons jerk and shove,
I stay up half the night
To see the land I love.

41. What is the poet doing?

(1) trying to sleep on a train
(2) watching scenery from a train
(3) conducting a train
(4) imagining a train ride
(5) guarding sleeping passengers on a train

① ② ③ ④ ⑤

42. Which of the following lines helps convey the idea that the train is moving rapidly?

(1) "Now as the train bears west"
(2) "Then a bleak wasted place"
(3) "I watch a beacon swing"
(4) "Mist deepens on the pane"
(5) "We rush into a rain"

① ② ③ ④ ⑤

43. Through which area might the poet be traveling?

(1) the Colorado Rocky Mountains
(2) the Arizona desert
(3) the Illinois prairie
(4) the New England coast
(5) the Washington rain forests

① ② ③ ④ ⑤

44. How does the poet make the reader feel?

(1) tired
(2) apprehensive
(3) romantic
(4) peaceful
(5) excited

① ② ③ ④ ⑤

45. What is the main effect of the last two lines of the poem?

(1) They contribute to a slow, even rhythm in the poem.
(2) They give the reader a clue that the train is stopping.
(3) They explain the poet's behavior in the rest of the poem.
(4) They help describe what the poet sees.
(5) They break up the mood established by the rest of the poem.

① ② ③ ④ ⑤

END OF EXAMINATION

TEST 5: MATHEMATICS POSTTEST

Directions

The Mathematics Posttest consists of 56 problems. Whenever possible, you should arrive at your own answer to a question before looking at the choices; otherwise, you may be misled by plausible mistakes.

You should take approximately 1½ hours to complete this test. There is no penalty for guessing. Try to answer as many questions as you can. Work rapidly but carefully, without spending too much time on any one question. If a question is too difficult for you, omit it and come back to it later.

For each answer, mark one answer space. See how the following example is done.

EXAMPLE

A secretary bought a desk calendar for $5.95 and a pencil container for $1.89. How much change did she get from a ten-dollar bill?

(1) $7.84
(2) $8.84
(3) $2.61
(4) $8.74
(5) $2.16

The amount is $2.16; therefore, answer space (5) has been marked.

Answers to the questions are in the Answer Key on page 677. Explanations for the answers are on pages 674–676.

Directions: Choose the one best answer to each problem.

1. One liter of fluid costs $2.00. To the nearest dollar, how much does 4 gallons cost if one gallon equals 3.78 liters?

(1) $26
(2) $27
(3) $28
(4) $29
(5) $30

(1) (2) (3) (4) (5)

2. Lou bought a satellite dish and 30 feet of wiring for installation. The dish had a radius of 4 feet, and he wanted to install it in his backyard which measured 14 feet by 20 feet. What is the circumference of the dish in feet?

(1) 8
(2) 12.56
(3) 25.12
(4) 34.7
(5) 80

(1) (2) (3) (4) (5)

3. Which is a solution of $2x > 19$?

(1) 10
(2) 9
(3) $\frac{17}{2}$
(4) 7
(5) $\frac{1}{23}$

(1) (2) (3) (4) (5)

4. Which of the following expresses 502.695 in scientific notation?

(1) 502695×10^{-3}
(2) 50.2695×10^{-2}
(3) 5.02695×10^{2}
(4) 5.02695×10^{3}
(5) 502695×10^{3}

(1) (2) (3) (4) (5)

5. Each semester the number of students in physics classes increases by 4% while the number of history students stays the same. In the fall semester, 350 students were in physics classes. How many students were in history classes in the spring?

(1) 14
(2) 138
(3) 262
(4) 379
(5) Insufficient data is given to solve the problem.

(1) (2) (3) (4) (5)

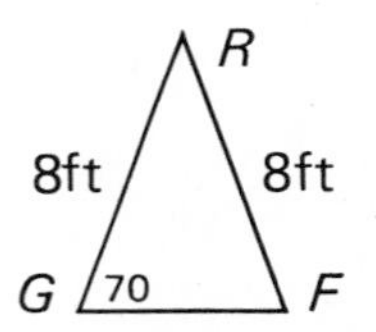

6. In triangle *GRF* how many degrees does angle *F* equal?

(1) 20
(2) 30
(3) 40
(4) 70
(5) 110

(1) (2) (3) (4) (5)

7. Mrs. Garguilo earned $1,329 a month, and Mr. Garguilo earned $1,295 a month. What was their combined annual income?

(1) $2,514
(2) $2,624
(3) $30,168
(4) $31,488
(5) $39,216

(1) (2) (3) (4) (5)

8. The quality control department found that 2 vacuum bottles leak in every shipment of 1,000 made from Hawthorne factory. Hank Dawson ordered 2 dozen bottles for his hardware store. What is the probability that a bottle bought at Hank's store will leak?

(1) 0.2%
(2) 0.48%
(3) 2%
(4) 7.3%
(5) 12%

(1) (2) (3) (4) (5)

GO ON TO THE NEXT PAGE.

9. If $2y = -12$ and $x + 2y = 5$, then what does x equal?

(1) -6
(2) -1
(3) 8
(4) 13
(5) 17

1 2 3 4 5

10. A room is 10½ feet square and has a 9 foot ceiling. How many *yards* of carpet molding will be needed to go around the room?

(1) 8¼
(2) 14
(3) 21
(4) 33
(5) 42

1 2 3 4 5

Items 11–13 refer to the following table.

Normal Monthly Precipitation (inches)

	Jan.	*Feb.*	*March*	*April*	*May*	*June*
Asheville	8.6	9.1	11.9	8.9	8.4	10.2
Birmingham	12.2	13.5	15.7	11.7	9.1	10.2
Dodge City	1.3	1.5	2.8	4.3	7.9	8.4
New York City	7.4	7.9	10.2	9.1	8.6	7.4
Miami	5.6	5.1	5.3	9.1	15.5	22.9
Honolulu	11.1	6.4	8.1	3.6	2.5	0.8

11. How many times more rain fell in Dodge City in June than in March?

(1) 1.5
(2) 3
(3) 5.6
(4) 7
(5) 11.2

1 2 3 4 5

12. How many fewer inches of rain did Honolulu have than Birmingham in the six months measured?

(1) 23.6
(2) 32.5
(3) 39.9
(4) 47.1
(5) 72.4

1 2 3 4 5

13. Which month had the most rainfall in all six cities?

(1) February
(2) March
(3) April
(4) May
(5) June

1 2 3 4 5

14. Simplify $3(2x + 5y) + 7x$.

(1) $6x + 5y + 7x$
(2) $6x + 15y + 7x$
(3) $6x + 12xy$
(4) $13x + 5y$
(5) $13x + 15y$

1 2 3 4 5

15. David Herbert has 4 pennies, 3 times as many nickels as pennies, and 4 times as many dimes as nickels. How much money does he have?

(1) \$0.59
(2) \$0.64
(3) \$1.28
(4) \$5.44
(5) \$7.31

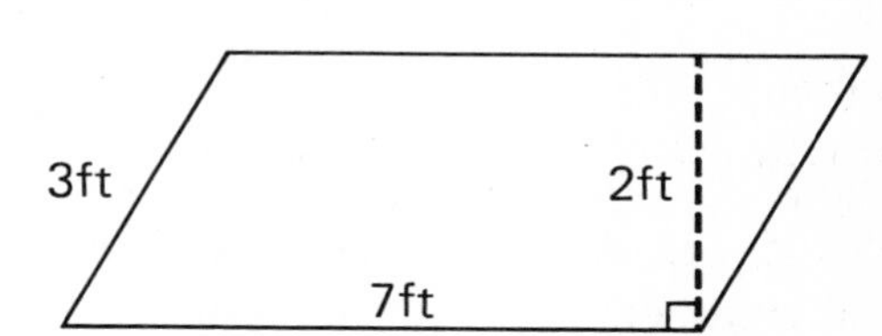

16. Mr. Chang built a flower bed that was shaped like a parallelogram alongside his garage. He wants to cover the bed with decorative bark chips. If one pound of chips covers 0.5 square foot, how many pounds of chips should Mr. Chang buy?

(1) 7
(2) 14
(3) 28
(4) 45
(5) 70

GO ON TO THE NEXT PAGE.

Items 17–18 refer to the diagram below.

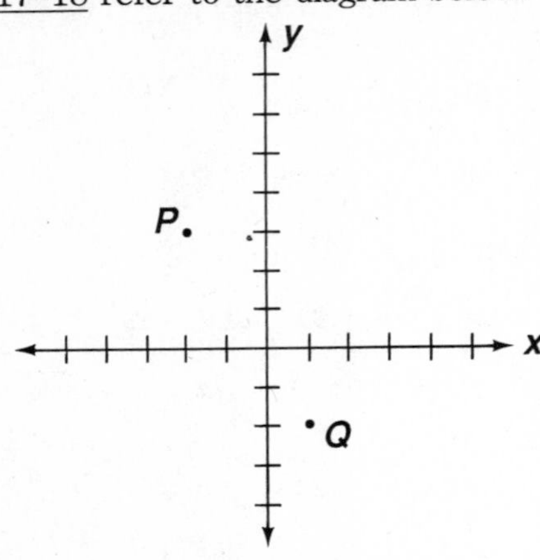

17. What is the distance from P to Q?

(1) $\sqrt{-6}$
(2) $\sqrt{6}$
(3) 5
(4) $\sqrt{34}$
(5) 34

① ② ③ ④ ⑤

18. What is the slope of line PQ?

(1) $-\frac{5}{3}$
(2) -1
(3) $-\frac{1}{3}$
(4) $\frac{1}{3}$
(5) $\frac{3}{5}$

① ② ③ ④ ⑤

19. The O'Callaghans purchased a 6 foot by 9 foot carpet priced at \$650. They borrowed money and repaid the loan in 2 years. Their total cost was \$741. What rate of interest did they pay?

(1) 4.5%
(2) 6.1%
(3) 7%
(4) 9.1%
(5) 14%

① ② ③ ④ ⑤

20. If $a = 12$ and $b = -2$, what is $\frac{1}{2}a - 3b + 2b^2$?

(1) -8
(2) -2
(3) 14
(4) 20
(5) 34

① ② ③ ④ ⑤

21. Alice bought two yards of fabric at \$3.00 per yard, one yard at \$4.50 per yard, and 6 yards at \$4.00 per yard. Which expression is the average cost per yard that she paid?

(1) $\dfrac{2(3.00) + 4.50 + 6(4.00)}{3.00 + 4.50 + 4.00}$

(2) $\dfrac{2(3.00) + 4.50 + 6(4.00)}{2 + 6}$

(3) $\dfrac{3.00 + 4.50 + 4.00}{2 + 1 + 6}$

(4) $\dfrac{2(3.00) + 4.50 + 6(4.00)}{2 + 1 + 6}$

(5) $2(3.00) + 4.50 + 6(4.00)$

① ② ③ ④ ⑤

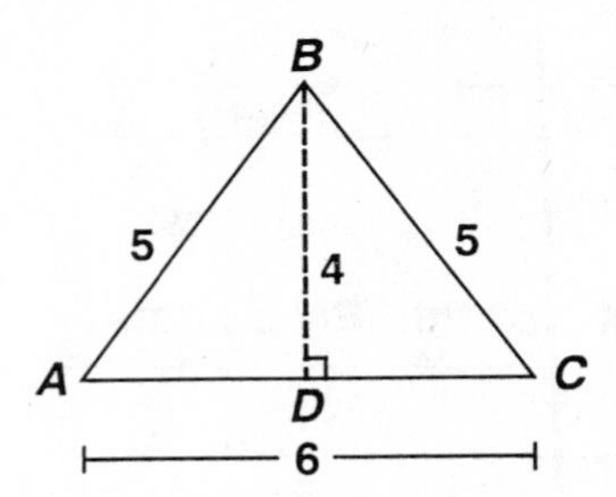

22. In triangle ABC the perpendicular line BD cuts line segment AC in half. What is the area of triangle ABD in square inches?

(1) 4
(2) 6
(3) 10
(4) 13
(5) 30

① ② ③ ④ ⑤

23. John got a one-year loan at 6% to buy a dining-room set that fit his 12 ft by 14 ft dining room. The total amount he paid for the loan was \$848. What was the price of the furniture?

(1) \$50.88
(2) \$600
(3) \$797.12
(4) \$800
(5) \$898.88

① ② ③ ④ ⑤

GO ON TO THE NEXT PAGE.

24. One square foot of linoleum costs \$4.92. What will 1⅓ square feet cost?

(1) \$1.64
(2) \$3.73
(3) \$6.31
(4) \$6.56
(5) \$65.97

(1) (2) (3) (4) (5)

25. If $x^2 - 2x - 3 = 0$, then $x =$

(1) -3 and 1
(2) $-\frac{1}{2}$ and $-\frac{3}{2}$
(3) $-\frac{1}{2}$ and $\frac{3}{2}$
(4) 3 and -1
(5) Insufficient data is given to solve the problem.

(1) (2) (3) (4) (5)

26. Solve $A = \pi r^2$ for r.

(1) $\sqrt{\frac{\pi}{A}}$
(2) $\sqrt{\frac{A}{\pi}}$
(3) $\frac{A}{\pi}$
(4) $\frac{\pi}{A}$
(5) $\frac{A^2}{\pi^2}$

(1) (2) (3) (4) (5)

27. The perimeter of a triangle is 27 ft. If the sides are in the ratio 1:2:3, what is the length of the longest side in feet?

(1) 4.5
(2) 6.75
(3) 9
(4) 13.5
(5) 27

(1) (2) (3) (4) (5)

Items 28–29 refer to the chart.

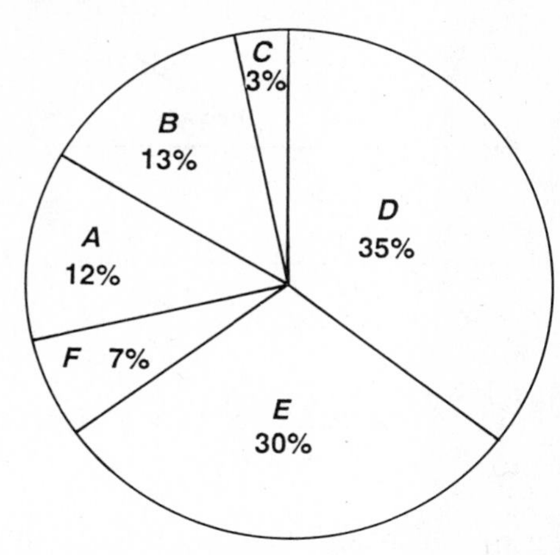

Average Time Spent on Each Machine Per Day

28. How many hours are spent on machine E in 7 work days of 8 hours each?

(1) 30
(2) 24
(3) 21
(4) 16.8
(5) 2.4

(1) (2) (3) (4) (5)

29. About how many hours in an eight-hour day are spent on machines A and B?

(1) 9
(2) 8
(3) 3
(4) 2
(5) 1

(1) (2) (3) (4) (5)

30. Twelve cases of motor oil cost \$40, and a set of four hubcaps is \$34.99. How much do 30 cases of motor oil cost?

(1) \$85
(2) \$95
(3) \$100
(4) \$110
(5) \$120

(1) (2) (3) (4) (5)

GO ON TO THE NEXT PAGE.

Items 31–33 refer to the following diagram.

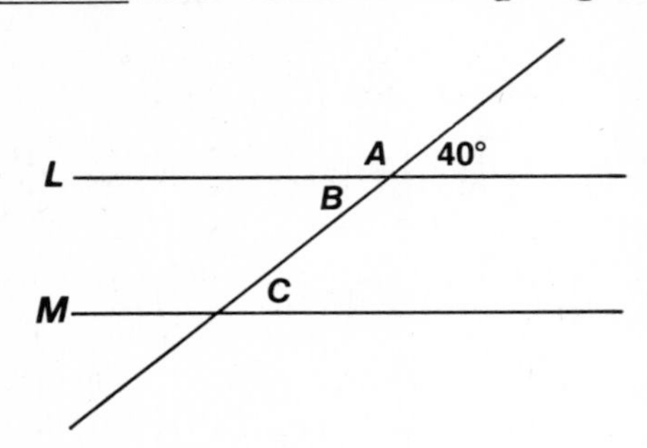

31. How many degrees does angle A measure?
    (1) 40
    (2) 50
    (3) 140
    (4) 180
    (5) 320

    (1) (2) (3) (4) (5)

32. The measure of angle B is
    (1) 40°
    (2) 50°
    (3) 140°
    (4) 180°
    (5) 320°

    (1) (2) (3) (4) (5)

33. How many degrees does angle C measure?
    (1) 40
    (2) 50
    (3) 140
    (4) 180
    (5) 320

    (1) (2) (3) (4) (5)

34. Mr. Tyndall wants to cover two windows in his kitchen with plastic, weather-protective sheeting. Each window is 36 inches wide and 66 inches long. How many *square feet* of plastic does he need?
    (1) $5\frac{1}{2}$
    (2) $8\frac{1}{2}$
    (3) 11
    (4) 33
    (5) 1,198

    (1) (2) (3) (4) (5)

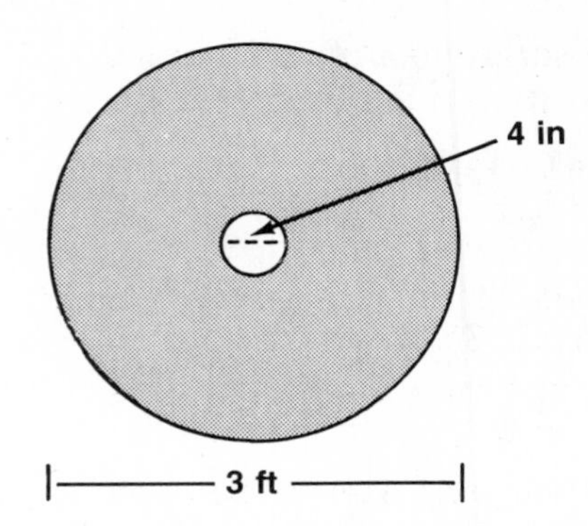

35. Laura had an umbrella table on her 5 foot square patio. The table measured 3 feet across and had a 4 inch hole in the center for the umbrella pole. Approximately how many *square inches* is the shaded area of the table?
    (1) 13
    (2) 310
    (3) 324
    (4) 1,005
    (5) 1,008

    (1) (2) (3) (4) (5)

Items 36–37 refer to the following graph.

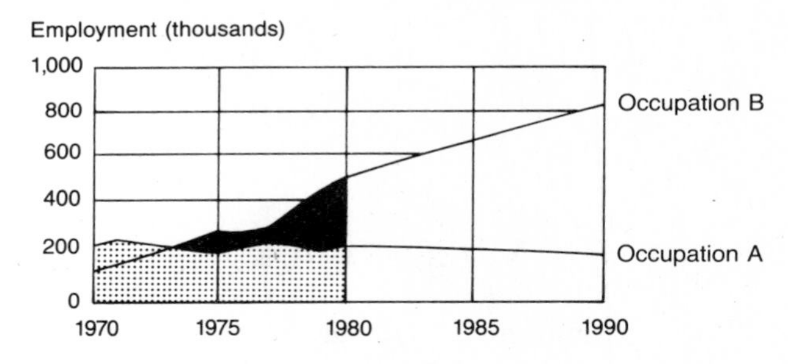

Source Bureau of Labor Statistics

36. Compare the number of employees in Occupation A and the number of employees in Occupation B in 1980. Which of the following statements is correct?
    (1) There are 300 fewer employees in Occupation A.
    (2) There are 500 fewer employees in Occupation A.
    (3) There are 30,000 fewer employees in Occupation A.
    (4) There are 300,000 more employees in Occupation B.
    (5) There are 500,000 more employees in Occupation B.

    (1) (2) (3) (4) (5)

GO ON TO THE NEXT PAGE.

37. By 1990, how many more employees will be in Occupation B than in Occupation A?

(1) about 600 more
(2) about 810,000 more
(3) about 4 times as many
(4) about 6 times as many
(5) about 600 times as many

① ② ③ ④ ⑤

38. Three rows of 4 lamps each can be packed in a crate. Each crate can hold two such layers. How many crates will be needed to pack 310 lamps?

(1) 12
(2) 13
(3) 24
(4) 26
(5) 52

① ② ③ ④ ⑤

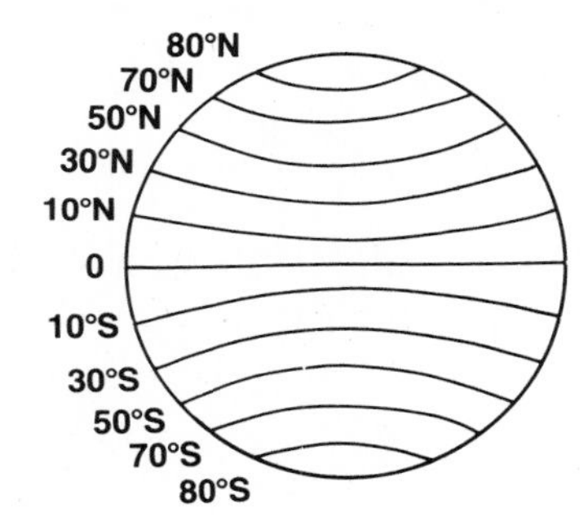

39. A plane flew from 30° south latitude to 10° north latitude. Through how many degrees of latitude did it travel?

(1) 10
(2) 20
(3) 25
(4) 30
(5) 40

① ② ③ ④ ⑤

40. The Kline family lived 32 miles from town in a 30-year-old house. The ages of the family were 16, 34, 37, 11, and 5. What is the median age?

(1) 5
(2) 11
(3) 16
(4) 34
(5) 37

① ② ③ ④ ⑤

Items 41–42 refer to the following situation.

Sarah's income last year was $20,000. She can deduct her charitable contributions from her income taxes in either of two ways: She can deduct 10% of income or 10% of total contributions. Last year she gave the United Fund $100, the Heart Fund $200, and she kept a pledge to contribute $150 a month to her college.

41. Since Sarah would like to deduct the greater amount from income taxes, what should be her deduction?

(1) $100
(2) $210
(3) $450
(4) $2,000
(5) $2,100

① ② ③ ④ ⑤

42. If Sarah were to increase all of her contributions next year by 20%, what would be the total amount she would give the college?

(1) $180
(2) $400
(3) $540
(4) $2,160
(5) $4,000

① ② ③ ④ ⑤

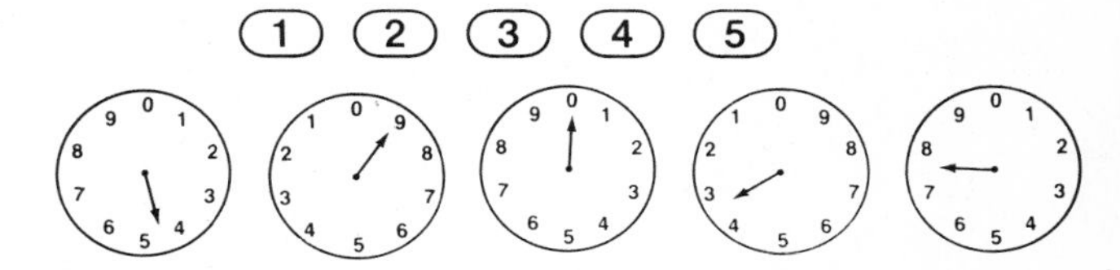

43. A utility meter shows the dials above with hands positioned as indicated. If the hand falls between two numbers, use the smaller one. What is the reading of the meter?

(1) 45,935
(2) 49,035
(3) 49,037
(4) 59,357
(5) 59,038

① ② ③ ④ ⑤

GO ON TO THE NEXT PAGE.

44. Marguerite has two bookcases that are 6 feet tall. Their total value is $250.00. Each bookcase has 4 shelves. How many of Marguerite's books can the bookcases hold?

(1) 70
(2) 192
(3) 250
(4) 380
(5) Insufficient data is given to solve the problem.

(1) (2) (3) (4) (5)

45. Mr. Pasko's monthly salary is $1,200. Mrs. Pasko's monthly salary is 10% higher because she works 5 more hours per week. How much do the Paskos earn in a year?

(1) $120
(2) $1,320
(3) $12,000
(4) $15,840
(5) $30,240

(1) (2) (3) (4) (5)

46. Solve $x^2 - x - 6$ for x.

(1) -2
(2) 3 or -2
(3) 2
(4) 3
(5) 2 or 3

(1) (2) (3) (4) (5)

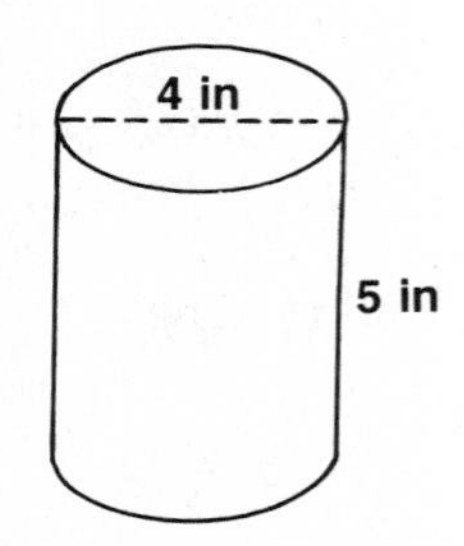

47. A glass measures 5 inches high from base to brim. The diameter is 4 inches, and the glass costs $0.60 or $5.89 per dozen. How many cubic inches does the glass hold?

(1) 12.56
(2) 20
(3) 37.7
(4) 49.3
(5) 62.8

(1) (2) (3) (4) (5)

48. A machine punches 6 holes every 30 seconds. The machine is overhauled after 1,400 hours of service. How many holes does it punch in 2 hours?

(1) 240
(2) 500
(3) 720
(4) 1,440
(5) 7,200

(1) (2) (3) (4) (5)

49. Kim had five bottles of different sizes. The bottles held 5.31 oz, 5.4 oz, 5.102 oz, 5.12 oz, and 5.2 oz. Which one was the next-to-smallest bottle?

(1) 5.102
(2) 5.12
(3) 5.2
(4) 5.31
(5) 5.4

(1) (2) (3) (4) (5)

50. Matt needed a ladder to reach the top of a 30 foot building. He planned to place the bottom of the ladder 16 feet away from the building. How many feet long must the ladder be?

(1) 30
(2) 31.6
(3) 34
(4) 42
(5) 49

(1) (2) (3) (4) (5)

GO ON TO THE NEXT PAGE.

51. On a map, Centerville and Middletown are 2.4 inches apart. If one inch on the map represents 25 miles, how many miles is Centerville from Middletown?

(1) 10.4
(2) 60
(3) 104
(4) 268
(5) 600

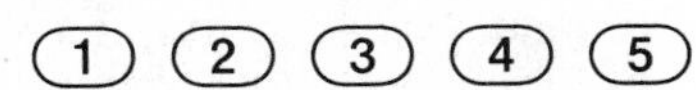

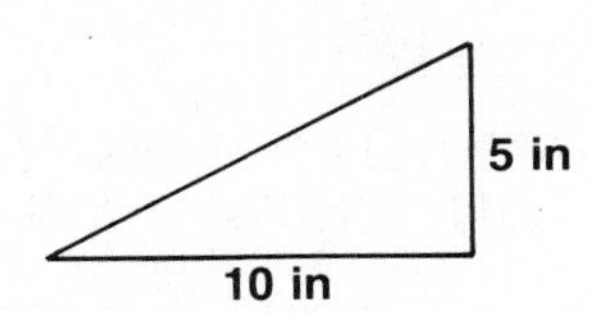

52. Mrs. Valdez wants to buy glass shelves to fit a corner cabinet with the dimensions in the diagram. If the price of glass is $1.15 per square inch, how much will three shelves cost?

(1) $25.00
(2) $28.75
(3) $50.00
(4) $86.25
(5) $93.50

① ② ③ ④ ⑤

53. A hotel held a banquet dinner. There were 17 tables set up; each table had 9 place settings. When everyone sat down for dinner, 8 people did not have seats. How many diners attended the banquet?

(1) 72
(2) 136
(3) 145
(4) 153
(5) 161

① ② ③ ④ ⑤

54. Juanita had 7 more than 6 times as many pens as Fred had. Ray had one-fourth as many as Fred. If x equals the number of pens Fred had, which expression shows the number of pens Ray had?

(1) x^4
(2) $\frac{x}{4}$
(3) $6x - 7$
(4) $4x$
(5) $6x + 7$

① ② ③ ④ ⑤

55. Last year, 22 fathers and 28 mothers were members of the PTA. At the March meeting, 18 fathers were present, but three-fourths of the mothers were not. What percent of the PTA parents attended the meeting?

(1) 78%
(2) 50%
(3) 39%
(4) 36%
(5) 23%

① ② ③ ④ ⑤

56. Fabiola worked 5 1/2 hours on Monday, 6 1/4 hours on Tuesday, 7 3/4 hours on Wednesday, 8 1/2 hours on Friday and 9 on Saturday. What was the average number of hours she worked a day?

(1) $7\frac{2}{5}$
(2) $7\frac{1}{2}$
(3) $8\frac{1}{4}$
(4) 9
(5) $37\frac{3}{5}$

① ② ③ ④ ⑤

END OF EXAMINATION

Posttest A Answer Explanations

Writing Skills
(pages 591–604)

1. (5) No error.

2. (2) A sentence fragment is another name for an incomplete sentence. *Counterfeiting in almost all kinds of consumer products* is a sentence fragment because it lacks a verb. *Counterfeiting* and *occurs* agree because they are both singular.

3. (5) No error. Since *They* is plural, it cannot substitute for *counterfeiting. Americans* is always capitalized.

4. (1) The noun *increase* and the verb *is* are both singular. *Analysts* is not the subject of the sentence.

5. (4) *Became* is not used with a helping verb. *Has become* is correct. *Government* is often misspelled because some people don't pronounce the *n* in the middle.

6. (4) *Education* is not spelled the way it sounds. *Will call* indicates that the act has not been put into effect. *But* and *or* do not logically connect the two sentences.

7. (3) These two complete thoughts are connected with a comma. A comma cannot be used to connect complete sentences. Since the ideas in the sentences are so closely related, you can use a semicolon to join them.

8. (2) *When buying something marked down more than 40 or 50 percent, be careful if the seller is suspect. You* is the understood subject of *be careful. When buying something marked down more than 40 or 50 percent* clearly refers to *you* and not to *care* or *the seller.*

9. (2) *You* is the pronoun used throughout this passage. It is good writing style to follow through with this usage and not to insert *one, them, it,* or *us.*

If someone mentioned the word "counterfeit," most people would automatically think of fake dollar bills. In the manufacturing and consumer worlds, counterfeit means everything from fake designer jeans to bogus microchips in heart pumps. Counterfeiting occurs in almost all kinds of consumer products. It costs Americans $20 billion a year and is responsible for the loss of over 750,000 jobs. The dramatic increase, analysts say, is due to the average consumer's obsession with brand names. To help combat this worldwide problem, the United States government has become involved. The Trademark Counterfeiting Act of 1984 calls for harsh penalties in the United States for product counterfeiting, and consumer education is stressed in programs provided by the International Anticounterfeiting Coalition. As a consumer, what can you do to protect yourself from buying fakes? It is important to shop at a store operated by a trustworthy merchant. Also, check for fuzzy or misspelled labels and tags; these are usually fake. When buying something marked down more than 40 or 50 percent, be careful if the seller is suspect. Counterfeiting will continue to be a major problem, but being an aware consumer will help you win the battle against fakes.

10. (4) *Talk* and *to think* are verb forms that do not match. *Think* is the only correct substitute for *to think.*

11. (1) *German* is a word that describes the teacher. It comes from *Germany,* which is also capitalized. Osten is followed by a comma because it is the last word in an interrupting descriptive phrase.

12. (5) No error. Removing the connecting word *but* would cause the sentence to be joined incorrectly by a comma.

13. (1) *Excited by the thought of a mathematical horse* is a long descriptive phrase at the beginning of the sentence. On the GED Test, a comma is required after such an introductory phrase. Because they often mispronounce it, many people incorrectly add an extra *h* to the end of height.

14. (1) *So* is the only option that shows the cause-and-effect relationship between the two parts of the sentence. In option (5), two complete sentences are incorrectly joined by a comma.

15. (5) No error. *They're* stands for *they are.* It is not logical to say *of they are tests.*

16. (2) *Would have leaned* suggests something that did *not* happen. It is a fact that Mr. Osten *did* lean forward. Option (5) is incorrect because *begun* cannot be used without a helping verb such as *has* or *had.*

17. (3) It is not clear whether *he* refers to Mr. Osten or the horse. To avoid using *the horse* twice in one sentence, it is good writing style to substitute *Clever Hans* for *it.*

18. (1) *Mr. Osten was terribly disappointed when he discovered that his horse was not really a mathematician. When* is the only option that correctly shows the time relationship between Mr. Osten's discovery and his disappointment. The original wording is awkward because it makes *disappointment,* rather than *Mr. Osten,* the subject of the sentence.

For centuries, people have tried to prove that animals can talk and think. In 1904, one such person, a German mathematics teacher names Osten, owned an unusually talented horse called Clever Hans. Clever Hans became a celebrity because not only could he do simple math, but he could also add and subtract fractions. Excited by the thought of a mathematical horse, people traveled from all over Europe to see Clever Hans, and at the height of his popularity he was the subject of many songs. Mr. Osten honestly believed in the intelligence of his horse, so one day he invited scientists to test Clever Hans. They discovered that when Mr. Osten knew the question before Clever Hans was asked it, the horse almost always knew the correct answer. When Mr. Osten did not know the question first, Clever Hans did not know the answer. The scientists then blindfolded the horse to see if he could answer questions correctly, but Clever Hans missed them all. After the scientists analyzed the results of their tests, they discovered that Mr. Osten gave nonverbal signals to the horse. Mr. Osten always would lean forward slightly when Clever Hans began tapping out the answer with his foot. When the horse had the correct answer, Mr. Osten would straighten up, and Clever Hans would stop tapping. Mr. Osten was terribly disappointed when he discovered that his horse was not really a mathematician.

19. (5) No error.

20. (2) *Equipment* is the correct spelling. No comma is needed to join *two* things (*pebbles* and *rocks*). *Which* refers to a thing *(pins),* and *who* refers to people.

21. (4) This sentence describes something that happened in the past. *Became* is a verb form used to show a past action. Option (2) is incorrect because the word *it* refers to *game. King* is capitalized only when it comes before a name.

22. (4) *Bowling* and *to practice* don't have matching endings. It is correct to say *bowling rather than practicing. Than* and *then* are often confused because of mispronunciation. *Than* is used to compare things; *then* shows time.

23. (1) *Archers* and *were* agree because they are both plural forms. According to the sentence, it was a fact that archers were needed for defense. *Could have been* indicates that they never were needed or that it was only a possibility that they were needed.

24. (3) The sentence tells about an action that happened in the past. *Was brought* is the correct past form of the verb.

25. (1) *An early form of bowling* is a descriptive phrase in the middle of the sentence and needs commas to set it off. *Its peak* is correct; *it's* stands for *it is.* It is not logical to say *it is peak.*

26. (2) A comma is not needed after the verb *passed* and the phrase coming after it, which explains more about the subject of the sentence *(law).* You wouldn't pause after *passed* if you were reading the sentence aloud.

27. (4) *The current game of tenpins was born when some enterprising person added a tenth pin to the game to circumvent the law. When* is the only connecting word among the options that logically shows the time relationship between tenpins being born and a person adding a tenth pin.

There's nothing like a Saturday night bowling tournament to create excitement among devoted bowlers. This popular sport actually began 7,000 years ago with Stone Age men and boys. Their sporting equipment included pebbles and rocks to knock down their pins, which were pointed stones or sheep joints. European bowling originated in German monasteries during the Middle Ages. It was part of a religious ritual to persuade peasants to lead a better life. The game next spread to England, where it became so popular that in 1366 the king passed a law forbidding participation in the game. His people had begun to spend their free time bowling rather than practicing their archery. At that time, expert archers were essential for military defense. Bowling was brought to America by Dutch settlers in New York and played upon a green called a "bowling green." In the 1840s ninepins, an early form of bowling, reached its peak, but controversy developed when people began betting on it. A law was passed forbidding ninepins but not the game of bowling. The current game of tenpins was born when some enterprising person added a tenth pin to the game to circumvent the law.

28. (4) *Scientists* is not capitalized because it does not refer to a particular person. Even though *stress* ends with *s,* it is singular. *Stress* and *has* agree.

29. (5) No error. *Are* is the correct verb because *heartbeat, pressure, temper, jags, sleeplessness,* and *stomach* are all the subjects, not *stress.* Adding *-e* to *stomach* is a common error. People often think of the word *ache* when they do this.

30. (4) *Stress can also weaken the body's ability to fight illness, making a person under stress ill more often than a relaxed person.* The wording of these sentences was cleaned up by making the second sentence a descriptive phrase. Option (2) may seem to be the correct answer, but it is not logical: *Stress, weakening the body's ability to fight illness, makes a person under stress ill more often than a relaxed person.* Stress alone does not make people ill. The fact that stress weakens the body's ability to fight illness does make a person ill.

31. (5) This is an example of misusing a comma alone to separate complete thoughts. The best revision is to use *when* to connect the two sentences. Option (2) is a run-on. Option (4) makes it impossible to phrase the sentence as a question.

32. (5) *Effects* is a noun and means more than one thing. *Affects* is a verb. No comma is needed after *victims* because there is no pause before the dependent part of the sentence.

33. (3) The two verbs, *must identify* and *will try,* do not match. *Try* is the only option that matches *identify.*

34. (5) No error. It is sometimes difficult to find the subject in a sentence beginning with *there. Sources* is the subject of this sentence. Option (1) is not correct because it is not logical to say *They are are.* Remember that *they're* stands for *they are.*

35. (2) The comma after *abuse* is not necessary. A comma does not separate a subject from a verb.

36. (4) Items in a series should match in form; *to relax* should parallel the form of *exercise* and *diet. Relaxation* is the parallel form.

Studies show that in some people stress causes physical and mental disorders. Stress has been studied by scientists for only fifty years. Among the symptoms of stress they have identified are rapid heartbeat, high blood pressure, short temper, crying jags, sleeplessness, and upset stomach. Stress can also weaken the body's ability to fight illness, making a person under stress ill more often than a relaxed person. But how can we possibly avoid stress when it is all around us? We need not be helpless victims because it is possible to lessen the effects of stress on our lives. We must first identify the sources of stress and then try to take measures to avoid its harmful results. There are many sources of stress. Family problems, an unfulfilling job, weight control, and drug abuse can all cause harmful stress. As we learn to recognize the causes of stress in our lives, we can also learn to control its effects with exercise, proper diet, and relaxation.

37. (4) *Looking for a job or reentering the working world might be a difficult task.* The original wording of this sentence is awkward because the verbs do not agree. *Looking* and *reentering* do agree. Options (1), (2), and (5) are not logical because the person in this sentence is not looking and finding, looking and planning, or looking and working.

38. (4) *And* cannot be used to join two unrelated sentences. Option (5) is a run-on.

39. (5) Many people might think *workers* is the subject of the sentence because it is so close to *challenge* and *stimulate. Variety* is the subject of the sentence, and since variety is singular, the verbs must agree with it. *Challenges* and *stimulates* agree with *variety.* Remember that verbs ending in *-s* usually agree with subjects that are singular.

40. (4) The complete names of holidays are usually capitalized. *Summer* is not capitalized because it is the name of a season.

41. (5) No error. Adding *which* to the sentence would make it a fragment. *Insurance* and *benefits* are two things joined by *and;* no comma is needed.

42. (3) *Expensive* is difficult to spell because it sounds as if an *s* should follow the *x.* The *ex* sound has an *s* "built into it" *(examine, exit, extra, extreme, exist).* Don't add an *s* to words beginning with *ex.*

43. (3) The original wording of the sentence is a run-on. Option (2) is also a run-on. Option (4) overworks the comma. The only correct option is to make two complete sentences out of the original run-on.

44. (4) *Which* refers only to things; *who* refers to people. In option (1), the subject *work* cannot be separated from the verb by a comma.

45. (3) *Like a flexible schedule, thrive on change,* and *need to explore different careers* are items in a series and should be separated by commas. *Risks* and *are* agree; they are both plural forms.

Looking for a job or reentering the working world might be a difficult task. There is a way, however, to ease this situation. Have you ever thought of working for a temporary employment agency? Temporary assignments let you explore the working world before you make up your mind. As a "temp," you can work in many different situations while learning new skills and meeting new people. The variety of working in a different place every day or week challenges and stimulates many workers. On the other hand, if you want to attend a computer seminar, lie in the sun on the first day of summer, or visit Aunt Grace on Columbus Day, you can easily take the day off. Some temporary agencies offer health insurance and other benefits to their workers. If the one you work for does not, you will find it expensive to provide your own health insurance. Another disadvantage to temporary work is that there is no guarantee of work. You do not automatically draw a paycheck every Friday. Temporary work may not be appropriate for people who crave security. There are risks involved with temporary work, but if you like a flexible schedule, thrive on change, or need to explore different careers, this approach might be for you.

46. (1) No error. When *and* connects two verbs (*have* microwave ovens and *must learn,*) a comma is not needed.

47. (2) Commas are placed around *then* because it interrupts the flow of the sentence. Read sentence 2 aloud and listen for the pauses before and after *then.* Options (4) and (5) each make a fragment from the group of words beginning with *then.*

48. (3) Two complete sentences cannot be connected with a comma. Option (2) is a run-on. Options (4) and (5) do not logically show the relationship between the two thoughts.

49. (3) *Don't* stands for *do not.* It is incorrect to write *air do not heat up very much.* Both *air* and *does* are singular forms. Therefore, option (3) is correct.

50. (2) *The waves bounce around inside the oven and pass through the food repeatedly.* In the original sentence, the verbs (*are passing* and *bounce*) do not agree in time. Both options (2) and (3) contain the verb *pass,* which matches the verb *bounce* in the revised sentence. In option (3), however, *bounce or pass* would change the meaning of the original sentence. Therefore, only option (2) is correct.

51. (5) No error. If you chose option (4), remember that a comma is needed after an introductory dependent part.

52. (3) *While microwaving is quick* is a phrase and not a complete sentence. It cannot stand alone. Option (2) is incorrect because it lacks a comma. Therefore, option (3) is correct.

53. (3) In this sentence, *we* cannot be a pronoun for *microwave owners. They* and *microwave owners* agree.

54. (3) There is no reason to capitalize *recipes.*

55. (4) There is no specific rule to help you spell *indispensable.* It's one of those words that you must memorize in order to spell it correctly. *Have* is correct because it agrees with *ovens. Become* is correct because it is used with a helper *(have).*

Today more and more people have microwave ovens and must learn a very different method of cooking. Let's look, then, at how microwave ovens work and how that affects their use with perishable goods. Microwaves are extra-short radio waves. The movement of these waves inside the oven does the actual cooking. The air in the oven usually doesn't heat up very much. The waves bounce around inside the oven and pass through the food repeatedly. This action causes cooking to begin just below the food's surface. As the heat begins to spread through the rest of the food, full cooking is achieved. While microwaving is quick, it does not always cook food evenly. Before new microwave owners master their ovens, they often find that some spots in a food will overcook, while others are still not completely cooked. To completely cook a particular food without overcooking these high-heat spots, many microwave recipes call for a 10- to 15-minute standing time after the power has been turned off. Because of their quick cooking times, microwave ovens have become indispensable to harried homemakers and other busy professionals.

Sample Essay

Today, it seems, almost every office and factory uses computers. Thousands of workers spend their days operating keyboard and screen to keep accounts, schedule appointments, fill orders, or carry out high-powered research.

Still, many people are holdouts from the computer revolution. They don't want to learn to work with computers. Secretly, they may believe that they couldn't learn if they tried.

Why do people feel this way? Computers remind some people of tasks they have found difficult. Computers tend to involve numbers, and some students had many problems with mathematics. Computers are a kind of machine, and some people feel that they and machines just don't get along.

Other people don't like computers because they seem so impersonal. These people would rather interact with another human being. The computer's messages leave them cold.

Actually, learning to use a computer *can* be difficult. Some users' manuals seem to be written in a strange language called "computerese." Some instructors are not much better.

Still, if people can drive a car with dozens of gauges, controls, and gadgets, they should be able to master computers. The machines are supposedly becoming "user friendly" (in other words, more people-oriented) in an effort to bridge the gap. With some effort on both sides, it is possible that computer phobics can become computer lovers.

Social Studies
(pages 605–624)

1. (4) The opening sentence tells you that the federal government aided the railroads with land and money grants. Options (1), (2), (3), and (5) are unrelated to the information in the passage.

2. (2) The passage states that new and faster production methods in the steel industry were the result of the growing demands of the rapidly expanding railroads. None of the other options can be supported by the information in the passage.

3. (2) The graph shows that the portions indicating senior citizen and mental health spending, when combined, occupy one-half of the graph. So they make up one-half of the total spending.

4. (1) Fewer senior citizens *might* result in a lower cost for services, but not necessarily. For example, fewer senior citizens could, in fact, need more services. Or the cost of certain services, such as medicine, might rise. So even if fewer services were needed, costs may not go down.

5. (4) When commissioner B says the county should take money from senior citizen services and give it to those who work and pay taxes, he is assuming that seniors don't work or pay taxes.

6. (5) Commissioner B implies that the young should get more services *because* they will work and pay taxes. In other words, he believes that productive citizens deserve more government help than the "unproductive."

7. (5) The sound of the key is the stimulus that causes the dog's response, rushing to greet its owner. In (1) and (3) there is a stimulus but no response, and in (2) and (4) there is no stimulus or response.

8. (4) The second paragraph states that soil erosion has increased since the introduction of agriculture and grazing.

9. (2) Planting only row crops leaves the land exposed to the elements. Options (1), (4), and (5) are identified in the article as causes of erosion, while (3) is not related to wind erosion.

10. (1) When an item is scarce, the price is likely to rise. If scarcity is corrected by costly methods, that cost is likely to be passed on to consumers. So, in either case, prices will rise.

11. (1) This is an important conclusion reached by the article. Options (4) and (5) are statements that support that conclusion. Options (2) and (3) are statements that illustrate the article's point that topsoil erosion is a serious and growing problem.

12. (3) Only this option could help farmers keep production high and costs low. Option (2) would increase costs. Options (1) and (4) are impractical in the Third World, where there are few industrial or technical jobs, food is needed, and land may be scarce. Option (5) would help only if the government used soil conservation methods.

13. (5) Other reasons for a slow rate of growth might include a high death rate or a high rate of emigration to other parts of the world.

14. (3) Food shortages would most likely occur where the population is greatest. The graph predicts that by 2000 Asia, Africa, and Oceania will have five times more people than other parts of the world.

15. (5) Migration is most likely to be from the areas of greatest population—Asia, Africa, Oceania—to areas of less population—America and Europe. Options (1)-(3) cannot be supported by data on the chart, and (4) is disproved by the data.

16. (2) The first sentence of the first paragraph and the first two sentences of the second paragraph alert you to the two main topics of the passage—improvements and liabilities, or drawbacks, of the New Deal—so option (2) is the correct one. Options (1), (3), (4), and (5) can be disproved by statements in the passage.

17. (4) The passage states that new programs, agencies, and a large bureaucracy were created. You may infer that large amounts of money would be needed to pay for these. Also, options (1)-(3) can be disproved by the passage, and (5) is not mentioned.

18. (3) Only this statement is supported by figures: "In 1930 the public debt was $16 billion; in 1940 it was $42 billion." The other statements are given but not supported with statistics or other information.

19. (4) Option (4) is correct because political parties are concerned mainly with elections. The passage provides no evidence to prove (1), (2), (3), or (5).

20. (3) You must understand the term *collective bargaining* and its functions in settling labor-management disagreements through give-and-take negotiations between the two sides to answer this question.

21. (1) Option (1) is correct because it implies that different justices at different times can and do change previous court rulings, as related in the passage. Options (2), (4), and (5) can be eliminated because they are contradicted by the passage, and (3) is not really discussed in the passage. The same justices may change their minds and reverse their ruling on an issue.

22. (3) In finding that "separate" schools are not "equal," the Supreme Court was supporting the idea that all people are guaranteed certain rights. If the court believed option (2) or (4) was more important, it could not have ruled as it did.

23. (1) To answer this question correctly, you need to study the key and be able to recognize the continents from their shapes.

24. (3) The line running across the map represents the equator. Countries north of it are in the Northern Hemisphere. You can see that there are more well-fed countries north of the equator. Option (2) can be neither proved nor disproved by the map, and options (1), (4), and (5) are disproved by the map.

25. (2) Since the map shows where hungry countries are located on the globe, it could be used to determine the path of a satellite. Once natural resources are located, those resources could be used to produce food or to produce goods that could be sold or traded for food.

26. (4) The table shows that the largest percent of increase among women workers has been in jobs where they are a minority, that is, jobs usually done by men. All the other options are contradicted by the figures on the table.

27. (3) A trend would mean that more and more women are doing jobs traditionally done by men. If women's incomes rise because of this, it must mean that those jobs, and the men who did them, earned more.

28. (5) Only people deciding who to train for what jobs could use these statistics. These statistics would be of no use in any of the other situations.

29. (5) The human trait described is the ability to solve problems in different and creative ways. Option (5) is the only example that shows people being creative. Options (1)-(4) show the opposite.

30. (2) The ability to solve problems in different and creative ways implies that people have the ability to change and adjust to different situations.

31. (2) As the map shows, the North had more roads and an extensive network of canals, so long-distance travel was probably easier there than in the South. All other options are shown by the map to be false.

32. (5) The map shows many navigable rivers and canals. Options (1) and (2) are shown by the map to be false, and options (3) and (4) are not really shown by the map.

33. (3) The map shows canals between Lake Erie and the Ohio River, and the Ohio flows by Louisville, Kentucky. Options (1) and (5) are statements not supported by the map, and options (2) and (4) are shown by the map to be untrue.

34. (1) The article states that 80 percent *do* know the facts; therefore, 20 percent do not.

35. (4) The second sentence states that most Americans already know a lot about how to keep their health. So education about how to stay healthy is probably not needed. Getting people to act on their knowledge is.

36. (4) By adding the percentages of those who said they are heavy, moderate, or light drinkers, you can see that 53 percent of Americans claimed to be drinkers. Options (1) and (2) are hypotheses, and options (3) and (5) are contradicted by the article.

37. (2) The article does not suggest any reasons that Americans break the rules of good health.

38. (3) The power of both federal and state governments to collect taxes and the cooperation of state and federal governments in highway building are both examples of the sharing of powers mentioned in the first sentence of the passage. Options (2) and (4) can be disproved by the passage; options (1) and (5) are not discussed in the passage.

39. (5) "Revenue sharing" is defined in the third sentence of the passage. According to the definition, federal money flowing to a city is an example of revenue sharing.

40. (4) State employees would have an interest in keeping their retirement benefits high. Since Delaware has the highest percentage of state employees, a law limiting their benefits would probably have the hardest time passing there.

41. (4) To answer this question correctly, you need to identify states by their outlines and locations. Arizona, in the Southwest (or lower left-hand side of the map), is in the 10.4%–11.4% range, which is considered average according to the question.

42. (5) Older people often live on fixed incomes. They would most likely favor a law that reduced their taxes. The state that had the greatest percentage of older people—Florida—would be the state where such a law would be most popular.

43. (5) Immigration was at its lowest during exactly those years when jobs and money were scarce. That fact strongly suggests that economics was a primary reason for coming to the United States. Options (1) and (2) are highly unlikely; and (3) and (4), while they may have had some impact on immigration figures, could not have brought immigration figures so low.

44. (4) If lake waters covered the highway and rail lines, special measures would be needed to move people and goods, and new roads and rail lines would have to be built. All this would cost a great deal of money, and this cost is what the legislature's action is meant to prevent.

45. (4) You will need to study the circle graphs to see that Republicans got the biggest percentage of votes in 1956. Options (1) and (2) are disproved by the graphs, (3) by the map, and (5) by the popular vote count.

46. (5) A look at the popular vote count shows that this option is true. Options (1), (3), and (4) are hypotheses that are neither proved nor disproved by the data, and option (2) is shown by the data to be false.

47. (4) As the maps show, the Great Plains states voted Republican in all four elections; the South voted Democratic in three of four elections. This suggests that regional interests did, at least in these elections, influence voters. Options (1), (2), and (5) are proved false by the data, and option (3) is not dealt with.

48. (3) An abundance of food sends food prices down. Farmers would have been paid less for what they grew. Abundant food could not have caused any of the consequences described in the other options.

49. (3) Richard is putting off doing something he doesn't want to do. This most closely resembles procrastination.

50. (1) Beth is taking out her anger on an innocent object. This fits the definition of displacement.

51. (2) As a smoker, Susan wouldn't want to accept the truth of the link between smoking and cancer. Her continuing to smoke is a denial of that information.

52. (5) Pete is finding a "good" reason—giving his ankle some needed exercise—to do what he knows is "bad"—ignoring his doctor's orders. That is rationalization.

53. (1) As the map shows, the North raised more food crops and had more mining and manufacturing than the South. The North would thus be better able to feed and arm its people during a war.

54. (2) The map does not indicate why there was little mining and steelmaking in the South. All the other options are supported by data on the map.

55. (2) The passage states that tradition and local election laws favor the two-party system. A change in those laws would, therefore, be needed to change the two-party system. Options (1) and (3) are disproved by the passage. Options (4) and (5) are impossible under the current system.

56. (1) The last two sentences of the passage state that in voting districts the *plurality* winner takes all the votes and the loser gets none from that district. If, for example, there are three candidates in an election, a candidate may get fewer than half the votes but have more votes than either of the other two, so he or she would win. Options (2)–(5) are all disproved by information in the passage.

57. (5) The sending of troops to put down communist-inspired threats to foreign governments was authorized by the Eisenhower Doctrine.

58. (3) The belief that Americans had a "mission" to "civilize" other people was part of the doctrine of Manifest Destiny.

59. (2) To claim the right to defend a nation of the Western Hemisphere (Venezuela) against a foreign power (England), President Cleveland would have used the Monroe Doctrine.

60. (1) In urging Americans not to becomed mixed up with foreign nations, Washington showed he believed in isolationism.

61. (2) Figures in the table show that the lowest percentage of voters who turned out for the 1964–1982 elections was in the 18 to 24 year old group.

62. (2) Look at the two lines comparing the percentage of male and female voters. Only in the 1980 presidential election did a larger percentage of women vote (59.4) than men (59.1). Options (1) and (5) cannot be proved by the information on the table. Options (3) and (4) are shown by the table to be untrue.

63. (4) The largest percentage of voters are aged 45–64, and the next largest are 65 and older. These groups, at the peak of their earning power and either in or looking toward retirement, are probably concerned about taxes and Social Security. Options (1) and (2) are more likely to concern the young. The kind of information that's on the table doesn't suggest whether (3) and (5) would be major concerns.

64. (5) Since voting percentages are reported beginning with age 18, you may infer that this is when Americans get the right to vote. No information on the table can help you determine (1) or (3). Options (2) and (4) are refuted by the figures.

Science
(pages 625–643)

1. (3) This information can be read directly from the graph.

2. (1) Water will seep 12 inches into the soil in less than 15 minutes. This information can be read directly from the diagram.

3. (1) Because deep water in the soil does not evaporate as readily as surface water, deep water will remain available to plants when no surface water is present. Plants that have been watered deeply develop deep roots and can reach deep water supplies. Options (2) and (5) are true but irrelevant.

4. (1) Covering the pot will increase the pressure inside the pot. If the pressure increases, we can lower the temperature and maintain the same cooking conditions. Only covering the pot and lowering the heat will maintain the temperature. Options (2) and (5) will increase the cooking temperature. Options (3) and (4) will allow the food to cool. Options (4) and (5) will allow all the moisture to evaporate.

5. (3) The air pressure in the mountains is lower. The water will boil at a lower temperature because there is less air pressure on the surface of the liquid to overcome. Because the noodles cook at a lower temperature, they must cook longer to reach the same degree of tenderness. Options (1) and (2) may be true; however, they are irrelevant. Options (4) and (5) are false.

6. (1) The defect could occur in either of the two cell types required for the process of cell growth and division. Only option (1) explains why the cells would *not* divide. All other options would have resulted in the T cells' growth and division.

7. (1) The figure shows that at "new moon" the side of the moon which is illuminated by the sun is entirely hidden from the earth. The side facing the earth is completely darkened and receives no light. All other answers are incorrect because they apply to other phases of the moon's cycle.

8. (4) It takes approximately 28 days for the moon to go through a complete cycle. Therefore, it will be about 28 days between one full moon and the next.

9. (2) The passage notes that the moon rises 51 minutes later each day of its cycle. If the moon rose in the evening during its first quarter phase, it will rise in the daytime sky during its last quarter phase. All other options are false statements, and no justification for them is given in the passage.

10. (4) The figure shows that only about one-half of the moon is lighted by the sun at any one time. This is referred to as the "light side." The unlighted side, the "dark side," remains cold. Based on this information, option (3) is a false statement. Options (1) and (2) are irrelevant because the "light" and "dark" sides are affected only by the moon's relationship with the sun, not with how it is observed from the earth. Option (5) is true but irrelevant.

11. (2) Dissolved materials are in a higher concentration inside the cell than in the surrounding distilled water. The animal swells because the water flows into the cell to try to equalize the concentration of dissolved molecules on both sides of the membrane. Reread the definition of osmosis.

12. (3) Only one of the sugars is found inside the cells because the cell does not contain a specific carrier molecule for the other one. This moving of only specially chosen molecules fits the definition of passive transport.

13. (1) The gas spreads evenly throughout the entire lung area. No carrier system, no membrane is involved.

14. (5) Reread the definition of secretion.

15. (4) Phagocytosis is the only process listed in which a cell can take a particle inside itself.

16. (5) Reread the definition of secretion.

17. (1) Reread paragraph 3. All other answer options are false.

18. (4) Paragraph 1 says that the reactivity of molybdenum is due to the ways its electrons are distributed around the nucleus. The properties named in the other options do not influence whether an element combines with other elements readily.

19. (1) Paragraph 3 lists the many non-steel uses of molybdenum. Options (2), (3), (4), and (5) are statements from the passage which support the conclusion listed in option (1).

20. (2) Molybdenum has many uses in steel and non-steel industries, but it also is an essential plant and animal nutrient as well as a preventer of tooth decay. All other options imply that chemical elements have a very limited number of uses and are false statements.

21. (2) The monoterpenes from the beetle larvae discourage adult beetles and other insects from eating the leaves that the larvae occupy. Option (1) is true, but it does not specify the relationships shown in the paragraph. It is too general. Options (3), (4), and (5) are false.

22. (1) The experiments showed that adult beetles and other insects avoided the leaves that the larvae were placed on, but they ate other nearby leaves. Therefore, in nature, they might eat from the same tree but never from the same leaf. Option (2) is true but irrelevant, because of option (1). According to the passage, options (3)–(5) must be false.

23. (3) Because the adults avoid the leaf on which the secretion has been placed, we know that some chemical in the secretion repels the adults. The fact that the adults avoided leaves on which whole larvae were placed does not indicate that the larvae *secrete* a chemical which options (1), (2), and (4) imply. Option (5) is an irrelevant statement.

24. (5) It must be shown that the other insects will eat untreated leaves before it can be shown that treating the leaves in some way deters the insects from eating them. Options (1)–(4) are all parts of the experiment that must be compared to the results obtained from option (5).

25. (1) This answer can be read directly from the table.

26. (5) In one hour of walking at this rate, 318 calories are burned.

$$\frac{3500 \text{ calories/pound}}{318 \text{ calories/hour}} = 11 \text{ hours/pound}$$

27. (3) This is the only general conclusion that can be drawn from the table. All other options state specific relationships that support this conclusion.

28. (4) This option stresses the person's desire to look attractive. All other options actually state health benefits that will result from the man's exercise program.

29. (4) The passage states that the glaciers tie up about 30 percent of the world's freshwater supply. If all the glaciers melt, more freshwater will be available. Option (1) is false because the glaciers cool the air above them, so the climate would warm up. With more water available, the ocean depths would increase, and present coastal lands would be flooded; these conclusions negate options (2) and (3). The passage states that the glaciers cause great dents in the earth. Since most of the glaciers are located in mountains, option (5) is also false.

30. (1) This is a conclusion which is supported by all the other options stated.

31. (2) In warm air the molecules are farther apart from each other than in cold air. Because the molecules are farther apart, fewer molecules occupy the same amount of room. The warm air is less dense and weighs less than cold air. It will rise because it is lighter. This eliminates option (4). Option (1) is true but irrelevant. Options (3) and (5) are false, because they do not take into account the important idea of number of molecules in a given amount of room.

32. (4) How well the cups retain heat will affect how quickly the coffee cools. If one cup is a better insulator, the coffee will cool more slowly. Option (1) is incorrect because both cups contained sugar. Option (2) is unlikely if both were poured at the same time. Options (3) and (5) are irrelevant.

33. (2) The physician assumes that too much salt and cholesterol will have harmful effects. Option (1) is too generalized; it is not restricted to only salt and cholesterol. Option (3) is a true statement, but if this were assumed, the physician would not put anyone on these restrictive diets. No relationship between salt and cholesterol has been stated as option (4) concludes. If option (5) were true, he would recommend no salt-no cholesterol diets.

34. (2) This information can be read directly from the chart.

35. (2) Scallops have 225 mg salt per serving, while beef has only 55. A person on a low-salt diet should select the foods having the lower amount of salt. In options (1), (3), (4), and (5), the person has selected food with a high salt content.

36. (5) Canned tomatoes have no cholesterol but have a high salt content. Raw tomatoes have no cholesterol and are very low in their salt content. If this observation can be generalized, the canned vegetables have a higher salt content than raw ones. All other options are false statements.

37. (3) Sodium saccharin serves no purpose in the toothpaste except to make it more pleasing to the buying public. All other options indicate ingredients which carry out part of the cleansing function of the toothpaste.

38. (4) The information states that isotopes contain the same number of protons but have a different atomic weight. Mass weight = number of protons + number of neutrons. Therefore, isotopes differ in their number of neutrons. All other options are false. The number of neutrons and the atomic number in an isotope may be either larger or less than the number in the element itself.

39. (1) Only this option shows that the number of protons must remain the same. Any iodine isotope will contain 53 protons.

40. (2) Only the immunization program decreased the number of causes of whooping cough. The passage states that options (1) and (3) had no effect. Option (4) is false because isolated cases of whooping cough still occur. Option (5) is an irrelevant false statement.

41. (5) All 3 statements are indicated by the passage to be true. For Statement A, reread paragraph 5, the last sentence. Statement B is implied in paragraph 4. Statement C is restated from the last paragraph, first two sentences.

42. (2) A safer vaccine with no harmful side effects would satisfy worried parents. They would allow their children to be vaccinated, and this would make the public health authorities happy. Option (1) would not satisfy the health authorities. Options (3) and (5) would not satisfy the parents. Option (4) would solve nothing; it is irrelevant.

43. (5) Admittedly, there are risks associated with the vaccines, but the serious side effects occur in less than 1 in 100,000 or more children. Options (1)–(4) indicate reasons that the immunization program should be enforced, despite the chance of risk involved.

44. (3) This graph indicates a high number of cases in 1940 with a dramatic decline shortly after this due to the immunization program. The disease continued at very low levels in the population until 1982 when some parents stopped having their children vaccinated because of possible side effects. Between 1982 and 1985, there has been an increase in the number of cases occurring yearly. None of the other graphs accurately reflect this pattern of disease occurrence. Option (1) indicates a very gradual decrease in the number of cases between 1940 and 1985. Option (2) indicates that no decrease occurred until 1980. Option (4) is accurate to 1982 but does not indicate that recently more cases have been occurring. Option (5) indicates an erratic, unpredictable pattern over this 45-year period.

45. (2) Throughout the passage "current", "flow of electrons," and "flow of current" are used interchangeably. The small transistors study how electric current behaves, allowing only one electron to pass through at a time. All other options are incorrect.

46. (3) The passage is concerned with describing the unexpected ways electrons behaved in the tiny transistors. All other options are important in understanding why the studies were begun, but they do not indicate what the findings were or why they were of special interest.

47. (1) Reread paragraphs 3 and 4. The physicists were surprised because single electrons did not behave as they appeared to in large scale transistors. Options (2) and (3) are false because in fact the experiments are designed to measure resistance at low levels in supercooled metals which are superconductors. Option (4) is false—chips are made of silicon, and transistors are placed on chips. Option (5) is a true statement stated in paragraph 1 and is irrelevant to the experiments.

48. (5) Taste is a matter of opinion. Options (1)–(4) could be confirmed through a chemical analysis of the baby food.

49. (2) The light wave changes direction as it leaves the air and enters the water. The pencil appears to bend. This fits the definition of refraction.

50. (1) The laser beam hits the mirror and is reflected back along the same path by which it traveled.

51. (5) The waves move away in a circular pattern from their source, which is the spot where the pebble landed. Reread the definition of radiation.

52. (3) The water condensing on the bathroom mirror makes the surface uneven. Threfore, no clear image forms due to diffusion.

53. (2) As the sun's rays pass from the air through the lens in the magnifying glass, they are bent and focus the image of the sun to a small spot.

54. (4) This is an often-repeated statement, but it would be quite difficult for any scientist to verify this by experimentation. The other options all indicate facts which can be verified by fossil records or by pedigree studies.

55. (4) A fever could be documented by taking the patient's temperature, the irritated throat and runny nose by a physical examination. Blood tests could confirm a diagnosis of a viral infection. A physician cannot document a patient's complaint of tiredness.

56. (1) Velocity and speed are the same in this question. Five seconds after the objects are dropped, the ball is falling at a speed of 160 ft/sec and the suitcase is falling at a speed of 138 ft/sec. These values can be read directly from the table. All other options are false.

57. (1) The answer to this question can be arrived at in 2 different ways. From the table: During seconds 1–3, the velocity increases from 32 to 95 feet/sec as option (1) indicates. The increase is 63 ft/sec. Option (2), change is 43 ft/sec. Option (3), change is 20 ft/sec. Option (4), 4 ft/sec. Option (5), 1 ft/sec. The answer can also be seen on the graph. The slope of the graph is the steepest during seconds 1–3. After 3 seconds, the slope decreases very quickly throughout the rest of the suitcase's fall.

58. (2) The wind resistance will be greater on the larger, bulkier suitcase. The hard, compact steel ball will offer little wind resistance, and its velocity will continue to increase at the same rate throughout the whole distance to the ground. All other options are incorrect. Air pressure and gravity will be the same on the two objects disproving options (1) and (3). Option (4), starting speed, is irrelevant in this situation. According to the student's assumption, the velocity of the two objects should be the same, regardless of weight disproving option (5).

two objects should be the same, regardless of weight disproving option (5).

59. (1) Every second the velocity of the ball increases by 32 ft/sec. This can be determined by subtracting the velocity values on the table for each one-second interval. An easier way to arrive at this is to look at the graph and see that the slope of the line for the velocity of the ball does not change over the entire 11 seconds recorded. A straight line indicates a constant rate of change.

60. (5) This statement is an opinion. All other options could be verified through a chemical analysis of the beans and/or the ground coffee.

61. (2) The chart does not indicate that various medications or disease states can alter the maximum heart rate. Anyone relying on the chart assumes that at a given age, all people have the same maximum heart rate. This explains why option (4) is a correct statement but an incorrect assumption. Options (1), (3), and (5) are irrelevant.

62. (2) This option indicates that people value what is rare, and that the amount of value was determined by a certain quality, luster. All other options could be verified by scientific analysis or experimentation.

63. (1) Only option (1) summarizes the controversy that has arisen about man's history as cannibals. Current scientific techniques have raised questions about whether "cannibals" ever existed so options (2), (3), and (5) are false. Option (4) is true but does not summarize the passage.

64. (3) The passage suggests that studies using new techniques indicate that primitive societies possibly were not cannibals but were called this by their neighbors or by more advanced societies. All other options are incorrect.

65. (3) If animal and human remains were treated in exactly the same way, scientists would conclude that people were treated as animals. Option (1), (2), and (5) are considered unreliable and are not scientifically valid proof. However, they often do support scientific findings. Option (4) indicates that people were recognized as something different from animals and would not support cannibalism.

66. (1) The accusers believed that human life was very important and that only the most primitive people would invent such a practice. Options (2)–(4) place no value on human life. These people would endorse cannibalism. Option (5) is irrelevant.

Interpreting Literature and the Arts
(pages 644–652)

1. (3) The author explains that people seldom realize the power of TV. Then he goes on to explain how one day he realized it. The phrase "came home to me" is used to describe this sudden realization.

2. (3) The author's last paragraph leads you to think he would welcome this option. The other options fail to inform and are all mainly for entertainment.

3. (4) You can find the answer to this question in the last sentence of the second paragraph (lines 19–22).

4. (4) In this example of figurative language, you need to figure out how the antennas were like trees in a forest. In this case, they were similar because they stood like trees and because there were so many of them.

5. (1) Option (5) is a fact, but it is not stated in the passage. Options (2), (3), and (4) are opinions from the passage. Unlike facts, they cannot be proved or disproved.

6. (2) The author uses "I," so the passage is not suitable for a textbook or advertising campaign. Yet the subject matter and writing style are not appropriate for an autobiography or novel.

7. (5) Context clues reveal the setting. Reference to the Mississippi River indicates a midwestern location; references to steamboats and minstrels indicate the 1800s as the time.

8. (3) The meaning of *transient* can be found by using context clues. Three examples from the author's childhood are given in the sentence following the word *transient* (lines 6–12). In the next sentence the author goes on to say, "These ambitions faded out."

9. (4) Whenever anything is said to be "best," you know an opinion is being stated. This option rewords the author's opinion stated in line 23: "Pilot was the grandest position of all." Options (1), (3), and (5) are facts that can be proved. Option (2) is incorrect because, while the author says a pilot makes much more money than a preacher, he says nothing about the amount of work involved.

10. (2) The modern-day job of airline captain is most like the old job of steamboat pilot, since both steer a vehicle and travel.

11. (3) The author is reminiscing about his childhood in a pleasant, nostalgic way. The humor in the passage helps keep the tone from becoming sad, serious, or angry, but it is not so strong that he would laugh loudly.

12. (2) Although the last sentence does reflect some of the author's feelings of envy and shows that he did daydream, it is primarily a humorous exaggeration. It isn't meant to be taken seriously.

13. (3) The poem uses a figure of speech in which the poet compares the moles' lives to his own life.

14. (3) Understanding the figure of speech in the poem helps you see that the main point the poet is trying to make is expressed in option (3). Options (1), (2), and (5) give too narrow a focus, and there is no evidence to suggest option (4).

15. (1) The word *root* can mean "to dig through the earth with one's snout." That is what the moles do—dig tunnels through the sunken earth to survive.

16. (5) The mood is the feeling that the poem creates. Since the poem talks about being weighted down and burdened by sorrows, it probably makes you feel depressed.

17. (4) Throughout the passage Arkady speaks of still being Russian. In the last paragraph he says, "Please, let me go back."

18. (2) Arkady tells Irina, "You're American now. . . . You're not Russian anymore." She feels at home because she has the same beliefs and attitudes that Americans have.

19. (5) First Arkady taps his chest and says, "The longer I'm here, the more Russian I am." Then Irina says, "No" and shakes her head angrily.

20. (1) This answer can be found in the last paragraph: "I'm not as brave as you are. . . ."

21. (3) Arkady tells Irina he is a "former Party member and chief investigator." None of the other questions is answered in the passage.

22. (1) You can tell from the details that the story is partly about two lovers who cannot remain together. That is usually a sad situation.

23. (2) The passage is a dialogue between two characters. That pattern of writing is often found in novels but not in articles, letters, editorials, or essays.

24. (4) Tom admits that he and Amanda "had dark ulterior motives." Tom invited the man to dinner, but it was really only an excuse for him to meet Laura.

25. (3) Since an oyster cannot talk at all, Amanda is saying that Tom is not eloquent when she compares him to one. There is no evidence in the passage to suggest options (2), (4), or (5).

26. (4) Tom comes right out and says Laura seems lovely and sweet because Amanda and he love her. Then he goes on to show concern because she is so shy and is considered peculiar.

27. (1) The topic is the subject that is talked about. Although each of the options is discussed in the passage, Laura's personality is the *main* topic of discussion.

28. (5) Tom tells Amanda that she must not expect too much of Laura when the guest comes for dinner. He then explains how "terribly shy" she is in the eyes of strangers. So if Laura acted in an outgoing manner, Tom would most likely be quite surprised.

29. (5) The statement and the conversation following it reveal that Amanda knows Laura is crippled but is uncomfortable facing the fact. Although the statement gives information and indicates some disagreement between Amanda and Tom, its primary effect is to reveal Amanda's feelings.

30. (2) The first four paragraphs describe what the speaker did to learn to read. Options (1) and (5) are incorrect because "Mr. Muhammad's teachings" refer to books he was learning from, not to actual classes.

31. (1) Details in the last paragraph suggest the speaker had time to do a lot of reading. All the other options are contradicted by details in the passage.

32. (3) The different details in the passage point to the idea that the speaker taught himself to read well, and that helped free his mind. Options (1) and (2) give too narrow a focus, option (4) doesn't include the idea of *how* he became free, and option (5) is never stated or suggested.

33. (3) You would usually expect a prisoner to feel the *opposite* of free. When you read a word where you would expect its opposite, you are reading irony.

34. (4) Details of the speaker's own experience suggest that he would support classes in which adults are given the chance to learn to read. Since he thought reading was desirable, he probably would not approve of book censorship, so option (3) is incorrect. The passage doesn't suggest how the speaker would feel about options (1), (2), or (5).

35. (5) The speaker is an ex-convict, and the "I" used throughout suggests an autobiography, a book written by someone about his or her own life. The passage is too personal for a manual, but too formal for a letter to a friend, so options (3) and (4) are incorrect.

36. (2) In the first paragraph, the author compares the story line of *The Fantasticks* to that of *Romeo and Juliet,* a classic play by William Shakespeare.

37. (4) The second paragraph says the play defied "bored critics." The fourth paragraph says the reviews were "tepid" for a while until the musical became a legend. Option (1) is contradicted in the first paragraph; options (2) and (3) in the fourth paragraph, and option (5) in the fifth paragraph.

38. (5) The second paragraph points out that the musical is a big success even with only a piano and harp as instrumentation. All the other opinions cannot be supported from *The Fantasticks.*

39. (1) The plot is what happens in the story, and the best idea of what the story is about is in the first paragraph. Although the last paragraph gives some musical lyrics, they do not tell you much about the plot.

40. (4) The author praises Noto's work and Noto as both a producer and actor, pointing out what a success *The Fantasticks* is. Option (3) is incorrect because, while the author says that the musical's success surprised many, she gives reasons for it: good acting, universality, an appealing story line.

41. (2) The poet is obviously in a sleeping car on a train, and the last two lines state that he is deliberately staying awake during the night to watch the scenery.

42. (5) The words "rush into a rain" give you a feeling of speed. The other lines do not give a feeling of the train's rapid motion. Usually the poet describes what he sees or what he is doing.

43. (1) This option is best because the train is going west and because the poet mentions mountain passes, gullies, ravines, lakes, and rain.

44. (5) Although the poet speaks of his love of the land, the mood is not really romantic. The vivid details presented, the rhyme and rhythm of the poem, and the feeling of speed show the poet's excitement about what he sees. This feeling is one that the reader also picks up as he reads through the poem.

45. (3) The last two lines explain that the poet is deliberately staying up through the night because he loves the land he is watching. What is said in each of the other options is incorrect.

Mathematics
(pages 653–661)

1. (5) $30.00

Multiply $2.00 by the number of liters in 4 gallons.
$\frac{\$2.00}{\text{liter}} \times 4(3.78) = \$30.24$ or, to the nearest dollar, $30.

2. (3) 25.12

Use the formula $C = \pi d$.
$C = 3.14 \times 8 = 25.12$ ft

3. (1) 10

Usually, solving the equation will be faster than trying all the options until you find one that isn't a solution.
$2x > 19$

$\frac{2x}{2} > \frac{19}{2}$

$x > \frac{19}{2}$

4. (3) 5.02695×10^2

In scientific notation, the first nonzero digit goes to the left of the decimal point, so the first part is 5.02695. Since we moved the decimal point to the *left* 2 places, use +2 for the exponent (positive exponents make the number large again). The scientific notation is 5.02695×10^2.

5. (5) Insufficient data

You don't know how many history students there were.

6. (4) 70

Note that two sides have the same length, 8 ft, so this is an isosceles triangle. Therefore, angles *B* and *C* are equal.

7. (4) $31,488

Their income each month is $1,329 + $1,295, so their income each year is 12 times as much.
12 ($1,329 + $1,295) =
12 ($2,624) = $31,488

8. (1) 0.2%

The number of bottles in the store doesn't affect the *percentage* of defective bottles. If 2 of every 1,000 break, $2/1{,}000 = 0.2\%$ is the probability that any bottle leaks.

9. (5) 17

Note that $2y$ appears in both equations making substitution for $2y$ easy. Since $2y = -12$.
$x + 2y = 5$
$x + (-12) = 5$
$x = 17$

10. (2) 14

The perimeter of a 10½ ft square is 4(10½). Convert to yards.
$$\frac{4(10\frac{1}{2})}{3} = \frac{42}{3} = 14$$

11. (2) 3

$8.4 \div 2.8 = 3$

12. (3) 39.9

Add the monthly totals for both cities, then subtract.

12.2	11.1	72.4
13.5	6.4	−32.5
15.7	8.1	39.9
11.7	3.6	
9.1	2.5	
+ 10.2	+ 0.8	
72.4	32.5	

13. (5) June

Compare the vertical columns of the table. June had the most rainfall—59.9 inches.

14. (5) $13x + 15y$

$3(2x + 5y) + 7x =$
$3(2x) + 3(5y) + 7x =$
$6x + 15y + 7x =$
$13x + 15y$

15. (4) $5.44

The value of 4 pennies is .04 dollars or 4 cents. The number of nickels is $3 \times 4 = 12$, so the value of the nickels is 12(5) = 60 cents. The number of dimes is $4 \times 12 = 48$, so the value of the dimes is 48 (10) = 480 cents. The total value is 4 + 60 + 480 cents or $5.44.

16. (3) 28

Use the formula $A = bh$.
$A = 2 \times 7 = 14$
Since 1 lb covers 0.5 sq ft, multiply the area of the garden by 0.5. $14 \times 0.5 = 28$ lb

17. (4) $\sqrt{34}$

There are two ways to solve this problem. The simpler method is to make a triangle from the points on the grid and use the Pythagorean Theorem to solve for the hypotenuse.

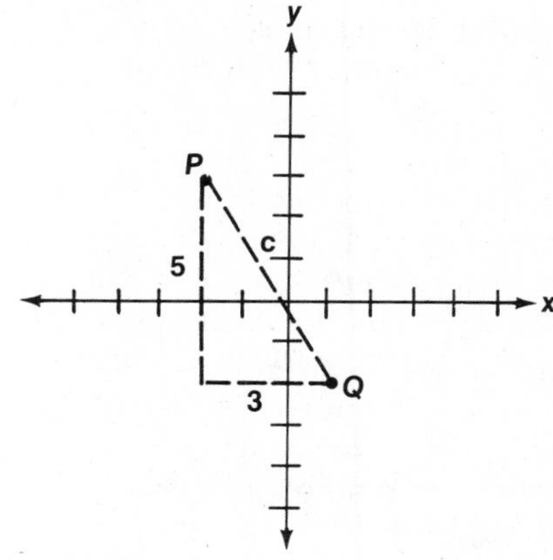

$a^2 + b^2 = c^2$
$5^2 + 3^2 = c^2$
$25 + 9 = \sqrt{34}$
$\sqrt{34} = c$
Or you can use the distance formula for finding the distance between two points in a plane.
$d = \sqrt{(x_2 - x_1)^2 + (y_2 - y_1)^2}$
where (x_1,y_1) and (x_2,y_2) are points on a plane.
$d = \sqrt{(-2 - 1)^2 + (3 - (-2))^2}$
as Point *P* is (−2,3) and Point *Q* is (1,−2).
$d = \sqrt{3^2 + 5^2}$
$d = \sqrt{9 + 25} = \sqrt{34}$

18. (1) $-\frac{5}{3}$

Use the slope formula for $P(-2,3)$ and $Q(1,-2)$.
$$m = \frac{y_2 - y_1}{x_2 - x_1}$$
$$m = \frac{3 - (-2)}{-2 - 1}$$
$$m = \frac{3 + 2}{-3} = -\frac{5}{3}$$

19. (3) 7%

Their interest amount is \$741 − 650 or \$91 for 2 years, so the amount for one year is \$91/2 = \$45.5. To find the rate of interest per year, divide the amount of interest by the amount borrowed.

$\frac{\$45.5}{\$650} = .07$ or 7%

20. (4) 20

Substitute the values for the variables.

$\frac{1}{2}a - 3b + 2b^2 =$

$\frac{1}{2}(12) - 3(-2) + 2(-2)^2 =$

$6 + 6 + 2(4) =$

$6 + 6 + 8 =$

20

21. (4) $\frac{2(3.00) + 4.50 + 6(4.00)}{2 + 1 + 6}$

Divide the amount Alice spent by the number of yards she bought to get the average cost per yard. Alice spent 2(3.00) + 4.50 + 6(4.00) dollars and the number of yards is 2 + 1 + 6. So the average cost is

$\frac{2(3.00) + 4.50 + 6(4.00)}{2 + 1 + 6}$

22. (2) 6

Since $\overline{BD}$ cuts $\overline{AC}$ in half, take half of 6 to find the length of $\overline{AD}$, 3 in. Then use the formula for area of a triangle, $A = \frac{1}{2}bh$.

$A = \frac{1}{2}(3)\,4$

$A = \frac{1}{2}\,12$

$A = 6$

23. (4) \$800

John paid back 100% of the loan plus 6% interest, so John paid 106% of the cost of the furniture.

$(1.06)x = \$848$

$x = \frac{\$848}{1.06}$

$x = \$800$

24. (4) \$6.56

$(1\frac{1}{3})(\$4.92) = \frac{4}{\cancel{3}}(\cancel{\$4.92})$ [1.64]

$= 4(1.64)$

$= 6.56$

25. (4) 3 and −1

You can factor this quadratic equation as follows:

$x^2 - 2x - 3 = 0$

$(x - 3)(x + 1) = 0$

$(x - 3) = 0$

$x = 3$

$(x + 1) = 0$

$x = -1$

26. (2) $\sqrt{\frac{A}{\pi}}$

$A = \pi r^2$

$\frac{A}{\pi} = r^2$

$\sqrt{\frac{A}{\pi}} = r$

27. (4) 13.5

Let one side be x. Then the other sides are $2x$ and $3x$.

$x + 2x + 3x = 27$

$6x = 27$

$x = 4.5$

Since $3x$ is the longest side, it is 3(4.5) ft = 13.5

28. (4) 16.8

Seven workdays is 7 × 8 = 56 hours .30 × 56 = 16.8 hours

29. (4) 2

The time on machines A and B is 12% + 13% = 25% or ¼. In an 8-hour day, this is ¼ × 8 = 2 hours.

30. (3) \$100

Each case of oil costs \$40/12, so 30 cases cost

$30\left(\frac{\$40}{12}\right) = \frac{1{,}200}{12} = \$100$

31. (3) 140

Angle A is the supplement of 40°, so $A = 180° - 40° = 140°$.

32. (1) 40°

Angle B and the 40° angle are vertical angles, so they are equal.

33. (1) 40

Angle C and the 40° angle are corresponding angles because lines L and M are parallel. Therefore angle C is 40°.

34. (4) 33

First change the window measurements from inches to feet, then find the area by using the formula $A = lw$

36 inches = 3 ft

66 inches = $5\frac{1}{2}$ ft

The area of the *two* windows is (note trick in multiplying):

$2 \times 3 \times 5\frac{1}{2} = 6 \times (5 + \frac{1}{2})$

$= 6(5) + 6\,(\frac{1}{2})$

$= 30 \times 3$

$= 33$ sq ft

35. (4) 1,005

You must subtract the area of the umbrella pole hole from the area of the table top. First, convert the diameter of the table from feet to inches. Use the formula $A = \pi r^2$ to find the area of the table and the umbrella hole.

Area of the umbrella hole:

$A = \pi r^2$

$A = 3.14 \times (2)^2$

$A = 3.14 \times 4$

$A = 12.56$

Area of the table:

$A = \pi r^2$

$A = 3.14 \times (18)^2$

$A = 3.14 \times 324$

$A = 1{,}017.36$

```
     3 24
     3.14
   1 2 96
   3 2 4
  97 2
 1,017.36
```

Subtract areas:

```
 1,017.36
 − 12.56
 1,004.80
```

Round up to 1,005

36. (4) There are 300,000 more employees in Occupation B.

Note that the vertical scale is in *thousands.* Find the vertical line for 1980. For occupation B, there are about 500,000, or about 300,000 more than the 200,000 employees in Occupation A.

37. (3) about 4 times as many

For 1990, about 800,000 are in Occupation B, and about 200,000 are in A.

38. (2) 13

Each layer has $3 \times 4 = 12$ lamps, so there are $2 \times 12 = 24$ lamps in each crate.

$\frac{310}{24} = 12.9$ but 13 crates will be *needed.*
One crate will not be full.

39. (5) 40

This problem is like going from -30 to $+10$ on a number line. The change is $10-(-30) = 40$.

40. (3) 16

The median is the middle number. Put the ages in order of youngest to oldest:
5, 11, 16, 34, 37
The middle number is 16.

41. (4) $2,000

Find 10% of her yearly income.
0.10 × \$20,000 = \$2,000
Sarah's total contribution for the year is:
\$100 + \$200 + 12(\$150) =
\$100 + \$200 + \$1,800 =
\$2,100
0.10 × \$2,100 = \$210
Sarah can deduct \$2,000 or \$210 from her income tax. She chooses the larger amount, \$2,000.

42. (4) $2,160

She contributed \$150 a month to the college last year.

12(150) = \$1,800
If she increases her contribution by 20%

.2(1,800) = 360
360 + 1,800 = 2,160

43. (3) 49,037

The hands on the first, fourth, and fifth dials are between two numbers, so choose the smaller number. The second and third dials clearly indicate 9 and 0.

44. (5) Insufficient data

You do not know how many books fit on each shelf.

45. (5) $30,240

Mrs. Pash's monthly salary is 110% of Mr. Pash's, or 1.10 × \$1,200 = \$1,320. Their combined monthly salary is \$1,200 + \$1,320 = \$2,520. Their income for one year is 12(\$2,520) = \$30,240.

46. (2) 3 or -2

To solve a quadratic equation, always try to factor. If factoring works, it's easier than using the quadratic formula.
$x^2 - x + 6 = 0$
$(x - 3)(x + 2) = 0$
Then $x - 3 = 0$ or $x + 2 = 0$,
so $x = 3$ or $x = -2$.

47. (5) 62.8

Use the formula $V = \pi r^2 h$.
$V = 3.14(2)^2 5$
$V = 12.56 \times 5$
$V = 62.8$ cu in

48. (4) 1,440

First, change 2 hours to seconds:

$2 \text{ hr} = 2 \not{\text{hr}} \times \frac{60 \not{\text{min}}}{1 \not{\text{hr}}} \times \frac{60 \text{ sec}}{1 \not{\text{min}}} = 7{,}200 \text{ sec}$
Next find how many periods of 30 sec this is:
$\frac{7{,}20\not{0}}{3\not{0}} = \frac{720}{3} = 240$ periods
In each period, 6 holes are punched, so the number of holes is
$6 \times 240 = 1{,}440$ holes.

49. (2) 5.12

Put the numbers in order from least to greatest amount.

50. (3) 34

$a = 30$ ft

$b = 16$ ft

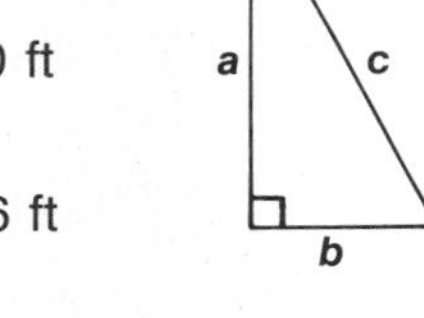

Use the Pythagorean Theorem. The length of the ladder is c.

$c^2 = (30)^2 + (16)^2$
$c^2 = 900 + 256$
$c^2 = 1{,}156$
$\sqrt{c} = \sqrt{1{,}156}$
$c = 34$

51. (2) 60 miles

Since each inch represents 25 miles, 2.4 inches represents 2.4 × 25 = 60 miles. You may also set up a proportion like this:
$\frac{1 \text{ inch}}{25 \text{ mi}} = \frac{2.4 \text{ inch}}{x \text{ miles}}$

52. (4) $86.25

Use the formula $A = ½bh$ to find the area of the triangular shelf.

$A = \frac{1}{2}(10 \times 5)$
$A = 25$ sq in
25 × \$1.15 = \$28.75,
the cost of one shelf
\$28.75 × 3 = \$86.25 for three shelves

53. (5) 161

If 8 were left over, the number of diners must be 8 *more* than 17 × 9. So $17 \times 9 + 8 = 153 + 8 = 161$.

54. (2) $\frac{x}{4}$

"One-fourth as many as Fred" is $\frac{1}{4}x$ or $\frac{x}{4}$.

55. (2) 50%

The number of mothers *present* is $\frac{1}{4} \times 28 = 7$. The total number of parents present is $18 + 7 = 25$. Since the number of parents who are members is $22 + 28 = 50$, the percent of parents who attended is $\frac{25}{50} = 50\%$.

56. (1) $7\frac{2}{5}$

To find an average of 5 numbers, add them and then divide by 5.

$5\frac{1}{2} + 6\frac{1}{4} + 7\frac{3}{4} + 8\frac{1}{2} + 9$
$= 5\frac{2}{4} + 6\frac{1}{4} + 7\frac{3}{4} + 8\frac{2}{4} + 9$
$= 35\frac{8}{4} = 37$
Then $37 \div 5 = 7.4$ or $7\frac{2}{5}$.

Answer Key—Posttest A

Writing Skills

1. (5)
2. (2)
3. (5)
4. (1)
5. (4)
6. (4)
7. (3)
8. (2)
9. (2)
10. (4)
11. (1)
12. (5)
13. (1)
14. (1)
15. (5)
16. (2)
17. (3)
18. (1)
19. (5)
20. (2)
21. (4)
22. (4)
23. (1)
24. (3)
25. (1)
26. (2)
27. (4)
28. (4)
29. (5)
30. (4)
31. (5)
32. (5)
33. (3)
34. (5)
35. (2)
36. (4)
37. (4)
38. (4)
39. (5)
40. (4)
41. (5)
42. (3)
43. (3)
44. (4)
45. (3)
46. (1)
47. (2)
48. (3)
49. (3)
50. (2)
51. (5)
52. (3)
53. (3)
54. (3)
55. (4)

Social Studies

1. (4)
2. (2)
3. (2)
4. (1)
5. (4)
6. (5)
7. (5)
8. (4)
9. (2)
10. (1)
11. (1)
12. (3)
13. (5)
14. (3)
15. (5)
16. (2)
17. (4)
18. (3)
19. (4)
20. (3)
21. (1)
22. (3)
23. (1)
24. (3)
25. (2)
26. (4)
27. (3)
28. (5)
29. (5)
30. (2)
31. (2)
32. (5)
33. (3)
34. (1)
35. (4)
36. (4)
37. (2)
38. (3)
39. (5)
40. (4)
41. (4)
42. (5)
43. (5)
44. (4)
45. (4)
46. (5)
47. (4)
48. (3)
49. (3)
50. (1)
51. (2)
52. (5)
53. (1)
54. (2)
55. (2)
56. (1)
57. (5)
58. (3)
59. (2)
60. (1)
61. (2)
62. (2)
63. (4)
64. (5)

Science

1. (3)
2. (1)
3. (1)
4. (1)
5. (3)
6. (1)
7. (1)
8. (4)
9. (2)
10. (4)
11. (2)
12. (3)
13. (1)
14. (5)
15. (4)
16. (5)
17. (1)
18. (4)
19. (1)
20. (2)
21. (2)
22. (1)
23. (3)
24. (5)
25. (1)
26. (5)
27. (3)
28. (4)
29. (4)
30. (1)
31. (2)
32. (4)
33. (2)
34. (2)
35. (2)
36. (5)
37. (3)
38. (4)
39. (1)
40. (2)
41. (5)
42. (2)
43. (5)
44. (3)
45. (2)
46. (3)
47. (1)
48. (5)
49. (2)
50. (1)
51. (5)
52. (3)
53. (2)
54. (4)
55. (4)
56. (1)
57. (1)
58. (2)
59. (1)
60. (5)
61. (2)
62. (2)
63. (1)
64. (3)
65. (3)
66. (1)

Interpreting Literature and the Arts

1. (3)
2. (3)
3. (4)
4. (4)
5. (1)
6. (2)
7. (5)
8. (3)
9. (4)
10. (2)
11. (3)
12. (2)
13. (3)
14. (3)
15. (1)
16. (5)
17. (4)
18. (2)
19. (5)
20. (1)
21. (3)
22. (1)
23. (2)
24. (4)
25. (3)
26. (4)
27. (1)
28. (5)
29. (5)
30. (2)
31. (1)
32. (3)
33. (3)
34. (4)
35. (5)
36. (2)
37. (4)
38. (5)
39. (1)
40. (4)
41. (2)
42. (5)
43. (1)
44. (5)
45. (3)

Mathematics

1. (5)
2. (3)
3. (1)
4. (3)
5. (5)
6. (4)
7. (4)
8. (1)
9. (5)
10. (2)
11. (2)
12. (3)
13. (5)
14. (5)
15. (4)
16. (3)
17. (4)
18. (1)
19. (3)
20. (4)
21. (4)
22. (2)
23. (4)
24. (4)
25. (4)
26. (2)
27. (4)
28. (4)
29. (4)
30. (3)
31. (3)
32. (1)
33. (1)
34. (4)
35. (4)
36. (4)
37. (3)
38. (2)
39. (5)
40. (3)
41. (4)
42. (4)
43. (3)
44. (5)
45. (5)
46. (2)
47. (5)
48. (4)
49. (2)
50. (3)
51. (2)
52. (4)
53. (5)
54. (2)
55. (2)
56. (1)

Finding Your Scores

Follow the same method for finding your scores that you did for the Pretest at the beginning of this book. Find the number of questions you answered correctly by crossing out the numbers on the Answer Key on page 677 of all the questions you answered incorrectly or did not answer at all.

Count how many questions you answered correctly on each test and write the number in the first column of the chart below, next to the name of that test.

Correct Answers	Test	Number of Correct Answers Needed for a Standard Score of											Your Standard Score
		25	30	35	40	45	50	55	60	65	70	75	
	Writing Skills — Multiple Choice	12	14	17	23	29	35	39	45	50	52	54	
	Writing Skills — *Essay	2	3	4	5	6	7	8	9	10	11	12	
	Social Studies	11	15	19	26	34	43	49	54	58	61	63	
	Science	12	14	19	24	31	38	46	53	58	61	64	
	Literature and the Arts	8	10	14	20	27	32	37	41	42	43	44	
	Mathematics	10	12	17	23	29	35	41	46	51	53	55	

*See page 679 for an explanation of how to determine your essay score.

Turn back to pages 4–5 of this book to the table listing the minimum scores for passing the GED Test required in your state. Check your standard scores against those requirements. See if your score on any one test is below the minimum score allowed. If it is, you probably will have difficulty with that subject in the actual GED Test. Study that subject section again where your score is low and take the Minitests one more time, carefully reading the answer explanations for those answers you miss.

If your scores on the Posttest are only a few points higher than the minimum required score for each test in your state, or if your score on any one test is below the minimum average score for all five tests, it would be a good idea to review that subject.

Scoring Your Essay If you're in a GED class, your teacher will be able to score your essay holistically, the way the GED Testing Service will have it scored. (See page 156. in the *Writing Skills* section for an explanation of holistic scoring if you haven't read that section yet.)

If you're studying by yourself, on the other hand, you will again need someone to help score your essay. It could be the same person who scored your Pretest essay. The person you choose will not be able to score your Posttest essay holistically because holistic scoring requires a period of training and guidance by an expert. However, if the two of you use the following method, you should be able to determine a score for your essay that will come close to what a holistic score would be.

First have your scorer preview the checklist below before you give him or her your essay to score.

Essay Scoring Checklist

To the scorer: Preview this entire checklist before you read and score the essay.

Read the essay topic on page 604. Next, read the essay written on that topic *quickly*. Take no more than two minutes. Try to achieve an overall impression of the writing. Then put the essay aside and, without referring back to it, rate it using the following checklist and scale. Six represents the highest score, one the lowest.

	1	2	3	4	5	6
Message— the presence of a clear, controlling idea	☐	☐	☐	☐	☐	☐
Details— the use of examples and specific details to support the message	☐	☐	☐	☐	☐	☐
Organization— a logical presentation of ideas	☐	☐	☐	☐	☐	☐
Expression— the clear, precise use of language to convey the message	☐	☐	☐	☐	☐	☐
Mechanics— knowledge of the conventions of standard English (grammar, punctuation, and so on)	☐	☐	☐	☐	☐	☐

Now take the checklist and find your score using this method: For each mark in a column, add the number of points at the top of the column. Your total should be from 5 to 30. Then multiply that total by $\frac{2}{5}$. That will give you your final essay score on a scale of from 2 to 12. Now find that score on the chart on page 678.

Posttest B

TEST 1: WRITING SKILLS POSTTEST

Directions

The Writing Skills Posttest consists of 55 multiple-choice questions and an essay. It is intended to measure your ability to use clear and effective English. It is a test of English as it is usually written, not as it might be spoken. Specific directions are given at the beginning of each part. Read these directions carefully before you begin.

You should take approximately 75 minutes to complete the multiple-choice questions. There is no penalty for guessing. Try to answer as many questions as you can. Work rapidly but carefully, without spending too much time on any one question. If a question is too difficult for you, skip it and come back to it later.

For each answer, mark one answer space.

EXAMPLE

The intelligens of computers is different from that of human beings.

What correction should be made to this sentence?

(1) change the spelling of intelligens to intelligence   
(2) change is to are
(3) change the spelling of different to diffrent
(4) insert a comma after that
(5) no correction is necessary

The correct answer is (1); therefore, answer space (1) has been marked.

You should take no more than 45 minutes to complete the essay section of the test. You can use a separate sheet of paper for writing your essay.

Answers to the questions are in the Answer Key on page 767. Explanations for the answers and a sample essay are on pages 752–755.

Part I

Directions: The following items are based on paragraphs that contain numbered sentences. Some of the sentences contain errors in sentence structure, usage, or mechanics. A few sentences, however, are correct as written. Read each paragraph and then answer the items based on it. For each item, choose the answer that would result in the most effective writing of the sentence or sentences. The best answer must be consistent with the meaning and tone of the rest of the paragraph.

Items 1–9 refer to the following passage.

(1) Many Americans are joining the fitness movement that is sweeping the country. (2) Blind and partially sighted people can also enjoy vigorous physical activity. (3) By learning cross-country skiing during week-long programs called Ski for Light. (4) Ski for Light is an exciting and unique program, it provides a week when experienced sighted skiers teach blind people to ski. (5) The goal of Ski for Light is to teach blind people an activity they can enjoy with sighted as well as blind friends'. (6) Blind skiers in this unusual program ranges in age from 18 to 72. (7) During this week of skiing fun, a volunteer Ski for Light guide uses accurate verbal descriptions of the terrain and skiing techniques to teach each blind skier. (8) At first, guides spend much of their time alerting the new cross-country skiers to changes in slopes upcoming trees, or turns. (9) Later, as the new skiers gain confidence, the guides can spend more time describing the beautiful winter scenery to their blind companions. (10) In many cities, organizations have been formed that also pair blind and sighted participants in many vigorous outdoor warm-whether activities. (11) Many of these sports clubs will have planned such activities as tandem biking, white-water rafting, swimming, and hiking. (12) Blind people and their sighted guides, through forming a partnership based on a love of outdoor athletic activities, can also participate in the move toward physical fitness.

1. Sentences 2 and 3: **Blind and partially sighted people can also enjoy vigorous physical activity. By learning cross-country skiing during week-long programs called Ski for Light.**

   Which of the following is the best way to write the underlined portion of these sentences? If you think the original is the best way, choose option (1).

   (1) activity. By learning
   (2) activity; by learning
   (3) activity by learning
   (4) activity, by learning
   (5) activity; however, by learning

   ① ② ③ ④ ⑤

2. Sentence 4: **Ski for Light is an exciting and unique program, it provides a week when experienced sighted skiers teach blind people to ski.**

   Which of the following is the best way to write the underlined portion of this sentence? If you think the original is the best way, choose option (1).

   (1) program, it provides
   (2) program, and it provides
   (3) program. Because it provides
   (4) program. It provides
   (5) program and

   ① ② ③ ④ ⑤

GO ON TO THE NEXT PAGE.

3. Sentence 5: **The goal of Ski for Light is to teach blind people an activity they can enjoy with sighted as well as blind friends'.**

   What correction should be made to this sentence?

   (1) insert so after activity
   (2) insert a comma after activity
   (3) replace they with you
   (4) insert a comma after enjoy
   (5) change friends' to friends

   (1) (2) (3) (4) (5)

4. Sentence 6: **Blind skiers in this unusual program ranges in age from 18 to 72.**

   What correction should be made to this sentence?

   (1) change skiers to Skiers
   (2) insert a comma after program
   (3) change ranges to range
   (4) change ranges to ranged
   (5) no correction is necessary

   (1) (2) (3) (4) (5)

5. Sentence 8: **At first, guides spend much of their time alerting the new cross-country skiers to changes in slopes upcoming trees, or turns.**

   What correction should be made to this sentence?

   (1) remove the comma after first
   (2) change spend to spending
   (3) insert a comma after slopes
   (4) insert a comma after or
   (5) no correction is necessary

   (1) (2) (3) (4) (5)

6. Sentence 9: **Later, as the new skiers gain confidence, the guides can spend more time describing the beautiful winter scenery to their blind companions.**

   What correction should be made to this sentence?

   (1) remove the comma after confidence
   (2) change spend to spends
   (3) change winter to Winter
   (4) replace their with there
   (5) no correction is necessary

   (1) (2) (3) (4) (5)

7. Sentence 10: **In many cities, organizations have been formed that also pair blind and sighted participants in many vigorous outdoor warm-whether activities.**

   What correction should be made to this sentence?

   (1) remove the comma after cities
   (2) change have to has
   (3) replace that with who
   (4) insert a comma after blind
   (5) change the spelling of whether to weather

   (1) (2) (3) (4) (5)

8. Sentence 11: **Many of these sports clubs will have planned such activities as tandem biking, white-water rafting, swimming, and hiking.**

   What correction should be made to this sentence?

   (1) insert a comma after clubs
   (2) change will have planned to plan
   (3) remove the comma after rafting
   (4) change hiking to hikes
   (5) no correction is necessary

   (1) (2) (3) (4) (5)

9. Sentence 12: **Blind people and their sighted guides, through forming a partnership based on a love of outdoor athletic activities, can also participate in the move toward physical fitness.**

   If you rewrote sentence 12 beginning with

   Through a partnership based on a love of outdoor athletic activities,

   the next words should be

   (1) blind people
   (2) the participation
   (3) physical fitness
   (4) getting a blind person
   (5) can also

   (1) (2) (3) (4) (5)

GO ON TO THE NEXT PAGE.

Items 10–18 refer to the following passage.

(1) In the early 1900s, a child of working parents were either locked in a room at home all day or left to wander in the streets. (2) Today day-care centers are commonplace. (3) Thanks to the pioneering work of Jane Addams, one of the most well-known social reformers of this century. (4) She was responsible for many welfare laws for workers, such as an eight-hour workday for women, factory safety inspections, and workmen's compensation. (5) She rented Hull House in 1889 and started the first social settlement house in America. (6) Jane Addams was interested in helping people from all walks of life and put her ideas for social reform into practical use. (7) For the many immigrants arriving in Chicago at the turn of the century she was indispensable in helping with job placement, English language lessons, and cultural adjustment. (8) Jane Addams was one of the founders of the National Association for the Advancement of Colored People, she also campaigned for woman suffrage. (9) In 1912 the suffragettes asked her to become a candidate for president of the United States, but she declined. (10) She works tirelessly for world peace and famine relief during World War I. (11) For her efforts to bring about world peace through disarmament and to free the world from hunger, she recieved the Nobel Peace Prize in 1931. (12) She invented social work and social welfare, and many people called her the greatest living American woman of her time.

10. Sentence 1: **In the early 1900s, a child of working parents were either locked in a room at home all day or left to wander in the streets.**

Which of the following is the best way to write the underlined portion of this sentence? If you think the original is the best way, choose option (1).

(1) parents were either
(2) parents was either
(3) parents either
(4) parents be either
(5) parents been either

1 2 3 4 5

11. Sentences 2 and 3: **Today day-care centers are commonplace. Thanks to the pioneering work of Jane Addams, one of the most well-known social reformers of this century.**

Which of the following is the best way to write the underlined portion of this sentence? If you think the original is the best way, choose option (1).

(1) commonplace. Thanks
(2) commonplace, and thanks
(3) commonplace; thanks
(4) commonplace thanks
(5) commonplace, but thanks

12. Sentence 6: **Jane Addams was interested in helping people from all walks of life and put her ideas for social reform into practical use.**

If you rewrote sentence 6 beginning with

Interested in helping people from all walks of life,

the next words should be

(1) Jane Addams
(2) her ideas
(3) social reform
(4) practical use
(5) her reforms

1 2 3 4 5

GO ON TO THE NEXT PAGE.

13. Sentence 7: **For the many immigrants arriving in Chicago at the turn of the century she was indispensable in helping with job placement, English language lessons, and cultural adjustment.**

What correction should be made to this sentence?

(1) change the spelling of immigrants to immigrance
(2) change Chicago to chicago
(3) insert a comma after century
(4) change century to Century
(5) change language to Language

(1) (2) (3) (4) (5)

14. Sentence 8: **Jane Addams was one of the founders of the National Association for the Advancement of Colored People, she also campaigned for woman suffrage.**

What correction should be made to this sentence?

(1) change was to were
(2) change founders to Founders
(3) remove the comma after People
(4) insert the word and before she
(5) change the spelling of campaigned to campained

(1) (2) (3) (4) (5)

15. Sentence 9: **In 1912 the suffragettes asked her to become a candidate for president of the United States, but she declined.**

What corrrection should be made to this sentence?

(1) insert the word who after suffragettes
(2) change asked to would ask
(3) change candidate to Candidate
(4) remove the comma after States
(5) no correction is necessary

(1) (2) (3) (4) (5)

16. Sentence 10. **She works tirelessly for world peace and famine relief during World War I.**

What correction should be made to this sentence?

(1) change works to worked
(2) insert a comma after peace
(3) replace and with or
(4) insert a comma after relief
(5) no correction is necessary

(1) (2) (3) (4) (5)

17. Sentence 11: **For her efforts to bring about world peace through disarmament and to free the world from hunger, she recieved the Nobel Peace Prize in 1931.**

What correction should be made to this sentence?

(1) insert a comma after efforts
(2) replace through with threw
(3) replace to free with freeing
(4) change the spelling of recieved to received
(5) no correction is necessary

(1) (2) (3) (4) (5)

18. Sentence 12: **She invented social work and social welfare, and many people called her the greatest living American woman of her time.**

Which of the following is the best way to write the underlined portion of this sentence? If you think the original is the best way, choose option (1).

(1) welfare, and
(2) welfare, although
(3) welfare; and
(4) welfare, but
(5) welfare, yet

(1) (2) (3) (4) (5)

GO ON TO THE NEXT PAGE.

Items 19–27 refer to the following passage.

(1) There are times when almost everyone has wanted to call the president either to complain about a policy decesion or to give him some encouragement. (2) Who takes all those calls from, for example kings, queens, celebrities, schoolchildren, and average citizens? (3) Eighteen female, and two male operators control the old-fashioned switchboard in the Old Executive Office Building adjacent to the White House. (4) On a normal day, the operators handle fifty thousand calls. (5) Of the calls they handle, thirty thousand are for the president. (6) The number doubles during emergencies. (7) The switchboard was flooded on the day Elvis Presley died, with calls from people suggesting that his birthday be made a national holiday. (8) Like the canadian Mounties, the White House operators are known for "getting their man," or woman, as the case may be. (9) They are famous for tracking down anyone either the president or the first lady want to reach. (10) They find them on ski slopes, on boats in the middle of the ocean, or on a barge floating down a river in France. (11) In 1908, the monthly phone bill is only $28.87, but today it averages $45,000.00 a month. (12) There is one thing, though, that the White House operators don't do they never accept collect calls.

19. Sentence 1: **There are times when almost everyone has wanted to call the president either to complain about a policy decesion or to give him some encouragement.**

    What correction should be made to this sentence?

    (1) change are to is
    (2) remove the word has
    (3) change the spelling of decesion to decision
    (4) change the spelling of decesion to desision
    (5) change the spelling of encouragement to encouragment

    (1) (2) (3) (4) (5)

20. Sentence 2: **Who takes all those calls from, for example kings, queens, celebrities, schoolchildren, and average citizens?**

    What correction should be made to this sentence?

    (1) change takes to take
    (2) insert a comma after example
    (3) change kings to Kings
    (4) change the spelling of citizens to citisens
    (5) no correction is necessary

    (1) (2) (3) (4) (5)

21. Sentence 3: **Eighteen female, and two male operators control the old-fashioned switchboard in the Old Executive Office Building adjacent to the White House.**

    What correction should be made to this sentence?

    (1) remove the comma after female
    (2) replace and with but
    (3) replace two with too
    (4) insert a comma after male
    (5) no correction is necessary

    (1) (2) (3) (4) (5)

22. Sentences 4 and 5: **On a normal day, the operators handle fifty thousand calls. Of the calls they handle, thirty thousand are for the president.**

    The most effective combination of sentences 4 and 5 would include which of the following groups of words?

    (1) thirty thousand of which
    (2) operators handle thirty thousand
    (3) fifty thousand, or thirty thousand
    (4) fifty thousand calls; however,
    (5) handle calls for the president

    (1) (2) (3) (4) (5)

GO ON TO THE NEXT PAGE.

23. Sentence 7: **The switchboard was flooded on the day Elvis Presley died, with calls from people suggesting that his birthday be made a national holiday.**

If you rewrote sentence 7 beginning with

When Elvis Presley died,

the next words should be

(1) flooding the switchboard
(2) with calls
(3) the switchboard
(4) a national holiday
(5) his birthday

① ② ③ ④ ⑤

24. Sentence 8: **Like the canadian Mounties, the White House operators are known for "getting their man," or woman, as the case may be.**

What correction should be made to this sentence?

(1) change canadian to Canadian
(2) remove the comma after Mounties
(3) insert a comma after operators
(4) change known to knowed
(5) replace their with there

① ② ③ ④ ⑤

25. Sentence 9: **They are famous for tracking down anyone either the president or the first lady want to reach.**

Which of the following is the best way to write the underlined portion of this sentence? If you think the original is the best way, choose option (1).

(1) want to reach
(2) wants to reach
(3) wanted to reach
(4) want to have reached
(5) had wanted to reach

① ② ③ ④ ⑤

26. Sentence 11: **In 1908, the monthly phone bill is only $28.87, but today it averages $45,000.00 a month.**

What correction should be made to this sentence?

(1) remove the comma after 1908
(2) change is to was
(3) remove the word but
(4) replace but with for
(5) no correction is necessary

① ② ③ ④ ⑤

27. Sentence 12: **There is one thing, though, that the White House operators don't do they never accept collect calls.**

Which of the following is the best way to write the underlined portion of this sentence? If you think the original is the best way, choose option (1).

(1) don't do they
(2) don't do, yet they
(3) don't do, even though they
(4) don't do. They
(5) don't do, they

① ② ③ ④ ⑤

GO ON TO THE NEXT PAGE.

Items 28–36 refer to the following passage.

(1) Do you dream of a romantic vacation in Hawaii? (2) In a recent survey, 19 million Americans chose Hawaii as their dream vacation spot. (3) Its soft climate, scenic mountains palm-fringed beaches, and clear blue water appeal to many visitors. (4) For many Americans, Hawaii possesses the glamour of a foriegn country. (5) Just think about all the things one can do in this land of aloha hospitality. (6) Diamond Head is Hawaii's most famous landmark, and it is an extinct volcanic crater that can be climbed for a stunning view of Waikiki. (7) The turquoise water of Hanauma bay attracts visitors wishing to snorkel or swim in the underwater park. (8) If you are adventurous, you can ride the big breakers at the Banzai Pipeline. (9) Or learn the unique dance of Hawaii, the hula. (10) Shoppers dressed in colorful cotton shirts or brightly flowered muumuus can browse in the 155 stores of the Ala Moana shopping mall. (11) The air of Hawaii is filled with the fragrance of exotic tropical flowers, and the sky abounds in rainbows, which are as commonplace as orchids. (12) All these things, plus the friendliness of its people, makes beautiful Hawaii the vacation destination of more than 4 million tourists a year.

28. Sentence 2: **In a recent survey, 19 million Americans chose Hawaii as their dream vacation spot.**

Which of the following is the best way to write the underlined portion of this sentence? If you think the original is the best way, choose option (1).

(1) Americans chose Hawaii
(2) Americans had chose Hawaii
(3) Americans will have chosen Hawaii
(4) Americans have chosen Hawaii
(5) Americans choose

(1) (2) (3) (4) (5)

29. Sentence 3: **Its soft climate, scenic mountains palm-fringed beaches, and clear blue water appeal to many visitors.**

What correction should be made to this sentence?

(1) replace Its with It's
(2) insert a comma after mountains
(3) insert a comma after water
(4) change appeal to appeals
(5) replace to with too

(1) (2) (3) (4) (5)

30. Sentence 4: **For many Americans, Hawaii possesses the glamour of a foriegn country.**

What correction should be made to this sentence?

(1) remove the comma after Americans
(2) change the spelling of possesses to posesses
(3) change the spelling of foriegn to foreign
(4) change country to Country
(5) no correction is necessary

(1) (2) (3) (4) (5)

31. Sentence 5: **Just think about all the things one can do in this land of aloha hospitality.**

Which of the following is the best way to write the underlined portion of this sentence? If you think the original is the best way, choose option (1).

(1) things one can do
(2) things you do
(3) things you can do
(4) things they can do
(5) things one does

(1) (2) (3) (4) (5)

GO ON TO THE NEXT PAGE.

32. Sentence 6: **Diamond Head is Hawaii's most famous landmark, and it is an extinct volcanic crater that can be climbed for a stunning view of Waikiki.**

If you rewrote sentence 6 beginning with

Hawaii's most famous landmark, Diamond Head,

the next word should be

(1) is
(2) and
(3) it
(4) can
(5) that

① ② ③ ④ ⑤

33. Sentence 7: **The turquoise water of Hanauma bay attracts visitors wishing to snorkel or swim in the underwater park.**

What correction should be made to this sentence?

(1) change bay to Bay
(2) insert a comma after bay
(3) change the spelling of attracts to attracks
(4) replace wishing with which wish
(5) replace swim with go swimming

① ② ③ ④ ⑤

34. Sentences 8 and 9: **If you are adventurous, you can ride the big breakers at the Banzai Pipeline. Or learn the unique dance of Hawaii, the hula.**

Which of the following is the best way to write the underlined portion of these sentences? If you think the original is the best way, choose option (1).

(1) pipeline. Or learn
(2) pipeline, or learn
(3) pipeline or learn
(4) pipeline or to learn
(5) pipeline; or, learn

① ② ③ ④ ⑤

35. Sentence 11: **The air of Hawaii is filled with the fragrance of exotic tropical flowers, and the sky abounds in rainbows, which are as commonplace as orchids.**

What correction should be made to this sentence?

(1) insert which after Hawaii
(2) remove the comma after flowers
(3) replace and with but
(4) change abounds to abounded
(5) no correction is necessary

① ② ③ ④ ⑤

36. Sentence 12: **All these things, plus the friendliness of its people, makes beautiful Hawaii the vacation destination of more than 4 million tourists a year.**

What correction should be made to this sentence?

(1) remove the comma after things
(2) replace its with it's
(3) remove the comma after people
(4) change makes to make
(5) change the spelling of beautiful to beutiful

① ② ③ ④ ⑤

GO ON TO THE NEXT PAGE.

Items 37–45 refer to the following passage.

(1) As a child, did you ever collect butterflies, stamps, or baseball cards? (2) One woman, knowen as the Hubcap Queen, began her collecting as an adult. (3) It all started in Tennessee when she needed a hubcap for her car. (4) She noticed many hubcaps lying along the side of the road, but began picking them up hoping to find a match for her missing hubcap. (5) At home, she cleaned them and hanged them on the garage walls. (6) People were fascinated by her unusual hobby, and they brought her hubcaps they had found. (7) People enjoyed looking at all the different kinds of hubcaps hanging in long rows along the walls. (8) Soon her collection grew too large for the walls of the garage, so she moved them to the old barn behind her house. (9) Before the move, someone occasionally asks to buy a hubcap, but she always replied that she could not part with any of her shiny friends. (10) However, it took so long to move them all to the barn that she knew it was time to sell a few. (11) Now when people ask to by her hubcaps, she happily sells them at a fair price. (12) Her unusual hobby has become a small but profitable business.

37. Sentence 2: **One woman, knowen as the Hubcap Queen, began her collecting as an adult.**

What correction should be made to this sentence?

(1) change the spelling of woman to women
(2) remove the comma after woman
(3) change the spelling of knowen to known
(4) change began to begun
(5) no correction is necessary

1 2 3 4 5

38. Sentence 3: **It all started in Tennessee when she needed a hubcap for her car.**

What correction should be made to this sentence?

(1) change Tennessee to tennessee
(2) replace when with because
(3) insert a comma after Tennessee
(4) change needed to will need
(5) no correction is necessary

1 2 3 4 5

39. Sentence 4: **She noticed many hubcaps lying along the side of the road, but began picking them up hoping to find a match for her missing hubcap.**

Which of the following is the best way to write the underlined portion of this sentence? If you think the original is the best way, choose option (1).

(1) road, but began
(2) road but began
(3) road and began
(4) road, and began
(5) road so began

1 2 3 4 5

40. Sentence 5: **At home, she cleaned them and hanged them on the garage walls.**

What correction should be made to this sentence?

(1) change cleaned to had cleaned
(2) insert a comma after them
(3) replace and with or
(4) change hanged to hung
(5) no correction is necessary

1 2 3 4 5

GO ON TO THE NEXT PAGE.

41. Sentence 6: **People were fascinated by her unusual hobby, and they brought her hubcaps they had found.**

Which of the following is the best way to write the underlined portion of this sentence? If you think the original is the best way, choose option (1).

(1) hobby, and they brought
(2) hobby because they brought
(3) hobby and they brought
(4) hobby, for they brought
(5) hobby, and brought

(1) (2) (3) (4) (5)

42. Sentence 8: **Soon her collection grew too large for the walls of the garage, so she moved them to the old barn behind her house.**

What correction should be made to this sentence?

(1) change grew to grown
(2) replace too with to
(3) replace so with even though
(4) replace so with but
(5) replace them with the hubcaps

(1) (2) (3) (4) (5)

43. Sentence 9: **Before the move, someone occasionally asks to buy a hubcap, but she always replied that she could not part with any of her shiny friends.**

Which of the following is the best way to write the underlined portion of this sentence? If you think the original is the best way, choose option (1).

(1) asks to buy
(2) asked to buy
(3) asking to buy
(4) asks to be buying
(5) will ask to buy

(1) (2) (3) (4) (5)

44. Sentence 10: **However, it took so long to move them all to the barn that she knew it was time to sell a few.**

If you rewrote sentence 10 beginning with

However, moving them all to the barn took so long

the next word should be

(1) that
(2) she
(3) it
(4) so
(5) to

(1) (2) (3) (4) (5)

45. Sentence 11: **Now when people ask to by her hubcaps, she happily sells them at a fair price.**

What correction should be made to this sentence?

(1) change ask to asked
(2) replace by with buy
(3) remove the comma after hubcaps
(4) change the spelling of happily to happly
(5) replace fair with fare

(1) (2) (3) (4) (5)

GO ON TO THE NEXT PAGE.

Items 46–55 refer to the following passage.

(1) Each year, Americans spend about $85 billion to buy more than 17 million used cars. (2) If you are buying a used car, the Federal Trade Commission's Used Car Rule may have helped you. (3) The rule requires all used-car dealers to place a large sticker a document called a "Buyers Guide," in the window of each used vehicle being offered for sale. (4) Whenever you purchase a used car from a dealer, you should receive the original or a copy of the Buyers Guide that apeared in the window of the vehicle you bought. (5) To help avoid desception, the Buyers Guide must reflect any changes in warranty coverage that you may negotiate with the dealer. (6) Dealers are required to post the Buyers Guide on all used vehicles, including used automobiles, light-duty vans, and light-duty trucks. (7) A "used vehicle" is one that has been driven more than the distance necessary to deliver a new car to the dealership or to test drive it. (8) "Demonstrator" cars are covered by the rule, motorcycles are excluded. (9) A major portion of the Buyers Guide gives you important information you can use when you select a used car. (10) In the past, lack of information and misunderstanding about warranties frequently was sources of consumer problems. (11) If dealers offer a warranty on a used vehicle, he must fill in the warranty portion of the Buyers Guide. (12) The Buyers Guide also contains useful information about manufacturers' warranties; it contains information about spoken promises; it also contains information on service contracts and consumer complaints.

46. Sentence 2: **If you are buying a used car, the Federal Trade Commission's Used Car Rule <u>may have helped you</u>.**

    Which of the following is the best way to write the underlined portion of this sentence? If you think the original is the best way, choose option (1).

    (1) may have helped you
    (2) had helped you
    (3) helped you
    (4) may help you
    (5) will have helped you

47. Sentence 3: **The rule requires all used-car dealers to place a large <u>sticker a document called</u> a "Buyers Guide," in the window of each used vehicle being offered for sale.**

    Which of the following is the best way to write the underlined portion of this sentence? If you think the original is the best way, choose option (1).

    (1) sticker a document called
    (2) sticker, a document called
    (3) sticker a document, called
    (4) sticker. A document called
    (5) sticker; a document called

48. Sentence 4: **Whenever you purchase a used car from a dealer, you should receive the original or a copy of the Buyers Guide that apeared in the window of the vehicle you bought.**

    What correction should be made to this sentence?

    (1) replace <u>Whenever</u> with <u>Since</u>
    (2) remove the comma after <u>dealer</u>
    (3) replace <u>you should</u> with <u>one should</u>
    (4) replace <u>that</u> with <u>which</u>
    (5) change the spelling of <u>apeared</u> to <u>appeared</u>

49. Sentence 5: **To help avoid desception, the Buyers Guide must reflect any changes in warranty coverage that you may negotiate with the dealer.**

    What correction should be made to this sentence?

    (1) change the spelling of <u>desception</u> to <u>deception</u>
    (2) remove the comma after <u>desception</u>
    (3) insert a comma after <u>coverage</u>
    (4) change <u>negotiate</u> to <u>negotiated</u>
    (5) no correction is necessary

GO ON TO THE NEXT PAGE.

50. Sentence 6: **Dealers are required to post the Buyers Guide on all used vehicles, including used automobiles, light-duty vans, and light-duty trucks.**

What correction should be made to this sentence?

(1) change are to is
(2) change are to be
(3) remove the comma after automobiles
(4) insert a comma after and
(5) no correction is necessary

① ② ③ ④ ⑤

51. Sentence 8: **"Demonstrator" cars are covered by the rule, motorcycles are excluded.**

What correction should be made to this sentence?

(1) change cars are to cars is
(2) change are covered to covered
(3) remove the comma after rule
(4) insert but after the comma
(5) change motorcycles to Motorcycles

① ② ③ ④ ⑤

52. Sentence 9: **A major portion of the Buyers Guide gives you important information you can use when you select a used car.**

Which of the following is the best way to write the underlined portion of this sentence? If you think the original is the best way, choose option (1).

(1) use when
(2) use even when
(3) use even if
(4) use because
(5) use once

① ② ③ ④ ⑤

53. Sentence 10: **In the past, lack of information and misunderstanding about warranties frequently was sources of consumer problems.**

What correction should be made to this sentence?

(1) remove the comma after past
(2) insert a comma after information
(3) change was to are
(4) change was to were
(5) change consumer to Consumer

① ② ③ ④ ⑤

54. Sentence 11: **If dealers offer a warranty on a used vehicle, he must fill in the warranty portion of the Buyers Guide.**

Which of the following is the best way to write the underlined portion of this sentence? If you think the original is the best, choose option (1).

(1) he
(2) it
(3) they
(4) you
(5) one

① ② ③ ④ ⑤

55. Sentence 12: **The Buyers Guide also contains useful information about manufacturers' warranties; it contains information about spoken promises; it also contains information on service contracts and consumer complaints.**

If you rewrote sentence 12 beginning with

Useful information about manufacturers' warranties, spoken promises, service contracts, and consumer complaints

the next word should be

(1) are
(2) is
(3) contain
(4) contains
(5) containing

① ② ③ ④ ⑤

GO ON TO THE NEXT PAGE.

Part II

Directions: This is a test to find out how well you write. The test has one question that asks you to present an opinion on an issue or to explain something. In preparing your answer for this question, you should take the following steps:

1. Read all of the information accompanying the question.
2. Plan your answer carefully before you write.
3. Use scratch paper to make any notes.
4. Write your answer.
5. Read carefully what you have written and make any changes that will improve your writing.
6. Check your paragraphing, sentence structure, spelling, punctuation, capitalization, and usage, and make any necessary corrections.

You will have 45 minutes to write on the question you are assigned. Write legibly and use a ballpoint pen.

Stress is a part of everyday life, and for many people it is increasing. Write a composition of 200 words that discusses the ways people deal with stress. You can discuss the negative ways, the positive ways, or both. Give examples, and be specific.

END OF EXAMINATION

TEST 2: SOCIAL STUDIES POSTTEST

Directions

The Social Studies Posttest consists of 64 multiple-choice questions. Some of the questions are based on maps, graphs, charts, cartoons, and short reading passages—all related to the social studies. Read the passage or study the material first and then answer the questions following it. You may refer to these materials as often as necessary to answer the questions. You will find that some of the questions will require considerable deliberation and frequent rereading of the passage or reexamination of the material presented.

This is in part a test of your background of general knowledge in the social studies, but it is also a "study test," that is, a test of your ability to understand the important meanings in what you see and read. In general, the test will not penalize you seriously for having forgotten many of the detailed facts you once knew, if you have retained the important generalizations and are able to use them intelligently.

You should take approximately 1½ hours to complete this test. There is no penalty for guessing. Try to answer as many questions as you can. Work rapidly but carefully, without spending too much time on any one question. If a question is too difficult for you, omit it and come back to it later.

For each answer, mark one answer space. See how the following example is done.

EXAMPLE

Zoning laws are passed by local governments to ensure the orderly development of land and property. Zoning boards divide cities into zones that group together similar uses. For example, there might be one zone for homes, another for business, another for industry, and so on. Certain types of construction are allowed in some zones but not in others.

According to the passage, which of the following cases would come under local zoning laws?

(1) A driver must pay toll charges to use a state highway.
(2) A property owner must pay taxes to the state.
(3) A mountainous region in Colorado is designated a wilderness area by the U.S. Department of the Interior.
(4) A homeowner must pay for garbage pickup.
(5) A department store wants to expand by building an addition.

① ② ③ ④ ●

Options (1), (2), and (3) concern state or national governments not local ones. Option (4) does not relate to zoning laws, but to sanitation. Only option (5), which involves construction, relates to zoning laws. Answer space (5) has been marked.

Answers to the questions are in the Answer Key on page 767. Explanations for the answers are on pages 755–758.

Directions: Choose the one best answer to each question.

1. Country X is highly industrialized and has a large GNP. It has skilled workers, trained managers, and the technology to produce goods ranging from electronic components to giant oceangoing tankers. The amount of usable farmland in Country X, however, is limited. Food production cannot meet the needs of the country's large population.

   Based on the information above, which of the following would you expect to be true of Country X?

   (1) Farmers are poorly trained.
   (2) Food products make up a large portion of its imports.
   (3) Food products are heavily taxed.
   (4) Managers and workers in industry are poorly fed.
   (5) Capital is in short supply.

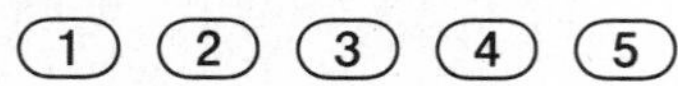

Reprinted by permission: Tribune Media Services

2. What does this cartoonist believe is true about the world's population?

   (1) The world's population will soon reach five billion.
   (2) It is unlikely that the world population will reach five billion.
   (3) The earth's resources cannot adequately support a population of five billion.
   (4) No matter what the world's population, the earth has the resources to support it.
   (5) Hunger and overcrowding should be eliminated now that the world's population has reached five billion.

(1) (2) (3) (4) (5)

Items 3–6 are based on the following information.

Listed below are five terms commonly used to describe a person's or group's political beliefs.

(1) liberal—favors legislative reform of the existing social, economic, or political system, prefers federal over state and local governments, and believes that government should regulate the economy

(2) conservative—wishes to maintain the existing social, political, or economic order, prefers local or state over federal government, and opposes government regulation of the economy

(3) left, left-wing—wants major changes in the existing order by either legislative reform or revolution. Usually pursues a more equal society by taking power from the rich and redistributing it to the general population

(4) right, right-wing—strongly opposes any change, especially of a liberal nature, and seeks to maintain, sometimes by force, the existing distribution of power

(5) reactionary—supports political or social change that represents a return to an earlier period

Decide which political view is best expressed in each of the following situations.

3. The military government of a Latin American country jails a newspaper editor for an article criticizing the government's inaction in the face of widespread poverty in the countryside.

   (1) liberal
   (2) conservative
   (3) left, left-wing
   (4) right, right-wing
   (5) reactionary

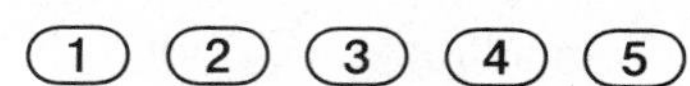

GO ON TO THE NEXT PAGE.

4. A candidate for the national assembly of a European nation declares that, if elected, she will work to reduce government regulation of the banking industry and restrictions on free trade.

   (1) liberal
   (2) conservative
   (3) left, left-wing
   (4) right, right-wing
   (5) reactionary

   (1) (2) (3) (4) (5)

5. A U.S. congressman proposes that the federal government fund and operate job training centers in cities with the highest unemployment.

   (1) liberal
   (2) conservative
   (3) left, left-wing
   (4) right, right-wing
   (5) reactionary

   (1) (2) (3) (4) (5)

6. During its first week in power, the revolutionary government of a small African country announces it will begin programs for free schooling, free health care, and land reform.

   (1) liberal
   (2) conservative
   (3) left, left-wing
   (4) right, right-wing
   (5) reactionary

   (1) (2) (3) (4) (5)

Items 7–8 are based on the article below.

In an experiment, hospitalized army and navy veterans of World War II were exposed to a repetitive gong, sounding at the rate of about 100 percussions a minute. This signal had been used as a call to battle stations aboard U.S. Navy ships during the war. When the navy veterans heard the gong, their nervous systems—the part that warns us of danger—quickly went into action. They became jumpy and nervous and charged up—even though 15 years had passed since this stimulus had signaled danger. The army veterans, however, showed little response. They had never been called to battle stations this way.

7. Which of the following is the most likely explanation of why the Navy veterans responded nervously to the gong stimulus?

   (1) In the past, the stimulus had signaled danger.
   (2) The veterans believed they were being called to battle stations.
   (3) The veterans were hospitalized for nervous disorders.
   (4) The response to a stimulus is never forgotten.
   (5) Repetitive sounds make many people nervous.

   (1) (2) (3) (4) (5)

8. Which of the following statements best describes what the experiment showed?

   (1) Soldiers should try to forget as much about their war experiences as possible.
   (2) Hospitals should be kept quiet because patients get nervous and jumpy when unexpected loud noises occur.
   (3) Responses to certain stimuli are retained after the response is necessary.
   (4) The armed forces have developed special signals to alert combat soldiers.
   (5) Navy veterans remembered their battle instructions better than army veterans.

   (1) (2) (3) (4) (5)

GO ON TO THE NEXT PAGE.

Items 9–13 are based on the map below.

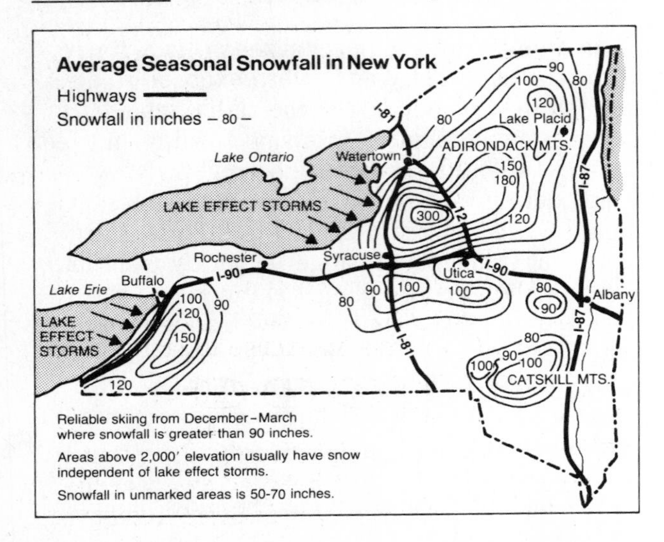

9. According to this map, which of the following will have reliable skiing from December through March?
   (1) Utica
   (2) Lake Placid
   (3) Watertown
   (4) Rochester
   (5) Albany

   (1) (2) (3) (4) (5)

10. What appears to be one result of lake effect storms?
    (1) They have prevented human settlement along the shores of the Great Lakes.
    (2) Their effect on weather is less than was previously believed.
    (3) They cause heavier snowfalls in the mountains than along the shorelines.
    (4) They contribute to heavy snowfalls on the shoreline directly in their path.
    (5) They prevent shipping on the Great Lakes after March.

    (1) (2) (3) (4) (5)

11. Based on the map, which of the following is a fact as opposed to an opinion?
    (1) There is usually better skiing at Lake Placid than in the Catskill Mountains.
    (2) Between December and March, deep snow often closes Highway I-90 between Buffalo and Syracuse.
    (3) Storms coming off the Great Lakes have little effect on snowfall in New York.
    (4) Lake-effect storms coming off Lake Ontario are less severe than those off Lake Erie.
    (5) The mean seasonal snowfall in Lake Placid is at least 100 inches.

    (1) (2) (3) (4) (5)

12. Which of the following statements is best supported by information on the map?
    (1) The economy of New York is heavily dependent on the winter sports industry.
    (2) The heavy snowfalls of northern New York prevent the building of a major highway through that region.
    (3) Lake-effect storms probably contribute to two of the state's areas of greatest snowfall, while elevation probably contributes to the other two.
    (4) In New York, the highest point above sea level is in the middle of the triangle made by Watertown, Utica, and Syracuse.
    (5) Skiing in the Catskill Mountains is not reliable between December and March.

    (1) (2) (3) (4) (5)

13. Which of the following groups could NOT make use of the information on this map?
    (1) skiers
    (2) state tourist offices
    (3) the state highway department
    (4) railroads and airlines
    (5) ships using New York City harbors

    (1) (2) (3) (4) (5)

GO ON TO THE NEXT PAGE.

Items 14–16 refer to the following passage.

Of all the events in the cold war, the Cuban missile crisis posed the most direct threat to the United States. In October of 1962, American planes discovered evidence that Soviet-built missiles were being installed on the island of Cuba. Americans were not accustomed to living with any military threat just 90 miles from their border. President Kennedy had to choose between risking war with the Soviet Union or allowing hostile weapons in America's backyard. He decided to surround Cuba with a naval blockade to halt approaching Soviet ships. For six terrifying days, the entire world waited and watched as Soviet ships steamed toward Cuba and a huge American invasion force gathered in Florida. Then, to the great relief of everyone involved, the Soviet ships turned around. The crisis finally ended when the Soviets agreed to dismantle the missiles already in place in Cuba. In return, the United States agreed not to invade the island.

14. Why was the Cuban missile crisis particularly upsetting to the United States?

    (1) Americans were opposed to stationing troops in Florida.
    (2) Hostile weapons were positioned close to U.S. borders.
    (3) Soviet missiles in Cuba caused the cold war.
    (4) Cuban planes were flying over Florida.
    (5) President Kennedy was young and inexperienced.

    (1) (2) (3) (4) (5)

15. In deciding to blockade Cuba, President Kennedy and his advisers must have believed that the approaching Soviet ships

    (1) brought the means to complete the Cuban missile bases
    (2) brought food and medicine to the threatened Cubans
    (3) carried an invasion force to overrun Cuba
    (4) would blockade Florida
    (5) would attack U.S. ships, giving the United States an excuse to start a war

    (1) (2) (3) (4) (5)

16. In this specific crisis situation, President Kennedy must have believed which of the following principles was most important?

    (1) a willingness to cooperate
    (2) a show of strength and determination
    (3) a desire to negotiate
    (4) a demonstration of goodwill
    (5) neutrality

    (1) (2) (3) (4) (5)

GO ON TO THE NEXT PAGE.

Items 17–20 are based on the following information.

The Military Retirement Act of 1986 changed the nation's military retirement system by increasing pensions for those with 30 years of military service and reducing pensions for those who retire after only 20 years. The law applies only to those entering the armed forces after August 1, 1986, and does not effect those who were in uniform or retired before that date.

The Pentagon estimated an annual savings of $3.2 billion. Senator X, a critic of the act, claimed that the law, while saving money, would cause a military manpower shortage. "A military that cuts its people's pensions can't expect those people to stay," said the Senator.

17. The Military Retirement Act of 1986 increased pensions for those who

(1) perform 20 years of military service
(2) retire after 30 years of service
(3) were retired before August 1, 1986
(4) were in uniform before August 1, 1986
(5) volunteer for the armed services

① ② ③ ④ ⑤

18. According to the act, a member of the armed forces, retiring on August 2, 1986, with 20 years of service received

(1) increased pension benefits
(2) decreased pension benefits
(3) no change in pension benefits
(4) less in Social Security retirement benefits
(5) a larger pension than a civilian retiree

① ② ③ ④ ⑤

19. What were the probable reasons for passing this act?

(1) to encourage early retirement from the military
(2) to increase pensions for those with 20 years of service
(3) to encourage an army of volunteers rather than draftees
(4) to encourage longer military service and to save money
(5) to save money and appease the Senate

① ② ③ ④ ⑤

20. What was wrong with the Senator's conclusion?

(1) The law would not save money, as he believed.
(2) The $3.2 billion saved would go toward raising basic military pay, thus encouraging people to stay in the military.
(3) The act did not reduce the pension of anyone already in the military.
(4) A cut in basic pay, not a cut in pensions, would cause military personnel to leave.
(5) The cuts applied only to those with 30 years' service who would have retired soon anyway.

① ② ③ ④ ⑤

GO ON TO THE NEXT PAGE.

Items 21–25 refer to the following graph.

The aging of America

U.S. population by age group
in percent change from 1985-2000

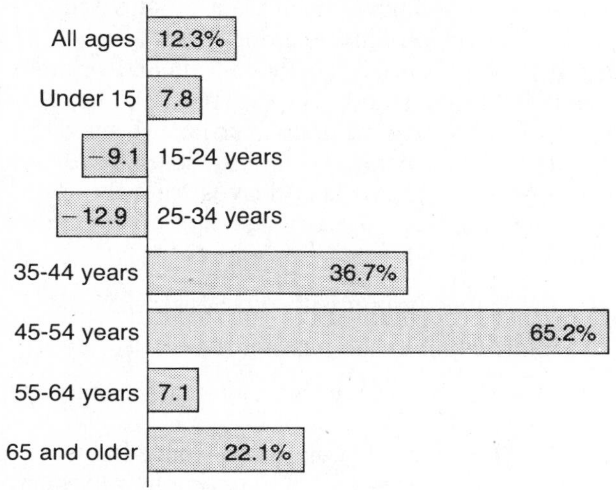

Source: American Demographics

21. According to this graph, which age group will have the greatest population increase between 1985 and 2000?

(1) 45 years and older
(2) 24 years and younger
(3) 44 years and younger
(4) 35–44 years of age
(5) 65 and older

22. Hospital administrators, deciding how best to meet the health needs of the population in the next 15 years, might infer from these statistics that hospitals should offer

(1) more therapies for drug and alcohol abuse
(2) more programs in nutrition
(3) more for the elderly services
(4) expanded emergency room
(5) fewer expensive therapies, such as organ transplants

1 2 3 4 5

23. A politician looking at this graph might conclude that, for the next decade or two, the social policy issue of most concern will be

(1) services for the handicapped
(2) Social Security retirement benefits
(3) day-care and early childhood education
(4) immigration
(5) national defense

24. Which of the following is a fact based on the graph and not a hypothesis or opinion?

(1) Between 1985 and 2000, the U.S. population is expected to increase by more than 12 percent.
(2) The number of retired people in the United States will increase between 1985 and 2000.
(3) The number of women of childbearing age will change very little in the near future.
(4) By the year 2000, the United States will spend less on education than it does now.
(5) Health care costs will increase as the U.S. population becomes older.

1 2 3 4 5

25. Which of the following statements is best supported by the information on the graph?

By the year 2000, the nation will need

(1) fewer farmers
(2) a larger percentage of teachers
(3) more doctors and other health-care workers
(4) fewer congressional representatives
(5) fewer bureaucrats

GO ON TO THE NEXT PAGE.

Items 26–27 refer to the passage below.

John D. Rockefeller was a bold and adventurous oilman. He was always ready to try new production techniques. By 1870, his Standard Oil Company of Cleveland was a major firm, and Rockefeller himself controlled about 40 percent of the oil industry. He let little stand in his way: he cut prices to eliminate competitors, made secret deals with railroads, bribed officials and politicians, and won numerous rate wars. By 1879, Rockefeller had taken over most of his competitors and controlled a full 90 percent of the industry. Soon oil prices soared. In 1882, Rockefeller capped his success by forming the Standard Oil Trust, a combination of 39 major oil companies that together controlled the production, refining, and marketing of oil in the United States.

26. Which of the following statements best summarizes the passage above?
    (1) Rockefeller's production techniques gave the oil industry its start.
    (2) Rockefeller led a fight for fair competition among the nation's growing industries.
    (3) Rockefeller succeeded in gaining a monopoly of the nation's oil industry.
    (4) Rockefeller confined his oil-industry interests to the distribution of oil products.
    (5) Rockefeller's success depended on his respect for politicians.

    (1) (2) (3) (4) (5)

27. According to the passage, what was one result of Rockefeller's almost total control of the oil industry?
    (1) Consumers paid more for oil.
    (2) Small companies controlled oil refining.
    (3) Oil prices remained steady.
    (4) Competition among oil companies became fierce.
    (5) Rate wars continued.

    (1) (2) (3) (4) (5)

Items 28–30 are based on the passage below.

People living on the island of Green Forest were bothered by an irritating skin disease. Farmer J discovered one day that rubbing fresh roots of a little-known bean plant on affected parts of his skin relieved the irritation. News of the discovery spread to other farms and communities. Merchants and townspeople were eager to acquire the new remedy. Farmer M found that bean plant yields could be doubled by fertilizing the soil with mulched leaves from the forest. News of his discovery also spread to other farms.

28. What prediction would you make from the information in the passage?
    (1) Farmers will grow only beans from now on.
    (2) The townspeople will become farmers.
    (3) More farmers will experiment with skin disease remedies.
    (4) Bean fields will be moved to forest areas.
    (5) Bean production will increase on the island.

    (1) (2) (3) (4) (5)

29. What important economic concept does this passage suggest?
    (1) law of supply and demand
    (2) recession
    (3) the business cycle
    (4) the modified market economy
    (5) industrialization and urbanization

    (1) (2) (3) (4) (5)

30. What does this passage illustrate regarding technology and productivity?
    (1) Technology in towns results in low levels of productivity.
    (2) Technology on farms decreases productivity.
    (3) Productivity and technology are unrelated.
    (4) Improved technology can increase production.
    (5) Island peoples usually have high levels of technology and productivity.

    (1) (2) (3) (4) (5)

GO ON TO THE NEXT PAGE.

Items 31–33 refer to the following information.

The Consumer Price Index (CPI) is a measure of changes in the cost of living that charts the price movements of more than 400 commodities, or goods, and services over a period of time.

Annual percentage changes for major categories of the Consumer Price Index and Producer Price Index, 1978–1985[1]

Consumer Price Index	1978	1979	1980	1981	1982	1983	1984	1985[2]
All items	9.0	13.3	12.4	8.9	3.9	3.8	4.0	3.8
Food	11.8	10.2	10.2	4.3	3.1	2.6	3.8	2.7
Energy	8.0	37.4	18.1	11.9	1.3	−.5	.2	1.8
Commodities excluding food and energy	7.6	8.8	9.9	5.9	5.8	5.0	3.1	2.1
Services excluding energy	9.4	13.6	14.1	12.9	3.4	4.8	5.6	5.7
Food and beverages	11.6	10.0	10.1	4.3	3.2	2.7	3.7	2.8
Housing	9.9	15.2	13.7	10.2	3.6	3.5	4.2	4.3
Apparel and upkeep	3.2	5.5	6.8	3.6	1.6	2.9	2.0	2.9
Transportation	7.7	18.2	14.7	11.0	1.7	3.9	3.1	2.6
Medical care	8.8	10.1	10.0	12.5	11.0	6.4	6.1	6.7
Entertainment	5.8	6.9	9.6	7.2	5.6	3.9	4.2	3.2
Other	6.4	7.9	10.1	9.8	12.1	8.0	6.1	6.3
Commodities	8.9	13.0	11.1	6.0	3.6	2.9	2.6	2.5
Services	9.3	13.7	14.2	13.0	4.3	4.8	5.4	5.1

31. Which of the following statements is not supported by the chart?

(1) In 1978, the cost of food was at its highest level.
(2) In 1981, the cost of services increased more than twice as much as the cost of commodities.
(3) In the years 1982–1985, consumer prices rose, but they rose at a slower rate than in the preceding four years.
(4) Only one item has fallen in price during the years covered by the chart.
(5) Between 1978–1985, the total price paid for services exceeded the total price paid for commodities.

(1) (2) (3) (4) (5)

32. After rising dramatically between 1978–1981, transportation costs showed only modest increases between 1982–1985. Which of the following is the most likely reason for that fact?

(1) The cost of servicing cars fell so people started driving again.
(2) The falling price of energy, which includes oil and gasoline, made transportation less expensive.
(3) In 1982, the government regulated the price of gasoline.
(4) American auto manufacturers lowered the price of new cars.
(5) Energy costs rose so dramatically that transportation ground to a halt.

(1) (2) (3) (4) (5)

33. Which of the following groups was probably hurt the most by the steeply rising prices of the late 1970s and early 1980s?

(1) students
(2) doctors
(3) Midwestern farmers
(4) retired people on fixed incomes
(5) union workers with cost-of-living clauses in their contracts

(1) (2) (3) (4) (5)

GO ON TO THE NEXT PAGE.

Items 34–37 are based on the following passage.

At the outbreak of World War II, thousands of Japanese Americans resided in the states located along America's West Coast. In a wave of concern that approached hysteria, many Americans in these states unjustifiably regarded Japanese Americans as a threat to national security.

Officials on the West Coast asked the U.S. government to move all Japanese Americans to other parts of the country. President Roosevelt authorized the immediate movement of some 112,000 persons of Japanese ancestry to relocation camps, where they were kept throughout most of the war. So sudden was this development, many Japanese Americans had to sell their homes and other property at sacrifice prices, causing financial ruin to thousands of families.

Although the loyalty of most was soon established, they were not allowed to return to their homes. Instead they were given the choice of moving to the interior of the country or joining the armed forces. About 36,000 took one of these options.

The controversy over the legality and justice of the relocation of the Japanese Americans continues even today. Some Americans view it as one of the greatest violations of civil liberties in American history. Others maintain that a wartime emergency places hardships on all Americans. According to this view, the relocation of the Japanese Americans, while probably not necessary, appeared so at the time and was therefore justified.

34. During World War II, many Japanese Americans were relocated because they were

(1) seen as a threat to national security
(2) needed in the armed forces
(3) causing financial ruin on the West Coast
(4) planning to return to Japan
(5) collaborating with the enemy

① ② ③ ④ ⑤

35. Which of the following was NOT a result of the relocation?

(1) Many Japanese Americans suffered financial ruin.
(2) Some were moved to the interior of the country.
(3) Some joined the armed forces.
(4) Most were quickly returned to their homes in West Coast states.
(5) They were kept in relocation camps throughout most of the war.

① ② ③ ④ ⑤

36. Which of the following is opinion not fact?

(1) At the outbreak of World War II, thousands of Japanese Americans resided in the states located along America's West Coast.
(2) West Coast officials asked the government to move all Japanese Americans to other areas of the country.
(3) President Roosevelt authorized the immediate transfer of 112,000 Japanese Americans to relocation camps.
(4) Many Japanese Americans had to sell their homes and other property quickly at sacrifice prices.
(5) The relocation of the Japanese Americans, while probably not necessary, appeared so at the time and was therefore justified.

① ② ③ ④ ⑤

GO ON TO THE NEXT PAGE.

37. Some Americans believe the relocation of Japanese Americans during World War II was justified. With which of the following statements would those Americans most likely agree?

    (1) There is no situation in which the violation of a U.S. citizen's civil liberties can be tolerated.
    (2) The civil liberties of U.S. citizens may be suspended during wartime emergencies.
    (3) Persons of foreign ancestry are not U.S. citizens.
    (4) The suspension of Japanese Americans' civil liberties should have been made permanent.
    (5) The protection of civil liberties and the defense of national security are of equal importance.

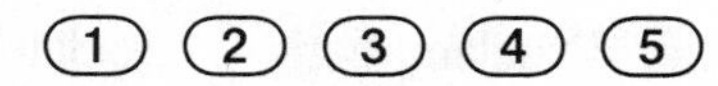

Items 38–40 are based on the following information.

A concept central to one theory of learning is that of *reinforcement.* Learning is reinforced when the stimulus that causes a response is likely to make that response occur again.

A reinforcing stimulus that gives pleasure to the subject is called a *positive reinforcement.* The subject learns that a certain behavior brings pleasure. On the other hand, a reinforcing stimulus that gives pain or displeasure is called a *negative reinforcement,* and the subject learns to avoid that behavior.

38. Which of the following is an example of positive reinforcement?

    (1) A child does poorly on a spelling test, so his father forbids him to watch television.
    (2) In an experiment, a laboratory rat learns that, when it presses a certain lever, a bell rings.
    (3) Workers on a factory assembly line are given cash bonuses whenever they increase production.
    (4) A soldier who is late reporting for duty is confined to base for the weekend.
    (5) A girl forgets to take out the trash as she was instructed, so her brother has to do it instead.

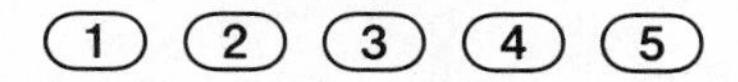

39. Which of the following is an example of negative reinforcement?

    (1) In an experiment, a pigeon learns that when it pecks a certain disk, it gets a small electric shock.
    (2) A mother promises her daughter that every time she cleans her room, she'll be allowed to go to the movies.
    (3) A daughter fails to clean her room one week, but her mother lets her go to the movies anyway.
    (4) A worker is threatened with dismissal if he's late again. He is late again and is fired.
    (5) In an experiment, a laboratory rat learns that, by pressing a lever, it receives food.

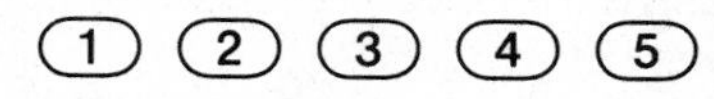

40. Positive and negative reinforcement might also be described as

    (1) peer pressure
    (2) involuntary reflex
    (3) reward and punishment
    (4) question and answer
    (5) supply and demand

GO ON TO THE NEXT PAGE.

Items 41–42 refer to the passage below.

School District 101 has a nearly $100,000 deficit, the superintendent revealed. The district's costs have risen dramatically while income, which comes almost entirely from property taxes, has not.

"It can only get worse," said the superintendent. "Figures show the district's population is increasing, so we can expect more students and increased costs. But the only way to increase income is to raise the property tax rate. I don't believe the voters will approve that," he added, "because so many of our property owners are older people without children."

41. What does the superintendent assume is true of district property owners?

    (1) They are unconcerned about their tax rate.
    (2) They are unwilling to pay for the education of other people's children.
    (3) They are moving out of the school district.
    (4) They are willing to see their taxes increased for education.
    (5) They will refuse to vote on the issue.

    (1) (2) (3) (4) (5)

42. Which of the following could the superintendent do to reduce the school district's deficit?

    (1) bus students from other district schools to District 101
    (2) offer new after-school programs for latch-key children
    (3) build another school to provide for the growing population
    (4) lay off teachers and increase the number of students per class
    (5) offer evening classes for working people

    (1) (2) (3) (4) (5)

Items 43–46 refer to the following information.

Listed below are the names and brief descriptions of five documents that are important in U.S. history.

(1) Mayflower Compact—an agreement signed by the male Pilgrim colonists to abide by a majority-rule government; the first step toward democratic government in the United States

(2) Declaration of Independence—the proclamation by the Second Continental Congress declaring the 13 American colonies independent from Great Britain

(3) Bill of Rights—the first ten amendments to the U.S. Constitution; a statement of the fundamental rights and liberties of the people of the nation

(4) Emancipation Proclamation—a proclamation by President Abraham Lincoln declaring the freedom of all slaves in territory at war with the Union

(5) Fourteenth Amendment—a change to the U.S. Constitution that gave citizenship to former slaves, provided ways to protect the rights of all citizens, canceled the three-fifths clause which determined how many representatives each state had in Congress, punished Confederate officers, and canceled Confederate debts

GO ON TO THE NEXT PAGE.

Read each quotation below and decide which of the documents it is from.

43. "Congress shall make no law respecting the establishment of religion, or prohibiting the free exercise thereof; or abridging the freedom of speech, or of the press; or the right of the people peaceably to assemble, and to petition the government for a redress of grievances."

(1) Mayflower Compact
(2) Declaration of Independence
(3) Bill of Rights
(4) Emancipation Proclamation
(5) Fourteenth Amendment

(1) (2) (3) (4) (5)

44. "We, whose names are underwritten . . . do enact, constitute, and frame, such just and equal laws, ordinances, acts, constitutions, and offices, . . . as shall be thought most meet (suitable) and convenient for the general good of the colony, unto which we promise all due submission and obedience."

(1) Mayflower Compact
(2) Declaration of Independence
(3) Bill of Rights
(4) Emancipation Proclamation
(5) Fourteenth Amendment

(1) (2) (3) (4) (5)

45. ". . . I do order and declare that all persons held as slaves within said designated States and parts of States are, and henceforward shall be, free; and that the Executive Government of the United States, including the military and naval authorities thereof, shall recognize and maintain the freedom of said persons."

(1) Mayflower Compact
(2) Declaration of Independence
(3) Bill of Rights
(4) Emancipation Proclamation
(5) Fourteenth Amendment

(1) (2) (3) (4) (5)

46. "When in the course of human events, it becomes necessary for one people to dissolve the political bands which have connected them with another, and to assume among the powers of the earth, the separate and equal station to which the laws of Nature and of Nature's God entitle them, a decent respect to the opinions of mankind requires that they should declare the causes which impel them to the separation."

(1) Mayflower Compact
(2) Declaration of Independence
(3) Bill of Rights
(4) Emancipation Proclamation
(5) Fourteenth Amendment

(1) (2) (3) (4) (5)

GO ON TO THE NEXT PAGE.

Items 47–49 refer to the following information.

Social Security
Cost of living increases

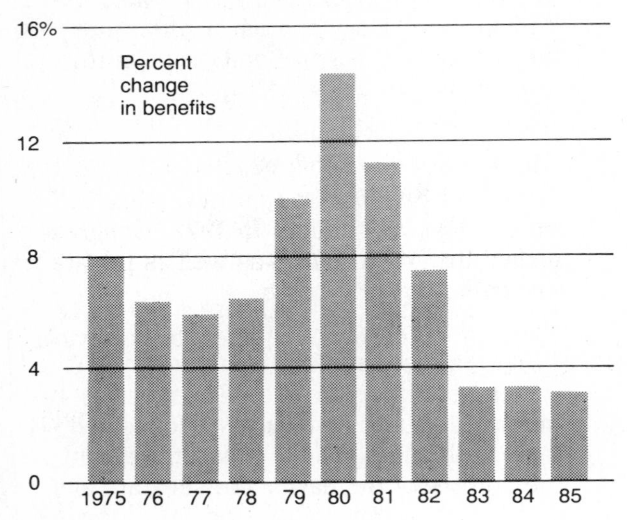

Source: Social Security Administration

A 1972 law provides for a cost-of-living adjustment (COLA) in Social Security retirement benefits when the inflation rate is three percent or more. If inflation falls below three percent, the increase is delayed until inflation rises above that level.

47. Based on the information above, which of the following is true?
    (1) Between 1975 and 1985, Social Security beneficiaries received a COLA in every year except one.
    (2) Social Security beneficiaries received almost 16 percent in cost-of-living increases in 1983.
    (3) Social Security beneficiaries received their highest COLA in 1980.
    (4) No COLA was paid in 1984.
    (5) Runaway inflation was finally brought under control beginning in 1979.

    (1) (2) (3) (4) (5)

48. If no Social Security COLA was paid in 1986, what must be true?
    (1) Consumer prices rose just three percent in 1986.
    (2) Inflation was higher than consumer prices in 1986.
    (3) Inflation was higher in 1986 than in 1985.
    (4) Since inflation increased by more than three percent in 1986, Congress must have repealed the 1972 law.
    (5) The inflation rate was less than three percent in 1986.

49. Which of the following statements is most likely true, according to the graph?
    (1) Social Security recipients did not receive a COLA in 1986.
    (2) Social Security recipients have had a COLA every year since the law was passed.
    (3) In any year when a COLA is paid, the amount of increase is three percent.
    (4) The amount of COLA paid in any year is in proportion to the amount of inflation during that year.
    (5) If the cost of living declines more than three percent in any year, Social Security benefits are reduced.

GO ON TO THE NEXT PAGE.

Items 50–52 are based on the following maps.

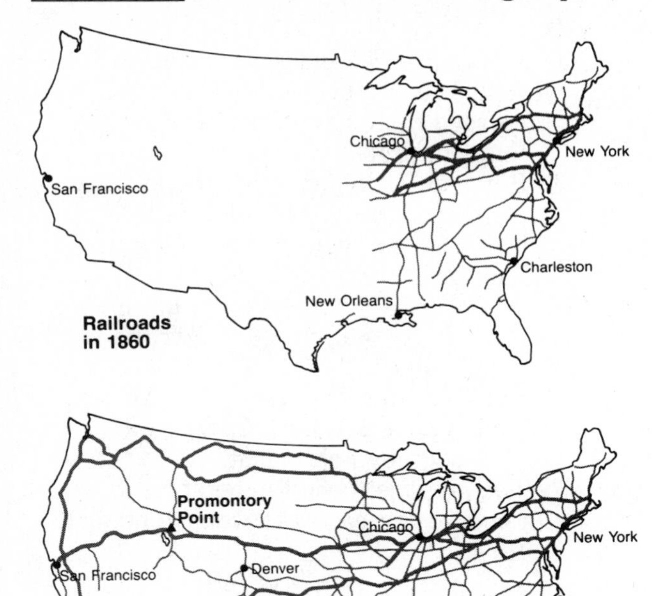

50. Based on what you see on the map of 1860, what major geographical feature was probably the western boundary of the most populous section of the country?

   (1) the Mississippi River
   (2) the Rocky Mountains
   (3) the Great Lakes
   (4) the Great Salt Lake
   (5) the Mojave Desert

   (1) (2) (3) (4) (5)

51. Which statement below is a hypothesis that could be drawn from the map?

   (1) A major railroad connected New York City and Chicago in 1860.
   (2) In 1860, one could travel by rail from New Orleans to New York.
   (3) Railroad expansion was not possible until the end of the Civil War in 1865.
   (4) In 1890, the U.S. had more than one coast-to-coast rail route.
   (5) In 1890, major railroads connected the East and West rather than the North and South.

   (1) (2) (3) (4) (5)

52. Which of the following could NOT have made use of the 1890 map?

   (1) a Texas cattle dealer
   (2) a Kansas grain farmer
   (3) the U.S. Postal Service
   (4) miners moving to California in 1849
   (5) immigrants arriving in New York harbor

   (1) (2) (3) (4) (5)

53. Title VII of the 1964 Civil Rights Act forbids job discrimination based on race, sex, national origin, or religion. In 1972, Congress applied the law to public as well as private employers.

   Which of the following appears to be a violation of Title VII?

   (1) A 55-year-old man is turned down for a job because the employer thinks he is "too old."
   (2) A black couple wanting to buy a house is shown property only in certain neighborhoods, although homes in other neighborhoods are for sale.
   (3) An Asian immigrant child who hasn't yet learned English is put into classes for slow learners.
   (4) A Mexican-American is denied a job because the employer said he "doesn't want any trouble with immigration."
   (5) A woman is fired for repeated absenteeism from the job.

   (1) (2) (3) (4) (5)

GO ON TO THE NEXT PAGE.

Items 54–57 are based on the following information.

Phoenix, Arizona, is one of the fastest growing metropolitan areas in the United States. In 1945, Phoenix had a population of 150,000; by 1984, it had grown to 1.8 million. Predictions are that, shortly after the year 2000, Phoenix will be a city of 3 million.

But the very thing that has attracted so many to Phoenix—its fine weather—is changing. Long-time residents say the weather is becoming less comfortable, certainly hotter, and they blame higher humidity (moisture in the air).

It is hotter, as the following chart demonstrates.

Summertime Temperatures in Phoenix

Decade	*Average Maximum (°F)*	*Average Minimum (°F)*	*Mean (°F)*
1940–49	104.1	72.6	88.4
1950–59	102.1	74.9	88.5
1960–69	102.8	74.1	88.5
1970–79	104.7	78.0	91.4
1980–84	104.4	80.3	92.3

But higher humidity is not a factor. Records show that, in fact, humidity is lower than it used to be. What is at fault, say scientists, is simply higher temperatures caused by the classic "heat island effect" of urban areas. Higher temperatures are the result of: (a) the ability of urban surfaces to absorb and store more radiant energy than soil or vegetation, (b) artificial heat sources, (c) low winds, and (d) the "blanket" effect of pollutants.

It is Phoenix's growth, then, and the resulting changes in land use, that have caused the city's higher, less comfortable temperatures.

54. Which of the following best summarizes the information on the chart?

(1) Between 1948 and 1984, average daytime temperatures in Phoenix have increased more than average nighttime temperatures.
(2) Between 1948 and 1984, the average mean temperature of Phoenix has increased by about four degrees Fahrenheit.
(3) The average mean temperature in Phoenix has not changed over the last four decades.
(4) Between 1980 and 1984, the average mean temperature in Phoenix was 92.3 degrees Fahrenheit.
(5) The average mean temperature in Phoenix decreased between 1960 and 1984.

1 2 3 4 5

55. Which of the following is NOT a cause of the temperature change in Phoenix?

(1) higher humidity
(2) urban surfaces
(3) artificial heat sources
(4) low winds
(5) pollutants

1 2 3 4 5

56. Which of the following is the main conclusion reached by the article?

(1) Phoenix is one of the fastest growing metropolitan areas in the United States.
(2) The thing that has attracted so many to Phoenix—its fine weather—is changing.
(3) Records show that the humidity is lower than it used to be.
(4) Higher temperatures are caused by the classic "heat island effect" of urban areas.
(5) Phoenix's growth, and the resulting changes in land use, have caused its higher, less comfortable temperatures.

GO ON TO THE NEXT PAGE.

57. Based on the information, what would you predict for Phoenix's weather?
    (1) Residents will place limits on the city's growth.
    (2) As Phoenix continues to grow, its weather will become hotter.
    (3) An increase in humidity will moderate the city's rising temperature.
    (4) City government will ask residents to limit their use of water and air conditioning.
    (5) Federal and state environmental protection agencies will curb the city's growth.

    (1) (2) (3) (4) (5)

Items 58–60 are based on the following study.

Raising the legal drinking age by one year significantly reduces the number of teenagers killed or injured in automobile accidents, according to a study at the University of Michigan.

The number of 18-year-olds seriously hurt or killed in one-vehicle accidents dropped 10.8 percent in Texas after passage of a 1981 state law raising the drinking age to 19 from 18, according to the study by the university's Transportation Research Institute. Accidents resulting in minor injury fell 14.3 percent, the study said.

The institute studied the effects of raising the drinking age to 21 from 18 in several states and found similar results. Texas raised its drinking age to 21 from 19 in 1986.

58. Lawmakers who vote to raise the legal drinking age probably believe which of the following is most important?
    (1) equal treatment of teenagers and adults
    (2) personal freedom
    (3) public safety
    (4) pedestrian safety
    (5) family responsibility

    (1) (2) (3) (4) (5)

59. According to the study, which of the following is a fact?
    (1) Raising the legal drinking age by one year will reduce the number of teenagers killed or injured in auto accidents by 10.8 percent.
    (2) Raising the legal drinking age from 18 to 21 will reduce the number of teenagers killed or injured in auto accidents by 25.1 percent.
    (3) In 1986, Texas raised its legal drinking age from 18 to 19.
    (4) After Texas raised its drinking age from 18 to 19, the number of 18-year-olds killed or seriously hurt in one-vehicle accidents in that state dropped 10.8 percent.
    (5) After Texas raised its drinking age from 18 to 19, the number of adults injured or killed in auto accidents involving teenager drivers fell by 14.3 percent.

    (1) (2) (3) (4) (5)

60. What result did Texas lawmakers expect when they raised the state's legal drinking age from 19 to 21?
    (1) Fewer people would be killed or injured in auto accidents.
    (2) The number of teenagers killed or injured in auto accidents would decrease by 10.8 percent.
    (3) Pedestrians would be safer from teens who drink and drive.
    (4) The number of teens killed or who suffered serious or minor injuries in auto accidents would fall by 14.3 percent.
    (5) The legal drinking age could be lowered once deaths and injuries from auto accidents had been reduced.

    (1) (2) (3) (4) (5)

GO ON TO THE NEXT PAGE.

Items 61–62 refer to the following passage.

The *recall,* which is a kind of "reverse election," is a way by which the people may remove public officials before the end of their term by petition and popular vote. Only thirteen states permit the recall of state officials, but it is much more widely available at the local level. The use of recall is restricted by the rather large number of signatures required on a recall petition (commonly 25 percent of the eligible voters) . . .

61. Which of the following is an example of the use of recall?
    (1) Citizens petition for a popular vote on whether to repeal a law passed by the state legislature.
    (2) The U.S. Congress votes to remove the President from office.
    (3) A city's voters petition for a vote on removing the mayor from office.
    (4) Citizens petition for a popular vote to pass a state law limiting the salaries of state employees.
    (5) A state legislature votes to raise the legal drinking age from 19 to 21 years.

    ① ② ③ ④ ⑤

62. Which of the following statements is NOT a fact, according to the passage?
    (1) The recall requires a citizens' petition, then a popular vote.
    (2) Thirty-seven states do not allow the recall of state officials.
    (3) Recall petitions commonly require the signatures of 25 percent of the eligible voters.
    (4) The only restriction on the use of recall is the large number of signatures required on the petition.
    (5) In thirteen states, the governor may be recalled by a popular vote.

    ① ② ③ ④ ⑤

Items 63–64 are based on the following passage.

Shortly after Theodore Roosevelt became President, disputes between the United Mine Workers union and mine owners closed the nation's coal mines. Roosevelt appointed a commission to work with both sides in order to settle the strike. The commission was successful. Each side was granted some but not all of its demands. This kind of settlement represented what Roosevelt later called a Square Deal. In a Square Deal, Roosevelt said, each side received what it deserved: fair treatment and consideration. Many miners felt disappointed at the outcome of their strike, but Roosevelt's actions did mark a turning point in labor history. For unlike his predecessors, Hayes and Cleveland, Roosevelt had played a role as mediator, not strikebreaker, in a labor dispute.

63. Based on the information in the passage, which of the following statements is true?
    (1) Presidents Hayes and Cleveland had tried and failed to achieve Square Deal measures in labor disputes.
    (2) Workers receiving Square Deal treatment could expect to realize all their demands.
    (3) Roosevelt used the term "Square Deal" to describe his role as strikebreaker in labor disputes.
    (4) Under Roosevelt's Square Deal, concerns of both labor and management received attention.
    (5) Roosevelt said it was a Square Deal for mine owners to feel disappointed.

    ① ② ③ ④ ⑤

64. Which of the following conclusions might be drawn from the passage?
    (1) Labor mediators represent the interests of management only.
    (2) The settlements of labor disputes after Roosevelt's administration were more orderly than they had been before.
    (3) Workers were afraid to call strikes during Roosevelt's presidency.
    (4) Roosevelt ignored labor disputes.
    (5) Mediation assures that both sides in a labor dispute receive full satisfaction.

    ① ② ③ ④ ⑤

END OF EXAMINATION

TEST 3: SCIENCE POSTTEST

Directions

The Science Posttest consists of 66 questions most of which contain reading passages. Each passage is followed by a number of multiple-choice questions related to its content. Read the passage first and then answer the questions following it. Refer to the passage as often as necessary to answer the questions.

You should take approximately 1½ hours to complete this test. There is no penalty for guessing. Try to answer as many questions as you can. Work rapidly but carefully, without spending too much time on any one question. If a question is too difficult for you, omit it and come back to it later.

For each answer, mark one answer space. See how the following example is done.

EXAMPLE

A physical change is one in which the chemical composition of a substance is not altered. A chemical change, in contrast, results in one or more new substances with different chemical makeups.

Which of the following is an example of a physical change?

(1) butter melting ● (2) 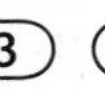  
(2) tarnish on silver
(3) gasoline being used in a car engine
(4) photographic film being developed
(5) photosynthesis in plants

The answer is "butter melting"; therefore, answer space (1) has been marked.

Answers to the questions are in the Answer Key on page 767. Explanations for the answers are on pages 758–760.

Directions: Choose the one best answer to each question.

Items 1–6 are based on the following information.

Matter can be described in terms of a number of different properties. Five properties are listed below.

(1) mole—an amount of matter containing a specific number of atoms or molecules of a substance
(2) concentration—the number of particles of a substance in a certain volume
(3) density—the weight of a certain volume of matter
(4) heat capacity—the amount of heat energy gained or lost as matter is heated or cooled
(5) equilibrium—the condition in which a chemical reaction seems to stop because the reactants and products are forming at the same rate

Each of the following items gives an example of one of the five terms defined above. For each item choose the one property that is best described by the example. Each of the terms above may be used more than once in the following set of items.

1. Forty-six grams of table salt and 272 grams of table sugar contain the same number of particles.

   The property that best explains why the salt and sugar have the same number of particles is

   (1) mole
   (2) concentration
   (3) density
   (4) heat capacity
   (5) equilibrium

   (1) (2) (3) (4) (5)

2. Hikers do very well when the air temperature is 6°C. However, if a fisherman in Alaska falls into 6°C water, he will die within 15 minutes if not rescued.

   The difference between these two situations is probably due to

   (1) mole
   (2) concentration
   (3) density
   (4) heat capacity
   (5) equilibrium

   (1) (2) (3) (4) (5)

3. One gram of styrofoam floats on water, but one gram of lead sinks in water.

   The property that accounts for this difference in the two materials is

   (1) mole
   (2) concentration
   (3) density
   (4) heat capacity
   (5) equilibrium

   (1) (2) (3) (4) (5)

4. When vinegar and baking soda are mixed together, a bubbling reaction occurs, but stops within a few seconds.

   The bubbling probably stops because of the property called

   (1) mole
   (2) concentration
   (3) density
   (4) heat capacity
   (5) equilibrium

   (1) (2) (3) (4) (5)

GO ON TO THE NEXT PAGE.

5. The owner of the fast-food drive-in discovers he can increase profits by using half the amount of syrup in 10-ounce soft drinks.

The property which is best described by the change in the amount of syrup used is

(1) mole
(2) concentration
(3) density
(4) heat capacity
(5) equilibrium

(1) (2) (3) (4) (5)

6. Water vapor rises over a pan of boiling water.

The vapor probably rises due to differences in

(1) mole
(2) concentration
(3) density
(4) heat capacity
(5) equilibrium

(1) (2) (3) (4) (5)

Items 7–8 are based on the following table.

Oceans and Seas

Name	Area (in sq mi)	Average depth (in ft)	Greatest known depth (in ft)
Pacific Ocean	64,000,000	13,215	37,782
Atlantic Ocean	31,815,000	12,880	30,246
Indian Ocean	25,300,000	13,002	24,460
Arctic Ocean	6,440,200	3,953	18,456
Mediterranean Sea[1]	1,145,100	4,688	15,197
Caribbean Sea	1,049,500	8,685	22,788
South China Sea	895,400	5,419	16,456
Bering Sea	884,900	5,075	15,659
Gulf of Mexico	615,000	4,874	12,425
Okhotsk Sea	613,800	2,749	12,001
East China Sea	482,300	617	9,126
Hudson Bay	475,800	420	600
Japan Sea	389,100	4,429	12,276
Andaman Sea	308,100	2,854	12,392
North Sea	222,100	308	2,165
Red Sea	169,100	1,611	7,254
Baltic Sea	163,000	180	1,380

1. Includes Black Sea and Sea of Azov.

7. Which body of water has no point as deep as 1,000 feet?

(1) Atlantic Ocean
(2) Baltic Sea
(3) East China Sea
(4) Hudson Bay
(5) Caribbean Sea

(1) (2) (3) (4) (5)

8. Which one of the following statements represents a conclusion that can be drawn from the above table?

(1) The Pacific Ocean has the deepest spot of all oceans.
(2) The area of the Atlantic Ocean is less than half the area of the Pacific.
(3) The average depth of the Pacific Ocean is more than three times that of the Arctic Ocean.
(4) The Pacific Ocean covers more area than any other ocean.
(5) The Pacific Ocean is the largest ocean.

(1) (2) (3) (4) (5)

GO ON TO THE NEXT PAGE.

9. An advertisement for a new sports car appeals strongly to the buyer's sense of values. Which of the following statements is actually a fact rather than an appeal to the emotions?

    (1) The streamlined body gives the car a classic appearance.
    (2) The engine delivers the "punch" you need.
    (3) Tinted glass reduces the sun's glare.
    (4) The suspension system gives the best handling you can imagine.
    (5) A spacious back seat allows plenty of room to stretch your legs.

    (1) (2) (3) (4) (5)

Items 10–11 are based on the following information.

Chromosomes, the tiny structures which carry the genetic information of the cell, are made up of DNA. DNA is one kind of large chemical molecule called a nucleic acid. When cells divide, the DNA must exactly duplicate itself so that each new cell contains DNA identical to the parent cell.

The DNA of the chromosomes contains the information for how proteins are to be assembled. When the body needs to make a particular protein, instructions must first be sent from the DNA to the ribosomes, the protein factories of the cell. This message is carried by another kind of nucleic acid called RNA.

10. Which of the following statements best summarizes the information given above?

    (1) DNA makes protein.
    (2) There are two kinds of nucleic acid.
    (3) Two kinds of nucleic acid are involved in making proteins.
    (4) DNA carries genetic information.
    (5) RNA is a messenger chemical.

    (1) (2) (3) (4) (5)

11. The cell makes a mistake when the RNA is being prepared from the DNA. Which of the following will most likely be the result of this mistake?

    (1) The protein will contain a mistake also.
    (2) The protein will be assembled correctly.
    (3) The protein will be able to carry out its intended purpose.
    (4) The mistake will cause a shortage in the DNA.
    (5) The mistake will become part of the ribosome.

    (1) (2) (3) (4) (5)

GO ON TO THE NEXT PAGE.

12. A woman usually weighs 120 pounds on her home scale. She goes on vacation, and after 3 days she weighs 125 pounds on the scale at the resort. She decides to go on a diet immediately. What assumption did she make?

(1) Both scales are accurate.
(2) The two scales are placed on the same type of flooring.
(3) The resort scale is less accurate than her home scale.
(4) Neither scale is accurate.
(5) The scales were not at zero before she weighed herself.

(1) (2) (3) (4) (5)

13. The label on a package of salt substitute contains the following information: "People with heart or kidney disease, diabetes, or persons receiving medical treatment should consult a physician before using this product."

What is the implication of this statement?

(1) Salt substitutes cannot be used by ill persons.
(2) People with kidney disease are not healthy.
(3) Diabetics should be under a physician's care.
(4) The product may be harmful to people with some medical disorders.
(5) Only healthy people can safely use this product.

(1) (2) (3) (4) (5)

Item 14 refers to the following diagram.

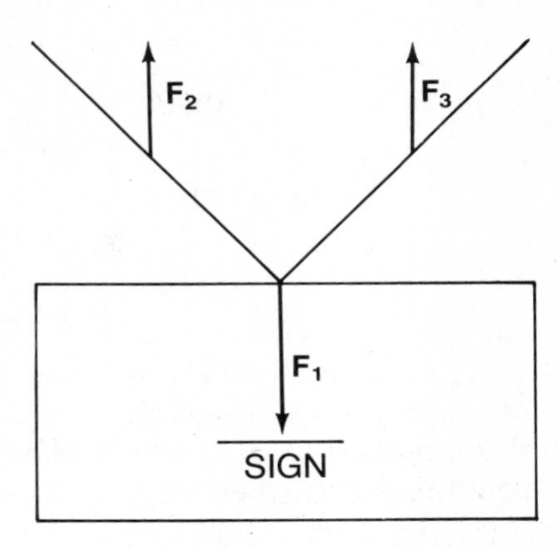

14. An object will remain motionless only if the sum of all the different forces acting on it is equal to zero.

A sign is hung from the ceiling as shown in the diagram. There are three forces acting on the sign which keep it at the same height. These forces are labeled F_1, F_2, and F_3. If the sign is to remain still rather than falling or sliding to one side, then what must be true about the forces?

(1) $F_2 + F_3 = F_1$
(2) F_1 is greater than $F_2 + F_3$
(3) F_1 is less than $F_2 + F_3$
(4) The three forces are equal.
(5) $F_2 = F_3$

(1) (2) (3) (4) (5)

GO ON TO THE NEXT PAGE.

Items 15–16 refer to the following table.

Mineral	Functions in the Body	Food Sources
calcium	• helps blood clot • helps maintain healthy teeth and bones	milk; cheese; green, leafy vegetables
iron	• combines with protein to build hemoglobin • needed to utilize oxygen in cells	red meat; egg yolk; nuts; legumes; dried fruits
iodine	• helps regulate the rate at which foods are burned	seafood; iodized salt
zinc	• needed for digestion and for carbohydrate metabolism	eggs; seafood; whole grains; meat; milk; liver
phosphorus	• helps build and maintain teeth and bones • helps nerves and muscles function	milk; cheese; whole grains; nuts; liver; fish; eggs
magnesium	• helps body use calcium and phosphorus	red meat; potatoes; cereals

15. Which of the following groups of minerals can be found in milk?

(1) calcium, iron, iodine
(2) calcium, zinc, phosphorus
(3) iodine, zinc, iron
(4) calcium, iodine, zinc
(5) phosphorus, iron, iodine

16. A severely overweight person suffers from a disease of the thyroid and does not utilize iodine properly.

Which of the following bodily functions is impaired?

(1) blood clotting
(2) nerve functioning
(3) muscle function
(4) hemoglobin production
(5) rate of food metabolism

(1) (2) (3) (4) (5)

Items 17–20 refer to the following passage.

Today finding sources of oil is more complicated and costly than ever. Surface oil is gone. To locate pools of oil underground, scientists are trying to learn how oil is formed. They have learned a great deal by observing old oil wells.

In an oil well a huge drill inside a pipe chews through rock. Pieces of the rock are then carried out of the hole and examined. By comparing the rocks from many oil wells, scientists have discovered that all the rocks show the same thing: rocks containing the shells of fossil protists are found on top of the pools of oil. Because most of the protists found in these rocks lived in oceans, scientists believe oil formed beneath oceans.

The presence of fossil protists in an area can help scientists locate underground oil. Scientists now theorize that the oil itself might have come from protists. Billions of protists floated in ancient oceans. These gleaming organisms captured some of the sun's energy in tiny drops of fatty oil and stored it in their shells. When the protists died, the shells sank to the ocean floor. Over millions of years, the oil drops from these protists changed to petroleum. The shells of the protists became part of the rock that formed above the pool of oil.

GO ON TO THE NEXT PAGE.

17. Which of the following statements best summarizes the passage?

    (1) Scientists are studying where oil came from in order to predict where it can be found.
    (2) Oil can be found beneath ancient oceans.
    (3) Rocks contain much information about a region's history.
    (4) Fossil protists formed oil.
    (5) Oil is found beneath the fossil remains of protists that once lived in ancient oceans.

    (1) (2) (3) (4) (5)

18. An area suspected of having large underground oil reserves is studied. No fossil protists are found. Assuming the ideas in the article are correct, the area probably

    (1) has no oil
    (2) is oil rich
    (3) will be the site of a major oil deposit in the future
    (4) was the site of a major oil deposit in the past
    (5) has limited oil supplies

    (1) (2) (3) (4) (5)

19. According to the passage, which one of the following is a hypothesis rather than a fact?

    (1) Petroleum may have come from drops of oil in the shells of protists.
    (2) Finding fossils of protists in an area suggests the presence of underground oil.
    (3) Oil deposits formed millions of years ago.
    (4) Rocks from many different oil wells have something in common.
    (5) The protists whose fossils were found in oil well rocks lived in oceans.

    (1) (2) (3) (4) (5)

20. According to the passage, pools of oil formed underneath layers of protists that died, sank, and became part of the rock at the bottom of ancient oceans.

    Which of the following statements might indicate a logical fallacy involved in this theory of oil formation?

    (1) Surface oil may have formed by a process different from underground oil.
    (2) Sunlight may not have reached the bottom of the ancient oceans.
    (3) Oil may have come from both the bodies and the shells of the protists.
    (4) If rock is solid, oil could not penetrate through it to collect in pools below.
    (5) The finding of deep underground oil suggests that the area was once an ocean floor.

    (1) (2) (3) (4) (5)

GO ON TO THE NEXT PAGE.

Items 21–22 are based on the following diagram.

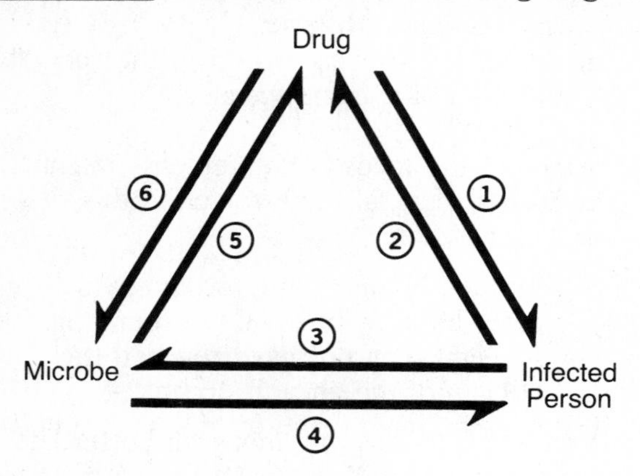

Any time a person who is ill takes a medication, many different interactions may occur.

21. The antibiotic tetracycline is rarely given to small children because it can damage nerves in the ear.

    Which of the relationships shown in the diagram does this example illustrate?

    (1) 1
    (2) 2
    (3) 3
    (4) 5
    (5) 6

22. Below are listed 5 statements which refer to the diagram above. Which one of the statements is a conclusion that can be drawn from the information presented?

    (1) The infected person usually develops some immunity to the microbe.
    (2) Some people are allergic to certain medications.
    (3) Bacteria may become resistant to some antibiotics.
    (4) Some drugs are quickly broken down by the body.
    (5) The drug, the infected person, and the microbe all affect each other in some way.

Items 23–25 refer to the following table.

Test tube	Contents	Reaction?
1	A + B	no
2	A + B + E	yes
3	A + B + E (boiled)	no
4	A + B + E (cold)	yes

Enzymes are proteins which are required for certain biological processes to take place. The table above shows the design and results of an experiment that was carried out to study enzymes.

Compound E was the enzyme used in the experiment. It was treated in different ways before being added to the experimental test tubes.

E (boiled) = enzyme was first boiled for 30 minutes

E (cold) = enzyme was placed on ice for 30 minutes

After all the chemicals were mixed together in the test tubes, the tubes were placed in a warm water bath for one hour. After this time the results were determined.

23. The purpose of the experiment was to establish whether enzymes are influenced by

    (1) reaction time
    (2) temperature
    (3) time and temperature
    (4) cold
    (5) proteins

24. The results of the experiment imply that

    (1) compound E is an enzyme
    (2) compound E is more reactive after it is boiled
    (3) cold treatment does not affect the function of enzymes
    (4) enzymes which have been chilled will not work
    (5) compound E works only in the cold

(1) (2) (3) (4) (5)

GO ON TO THE NEXT PAGE.

25. A lab technician is told to store an enzyme preparation for future use. Judging from the results of this experiment, she should avoid storing the enzyme

(1) in a freezer
(2) under a bright light
(3) in dark room
(4) at room temperature
(5) in a boiling water bath

① ② ③ ④ ⑤

Items 26–28 refer to the following passage.

The monarch butterfly is a graceful creature that weighs much less than a dime. It may be surprising to learn, then, that most of the migrating monarch butterflies in the eastern United States travel a round-trip distance of 2,500 miles during a life span that is only nine months long.

In early summer most female monarchs lay their eggs on milkweed plants. After several stages of development, adult monarchs emerge about three weeks later. The adult monarchs mate, eggs are laid, and a new generation of monarchs begins.

This reproduction cycle is repeated several times during the summer. As the days shorten and cool in the fall, however, a change takes place. The newly hatched monarchs in the fall generation do not mate. These butterflies store their food as energy-rich fats in their bodies. By September, when it is still warm enough to fly, the monarch population has begun to migrate south to Mexico.

In the mountains of Mexico huge colonies of monarch butterflies cling to trees in the cool, moist mountain air and wait out the northern winter. The butterflies are largely inactive during their stay in Mexico, burning up little of the fat reserves needed for the flight back north.

As spring approaches and the days lengthen in the Mexican sunshine, the cycle reverses. The monarchs that have been inactive all winter begin to fly and swarm. Their reproductive systems begin to function. Soon they start the long journey north. Many will not survive the trip. But along the way, they will lay the eggs that will become the first monarch generation for the coming year.

26. Which of the following is true of monarch butterflies in the summer?

(1) They repeat a cycle of egg laying, hatching, and mating.
(2) They accumulate fat deposits.
(3) They live in the cool mountains of Mexico.
(4) Their reproductive systems do not function.
(5) They are largely inactive.

① ② ③ ④ ⑤

27. A researcher studying monarch butterflies wants to see if he can make the early summer monarchs behave like the autumn monarchs. Based on the information in the passage, what conditions would he have to mimic in their environment to stimulate the change?

(1) cooling and shortening of days
(2) warm long days
(3) decreasing milkweed supplies
(4) three weeks of cold weather
(5) cool, moist mountain air

① ② ③ ④ ⑤

28. Which of the following represents a conclusion that can be drawn from the passage?

(1) Biological adjustments are necessary to insure the survival of the monarch butterfly species.
(2) Summer monarchs have fewer fat reserves.
(3) Autumn monarchs do not mate early in adulthood.
(4) Autumn monarchs migrate hundreds of miles to find warm winter weather.
(5) Monarchs would live longer if they did not migrate so far.

① ② ③ ④ ⑤

GO ON TO THE NEXT PAGE.

Items 29–33 are based on the following information.

Several factors may determine whether an organism lives in a given area. Temperature, moisture, soil, and water chemistry are obvious physical influences. Listed below are five other factors.

(1) dispersal—transport; ability of an organism to reach an area

(2) behavior—the species actually chooses where it will and will not live

(3) predation—one organism captures or feeds on others

(4) allelopathy—substances secreted by one organism have harmful effects on another

(5) competition—closely related species that eat the same types of food and live in the same sorts of places struggle against each other for a place to live

The following items describe situations that reflect the factors listed above. For each situation, choose the one factor that best explains how the organisms came to live where they do. Any factor may describe more than one situation.

29. In 1883 the island of Krakatau was completely destroyed by a volcanic eruption. All that remained of the island was a sterilized, ash-covered peak. Nine months after eruption, only one species, a spider, was present on the island. Three years later blue-green algae, ferns, and some flowering plants could be found. Ten years later there were coconut trees, and after 25 years there were 263 species of animals.

    The factor being described is

    (1) dispersal
    (2) behavior
    (3) predation
    (4) allelopathy
    (5) competition

    ① ② ③ ④ ⑤

30. In southern California some chaparral shrubs are often separated from grasslands by a bare area 1–2 meters wide. Chemicals produced by the shrubs evaporate easily from the leaves and inhibit the growth of nearby grasses.

    The factor which best describes the effect of the shrubs on the grasses is

    (1) dispersal
    (2) behavior
    (3) predation
    (4) allelopathy
    (5) competition

    ① ② ③ ④ ⑤

31. The tree pipit and the meadow pipit are similar types of birds. Both build nests on the ground, eat the same foods, and sing similar mating songs. However, the meadow pipit jumps to the ground to end its song, while the tree pipit ends its song perched in a tree. Therefore, tree pipits are found only in areas having tall trees.

    The areas where the tree pipit lives are limited by

    (1) dispersal
    (2) behavior
    (3) predation
    (4) allelopathy
    (5) competition

    ① ② ③ ④ ⑤

32. Penicillin produced by the mold *Penicillium* is an antibiotic that inhibits the growth of certain bacteria near the mold.

    The action of penicillin is an example of the factor called

    (1) dispersal
    (2) behavior
    (3) predation
    (4) allelopathy
    (5) competition

    ① ② ③ ④ ⑤

GO ON TO THE NEXT PAGE.

33. Redwings and tricolors are two closely related species of blackbird in western North America. Very early in the spring individual male redwings build nests in marshy areas. Later, when large numbers of tricolors move into a redwing territory to set up their colonies, the male redwings become very aggressive. The redwings eventually lose their territory simply because there are so many more tricolors.

The factor being described is

(1) dispersal
(2) behavior
(3) predation
(4) allelopathy
(5) competition

(1) (2) (3) (4) (5)

34. A local medical group offers to finance a research project to study burn trauma and tissue repair in mice. The researcher decides not to accept their offer for several different reasons. Which of the following statements shows that his personal values have influenced his decision not to do the study?

(1) He does not have the research equipment necessary to do the project well.
(2) He does not have adequate housing and care for the animals.
(3) He does not want to cause severe injury to the mice.
(4) He does not have an assistant to help with the project.
(5) The project would cost more than the local group is offering to pay.

(1) (2) (3) (4) (5)

35. Below are five statements which refer to clouds. Which of the following statements represents an opinion rather than a fact that can be verified?

(1) Clouds contain moisture.
(2) On cloudy days ultraviolet light can still reach the earth and cause sunburn.
(3) Clouds can trap the earth's heat and prevent it from radiating away.
(4) Clouds contain particles of dust.
(5) Even when the sky is cloudy, people should use sunscreens to prevent sunburn.

(1) (2) (3) (4) (5)

36. A newscast announcing an earthquake in Peru contained the following statements.

A. This quake is the greatest disaster the people of this country have ever experienced.
B. This earthquake has the highest Richter scale reading ever recorded here.
C. Cracks and fissures developed throughout the country.
D. Buildings were toppled throughout the capital city.
E. The extent of the damage exceeds anyone's prediction.

Which of the above statements could be scientifically verified?

(1) A and B
(2) C and D
(3) B, C, and D
(4) B, C, and E
(5) A, B, C, and D

(1) (2) (3) (4) (5)

GO ON TO THE NEXT PAGE.

37. Thermometers may be filled with mercury, a liquid metal which expands when heated.

The following experiment was performed. The expansion of mercury in a thermometer was determined in three different solutions. The results are shown below.

Solution	Expansion of mercury in thermometer
1	1 cm
2	2 cm
3	3 cm

The conclusion was drawn that the temperature difference between solutions 1 and 2 is the same as the difference between solutions 2 and 3.

In stating this conclusion, what assumption is made?

(1) The solutions were at different temperatures.
(2) The molecules in the mercury are moving faster at higher temperatures.
(3) Temperature causes the mercury to rise.
(4) Mercury expands the same amount for equal changes in temperature.
(5) Mercury will expand differently in the different solutions.

Items 38–41 are based on the following passage.

The sound, color, and sparkle of fireworks have fascinated humans for centuries. Fireworks were probably invented in China in the twelfth century. A mixture of potassium nitrate, sulfur, and carbon was found to be useful for two quite different purposes: gunpowder and fireworks. Since then, firecrackers, Roman candles, cherry bombs, and rockets have been used to celebrate important events throughout the world.

However, fireworks are, after all, explosives. The composition of a Roman candle is not much different from that of a small bomb. Compounds containing nitrate ions (NO_3^-), chlorate ions (ClO_3^-), sulfur, and charcoal provide the explosion that sends the rocket into the air and then blows it apart.

Powdered metals—iron, steel, magnesium, aluminum, and titanium—catch fire and produce the sparks and flames. Metallic compounds add color to the sparks. Sodium compounds produce a yellow color; calcium compounds, red; strontium compounds, scarlet; barium compounds, green; and copper compounds, bluish-green. Ammonium compounds change the shades of these colors. Picric acid and sulfur make the colors more brilliant.

38. According to the passage, the explosion heard when fireworks go off is due in part to the presence of

(1) iron
(2) sulfur
(3) powdered metals
(4) copper
(5) ammonium

(1) (2) (3) (4) (5)

GO ON TO THE NEXT PAGE.

39. A chemist is given a chemical compound to analyze. She does not know what elements it contains, but some preliminary tests suggest it contains barium. How could she test this hypothesis?

(1) Dissolve the compound in a nitrate solution.
(2) Mix it with an ammonium compound.
(3) Add some chlorate ions.
(4) See what color it produces when it is burned.
(5) Combine with magnesium.

① ② ③ ④ ⑤

40. Two different fireworks samples are sent to a factory for comparison. They are identical in their content of powdered metals, metallic compounds, and ammonium compounds. One also contains picric acid and sulfur.

What would distinguish the one containing picric acid and sulfur?

(1) intense vivid colors over a wide range
(2) few greens, vivid blues
(3) predominantly red
(4) wide variety of dull colors
(5) intense colors with little shade variation

① ② ③ ④ ⑤

41. Which of the following statements could not be proven in a chemical analysis?

(1) Fireworks are explosives.
(2) Beautifully colored fireworks displays are fascinating to watch.
(3) Gunpowder and fireworks are made from similar ingredients.
(4) Metallic compounds emit colors when they catch fire.
(5) Powdered metals burn easily and produce sparks.

① ② ③ ④ ⑤

42. When a virus infects a person, special white blood cells produce a protein called interferon. Interferon triggers other cells to produce substances which help to make the body more resistant to immediate infection by a second virus.

A person has a summer cold. Before it clears, a viral flu epidemic begins in his community. Based on the information given above, which of the following will probably happen?

(1) He will have an extremely severe case of flu.
(2) His cold will become much worse.
(3) He will have at most a mild case of flu.
(4) The cold will clear immediately.
(5) The cold will disappear and the flu will last for a long time.

① ② ③ ④ ⑤

43. Which of the following claims about a new diet soft drink is based only on opinion?

(1) sweetened with saccharine
(2) sugar free
(3) 100 percent caffeine free
(4) no artificial coloring
(5) sweet, natural sugar taste

① ② ③ ④ ⑤

GO ON TO THE NEXT PAGE.

Items 44–48 refer to the following graph

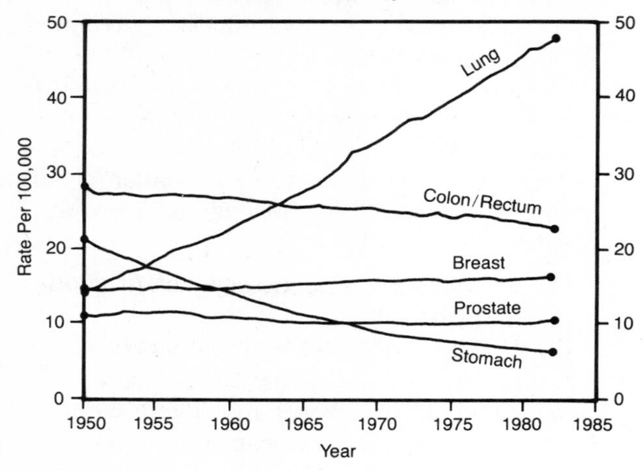

44. The type of cancer which accounted for the greatest number of deaths in 1960 is

(1) breast
(2) colon/rectum
(3) lung
(4) prostate
(5) stomach

(1) (2) (3) (4) (5)

45. Which of the following statements best summarizes the information on the graph?

(1) The death rate due to cancer has not declined noticeably over the past 35 years.
(2) Lung cancer claimed more lives in 1982 than in 1950.
(3) The number of women dying of breast cancer has remained unchanged since 1950.
(4) The increase in deaths due to lung cancer over the past 35 years is greater than the decrease in deaths due to stomach or colon/rectum cancer.
(5) The death rate due to stomach cancer has declined noticeably since 1950.

(1) (2) (3) (4) (5)

46. This graph indicates deaths per 100,000 individuals due to five types of cancer. Which of the following can NOT be calculated from the graph?

(1) the type of cancer which accounted for the most deaths each year
(2) the number of cases per 100,000 people of each cancer type for a given year
(3) the change in death rate for stomach cancer from 1950 to 1975
(4) the year by year change in the mortality rate due to these cancer types
(5) the year in which the total death rate due to these five types of cancer was the highest

(1) (2) (3) (4) (5)

47. According to the data presented, one can conclude that no progress has been made against cancer. Which of the following statements would be the basis of a logical fallacy to this conclusion?

(1) Approximately the same number of people died of cancer in 1982 as in 1950.
(2) The number of lung cancer deaths is increasing.
(3) Over the past 30 years, the number of cancer cases occurring has increased greatly and so has the number of cures.
(4) The number of deaths from breast and prostate cancer are unchanged.
(5) No particular type of cancer has been eliminated.

(1) (2) (3) (4) (5)

GO ON TO THE NEXT PAGE.

48. The massive research effort in the area of cancer has not produced cures.

Which of the following statements justify the conclusion above?

(1) Many drugs have been developed which are not yet routinely available because of required testing periods.
(2) New techniques are allowing physicians to detect cancer at an earlier stage.
(3) The dramatic increase in lung cancer is due to the increased number of women smokers.
(4) Many more cases of cancer are being detected now than in 1950.
(5) Approximately the same number of people died of cancer in 1975 as in 1982.

49. A force was applied to a book to move it along a horizontal surface. The same force was applied in each case. The results of the experiment are shown below.

Surface	Distance book moved
smooth tabletop	6 ft
rough picnic tabletop	2 ft
log	2 in

What is the hypothesis being tested in this experiment?

(1) An object will not move unless a force is applied to it.
(2) Friction operates in all directions.
(3) The distance an object moves is determined by the initial force applied to it.
(4) The force of friction will be greater when an object moves on a rough surface.
(5) All objects come to rest sooner or later.

50. Vitamins are substances which are necessary for all metabolic processes but cannot be manufactured by the body.

A woman takes a multivitamin tablet each day. In addition, she takes vitamin A, vitamin B_6, vitamin B_{12}, vitamin C, and vitamin E. Four of the statements listed below indicate that there is a fallacy in her reasoning.

Which one of the following statements actually does support her action?

(1) Vitamins are a necessary part of good nutrition.
(2) Excess vitamins are rarely stored for future use by the body.
(3) Vitamins are required by the body in very small amounts.
(4) An excess of vitamin A over a long period of time can cause some metabolic problems.
(5) A multivitamin tablet usually contains 100 percent of the amount of each vitamin required daily.

GO ON TO THE NEXT PAGE.

Items 51–53 are based on the following passage.

Astronauts floating weightlessly through their spaceship have become a common sight on television news programs. Gravity is present within the spaceship, but it is accelerating the spaceship and all the objects in it—including the astronauts—equally. This condition of equal acceleration is called microgravity.

Human beings have adapted to the earth's force of gravity. To date, only astronauts have lived and worked in a condition of microgravity. Doctors have observed no serious health problems in astronauts returning from space. Human bones may lose small amounts of calcium and other minerals. Temporary dizziness and difficulty in standing may also be experienced because blood may have collected in the lower parts of the body.

Plans are currently being designed for larger space stations housing thousands of people. Floating in space above the earth or moon, these space colonists would not feel the gravitational pull of the earth or moon. A constant condition of microgravity would exist unless the environment were made more habitable for humans. To accomplish this, the space station could be made to spin slowly. This movement would not create gravity, but it would seem to "push" people against the floor of the space station. To the colonists, the effect would be the same as that of gravity.

51. Which of the following statements is implied by the passage?

(1) Gravity is the same at all places in space.
(2) Gravity and the effect of rotation appear to be the same to an observer.
(3) Gravity is due to slow spinning movement.
(4) Gravity does not affect health.
(5) Gravity is necessary for strong bones.

① ② ③ ④ ⑤

52. Which of the following represents an assumption made in the passage?

(1) Working in space would be easier if a gravitational force were created.
(2) There are some tasks which are best performed by people on space stations.
(3) The effects of gravity can be mimicked.
(4) Dizziness and difficulty in standing due to microgravity may be temporary.
(5) Space stations of the future will be much larger.

① ② ③ ④ ⑤

53. As the distance between objects increases, the gravitational force between them decreases. Which of the following statements supports this conclusion?

(1) Larger space stations are needed in the future.
(2) Gravity is present everywhere.
(3) Out in space very little gravitational force is felt.
(4) The moon does not have gravitational pull.
(5) Gravity cannot be created.

① ② ③ ④ ⑤

GO ON TO THE NEXT PAGE.

54. A description found in a floral catalog lists several different features of a particular plant. Which of the following statements could be confirmed through scientific experimentation?

(1) The plant requires temperatures warmer than 65°F.
(2) The beautiful variegated leaves give color in any setting.
(3) The thornless stems make the plant ideal for cut arrangements.
(4) The fragrance is delicate and pleasing.
(5) The perfectly formed buds open into dazzling displays of color.

(1) (2) (3) (4) (5)

Items 55–56 refer to the following graph.

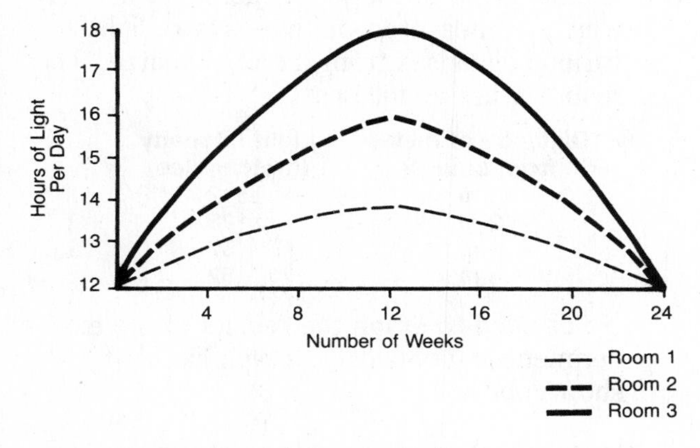

A nurseryman wanted to study the effects of different light cycles on the growth of plants. Three experimental rooms received artificial lighting that duplicated the light patterns of growing seasons in three different locations.

55. Plant 1 requires 15 hours of light each day for at least three weeks if the leaves are to turn brilliant red. The leaves will turn red in room

(1) 1
(2) 2
(3) 1 and 2
(4) 2 and 3
(5) 1, 2, and 3

(1) (2) (3) (4) (5)

56. Plant 3 forms flowers and seeds only when the days have no more than 15 hours of daylight. This plant will probably grow naturally in areas that have light patterns like those in room

(1) 1
(2) 2
(3) 1 and 2
(4) 2 and 3
(5) 1, 2, and 3

(1) (2) (3) (4) (5)

GO ON TO THE NEXT PAGE.

57. In dry climates "evaporative coolers" are often used instead of refrigerated air conditioners. In an evaporative cooler, a large fan draws air in through straw pads which are kept wet by water trickling over them. Air drawn in through the wet pads is cooled, and this cooled air is circulated through the house.

Which of the following statements best explains how an evaporative cooler works?

(1) Air absorbs moisture from the water.
(2) Water in the pads evaporates into the outside air.
(3) The air is cooled because it is circulated by the fan.
(4) Hot air is cooled because it gives up its heat to evaporate the water.
(5) Wet air is colder than dry air.

(1) (2) (3) (4) (5)

58. Which of the following statements about cockroaches represents an opinion rather than a fact?

(1) Cockroaches are insects.
(2) Cockroaches can detect light.
(3) Cockroaches are most active in the dark.
(4) Cockroaches would be eliminated if people would keep their houses clean.
(5) Cockroaches have antennae and three body parts.

(1) (2) (3) (4) (5)

59. Some babies drink formula rather than cow's milk for the first 6 to 12 months of their lives. When they begin to drink cow's milk, pediatricians recommend that the baby be given 2 percent lowfat milk rather than skim no-fat milk. The two milk sources differ only in their fat content.

What is the implication of the pediatrician's instructions?

(1) Skim milk contains products harmful to the baby.
(2) Babies over 12 months of age should never drink formula.
(3) Skim milk is more nutritious than lowfat milk.
(4) Babies require some fat in their diet.
(5) Fat should be eliminated from the diet of young babies.

(1) (2) (3) (4) (5)

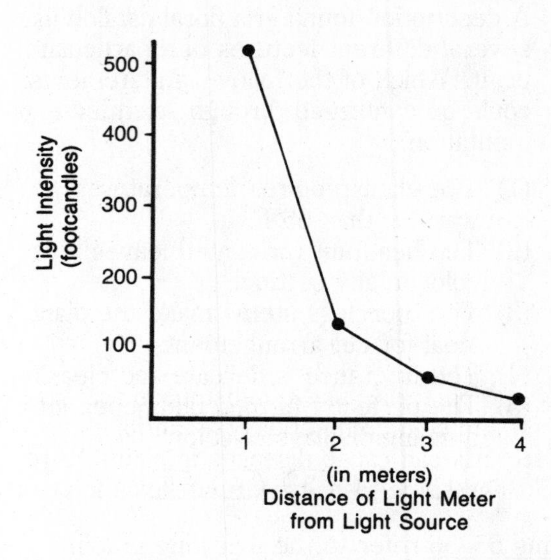

60. A student performed an experiment in which he measured the intensity of light at various distances from the light source. The results were as follows:

Distance of meter from source	Light intensity (footcandles)
1 m	512
2 m	128
3 m	57
4 m	32

He decided to graph the results of the experiment and obtained a graph like that shown above.

He graphed the data to show that

(1) the light meter was accurate
(2) intensity and distance are unrelated
(3) intensity became greater with distance
(4) there is a mathematical relationship between distance and intensity
(5) the experiment was a success

GO ON TO THE NEXT PAGE.

Items 61–64 are based on the following passage.

What many people think of when the word "bacteria" is mentioned are pathogens—bacteria that cause disease. Pathogens damage living tissues and produce toxic materials that poison the body. Pathogenic bacteria cause hundreds of diseases, including strep throat, pneumonia, tuberculosis, and tetanus in humans and in other organisms. But bacteria can act in many other ways besides producing disease. Some bacteria produce chemical substances which kill other types of bacteria. These substances are produced and sold commercially as antibiotics.

Bacteria can cause diseases in plants. Fireblight and some plant tumors are examples of bacterial infections. Bacteria can also help plants to grow by forming nitrate fertilizers in the soil that plants can easily use. Bacteria can also produce poisons which kill certain kinds of insects. These are natural insecticides and help to control insect populations.

Bacteria are needed to decompose wastes. They do this by using the nutrients in the wastes for food. However, dumping large amounts of wastes into lakes and rivers provides bacteria with a more than ample food supply. With so much food, the bacteria grow and reproduce rapidly. The huge numbers of bacteria use up the oxygen dissolved in the water which causes fish and other organisms to suffocate.

Bacteria are used to make certain food, such as cheese and yogurt. But bacteria are also the cause of large food losses through decay and spoilage.

61. Which of the following statements best summarizes the passage?

(1) Antibiotics are the main commercial value of bacteria.
(2) Man has learned to utilize bacteria to his advantage.
(3) Bacteria cause many problems such as water pollution and disease.
(4) The ways in which bacteria help people far outnumber the ways they are harmful.
(5) Bacteria affect many different aspects of our daily lives.

(1) (2) (3) (4) (5)

62. Which of the following statements represents a conclusion which can be drawn from the passage?

(1) Bacteria are used in the production of many foods.
(2) Man has found many ways to use bacteria to his advantage.
(3) Water treatment systems depend on bacteria for the breakdown of wastes.
(4) Poisons produced by some bacteria are used on a wide scale to control insect pests which damage crops.
(5) Antibiotics produced by some bacteria are useful drugs in disease treatment.

(1) (2) (3) (4) (5)

63. If there were no bacteria, which one of the following effects might be observed?

(1) Soils would be nutritionally richer for plants.
(2) Lakes would be free of pollution.
(3) Fewer varieties of food would be available.
(4) Disease would be eliminated.
(5) Some insect populations would disappear.

(1) (2) (3) (4) (5)

64. As Lake Erie became more and more polluted, the fish in the lake died due to lack of oxygen in the water. Which of the following statements could be used to support this conclusion?

(1) Bacteria multiply rapidly in polluted waters.
(2) Bacteria break down waste for food.
(3) Water pollution results from more and more wastes being added to the water supply.
(4) Bacteria carry out many of the decay processes in our environment.
(5) Bacteria in the lake produced chemical substances which killed the fish.

(1) (2) (3) (4) (5)

GO ON TO THE NEXT PAGE.

65. A rain gauge is a device similar to a measuring cup. A weather reporter places a rain gauge outside during a rainstorm. When the storm ends, the gauge contains one-half inch of rain. She concludes that the city received one-half inch of rain.

Which of the following assumptions did she make in reaching this conclusion?

A. The rainfall was the same in all parts of the city.
B. The gauge was oriented in a vertical direction.
C. The wind was not strong enough to blow the rain sideways.

(1) A
(2) B
(3) A and B
(4) B and C
(5) A, B, and C

(1) (2) (3) (4) (5)

66. "Genetically engineered" organisms are life-forms such as bacteria which have had their genetic material altered in the laboratory. Often, the reason for changing an organism is to create a new organism that possesses useful traits. For example, the human genetic material that codes instructions for making growth hormone can be placed inside yeast cells. These genetically engineered yeast cells will now produce the rare and valuable human growth hormone.

Some concerns have been raised about genetic engineering. Which of the following questions reflect how values influence the decisions made about this process?

(1) Will the genetically engineered yeast actually produce the needed material?
(2) Will the process of genetic engineering alter the characteristics of the yeast in some unpredictable way?
(3) Will the product of genetic engineering have fewer side effects than materials produced under other conditions?
(4) Will the material produced by genetic engineering actually work in the patient?
(5) Is the effort needed to produce the drug worthwhile if very few people need it?

(1) (2) (3) (4) (5)

END OF EXAMINATION

TEST 4: INTERPRETING LITERATURE AND THE ARTS

POSTTEST

Directions

The Interpreting Literature and the Arts Posttest consists of 45 multiple-choice questions based on selections from various kinds of reading materials. The selections are from literary works such as books, journals, and magazine or newspaper commentaries. One or more questions follow each selection. The best procedure for you to follow is to read the selection through once, then read all the questions based on the selection, answering as many questions as you can. Then reread the selection as many times as necessary to answer the more difficult questions.

You should take approximately 65 minutes to complete this test. There is no penalty for guessing. Try to answer as many questions as you can. Work rapidly but carefully, without spending too much time on any one question. If a question is too difficult for you, skip it and come back to it later.

For each answer, mark one answer space. See how the following example is done.

EXAMPLE

Often I think of the beautiful town
That is seated by the sea;
Often in thought go up and down
The pleasant streets of that dear old town,
  And my youth comes back to me.

In the poem above, the author is writing about

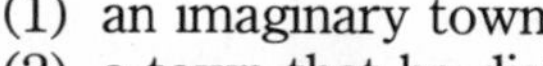

(1) an imaginary town
(2) a town that he dislikes
(3) the town he lives in
(4) a town he once visited
(5) the town he grew up in

The answer is "the town he grew up in"; therefore, answer space (5) has been marked.

Answers to the questions are in the Answer Key on page 767. Explanations for the answers are on pages 760–762.

Directions: Choose the one best answer to each question.

Items 1–6 are based on the following passage.

Do you think Florence will succeed in her plan?

There, outside, beyond the slowly rising mist, and farther off than her eyes could see, her life awaited her. The woman on the bed was old, her life was fading as the mist rose. She thought of her mother as already in the grave; and she would not let herself be strangled by the hands of the dead.

"I'm going, Ma," she said. "I got to go."

Her mother leaned back, face upward to the light, and began to cry. Gabriel moved to Florence's side and grabbed her arm. She looked up into his face and saw that his eyes were full of tears.

"You can't go," he said. "You can't go. You can't go and leave your mother thisaway. She need a woman, Florence, to help look after her. What she going to do here, all alone with me?"

She pushed him from her and moved to stand over her mother's bed.

"Ma," she said, "don't be like that. Ain't a blessed thing for you to cry about so. Ain't a thing can happen to me up North can't happen to me here. God's everywhere, Ma. Ain't no need to worry."

She knew that she was mouthing words; and she realized suddenly that her mother scorned to dignify these words with her attention.

1. What had Florence decided to do?

(1) take a vacation
(2) move away from home
(3) go home for the night
(4) take her mother north
(5) get married

① ② ③ ④ ⑤

2. Though the story is not told by any of the characters, it is told as if seen by whom?

(1) Florence
(2) Gabriel
(3) Florence's mother
(4) all three characters
(5) an outsider

① ② ③ ④ ⑤

3. How did Gabriel react to Florence's decision?

(1) He worried that she would be in danger.
(2) He became angry that he couldn't go with her.
(3) He was greatly relieved by her decision.
(4) He was proud of her independence.
(5) He worried about himself and Florence's mother.

① ② ③ ④ ⑤

4. The phrase "knew that she was mouthing words" in line 27 means that Florence realized she was

(1) opening her mouth but making no sound
(2) talking without paying much attention to what she was saying
(3) showing disrespect for her mother by talking back
(4) speaking for both herself and Gabriel
(5) boasting about her decision

① ② ③ ④ ⑤

5. Why did the mother remain silent at the end of the passage?

(1) She knew Gabriel would take good care of her.
(2) She felt both angry and resentful toward Florence.
(3) She was too ill to talk.
(4) She was trying to think of a way to make Florence stay.
(5) She became afraid of Florence.

① ② ③ ④ ⑤

6. If one of Florence's friends had decided to place her own mother in a nursing home, which of the following would most likely describe Florence's reaction?

(1) disappointed
(2) angry
(3) delighted
(4) supportive
(5) uncaring

① ② ③ ④ ⑤

GO ON TO THE NEXT PAGE.

Items 7–12 are based on the following poem.

How do the three people at tea feel about each other?

At Tea

The kettle descants in a cosy drone,
And the young wife looks in her husband's face,
And then at her guest's, and shows in her own
Her sense that she fills an envied place;
And the visiting lady is all abloom,
And says there was never so sweet a room.

And the happy young housewife does not know
That the woman beside her was first his choice,
Till the fates ordained it could not be so. . . .
Betraying nothing in look or voice
The guest sits smiling and sips her tea,
And he throws her a stray glance yearningly.

7. In lines 3 and 4, the poet is telling the reader that the wife believes that

(1) she envies the guest
(2) the guest envies the husband
(3) the husband envies the guest
(4) the guest envies her
(5) she envies her husband

① ② ③ ④ ⑤

8. Which of the following descriptions of the guest is directly supported by the poem?

(1) complimentary
(2) rude
(3) snobbish
(4) honest
(5) talkative

① ② ③ ④ ⑤

9. Which of the following statements about the young wife is true?

(1) She is disappointed because she is a housewife.
(2) She is unaware that her husband preferred the other woman.
(3) She is a hypocrite because she offers the lady tea.
(4) She is mistrustful of the visiting lady.
(5) She is resentful of her husband because he loves the visitor.

① ② ③ ④ ⑤

10. If the guest had written an account in a diary about the afternoon at tea, she might have sounded

(1) hopeful
(2) sad
(3) enthusiastic
(4) frightened
(5) ashamed

① ② ③ ④ ⑤

11. How is the poet describing the situation?

(1) grimly
(2) angrily
(3) ironically
(4) wistfully
(5) praisingly

① ② ③ ④ ⑤

12. What is the effect of the last line of the poem?

(1) It answers a question in the reader's mind.
(2) It reveals a conflict between the wife and her husband.
(3) It convinces the reader not to take the poem too seriously.
(4) It brings the poem to a very abrupt end.
(5) It shows that a secret will soon be revealed.

① ② ③ ④ ⑤

GO ON TO THE NEXT PAGE.

Items 13–18 are based on the following passage.

To whom would this artist's paintings appeal?

Autograph seekers besiege him [Charles Wysocki] and students flood him with mail. As fast as his acrylic originals leave his studio in the San Bernardino mountains (about once every six weeks), they're sold to collectors for as much as $30,000 apiece. *An American Celebration: The Art of Charles Wysocki* sold out within three months of publication, and Wysocki's annual *Americana Calendar* . . . and posters are best-sellers as well. All this activity has added up to $7.25 million in sales since 1979.

Wysocki's only beef is never having had his work reviewed by art critics, a complaint that makes William Wilson of the *Los Angeles Times* testy. Says Wilson: "If they're inside the art system, they don't get ignored." That verdict doesn't keep other painters from following in Wysocki's brush strokes. "There are probably a half dozen artists all trying to do what Chuck does," says Dave Usher, who publishes Wysocki's work. "But none can touch him."

Wysocki began painting his rural scenes 22 years ago, after discovering the San Fernando countryside and the pristine timelessness of New England. His work evokes not only the stylized sentimentality of Norman Rockwell but also the simplicity of Grandma Moses, and yet manages to defy categorizing. "I'm too citified to be folk and too trained to be primitive," says Wysocki.

The results are paeans to the past: colloquial scenes of neat clapboard houses and industrious apple-cheeked families working and frolicking under wind-stiff star spangled banners. Into these scenes Wysocki inserts familiar details—window boxes, doorsteps and lanterns, a cat on a sill, a vase on a table, tiny children's drawings in the panes of a schoolhouse window. . . .

He prefers to think that his work is a vision of America as he'd like it to be. "In my paintings you don't see empty bottles or rags lying on the road," he says. "I don't think nostalgia has to be grubby. Maybe secretly I'm an environmentalist and would like to clean up America."

Born and reared in a working-class neighborhood of Detroit, Wysocki remembers that "walking down the street on holidays was like walking through a tunnel of red, white and blue. As I started painting, these memories came through the brush and into the painting. That's one of the reasons I feel very patriotic. It's a reversion to my youth."

13. What does the author mean by stating, "The results are paeans to the past" (line 33)?

(1) Wysocki's popularity is largely among older people.
(2) Wysocki's style has been copied from past artists.
(3) Wysocki's artwork praises the life of long ago.
(4) Wysocki developed his personal style long ago.
(5) The lack of a distinct style in Wysocki's art is a result of his past.

(1) (2) (3) (4) (5)

14. How would Wysocki describe his paintings?

(1) highly realistic
(2) plain and without detail
(3) easy to describe and categorize
(4) a personal dream
(5) very similar to Norman Rockwell's paintings

(1) (2) (3) (4) (5)

15. What does William Wilson suggest about Wysocki?

(1) Wysocki is as good a painter as Norman Rockwell.
(2) Wysocki is very temperamental.
(3) Art critics give Wysocki's paintings good reviews.
(4) Wysocki is not really a part of the art system.
(5) Wysocki is so good that others try to imitate him.

GO ON TO THE NEXT PAGE.

16. Which of the following would you think Wysocki painted?

(1) Summer in San Diego
(2) Detroit: An Exciting City
(3) Bunker Hill: Soldiers in Battle
(4) City Factories
(5) Independence Day: Enterprising Immigrants

① ② ③ ④ ⑤

17. Which of the following devices used by the author is LEAST helpful to the reader in visualizing Wysocki's paintings?

(1) having Wysocki describe his work
(2) describing Wysocki's popularity
(3) comparing Wysocki to Norman Rockwell
(4) describing Wysocki's painting of a schoolhouse
(5) having Wysocki describe his past

① ② ③ ④ ⑤

18. What kind of mood does Wysocki create for the viewer?

(1) sentimental
(2) industrious
(3) sad
(4) humorous
(5) carefree

① ② ③ ④ ⑤

<u>Items 19–23</u> are based on the following poem.

What is happening this morning?

Snowy Morning

Wake
gently this morning
to a different day
Listen.

There is no bray
of buses,
no brake growls,
no siren howls and
no horns
blow.
There is only
the silence
of a city
hushed
by snow.

—*by Lilian Moore*

19. Which of the following best states the meaning of lines 1–3?

(1) It is time to get up.
(2) Make changes in your life today.
(3) When you awaken, you will find that something has changed.
(4) Nothing stays the same.
(5) Don't rush out of bed.

① ② ③ ④ ⑤

20. What is the main idea of the poem?

(1) Things look different after it has snowed.
(2) Snow quiets city noises.
(3) Every morning begins a new and different day.
(4) Snow causes traffic jams in the city.
(5) Today is an unusual day.

① ② ③ ④ ⑤

21. To what does the poet compare a bus?

(1) grinding machine
(2) fire engine
(3) donkey
(4) brake
(5) honking car

① ② ③ ④ ⑤

22. Which of the following places could the poet be describing?

(1) a farm
(2) Los Angeles
(3) a hospital
(4) a suburb
(5) New York

① ② ③ ④ ⑤

23. What kind of mood does the poem create for the reader?

(1) quiet
(2) depressing
(3) tense
(4) bitter
(5) joyful

① ② ③ ④ ⑤

GO ON TO THE NEXT PAGE.

Items 24–28 are based on the following passage.

Is this movie a successful sequel?

The Karate Kid was one of 1984's smashes, grossing more than $100 million to date. That tale of the underdog overcoming tremendous odds was based on the relationship between the teenage Daniel (Ralph Macchio) and his personal martial arts mentor Mr. Miyagi (Noriyuki "Pat" Morita). With enough action to satisfy the popcorn gobblers, it was a complete summer movie. *Part II* was born with an obvious predicament for director John Avildsen: how to reestablish yet broaden Macchio's and Morita's story without rehashing the original. It was a losing battle. In this sequel, Morita humbles his nemesis from the original movie (Martin Kove), and six months later Macchio announces that his mother is moving and his girlfriend has left him. So when Morita receives a letter telling of his father's illness, he heads for his native Okinawa, with Macchio in tow. They find that all is not as Morita left it 45 years before. For starters, his village is now part of a U.S. air base. Morita also has trouble with the local landlord (veteran character actor Danny Kamekona). Long ago, the landlord lost his honor when Morita stole his wife to be (Nobu McCarthy). "In Okinawa, honor has no time limit," says Morita, explaining why his former friend still holds the grudge and intends to fight him to the death over it. Despite the inevitable confrontations—one of them matches Macchio against Kamekona's nephew (Yuji Okumoto)—the fighting is again not at the film's heart. Honor, custom and tradition are its focus, and the decidedly slow pace and beautiful village scenes, shot in Hawaii, lend some integrity to the plot. Morita also returns to his first love (McCarthy), while Macchio finds a new one (Tamlyn Tomita). Morita brings the same charm to the role that won him an Oscar nomination, and Macchio and the rest of the cast are workmanlike. But the film is ultimately too predictable, even somewhat tiresome, and *Karate Kid Part II* goes down kicking. (PG)

24. How is *Karate Kid Part II* different from *Part I?*

(1) The two main actors are not the same in *Part II.*
(2) Fighting is at the heart of the film in *Part II.*
(3) One of the characters has a new love interest in *Part II.*
(4) It cost much more money to make *Part II.*
(5) The action is much faster in *Part II.*

1 2 3 4 5

25. In the movie, why does the character played by Morita return to Okinawa?

(1) A family member is ill.
(2) His mother is moving.
(3) He is afraid the U.S. air base has changed his old home.
(4) He wants to help Macchio forget his problems.
(5) He wants to confront a man who has a grudge against him.

1 2 3 4 5

26. Which of the following movie themes does *Karate Kid Part II* have as one of its main themes?

(1) ambition
(2) love and romance
(3) vengeance
(4) acceptance of fate
(5) honor

1 2 3 4 5

27. According to the author, which of the following problems is likely to occur with most movie sequels?

(1) getting the same actors to play their original roles
(2) overcoming audience prejudice against sequels
(3) including enough action in the sequel
(4) reestablishing the original story without repeating it
(5) choosing an appropriate setting in which to film the sequel

1 2 3 4 5

GO ON TO THE NEXT PAGE.

28. What is the author's attitude toward *Part II?*

(1) enthusiastic
(2) disappointed
(3) confused
(4) scornful
(5) indifferent

1 2 3 4 5

Items 29–34 are based on the following passage.

What problems did the author experience at school?

I wanted to be accepted. It must have been in sixth grade. It was just before the Fourth of July. They were trying out students for this patriotic play. I wanted to do Abe Lincoln, so I learned the Gettysburg Address inside and out. I'd be out in the fields pickin' the crops and I'd be memorizin'. I was the only one who didn't have to read the part, 'cause I learned it. The part was given to a girl who was a grower's daughter. She had to read it out of a book, but they said she had better diction. I was very disappointed. I quit about eighth grade.

Anytime anybody'd talk to me about politics, about civil rights, I would ignore it. It's a very degrading thing because you can't express yourself. They wanted us to speak English in the school classes. We'd put out a real effort. I would get into a lot of fights because I spoke Spanish and they couldn't understand it. I was punished. I was kept after school for not speaking English.

29. According to the passage, what is the ethnic background of the author?

(a) American Indian
(2) black
(3) Hispanic
(4) English
(5) a field worker

1 2 3 4 5

30. How does the author feel about the childhood he discusses?

(1) confused
(2) proud
(3) sad
(4) bitter
(5) hopeful

1 2 3 4 5

31. When did the author quit school?

(1) when he was not selected to play the part of Abe Lincoln
(2) about two years after the incident involving the patriotic play
(3) when he was expelled
(4) at the age of sixteen
(5) when all his friends quit

1 2 3 4 5

32. Which of the following conclusions might be drawn from the passage?

(1) The author didn't try very hard to succeed in school.
(2) It is a handicap to be unable to speak English well.
(3) Sixth-grade boys get into a lot of fights.
(4) Political discussions were discouraged at the author's school.
(5) Spanish was accepted in the schools.

1 2 3 4 5

33. Why did the author ignore discussions about politics and civil rights?

(1) He didn't have an opinion about these matters.
(2) He was denied the right of free speech.
(3) He found it difficult to express his ideas in English.
(4) Everyone was speaking Spanish.
(5) No one listened to him anyway.

1 2 3 4 5

34. Who of the following would be most able to identify with the feelings and experiences of the author?

(1) a juvenile delinquent
(2) a struggling actor
(3) a welfare recipient
(4) a farmer
(5) a naturalized citizen

1 2 3 4 5

GO ON TO THE NEXT PAGE.

Items 35–40 are based on the following passage.

What kind of town is Poker Flat?

As Mr. John Oakhurst, gambler, stepped into the main street of Poker Flat on the morning of the twenty-third of November, 1850, he was conscious of a change in its moral atmosphere since the preceding night. Two or three men, conversing earnestly together, ceased as he approached, and exchanged significant glances. There was a Sabbath lull in the air, which, in a settlement unused to Sabbath influences, looked ominous.

Mr. Oakhurst's calm, handsome face betrayed small concern in these indications. Whether he was conscious of any predisposing cause, was another question. "I reckon they're after somebody," he reflected; "likely it's me." He returned to his pocket the handkerchief with which he had been whipping away the red dust of Poker Flat from his neat boots, and quietly discharged his mind of any further conjecture.

In point of fact, Poker Flat was "after somebody." It had lately suffered the loss of several thousand dollars, two valuable horses, and a prominent citizen. It was experiencing a spasm of virtuous reaction, quite as lawless and ungovernable as any of the acts that had provoked it. A secret committee had determined to rid the town of all improper persons. This was done permanently in regard of two men who were then hanging from the boughs of a sycamore in the gulch, and temporarily in the banishment of certain other objectionable characters. . . .

Mr. Oakhurst was right in supposing that he was included in this category. A few of the committee had urged hanging him as a possible example, and a sure method of reimbursing themselves from his pockets of the sums he had won from them. "It's agin justice," said Jim Wheeler, "to let this yer young man from Roaring Camp—an entire stranger—carry away our money." But a crude sentiment of equity residing in the breasts of those who had been fortunate enough to win from Mr. Oakhurst overruled this narrower local prejudice.

Mr. Oakhurst received his sentence with philosophic calmness, none the less coolly that he was aware of the hesitation of his judges. He was too much of a gambler not to accept Fate. With him life was at best an uncertain game, and he recognized the usual percentage in favor of the dealer.

A body of armed men accompanied the deported wickedness of Poker Flat to the outskirts of the settlement.

35. What is happening to John Oakhurst?

(1) Oakhurst has just witnessed a hanging.
(2) Oakhurst has just been told about a secret committee.
(3) Oakhurst and other undesirables are being banished from Poker Flat.
(4) Oakhurst has just won a great deal of money.
(5) Oakhurst knows he is going to be killed.

(1) (2) (3) (4) (5)

GO ON TO THE NEXT PAGE.

36. Which of the following statements is true of the townspeople of Poker Flat?
    (1) They act inconsistently in enforcing moral rules.
    (2) They are against gambling.
    (3) They are deeply religious people.
    (4) They are philosophical and calm.
    (5) They avoid fights and confrontations.

    (1) (2) (3) (4) (5)

37. To what does John Oakhurst compare life?
    (1) a sentence from a judge
    (2) a child's game
    (3) a committee decision
    (4) a card game
    (5) fate

    (1) (2) (3) (4) (5)

38. To what historical event can the treatment of Oakhurst and others be compared?
    (1) Watergate trials
    (2) Vietnam War
    (3) Great Depression
    (4) Salem witchcraft trials
    (5) civil rights marches

    (1) (2) (3) (4) (5)

39. Which of the following purposes does the first paragraph serve?
    (1) introduces the major characters
    (2) gives information about the setting
    (3) outlines the plot
    (4) describes a major conflict
    (5) provides an unimportant distraction

    (1) (2) (3) (4) (5)

40. Who is telling this story?
    (1) John Oakhurst
    (2) a person on the secret committee
    (3) an outside narrator with no knowledge of the thoughts and feelings of the characters
    (4) an outside narrator with knowledge of the thoughts and feelings only of John Oakhurst
    (5) an outside narrator with knowledge of the thoughts and feelings of all the characters

    (1) (2) (3) (4) (5)

GO ON TO THE NEXT PAGE.

Items 41–45 are based on the following passage from a play.

What does Iris do with the gift she is offered?

(Music and Lights up. Sidney and Iris are seated . . . with the audition book for South Pacific. There is a loud knocking at the door and Iris opens it to Mavis Bryson—an older, heavier, more fashionable version of herself—and without a moment's pause, demonstratively, shuts and bars it with her body.)

IRIS. I don't need it—*(Meaning the dress box which her sister is carrying)*—I don't want it—and I won't take it.

MAVIS. Just try it on. That's all I ask. *(Iris reluctantly opens the door to admit her.)* Hello, Sid, darling.

SIDNEY. Hello, Mav.

MAVIS. *(Blithely opening the box)* Could you conceivably have the hootenanny at another time? *(She turns off the phonograph.)*

IRIS. We don't go to cocktail parties, Mavis. At least the kind where you wear a dress like *that.* I want to tell you from the top, Mavis. This is not a good time. I am in no mood for the big sister–little sister hassle today. That's all I—*(Mavis crosses and maternally stops Iris's mouth in midspeech with one hand.)*

MAVIS. Just slip it on; I had it taken up for you. You'll look stunning in it. *(Confidentially, as she zips and buttons)* What have you heard from Gloria?

IRIS. Not a word.

MAVIS. Here, let me smooth it down on you. Now, really, I can't tell a thing with those sticking out—*(Iris pulls up her jeans as far as possible under the dress)* It's stunning! Now all you'll need for Easter is a new pair of sneakers.

41. How are Iris and Mavis related to each other?

(1) They are not related.
(2) They are mother and daughter.
(3) They are sisters-in-law.
(4) They are sisters.
(5) They are aunt and niece.

① ② ③ ④ ⑤

42. What is Mavis planning to give Iris?

(1) a floor-length party dress
(2) a pair of jeans
(3) a new pair of sneakers
(4) an elaborate gift box
(5) a hand-me-down dress

① ② ③ ④ ⑤

43. What does this passage suggest about Sidney?

(1) Sidney is attracted to Mavis.
(2) Sidney never goes to cocktail parties.
(3) Sidney doesn't interfere in disagreements between the sisters.
(4) Sidney resents having his evening interrupted by Mavis.
(5) Sidney and Iris have been married for many years.

① ② ③ ④ ⑤

44. Which of the following statements best describes Iris's attitude toward Mavis?

(1) Iris feels she needs Mavis's help.
(2) Iris cares deeply for Mavis.
(3) Iris is critical of Mavis.
(4) Iris pities Mavis.
(5) Iris wishes she were more like Mavis.

① ② ③ ④ ⑤

45. Which of the following stage directions gives the most insight into Mavis's character?

(1) "(. . . There is a loud knocking at the door and Iris opens it to Mavis Bryson—an older, heavier, more fashionable version of herself. . . .)
(2) "*(Iris reluctantly opens the door to admit her.)*"
(3) "*(Blithely opening the box)*"
(4) "*(Mavis crosses and maternally stops Iris's mouth in midspeech with one hand.)*"
(5) "*(Confidentially, as she zips and buttons)*"

① ② ③ ④ ⑤

END OF EXAMINATION

TEST 5: MATHEMATICS POSTTEST

Directions

The Mathematics Posttest consists of 56 problems. Whenever possible, you should arrive at your own answer to a question before looking at the choices; otherwise, you may be misled by plausible mistakes. You may refer to the formula page on the inside back cover of this book.

You should take approximately 1½ hours to complete this test. There is no penalty for guessing. Try to answer as many questions as you can. Work rapidly but carefully, without spending too much time on any one question. If a question is too difficult for you, skip it and come back to it later.

For each answer, mark one answer space. See how the following example is done.

EXAMPLE

A secretary bought a desk calendar for $5.95 and a pencil container for $1.89. How much change did she get from a $10 bill?

(1) $2.16
(2) $2.61
(3) $7.84
(4) $8.74
(5) $8.84

● ② ③ ④ ⑤

The amount is $2.16; therefore, answer space (1) has been marked.

Answers to the questions are in the Answer Key on page 767. Explanations for the answers are on pages 762–766.

Directions: For each problem choose the one best answer.

Plane A

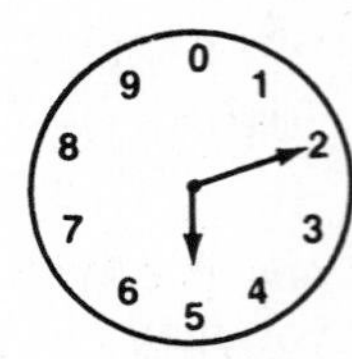

Plane B

1. On an altimeter the shorter hand indicates thousands of feet above sea level. The longer hand indicates hundreds of feet above sea level. How many feet higher above sea level is Plane B flying than Plane A?

(1) 4
(2) 32
(3) 400
(4) 3,200
(5) 10,000

2. Coffee priced at $4 per pound will be specially discounted 8%. How much will $1\frac{1}{2}$ pounds cost?

(1) $3.68
(2) $4.80
(3) $5.52
(4) $6.00
(5) Insufficient data is given to solve the problem.

3. A woman had car trouble and missed 10 hours of work. If she earns $321 for a 40-hour week, how much did she lose while her car was not running?

(1) $8.03
(2) $32.10
(3) $80.25
(4) $240.75
(5) $311.00

4. What is the area in square inches of a wheel that is 30 inches in diameter?

(1) 222
(2) 503.25
(3) 647
(4) 706.5
(5) 824

5. When it's noon Eastern Standard Time in Miami, it's 9 A.M. Pacific Standard Time in Seattle. If a person in Miami calls a relative in Seattle at 8:05 P.M. Eastern Standard Time and talks for 67 minutes, what time will it be in Seattle when he hangs up?

(1) 5:12 P.M.
(2) 5:42 P.M.
(3) 6:12 P.M.
(4) 9:12 P.M.
(5) 12 minutes after midnight

6. An advertising agency can produce a 30-second radio commercial from 15 minutes of tape. Each minute of taping costs the agency $188. How many 15-minute taping sessions can be made during $4\frac{1}{2}$ hours?

(1) 12
(2) 14
(3) 16
(4) 18
(5) 21

7. A shoe store had 500 dozen pairs of shoes when it advertised a 50% off sale. All but 65 dozen were dress shoes, and the others were work boots. How many pairs of dress shoes did the store mark down?

(1) 435
(2) 1,870
(3) 2,610
(4) 5,220
(5) Insufficient data is given to solve the problem

8. Anita Gomez wants to send a globe as a gift. She has a rectangular box with inside measurements of 10 inches by 8 inches by 12 inches. Which of the following is the diameter of the largest globe that will fit inside the box?

(1) 12
(2) 11.5
(3) 10.5
(4) 10
(5) 8

GO ON TO THE NEXT PAGE.

9. In 1976 a 2-bedroom house was worth $33,400. In 1986 the house had increased in value by 289% over the 1976 value. What was the house worth in 1986?

(1) $33,689
(2) $43,052
(3) $96,526
(4) $129,926
(5) $6,762,600

① ② ③ ④ ⑤

10. The Andersons bought a used car for $2,400. They agreed to a loan in which they must make 24 equal monthly payments of $116 each. How much was the finance charge on the loan?

(1) $184
(2) $384
(3) $984
(4) $2,784
(5) $3,384

① ② ③ ④ ⑤

11. A stock showed the following activity during one business week:

A. Monday $+\frac{1}{2}$
B. Tuesday $+\frac{5}{8}$
C. Wednesday $+\frac{1}{4}$
D. Thursday $+\frac{3}{8}$
E. Friday $+\frac{3}{4}$

Which of the following shows the order of gains from least to most during the week?

(1) E,B,A,D,C
(2) C,D,A,B,E
(3) C,B,A,D,E
(4) E,A,B,D,C
(5) A,E,D,B,C

① ② ③ ④ ⑤

12. If a woman paid $80.50 in interest on a loan at 11.5%, how much money had she borrowed?

(1) $925
(2) $850
(3) $750
(4) $700
(5) Insufficient data is given to solve the problem.

① ② ③ ④ ⑤

13. A runner prepared for a race by running around a quarter-mile track. Over 5 days she ran $5\frac{1}{2}$ miles, $6\frac{1}{4}$ miles, $7\frac{3}{4}$ miles, $8\frac{1}{2}$ miles, and 9 miles. What was the mean number of miles that she ran?

(1) $7\frac{1}{10}$
(2) $7\frac{1}{5}$
(3) $7\frac{3}{10}$
(4) $7\frac{2}{5}$
(5) $7\frac{1}{2}$

① ② ③ ④ ⑤

14. A keyboard operator averages 60 words a minute in the morning but only 56 words a minute in the afternoon. Which of the following expressions shows the number of words she averages in a day if she works 4 hours in the morning and 3.5 hours after lunch?

(1) $60(60)4 + 60(56)3.5$
(2) $60(60 + 56) \times (4 + 3.5)$
(3) $(60 + 56 + 4 + 3.5)60$
(4) $\frac{60 \times 60}{4} + \frac{60 \times 56}{3.5}$
(5) Insufficient data is given to solve the problem.

① ② ③ ④ ⑤

15. Carmen Morales bought some land 4 years ago for $8,500. This year the land is worth $13,000. What is the approximate percentage increase in the value of the land?

(1) 53%
(2) 51%
(3) 49%
(4) 28%
(5) Insufficient data is given to solve the problem.

① ② ③ ④ ⑤

GO ON TO THE NEXT PAGE.

Items 16–21 refer to the following table and diagram.

Floor area (sq ft)	Size of air conditioner (British Thermal Units)
100–200	5,500–6,000
200–300	6,000–7,500
300–400	7,500–9,000
400–500	9,000–11,000
500–750	11,000–14,500
750–900	14,500–16,500
900–1,000	16,500–18,000
1,000 and over	18,000 and over

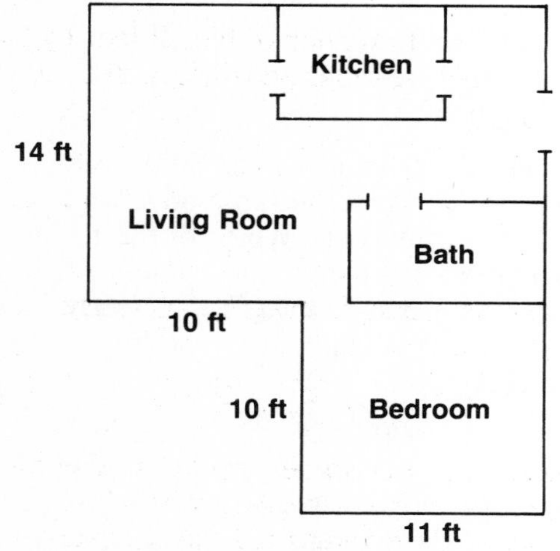

Charlie plans to buy an air conditioner, but he needs to find out what size will best cool his apartment. He found that a room-sized air conditioner costs $340, while one that would cool the entire apartment is $500. The larger air conditioner is 30% more efficient than the room-sized one.

16. What size air conditioner should Charlie get for his bedroom?

(1) 5,500–6,000
(2) 6,000–7,500
(3) 7,500–9,000
(4) 9,000–11,000
(5) 11,000–14,500

(1) (2) (3) (4) (5)

17. What size air conditioner should he look for to cool his entire apartment?

(1) 5,500–6,000
(2) 6,000–7,500
(3) 7,500–9,000
(4) 9,000–11,000
(5) 11,000–14,500

(1) (2) (3) (4) (5)

18. What is the difference in square feet between Charlie's bedroom and his apartment?

(1) 96
(2) 137
(3) 198
(4) 266
(5) 294

(1) (2) (3) (4) (5)

19. What is the approximate percentage difference in price for the two sizes of air conditioner?

(1) 22%
(2) 38%
(3) 47%
(4) 53%
(5) 160%

(1) (2) (3) (4) (5)

20. If the efficiency rating for a room air conditioner is 22.0 based on a scale of 1 to 100, what is the rating for the larger model? (Round the number to tenths.)

(1) 6.6
(2) 12.0
(3) 19.3
(4) 22.0
(5) 28.6

(1) (2) (3) (4) (5)

21. If the smaller air conditioner cost $0.45 an hour to use, how much would Charlie pay if he left it running for 2 days?

(1) $10.80
(2) $21.60
(3) $33.40
(4) $40.32
(5) $48.00

(1) (2) (3) (4) (5)

22. Tyrone wants to frame 2 posters for his bedroom. Each poster is 36.5 inches wide and 64 inches long. The framing costs $2.78 per inch. How many inches of framing does he need?

(1) 100.5
(2) 201
(3) 350
(4) 380.5
(5) 402

(1) (2) (3) (4) (5)

GO ON TO THE NEXT PAGE.

23. A community group sponsored a flea market. It spent \$400 to rent a lot and charged each seller \$50 for a 10 foot by 10 foot booth. The group computed its profit at \$700. How many sellers participated in the market?

(1) 150
(2) 30
(3) 22
(4) 14
(5) 8

(1) (2) (3) (4) (5)

24. Ed and James have 25 grandchildren between them. Ed has 11 more than James. How many grandchildren does Ed have?

(1) 7
(2) 10
(3) 14
(4) 18
(5) 36

(1) (2) (3) (4) (5)

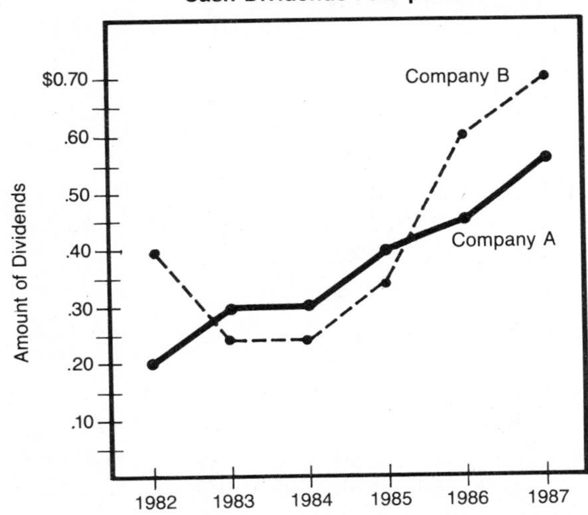

25. If a woman had 150 shares of stock in Company B during the years 1982 through 1986, what amount of money did she receive in dividends?

(1) \$425.00
(2) \$385.25
(3) \$288.50
(4) \$268.50
(5) \$185.00

(1) (2) (3) (4) (5)

26. A bank sign showed the afternoon temperature as 35° Celsius and the time as 2:50. The formula for converting Celsius degrees to Fahrenheit is $F = \frac{9C}{5} + 32$. How many degrees Fahrenheit was it?

(1) 67
(2) 78
(3) 83
(4) 95
(5) 112

(1) (2) (3) (4) (5)

27. What is the least number of tiles 2 feet by 2 feet that will be required to tile a kitchen 16 feet long?

(1) 4
(2) 16
(3) 48
(4) 64
(5) Insufficient data is given to solve the problem.

(1) (2) (3) (4) (5)

28. A company had 60 women workers. The ratio of men to women workers was 4 to 1. How many men workers did the company employ?

(1) 15
(2) 64
(3) 180
(4) 240
(5) 300

(1) (2) (3) (4) (5)

29. Which of the following has the greatest value?

A. a box containing 10 quarters
B. a box containing 20 dimes
C. a box containing 550 pennies
D. a box containing 30 half dollars
E. a box containing a \$10 bill

(1) A
(2) B
(3) C
(4) D
(5) E

(1) (2) (3) (4) (5)

GO ON TO THE NEXT PAGE.

30. A retiree works part-time at a fast-food restaurant. He makes \$5 an hour. On Monday he worked 6 hours, on Wednesday 5 hours, and on Friday 6 hours. Which of the following expressions shows the amount of money that the retiree made for these 3 days?

(1) \$5(5) + 6 + 6
(2) \$5(5 + 6 + 6)
(3) \$5 + (6) × (5) × (6)
(4) (\$5 × 6) + 6 + 5
(5) $\frac{6 + 5 + 6}{\$5}$

① ② ③ ④ ⑤

Items 31–32 refer to the following graph.

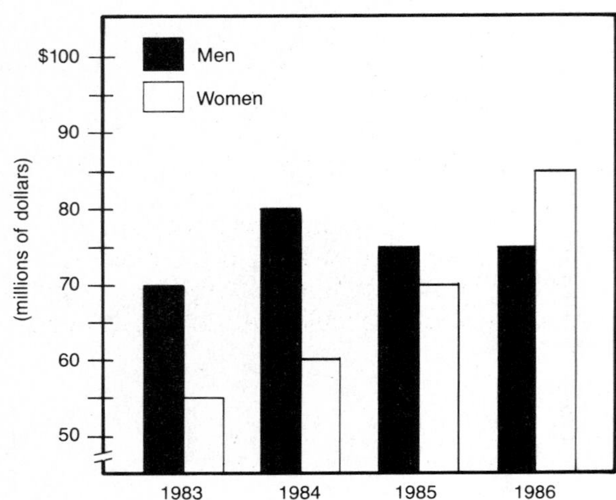

31. What is the difference between the total credit card usage in 1983 and in 1986?

(1) \$35,000
(2) \$185,000
(3) \$35,000,000
(4) \$125,000,000
(5) \$160,000,000

① ② ③ ④ ⑤

32. What is the ratio of the expenditure by men to the expenditure by women in 1984?

(1) 7:5
(2) 6:8
(3) 4:3
(4) 3:4
(5) 3:2

① ② ③ ④ ⑤

33. A radio station is running a contest. First prize is a car; the second, third, and fourth prizes are trips; and the fifth prize is \$500. In all, 4,500 listeners have entered the contest. What is the probability that Joe Edwards will win a trip?

(1) 3/5
(2) 1/1,500
(3) 1/4,500
(4) 5/4,500
(5) Insufficient data is given to solve the problem

① ② ③ ④ ⑤

34. If 5 pounds of cookies cost \$3.50, how much do 6 pounds cost?

(1) \$0.70
(2) \$2.92
(3) \$4.20
(4) \$17.50
(5) \$21.00

① ② ③ ④ ⑤

35. What is the value of $6^4 - 6^2$?

(1) 4,032
(2) 1,260
(3) 36
(4) 12
(5) 4

① ② ③ ④ ⑤

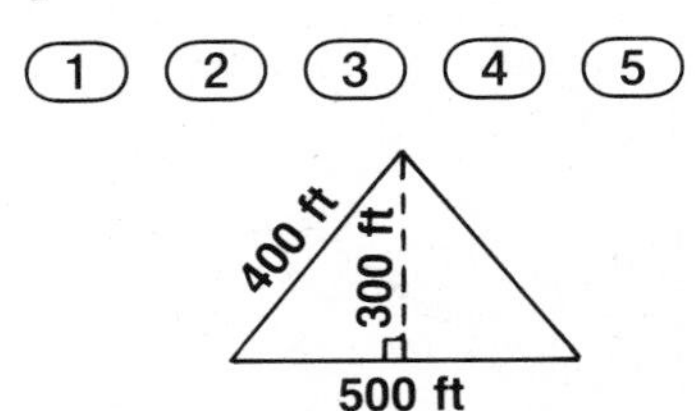

36. A paving crew must figure out the amount of blacktopping it needs to pave the parking lot shown above. Which of the following expressions could it use to determine the square measure of the lot?

(1) 300 × 400 × 500
(2) 300 + 400 + 500
(3) $\frac{1}{2}$ (500) (300)
(4) $\frac{1}{2}$ (400) (300)
(5) Insufficient data is given to solve the problem.

① ② ③ ④ ⑤

GO ON TO THE NEXT PAGE.

37. Simplify $5m + 8 - 13 - 2m$.

(1) $3m + 21$
(2) $21 + (-3m)$
(3) $7m + 5$
(4) $3m - 5$
(5) $10m - 5$

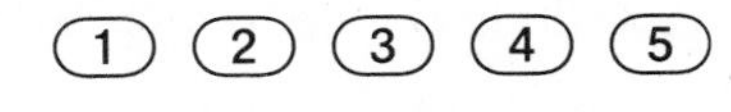

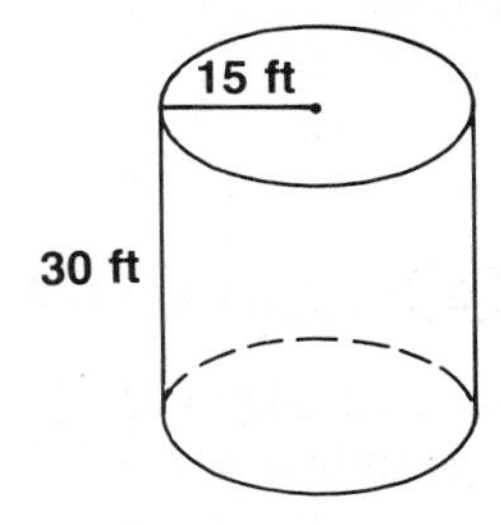

38. How much grain in cubic feet can a farmer store in the silo shown above before he must rent another one?

(1) 450
(2) 2,826
(3) 6,750
(4) 21,195
(5) 42,390

39. A husband and wife together have \$78 one morning. The wife needs twice as much money as the husband that day because she will go grocery shopping after work. How much money will each one get?

(1) the wife \$29; the husband \$29
(2) the wife \$40; the husband \$38
(3) the wife \$38; the husband \$40
(4) the wife \$26; the husband \$52
(5) the wife \$52; the husband \$26

(1) (2) (3) (4) (5)

40. The batting average of a player is the ratio of the number of hits to the number of times at bat. If the average of a player is .280 and he has been to bat 150 times, which of the following expressions could be used to determine how many hits he has?

(1) $\frac{.280}{150}$
(2) $\frac{150}{.280}$
(3) $150 - .280$
(4) $\sqrt{.280 - 150}$
(5) $.280 \times 150$

(1) (2) (3) (4) (5)

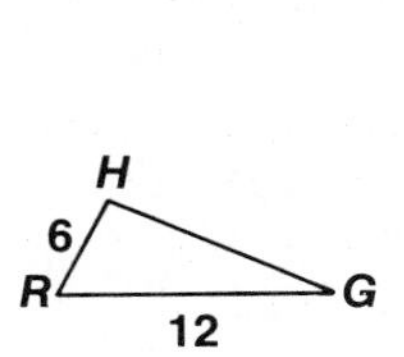

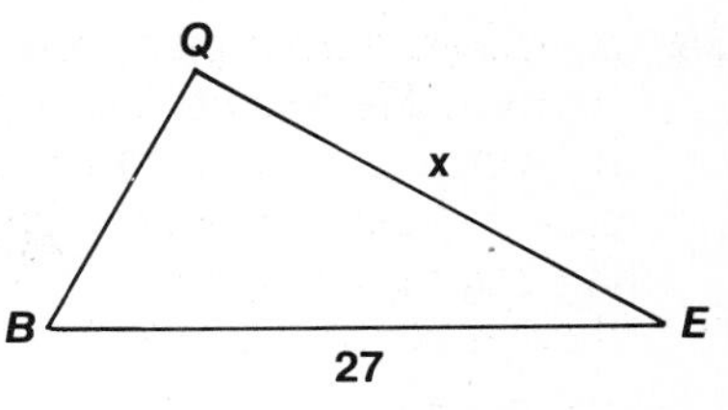

41. If triangle RHG and triangle BQE are similar, how long is side QE?

(1) 8
(2) 13.5
(3) 15
(4) 21
(5) Insufficient data is given to solve the problem.

(1) (2) (3) (4) (5)

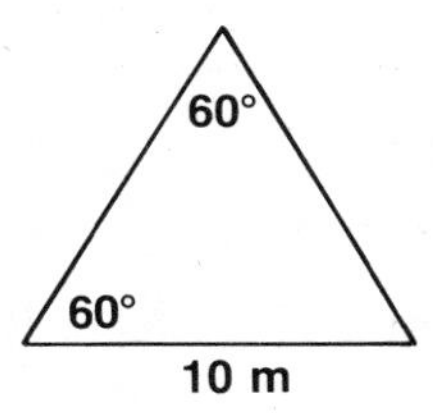

42. The Triangle Restaurant wants to string lights around its new sign. If the dimensions of the sign are as shown above, how many meters of lights should the restaurant owner purchase?

(1) 30
(2) 60
(3) 130
(4) 180
(5) Insufficient data is given to solve the problem.

(1) (2) (3) (4) (5)

43. What is the value of $s(p + r)$ if $s = \frac{1}{2}$, $p = 6$, and $r = 4$?

(1) 5
(2) 7
(3) 10
(4) 12
(5) 24

(1) (2) (3) (4) (5)

GO ON TO THE NEXT PAGE.

Items 44–46 refer to the following diagram.

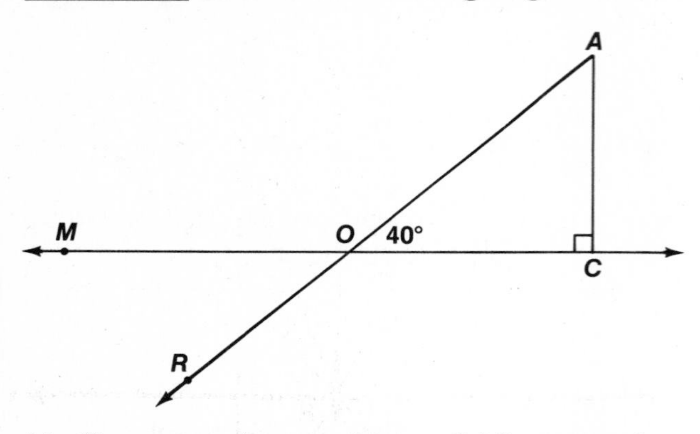

44. How many degrees does $\angle CAO$ measure?
(1) 140
(2) 60
(3) 55
(4) 50
(5) 40

1 2 3 4 5

45. What is the measure of $\angle AOM$?
(1) 140
(2) 60
(3) 55
(4) 50
(5) 40

46. How many degrees does $\angle MOR$ measure?
(1) 140
(2) 60
(3) 55
(4) 50
(5) 40

1 2 3 4 5

47. Which of the following is a correct factoring of the equation $x^2 + 7x + 12 = 0$?
(1) $(x + 4)(x - 3)$
(2) $(x + 3)(x - 4)$
(3) $(x + 7)(x + 12)$
(4) $(x - 7)(x - 12)$
(5) $(x + 4)(x + 3)$

1 2 3 4 5

48. A particular home computer was advertised by four different stores as follows:
A. \$40 down and \$40 a month for $1\frac{1}{2}$ years
B. 12% off the normal price of \$700
C. \$660 with a rebate of \$50
D. \$100 a month for 5 months and a balloon payment of \$200 in the sixth month

Which would be the best buy?
(1) A
(2) B
(3) C
(4) D
(5) Insufficient data is given to solve the problem.

1 2 3 4 5

49. The moon is an average of 237,000 miles from earth. In scientific notation, approximately how far would a spacecraft from earth travel during a round trip to the moon?
(1) 2.37×10^5
(2) 237×10^5
(3) 4.74×10^5
(4) 474×10^3
(5) 5.74×10^3

1 2 3 4 5

50. The surface area of a circular garden is 314 square feet. How many feet of rope would be needed to rope off the garden around its edge?
(1) 3.14
(2) 31.4
(3) 62.8
(4) 628
(5) Insufficient data is given to solve the problem.

1 2 3 4 5

GO ON TO THE NEXT PAGE.

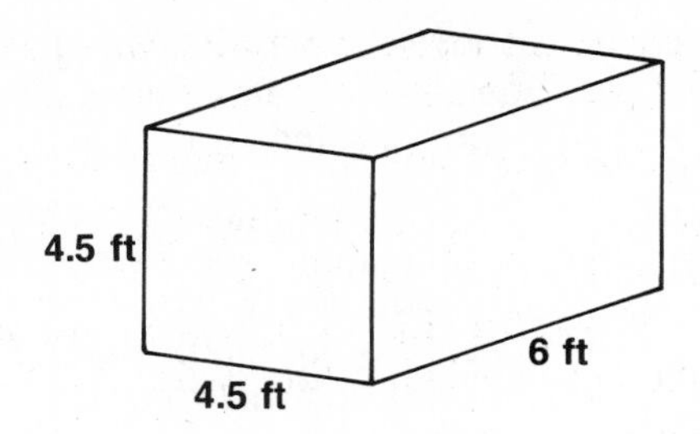

51. A moving company charges $13.20 for the packing carton shown above. What is the capacity in *cubic yards* of the carton?

(1) 4.5
(2) 15.0
(3) 59.4
(4) 121.5
(5) 134.7

① ② ③ ④ ⑤

52. Which of the following is a correct solution to $x < (5 + 1)2$?

(1) 5
(2) 12
(3) 14
(4) 17
(5) 20

① ② ③ ④ ⑤

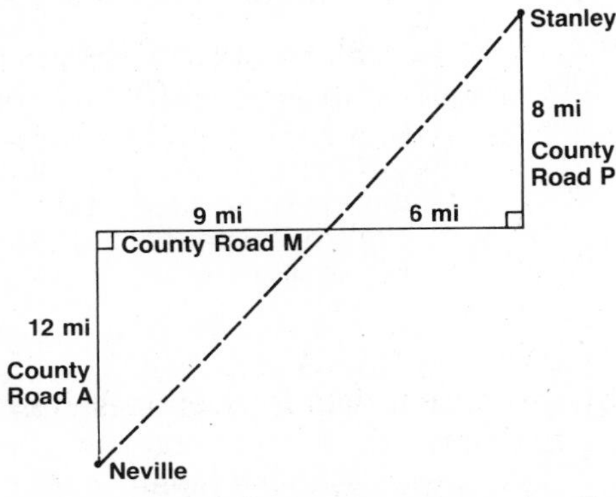

53. A new road is being planned to run directly from the town of Neville to the town of Stanley. How many miles long will the new road be?

(1) 10
(2) 15
(3) 25
(4) $\sqrt{35}$
(5) Insufficient data is given to solve the problem.

① ② ③ ④ ⑤

Items 54–56 refer to the following coordinate grid.

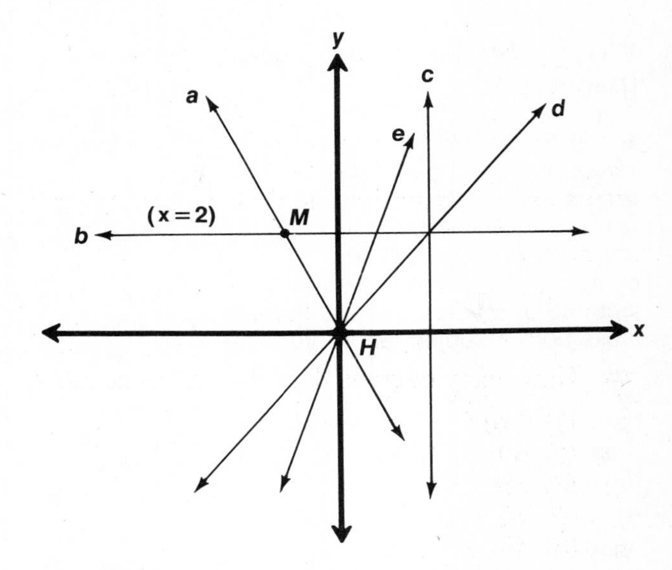

54. Which line has a slope equal to 0?

(1) *a*
(2) *b*
(3) *c*
(4) *d*
(5) *e*

① ② ③ ④ ⑤

55. What is the midpoint of the distance between point *M* and point *H* (0,0)?

(1) 1
(2) 2
(3) $\sqrt{2}$
(4) $\sqrt{5}$
(5) Insufficient data is given to solve the problem.

① ② ③ ④ ⑤

56. What is the point of intersection of lines *b* $(x = 2)$ and *d* $(x = y)$?

(1) (0,2)
(2) (2,0)
(3) (0,4)
(4) (2,2)
(5) (4,0)

① ② ③ ④ ⑤

END OF EXAMINATION

Posttest B Answer Explanations

Writing Skills
(pages 681–694)

1. (3) *By learning cross-country skiing during week-long programs called Ski for Light* is a sentence fragment. A *sentence fragment* does not present a complete thought; it lacks a subject and/or a verb. This fragment lacks both a subject and a verb. Option (5) is incorrect because a semicolon and *however* can be used only to join two complete thoughts. *Each* sentence must have a subject and a verb.

2. (4) A comma is not a strong enough punctuation mark to join two sentences. *And* (option 2) should be used only to connect two closely related ideas. Option (4) is the best choice.

3. (5) *Friends* is simply a plural word. It does not need an apostrophe, which is used to show possession.

4. (3) *Skiers* is the subject, not *program.* Since *skiers* is a plural, it needs a matching plural verb. Don't be fooled by words that come between a subject and verb. *Ranged* is incorrect because it indicates an action in the past. The skiing program still exists.

5. (3) This is a series of three items: *changes in slopes, upcoming trees,* or *turns.* Commas are needed to separate items in a series. Changing *spend* to *spending* makes the sentence a fragment.

6. (5) No error. Seasons of the year usually are not capitalized.

7. (5) *Whether* indicates a choice. *Weather* refers to outside conditions.

8. (2) *Will have planned* suggests something that has not yet happened. *Plan* shows present time. Changing *hiking* to *hikes* makes the list of activities mismatched. *Biking, rafting, swimming,* and *hikes* do not match. As in the original wording, all the items must end in *-ing.*

9. (1) *Through a partnership based on a love of outdoor athletic activities, blind people and their sighted guides can participate in the move toward physical fitness.* The phrase at the beginning now clearly describes blind people and sighted guides. In the original wording, it is not clear if the blind people *and* their guides are forming a partnership or *just* the guides.

Many Americans are joining the fitness movement that is sweeping the country. Blind and partially sighted people can also enjoy vigorous physical activity by learning cross-country skiing during week-long programs called Ski for Light. Ski for Light is an exciting and unique program. It provides a week when experienced sighted skiers teach blind people to ski. The goal of Ski for Light is to teach blind people an activity they can enjoy with sighted as well as blind friends. Blind skiers in this unusual program range in age from 18 to 72. During this week of skiing fun, a volunteer Ski for Light guide uses accurate verbal descriptions of the terrain and skiing techniques to teach each blind skier. At first, guides spend much of their time alerting the new cross-country skiers to changes in slopes, upcoming trees, or turns. Later, as the new skiers gain confidence, the guides can spend more time describing the beautiful winter scenery to their blind companions. In many cities, organizations have been formed that also pair blind and sighted participants in many vigorous outdoor warm-weather activities. Many of these sports clubs plan such activities as tandem biking, white-water rafting, swimming, and hiking. Through a partnership based on a love of outdoor athletic activities, blind people and their sighted guides can participate in the move toward physical fitness.

10. (2) The subject is *child,* and it means just one person. *Child* and *was* agree. *Of working parents* is a phrase between the subject and the verb. Don't be tricked by a word meaning more than one *(parents)* that comes between the subject and the verb.

11. (4) *Thanks to the pioneering work of Jane Addams, one of the most well-known social reformers of this century* is a sentence fragment. It lacks a subject and a verb. Option (4) is the simplest way to combine the two.

12. (1) *Interested in helping people from all walks of life, Jane Addams put her ideas for social reform into practical use. Interested* describes Jane Addams and not her ideas or her reforms. Using a descriptive phrase at the beginning of a sentence is one way of adding variety to your writing. Just make sure the phrase describes the correct word in the sentence.

13. (3) Since *For many immigrants arriving in Chicago at the turn of the century* is a long introductory phrase, it's best to use a comma after it. *Chicago* is capitalized because it is the name of a city.

14. (4) Two complete thoughts cannot be joined with a comma. *And* can be used to join the two closely related thoughts. Since *Jane Addams* means one and not more than one person, option (1) is incorrect. Don't be fooled by names that end in *s (Jones, Bass, Kansas).* They indicate one person or place.

15. (5) No error. Remember that commas are used before a connecting word *(but)* joining two sentences.

16. (1) World War I happened in the past. *Worked* is correct because it shows past time. Option (2) is incorrect because a comma is not used between two things joined by *and.*

17. (4) The correct spelling is *received.* The rule is "*i* before *e* except after *c.*" *Through* and *threw* are commonly confused; *threw* is a form of the verb *throw.*

18. (1) A comma is placed between two complete thoughts joined by *and, or, nor, for, but, so,* or *yet. Although, but,* and *yet* do not correctly show the relationship between the two ideas.

In the early 1900s, a child of working parents was either locked in a room at home all day or left to wander in the streets. Today day-care centers are commonplace thanks to the pioneering work of Jane Addams, one of the most well-known social reformers of this century. She was responsible for many welfare laws for workers, such as an eight-hour workday for women, factory safety inspections, and workmen's compensation. She rented Hull House in 1889 and started the first social settlement house in America. Interested in helping people from all walks of life, Jane Addams put her ideas for social reform into practical use. For the many immigrants arriving in Chicago at the turn of the century, she was indispensable in helping with job placement, English language lessons, and cultural adjustment. Jane Addams was one of the founders of the National Association for the Advancement of Colored People, and she also campaigned for woman suffrage. In 1912 the suffragettes asked her to become a candidate for president of the United States, but she declined. She worked tirelessly for world peace and famine relief during World War I. For her efforts to bring about world peace through disarmament and to free the world from hunger, she received the Nobel Peace Prize in 1931. She invented social work and social welfare, and many people called her the greatest living American woman of her time.

19. (3) *Decision* is the correct spelling. *Are* is correct because *times* is the subject *(times are). Times* and *are* agree because they are both plural forms.

20. (2) Since *for example* is an interrupting phrase, it must be separated from the rest of the sentence by commas.

21. (1) No comma is needed between two things joined by *and.*

22. (1) *On a normal day, the operators handle fifty thousand calls, thirty thousand of which are for the president.* This option gets rid of unnecessary words to combine the two sentences most effectively.

23. (3) *When Elvis Presley died, the switchboard was flooded with calls from people suggesting that his birthday be made a national holiday.*

24. (1) *Canadian* is a word that describes *Mounties;* it comes from *Canada,* which is capitalized. *Their* shows ownership, while *there* indicates place.

25. (2) When two subjects are joined with *either/or,* the verb agrees with the subject closer to it. *First lady* is singular, so the verb should also be singular *(wants).* Remember that verbs ending in *s* agree with subjects that mean one person or thing.

26. (2) *Was* is used to indicate past time; *in 1908* is the clue that tells you that the first part of the sentence is about something that happened in the past. Removing *but* is incorrect. Two complete thoughts cannot be joined with just a comma.

27. (4) The original wording is a run-on. *Yet* and *even though* do not accurately express the relationship between the two complete thoughts.

There are times when almost everyone has wanted to call the president either to complain about a policy decision or to give him some encouragement. Who takes all those calls from, for example, kings, queens, celebrities, schoolchildren, and average citizens? Eighteen female and two male operators control the old-fashioned switchboard in the Old Executive Office Building adjacent to the White House. On a normal day, the operators handle fifty thousand calls, thirty thousand of which are for the president. The number doubles during emergencies. When Elvis Presley died, the switchboard was flooded with calls from people suggesting that his birthday be made a national holiday. Like the Canadian Mounties, the White House operators are known for "getting their man" or woman, as the case may be. They are famous for tracking down anyone either the president or the first lady wants to reach. They find them on ski slopes, on boats in the middle of the ocean, or on a barge floating down a river in France. In 1908, the monthly phone bill was only $28.87, but today it averages $45,000.00 a month. There is one thing, though, that the White House operators don't do. They never accept collect calls.

28. (1) If you did not choose option (1), you didn't choose the correct time for the verb. *In a recent survey* is a clue to past time.

29. (2) *Climate, mountains, beaches,* and *water* are items in a series. They should be separated by commas. Since all four of these things are the subject, the subject is plural, and the verb *appeal* must agree. *Appeals* is used only with a singular subject.

30. (3) *Foreign* is an exception to the rule "*i* before *e* except after *c.*"

31. (3) The pronoun *you* is used throughout this passage. Option (3) is the only option that correctly follows through with this usage.

32. (1) *Hawaii's most famous landmark, Diamond Head, is an extinct volcanic crater that can be climbed for a stunning view of Waikiki.* The best way to revise this sentence is to get rid of the unnecessary words *and it is.*

33. (1) *Bay* is part of the place name and as such should be capitalized. Option (5) is incorrect because *snorkel* and *go swimming* are not parallel; they do not match in construction.

34. (3) *Or learn the unique dance of Hawaii, the hula* is a sentence fragment because it lacks a subject. The best way to revise these sentences is to combine the complete verbs of the sentences. Option (4) is incorrect because *can ride* does not match *to learn.*

35. (5) No error. Inserting *which* changes the sentence to a fragment. Option (4) is incorrect because *is* and *abounded* do not match.

36. (4) *Things,* not *friendliness,* is the subject of this sentence. *Things make* is correct because subject and verb agree. Don't be misled by words that come between the subject and the verb.

Do you dream of a romantic vacation in Hawaii? In a recent survey, 19 million Americans chose Hawaii as their dream vacation spot. Its soft climate, scenic mountains, palm-fringed beaches, and clear blue water appeal to many visitors. For many Americans, Hawaii possesses the glamour of a foreign country. Just think about all the things you can do in this land of aloha hospitality. Hawaii's most famous landmark, Diamond Head, is an extinct volcanic crater that can be climbed for a stunning view of Waikiki. The turquoise water of Hanauma Bay attracts visitors wishing to snorkel or swim in the underwater park. If you are adventurous, you can ride the big breakers at the Banzai Pipeline or learn the unique dance of Hawaii, the hula. Shoppers dressed in colorful cotton shirts or brightly flowered muumuus can browse in the 155 stores of the Ala Moana shopping mall. The air of Hawaii is filled with the fragrance of exotic tropical flowers, and the sky abounds in rainbows, which are as commonplace as orchids. All these things, plus the friendliness of its people, make beautiful Hawaii the vacation destination of more than 4 million tourists a year.

37. (3) Careless pronunciation can cause *known* to be spelled incorrectly as *knowen. Begun* (option 4) cannot be used without a helping verb such as *had* or *have.*

38. (5) No error. *It all started* is the clue to using a connecting word that shows time *(when). Will need* is incorrect because it refers to something that has not yet happened.

39. (3) *But* shows contrast. There is no contrast between noticing the hubcaps and picking them up. *And* is the correct way to join the two verbs *noticed* and *began.*

40. (4) *Hanged* refers to "hanging by the neck." *Hung* means to put or place one object on another.

41. (1) Commas are used before *and, or, nor, for, but, so,* and *yet* when they join two complete thoughts. Option (5) would be correct if you omitted the comma after *hobby.*

42. (5) In the original wording, it is not clear what *them* refers to. Replacing *them* with *the hubcaps* makes it clear that she moved the hubcaps and not something else.

43. (2) *Asked* refers to something that has already happened. *Before the move* is the clue that you need such a verb in the past.

44. (1) *However, moving them all to the barn took so long that she knew it was time to sell a few.* A connecting word must be used to join the phrase *moving them all to the barn* to the rest of the sentence. *That* and *so* are the only connecting words in the options. *So* can only be used to connect two complete thoughts and not a phrase and a sentence. *That* can be used to connect a phrase to a sentence.

45. (2) *Buy* means "to purchase." *By* usually indicates nearness or direction.

As a child, did you ever collect butterflies, stamps, or baseball cards? One woman, known as the Hubcap Queen, began her collecting as an adult. It all started in Tennessee when she needed a hubcap for her car. She noticed many hubcaps lying along the side of the road and began picking them up hoping to find a match for her missing hubcap. At home, she cleaned them and hung them on the garage walls. People were fascinated by her unusual hobby, and they brought her hubcaps they had found. People enjoyed looking at all the different kinds of hubcaps hanging in long rows along the walls. Soon her collection grew too large for the walls of the garage, so she moved the hubcaps to the old barn behind her house. Before the move, someone occasionally asked to buy a hubcap, but she always replied that she could not part with any of her shiny friends. However, moving them all to the barn took so long that she knew it was time to sell a few. Now when people ask to buy her hubcaps, she happily sells them at a fair price. Her unusual hobby has become a small but profitable business.

46. (4) *May help* expresses an action that might happen. Options (1), (2), (3), and (5) express past time. The verb in the dependent part *(are buying)* shows an action that could happen in present time. Therefore, option (4) and *are buying* agree.

47. (2) *A document called a "Buyers Guide"* is a group of words that gives additional information about the word *sticker.* Option (2) is correct because a comma must come before and after a phrase that gives additional information.

48. (5) *Appeared* is the correct spelling. Option (3) is incorrect because *one should* does not match *you purchase.* Remember that matching pronouns must be used throughout a passage.

49. (1) *Deception* is spelled without an *s.* Remember that commas are not used before *that.*

50. (5) No error. *Dealers* and *are* agree. *Dealers be* is nonstandard English.

51. (4) This is an example of misusing a comma; you need to use a connecting word with it. Option (4) contains the connecting word *but.* Both *cars* and *motorcycles* agree with *are.*

52. (1) The original wording of the sentence is correct. The connecting words in options (2), (3), (4), and (5) do not logically express the relationship between the dependent part and the main part of the sentence.

53. (4) Sentence 10 has two subjects, *lack* and *misunderstanding.* Because it has two subjects, the verb must agree; it must be a plural verb. Therefore, option (4) is correct because *were* refers to more than one thing. If you chose option (3), you probably overlooked the time clue *(In the past). Are* shows present time; *were* shows past time.

54. (3) *He* is incorrect because it does not match the word it replaces *(dealers). They* is the only pronoun in the options that means more than one thing.

55. (2) *Useful information about manufacturers' warranties, spoken promises, service contracts, and consumer complaints is contained in the Buyers Guide.* Since *information* is the singular subject of the revised sentence, the verb *is* (not *are*) agrees with it. Option (5) makes the revision a fragment. Options (3) and (4) would not be logical verb choices.

Each year, Americans spend about $85 billion to buy more than 17 million used cars. If you are buying a used car, the Federal Trade Commission's Used Car Rule may help you. The rule requires all used-car dealers to place a large sticker, a document called a "Buyers Guide," in the window of each used vehicle being offered for sale. Whenever you purchase a used car from a dealer, you should receive the original or a copy of the Buyers Guide that appeared in the window of the vehicle you bought. To help avoid deception, the Buyers Guide must reflect any changes in warranty coverage that you may negotiate with the dealer. Dealers are required to post the Buyers Guide on all used vehicles, including used automobiles, light-duty vans, and light-duty trucks. A "used vehicle" is one that has been driven more than the distance necessary to deliver a new car to the dealership or to test drive it. "Demonstrator" cars are covered by the rule, but motorcycles are excluded. A major portion of the Buyers Guide gives you important information you can use when you select a used car. In the past, lack of information and misunderstanding about warranties frequently were sources of consumer problems. If dealers offer a warranty on a used vehicle, they must fill in the warranty portion of the Buyers Guide. Useful information about manufacturers' warranties, spoken promises, service contracts, and consumer complaints is contained in the Buyers Guide.

Sample Essay

Stress is a part of everyday life, but many people today are overstressed. For example, they may have too much work to do—or be out of work. The high divorce rate and other changes in family life also add to stress for some people.

Some ways of handling stress are helpful, and some are not. Smoking, eating, or drinking too much are no real help. Some people become irritable and hard to get along with when they are under pressure, and this behavior only adds to their problems.

There are ways to help ease the problems of stress. Doctors have learned that such problems tend to be worse when people feel they do not have control over their lives. Working to gain more control over what is happening will help ease stress. If the situation cannot be controlled, it helps at least to understand it.

Exercise is another good way to deal with stress. Regular workouts, running, tennis, or even fast walking can ease tensions. Relaxation routines also help. For example, a person can lean back and imagine he or she is in a beautiful, restful place.

Constant stress is bad for both physical and mental health. Everyone, no matter how busy, needs to take time to relax and unwind. People may live longer lives as a result, and they will surely be happier.

Social Studies
(pages 695–712)

1. (2) Since Country X cannot produce enough to feed its people, yet is highly advanced in technology, it would be both necessary and possible for it to buy food from other nations.

2. (3) The earth, having just become the parent of its five billionth child, admits that the child will be hungry and crowded. The cartoonist evidently believes the earth hasn't the resources to care for that many people.

3. (4) The use of force against those who want change would be characteristic of an extreme right-wing government.

4. (2) The opposition to government regulation of economic matters is a conservative political view.

5. (1) The belief that the federal government can best solve social or economic problems is a liberal one.

6. (3) The belief in revolution and in the redistribution of power are characteristic of an extreme left-wing political view.

7. (1) The passage tells you that, in the past, the Navy veterans were called to battle by the same sound. Their nervous response in the hospital was similar to the one they would have had in the past.

8. (3) Option (3) states the central purpose of the study. Options (1) and (2) are opinions. Option (4) may be true, but it does not answer the question. Option (5) can be neither proved nor disproved.

9. (2) The map's key states that there is reliable skiing from December through March in areas where snowfall is greater than 90 inches.

10. (4) Arrows show the direction of lake-effect storms, and directly in their path along the shorelines are two areas of heavy snow. Options (1) and (3) can be disproved by the map. Options (2) and (5) can be neither proved nor disproved.

11. (5) The symbol for Lake Placid shows it slightly above the line indicating 100 inches of snow. All the other options may or may not be true, but they cannot be demonstrated by the map.

12. (3) The map shows four areas of heavy snowfall. Two are directly in the path of lake-effect storms; two are in areas labeled *mountains.* The map's key suggests that both lake-effect storms and elevation affect snowfall.

13. (5) The map does not suggest any relationship between snow and shipping in New York harbor. Railroads, airlines, and highways would be affected by snow, as would skiers and tourist offices that inform people interested in winter sports or travel.

14. (2) According to the third sentence of the passage, Soviet missiles were only 90 miles from U.S. shores, hence posing a new and dangerous threat.

15. (1) The passage states that missile bases were being installed and that the President risked war to keep the missiles out of Cuba. This strongly implies that the Soviet ships were bringing the means to complete the bases.

16. (2) The President demonstrated a determination to maintain the blockade and a willingness to use force if the Soviet ships didn't turn around. All other options are contradicted by the passage.

17. (2) The passage states that pensions would increase for those serving 30 years.

18. (3) Since the law applied only to those *entering* the armed forces after August 1, 1986, this person was not affected.

19. (4) By rewarding those with longer service, the military tried to encourage people to serve longer. Since the Pentagon noted how much money would be saved, this was probably also a reason for the law.

20. (3) The Senator said that people who had their pensions reduced would leave the armed forces because of that. But those already in the military would not have pensions reduced, and those to whom the reduction applied would know what pension to expect.

21. (1) Quick addition will tell you that the 45 and older group will increase by a larger percentage than the other options.

22. (3) The graph shows that there will be a larger increase in older people than in younger. More services for the elderly would seem to be in order.

23. (2) Since there will be more older people, retirement security will probably be a major concern.

24. (1) The top bar of the graph shows the population for all ages increasing by 12.3 percent. The other options may be true, but they are opinions.

25. (3) Since the greater part of the population will be older and older people tend to have more health problems, you may infer that the nation will need more health-care workers.

26. (3) Remember that *monopoly* means having almost total control of the means of producing and selling an item, as Rockefeller did in the oil industry.

27. (1) The next to the last sentence in the passage states that "oil prices soared." Options (2), (3), (4), and (5) can be disproved by the passage.

28. (5) Since there is a need and a new desire for the roots of the bean plants, and the means to produce them in increased quantities exist, it is predictable that farmers on the island will grow more beans to meet the increased demand.

29. (1) To answer this question, you will need to recall the law of supply and demand—that supply will increase or decrease in proportion to increased or decreased demand. Options (2), (3), (4), and (5) list important economic concepts, but none of them applies to this passage.

30. (4) The use of fertilizers in agriculture is a technological measure. Since the farmers improved their production levels through the use of fertilizer, it is demonstrated by the passage that technology can increase agricultural production.

31. (5) Option (5) may or may not be true. The table does not show how much is paid for goods or services; it only shows the percentage of change in price. Options (1), (2), and (3) are facts; option (4) is a fact that is disproved by the table.

32. (2) The price of energy would have a direct effect on the price of transportation, and the chart does show the two items' costs rising and falling together. Other options are highly unlikely.

33. (4) People whose incomes cannot increase would be hurt most. It is difficult to say how students (1) or farmers (3) might be affected. Doctors (2) might raise their fees, and those with cost-of-living increases (5) would not be hurt by rising costs.

34. (1) The second sentence states that many Americans unjustifiably regarded Japanese Americans as a threat to national security.

35. (4) The third paragraph states that although their loyalty was soon established, Japanese Americans were not allowed to return home. Options (1), (2), (3), and (5) were results of the relocation.

36. (5) The last paragraph states that this is only one opinion of the relocation. Options (1), (2), (3), and (4) are facts.

37. (2) Those who believe relocation was justified must agree with option (2) since it restates what occurred. Agreement with options (1) and (5) would mean the relocation was not justified. Option (3) is a misstatement of fact. The passage implies the relocation was unconstitutional, but it does not discuss its legality (4).

38. (3) You may infer that the stimulus, cash, gives the workers pleasure, and that it is likely to make their response, increased production, occur again. Options (1) and (4) are examples of negative reinforcement. We don't know if the bell in (2) is a pleasant or an unpleasant experience. There is no stimulus and response, no cause and effect relationship, in option (5).

39. (1) You may infer that the shock stimulus is unpleasant and likely to make the pigeon avoid pecking that disk again. Options (2) and (5) are examples of positive reinforcement. In (3) and (4) there is no reinforcing stimulus.

40. (3) When a reinforcing stimulus gives pleasure, this is a reward; when it gives pain or displeasure, this could be called punishment. None of the other options apply.

41. (2) When the superintendent claims that people without children won't want their taxes raised to pay for education, he is saying that people are unwilling to pay for educating other people's children.

42. (4) Options (1), (2), (3), and (5) would all increase the costs to be paid by the school district, thereby increasing the deficit. Only option (4) would lower expenses and, thus, the deficit.

43. (3) This statement defines people's rights and the limits of government. It is the first amendment to the U.S. Constitution and is contained in the Bill of Rights.

44. (1) The signer of this document agreed to abide by "just and equal laws, . . . for the general good of the colony." This is from the Mayflower Compact.

45. (4) The writer of this document announced "that all persons held as slaves . . . are, . . . and shall be, free." This is from the Emancipation Proclamation.

46. (2) The writers of this statement are dissolving "the political bands which have connected them with another," and declaring a "separation." This is from the Declaration of Independence.

47. (3) The graph shows the highest percent of increase in benefits in 1980. All the other options are untrue according to the graph.

48. (5) According to the 1972 law, a COLA must be paid when the inflation rate is 3% or more. If no COLA was paid in 1986, then the inflation rate must have been less than 3%.

49. (4) Variation in the cost of living adjustments paid in different years suggests that the amounts are determined according to the inflation rate. Options (1) and (2) cannot be determined by the graph. Option (3) is disproved by the graph, and (5) is not a feature of the laws as stated.

50. (1) Your knowledge of U.S. geography can help you see that, in 1860, the railroads ended at just the place where the Mississippi River would be if it were shown on the map.

51. (3) While this option may be true, it is an expression of opinion that cannot be substantiated by the map. All other options are facts.

52. (4) You may recall that the Forty-Niners took part in the California gold rush of 1849, too early to use the railroads. All the other groups could and did use the railroads.

53. (4) This person is denied a job because she may be suspected of being an illegal immigrant, although she may not be. This is a case of job discrimination based on national origin. Option (1) may be age discrimination, which is not covered by Title VII. Options (2) and (3) show discrimination in housing and education, which are not covered by Title VII. Option (5) shows no discrimination.

54. (2) This is probably the best summary of the graph's information. Option (1) can't be proved because the graph doesn't specify daytime and nighttime temperatures. Options (3) and (5) are disproved by the graph. Option (4) is only one fact from the graph and does not represent a summary.

55. (1) The third paragraph states that higher humidity is not a factor in Phoenix's higher temperatures.

56. (5) This statement sums up all the information in the article. Options (1), (2), (3), and (4) all support that conclusion.

57. (2) Since the city's growth has made it hotter, its continued growth, which is predicted, will probably make it hotter still. Any of the other options is possible, but none of them could be predicted from the passage.

58. (3) In this situation, they must believe that public safety is the primary consideration. If they believed (1) or (2) were most important, they could not vote to raise the legal drinking age. Lawmakers' thoughts about (4) and (5) are unclear since they are vaguely related to the issue of teenage drinking.

59. (4) This is an exact statement of the results of the study. Options (1) and (2) are predictions which may or may not come true and can't be supported by the study. Options (3) and (5) are not true, according to the passage.

60. (1) Based on the study, this is the only reliable prediction they could make. They could not expect the exact percentages in (2) and (4). They could make no predictions regarding (3). Option (5) is unlikely since it would reverse the trend.

61. (3) This fits the definition of *recall:* The people remove a public official by petitioning for a popular vote. Options (1) and (4) deal with citizen petitions and votes on laws not officials. Options (2) and (5) are legislative votes, not popular votes.

62. (4) The passage doesn't say this is the *only* restriction. All the other options are facts either stated or implied in the passage.

63. (4) According to the fifth sentence, Roosevelt's concept of a Square Deal meant that each side received fair treatment and consideration. Options (1), (2), (3), and (5) can be disproved by the information in the passage.

64. (2) The last two sentences state that Roosevelt's actions marked "a turning point in labor history" and that his role as "mediator" rather than "strikebreaker" differed from that of past Presidents. Options (1), (3), (4), and (5) can be disproved by the passage.

Science
(pages 713–732)

1. (1) Mole is the only property which is restricted to a certain number of particles. No volume is specified in (2) and (3).

2. (4) Water has a greater heat capacity than air. Water will draw more heat from a person's body than air will when they are at the same temperature.

3. (3) There is one gram of each substance, yet one sinks and one floats. Therefore, one must occupy a larger volume. Density is defined as the weight in a given volume of material.

4. (5) The bubbling indicates that a chemical reaction is going on. When the bubbling stops, the chemical reaction appears to stop because the products and reactants are forming at the same rate.

5. (2) By using more water and less syrup in the drinks, the owner decreases the concentration of syrup. The drinks contain fewer syrup molecules in a 10-ounce volume.

6. (3) The water vapor rises because it is less dense than the air around it.

7. (4) The deepest point in Hudson Bay is only 600 feet.

8. (5) Only Option (5) actually represents a conclusion.

9. (3) How much the tinted glass reduces the sun's glare can actually be measured and verified by scientific means. All other options appeal to the buyer.

10. (3) Options (2)–(5) are true statements which can be found in the passage. However, (3) is the only one which adequately summarizes the information contained above. Option (1) is false.

11. (1) The RNA contains the information for preparing the protein. This is the only instruction the ribosome will receive. If the instructions are wrong, the protein will not be assembled correctly (2). The protein will probably not be able to function properly if there is a mistake in its structure (3). A mistake in RNA is not transmitted to the DNA (4) nor will it change the structure of the ribosomes. Therefore, option (5) is incorrect.

12. (1) The weight difference means nothing if the two scales are not accurate. The woman believed that the two different readings actually did mean that she had gained 5 pounds. Option (2) is irrelevant. If she assumed options (3), (4), or (5), she would not have been concerned over the weight difference.

13. (4) The package information implies that people who suffer medical disorders should ask their physicians if this product will have any harmful effects on their conditions. Contrary to options (1) and (5), many people under a physician's care use salt substitutes. The label does not discuss who is considered healthy as options (2) and (3) suggest.

14. (1) Forces 2 and 3 are upward forces; Force 1 is a downward force. If the sign is to remain still, the upward forces must equal the downward forces.

15. (2) The information is contained in the table.

16. (5) Iodine helps regulate the rate at which foods are burned, or the metabolic rate. If iodine is not used properly by the body, then this function will not be carried out adequately.

17. (1) Options (2)–(5) all contain information which can be found in the passage. However, option (1) is the only statement which actually summarizes the entire passage.

18. (1) The passage says that rocks containing the shells of fossil protists are found on top of pools of oil. The absence of shells of fossil protists would indicate that no oil is present.

19. (1) The passage states that scientists theorize that oil formed in this way. Options (2)–(5) are facts according to the passage.

20. (4) The protist shells are part of the rock that formed above the pools of oil. All other options are unrelated to the question asked.

21. (1) This shows an effect the drug will have on the ill person who takes the medication. Options (2)–(5) are incorrect.

22. (5) This is the only statement which summarizes the material presented in the diagram. All the other options represent a specific relationship.

23. (2) The experiment determined whether chilling or boiling affects the enzyme's ability to function in a reaction. Because the reaction time is the same for all tubes, (1) and (3) are incorrect. Option (4) is true, but it does not adequately summarize the entire experiment. Option (5) is incorrect.

24. (3) The results obtained in tubes 2 and 4 indicate that the enzyme functions normally after cold treatment. Option (4), then, is incorrect. Option (2) is false because no reaction occurs in tube 3. Option (5) is false because the reaction itself was carried out in a warm-water bath, not in the cold.

25. (5) Tube 3 indicates that boiling destroys the enzyme's ability to help in the reaction. Cold has no effect (1)–(3), as shown in tube 4. Option (4) is a condition not considered in the experiment.

26. (1) This is the only statement which is true of the summer generations of monarchs. All other options are true only of the autumn butterflies.

27. (1) It is the cooling and shortening of days that announce the coming of autumn and trigger a change in the butterfly generations. Reread paragraph 3. All other options are incorrect.

28. (1) Only this statement is a generalization, a conclusion about the changes which occur between the summer and autumn butterflies. All the other options support this conclusion.

29. (1) All life on the island was destroyed by the eruption. All organisms had to be reintroduced to the island, finding their way from nearby land.

30. (4) The shrubs produce chemicals which have a harmful effect on the grasses. This fits the definition of *allelopathy.*

31. (2) The tree pipit can live only in areas having a tall tree because of his singing *behavior.*

32. (4) The mold secretes penicillin, a substance which is harmful to bacteria.

33. (5) The two blackbird species struggle for the same territory.

34. (3) The scientist's values will not allow him to inflict severe pain and injury on the mice. All other options reflect concrete problems he would run into in doing the project.

35. (5) This statement is an opinion which has some basis in fact. As expressed, however, it is an opinion. Options (1)–(4) are facts which can be scientifically verified.

36. (3) Statements B, C, and D could be verified by scientific observation and analysis. It is common knowledge that the Richter scale is the scale on which the intensity of earthquakes is measured. Statements A and E could not be verified. Statement A is an opinion. Statement E is too broad.

37. (4) The experimenter assumes that every centimeter of expansion in the mercury represents an equal change in temperature. If this assumption were not made, the stated conclusion could not be drawn. Option (5) states the opposite and cannot be correct. Options (1) and (2) are irrelevant. Option (3) is incomplete; *change* in temperature causes the mercury to rise.

38. (2) This information is found in the passage.

39. (4) The final paragraph tells us that different metals produce different characteristic colors in the sparks. No other option states any distinctive characteristic about a particular metal.

40. (1) The final paragraph indicates that ammonium compounds cause a variety of color shades, while picric acid and sulfur make the colors more intense. Fireworks which contain all of these compounds will have many variations in color which are quite intense. The sample lacking picric acid and sulfur will have many dull colors.

41. (2) This statement is an opinion. All other options are scientifically verifiable.

42. (3) Because interferon makes the body less susceptible to a second infection, any flu infection he suffers will be mild.

43. (5) Taste is a matter of opinion. Options (1)–(4) could be confirmed in a chemical analysis.

44. (2) This information is derived from the graph.

45. (1) Only this statement summarizes the information on the graph. All other options are details.

46. (2) The graph does not indicate how many new cases of cancer occurred each year. It gives only information about how many people died (1), (3), (4), and (5).

47. (3) If more cases of cancer are being diagnosed each year, but the number of deaths does not change, more cures are taking place. Option (3) tells us this. All other options emphasize the fact that no dramatic change in death rates is occurring.

48. (5) This answer emphasizes the death rate. Options (1), (2), and (4) indicate that much progress has been made against cancer in the areas of medications, detection, and diagnosis. Option (3) indicates a reason for the rise in lung cancer, the only cancer type which has increased dramatically.

the book will move is friction. The book moves a shorter distance on a rough surface, so the force of friction must be greater. Option (1) is incorrect; a force was applied in all cases. The experiment does not study direction of the frictional force (2). The same force is applied in all three cases (3). Option (5) does not consider the differences in the surfaces.

50. (1) All options are true statements. Only option (1) indicates she is practicing good nutrition by taking vitamins. Options (2)–(5) suggest that she receives no benefit from taking excessive amounts of vitamins.

51. (2) The effects of gravity can be mimicked by spinning the space stations (3). No others are implied in the passage. Option (1) is a false statement. Option (4) is clearly stated in the passage. Another implication of the passage might be stated as "The small amount of minerals lost from bone does not pose a serious health problem" (5).

52. (1) The passage merely states that thousands of people will be floating in space stations (2). The passages cites doctors' reports that there are no problems associated with living under conditions of microgravity (4). Option (3) is stated. Option (5) is refuted.

53. (3) Little gravitational force is felt because when one is out in space, he or she is a very great distance from other objects. Option (1) is irrelevant. Options (2) and (4) are false statements. Option (5) is true, but does not support the given statement.

54. (1) Temperature requirements of a plant can be experimentally determined. All other options express opinions.

55. (4) This information can be read from the graph. The light in room 1 never shines for 15 hours a day. Room 2 receives 15 or more hours of light each day between weeks 8 and 16. The plants in room 3 receive at least 15 hours of light per day for 16 weeks (between weeks 4 and 20). The plant leaves will turn red in both rooms 2 and 3.

56. (1) The light in room 1 never shines for 15 hours a day.

57. (4) Energy is required to change water from a liquid to a gas. The energy required to evaporate the water is supplied by the hot air. In the process, the air gives up its heat and becomes cool. Options (1) and (5) are irrelevant statements. Option (2) may be true, but it would not explain why the house is cooled. Option (3) is false; if anything, the circulation process would heat up the air.

58. (4) This statement is an opinion. All other options could be verified by scientific procedures.

59. (4) The passage states that the two kinds of milk differ only in their fat content. If 2 percent fat in milk is better for babies than milk with no fat at all, fat in the milk must be desirable. Options (1), (3), and (5) can be eliminated on the basis of this discussion. Option (2) is both false and irrelevant.

60. (4) The purpose of a graph is to indicate a relationship between two different factors. He would not have graphed the results if he did not believe that a relationship existed (2). He may have assumed option (1) when he began the experiment, but it did not contribute to his decision to graph the data. Option (3) is false based on the experimental results.

61. (5) Only this option summarizes the ideas that bacteria both help and hinder us in many commonplace ways. Options (1)–(3) are true statements but present a one-sided view of the information in the passage. Option (4) is never discussed in the passage.

62. (2) Only this statement represents a conclusion which can be drawn from the passage. All other options are true statements supporting this conclusion.

63. (3) Bacteria are involved in many food processes. All other options express the opposite of what would occur if there were no bacteria.

64. (1) The passage says that the bacteria multiply rapidly when large amounts of wastes are available. The huge numbers of bacteria use up the available oxygen. This relationship is well stated in paragraph 3. Options (2)–(4) are true statements, but they do not directly support the statement about Lake Erie. Option (5) is false and contradicts the statement itself.

65. (5) She made all three assumptions. She assumed statement A when she said the whole city received the same amount of rain as was collected at her particular location. Statement B must be assumed if the gauge is to catch any rain. If strong wind blows the rain sideways, it will not collect in the gauge (assumption C).

66. (5) The decision to invest time, effort, and money to benefit a few people cannot be made on the basis of scientific evidence. The answer to this question involves both economics and ethics. All other options can be answered through scientific methods.

Interpreting Literature and the Arts
(pages 733–742)

1. (2) The passage doesn't tell you outright what Florence was going to do. But context clues such as "her life awaited her," "I'm going, Ma," and "up North" help you guess that Florence was going to leave home.

2. (1) Although not told by Florence, the story reveals the inner thoughts, feelings, and opinions only of Florence. Although the narrator reports words and actions of all the characters, option (5) is not correct because an outside observer would not know how Florence sees things.

3. (5) Gabriel's tears and his attempts to persuade her not to go contradict options (3) and (4). His remarks about her mother and himself show that he is worried about *them,* not about Florence. There is not enough evidence in the passage to support option (2).

4. (2) The surrounding words provide context clues to help you see that Florence was speaking just for the sake of saying something.

5. (2) The phrase "scorned to dignify these words with her attention" indicates the mother's attitude. The passage does not give sufficient evidence to support any of the other options.

6. (4) Florence seems to feel that people must do certain things for themselves, even if it means not being able to help family members. She would therefore most likely support her friend's decision.

7. (4) Lines 3 and 4 of the poem say that the wife has a sense of her place—"she fills an envied place." That "place" is her position as wife; it is also the one she believes the guest envies.

8. (1) The phrase "says there was never so sweet a room" in the sixth line of the poem is a compliment from the guest. So option (1) is directly supported by the poem.

9. (2) The poem says that "the happy young housewife does not know/That the woman beside her was first his choice." There is no evidence in the poem to support any of the other options.

10. (2) The guest is very gracious and complimentary, and the wife remains ignorant of the feelings that the guest and the husband have for each other (despite the husband's glances). So it is unlikely that the guest would sound hopeful, enthusiastic, frightened, or ashamed. She would, however, be sad not to be in the wife's position.

11. (3) The tone is certainly not grim, angry, wistful, or praising, so options (1), (2), (4), and (5) can be eliminated. The tone is gently ironic, for the young housewife probably would not be quite as happy if she knew what you have discovered.

12. (1) Line 12 answers the question of how the husband feels about his guest. This line fits in with the rhyme and rhythm of the poem, making the ending more serious and ironic, but not too abrupt. Thus, options (3) and (4) are eliminated. There is no evidence in the poem to support the other options.

13. (3) Even if you don't know what the word *paeans* means, you can figure it out by picking the option that fits the context of the passage. Since the author tells how Wysocki's paintings express his patriotism and appreciation for America's past, option (3) is best. None of the other options fits in the context of the passage.

14. (4) In the second to the last paragraph, Wysocki says his work is a vision of America as he'd like it to be. Thus, his paintings, an attempt to "clean up" America, are not totally realistic. His own remarks about his work contradict the opinions in the other options.

15. (4) Wilson says that if Wysocki were inside the art system, he would be reviewed and not ignored. Thus, since Wysocki is not reviewed by critics, you can conclude that Wilson thinks Wysocki is not really a part of the system.

16. (5) Since Wysocki paints rural scenes, he is not likely to paint a work with the title of option (1), (2), or (4). Options (3) and (5) reflect the painter's patriotism, but since Wysocki prefers neat scenes without mess, he is not likely to paint a battle scene, so option (3) is incorrect.

17. (2) The description of Wysocki's popularity and success does not help the reader visualize his paintings, but all the other devices or descriptions do. Wysocki gives clues to what his paintings are like when he describes both his work and his past, since he paints by remembering scenes from his past.

18. (1) The passage is full of details about Wysocki's nostalgic paintings of the past and of how he enjoys painting America as he'd like it to be. The passage gives the reader the idea that viewers of Wysocki's art would be in a nostalgic and sentimental mood.

19. (3) This choice takes into account the two important ideas in lines 1–3: waking up and finding that something is different.

20. (2) The first stanza ends with "Listen." The last stanza ends with "the silence/of a city/hushed/by snow." That is the main idea of the poem.

21. (3) The words "the bray of buses" suggest that a bus can be compared to a braying donkey.

22. (5) The poem describes a busy *city* that has had a snowstorm. New York is the only likely option. Los Angeles seldom gets snow, and suburbanites do not usually hear so much everyday noise.

23. (1) The main idea of the poem, together with the word "hushed" and the soft sound of *s* used often in the last five lines, creates a quiet mood.

24. (3) This fact is mentioned near the end of the review. There is no evidence to suggest option (4), and options (1), (2), and (5) are all contradicted by the review.

25. (1) Option (2) is incorrect because it is the mother of the character played by Macchio who moves. Although the other reasons may also have motivated Morita's character to go to Okinawa, the review says that he left after getting a letter telling of his father's illness. You can infer that that is the main reason for his going.

26. (5) Though romance and vengeance figure in the plot, the author says that honor, custom, and tradition are the film's focus.

27. (4) This is the only option mentioned by the author (lines 10–13) as a problem. Although the problems mentioned in the other options may occur in making some sequels, none are common to most sequels.

28. (2) The author says too many positive things about the movie to be scornful. But his last sentence and other critical remarks such as "It was a losing battle" indicate that he was disappointed in the sequel.

29. (3) This is the best conclusion based on the information in the passage, since it tells that the native language of the author was Spanish. Options (1) and (2) have no basis for support in the passage; option (5) is not an example of "ethnic background" as asked for in the question.

30. (4) Because the author discusses his failure to be accepted and the unfairness he experienced at school, and because he got into fights and quit school, you can assume he is more angry and bitter than sad or confused. None of the events described by the author would give him reason to feel proud or hopeful about his childhood.

31. (2) The author states that he was in sixth grade when he tried out to be Abe Lincoln and quit school in about eighth grade, which would be about two years later. Although you may infer that not getting the part was *one* of the experiences that led to the author's quitting school, no direct relationship is indicated in the passage.

32. (2) The author states that he felt frustrated and less capable because of his inability to speak English. Option (4) is not correct because, while the author says he did not participate in discussions on politics and civil rights, he mentions them and never suggests that such discussions were discouraged. Option (3) is incorrect; the boy got into fights because he spoke Spanish, not because he was in sixth grade. Options (1) and (5) are incorrect because both contradict statements made in the passage.

33. (3) Answering this question requires careful attention to detail. In Lines 16–18, the author explains his hesitation in speaking about politics and civil rights: "It's a very degrading thing because you can't express yourself."

34. (5) Although the author experienced poverty, punishments, and school conflicts, only a naturalized citizen with a different native language would identify with similar language barriers and educational struggles.

35. (3) The third and fourth paragraph and the last sentence talk about the secret committee's plan to banish undesirable people, a category that includes Oakhurst. These parts of the passage also talk about the committee's escorting the undesirables out of town.

36. (1) The author says that in Poker Flat there was "a change in its moral atmosphere since the preceding night," that it was "a settlement unused to Sabbath influences," and that it "was experiencing a spasm of virtuous reaction." These words give clues that the people's concern for "morality" were not consistent. The committee and its decisions were new and unexpected.

37. (4) Life is called "an uncertain game." It is obviously a card game because of the reference to gamblers and to "the dealer."

38. (4) During the historic era of the Salem witchcraft trials, people suspected of being evil or dangerous were often killed, punished, or banished without a fair trial.

39. (2) The description in the opening paragraph helps set the scene. Since only one character, John Oakhurst, is mentioned, option (1) is not valid. Nor has the paragraph carried out the purposes in options (3), (4), or (5).

40. (5) The person telling the story reveals a knowledge of the thoughts, motives, and feelings of Oakhurst, of several of the gamblers, and even of the townspeople as a whole.

41. (4) The stage directions for Iris's first lines indicate that the two characters are sisters.

42. (5) The stage directions in Iris's first lines mention a "dress box," which would eliminate options (2), (3), and (4). Option (1) can be eliminated because the final stage directions have Iris pulling up her jeans under the dress. And Mavis's size, mentioned in the opening stage directions, combined with her comment that she had the dress "taken up," would indicate that option (5) is the correct answer.

43. (3) Sidney makes no comments except to return Mavis's greeting. Iris acknowledges that they *do* go to some cocktail parties, so option (2) is incorrect. There is not enough evidence to support options (1), (4), or (5).

44. (3) Iris's first comments eliminate option (1). Her rude treatment of Mavis and her comments about the style of dress, cocktail parties, and the "big sister–little sister hassle" eliminate option (2) and reveal a tense relationship. Nothing in the passage suggests options (4) or (5).

45. (4) Option (4) suggests that Mavis is dominating. Option (1) describes only Mavis's physical appearance, not her inner character.

Mathematics
(pages 743–751)

1. (3) 400

Plane A is flying at 4,800 ft: $(4 \times 1{,}000) + (8 \times 100)$. Plane B is flying at 5,200 ft: $(5 \times 1{,}000) + (2 \times 100)$. Find the difference between the two by subtracting.

$5{,}200 - 4{,}800 = 400$

2. (3) $5.52

First find the price per pound with the special discount.

```
$ 4.00      $ 4.00
x   .08     −  .32
 .3200        3.68
```

Then find the price for $1\frac{1}{2}$ lb.

```
 $ 3.68
 x  1.5 ←convert 1½ to a
 1,840   decimal
 3 68
$5.520
```

3. (3) $80.25

Solve this problem by setting up a proportion: 40 hours of work is to $321 as 10 hours of work is to an unknown number of dollars. Set up the proportion.

10	
40	321

$$\frac{10}{40} = \frac{x}{321}$$

Multiply the diagonals.

$10 \times 321 = 3{,}210$

Divide by the remaining number.

```
      $80.25
40)$3,210.00
    3 20
      10 0
       8 0
       2 00
```

4. (4) 706.5

The radius (r) is equal to ½ the diameter. Since the diameter is 30 inches, the radius is 15 inches. Use the formula for computing the area of a circle to solve this problem.

$A = 3.14\ (15)^2$
$A = 3.14\ (225)$
$A = 706.5$ square inches

5. (3) 6:12 P.M.

Add the length of the call, 67 minutes, to the 8:05 P.M. starting time.

```
 8:05
+  67
 8:72 = 9:12 P.M.
```

The call ends at 9:12 P.M. Eastern Standard Time, so subtract 3 hours to find Pacific Standard Time: 6:12 P.M.

6. (4) 18

To find how many 15-minute periods there are in 4½ hours, divide 4½ hours by 15 minutes. 15 minutes is ¼ of an hour, so divide 4½ hours by ¼.

$4\frac{1}{2} \div \frac{1}{4} = \frac{9}{2} \div \frac{1}{4} = \frac{9}{\not{2}} \times \frac{\not{4}}{1} = 18$

The information about the cost of the taping is not needed to answer the question.

7. (4) 5,220

First find the number of dozens of pairs of dress shoes the store carried.

```
  500 dozen pairs total
−  65 dozen pairs nondress
  435 dozen pairs dress
```

Then multiply the number of dozen pairs of dress shoes by 12 to find the total number of *pairs* of dress shoes.

```
  435  dozen pairs of dress
x  12  shoes
  870  number in a dozen
 4 35
5,220  pairs of dress shoes
```

8. (5) 8 in

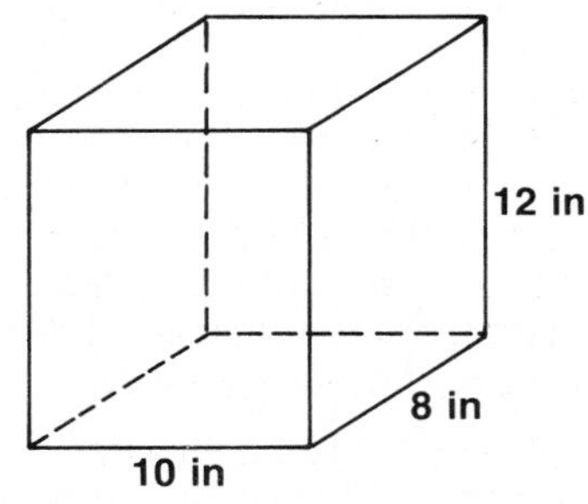

A globe could not be any wider than the shortest side of the box. Therefore, the largest globe could be only 8 inches in diameter.

9. (3) $96,526

To find the 1986 value of a house that increased in value by 289% since 1976, multiply the 1976 value by the amount of increase, 289% (or 2.89).

```
   $33,400
      2.89
   3 006 00
  26 720 0
  66 800
$96,526.00
```

10. (2) $384

First multiply 24 by 116 to find the total amount the Andersons had to pay.

$24 \times 116 = \$2{,}784$

Then subtract $2,400 from this total. The difference between the total amount paid and $2,400 equals the finance charge.

```
$ 2,784 total of payments
− 2,400 purchase price
$   384 finance charge
```

11. (2) C, D, A, B, E

Choose the least common denominator (8) and change each fraction to one with a denominator of 8.

$\frac{1}{2} = \frac{4}{8} \qquad \frac{1}{4} = \frac{2}{8} \qquad \frac{3}{4} = \frac{6}{8}$

Then compare the numerators of the fractions and order them from least to most.

12. (5) Insufficient data

You need to know the time of the loan (t) before you can use the formula to find how much money she had borrowed.

13. (4) $7\frac{2}{5}$

To solve this problem, first find a common denominator and add.

$5\frac{1}{2} = 5\frac{2}{4}$
$6\frac{1}{4} = 6\frac{1}{4}$
$7\frac{3}{4} = 7\frac{3}{4}$
$8\frac{1}{2} = 8\frac{2}{4}$
$9 = \underline{\quad 9 \quad}$
$\quad\ \ 35\frac{8}{4} = 37$

Then divide the total by 5.

$37 \div 5 = 7\frac{2}{5}$

14. (1) 60(60)4 + 60(56)3.5

Multiply the average number of words she enters in the morning per minute (60) by the number of minutes in an hour (60) by the number of morning hours she works (4). Add that total to the average number of words she enters in the afternoon per minute (56) multiplied by the number of minutes in an hour (60) and by the number of afternoon hours she works (3.5).

15. (1) 53%

First find the amount of increase.

$$\begin{array}{r} \$13{,}000 \\ -\ \ 8{,}500 \\ \hline 4{,}500 \end{array}$$

Then find the percent of 8,500 this increase is.

4,500	
8,500	100

4,500 × 100 = 450,000

$$\begin{array}{r} 52.9 \\ 8{,}500\overline{)450{,}000.} \\ 425\ 00 \\ \hline 25\ 000 \\ 17\ 000 \\ \hline 8\ 000\ 0 \end{array}$$

16. (1) 5,500–6,000

Find the floor area of his bedroom by multiplying the length by the width.

10 ft × 11 ft = 110 sq ft

Then find 110 sq ft on the chart and read across to see which size air conditioner he needs.

17. (4) 9,000–11,000

First find the area of his entire apartment. You can find the length of the apartment by adding the length of the living room (14) and that of the bedroom (10). You can find the width by adding the width of the living room (10) and that of the bedroom (11).

length = 14 + 10 = 24
width = 10 + 11 = 21
A = 24 × 21 = 504

However, the apartment is L-shaped, so you have to subtract the area in the lower-left corner that is not actually part of his apartment. Its dimensions are 10 by 10.

10 × 10 = 100
504 − 100 = 404

The floor area of Charlie's entire apartment is 404 sq ft, so he should look for an air conditioner from 9,000 to 11,000 Btu's.

18. (5) 294

The square measure of his bedroom is 110. The square measure of his apartment is 404. Subtract to find the difference.

404 − 110 = 294

19. (3) 47%

Take the difference in the two costs.

$$\begin{array}{r} \$\ 500 \\ -\ 340 \\ \hline 160 \end{array}$$

Then use the grid method to find what percent $160 is of $340.

160	
340	100

160 × 100 = 16,000

$$\begin{array}{r} 47 \\ 340\overline{)16{,}000} \\ 13\ 60 \\ \hline 2\ 400 \\ 2\ 380 \\ \hline 20 \end{array}$$

20. (5) 28.6

First find 30% of 22.

	30
22	100

30 × 22 = 660

$$\begin{array}{r} 6.6 \\ 100\overline{)660.} \\ 600 \\ \hline 60\ 0 \end{array}$$

Add that onto the rating of the smaller unit.

$$\begin{array}{r} 22.0 \\ +\ 6.6 \\ \hline 28.6 \end{array}$$

21. (2) $21.60

There are 24 hours in one day and so 48 hours in 2 days.

$$\begin{array}{r} 48 \\ 0.45 \\ \hline 2\ 40 \\ 19\ 2\ \ \\ \hline 21.60 \end{array}$$

22. (5) 402

The information about the cost is not needed. You can solve this problem in a number of ways. Here's one. Use the perimeter formula to find the distance around one poster.

P = 2(64) + 2(36.5)
P = 128 + 73

one poster: $\begin{array}{r} 128 \\ +\ 73 \\ \hline 201 \end{array}$ two posters: $\begin{array}{r} 201 \\ \times\ \ 2 \\ \hline 402 \end{array}$

23. (3) 22

The group netted $700. They also made $400 in addition to that, which they had to spend on the rent. So their gross profits were the two sums added together ($1,100). To find how many sellers there were, divide the gross profits by the amount each seller had to pay.

$$\begin{array}{r} 22 \\ 50\overline{)1{,}100} \\ 1\ 00 \\ \hline 100 \end{array}$$

24. (4) 18

The total number of grandchildren is 25, so you can write an equation like this, where e equals the number Ed has and j the number James has.

$e + j = 25$

The number Ed has (e) is 11 more than the number James has (j), so this second equation shows that relationship.

$e - 11 = j$

Now substitute $e - 11$ for j in the first equation to find how many grandchildren Ed (e) has.